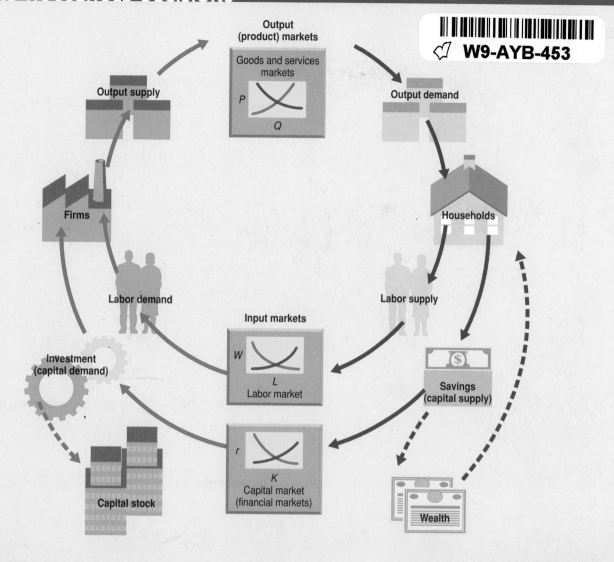

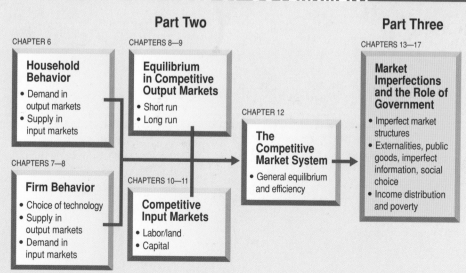

Part Two

Part Three

CHAPTER 6

Household Behavior
- Demand in output markets
- Supply in input markets

CHAPTERS 8—9

Equilibrium in Competitive Output Markets
- Short run
- Long run

CHAPTER 12

The Competitive Market System
- General equilibrium and efficiency

CHAPTERS 13—17

Market Imperfections and the Role of Government
- Imperfect market structures
- Externalities, public goods, imperfect information, social choice
- Income distribution and poverty

CHAPTERS 7—8

Firm Behavior
- Choice of technology
- Supply in output markets
- Demand in input markets

CHAPTERS 10—11

Competitive Input Markets
- Labor/land
- Capital

FIFTH EDITION

PRINCIPLES OF
ECONOMICS

FIFTH EDITION

PRINCIPLES OF
ECONOMICS

Karl E. Case
WELLESLEY COLLEGE

Ray C. Fair
YALE UNIVERSITY

Prentice Hall, Upper Saddle River, New Jersey 07458

Acquisitions Editor:	Rod Banister
Developmental Editor:	Michael Elia
Assistant Editor:	Gladys Soto
Editorial Assistant:	William Becher
Editor-in-Chief:	James Boyd
Marketing Manager:	Patrick Lynch
Associate Managing Editor:	David Salierno
Permissions Coordinator:	Jennifer Rella
Managing Editor:	Dee Josephson
Manufacturing Supervisor:	Arnold Vila
Manufacturing Manager:	Vincent Scelta
Electronic Artist:	Warren Fischbach
Senior Production Manager:	Lorraine Patsco
Designer:	Ann France
Design Manager:	Patricia Smythe
Photo Research Supervisor:	Melinda Lee Reo
Image Permission Supervisor:	Kay Dellosa
Photo Researcher:	Melinda Alexander
Cover Illustration:	Theo Rudnak
Project Management/Composition:	TSI Graphics

 Copyright ©1999, 1996, 1994, 1992, 1989 by Prentice-Hall, Inc.
A Simon & Schuster Company
Upper Saddle River, New Jersey 07458

Library of Congress Cataloging-in-Publication Data

Case, Karl E.
  Principles of economics / Karl E. Case, Ray C. Fair. — 5th ed.
    p. cm.
  Includes bibliographical references and index.
  ISBN 0-13-095710-0 (alk. paper)
    1. Economics. I. Fair, Ray C. II. Title.
  HB171.5.C3123 1999
  330—dc21   98-23823
                                                                    CIP

Prentice-Hall International (UK) Limited, London
Prentice-Hall of Australia Pty. Limited, Sydney
Prentice-Hall Canada, Inc., Toronto
Prentice-Hall Hispanoamericana, S.A., Mexico
Prentice-Hall of India Private Limited, New Delhi
Prentice-Hall of Japan, Inc., Tokyo
Simon & Schuster Asia Pte. Ltd., Singapore
Editora Prentice-Hall do Brasil, Ltda., Rio de Janeiro

Printed in the United States of America

10 9 8 7 6 5 4 3

To
Professor Richard A. Musgrave
and
Professor Robert M. Solow

BRIEF CONTENTS

CONTENTS

MICROECONOMICS

MACROECONOMICS

INTERNATIONAL ECONOMICS

GLOBAL COVERAGE

Because the study of economics crosses national boundaries, this book includes international examples in almost every chapter. The following list is a summary of global examples and discussions in the text.

GLOBAL COVERAGE

PREFACE

AS THIS FIFTH edition is being prepared to go on press, we are into the 28th consecutive quarter of expansion in the U.S. economy. Unemployment is at its lowest in nearly 30 years. A number of Asian economies, including Korea, Thailand, and Indonesia, have suffered sharp economic downturns, and even Japan, the world's second largest economy, is suffering through recession and slow growth. Much of Europe is set to adopt a common currency. Hong Kong has become part of China. Congress passed the Taxpayer Relief Act and welfare reform has become reality. The Russian economy has begun to grow. (When our first edition was published in 1989, the Berlin Wall had not yet fallen, the Cold War still chilled international relations, and Iraq had not yet invaded Kuwait.) How rapidly the world is changing!

The degree to which the economic landscape has changed since our fourth edition was published has led to hundreds of changes—some large, some not so large, some you might expect, some not—in this revision. One way of reflecting many of those changes in the landscape is through the new Fast Facts feature we added to every chapter. Each Fast Fact contains some additional data or current example that describes a significant change in the economy. This feature adds depth to the text but does not add bulk, because each Fast Fact is concise and most are written to fit in the margin column.

Revising a book involves adding new material, and there is a tendency for textbooks to grow in volume over time. However, student time is a scarce resource, and longer books are more costly to produce. Therefore, our goal throughout was to update, refine, and add material where needed, but to end up cutting excess baggage and obsolete material wherever possible. The bottom line is that the fifth edition is a shorter book.

All tables and figures have been updated with the most recent data available, and the case studies that end each part are completely new. Although we continue to cover the core of economic theory, we have added new material on important topics that have only recently emerged as major economic issues. These include health-care reform, immigration, urban problems and crime, the balanced budget amendment, welfare reform, the new trade treaties, several countries' recent problems with volatile exchange rates, and the experiences of transitional economies.

In addition, the fifth edition contains more international material than any previous edition. Almost every chapter contains a global application or example. A complete list of global examples follows the detailed table of contents. We've also added many new problems to the end of each chapter and included solutions to the even-numbered problems at the end of the text.

To date, more than 400,000 students and professors have used *Principles of Economics* or one of its split volumes. In this new edition, we have made every effort to be responsive to our readers' suggestions while maintaining the book's basic focus and pedagogical organization. To make the book accessible to a wider range of students, we have cut a great deal of extraneous material, simplified several of the more analytical sections, and redrawn many of the more technical graphs using numbers rather than variable names. Also, to make the book more appealing to today's visual learners, we've completely revised the art, photo, and illustration program. The result, we hope, is a principles book that students will keep on their shelves and use throughout college and beyond.

THE PLAN OF THE FIFTH EDITION

Despite major revisions and new features, the themes of the fifth edition are the same themes of the first four editions. The purpose of this book is to introduce the discipline of economics and to provide a basic understanding of how economies function. This requires a blend of economic theory, institutional material, and real-world applications. We have tried to maintain a reasonable balance between these ingredients in every chapter in this book. Like the first four editions, the fifth edition also attempts to present differing theoretical views in an evenhanded way.

Although we have chosen to present microeconomics first, we have designed the text so that professors may proceed directly to macroeconomics after teaching the five introductory chapters.

MICROECONOMICS

Market research and comments from users of the third edition convinced us that the organization of the microeconomic material is pedagogically sound. For this reason, we have not altered the presentation drastically.

The organization of the microeconomic material continues to reflect our belief that the best way to understand how market economies operate—and the best way to understand basic economic theory—is to work through the perfectly competitive model first, including discussions of output *and* input markets and the connections between them, before turning to noncompetitive market structures. When students understand how a simple competitive system works, they can start thinking about how the pieces of the economy "fit together." We think this is a better approach to teaching economics than some of the more traditional approaches, which encourage students to think of economics as a series of disconnected alternative market models.

Doing competition first also allows students to see the power of the market system. It is impossible to discuss the things that markets do well until students have seen how a simple system determines the allocation of resources. This is our purpose in chapters 6–11. Chapter 12 remains a pivotal chapter that links the world of perfect competition with the imperfect world of noncompetitive markets, externalities, imperfect information, and poverty, all of which we discuss in chapters 13–17. In chapters 18–20, students use everything they've learned in chapters 6–17 to take a closer look at some of the fields of applied microeconomics (the economics of taxation, labor economics, and the economics of health care, immigration, and the urban problems).

MACROECONOMICS

Several new textbooks have shifted the emphasis in the presentation of macroeconomics from short-run income determination to long-run growth while de-emphasizing business cycles, the role of countercyclical policy, and the problems of unemployment and inflation. Although we agree that growth deserves more attention in macroeconomics, we have chosen *not* to follow their lead. We remain convinced that the basic structure of aggregate supply and aggregate demand provides a very powerful pedagogical framework within which students can come to understand the nature of the debates that now permeate the professional literature, including the efficacy of monetary and fiscal policy, the role of the Fed, and the factors that determine growth and the cyclical behavior of the economy. We are also convinced that unemployment and inflation remain serious potential problems for economies in the United States and across the world.

Although we have made a number of changes to the content of the macroeconomic material, we remain committed to the view that it is a mistake simply to throw aggregate demand and aggregate supply curves at students in the first few chapters of a principles book. To understand the *AS* and *AD* curves, they need to know about the functioning of the goods market and the money market. The logic behind the simple demand curve is simply wrong when applied to the relationship between aggregate demand and the price level. Similarly, the logic behind the simple supply curve is wrong when applied to the relationship between aggregate supply and the price level.

Part of teaching economics is teaching economic reasoning. Our discipline is built around deductive logic. Once we teach students a pattern of logic, we want and expect them to apply it to new circumstances. When they apply the logic of a simple demand curve or simple supply curve to the aggregate demand or aggregate supply curve, the logic does not fit. We believe the best way to teach the reasoning embodied in the aggregate demand and aggregate supply curves without creating serious confusion is to build up to them carefully.

Organization As in the fourth edition, the macroeconomics section begins with three introductory chapters (21–23) that introduce students to macroeconomic tools, national income accounting, and inflation and unemployment (both in the United States and abroad). These chapters are followed by two chapters that present the basic functioning of the goods market (chapters 24 and 25) and two chapters that present the basic functioning of the money market (chapters 26 and 27). It is these four chapters that students are introduced to the concepts of fiscal and monetary policy. These chapters are followed by a chapter that brings the two markets together. This chapter, chapter 28, does in essence a very simplified version of *IS/LM* analysis verbally. (The *IS* and *LM* curves are included in an appendix to chapter 28 for those instructors who are interested in teaching them.)

Given the groundwork that has been laid in chapter 28, chapter 29 proceeds directly to derive the aggregate demand curve and then the aggregate supply curve. The two curves are then put together to determine the aggregate price level and to discuss the various theories of inflation.

Following the development of the *AD* and *AS* curves, we turn to a more detailed look at the labor market in chapter 30 and discuss various theories of unemployment. By the end of chapter 30, students have put the goods market, the money market, and the labor market together, and they have analyzed inflation, unemployment, and monetary and fiscal policy. Chapter 31 uses the material learned earlier to analyze a number of current macroeconomic issues, including proposed balanced-budget legislation and business cycles in Europe and Asia.

In chapter 32, we take a closer look at the behavior of households and firms in the macroeconomy. It can be skipped without losing the flow of the material. We close the macro section of the book by looking at some current debates in macroeconomics (chapter 33) and economic growth and productivity (chapter 34).

Content In preparing the fifth edition, we have maintained the two innovations we introduced in the second edition. The first of these is the treatment of aggregate supply. Clearly, there is strong disagreement among economists and across economics textbooks on the exact nature of the aggregate supply curve. All economists agree that if input prices rise at the same rate as output prices, the aggregate supply curve is vertical; firms have no incentive to change output if their costs and revenues change at the same rate. For the *AS* curve to have a positive slope in the short run, input prices must either be constant or there must be some lag in their adjustment.

Some textbooks assume that input prices are constant when the overall price level changes, essentially treating the aggregate supply curve as if it were the sum of individual market supply curves. This assumption of constant input prices is obviously unrealistic, and in the second edition we changed our description of the short-run *AS* curve to one that assumes some lag in input price adjustment when the overall private level changes. In addition, we clarified and expanded our description of the long-run aggregate supply curve, incorporating the concept of potential GDP.

Second, we continue to distinguish between inflation (a change in the overall price level) and *sustained* inflation (an increase in the overall price level that continues for some period of time). There can be confusion in students' minds as to what inflation is and whether or not it is a purely monetary phenomenon, and we think that this distinction helps to clarify our discussions.

Highlights
of the Fifth Edition

NEW FAST FACTS IN EVERY CHAPTER

An important new feature of the fifth edition is that several Fast Facts have been added to every chapter. Each is either a new table of data, an additional example, a research result, or simply an illustration of a point made in the text. Although brief and not as involved as a box, we believe these will add depth and richness to the material. As an example, in the discussion of elasticity, we obtained some current estimates of price elasticity of demand for a number of common goods from Regional Financial Associates, a first-rate forecasting and modelling firm in Philadelphia.

Other examples include a brief discussion of the Three Gorges Dam under construction in China, the current U.S.-dollar exchange rates against several currencies, and a table showing the cumulative effects of alternative growth rates over 10- and 20-year time periods.

RECENT DATA, EXAMPLES, EVENTS, AND TOPICS

Every chart, table, and graph in the book has been revised with the most recent data available. In addition, we have integrated topics that have generated a great deal of attention over the last few years—the economics of crime, immigration and health care, the Justice Department's assault on Microsoft, the recent experiences of Russia and the economies of Eastern Europe, the continuing economic problems of Asia, the adoption of a common currency in Europe, the debate about shifting to a consumption tax, and the decline of the "natural monopolies" and consequent deregulation of electricity rates, to name just a few.

THE BEA'S NEW PROCEDURE

The Bureau of Economic Analysis (BEA) make a major change at the end of 1995 in its presentation of the national income and product accounts. The focus is no longer on constant-dollar magnitudes and on implicit price deflators, but instead on "chain-type annual weights" quantity and price indexes. This change is much more important than the BEA's change in focus a few years ago from GNP to GDP.

Unfortunately, our enthusiasm to get the description of the new and complex chain index into the fourth edition led us to pitch the discussion too high. We heard from many students and instructors that the presentation was too hard. Therefore, we have completely rewritten that section and lowered the level of the discussion. The topic remains a difficult one for students to understand, however, and some may wish to skip it altogether.

INCREASED COVERAGE OF INTERNATIONAL MATERIAL

We have increased our coverage of international material in three ways. First, we have added many new Global Perspective boxes throughout the text. These boxes are designed to illustrate economic logic with global examples and to emphasize today's global economy. Second, we introduce imports and exports into the simple goods market model early in macroeconomics. (We do, however, continue to believe that a complete treatment of open market macroeconomics should not be taught until students have mastered the logic of a simple closed macroeconomy. For this reason, we have chosen to place the "open-economy macro" chapter in International Economics, the final section of the book.) Finally, we have integrated international examples directly into the text whenever appropriate. All international examples are listed in a table following the book's detailed table of contents.

OPTIONAL CHAPTERS

We have tried to keep uppermost in our minds that time is always tight in a principles course. For this reason, we have made sure that certain chapters can be skipped without losing the flow of the material. In microeconomics, chapter 11 (on the capital market) can be skipped because chapter 10 (on input markets in general) covers the basics of the capital market. Similarly, the "topics" chapters in Part Four can be skipped if time is short.

In macroeconomics, chapters 32–34 are optional. The chapters in the international section, with the exception of chapter 36, can be taught at any time that the instructor deems appropriate.

STUDENT LEARNING AIDS

Each chapter begins with a brief overview of what the student has learned in the previous chapter and ends with a brief "look ahead" to the following chapter. To help students study, key terms have been printed in boldface and glossed to the margins. Each chapter ends with a point-by-point summary of the chapter, a list of review terms and concepts (cross-referenced to text page), and a problem set.

Because many believe that economics must be relevant to be interesting, we have included three types of boxes for the fifth edition. Global Perspective boxes provide economic examples from around the world. Application boxes apply the theory learned in the text to real-world events and situations. Issues and Debates boxes examine many of the economic issues currently under debate.

In addition, we have set the major principles of economics off from the text in such a way as to highlight their importance. These highlights flow logically from the preceding text and into the text that follows. Students tell us that they find these very useful as a way of reviewing the key points in each chapter to prepare for exams.

PROBLEM SETS AND SOLUTIONS

Each chapter and appendix ends with a problem set that asks students to think about what they've learned in the chapter. These problems are not simple memorization questions. Rather, they ask students to perform graphical analysis or to apply economics to a real-world situation or policy decision. Approximately 40 percent of the problems are new to this edition. More challenging problems are indicated by an asterisk. The solutions to all even-numbered problems appear at the back of the book. The solutions to all odd-numbered problems, as well as additional problem sets, are available in the Instructor's Resource Manual.

CASE STUDIES

The end-of-part case studies continue to be quite popular. The fifth edition features nine new case studies on topics ranging from the spotted owl and new homes to making your own money.

Each case study is accompanied by questions for analytical thinking. The cases are not simply additional problems, and they are not simple extensions of the text material. They are meant to be applications of some of the *ideas* that the part was designed to teach and are designed to foster critical thinking and "thinking like an economist." They might be used as assignments or for class discussion.

TEACHING AND LEARNING TOOLS

The ancillary package for the fifth edition reflects changes in technology and utilizes new ways of disseminating information. A customized Web site links with Prentice Hall Learning on the Internet Partnership (PHLIP) to offer a comprehensive Internet package for the student and the instructor. An integrated package of software, printed supplements, videos, and reference guides completes the total teaching and learning package. Please contact your Prentice Hall sales representative for information on any of the Case and Fair supplements.

INTERNET RESOURCES (WWW.PRENHALL.COM/CASEFAIR)

The Case and Fair Web site offers students another opportunity to sharpen their problem-solving skills and to assess their understanding of the text material. Just go to the Case and Fair site and click on the Online Study Guide for additional true/false, multiple-choice, fill-in-the-blanks, and essay questions. The site also connects the student to the Take It to the Net web-destination exercises cited at the end of each chapter in the text. The online study guide has a built-in grading feature; students take the exams and receive immediate feedback.

From the Case and Fair Web site, the student and the instructor can link to PHLIP. Developed by Dan Cooper at Marist College, PHLIP provides academic support for faculty and students using the fifth edition. The student section of PHLIP offers some downloadable supplements as well as PHLIPing through the News, a review of current-events articles keyed to topics in the text. Scott Simkins (North Carolina A&T State University) and Jim Barbour (Elon

College) update the articles biweekly and provide summaries with discussion questions and research ideas. The faculty section of PHLIP requires a user name and password—please contact your Prentice Hall sales representative.

ECONOMICS EXPLORER RUNTIME MULTIMEDIA

The *Economics Explorer* CD-ROM, developed by Prentice Hall and Logal Software, Inc., combines video, animation, and spreadsheet capabilities to bring economics to life. Logal has taken the basic economic models from the textbook and created a series of dynamic, interactive simulations that help students visualize how math, graphs, and economic intuition are connected.

Once students have learned to use the simulation, they can design their own experiments and test their own conjectures. Using *Economics Explorer,* students can test the limits of economic models, input their own data to recreate events from economic history, and (using spreadsheet capabilities) record the results and display them in graphs like those from their textbook.

The fifth edition Instructor's Manual provides tips for integrating *Economics Explorer* into the course. The Study Guide alerts the students to relevant exercises tied to topics in the text.

STUDY GUIDES

Two comprehensive study guides, one for microeconomics and one for macroeconomics, have been prepared by Thomas Beveridge of North Carolina State University. These study aids reinforce the textbook and provide students with additional applications and exercises. Each chapter contains the following elements:

- *Point-by-Point Objectives.* A list of learning goals for the chapter, along with a brief summary of the material, helpful study hints, practice questions with solutions, and page references to the text.
- *Practice Tests.* Approximately 20 multiple-choice questions and their answers.
- *Application Questions.* A series of multiple-choice questions that require the use of graphic or numerical analysis to solve economic problems.
- *Solutions.* Worked-out solutions to all questions in the Study Guide, complete with page references to the text.
- *Comprehensive Part Exams.* Nine part exams to test the students' overall comprehension consisting of up to 25 multiple-choice questions, extended examples, and problem questions where appropriate.

The study Guide also references the Take It to the Net Web exercises from the text and alerts the student to relevant applications in the *Economics Explorer* software.

INSTRUCTOR'S MANUALS

Two innovative instructor's manuals, *Principles of Microeconomics* and *Principles of Macroeconomics,* were written by Mary Lesser at Iona College. The manuals are designed to help the instructor incorporate applicable elements of the fifth edition supplement package. The manuals include:

- Detailed chapter outlines with key terminology, teaching notes, and lecture suggestions.
- Video Guide for the 1998/99 Economics Video Library.
- Class Tips from Students, which feature real-world ideas from the students' point of view.
- Teaching Tips on incorporating the Take It to the Net Web exercises and *Economics Explorer* software.
- Additional Problems with solutions.
- Extended Applications, which include exercises, activities, and experiments to help make economics relevant to students.
- Solutions to all odd-numbered problems from the text.
- Case Study Solutions for the analytical thinking questions that accompany cases from the fifth edition text.

TEST ITEM FILES

The fifth edition test bank, completely revised and updated by Timothy Duy of the University of Oregon, contains almost 7,000 true/false, multiple-choice, short-answer, and essay questions. Also included are Problem Sets, a series of questions based on a scenario or graph. Each question in the test bank is page-referenced and coded for level of difficulty (easy, moderate, challenging, and honors). Questions are also classified as fact, definition, single, and multi. Questions classified as single require the student to use a single-step analytical process to answer, whereas the questions classified as multi require the student to perform numerous steps in the analytical process.

A test item file is available for both microeconomics and macroeconomics, in printed form or in a computerized version.

PH CUSTOM TESTS

Available for Windows and Macintosh, PH Custom is the computerized version of the test item files. The test program allows professors to edit, add or delete questions from the test item file, edit existing graphics and create new graphics, and export files to word processing programs.

POWERPOINT LECTURE PRESENTATION

An all-new PowerPoint presentation, by Mark Karscig of Central Missouri State University, offers summaries and necessary reinforcement of important text material. Many important graphs "build" over a sequencing of slides so that students may see the step-by-step process involved in economic analysis. The package will allow for instructors to make full-color, professional-looking presentations while providing the ability for custom handouts to be provided to the students.

COLOR TRANSPARENCIES

All figures and tables from the text are reproduced as full-page, four-color acetates.

ABC NEWS/PRENTICE HALL VIDEO LIBRARY   **ABCNEWS**

ABC News and Prentice Hall combine their individual expertise in academic publishing and global reporting to provide a comprehensive video ancillary to the fifth edition. The 1998/99 Economics Video Library contains 23 news clips from *Nightline*, *World News Tonight*, *Wall Street Journal Report*, and *20/20*. Each clip illustrates the vital, ongoing connections between what is learned in the classroom and what is happening in the world around us. All the videos are timely or timeless, and many can be used at different points in the course. The instructor's manuals provide suggestions on where and how to integrate each video.

THE NEW YORK TIMES "THEMES OF THE TIMES"

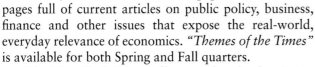

The New York Times, Inc., and Prentice Hall collaborate to offer *Economic Themes of the Times*—12 newspaper pages full of current articles on public policy, business, finance and other issues that expose the real-world, everyday relevance of economics. *"Themes of the Times"* is available for both Spring and Fall quarters.

The New York Times offers a reduced subscription rate for students and professors. For more information, call 1-800-631-1222.

SURFING FOR SUCCESS INTERNET GUIDE

Surfing for Success in Economics 1998/99 is an invaluable guide on using Internet resources. Scott Simkins and Jim Barbour join Andrew Stull in creating a reference that not only helps beginning students learn their way around the Internet, but lists economics-related sites and Your Turn Web-destination exercises to make surfing the Internet a natural part of the economics classroom.

THE SECOND YEAR SUPPLEMENT PACKAGE

A new wave of supplements will be available to help the instructor in the second year of using the fifth edition textbook:

- A brand new Test Item File, written by Mary Lesser, Iona College.
- 1999/2000 Economics Video Library and Video Guide.
- Presentation Manager.

ACKNOWLEDGMENTS

We are grateful to many people for help on the fifth edition. We are most grateful to Mike Elia, Senior Developmental Editor for Business Publishing at Prentice Hall, for stepping in to oversee the entire project. The quality of the book owes much to his guidance, and we owe much to his good humor. Gladys Soto, Assistant Editor, indefatigability marshalled the extensive array of supplements to accompany this text. We also owe much to Rod Banister, Executive Editor for Economics at Prentice Hall, for his help and enthusiasm.

We are also indebted to Elena Ranguelova, David Lindauer, Jack Triplett of the BEA, and Susan Skeath. We want to thank Peter Scott and Elizabeth Gill for their research assistance and proofreading of the manuscript.

We also owe a debt of gratitude to those who reviewed the fifth edition and provided us with a valuable insight as we prepared the new edition:

- Alex Anas, SUNY at Buffalo
- Charles A. Bennett, Gannon University
- Minh Quang Dao, Eastern Illinois University
- Douglas A. Greenley, Moorhead State University
- Cynthia S. McCarty, Jacksonville State Univerity
- James J. McLain, University of New Orleans
- Martha L. Olney, University of California-Berkeley
- Ben Young, University of Missouri-Kansas City
- Darrel Young, University of Texas

We are extremely indebted to James Shope and Michael Krause for reviewing the entire manuscript for this revision.

Last but not least, the following individuals were of immense help in reviewing all or part of this book and the teaching/learning package in various stages of development:

Lew Abernathy, University of North Texas • Jack Adams, University of Maryland • Doulas Agbetsiafa, Indiana University at

South Bend • Sam Alapati, Rutgers University • Polly Allen, University of Connecticut • Stuart Allen, University of North Carolina at Greensboro • Jim Angresano, Hampton-Sydney College • Kenneth S. Arakelian, University of Rhode Island • Harvey Arnold, Indian River Community College • Nick Apergis, Fordham University • Kidane Asmeron, Pennsylvania State University • James Aylesworth, Lakeland Community College • Kari Battaglia, University of North Texas • Daniel K. Benjamin, Clemson University • Bruce Bolnick, Northeastern University • G. E. Breger, University of South Carolina • Dennis Brennan, William Rainey Harper Junior College • Lindsay Caulkins, John Carroll University • Atreya Chakraborty, Boston College • Harold Christensen, Centenary College • Daniel Christiansen, Albion College • Samuel Kim-Liang Chuah, Walla Walla College • David Colander, Middlebury College • Daniel Condon, University of Illinois at Chicago; Moraine Valley Community College • David Cowen, University of Texas at Austin • Michael Donihue, Colby College • Robert Driskill, Ohio State University • Gary Dymski, University of Southern California • Jay Egger, Towson State University • Noel J. J. Farley, Bryn Mawr College • Mosin Farminesh, Temple University • Dan Feaster, Miami University of Ohio • Susan Feiner, Virginia Commonwealth University • Getachew Felleke, Albright College • Lois Fenske, South Puget Sound Community College • William Field, DePauw University • Bill Foeller, State University of New York at Fredonia • Roger Nils Folsom, San Jose State University • Sean Fraley, College of Mount Saint Joseph • N. Galloro, Chabot College • Tom Gausman, Northern Illinois University, DeKalb • Shirley J. Gedeon, University of Vermont • Gary Gigliotti, Rutgers University • Lynn Gillette, Texas A&M University • Sarah L. Glavin, Boston College • Devra Golbe, Hunter College • Roger Goldberg, Ohio Northern University • Douglas Greenley, Morrhead State University • Lisa M. Grobar, California State University at Long Beach • Benjamin Gutierrez, Indiana University at Bloomington • A. R. Gutowsky, California State University at Sacramento • David R. Hakes, University of Missouri at St. Louis • Stephen Happel, Arizona State University • Mitchell Harwitz, State University of New York at Buffalo • David Hoaas, Centenary College • Harry Holzer, Michigan State University • Bobbie Horn, University of Tulsa • John Horowitz, Ball State University • Janet Hunt, University of Georgia • Fred Inaba, Washington State University • Richard Inman, Boston College • Shirley Johnson, Vassar College • Farhoud Kafi, Babson College • R. Kallen, Roosevelt University • Arthur E. Kartman, San Diego State University • Hirshel Kasper, Oberlin College • Bruce Kaufman, Georgia State University • Dominique Khactu, The University of North Dakota • Phillip King, San Francisco State University • Barbara Kneeshaw, Wayne County Community College • Barry Kotlove, Elmira College • David Kraybill, University of Georgia at Athens • Rosung Kwak, University of Texas at Austin • Melissa Lam, Wellesley College • Jim Lee, Fort Hays State University • Judy Lee, Leeward Community College • Gary Lemon, DePauw University • Alan Leonard, Northern Illinois University • George Lieu, Tuskegee University • Stephen E. Lile, Western Kentucky University • Jane Lillydahl, University of Colorado at Boulder • Al Link, University of North Carolina at Greensboro • Robert Litro, U. S. Air Force Academy, Wallingford, CT • Burl F. Long, University of Florida • Gerald Lynch, Purdue University • Karla Lynch, University of North Texas • Michael Magura, University of Toledo • Don Maxwell, Central State University • Nan Maxwell, California State University at Hayward • J. Harold McClure, Jr., Villanova University • Rick McIntyre, University of Rhode Island • K. Mehtaboin, College of St. Rose • Shahruz Mohtadi, Suffolk University • Joe L. Moore, Arkansas Technical University • Robert Moore, Occidental College • Doug Morgan, University of California at Santa Barbara • Norma C. Morgan, Curry College • John Murphy, North Shore Community College, Massachusetts • Veena Nayak, State University of New York at Buffalo • Randy Nelson, Colby College • David Nickerson, University of British Columbia • Rachel Nugent, Pacific Lutheran University • Akorlie A. Nyatepe-Coo, University of Wisconsin at LaCrosse • Norman P. Obst, Michigan State University • William C. O'Connor, Western Montana College • Kent Olson, Oklahoma State University • Carl Parker, Fort Hays State University • Spirog Patton, Neumann College • Tony Pizelo, Spokane Community College • Michael Rendich, Westchester Community College • Lynn Rittenoure, University of Tulsa • David C. Rose, University of Missouri at St. Louis • Richard Rosenberg, Pennsylvania State University • Mark Rush, University of Florida at Gainesville • Dereka Rushbrook, Ripon College • David L. Schaffer, Haverford College • Gary Sellers, University of Akron • Jean Shackleford, Bucknell University • Linda Shaffer, California State University at Fresno • Geoff Shepherd, University of Massachusetts at Amherst • Bih-Hay Sheu, University of Texas at Austin • Alden Shiers, California Polytechnic State University • Sue Skeath, Wellesley College • Paula Smith, Central State University, Oklahoma • John Solow, University of Iowa at Iowa City • Susan Stojanovic, Washington University, St. Louis • Ernst W. Stromsdorfer, Washington State University • Michael Taussig, Rutgers University • Timothy Taylor, Stanford University • Sister Beth Anne Tercek, SND, Notre Dame College of Ohio • Jack Trierweler, Northern State University • Brian M. Trinque, University of Texas at Austin • Ann Velenchik, Wellesley College • Chris Waller, Indiana University at Bloomington • Walter Wessels, North Carolina State University • Joan Whalen-Ayyappan, DeVry Institute of Technology • Robert Whaples, Wake Forest University • Leonard A. White, University of Arkansas • Abera Zeyege, Ball State University • James Ziliak, Indiana University at Bloomington

We welcome comments about the fifth edition. Please write to us care of Economics Editor, Prentice Hall Higher Education Division, One Lake Street, Upper Saddle River, N.J. 07458.

Karl E. Case
Ray C. Fair

Save a Tree!

Many of the components of the teaching and learning package are available in electronic format. Disk-based supplements conserve paper and allow you to select and print only the material you plan to use. For more information, please ask your Prentice Hall sales representative.

ABOUT THE AUTHORS

Karl E. Case

is the Marion Butler McLean Professor in the History of Ideas and Professor of Economics at Wellesley College. He also lectures on economics and tax policy in the International Tax Program at Harvard Law School and is a visiting scholar at the Federal Reserve Bank of Boston. He received his B.A. from Miami University in 1968, spent 3 years in the army, and received his M.A. and Ph.D. from Harvard University. In 1980 and 1981, he was Fellow in Law and Economics at Harvard Law School.

Professor Case's research has been in the areas of public finance, taxation, and housing. He is the author or coauthor of four other books, including *Economics and Tax Policy* and *Property Taxation: The Need for Reform*, as well as numerous articles in professional journals.

For the past 21 years, he has taught at Wellesley College. Before coming to Wellesley, he served as Head Tutor (director of undergraduate studies) at Harvard, where he won the Allyn Young Teaching Prize. He has been a member of the AEA's Committee on Economic Education and was Associate Editor of the *Journal of Economic Education*, responsible for the section on innovations in teaching. He teaches at least one section of the principles course every year.

Ray C. Fair

is Professor of Economics at Yale University. He is a member of the Cowles Foundation at Yale and a Fellow of the Econometric Society. He received a B.A. in economics from Fresno State College in 1964 and a Ph.D. in economics from M.I.T. in 1968. He taught at Princeton University from 1968 to 1974 and has been at Yale since 1974.

Professor Fair's research has primarily been in the areas of macroeconomics and econometrics, with particular emphasis on macroeconometric model building. His publications include *Specification, Estimation, and Analysis of Macroeconometric Models* (Harvard Press, 1984) and *Testing Macroeconometric Models* (Harvard Press, 1994).

Professor Fair has taught introductory and intermediate economics at Yale. He has also taught graduate courses in macroeconomic theory and macroeconometrics.

Professor Fair's United States and multicountry models are available for use on the Internet free of charge. The address is **http://fairmodel.econ.yale.edu.** Many teachers have found that having students work with the United States model on the Internet is a useful complement to even an introductory macroeconomics course.

INTRODUCTION
PART ONE

INTRODUCTION TO ECONOMICS

THE SCOPE AND METHOD OF ECONOMICS

THE STUDY OF ECONOMICS should begin with a sense of wonder. Pause for a moment and consider a typical day in your life. For breakfast you might have bread made in a local bakery with flour produced in Minnesota from wheat grown in Kansas and bacon from pigs raised in Ohio packaged in plastic made in New Jersey. You spill coffee from Colombia on your shirt made in Texas from textiles shipped from South Carolina.

After class you drive with a friend in a Japanese car on an interstate highway system that took 20 years and billions of dollars to build. You stop for gasoline refined in Louisiana from Saudi Arabian crude oil brought to the United States on a supertanker that took three years to build at a shipyard in Maine.

At night you call your brother in Mexico City. The call travels over fiber-optic cable to a powerful antenna that sends it to a transponder on one of over 1,000 communications satellites orbiting the earth.

You use or consume tens of thousands of things, both tangible and intangible, every day: buildings, the music of a rock band, the compact disc it is recorded on, telephone services, staples, paper, toothpaste, tweezers, soap, a digital watch, fire protection, antacid tablets, banks, electricity, eggs, insurance, football fields, computers, buses, rugs, subways, health services, sidewalks, and so forth. Somebody made all these things. Somebody decided to organize men and women and materials to produce them and distribute them. Thousands of decisions went into their completion. Somehow they got to you.

One hundred thirty-one million people in the United States—almost half the total population—work at hundreds of thousands of different jobs producing over $8 trillion worth of goods and services every year. Some cannot find work; some choose not to work. Some are rich; others are poor.

The United States imports over $140 billion worth of automobiles and parts and about $70 billion worth of petroleum and petroleum products each year; it exports around $55 billion worth of agricultural products, including food. High-rise office buildings go up in central cities. Condominiums and homes are built in the suburbs. In other places homes are abandoned and boarded up.

Some countries are wealthy. Others are impoverished. Some are growing. Some are stagnating. Some businesses are doing well. Others are going bankrupt.

At any moment in time every society faces constraints imposed by nature and by previous generations. Some societies are handsomely endowed by nature with fertile land, water, sunshine, and natural resources. Others have deserts and few mineral resources. Some societies receive much from previous generations—art, music, technical knowledge, beautiful buildings, and productive factories. Others are left with overgrazed, eroded land, cities leveled by war, or polluted natural environments. *All* societies face limits.

economics *The study of how individuals and societies choose to use the scarce resources that nature and previous generations have provided.*

Economics is the study of how individuals and societies choose to use the scarce resources that nature and previous generations have provided. The key word in this definition is *choose*. Economics is a behavioral, or social, science. In large measure it is the study of how people make choices. The choices that people make, when added up, translate into societal choices.

The purpose of this chapter and the next is to elaborate on this definition and to introduce the subject matter of economics. What is produced? How is it produced? Who gets it? Why? Is the result good or bad? Can it be improved?

WHY STUDY ECONOMICS?

There are four main reasons to study economics: to learn a way of thinking, to understand society, to understand global affairs, and to be an informed voter.

TO LEARN A WAY OF THINKING

Probably the most important reason for studying economics is to learn a way of thinking. A good way to introduce economics is to review three of its most fundamental concepts: *opportunity cost*, *marginalism*, and *efficient markets*. If your study of economics is successful, you will use these concepts every day in making decisions.

▶ **Opportunity Cost** What happens in an economy is the outcome of thousands of individual decisions. Households must decide how to divide their incomes among all the goods and services available in the marketplace. People must decide whether to work or not to work, whether to go to school, and how much to save. Businesses must decide what to produce, how much to produce, how much to charge, and where to locate. It is not surprising that economic analysis focuses on the process of decision making.

Nearly all decisions involve trade-offs. A key concept that recurs in analyzing the decision-making process is the notion of *opportunity cost*. The full "cost" of making a specific choice includes what we give up by not making the alternative choice. That which we forgo, or give up, when we make a choice or a decision is called the **opportunity cost** of that decision.

opportunity cost *That which we forgo, or give up, when we make a choice or a decision.*

This concept applies to individuals, businesses, and entire societies. The opportunity cost of going to a movie is the value of the other things you could have done with the same money and time. If you decide to take time off from work, the opportunity cost of your leisure is the pay that you would have earned had you worked. Part of the cost of a college education is the income you could have earned by working full time instead of going to school. If a firm purchases a new piece of equipment for $3,000, it does so because it expects that equipment to generate more profit. There is an opportunity cost, however, because that $3,000 could have been deposited in an interest-earning account. To a society, the opportunity cost of using resources to put astronauts on the moon is the value of the private/civilian goods that could have been produced with the same resources.

Opportunity costs arise because resources are scarce. *Scarce* simply means "limited." Consider one of our most important resources—time. There are only 24 hours in a day, and we must live our lives under this constraint. A farmer in rural Brazil must decide whether it is better to continue to farm or to go to the city and look for a job. A hockey player at the University of Vermont must decide whether she will play on the varsity team or spend more time improving her academic work.

▶ **Marginalism and Sunk Costs**   A second key concept used in analyzing choices is the notion of *marginalism*. In weighing the costs and benefits of a decision, it is important to weigh only the costs and benefits that arise from the decision. Suppose, for example, that you live in New Orleans and that you are weighing the costs and benefits of visiting your mother in Iowa. If business required that you travel to Kansas City, the cost of visiting Mom would be only the additional, or *marginal*, time and money cost of getting to Iowa from Kansas City.

Consider the cost of producing this book. Assume that 10,000 copies are produced. The total cost of producing the copies includes the cost of the authors' time in writing the book, the cost of editing, the cost of making the plates for printing, and the cost of the paper and ink. If the total cost were $600,000, then the average cost of one copy would be $60, which is simply $600,000 divided by 10,000.

Although average cost is an important concept, a book publisher must know more than simply the average cost of a book. For example, suppose a second printing is being debated. That is, should another 10,000 copies be produced? In deciding whether to proceed, the costs of writing, editing, making plates, and so forth are irrelevant. Why? Because they have already been incurred—they are *sunk costs*. **Sunk costs** are costs that cannot be avoided, regardless of what is done in the future, because they have already been incurred. All that matters are the costs associated with the additional, or marginal, books to be printed. Technically, *marginal cost* is the cost of producing one more unit of output.

There are numerous examples in which the concept of marginal cost is useful. For an airplane that is about to take off with empty seats, the marginal cost of an extra passenger is essentially zero; the total cost of the trip is essentially unchanged by the addition of an extra passenger. Thus, setting aside a few seats to be sold at big discounts can be profitable even if the fare for those seats is far below the average cost per seat of making the trip. As long as the airline succeeds in filling seats that would otherwise have been empty, doing so is profitable.

▶ **Efficient Markets—No Free Lunch**   Suppose you are driving on a three-lane highway and you come upon a toll plaza with six toll booths. Three toll booths are straight ahead in the three lanes of traffic, and the three other booths are off to the right. Which lane should you choose? It is usually the case that the wait time is approximately the same no matter what you do. If one line is much shorter than the others, cars will quickly move into it until the lines are equalized.

As you will see later, the term *profit* in economics has a very precise meaning. Economists, however, often loosely refer to "good deals" or risk-free ventures as *profit opportunities*. Using the term loosely, a profit opportunity exists at the toll booths if one line is shorter than the others. In general, such profit opportunities are rare. At any one time there are many people searching for them, and, as a consequence, few exist. Markets like this, where any profit opportunities are eliminated almost instantaneously, are said to be **efficient markets**. (We discuss *markets*, the institutions through which buyers and sellers interact and engage in exchange, in detail in chapter 2.)

The common way of expressing the efficient markets concept is "there's no such thing as a free lunch." How should you react when a stockbroker calls up with a hot tip on the stock market? With skepticism. There are thousands of individuals each day looking for hot tips in the market, and if a particular tip about a stock is valid there will be an immediate rush to buy the stock, which will quickly drive its price up.

sunk costs *Costs that cannot be avoided, regardless of what is done in the future, because they have already been incurred.*

efficient market *A market in which profit opportunities are eliminated almost instantaneously.*

This economists' view that very few profit opportunities exist can, of course, be carried too far. There is a story about two people walking along, one an economist and one not. The noneconomist sees a twenty-dollar bill on the sidewalk and says, "There's a twenty-dollar bill on the sidewalk." The economist replies, "That is not possible. If there were, somebody would already have picked it up."

There are clearly times when profit opportunities exist. Someone has to be first to get the news, and some people have quicker insights than others. Nevertheless, news travels fast, and there are thousands of people with quick insights. The general view that profit opportunities are rare is close to the mark.

> The study of economics teaches us a way of thinking and helps us make decisions.

TO UNDERSTAND SOCIETY

Another reason for studying economics is to understand society better. Clearly, past and present economic decisions have an enormous influence on the character of life in a society. The current state of the physical environment, the level of material well-being, and the nature and number of jobs are all products of the economic system.

To get a sense of the ways in which economic decisions have shaped our environment, imagine looking out of a top-floor window of a high-rise office building in any large city. The workday is about to begin. All around you are other tall glass and steel buildings full of workers. In the distance you see the smoke of factories. Looking down, you see thousands of commuters pouring off trains and buses, and cars backed up on freeway exit ramps. You see trucks carrying goods from one place to another. You also see the face of urban poverty: Just beyond the freeway is a large public housing project and, beyond that, burned-out and boarded-up buildings.

What you see before you is the product of millions of economic decisions made over hundreds of years. People at some point decided to spend time and money building those buildings and factories. Somebody cleared the land, laid the tracks, built the roads, and produced the cars and buses.

Not only have economic decisions shaped the physical environment, they have determined the character of society as well. At no time has the impact of economic change on a society been more evident than in England during the late eighteenth and early nineteenth centuries, a period that we now call the **Industrial Revolution**. Increases in the productivity of agriculture, new manufacturing technologies, and the development of more efficient forms of transportation led to a massive movement of the British population from the countryside to the city. At the beginning of the eighteenth century, approximately two out of three people in Great Britain worked in agriculture. By 1812, only one in three remained in agriculture, and by 1900 the figure was fewer than one in ten. People jammed into overcrowded cities and worked long hours in factories. The world had changed completely in two centuries—a period that, in the run of history, was nothing more than the blink of an eye.

It is not surprising that the discipline of economics began to take shape during this period. Social critics and philosophers looked around them and knew that their philosophies must expand to accommodate the changes. Adam Smith's *Wealth of Nations* appeared in 1776. It was followed by the writings of David Ricardo, Karl Marx, Thomas Malthus, and others. Each tried to make sense out of what was happening. Who was building the factories? Why? What determined the level of wages paid to workers or the price of food? What would happen in the future, and what *should* happen? The people who asked these questions were the first economists.

Similar changes continue to affect the character of life today. In 1997 the number of jobs in the United States increased by more than 3 million, but nearly 7 million people who wanted a job could not find one. While the economy was growing, the wages of many workers were falling relative to the cost of living. While the Mexican economy has been growing since the United States and Mexico signed a trade treaty in 1993, thousands of Mexicans continue to pour into the United States. How does one make sense of all of this? Why do we have unemployment? What forces determine wages? What are the ramifications of continued immigration into the United States?

The study of economics is an essential part of the study of society.

TO UNDERSTAND GLOBAL AFFAIRS

A third reason for studying economics is to understand global affairs. News headlines are filled with economic stories. Great Britain and the rest of the European Union (a European trading bloc) struggle with the implications of their agreement to adopt a common currency, the Euro. The nations of the former Soviet Union are wrestling with a new phenomenon that clouds their efforts to "privatize" state-owned industries: organized crime. A new government in the Democratic Republic of Congo, formerly Zaire, is trying to reverse decades of stagnation.

All countries are part of a world economy, and understanding international relations begins with a basic knowledge of the economic links among countries. For centuries countries have attempted to protect their industries and workers from foreign competition by taxing and limiting the number of imports. Most economists argue, however, that unrestricted trade is in the long-run interest of all countries. Just after World War II many countries signed the General Agreement on Tariffs and Trade (GATT), in which they committed to lowering trade barriers. The process continues today as the Congress debates the most recent version of the GATT. The issue is a passionate one. French farmers, fearing the effects of cheap imports on their livelihood, protested strongly when France committed to signing the new GATT. Labor unions in the United States vowed to defeat any politicians who voted to ratify the North American Free Trade Agreement (NAFTA) with Mexico in 1993 and the new GATT in 1995.

Americans are investing heavily in industries in countries like Indonesia and China. During the 1980s the Japanese bought billions of dollars' worth of U.S. real estate, shares of corporate stocks, and government bonds. In recent years the Japanese, suffering economic problems at home, have pulled back, with important consequences for the United States. The end of the apartheid laws that legally separated the races in South Africa has created a new climate for international investment in that country. Meanwhile, the countries of Eastern Europe are struggling to create from the ground up economic and social institutions that took centuries to build in the West.

Another important issue in today's world is the widening gap between rich and poor nations. In 1998, world population was about 6 billion. Of that number, 4.5 billion lived in less-developed countries and 1.5 billion lived in more-developed countries.

WORRIES THAT FREE TRADE POLICIES WILL COST JOBS OFTEN BRING PROTESTS BY WORKERS.

The 75 percent of the world's population that lives in the less-developed countries receives less than 20 percent of the world's income. In dozens of countries, per capita income is only a few hundred dollars a year.

An understanding of economics is essential to an understanding of global affairs.

TO BE AN INFORMED VOTER

A knowledge of economics is essential to be an informed voter. During the last 25 years, the U.S. economy has been on a roller coaster. In 1973–1974, the Organization of Petroleum Exporting Countries (OPEC) succeeded in raising the price of crude oil by 400 percent. Simultaneously, a sequence of events in the world food market drove food prices up by 25 percent. By mid-1974, prices in the United States were rising across the board at a very rapid rate. Partially as a result of government policy to fight runaway inflation, the economy went into a recession in 1975. (An *inflation* is an increase in the overall price level in the economy; a *recession* is a period of decreasing output and rising unemployment.) The recession succeeded in slowing price increases, but in the process millions found themselves unemployed.

From 1979 through 1983, it happened all over again. Prices rose rapidly, the government reacted with more policies designed to stop prices from rising, and the United States ended up with an even worse recession in 1982. By the end of that year, 10.8 percent of the workforce was unemployed. Then, in mid-1990—after almost eight years of strong economic performance—the U.S. economy went into another recession. During the third and fourth quarters of 1990 and the first quarter of 1991, gross domestic product (GDP, a measure of the total output of the U.S. economy) fell, and unemployment again increased sharply. The recession of 1990–1991 was followed by a very slow recovery, which became the key issue in the 1992 presidential election. The 1994 congressional elections and the 1996 contest between Bob Dole and Bill Clinton focused on deficit reduction, tax reform, and welfare reform. The economic viability of "entitlement" programs, such as Social Security and Medicare, were also big issues. In 1997, the British election was dominated by the debate over Britain's full participation in the scheduled conversion to a common European currency. In the United States and throughout the world, economic issues continue to play a major role in the political process.

When we participate in the political process, we are voting on issues that require a basic understanding of economics.

THE SCOPE OF ECONOMICS

Most students taking economics for the first time are surprised by the breadth of what they study. Some think that economics will teach them about the stock market or what to do with their money. Others think that economics deals exclusively with problems like inflation and unemployment. In fact, it deals with all these subjects, but they are pieces of a much larger puzzle.

Economics has deep roots in, and close ties to, social philosophy. An issue of great importance to philosophers, for example, is distributional justice. Why are some people rich and others poor, and, whatever the answer, is this fair? A number of nineteenth-century social philosophers wrestled with these questions, and out of their musings economics as a separate discipline was born.

The easiest way to get a feel for the breadth and depth of what you will be studying is to explore briefly the way economics is organized. First of all, there are two major divisions of economics: microeconomics and macroeconomics.

MICROECONOMICS AND MACROECONOMICS

Microeconomics deals with the functioning of individual industries and the behavior of individual economic decision-making units: business firms and households. Firms' choices about what to produce and how much to charge, and households' choices about what and how much to buy, help to explain why the economy produces the things it does.

Another big question addressed by microeconomics is who gets the things that are produced. Wealthy households get more than poor households, and the forces that determine this distribution of output are the province of microeconomics. Why does poverty exist? Who is poor? Why do some jobs pay more than others?

Think again about all the things you consume in a day, and then think back to that view over a big city. Somebody decided to build those factories. Somebody decided to construct the roads, build the housing, produce the cars, and smoke the bacon. Why? What is going on in all those buildings? It is easy to see that understanding individual micro decisions is very important to any understanding of society.

Macroeconomics looks at the economy as a whole. Instead of trying to understand what determines the output of a single firm or industry or the consumption patterns of a single household or group of households, macroeconomics examines the factors that determine national output, or national product. Microeconomics is concerned with *household* income; macroeconomics deals with *national* income.

Whereas microeconomics focuses on individual product prices and relative prices, macroeconomics looks at the overall price level and how quickly (or slowly) it is rising (or falling). Microeconomics questions how many people will be hired (or fired) this year in a particular industry or in a certain geographical area, and the factors that determine how much labor a firm or industry will hire. Macroeconomics deals with *aggregate* employment and unemployment: how many jobs exist in the economy as a whole, and how many people who are willing to work are not able to find work.

To summarize:

> Microeconomics looks at the individual unit—the household, the firm, the industry. It sees and examines the "trees." Macroeconomics looks at the whole, the aggregate. It sees and analyzes the "forest."

Table 1.1 summarizes these divisions and some of the subjects with which they are concerned.

microeconomics *The branch of economics that examines the functioning of individual industries and the behavior of individual decision-making units—that is, business firms and households.*

macroeconomics *The branch of economics that examines the economic behavior of aggregates—income, employment, output, and so on—on a national scale.*

TABLE 1.1	EXAMPLES OF MICROECONOMIC AND MACROECONOMIC CONCERNS			
DIVISION OF ECONOMICS	**PRODUCTION**	**PRICES**	**INCOME**	**EMPLOYMENT**
Microeconomics	*Production/Output in individual industries and businesses* How much steel How much office space How many cars	*Price of individual goods and services* Price of medical care Price of gasoline Food prices Apartment rents	*Distribution of income and wealth* Wages in the auto industry Minimum wage Executive salaries Poverty	*Employment by individual businesses and industries* Jobs in the steel industry Number of employees in a firm Number of accountants
Macroeconomics	*National Production/Output* Total industrial output Gross domestic product Growth of output	*Aggregate price level* Consumer prices Producer prices Rate of inflation	*National income* Total wages and salaries Total corporate profits	*Employment and unemployment in the economy* Total number of jobs Unemployment rate

THE DIVERSE FIELDS OF ECONOMICS

Individual economists focus their research and study in many diverse areas. Many of these specialized fields are reflected in the advanced courses offered at most colleges and universities. Some are concerned with economic history or the history of economic thought. Others focus on international economics or growth in less-developed countries. Still others study the economics of cities (urban economics) or the relationship between economics and law. (See the Application box titled "The Fields of Economics" for more details.)

Economists also differ in the emphasis they place on theory. Some economists specialize in developing new theories, whereas others spend their time testing the theories of others. Some economists hope to expand the frontiers of knowledge, whereas others are more interested in applying what is already known to the formulation of public policies.

As you begin your study of economics, look through your school's course catalog and talk to the faculty about their interests. You will discover that economics encompasses a broad range of inquiry and is linked to many other disciplines.

THE METHOD OF ECONOMICS

Economics asks and attempts to answer two kinds of questions, positive and normative. **Positive economics** attempts to understand behavior and the operation of economic systems *without making judgments* about whether the outcomes are good or bad. It strives to describe what exists and how it works. What determines the wage rate for unskilled workers? What would happen if we abolished the corporate income tax? The answers to such questions are the subject of positive economics.

positive economics *An approach to economics that seeks to understand behavior and the operation of systems without making judgments. It describes what exists and how it works.*

In contrast, **normative economics** looks at the outcomes of economic behavior and asks if they are good or bad and whether they can be made better. Normative economics involves judgments and prescriptions for courses of action. Should the government subsidize or regulate the cost of higher education? Should medical benefits to the elderly under Medicare be available to those with incomes below some threshold? Should the United States allow importers to sell foreign-produced goods that compete with U.S.-produced products? Should we reduce inheritance taxes? Normative economics is often called *policy economics*.

normative economics *An approach to economics that analyzes outcomes of economic behavior, evaluates them as good or bad, and may prescribe courses of action. Also called policy economics.*

Of course, most normative questions involve positive questions. To know whether the government *should* take a particular action, we must know first if it *can* and second what the consequences are likely to be. (For example, if we lower import fees, will there be more competition and lower prices?)

Some claim that positive, value-free economic analysis is impossible. They argue that analysts come to problems with biases that cannot help but influence their work. Furthermore, even in choosing what questions to ask or what problems to analyze, economists are influenced by political, ideological, and moral views.

Although this argument has some merit, it is nevertheless important to distinguish between analyses that attempt to be positive and those that are intentionally and explicitly normative. Economists who ask explicitly normative questions should be forced to specify their grounds for judging one outcome superior to another.

descriptive economics *The compilation of data that describe phenomena and facts.*

▶ **Descriptive Economics and Economic Theory**   Positive economics is often divided into descriptive economics and economic theory. **Descriptive economics** is simply the compilation of data that describe phenomena and facts. Examples of such data appear in the *Statistical Abstract of the United States*, a large volume of data published by the Department of Commerce every year that describes many features of the U.S. economy. Massive volumes of data can now also be found on the World Wide Web.

THE FIELDS OF ECONOMICS

A good way to convey the diversity of economics is to describe some of its major fields of study and the issues that economists address.

- **INDUSTRIAL ORGANIZATION** looks carefully at the structure and performance of industries and firms within an economy. How do businesses compete? Who gains and who loses?

- **URBAN AND REGIONAL ECONOMICS** studies the spatial arrangement of economic activity. Why do we have cities? Why are manufacturing firms locating farther and farther from the center of urban areas?

- **ECONOMETRICS** applies statistical techniques and data to economic problems in an effort to test hypotheses and theories. Most schools require economics majors to take at least one course in statistics or econometrics.

- **COMPARATIVE ECONOMIC SYSTEMS** examines the ways alternative economic systems function. What are the advantages and disadvantages of different systems? What is the best way to convert the planned economies of the former Soviet Union to market systems?

- **ECONOMIC DEVELOPMENT** focuses on the problems of poor countries. What can be done to promote development in these nations? Important concerns of development economists include population growth and control, provision for basic needs, and strategies for international trade.

- **LABOR ECONOMICS** deals with the factors that determine wage rates, employment, and unemployment. How do people decide whether to work, how much to work, and at what kind of job? How have the roles of unions and management changed in recent years?

- **FINANCE** examines the ways in which households and firms actually pay for, or finance, their purchases. It involves the study of capital markets (including the stock and bond markets), futures and options, capital budgeting, and asset valuation.

- **INTERNATIONAL ECONOMICS** studies trade flows among countries and international financial institutions. What are the advantages and disadvantages for a country that allows its citizens to buy and sell freely in world markets? Why is the dollar strong or weak?

- **PUBLIC ECONOMICS** examines the role of government in the economy. What are the economic functions of government, and what should they be? How should the government finance the services that it provides? What kinds of government programs should confront the problems of poverty, unemployment, and pollution?

- **ECONOMIC HISTORY** traces the development of the modern economy. What economic and political events and scientific advances caused the Industrial Revolution? What explains the tremendous growth and progress of post-World War II Japan? What caused the Great Depression of the 1930s?

SEVERAL OF THE FIELDS OF ECONOMICS ARE CONCERNED WITH POVERTY IN DEVELOPING COUNTRIES.

- **LAW AND ECONOMICS** analyzes the economic function of legal rules and institutions. How does the law change the behavior of individuals and businesses? Do different liability rules make accidents and injuries more, or less, likely? What are the economic costs of crime?

- **THE HISTORY OF ECONOMIC THOUGHT**, which is grounded in philosophy, studies the development of economic ideas and theories over time, from Adam Smith in the eighteenth century to the works of economists such as Thomas Malthus, Karl Marx, and John Maynard Keynes. Because economic theory is constantly developing and changing, studying the history of ideas helps give meaning to modern theory and puts it in perspective.

For more on the fields of economics, see the Case and Fair Web page at
http://www.prenhall.com/casefair.

Where do all these data come from? The Census Bureau produces an enormous amount of raw data every year, as do the Bureau of Labor Statistics, the Bureau of Economic Analysis, and nongovernment agencies such as the University of Michigan Survey

Research Center. One important study now published annually is the *Survey of Consumer Expenditure*, which asks individual households to keep careful records of all their expenditures over a long period of time. Another is the *National Longitudinal Survey of Labor Force Behavior*, conducted over many years by the Center for Human Resource Development at Ohio State University.

Economic theory attempts to generalize about data and interpret them. An **economic theory** is a statement or set of related statements about cause and effect, action and reaction. One of the first theories you will encounter in this text is the *law of demand*, which was most clearly stated by Alfred Marshall in 1890: When the price of a product rises, people tend to buy less of it; when the price of a product falls, they tend to buy more.

Theories do not always arise out of formal numerical data. All of us have been collecting observations of people's behavior and their responses to economic stimuli for most of our lives. We may have observed our parents' reaction to a sudden increase—or decrease—in income or to the loss of a job or the acquisition of a new one. We all have seen people standing in line waiting for a bargain. And, of course, our own actions and reactions are another important source of data.

THEORIES AND MODELS

In many disciplines, including physics, chemistry, meteorology, political science, and economics, theorists build formal models of behavior. A **model** is a formal statement of a theory. It is usually a mathematical statement of a presumed relationship between two or more variables.

A **variable** is a measure that can change from time to time or from observation to observation. Income is a variable—it has different values for different people, and different values for the same person at different times. The rental price of a movie on a videocassette is a variable; it has different values at different stores and at different times. There are countless other examples.

Because all models simplify reality by stripping part of it away, they are abstractions. Critics of economics often point to abstraction as a weakness. Most economists, however, see abstraction as a real strength.

The easiest way to see how abstraction can be helpful is to think of a map. A map is a representation of reality that is simplified and abstract. A city or state appears on a piece of paper as a series of lines and colors. The amount of reality that the map maker can strip away before the map loses something essential depends on what the map will be used for. If I want to drive from St. Louis to Phoenix, I need to know only the major interstate highways and roads. I lose absolutely nothing and gain clarity by cutting out the local streets and roads. However, if I need to get around in Phoenix, I may need to see every street and alley.

Most maps are two-dimensional representations of a three-dimensional world; they show where roads and highways go but do not show hills and valleys along the way. Trail maps for hikers, however, have "contour lines" that represent changes in elevation. When you are in a car, changes in elevation matter very little; they would make a map needlessly complex and much more difficult to read. But if you are on foot carrying a 50-pound pack, a knowledge of elevation is crucial.

Like maps, economic models are abstractions that strip away detail to expose only those aspects of behavior that are important to the question being asked. The principle that irrelevant detail should be cut away is called the principle of **Ockham's razor** after the fourteenth-century philosopher William of Ockham.

But be careful. Although abstraction is a powerful tool for exposing and analyzing specific aspects of behavior, it is possible to oversimplify. Economic models often strip away a good deal of social and political reality to get at underlying concepts. When an economic theory is used to help formulate actual government or institutional policy, political and social reality must often be reintroduced if the policy is to have a chance of working.

economic theory *A statement or set of related statements about cause and effect, action and reaction.*

model *A formal statement of a theory. Usually a mathematical statement of a presumed relationship between two or more variables.*

variable *A measure that can change from time to time or from observation to observation.*

MAPS ARE USEFUL ABSTRACT REPRESENTATIONS OF REALITY.

Ockham's razor *The principle that irrelevant detail should be cut away.*

The key here is that the appropriate amount of simplification and abstraction depends upon the use to which the model will be put. To return to the map example: You don't want to walk around San Francisco with a map made for drivers—there are too many very steep hills!

▶ **All Else Equal: *Ceteris Paribus*** It is almost always true that whatever you want to explain with a model depends on more than one factor. Suppose, for example, that you want to explain the total number of miles driven by automobile owners in the United States. The number of miles driven will change from year to year or month to month; it is a variable. The issue, if we want to understand and explain changes that occur, is what factors cause those changes.

Obviously, many things might affect total miles driven. First, more or fewer people may be driving. This number, in turn, can be affected by changes in the driving age, by population growth, or by changes in state laws. Other factors might include the price of gasoline, the household's income, the number and age of children in the household, the distance from home to work, the location of shopping facilities, and the availability and quality of public transport. When any of these variables change, the members of the household may drive more or less. If changes in any of these variables affect large numbers of households across the country, the total number of miles driven will change.

Very often we need to isolate or separate out these effects. For example, suppose we want to know the impact on driving of a higher tax on gasoline. This change would raise the price of gasoline at the pump, but would not (at least in the short run) affect income, workplace location, number of children, and so forth.

To isolate the impact of one single factor, we use the device of ***ceteris paribus***, or **all else equal**. We ask: What is the impact of a change in gasoline price on driving behavior, *ceteris paribus*, or assuming that nothing else changes? If gasoline prices rise by 10 percent, how much less driving will there be, assuming no simultaneous change in anything else—that is, assuming that income, number of children, population, laws, and so on all remain constant?

ceteris paribus, or all else equal
A device used to analyze the relationship between two variables while the values of other variables are held unchanged.

> Using the device of *ceteris paribus* is one part of the process of abstraction. In formulating economic theory, the concept helps us simplify reality in order to focus on the relationships that we are interested in.

▶ **Expressing Models in Words, Graphs, and Equations** Consider the following statements: "Lower airline ticket prices cause people to fly more frequently." "Higher interest rates slow the rate of home sales." "When firms produce more output, employment increases." "Higher gasoline prices cause people to drive less and to buy more fuel-efficient cars."

Each of these statements expresses a relationship between two variables that can be quantified. In each case there is a stimulus and a response, a cause and an effect. Quantitative relationships can be expressed in a variety of ways. Sometimes words are sufficient to express the essence of a theory, but often it is necessary to be more specific about the nature of a relationship or about the size of a response. The most common method of expressing the quantitative relationship between two variables is *graphing* that relationship on a two-dimensional plane. In fact, we will use graphical analysis extensively in chapter 2 and beyond. Because it is essential that you be familiar with the basics of graphing, the appendix to this chapter presents a careful review of graphing techniques.

Quantitative relationships between variables can also be presented through *equations*. For example, suppose we discovered that over time, U.S. households collectively spend, or consume, 90 percent of their income and save 10 percent of their income. We could then write:

$$C = .90Y \text{ and } S = .10Y$$

where C is consumption spending, Y is income, and S is saving. Writing explicit algebraic expressions like these helps us understand the nature of the underlying process of decision making. Understanding this process is what economics is all about.

➤ **Cautions and Pitfalls**   In formulating theories and models, it is especially important to avoid two pitfalls: the post hoc fallacy and the fallacy of composition.

The Post Hoc Fallacy   Theories often make statements, or sets of statements, about cause and effect. It can be quite tempting to look at two events that happen in sequence and assume that the first caused the second to happen. Clearly, this is not always the case. This common error is called the **post hoc, ergo propter hoc** (or "after this, therefore because of this") fallacy.

post hoc, ergo propter hoc
Literally, "after this (in time), therefore because of this." A common error made in thinking about causation: If Event A happens before Event B, it is not necessarily true that A caused B.

There are thousands of examples. The Colorado Rockies have won seven games in a row. Last night, I went to the game and they lost. I must have "jinxed" them. They lost *because* I went to the game.

Stock market analysts indulge in what is perhaps the most striking example of the post hoc fallacy in action. Every day the stock market goes up or down, and every day some analyst on some national news program singles out one or two of the day's events as *the* cause of some change in the market: "Today the Dow Jones industrial average rose five points on heavy trading; analysts say that the increase was due to progress in talks between the United States and Cuba." Research has shown that daily changes in stock market averages are very largely random. While major news events clearly have a direct influence on certain stock prices, most daily changes cannot be directly linked to specific news stories.

Very closely related to the post hoc fallacy is the often erroneous link between correlation and causation. Two variables are said to be *correlated* if one variable changes when the other variable changes. But correlation does not imply causation. Cities that have high crime rates also have lots of automobiles, so there is a very high degree of correlation between number of cars and crime rates. Can we argue, then, that cars *cause* crime? No. The reason for the correlation may have nothing to do with cause and effect. Big cities have lots of people, lots of people have lots of cars, and therefore big cities have lots of cars. Big cities also have high crime rates for many reasons—crowding, poverty, anonymity, unequal distribution of wealth, and the ready availability of drugs, to mention only a few. But the presence of cars is probably not one of them.

This caution must also be viewed in reverse. Sometimes events that seem entirely unconnected actually *are* connected. In 1978 Governor Michael Dukakis of Massachusetts ran for reelection. Still quite popular, Dukakis was nevertheless defeated in the Democratic primary that year by a razor-thin margin. The weekend before, the Boston Red Sox, in the thick of the division championship race, had been badly beaten by the New York Yankees in four straight games. Some very respectable political analysts believe that hundreds of thousands of Boston sports fans vented their anger on the incumbent governor the following Tuesday.

The Fallacy of Composition   To conclude that what is true for a part is necessarily true for the whole is to fall into the **fallacy of composition.** Suppose that a large group of cattle ranchers graze their cattle on the same range. To an individual rancher, more cattle and more grazing mean a higher income. But because its capacity is limited, the land can support only so many cattle. If every cattle rancher increased the number of cattle sent out to graze, the land would become overgrazed and barren, and everyone's income would fall. In short:

fallacy of composition *The erroneous belief that what is true for a part is necessarily true for the whole.*

Theories that seem to work well when applied to individuals or households often break down when they are applied to the whole.

➤ **Testing Theories and Models: Empirical Economics** In science, a theory is rejected when it fails to explain what is observed or when another theory better explains what is observed. Prior to the sixteenth century almost everyone believed that the earth was the center of the universe and that the sun and stars rotated around it. The astronomer Ptolemy (A.D. 127–151) built a model that explained and predicted the movements of the heavenly bodies in a geocentric (earth-centered) universe. Early in the sixteenth century, however, the Polish astronomer Nicholas Copernicus found himself dissatisfied with the Ptolemaic model and proposed an alternative theory or model, placing the sun at the center of the known universe and relegating the earth to the status of one planet among many. The battle between the competing models was waged, at least in part, with data based on observations—actual measurements of planetary movements. The new model ultimately predicted much better than the old, and in time it came to be accepted.

In the seventeenth century, building on the works of Copernicus and others, Sir Isaac Newton constructed yet another body of theory that seemed to predict planetary motion with still more accuracy. Newtonian physics became the accepted body of theory, relied on for almost 300 years. Then Albert Einstein's theory of relativity replaced Newtonian physics because it was able to explain some things that earlier theories could not.

Economic theories are also confronted with new and often conflicting data from time to time. The collection and use of data to test economic theories is called **empirical economics**.

Numerous large data sets are available to facilitate economic research. For example, economists studying the labor market can now test behavioral theories against the actual working experiences of thousands of randomly selected people who have been surveyed continuously since the 1960s by economists at Ohio State University. Macro-economists continuously monitoring and studying the behavior of the national economy pass thousands of items of data, collected by both government agencies and private companies, back and forth on diskettes and over the Internet. Housing market analysts analyze data tapes containing observations recorded in connection with millions of home sales.

All scientific research needs to isolate and measure the responsiveness of one variable to a change in another variable *ceteris paribus*. Physical scientists, such as physicists and geologists, can often impose the condition of *ceteris paribus* by conducting controlled experiments. They can, for example, measure the effect of one chemical on another while literally holding all else constant in an environment that they control completely. Social scientists, who study people, rarely have this luxury.

Although controlled experiments are difficult in economics and other social sciences, they are not impossible. Researchers can isolate and measure the effect of one variable on another. There are a number of ways to do this. One way is to observe the behavior of groups of similar people under different circumstances. For example, suppose you wanted to estimate the effect of the tax rate increases enacted by Congress in 1993 on the amount that households save, an important tax policy issue. Of course, you could look at household saving before and after the change. But who's to say that what you observe is not due to changes in income that occurred at the same time? To isolate the tax effect, you could look at a set of households whose income did not change. Sophisticated computer programs are now allowing economists to isolate such effects more easily than ever before.

empirical economics *The collection and use of data to test economic theories.*

ECONOMIC POLICY

Economic theory helps us understand how the world works, but the formulation of *economic policy* requires a second step. We must have objectives. What do we want to change? Why? What is good and what is bad about the way the system is operating? Can we make it better?

Such questions force us to be specific about the grounds for judging one outcome superior to another. What does it mean to be better? Four criteria are frequently applied in making these judgments:

Criteria for Judging Economic Outcomes:
1. Efficiency
2. Equity
3. Growth
4. Stability

➤ **Efficiency** In physics, "efficiency" refers to the ratio of useful energy delivered by a system to the energy supplied to it. An efficient automobile engine, for example, is one that uses up a small amount of fuel per mile for a given level of power.

In economics, **efficiency** means *allocative efficiency*. An efficient economy is one that produces what people want at the least possible cost. If the system allocates resources to the production of things that nobody wants, it is inefficient. If all members of a particular society were vegetarian and somehow half of all that society's resources were used to produce meat, the result would be inefficient. It is inefficient when steel beams lie in the rain and rust because somebody fouled up a shipping schedule. If a firm could produce its product using 25 percent less labor and energy without sacrificing quality, it too is inefficient.

The clearest example of an efficient change is a voluntary exchange. If you and I each want something that the other has and we agree to exchange, we are both better off, and no one loses. When a company reorganizes its production or adopts a new technology that enables it to produce more of its product with fewer resources, without sacrificing quality, it has made an efficient change. At least potentially, the resources saved could be used to produce more of something.

Inefficiencies can arise in numerous ways. Sometimes they are caused by government regulations or tax laws that distort otherwise sound economic decisions. Suppose that land in Ohio is best suited for corn production and that land in Kansas is best suited for wheat production. Clearly, a law that requires Kansas to produce only corn and Ohio to produce only wheat would be inefficient. If firms that cause environmental damage are not held accountable for their actions, the incentive to minimize those damages is lost, and the result is inefficient.

Because most changes that can be made in an economy will leave some people better off and others worse off, we must have a way of comparing the gains and losses that may result. Most often we simply compare their sizes in dollar terms. A change is efficient if the value of the resulting gains exceeds the value of the resulting losses. In this case the winners can potentially compensate the losers, and they would still be better off.

➤ **Equity** While efficiency has a fairly precise definition that can be applied with some degree of rigor, **equity** (fairness) lies in the eye of the beholder. To many, fairness implies a more equal distribution of income and wealth. Fairness may imply alleviating poverty, but the extent to which the poor should receive cash benefits from the government is the subject of enormous disagreement. For thousands of years philosophers have wrestled with the principles of justice that should guide social decisions. They will probably wrestle with such questions for thousands of years to come.

Despite the impossibility of defining equity or fairness universally, public policy makers judge the fairness of economic outcomes all the time. Rent control laws were passed because some legislators thought that landlords treated low-income tenants unfairly. Certainly most social welfare programs are created in the name of equity.

efficiency *In economics, allocative efficiency. An efficient economy is one that produces what people want at the least possible cost.*

equity *Fairness.*

> **Growth** As the result of technological change, the building of machinery, and the acquisition of knowledge, societies learn to produce new things and to produce old things better. In the early days of the U.S. economy, it took nearly half the population to produce the required food supply. Today less than 2.5 percent of the country's population works in agriculture.

When we devise new and better ways of producing the things we use now and develop new products and services, the total amount of production in the economy increases. **Economic growth** is an increase in the total output of an economy. If output grows faster than the population, output per capita rises and standards of living increase. Presumably, when an economy grows there is more of what people want. Rural and agrarian societies become modern industrial societies as a result of economic growth and rising per capita output.

economic growth *An increase in the total output of an economy.*

Some policies discourage economic growth and others encourage it. Tax laws, for example, can be designed to encourage the development and application of new production techniques. Research and development in some societies are subsidized by the government. Building roads, highways, bridges, and transport systems in developing countries may speed up the process of economic growth. If businesses and wealthy people invest their wealth outside their country rather than in its own industries, growth in their home country may be slowed.

> **Stability** Economic **stability** refers to the condition in which national output is steady or growing, with low inflation and full employment of resources. An economy may at times be unstable. During the 1950s and 1960s, the U.S. economy experienced a long period of relatively steady growth, stable prices, and low unemployment. Between 1951 and 1969, consumer prices never rose more than 5 percent in a single year, and in only two years did the number of unemployed exceed 6 percent of the labor force. The decades of the 1970s and 1980s, however, were unstable. The United States experienced two periods of rapid price inflation (over 10 percent) and two periods of severe unemployment. In 1982, for example, 12 million people (10.8 percent of the workforce) were looking for work. The beginning of the 1990s was another period of instability, with a recession occurring in 1990–1991. In 1997 the economy was growing at a large enough rate that fears of inflation began to arise. In response, the Federal Reserve System (the U.S. central bank) acted to raise interest rates with a goal of slowing the country's growth rate. The causes of instability and the ways in which governments have attempted to stabilize the economy are the subject matter of macroeconomics.

stability *A condition in which output is steady or growing, with low inflation and full employment of resources.*

AN INVITATION

This chapter is meant to prepare you for what is to come. The first part of the chapter invited you into an exciting discipline that deals with important issues and questions. You cannot begin to understand how a society functions without knowing something about its economic history and its economic system.

The second part of the chapter introduced the method of reasoning that economics requires and some of the tools that economics uses. We believe that learning to think in this very powerful way will help you better understand the world.

As you proceed, it is important that you keep track of what you've learned in earlier chapters. This book has a plan; it proceeds step by step, each section building on the last. It would be a good idea to read through each chapter's table of contents and flip through each chapter before you read it to be sure you understand where it fits in the big picture.

SUMMARY

1. *Economics* is the study of how individuals and societies choose to use the scarce resources that nature and previous generations have provided.

WHY STUDY ECONOMICS?

2. There are many reasons to study economics, including (a) to learn a way of thinking, (b) to understand society, (c) to understand global affairs, and (d) to be an informed voter.

3. That which we forgo when we make a choice or a decision is the *opportunity cost* of that decision.

THE SCOPE OF ECONOMICS

4. *Microeconomics* deals with the functioning of individual markets and industries and with the behavior of individual decision-making units: firms and households.

5. *Macroeconomics* looks at the economy as a whole. It deals with the economic behavior of aggregates—national output, national income, the overall price level, and the general rate of inflation.

6. Economics is a broad and diverse discipline with many special fields of inquiry. These include economic history, international economics, and urban economics.

THE METHOD OF ECONOMICS

7. Economics asks and attempts to answer two kinds of questions: positive and normative. *Positive economics* attempts to understand behavior and the operation of economies without making judgments about whether the outcomes are good or bad. *Normative economics* looks at the results

of economic behavior and asks if they are good or bad and whether they can be improved.

8. Positive economics is often divided into two parts. *Descriptive economics* involves the compilation of data that accurately describe economic facts and events. *Economic theory* attempts to generalize and explain what is observed. It involves statements of cause and effect—of action and reaction.

9. An economic *model* is a formal statement of an economic theory. Models simplify and abstract from reality.

10. It is often useful to isolate the effects of one variable or another while holding "all else constant." This is the device of *ceteris paribus*.

11. Models and theories can be expressed in many ways. The most common ways are in words, in graphs, and in equations.

12. Because one event happens before another, the second event does not necessarily happen as a result of the first. To assume that "after" implies "because" is to commit the fallacy of *post hoc, ergo propter hoc*. The erroneous belief that what is true for a part is necessarily true for the whole is the *fallacy of composition*.

13. *Empirical economics* involves the collection and use of data to test economic theories. In principle, the best model is the one that yields the most accurate predictions.

14. To make policy, one must be careful to specify criteria for making judgments. Four specific criteria are used most often in economics: *efficiency*, *equity*, *growth*, and *stability*.

REVIEW TERMS AND CONCEPTS

ceteris paribus, 11
descriptive economics, 8
economic growth, 15
economic theory, 10
economics, 2
efficiency, 14
efficient market, 3
empirical economics, 13

equity, 14
fallacy of composition, 12
Industrial Revolution, 4
macroeconomics, 7
microeconomics, 7
model, 10
normative economics, 8

Ockham's razor, 10
opportunity cost, 2
positive economics, 8
post hoc, ergo propter hoc, 12
stability, 15
sunk costs, 3
variable, 10

PROBLEM SET

1. One of the scarce resources that constrain our behavior is time. Each of us has only 24 hours in a day. How do you go about allocating your time in a given day among competing alternatives? How do you go about weighing the alternatives? Once you choose a most important use of time, why do you not spend all your time on it? Use the notion of opportunity cost in your answer.

2. Which of the following statements are examples of positive economic analysis? Which are examples of normative analysis?

a. The 1997 cut in the federal inheritance tax is likely to cause a moderate increase in saving by higher-income households and a decline in donations to charity.

b. The inheritance tax should be repealed because it is unfair.

c. President Clinton proposed allowing Chile to join the North American Free Trade Agreement (NAFTA) in 1998. (NAFTA is an agreement signed by the United States, Mexico, and Canada in which the countries agreed to establish all of North America as a free-trade zone.) Admission of Chile should not be allowed because Chile's environmental standards are not up to those in the United States, which would give Chilean firms a cost advantage in competing with U.S. firms.

d. Allowing Chile to join NAFTA would cause wine prices in the United States to drop.

e. The establishment of a new political regime in the Democratic Republic of Congo (DRC, formerly Zaire) in 1997 will cause the world price of diamonds to drop because the supply of diamonds from the DRC to world markets will increase.

f. The first priorities of the new regime in the Democratic Republic of Congo should be to rebuild schools and highways and to provide basic health care.

3. Selwyn signed up with an Internet provider for a fixed fee of $19.95 per month. For this fee he gets unlimited access to the World Wide Web. During the average month in 1998, he was logged onto the Web for 17 hours. What is the average cost of an hour of Web time to Selwyn? What is the marginal cost of an additional hour?

4. Describe one of the major economic issues facing the government of your city or your state. (*Hint:* You might look at a local newspaper. Most issues that make it into the paper will have an impact on people's lives.) Who will be affected by the resolution of this issue? What alternative actions have been proposed? Who will be the winners? The losers?

5. Suppose that all of the 10,000 voting-age citizens of Lumpland are required to register to vote every year. Suppose also that the citizens of Lumpland are fully employed and that they each value their time at $10 per hour. In addition, assume that nonvoting high-school students in Lumpland are willing to work for $5 per hour. The government has two choices: (1) It can hire 200 students to work at registration locations for 5 hours per day for 10 days, or (2) it can hire 400 students for 5 hours per day for 10 days. If the government hires 200 students, each of the 10,000 citizens will have to wait in line for an hour to register. If the government hires 400 students, there will be no waiting time.

Assume that the cost of paying the students is obtained by taxing each voting-age citizen equally. The current government is very conservative and has decided to hold taxes down by hiring only 200 students. Do you agree with this decision? Why or why not? Is it efficient? Is it fair?

6. Suppose that a city is considering building a bridge across a river. The bridge will be financed by tax dollars. The city gets these revenues from a sales tax imposed on things sold in the city. The bridge would provide more direct access for commuters and shoppers. It would also alleviate the huge traffic jam that occurs every morning at the bridge down the river in another city.

a. Who would gain if the bridge were built? Could those gains be measured? How?

b. Who would be hurt if the bridge were built? Could those costs be measured? How?

c. How would you determine if it were efficient to build the bridge?

7. A question facing many U.S. states is whether to allow casino gambling. States with casino gambling have seen a substantial increase in tax revenue flowing to state government. This revenue can be used to finance schools, repair roads, maintain social programs, or reduce other taxes.

a. Recall that efficiency means producing what people want at least cost. Can you make an efficiency argument in favor of allowing casinos to operate?

b. What nonmonetary costs might be associated with gambling? Would these costs have an impact on the efficiency argument you presented in part a?

c. Using the concept of equity, argue for or against the legalization of casino gambling.

8. For each of the following situations, identify the full cost (opportunity costs) involved:

a. A worker earning an hourly wage of $8.50 decides to cut back to half time in order to attend Houston Community College.

b. Sue decides to drive to Los Angeles from San Francisco to visit her son, who attends UCLA.

c. Tom decides to go to a wild fraternity party and stays out all night before his physics exam.

d. Annie spends $200 on a new dress.

e. The Confab Company spends $1 million to build a new branch plant that will probably be in operation for at least 10 years.

f. Alex's father owns a small grocery store in town. Alex works 40 hours a week in the store but receives no compensation.

TAKE IT TO THE NET

We invite you to visit the Case and Fair page on the Prentice Hall Web site:

http://www.prenhall.com/casefair

for this chapter's World Wide Web exercise.

HOW TO READ AND UNDERSTAND GRAPHS

Economics is the most quantitative of the social sciences. If you flip through the pages of this or any other economics text, you will see countless tables and graphs. These serve a number of purposes. First, they illustrate important economic relationships. Second, they make difficult problems easier to understand and analyze. Finally, patterns and regularities that may not be discernible in simple lists of numbers can often be seen when those numbers are laid out in a table or on a graph.

A **graph** is a two-dimensional representation of a set of numbers, or data. There are many ways that numbers can be illustrated by a graph.

TIME SERIES GRAPHS

It is often useful to see how a single measure or variable changes over time. One way to present this information is to plot the values of the variable on a graph, with each value corresponding to a different time period. A graph of this kind is called a **time series graph**. On a time series graph, time is measured along the horizontal scale and the variable being graphed is measured along the vertical scale. Figure 1A.1 is a time series graph that presents the total disposable income in the U.S. economy for each year between 1975 and 1997.[1] This graph is based on the data found in Table 1A.1. By displaying these data graphically, we can see clearly that (1) total personal disposable income has been increasing steadily since 1975, and (2) during certain periods, disposable income was increasing at a faster rate than during other periods.

GRAPHING TWO VARIABLES ON A CARTESIAN COORDINATE SYSTEM

More important than simple graphs of one variable are graphs that contain information on two variables at the same time. The most common method of graphing two variables is the **Cartesian coordinate system**. This system is constructed by simply drawing two perpendicular lines: a horizontal line, or **X axis**, and a vertical

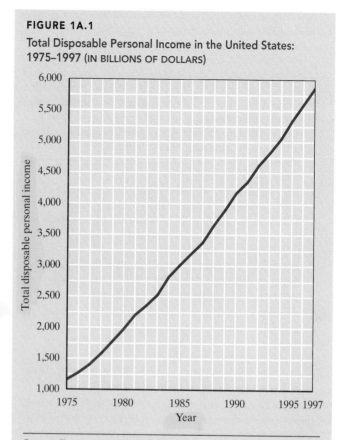

FIGURE 1A.1

Total Disposable Personal Income in the United States: 1975–1997 (IN BILLIONS OF DOLLARS)

Source: Economic Report of the President, 1998, p. 317.

line, or **Y axis**. The axes contain measurement scales that intersect at 0 (zero). This point is called the **origin**. On the vertical scale, positive numbers lie above the horizontal axis (that is, above the origin) and negative numbers lie below it. On the horizontal scale, positive numbers lie to the right of the vertical axis (to the right of the origin) and negative numbers lie to the left of it. The point at which the graph intersects the Y axis is called the **Y-intercept**.

When two variables are plotted on a single graph, each point represents a *pair* of numbers. The first number is measured on the X axis and the second number is measured on the Y axis. For example, the following points

---

[1]The measure of income presented in Table 1A.1 and in Figure 1A.1 is disposable income in billions of dollars. It is the total personal income received by all households in the United States minus the taxes that they pay.

TABLE 1A.1

TOTAL DISPOSABLE PERSONAL INCOME IN THE UNITED STATES, 1975–1997 (IN BILLIONS OF DOLLARS)

YEAR	TOTAL DISPOSABLE PERSONAL INCOME
1975	1,162.6
1976	1,277.1
1977	1,406.1
1978	1,585.8
1979	1,775.7
1980	1,980.5
1981	2,208.3
1982	2,355.8
1983	2,531.5
1984	2,819.8
1985	3,012.1
1986	3,198.5
1987	3,374.6
1988	3,652.6
1989	3,906.1
1990	4,179.4
1991	4,356.8
1992	4,626.7
1993	4,829.2
1994	5,052.7
1995	5,355.7
1996	5,608.3
1997	5,886.6

Source: Economic Report of the President, 1998, p. 317.

FIGURE 1A.2

A Cartesian Coordinate System

A Cartesian coordinate system is constructed by drawing two perpendicular lines: a vertical axis (the Y axis) and a horizontal axis (the X axis). Each axis is a measuring scale.

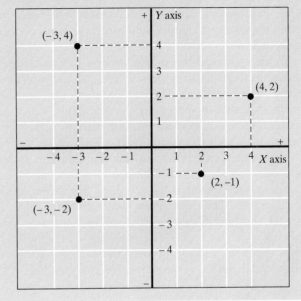

those households, ranked by income. For example, the average income for the top fifth (20 percent) of the households was $76,660. The average spending for the top 20 percent was $55,411.

TABLE 1A.2

CONSUMPTION EXPENDITURES AND INCOME, 1990[a]

	AVERAGE INCOME	AVERAGE CONSUMPTION EXPENDITURES
Bottom fifth	$ 5,637	$12,908
2nd fifth	14,115	17,924
3rd fifth	24,500	24,673
4th fifth	38,376	34,247
Top fifth	76,660	55,411

[a]Income and consumption data are for consumer units. Consumer units are defined as (1) all members of a particular household related by blood, marriage, adoption, or other legal arrangements, (2) a person living alone or sharing a household with others, but who is financially independent, or (3) two or more persons living together who pool their incomes.

Source: Statistical Abstract of the United States, 1992, p. 442.

(X, Y) are plotted on the set of axes drawn in figure 1A.2: (4, 2), (2, –1), (–3, 4), (–3, –2). Most, but not all, of the graphs in this book are plots of two variables where both values are positive numbers (such as [4, 2] in Figure 1A.2). On these graphs, only the upper right quadrant of the coordinate system (i.e., the quadrant in which all X and Y values are positive) will be drawn.

PLOTTING INCOME AND CONSUMPTION DATA FOR HOUSEHOLDS

Table 1A.2 presents some data collected by the Bureau of Labor Statistics (BLS). In a recent survey, 5,000 households were asked to keep careful track of all their expenditures. The table shows average income and average spending for

Figure 1A.3 presents the numbers from Table 1A.2 graphically using the Cartesian coordinate system. Along the horizontal scale, the X axis, we measure average income. Along the vertical scale, the Y axis, we measure average consumption spending. Each of the five pairs of numbers from the table is represented by a point on the graph. Because all numbers are positive numbers, we need to show only the upper right quadrant of the coordinate system.

To help you read this graph, we have drawn a dotted line connecting all the points where consumption and income would be equal. *This 45° line does not represent any data.* Rather, it represents the line along which all variables on the X axis correspond exactly to the variables on the Y axis (for example, [1, 1], [2, 2], [3.7, 3.7], etc.). The heavy blue line traces out the data; the dotted line is only to help you read the graph.

There are several things to look for when reading a graph. The first thing you should notice is whether the line slopes upward or downward as you move from left to right. The blue line in Figure 1A.3 slopes upward, indicating that there seems to be a **positive relationship** between income and spending: The

higher a household's income, the more a household tends to consume. If we had graphed the percentage of each group receiving welfare payments along the Y axis, the line would presumably slope downward, indicating that welfare payments are lower at higher income levels. The income level/welfare payment relationship is thus a **negative** one.

SLOPE

The **slope** of a line or curve is a measure that indicates whether the relationship between the variables is positive or negative and how much of a response there is in Y (the variable on the vertical axis) when X (the variable on the horizontal axis) changes. The slope of a line between two points is the change in the quantity measured on the Y axis divided by the change in the quantity measured on the X axis. We will normally use Δ (the Greek letter *delta*) to refer to a change in a variable. In Figure 1A.4, the slope of the line between points A and B is ΔY divided by ΔX. Sometimes it's easy to remember slope as "the rise over the run," indicating the vertical change over the horizontal change.

To be precise, ΔX between two points on a graph is simply X_2 minus X_1, where X_2 is the X value for the second point and X_1 is the X value for the first point. Similarly, ΔY is defined as Y_2 minus Y_1, where Y_2 is the Y value for the second point and Y_1 is the Y value for the first point. Slope is equal to

$$\frac{\Delta Y}{\Delta X} = \frac{Y_2 - Y_1}{X_2 - X_1}.$$

As we move from A to B in Figure 1A.4(a), both X and Y increase; the slope is thus a positive number. However, as we move from A to B in Figure 1A.4(b), X increases [$(X_2 - X_1)$ is a positive number], but Y decreases [$(Y_2 - Y_1)$ is a negative number]. The slope in Figure 1A.4(b) is thus a negative number, as a negative number divided by a positive number gives a negative quotient.

To calculate the numerical value of the slope between points A and B in Figure 1A.4, we need to calculate ΔY and ΔX. Since consumption is measured on the Y axis, ΔY is 5,016 [$(Y_2 - Y_1) = (17,924 - 12,908)$]. Because income is measured along the X axis, ΔX is 8,478 [$(X_2 - X_1) = (14,115 - 5,637)$]. The slope between A and B is $\Delta Y/\Delta X = 5,016/8,478 = +.592$.

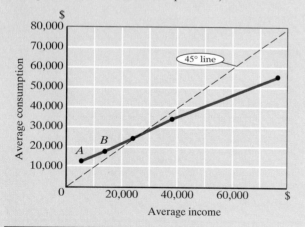

FIGURE 1A.3

Household Consumption and Income

A graph is a simple two-dimensional geometric representation of data. This graph displays the data from Table 1A.2. Along the horizontal scale (X axis), we measure household income. Along the vertical scale (Y axis), we measure household consumption. *Note:* At point A, consumption equals $12,908 and income equals $5,637. At point B, consumption equals $17,924 and income equals $14,115.

Source: Statistical Abstract of the United States, 1992, p. 442.

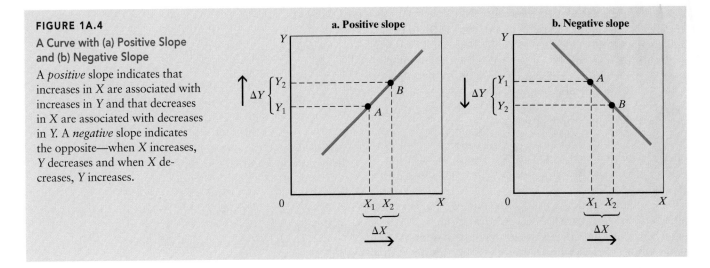

FIGURE 1A.4

A Curve with (a) Positive Slope and (b) Negative Slope

A *positive* slope indicates that increases in X are associated with increases in Y and that decreases in X are associated with decreases in Y. A *negative* slope indicates the opposite—when X increases, Y decreases and when X decreases, Y increases.

Another interesting thing to note about the data graphed in Figure 1A.3 is that all the points lie roughly along a straight line. (If you look very closely, however, you can see that the slope declines as one moves from left to right; the line becomes slightly less steep.) A straight line has a constant slope. That is, if you pick any two points along it and calculate the slope, you will always get the same number. A horizontal line has a zero slope (ΔY is zero); a vertical line has an "infinite" slope, because ΔY is too big to be measured.

Unlike the slope of a straight line, the slope of a *curve* is continually changing. Consider, for example, the curves in Figure 1A.5. Figure 1A.5(a) shows a curve with a positive slope that decreases as you move from left

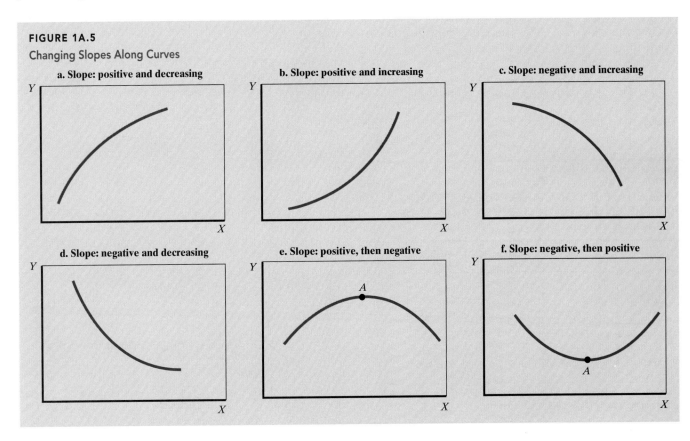

FIGURE 1A.5

Changing Slopes Along Curves

to right. The easiest way to think about the concept of increasing or decreasing slope is to imagine what it is like walking up a hill from left to right. If the hill is steep, as it is in the first part of Figure 1A.5(a), you are moving a lot in the Y direction for each step you take in the X direction. If the hill is less steep, as it is further along in Figure 1A.5(a), you are moving less in the Y direction for every step you take in the X direction. Thus, when the hill is steep, slope ($\Delta Y/\Delta X$) is a larger number than it is when the hill is flatter. The curve in Figure 1A.5(b) has a positive slope, but its slope *increases* as you move from left to right.

The same analogy holds for curves that have a negative slope. Figure 1A.5(c) shows a curve with a negative slope that increases (in absolute value) as you move from left to right. This time think about skiing down a hill. At first, the descent in Figure 1A.5(c) is gradual (low slope), but as you proceed down the hill (to the right), you descend more quickly (high slope). Figure 1A.5(d) shows a curve with a negative slope that *decreases* in absolute value as you move from left to right.

In Figure 1A.5(e), the slope goes from positive to negative as X increases. In 1A.5(f), the slope goes from negative to positive. At point A in both, the slope is zero. (Remember, slope is defined as $\Delta Y/\Delta X$. At point A, Y is not changing [$\Delta Y = 0$]. Therefore slope at point A is zero.)

SOME PRECAUTIONS

When you read a graph, it is important to think carefully about what the points in the space defined by the axes represent. Table 1A.3 and Figure 1A.6 present a graph of consumption and income that is very different from the one in Table 1A.2 and Figure 1A.3. First, each point in Figure 1A.6 represents a different year; in Figure 1A.3, each point represented a different group of households at the *same* point in time (1990). Second, the points in Figure 1A.6 represent *aggregate* consumption and income for the whole nation measured in *billions* of dollars; in Figure 1A.3, the points represented average *household* income and consumption measured in dollars.

It is interesting to compare these two graphs. All points on the aggregate consumption curve in Figure 1A.6 lie below the 45° line, which means that aggregate consumption is always less than aggregate income. However, the graph of average household income and consumption in Figure 1A.3 crosses the 45° line, implying that for some households consumption is larger than income.

TABLE 1A.3

AGGREGATE INCOME AND CONSUMPTION FOR THE ENTIRE UNITED STATES, 1930–1990 (IN BILLIONS OF DOLLARS)

	AGGREGATE NATIONAL INCOME	AGGREGATE CONSUMPTION
1930	75.3	70.2
1940	81.1	71.2
1950	241.7	192.7
1960	429.8	332.2
1970	840.6	648.1
1980	2,244.5	1,760.4
1990	4,652.1	3,839.3

Source: U.S. Department of Commerce, *Survey of Current Business,* August 1997, pp. 148, 164.

FIGURE 1A.6

National Income and Consumption

It is important to think carefully about what is represented by points in the space defined by the axes of a graph. In this graph, we have income graphed with consumption, as in Figure 1A.3, but here each observation point is national income and aggregate consumption in *different years*, measured in billions of dollars.

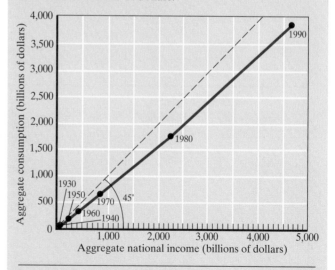

Source: See Table 1A.3.

SUMMARY

1. A *graph* is a two-dimensional representation of a set of numbers, or data. A *time series graph* illustrates how a single variable changes over time.

2. The most common method of graphing two variables on one graph is the *Cartesian coordinate system,* which includes an X (horizontal) *axis* and a Y (vertical) *axis.* The points at which the two axes intersect is called the *origin.* The point at which a graph intersects the Y axis is called the *Y-intercept.*

3. The *slope* of a line or curve indicates whether the relationship between the two variables graphed on a Cartesian coordinate system is positive or negative and how much of a response there is in Y (the variable on the vertical axis) when X (the variable on the horizontal axis) changes. The slope of a line between two points is the change in the quantity measured on the Y axis divided by the change in the quantity measured on the X axis.

REVIEW TERMS AND CONCEPTS

Cartesian coordinate system A common method of graphing two variables that makes use of two perpendicular lines against which the variables are plotted.   18

graph A two-dimensional representation of a set of numbers, or data.   18

negative relationship A relationship between two variables, X and Y, in which a decrease in X is associated with an increase in Y, and an increase in X is associated with a decrease in Y.   20

origin On a Cartesian coordinate system, the point at which the horizontal and vertical axes intersect.   18

positive relationship A relationship between two variables, X and Y, in which a decrease in X is associated with a decrease in Y, and an increase in X is associated with an increase in Y.   20

slope A measurement that indicates whether the relationship between variables is positive or negative and how much of a response there is in Y (the variable on the vertical axis)

when X (the variable on the horizontal axis) changes.   20

times series graph A graph illustrating how a variable changes over time.   18

X axis On a Cartesian coordinate system, the horizontal line against which a variable is plotted.   18

Y axis On a Cartesian coordinate system, the vertical line against which a variable is plotted.   18

Y-intercept The point at which a graph intersects the Y axis.   18

PROBLEM SET

1. Graph each of the following sets of numbers. Draw a line through the points and calculate the slope of each line.

1		2		3		4		5		6	
X	Y	X	Y	X	Y	X	Y	X	Y	X	Y
1	5	1	25	0	0	0	40	0	0	0.1	100
2	10	2	20	10	10	10	30	10	10	0.2	75
3	15	3	15	20	20	20	20	20	20	0.3	50
4	20	4	10	30	30	30	10	30	10	0.4	25
5	25	5	5	40	40	40	0	40	0	0.5	0

2. For each of the graphs in Figure 1 on page 24, say whether the curve has a positive or negative slope. Give an intuitive explanation for the slope of each curve.

3. For each of the following equations, graph the line and calculate its slope.
   a. $P = 10 - 2q_D$ (Put q_D on the X axis)
   b. $P = 100 - 4q_D$ (Put q_D on the X axis)
   c. $P = 50 + 6q_S$ (Put q_S on the X axis)
   d. $I = 10,000 - 500r$ (Put I on the X axis)

FIGURE 1

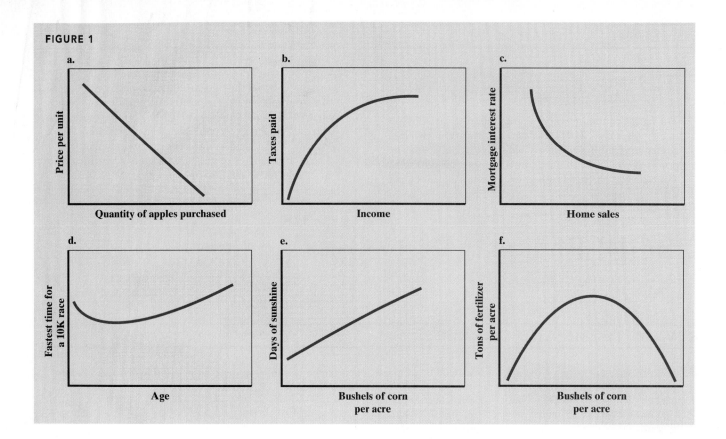

THE ECONOMIC PROBLEM: SCARCITY AND CHOICE

CHAPTER 1 BEGAN with a broad definition of economics. As you saw there, every society has some system or mechanism that transforms what nature and previous generations provide into useful form. Economics is the study of that process and its outcomes. Economists attempt to answer these questions: What gets produced? How is it produced? Who gets it? Why? Is it good or bad? Can it be improved?

This chapter explores these questions further. In a sense, this entire chapter *is* the definition of economics. It lays out the central problems addressed by the discipline and provides the framework that will guide you through the rest of the book.

Human wants are unlimited, but resources are not. Limited, or scarce, resources force individuals and societies to choose. The central function of any economy, no matter how simple or how complex, is to transform resources into useful form in accordance with those choices. The process by which this transformation takes place is called **production**.

The term **resources** is very broad. Some resources are the product of nature: land, wildlife, minerals, timber, energy, even the rain and the wind. At any given time, the resources, or **inputs**, available to a society also include those things that have been produced by previous generations, such as buildings and equipment. Things that are produced and then used to produce other valuable goods or services later on are called *capital resources*, or simply **capital**. Buildings, machinery, equipment, tables, roads, bridges, desks, and so forth are part of the nation's capital stock. *Human resources*—labor, skills, and knowledge—are also an important part of a nation's resources.

Producers are those who take resources and transform them into usable products, or **outputs**. Private manufacturing firms purchase resources and produce products for the market. Governments do so as well. National defense, the justice system, police and fire protection, and sewer services are all examples of outputs produced by the government, which is sometimes called the *public sector*.

Individual households often produce products for themselves. A household that owns its own home is in essence using land and a structure (capital)

production *The process by which resources are transformed into useful forms.*

resources or **inputs** *Anything provided by nature or previous generations that can be used directly or indirectly to satisfy human wants.*

capital *Things that have already been produced that are in turn used to produce other goods and services.*

producers *Those people or groups of people, whether private or public, who transform resources into usable products.*

outputs *Usable products.*

25

to produce "housing services" that it consumes itself. The Chicago Symphony Orchestra is no less a producer than General Motors. An orchestra takes capital resources—a building, musical instruments, lighting fixtures, musical scores, and so on—and combines them with land and highly skilled labor to produce performances.

SCARCITY, CHOICE, AND OPPORTUNITY COST

In the second half of this chapter, we discuss the global economic landscape. But before you can understand the different types of economic systems, it is important to understand the basic economic concepts of scarcity, choice, and opportunity cost.

THE THREE BASIC QUESTIONS

three basic questions
The questions that all societies must answer: (1) What will be produced? (2) How will it be produced? (3) Who will get what is produced?

All societies must answer **three basic questions:**

1. What will be produced?
2. How will it be produced?
3. Who will get what is produced?

Stated a slightly different way, the economic system must determine the *mix of output*, the *allocation of scarce resources* among producers, and the *distribution of that output* (Figure 2.1).

➤ **Scarcity and Choice in a One-Person Economy** The simplest economy is one in which a single person lives alone on an island. Consider Bill, the survivor of a plane crash, who finds himself cast ashore in such a place. Here, individual and society are one; there is no distinction between social and private. *Nonetheless, nearly all of the basic decisions that characterize complex economies must be made.* That is, although Bill himself will get whatever he produces, he still must decide how to allocate the island's resources, what to produce, and how and when to produce it.

First, Bill must decide *what* he wants to produce. Notice that the word *needs* does not appear here. Needs are absolute requirements, but beyond just enough water, basic nutrition, and shelter to survive, they are very difficult to define. What is an "absolute necessity" for one person may not be for another. In any case, Bill must put his wants in some order of priority and make some choices.

Next he must look at the *possibilities*. What can he do to satisfy his wants, given the limits of the island? In every society, no matter how simple or complex, people are constrained in what they can do. In this society of one, Bill is constrained by time, his physical condition, his knowledge, his skills, and the resources and climate of the island.

FIGURE 2.1

The Three Basic Questions

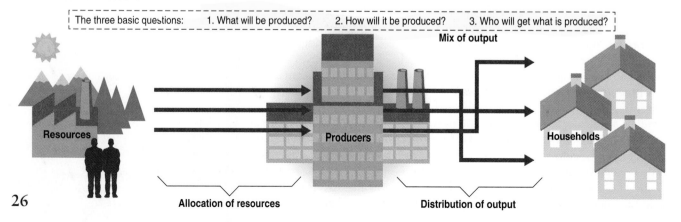

26

Given that resources are limited, Bill must decide *how* to use them best to satisfy his hierarchy of wants. Food would probably come close to the top of his list. Should he spend his time simply gathering fruits and berries? Should he hunt for game? Should he clear a field and plant seeds? Clearly, the answers to these questions depend on the character of the island, its climate, its flora and fauna (*are* there any fruits and berries?), the extent of his skills and knowledge (does he know anything about farming?), and his preferences (he may be a vegetarian).

▶ **Opportunity Cost**   The concepts of *constrained choice* and *scarcity* are central to the discipline of economics. They can be applied when discussing the behavior of individuals like Bill and when analyzing the behavior of large groups of people in complex societies.

Given the scarcity of time and resources, Bill has less time to gather fruits and berries if he chooses to hunt—he trades more meat for less fruit. There is a trade-off between food and shelter, too. If Bill likes to be comfortable, he may work on building a nice place to live, but that may require giving up the food he might have produced. As we noted in chapter 1, that which we forgo when we make a choice is the **opportunity cost** of that choice.

opportunity cost *That which we give up, or forgo, when we make a choice or a decision.*

Bill may occasionally decide to rest, to lie on the beach and enjoy the sun. In one sense, that benefit is free—he doesn't have to pay for the privilege. In reality, however, it does have an opportunity cost. The true cost of that leisure is the value of the other things Bill could have produced, but did not, during the time he spent on the beach.

In the 1960s, the United States decided to put a human being on the moon. To do so required devoting enormous resources to the space program, resources that could have been used to produce other things. Among other possibilities, taxes might have been lower. That would have meant more income for all of us to spend on goods and services. Those same resources could also have been used for medical research, to improve education, to repair roads and bridges, to aid the poor, or to support the arts.

In making everyday decisions it is often helpful to think about opportunity costs. Should I go to the dorm party or not? First, it costs $4 to get in. When I pay money for anything, I give up the other things that I could have bought with that money. Second, it costs two or three hours. Clearly, time is a valuable commodity for a college student. I have exams next week and I need to study. I could go to a movie instead of the party. I could go to another party. I could sleep. Just as Bill must weigh the value of sunning on the beach against more food or better housing, so I must weigh the value of the fun I may have at the party against everything else I might otherwise do with the time and money.

▶ **Scarcity and Choice in an Economy of Two or More**   Now suppose that another survivor of the crash, Colleen, appears on the island. Now that Bill is not alone things are more complex, and some new decisions must be made. Bill's and Colleen's preferences about what things to produce are likely to be different. They will probably not have the same knowledge or skills. Perhaps Colleen is very good at tracking animals, and Bill has a knack for building things. How should they split the work that needs to be done? Once things are produced, they must decide how to divide them. How should their products be distributed?

The mechanism for answering these fundamental questions is clear when Bill is alone on the island. The "central plan" is his; he simply decides what he wants and what to do about it. The minute someone else appears, however, a number of decision-making arrangements immediately become possible. One or the other may take charge, in which case that person will decide for both of them. The two may agree to cooperate, with each having an equal say, and come up with a joint plan. Or they may agree to split the planning, as well as the production duties. Finally, they may go off to live alone at opposite ends of the island. Even if they live apart, however, they may take advantage of each other's presence by specializing and trading.

Modern industrial societies must answer exactly the same questions that Colleen and Bill must answer, but the mechanics of larger economies are naturally more complex. Instead of two people living together, the United States has over 268 million. Still decisions must be made about what to produce, how to produce it, and who gets it.

➤ Specialization, Exchange, and Comparative Advantage The idea that members of society benefit by specializing in what they do best has a long history and is one of the most important and powerful ideas in all of economics. David Ricardo, a major nineteenth-century British economist, formalized the point precisely. According to Ricardo's **theory of comparative advantage**, specialization and free trade will benefit all trading parties, even when some are "absolutely" more efficient producers than others. Ricardo's basic point applies just as much to Colleen and Bill as it does to different nations.

theory of comparative advantage *Ricardo's theory that specialization and free trade will benefit all trading parties, even those that may be absolutely more efficient producers.*

To keep things simple, suppose that Colleen and Bill have only two tasks to accomplish each week: gathering food to eat and cutting logs to be used in constructing a house. If Colleen could cut more logs than Bill in one day, and Bill could gather more nuts and berries than Colleen could, specialization would clearly lead to more total production. Both would benefit if Colleen only cuts logs and Bill only gathers nuts and berries. But suppose that Bill is slow and somewhat clumsy in his nut-gathering and that Colleen is better at both cutting logs *and* gathering food. Ricardo points out that it still pays for them to specialize and exchange.

Suppose that Colleen can cut 10 logs per day and that Bill can cut only 5. Also suppose that Colleen can gather 10 bushels of food per day and that Bill can gather only 8 (see table embedded in Figure 2.2). Assume also that Bill and Colleen value bushels of food and logs equally. How then can the two gain from specialization and exchange? Think of opportunity costs. When Colleen gives up a day of food production to work on the house, she cuts 10 logs and sacrifices 10 bushels of food. The opportunity cost of 10 logs is thus 10 bushels of food if Colleen switches from food to logs. But because Bill can cut only 5 logs in a day, he has to work for 2 days to cut 10 logs. In 2 days, Bill could have produced 16 bushels of food (2 days × 8 bushels per day). The opportunity cost of 10 logs is thus 16 bushels of food if Bill switches from food to logs.

As Figure 2.2 makes clear, even though Colleen is *absolutely* more efficient at food production than Bill, she should specialize in logs and Bill should specialize in food. This way, the maximum number of logs and bushels are produced. A person or a country is said to have a comparative advantage in producing a good or service if it is *relatively* more efficient than a trading partner at doing so.

Looking at the same situation from the standpoint of food production leads to exactly the same conclusion. If Colleen were to switch from cutting logs to gathering food, she would sacrifice 10 logs to produce only 10 bushels of food. But if Bill were to switch from cutting logs to gathering food, he would sacrifice 10 logs to produce a full 16 bushels! Even though Colleen has an *absolute advantage* in both cutting logs and producing food, Bill has a *comparative advantage* producing food because, for the same sacrifice of logs, Bill produces much more food.

The theory of comparative advantage shows that trade and specialization work to raise productivity. But specialization may also lead to the development of skills that enhance productivity even further. By specializing in log cutting, Colleen will get even stronger shoulders. By spending more time at gathering food, Bill will refine his food-finding skills. The same applies to countries that engage in international trade.

The degree of specialization in modern industrial societies is breathtaking. Once again let your mind wander over the range of products and services available or under development today. As knowledge expands, specialization becomes a necessity. This is true not only for scientists and doctors but also in every career from tree surgeon to

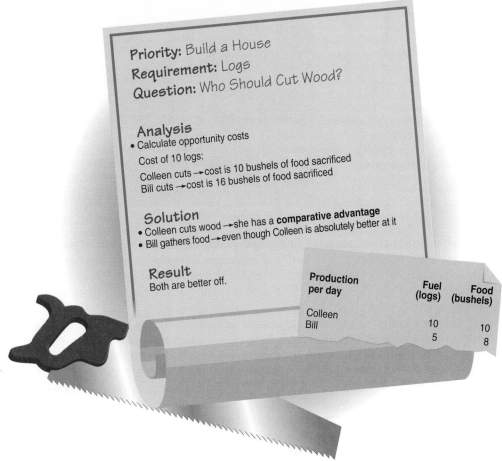

Priority: Build a House
Requirement: Logs
Question: Who Should Cut Wood?

Analysis
• Calculate opportunity costs

Cost of 10 logs:
Colleen cuts → cost is 10 bushels of food sacrificed
Bill cuts → cost is 16 bushels of food sacrificed

Solution
• Colleen cuts wood → she has a **comparative advantage**
• Bill gathers food → even though Colleen is absolutely better at it

Result
Both are better off.

Production per day	Fuel (logs)	Food (bushels)
Colleen	10	10
Bill	5	8

FIGURE 2.2
Comparative Advantage and Opportunity Costs

divorce lawyers. Understanding specialization and trade will help you to explain much of what goes on in today's global economy.

➤ **Weighing Present and Expected Future Costs and Benefits** Very often we find ourselves weighing benefits available today against benefits available tomorrow. Here too the notion of opportunity cost is helpful.

While alone on the island, Bill had to choose between cultivating a field and just gathering wild nuts and berries. Gathering nuts and berries provides food now; gathering seeds and clearing a field for planting will yield food tomorrow, if all goes well. Using today's time to farm may well be worth the effort if doing so will yield more food than Bill would otherwise have in the future. By planting, Bill is trading present value for future values.

The simplest example of trading present for future benefits is the act of saving. When I put income aside today for use in the future, I give up some things that I could have had today in exchange for something tomorrow. Because nothing is certain, some judgment about future events and expected values must be made. What will my income be in 10 years? How long am I likely to live?

We trade off present and future benefits in small ways all the time. If you decide to study rather than go to the dorm party, you are trading present fun for the expected future benefits of higher grades. If you decide to go outside on a very cold day and run five miles, you are trading discomfort in the present for being in better shape later on.

LEISURE IS NOT "COSTLESS." IT HAS AN OPPORTUNITY COST. LYING IN A HAMMOCK USES TIME THAT COULD HAVE BEEN USED TO DO OTHER THINGS.

> **Capital Goods and Consumer Goods** A society trades present for expected future benefits when it devotes a portion of its resources to research and development or to investment in capital. As we said earlier in this chapter, *capital* in its broadest definition is anything that has already been produced that will be used to produce other valuable goods or services over time.

Building capital means trading present benefits for future ones. Bill and Colleen might trade gathering berries or lying in the sun for cutting logs to build a nicer house in the future. In a modern society, resources used to produce capital goods could have been used to produce **consumer goods**—that is, goods for present consumption. Heavy industrial machinery does not directly satisfy the wants of anyone, but producing it requires resources that could instead have gone into producing things that do satisfy wants directly—food, clothing, toys, or golf clubs.

consumer goods *Goods produced for present consumption.*

Capital is everywhere. A road is capital. Once built, we can drive on it or transport goods and services over it for many years to come. A house is also capital. Before a new manufacturing firm can start up, it must put some capital in place. The buildings, equipment, and inventories that it uses are its capital. As it contributes to the production process, this capital yields valuable services through time.

In chapter 1 we talked about the enormous amount of capital—buildings, factories, housing, cars, trucks, telephone lines, and so forth—that you might see from a window high in a skyscraper. Much of it was put in place by previous generations, yet it continues to provide valuable services today; it is part of this generation's endowment of resources. To build every building, every road, every factory, every house, every car or truck, society must forgo using resources to produce consumer goods today. To get an education, I pay tuition and put off joining the workforce for a while.

Capital need not be tangible. When you spend time and resources developing skills or getting an education, you are investing in human capital—your own human capital. This capital will continue to exist and yield benefits to you for years to come. A computer program produced by a software company may come on a tangible disk that costs 75¢ to make, but its true intangible value comes from the ideas embodied in the program itself, which will drive computers to do valuable, time-saving tasks over time. It too is capital.

investment *The process of using resources to produce new capital.*

The process of using resources to produce new capital is called **investment**. (In everyday language, the term *investment* often refers to the act of buying a share of stock or a bond, as in "I invested in some Treasury bonds." In economics, however, investment *always* refers to the creation of capital: the purchase or putting in place of buildings, equipment, roads, houses, and the like.) A wise investment in capital is one that yields future benefits that are more valuable than the present cost. When you spend money for a house, for example, presumably you value its future benefits. That is, you expect to gain more from living in it than you would from the things you could buy today with the same money.

Because resources are scarce, the opportunity cost of every investment in capital is forgone present consumption.

THE PRODUCTION POSSIBILITY FRONTIER

A simple graphical device called the **production possibility frontier** (ppf) illustrates the principles of constrained choice, opportunity cost, and scarcity. The ppf is a graph that shows all the combinations of goods and services that can be produced if all of society's resources are used efficiently. Figure 2.3 shows a ppf for a hypothetical economy.

On the *Y* axis we measure the quantity of capital goods produced, and on the *X* axis, the quantity of consumer goods. All points below and to the left of the curve (the shaded area) represent combinations of capital and consumer goods that are possible for the society given the resources available and existing technology. Points above and to the right of the curve, such as point *G*, represent combinations that cannot be reached. If an economy were to end up at point *A* on the graph, it would be producing no consumer goods at all; all resources would be used for the production of capital. If an economy were to end up at point *B*, it would be devoting all of its resources to the production of consumer goods and none of its resources to the formation of capital.

While all economies produce some of each kind of good, different economies emphasize different things. About 16 percent of gross output in the United States in 1995 was new capital. In Japan, capital accounted for about 29 percent of gross output in 1995, while in Haiti the figure was 2 percent. Japan is closer to point *A* on its ppf, Haiti closer to *B*, and the United States is somewhere in between.

Points that are actually on the production possibility frontier are points of both full resource employment and production efficiency. (Recall from chapter 1 that an efficient economy is one that produces the things that people want at least cost. *Production efficiency* is a state in which a given mix of outputs is produced at least cost.) Resources are not going unused, and there is no waste. Points that lie within the shaded area, but that are not on the frontier, represent either unemployment of resources or production inefficiency. An economy producing at point *D* in Figure 2.3 can produce

production possibility frontier (ppf) *A graph that shows all the combinations of goods and services that can be produced if all of society's resources are used efficiently.*

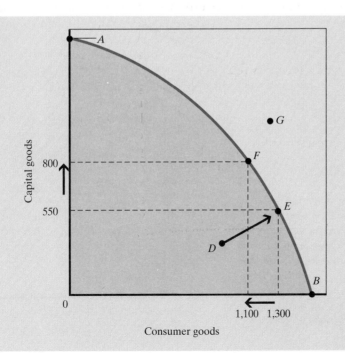

FIGURE 2.3
Production Possibility Frontier

The production possibility frontier illustrates a number of economic concepts. One of the most important is *opportunity cost*. The opportunity cost of producing more capital goods is fewer consumer goods. Moving from *E* to *F*, the number of capital goods increases from 550 to 800. But the number of consumer goods decreases from 1,300 to 1,100.

31

more capital goods and more consumer goods, for example, by moving to point *E*. This is possible because resources are not fully employed at point *D* or are not being used efficiently.

▶ **Unemployment**   During the Great Depression of the 1930s, the U.S. economy experienced prolonged unemployment. Millions of workers found themselves without jobs. In 1933, 25 percent of the civilian labor force was unemployed. This figure stayed above 14 percent until 1940, when increased defense spending by the United States created millions of jobs. In June of 1975, the unemployment rate went over 9 percent for the first time since the 1930s. In December of 1982, when the unemployment rate hit 10.8 percent, nearly 12 million were out looking for work. In June of 1992, the number of unemployed rose to just under 10 million.

In addition to the hardship that falls on the unemployed themselves, unemployment of labor means unemployment of capital. During downturns or recessions, industrial plants run at less than their total capacity. Clearly, when there is unemployment of labor and capital, we are not producing all that we can.

Periods of unemployment correspond to points inside the production possibility frontier, points like *D* in Figure 2.3. Moving onto the frontier from a point like *D* means achieving full employment of resources.

▶ **Inefficiency**   Although an economy may be operating with full employment of its land, labor, and capital resources, it may still be operating inside its production possibility frontier (at a point like *D* in Figure 2.3). It could be using those resources *inefficiently*.

Clearly, waste and mismanagement are the results of a firm operating below its potential. If I am the owner of a bakery and I forget to order flour, my workers and ovens stand idle while I figure out what to do. In 1997, Great Lakes Airways had to shut down operations for several weeks because its maintenance staff had been improperly trained.

Sometimes, inefficiency results from mismanagement of the economy rather than mismanagement of individual private firms. Suppose, for example, that the land and climate in Ohio are best suited for corn production, and the land and climate in Kansas are best suited for wheat production. If Congress passes a law forcing Ohio farmers to plant 50 percent of their acreage in wheat and Kansas farmers to plant 50 percent in corn, neither corn nor wheat production will be up to potential. The economy will be at a point like *A* in Figure 2.4—inside the production possibility frontier. Allowing

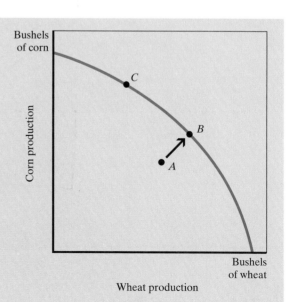

FIGURE 2.4

Inefficiency from Misallocation of Land in Farming

Society can end up inside its production possibility frontier at a point like *A* by using its resources inefficiently. If, for example, Ohio's climate and soil were best suited for corn production and those of Kansas were best suited for wheat production, a law forcing Kansas farmers to produce corn and Ohio farmers to produce wheat would result in less of both. In such a case, society might be at point *A* rather than point *B*.

each state to specialize in producing the crop that it produces best increases the production of both crops and moves the economy to a point like *B* in Figure 2.4.

> **The Efficient Mix of Output** To be efficient, an economy must produce what people want. This means that, in addition to operating *on* the ppf, the economy must be operating at the *right point* on the ppf. Suppose that an economy devotes 100 percent of its resources to beef production and that the beef industry runs efficiently, using the most modern techniques. But also suppose that everyone in the society is a vegetarian. The result is a total waste of resources (assuming that the society cannot trade its beef for vegetables produced in another country.)

Both points *B* and *C* in Figure 2.4 are points of production efficiency and full employment. Whether *B* is more or less efficient than *C*, however, depends on the preferences of members of society.

> **Negative Slope and Opportunity Cost** As we've seen, points that lie on the production possibility frontier represent points of full resource employment and production efficiency. But society can choose only one point on the curve. Because a society's choices are constrained by available resources and existing technology, when those resources are fully and efficiently employed it can produce more capital goods only by reducing production of consumer goods. The opportunity cost of the additional capital is the forgone production of consumer goods.

The fact that scarcity exists is illustrated by the negative slope of the production possibility frontier. (If you need a review of slope, see the appendix to chapter 1.) In moving from point *E* to point *F* in Figure 2.3, capital production *increases* by $800 - 550 = 250$ units (a positive change), but that increase in capital can be achieved only by shifting resources out of the production of consumer goods. Thus, in moving from point *E* to point *F* in Figure 2.3, consumer good production *decreases* by $1300 - 1100 = 200$ units of the consumer good (a negative change). The slope of the curve, the ratio of the change in capital goods to the change in consumer goods, is negative.[1]

> **The Law of Increasing Opportunity Costs** The negative slope of the ppf indicates the trade-off that a society faces between two goods. We can learn something further about the shape of the frontier and the terms of this trade-off. Let us look at the trade-off between corn and wheat production in Ohio and Kansas. In a recent year Ohio and Kansas together produced 510 million bushels of corn and 380 million bushels of wheat. Table 2.1 presents these two numbers, plus some hypothetical combinations of corn and wheat production that might exist for Ohio and Kansas together. Figure 2.5 graphs the data from Table 2.1.

TABLE 2.1 PRODUCTION POSSIBILITY SCHEDULE FOR TOTAL CORN AND WHEAT PRODUCTION IN OHIO AND KANSAS

POINT ON PPF	TOTAL CORN PRODUCTION (MILLIONS OF BUSHELS PER YEAR)	TOTAL WHEAT PRODUCTION (MILLIONS OF BUSHELS PER YEAR)
A	700	100
B	650	200
C	510	380
D	400	500
E	300	550

[1]The value of the slope of a society's production possibility frontier is called the *marginal rate of transformation (MRT)*. In Figure 2.3, the MRT between point *E* and point *F* is simply the ratio of the change in capital goods (a positive number) to the change in consumer goods (a negative number).

FIGURE 2.5

Corn and Wheat Production in Ohio and Kansas

The ppf illustrates that the opportunity cost of corn production increases as we shift resources from wheat production to corn production. Moving from *E* to *D*, we get an additional 100 million bushels of corn at a cost of 50 million bushels of wheat. Moving from *B* to *A*, we get only 50 million bushels of corn at a cost of 100 million bushels of wheat. The cost *per bushel* of corn—measured in lost wheat—has increased.

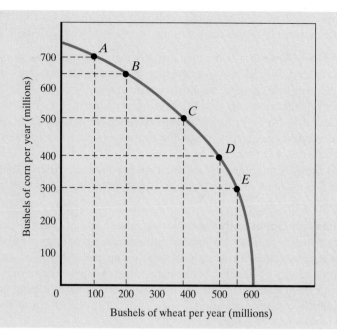

Suppose that society's demand for corn dramatically increases. If this happens, farmers would probably shift some of their acreage from wheat production to corn production. Such a shift is represented by a move from point *C* (where corn = 510, and wheat = 380) up and to the left along the ppf toward points *A* and *B* in Figure 2.5. As this happens, it becomes more and more difficult to produce additional corn. The best land for corn production was presumably already in corn, and the best land for wheat production already in wheat. As we try to produce more and more corn, the land is less and less well suited to that crop. And as we take more and more land out of wheat production, we will be taking increasingly better wheat-producing land. All of this is to say that the opportunity cost of more corn, measured in terms of wheat, increases.

Moving from *E* to *D*, Table 2.1 shows that we can get 100 million bushels of corn (400 − 300) by sacrificing only 50 million bushels of wheat (550 − 500)—that is, we get two bushels of corn for every bushel of wheat.[2] However, when we are already stretching the ability of the land to produce corn, it becomes more difficult to produce more, and the opportunity cost goes up. Moving from *B* to *A*, we can get only 50 million bushels of corn (700 − 650) by sacrificing 100 million bushels of wheat (200 − 100). For every bushel of wheat, we now get only half a bushel of corn. However, if the demand for *wheat* were to increase substantially and we were to move down and to the right along the production possibility frontier, it would become increasingly difficult to produce wheat, and the opportunity cost of wheat, in terms of corn, would rise. This is the *law of increasing opportunity cost*.

It is important to remember that the ppf represents choices available within the constraints imposed by the current state of agricultural technology. In the long run, technology may improve, and when that happens we have *growth*.

economic growth *An increase in the total output of an economy. It occurs when a society acquires new resources or when it learns to produce more using existing resources.*

▶ **Economic Growth** **Economic growth** is characterized by an increase in the total output of an economy. It occurs when a society acquires new resources or when society learns to produce more with existing resources. New resources may mean a larger

---

[2]This implies that the marginal rate of transformation is −2 between *D* and *E*. Change in corn = + 100; change in wheat = −50. MRT = +100/ −50 = −2.

TABLE 2.2 INCREASING PRODUCTIVITY IN CORN AND WHEAT PRODUCTION IN THE UNITED STATES, 1935–1995

	CORN		WHEAT	
	Yield Per Acre (Bushels)	Labor Hours Per 100 Bushels	Yield Per Acre (Bushels)	Labor Hours Per 100 Bushels
1935–1939	26.1	108	13.2	67
1945–1949	36.1	53	16.9	34
1955–1959	48.7	20	22.3	17
1965–1969	78.5	7	27.5	11
1975–1979	95.3	4	31.3	9
1981–1985	107.2	3	36.9	7
1985–1990	112.8	NA*	38.0	NA*
1990–1995	120.6	NA*	38.1	NA*

*Data not available.

Sources: U.S. Department of Agriculture, Economic Research Service, Agricultural Statistics, 1992; Statistical Abstract of the United States, 1996, Table 1105, p. 675.

labor force or an increased capital stock. The production and use of new machinery and equipment (capital) increases workers' productivity. (Give a man a shovel and he can dig a bigger hole; give him a steam shovel and wow!) Improved productivity also comes from technological change and *innovation*, the discovery and application of new, efficient production techniques.

The last 30 years have seen dramatic increases in the productivity of U.S. agriculture. Based on data compiled by the Department of Agriculture, Table 2.2 shows that yield per acre in corn production has increased fivefold since the late 1930s, while the labor required to produce it has dropped dramatically. Productivity in wheat production has also increased, at only a slightly less remarkable rate: Output per acre has almost tripled, while labor requirements are down nearly 90 percent. These increases are the result of more efficient farming techniques, more and better capital (tractors, combines, and other equipment), and advances in scientific knowledge and technological change (hybrid seeds, fertilizers, and so forth). As you can see in Figure 2.6, increases such as these shift the ppf up and to the right.

▶ **Sources of Growth and the Dilemma of the Poor Countries** Economic growth arises from many sources, the two most important of which, over the years, have been the accumulation of capital and technological advances. For poor countries, capital is essential; they must build the communication networks and transportation systems necessary to develop industries that function efficiently. They also need capital goods to develop their agricultural sectors.

Recall that capital goods are produced only at a sacrifice of consumer goods. The same can be said for technological advances. Technological advances come from research and development that uses resources; thus they too must be paid for. The resources used to produce capital goods—to build a road, a tractor, or a manufacturing plant—*and* to develop new technologies could have been used to produce consumer goods.

When a large part of a country's population is very poor, taking resources out of the production of consumer goods (such as food and clothing) is very difficult. In addition, in some countries those wealthy enough to invest in domestic industries choose instead to invest abroad because of political turmoil at home. As a result, it often falls to the governments of poor countries to generate revenues for capital production and research out of tax collections.

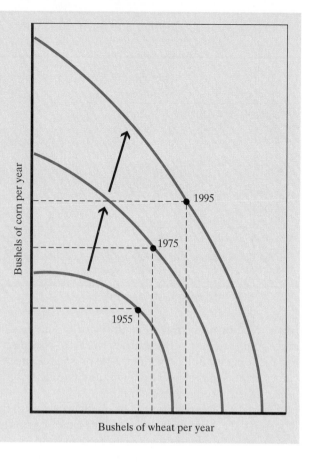

FIGURE 2.6

Economic Growth Shifts the ppf Up and to the Right
Productivity increases have enhanced the ability of the United States to produce both corn and wheat. As Table 2.2 shows, productivity increases were more dramatic for corn than for wheat. The shifts in the ppf were thus not parallel.

Note: The ppf also shifts if the amount of land or labor in corn and wheat production changes. Although we emphasize productivity increases here, the actual shifts between years were in part due to land and labor changes.

All these factors have contributed to the growing gap between some poor and rich nations. Figure 2.7 graphs the result, using production possibility frontiers. On the left, the rich country devotes a larger portion of its production to capital, while the poor country produces mostly consumer goods. On the right, you see the result: The ppf of the rich country shifts up and out farther and faster.

> Although it exists only as an abstraction, the production possibility frontier illustrates a number of very important concepts that we shall use throughout the rest of this book: scarcity, unemployment, inefficiency, opportunity cost, the law of increasing opportunity cost, and economic growth.

THE ECONOMIC PROBLEM

Recall the three basic questions facing all economic systems: (1) What will be produced? (2) How will it be produced? and (3) Who will get it?

When Bill was alone on the island, the mechanism for answering these questions was simple: He thought about his own wants and preferences, looked at the constraints imposed by the resources of the island and his own skills and time, and made his decisions. As he set about his work, he allocated available resources quite simply, more or less by dividing up his available time. Distribution of the output was irrelevant. Because Bill was the society, he got it all.

Introducing even one more person into the economy—in this case, Colleen—changed all that. With Colleen on the island, resource allocation involves deciding not only how each person spends time but also who does what; and now there are two sets of wants and preferences. If Bill and Colleen go off on their own and form two completely

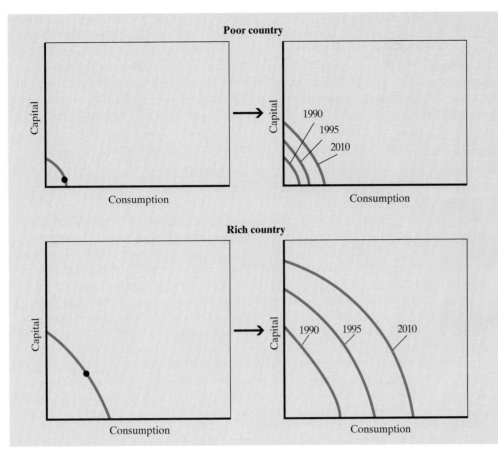

FIGURE 2.7

Capital Goods and Growth in Poor and Rich Countries

Rich countries find it easier to devote resources to the production of capital than poor countries do. But the more resources that flow into capital production, the faster the rate of economic growth. Thus the gap between poor and rich countries has grown over time.

Figure labels (clockwise): Poor country; Capital; Consumption; 1990, 1995, 2010; Rich country; Capital; Consumption; 1990, 1995, 2010.

separate self-sufficient economies, there will be lost potential. Clearly, two people can do many more things together than one person can do alone. They may use their comparative advantages in different skills to specialize. Cooperation and coordination may give rise to gains that would otherwise not be possible.

When a society consists of millions of people, the problem of coordination and cooperation becomes enormous, but so does the potential for gain. In large, complex economies, specialization can go wild, with people working in jobs as different in their detail as an impressionist painting is from a blank page. The range of products available in a modern industrial society is beyond anything that could have been imagined a hundred years ago, and so is the range of jobs.

The amount of coordination and cooperation in a modern industrial society is almost impossible to imagine. Yet something seems to drive economic systems, if sometimes clumsily and inefficiently, toward producing the things that people want. Given scarce resources, how, exactly, do large, complex societies go about answering the three basic economic questions? This is the **economic problem**, and this is what this text is about.

ECONOMIC SYSTEMS

Now that you understand the economic problem, we can explore how different economic systems go about answering the three basic questions.

COMMAND ECONOMIES

In a pure **command economy**, the basic economic questions are answered by a central government. Through a combination of government ownership of state enterprises and central planning, the government, either directly or indirectly, sets output targets, incomes, and prices.

economic problem *Given scarce resources, how exactly do large, complex societies go about answering the three basic economic questions?*

command economy *An economy in which a central government either directly or indirectly sets output targets, incomes, and prices.*

It is an understatement to say that planned economies have not fared well over the last decade. In fact, the planned economies of Eastern Europe and the former Soviet Union—including the Russian Republic—have completely collapsed. (Another former command economy, that of Poland, is doing somewhat better.) China remains committed to many of the principles of a planned economy, but reforms have moved it sharply away from pure central planning. For further information on the recent progress in Eastern Europe, see the Global Perspective feature, "Eastern Europe and Russia: A Mixed Progress Report."

LAISSEZ-FAIRE ECONOMIES: THE FREE MARKET

At the opposite end of the spectrum from the command economy is the **laissez-faire economy**. The term *laissez faire*, which, translated literally from French, means "allow [them] to do," implies a complete lack of government involvement in the economy. In this type of economy, individuals and firms pursue their own self-interest without any central direction or regulation; the sum total of millions of individual decisions ultimately determines all basic economic outcomes. The central institution through which a laissez-faire system answers the basic questions is the **market,** a term that is used in economics to mean an institution through which buyers and sellers interact and engage in exchange.

The interactions between buyers and sellers in any market range from simple to complex. Early explorers of the North American Midwest who wished to exchange with Native Americans did so simply by bringing their goods to a central place and trading them. Today, a jewelry maker in Maine may sell gold necklaces to a buyer through the Home Shopping Network that shows the product on television—customers call in orders and pay with a credit card. Ultimately, funds are transferred through a complicated chain of financial transactions. The result is that a buyer in Oakland, California, buys a necklace from an unseen jewelry producer in Maine.

In short:

> Some markets are simple and others are complex, but they all involve buyers and sellers engaging in exchange. The behavior of buyers and sellers in a laissez-faire economy determines what gets produced, how it is produced, and who gets it.

The following chapters explore market systems in great depth. A quick preview is worthwhile here, however.

➤ **Consumer Sovereignty** In a free, unregulated market, goods and services are produced and sold only if the supplier can make a profit. In simple terms, making a *profit* means selling goods or services for more than it costs to produce them. Clearly, you can't make a profit unless someone wants the product that you are selling. This logic leads to the notion of **consumer sovereignty:** The mix of output found in any free market system is dictated ultimately by the tastes and preferences of consumers, who "vote" by buying or not buying. Businesses rise and fall in response to consumer demands. No central directive or plan is necessary.

➤ **Individual Production Decisions: Free Enterprise** Under a free market system, individual producers must also figure out how to organize and coordinate the actual production of their products or services. The owner of a small shoe repair shop must buy the equipment and tools that she needs, hang signs, and set prices by herself. In a big corporation, so many people are involved in planning the production process that in many ways corporate planning resembles the planning in a command economy. In a free market economy, producers may be small or large. One person who hand paints eggshells may start to sell them as a business; a woman who has been showing her poodle may start handling other people's dogs in the show ring. On a larger scale, a group of furniture designers may put together a large portfolio of sketches, raise several million dollars, and start a bigger business. At the extreme are huge corporations like

EASTERN EUROPE AND RUSSIA: A MIXED PROGRESS REPORT

During the late 1980s, the command economies of Eastern Europe collapsed like a row of dominoes. The process began in November 1989, when the Berlin Wall, which had separated the communist East from the capitalist West for nearly 30 years, was torn down. Finally, in 1991, the once mighty Soviet Union disintegrated, ending 75 years of communism and nearly a half century of Cold War with the West.

A decade has passed, and the transition to a set of independent economies oriented to the market is nearly complete. But the road to prosperity has been uneven and quite rocky. Some countries, including Poland, Hungary, and the Czech Republic, are doing quite well. Poland, which was the first of the group to begin recording positive growth (in 1992), was growing at an annual rate of 7.3 percent in early 1997. However, poorer countries like Albania, Bulgaria, and Romania were still waiting for the first signs of growth:

With fading memories of the jubilation at the collapse of Communism seven years ago, there is a new divide—some call it the latter-day iron curtain—between have and have-not nations of Central and Eastern Europe. Only in the former does the joy remain.

The 1996 economic data show the division clearly. Foreign investment and rising buying power have transformed the larger cities of Hungary, the Czech Republic and Poland into places with many of the accouterments of the West: fast-food restaurants, self-service gas stations, Benetton stores and apartment complexes outfitted with satellite dishes.

More than $15 billion in foreign investment has poured into Hungary since 1990. In neighboring Romania, which has more than twice the people, only $2 billion has come in, and in Bulgaria, a paltry $700 million.

The average monthly wage in Poland is now well over $300, and people have access to adequate and cheap medical care. In chaotic Bulgaria . . . many hospitals lack even such basics as X-ray film.[a]

The biggest country making the transition was, of course, Russia. While slumping through the early and mid-1990s, Russia showed signs of life for the first time in 1997 when aggregate output rose. But deep problems and much uncertainty remain:

The officially recorded economy has been contracting for eight years in a row, leaving it at the end of 1996 at about half its size in 1989—a steeper fall than in America at the time of the Great Depression (though the black economy has expanded).

Meanwhile prices, unemployment and the tally of unpaid wages have been rising.

[Russia's] is now a market economy, whatever its imperfections. Moreover, much of the pain necessary to achieve such an economy may at last be over. In particular, inflation—enemy of the poor and destroyer of social stability—has dropped from 2,505% in 1992 to an annual rate of 15% in April this year.

Even more notable is the transfer of property into private hands—the biggest in history. In just three years after 1991, 120,000 enterprises changed from state to private ownership.

What all this adds up to is that 22% of Russians, or 32m people, are living below the official poverty line (defined as a minimum subsistence level of 394,000 rubles— $70—a month). Among other things, as Communists like to point out, this means falling meat and milk consumption: the average salary buys only about two-thirds as much meat as in Soviet days, and only about one-third as much milk.[b]

Sources: [a]Jane Perlez, "New Bricks, Same Old Walls for Europe's Poor Nations," *The New York Times*, Jan. 24, 1997, p. 1. Copyright © 1997 by The New York Times Co. Reprinted by permission. [b]"A Survey of Russia," *The Economist*, July 12, 1997, pp. 1–19.

 For more on the economies of Eastern Europe and Russia, see the Case and Fair Web page at http://www.prenhall.com/casefair.

IBM, Mitsubishi, and Exxon, each of which sells tens of billions of dollars' worth of products every year. Whether the firms are large or small, however, production decisions in a market economy are made by separate private organizations acting in what they perceive to be their own interests.

In a market economy, individuals seeking profits are free to start new businesses. Because new businesses require capital investment before they can begin operation, starting a new business involves risk. A well-run business that produces a product for which demand exists will succeed; a poorly run business or one that produces a product for which little demand exists is likely to fail. It is through *free enterprise* that new products and new production techniques find their way into use.

FREE ENTERPRISE "AFLOAT" IN SOUTHEAST ASIA.

price *The amount that a product sells for per unit. It reflects what society is willing to pay.*

Proponents of free market systems argue that free enterprise leads to more efficient production and better response to diverse and changing consumer preferences. If a producer produces inefficiently, competitors will come along, fight for the business, and eventually take it away. Thus in a free market economy, competition forces producers to use efficient techniques of production. It is competition, then, that ultimately dictates how outputs are produced.

➤ **Distribution of Output** In a free market system, the distribution of output—who gets what—is also determined in a decentralized way. The amount that any one household gets depends on its income and wealth. *Income* is the amount that a household earns each year. It comes in a number of forms: wages, salaries, interest, and the like. *Wealth* is the amount that households have accumulated out of past income through saving or inheritance.

To the extent that income comes from working for a wage, it is at least in part determined by individual choice. You will work for the wages available in the market only if these wages (and the things they can buy) are sufficient to compensate you for what you give up by working. Your leisure certainly has a value also. You may discover that you can increase your income by getting more education or training. You *can't* increase your income, however, if you acquire a skill that no one wants.

➤ **Price Theory** The basic coordinating mechanism in a free market system is price. A **price** is the amount that a product sells for per unit, and it reflects what society is willing to pay. Prices of inputs—labor, land, capital—determine how much it costs to produce a product. Prices of various kinds of labor, or *wage rates*, determine the rewards for working in different jobs and professions. Many of the independent decisions made in a market economy involve the weighing of prices and costs, so it is not surprising that much of economic theory focuses on the factors that influence and determine prices. This is why microeconomic theory is often simply called *price theory*.

In sum:

> In a free market system, the basic economic questions are answered without the help of a central government plan or directives. This is what the "free" in free market means—the system is left to operate on its own, with no outside interference. Individuals pursuing their own self-interest will go into business and produce the products and services that people want; others will decide whether to acquire skills or not, whether to work or not, and whether to buy, sell, invest, or save the income that they earn. The basic coordinating mechanism is price.

MIXED SYSTEMS, MARKETS, AND GOVERNMENTS

The differences between command economies and laissez-faire economies in their pure forms are enormous. But in fact these pure forms do not exist in the world; all real systems are in some sense "mixed." That is, individual enterprise exists and independent choice is exercised even in economies in which the government plays the major role.

Conversely, no market economies exist without government involvement and government regulation. The United States has basically a free market economy, but government purchases accounted for about 18 percent of its total production in 1997. The U.S. government directly employs about 16 percent of all workers, and taxes are about a third of the total income of the economy. The government also redistributes income by means of taxation and social welfare expenditures, and it regulates many economic activities.

One of the major themes in this book, and indeed in economics, is the tension between the advantages of free, unregulated markets and the need for government involvement. Advocates of free markets argue that such markets work best when left to themselves. They produce only what people want; without buyers, sellers go out of business. Competition forces firms to adopt efficient production techniques. Wage differentials lead people to acquire needed skills. Competition also leads to innovation in both production techniques and products. The result is quality and variety. But market systems have problems too.

> Even staunch defenders of the free enterprise system recognize that market systems are not perfect. First, they do not always produce what people want at lowest cost—there are inefficiencies. Second, rewards (income) may be unfairly distributed, and some groups may be left out. Third, periods of unemployment and inflation recur with some regularity.

Many people point to these problems as reasons for government involvement. Indeed, for some problems government involvement may be the only solution. But government decisions are made by people who presumably, like the rest of us, act in their own self-interest. While governments may indeed be called upon to improve the functioning of the economy, there is no guarantee that they will do so. Just as markets may fail to produce an allocation of resources that is perfectly efficient and fair, governments may fail to improve matters. We return to this debate many times throughout this text.

LOOKING AHEAD

This chapter has described the economic problem in broad terms. We have outlined the questions that all economic systems must answer. We also discussed very broadly the two kinds of economic systems. In the next chapter we turn from the general to the specific. There we discuss in some detail the institutions of U.S. capitalism: how the private sector is organized, what the government actually does, and how the international sector operates. Chapters 4 and 5 then begin the task of analyzing the way market systems work.

SUMMARY

1. Every society has some system or mechanism for transforming what nature and previous generations have provided into useful form. Economics is the study of that process and its outcomes.

2. *Producers* are those who take resources and transform them into usable products, or *outputs*. Private firms, households, and governments all produce something.

SCARCITY, CHOICE, AND OPPORTUNITY COST

3. All societies must answer *three basic questions:* What will be produced? How will it be produced? Who will get what is produced? These three questions make up the *economic problem.*

4. One person alone on an island must make the same basic decisions that complex societies make. When a society consists of more than one person, questions of distribution, cooperation, and specialization arise.

5. Because resources are scarce relative to human wants in all societies, using resources to produce one good or service implies *not* using them to produce something else. This

concept of *opportunity cost* is central to an understanding of economics.

6. Using resources to produce *capital* that will in turn produce benefits in the future implies *not* using those resources to produce consumer goods in the present.

7. Even if one individual or nation is absolutely more efficient at producing goods than another, all parties will gain if they specialize in producing goods in which they have a *comparative advantage.*

8. A *production possibility frontier* (ppf) is a graph that shows all the combinations of goods and services that can be produced if all of society's resources are used efficiently. The production possibility frontier illustrates a number of important economic concepts: scarcity, unemployment, inefficiency, increasing opportunity cost, and economic growth.

9. *Economic growth* occurs when society produces more, either by acquiring more resources or by learning to produce more with existing resources. Improved productivity may come from additional capital, or from the discovery and application of new, more efficient, techniques of production.

ECONOMIC SYSTEMS

10. In some modern societies, government plays a big role in answering the three basic questions. In pure *command economies*, a central authority directly or indirectly sets output targets, incomes, and prices.

11. A *laissez-faire economy* is one in which individuals independently pursue their own self-interest, without any central direction or regulation and ultimately determine all basic economic outcomes.

12. A *market* is an institution through which buyers and sellers interact and engage in exchange. Some markets involve simple face-to-face exchange; others involve a complex series of transactions, often over great distance or electronically.

13. There are no purely planned economies and no pure laissez-faire economies; all economies are mixed. Individual enterprise, independent choice, and relatively free markets exist in centrally planned economies, and there is significant government involvement in market economies such as that of the United States.

14. One of the great debates in economics revolves around the tension between the advantages of free, unregulated markets and the need for government involvement in the economy. Free markets produce what people want, and competition forces firms to adopt efficient production techniques. The need for government intervention arises because free markets are characterized by inefficiencies and an unequal distribution of income and experience regular periods of inflation and unemployment.

REVIEW TERMS AND CONCEPTS

capital, 25
command economy, 37
comparative advantage, theory of, 28
consumer goods, 30
consumer sovereignty, 38
economic growth, 34
economic problem, 37

investment, 30
laissez-faire economy, 38
market, 38
opportunity cost, 27
outputs, 25
price, 40

producers, 25
production, 25
production possibility frontier (ppf), 31
resources or inputs, 25
three basic questions, 26

PROBLEM SET

1. Define *capital*. What distinguishes land from capital? Is a tree capital?

2. "Studying economics instead of going to town and partying is like building a boat instead of lying on the beach." Explain this statement carefully, using the concepts of capital and opportunity cost.

3. Kristen and Anna live in the beach town of Santa Monica. They own a small business in which they make wristbands and potholders and sell them to people on the beach. Kristen can make 15 wristbands per hour, but only 3 potholders. Anna is a bit slower and can make only 12 wristbands or 2 potholders in an hour.

	OUTPUT PER HOUR	
	KRISTEN	ANNA
Wristbands	15	12
Potholders	3	2

  a. For Kristen, what is the opportunity cost of a potholder? For Anna? Who has a comparative advantage in the production of potholders? Explain.

  b. Who has a comparative advantage in the production of wristbands? Explain.

  c. Assume that Kristen works 20 hours per week in the business. If Kristen were in business on her own, graph the possible combinations of potholders and wristbands that she could produce in a week. Do the same for Anna.

  d. If Kristen devoted half of her time (10 out of 20 hours) to wristbands and half of her time to potholders, how many of each would she produce in a week? If Anna did the same thing, how many of each would she produce? How many wristbands and potholders would be produced in total?

  e. Suppose that Anna spent all 20 hours of her time on wristbands and Kristen spent 17 hours on potholders and 3 hours on wristbands. How many of each would be produced?

  f. Suppose that Kristen and Anna can sell all their wristbands for $1 each and all their potholders for $5.50 each. If each of them worked 20 hours per week, how should they split their time between wristbands and potholders? What is their maximum joint revenue?

4. Briefly describe the trade-offs involved in each of the following decisions. Specifically, list some of the opportunity costs associated with the decision, paying particular attention to the trade-offs between present and future consumption.
   a. After a stressful senior year in high school, Sherice decides to take the summer off rather than work before going on to college.
   b. Frank is overweight and decides to work out every day and to go on a diet.
   c. Mei is very diligent about taking her car in for routine maintenance, even though it takes two hours of her time and costs $100 four times each year.
   d. Jim is in a big hurry. He runs a red light on the way to work.

5. "If an economy is operating at a point inside its production possibility frontier, it must be the case that resources are unemployed." Do you agree or disagree?

6. Suppose that a simple society has an economy with only one resource, labor. Labor can be used to produce only two commodities—X, a necessity good (food), and Y, a luxury good (music and merriment). Suppose that the labor force consists of 100 workers. One laborer can produce either 5 units of necessity per month (by hunting and gathering) or 10 units of luxury per month (by writing songs, playing the guitar, dancing, and so on).
   a. On a graph, draw the economy's production possibility frontier. Where does the ppf intersect the Y axis? Where does it intersect the X axis? What meaning do those points have?
   b. Suppose the economy ended up producing at a point *inside* the ppf. Give at least two reasons why this could occur. What could be done to move the economy to a point *on* the ppf?
   c. Suppose you succeeded in lifting your economy to a point on its ppf. What point would you choose? How might your small society decide the point at which it wanted to be?
   d. Once you have chosen a point on the ppf, you still need to decide how your society's product will be divided up. If you were a dictator, how would you decide? What would happen if you left product distribution to the free market?

7. What progress has been made during the last year in Eastern Europe? Which countries are growing? Which are in decline? What factors seem to have contributed to the differences in success across countries?

*8. Match each diagram in Figure 1 with its description. Assume that the economy is producing or attempting to produce at point A, and most members of society like meat and not fish. Some descriptions apply to more than one diagram, and some diagrams have more than one description.

*Throughout the book, an asterisk designates a more challenging problem, as explained in the Preface.

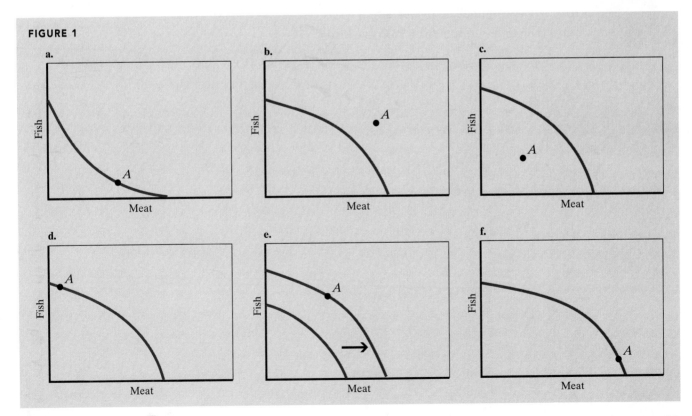

FIGURE 1

a. Inefficient production of meat and fish.
b. Productive efficiency.
c. An inefficient mix of output.
d. Technological advances in the production of meat and fish.
e. The law of increasing opportunity costs.
f. An impossible combination of meat and fish.

9. A nation with fixed quantities of resources is able to produce any of the following combinations of bread and ovens:

LOAVES OF BREAD (MILLIONS)	OVENS (THOUSANDS)
75	0
60	12
45	22
30	30
15	36
0	40

These figures assume that a certain number of previously produced ovens are available in the current period for baking bread.

a. Using the data in the table, graph the production possibilities frontier (with ovens on the vertical axis).

b. Does the principle of "increasing opportunity cost" hold in this nation? Explain briefly. (*Hint*: What happens to the opportunity cost of bread—measured in number of ovens—as bread production increases?)

c. If this country chooses to produce both ovens and bread, what will happen to the production possibilities frontier over time? Why?

d. A politician running for national office wants to reallocate resources to produce the maximum possible quantity of bread, with no production of ovens. His slogan is: "You can't eat ovens!" If this politician is successful, explain what will happen to the production possibilities curve over time. Why?

Now suppose that a new technology is discovered that allows twice as many loaves of bread to be baked in each existing oven.

e. Illustrate (on your original graph) the effect of this new technology on the production possibilities curve.

f. Suppose that before the new technology is introduced, the nation produces 22 ovens. After the new technology is introduced, the nation produces 30 ovens. What is the effect of the new technology on the production of bread? (Give the number of loaves before and after the change.)

TAKE IT TO THE NET

We invite you to visit the Case and Fair page on the Prentice Hall Web site:

http://www.prenhall.com/casefair

for this chapter's World Wide Web exercise.

Chapter 3

THE STRUCTURE OF THE U.S. ECONOMY: THE PRIVATE, PUBLIC, AND INTERNATIONAL SECTORS

THE PREVIOUS CHAPTER described the economic problem. All societies are endowed by nature and by previous generations with scarce resources. The production process combines and transforms these resources into goods and services that are demanded by the members of society.

At the end of chapter 2, we briefly described the economic systems that exist in the world today. This chapter describes the basic institutional structure of the U.S. economy in more detail. Because most production is undertaken by private individuals and organizations, we first look at the private sector. The **private sector** is made up of independently owned firms that exist to make a profit, nonprofit organizations, and individual households. It includes Chrysler Corporation, Occidental College, the Catholic Church, soybean farms in Iowa, the corner drugstore, and the babysitter down the street. The private sector is defined by independent ownership and control. In essence, it includes all the decision-making units within the economy that are not part of the government.

Next, we turn to a discussion of the public sector. The **public sector** is the government and its agencies at all levels—federal, state, and local. Government employees—tax assessors, public school teachers, post office workers, colonels in the army, Supreme Court justices, and the president—work in the public sector. Just as the Ford Motor Company uses land, labor, and capital to produce automobiles, the public sector uses land, labor, and capital to produce goods and services such as police and fire protection, education, and national defense. The public sector in the United States also produces some things that are simultaneously produced by the private sector. The post office provides overnight express-mail service that competes directly with similar services provided by private firms such as

private sector *Includes all independently owned profit-making firms, nonprofit organizations, and households; all the decision-making units in the economy that are not part of the government.*

public sector *Includes all agencies at all levels of government—federal, state, and local.*

FedEx and United Parcel Service. The University of Michigan, part of the public sector, directly competes for "buyers" of its "product" with private sector schools such as Northwestern University and Colorado College.

Finally, we provide a brief introduction to the **international sector** and discuss the importance of imports and exports to the U.S. economy. From any one country's perspective, the international sector consists of the economies of the rest of the world. Over the last several decades, the U.S. economy has become increasingly influenced by events abroad. The adoption of a common currency in Europe, the transfer of Hong Kong to the People's Republic of China, the elimination of farm subsidies in France, the end of a recession in Japan, and other global events all have important implications for the functioning of the U.S. economy. In a very real sense there is only one economy: the world economy.

Recall the distinction drawn in chapter 1 between descriptive economics and economic theory, and then notice what this chapter is not. We do not analyze behavior in this chapter. Here we describe institutions only as they exist. We also avoid normative distinctions. We do not talk about proper or improper roles of government in the economy, for example, or the things that governments might do to make the economy more efficient or fair.

international sector *From any one country's perspective, the economies of the rest of the world.*

THE PRIVATE SECTOR: U.S. BUSINESS AND INDUSTRIAL ORGANIZATION

How is business organized in the United States? Let us see first how the law permits *individual firms* to be organized. Then we can talk about the different ways that *industries* are structured. An individual firm's behavior depends on both its own legal structure and its relationship to other firms in its industry.

THE LEGAL ORGANIZATION OF FIRMS

Most private sector activity takes place within business firms that exist to make a profit. Some other private sector organizations that exist for reasons other than profit—clubs, cooperatives, and nonprofit organizations, for example—do produce goods or services. But because these organizations represent a small fraction of private sector activity, we focus here on profit-making firms.

> A business set up to make profits may be organized in one of three basic legal forms: (1) a proprietorship, (2) a partnership, or (3) a corporation. A single business may pass through more than one of these forms of organization during its development.

▶ **The Proprietorship**   The least complex and most common form a business can take is the simple **proprietorship**. There is no legal process involved in starting a proprietorship. You simply start operating. You must, however, keep records of revenues and costs and pay personal income taxes on your profit.

A professor who does consulting on the side, for example, receives fees and has costs (computer expenses, research materials, and so forth). This consulting business is a proprietorship, even though the proprietor is the only employee and the business is very limited. A large restaurant that employs hundreds of people may also be a proprietorship if it is owned by a single person. Many doctors and lawyers in private practice report their incomes and expenses as proprietors.

In a proprietorship, one person owns the firm. In a sense, that person *is* the firm. If the firm owes money, the proprietor owes the money; if the firm earns a profit, the proprietor earns a profit. There is no wall of protection between a proprietor and her business, as we will see there is between corporations and their owners.

proprietorship *A form of business organization in which a person simply sets up a business to provide goods or services at a profit. In a proprietorship, the proprietor (or owner) is the firm. The assets and liabilities of the firm are the owner's assets and liabilities.*

TABLE 3.1 NUMBER OF FIRMS AND SALES BY TYPE OF BUSINESS, 1993

	NUMBER OF FIRMS (THOUSANDS)	PERCENT OF TOTAL FIRMS	TOTAL SALES ($ BILLIONS)	PERCENT OF TOTAL SALES
Proprietorships	15,848	74.5	757	5.7
Partnerships	1,467	6.9	627	4.8
Corporations	3,965	18.6	11,814	89.5
Total	21,280	100.0	13,198	100.0

Source: Statistical Abstract of the United States, 1997, Table 833.

The Internal Revenue Service (IRS) estimates that there are over 15.8 million proprietorships in the United States. That is one for every 16 adults in the country. Most of these proprietorships are small; while they make up over 70 percent of all businesses, they account for only 5.7 percent of total sales (Table 3.1).

▶ **The Partnership** A **partnership** is a proprietorship with more than one proprietor. When two or more people agree to share the responsibility for a business, they form a partnership. Although no formal legal process is required to start this kind of business, most partnerships are based on agreements signed by all the partners. These agreements detail who pays what part of the costs and how profits shall be divided. Because profits from partnerships are taxable, accurate records of receipts and expenditures must be kept and each party's profits must be reported to the Internal Revenue Service.

In a partnership, as in a proprietorship, there is no limit to the liability of the owners (that is, the partners) for the firm's debts. But with a partnership each partner is both *jointly* and *separately* liable for all the debts of the partnership. What does this mean? If you own one third of a partnership that goes out of business with a debt of $300,000, you owe your creditors $100,000, and so does each of your partners. But if your partners skip town, you owe the entire $300,000.

Just under 7 percent of all firms in the United States are partnerships, and they account for only 4.8 percent of total sales (see again Table 3.1).

▶ **The Corporation** A **corporation** is a formally established legal entity that exists separately from those who establish it and those who own it. To establish a corporation, a corporate charter must be obtained from a state government. In most states this is quite easily accomplished. A lawyer simply fills out the appropriate paperwork and files it with the right state agency, along with certain fees. When a corporation is formed, **shares of stock** (certificates of partial ownership) are issued and either sold or assigned. A corporation is owned by its shareholders, who are in a sense partners in the firm's success or failure. Each share of stock entitles the holder to a portion of the corporation's profits. Shareholders differ from simple partners, however, in two important ways. First, the liability of shareholders is limited to the amount they paid for the stock. If the company goes out of business or bankrupt, the shareholders may lose what they have invested, but no more than that. They are *not* liable for the corporation's debts beyond the amount they invested. Second, the federal government and all but four states levy special taxes on corporations. These government bodies do not levy special taxes on proprietors and partners.

The federal corporate income tax is a tax on the **net income**, or profits, of corporations. The tax is 15 percent of net income on the first $50,000, but it rises to 25 percent for taxable income between $50,000 and $75,000 and to 34 percent after income exceeds $75,000. (In 1993, as part of President Clinton's deficit reduction package, the top rate was raised to 35 percent on taxable net income over $10 million.) Actually,

partnership *A form of business organization in which there is more than one proprietor. The owners are responsible jointly and separately for the firm's obligations.*

corporation *A form of business organization resting on a legal charter that establishes the corporation as an entity separate from its owners. Owners hold shares and are liable for the firm's debts only up to the limit of their investment, or share, in the firm.*

share of stock *A certificate of partial ownership of a corporation. Entitles the holder to a portion of the corporation's profits.*

net income *The profits of a firm.*

TABLE 3.2   THE DISTRIBUTION OF CORPORATE PROFITS IN 1997

	BILLIONS OF DOLLARS	PERCENT OF BEFORE-TAX PROFIT
Profits before tax	729.8	100.0
Minus profits tax liability	−249.4	−34.2
Profits after tax	480.4	65.8
Minus dividends paid	−336.1	−46.1
Undistributed profits	144.3	19.7

Source: U.S. Department of Commerce, Bureau of Economic Analysis.

dividends *The portion of a corporation's profits that the firm pays out each period to shareholders. Also called* distributed profits.

99 percent of all corporate net income is taxed at the 35 percent rate. In essence, this means that tax is paid twice on corporate net income: once by the corporation when it pays tax on its profits, and again by the shareholders when they pay personal income tax on their **dividends**—that is, the share of profits they receive from the corporation each period.

The special privilege granted to corporations limiting their liability is often called a *franchise*. Some view the corporate tax as a payment to the government in exchange for limited liability status. In New York State, the state corporation tax is actually called the franchise tax.

Corporate net income is usually divided into three pieces. Some of it is paid to federal and state governments in the form of taxes. Some of it is paid out to shareholders as dividends (sometimes called *distributed profits*). And some of it usually stays within the corporation to be used for the purchase of capital assets. This part of corporate profits is called **retained earnings**, or *undistributed profits*.

retained earnings *The profits that a corporation keeps, usually for the purchase of capital assets. Also called* undistributed profits.

In 1997, U.S. corporations earned total profits of $729.8 billion. Out of this, $249.4 billion in taxes were paid, leaving $480.4 billion in after-tax profits. Of this amount, $336.1 billion was paid out to shareholders and the rest, $144.3 billion, was retained. In percentage terms, taxes accounted for 34.2 percent, while shareholders directly received 46.1 percent of total profits (Table 3.2). Turning again to Table 3.1, in 1993 there were about 4 million corporations, just under 20 percent of all firms. But these 4 million firms accounted for almost 90 percent of total sales.

Many corporations are very large. Each year *Fortune* magazine publishes a list of the 500 largest industrial corporations in the United States. Topping the *Fortune* 500 in 1997 was General Motors. GM's total sales in 1996 were more than $168 billion. The company employed over 647,000 people that year!

The internal organization of a firm, whether it is a proprietorship, a partnership, or a corporation, affects its behavior and the behavior of potential investors. For example, because they are protected by a corporation's limited liability status, potential investors may be more likely to back high-risk but potentially high-payoff corporate ventures.

Although a firm's internal structure is important, it is less important to an understanding of a firm's behavior than the organization of the industry or the market in which the firm competes. For example, whether it is a proprietorship or a corporation, a firm with little or no competition is likely to behave differently from a firm facing stiff competition from many rivals. With this in mind, we now expand our focus from the individual firm to the industry.

industry *A group of firms that produce a similar product. The boundaries of a "product" can be drawn very widely ("agricultural products"), less widely ("dairy products"), or very narrowly ("cheese"). The term* industry *can be used interchangeably with the term* market.

THE ORGANIZATION OF INDUSTRIES

The term **industry** is used loosely to refer to groups of firms that produce similar products. Industries can be defined narrowly or broadly, depending on the issue being discussed. For example, a company that produces and packages cheese is a part of the

PART ONE
*Introduction
to Economics*

cheese industry, the dairy products industry, the food products industry, and the agricultural products industry.[1]

Whether we define industries broadly or narrowly, how firms within any industry behave depends on how that industry is organized. When we speak of **market organization** we refer to the way an industry is structured: how many firms there are in an industry, whether products are virtually the same or differentiated, whether or not firms in the industry can control prices or wages, whether or not competing firms can freely enter and leave the industry, and so forth. The kind of industry—or *market*—in which a firm operates determines, in large part, how it will behave.

In the discussion that follows, we analyze industries as if their structures fit their definitions precisely. In reality, however, industries are not always easy to categorize. Nonetheless, these categories provide a useful and convenient framework.

▶ **Perfect Competition**   At one end of the market-organization spectrum is the competitive industry, in which many relatively small firms produce nearly identical products. **Perfect competition** is a very precisely defined form of industry structure. (The word *perfect* here does not refer to virtue. It simply means "total," or "complete.") In a perfectly competitive industry, no single firm has any control over prices. That is, no single firm is large enough to affect the market price of its product or the prices of the inputs that it buys. This crucial observation follows from two characteristics of competitive industries. First, a competitive industry is composed of many firms, each small relative to the size of the industry. Second, every firm in a perfectly competitive industry produces exactly the same product; the output of one firm cannot be distinguished from the output of the others. Products in a perfectly competitive industry are said to be **homogeneous**.

These characteristics limit the decisions open to competitive firms and simplify the analysis of competitive behavior. Because all firms in a perfectly competitive industry produce virtually identical products, and because each firm is small relative to the market, perfectly competitive firms have no control over the prices at which they sell their output. Taking prices as a given, then, each firm can decide only how much output to produce and how to produce it.

Consider agriculture, the classic example of a perfectly competitive industry. A wheat farmer in South Dakota has absolutely no control over the price of wheat. Prices are determined not by the individual farmers but rather by the interaction of many suppliers and many demanders. The only decisions left to the wheat farmer are how much wheat to plant and when and how to produce the crop.

Another mark of perfectly competitive industries is ease of entry. *Ease of entry* means that new firms can easily enter a market and compete for profits. No barriers exist to prevent new firms from competing. New firms can, and do, frequently enter such industries in search of profits, whereas others go out of business when they suffer losses. For example, anyone who has been to Seattle, Washington, recently knows the importance of coffee. Several years ago, a firm called Starbucks opened a series of gourmet coffee shops in the city. Within a short while, business was booming, and Starbucks was making enormous profits. The success of Starbucks attracted competition, and hundreds of new firms entered the market during the 1990s. Entry was easy: After all, to sell coffee all you need is a place to do business, a coffee maker, perhaps an espresso machine, and some effort. Today, Seattle's landscape is filled with coffee and espresso signs; even McDonald's sells gourmet coffee there. Starbucks has expanded nationwide, and it is likely to attract competition wherever it goes because entry into the market is easy.

When a firm *exits* an industry, it simply stops producing a product. Sometimes an exiting firm goes out of business altogether. During the last 10 years, for example,

---

[1]The U.S. Department of Commerce has devised a code system, the Standard Industrial Classification (S.I.C.) System, which defines industries at various levels of detail.

market organization *The way an industry is structured. Structure is defined by how many firms there are in an industry, whether products are differentiated or are virtually the same, whether or not firms in the industry can control prices or wages, and whether or not competing firms can enter and leave the industry freely.*

perfect competition *An industry structure in which there are many firms, each small relative to the industry, producing virtually identical products and in which no firm is large enough to have any control over prices. In perfectly competitive industries, new competitors can freely enter and exit the market.*

homogeneous products *Undifferentiated outputs; products that are identical to, or indistinguishable from, one another.*

FAST FACTS

The percentage of U.S. workers employed in agriculture has dropped steadily over the years. In 1840, the figure was above 68%. By 1997, it had dropped to 2.6%:

1840	68.6%
1870	53.0%
1900	37.5%
1940	20.1%
1950	12.2%
1960	8.3%
1970	4.4%
1980	3.4%
1990	2.7%
1997	2.6%

Sources: Historical Statistics of the United States, 1789–1945, Tables D1–10 (For 1840–1900 data); Economic Report of the President, 1998, p. 322 (For 1940–1997 data).

IN COMPETITIVE MARKETS, NEW FIRMS CAN ENTER AN INDUSTRY WITH RELATIVE EASE AND COMPETE FOR PROFITS. HUNDREDS OF NEW UPSCALE COFFEE SHOPS HAVE ENTERED THE MARKET TO COMPETE WITH STARBUCKS.

thousands of small farmers have gone out of business, sold off their assets, paid what bills they could, and disappeared.

To summarize:

> Perfectly competitive industries are made up of many firms, each small relative to the size of the total market. In these industries, individual firms do not distinguish or differentiate their products from those of their competitors. Product prices are determined by market forces and are virtually unaffected by decisions of any single firm. Entry into and exit from the market are relatively easy.

monopoly *An industry structure in which there is only one large firm that produces a product for which there are no close substitutes. Monopolists can set prices but are subject to market discipline. For a monopoly to continue to exist, something must prevent potential competitors from entering the industry and competing for profits.*

barrier to entry *Something that prevents new firms from entering and competing in an industry.*

➤ **Monopoly** At the other end of the spectrum is **monopoly**, a market or industry in which only one firm produces a product for which there are no close substitutes.

When there is only one firm in a market, that firm sets the price of its product. This does not mean, however, that monopolies can set any price they please. Even if a firm produces a product that everyone likes, the firm gains nothing if it charges a price so high that no one buys it. Thus, even a monopolist is subject to discipline imposed by the market.

For a monopoly to remain a monopoly, it must find some way to keep other firms from entering its market and competing for profits. Often governments erect such **barriers to entry**. Sometimes they grant an exclusive license to one producer. In Taiwan, for example, the national government licensed only one company to produce beer and prohibited beer imports until 1987. In the United States, public utilities—electric power and gas companies, for example, most of which are privately owned—have traditionally been shielded by the government from competition. For many years the American Telephone and Telegraph Company was essentially the exclusive producer of telephone services, both local and long distance. However, dramatic changes in the telecommunications industry, including the breakup of AT&T by the courts in 1983, have made that market much more competitive. In 1998, competition was even introduced into increasingly deregulated electricity and natural gas markets.

Sometimes monopolies are specific to a particular time and location. Professional sports teams sign exclusive vendor agreements for games. Most often, for example, a single vendor will be responsible for food and beverage sales at a pro football game. Because most stadiums do not permit you to bring food and beverages into a game, the vendor is providing a service for which there is no close substitute, and entry is blocked. Have you ever noticed the price of food and drinks at a pro ballgame?

In sum:

> A monopoly is a one-firm industry that produces a product for which there are no close substitutes. Such a firm can set price, but its pricing behavior is constrained by its market: It can sell a product only if people are willing to buy it. A monopolist is protected from competition by barriers to entry.

▶ **Monopolistic Competition** Somewhere between monopoly and competition, but much closer to competition, is a very common hybrid market organization called **monopolistic competition**. In a monopolistically competitive industry, many firms compete for essentially the same customers, but each firm produces a slightly different product. If these firms can *differentiate* their products successfully, they establish a *brand loyalty* that allows them to enjoy the benefits of a monopoly. Procter & Gamble is the only producer of Ivory Soap—it "monopolizes" the market for Ivory—but the soap business is still very competitive because many close substitutes are available. Prentice Hall is the only company that can sell this book, but there are many other economics texts.

Although individual firms in perfectly competitive markets have no control over price, monopolistic competitors do exercise some price-setting power. That control is quite limited, however, because of the many close substitutes available. Monopolistically competitive firms are thus subject to a great deal of "market discipline."

A good example of monopolistic competition can be found in the music industry. Every rock band has a unique style; each has its own name. Entry is relatively inexpensive; all you need are musicians, instruments, amplifiers, and a P.A. system. Thinking of each band as a small firm, management differentiates the product in an attempt to compete, and the competition is fierce. Very successful rock bands are more like monopolies, however; there are no "close" substitutes for R.E.M., U2, or the Rolling Stones.

In monopolistically competitive industries, there is both price and quality competition. Firms often enter these industries because they have an idea for a new product that represents a slight variation or improvement on an old one. Perhaps the purest example of a monopolistically competitive market is the restaurant industry. Every major city in the world contains hundreds and hundreds of restaurants, each producing a slightly differentiated product in a highly competitive way. The cosmetics and clothing industries are also monopolistically competitive. Firms in such industries must decide on output, price, and quality of product.

Free, or at least relatively easy, entry and exit characterize monopolistic competition. When a firm enjoys success in one of its product lines, its profits invite new firms to come into its market with new brands or styles. Many new restaurants are born every year and many unsuccessful ones quietly expire.

To summarize:

> Monopolistically competitive firms contain large numbers of relatively small firms. Unlike firms in perfectly competitive industries, monopolistically competitive firms differentiate their products. Individual firms produce unique products and thus, despite their small size, exercise some control over price. Entry and exit are relatively easy.

▶ **Oligopoly** An industry in which there are only a small number of firms is an **oligopoly**. For example, the automobile industry in the United States has only three major U.S. competitors and a few smaller ones. A total of eight firms produce 100 percent of all the primary copper produced in the United States, and four large firms control 87 percent of the breakfast cereal industry. Except for the fact that each contains only a few competitors, however, oligopolistic industries have little in common. In some, products are highly differentiated (automobiles and cereal, for example); in others,

monopolistic competition
An industry structure in which many firms compete, producing similar but slightly differentiated products. There are close substitutes for the product of any given firm. Monopolistic competitors have some control over price. Price and quality competition follows from product differentiation. Entry and exit are relatively easy, and success invites new competitors.

oligopoly *An industry structure with a small number of (usually) large firms producing products that range from highly differentiated (automobiles) to standardized (copper). In general, entry of new firms into an oligopolistic industry is difficult but possible.*

TABLE 3.3 CHARACTERISTICS OF DIFFERENT MARKET ORGANIZATIONS

	NUMBER OF FIRMS	PRODUCTS DIFFERENTIATED OR HOMOGENEOUS	FIRMS HAVE PRICE-SETTING POWER	EASY ENTRY	DISTINGUISHING CHARACTERISTICS	EXAMPLES
Perfect competition	Many	Homogeneous	No	Yes	Price competition only	Wheat farmer Textile firm
Monopolistic competition	Many	Differentiated	Yes, but limited	Yes	Price and quality competition	Restaurants Music industry
Oligopoly	Few	Either	Yes	Limited	Strategic behavior	Breakfast cereal Primary copper
Monopoly	One	A unique, single product	Yes	No	Still constrained by market demand	Public utility Beverage vendor at a pro football game

they are not (the steel industry, for example). In some, the industry is dominated by one very large firm; in others, the participating firms are of roughly equal size and have roughly equal power.

Oligopolies behave unpredictably. In markets where two or three large rivals compete head-on, the competing firms often execute strategies that anticipate counterstrategies. In setting price, for example, one firm must take into account how its competitors in the oligopoly are likely to react. One firm's action usually triggers a reaction from another, which in turn triggers still another reaction, and so on. The strategies and counterstrategies employed by these firms determine who gets the sales. As a result, oligopolies are characterized by a great deal of uncertainty, and it is difficult to generalize about their behavior.

Entry into an oligopolistic industry is usually possible, but difficult. Because firms in oligopolies are generally large, a large initial investment is usually required to break in.

In sum:

> Oligopolies are industries with a few large firms, but beyond that it is hard to generalize. In some oligopolies, firms differentiate their products; in others, they do not. Individual firms do exercise control over prices and generally behave "strategically" with respect to one another.

The four main kinds of market organization in the United States are summarized in Table 3.3.

HOW COMPETITIVE IS THE U.S. ECONOMY?

In an article published in the early 1980s, William G. Shepherd provides some evidence on the extent of competition in the U.S. economy.[2] Shepherd defines four market types that correspond roughly to the categories we have just defined: (1) pure monopolies, (2) industries with dominant firms, (3) tight oligopolies, and (4) effectively competitive industries.

In Shepherd's classification scheme, monopolies are just as we described them. One firm accounts for 100 percent (or nearly 100 percent) of an industry's total sales. No close substitutes for its product exist and entry to the market is blocked. Industries with dominant firms are near monopolies. In such industries, the dominant firm accounts for 50 percent to 90 percent of total industry sales, no close

[2]William G. Shepherd, "Causes of Increased Competition in the U.S. Economy, 1939–1980," *Review of Economics and Statistics* LXIV (November 1982), 613–626.

TABLE 3.4 TRENDS IN COMPETITION IN THE U.S. ECONOMY, 1939–1980

	1939	1958	1980
Pure monopoly	6.2	3.1	2.5
Dominant firm	5.0	5.0	2.8
Tight oligopoly	36.4	35.6	18.0
Effectively competitive firms	52.4	56.3	76.7
Total	100.0	100.0	100.0

Note: Percentage share of national income by industry category.

Source: William G. Shepherd, "Causes of Increased Competition in the U.S. Economy, 1939–1980," *Review of Economics and Statistics* LXIV (November 1982), 613–626.

rivals exist, and entry to the market is difficult. Tight oligopolies are industries in which the top four firms account for over 60 percent of total sales and in which entry barriers are high. Shepherd lumps all other firms together in the "effectively competitive" category.

The classification "effectively competitive" signifies more than just perfect competition. It also includes all of what we described as monopolistic competition. In Shepherd's effectively competitive group, the top four firms control less than 40 percent of the market, and entry barriers are low.

Table 3.4, based on Shepherd's estimates, shows what happened to the level of competition in the U.S. economy between 1939 and 1980. Pure monopolies, a category that includes most public utilities and some patented goods, accounted for only 2.5 percent of total national income in 1980, down from 6.2 percent in 1939. In fact, purely monopolistic and dominant-firm industries together accounted for just a little over 5 percent of national income in 1980. In contrast, 76.7 percent of national income originated in sectors that Shepherd classifies as effectively competitive, up from 52.4 percent in 1939. The estimates indicate that the percentage of national income originating in tight oligopolies was cut in half between 1958 and 1980.

The U.S. economy has apparently become more competitive over the years. A number of factors may have contributed to this change. Without going into detail here, these factors include increased competition from imports, deregulation (particularly in the trucking, airline, and telecommunications industries), and enforcement of antimonopoly laws.

STRUCTURAL CHANGE SINCE 1970

Table 3.5 gives a breakdown of employment by major product type or industry. These data point to a number of important changes. First, the percentage of the total employment accounted for by manufacturing has been continuously shrinking for 30 years.

TABLE 3.5 PERCENTAGE OF NONAGRICULTURAL EMPLOYMENT BY SECTOR, 1970–1997

	MANUFACTURING	WHOLESALE AND RETAIL TRADE	SERVICES	GOVERNMENT	CONSTRUCTION	FINANCIAL INSURANCE AND REAL ESTATE	OTHER
1970	28.3	21.1	16.1	17.7	4.6	5.1	7.1
1980	23.1	22.5	19.3	18.0	4.6	5.6	6.9
1990	17.7	23.7	25.2	17.0	4.5	6.1	5.8
1997	15.3	23.7	28.8	16.4	4.3	5.9	5.6

Source: Department of Labor, Bureau of Labor Statistics, 1997 Benchmark Revisions; authors' tabulation.

The decline since 1970 has been due in part to increased competition from abroad: Americans buy a tremendous number of products, including automobiles, textiles, televisions, VCRs, cameras, and machine tools, from Korea, Japan, and Taiwan. One of the biggest-selling new manufactured items in the United States today is the fax machine. But even though the fax machine was invented in the United States, not a single machine is currently manufactured in the United States. By 1997, manufacturing had dropped to only 15.3 percent of U.S. nonagricultural jobs.

The fastest growing sector of the U.S. economy has been the service sector. Americans eat at restaurants, stay at hotels, and consume recreation, entertainment, and personal services at a far greater rate than ever before. In addition to personal services, business services are an important part of the service sector. Business services include consulting, software production, and legal services—all of which have been growing in recent years.

One frequently voiced concern is that "good" jobs are being lost and replaced by "bad" ones. Manufacturing in the United States has traditionally been a high-wage sector. Most people who work in plants receive substantial hourly wages. As manufacturing has declined, though, more and more jobs have opened up in the expanding service sector, where hourly wages have traditionally been lower. But recent data show that this situation is changing. The service sector is now generating more high-paying jobs. For more details, see the Application feature titled "The Changing Mix of Jobs in the United States."

Although some people are deeply concerned over this structural change in the U.S. economy, others see it as a natural consequence of continued economic growth and progress. As recently as 1870, agriculture accounted for 22 percent of national income and more than half of employment. But as farmers learned more and more productive farming methods, the need for farm labor declined, and so did food prices. With lower food prices, people could spend their incomes on other things—manufactured goods and services. Because agriculture needed fewer workers, labor was available for employment in the new expanding sectors. By 1997, fewer than 3 percent of American workers were in agriculture. Thus as the U.S. economy grew and developed, some sectors, such as agriculture, shrank in relative importance and others, such as manufacturing and services, grew in relative importance.

THE SERVICE SECTOR HAS BEEN GROWING FASTER THAN MANUFACTURING OVER THE LAST SEVERAL DECADES. HOWEVER, THE SERVICE SECTOR IS MORE THAN JUST FAST FOOD. SOFTWARE DEVELOPMENT IS PART OF THE SERVICE SECTOR, AND IT REQUIRES SKILLED WORKERS AND PAYS HIGH WAGES.

THE CHANGING MIX OF JOBS IN THE UNITED STATES

As the following excerpt from a recent article from the *New York Times* points out, you shouldn't believe everything you hear about the current job situation in the United States:

> The notion that Americans are working more for less pay is firmly embedded in public rhetoric. And it is practically gospel that the growing American economy cannot deliver the higher pay that American workers want.
>
> No doubt many Americans are losing ground economically. But in fact most of the jobs the economy has added in the last [few] years are in occupations that pay more, not less, than the average, which is now about $15.50 an hour.
>
> [In 1994 alone], 72 percent of the 2.5 million new jobs [were] for managers, from the chief executive to the branch sales manager, and for professionals, from surgeons and nurses to software programmers, accountants and high school teachers. And despite its reputation for low wages, the service sector is adding most of the higher-wage jobs.
>
> As a result, average hourly pay for all employees . . . is slowly rising, government data show, not falling as so many politicians and commentators have been saying. Average hourly compensation, which includes health benefits, paid vacations, pensions and other benefits, is also rising. . . .
>
> The source of much of the improvement is the service sector, which is supposed to have been producing only low-wage jobs like hamburger flipping and baby-sitting.

Source: Sylvia Nasar, "Statistics Reveal Bulk of New Jobs Pay Over Average," *The New York Times,* Oct. 17, 1994, p. A1. Copyright © 1994 by The New York Times Co. Reprinted by permission.

For more on the changing mix of jobs in the United States, see the Case and Fair Web page at **http://www.prenhall.com/casefair.**

Modern economies are in a continuous state of change. Resources are always moving. In the process, the basic industrial structure changes. The purpose of this book is to help you understand this process. Why are new firms formed? Why do others go out of business? Why are some sectors expanding while others are contracting?

THE PUBLIC SECTOR: TAXES AND GOVERNMENT SPENDING

Thus far we have talked only about the sets of decisions facing private firms. But this is only part of the story. Although the U.S. economy is basically a market economy, it also has a public sector that plays a major role in determining the allocation of resources, the mix of output, and the distribution of rewards. To understand the workings of any economic system, it is necessary to understand the role of government—the public sector.

Government in the United States operates on three different levels—federal, state, and local. Each of these levels has assumed a different set of functions and responsibilities over the years, and although there is some overlap, each level derives its main revenues from different sources. How big is this public sector? What does it spend its money on, and where does it get its money?

THE SIZE OF THE PUBLIC SECTOR

An economy's **gross domestic product**, or **GDP**, is the total value of all goods and services produced in the economy in a given period of time, say, a year. The concept of GDP is used extensively in macroeconomics. Here it is enough to say that GDP is used as a measure of a nation's total annual output. As you can see from Figure 3.1, public expenditure at all levels, as a percentage of GDP, increased from 19.3 percent in 1940 to 34.8 percent in 1990, then dropping slightly to 33.8 percent in 1997. The federal portion of total expenditures increased more rapidly, more than doubling

gross domestic product (GDP) *The total value of all goods and services produced by a national economy within a given time period.*

FIGURE 3.1

Total Government Expenditure as a Percentage of GDP, 1940–1997

Total government expenditures grew from 19.3% of GDP in 1940 to 34.8% in 1990. Since 1990, the percentage has fallen slightly. The share of state and local governments grew only slightly, but the federal share more than doubled.

Sources: U.S. Department of Commerce, Bureau of Economic Analysis. Grants to states and localities included in federal.

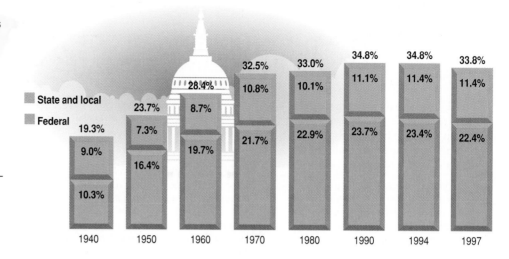

government consumption and investment *A category of government spending that includes the portion of national output that the government uses directly—ships for the navy, memo pads for the FBI, salaries for government employees.*

government transfer payments *Cash payments made by the government directly to households for which no current services are received in return. They include social security benefits, unemployment compensation, and welfare payments.*

government interest payments *Cash payments made by the government to those who own government bonds.*

since 1940, whereas the state and local share grew only from 9.0 percent of GDP to 11.4 percent in the same period.[3]

Government spending can be broken into three major categories: consumption and investment, transfer payments to households, and interest payments. **Consumption and investment** make up that portion of national output that government actually uses directly. They include the airplanes purchased from McDonnell Douglas by the air force, the new Senate office building (in the year that it was built), and the paper, books, and pens produced by private companies that are used by government employees. This category also includes the wages and salaries paid for the services of government employees. Table 3.6 shows that government nondefense consumption and investment as a percentage of GDP have remained roughly constant since 1970. Government defense consumption and investment as a percentage of GDP have decreased substantially since 1960.

Transfer payments are cash payments made directly to households—social security benefits, unemployment compensation payments, welfare payments, and so forth. The government receives no current services in return for these payments. **Interest payments** are also cash payments, but they are paid to those who own government bonds. Table 3.6 shows that both transfer payments and interest payments as a percentage of GDP have increased sharply since 1960.

The increase in the size of the social security system accounts for much of the increase in transfer payments. Social security is a self-financing system in which benefits are paid out of taxes contributed by workers and their employers. Some have argued that because workers who have contributed will ultimately be entitled to benefits, the system should be separated from other federal receipts and expenditures for accounting purposes, but this has not been done so far.

As Table 3.6 shows, interest payments in 1990 almost doubled as a percentage of GDP over the 1980 level. This is because of the huge deficits run up during the early 1980s. When the government spends more than it taxes, it must borrow. It does so by issuing bonds, and it must pay interest on the bonds. The percentage has dropped slightly since 1990.

Another way to look at the relative size of the public sector is to look at government employment as a percentage of total employment (see again Table 3.6). In 1997, federal government civilian employment was only 2.1 percent of total employment. In addition,

[3]Federal grants to state and local governments are included as a federal expenditure rather than a state and local expenditure because they are paid for out of federal tax revenues.

TABLE 3.6 THE SIZE OF THE PUBLIC SECTOR, 1940–1997

Government Expenditure as a Percentage of GDP

	1940	1950	1960	1970	1980	1990	1994	1997
Total	19.3	23.7	28.4	32.5	33.0	34.8	34.8	33.8
Consumption and investment, nondefense	12.3	9.2	11.1	14.0	14.3	14.0	13.9	13.6
Consumption and investment, defense	2.5	6.8	10.4	8.7	6.3	6.5	5.0	4.3
Transfer payments	2.7	6.1	5.6	8.1	11.4	11.8	13.6	13.7
Interest payments (net)	1.2	1.5	1.3	1.2	1.2	2.2	2.1	2.0

Government Employment as a Percentage of Total Employment (Excluding Military) in the Economy

	1950	1960	1970	1980	1990	1994	1997
Total	13.3	15.4	17.7	18.0	16.6	16.8	15.3
Federal	4.2	4.2	3.8	3.2	2.8	2.5	2.1
State and local	9.1	11.2	13.9	14.8	13.8	14.3	13.2

Sources: U.S. Department of Commerce, Bureau of Economic Analysis and Bureau of Labor Statistics.

federal civilian employment as a percentage of total employment in the United States has fallen steadily since 1950. State and local government employment grew steadily as a fraction of total employment in the economy through 1980. Since 1980, however, it has dropped back to about the 1970 level. Total government employment in 1997 was 15.3 percent of total employment in the economy, down from 18.0 percent in 1980.

How big is the public sector in the United States relative to the public sectors in other countries? Good statistics on employment and spending are not easy to find, but Figure 3.2 presents some international comparisons based on taxes collected. (Taxes

FIGURE 3.2

Taxes as a Percentage of Gross Domestic Product, 1980 and 1994

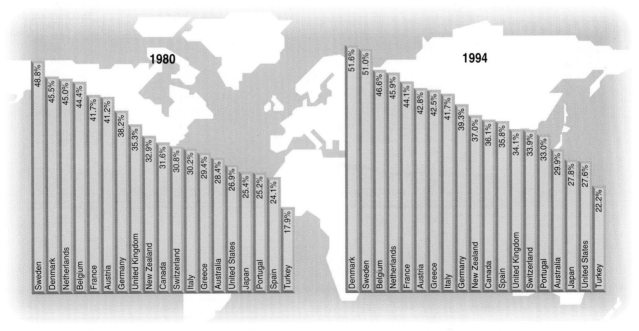

Source: Statistical Abstract of the United States, 1994, p. 867, 1997, p. 844.

are used as the basis of comparison because they support the public sector's activities, and tax data are easy to find.) The figure shows total national and local taxes as a percentage of gross domestic product (GDP).

In 1980, U.S. federal, state, and local taxes amounted to 26.9 percent of GDP. This placed the United States fifteenth among the 19 countries in the comparison. Between 1980 and 1994, taxes as a percentage of GDP increased in all 19 countries except the United Kingdom. The smallest increase for the 18 countries that had increases was registered in the United States, where taxes as a percentage of GDP rose only .7 percentage points. As of 1994, only Turkey, among this group of more developed countries, had lower taxes as a percentage of GDP than the United States.

GOVERNMENT EXPENDITURES

The detailed breakdown of federal expenditures for fiscal year 1997 in Table 3.7 shows that the top six categories account for over 88 percent of the total. National defense and social security alone account for nearly 40 percent of federal spending. Table 3.8 compares the same categories for 1985 and 1997. With the end of the Cold War, expenditures for national defense have been shrinking sharply. Expenditures for Medicare and health have been growing rapidly. The crisis in health-care costs that is such an important issue today is evident in these numbers. Medicare and health-care expenditures taken together rose from 10.5 percent of total expenditures in 1985 to 19.7 percent of total expenditures in 1997.

TABLE 3.7   FEDERAL EXPENDITURES BY FUNCTION, 1997

	BILLIONS OF DOLLARS	PERCENTAGE OF TOTAL
Social security	367.7	22.5
National defense	267.2	16.4
Net interest	247.4	15.2
Income security	238.9	14.6
Medicare	194.3	11.9
Health	127.6	7.8
Education, training, employment	51.3	3.1
Veterans benefits	39.7	2.4
Transportation	39.3	2.4
Natural resources environment	22.8	1.4
Administration of justice	20.8	1.3
Science, space, and technology	16.6	1.0
International affairs	14.8	.9
General governments	13.1	.8
Community and regional development	12.8	.8
Agriculture	10.3	.6
Miscellaneous and offsetting receipts	−53.6	−3.1
Total	1631.0	100.0

Source: Statistical Abstract of the United States, 1997, Table 520.

PART ONE
*Introduction
to Economics*

TABLE 3.8

FEDERAL EXPENDITURES BY FUNCTION:
PERCENTAGE SHARES OF TOTAL
COMPARED FOR 1985 AND 1997

	1985	1997	CHANGE IN SHARE
National defense	26.7	16.4	−10.3
Social security	19.9	22.5	+2.6
Net interest	13.7	15.2	+1.5
Income security	13.5	14.6	+1.1
Medicare	7.0	11.9	+4.9
Health	3.5	7.8	+4.3
All other	15.7	11.6	−4.1
Total	100.0	100.0	

Source: Statistical Abstract of the United States, 1997, Table 520, 1994, Table 509.

Table 3.9 shows state and local government spending by category in 1994. In that year, 32.9 percent of all state and local spending went for education—mostly public elementary and secondary education, although all states spend money on higher education as well. Since 1980, education and highways have contracted as a portion of total spending, while interest on debt, public welfare, and health and hospitals have assumed a significantly larger share.

SOURCES OF GOVERNMENT REVENUE

A breakdown of the sources of federal tax revenues appears in Table 3.10. The biggest single source of revenue for the federal government is the *individual income tax*, which accounted for 44.5 percent of total revenues in 1980. That figure dropped slightly to 43.7 percent in 1997. Federal income tax is withheld from most people's pay each week by their employers, who send it to the Internal Revenue Service. Self-employed people are responsible for sending in their own estimated taxes four times each year.

TABLE 3.9 STATE AND LOCAL EXPENDITURES BY FUNCTION, 1980 AND 1994

	PERCENTAGE OF TOTAL, 1980	PERCENTAGE OF TOTAL, 1994	BILLIONS OF DOLLARS, 1994
Education	36.3	32.9	353.3
Public welfare	12.4	16.7	179.8
Health and hospitals	8.8	9.3	100.4
Highways	9.1	6.7	72.1
Interest on debt	4.0	5.1	55.0
Police and fire	5.2	5.1	54.8
General administration	1.8	1.9	20.6
Other[a]	22.4	22.3	238.0
Total	100.0	100.0	1,074.0

[a]*Includes parks, sanitation, and housing, among other areas.*

Source: Statistical Abstract of the United States, 1997, p. 304.

TABLE 3.10 FEDERAL RECEIPTS BY SOURCE, 1980 AND 1997

	1980		1997	
	Billions of Dollars	Percent	Billions of Dollars	Percent
Individual income taxes	249.7	44.5	753.8	43.7
Corporate income taxes	70.3	12.5	211.9	12.3
Social insurance taxes	195.3	34.8	645.9	37.5
Excise taxes	32.5	5.8	71.6	4.2
Gift and estate taxes	6.5	1.2	20.6	1.2
Customs duties	7.2	1.2	19.7	1.1
Total	561.5	100.0	1,723.5	100.0

Source: U.S. Department of Commerce, Bureau of Economic Analysis.

social insurance, or payroll, taxes *Taxes levied at a flat rate on wages and salaries. Proceeds support various government-administrated social-benefit programs, including the social security system and the unemployment benefits system.*

Social insurance taxes are levied at a flat rate on wages and salaries up to a maximum amount. Because these taxes are figured as a percentage of wages and salaries and are levied on both employers and employees, they are also known as **payroll taxes.** The payroll tax is levied at a flat rate of 7.65 percent on employees and another 7.65 percent on employers. Self-employed persons pay between 12.8 percent and 14.2 percent depending on their income.

Social insurance taxes go into one of several trust funds that pay social security cash and health benefits to retirees, the disabled, and the survivors of workers who paid into the system. Payroll taxes also fund the unemployment compensation system.

Payroll taxes now account for a much larger portion of federal revenues than they have in the past. In 1997, they brought in 37.5 percent of total federal revenues, up from 34.8 percent in 1980. In 1965, they brought in only 21 percent of total revenues (not shown in Table 3.10). The payroll tax rate has been increased steadily because of worries about the future solvency of the system. A huge number of people will reach retirement age soon after the year 2000. At the same time, the labor force will be smaller. Because the tax rate required to support the increasing number of elderly then would be intolerable, the rate was sharply increased during the 1970s. It continues to increase now, in order to generate a surplus in the social security trust funds that should prevent the system's collapse in the future.

corporate income taxes *Taxes levied on the net incomes of corporations.*

Corporate income taxes are levied on the net income of corporations only, not on the profits of other forms of business organization (proprietorships and partnerships), which are taxed directly as ordinary personal income to the owners. Although payroll taxes have been increasing as a share of total tax revenues, corporate income taxes have had their ups and downs. In 1960, they accounted for about 22 percent of federal revenues. Table 3.10 shows that they accounted for 12.5 percent in 1980 and 12.3 percent in 1997. Big cuts came in 1981 when Congress enacted the Economic Recovery Tax Act, designed to stimulate business investment. The Tax Reform Act of 1986 sharply reduced personal income taxes and partly offset the lost revenues by increasing the corporation tax. The net effect is that the share of corporate taxes was about the same in 1997 as in 1980.

excise taxes *Taxes on specific commodities.*

Excise taxes make up only about 4.2 percent of the federal total. These are taxes on specific commodities like cigarettes, alcoholic beverages, gasoline, tires and tubes, and telephone service.

The sources of state and local revenues in 1997 appear in Table 3.11. Sales taxes, levied primarily by states, account for 23.6 percent of the total. Property taxes, 19.1

TABLE 3.11 STATE AND LOCAL TAX RECEIPTS, 1997

	BILLIONS OF DOLLARS	PERCENT OF TOTAL TAXES
Sales taxes	257.4	23.6
Property taxes	208.8	19.1
Personal income taxes	159.8	14.7
Social insurance taxes	86.2	7.9
Corporate taxes	37.6	3.4
Federal grants	224.2	20.6
Other	116.5	10.7
Total	1,090.5	100.0

Sources: U.S. Department of Commerce, Bureau of Economic Analysis.

percent of the total, are levied primarily by local governments (such as counties, cities, and towns) on the estimated, or "assessed," value of commercial, industrial, and residential property. Personal income taxes account for 14.7 percent of state and local revenues, social insurance taxes 7.9 percent and corporate taxes 3.4 percent. Of total state and local revenue, 20.6 percent comes in the form of federal grants.

THE INTERNATIONAL SECTOR: IMPORTS AND EXPORTS

One of the great economic lessons of the 1970s and 1980s was that all economies, regardless of their size, depend to some extent on other economies and are affected by events outside their borders. Ask anyone in Iowa about the impact of foreign trade on farm prices and, therefore, on the well-being of U.S. farmers. Or ask steelworkers in Pittsburgh and Youngstown about the effect of cheap German and Japanese steel on the economies of those towns. One of the most controversial trade issues in recent years was the North American Free Trade Agreement (NAFTA), which was signed by President Bush in December 1992, and approved by the Congress in 1993. The purpose of NAFTA is to reduce trade barriers between the United States, Canada, and Mexico. In 1995, the Congress ratified the General Agreement on Tariffs and Trade (GATT), also designed to reduce trade barriers, after extended and often bitter debate.

The U.S. economy is by no means "closed." Thousands of transactions between the United States and virtually every country in the world take place daily. In 1997 the United States sold $51.3 billion in agricultural products to the rest of the world and bought about $70.8 billion in petroleum products from other countries. Overall, the United States imported $1,058.8 billion worth of goods and services in 1997, 13.1 percent of its GDP.

The growth of the international sector of the U.S. economy is a relatively recent phenomenon. Prior to 1970, imports and exports of goods and services accounted for a relatively small and stable fraction of U.S. GDP. Table 3.12 shows imports and exports for selected years since 1929. Between 1929 and 1970, imports were less than 6 percent of GDP. During the Depression and immediately following World War II, imports were even below 4 percent of GDP.

TABLE 3.12 U.S. IMPORTS AND EXPORTS OF GOODS AND SERVICES, 1929–1997

	EXPORTS OF GOODS AND SERVICES		IMPORTS OF GOODS AND SERVICES	
	Billions of Dollars	Percentage of GDP	Billions of Dollars	Percentage of GDP
1929	5.9	5.7	5.6	5.4
1933	2.0	3.6	1.9	3.4
1945	6.7	3.0	7.5	3.4
1955	17.6	4.2	17.2	4.1
1960	25.3	4.8	22.8	4.3
1965	35.4	4.9	31.5	4.4
1970	57.0	5.5	55.8	5.4
1974	124.3	8.3	127.5	8.5
1976	148.9	8.2	151.1	8.3
1978	186.1	8.1	212.3	9.3
1980	278.9	10.0	293.8	10.6
1981	302.8	9.7	317.8	10.2
1982	282.6	8.7	303.2	9.4
1983	277.0	7.9	328.6	9.3
1984	303.1	7.8	405.1	10.4
1985	303.0	7.2	417.2	10.0
1986	320.7	7.3	452.2	10.2
1987	365.7	7.8	507.9	10.8
1988	447.2	8.9	553.2	11.0
1989	509.3	9.4	589.7	10.8
1990	557.3	9.7	628.6	10.9
1991	601.8	10.2	622.3	10.5
1992	639.4	10.2	669.0	10.7
1993	658.6	10.0	719.3	11.0
1994	721.2	10.4	812.1	11.7
1995	818.4	11.3	904.5	12.4
1996	870.9	11.4	965.7	12.6
1997	958.0	11.9	1,058.8	13.1

Source: U.S. Department of Commerce, Bureau of Economic Analysis.

Beginning in 1970, however, the volume of international trade increased significantly. Imports and exports doubled as a percentage of GDP by the end of the 1970s. Imports reached more than 10 percent by 1980. Exports dropped to 7.2 percent in 1985, but rebounded to 10 percent by 1991. There has been a substantial increase in both exports and imports since 1994.

▶ **The Composition of U.S. Trade** Table 3.13 lists the types of merchandise the United States imported and exported in 1997. Perhaps the most surprising thing about this merchandise is its tremendous diversity.

The largest category—42.9 percent of U.S. exports and 28.6 percent of U.S. imports—is capital goods except automotive, a very broad category that includes many specialized and diverse products. The second most important category of U.S. exports is industrial supplies and materials—$152.7 billion in 1997. In third place is consumer goods except automotive, followed in fourth place by automobiles.

TABLE 3.13 MAJOR CATEGORIES OF MERCHANDISE IMPORTS AND EXPORTS BY THE UNITED STATES, 1997

EXPORTS	BILLIONS OF DOLLARS	PERCENTAGE OF TOTAL
Agricultural products	58.3	8.5
Nonagricultural products	628.2	91.5
Total	686.5	100.0
Food, feeds, and beverages	51.0	7.4
Industrial supplies and materials	152.7	22.2
Capital goods except automotive (machinery, aircraft, etc.)	294.5	42.9
Automobiles, vehicles, parts, and engines	73.7	10.8
Consumer goods except automotive	77.5	11.3
All other	37.1	5.4
Total	686.5	100.0

IMPORTS	BILLIONS OF DOLLARS	PERCENTAGE OF TOTAL
Petroleum and petroleum products	72.1	8.1
Nonpetroleum products	816.6	91.9
Total	888.7	100.0
Petroleum and petroleum products	72.1	8.1
Food, feeds, and beverages	39.7	4.5
Industrial supplies and materials	135.1	15.2
Capital goods except automotive (machinery, aircraft, etc.)	254.1	28.6
Automobiles, vehicles, parts, and engines	141.3	15.9
Consumer goods except automotive	192.9	21.7
All other	53.5	6.0
Total	888.7	100.0

Sources: U.S. Department of Commerce, Bureau of Economic Analysis.

Prior to 1970, imports of petroleum and petroleum products never amounted to more than $3 billion annually and were never more than 10 percent of total imports. The rapid increase in oil prices in 1973 to 1974 changed all this. By 1980 crude oil accounted for nearly a third of total imports. But in the early 1980s the United States began to cut its consumption of petroleum. By 1988, petroleum and natural gas accounted for only 8.8 percent of total imports. With the 1990 invasion of Kuwait, oil prices rose and the dollar volume of imports jumped back to over 12 percent of the total. After the Persian Gulf War, prices again fell and the figure dropped back to 8.1 percent in 1997.

Another important category of imports that has received a great deal of attention because of its impact on major U.S. industries is automobiles. In 1997 imports of automobiles and parts totaled $141.3 billion.

FROM INSTITUTIONS TO THEORY

This chapter has sketched the institutional structure of the U.S. economy. As we turn to economic theory, both positive and normative, you should reflect on the basic realities of economic life in the United States presented here. Why is the service sector expanding and the manufacturing sector contracting? Why is the public sector as large as it is? What economic functions does it perform? What determines the level of imports and exports? What effects do cheap foreign products have on the U.S. economy?

One of the most important questions in economics concerns the relative merits of public sector involvement in the economy. Should the government be involved in the economy, or should the market be left to its own devices? Before we can confront these and other important issues, we need to establish a theoretical framework. Our study of the economy and its operation begins in chapter 4 with the behavior of suppliers and demanders in private markets.

SUMMARY

1. The *private sector* is made up of privately owned firms that exist to make a profit, nonprofit organizations, and individual households. The *public sector* is the government and its agencies at all levels—federal, state, and local. The *international sector* is the global economy. From any one country's perspective, the international sector consists of the economies of the rest of the world.

THE PRIVATE SECTOR: U.S. BUSINESS AND INDUSTRIAL ORGANIZATION

2. A *proprietorship* is a firm with a single owner. A *partnership* has two or more owners. Proprietors and partners are fully liable for all the debts of the business. A *corporation* is a formally established legal entity that limits the liability of its owners. The owners are not responsible for the debts of the firm beyond what they invest.

3. The term *industry* is used loosely to refer to groups of firms that produce similar products. Industries can be broadly or narrowly defined. A company that produces cheese belongs to the cheese industry, the dairy industry, the food products industry, and the agricultural products industry.

4. In *perfect competition*, no single firm has any control over prices. This follows from two characteristics of this industry structure: (1) Perfectly competitive industries are composed of many firms, each small relative to the size of the industry, and (2) each firm in a perfectly competitive industry produces exactly the same product—that is, products are *homogeneous*.

5. A *monopoly* is an industry structure in which only one firm produces a product for which there are no close substitutes. To remain a monopoly in a profitable industry, a firm must be able to block the entry of competing firms.

6. In *monopolistic competition*, many firms compete, but each firm produces a slightly different product. Although each firm's product is unique, there are many close substitutes. Entering and exiting monopolistically competitive industries are relatively easy.

7. An *oligopoly* is an industry with a small number of firms. In general, entry of new firms into an oligopolistic industry is difficult but possible.

THE PUBLIC SECTOR: TAXES AND GOVERNMENT SPENDING

8. Public expenditures at all levels increased from 19.3 percent of GDP in 1940 to 33.8 percent in 1997. The federal portion of total expenditures grew more rapidly than the state and local portion, more than doubling since 1940.

9. Other measures of the size of the public sector have not increased as rapidly. Government employment increased slightly, from 13.3 percent of total employment in 1950 to 15.3 percent in 1997.

10. National defense and social security account for nearly 40 percent of federal spending. The top four categories of state and local spending are education, public welfare, health and hospitals, and highways.

11. Individual income taxes and social insurance taxes together accounted for about 81 percent of federal revenues in 1997. Over the last quarter century, social insurance taxes have increased dramatically as a portion of total federal revenues. Sales taxes and property taxes accounted for about 43 percent of state and local revenues in 1997.

THE INTERNATIONAL SECTOR: IMPORTS AND EXPORTS

12. Thousands of transactions between the United States and virtually every other country in the world take place daily. This has led to the increased importance of the international sector in the U.S. economy. In 1997, the United States imported $1,058.8 billion worth of goods and services, 13.1 percent of its GDP.

REVIEW TERMS AND CONCEPTS

barrier to entry, 50

corporate income taxes, 60

corporation, 47

dividends, 48

excise taxes, 60

government consumption and investment, 56

government interest payments, 56

government transfer payments, 56

gross domestic product (GDP), 55

homogeneous products, 49

industry, 48

international sector, 46

market organization, 49

monopolistic competition, 51

monopoly, 50

net income, 47

oligopoly, 51

partnership, 47

perfect competition, 49

private sector, 45

proprietorship, 46

public sector, 45

retained earnings, 48

share of stock, 47

social insurance, or payroll, taxes, 60

PROBLEM SET

1. Health care continues to be a major issue in U.S. society. Look up the latest figures on health-care expenditures as a percentage of GDP. What share of total government expenditure (federal, state, and local) is devoted to health care?

2. The figures presented in Table 3.4 suggest that the U.S. economy is becoming more competitive. Does your experience over the last few years seem to support this conclusion? Can you think of specific industries or markets that have become or are becoming more competitive?

3. Do a short research project on one of the following large government programs. What does the program accomplish or hope to accomplish? What is the basic logic for government involvement? How much was spent on the program in 1998 compared to 1980?
   a. Medicare
   b. Medicaid
   c. Social security
   d. State colleges and universities
   e. Student financial aid
   f. Aid to Families with Dependent Children (AFDC)
   g. Food stamps
   h. Interstate highways

4. The Congress debated the GATT in 1994 and approved it in 1995. What groups in the United States were opposed to its passage? Why? What are the basic arguments in favor of the GATT? The basic arguments against it?

5. State whether each of the following industries is essentially competitive, monopolistically competitive, oligopolistic, or monopolistic. Your answer should be based on your impressions as a buyer of goods or services or on what you know about the industry, not on research. Briefly explain your answer.
   a. The hotel/motel industry
   b. The cable television industry
   c. The shampoo industry
   d. The airline industry
   e. The hamburger industry
   f. The higher education (college and university) industry

6. The chapter contains conflicting evidence on whether the public sector has expanded relative to the rest of the economy in the last 20 to 30 years. What figures might be quoted in support of the proposition that it has expanded? Do they tell the whole story? Discuss.

7. What are the differences between a proprietorship and a corporation? If you were going to start a small business, which form of organization would you choose? What are the advantages and disadvantages of the two forms of organization?

8. "Most firms are corporations, but they account for a relatively small portion of total output in the United States." Do you agree or disagree with this statement? Explain your answer.

9. In 1997 shareholders directly received only 37.8 percent of total corporate profits. What happened to the rest?

10. Perfectly competitive industries are made up of large numbers of firms, each small relative to the size of the industry and each producing homogeneous products. What does this imply about an individual firm's ability to influence price? Explain your answer.

11. How is a monopolistically competitive industry like a monopoly? In what ways is it like a perfectly competitive industry?

12. How is it possible for government spending to increase as a percentage of GDP while taxes and government employment are both decreasing?

13. Why is the federal government spending much more on interest payments now than it was a decade ago? Explain.

14. Of the items that you buy frequently or services that you spend money on, which ones are produced in the United States and which are imported? Of the major industries in your home state, which produce products or services that are exported?

15. It is sometimes argued that the government's practice of awarding patents (exclusive rights) to inventors and producers of products creates monopoly power and deprives consumers of the advantages of free competition. The argument surfaces frequently in discussions about the prescription drug market. For example, if a researcher were to discover a cure for AIDS and procure a patent, she would be a monopolist, and she'd be able to charge a very high price for her product. Do you agree with this argument? What is the rationale for issuing patents? If you were to procure a patent on a new formula for a lovely new perfume, would you be a monopolist? Explain your answers.

TAKE IT TO THE NET

We invite you to visit the Case and Fair page on the Prentice Hall Web site:

http://www.prenhall.com/casefair

for this chapter's World Wide Web exercise.

Chapter 4

DEMAND, SUPPLY, AND MARKET EQUILIBRIUM

CHAPTERS 1 AND 2 INTRODUCED the discipline, methodology, and subject matter of economics. Chapter 3 described the institutional landscape of the U.S. economy—its private, public, and international sectors. We now begin the task of analyzing how a market economy actually works. This chapter and the next present an overview of the way individual markets work. They introduce some of the concepts needed to understand both microeconomics and macroeconomics.

As we proceed to define terms and make assumptions, it is important to keep in mind what we are doing. In chapter 1 we explained what economic theory attempts to do. Theories are abstract representations of reality, like a map that represents a city. We believe that the models presented here will help you understand the workings of the economy just as a map helps you find your way around a city. But just as a map presents one view of the world, so too does any given theory of the economy. Alternatives exist to the theory that we present. We believe, however, that the basic model presented here, while sometimes abstract, is useful in gaining an understanding of how the economy works.

In the simple island society discussed in chapter 2, Bill and Colleen solved the economic problem directly. They allocated their time and used the island's resources to satisfy their wants. Bill might be a farmer, Colleen a hunter and carpenter. He might be a civil engineer, she a doctor. Exchange occurred, but complex markets were not necessary.

In societies of many people, however, production must satisfy wide-ranging tastes and preferences. Producers therefore specialize. Farmers produce more food than they can eat in order to sell it to buy manufactured goods. Physicians are paid for specialized services, as are attorneys, construction workers, and editors. When there is specialization, there must be exchange, and *markets* are the institutions through which exchange takes place.

This chapter begins to explore the basic forces at work in market systems. The purpose of our discussion is to explain how the individual decisions of households and firms together, without any central planning or direction, answer the three basic questions: What will be produced, how will it be produced, and who will get what is produced? We begin with some definitions.

FIRMS AND HOUSEHOLDS: THE BASIC DECISION-MAKING UNITS

Throughout this book, we discuss and analyze the behavior of two fundamental decision-making units: *firms*—the primary producing units in an economy—and *households*—the consuming units in an economy. Both are made up of people performing different functions and playing different roles. In essence, then, what we are developing is a theory of human behavior.

A **firm** exists when a person or a group of people decides to produce a product or products by transforming *inputs* (that is, resources in the broadest sense) into *outputs* (the products that are sold in the market). Some firms produce goods; others produce services. Some are large, some are small, and some are in between. But all firms exist to transform resources into things that people want. The Colorado Symphony Orchestra takes labor, land, a building, musically talented people, electricity, and other inputs and combines them to produce concerts. The production process can be extremely complicated. For example, the first flutist in the orchestra uses training, talent, previous performance experience, a score, an instrument, the conductor's interpretation, and her own feelings about the music to produce just one contribution to an overall performance.

Most firms exist to make a profit for their owners, but some do not. Columbia University, for example, fits the description of a firm: It takes inputs in the form of labor, land, skills, books, and buildings and produces a service that we call education. Although it sells that service for a price, it does not exist to make a profit, but rather to provide education of the highest quality possible.

Still, most firms exist to make a profit. They engage in production because they can sell their product for more than it costs to produce it. The analysis of firm behavior that follows rests on the assumption that *firms make decisions in order to maximize profits*.

An **entrepreneur** is one who organizes, manages, and assumes the risks of a firm. When a new firm is created—whether a proprietorship, a partnership, or a corporation—someone must organize the new firm, arrange financing, hire employees, and take risks. That person is an entrepreneur. Sometimes existing companies introduce new products, and sometimes new firms develop or improve on an old idea, but at the root of it all is entrepreneurship, which some see as the core of the free enterprise system.

At the root of the debate about the potential of free enterprise in formerly socialist Eastern Europe is the question of entrepreneurship. Does an entrepreneurial spirit exist in that part of the world? If not, can it be developed? Without it, the free enterprise system breaks down.

The consuming units in an economy are **households**. A household may consist of any number of people: a single person living alone, a married couple with four children, or 15 unrelated people sharing a house. Household decisions are presumably based on individual tastes and preferences. The household buys what it wants and can afford. In a large, heterogeneous, and open society such as the United States, wildly different tastes find expression in the marketplace. A six-block walk in any direction on any street in Manhattan or a drive from the Chicago Loop south into rural Illinois should be enough to convince anyone that it is difficult to generalize about what people like and do not like.

Even though households have wide-ranging preferences, they also have some things in common. All—even the very rich—have ultimately limited incomes, and all must pay in some way for the things they consume. Although households may have some control over their incomes—they can work more or less—they are also constrained by the availability of jobs, current wages, their own abilities, and their accumulated and inherited wealth (or lack thereof).

firm *An organization that transforms resources (inputs) into products (outputs). Firms are the primary producing units in a market economy.*

entrepreneur *A person who organizes, manages, and assumes the risks of a firm, taking a new idea or a new product and turning it into a successful business.*

households *The consuming units in an economy.*

INPUT MARKETS AND OUTPUT MARKETS: THE CIRCULAR FLOW

Households and firms interact in two basic kinds of markets: product (or output) markets and input (or factor) markets. Goods and services that are intended for use by households are exchanged in **product** or **output markets**. In output markets, firms *supply* and households *demand*.

To produce goods and services, firms must buy resources in **input** or **factor markets**. Firms buy inputs from households, which supply these inputs. When a firm decides how much to produce (supply) in output markets, it must simultaneously decide how much of each input it needs to produce the desired level of output. To produce automobiles, Chrysler Corporation must use many inputs, including tires, steel, complicated machinery, and many different kinds of labor.

Figure 4.1 shows the *circular flow* of economic activity through a simple market economy. Note that the flow reflects the direction in which goods and services flow through input and output markets. For example, goods and services flow from firms to households through output markets. Labor services flow from households to firms through input markets. Payment (most often in money form) for goods and services flows in the opposite direction.

In input markets, households *supply* resources. Most households earn their incomes by working—they supply their labor in the **labor market** to firms that demand labor and pay workers for their time and skills. Households may also loan their accumulated or inherited savings to firms for interest, or exchange those savings for claims to future profits, as when a household buys shares of stock in a corporation. In the **capital market**, households supply the funds that firms use to buy capital goods. Households may also supply land or other real property in exchange for rent in the **land market**.

Inputs into the production process are also called **factors of production**. Land, labor, and capital are the three key factors of production. Throughout this text, we use the terms *input* and *factor of production* interchangeably. Thus, input markets and factor markets mean the same thing.

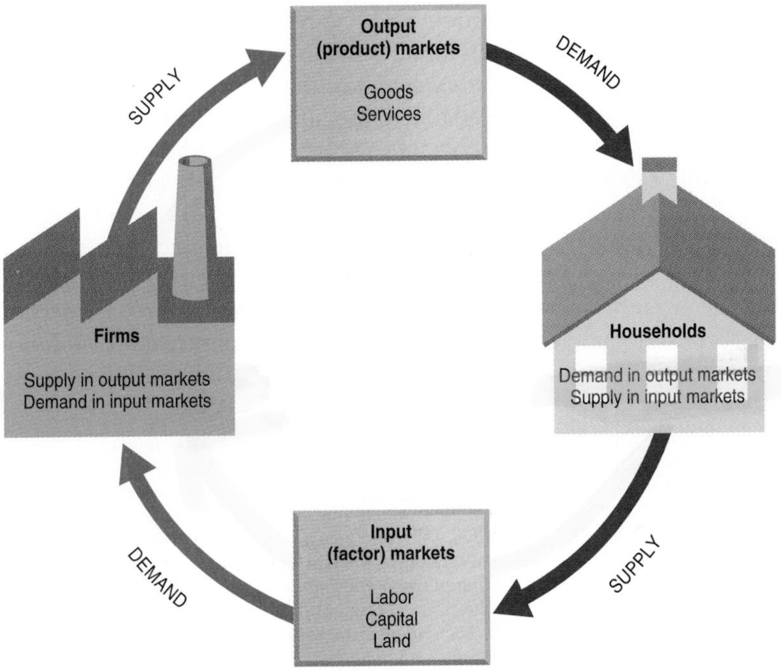

product or **output markets**
The markets in which goods and services are exchanged.

input or **factor markets**
The markets in which the resources used to produce products are exchanged.

labor market *The input/factor market in which households supply work for wages to firms that demand labor.*

capital market *The input/factor market in which households supply their savings, for interest or for claims to future profits, to firms that demand funds in order to buy capital goods.*

land market *The input/factor market in which households supply land or other real property in exchange for rent.*

factors of production *The inputs into the production process. Land, labor, and capital are the three key factors of production.*

FIGURE 4.1

The Circular Flow of Economic Activity

Diagrams like this one show the circular flow of economic activity, hence the name *circular flow diagram*. Here, goods and services flow clockwise: Labor services supplied by households flow to firms, and goods and services produced by firms flow to households. Money (not pictured here) flows in the opposite (counterclockwise) direction: Payment for goods and services flows from households to firms, and payment for labor services flows from firms to households.

Note: Color Guide—In Figure 4.1 households are depicted in *blue* and firms are depicted in *red*. From now on all diagrams relating to the behavior of households will be blue or shades of blue, and all diagrams relating to the behavior of firms will be in red or shades of red.

Early economics texts included entrepreneurship as a type of input, just like land, labor, and capital. Treating entrepreneurship as a separate factor of production has fallen out of favor, however, partially because it is unmeasurable. Most economists today implicitly assume that it is in plentiful supply. That is, if profit opportunities exist, it is likely that entrepreneurs will crop up to take advantage of them. This assumption has turned out to be a good predictor of actual economic behavior and performance.

The supply of inputs and their prices ultimately determine households' income. The amount of income a household earns thus depends on the decisions it makes concerning what types of inputs it chooses to supply. Whether to stay in school, how much and what kind of training to get, whether to start a business, how many hours to work, whether to work at all, and how to invest savings are all household decisions that affect income.

As you can see, then:

> Input and output markets are connected through the behavior of both firms and households. Firms determine the quantities and character of outputs produced and the types of quantities of inputs demanded. Households determine the types and quantities of products demanded and the quantities and types of inputs supplied.[1]

The following analysis of demand and supply will lead up to a theory of how market prices are determined. Prices are determined by the interaction between demanders and suppliers. To understand this interaction, we first need to know how product prices influence the behavior of demanders and suppliers *separately*. We therefore discuss output markets by focusing first on demanders, then on suppliers, and then on the interaction.

DEMAND IN PRODUCT/OUTPUT MARKETS

In real life, households make many decisions at the same time. To see how the forces of demand and supply work, however, let us focus first on the amount of a *single* product that an *individual* household decides to consume within some given period of time, such as a month or a year.

> A household's decision about what quantity of a particular output, or product, to demand depends upon a number of factors:
>
> - The *price of the product* in question.
> - The *income available* to the household.
> - The household's *amount of accumulated wealth*.
> - The *prices of other products* available to the household.
> - The household's *tastes and preferences*.
> - The household's *expectations* about future income, wealth, and prices.

quantity demanded *The amount (number of units) of a product that a household would buy in a given period if it could buy all it wanted at the current market price.*

Quantity demanded is the amount (number of units) of a product that a household would buy in a given period *if it could buy all it wanted at the current market price*.

Of course, the amount of a product that households finally purchase depends on the amount of product actually available in the market. The phrase *if it could buy all it wanted* is critical to the definition of quantity demanded because it allows for the possibility that quantity supplied and quantity demanded are unequal.

---

[1] Our description of markets begins with the behavior of firms and households. Modern orthodox economic theory essentially combines two distinct but closely related theories of behavior. The "theory of household behavior," or "consumer behavior," has its roots in the works of nineteenth-century utilitarians such as Jeremy Bentham, William Jevons, Carl Menger, Leon Walras, Vilfredo Pareto, and F. Y. Edgeworth. The "theory of the firm" developed out of the earlier classical political economy of Adam Smith, David Ricardo, and Thomas Malthus. In 1890 Alfred Marshall published the first of many editions of his *Principles of Economics*. That volume pulled together the main themes of both the classical economists and the utilitarians into what is now called "neoclassical economics." While there have been many changes over the years, the basic structure of the model that we build can be found in Marshall's work.

> **Changes in Quantity Demanded versus Changes in Demand**   The most important relationship in individual markets is that between market price and quantity demanded. For this reason, we need to begin our discussion by analyzing the likely response of households to changes in price using the device of *ceteris paribus*, or "all else equal." That is, we will attempt to derive a relationship between the quantity demanded of a good per time period and the price of that good, holding income, wealth, other prices, tastes, and expectations constant.

It is very important to distinguish between price changes, which affect the quantity of a good demanded, and changes in other factors (such as income), which change the entire relationship between price and quantity. For example, if a family begins earning a higher income, it might buy more of a good at every possible price. To be sure that we distinguish between changes in price and other changes that affect demand, we will throughout the rest of the text be very precise about terminology. Specifically:

> Changes in the price of a product affect the *quantity demanded* per period. Changes in any other factor, such as income or preferences, affect *demand*. Thus we say that an increase in the price of Coca-Cola is likely to cause a decrease in the *quantity of Coca-Cola demanded*. However, we say that an increase in income is likely to cause an increase in the *demand* for most goods.

PRICE AND QUANTITY DEMANDED: THE LAW OF DEMAND

A **demand schedule** shows the quantities of a product that a household would be willing to buy at different prices. Table 4.1 presents a hypothetical demand schedule for Anna, a student who went off to college to study economics while her boyfriend went to art school. If telephone calls were free (a price of zero), Anna would call her boyfriend every day, or 30 times a month. At a price of $.50 per call, she makes 25 calls a month. When the price hits $3.50, she cuts back to seven calls a month. This same information presented graphically is called a **demand curve**. Anna's demand curve is presented in Figure 4.2.[2]

You will note in Figure 4.2 that *quantity* is measured along the horizontal axis, and *price* is measured along the vertical axis. This is the convention we follow throughout this book.

> **Demand Curves Slope Downward**   The data in Table 4.1 show that at lower prices, Anna calls her boyfriend more frequently; at higher prices, she calls less frequently. There is thus a *negative, or inverse, relationship between quantity demanded and price.* When price rises, quantity demanded falls, and when price falls, quantity demanded rises. Thus demand curves always slope downward. This negative relationship between price and quantity demanded is often referred to as the **law of demand**, a term first used by economist Alfred Marshall in his 1890 textbook.

Some people are put off by the abstractness of demand curves. Of course, we don't actually draw our own demand curves for products. When we want to make a purchase, we usually face only a single price, and how much we would buy at other prices is irrelevant. But demand curves help analysts understand the kind of behavior that households are *likely* to exhibit if they are actually faced with a higher or lower price. We know, for example, that if the price of a good rises enough, the quantity demanded

TABLE 4.1

ANNA'S DEMAND SCHEDULE FOR TELEPHONE CALLS

PRICE (PER CALL)	QUANTITY DEMANDED (CALLS PER MONTH)
$ 0	30
.50	25
3.50	7
7.00	3
10.00	1
15.00	0

demand schedule *A table showing how much of a given product a household would be willing to buy at different prices.*

demand curve *A graph illustrating how much of a given product a household would be willing to buy at different prices.*

law of demand *The negative relationship between price and quantity demanded: As price rises, quantity demanded decreases. As price falls, quantity demanded increases.*

---

[2]Drawing a smooth curve, as we do in Figure 4.2, suggests that Anna can make a quarter of a phone call or half of a phone call. For example, according to the graph, at a price of $12 per call, Anna would make half a call and at $9 per call, about a call and a half. While fractional purchases can be made for goods that are *divisible*, such as phone calls—you might talk for one minute instead of two minutes—and products sold by weight, they are impossible for large purchases, such as automobiles. We use the term *lumpy* to describe goods that cannot be divided. You would not draw a smooth, downward sloping curve of a household's demand for automobiles, for example, because there might be only one (or at most two) points, and any points in between would be meaningless. Whenever we draw a smooth demand curve, we are assuming divisibility.

FIGURE 4.2

Anna's Demand Curve

The relationship between price and quantity demanded presented graphically is called a *demand curve*. Demand curves have a negative slope, indicating that lower prices cause quantity demanded to increase. Note that Anna's demand curve is blue; demand in product markets is determined by household choice.

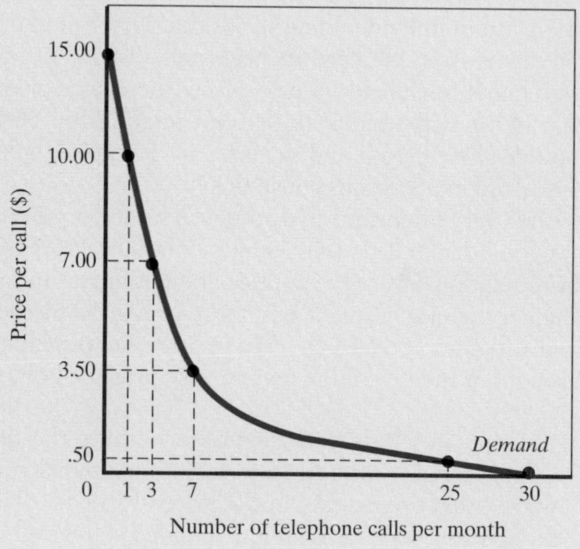

Price per call ($)

- 15.00
- 10.00
- 7.00
- 3.50
- .50

Demand

0 1 3 7   25 30

Number of telephone calls per month

must ultimately drop to zero. The demand curve is thus a tool that helps us explain economic behavior and predict reactions to possible price changes.

Marshall's definition of a social "law" captures the idea:

> The term "law" means nothing more than a general proposition or statement of tendencies, more or less certain, more or less definite . . . a *social law* is a statement of social tendencies; that is, that a certain course of action may be expected from the members of a social group under certain conditions.[3]

It seems reasonable to expect that consumers will demand more of a product at a lower price and less of it at a higher price. Households must divide their incomes over a wide range of goods and services. If I spend $4.50 for a pound of prime beef, I am sacrificing the other things that I might have bought with that $4.50. If the price of prime beef were to jump to $7 per pound, while chicken breasts remained at $1.99 (remember *ceteris paribus*—we are holding all else constant), I would have to give up more chicken and/or other items to buy that pound of beef. So I would probably eat more chicken and less beef. Anna calls her boyfriend three times when phone calls cost $7 each. A fourth call would mean sacrificing $7 worth of other purchases. At a price of $3.50, however, the opportunity cost of each call is lower, and she calls more frequently.

Another explanation behind the fact that demand curves are very likely to slope downward rests on the notion of *utility*. Economists use the concept of *utility* to mean happiness or satisfaction. Presumably we consume goods and services because they give us utility. But as we consume more of a product within a given period of time, it is likely that each additional unit consumed will yield successively less satisfaction. The utility I gain from a second ice cream cone is likely to be less than the utility I gained from the first; the third is worth even less, and so forth. This *law of diminishing marginal utility* is an important concept in economics. If each successive unit of a good is worth less to me, I am not going to be willing to pay as much for it. It is thus reasonable to expect a downward slope in the demand curve for that good.

The idea of diminishing marginal utility also helps to explain Anna's behavior. The demand curve is a way of representing what she is willing to pay per phone call. At a

PART ONE
*Introduction
to Economics*

72

[3]Alfred Marshall, *Principles of Economics*, 8th ed. (New York: Macmillan, 1948), p. 33. (The first edition was published in 1890.)

price of $7, she calls her boyfriend three times per month. A fourth call, however, is worth less than the third—that is, the fourth call is worth less than $7 to her, so she stops at three. If the price were only $3.50, however, she would keep right on calling. But even at $3.50, she would stop at seven calls per month. This behavior reveals that the eighth call has less value to Anna than the seventh.

Thinking about the ways that people are affected by price changes also helps us see what is behind the law of demand. Consider this example: Luis lives and works in Mexico City. His elderly mother lives in Santiago, Chile. Last year, the airlines servicing South America got into a price war, and the price of flying between Mexico City and Santiago dropped from 20,000 pesos to 10,000 pesos. How might Luis's behavior change?

First, he is better off. Last year he flew home to Chile three times at a total cost of 60,000 pesos. This year he can fly to Chile the same number of times, buy exactly the same combination of other goods and services that he bought last year, and have 30,000 pesos left over! Because he is better off—his income can buy more—he may fly home more frequently. Second, the opportunity cost of flying home has changed. Before the price war, Luis had to sacrifice 20,000 pesos worth of other goods and services each time he flew to Chile. After the price war he must sacrifice only 10,000 pesos worth of other goods and services for each trip. The trade-off has changed. Both of these effects are likely to lead to a higher quantity demanded in response to the lower price.

In sum:

It is reasonable to expect quantity demanded to fall when price rises, *ceteris paribus*, and to expect quantity demanded to rise when price falls, *ceteris paribus*. Demand curves have a negative slope.

▶ **Other Properties of Demand Curves**   Two additional things are notable about Anna's demand curve. First, it intersects the Y, or price, axis. This means that there is a price above which no calls will be made. In this case, Anna simply stops calling when the price reaches $15 per call.

As long as households have limited incomes and wealth, all demand curves will intersect the price axis. For any commodity, there is always a price above which a household will not, or cannot, pay. Even if the good or service is very important, all households are ultimately constrained, or limited, by income and wealth.

Second, Anna's demand curve intersects the X, or quantity, axis. Even at a zero price, there is a limit to the number of phone calls Anna will make. If telephone calls were free, she would call 30 times a month, but not more.

That demand curves intersect the quantity axis is a matter of common sense. Demands for most goods are limited, if only by time, even at a zero price.

To summarize what we know about the shape of demand curves:

1. They have a negative slope. An increase in price is likely to lead to a decrease in quantity demanded, and a decrease in price is likely to lead to an increase in quantity demanded.
2. They intersect the quantity (X) axis, a result of time limitations and diminishing marginal utility.
3. They intersect the price (Y) axis, a result of limited incomes and wealth.

But that's all we can say; it is not possible to generalize further. The actual shape of an individual household demand curve—whether it is steep or flat, whether it is bowed in or bowed out—depends on the unique tastes and preferences of the household and other factors. Some households may be very sensitive to price changes; other households may respond little to a change in price. In some cases, plentiful substitutes are available; in other cases they are not. Thus, to fully understand the shape and position of demand curves, we must turn to the other determinants of household demand.

OTHER DETERMINANTS OF HOUSEHOLD DEMAND

Of the many factors likely to influence a household's demand for a specific product, we have considered only the price of the product itself. Other determining factors include household income and wealth, the prices of other goods and services, tastes and preferences, and expectations.

➤ **Income and Wealth**   Before we proceed, we need to define two terms that are often confused, *income* and *wealth*. A household's **income** is the sum of all the wages, salaries, profits, interest payments, rents, and other forms of earnings received by the household *in a given period of time*. Income is thus a *flow* measure: We must specify a time period for it—income *per month* or *per year*. You can spend or consume more or less than your income in any given period. If you consume less than your income, you save. To consume more than your income in a period, you must either borrow or draw on savings accumulated from previous periods.

Wealth is the total value of what a household owns less what it owes. Another word for wealth is **net worth**—the amount a household would have left if it sold off all its possessions and paid off all its debts. Wealth is a *stock* measure: It is measured at a given point in time. If, in a given period, you spend less than your income, you save; the amount that you save is added to your wealth. Saving is the flow that affects the stock of wealth. When you spend more than your income, you *dissave*—you reduce your wealth.

Clearly, households with higher incomes and higher accumulated savings or inherited wealth can afford to buy more things. In general, then, we would expect higher demand at higher levels of income/wealth and lower demand at lower levels of income/wealth. Goods for which demand goes up when income is higher and for which demand goes down when income is lower are called **normal goods**. Movie tickets, restaurant meals, telephone calls, and shirts are all normal goods.

But generalization in economics can be hazardous. Sometimes demand for a good falls when household income rises. Consider, for example, the various qualities of meat available. When a household's income rises, it is likely to buy higher quality meats—its demand for filet mignon is likely to rise—but its demand for lower quality meats—chuck steak, for example—is likely to fall. Transportation is another example. At higher incomes, people can afford to fly. People who can afford to fly are less likely to take the bus long distances. Thus higher income may reduce the number of times someone takes a bus. Goods for which demand tends to fall when income rises are called **inferior goods**.

➤ **Prices of Other Goods and Services**   No consumer decides in isolation on the amount of any one commodity to buy. Rather, each decision is part of a larger set of decisions that are made simultaneously. Households must apportion their incomes over many different goods and services. As a result, the price of any one good can and does affect the demand for other goods.

This is most obviously the case when goods are substitutes for one another. To return to our lonesome first-year student: If the price of a telephone call rises to $10, Anna will call her boyfriend only once a month (see Table 4.1). But, of course, she can get in touch with him in other ways. Presumably she substitutes some other, less costly, form of communication, such as writing more letters or sending more E-mails.

When an *increase* in the price of one good causes demand for another good to *increase* (a positive relationship), we say that the goods are **substitutes**. A *fall* in the price of a good causes a *decline* in demand for its substitutes. Substitutes are goods that can serve as replacements for one another.

---

income *The sum of all a household's wages, salaries, profits, interest payments, rents, and other forms of earnings in a given period of time. It is a flow measure.*

wealth or **net worth** *The total value of what a household owns minus what it owes. It is a stock measure.*

A major portion of household wealth, one determinant of demand, is made up of financial assets. At the end of 1996, financial assets of households was about $23 trillion: 16% was held in bank deposits, 28% in pension funds, 21% in shares of stock, 9% in bonds and other fixed-income investments, 7% in mutual funds, and the remaining 19% in other forms.

Source: Flow of Funds Accounts of the United States.

normal goods *Goods for which demand goes up when income is higher and for which demand goes down when income is lower.*

inferior goods *Goods for which demand tends to fall when income rises.*

substitutes *Goods that can serve as replacements for one another; when the price of one increases, demand for the other goes up.*

To be substitutes, two products need not be identical. Identical products are called **perfect substitutes**. Japanese cars are not identical to American cars. Nonetheless, all have four wheels, are capable of carrying people, and run on gasoline. Thus, significant changes in the price of one country's cars can be expected to influence demand for the other country's cars. Compact discs are substitutes for records and tapes, restaurant meals are substitutes for meals eaten at home, and flying from New York to Washington is a substitute for taking the train.

Often, two products "go together"—that is, they complement each other. Our lonesome letter writer, for example, will find her demand for stamps and stationery rising as she writes more letters, and her demand for Internet access rising as she sends more E-mails. Bacon and eggs are **complementary goods,** as are cars and gasoline, and cameras and film. During a price war among the airlines in the summer of 1994 when travel became less expensive, the demand for taxi service to and from airports and for luggage increased across the country. When two goods are complements, a *decrease* in the price of one results in *increase* in demand for the other, and vice versa.

Because any one good may have many potential substitutes and complements at the same time, a single price change may affect a household's demands for many goods simultaneously; the demand for some of these products may rise while the demand for others may fall. For example, one of the newest technologies for personal computers is the CD-ROM. Massive amounts of data can now be stored digitally on compact disks that can be read by personal computers with a CD-ROM drive. When these drives first came on the market they were quite expensive, selling for several hundred dollars each. Now they are much less expensive, and most new computers have them built in. As a result, the demand for the CD-ROM disks (complementary goods) is soaring. As more and more students adopt the CD technology and the price of CDs and CD hardware falls, fewer people will be buying things like encyclopedias printed on paper (substitute goods).

> **Tastes and Preferences** Income, wealth, and the prices of things available are the three factors that determine the combinations of things that a household is *able* to buy. You know that you cannot afford to rent an apartment at $1,200 per month if your monthly income is only $400. But within these constraints, you are more or less free to choose what to buy. Your final choice depends on your individual tastes and preferences.

Changes in preferences can and do manifest themselves in market behavior. Twenty-five years ago the major big-city marathons drew only a few hundred runners. Now tens of thousands enter and run. The demand for running shoes, running suits, stopwatches, and other running items has greatly increased. For many years, people drank soda for refreshment. Today convenience stores are filled with a dizzying array of iced teas, fruit juices, natural beverages, and mineral waters.

Within the constraints of prices and incomes, it is preference that shapes the demand curve. But it is difficult to generalize about tastes and preferences. First of all, they are volatile: Five years ago, more people smoked cigarettes and fewer people had computers. Second, they are idiosyncratic: Some people like to talk on the telephone, while others prefer the written word; some people prefer dogs, while others are crazy about cats; some people like chicken wings, while others prefer legs. The diversity of individual demands is almost infinite.

> **Expectations** What you decide to buy today certainly depends on today's prices and your current income and wealth. But you also have expectations about what your position will be in the future. You may have expectations about future changes in prices, too, and these may affect your decisions today.

There are many examples of the ways expectations affect demand. When people buy a house or a car, they often must borrow part of the purchase price and pay it back over a number of years. In deciding what kind of house or car to buy, they presumably must think about their income today, as well as what their income is likely to be in the future.

perfect substitutes *Identical products.*

complements, complementary goods *Goods that "go together"; a decrease in the price of one results in an increase in demand for the other, and vice versa.*

PERFECT SUBSTITUTES? ON A HOT DAY IN THE DESERT, ONE BRAND IS AS GOOD AS ANOTHER.

As another example, consider a student in his final year of medical school living on a scholarship of $12,000. Compare him with another person earning $6 an hour at a full-time job, with no expectation of a significant change in income in the future. The two have virtually identical incomes. But even if they had the same tastes, the medical student is likely to demand different things, simply because he expects a major increase in income later on.

Increasingly, economic theory has come to recognize the importance of expectations. We will devote a good deal of time to discussing how expectations affect more than just demand. For the time being, however, it is important to understand that demand depends on more than just *current* incomes, prices, and tastes.

SHIFT OF DEMAND VERSUS MOVEMENT ALONG A DEMAND CURVE

Recall that a demand curve shows the relationship between quantity demanded and the price of a good. Such demand curves are derived while holding income, tastes, and other prices constant. If this condition of *ceteris paribus* were relaxed, we would have to derive an entirely new relationship between price and quantity.

Let us return once again to Anna (Table 4.1 and Figure 4.2). Suppose that when we derived the demand schedule in Table 4.1, Anna had a part-time job that paid $200 per month. Now suppose that her parents inherit some money and begin sending her an additional $200 per month. Assuming that she keeps her job, Anna's income is now $400 per month.[4]

With her higher income, Anna would probably call her boyfriend more frequently, regardless of the price of a call. Table 4.2 and Figure 4.3 present Anna's original-income schedule (D_1) and increased-income demand schedule (D_2). At $.50 per call, the frequency of her calls (the quantity she demands) increases from 25 to 33 calls per month; at $3.50 per call, frequency increases from 7 to 18 calls per month; at $10 per call, frequency increases from one to seven calls per month. (Note in Figure 4.3 that even if calls are free, Anna's income matters; at zero price, her demand increases. With a higher income, she may visit her boyfriend more, for example, and more visits might mean more phone calls to organize and plan.)

The conditions that were in place at the time we drew the original demand curve have now changed. In other words, a factor that affects Anna's demand for telephone calls

TABLE 4.2 SHIFT OF ANNA'S DEMAND SCHEDULE DUE TO INCREASE IN INCOME

Price (Per Call)	SCHEDULE D_1 Quantity Demanded (Calls Per Month at an Income of $200 Per Month)	SCHEDULE D_2 Quantity Demanded (Calls Per Month at an Income of $400 Per Month)
$ 0	30	35
.50	25	33
3.50	7	18
7.00	3	12
10.00	1	7
15.00	0	2
20.00	0	0

[4]The income from home may affect the amount of time Anna spends working. In the extreme, she may quit her job and her income will remain at $200. In essence, she would be spending the entire $200 on leisure. Here we assume that she keeps the job and that her income is higher. The point is that because labor supply decisions affect income, they are closely tied to output demand decisions. In a sense, the two decisions are made simultaneously.

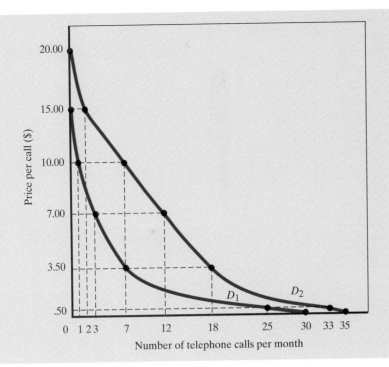

FIGURE 4.3

Shift of a Demand Curve Following a Rise in Income
When the price of a good changes, we move *along* the demand curve for that good. When any other factor that influences demand changes (income, tastes, etc.), the relationship between price and quantity is different; there is a *shift* of the demand curve, in this case from D_1 to D_2.

(in this case, her income) has changed, and there is now a new relationship between price and quantity demanded. Such a change is referred to as a **shift of the demand curve.**

It is very important to distinguish between a change in quantity demanded—that is, some movement *along* a demand curve—and a shift of demand. Demand schedules and demand curves show the relationship between the price of a good or service and the quantity demanded per period, *ceteris paribus*. If price changes, quantity demanded will change—this is a **movement along the demand curve.** When any of the *other* factors that influence demand change, however, a new relationship between price and quantity demanded is established—this is a *shift of the demand curve.* The result, then, is a *new* demand curve. Changes in income, preferences, or prices of other goods cause the demand curve to shift:

shift of a demand curve
The change that takes place in a demand curve corresponding to a new relationship between quantity demanded of a good and the price of that good. The shift is brought about by a change in the original conditions.

movement along a demand curve *The change in quantity demanded brought about by a change in price.*

Change in price of a good or service

   leads to

      ⟶ Change in *quantity demanded* (**Movement along the demand curve**).

Change in income, preferences, or prices of other goods or services

   leads to

      ⟶ Change in *demand* (**Shift of demand curve**).

Figure 4.4 illustrates the differences between movement along a demand curve and shifting demand curves. In Figure 4.4a, an increase in household income causes demand for hamburger (an inferior good) to decline, or shift to the left from D_1 to D_2. (Because quantity is measured on the horizontal axis, a decrease means a shift to the left.) In contrast, demand for steak (a normal good) increases, or shifts to the right, when income rises.

In Figure 4.4b, an increase in the price of hamburger from \$1.49 to \$3.09 a pound causes a household to buy less hamburger each month. In other words, the higher price causes the *quantity demanded* to decline from 10 pounds to 5 pounds per month. This change represents a movement *along* the demand curve for hamburger. In place

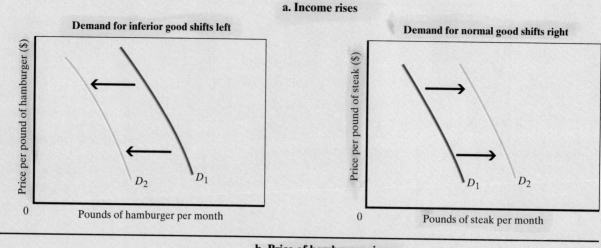

a. Income rises

Demand for inferior good shifts left

Price per pound of hamburger ($) — vertical axis

D_2 D_1

Pounds of hamburger per month

Demand for normal good shifts right

Price per pound of steak ($) — vertical axis

D_1 D_2

Pounds of steak per month

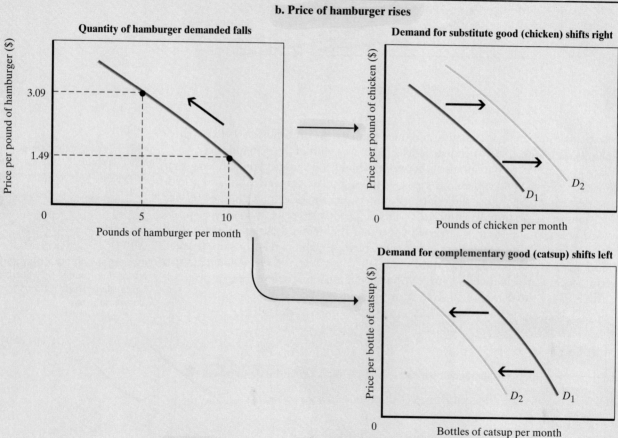

b. Price of hamburger rises

Quantity of hamburger demanded falls

Price per pound of hamburger ($) — vertical axis

3.09

1.49

0   5   10

Pounds of hamburger per month

Demand for substitute good (chicken) shifts right

Price per pound of chicken ($) — vertical axis

D_1 D_2

Pounds of chicken per month

Demand for complementary good (catsup) shifts left

Price per bottle of catsup ($) — vertical axis

D_2 D_1

Bottles of catsup per month

FIGURE 4.4

Shifts versus Movement along a Demand Curve

a. When income increases, the demand for inferior goods *shifts to the left* and the demand for normal goods *shifts to the right*. **b.** If the price of hamburger rises, the quantity of hamburger demanded declines—this is a movement along the demand curve. The same price rise for hamburger would shift the demand for chicken (a substitute for hamburger) to the right and the demand for catsup (a complement to hamburger) to the left.

of hamburger, the household buys more chicken. The household's demand for chicken (a substitute for hamburger) rises—the demand curve shifts to the right. At the same time, the demand for catsup (a good that complements hamburger) declines—its demand curve shifts to the left.

FROM HOUSEHOLD DEMAND TO MARKET DEMAND

Market demand is simply the sum of all the quantities of a good or service demanded per period by all the households buying in the market for that good or service. Figure 4.5 shows the derivation of a market demand curve from three individual demand curves. (Although this market demand curve is derived from the behavior of only three people, most markets have thousands or even millions of demanders.) As the table in Figure 4.5 shows, when the price of a pound of coffee is $3.50, both A and C would purchase 4 pounds per month, while B would buy none. At that price, presumably, B drinks tea. Market demand at $3.50 would thus be a total of 4 + 4 or 8 pounds. At a price of $1.50 per pound, however, A would purchase 8 pounds per month, B 3 pounds, and C 9 pounds. Thus, at $1.50 per pound, market demand would be 8 + 3 + 9, or 20 pounds of coffee per month.

The total quantity demanded in the marketplace at a given price, then, is simply the sum of all the quantities demanded by all the individual households shopping in the

market demand *The sum of all the quantities of a good or service demanded per period by all the households buying in the market for that good or service.*

FIGURE 4.5

Deriving Market Demand from Individual Demand Curves

Total demand in the marketplace is simply the sum of the demands of all the households shopping in a particular market. It is the sum of all the individual demand curves—that is, the sum of all the individual quantities demanded at each price.

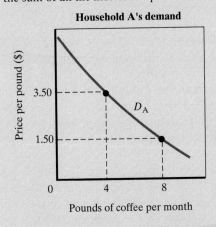

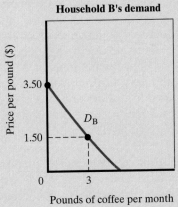

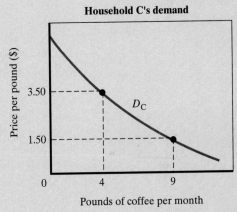

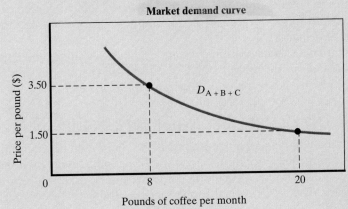

Price	Quantity (q) demanded by			Market demand (Q)
	A	B	C	
$3.50	4	+ 0	+ 4	→ 8
1.50	8	+ 3	+ 9	→ 20

market *at that price*. A market demand curve shows the total amount of a product that would be sold at each price if households could buy all they wanted at that price. As Figure 4.5 shows, the market demand curve is the sum of all the individual demand curves—that is, the sum of all the individual quantities demanded at each price. The market demand curve thus takes its shape and position from the shapes, positions, and number of individual demand curves. If more people decide to shop in a market, more demand curves must be added, and the market demand curve will shift to the right. Market demand curves may also shift as a result of preference changes, income changes, or changes in the number of demanders.

As a general rule throughout this book, capital letters refer to the entire market and lowercase letters refer to individual households or firms. Thus, in Figure 4.5, Q refers to total quantity demanded in the market, while q refers to the quantity demanded by individual households.

SUPPLY IN PRODUCT/OUTPUT MARKETS

In addition to dealing with households' demands for outputs, economic theory deals with the behavior of business firms, which supply in output markets and demand in input markets (see again Figure 4.1). Firms engage in production, and we assume that they do so for profit. Successful firms make profits because they are able to sell their products for more than it costs to produce them.

Supply decisions can thus be expected to depend on profit potential. Because **profit** is the simple difference between revenues and costs, supply is likely to react to changes in revenues and changes in production costs. The amount of revenue earned by a firm depends on the price of its product in the market and on how much it sells. Costs of production depend on many factors, the most important of which are (1) the kinds of inputs needed to produce the product, (2) the amount of each input required, and (3) the prices of inputs.

The supply decision is just one of several decisions that firms make in order to maximize profit. There are usually a number of ways to produce any given product. A golf course can be built by hundreds of workers with shovels and grass seed or by a few workers with heavy earth-moving equipment and sod blankets. Hamburgers can be individually fried by a short-order cook or grilled by the hundreds on a mechanized moving grill. Firms must choose the production technique most appropriate to their products and projected levels of production. The best method of production is the one that minimizes cost, thus maximizing profit.

Which production technique is best, in turn, depends on the prices of inputs. Where labor is cheap and machinery is expensive and difficult to transport, firms are likely to choose production techniques that use a great deal of labor. Where machines are available and labor is scarce or expensive, they are likely to choose more capital-intensive methods. Obviously, the technique ultimately chosen determines input requirements. Thus, by choosing an output supply target and the most appropriate technology, firms determine which inputs to demand.

With the caution that no decision exists in a vacuum, let us begin our examination of firm behavior by focusing on the output supply decision and the relationship between quantity supplied and output price, *ceteris paribus*.

PRICE AND QUANTITY SUPPLIED: THE LAW OF SUPPLY

Quantity supplied is the amount of a particular product that a firm would be willing and able to offer for sale at a particular price during a given time period. A **supply schedule** shows how much of a product a firm will supply at alternative prices. Table 4.3 itemizes the quantities of soybeans that an individual farmer such as Clarence Brown might

profit *The difference between revenues and costs.*

quantity supplied *The amount of a particular product that a firm would be willing and able to offer for sale at a particular price during a given time period.*

supply schedule *A table showing how much of a product firms will supply at different prices.*

supply at various prices. If the market paid $1.50 or less a bushel for soybeans, Brown would not supply any soybeans. For one thing, it costs more than $1.50 to produce a bushel of soybeans; for another, Brown can use his land more profitably to produce something else. At $1.75 per bushel, however, at least some soybean production takes place on Brown's farm, and a price increase from $1.75 to $2.25 per bushel causes the quantity supplied by Brown to increase from 10,000 to 20,000 bushels per year. The higher price may justify shifting land from wheat to soybean production or putting previously fallow land into soybeans. Or it may lead to more intensive farming of land already in soybeans, using expensive fertilizer or equipment that was not cost-justified at the lower price.

Generalizing from Farmer Brown's experience, we can reasonably expect an increase in market price, *ceteris paribus*, to lead to an increase in quantity supplied. In other words, there is a positive relationship between the quantity of a good supplied and price. This statement sums up the **law of supply**: An increase in market price will lead to an increase in quantity supplied, and a decrease in market price will lead to a decrease in quantity supplied.

The information in a supply schedule may be presented graphically in a **supply curve**. Supply curves slope upward. The upward, or positive, slope of Brown's curve in Figure 4.6 reflects this positive relationship between price and quantity supplied.

Note in Brown's supply schedule, however, that when price rises from $4 to $5, quantity supplied no longer increases. Often an individual firm's ability to respond to an increase in price is constrained by its existing scale of operations, or capacity, in the short run. For example, Brown's ability to produce more soybeans depends on the size of his farm, the fertility of his soil, and the types of equipment he has. The fact that output stays constant at 45,000 bushels per year suggests that he is running up against the limits imposed by the size of his farm, the quality of his soil, and his existing technology.

TABLE 4.3

CLARENCE BROWN'S SUPPLY SCHEDULE FOR SOYBEANS

PRICE (PER BUSHEL)	QUANTITY SUPPLIED (BUSHELS PER YEAR)
$1.50	0
1.75	10,000
2.25	20,000
3.00	30,000
4.00	45,000
5.00	45,000

law of supply *The positive relationship between price and quantity of a good supplied: An increase in market price will lead to an increase in quantity supplied, and a decrease in market price will lead to a decrease in quantity supplied.*

supply curve *A graph illustrating how much of a product a firm will supply at different prices.*

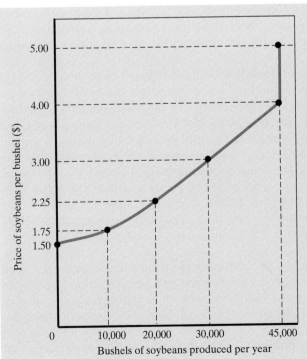

FIGURE 4.6

Clarence Brown's Individual Supply Curve

A producer will supply more when the price of output is higher. The slope of a supply curve is positive. Note that the supply curve is red: Supply is determined by choices made by firms.

In the longer run, however, Brown may acquire more land, or technology may change, allowing for more soybean production. The terms *short run* and *long run* have very precise meanings in economics; we will discuss them in detail later. Here it is important only to understand that time plays a critical role in supply decisions. When prices change, firms' immediate response may be different from what they are able to do after a month or a year. Short-run and long-run supply curves are often different.

OTHER DETERMINANTS OF FIRM SUPPLY

Of the factors we've listed that are likely to affect the quantity of output supplied by a given firm, we have thus far discussed only the price of output. Other factors that affect supply include the cost of producing the product and the prices of related products.

➤ **The Cost of Production** Regardless of the price that a firm can command for its product, price must exceed the cost of producing the output for the firm to make a profit. Thus, the supply decision is likely to change in response to changes in the cost of production. Cost of production depends on a number of factors, including the available technologies and the price of the inputs needed by the firm (labor, land, capital, energy, and so forth).

Technological change can have an enormous impact on the cost of production over time. Consider agriculture. The introduction of fertilizers, the development of complex farm machinery, and the use of bioengineering to increase the yield of individual crops have all powerfully affected the cost of producing agricultural products. Farm productivity in the United States has been increasing dramatically for decades. Yield per acre of corn production has increased fivefold since the late 1930s, and the amount of labor required to produce 100 bushels of corn has fallen from 108 hours in the late 1930s, to 20 hours in the late 1950s, to less than 3 hours today.

When a technological advance lowers the cost of production, output is likely to increase. When yield per acre increases, individual farmers can and do produce more. The output of the Ford Motor Company increased substantially after the introduction of assembly line techniques. The production of electronic calculators, and later personal computers, boomed with the development of inexpensive techniques to produce microprocessors.

Cost of production is also affected directly by the price of the factors of production. During 1994 timber prices in the United States rose dramatically. As a result, the cost of building new homes jumped significantly and the supply of new homes dropped. Also, in 1996, due to a very cold winter in the United States and Europe, demand pushed the world price of oil from around $17 a barrel to around $26. As a result, cab drivers faced higher gasoline prices, airlines faced higher fuel costs, and manufacturing firms faced higher heating bills. The result: Cab drivers probably spent less time driving around looking for fares, airlines cut a few low-profit routes, and some manufacturing plants stopped running extra shifts. The moral of this story: Increases in input prices raise costs of production and are likely to reduce supply.

➤ **The Prices of Related Products** Firms often react to changes in the prices of related products. For example, if land can be used for either corn or soybean production, an increase in soybean prices may cause individual farmers to shift acreage out of corn production and into soybeans. Thus, an increase in soybean prices actually affects the amount of corn supplied.

Similarly, if beef prices rise, producers may respond by raising more cattle. But leather comes from cowhide. Thus, an increase in beef prices may actually increase the supply of leather.

To summarize:

> Assuming that its objective is to maximize profits, a firm's decision about what quantity of output, or product, to supply depends on
>
> 1. The price of the good or service
> 2. The cost of producing the product, which in turn depends on
>   - The price of required inputs (labor, capital, and land), and
>   - The technologies that can be used to produce the product
> 3. The prices of related products

SHIFT OF SUPPLY VERSUS MOVEMENT ALONG A SUPPLY CURVE

A supply curve shows the relationship between the quantity of a good or service supplied by a firm and the price that good or service brings in the market. Higher prices are likely to lead to an increase in quantity supplied, *ceteris paribus*. Remember: The supply curve is derived holding everything constant except price. When the price of a product changes *ceteris paribus*, a change in the quantity supplied follows—that is, a *movement along* the supply curve takes place. But, as you have seen, supply decisions are also influenced by factors other than price. New relationships between price and quantity supplied come about when factors other than price change, and the result is a *shift* of the supply curve. When factors other than price cause supply curves to shift, we say that there has been a *change in supply*.

Recall that the cost of production depends on the price of inputs and the technologies of production available. Now suppose that a major breakthrough in the production of soybeans has occurred: Genetic engineering has produced a superstrain of disease- and pest-resistant seed. Such a technological change would enable individual farmers to supply more soybeans at *any* market price. Table 4.4 and Figure 4.7 describe this change. At $3 a bushel, farmers would have produced 30,000 bushels from the old seed (schedule S_1 in Table 4.4); with the lower cost of production and higher yield resulting from the new seed, they produce 40,000 bushels (schedule S_2 in Table 4.4). At $1.75 per bushel, they would have produced 10,000 bushels from the old seed; but with the lower costs and higher yields, output rises to 23,000 bushels.

Increases in input prices may also cause supply curves to shift. If Farmer Brown faces higher fuel costs, for example, his supply curve will shift to the left—that is, he will produce less at any given market price. If Brown's soybean supply curve shifted far enough to the left, it would intersect the price axis at a higher point, meaning that it would take a higher market price to induce Brown to produce any soybeans at all.

TABLE 4.4 SHIFT OF SUPPLY SCHEDULE FOR SOYBEANS FOLLOWING DEVELOPMENT OF A NEW DISEASE-RESISTANT SEED STRAIN

Price (Per Bushel)	SCHEDULE S_1 Quantity Supplied (Bushels Per Year Using Old Seed)	SCHEDULE S_2 Quantity Supplied (Bushels Per Year Using New Seed)
$1.50	0	5,000
1.75	10,000	23,000
2.25	20,000	33,000
3.00	30,000	40,000
4.00	45,000	54,000
5.00	45,000	54,000

FIGURE 4.7

Shift of Supply Curve for Soybeans Following Development of a New Seed Strain

When the price of a product changes, we move *along* the supply curve for that product; the quantity supplied rises or falls. When any other factor affecting supply changes, the supply curve *shifts*.

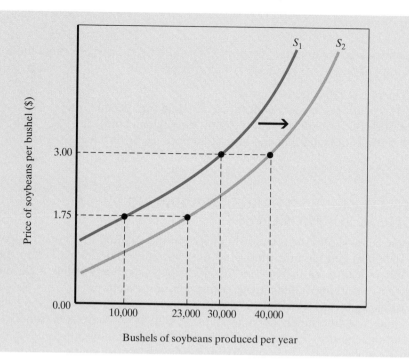

As with demand, it is very important to distinguish between *movements along* supply curves (changes in quantity supplied) and *shifts in* supply curves (changes in supply):

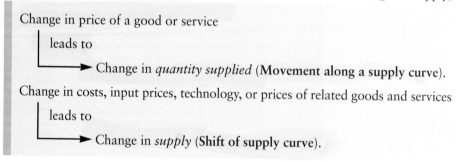

Change in price of a good or service

    leads to

      → Change in *quantity supplied* (**Movement along a supply curve**).

Change in costs, input prices, technology, or prices of related goods and services

    leads to

      → Change in *supply* (**Shift of supply curve**).

FROM INDIVIDUAL FIRM SUPPLY TO MARKET SUPPLY

market supply *The sum of all that is supplied each period by all producers of a single product.*

Market supply is determined in the same fashion as market demand. It is simply the sum of all that is supplied each period by all producers of a single product. Figure 4.8 derives a market supply curve from the supply curves of three individual firms. (In a market with more firms, total market supply would be the sum of the amounts produced by each of the firms in that market.) As the table in Figure 4.8 shows, at a price of $3 farm A supplies 30,000 bushels of soybeans, farm B supplies 10,000 bushels, and farm C supplies 25,000 bushels. At this price, the total amount supplied in the market is 30,000 + 10,000 + 25,000, or 65,000 bushels. At a price of $1.75, however, the total amount supplied is only 25,000 bushels (10,000 + 5,000 + 10,000). The market supply curve is thus the simple addition of the individual supply curves of all the firms in a particular market—that is, the sum of all the individual quantities supplied at each price.

The position and shape of the market supply curve depend on the positions and shapes of the individual firms' supply curves from which it is derived. But they also depend on the number of firms that produce in that market. If firms that produce for a particular market are earning high profits, other firms may be tempted to go into that line of business. When the technology to produce computers for home use became available,

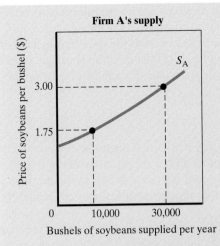

Firm A's supply

Price of soybeans per bushel ($)

3.00

1.75

S_A

0   10,000   30,000

Bushels of soybeans supplied per year

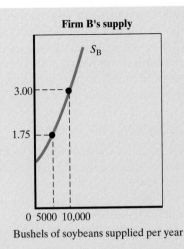

Firm B's supply

S_B

3.00

1.75

0 5000 10,000

Bushels of soybeans supplied per year

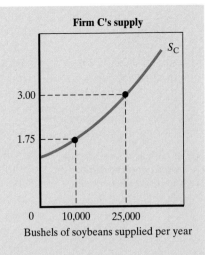

Firm C's supply

S_C

3.00

1.75

0   10,000   25,000

Bushels of soybeans supplied per year

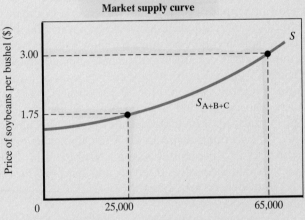

Market supply curve

Price of soybeans per bushel ($)

S

3.00

1.75

S_{A+B+C}

0   25,000   65,000

Bushels of soybeans supplied per year

Price	Quantity (q) supplied by			Market supply (Q)
	A	B	C	
$3.00	30,000 +	10,000 +	25,000	→ 65,000
1.75	10,000 +	5,000 +	10,000	→ 25,000

FIGURE 4.8

Deriving Market Supply from Individual Firm Supply Curves

Total supply in the marketplace is the sum of all the amounts supplied by all the firms selling in the market. It is the sum of all the individual quantities supplied at each price.

literally hundreds of new firms got into the act. The popularity and profitability of professional football has three times led to the formation of new leagues. When new firms enter an industry, the supply curve shifts to the right. When firms go out of business, or "exit" the market, the supply curve shifts to the left.

MARKET EQUILIBRIUM

So far we have identified a number of factors that influence the amount that households demand and the amount that firms supply in product (output) markets. The discussion has emphasized the role of market price as a determinant both of quantity demanded and quantity supplied. We are now ready to see how supply and demand in the market interact to determine the final market price.

We have been very careful in our discussions thus far to separate household decisions about how much to demand from firm decisions about how much to supply. The operation of the market, however, clearly depends on the interaction between suppliers and demanders. At any moment, one of three conditions prevails in every market: (1) The quantity demanded exceeds the quantity supplied at the current price, a situation called *excess demand*; (2) The quantity supplied exceeds the quantity demanded at the current price, a situation called *excess supply*; or (3) the quantity supplied equals the quantity demanded at the current price, a situation called **equilibrium**. At equilibrium, no tendency for price to change exists.

equilibrium *The condition that exists when quantity supplied and quantity demanded are equal. At equilibrium, there is no tendency for price to change.*

excess demand or **shortage** *The condition that exists when quantity demanded exceeds quantity supplied at the current price.*

EXCESS DEMAND

Excess demand, or a **shortage,** exists when quantity demanded is greater than quantity supplied at the current price. Figure 4.9, which plots both a supply curve and a demand curve on the same graph, illustrates such a situation. As you can see, market demand at $1.75 per bushel (50,000 bushels) exceeds the amount that farmers are currently supplying (25,000 bushels).

When excess demand occurs in an unregulated market, there is a tendency for price to rise as demanders compete against each other for the limited supply. The adjustment mechanisms may differ, but the outcome is always the same. For example, consider the mechanism of an auction. In an auction, items are sold directly to the highest bidder. When the auctioneer starts the bidding at a low price, many people bid for the item. At first there is a shortage: Quantity demanded exceeds quantity supplied. As would-be buyers offer higher and higher prices, bidders drop out, until the one who offers the most ends up with the item being auctioned. Price rises until quantity demanded and quantity supplied are equal.

At a price of $1.75 (see Figure 4.9 again), farmers produce soybeans at a rate of 25,000 bushels per year, but at that price the demand is for 50,000 bushels. Most farm products are sold to local dealers who in turn sell large quantities in major market centers, where bidding would push prices up if quantity demanded exceeded quantity supplied. As price rises above $1.75, two things happen: (1) The quantity demanded falls as buyers drop out of the market and perhaps choose a substitute, and (2) the quantity supplied increases as farmers find themselves receiving a higher price for their product and shift additional acres into soybean production.[5]

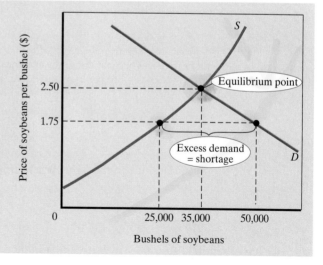

FIGURE 4.9

Excess Demand, or Shortage
At a price of $1.75 per bushel, quantity demanded exceeds quantity supplied. When *excess demand* arises, there is a tendency for price to rise. When quantity demanded equals quantity supplied, excess demand is eliminated and the market is in equilibrium. Here, the equilibrium price is $2.50, and the equilibrium quantity is 35,000 bushels.

[5]Once farmers have produced in any given season, they cannot change their minds and produce more, of course. When we derived Clarence Brown's supply schedule in Table 4.3, we imagined him reacting to prices that existed at the time he decided how much land to plant in soybeans. In Figure 4.9, the upward slope shows that higher prices justify shifting land from other crops. Final price may not be determined until final production figures are in. For our purposes here, however, we have ignored this timing problem. The best way to think about it is that demand and supply are *flows*, or *rates*, of production—that is, we are talking about the number of bushels produced *per production period*. Adjustments in the rate of production may take place over a number of production periods.

BIDDING AT AN AUCTION IS ONE WAY TO QUICKLY ELIMINATE EXCESS DEMAND.

This process continues until the shortage is eliminated. In Figure 4.9, this occurs at $2.50, where quantity demanded has fallen from 50,000 to 35,000 bushels per year and quantity supplied has increased from 25,000 to 35,000 bushels per year. When quantity demanded and quantity supplied are equal and there is no further bidding, the process has achieved an equilibrium, a situation in which *there is no natural tendency for further adjustment*. Graphically, the point of equilibrium is the point at which the supply curve and the demand curve intersect.

The process through which excess demand leads to higher prices is different in different markets. Consider the market for houses in the hypothetical town of Boomville with a population of 25,000 people, most of whom live in single-family homes. Normally about 75 homes are sold in the Boomville market each year. But last year, a major business opened a plant in town, creating 1,500 new jobs that pay good wages. This attracted new residents to the area, and real estate agents now have more buyers than there are properties for sale. Quantity demanded now exceeds quantity supplied. In other words, there is a shortage.

Auctions are not unheard of in the housing market, but they are rare. This market usually works more subtly, but the outcome is the same. Properties are sold very quickly and housing prices begin to rise. Boomville sellers soon learn that there are more buyers than usual, and they begin to hold out for higher offers. As prices for Boomville houses rise, quantity demanded eventually drops off and quantity supplied increases. Quantity supplied increases in at least two ways: (1) Encouraged by the high prices, builders begin constructing new houses, and (2) some people, attracted by the higher prices their homes will fetch, put their houses on the market. Discouraged by higher prices, however, some potential buyers (demanders) may begin to look for housing in neighboring towns and settle on commuting. Eventually, equilibrium will be reestablished, with the quantity of houses demanded just equal to the quantity of houses supplied.

Although the mechanics of price adjustment in the housing market differ from the mechanics of an auction, the outcome is exactly the same:

When quantity demanded exceeds quantity supplied, price tends to rise. When the price in a market rises, quantity demanded falls and quantity supplied rises until an equilibrium is reached at which quantity demanded and quantity supplied are equal.

This process is called *price rationing*. When a shortage exists, some people will be satisfied and some will not. When the market operates without interference, price increases will distribute what is available to those who are willing and able to pay the most. As long as there is a way for buyers and sellers to interact, those who are willing to pay more will make that fact known somehow. (We discuss the nature of the price system as a rationing device in detail in chapter 5.)

EXCESS SUPPLY

excess supply or **surplus**
The condition that exists when quantity supplied exceeds quantity demanded at the current price.

Excess supply, or a **surplus,** exists when the quantity supplied exceeds the quantity demanded at the current price. As with a shortage, the mechanics of price adjustment in the face of a surplus can differ from market to market. For example, if automobile dealers find themselves with unsold cars in the fall when the new models are coming in, you can expect to see price cuts. Sometimes dealers offer discounts to encourage buyers; sometimes buyers themselves simply offer less than the price initially asked. In any event, products do no one any good sitting in dealers' lots or on warehouse shelves. The auction metaphor introduced earlier can also be applied here: If the initial asking price is too high, no one bids, and the auctioneer tries a lower price. It's almost always true, and 1997 was no exception, that certain items do not sell as well as anticipated during the Christmas holidays. After Christmas, most stores have big sales during which they lower the prices of overstocked items. Quantities supplied exceeded quantities demanded at the current prices, so stores cut prices.

Across the state from Boomville is Bustville, where last year a drug manufacturer shut down its operations and 1,500 people found themselves out of work. With no other prospects for work, many residents decided to pack up and move. They put their houses up for sale, but there were few buyers. The result was an excess supply, or surplus, of houses: The quantity of houses supplied exceeded the quantity demanded at the current prices.

As houses sit unsold on the market for months, sellers start to cut their asking prices. Potential buyers begin offering considerably less than sellers are asking. As prices fall, two things are likely to happen. First, the low housing prices may attract new buyers. People who might have bought in a neighboring town see that there are housing bargains to be had in Bustville, and quantity demanded rises in response to price decline. Second, some of those who put their houses on the market may be discouraged by the lower prices and decide to stay in Bustville. Developers are certainly not likely to be building new housing in town. Lower prices thus lead to a decline in quantity supplied as potential sellers pull their houses from the market. This was exactly the situation in New England and California in the early 1990s.

Figure 4.10 illustrates another excess supply/surplus situation. At a price of $3 per bushel, farmers are supplying soybeans at a rate of 40,000 bushels per year, but buyers demand only 20,000. With 20,000 (40,000 minus 20,000) bushels of soybeans going unsold, the market price falls. As price falls from $3 to $2.50, quantity supplied decreases from 40,000 bushels per year to 35,000. The lower price causes quantity demanded to rise from 20,000 to 35,000. At $2.50, quantity demanded and quantity supplied are equal. For the data shown here, then, $2.50 and 35,000 bushels are the equilibrium price and quantity.

Early in 1994, crude oil production worldwide exceeded the quantity demanded, and prices fell significantly as competing producer countries tried to maintain their share of world markets. Although the mechanism by which price is adjusted is different for automobiles, housing, soybeans, and crude oil, the outcome is the same:

> When quantity supplied exceeds quantity demanded at the current price, the price tends to fall. When price falls, quantity supplied is likely to decrease and quantity demanded is likely to increase until an equilibrium price is reached where quantity supplied and quantity demanded are equal.

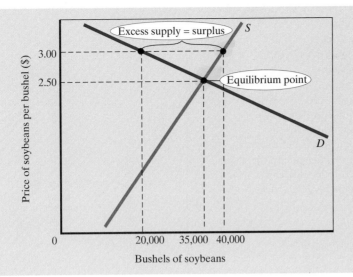

FIGURE 4.10

Excess Supply, or Surplus

At a price of $3, quantity supplied exceeds quantity demanded by 20,000 bushels. This excess supply will cause price to fall.

CHANGES IN EQUILIBRIUM

When supply and demand curves shift, the equilibrium price and quantity change. The following example will help to illustrate this point.

South America is a major producer of coffee beans. A cold snap there can reduce the coffee harvest enough to affect the world price of coffee beans. In the summer of 1994, a major freeze hit Brazil and Colombia and drove up the price of coffee on world markets to a record $2.40 per pound.

Figure 4.11 illustrates how the freeze pushed up coffee prices. Initially, the market was in equilibrium at a price of $1.20. At that price, the quantity demanded was equal to quantity supplied (13.2 billion pounds). At a price of $1.20 and a quantity of 13.2 billion pounds, the demand curve (labeled D) intersected the initial supply curve (labeled S_1). (Remember that equilibrium exists when quantity demanded equals quantity supplied—the point at which the supply and demand curves intersect.)

The freeze caused a decrease in the supply of coffee beans. That is, it caused the supply curve to shift to the left. In Figure 4.11, the new supply curve (the supply curve that shows the relationship between price and quantity supplied after the freeze) is labeled S_2.

At the initial equilibrium price, $1.20, there is now a shortage of coffee. If the price were to remain at $1.20, quantity demanded would not change; it would remain at 13.2 billion pounds. But at that price, quantity supplied would drop to 6.6 billion pounds. At a price of $1.20, quantity demanded is greater than quantity supplied.

When excess demand exists in a market, price can be expected to rise, and rise it did. As the figure shows, price rose to a new equilibrium at $2.40. At $2.40, quantity demanded is again equal to quantity supplied, this time at 9.9 billion pounds—the point at which the new supply curve (S_2) intersects the demand curve.

Notice that as the price of coffee rose from $1.20 to $2.40, two things happened. First, the quantity demanded declined (a movement along the demand curve) as people shifted to substitutes such as tea and hot cocoa. Second, the quantity supplied began to rise, but within the limits imposed by the damage from the freeze. (It might also be that some countries or areas with high costs of production, previously unprofitable, came into production and shipped to the world market at the higher price.) That is, the quantity supplied increased in response to the

FIGURE 4.11

The Coffee Market: A Shift of Supply and Subsequent Price Adjustment

Before the freeze, the coffee market was in equilibrium at a price of $1.20. At that price, quantity demanded equaled quantity supplied. The freeze shifted the supply curve to the left (from S_1 to S_2), increasing equilibrium price to $2.40.

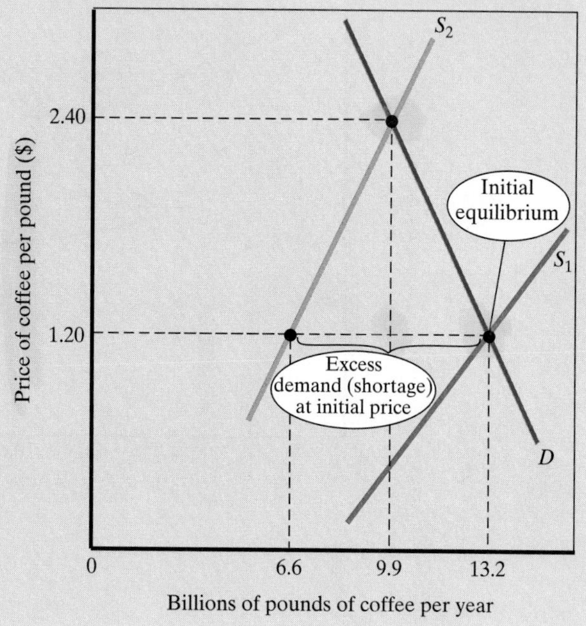

higher price *along* the new supply curve, which lies to the left of the old supply curve. The final result was a higher price ($2.40), a smaller quantity finally exchanged in the market (9.9 billion pounds), and coffee bought only by those willing to pay $2.40 per pound.

Figure 4.12 presents 10 examples of supply and demand shifts and the resulting changes in equilibrium price and quantity. Be sure to go through each graph carefully and ensure that you understand each.

DEMAND AND SUPPLY IN PRODUCT MARKETS: A REVIEW

As you continue your study of economics, you will discover that it is a discipline full of controversy and debate. There is, however, little disagreement about the basic way that the forces of supply and demand operate in free markets. If you hear that a freeze in Florida has destroyed a good portion of the citrus crop, you can bet that the price of oranges will rise.[6] If you read that the weather in the Midwest has been good and a record corn crop is expected, you can bet that corn prices will fall. When fishermen in Massachusetts go on strike and stop bringing in the daily catch, you can bet that the price of fish will go up. For additional examples of how the forces of supply and demand work, see the Application feature titled "Supply and Demand in the News."

---

[6]In economics you have to think twice, however, even about a "safe" bet. If you bet that the price of frozen orange juice will rise after a freeze, you will lose your money. It turns out that much of the crop that is damaged by a freeze can be used, but for only one thing—to make frozen orange juice. Thus, a freeze actually *increases* the supply of frozen juice on the national market. Following the last two hard freezes in Florida, the price of oranges shot up, but the price of orange juice fell sharply!

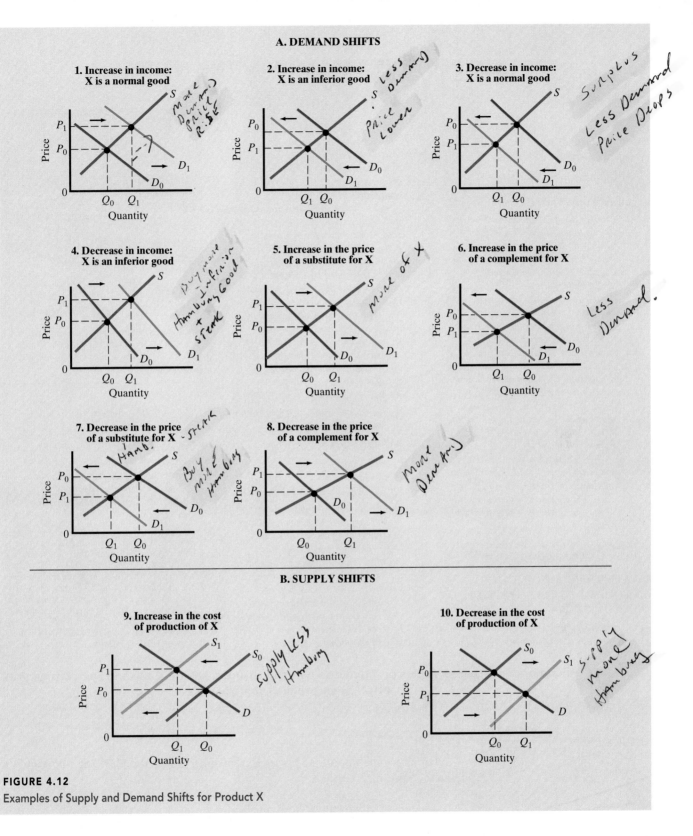

A. DEMAND SHIFTS

1. Increase in income: X is a normal good

2. Increase in income: X is an inferior good

3. Decrease in income: X is a normal good

4. Decrease in income: X is an inferior good

5. Increase in the price of a substitute for X

6. Increase in the price of a complement for X

7. Decrease in the price of a substitute for X

8. Decrease in the price of a complement for X

B. SUPPLY SHIFTS

9. Increase in the cost of production of X

10. Decrease in the cost of production of X

FIGURE 4.12

Examples of Supply and Demand Shifts for Product X

SUPPLY AND DEMAND IN THE NEWS

The basic forces of supply and demand are at work all around us, as the following news articles illustrate.

1. Supply shifts to the right:

ORANGE JUICE HITS 4-YEAR LOW

Orange juice . . . prices sank yesterday to their lowest level in four years after the Government said a freeze last month would not reduce a record Florida orange crop. . . .

The Department of Agriculture's third forecast since October once again predicted that 220 million boxes of oranges would be harvested in Florida this year. Last year, the state yielded 203.2 million boxes.

The report surprised traders, who expected the agency to lower its forecast by as many as 15 million boxes after the freeze. The agency even raised its estimate for the amount of juice each box would yield, to 1.54 gallons from 1.53 last month.

"The crop is bigger and the yields are higher," said Walter Spilka, an analyst at Smith Barney in New York. "There's no problem in Florida. There's an ocean of orange juice and prices are going to go lower."[a]

2. Demand shifts to the right; supply is expected to shift to the left:

WHETHER CUP OF JOE OR GOURMET'S CAFÉ, ITS PRICE IS SOARING

From a cappuccino grande at Starbucks to a plain cup of black no-sugar at a street vendor's cart, from a pound of Swiss water-processed decaf beans at Zabar's to a can of ground Folgers at the grocery store, the price of coffee is going up. . . .

The price increase, caused in part by increased demand for good coffee and shortages in stockpiles, is the longest sustained price rise in 20 years, and its impact is being felt across the board by importers and roasters, as well as small specialty retailers and consumers. . . .

The price surge began when industry forecasters began projecting smaller crops in Central America during the current season, and in South America in the coming season.[b]

3. Demand shifts to the right, causing short-run inventories to fall; higher prices should increase quantity supplied:

COPPER PRICES MOVE HIGHER

Copper prices rose yesterday after a larger-than-expected drop in stockpiles renewed expectations that demand would keep supplies lean. . . .

Builders are the largest consumers of copper, and last week, the Commerce Department reported that American construction spending rose 2.3 percent in February, the second consecutive increase.

GOOD WEATHER IN FLORIDA MEANS A GOOD HARVEST. SUPPLY SHIFTS TO THE RIGHT AND CAUSES ORANGE PRICES TO DROP.

"Stockpiles are falling because demand in the U.S. is still fairly good and the recent economic data are very constructive," said William O'Neill, director of futures research at Merrill Lynch in New York.[c]

Sources: [a]"Orange Juice Hits 4-Year Low; Crude Oil Slips as Stocks Rise," *The New York Times,* Feb. 13, 1997, p. D15; [b]David Halbfinger, "Whether Cup of Joe or Gourmet's Café, Its Price is Soaring," *The New York Times,* May 13, 1997, p. A1; [c]"Copper Prices Move Higher As Drop in Supply Accelerates," *The New York Times,* April 9, 1997, p. D15. Copyright © 1997 by The New York Times Co. Reprinted by permission.

 For more on recent examples of supply and demand changes, see the Case and Fair Web page at **http://www.prenhall.com/casefair.**

Here are some important points to remember about the mechanics of supply and demand in product markets:

1. A demand curve shows how much of a product a household would buy if it could buy all it wanted at the given price. A supply curve shows how much of a product a firm would supply if it could sell all it wanted at the given price.
2. Quantity demanded and quantity supplied are always per time period—that is, per day, per month, or per year.

3. The demand for a good is determined by price, household income and wealth, the prices of other goods and services, tastes and preferences, and expectations.

4. The supply of a good is determined by price, costs of production, and the prices of related products. Costs of production are determined by available technologies of production and input prices.

5. Be careful to distinguish between movements along supply and demand curves and shifts of these curves. When the price of a good changes, the quantity of that good demanded or supplied changes—that is, a movement occurs along the curve. When any other factor changes, the curves shift, or change position.

6. Market equilibrium exists only when quantity supplied equals quantity demanded at the current price.

LOOKING AHEAD: MARKETS AND THE ALLOCATION OF RESOURCES

You can already begin to see how markets answer the basic economic questions of what is produced, how it is produced, and who gets what is produced. A firm will produce what is profitable to produce. If it can sell a product at a price that is sufficient to leave a profit after production costs are paid, it will in all likelihood produce that product. Resources will flow in the direction of profit opportunities.

■ Demand curves reflect what people are willing and able to pay for products; they are influenced by incomes, wealth, preferences, the prices of other goods, and expectations. Because product prices are determined by the interaction of supply and demand, prices reflect what people are willing to pay. If people's preferences or incomes change, resources will be allocated differently. Consider, for example, an increase in demand—a shift in the market demand curve. Beginning at an equilibrium, households simply begin buying more. At the equilibrium price, quantity demanded becomes greater than quantity supplied. When there is excess demand, prices will rise, and higher prices mean higher profits for firms in the industry. Higher profits, in turn, provide existing firms with an incentive to expand and new firms with an incentive to enter the industry. Thus, the decisions of independent private firms responding to prices and profit opportunities determine *what* will be produced. No central direction is necessary.

Adam Smith saw this self-regulating feature of markets more than 200 years ago:

> Every individual . . . by pursuing his own interest . . . promotes that of society. He is led . . . by an invisible hand to promote an end which was no part of his intention.[7]

The term Smith coined, the *invisible hand*, has passed into common parlance and is still used by economists to refer to the self-regulation of markets.

■ Firms in business to make a profit have a good reason to choose the best available technology—lower costs mean higher profits. Thus, individual firms determine *how* to produce their products, again with no central direction.

■ So far we have barely touched on the question of distribution—*who* gets what is produced? But you can see part of the answer in the simple supply and demand diagrams. When a good is in short supply, price rises. As it does, those who are willing and able to continue buying do so; others stop buying.

The next chapter begins with a more detailed discussion of these topics. How, exactly, is the final allocation of resources (the mix of output and the distribution of output) determined in a market system?

---

[7]Adam Smith, *The Wealth of Nations*, p. 456.

SUMMARY

1. In societies with many people, production must satisfy wide-ranging tastes and preferences, and producers must therefore specialize.

FIRMS AND HOUSEHOLDS: THE BASIC DECISION-MAKING UNITS

2. A *firm* exists when a person or a group of people decides to produce a product or products by transforming resources, or *inputs*, into *outputs*—the products that are sold in the market. Firms are the primary producing units in a market economy. We assume firms make decisions to maximize profits.

3. *Households* are the primary consuming units in an economy. All households' incomes are subject to constraints.

INPUT MARKETS AND OUTPUT MARKETS: THE CIRCULAR FLOW

4. Households and firms interact in two basic kinds of markets: *product* or *output markets* and *input* or *factor markets*. Goods and services intended for use by households are exchanged in output markets. In output markets, competing firms supply and competing households demand. In input markets, competing firms demand and competing households supply.

5. Ultimately, firms determine the quantities and character of outputs produced, the types and quantities of inputs demanded, and the technologies used in production. Households determine the types and quantities of products demanded and the types and quantities of inputs supplied.

DEMAND IN PRODUCT/OUTPUT MARKETS

6. The quantity demanded of an individual product by an individual household depends on (1) price, (2) income, (3) wealth, (4) the prices of other products, (5) tastes and preferences, and (6) expectations about the future.

7. Quantity demanded is the amount of a product that an individual household would buy in a given period if it could buy all it wanted at the current price.

8. A *demand schedule* shows the quantities of a product that a household would buy at different prices. The same information can be presented graphically in a *demand curve*.

9. The *law of demand* states that there is a negative relationship between price and quantity demanded: As price rises, quantity demanded decreases, and vice versa. Demand curves slope downward.

10. All demand curves eventually intersect the price axis because there is always a price above which a household cannot, or will not, pay. All demand curves also eventually intersect the quantity axis because demand for most goods is limited, if only by time, even at a zero price.

11. When an increase in income causes demand for a good to rise, that good is a *normal good*. When an increase in income causes demand for a good to fall, that good is an *inferior good*.

12. If a rise in the price of good X causes demand for good Y to increase, the goods are *substitutes*. If a rise in the price of X causes demand for Y to fall, the goods are *complements*.

13. Market demand is simply the sum of all the quantities of a good or service demanded per period by all the households buying in the market for that good or service. It is the sum of all the individual quantities demanded at each price.

SUPPLY IN PRODUCT/OUTPUT MARKETS

14. Quantity supplied by a firm depends on (1) the price of the good or service, (2) the cost of producing the product, which includes the prices of required inputs and the technologies that can be used to produce the product, and (3) the prices of related products.

15. Market supply is the sum of all that is supplied each period by all producers of a single product. It is the sum of all the individual quantities supplied at each price.

16. It is very important to distinguish between *movements* along demand and supply curves and *shifts* of demand and supply curves. The demand curve shows the relationship between price and quantity demanded. The supply curve shows the relationship between price and quantity supplied. A change in price is a movement along the curve. Changes in tastes, income, wealth, expectations, or prices of other goods and services cause demand curves to shift; changes in costs, input prices, technology, or prices of related goods and services cause supply curves to shift.

MARKET EQUILIBRIUM

17. When quantity demanded exceeds quantity supplied at the current price, *excess demand* (or a *shortage*) exists and the price tends to rise. When prices in a market rise, quantity demanded falls and quantity supplied rises until an equilibrium is reached at which quantity supplied and quantity demanded are equal. At *equilibrium*, there is no further tendency for price to change.

18. When quantity supplied exceeds quantity demanded at the current price, *excess supply* (or a *surplus*) exists and the price tends to fall. When price falls, quantity supplied decreases and quantity demanded increases until an equilibrium price is reached where quantity supplied and quantity demanded are equal.

REVIEW TERMS AND CONCEPTS

capital market, 69
complements, complementary goods, 75
demand curve, 71
demand schedule, 71
entrepreneur, 68
equilibrium, 86
excess demand or shortage, 86
excess supply or surplus, 88
factors of production, 69
firm, 68
households, 68

income, 74
inferior goods, 74
input or factor markets, 69
labor market, 69
land market, 69
law of demand, 71
law of supply, 81
market demand, 79
market supply, 84
movement along a demand curve, 77
normal goods, 74

perfect substitutes, 75
product or output markets, 69
profit, 80
quantity demanded, 70
quantity supplied, 80
shift of a demand curve, 77
substitutes, 74
supply curve, 81
supply schedule, 80
wealth or net worth, 74

PROBLEM SET

1. Illustrate the following with supply and demand curves:
   a. In 1997 and 1998, the economy expanded, increasing the demand for labor and pushing up wages.
   b. In the mid-1990s, more and more people decided to lease their cars rather than buy them. When leases expire, people usually turn in their cars and lease new ones. During 1997, there was a big increase in used cars available for sale, and the price of used cars dropped sharply.
   c. As more and more people bought home computers during the 1990s, the demand for access to the World Wide Web and the Internet increased sharply. At the same time, new companies like Erol's began to enter the Internet-access market, competing with older, more established services such as America Online. Despite a massive increase in demand, the price of access to the Web actually declined.
   d. Before economic reforms were implemented in the countries of Eastern Europe, regulation held the price of bread substantially below equilibrium. When reforms were implemented, prices were deregulated and they rose dramatically. As a result, the quantity of bread demanded fell and the quantity of bread supplied rose sharply.
   e. Good weather in the Midwest during 1997 produced a very large wheat crop and pushed wheat prices down to below $3.50 per bushel.

2. During the summer of 1997, the Baltimore Orioles and the New York Yankees were battling it out for first place in the American League East. Meanwhile, the Detroit Tigers were in last place. When the Yankees came to Baltimore on September 11 to play the Orioles at Camden Yard (the Baltimore stadium), all 48,000 tickets to the game were sold out months in advance, and many of the fans who wanted tickets couldn't get them. In contrast, a few weeks earlier, the Orioles had travelled to Detroit to play the Tigers in Tiger Stadium, and the game set a record for low attendance. In fact, only 15,000 went to the game in a stadium that holds 52,000. Assume for simplicity that all tickets to both games sold for $20 each.

   a. Draw supply and demand curves for tickets to each of the two games. Draw one graph for each game. Label the excess demand or excess supply, where appropriate. (*Hint*: Supply is fixed. It does not change with price.)
   b. Is there a pricing policy that would have filled Tiger Stadium for the Detroit game?
   c. The price system was not allowed to work to ration the Yankee tickets to those who would pay the most for them. How do you know this? What might have determined who got the tickets?

3. During 1997, Orlando, Florida was growing rapidly, with new jobs luring young people into the area. Despite increases in population and income growth that expanded demand for housing, the price of existing houses barely increased. Why? Illustrate your answer with supply and demand curves.

4. Do you agree or disagree with each of the following statements? Briefly explain your answers.
   a. The price of a good rises, causing the demand for another good to fall. The two goods are therefore substitutes.
   b. A shift in supply causes the price of a good to fall. The shift must have been an increase in supply.
   c. During 1997, incomes rose sharply for most Americans. This change would likely lead to an increase in the prices of both normal and inferior goods.
   d. Two normal goods cannot be substitutes for each other.
   e. If demand increases and supply increases at the same time, price will clearly rise.
   f. The price of Good A falls. This causes an increase in the price of Good B. Goods A and B are therefore complements.

5. The U.S. government administers two programs that affect the market for cigarettes. Media campaigns and labeling requirements are aimed at making the public aware of the health dangers of cigarettes. At the same time, the Department of Agriculture maintains price supports for

tobacco. Under this program, the supported price is above the market equilibrium price, and the government limits the amount of land that can be devoted to tobacco production. Are these two programs at odds with respect to the goal of reducing cigarette consumption? As a part of your answer, illustrate graphically the effects of both policies on the market for cigarettes.

6. Housing prices in Boston and Los Angeles have been on a roller coaster ride. Illustrate each of the following situations with supply and demand curves:
   a. In both cities an increase in income combined with expectations of a strong market shifted demand and caused prices to rise rapidly during the mid- to late 1980s.
   b. By 1990, the construction industry boomed as more and more developers started new residential projects. But those new projects expanded the supply of housing just as demand was shifting as a result of falling incomes and expectations during the 1990 to 1991 recession.
   c. In 1997, housing in higher-income towns in the Boston area was experiencing price increases at the same time as housing prices in lower income towns were experiencing price decreases. In part this effect was due to "trade-up" buyers selling houses in lower-income areas and buying houses in higher-income areas.
   d. Despite falling incomes, housing markets in lower-income areas in Los Angeles were actually experiencing some price increases in 1994 and 1995 as immigration of lower-income households continued.

7. The following two sets of statements contain common errors. Identify and explain each.
   a. Demand increases, causing prices to rise. Higher prices cause demand to fall. Therefore, prices fall back to their original levels.
   b. The supply of meat in Russia increases, causing meat prices to fall. Lower prices mean that Russian households spend more on meat.

8. For each of the following, draw a diagram that illustrates the likely effect on the market for eggs. Indicate in each case the impact on equilibrium price and equilibrium quantity.
   a. A surgeon general warning that high-cholesterol foods cause heart attacks.
   b. A decrease in the price of bacon, a complementary product.
   c. An increase in the price of chicken feed.
   d. Caesar salads become trendy at dinner parties. (The dressing is made with raw eggs.)
   e. A technological innovation that reduces egg breakage during packing.

9. "An increase in demand causes an increase in price. But an increase in price causes a decrease in demand. Increases in demand, therefore, largely cancel themselves out." Comment.

*10. Suppose the demand and supply curves for eggs in the United States are given by the following equations:

$$Q_d = 100 - 20P$$
$$Q_s = 10 + 40P$$

where Q_d = millions of dozens of eggs Americans would like to buy each year; Q_s = millions of dozens of eggs U.S. farms would like to sell each year; P = price per dozen eggs.
   a. Fill in the following table:

PRICE (PER DOZEN)	QUANTITY DEMANDED (Q_d)	QUANTITY SUPPLIED (Q_s)
$ .50	_____	_____
$1.00	_____	_____
$1.50	_____	_____
$2.00	_____	_____
$2.50	_____	_____

   b. Use the information in the table to find the equilibrium price and equilibrium quantity.
   c. Graph the demand and supply curves, and identify the equilibrium price and quantity.

*11. Housing policy analysts debate the best way to increase the number of housing units available to low-income households. One strategy—the demand-side strategy—is to provide people with housing "vouchers," paid for by the government, that can be used to rent housing supplied by the private market. Another—a supply-side strategy—is to have the government subsidize housing suppliers or to build public housing.
   a. Illustrate supply- and demand-side strategies using supply and demand curves. Which results in higher rents?
   b. Critics of housing vouchers (the demand-side strategy) argue that because the supply of housing to low-income households is limited and will not respond at all to higher rents, demand vouchers will serve only to drive up rents and make landlords better off. Illustrate their point with supply and demand curves.

*12. Suppose the market demand for pizza is given by $Q_d = 300 - 20P$ and the market supply for pizza is given by $Q_s = 20P - 100$, where P = price (per pizza).
   a. Graph the supply and demand schedules for pizza using $5 through $15 as the value of P.
   b. In equilibrium, how many pizzas would be sold and at what price?
   c. What would happen if suppliers set the price of pizza at $15? Explain the market adjustment process.
   d. Suppose the price of hamburgers, a substitute for pizza, doubles. This leads to a doubling of the demand for pizza (at each price consumers demand twice as much pizza as before). Write the equation for the new market demand for pizza.
   e. Find the new equilibrium price and quantity of pizza.

_____

*Note: Problems marked with an asterisk are more challenging.

TAKE IT TO THE NET

We invite you to visit the Case and Fair page on the Prentice Hall Web site:

http://www.prenhall.com/casefair

for this chapter's World Wide Web exercise.

THE PRICE SYSTEM, SUPPLY AND DEMAND, AND ELASTICITY

EVERY SOCIETY has a system of institutions that determines what is produced, how it is produced, and who gets what is produced. In some societies, these decisions are made centrally, through planning agencies or by government directive. But in every society many decisions are made in a *decentralized* way, through the operation of markets.

Markets exist in all societies, and chapter 4 provided a bare-bones description of how markets operate. In this chapter, we continue our examination of supply, demand, and the price system.

THE PRICE SYSTEM: RATIONING AND ALLOCATING RESOURCES

The market system, also called the *price system*, performs two important and closely related functions. First, it provides an automatic mechanism for distributing scarce goods and services. That is, it serves as a **price rationing** device for allocating goods and services to consumers when the quantity demanded exceeds the quantity supplied. Second, the price system ultimately determines both the allocation of resources among producers and the final mix of outputs.

PRICE RATIONING

Consider first the simple process by which the price system eliminates a shortage. Figure 5.1 shows hypothetical supply and demand curves for lobsters caught off the coast of New England.

Lobsters are considered a delicacy. Maine produces most of the lobster catch in the United States, and anyone who drives up the Maine coast cannot avoid the hundreds of restaurants selling lobster rolls, steamed lobster, and baked stuffed lobster.

As Figure 5.1 shows, the equilibrium price of live New England lobsters was $3.27 per pound in 1998. At this price, lobster boats brought in lobsters at a rate of 47 million pounds per year—an amount that was just enough to satisfy demand.

price rationing *The process by which the market system allocates goods and services to consumers when quantity demanded exceeds quantity supplied.*

97

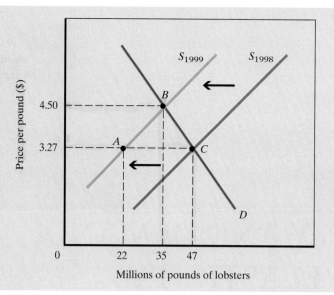

FIGURE 5.1

The Market for Lobsters

Suppose that in 1999, 20,000 square miles of lobstering waters off the coast of Maine are closed. The supply curve shifts to the left. Before the waters are closed, the lobster market is in equilibrium at the price of $3.27 and a quantity of 47 million pounds. The decreased supply of lobster leads to higher prices, and a new equilibrium is reached at $4.50 and 35 million pounds.

Market equilibrium existed at $3.27 per pound, because at that price quantity demanded was equal to quantity supplied. (Remember that equilibrium occurs at the point where the supply and demand curves intersect. In Figure 5.1, this occurs at point C.)

Now suppose that in 1999 the waters off a section of the Maine coast become contaminated with a poisonous parasite. As a result, the Department of Agriculture is forced to close 20,000 square miles of the most productive lobstering areas. Even though many of the lobster boats shift their trapping activities to other waters, there is a sharp reduction in the quantity of lobster supplied. The supply curve shifts to the left, from S_{1998} to S_{1999}. This shift in the supply curve creates a situation of excess demand at $3.27. At that price, the quantity demanded is 47 million pounds and the quantity supplied is 22 million pounds. Quantity demanded exceeds quantity supplied by 25 million pounds.

The reduced supply causes the price of lobster to rise sharply. As the price rises, the available supply is "rationed." Who gets it? Those who are willing and able to pay the most.

You can see the market's price rationing function clearly in Figure 5.1. As the price rises from $3.27, the quantity demanded declines along the demand curve, moving from point C (47 million pounds) toward point B (35 million pounds). The higher prices mean that restaurants must charge much more for lobster rolls and stuffed lobsters. As a result, many people simply stop buying lobster or order it less frequently when they dine out. Some restaurants drop it from the menu entirely, and some shoppers at the fish counter turn to lobster substitutes such as swordfish and salmon.

As the price rises, lobster trappers (suppliers) also change their behavior. They stay out longer and put out more traps than they did when the price was $3.27 per pound. Quantity supplied increases from 22 million pounds to 35 million pounds. This increase in price brings about a movement along the 1999 supply curve from point A to point B.

Finally, a new equilibrium is established at a price of $4.50 per pound and a total output of 35 million pounds. The market has determined who gets the lobsters: *The lower total supply is rationed to those who are willing and able to pay the higher price.*

This idea of "willingness to pay" is central to the distribution of available supply, and willingness depends on both desire (preferences) and income/wealth. Willingness to pay does not necessarily mean that only the very rich will continue to buy lobsters when the price increases. Lower-income people may continue to buy some lobster, but they will have to be willing to sacrifice more of other goods to do so.

In sum:

> The adjustment of price is the rationing mechanism in free markets. Price rationing means that whenever there is a need to ration a good—that is, when a shortage exists—in a free market, the price of the good will rise until quantity supplied equals quantity demanded—that is, until the market clears.

There is some price that will clear any market you can think of. Consider the market for a famous painting such as van Gogh's *Portrait of Dr. Gachet,* illustrated in Figure 5.2. At a low price, there would be an enormous excess demand for such an important painting. The price would be bid up until there was only one remaining demander. Presumably, that price would be very high. In fact, van Gogh's *Portrait of Dr. Gachet* sold for a record $82.5 million in 1990. If the product is in strictly scarce supply, as a single painting is, its price is said to be *demand determined.* That is, its price is determined solely and exclusively by the amount that the highest bidder or highest bidders are willing to pay.

One might interpret the statement that "there is some price that will clear any market" to mean "everything has its price." But that is not exactly what it means. Suppose you own a small silver bracelet that has been in your family for generations. It is quite possible that you wouldn't sell it for *any* amount of money. Does this mean that the market is not working, or that quantity supplied and quantity demanded are not equal? Not at all. It means simply that *you* are the highest bidder. By turning down all bids, you must be willing to forgo what anybody offers for it.

WHEN SUPPLY IS FIXED OR SOMETHING FOR SALE IS UNIQUE, ITS PRICE IS *DEMAND DETERMINED.* PRICE IS WHAT THE HIGHEST BIDDER IS WILLING TO PAY. IN 1990, THE HIGHEST BIDDER WAS WILLING TO PAY $82.5 MILLION FOR VAN GOGH'S *PORTRAIT OF DR. GACHET.*

CONSTRAINTS ON THE MARKET AND ALTERNATIVE RATIONING MECHANISMS

On occasion, both governments and private firms decide to use some mechanism other than the market system to ration an item for which there is excess demand at the current price. (This was often the case in the former Soviet Union and other Communist nations like China, Cuba, Poland, and East Germany. For more information, see the Global Perspective box titled "The Market Comes to China.") Policies designed to stop price rationing are commonly justified in a number of ways.

The rationale most often used is fairness. It is not "fair" to let landlords charge high rents, not "fair" for oil companies to run up the price of gasoline, not "fair" for insurance companies to charge enormous premiums, and so on. After all, the argument goes, we have no choice but to pay—housing and insurance are necessary, and one

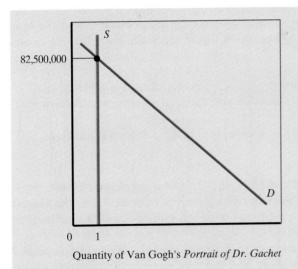

Quantity of Van Gogh's *Portrait of Dr. Gachet*

FIGURE 5.2

Market for a Rare Painting

There is some price that will clear any market, even if supply is strictly limited. In an auction for a unique painting, the price (bid) will rise to eliminate excess demand until there is only one bidder willing to purchase the single available painting.

THE MARKET COMES TO CHINA

Price rationing allocates goods and services to those who are willing and able to pay for them. One of the central premises of communism is that price rationing for basic necessities, such as food, is unfair; everyone should be able to afford such items as food and shelter. But regulating prices to "fair" levels below equilibrium means that quantity supplied will be less than quantity demanded.

In addition, preventing the price mechanism from operating requires that some device other than price be used to ration the available goods. Before the collapse of communism in the Soviet Union and Eastern Europe, people waited in long lines at state stores, which could not meet the citizens' demands. The stores were not well stocked in part because farmers could get a much better price for their goods on the illegal black market. The biggest problem with regulated prices, however, is that the incentive to produce is lost.

In 1997, China's paramount leader Deng Xiaoping died. More than any other leader in the communist world, Deng understood the importance of market prices as an incentive. In 1978, local officials associated with Deng began allowing poor rural peasants to grow grain on their own individual plots of land. The peasants could not own the land, and the government took a fixed amount of the grain they produced as a tax. But they were permitted to sell all surpluses in private markets at market prices. This policy had a dramatic effect on the level of output. As prices increased, so did the quantity supplied.

Productivity soared, and Chinese agriculture began to grow dramatically.

Deng also knew that the industrial sector could not function without market prices playing a role. As of 1997, markets—not bureaucracies—determined the prices of nearly nine-tenths of all finished goods in China.

For the 75 percent of Chinese who make their living from the land, incomes have gone up over 200 percent since 1978, to $1,000 per year. Industrial incomes have risen even more. China's economy has grown at an average rate of over 9 percent since 1982. In 1997, it grew at an impressive 10 percent annual rate.

Source: "Deng's China," *The Economist,* February, 1997.

For more on recent changes in China, see the Case and Fair Web page at
http://www.prenhall.com/casefair.

---

needs gasoline to get to work. While it is not precisely true that price rationing allocates goods and services solely on the basis of income and wealth, income and wealth do constrain our wants. Why should all the gasoline or all the tickets to the World Series go just to the rich?

Various schemes to keep price from rising to equilibrium are based on several perceptions of injustice, among them (1) that price-gouging is bad, (2) that income is unfairly distributed, and (3) that some items are necessities, and everyone should be able to buy them at a "reasonable" price. Regardless of the rationale, the following examples will make two things clear:

1. Attempts to bypass price rationing in the market and to use alternative rationing devices are much more difficult and costly than they would seem at first glance.
2. Very often, such attempts distribute costs and benefits among households in unintended ways.

➤ **Oil, Gasoline, and OPEC** In 1973 and 1974, the Organization of Petroleum Exporting Countries (OPEC) imposed an embargo on shipments of crude oil to the United States. What followed was a drastic reduction in the quantity of gasoline available at local gas pumps.

Had the market system been allowed to operate, refined gasoline prices would have increased dramatically until quantity supplied was equal to quantity demanded.

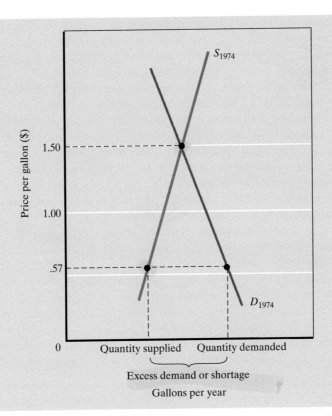

FIGURE 5.3

Excess Demand (Shortage)
Created by a Price Ceiling

In 1974, a ceiling price of 57¢
per gallon of leaded regular
gasoline was imposed. If the
price had instead been set by
the interaction of supply and
demand, it would have
increased to approximately
$1.50 per gallon. At 57¢ per
gallon, the quantity demanded
exceeded the quantity supplied.
Because the price system was
not allowed to function, an
alternative rationing system
had to be found to distribute
the available supply of gasoline.

But the government decided that rationing gasoline to only those who were willing and able to pay the most was unfair, and Congress imposed a **price ceiling**, or maximum price, of 57¢ per gallon of leaded regular gasoline. That price ceiling was intended to keep gasoline "affordable," but it also perpetuated the shortage. At the restricted price, quantity demanded remained greater than quantity supplied, and the available gasoline had to be divided up somehow among all potential demanders.

You can see the effects of the price ceiling by looking carefully at Figure 5.3. If the price had been set by the interaction of supply and demand, it would have increased to approximately $1.50 per gallon. Instead, Congress made it illegal to sell gasoline for more than 57¢ per gallon. At that price, quantity demanded exceeded quantity supplied and a shortage existed. Because the price system was not allowed to function, an alternative rationing system had to be found to distribute the available supply of gasoline.

Several devices were tried. The most common of all nonprice rationing systems is **queuing**, a term that simply means waiting in line. During 1974 very long lines began to appear at gas stations, starting as early as 5 A.M. Under this system, gasoline went to those who were willing to pay the most, but the sacrifice was measured in hours and aggravation rather than in dollars.[1]

price ceiling *A maximum price that sellers may charge for a good, usually set by government.*

queuing *Waiting in line as a means of distributing goods and services; a nonprice rationing mechanism.*

---

[1]You can also show formally that the result is inefficient—that there is a resulting net loss of total value to society. First, there is the cost of waiting in line. Time has a value. With price rationing, no one has to wait in line and the value of that time is saved. Second, there may be additional lost value if the gasoline ends up in the hands of someone who places a lower value on it than someone else who gets no gas. Suppose, for example, that the market price of gasoline if unconstrained would rise to $2, but that the government has it fixed at $1. There will be long lines to get gas. Imagine that to motorist A, ten gallons of gas is worth $35 but that she fails to get it because her time is too valuable to wait in line. To motorist B, ten gallons is worth only $15, but his time is worth much less, so he gets the gas. Clearly, in the end, A could pay B for the gas and both could be better off. If A pays B $30 for the gas, A is $5 better off and B is $15 better off. In addition, A doesn't have to wait in line. Thus, the allocation that results from nonprice rationing involves a net loss of value. Such losses are called dead weight losses.

favored customers *Those who receive special treatment from dealers during situations of excess demand.*

ration coupons *Tickets or coupons that entitle individuals to purchase a certain amount of a given product per month.*

black market *A market in which illegal trading takes place at market-determined prices.*

Gasoline prices were a major concern in the 1970s. Since 1980, however, gasoline prices have been remarkably stable:

	% Change in:	
	Prices in General	The Price of Gasoline
1980–85	+30.6%	+1.3%
1985–90	+21.5%	+2.5%
1990–95	+16.6%	−1.2%

A second nonprice rationing device used during the gasoline crisis was that of **favored customers**. Many gas station owners decided not to sell gasoline to the general public at all but to reserve their scarce supplies for friends and favored customers. Not surprisingly, many customers tried to become "favored" by offering side payments to gas station owners. Owners also charged high prices for service. By doing so, they increased the real price of gasoline but hid it in service overcharges to get around the ceiling.

Yet another method of dividing up available supply is the use of **ration coupons**. It was suggested in both 1974 and 1979 that families be given ration tickets, or coupons, that would entitle them to purchase a certain number of gallons of gasoline each month. That way, everyone would get the same amount, regardless of income. Such a system had been employed in the United States during the 1940s, when wartime price ceilings on meat, sugar, butter, tires, nylon stockings, and many other items were imposed.

When ration coupons are used with no prohibition against trading them, however, the result is almost identical to a system of price rationing. Those who are willing and able to pay the most simply buy up the coupons and use them to purchase gasoline, chocolate, fresh eggs, or anything else that is sold at a restricted price.[2] This means that the price of the restricted good will effectively rise to the market-clearing price. For instance, suppose that you decide not to sell your ration coupon. You are then forgoing what you would have received by selling the coupon. Thus the "real" price of the good you purchase will be higher (if only in opportunity cost) than the restricted price. Even when trading coupons is declared illegal, it is virtually impossible to stop black markets from developing. In a **black market**, illegal trading takes place at market-determined prices.

▶ **The World Cup, 1994** Another way to understand the price system's rationing function is to look at the ways in which tickets to popular sporting events and concerts are sold and distributed. One of the most interesting recent examples is the 1994 World Cup soccer tournament.

In the summer of 1994, the World Cup came to the United States. The matches took place in nine cities, including Boston, Washington, Chicago, and Los Angeles. A total of 52 games were played among qualifying teams representing 24 countries. The final game between Italy and Brazil was played on July 17 in the Rose Bowl in Pasadena, California. (Brazil won.)

A total of 3.6 million tickets were available for the games. Demand for soccer tickets was very high. Soccer is without question the most popular sport in the world, and it is literally true that wars have been fought because of the outcome of matches. With national pride at stake, tens of thousands of people flocked to the United States. In addition, the sport's growing popularity in the United States led to high ticket demand by U.S. residents. Rather than charging market-clearing prices, the event's organizers decided to charge "fair" prices and set the average ticket price at about $58.

This price was below equilibrium, and there was excess demand for the tickets almost from the time that they went on sale. Interestingly, organizers of similar high-interest sporting events (like the Super Bowl, the NBA playoffs, and the World Series) almost always price tickets below the level that would just fill the stadiums. Why? In their words, to do otherwise would be "unfair." As Alan Rothenberg, chairman of World Cup USA put it: "We definitely could have charged more. . . . Obviously we wanted to price the tickets high enough so we can pay for the event. . . . but at the same time not be unfair to the public."

We have seen, however, that if the price system is not going to be used to allocate the tickets among demanders, another method must be found. One method gives the tickets to certain favored customers. The *Washington Post* (December 25, 1993) reported that 25 percent to 30 percent of the tickets were committed to "corporate sponsors, city

[2] Of course, if you are assigned a number of tickets, and you sell them, you are better off than you would be with price rationing. Ration tickets thus serve as a way of redistributing income.

IF U.S. FANS WERE WILLING TO PAY $3,000 FOR A TICKET TO THE WORLD CUP IN LOS ANGELES IN 1994, WHAT DO YOU THINK THE MORE FRENZIED SOCCER FANS IN EUROPE WILL PAY FOR A TICKET TO THE 1998 FINALS AT THE NEWLY BUILT STADIA FRANCE JUST OUTSIDE OF PARIS?

officials, members of Congress, and other dignitaries." Another 15 percent were held for soccer's world governing body, and yet another 15 percent were held for the "U.S. soccer community"—coaches, officials, and players. The remaining tickets were sold through a mail lottery and, in some cities, by queuing.

The distribution of tickets was not really over until the final match was played. Consider the demand for tickets to the final match that were distributed to fans months earlier. The organizing body did charge more for final game tickets—the price of the cheapest ticket was $180 and the most expensive $475, with the average around $300. But consider the potential demand! As *Worth* magazine (May 1994) put it, "Foreign fans will be waving huge wads of bills near game day." Because the Rose Bowl holds only 91,794 people, by some estimates the equilibrium ticket price was in the vicinity of $3,000!

Figure 5.4 illustrates the situation. The supply curve is vertical at 91,794 tickets—the fixed number of seats available. As the demand curve shows, some people were willing to pay prices far in excess of $3,000—and many did. The *Los Angeles Times* reported that one man paid $250,000 for a set (unspecified number) of tickets. Even before tickets were issued, an extensive and complicated black market had begun operating.

Now consider someone who paid $180 for a final game ticket and went to the game. What price did she really pay to go to the game? The answer: A lot more than $180. By not selling her ticket, she revealed that going to the game was worth more to her than all the other things that $3,000 or $4,000 could buy.

What, then, can we conclude about alternatives to the price rationing system?

No matter how good the intentions of private organizations and governments, it is very difficult to prevent the price system from operating and to stop willingness to pay from asserting itself. Every time an alternative is tried, the price system seems to sneak in the back door. With favored customers and black markets, the final distribution may be even more unfair than that which would result from simple price rationing.

PRICES AND THE ALLOCATION OF RESOURCES

Thinking of the market system as a mechanism for allocating scarce goods and services among competing demanders is very revealing. But the market determines much more than just the distribution of final outputs. It also determines what gets produced and how resources are allocated among competing uses.

FIGURE 5.4

Supply of and Demand for World Cup Final Game Tickets
World Cup 1994 final game tickets were initially sold for an average face price of about $300. The Rose Bowl in Pasadena holds 91,794 people. Thus, the supply curve is vertical at 91,794 tickets. At $300, the quantity demanded far exceeded the quantity supplied. The result was enormous excess demand.

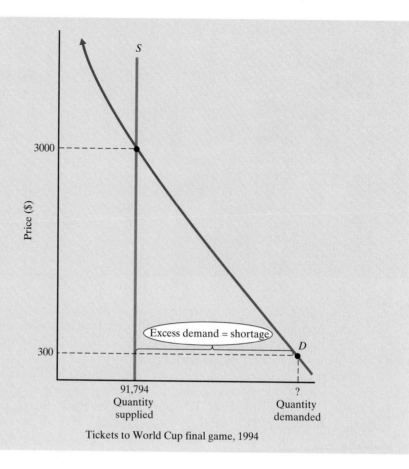

Excess demand = shortage

Tickets to World Cup final game, 1994

Consider a change in consumer preferences that leads to an increase in demand for a specific good or service. During the 1970s, for example, people began going to restaurants much more frequently than before. Researchers think that this trend, which continues today, is partially the result of social changes (such as a dramatic rise in the number of two-earner families) and partially the result of rising incomes. The market responded to this change in demand by shifting resources, both capital and labor, into more and better restaurants.

With the increase in demand for restaurant meals, the price of eating out rose, and the restaurant business became more profitable. The higher profits attracted new businesses and provided old restaurants with an incentive to expand. As new capital, seeking profits, flowed into the restaurant business, so too did labor. New restaurants need chefs. Chefs need training, and the higher wages that came with increased demand provided an incentive for them to get it. In response to the increase in demand for training, new cooking schools opened and existing schools began to offer courses in the culinary arts.

This story could run on and on, but the point is clear:

Price changes resulting from shifts of demand in output markets cause profits to rise or fall. Profits attract capital; losses lead to disinvestment. Higher wages attract labor and encourage workers to acquire skills. At the core of the system, supply, demand, and prices in input and output markets determine the allocation of resources and the ultimate combinations of things produced.

SUPPLY AND DEMAND ANALYSIS: AN OIL IMPORT FEE

The basic logic of supply and demand is a powerful tool of analysis. As an extended example of the power of this logic, we will consider a recent proposal to impose a tax on imported oil. The idea of raising the federal gasoline tax is hotly debated, with many arguing strongly for such a tax. Many economists, however, believe that a fee on imported crude oil, which is used to produce gasoline, would have better effects on the economy than would a gasoline tax.

Consider the facts. Between 1985 and 1989, the United States increased its dependence on oil imports dramatically. In 1989, total U.S. demand for crude oil was 13.6 million barrels per day. Of that amount, only 7.7 million barrels per day (57 percent) were supplied by U.S. producers, with the remaining 5.9 million barrels per day (43 percent) imported. The price of oil on world markets that year averaged about $18. This heavy dependence on foreign oil left the United States vulnerable to the price shock that followed the Iraqi invasion of Kuwait in August 1990. In the months following the invasion, the price of crude oil on world markets shot up to $40 per barrel.

Even before the invasion, many economists and some politicians had recommended a stiff oil import fee (or tax) that would, it was argued, reduce the U.S. dependence on foreign oil by (1) reducing overall consumption and (2) providing an incentive for increased domestic production. An added bonus would be improved air quality from the reduction in driving.

Supply and demand analysis makes the arguments of the import fee proponents easier to understand. Part a of Figure 5.5 shows the U.S. market for oil. The world price of oil is assumed to be $18, and the United States is assumed to be able to buy all the oil that it wants at this price. This means that domestic producers cannot get away with charging any more than $18 per barrel. The curve labeled $Supply_{US}$ shows the amount that domestic suppliers will produce at each price level. At a price of $18, domestic production is 7.7 million barrels. Stated somewhat differently, U.S. producers will produce at point A on the supply curve. The total quantity of oil demanded in the United States in 1989 was 13.6 million barrels per day. At a price of $18, the quantity demanded in the United States is point B on the demand curve.

The difference between the total quantity demanded (13.6 million barrels per day) and domestic production (7.7 million barrels per day) is total imports (5.9 million barrels per day).

Now suppose that the government levies a tax of 33 percent on imported oil. Because the import price is $18, a tax of $6 (or .33 × $18) per barrel means that importers of oil in the United States will pay a total of $24 per barrel ($18 + $6). This new higher price means that U.S. producers can also charge up to $24 for a barrel of crude. Note, however, that the tax is paid only on imported oil. Thus the entire $24 paid for domestic crude goes to domestic producers.

Figure 5.5b shows the result of the tax. First, because of higher price the quantity demanded drops to 12.2 million barrels per day. This is a movement *along* the demand curve from point B to point D. At the same time, the quantity supplied by domestic producers increases to 9.0 million barrels per day. This is a movement *along* the supply curve from point A to point C. With an increase in domestic quantity supplied and a decrease in domestic quantity demanded, imports decrease to 3.2 million barrels per day (12.2 − 9.0).[3]

---

[3]These figures were not chosen randomly. It is interesting to note that in 1985 the world price of crude oil averaged about $24 a barrel. Domestic production was 9.0 million barrels per day, and domestic consumption was 12.2 million barrels per day, with imports of only 3.2 million. The drop in the world price between 1985 and 1989 increased imports to 5.9 million, an 84% increase.

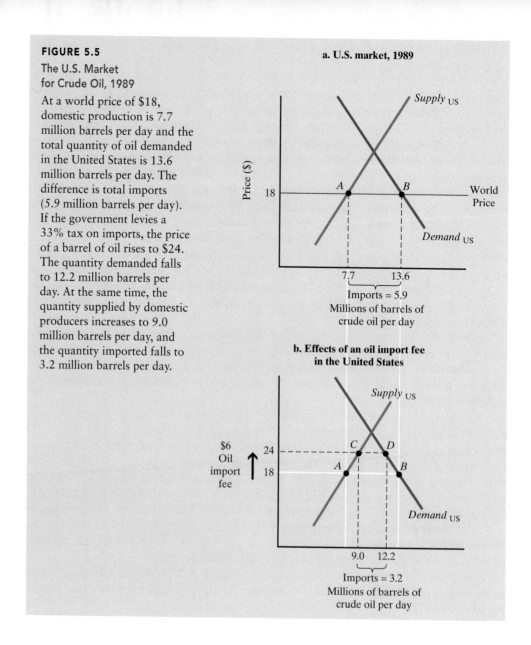

FIGURE 5.5

The U.S. Market for Crude Oil, 1989

At a world price of $18, domestic production is 7.7 million barrels per day and the total quantity of oil demanded in the United States is 13.6 million barrels per day. The difference is total imports (5.9 million barrels per day). If the government levies a 33% tax on imports, the price of a barrel of oil rises to $24. The quantity demanded falls to 12.2 million barrels per day. At the same time, the quantity supplied by domestic producers increases to 9.0 million barrels per day, and the quantity imported falls to 3.2 million barrels per day.

a. U.S. market, 1989

Supply US

Demand US

Price ($)

18   A   B   World Price

7.7   13.6

Imports = 5.9

Millions of barrels of crude oil per day

b. Effects of an oil import fee in the United States

Supply US

Demand US

$6 Oil import fee

24   C   D

18   A   B

9.0   12.2

Imports = 3.2

Millions of barrels of crude oil per day

The tax also generates revenues for the federal government. The total tax revenue collected is equal to the tax per barrel ($6) times the number of imported barrels. When the quantity imported is 3.2 million barrels per day, total revenue is $6 × 3.2 million, or $19.2 million *per day* (about $7 billion per year).

What does all of this mean? In the final analysis, an oil import fee would (1) increase domestic production and (2) reduce overall consumption. This would in turn help with the problem of air pollution and simultaneously reduce U.S. dependence on foreign oil.

ELASTICITY

The principles of supply and demand enable us to make certain predictions about how households and firms are likely to behave in both national and international markets. When the price of a good rises, for example, households are likely to purchase less of it

TRAFFIC CONGESTION AND ORGAN DONATIONS

We can now use what we've learned about the price system to examine two topics of current interest: traffic congestion and organ donations.

TRAFFIC CONGESTION

Very few people in the United States have not had the frustrating experience of sitting in traffic. Indeed, traffic jams are by no means unique to the United States. Some of the worst traffic congestion in the world can be found in Bangkok (Thailand) and Taipei (Taiwan).

Traffic jams are costly. Clearly, time has a value, and the opportunity cost of sitting in traffic for two hours can be significant. A recent study estimated the cost of the morning rush hour in a major U.S. city at over $13 million.

You can think of congestion as "excess demand for road space." That is, at the current price, the quantity demanded exceeds the quantity supplied. The way we currently ration that shortage of space is by waiting in line to use it.

Can we use the price mechanism to help? While this idea goes back at least 100 years, most credit the late Nobel Prize-winning economist William Vickrey for pushing an idea whose time may have finally come. The idea is simple: Charge people a price to use highways . . . a price high enough to keep the traffic flowing. As the price is raised, those who live near public transportation and those who might be able to avoid travelling altogether

would avoid the congested roads, at least during peak hours. In essence, quantity demanded will drop. Those who must continue to use the roads will pay, but they will not waste time waiting in traffic.

How might such a price be collected? One obvious answer is a toll. Many states impose tolls for the use of bridges, turnpikes, and thruways, but most prices are low enough that they have little impact on highway use. The city-state of Singapore requires car owners to purchase a very expensive license (mounted on the car's windshield) if they want to drive on downtown streets during peak hours. This system has helped Singapore's congestion problems greatly. Professor Vickrey proposed that every car be equipped with a radio signal that would ring up a charge every time the car passes a designated street corner. The charges could be changed depending on the time of day and the degree of congestion in the area.

With today's small powerful microprocessors, the necessary technology is already here; it is being used by a number of states to speed traffic through toll booths. Many are betting that the next few years will see a dramatic increase in road prices.[a]

ORGAN DONATIONS

Improved medical technology has led to a dramatic increase in the number of organ transplants performed in the

United States and elsewhere in the world. The availability of organs is constraining the use of transplants, however. In simple terms, the quantity demanded is far greater than the quantity supplied. For example, there were about 10,000 kidney transplants in 1995 while over 30,000 people were awaiting the procedure.

The supply of available organs comes primarily from people who donate them for use in transplants after they die. Some states ask people to indicate on their driver's license whether they agree to the use of their organs after an accidental death, but so far (despite a recent campaign supported by Michael Jordan) persuasion hasn't solved the problem.

Can the market help? A recent proposal by Nobel Prize-winning economist Gary Becker argues that potential organ donors should be paid a price to induce them to register as a potential organ donor. Such a price, he argues, would increase the quantity supplied sharply, because today the price is zero![b]

Sources: [a]Kim Clark, "How to Make Traffic Jams a Thing of the Past," Fortune, March 31, 1997; William Vickrey, "Pricing as a Tool in Coordination of Local Transportation," in Transportation Economics (New York: National Bureau of Economic Research, 1965); and [b]Gary Becker, "How Uncle Sam Could Ease the Organ Shortage," Business Week, January 20, 1997.

For more on the use of the price system, see the Case and Fair Web page at
http://www.prenhall.com/casefair.

and firms are likely to supply more of it. When costs of production fall, firms are likely to supply more—supply will increase, or shift to the right. When the price of a good falls, households are likely to buy fewer substitutes—demand for substitutes is likely to decrease, or shift to the left.

The size, or magnitude, of these reactions can be very important. You have already seen that during the oil embargo of the early 1970s, the Organization of Petroleum Exporting Countries (OPEC) succeeded in increasing the price of crude oil substantially.

Because this strategy raised revenues to the oil producing countries, we might expect this strategy to work for everyone. But if the banana exporting countries, which we will call OBEC, had done the same thing, the strategy would not have worked.

Why? Suppose the banana exporting countries decide to cut production by 30 percent in order to drive up the world price of bananas. At first, when the quantity of bananas supplied declines, the quantity demanded is greater than the quantity supplied, and the world price rises. The issue for OBEC, however, is *how much* the world price will rise. That is, how much will people be willing to pay to continue consuming bananas? Unless the percentage *increase* in price is greater than the percentage *decrease* in output, the OBEC countries will lose revenues. And a little research shows us that the news is not good for OBEC. There are many reasonable substitutes for bananas. As the price of bananas rises, people simply eat fewer bananas and eat more pineapples or oranges. Many people are simply not willing to pay a higher price for bananas. The quantity of bananas demanded declines 30 percent—to the new quantity supplied—after only a modest price rise, and OBEC fails in its mission; its revenues decrease instead of increase.

The quantity of oil demanded is not nearly as responsive to a change in price because no substitutes for oil are readily available. When the price of crude oil went up in the early 1970s, 130 million motor vehicles, getting an average of 12 miles per gallon and consuming over 100 billion gallons of gasoline each year, were on the road in the United States. Millions of homes were heated with oil, and industry ran on equipment that used petroleum products. When OPEC cut production, the price of oil rose sharply. Quantity demanded fell somewhat, but price increased over 400 percent. What makes the cases of OPEC and OBEC different is the *magnitude* of the response in the quantity demanded to a change of price.

The importance of actual measurement cannot be overstated. Without the ability to measure and predict how much people are likely to respond to economic changes, all the economic theory in the world would be of little help to policy makers. In fact, most of the research being done in economics today involves the collection and analysis of quantitative data that measure behavior. This is a dramatic change in the discipline of economics that has taken place only in the last 30 years.

Economists commonly measure responsiveness using the concept of **elasticity**. Elasticity is a general concept that can be used to quantify the response in one variable when another variable changes. If some variable A changes in response to changes in another variable B, the elasticity of A with respect to B is equal to the percentage change in A divided by the percentage change in B:

elasticity *A general concept used to quantify the response in one variable when another variable changes.*

$$\text{elasticity of } A \text{ with respect to } B = \frac{\%\Delta A}{\%\Delta B}$$

We may speak of the elasticity of demand or supply with respect to price, of the elasticity of investment with respect to the interest rate, or of the elasticity of tax payments with respect to income. We begin with a discussion of price elasticity of demand.

PRICE ELASTICITY OF DEMAND

You have already seen the law of demand at work. Recall that, *ceteris paribus,* when prices rise, quantity demanded can be expected to decline. When prices fall, quantity demanded can be expected to rise. The normal negative relationship between price and quantity demanded is reflected in the downward slope of demand curves.

▶ **Slope and Elasticity** The slope of a demand curve may in a rough way reveal the responsiveness of the quantity demanded to price changes, but slope can be quite misleading. In fact, it is not a good formal measure of responsiveness.

Consider the two identical demand curves in Figure 5.6. The only difference between the two is that quantity demanded is measured in pounds in the graph on the left

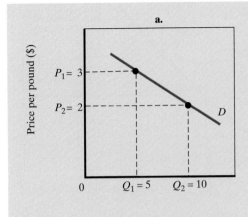

a.

b.

FIGURE 5.6
Slope Is Not a Useful Measure of Responsiveness
Changing the unit of measure from pounds to ounces changes the measured slope of the demand curve dramatically. But the behavior of buyers in the two diagrams is identical.

Pounds of steak per month

Slope: $\dfrac{\Delta Y}{\Delta X} = \dfrac{P_2 - P_1}{Q_2 - Q_1}$

$= \dfrac{2 - 3}{10 - 5} = -\dfrac{1}{5}$

Ounces of steak per month

Slope: $\dfrac{\Delta Y}{\Delta X} = \dfrac{P_2 - P_1}{Q_2 - Q_1}$

$= \dfrac{2 - 3}{160 - 80} = -\dfrac{1}{80}$

and in ounces in the graph on the right. When we calculate the numerical value of each slope, however, we get very different answers. The curve on the left has a slope of $-1/5$, and the curve on the right has a slope of $-1/80$, yet the two curves represent the *exact same behavior*. If we had changed dollars to cents on the Y axis, the two slopes would be -20 and -1.25 respectively. (Review the appendix to chapter 1 if you don't understand how these numbers are calculated.)

The problem is that the numerical value of slope depends on the units used to measure the variables on the axes. To correct this problem, we must convert the changes in price and quantity to percentages. The price increase in Figure 5.6 leads to a decline of 5 pounds, or 80 ounces, in the quantity of steak demanded—a decline of 50 percent from the initial 10 pounds, or 160 ounces, whether we measure the steak in pounds or ounces.

We define **price elasticity of demand**, then, simply as the ratio of the percentage change in quantity demanded to the percentage change in price. Stated mathematically:

price elasticity of demand
The ratio of the percentage change in quantity demanded to the percentage change in price; measures the responsiveness of demand to changes in price.

$$\text{price elasticity of demand} = \frac{\%\ \text{change in quantity demanded}}{\%\ \text{change in price}}$$

Percentage changes should always carry the sign (plus or minus) of the change. Positive changes, or increases, take a $(+)$. Negative changes, or decreases, take a $(-)$. The law of demand implies that price elasticity of demand is nearly always a negative number: Price increases $(+)$ will lead to decreases in quantity demanded $(-)$, and vice versa. Thus, the numerator and denominator should have opposite signs, resulting in a negative ratio.

▶ **Types of Elasticity** Table 5.1 gives the hypothetical responses of demanders to a 10 percent price increase in four markets. Insulin is absolutely necessary to an insulin-dependent diabetic, and the quantity demanded is unlikely to respond to an increase in price. When the quantity demanded does not respond at all to a price change, the percentage change in quantity demanded is zero, and the elasticity is zero. In this case, we say that the demand for the product is **perfectly inelastic**. Figure 5.7a illustrates the perfectly inelastic demand for insulin. Because quantity demanded does not change *at all* when price changes, the demand curve is simply a vertical line.

perfectly inelastic demand
Demand in which quantity demanded does not respond at all to a change in price.

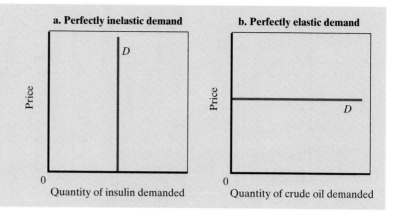

FIGURE 5.7

Perfectly Elastic and Perfectly Inelastic Demand Curves

Figure 5.7a shows a perfectly inelastic demand curve for insulin. Price elasticity of demand is zero. Quantity demanded is fixed; it does not change at all when price changes. Figure 5.7b shows a perfectly elastic demand curve for crude oil. A tiny price increase drives the quantity demanded to zero. In essence, perfectly elastic demand implies that individual producers can sell all they want at the going market price but cannot charge a higher price.

Unlike insulin, basic telephone service is generally considered a necessity, but not an absolute necessity. If a 10 percent increase in telephone rates results in a 1 percent decline in the quantity of service demanded, demand elasticity is $(-1 \div 10) = -.1$.

When the percentage change in quantity demanded is smaller in absolute size than the percentage change in price, as is the case with telephone service, then elasticity is less than 1 in absolute size.[4] When a product has an elasticity between zero and minus (negative) one, we say that demand is **inelastic**. The demand for basic telephone service is inelastic at $-.1$. Stated simply, inelastic demand means that there is some responsiveness of demand, but not a great deal, to a change in price.

inelastic demand *Demand that responds somewhat, but not a great deal, to changes in price. Inelastic demand always has a numerical value between zero and −1.*

A warning: You must be very careful about signs. Because it is generally understood that demand elasticities are negative (demand curves have a negative slope), they are often reported and discussed without the negative sign. For example, a technical paper might report that the demand for housing "appears to be inelastic with respect to price, or less than one (.6)." What the writer means is that the estimated elasticity is $-.6$, which is between zero and -1. Its absolute value is less than 1.

unitary elasticity *A demand relationship in which the percentage change in quantity of a product demanded is the same as the percentage change in price in absolute value (a demand elasticity of −1).*

Returning to Table 5.1, we see that a 10 percent increase in beef prices drives down the quantity of beef demanded by 10 percent. Demand elasticity is thus $(-10 \div 10) = -1$. When the percentage change in quantity of product demanded is the same as the percentage change in price in absolute value, we say that the demand for that product has **unitary elasticity**. The elasticity of a unitarily elastic product is always minus one (-1). As Table 5.1 shows, the demand for beef has unitary elasticity.

TABLE 5.1   HYPOTHETICAL DEMAND ELASTICITIES FOR FOUR PRODUCTS

PRODUCT	% CHANGE IN PRICE (%ΔP)	% CHANGE IN QUANTITY DEMANDED (%ΔQ_D)	ELASTICITY (%ΔQ_D ÷ %ΔP)	
Insulin	+10%	0%	0 ⟶	Perfectly inelastic
Basic telephone service	+10%	−1%	−.1 ⟶	Inelastic
Beef	+10%	−10%	−1.0 ⟶	Unitarily elastic
Bananas	+10%	−30%	−3.0 ⟶	Elastic

[4]The term *absolute size* or *absolute value* means ignoring the sign. The absolute value of -4 is 4; the absolute value of -3.8 is greater than the absolute value of 2.

When the percentage decrease in quantity demanded is larger than the percentage increase in price in absolute size, we say that demand is **elastic**. The demand for bananas, for example, is likely to be quite elastic because there are many substitutes for bananas (other fruits, for instance). If a 10 percent increase in the price of bananas leads to a 30 percent decrease in the quantity of bananas demanded, the price elasticity of demand for bananas is $(-30 \div 10) = -3$. When the absolute value of elasticity exceeds 1, demand is elastic.

Finally, if a small increase in the price of a product causes the quantity demanded to drop immediately to zero, demand for that product is said to be **perfectly elastic**. Suppose, for example, that you produce a product that can be sold only at a predetermined, fixed price. If you charged even one penny more, no one would buy your product because people would simply buy from another producer who hadn't raised the price. This is very close to reality for domestic oil producers, who cannot charge more than the world price for crude oil, and for farmers, who cannot charge more than the current market price for their crops.

A perfectly elastic demand curve is illustrated in Figure 5.7b. Because the quantity demanded drops to zero above a certain price, the demand curve for a perfectly elastic good is a horizontal line. Perfect elasticity implies that individual producers can sell all they want at a fixed price but cannot charge a higher price.

elastic demand *A demand relationship in which the percentage change in quantity demanded is larger in absolute value than the percentage change in price (a demand elasticity with an absolute value greater than 1).*

perfectly elastic demand *Demand in which quantity demanded drops to zero at the slightest increase in price.*

CALCULATING ELASTICITIES

Elasticities must be calculated cautiously. Return for a moment to the demand curves in Figure 5.6. The fact that these two identical demand curves have dramatically different slopes should be enough to convince you that slope is a poor measure of responsiveness.

The concept of elasticity circumvents the measurement problem posed by the graphs in Figure 5.6 by converting the changes in price and quantity into percentage changes. Recall that elasticity of demand is the *percentage* change in quantity demanded divided by the *percentage* change in price.

▶ **Calculating Percentage Changes** Because we need to know percentage changes to calculate elasticity, let's begin our example by calculating the percentage change in quantity demanded. Figure 5.6a, reproduced in the margin here, shows that the quantity of steak demanded increases from 5 pounds (Q_1) to 10 pounds (Q_2) when price drops from $3 to $2 per pound. Thus, the change in quantity demanded is equal to $Q_2 - Q_1$, or 5 pounds.

To convert this change into a percentage change, we must decide on a *base* against which to calculate the percentage. It is often convenient to use the initial value of quantity demanded (Q_1) as the base.

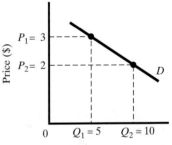

Pounds of steak per month

FAST FACTS

Many economists have advocated the legalization of drugs on the grounds that legalization would take the profit out of drug trafficking and reduce crime. However, lower prices would lead to higher usage. Some argue that because many drugs are addictive, demand is likely to be quite inelastic. A few studies show the opposite. One study found that the price elasticity of demand for marijuana is between -1.0 and -1.5. A more recent historical study finds that the price elasticity of demand for opium in Indonesia between 1923 and 1938 was -0.7 in the short run and -1.0 in the long run.

Sources: Jan van Ours, "The Price Elasticity of Hard Drugs: The Case of Opium in the West Indies, 1923–1938," *Journal of Political Economy*, April, 1995; Charles T. Nisbet and Firouz Vakil, "Some Estimates of Price and Expenditure Elasticities of Demand for Marijuana Among U.C.L.A. Students," *Review of Economics and Statistics*, November, 1972.

To calculate percentage change in quantity demanded using the initial value as the base, the following formula is used:

$$\% \text{ change in quantity demanded} = \frac{\text{change in quantity demanded}}{Q_1} \times 100\%$$

$$= \frac{Q_2 - Q_1}{Q_1} \times 100\%.$$

In Figure 5.6, $Q_2 = 10$ and $Q_1 = 5$. Thus:

$$\% \text{ change in quantity demanded} = \frac{10 - 5}{5} \times 100\% = \frac{5}{5} \times 100\% = 100\%.$$

Expressing this equation verbally, we can say that an increase in quantity demanded from 5 pounds to 10 pounds is a 100 percent increase from 5 pounds. Note that you arrive at exactly the same result if you use the diagram in Figure 5.6b, in which quantity demanded is measured in ounces. An increase from Q_1 (80 ounces) to Q_2 (160 ounces) is a 100 percent increase.

We can calculate the percentage change in price in a similar way. Once again, let's use the initial value of P (that is, P_1) as the base for calculating the percentage. Using P_1 as the base, the formula for calculating the percentage change in P is simply:

$$\% \text{ change in price} = \frac{\text{change in price}}{P_1} \times 100\%$$

$$= \frac{P_2 - P_1}{P_1} \times 100\%.$$

In Figure 5.6a, P_2 equals 2, and P_1 equals 3. Thus, the change in P, or ΔP, is a negative number: $P_2 - P_1 = 2 - 3 = -1$. This is true because the change is a decrease in price. Plugging the values of P_1 and P_2 into the equation above, we get:

$$\% \text{ change in price} = \frac{2 - 3}{3} \times 100\% = \frac{-1}{3} \times 100\% = -33.3\%.$$

In other words, decreasing price from \$3 to \$2 is a 33.3 percent decline.

▶ **Elasticity Is a Ratio of Percentages** Once all the changes in quantity demanded and price have been converted into percentages, calculating elasticity is a matter of simple division. Recall the formal definition of elasticity:

$$\text{price elasticity of demand} = \frac{\% \text{ change in quantity demanded}}{\% \text{ change in price}}$$

If demand is elastic, the ratio of percentage change in quantity demanded to percentage change in price will have an absolute value greater than 1. If demand is inelastic, the ratio will have an absolute value between zero and 1. If the two percentages are exactly equal, so that a given percentage change in price causes an equal percentage change in quantity demanded, elasticity is equal to -1; this is unitary elasticity.

Substituting the percentages calculated above, we see that a 33.3 percent decrease in price leads to a 100 percent increase in quantity demanded; thus:

$$\text{price elasticity of demand} = \frac{+100\%}{-33.3\%} = -3.0.$$

According to these calculations, the demand for steak is elastic.

▶ **The Midpoint Formula** Although simple, the use of the initial values of P and Q as the bases for calculating percentage changes can be misleading. Let's return to the example of demand for steak in Figure 5.6a, where we have a change in quantity demanded of 5 pounds. Using the initial value Q_1 as the base, we calculated that this change represents a 100 percent increase over the base. Now suppose that the price of steak rises back to $3, causing the quantity demanded to drop back to 5 pounds. How much of a percentage decrease in quantity demanded is this? We now have $Q_1 = 10$ and $Q_2 = 5$. Using the same formula we used above, we get:

$$\% \text{ change in quantity demanded} = \frac{\text{change in quantity demanded}}{Q_1} \times 100\%$$

$$= \frac{Q_2 - Q_1}{Q_1} \times 100\%$$

$$= \frac{5 - 10}{10} \times 100\% = -50\%.$$

Thus, an increase from 5 pounds to 10 pounds is a 100 percent increase (because the initial value used for the base is 5), but a decrease from ten pounds to five pounds is only a 50 percent decrease (because the initial value used for the base is 10). This does not make much sense because in both cases we are calculating elasticity on the same interval on the demand curve. Changing "direction" of the calculation should not change the elasticity.

To describe percentage changes more accurately, a simple convention has been adopted. Instead of using the initial values of Q and P as the bases for calculating percentages, we use these values' *midpoints* as the bases. That is, we use the value halfway between P_1 and P_2 for the base in calculating the percentage change in price, and the value halfway between Q_1 and Q_2 as the base for calculating percentage change in quantity demanded.

Thus, the **midpoint formula** for calculating the percentage change in quantity demanded becomes:

$$\% \text{ change in quantity demanded} = \frac{\text{change in quantity demanded}}{(Q_1 + Q_2)/2} \times 100\%$$

$$= \frac{Q_2 - Q_1}{(Q_1 + Q_2)/2} \times 100\%.$$

midpoint formula *A more precise way of calculating percentages using the value halfway between P_1 and P_2 for the base in calculating the percentage change in price, and the value halfway between Q_1 and Q_2 as the base for calculating the percentage change in quantity demanded.*

Substituting the numbers from the original Figure 5.6a, we get:

$$\% \text{ change in quantity demanded} = \frac{10 - 5}{(5 + 10)/2} \times 100\% = \frac{5}{7.5} \times 100\% = 66.7\%.$$

Using the point halfway between P_1 and P_2 as the base for calculating the percentage change in price, we get:

$$\% \text{ change in price} = \frac{\text{change in price}}{(P_1 + P_2)/2} \times 100\%$$

$$= \frac{P_2 - P_1}{(P_1 + P_2)/2} \times 100\%.$$

Substituting the numbers from the original Figure 5.6a yields:

$$\% \text{ change in price} = \frac{2 - 3}{(3 + 2)/2} \times 100\% = \frac{-1}{2.5} \times 100\% = -40.0\%.$$

TABLE 5.2   CALCULATING PRICE ELASTICITY WITH THE MIDPOINT FORMULA

FIRST, CALCULATE PERCENTAGE CHANGE IN QUANTITY DEMANDED (%ΔQ_D):

$$\% \text{ change in quantity demanded} = \frac{\text{change in quantity demanded}}{(Q_1 + Q_2)/2} \times 100\% = \frac{Q_2 - Q_1}{(Q_1 + Q_2)/2} \times 100\%$$

Substituting the numbers from Figure 5.6a:

$$\% \text{ change in quantity demanded} = \frac{10 - 5}{(5 + 10)/2} \times 100\% = \frac{5}{7.5} \times 100\% = 66.7\%$$

NEXT, CALCULATE PERCENTAGE CHANGE IN PRICE (%ΔP):

$$\% \text{ change in price} = \frac{\text{change in price}}{(P_1 + P_2)/2} \times 100\% = \frac{P_2 - P_1}{(P_1 + P_2)/2} \times 100\%$$

Substituting the numbers from Figure 5.6a:

$$\% \text{ change in price} = \frac{2 - 3}{(3 + 2)/2} \times 100\% = \frac{-1}{2.5} \times 100\% = -40.0\%$$

PRICE ELASTICITY COMPARES THE PERCENTAGE CHANGE IN QUANTITY DEMANDED AND THE PERCENTAGE CHANGE IN PRICE:

$$\frac{\%\Delta Q_D}{\%\Delta P} = \frac{66.7\%}{-40.0\%}$$
$$= -1.67$$
$$= \text{PRICE ELASTICITY OF DEMAND}$$

DEMAND IS ELASTIC.

We can thus say that a change from a quantity of 5 to a quantity of 10 is a +66.7 percent change using the midpoint formula, and a change in price from $3 to $2 is a −40 percent change using the midpoint formula.

Using these percentages to calculate elasticity yields:

$$\text{price elasticity of demand} = \frac{\% \text{ change in quantity demanded}}{\% \text{ change in price}} = \frac{66.6\%}{-40.0\%} = -1.67.$$

Using the midpoint formula in this case gives a lower demand elasticity, but the demand remains elastic because the percentage change in quantity demanded is still greater than the percentage change in price in absolute size.

The calculations based on the midpoint approach are summarized in Table 5.2.

> **Elasticity Changes along a Straight-Line Demand Curve**   An interesting and important point is that elasticity changes from point to point along a demand curve even if the slope of that demand curve does not change—that is, even along a straight-line demand curve. Indeed, the differences in elasticity along a demand curve can be quite large.

Consider the demand schedule shown in Table 5.3 and the demand curve in Figure 5.8. Herb works about 22 days per month in a downtown San Francisco office tower. On the top floor of the building is a nice dining room. If lunch in the dining room costs $10, Herb would eat there only twice a month. If the price of lunch falls to $9, he would eat there four times a month. (Herb would bring his lunch to work on other days.) If lunch were only a dollar, he would eat there 20 times a month.

Let's calculate price elasticity of demand between points *A* and *B* on the demand curve in Figure 5.8. Moving from *A* to *B*, the price of a lunch drops from $10 to $9 (a decrease of $1) and the number of dining room lunches that Herb eats per month increases from two to four (an increase of two). We will use the midpoint approach.

First, we calculate the percentage change in quantity demanded:

$$\% \text{ change in quantity demanded} = \frac{Q_2 - Q_1}{(Q_1 + Q_2)/2} \times 100\%.$$

Substituting the numbers from Figure 5.8, we get:

$$\% \text{ change in quantity demanded} = \frac{4 - 2}{(2 + 4)/2} \times 100\% = \frac{2}{3} \times 100\% = 66.7\%$$

TABLE 5.3

DEMAND SCHEDULE FOR OFFICE DINING ROOM LUNCHES

PRICE (PER LUNCH)	QUANTITY DEMANDED (LUNCHES PER MONTH)
$11	0
10	2
9	4
8	6
7	8
6	10
5	12
4	14
3	16
2	18
1	20
0	22

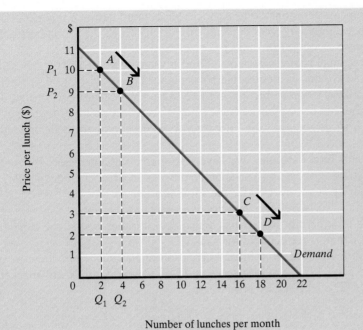

FIGURE 5.8

Demand Curve for Lunch
at the Office Dining Room

Between points A and B,
demand is quite elastic at
−6.4. Between points C and
D, demand is quite inelastic
at −0.294.

Next, we calculate the percentage change in price:

$$\% \text{ change in price} = \frac{P_2 - P_1}{(P_1 + P_2)/2} \times 100\%.$$

Substituting the numbers from Figure 5.8:

$$\% \text{ change in price} = \frac{9 - 10}{(10 + 9)/2} \times 100\% = \frac{-1}{9.5} \times 100\% = -10.5\%.$$

Finally, we calculate elasticity by comparing the two ratios as:

$$\text{elasticity of demand} = \frac{\% \text{ change in quantity demanded}}{\% \text{ change in price}}$$

$$= \frac{66.7\%}{-10.5\%} = -6.4.$$

The percentage change in quantity demanded is 6.4 times larger than the percentage change in price. In other words, Herb's demand between points A and B is quite responsive; his demand between points A and B is elastic.

Now consider a different movement along the same demand curve in Figure 5.8. Moving from point C to point D, the graph indicates that at a price of $3, Herb eats in the office dining room 16 times per month. If the price drops to $2, he eats there 18 times per month. These changes expressed in numerical terms are exactly the same as the price and quantity changes between points A and B in the figure—price falls $1, and quantity demanded increases by two meals. Expressed in percentage terms, however, these changes are very different.

Using the midpoints as the base, the $1 price decline is only a 10.5 percent reduction when price is up around $9.50, between points A and B. The same $1 price decline is a 40 percent reduction when price is down around $2.50, between points C and D. The two-meal increase in quantity demanded is a 66.7 percent increase when Herb averages only three meals per month, but it is only an 11.76 percent increase when he averages 17 meals per month. The elasticity of demand between points C and D is thus 11.76 percent divided by -40 percent, or $-.294$. (Work these numbers out for yourself by using the midpoint formula.)

The percentage changes between A and B are very different from those between C and D, and so are the elasticities. Herb's demand is quite elastic (-6.4) between points A and B; a 10.5 percent reduction in price caused a 66.7 percent increase in quantity demanded. But his demand is inelastic ($-.294$) between points C and D; a 40 percent decrease in price caused only an 11.8 percent increase in quantity demanded.

➤ **Elasticity and Total Revenue** We have seen that OPEC increased its revenues in the 1970s by restricting supply and pushing up the market price of crude oil. We also argued that a similar strategy by OBEC, the Organization of Banana Exporting Countries, would probably fail. Why? The quantity of oil demanded is not as responsive to a change in price as is the quantity of bananas demanded. In other words, the demand for oil is more inelastic than is the demand for bananas.

We can now use the more formal definition of elasticity to make more precise our argument of why OPEC would succeed and OBEC would fail. In any market, $P \times Q$ is total revenue (TR) received by producers:

$$TR = P \times Q$$
$$\text{total revenue} = \text{price} \times \text{quantity}$$

OPEC's total revenue is the price per barrel of oil (P) times the number of barrels its participant countries sell (Q). To banana producers, total revenue is the price per bunch times the number of bunches sold.

When price increases in a market, quantity demanded declines. As we've seen, when price (P) declines, quantity demanded (Q_D) increases. The two factors, P and Q_D, move in opposite directions:

$$\begin{array}{cc} \text{Effects of price changes} & P\uparrow \rightarrow Q_D\downarrow \\ \text{on quantity demanded:} & \text{and} \\ & P\downarrow \rightarrow Q_D\uparrow \end{array}$$

Because total revenue is the product of P and Q, whether TR rises or falls in response to a price increase depends on which is bigger, the percentage increase in price or the percentage decrease in quantity demanded. If the percentage decrease in quantity demanded is smaller than the percentage increase in price, total revenue will rise. This occurs when demand is *inelastic*. In this case, the percentage price rise simply outweighs the percentage quantity decline, and $P \times Q = (TR)$ rises:

$$\begin{array}{cc} \text{Effect of price increase on} & \\ \text{a product with inelastic demand:} & \uparrow P \times Q_D\downarrow = TR\uparrow \end{array}$$

If, however, the percentage decline in quantity demanded following a price increase is larger than the percentage increase in price, total revenue will fall. This occurs when demand is *elastic*. The percentage price increase is outweighed by the percentage quantity decline:

$$\begin{array}{cc} \text{Effect of price increase on} & \\ \text{a product with elastic demand:} & \uparrow P \times Q_D\downarrow = TR\downarrow \end{array}$$

The opposite is true for a price cut. When demand is elastic, a cut in price increases total revenues:

Effect of price cut on a product with elastic demand:	$\downarrow P \times Q_D \uparrow = TR \uparrow$

When demand is inelastic, a cut in price reduces total revenues:

Effect of price cut on a product with inelastic demand:	$\downarrow P \times Q_D \uparrow = TR \downarrow$

Review the logic of these equations to make sure you understand the reasoning thoroughly.

With this knowledge, we can now easily see why the OPEC cartel was so effective. The demand for oil is inelastic. Restricting the quantity of oil available led to a huge increase in the price of oil—the percentage increase was larger in absolute value than the percentage decrease in the quantity of oil demanded. Hence, OPEC's total revenues went up. In contrast, an OBEC cartel would not be effective because the demand for bananas is elastic. A small increase in the price of bananas results in a large decrease in the quantity of bananas demanded and thus causes total revenues to fall. For some details on the elasticity experiences of some other businesses, see the Application feature titled "London Newspapers and New York Restaurants Learn about Elasticity."

THE DETERMINANTS OF DEMAND ELASTICITY

Elasticity of demand is a way of measuring the responsiveness of consumers' demand to changes in price. As a measure of behavior, it can be applied to individual households or to market demand as a whole. I love peaches and I would hate to give them up. My demand for peaches is therefore inelastic. But not everyone is crazy about peaches, and, in fact, the market demand for peaches is relatively elastic. Because no two people have exactly the same preferences, reactions to price changes will be different for different people, and this makes generalizations hazardous. Nonetheless, a few principles do seem to hold.

➤ **Availability of Substitutes** Perhaps the most obvious factor affecting demand elasticity is the availability of substitutes. Consider a number of farm stands lined up along a country road. If every stand sells fresh corn of roughly the same quality, Mom's Green Thumb will find it very difficult to charge a price much higher than the competition charges, because a nearly perfect substitute is available just down the road. The demand for Mom's corn is thus likely to be very elastic: An increase in price will lead to a rapid decline in the quantity demanded of Mom's corn.

In Table 5.1, we considered two products that have no readily available substitutes, local telephone service and insulin for diabetics. There are many others. Demand for these products is likely to be quite inelastic.

➤ **The Importance of Being Unimportant** When an item represents a relatively small part of our total budget, we tend to pay little attention to its price. For example, if I pick up a pack of mints once in a while, I might not notice an increase in price from 25¢ to 35¢. Yet this is a 40 percent increase in price (33.3 percent using the midpoint formula). In cases such as these, we are not likely to respond very much to changes in price, and demand is likely to be inelastic.

➤ **The Time Dimension** When the OPEC nations cut output and succeeded in pushing up the price of crude oil in the early 1970s, few substitutes were immediately available. Demand was relatively inelastic, and prices rose substantially. During the last 30 years,

LONDON NEWSPAPERS AND NEW YORK RESTAURANTS LEARN ABOUT ELASTICITY

Businesses must carefully consider the demand elasticity for their products when adjusting prices. Consider these two examples:

1. The London *Independent* Recently, the *Independent*, a daily newspaper printed in London, announced a price cut to 30 pence from 50 pence. As a result, daily circulation increased from 240,000 copies to 280,000 copies. At first glance, the price cut might seem successful, but look closely at the result.

A price cut from 50 pence to 30 pence is a 40 percent reduction (50 percent using the midpoint formula). The increase in circulation each day is only 16.6 percent (15.4 percent using the midpoint formula). Thus, demand is *inelastic*:

$$\text{Elasticity} = \frac{+15.4\%}{-50.0\%} = -.31$$

When demand is inelastic, a cut in price leads to a reduction in daily revenues.

Before: 50 pence × 240,000 copies = 12,000,000 pence in revenue

After: 30 pence × 280,000 copies = 8,400,000 pence in revenue

2. Restaurants in New York City In the early 1990s, New York City was experiencing economic hard

NEW YORK'S EXPENSIVE RESTAURANTS HAVE FOUND THAT THE DEMAND FOR MEALS CAN BE QUITE ELASTIC. WHEN THEY LOWERED PRICES IN 1992, DEMAND INCREASED ENOUGH TO INCREASE TOTAL REVENUES.

times. Unemployment was up, incomes were down, and there was great uncertainty about the future. Like other businesses, restaurants were suffering. Fewer people were dining out, and those who were avoided the most expensive restaurants.

The 1992 Democratic National Convention in July brought thousands of visiting delegates and journalists to the city. But many feared the out-of-town visitors would suffer "sticker shock" and avoid the city's most expensive restaurants. (Prices in New York are much higher than in most other parts of the country.)

And so a plan was hatched. A group of 100 restaurants got together and offered lunch for $19.92, and a number of them added special dinner menus with meals priced at $24.92. These prices may sound high to you, but they were a substantial reduction for most of the participating restaurants!

The result: Revenues were up during the convention. But what happened after the delegates left? Many restaurants decided to keep their prices down and got a real surprise: Local demand was elastic. Lower prices brought in more total revenue.

For additional current applications of elasticity, see the Case and Fair Web page at **http://www.prenhall.com/casefair**.

however, we have had time to adjust our behavior in response to the higher price, and the quantity of oil demanded has fallen dramatically. Automobiles manufactured today get more miles per gallon, and some drivers have cut down on their driving. Millions have insulated their homes, most have turned down their thermostats, and some have explored alternative energy sources.

All this illustrates a very important point:

The elasticity of demand in the short run may be very different from the elasticity of demand in the long run. In the longer run, demand is likely to become more elastic, or responsive, simply because households make adjustments over time and producers develop substitute goods.

OTHER IMPORTANT ELASTICITIES

So far we have been discussing price elasticity of demand, which measures the responsiveness of quantity demanded to changes in price. However, as we noted earlier, elasticity is a perfectly general concept. If B causes a change in A and we can measure the change in both, we can calculate the elasticity of A with respect to B. Let us look briefly at three other important types of elasticity.

▶ **Income Elasticity of Demand** **Income elasticity of demand**, which measures the responsiveness of demand to changes in income, is defined as:

$$\text{income elasticity of demand} = \frac{\% \text{ change in quantity demanded}}{\% \text{ change in income}}$$

income elasticity of demand *Measures the responsiveness of demand to changes in income.*

Measuring income elasticity is important for many reasons. Government policy makers spend a great deal of time and money weighing the relative merits of different policies. During the 1970s, for example, the Department of Housing and Urban Development (HUD) conducted a huge experiment in four cities to estimate the income elasticity of housing demand. In this "housing allowance demand experiment," low-income families received housing vouchers over an extended period of time, and researchers watched their housing consumption for several years. Most estimates, including the ones from the HUD study, put the income elasticity of housing demand between .5 and .8. That is, a 10 percent increase in income can be expected to raise the quantity of housing demanded by a household by 5 to 8 percent.

▶ **Cross-Price Elasticity of Demand** **Cross-price elasticity of demand**, which measures the response of quantity of one good demanded to a change in the price of another good, is defined as:

$$\text{cross-price elasticity of demand} = \frac{\% \text{ change in quantity of } Y \text{ demanded}}{\% \text{ change in price of } X}$$

cross-price elasticity of demand *A measure of the response of the quantity of one good demanded to a change in the price of another good.*

Like income elasticity, cross-price elasticity can be either positive or negative. A *positive* cross-price elasticity indicates that an increase in the price of X causes the demand for Y to rise. This implies that the goods are substitutes. If cross-price elasticity turns out to be *negative*, an increase in the price of X causes a decrease in the demand for Y. This implies that the goods are complements.

▶ **Elasticity of Supply** **Elasticity of supply**, which measures the response of quantity of a good supplied to a change in price of that good, is defined as:

$$\text{elasticity of supply} = \frac{\% \text{ change in quantity supplied}}{\% \text{ change in price}}$$

elasticity of supply *A measure of the response of quantity of a good supplied to a change in price of that good. Likely to be positive in output markets.*

In output markets, the elasticity of supply is likely to be a positive number—that is, a higher price leads to an increase in the quantity supplied, *ceteris paribus*. (Recall our discussion of upward-sloping supply curves in this chapter and the last.)

elasticity of labor supply *A measure of the response of labor supplied to a change in the price of labor.*

In input markets, however, some interesting problems crop up. Perhaps the most studied elasticity of all is the **elasticity of labor supply**, which measures the response of labor supplied to a change in the price of labor. Economists have examined household labor supply responses to such government programs as welfare, social security, the income tax system, need-based student aid, and unemployment insurance, among others.

In simple terms, the elasticity of labor supply is defined as:

$$\text{elasticity of labor supply} = \frac{\% \text{ change in quantity of labor supplied}}{\% \text{ change in the wage rate}}$$

It seems reasonable at first glance to assume that an increase in wages increases the quantity of labor supplied. That would imply an upward-sloping supply curve and a positive labor supply elasticity. But this is not necessarily so. An increase in wages makes workers better off: They can work the same amount and have higher incomes. One of the things that they might like to "buy" with that higher income is more leisure time. "Buying" leisure simply means working fewer hours, and the "price" of leisure is the lost wages. Thus it is quite possible that an increase in wages to some groups will lead to a reduction in the quantity of labor supplied.

LOOKING AHEAD

We have now examined the basic forces of supply and demand and discussed the market/price system. These basic concepts will serve as building blocks for what comes next. Whether you are studying microeconomics or macroeconomics, you will be studying the functions of markets and the behavior of market participants in more detail in the following chapters.

Because the concepts presented in the first five chapters are so important to your understanding of what is to come, this might be a good point for a brief review of part 1.

SUMMARY

THE PRICE SYSTEM: RATIONING AND ALLOCATING RESOURCES

1. In a market economy, the market system (or price system) serves two functions. It determines the allocation of resources among producers and the final mix of outputs. It also distributes goods and services on the basis of willingness and ability to pay. In this sense, it serves as a *price rationing* device.

2. Governments, as well as private firms, sometimes decide not to use the market system to ration an item for which there is excess demand. Examples of nonprice rationing systems include *queuing, favored customers,* and *ration coupons.* The most common rationale for such policies is "fairness."

3. Attempts to bypass the market and use alternative nonprice rationing devices are much more difficult and costly than it would seem at first glance. Schemes that open up opportunities for favored customers, black markets, and side payments often end up less "fair" than the free market.

SUPPLY AND DEMAND ANALYSIS: AN OIL IMPORT FEE

4. The basic logic of supply and demand is a powerful tool for analysis. For example, supply and demand analysis shows that an oil import tax will reduce quantity of oil demanded, increase domestic production, and generate revenues for the government.

ELASTICITY

5. *Elasticity* is a general measure of responsiveness that can be used to quantify many different relationships. If one variable A changes in response to changes in another variable B, the elasticity of A with respect to B is equal to the percentage change in A divided by the percentage change in B.

6. The slope of a demand curve is an inadequate measure of responsiveness, because its value depends on the units of measurement used. For this reason, elasticities are calculated using percentages.

7. *Price elasticity of demand* is the ratio of the percentage change in quantity demanded of a good to the percentage change in price of that good. *Perfectly inelastic* demand is demand whose quantity demanded does not respond at all to changes in price; its numerical value is zero. *Inelastic* demand is demand whose quantity demanded responds somewhat, but not a great deal, to changes in price; its numerical value is between zero and -1. *Elastic* demand is demand in which the percentage change in quantity demanded is larger in absolute value than the percentage change in price. Its absolute value is greater than 1. *Unitary elasticity* of demand describes a relationship in which the percentage change in the quantity of a product demanded is the same as the percentage change in price; unitary elasticity has a numerical value of -1. *Perfectly elastic* demand describes a relationship in which a small increase in the price of a product causes the quantity demanded for that product to drop to zero.

8. If demand is elastic, a price increase will reduce the quantity demanded by a larger percentage than the percentage increase in price, and total revenue ($P \times Q$) will fall. If demand is inelastic, a price increase will increase total revenue.

9. If demand is elastic, a price cut will cause quantity demanded to increase by a greater percentage than the percentage decrease in price, and total revenue will rise. If demand is inelastic, a price cut will cause quantity demanded to increase by a smaller percentage than the percentage decrease in price, and total revenue will fall.

10. The elasticity of demand depends on (1) the availability of substitutes, (2) the importance of the item in individual budgets, and (3) the time frame in question.

11. There are several important elasticities. *Income elasticity of demand* measures the responsiveness of the quantity demanded with respect to changes in income. *Cross-price elasticity of demand* measures the response of quantity of one good demanded to a change in the price of another good. *Elasticity of supply* measures the response of quantity of a good supplied to a change in the price of that good. The *elasticity of labor supply* measures the response of the quantity of labor supplied to a change in the price of labor.

REVIEW TERMS AND CONCEPTS

PROBLEM SET

1. Illustrate the following with supply and/or demand curves:
   a. A situation of excess labor supply (unemployment) caused by a "minimum wage" law.
   b. The effect of a sharp increase in heating oil prices on the demand for insulation material.

2. The scalping of tickets to sporting events and concerts, which is illegal in most states, may in fact serve a useful function. Do you agree or disagree? Write an essay explaining your answer.

3. In an effort to "support" the price of some agricultural goods, the Department of Agriculture pays farmers a subsidy in cash for every acre that they leave *unplanted*. The Agriculture Department argues that the subsidy increases the "cost" of planting and that it will reduce supply and increase the price of competitively produced agricultural goods. Critics argue that because the subsidy is a payment to farmers, it will reduce costs and lead to lower prices. Which argument is correct? Explain.

4. Illustrate the following with supply and/or demand curves:
   a. The federal government "supports" the price of wheat by paying farmers not to plant wheat on some of their land.
   b. The impact of an increase in the price of chicken on the price of hamburger.
   c. Incomes rise, shifting the demand for gasoline. Crude oil prices rise, shifting the supply of gasoline. At the new equilibrium, the quantity of gasoline sold is less than it was before. (Crude oil is used to produce gasoline).

5. "The price of blue jeans has risen substantially in recent years. Demand for blue jeans has also been rising. This is hard to explain because the law of demand says that higher prices should lead to lower demand." Do you agree?

6. Illustrate the following with supply and demand curves:
   a. The economy was doing very well in 1997. Income was rising and the stock market hit new record highs. As a result, the price of housing rose.

b. In 1996, several cows in Great Britain came down with "mad cow disease." As a result, the countries of the European Union banned the import of British beef. The result was higher beef prices in Continental Europe.

c. In 1997, the mayor of New York City and the governor of New York State negotiated a slow phaseout of rent control in the city. Under rent control, rents are held by law below their equilibrium levels. The result will be higher rents.

d. In 1998, a survey of plant stores indicated that the demand for houseplants was rising sharply. At the same time, dozens of low-cost producers started growing plants for sale. The net result was a decline in the average price of houseplants.

7. Suppose that the world price of oil is $16 per barrel, and suppose that the United States can buy all the oil it wants at this price. Suppose also that the demand and supply schedules for oil in the United States are as follows:

PRICE ($ PER BARREL)	U.S. QUANTITY DEMANDED	U.S. QUANTITY SUPPLIED
14	16	4
16	15	6
18	14	8
20	13	10
22	12	12

a. On graph paper, draw the supply and demand curves for the United States.

b. With free trade in oil, what price will Americans pay for their oil? What quantity will Americans buy? How much of this will be supplied by American producers? How much will be imported? Illustrate total imports on your graph of the U.S. oil market.

c. Suppose the United States imposes a tax of $4 per barrel on imported oil. What quantity would Americans buy? How much of this would be supplied by American producers? How much would be imported? How much tax would the government collect?

d. Briefly summarize the impact of an oil-import tax by explaining who is helped and who is hurt among the following groups: domestic oil consumers, domestic oil producers, foreign oil producers, the U.S. government.

8. Use the data in problem 7 to answer the following questions. But now suppose that the United States allows no oil imports.

a. What is the equilibrium price and quantity for oil in the United States?

b. If the United States imposed a price ceiling of $18 per barrel on the oil market, would there be an excess supply or an excess demand for oil? How much?

c. Under the price ceiling, quantity supplied and quantity demanded differ. Which of the two will determine how much oil is purchased? Briefly explain why.

9. A sporting goods store has estimated the demand curve for Brand A running shoes as a function of price. Use the following diagram to answer the questions below:

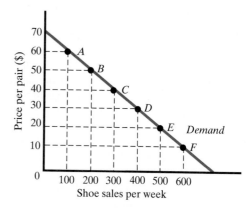

a. Calculate demand elasticity using the midpoint formula between points *A* and *B*, between points *C* and *D*, and between points *E* and *F*.

b. If the store currently charges a price of $50, then increases this price to $60, what happens to total revenue from shoe sales (calculate $P \times Q$ before and after the price change)? Repeat the exercise for initial prices being increased to $40 and $20, respectively.

c. Explain why the answers to a. can be used to predict the answers to b.

10. Taxicab fares in most cities are regulated. Several years ago, taxicab drivers in Boston obtained permission to raise their fares 10 percent, and they anticipated that revenues would increase by about 10 percent as a result. They were disappointed, however. When the commissioner granted the 10 percent increase, revenues increased by only about 5 percent. What can you infer about the elasticity of demand for taxicab rides? What were taxicab drivers assuming about the elasticity of demand?

11. Using the midpoint formula, calculate elasticity for each of the following changes in demand by a household:

	P_1	P_2	Q_1	Q_2
Demand for:				
a. Long-distance telephone service	$ .25 per minute	$ .15 per minute	300 min. per month	400 min. per month
b. Orange juice	$1.49 per quart	$1.89 per quart	14 qts. per month	12 qts. per month
c. Big Macs	$2.89	$1.00	3 per week	6 per week
d. Cooked shrimp	$9.00 per pound	$12.00 per pound	2 lbs. per month	1.5 lbs. per month

12. Fill in the missing amounts in the following table:

	% CHANGE IN PRICE	% CHANGE IN QUANTITY DEMANDED	ELASTICITY
Demand for Ben & Jerry's Ice Cream	+10%	−12%	a.
Demand for beer at San Francisco 49ers football games	−20%	b.	−.5
Demand for Broadway theater tickets in New York	c.	−15%	−1.0
Supply of chickens	+10%	d.	+1.2
Supply of beef cattle	−15%	−10%	e.

13. Use the table in question 12 to defend your answers to the following questions:
   a. Would you recommend that Ben & Jerry's move forward with a plan to raise prices if the company's only goal is to increase revenues?
   b. Would you recommend that beer stands cut prices to increase revenues at 49ers games next year?

*14. Studies have fixed the short-run price elasticity of demand for gasoline at the pump at −0.20. Suppose that international hostilities lead to a sudden cutoff of crude oil supplies. As a result, U.S. supplies of refined gasoline drop 10 percent.
   a. If gasoline was selling for $1.40 per gallon before the cutoff, how much of a price increase would you expect to see in the coming months?

b. Suppose that the government imposes a price ceiling on gas at $1.40 per gallon. How would the relationship between consumers and gas station owners change?

*15. For each of the following, say whether you agree or disagree and explain your answer.
   a. The demand curve pictured below is elastic.

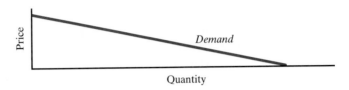

   b. If supply were to increase somewhat in the diagram below, prices would fall and firms would earn less revenue.

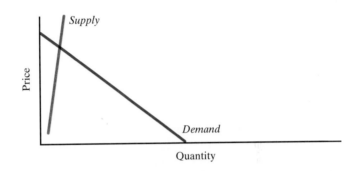

TAKE IT TO THE NET

We invite you to visit the Case and Fair page on the Prentice Hall Web site:

http://www.prenhall.com/casefair

for this chapter's World Wide Web exercise.

THE SPOTTED OWL, THE LUMBER INDUSTRY, AND THE MARKET FOR NEW HOMES

The housing industry is an important sector of the U.S. economy. Federal Reserve officials monitor this industry because of the possible economy-wide effects of changes in housing market activity. Bank managers closely watch the housing market because bank lending can be affected by fluctuations in the number of housing sales. In the labor market, fluctuations in new home construction can cause similar fluctuations in the number of employed individuals in the home construction industry. A variety of local businesses can also be affected by changes in housing market conditions because new home owners buy, among other things, new appliances. And the spending of individuals can change as changes in housing prices affect individuals' wealth.

The price of newly constructed homes is determined by supply and demand in that market. The supply of new homes is affected by changes in labor costs in the construction industry, other construction costs (for example, lumber prices), and the price of land. The demand for new homes is determined by changes in income, interest rates (which determine the cost of financing the purchase of a new home), demographics, and, in some cases, prospective home buyers' expectations of future home prices. A change in any one of these determinants of supply and demand will cause changes in the price and number of new homes.

In the early 1990s, the market for new homes was affected by the impact of regulatory actions taken to protect the northern spotted owl. By 1990, an estimated 4,000 to 6,000 spotted owls were believed to exist in the old-growth forests of northern California, Oregon, and Washington; old-growth forests include trees that are 200 to more than 1,000 years old. Over time, the spotted owl had become dependent on the food species found in these forests and, therefore, could not exist elsewhere. On June 22, 1990, the U.S. Fish and Wildlife Service declared the northern spotted owl a threatened species, placing it under the protection of the Endangered Species Act.

One federal study indicated 8.4 million acres of old-growth forest were needed for the spotted owl's survival. With approximately 5.4 million

acres already off limits to timber harvesting, this meant an additional 3 million acres would need to be removed from logging. The declaration of the spotted owl as a threatened species placed it in the middle of a debate between those concerned about the possible loss of a species and those concerned about the effects of logging restrictions on timber supplies and on the economies of the Pacific Northwest.

Logging restrictions on federal, state, and privately owned land were ordered in 1991, limiting the amount of timber that could be harvested. Critics of these restrictions cited a number of costs of protecting the spotted owl:

1. significant timber-related job losses (with some estimates of job losses in excess of 100,000).
2. the possible closure of local sawmills.
3. increased prices of wood products as a result of reductions in timber supply.
4. reductions in government revenues caused by reduced timber sales from federally owned land.
5. increased costs to the government in the form of, for example, increased unemployment claims in regions affected by harvesting restrictions.

Proponents of the policy to limit harvesting argued that endangered species must be protected from extinction. They also argued that the effects of restrictions on timber-dependent industries would not be nearly as severe as critics claimed because, for example, firms would respond to these restrictions by seeking alternative sources of timber. Some environmentalists even proposed a ban on the export of logs from federal and state lands. The sale of logs to foreign sawmills, it was argued, caused reductions in the number of jobs at local sawmills.

By 1991, these logging restrictions appeared to affect wood and lumber prices (see Figure 1). The prices of some wood products, such as two-by-fours and half-inch plywood, increased by nearly 20 percent over a two-week period in the spring of 1991. Although these logging restrictions caused layoffs and the closure of some sawmills, adversely affecting some communities in the Pacific Northwest, some firms benefited from the restrictions. For example, the Weyerhaeuser Corporation, a forest products company, owned 5.6 million acres of timber not affected by the logging restrictions. As timber prices increased because of the logging restrictions, Weyerhaeuser was able to harvest its own timber and sell logs and lumber at higher prices. Furthermore, as some timber mills closed, other "leaner," more efficient mills increased hiring during the period as they successfully made the transition to the harvesting of smaller trees.

Questions for Analytical Thinking

1. a. Using supply and demand curves, graphically illustrate and explain the effects of timber harvest restrictions on lumber prices. Explain how the lumber price effects of logging restrictions might change as logging companies have more time to respond to the effects of these restrictions.
   b. In 1994, federal judge William Dwyer lifted the logging ban on some of the federally owned land. What effect, if any, do you think this action might have had on the supply of lumber and wood products and, therefore, on lumber product prices? Explain.
   c. Are your conclusions in parts a and b consistent with the actual movements in lumber and wood product prices found in Figure 1? Explain.

2. A June 21, 1991, editorial in the *Wall Street Journal* referred to the possible effects of logging restrictions on new home prices as a "spotted owl surcharge."
   a. Using supply and demand curves for new homes, graphically illustrate and explain the effects of logging restrictions on the market for new homes. Based on your analysis, what do you think happened to the demand for new homes as a result of these restrictions? Explain.
   b. As the price of new homes changed due to logging restrictions, how might potential new home buyers have responded in their search for housing services?
   c. New homes and existing homes are likely viewed as substitutes by

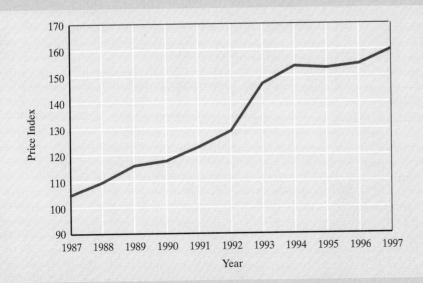

FIGURE 1

Producer Price Index for Lumber and Wood Products (excluding furniture)

Base Year: 1982

home buyers. Given your previous analysis, explain what effect, if any, these logging restrictions might have had on the market for existing homes. Use supply and demand curves in your analysis.

d. And finally, how might home builders (contractors) have changed their behavior as lumber prices increased? Explain.

3. Between 1990 and 1995, the median price of existing homes in the Hartford, Connecticut, area fell each year. During this same period, lumber and wood product prices increased each year. Are these two observations inconsistent with our understanding of the ability of the supply and demand model to explain the price of existing homes? Explain.

4. The share price of a company's stock generally reflects investors' expectations of the company's current and future profitability. When proposals to limit timber harvesting in the Pacific Northwest were being discussed in the spring of 1991, the price of Weyerhaeuser stock actually increased. Why do you think this occurred?

5. When policy makers examine proposals to protect a particular species (or some other natural resource), what costs and benefits do you think they should consider when making this decision?

Sources: Karl E. Case, "The Real Estate Cycle and the Economy: Consequences of the Massachusetts Boom of 1984–87," *New England Economic Review*, Federal Reserve Bank of Boston, Sept./Oct. 1991, pp. 37–46; Timothy Egan, "Oregon, Foiling Forecasters, Thrives as It Protects Owls," *New York Times*, October 11, 1994; Daniel A. Hagen, James W. Vincent, and Patrick B. Welle, "Benefits of Preserving Old-Growth Forests and the Spotted Owl," *Contemporary Policy Issues*, April 1992, pp. 13–26; Bill Richards, "Owls, of All Things, Help Weyerhaeuser Cash In on Timber," *Wall Street Journal*, June 24, 1992; David Schaefer and Sylvia Nogaki, "Threatened—Wildlife Agency Makes It Official on Spotted Owl," *Seattle Times*, June 22, 1990.

MICROECONOMICS

PART TWO

FOUNDATIONS OF MICROECONOMICS: CONSUMERS AND FIRMS

HOUSEHOLD BEHAVIOR AND CONSUMER CHOICE

NOW THAT WE have discussed the basic forces of supply and demand, we can explore the underlying behavior of the two fundamental decision-making units in the economy, households and firms.

Figure 6.1 presents a diagram of a simple competitive economy. The figure is an expanded version of the circular flow diagram first presented in Figure 4.1. It is designed to guide you through part two (chapters 6 through 12) of this book. You will see the "big picture" much more clearly if you follow this diagram closely as you work your way through this part of the book. (For your convenience, the diagram will be repeated several times in the next few chapters.)

Recall that households and firms interact in two kinds of markets: output (product) markets, shown at the top of Figure 6.1, and input (factor) markets, shown at the bottom. Households *demand* outputs and *supply* inputs. In contrast, firms *supply* outputs and *demand* inputs. This chapter explores the behavior of households, focusing first on household demand for outputs and then on household supply in labor and capital markets.

The remaining chapters in part two focus on firms and the interaction between firms and households. Chapters 7 through 9 analyze the behavior of firms in output markets in both the short run and the long run. Chapter 10 focuses on the behavior of firms in input markets in general, especially the labor and land markets. Chapter 11 discusses the capital market in more detail. Chapter 12 puts all the pieces together and analyzes the functioning of a complete market system. Following chapter 12, part three of the book relaxes many assumptions and analyzes market imperfections, as well as the potential for and pitfalls of government involvement in the economy. The plan for chapters 6 through 17 is outlined in Figure 6.2.

Recall that throughout this book, all diagrams that describe the behavior of households are drawn or highlighted in *blue*. All diagrams that describe the behavior of firms are drawn or highlighted in *red*. Look carefully at the supply and demand diagrams in Figure 6.1, and notice that in both the labor and capital markets, the supply curves are blue. This is because labor and

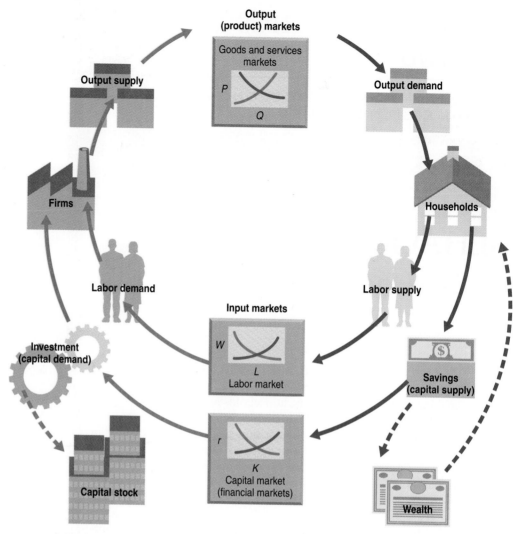

FIGURE 6.1

Firm and Household Decisions

Households demand in output markets and supply labor and capital in input markets. To simplify our analysis, we have not included the government and international sectors in this circular flow diagram. These topics will be discussed in detail later.

capital are supplied by households. The demand curves for labor and capital are red because firms demand these inputs for production.

➤ **Assumptions** Before we proceed with our discussion of household choice, we need to make a few basic assumptions. The key assumption that we make in chapters 6 through 12 is that all markets are perfectly competitive. Recall from chapter 3 that a *perfectly competitive* market is one in which no single firm is large enough to have any control over the price of its products or the prices of the inputs that it buys. Similarly, no single household in a perfectly competitive market has any control over the prices of the products that it buys or the prices of the inputs (labor and capital) that it sells.

We also assume that households and firms possess all the information they need to make market choices. Specifically, we assume that households possess knowledge of the qualities and prices of everything available in the market. Firms know all that there is to know about wage rates, capital costs, and output prices. This assumption is often called the assumption of **perfect knowledge.**

perfect knowledge *The assumption that households possess a knowledge of the qualities and prices of everything available in the market, and that firms have all available information regarding wage rates, capital costs, and output prices.*

FIGURE 6.2

Understanding the Microeconomy
and the Role of Government

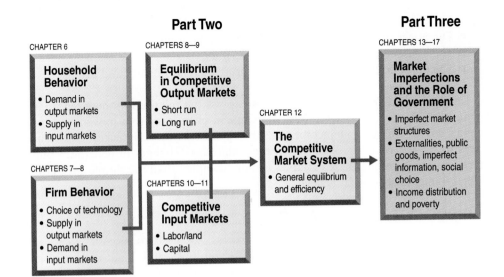

Part Two

CHAPTER 6

Household Behavior
- Demand in output markets
- Supply in input markets

CHAPTERS 7—8

Firm Behavior
- Choice of technology
- Supply in output markets
- Demand in input markets

CHAPTERS 8—9

Equilibrium in Competitive Output Markets
- Short run
- Long run

CHAPTERS 10—11

Competitive Input Markets
- Labor/land
- Capital

CHAPTER 12

The Competitive Market System
- General equilibrium and efficiency

Part Three

CHAPTERS 13—17

Market Imperfections and the Role of Government
- Imperfect market structures
- Externalities, public goods, imperfect information, social choice
- Income distribution and poverty

By the end of chapter 12 we will have a complete picture of an economy, but it will be based on this set of fairly restrictive assumptions. At first, this may seem unrealistic to you. Keep the following in mind, however:

Much of the economic analysis in the chapters that follow applies to all forms of market structure. Indeed, much of the power of economic reasoning is that it is quite general. Because monopolists, oligopolists, monopolistic competitors, and perfect competitors share the objective of maximizing profits, it should not be surprising that their behavior is in many ways similar. We focus here on perfect competition because many of these basic principles are easier to learn in the simplest of cases first.

HOUSEHOLD CHOICE IN OUTPUT MARKETS

Every household must make three basic decisions:

1. How much of each product, or output, to demand;
2. How much labor to supply; and
3. How much to spend today and how much to save for the future.

In the pages that follow, we examine each of these decisions.

As we begin our look at demand in output markets, you must keep in mind that the choices underlying the demand curve are only part of the larger household-choice problem. Closely related decisions about how much to work and how much to save are equally important and must be made simultaneously with output-demand decisions.

THE DETERMINANTS OF HOUSEHOLD DEMAND

As we saw in chapter 4,

Several factors influence the quantity of a given good or service demanded by a single household:

- The price of the product
- The income available to the household
- The household's amount of accumulated wealth

- The prices of other products available to the household
- The household's tastes and preferences, and
- The household's expectations about future income, wealth, and prices.

Demand schedules and demand curves express the relationship between quantity demanded and price, *ceteris paribus*. A change in price leads to a movement along a demand curve. Changes in income, in other prices, or in preferences shift demand curves to the left or right. We refer to these shifts as "changes in demand." But the interrelationship among these variables is more complex than the simple exposition in chapter 4 might lead you to believe.

THE BUDGET CONSTRAINT

Before we examine the household choice process, we need to discuss exactly what choices are open or not open to households. If you look carefully at the list of items that influence household demand, you will see that the first four actually define the set of options available:

Information on a household's income and wealth, together with information on product prices, makes it possible to distinguish those combinations of goods and services that are affordable from those that are not.[1]

budget constraint *The limits imposed on household choices by income, wealth, and product prices.*

Income, wealth, and prices thus define what we call a household's **budget constraint**. The budget constraint facing any household results primarily from limits imposed externally by one or more markets. In competitive markets, for example, households cannot control prices; they must buy goods and services at market-determined prices. A household has some control over its income: Its members can choose to work or not, and they can sometimes decide how many hours to work and how many jobs to hold. But constraints exist in the labor market, too. The amount that household members are paid is limited by current market wage rates. Whether they can get a job is determined by the availability of jobs.

While income does in fact depend, at least in part, on the choices that households make, we will treat it as a given for now. Later on in this chapter we will relax this assumption and explore labor supply choices in more detail.

The income, wealth, and price constraints that surround choice are best illustrated with an example. Consider Barbara, a recent graduate of a midwestern university, who takes a job as an account manager at a public relations firm. Let's assume that she receives a salary of $1,000 per month (after taxes), and that she has no wealth and no credit. Barbara's monthly expenditures are limited to her flow of income. Table 6.1 summarizes some of the choices open to her.

A careful search of the housing market reveals four vacant apartments. The least expensive is a one-room studio with a small kitchenette that rents for $400 per month, including utilities (Option A). If she lived there, Barbara could afford to spend $250 per month on food and still have $350 left over for other things.

About four blocks away is a one-bedroom apartment with wall-to-wall carpeting and a larger kitchen. It has much more space, but the rent is $600, including utilities. If Barbara took this apartment, she might cut her food expenditures by $50 per month and have only $200 per month left for everything else.

In the same building as the one-bedroom apartment is an identical unit on the top floor of the building with a balcony facing west toward the sunset. The balcony and

[1]Remember that we drew the distinction between income and wealth in chapter 4. *Income* is the sum of a household's earnings within a given period; it is a flow variable. In contrast, *wealth* is a stock variable; it is what a household owns minus what it owes at a given point in time.

OPTION	MONTHLY RENT	FOOD	OTHER EXPENSES	TOTAL	AVAILABLE?
A	$400	$250	$350	$1,000	Yes
B	600	200	200	1,000	Yes
C	700	150	150	1,000	Yes
D	1,000	100	100	1,200	No

view add $100 to the monthly rent. To live there, Barbara would be left with only $300 to split between food and other expenses.

Just because she was curious, Barbara took a look at a townhouse in the suburbs that was renting for $1,000 per month. Obviously, unless she could get along without eating or doing anything else that costs money, she could not afford it. The combination of the townhouse and any amount of food is outside her budget constraint.

Notice that we have used the information that we have on income and prices to identify different combinations of housing, food, and other items that are available to a single-person household with an income of $1,000 per month. We have said nothing about the process of choosing. Rather, we have carved out what is called a **choice set** or **opportunity set**, the set of options that is defined and limited by Barbara's budget constraint.

choice set or **opportunity set** *The set of options that is defined and limited by a budget constraint.*

▶ **Preferences, Tastes, Trade-Offs, and Opportunity Cost** So far, we have identified only the combinations of goods and services that are available to Barbara and those that are not. Within the constraints imposed by limited incomes and fixed prices, however, households are free to choose what they will buy and what they will not buy. Their ultimate choices are governed by their individual preferences and tastes.

It will help you to think of the household-choice process as a process of allocating income over a large number of available goods and services. A household's final demand for any single product is just one of many outcomes that result from the decision-making process. Think, for example, of a demand curve that shows a household's reaction to a drop in the price of air travel. During certain periods when people travel less frequently, special fares flood the market and many people decide to take trips that they otherwise would not have taken. But if I live in Florida and decide to spend $400 to visit my mother in Nashville, I cannot spend that $400 on new clothes, dinners at a restaurant, or a new set of tires.

A change in the price of a single good changes the constraints within which households choose, and this may change the entire allocation of income. Demand for some

PREFERENCES PLAY A KEY ROLE
IN DETERMINING DEMAND.
SOME PEOPLE LIKE FROSTED
FLAKES, WHEREAS OTHERS WILL
ONLY EAT GRANOLA WITH
NATURAL DRIED FRUITS.

goods and services may rise while demand for others falls. A complicated set of trade-offs lies behind the shape and position of a household's demand curve for a single good. Whenever a household makes a choice, it is really weighing the good or service it chooses against all the other things that the same money could buy. For more information on the ways choice sets have changed over the years, see the Application feature titled: "Opportunity Costs—Then and Now."

Consider again our young account manager and her options as listed in Table 6.1. If she hates to cook, likes to eat at restaurants, and goes out three nights a week, she will probably trade off some housing for dinners out and money to spend on clothes and other things. She will probably rent the studio for $400. But she may love to spend long evenings at home reading, listening to classical music, and sipping tea while watching the sunset. In that case, she will probably trade off some restaurant meals, evenings out, and travel expenses for the added comfort of the larger apartment with the balcony and the view.

> As long as a household faces a limited budget—and all households ultimately do—the real cost of any good or service is the value of the other goods and services that could have been purchased with the same amount of money. The real cost of a good or service is its opportunity cost, and opportunity cost is determined by relative prices.

> **The Budget Constraint More Formally** Ann and Tom are struggling graduate students in economics at the University of Virginia. Their tuition is completely paid by graduate fellowships. They live as resident advisers in a first-year dormitory, in return for which they receive an apartment and meals. Their fellowships also give them $200 each month to cover all their other expenses. To simplify things, let's assume that Ann and Tom spend their money on only two things: meals at the local Thai restaurant and nights at the local jazz club, The Hungry Ear. Thai meals go for a fixed price of $20 per couple. Two tickets to the jazz club, including espresso, are $10.

As Figure 6.3 shows, we can graphically depict the choices that are available to our dynamic duo. The axes measure the *quantities* of the two goods that Ann and Tom buy. The horizontal axis measures the number of Thai meals consumed per month, and

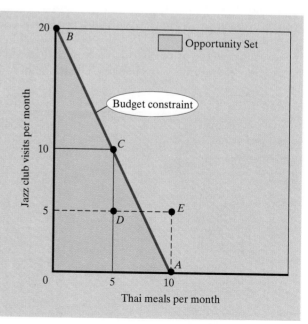

FIGURE 6.3

Budget Constraint and Opportunity Set for Ann and Tom

A budget constraint separates those combinations of goods and services that are available, given limited income, from those that are not. The available combinations make up the opportunity set.

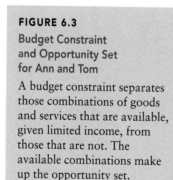

OPPORTUNITY COSTS—THEN AND NOW

The real cost of buying a $15 compact disc is the total of all the other things you could have bought with that $15. In other words, the real cost of a good or service is its *opportunity cost*.

A good's opportunity cost is determined by the price of that good *relative to* the prices of other goods and services. If a sandwich at your favorite eatery costs $5, and sandwiches are your second choice after CDs, the real cost of a CD is 3 sandwiches. As relative prices have changed over the years, so have the trade-offs among goods and services:

	PRICE IN 1970	PRICE IN 1997	PERCENT CHANGE
Prices in general[a]	1.00	4.09	309%
Long-playing album/compact disc	$4	$13	225%
Standard 20″ color TV	$325	$300	−8%
Big Mac at McDonald's	$.55	$2.39	335%
Basic Ford automobile[b]	$2,850	$18,000	532%
Tuition[c] at the University of Michigan:			
for a resident	$1,073	$11,664	987%
for an out-of-state student	$2,935	$23,870	713%
Standard refrigerator	$220	$600	173%
Ticket to a Broadway show	$9	$60	567%
Half gallon of milk	$.57	$1.48	160%
One pound of sirloin steak	$1.35	$3.99	195%

Note: Incomes have gone up too—by one measure (after-tax personal income per capita) income went from $3,545 in 1970 to $21,940 in June 1997, an increase of 519 percent.

[a]*As measured by the consumer price index*

[b]*1970 Fairlane/1997 Taurus*

[c]*Including room and board*

For more on opportunity costs see the Case and Fair Web page at
http://www.prenhall.com/casefair.

the vertical axis measures the number of trips to The Hungry Ear. (Note that price is not on the vertical axis here.) Every point in the space between the axes represents some combination of Thai meals and nights at the jazz club. The question is: Which of these points can Ann and Tom purchase with a fixed budget of $200 per month? That is, which points are in the opportunity set and which are not?

One possibility is that the kids in the dorm are driving Ann and Tom crazy. The two grad students want to avoid the dining hall at all costs. Thus they might decide to spend all their money on Thai food and none of it on jazz. This decision would be represented by a point *on* the horizontal axis because all the points on that axis are points at which Ann and Tom make no jazz club visits. How many meals can Ann and Tom afford? The answer is simple: If income is $200 and the price of Thai meals is $20, they can afford $200 ÷ $20 = 10 meals. This point is labeled *A* on the budget constraint in Figure 6.3.

Another possibility is that general exams are coming up and Ann and Tom decide to chill out at The Hungry Ear to relieve stress. Suppose that they choose to

CHAPTER SIX
*Household Behavior
and Consumer Choice* **133**

spend all their money on jazz and none of it on Thai food. This decision would be represented by a point *on* the vertical axis because all the points on this axis are points at which Ann and Tom eat no Thai meals. How many jazz club visits can they afford? Again, the answer is simple: With an income of $200 and with the price of jazz/espresso at $10, they can go to The Hungry Ear $200 ÷ $10 = 20 times. This is the point labeled *B* in Figure 6.3. The line connecting points *A* and *B* is Ann and Tom's budget constraint.

What about all the points between *A* and *B* on the budget constraint? Starting from point *B*, suppose Ann and Tom give up trips to the jazz club to buy more Thai meals. Each additional Thai meal "costs" two trips to the Hungry Ear. The opportunity cost of a Thai meal is two jazz club trips.

Point *C* on the budget constraint represents a compromise. Here Ann and Tom go to the club 10 times and eat at the Thai restaurant 5 times. To verify that point *C* is on the budget constraint, price it out: 10 jazz club trips cost a total of $10 × 10 = $100, and 5 Thai meals cost a total of $20 × 5 = $100. The total is thus $100 + $100 = $200.[2]

The budget constraint divides all the points between the axes into two groups: those that can be purchased for $200 or less (the opportunity set) and those that are unavailable. Point *D* on the diagram costs less than $200; point *E* costs more than $200. (Verify that this is true.) The opportunity set is the shaded area in Figure 6.3.

▶ **Budget Constraints Change When Prices Rise or Fall** Now suppose that the Thai restaurant is offering two-for-one certificates good during the month of November. In effect, this means that the price of Thai meals drops to $10 for Ann and Tom. How would the budget constraint in Figure 6.3 change?

First, point *B* would not change. If Ann and Tom spend all their money on jazz, the price of Thai meals is irrelevant. Ann and Tom can still afford only 20 trips to the jazz club. What has changed is point *A*, which moves to point *A'* in Figure 6.4. At the new lower price of $10, if Ann and Tom spent all their money on Thai meals, they

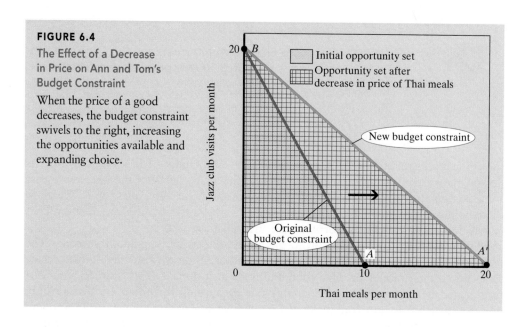

FIGURE 6.4

The Effect of a Decrease in Price on Ann and Tom's Budget Constraint

When the price of a good decreases, the budget constraint swivels to the right, increasing the opportunities available and expanding choice.

[2]The budget constraint can be written $20X + $10Y = $200, which is the equation of the line in Figure 6.3. This equation simply tells you to multiply the number of units of X consumed by $20, then multiply the number of units of Y consumed by $10; the sum of these two products should equal $200.

could buy twice as many, $200 \div $10 = 20$. The budget constraint *swivels*, as shown in Figure 6.4.

The new, flatter budget constraint reflects the new trade-off between Thai meals and Hungry Ear visits. Now, after the price of Thai meals drops to $10, the opportunity cost of a Thai meal is only one jazz club visit. The opportunity set has expanded because at the lower price more combinations of Thai meals and jazz are available.

Figure 6.4 thus illustrates a very important point. When the price of a single good changes, more than just the quantity demanded of that good may be affected. The household now faces an entirely different choice problem—the opportunity set has expanded. At the same income of $200, the new lower price means that Ann and Tom might choose more Thai meals, more jazz club visits, or more of both! They are clearly better off.

> The budget constraint is defined by income, wealth, and prices. Within those limits, households are free to choose, and the household's ultimate choice depends on its own likes and dislikes.

The range of goods and services available in a modern society is as vast as consumer tastes are variable, and this makes any generalization about the household choice process hazardous. Nonetheless, the theory of household behavior that follows is an attempt to derive some logical propositions about the way households make choices.

THE BASIS OF CHOICE: UTILITY

Somehow, from the millions of things that are available, each of us manages to sort out a set of goods and services to buy. When we make our choices, we make specific judgments about the relative worth of things that are very different.

During the nineteenth century, the weighing of values was formalized into a concept called utility. Whether one item is preferable to another depends upon how much **utility**, or satisfaction, it yields relative to its alternatives. How do we decide on the relative worth of a new puppy or a stereo? A trip to the mountains or a weekend in New York City? Working or not working? As we make our choices, we are effectively weighing the utilities we would receive from all the possible available goods.

Certain problems are implicit in the concept of utility. First, it is impossible to measure utility completely and accurately. Second, it is impossible to compare the utilities of different people—that is, one cannot say whether person A or person B has a higher level of utility. Despite these problems, however, the idea of utility helps us understand the process of choice better.

DIMINISHING MARGINAL UTILITY

In making their choices, most people spread their incomes over many different kinds of goods. One reason people prefer variety is that consuming more and more of any one good reduces the marginal, or extra, satisfaction they get from further consumption of the same good. Formally, **marginal utility (MU)** is the additional satisfaction gained by the consumption or use of *one more* unit of something.

It is important to distinguish marginal utility from total utility. **Total utility** is the total amount of satisfaction obtained from consumption of a good or service. Marginal utility comes only from the *last unit* consumed; total utility comes from *all* units consumed.

Suppose that you live next to a store that sells homemade ice cream that you are crazy about. But even though you get a great deal of pleasure from eating ice cream,

utility *The satisfaction, or reward, a product yields relative to its alternatives. The basis of choice.*

marginal utility (MU) *The additional satisfaction gained by the consumption or use of one more unit of something.*

total utility *The total amount of satisfaction obtained from consumption of a good or service.*

TRIPS TO CLUB	TOTAL UTILITY	MARGINAL UTILITY
1	12	12
2	22	10
3	28	6
4	32	4
5	34	2
6	34	0

law of diminishing marginal utility *The more of any one good consumed in a given period, the less satisfaction (utility) generated by consuming each additional (marginal) unit of the same good.*

you don't spend your entire income on it. The first cone of the day tastes heavenly. The second is merely delicious. The third is still very good, but it's clear that the glow is fading. Why? Because the more of any one good we consume in a given period, the less satisfaction, or utility, we get from each additional, or marginal, unit. In 1890 Alfred Marshall called this "familiar and fundamental tendency of human nature" the **law of diminishing marginal utility**.[3]

Consider this simple example. Frank loves country music, and a country band is playing seven nights a week at a club near his house. Table 6.2 shows how the utility he derives from the band might change as he goes to the club more and more frequently. The first visit generates 12 "utils," or units of utility. If Frank goes again another night he enjoys it, but not quite as much as the first night. The second night by itself yields 10 additional utils. *Marginal utility* is 10, while the *total utility* derived from two nights at the club is 22. Three nights per week at the club provide 28 total utils; the marginal utility of the third night is 6, because total utility rose from 22 to 28. Figure 6.5 graphs

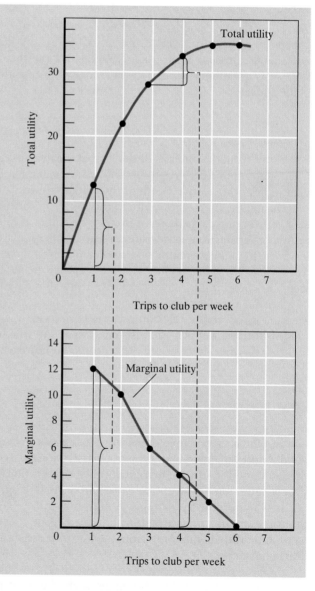

FIGURE 6.5

Graphs of Frank's Total and Marginal Utility

Marginal utility is the additional utility gained by consuming one additional unit of a commodity—in this case, trips to the club. When marginal utility is zero, total utility stops rising.

[3]Alfred Marshall, *Principles of Economics*, 8th ed. (New York: Macmillan, 1948), p. 93 (1st ed., 1890).

TABLE 6.3 ALLOCATION OF FIXED EXPENDITURE PER WEEK BETWEEN TWO ALTERNATIVES

(1) TRIPS TO CLUB PER WEEK	(2) TOTAL UTILITY	(3) MARGINAL UTILITY (MU)	(4) PRICE (P)	(5) MARGINAL UTILITY PER DOLLAR (MU/P)
1	12	12	$3.00	4.0
2	22	10	3.00	3.3
3	28	6	3.00	2.0
4	32	4	3.00	1.3
5	34	2	3.00	0.7
6	34	0	3.00	0

(1) BASKETBALL GAMES PER WEEK	(2) TOTAL UTILITY	(3) MARGINAL UTILITY (MU)	(4) PRICE (P)	(5) MARGINAL UTILITY PER DOLLAR (MU/P)
1	21	21	$6.00	3.5
2	33	12	6.00	2.0
3	42	9	6.00	1.5
4	48	6	6.00	1.0
5	51	3	6.00	.5
6	51	0	6.00	0

total and marginal utility using the data in Table 6.2. Total utility increases up through Frank's fifth trip to the club, but levels off on the sixth night. Marginal utility, which has declined from the beginning, is now at zero.

ALLOCATING INCOME TO MAXIMIZE UTILITY

How many times in one week would Frank go to the club to hear his favorite band? The answer depends on three things: Frank's income, the price of admission to the club, and the alternatives available. If the price of admission were zero and no alternatives existed, he would probably go to the club five nights a week. (Remember, the sixth does not increase his utility, so why should he bother to go?) But Frank is also a basketball fan. His city has many good high school and college teams, and he can go to games six nights a week if he wants to.

Let us say for now that admission to both the country music club and the basketball games is free—that is, there is no price/income constraint. There is a time constraint, however, because there are only seven nights in a week. Table 6.3 lists Frank's total and marginal utilities from attending basketball games and going to country music clubs. From column 3 of the table we can conclude that on the first night Frank will go to a basketball game. The game is worth far more to him (21 utils) than a trip to the club (12 utils).

On the second night, Frank's decision is not so easy. Because he has been to one basketball game this week, the second is worth less (12 utils, as compared to 21 for the first basketball game). In fact, it is worth exactly the same as a first trip to the club, so he is indifferent to whether he goes to the game or the club. So he splits the next two nights: One night he sees ball game number two (12 utils), the other he spends at the club (12 utils). At this point, Frank has been to two ball games and spent one night at the club. Where will Frank go on evening four? To the club again, because the marginal utility from a second trip to the club (10 utils) is greater than the marginal utility from attending a third basketball game (9 utils).

Frank is splitting his time between the two activities in order to maximize total utility. At each successive step, he chooses the activity that yields the most marginal utility. Continuing with this logic, you can see that spending three nights at the club and four nights watching basketball produces total utility of 76 utils each week (28 plus 48). No other combination of games and club trips can produce as much utility.

So far, the only cost of a night of listening to country music is a forgone basketball game, and the only cost of a basketball game is a forgone night of country music. Now let's suppose that it costs $3 to get into the club and $6 to go to a basketball game. Suppose further that after paying rent and taking care of other expenses Frank has only $21 left over to spend on entertainment. Typically, consumers allocate limited incomes, or budgets, over a large set of goods and services. Here we have a limited income ($21) being allocated between only two goods, but the principle is the same. Income ($21) and prices ($3 and $6) define Frank's budget constraint. Within that constraint, Frank chooses in order to maximize utility.

Because the two activities now cost different amounts, we need to find the *marginal utility per dollar* spent on each activity. If Frank is to spend his money on the combination of activities lying within his budget constraint that gives him the most total utility, each night he must choose the activity that gives him the *most utility per dollar spent*. As you can see from column 5 in Table 6.3, Frank gets 4 utils per dollar on the first night he goes to the club (12 utils ÷ $3 = 4 utils per dollar). On night two he goes to a game and gets 3.5 utils per dollar (21 utils ÷ $6 = 3.5 utils per dollar). On night three it's back to the club. Then what happens? When all is said and done—work this out for yourself—Frank ends up going to two games and spending three nights at the club. No other combination of activities that $21 will buy yields more utility.

OPTIONAL MATERIAL

THE UTILITY-MAXIMIZING RULE

In general, a utility-maximizing consumer spreads out his or her expenditures until the following condition holds:

> Utility-Maximizing Rule: $\dfrac{MU_X}{P_X} = \dfrac{MU_Y}{P_Y}$ for all pairs of goods

where MU_X is the marginal utility derived from the last unit of X consumed, MU_Y is the marginal utility derived from the last unit of Y consumed, P_X is the price per unit of X, and P_Y is the price per unit of Y.

To see why this utility-maximizing rule is true, think for a moment about what would happen if it were *not* true. For example, suppose MU_X/P_X were greater than MU_Y/P_Y; that is, suppose that a consumer purchased a bundle of goods so that the marginal utility from the last dollar spent on X were greater than the marginal utility from the last dollar spent on Y. This would mean that the consumer could increase her or his utility by spending a dollar less on Y and a dollar more on X. But as a consumer shifts to buying more X and less Y, she runs into diminishing marginal utility. Buying more units of X *decreases* the marginal utility derived from consuming additional units of X. As a result, the marginal utility of another dollar spent on X falls. Now *less* is being spent on Y and that means its marginal utility *increases*. This process continues until $MU_X/P_X = MU_Y/P_Y$. When this condition holds, there is no way for the consumer to increase his or her utility by changing the bundle of goods purchased.

You can see how the utility-maximizing rule works in Frank's choice between country music and basketball. At each stage, Frank chooses the activity that gives him the most utility per dollar. If he goes to a game, the utility he will derive from the next game—marginal utility—falls. If he goes to the club, the utility he will derive from his next visit falls, and so forth.

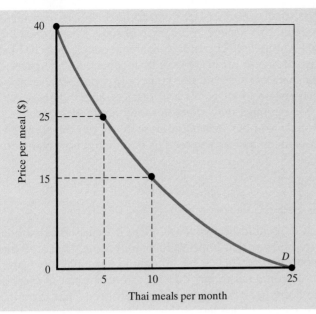

FIGURE 6.6

Diminishing Marginal Utility and Downward-Sloping Demand

At a price of $40, the utility gained from even the first Thai meal is not worth the price. However, a lower price of $25 lures Ann and Tom into the Thai restaurant 5 times a month. (The utility from the sixth meal is not worth $25.) If the price is $15, Ann and Tom will eat Thai meals 10 times a month—until the marginal utility of a Thai meal drops below the utility they could gain from spending $15 on other goods. At 25 meals a month, they cannot tolerate the thought of another Thai meal even if it is free!

DIMINISHING MARGINAL UTILITY AND DOWNWARD-SLOPING DEMAND

The concept of diminishing marginal utility offers us one reason why people spread their incomes over a variety of goods and services rather than spend them all on one or two items. It also leads us to conclude that demand curves slope downward.

To see why this is so, let's return to our friends Ann and Tom, the struggling graduate students. Recall that they chose between meals at a Thai restaurant and trips to a jazz club. Now think about their demand curve for Thai meals, shown in Figure 6.6. When the price of a meal is $40, they decide not to buy any Thai meals. What they are really deciding is that the utility gained from even that first scrumptious meal each month isn't worth the utility that would come from the other things that $40 can buy.

Now consider a price of $25. At this price, Ann and Tom buy five Thai meals. Clearly the first, second, third, fourth, and fifth meals each generate enough utility to justify the price. Tom and Ann "reveal" this by buying five meals. But after the fifth meal, the utility gained from the next meal is not worth $25.

Ultimately, every demand curve hits the quantity (horizontal) axis as a result of diminishing marginal utility—in other words, demand curves slope downward. How many times will Ann and Tom go to the Thai restaurant if meals are free? Twenty-five times. After 25 times a month, they are so sick of Thai food that they will not eat any more even if it is free! That is, marginal utility—the utility gained from the last meal—has dropped to zero. If you think this is unrealistic, ask yourself how much water you drank today.

INCOME AND SUBSTITUTION EFFECTS

Although the idea of utility is, we believe, a helpful way of thinking about the choice process, there is an explanation for downward-sloping demand curves that does not rely on the concept of utility or the assumption of diminishing marginal utility. This explanation centers on income and substitution effects.

Keeping in mind that consumers face constrained choices, consider the probable response of a household to a decline in the price of some heavily used product, *ceteris paribus*. How might a household currently consuming many goods be likely to respond to a fall in the price of one of those goods if its income, its preferences, and all other prices remained unchanged? Clearly, the household would face a new budget constraint, and its final choice of all goods and services might change. A decline in the price of gasoline, for example, may affect not only how much gasoline you purchase but also the kind of car you buy, when and how much you travel, where you go, and (not so directly) how many movies you see this month and how many projects around the house you get done.

THE INCOME EFFECT

Price changes affect households in two ways. First, if we assume that households confine their choices to products that improve their well-being, then a decline in the price of any product, *ceteris paribus*, makes the household unequivocally better off. In other words, if a household continues to buy the exact same amount of every good and service after the price decrease, it will have income left over. That extra income may be spent on the product whose price has declined, hereafter called good *X*, or on other products. The change in consumption of *X* due to this improvement in well-being is called the **income effect of a price change**.

Suppose that I live in Florida and that four times a year I fly to Nashville to visit my mother. Suppose further that last year a round-trip ticket to Nashville cost $400. Thus, I spend a total of $1,600 per year on trips to visit Mom. This year, however, increased competition among the airlines has led one airline to offer round-trip tickets to Nashville for $200. Assuming that the price remains at $200 all year, I can now fly home exactly the same number of times, and I will have spent $800 less for airline tickets than I did last year. Now that I'm better off, I have additional opportunities. I could fly home a fifth time this year, leaving $600 ($800 − $200) to spend on other things, or I could fly home the same number of times (four) and spend all of the extra $800 on other things.

> When the price of something we buy falls, we are *better off*. When the price of something we buy rises, we are *worse off*.

Look back at Figure 6.4. When the price of Thai meals fell, the opportunity set facing Tom and Ann expanded—they were able to afford more Thai meals, more jazz club trips, or more of both. They were unequivocally better off because of the price decline. In a sense, their "real" income was higher.

Now recall from chapter 4 the definition of a *normal good*. When income rises, demand for normal goods increases. Most goods are normal goods. Because of the price decline, Tom and Ann can afford to buy more. If Thai food is a normal good, a decline in the price of Thai food should lead to an increase in the quantity demanded of Thai food.

THE SUBSTITUTION EFFECT

The fact that a price decline leaves households better off is only part of the story. When the price of a product falls, that product also becomes *relatively* cheaper. That is, it becomes more attractive relative to potential substitutes. A fall in the price of product *X* might cause a household to shift its purchasing pattern away from substitutes toward *X*. This shift is called the **substitution effect of a price change**.

Earlier, we made the point that the "real" cost or price of a good is what one must sacrifice in order to consume it. This opportunity cost is determined by relative prices.

To see why this is so, consider again the choice that I face when a round-trip ticket to Nashville costs $400. Each trip that I take requires a sacrifice of $400 worth of other goods and services. When the price drops to $200, the opportunity cost of a ticket has dropped by $200. In other words, after the price decline, I have to sacrifice only $200 (rather than $400) worth of other goods and services to visit Mom.

To clarify the distinction between the income and substitution effects in your mind, imagine how I would be affected if two things happened to me at the same time. First, the price of round-trip air travel between Florida and Nashville drops from $400 to $200. Second, my income is reduced by $800. I am now faced with new relative prices, but—assuming I flew home four times last year—I am no better off now than I was before the price of a ticket declined. The decrease in the price of air travel has exactly offset my decrease in income.

I am still likely to take more trips home. Why? Because the opportunity cost of a trip home is now lower, *ceteris paribus* (that is, assuming no change in the prices of other goods and services). A trip to Nashville now requires a sacrifice of only $200 worth of other goods and services, not the $400 worth that it did before. Thus, I will substitute away from other goods toward trips to see my mother.

Everything works in the opposite direction when a price rises, *ceteris paribus*. A price increase makes households worse off. If income and other prices don't change, spending the same amount of money buys less, and households will be forced to buy less. This is the income effect. In addition, when the price of a product rises, that item becomes more expensive relative to potential substitutes, and the household is likely to substitute other goods for it. This is the substitution effect. (For another example of the income and substitution effects, see the Application box titled "The Tax Laws and the Income and Substitution Effects.")

What do the income and substitution effects tell us about the demand curve?

Both the income and substitution effects imply a negative relationship between price and quantity demanded—in other words, downward-sloping demand. When the price of something falls, *ceteris paribus*, we are better off, and we are likely to buy more of that good and other goods (income effect). And because lower price also means "less expensive relative to substitutes," we are likely to buy more of the good (substitution effect). When the price of something rises, we are worse off, and we will buy less of it (income effect). Higher price also means "more expensive relative to substitutes," and we are likely to buy less of it and more of other goods (substitution effect).[4]

Figure 6.7 summarizes the income and substitution effects of a price change.

---

[4]For some goods, the income and substitution effects work in opposite directions. When our income rises, we may buy less of some goods. In chapter 4, we called such goods *inferior goods*.

When the price of an inferior good rises, it is, like any other good, more expensive relative to substitutes, and we are likely to replace it with lower-priced substitutes. However, when we are worse off we increase our demand for inferior goods. Thus, the income effect could lead us to buy more of the good, partially offsetting the substitution effect.

Even if a good is "very inferior," demand curves will slope downward as long as the substitution effect is larger than the income effect. But it is possible, at least in theory, for the income effect to be larger. In such a case, a price increase would actually lead to an increase in quantity demanded. This possibility was pointed out by Alfred Marshall in *Principles of Economics*. Marshall attributes the notion of an upward-sloping demand curve to Sir Robert Giffen, and for this reason the notion is often referred to as *Giffen's paradox*. Fortunately or unfortunately, no one has ever demonstrated that a Giffen good has ever existed.

FIGURE 6.7

Income and Substitution Effects of a Price Change

For normal goods, the income and substitution effects work in the same direction. Higher prices lead to a lower quantity demanded, and lower prices lead to a higher quantity demanded.

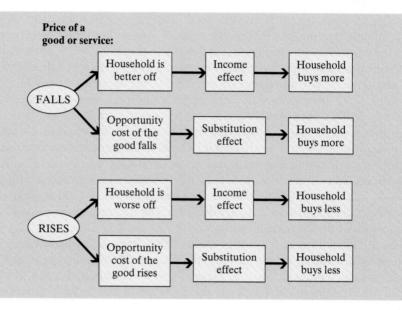

Price of a good or service:

CONSUMER SURPLUS

The argument, made several times already, that the market forces us to reveal a great deal about our personal preferences is an extremely important one, and it bears repeating at least once more here. If you are free to choose within the constraints imposed by prices and your income, and you decide to buy (say) a hamburger for $2.50, you have "revealed" that a hamburger is worth at least $2.50 to you.

A simple market demand curve such as the one in Figure 6.8a illustrates this point quite clearly. At the current market price of $2.50, consumers will purchase 7 million hamburgers per month. There is only one price in the market, and the demand curve tells us how many hamburgers households would buy if they could purchase all they wanted at the posted price of $2.50. Anyone who values a hamburger at $2.50 or more will buy it. Anyone who does not value it that highly will not.

Some people, however, value hamburgers at more than $2.50. As Figure 6.8a shows, even if the price were $5.00, consumers would still buy one million hamburgers. If these

FIGURE 6.8

Market Demand, Revealed Preference, and Consumer Surplus

The difference between the maximum amount that a person is willing to pay for a good and its current market price is the person's *consumer surplus*. The total consumer surplus suggested by the data in Figure 6.8a is represented by the shaded area in Figure 6.8b.

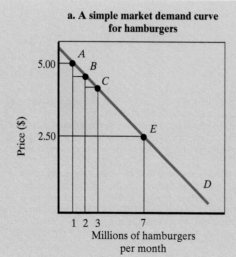

a. A simple market demand curve for hamburgers

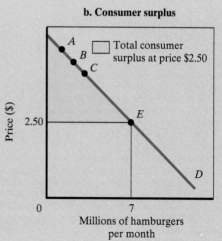

b. Consumer surplus

THE TAX LAWS AND THE INCOME AND SUBSTITUTION EFFECTS

Charitable contributions are an important source of revenue for the nonprofit sector. In 1995, individuals in the United States contributed more than $100 billion to such tax-exempt nonprofit organizations as museums, churches, and colleges.

Charitable contributions are afforded special treatment in the U.S. tax code. Individuals, families, and corporations are permitted to deduct their contributions to most nonprofit organizations from their taxable income. Thus, for every dollar donated to such an organization, there is a tax saving. Changes in the tax laws during the 1980s were not favorable to charitable giving, however. A classic paper by Charles Clotfelter examines the effects of the revised tax laws on charitable contributions in the 1980s. The income and substitution effects are critical to understand how taxes affect charitable giving.

HOW TAXES CAN AFFECT BEHAVIOR

Almost everyone must file a tax return each year. Filers are permitted either to take a standard deduction of a specified amount or to "itemize." The itemized expenditures that can be deducted from income include charitable contributions.

When deductions are itemized, the amount of tax saving from a deduction depends on the taxpayer's tax rate bracket. Before the 1981 Economic Recovery Tax Act, the highest tax bracket was 70 percent. This meant that if someone in that bracket donated $1,000 to the Red Cross, the net cost of that gift to the donor was only $300. Why? Because a tax rate of 70 percent

meant that deducting a gift of $1,000 from taxable income saved the donor $700 in taxes.

In 1981, the highest tax rate was reduced to 50 percent. Worried nonprofit organizations were quick to point out that this tax cut increased the "cost" of giving substantially. When the top tax rate decreased from 70 percent to 50 percent, the net cost of the $1,000 gift rose from $300 to $500—an increase of 66.7 percent!

The Tax Reform Act of 1986 reduced the rate affecting the highest-income households even further, from 50 percent to 28 percent over a few years. Thus, the net cost of the $1,000 contribution for those who pay the top rate rose from $300 before 1981, to $500 between 1981 and 1986, to $720 a few years later.

THE PREDICTED EFFECTS

How might we expect households to respond to the lower tax rates? First, because tax rates were decreased, households had more disposable income after the cuts. Assuming that charitable giving is a normal good, this income effect should lead to more giving. But giving to charity is now more expensive relative to other goods. The opportunity cost of a $1,000 donation before 1981 was $300; in 1986 it was $500. This substitution effect, which should lead to fewer charitable contributions, is what the nonprofit sector worried about.

WHAT REALLY HAPPENED?

Clotfelter found that the overall effects of lower tax rates on charitable giving were relatively small over the period

he studied but were generally in line with the predictions of theory. For example, he found the largest reductions in giving among the highest-income households facing the highest tax brackets. These people had the largest substitution effects. In contrast, nonitemizers (i.e., those who took the standard deduction) actually increased their giving somewhat. This result is exactly what theory would predict. Those who do not itemize their deductions do not receive any tax benefits from giving to charity. Thus, for those who took the standard deduction, the tax cut had an income effect but no substitution effect. We would expect a strong income effect that is not accompanied by an offsetting substitution effect to lead to increased charitable donations, and this is exactly what happened.

RECENT CHANGE

In 1993, the Congress passed the Omnibus Budget Reconciliation Act, which raised the top marginal rate under the income tax back to 39.6 percent for incomes above $250,000. Using the logic above, the "price" of a $1,000 contribution for someone earning over $250,000 fell from a high of $720 to $604. How would we expect this change to affect charitable contributions?

Source: Based on Charles T. Clotfelter, "The Impact of Tax Reform on Charitable Giving: A 1989 Perspective," the Office of Tax Policy Research, Working Paper Series, Working Paper No. 90-7, School of Business Administration, University of Michigan (Ann Arbor), December 1, 1989.

For more on the income and substitution effects, see the Case and Fair Web page at http://www.prenhall.com/casefair.

consumer surplus *The difference between the maximum amount a person is willing to pay for a good and its current market price.*

people were able to buy the good at a price of $2.50, they would earn a **consumer surplus.** Consumer surplus is the difference between the maximum amount a person is willing to pay for a good and its current market price. The consumer surplus earned by the people willing to pay $5.00 for a hamburger is approximately equal to the shaded area between point *A* and the price, $2.50.

The second million hamburgers in Figure 6.8a are valued at more than the market price as well, although the consumer surplus gained is slightly less. Point *B* on the market demand curve shows the maximum amount that consumers would be willing to pay for the second million hamburgers. The consumer surplus earned by these people is equal to the shaded area between *B* and the price, $2.50. Similarly, for the third million hamburgers, maximum willingness to pay is given by point *C*; consumer surplus is a bit lower than it is at points *A* and *B*, but it is still significant.

The total value of the consumer surplus suggested by the data in Figure 6.8a is roughly equal to the area of the shaded triangle in Figure 6.8b. To understand why this is so, think about offering hamburgers to consumers at successively lower prices. If the good were actually sold for $2.50, those near point *A* on the demand curve would get a large surplus; those at point *B* would get a smaller surplus. Those at point *E* would get none.

The idea of consumer surplus helps to explain an old paradox that dates back to Plato. Adam Smith wrote about it in 1776:

diamond/water paradox *A paradox stating that (1) the things with the greatest value in use frequently have little or no value in exchange, and (2) the things with the greatest value in exchange frequently have little or no value in use.*

> The things which have the greatest value in use have frequently little or no value in exchange; and on the contrary, those which have the greatest value in exchange have frequently little or no value in use. Nothing is more useful than water: but it will purchase scarce any thing; scarce anything can be had in exchange for it. A diamond, on the contrary, has scarce any value in use; but a very great quantity of other goods may frequently be had in exchange for it.[5]

Although diamonds have arguably more than "scarce any value in use" today (they are used to cut glass, for example), Smith's **diamond/water paradox** is still instructive, at least where water is concerned.

The low price of water owes much to the fact that it is in plentiful supply. Even at a price of zero we do not consume an infinite amount of water. We consume up to the point where *marginal* utility drops to zero. The *marginal* value of water is zero. Each of us enjoys an enormous consumer surplus when we consume nearly free water. We tend to take water for granted, but imagine what would happen to its price if there were simply not enough for everyone. It would command a high price indeed. As the figure in the margin shows, at a price of zero, the "value" of water is the entire shaded area.

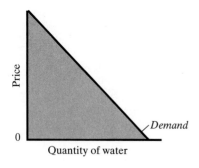

cost-benefit analysis *The formal technique by which the benefits of a public project are weighed against its costs.*

Consumer surplus measurement is a key element in **cost-benefit analysis,** the formal technique by which the benefits of a public project are weighed against its costs. To decide whether to build a new electrical power plant, we need to know the value, to consumers, of the electricity that it will produce. Just as the value of water to consumers is not just its price times the quantity that people consume, the value of electricity generated is not just the price of electricity times the quantity the new plant will produce. The total value that should be weighed against the costs of the plant includes the consumer surplus that electricity users will enjoy if the plant is built.

HOUSEHOLD CHOICE IN INPUT MARKETS

So far, we have focused on the decision-making process that lies behind output demand curves. Households with limited incomes allocate those incomes across various combinations of goods and services that are available and affordable. In looking at the factors

[5]Adam Smith, *The Wealth of Nations*, Modern Library Edition (New York: Random House, 1937), p. 28 (1st ed. 1776). The cheapness of water is referred to by Plato in *Euthydem.*, 304B.

affecting choices in the output market, we assumed that income was fixed, or given. We noted at the outset, however, that income is in fact partially determined by choices that households make in input markets (look back at Figure 6.1). We now turn to a brief discussion of the two decisions households make in input markets: the labor supply decision and the saving decision.

THE LABOR SUPPLY DECISION

Most income in the United States is wage and salary income paid in compensation for labor. Household members supply labor in exchange for wages or salaries. As in output markets, households face constrained choices in input markets. They must decide:

1. Whether to work,
2. How much to work, and
3. What kind of a job to work at.

In essence, household members must decide how much labor to supply. The choices they make are affected by:

1. The availability of jobs,
2. Market wage rates, and
3. The skills they possess.

As with decisions in output markets, the labor supply decision involves a set of trade-offs. There are basically two alternatives to working for a wage: (1) not working, and (2) unpaid work. If I don't work, I sacrifice income for the benefits of staying at home and reading, watching TV, swimming, or sleeping. Another option is to work, but not for a money wage. In this case, I sacrifice money income for the benefits of growing my own food, bringing up my children, or taking care of my house.

As with the trade-offs in output markets, my final choice depends on how I value the alternatives available. If I work, I earn a wage that I can use to buy things. Thus, the trade-off is between the value of the goods and services I can buy with the wages I earn versus the value of things I can produce at home (home-grown food, manageable children, clean clothes, and so on) or the value I place on leisure. This choice is illustrated in Figure 6.9. In general, then:

The wage rate can be thought of as the price—or the opportunity cost—of the benefits of either unpaid work or leisure.

THE PRICE OF LEISURE

In our analysis in the early part of this chapter, households had to allocate a limited budget across a set of goods and services. Now they must choose among goods, services, and *leisure*.

When we add leisure to the picture, we do so with one important distinction. Trading off one good for another involves buying less of one and more of another, so households simply reallocate *money* from one good to the other. "Buying" more leisure, however, means reallocating *time* between work and nonwork activities. For each hour of leisure that I decide to consume, I give up one hour's wages. Thus the wage rate is the *price of leisure*.

Conditions in the labor market determine the budget constraints and final opportunity sets that face households. The availability of jobs and these jobs' wage rates determine the final combinations of goods and services that a household can afford. The

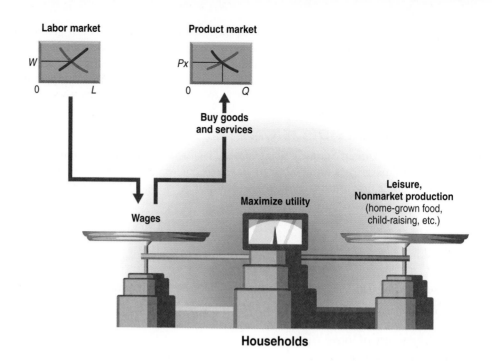

FIGURE 6.9

The Trade-Off Facing Households
The decision to enter the workforce involves a trade-off between wages (and the goods and services that wages will buy) on the one hand, and leisure and the value of nonmarket production on the other.

final choice within these constraints depends on each household's unique tastes and preferences. Different people place more or less value on leisure—but everyone needs to put food on the table.

INCOME AND SUBSTITUTION EFFECTS OF A WAGE CHANGE

labor supply curve *A diagram that shows the quantity of labor supplied at different wage rates. Its shape depends on how households react to changes in the wage rate.*

A **labor supply curve** shows the quantity of labor supplied at different wage rates. The shape of the labor supply curve depends on how households react to changes in the wage rate.

Consider an increase in wages. First, an increase in wages makes households better off. If they work the same number of hours—that is, if they supply the same amount of labor—they will earn higher incomes and be able to buy more goods and services. But they can also buy more leisure. If leisure is a normal good (that is, a good for which demand increases as income increases), an increase in income will lead to a higher demand for leisure and a lower labor supply. This is the *income effect of a wage increase*.

However, there is also a potential *substitution effect of a wage increase*. A higher wage rate means that leisure is more expensive. If you think of the wage rate as the price of leisure, each individual hour of leisure consumed at a higher wage costs more in forgone wages. As a result, we would expect households to substitute other goods for leisure. This means working more, or a lower quantity demanded of leisure and a higher quantity supplied of labor.

Note that in the labor market the income and substitution effects work in *opposite* directions when leisure is a normal good. The income effect of a wage increase implies buying more leisure and working less; the substitution effect implies buying less leisure and working more. Whether households will supply more labor overall or less labor overall when wages rise depends on the relative strength of both the income and the substitution effects.

If the substitution effect is greater than the income effect, the wage increase will increase labor supply. This suggests that the labor supply curve slopes upward, or has a positive slope, like the one in Figure 6.10a. If the income effect outweighs the substitution effect, however, a higher wage will lead to added consumption of leisure, and labor supply will decrease. This implies that the labor supply curve "bends back," as the one in Figure 6.10b does.

During the early years of the Industrial Revolution in late eighteenth-century Great Britain, the textile industry operated under what was called the "putting-out" system. Spinning and weaving were done in small cottages to supplement the family farm income, hence the term "cottage industry." During that period, wages and household incomes rose considerably. Some economic historians claim that this higher income actually led many households to take more leisure and work fewer hours; the empirical evidence suggests a backward-bending labor supply curve.

Just as income and substitution effects helped us understand household choices in output markets, they now help us understand household choices in input markets. The point here is simple:

> When leisure is added to the choice set, the line between input and output market decisions becomes blurred. In fact, households decide simultaneously how much of each good to consume and how much leisure to consume.

SAVING AND BORROWING: PRESENT VERSUS FUTURE CONSUMPTION

We began this chapter by examining the way households allocate a fixed income over a large number of goods and services. We then pointed out that, at least in part, choices made by households determine income levels. Within the constraints imposed by the market, households decide whether to work and how much to work.

So far, however, we have talked about only the current period—the allocation of current income among alternative uses and the work/leisure choice *today*. But households can also (1) use present income to finance future spending—they can *save*—or (2) use future income to finance present spending—they can *borrow*.

When a household decides to save, it is using current income to finance future consumption. That future consumption may come in three years, when you use your savings to buy a car; in 10 years, when you sell stock to put a deposit on a house; or in 45 years, when you retire and begin to receive money from your pension plan. But most people cannot finance large purchases—a house or condominium, for example—out of current income and savings. They almost always borrow money and sign a mortgage. When a household borrows, it is, in essence, financing a current purchase with future income. It pays back the loan out of future income.

Even in simple economies such as the two-person, desert-island economy of Colleen and Bill (see chapter 2), people must make decisions about *present versus future consumption*. Colleen and Bill could (1) produce goods for today's consumption by hunting and gathering, (2) consume leisure by sleeping on the beach, or (3) work on projects to enhance future consumption opportunities. Building a house or a boat over a five-year period is trading present consumption for future consumption.

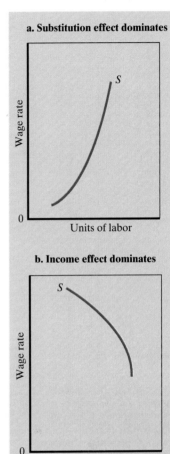

a. Substitution effect dominates

b. Income effect dominates

FIGURE 6.10

Two Labor Supply Curves
When the substitution effect outweighs the income effect, the labor supply curve slopes upward (a). When the income effect outweighs the substitution effect, the result is a "backward-bending" labor supply curve: The labor supply curve slopes downward (b).

When a household saves, it usually puts the money into something that will generate income. There is no sense in putting money under your mattress when you can make it work in so many ways: savings accounts, money market funds, stocks, corporate bonds, and so forth—many of which are virtually risk free. When you put your money in any of these places, you are actually lending it out, and the borrower pays you a fee for its use. This fee usually takes the form of *interest*.

Just as changes in wage rates affect household behavior in the labor market, so do changes in interest rates affect household behavior in capital markets. Higher interest rates mean that borrowing is more expensive—required monthly payments on a newly purchased house or car will be higher. But higher interest rates also mean that saving will earn a higher return: $1,000 invested in a 5 percent savings account or bond yields $50 per year. If rates rise to 10 percent, the annual interest rises to $100.

But what impact do interest rates have on saving behavior? As with the effect of wage changes on labor supply, the effect of changes in interest rates on saving can best be understood in terms of income and substitution effects. Suppose, for example, that I have been saving for a number of years for retirement. Will an increase in interest rates lead to an increase or a decrease in my saving? The answer is not obvious. First, because each dollar saved will earn a higher rate of return, the "price" of spending today in terms of forgone future spending is higher. That is, each dollar that I spend today (instead of saving) costs me more in terms of future consumption because my saving will now earn a higher return. On this score I will be led to save *more*, and this is the substitution effect at work.

But note that I will also earn more on all the saving that I have done to date, and in this sense I am better off. I will not need to save as much for retirement or future consumption as I did before. Consequently, I will be led to save *less*, and this is the income effect at work. The final impact of a change in interest rates depends on the relative size of the income and substitution effects.

> Most empirical evidence indicates that saving tends to increase as the interest rate rises. In other words, the substitution effect is larger than the income effect.

Saving and investment decisions involve a huge and complex set of institutions, the **financial capital market**, in which the suppliers of capital (households that save) and the demand for capital (business firms that want to invest) interact. The amount of capital investment in an economy is constrained in the long run by that economy's saving rate. You can think of household *saving*, then, as the economy's supply of capital. When a firm borrows to finance a capital acquisition, it is almost as if households have supplied the capital for the fee we call interest. We treat capital markets in detail in chapter 11.[6]

financial capital market *The complex set of institutions in which suppliers of capital (households that save) and the demand for capital (business firms wanting to invest) interact.*

A REVIEW: HOUSEHOLDS IN OUTPUT AND INPUT MARKETS

In probing the behavior of households in both input and output markets and examining the nature of constrained choice, we went behind the household demand curve, using the simplifying assumption that income was fixed and given. Income, wealth, and prices set the limits, or *constraints*, within which households make their choices in

---

[6]Here we are looking at a country as if it were isolated from the rest of the world. Very often, however, capital investment is financed by funds loaned or provided by foreign citizens or governments. For example, in recent years a substantial amount of Japanese savings has found its way into the United States to buy stocks, bonds, and other financial instruments. In part, these flows finance capital investment. Also, the United States and other countries that contribute funds to the World Bank and the International Monetary Fund have provided billions in out-right grants and loans to help developing countries produce capital. For more information on these institutions, see the last chapter of this text.

output markets. Within those limits, households make their choices on the basis of personal tastes and preferences.

The notion of *utility* helps to explain the process of choice. The law of *diminishing marginal utility* partly explains why people seem to spread their incomes over many different goods and services and why demand curves have a negative slope. Another important explanation behind the negative relationship between price and quantity demanded lies in *income effects* and *substitution effects*.

As we turned to input markets, we relaxed the assumption that income was fixed and given. In the labor market, households are forced to weigh the value of leisure against the value of goods and services that can be bought with wage income. Once again, we found household preferences for goods and leisure operating within a set of constraints imposed by the market. Households also face the problem of allocating income and consumption over more than one period of time. They can finance spending in the future with today's income by saving and earning interest, or they can spend tomorrow's income today by borrowing.

We now have a rough sketch of the factors that determine output demand and input supply. (You can review these in Figure 6.1.) In the next three chapters, we turn to firm behavior and explore in detail the factors that affect output supply and input demand.

SUMMARY

1. In perfectly competitive markets, prices are determined by the forces of supply and demand, and no single household or firm has any control over them. The assumption of a perfectly competitive market underlies all of our discussions through chapter 12. Much of what we say in these chapters, however, can be generalized to the other forms of market structure. We also assume that households possess *perfect knowledge* of the qualities and prices of everything available in the market.

HOUSEHOLD CHOICE IN OUTPUT MARKETS

2. Every household must make three basic decisions: (1) how much of each product, or output, to demand; (2) how much labor to supply; and (3) how much to spend today and how much to save for the future.

3. Income, wealth, and prices define a household's *budget constraint*. The budget constraint separates those combinations of goods and services that are available from those that are not. All the points below and to the left of a graph of a household's budget constraint make up its *choice set*, or *opportunity set*.

4. It is best to think of the household choice problem as one of allocating income over a large number of goods and services. A change in the price of one good may change the entire allocation. Demand for some goods may rise while demand for others may fall.

5. As long as a household faces a limited income, the real cost of any single good or service is the value of the *other* goods and services that could have been purchased with the same amount of money.

6. Within the constraints of prices, income, and wealth, household decisions ultimately depend on preferences—likes, dislikes, and tastes.

THE BASIS OF CHOICE: UTILITY

7. Whether one item is preferable to another depends on how much *utility*, or satisfaction, it yields relative to its alternatives.

8. The *law of diminishing marginal utility* says that the more of any good we consume in a given period of time, the less satisfaction, or utility, we get out of each additional (or marginal) unit of that good.

9. Households allocate income among goods and services in order to maximize utility. This implies choosing activities that yield the highest marginal utility per dollar. In a two-good world, households will choose so as to equate the marginal utility per dollar spent on X with the marginal utility per dollar spent on Y. This is the *utility-maximizing rule*.

INCOME AND SUBSTITUTION EFFECTS

10. The fact that demand curves have a negative slope can be explained in two ways: (1) Marginal utility for all goods diminishes, and (2) for most normal goods both the *income and substitution effects* of a price decline lead to more consumption of the good.

CONSUMER SURPLUS

11. When any good is sold at a fixed price, households must "reveal" whether that good is worth the price being asked. For many people who buy in a given market, the product is worth more than its current price. Those people receive a *consumer surplus*.

HOUSEHOLD CHOICE IN INPUT MARKETS

12. In the labor market, a trade-off exists between the value of the goods and services that can be bought in the market or produced at home and the value that one places on leisure. The opportunity cost of paid work is leisure and unpaid work. The wage rate is the price, or opportunity cost, of the benefits of unpaid work or of leisure.

13. The income and substitution effects of a change in the wage rate work in opposite directions. Higher wages mean that (1) leisure is more expensive (likely response: people work *more*—substitution effect), and (2) more income is earned in a given number of hours, so some time may be spent on leisure (likely response: people work *less*—income effect).

14. In addition to deciding how to allocate its present income among goods and services, a household may also decide to save or borrow. When a household decides to save part of its current income, it is using current income to finance future spending. When a household borrows, it finances current purchases with future income.

15. An increase in interest rates has a positive effect on saving if the substitution effect dominates the income effect, and a negative effect if the income effect dominates the substitution effect. Most empirical evidence shows that the substitution effect dominates here.

REVIEW TERMS AND CONCEPTS

budget constraint, 130
choice set or opportunity set, 131
consumer surplus, 144
cost-benefit analysis, 144
diamond/water paradox, 144

financial capital market, 148
income effect of a price change, 140
labor supply curve, 146
law of diminishing marginal utility, 136
marginal utility (*MU*), 135

perfect knowledge, 128
substitution effect of a price change, 140
total utility, 135
utility, 135
utility-maximizing rule, 138

PROBLEM SET

1. For each of the following events, consider how you might react. What things might you consume more or less of? Would you work more or less? Would you increase or decrease your saving? Are your responses consistent with the discussion of household behavior in this chapter?
   a. Tuition at your college is cut 25 percent.
   b. You receive an award that pays you $300 per month for the next five years.
   c. The price of food doubles. (If you are on a meal plan, assume that your board charges double.)
   d. A new business opens up nearby offering part-time jobs at $20 per hour.

2. The following table gives a hypothetical total utility schedule for the Cookie Monster:

NUMBER OF COOKIES	TOTAL UTILITY
0	0
1	100
2	200
3	275
4	325
5	350
6	360
7	360

Calculate the CM's marginal utility schedule. Draw a graph of total and marginal utility. If cookies cost the CM five cents each, what is the maximum number of cookies he would most likely eat?

3. Kamika lives in Chicago but goes to school in Tucson, Arizona. For the last two years, she has made four trips home each year. During 1999, the price of a round-trip ticket from Chicago to Tucson increased from $350 to $600. As a result, Kamika bought five fewer CDs that year and decided not to drive to Phoenix with friends for an expensive rock concert.
   a. Explain how Kamika's demand for CDs and concert tickets can be affected by an increase in air travel prices.
   b. Using this example, explain why both income and substitution effects might be expected to reduce the number of trips home that Kamika takes.

4. Sketch the following budget constraints:

	P_X	P_Y	INCOME
a.	$20	$50	$1,000
b.	40	50	1,000
c.	20	100	1,000
d.	20	50	2,000
e.	.25	.25	7.00
f.	.25	.50	7.00
g.	.50	.25	7.00

5. On January 1, Professor Smith made a resolution to lose some weight and save some money. He decided that he would strictly budget $100 for lunches each month. For lunch he has only two choices: the faculty club, where the price of a lunch is $5, and Alice's Restaurant, where the price of a lunch is $10. Every day that he doesn't eat lunch, he runs 5 miles.
   a. Assuming that Professor Smith spends the entire $100 each month at either Alice's or the club, sketch his budget constraint. Show actual numbers on the axes.
   b. Last month Professor Smith chose to eat at the club 10 times and at Alice's 5 times. Does this choice fit within his budget constraint?
   c. Last month, Alice ran a half-price lunch special all month. All lunches were reduced to $5. Show the effect on Professor Smith's budget constraint.

6. Reform of the U.S. welfare system has been a goal of many administrations, including President Clinton's. The major thrust of welfare reform proposals over the last two decades has been to restore the incentive to work. Because welfare programs are for low-income families, those who earn income lose their eligibility for welfare. This acts as a stiff "tax" on working.
   In 1981, President Reagan proposed and the Congress approved significant cuts in welfare expenditures. Cutting benefits would make living on welfare less attractive, it was argued, and lead to an expansion of the labor supply. But the way the welfare changes were enacted led to a second effect. Before the cuts, a welfare recipient's benefits were reduced by $.50 for every dollar he or she earned. For example, someone who earned $200 per month would lose $100 in welfare benefits; thus, his or her final income would rise by only $100. After the cuts, the implicit tax rate went up to 80 percent: Benefits were reduced by $.80 for every dollar earned. For example, after the cuts, a person earning $200 would lose $160 in benefits. This meant that final income would rise by only $40.
   Using the income and substitution effects, explain how the Reagan cuts could lead to either an increase or a decrease in labor supply.

7. Assume that Mei has $100 per month to divide between dinners at a Chinese restaurant and nights at Zanzibar, a local pub. Assume that going to Zanzibar costs $20 and eating at the Chinese restaurant costs $10. Suppose that Mei spends two nights at Zanzibar and eats six times at the Chinese restaurant.
   a. Draw Mei's budget constraint and show that she can afford six meals and two nights at Zanzibar.
   b. Assume that Mei comes into some money and can now spend $200 per month. Draw her new budget constraint.
   c. As a result of the increase in income, Mei decides to spend eight nights at Zanzibar and eat at the Chinese restaurant four times. What kind of a good is Chinese food? What kind of a good is a night at Zanzibar?
   d. What part of the increase in Zanzibar trips is due to the income effect, and which part is due to the substitution effect? Explain your answer.

8. Assume that as a result of two recent hijackings and bombings, people's desire to fly diminishes significantly. Describe and graph (using supply and demand curves) how you might expect the air travel market to react. What might happen to the price of airline tickets?

9. Say whether you agree or disagree with each of the following statements, and explain your reason:
   a. "If the income effect of a wage change dominates the substitution effect for a given household, and the household works longer hours following a wage change, wages must have risen."
   b. "In product markets when a price falls, the substitution effect leads to more consumption, but for normal goods, the income effect leads to less consumption."

10. For this problem, assume that Joe has $80 to spend on books and movies each month, and that both goods must be purchased whole (no fractional units). Movies cost $8 each, while books cost $20 each. Joe's preferences for movies and books are summarized by the information on the next page:

	MOVIES				BOOKS		
# PER MONTH	TU	MU	MU/$	# PER MONTH	TU	MU	MU/$
1	50			1	22		
2	80			2	42		
3	100			3	52		
4	110			4	57		
5	116			5	60		
6	121			6	62		
7	123			7	63		

a. Fill in the figures for marginal utility and marginal utility per dollar for both movies and books.

b. Are these preferences consistent with the "law of diminishing marginal utility"? Explain briefly.

c. Given the budget of $80, what quantity of books and what quantity of movies will maximize Joe's level of satisfaction? Explain briefly.

d. Draw the budget constraint (with books on the horizontal axis) and identify the optimal combination of books and movies as point A.

e. Now suppose the price of books falls to $10. Which of the columns in the table must be recalculated? Do the required recalculations.

f. After the price change, how many movies and how many books will Joe purchase?

g. Draw in the new budget constraint and identify the new optimal combination of books and movies as point B.

h. If you calculated correctly, you have found that a decrease in the price of books has caused this person to buy more movies as well as more books. How can this be?

11. In most countries, an auction has bidders starting at low prices and bidding progressively higher. In Holland, the process is reversed: the auctioneer starts at a high price and bids down. The first person to agree to an announced price will get the good. Which method is more effective at reducing consumer surplus? Why?

12. If leisure is a normal good, would you expect a large inheritance to cause an increase or a decrease in the number of hours a person wants to work? Why? How would a 100 percent tax rate on large inheritances affect total desired working hours in the economy?

TAKE IT TO THE NET

We invite you to visit the Case and Fair page on the Prentice Hall Web site:

http://www.prenhall.com/casefair

for this chapter's World Wide Web exercise.

INDIFFERENCE CURVES

Early in this chapter, we saw how a consumer choosing between two goods is constrained by the prices of those goods and by his or her income. This appendix returns to that example and analyzes the process of choice more formally. (Before we proceed, review carefully the text under the heading "The Budget Constraint More Formally.")

ASSUMPTIONS

We base the following analysis on four assumptions:

1. We assume that this analysis is restricted to goods that yield positive marginal utility, or, more simply, that "more is better." One way to justify this assumption is to say that if more of something actually makes you worse off, you can simply throw it away at no cost. This is the assumption of free disposal.

2. The **marginal rate of substitution** is defined as MU_X/MU_Y, or the ratio at which a household is willing to substitute Y for X. When MU_X/MU_Y is equal to four, for example, I would be willing to trade four units of Y for one additional unit of X.

   We assume a diminishing marginal rate of substitution. That is, as more of X and less of Y is consumed, MU_X/MU_Y declines. As you consume more of X and less of Y, X becomes less valuable in terms of units of Y, or Y becomes more valuable in terms of X. This is almost, but not precisely, equivalent to assuming diminishing marginal utility.

3. We assume that consumers have the ability to choose among the combinations of goods and services available. Confronted with the choice between two alternative combinations of goods and services, A and B, a consumer will respond in one of three ways: (1) She prefers A over B, (2) she prefers B over A, or (3) she is indifferent between A and B—that is, she likes A and B equally.

4. We assume that consumer choices are consistent with a simple assumption of rationality. If a consumer shows that he prefers A to B and subsequently shows that he prefers B to a third alternative, C, he should prefer A to C if confronted with a choice between the two.

DERIVING INDIFFERENCE CURVES

If we accept these four assumptions, we can construct a "map" of a consumer's preferences. These preference maps are made up of indifference curves. An **indifference curve** is a set of points, each point representing a combination of goods X and Y, all of which yield the same total utility.

Figure 6A.1 shows how we might go about deriving an indifference curve for a hypothetical consumer. Each point in the diagram represents some amount of X and some amount of Y. Point A in the diagram, for example, represents X_A units of X and Y_A units of Y. Now suppose that we take some amount of Y away from our hypothetical consumer, moving him to A'. At A' he has the same amount of X—that is, X_A units—but less Y; he now has only Y_C units of Y. Because "more is better," our consumer is unequivocally worse off at A' than he was at A.

To compensate for the loss of Y, we now begin giving our consumer some more X. If we give him just a little, he will still be worse off than he was at A; if we give him lots of X, he will be better off. But there must be some quantity of X that will just compensate for the loss of Y. By giving him that amount, we will have put together a bundle, Y_C and X_C, that yields the exact same total utility as bundle A. This is bundle C in Figure 6A.1. If confronted with a choice between bundles A and C, our consumer will say "Either one; I don't care." In other

---

FIGURE 6A.1

An Indifference Curve

An indifference curve is a set of points, each representing a combination of some amount of good X and some amount of good Y, that all yield the same amount of total utility. The consumer depicted here is indifferent between bundles A and B, B and C, and A and C.

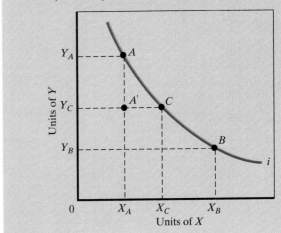

words, he is *indifferent* between *A* and *C*. When confronted with a choice between bundles *C* and *B* (which represents X_B and Y_B units of *X* and *Y*), he is also indifferent. The points along the curve labeled *i* in Figure 6A.1 represent all the combinations of *X* and *Y* that yield the same total utility to our consumer. That curve is thus an indifference curve.

Each consumer has a whole set of indifference curves. Return for a moment to Figure 6A.1. Starting at point *A* again, imagine that we give the consumer a tiny bit more *X* *and* a tiny bit more *Y*. Because more is better, we know that the new bundle will yield a higher level of total utility, and the consumer will be better off. Now, just as we constructed the first indifference curve, we can construct a second one. What we get is an indifference curve that is *higher* and to the *right* of the first curve. Because utility along an indifference curve is constant at all points, every point along the new curve represents a higher level of total utility than every point along the first.

Figure 6A.2 shows a set of four indifference curves. The curve labeled i_4 represents the combinations of *X* and *Y* that yield the highest level of total utility among the four. Many other indifference curves exist between those shown on the diagram; in fact, their number is infinite. Notice that as you move up and to the right, utility increases.

The shapes of the indifference curves depend on the preferences of the consumer, and the whole set of indifference curves is called a **preference map**. Each consumer has a unique preference map.

PROPERTIES OF INDIFFERENCE CURVES

The indifference curves shown in Figure 6A.2 are drawn bowing in toward the origin, or zero point, on the axes. In other words, the absolute value of the slope of the indifference curves decreases, or the curves get flatter, as we move to the right. Thus, we say that indifference curves are convex toward the origin. This shape follows directly from the assumption of diminishing marginal rate of substitution and makes sense if you remember the law of diminishing marginal utility.

To understand the convex shape, compare the segment of curve i_1 between *A* and *B* with the segment of the same curve between *C* and *D*. Moving from *A* to *B*, the consumer is willing to give up a substantial amount of *Y* to get a small amount of *X*. (Remember that total utility is constant along an indifference curve; the consumer is therefore indifferent between *A* and *B*.) Moving from *C* and *D*, however, the consumer is willing to give up only a small amount of *Y* to get more *X*.

This changing trade-off makes complete sense when you remember the law of diminishing marginal utility. Notice that between *A* and *B*, a lot of *Y* is consumed, and the marginal utility derived from a unit of *Y* is likely to be small. At the same time, though, only a little of *X* is being consumed, so the marginal utility derived from consuming a unit of *X* is likely to be high.

Suppose, for example, that *X* is pizza and *Y* is soda. Near *A* and *B*, a thirsty, hungry football player who has 10 sodas in front of him but only 1 slice of pizza will trade several sodas for another slice. Down around *C* and *D*, however, he has 20 slices of pizza and only a single soda. Now he will trade several slices of pizza to get an additional soda.

We can show how the trade-off changes more formally by deriving an expression for the slope of an indifference curve. Let's look at the arc (i.e., the section of the curve) between *A* and *B*. We know that in moving from *A* to *B*, total utility remains constant. That means that the utility lost as a result of consuming less *Y* must be matched by the utility gained from consuming more *X*. We can approximate the loss of utility by multiplying the marginal utility of *Y* (MU_Y) by the number of units by which consumption of *Y* is curtailed (ΔY). Similarly, we can approximate the utility gained from consuming more *X* by multiplying the marginal utility of *X* (MU_X) by the number of additional units of *X* consumed (ΔX).

FIGURE 6A.2

A Preference Map: A Family of Indifference Curves

Each consumer has a unique family of indifference curves called a preference map. Higher indifference curves represent higher levels of total utility.

$$\text{Slope:} = \frac{\Delta Y_1}{\Delta X_1} = -\frac{MU_X}{MU_Y}$$

Remember: Because the consumer is indifferent between points A and B, total utility is the same at both points. Thus, these two must be equal in magnitude—that is, the gain in utility from consuming more X must equal the loss in utility from consuming less Y. Since ΔY is a negative number (because consumption of Y decreases from A to B), it follows that:

$$MU_X \cdot \Delta X = -(MU_Y \cdot \Delta Y).$$

If we divide both sides by MU_Y and by ΔX, we obtain:

$$\frac{\Delta Y}{\Delta X} = -\left(\frac{MU_X}{MU_Y}\right).$$

Recall that the slope of any line is calculated by dividing the change in Y (that is, ΔY) by the change in X (that is, ΔX). This leads us to conclude that:

> The slope of an indifference curve is the ratio of the marginal utility of X to the marginal utility of Y, and it is negative.

Now let's return to our pizza (X) and soda (Y) example. As we move down from the $A{:}B$ area to the $C{:}D$ area, our football player is consuming less soda and more pizza. The marginal utility of pizza (MU_X) is falling and the marginal utility of soda (MU_Y) is rising. That means that MU_X/MU_Y (**the marginal rate of substitution**) is falling, and the absolute value of the slope of the indifference curve is declining. And, indeed, it does get flatter.

CONSUMER CHOICE

As you recall, demand depends on income, the prices of goods and services, and preferences or tastes. We are now ready to see how preferences as embodied in indifference curves interact with budget constraints to determine how the final quantities of X and Y will be chosen.

In Figure 6A.3, a set of indifference curves is superimposed on a consumer's budget constraint. Recall that the budget constraint separates those combinations of X and Y that are available from those that are not. The constraint simply shows those combinations that can be purchased with an income of I at prices P_X and P_Y. The budget constraint crosses the X axis at I/P_X, or the number of units of X that can be purchased with I if nothing is spent on Y. Similarly, the budget constraint crosses the Y axis at I/P_Y, or the number of units of Y that can be purchased with an income of I if nothing is spent on X. The shaded area is the consumer's opportunity set. The slope of a budget constraint is $-P_X/P_Y$.

Consumers will choose from among available combinations of X and Y the one that maximizes utility. In graphic terms, the consumer will move along the budget constraint until he or she is on the highest possible indifference curve. Utility rises by moving from points such as A or C (which lie on i_1) toward B (which lies on i_2). Any movement away from point B moves the consumer to a lower indifference curve—a lower level of utility. In this case, utility is maximized when our consumer buys X^* units of X and Y^* units of Y. At point B, the budget constraint is just tangent to (that is, just touches) indifference curve i_2.

> As long as indifference curves are convex to the origin, utility maximization will take place at that point at which the indifference curve is just tangent to the budget constraint.

The tangency condition has important implications. Where two curves are tangent, they have the same slope, which implies that the slope of the indifference curve is

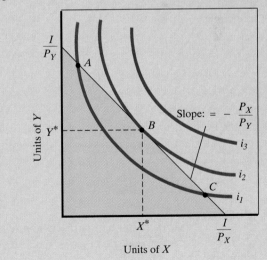

FIGURE 6A.3

Consumer Utility-Maximizing Equilibrium

Consumers will choose the combination of X and Y that maximizes total utility. Graphically, the consumer will move along the budget constraint until the highest possible indifference curve is reached. At that point, the budget constraint and the indifference curve are tangent. This point of tangency occurs at X^* and Y^* (point B).

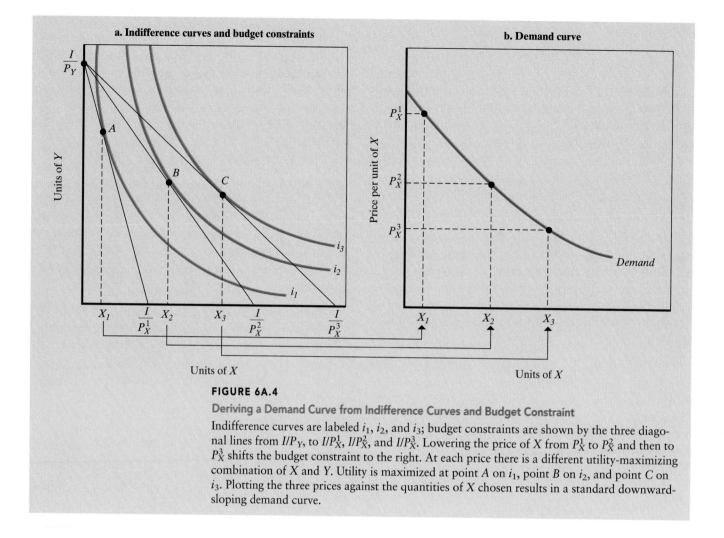

a. Indifference curves and budget constraints

b. Demand curve

FIGURE 6A.4

Deriving a Demand Curve from Indifference Curves and Budget Constraint

Indifference curves are labeled i_1, i_2, and i_3; budget constraints are shown by the three diagonal lines from I/P_Y, to I/P_X^1, I/P_X^2, and I/P_X^3. Lowering the price of X from P_X^1 to P_X^2 and then to P_X^3 shifts the budget constraint to the right. At each price there is a different utility-maximizing combination of X and Y. Utility is maximized at point A on i_1, point B on i_2, and point C on i_3. Plotting the three prices against the quantities of X chosen results in a standard downward-sloping demand curve.

exactly equal to the slope of the budget constraint at the point of tangency:

$$-\frac{MU_X}{MU_Y} = -\frac{P_X}{P_Y}.$$

slope of indifference curve = slope of budget constraint

By multiplying both sides of this equation by MU_Y and dividing both sides by P_Y, we can rewrite this utility-maximizing rule as:

$$\frac{MU_X}{P_X} = \frac{MU_Y}{P_Y}.$$

This is the same rule derived in our earlier discussion without using indifference curves. We can describe this rule intuitively by saying that consumers maximize their total

utility by equating the marginal utility per dollar spent on X with the marginal utility per dollar spent on Y. If this rule did not hold, utility could be increased by shifting money from one good to the other.

DERIVING A DEMAND CURVE FROM INDIFFERENCE CURVES AND BUDGET CONSTRAINTS

We now turn to the task of deriving a simple demand curve from indifference curves and budget constraints. A demand curve shows the quantity of a single good, X in this case, that a consumer will demand at various prices. To derive the demand curve, we need to confront our consumer with several alternative prices for X while keeping other prices, income, and preferences constant.

Figure 6A.4 shows the derivation. We begin with price P_X^1. At that price, the utility-maximizing point is A, where the consumer demands X_1 units of X. Therefore, in the right-hand diagram, we plot P_X^1 against X_1. This is the first point on our demand curve.

Now we lower the price of X to P_X^2. Lowering the price expands the opportunity set, and the budget constraint shifts to the right. Because the price of X has fallen, if our consumer spends all of his income on X, he can buy more of it. He is also better off, because he can move to a higher indifference curve. The new utility-maximizing point is B, where the consumer demands X_2 units of X. Because the consumer demands X_2 units of X at a price of P_X^2, we plot P_X^2 against X_2 in the right-hand diagram. A second price cut to P_X^3 moves our consumer to point C, where he demands X_3 units of X, and so on. Thus, we see how the demand curve can be derived from a consumer's preference map and budget constraint.

SUMMARY

1. An *indifference curve* is a set of points, each point representing a combination of goods X and Y, all of which yield the same total utility. A particular consumer's set of indifference curves is called a *preference map.*

2. The slope of an indifference curve is the ratio of the marginal utility of X to the marginal utility of Y, and it is negative.

3. As long as indifference curves are convex to the origin, utility maximization will take place at that point at which the indifference curve is just tangent to (that is, just touches) the budget constraint. The utility-maximizing rule can also be written as $MU_X/P_X = MU_Y/P_Y$.

REVIEW TERMS AND CONCEPTS

indifference curve A set of points, each point representing a combination of goods X and Y, all of which yield the same total utility. 153

marginal rate of substitution MU_X/MU_Y; the ratio at which a household is willing to substitute good Y for good X. 153

preference map A consumer's set of indifference curves. 154

PROBLEM SET

1. Which of the four assumptions that were made at the beginning of the appendix are violated by the indifference curves in Figure 1? Explain.

2. Assume that a household receives a weekly income of $100. If Figure 2 on p. 158 represents that household's choices as the price of X changes, plot three points on the household's demand curve.

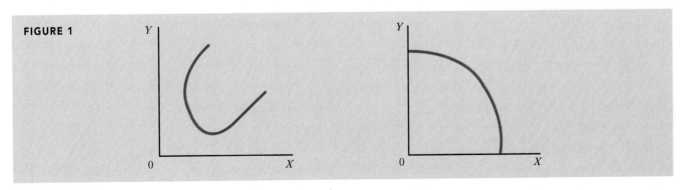

FIGURE 1

FIGURE 2

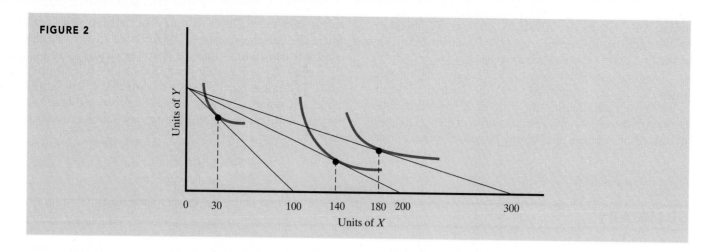

*3. If Ann's marginal rate of substitution of Y for X is 5 (that is, $MU_X/MU_Y = 5$), the price of X is $9.00, and the price of Y is $2.00, she is spending too much of her income on Y. Do you agree or disagree? Explain your answer using a graph.

*4. Assume that Jim is a rational consumer who consumes only two goods, apples (A) and nuts (N). Assume that his marginal rate of substitution of apples for nuts is given by the following formula:

$$MRS = MU_N/MU_A = A/N$$

That is, Jim's *MRS* is simply equal to the ratio of the number of apples consumed to the number of nuts consumed.

a. Assume that Jim's income is $100, the price of nuts is $5, and the price of apples is $10. What quantities of apples and nuts will he consume?

b. Find two additional points on his demand curve for nuts ($P_N = 10 and $P_N = 2).

c. Sketch one of the equilibrium points on an indifference curve graph.

Chapter 7

THE PRODUCTION PROCESS: THE BEHAVIOR OF PROFIT-MAXIMIZING FIRMS

IN CHAPTER 6, we took a brief look at the household decisions that lie behind supply and demand curves. We spent some time discussing household choices: how much to work and how to choose among the wide range of goods and services available within the constraints of prices and income. We also identified some of the influences on household demand in output markets, as well as some of the influences on household supply behavior in input markets.

We now turn to the other side of the system and examine the behavior of firms. Business firms purchase inputs in order to produce and sell outputs. In other words, they *demand* factors of production in input markets and *supply* goods and services in output markets. Figure 7.1 repeats the now familiar circular flow diagram you first encountered in chapter 6. Here in chapter 7 we look inside the firm at the production process that transforms inputs into outputs.

Although chapters 7 through 12 describe the behavior of perfectly competitive firms, much of what we say in these chapters also applies to firms that are not perfectly competitive. For example, when we turn to monopoly in chapter 13, we will be describing firms that are similar to competitive firms in many ways. All firms, whether competitive or not, demand inputs, engage in production, and produce outputs. All firms have an incentive to maximize profits and thus to minimize costs.

Central to our analysis is **production,** the process by which inputs are combined, transformed, and turned into outputs. Firms vary in size and internal organization, but they all take inputs and transform them into things for which there is some demand. For example, an independent accountant combines labor, paper, telephone service, time, learning, and a personal computer to provide help to confused taxpayers. An automobile plant uses

production *The process by which inputs are combined, transformed, and turned into outputs.*

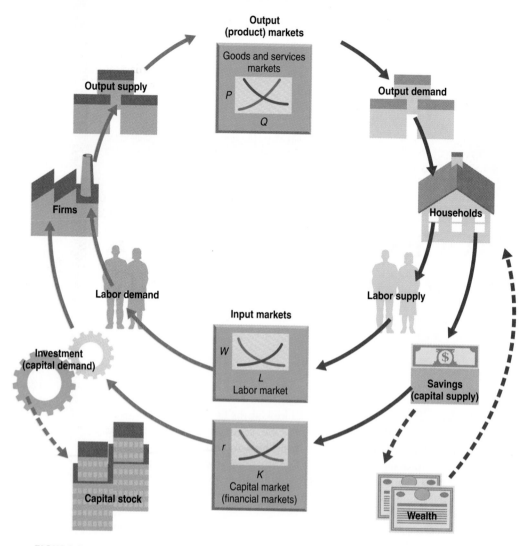

FIGURE 7.1

Firm and Household Decisions

steel, labor, plastic, electricity, machines, and countless other inputs to produce cars. Before we begin our discussion of the production process, however, we need to clarify some of the assumptions on which our analysis is based.

➤ **Production Is Not Limited to Firms** Although our discussions in the next several chapters focus on profit-making business firms, it is important to understand that production and productive activity are not confined to private business firms. Households also engage in transforming factors of production (labor, capital, energy, natural resources, etc.) into useful things. When I work in my garden, I am combining land, labor, fertilizer, seeds, and tools (capital) into the vegetables I eat and the flowers I enjoy. The government also combines land, labor, and capital to produce public services for which demand exists: national defense, police and fire protection, and education, to name a few.

Private business firms are set apart from other producers, such as households and government, by their purpose. A **firm** exists when a person or a group of people decides to produce a good or service to meet a perceived demand. They engage in production

firm *An organization that comes into being when a person or a group of people decides to produce a good or service to meet a perceived demand. Most firms exist to make a profit.*

(that is, they transform inputs into outputs) because they can sell their products for more than it costs to produce them.

Even among firms that exist to make a profit, however, there are many important differences. A firm's behavior is likely to depend on how it is organized internally and on its relationship to the firms with which it competes. How many competitors are there? How large are they? How do they compete?

In chapter 3 we discussed the different ways that businesses can organize—as proprietorships, as partnerships, or as corporations. We also discussed the different forms of industry in the U.S. economy—perfect competition, monopolistic competition, oligopoly, and monopoly. Before we finish with microeconomics, we will analyze the behavior of all four of these industry types. But it is logical to start with the simplest. Thus, the next three chapters will deal exclusively with the behavior of firms in perfectly competitive industries.

▶ **Perfect Competition** As you learned in chapter 3, **perfect competition** exists in an industry that contains many relatively small firms producing identical products. In a perfectly competitive industry, no single firm has any control over prices. In other words, an individual firm cannot affect the market price of its product or the prices of the inputs that it buys. This important characteristic follows from two assumptions. First, a competitive industry is composed of many firms, each small relative to the size of the industry. Second, every firm in a perfectly competitive industry produces **homogeneous products**, which means that one firm's output cannot be distinguished from the output of the others.

These assumptions limit the decisions open to competitive firms and simplify the analysis of competitive behavior. Firms in perfectly competitive industries do not differentiate their products, nor do they make decisions about price. Rather, each firm takes prices as given—that is, as determined in the market by the laws of supply and demand—and decides only how much to produce and how to produce it.

The idea that competitive firms are "price-takers" is central to our discussion. Of course, we do not mean that firms cannot affix price tags to their merchandise; all firms have this ability. We simply mean that, given the availability of perfect substitutes, any product priced over the market price will not be sold.

These assumptions also imply that the demand for the product of a competitive firm is perfectly elastic (see chapter 5). For example, consider the Ohio corn farmer whose situation is shown in Figure 7.2. The left side of the diagram represents the

perfect competition *An industry structure in which there are many firms, each small relative to the industry, producing virtually identical products and in which no firm is large enough to have any control over prices. In perfectly competitive industries, new competitors can freely enter and exit the market.*

homogeneous products *Undifferentiated products; products that are identical to, or indistinguishable from, one another.*

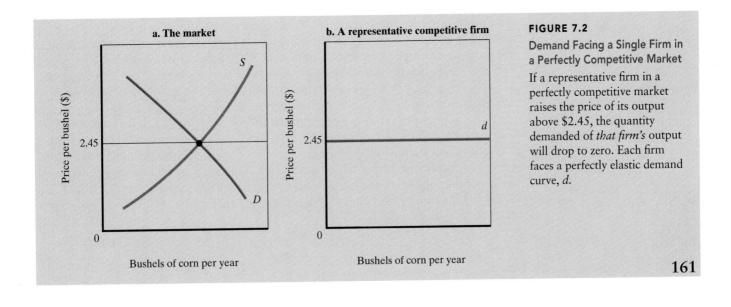

a. The market   b. A representative competitive firm

FIGURE 7.2

Demand Facing a Single Firm in a Perfectly Competitive Market

If a representative firm in a perfectly competitive market raises the price of its output above $2.45, the quantity demanded of *that firm's* output will drop to zero. Each firm faces a perfectly elastic demand curve, *d*.

current conditions in the market. Corn is currently selling for $2.45 per bushel.[1] The right side of the diagram shows the demand for corn as the farmer sees it. If she were to raise her price, she would sell no corn at all; because there are perfect substitutes available, the quantity demanded of her corn would drop to zero. To lower her price would be silly because she can sell all she wants at the current price. (Remember, each farmer's production is very small relative to the entire corn market.)

In perfect competition we also assume easy entry—that firms can easily enter and exit the industry. If firms in an industry are earning high profits, new firms are likely to spring up. There are no barriers that prevent a new firm from competing. Fast food restaurants are quick to spring up when a new shopping center opens, and new gas stations appear when a housing development or a new highway is built.

We also assume *easy exit*. When a firm finds itself suffering losses or earning low profits, one option is to go out of business, or exit the industry. Everyone knows a favorite restaurant that went out of business. Changes in cost of production, falling prices from international or regional competition, and changing technology may all turn business profits into losses and failure.

As you saw in chapter 3, the best examples of perfect competition are probably found in agriculture. In that industry, products are absolutely homogeneous—it is impossible to distinguish one farmer's wheat from another's—and prices are set by the forces of supply and demand in a huge national market.

THE BEHAVIOR OF PROFIT-MAXIMIZING FIRMS

All firms must make several basic decisions to achieve what we assume to be their primary objective—maximum profits. Figure 7.3 shows three basic decisions.

> The Three Decisions That All Firms Must Make:
>
> 1. How much output to supply (quantity of product);
> 2. How to produce that output (which production technique/technology to use); and
> 3. How much of each input to demand.

The first and last choices are linked by the second choice. Once a firm has decided how much to produce, the choice of a production method determines the firm's input requirements. If a sweater company decides to produce 5,000 sweaters this month, it knows how many production workers it will need, how much electricity it will use, how much raw yarn to purchase, and how many sewing machines to run.

Similarly, given a technique of production, any set of input quantities determines the amount of output that can be produced. Certainly the number of machines and workers employed in a sweater mill determines how many sweaters can be produced.

Changing the *technology* of production will change the relationship between input and output quantities. An apple orchard that uses expensive equipment to raise pickers up into the trees will harvest more fruit with fewer workers in a given period of time than an orchard in which pickers use simple ladders. It is also possible that two different technologies can produce the same quantity of output. For example, a fully computerized textile mill with only a few workers running the machines may produce the same number of sweaters as a mill with no sophisticated machines but many workers. A profit-maximizing firm chooses the technology that minimizes its costs for a given level of output.

1. How much output to supply
2. Which production technology to use
3. How much of each input to demand

FIGURE 7.3

The Three Decisions That All Firms Must Make

---

[1]Capital letters refer to the entire market and lower-case letters refer to representative firms. For example, in Figure 7.2, the market demand curve is labeled *D* and the demand curve facing the firm is labeled *d*.

Remember as we proceed that we are discussing and analyzing the behavior of *perfectly competitive* firms. Thus, we will say nothing about price-setting behavior, product quality, and other characteristics of the product—choices that lead to product differentiation. In perfect competition, both input and output prices are beyond a firm's control—they are determined in the market and are not the decisions of any individual firm. And remember that all firms in a given industry produce the same exact product. When we analyze the behavior of firms in other kinds of markets (in chapters 13 and 14), the three basic decisions will be expanded to include the setting of prices and the determination of product quality.

PROFITS AND ECONOMIC COSTS

We assume that firms are in business to make a profit and that a firm's behavior is guided by the goal of maximizing profits. What is profit? **Profit** is the difference between total revenue and total cost:

profit *The difference between total revenue and total cost.*

> Profit = Total revenue − Total cost

Total revenue is the amount received from the sale of the product; it is equal to the number of units sold (q) times the price received per unit (P). Total cost is less straightforward to define. We define **total cost** here to include (1) out-of-pocket costs, (2) a normal rate of return on capital, (3) the opportunity cost of each factor of production. This definition of profit thus takes into account the opportunity cost of capital, because total cost includes a normal rate of return on capital. This definition of profit differs from the accounting definition of profit, which does not include a normal rate of return on capital in total cost. Unless otherwise stated, we will use this definition of profit, not the accounting definition, in what follows.

total revenue *The amount received from the sale of the product (q × P).*

total cost *The total of (1) out-of-pocket costs, (2) a normal rate of return on capital, and (3) the opportunity cost of each factor of production.*

▶ **Normal Rate of Return** When someone decides to start a firm, he or she must commit resources. To operate a manufacturing firm, you need a plant and some equipment. To start a restaurant, you need to buy grills, ovens, tables, chairs, and so forth. In other words, you must invest in capital. Such investment requires resources that stay tied up in the firm as long as it operates. Even firms that have been around a long time must continue to invest. Plant and equipment wear out and must be replaced. Firms that decide to expand must put new capital in place. This is as true of proprietorships, where the resources come directly from the proprietor, as it is of corporations, where the resources needed to make investments come from shareholders.

Whenever resources are used to invest in a business, there is an opportunity cost. Instead of opening a candy store, I could put my funds into an alternative use such as a certificate of deposit or a government bond, both of which earn interest. Instead of using its retained earnings to build a new plant, a firm could simply earn interest on those funds or pay them out to shareholders.

A **normal rate of return** is the rate that is just sufficient to keep owners and investors satisfied. If the rate of return were to fall below normal, it would be difficult or impossible for managers to raise resources needed to purchase new capital. Owners of the firm would be receiving a rate of return that was lower than they could receive elsewhere in the economy, and they would have no incentive to invest in the firm.

normal rate of return *A rate of return on capital that is just sufficient to keep owners and investors satisfied. For relatively risk-free firms, it should be nearly the same as the interest rate on risk-free government bonds.*

If the firm has fairly steady revenues and the future looks secure, the normal rate of return should be very close to the interest rate on risk-free government bonds. I certainly won't keep investors interested in my firm if I don't pay them a rate of return at least as high as they can get from a risk-free government or corporate bond. If my firm is rock solid and the economy is steady, I may not have to pay a much higher rate. But if my firm is in a very speculative industry and the future of the economy is shaky, I may have to pay substantially more to keep my shareholders happy. In exchange for taking such a risk, they will expect a higher return.

A normal rate of return is considered a part of the total cost of a business. Adding a normal rate of return to total cost has an important meaning: When a firm earns exactly a normal rate of return, it is earning a zero profit as we have defined profit. If the level of profit is positive, the firm is earning an above-normal rate of return on capital.

A simple example will illustrate the concepts of a normal rate of return being part of total cost. Suppose that Sue and Ann decide to start a small business selling turquoise belts in the Denver airport. To get into the business they need to invest in a fancy pushcart. The price of the pushcart is $20,000 with all the displays and attachments built in. Suppose that Sue and Ann estimate that they will sell 3,000 belts each year for $10 each. Further, assume that each belt costs $5 from the supplier. Finally, the cart must be staffed by one clerk, who works for an annual wage of $14,000. Is this business going to make a profit?

To answer this question, we must determine total revenue and total cost. First, annual revenue is simply $30,000 (3,000 belts × $10). Total cost includes the cost of the belts—$15,000 (3,000 belts × $5)—plus the labor cost of $14,000, for a total of $29,000. Thus, on the basis of the annual revenue and cost flows, the firm *seems* to be making a profit of $1,000 ($30,000 − $29,000).

But what about the $20,000 initial investment in the pushcart? This investment is *not* a direct part of the cost of Sue and Ann's firm. If we assume that the cart maintains its value over time, *the only thing that Sue and Ann are giving up is the interest that they might have earned had they not tied up their funds in the pushcart.* That is, the only real "cost" is the opportunity cost of the investment, which is the forgone interest on the $20,000.

Now suppose that Sue and Ann want a minimum return equal to 10 percent—which is, say, the rate of interest that they could have gotten by purchasing corporate bonds. This implies a normal return of 10 percent, or $2,000 annually (= $20,000 × .10) on the $20,000 investment. But, as we determined above, Sue and Ann will earn only $1,000 annually. This is only a 5 percent return on their investment. Thus, they are really earning a below-normal return. Recall that the opportunity cost of capital must be added to total cost in calculating profit. Thus, the total cost in this case is $31,000 ($29,000 + $2,000 in forgone interest on the investment). The level of profit is negative: $30,000 minus $31,000 equals −$1,000. These calculations are summarized in Table 7.1. Because the level of profit is negative, Sue and Ann are actually suffering a *loss* on their belt business.

When a firm earns a *positive* level of profit, it is earning more than is sufficient to retain the interest of investors. In fact, positive profits are likely to attract new firms into an industry and cause existing firms to expand.

TABLE 7.1 CALCULATING TOTAL REVENUE, TOTAL COST, AND PROFIT

INITIAL INVESTMENT: MARKET INTEREST RATE AVAILABLE:	$20,000 .10 OR 10%
Total revenue (3,000 belts × $10 each):	$30,000
Costs:	
Belts from supplier	$15,000
Labor cost	14,000
Normal return/Opportunity cost of capital ($20,000 × .10)	+ 2,000
Total cost:	$31,000
Profit = Total revenue − Total cost =	−$ 1,000
●There is a loss of $1,000.	

When a firm suffers a *negative* level of profit—that is, when it incurs a loss—it is earning at a rate below that required to keep investors happy. Such a loss may or may not be a loss as an accountant would measure it. Even if I earn a rate of return of 10 percent on my assets, I am earning a below normal rate of return, or a loss, if a normal return for my industry is 15 percent. Losses may cause some firms to exit the industry; others will contract in size. Certainly new investment will not flow into such an industry.

▶ **Opportunity Costs of All Inputs** Total cost includes the opportunity cost of all inputs, not just out-of-pocket costs. If you open a restaurant and work 40 hours a week helping to run it, the cost of running the restaurant includes the cost of your time, even if you do not pay yourself a formal wage. (If you don't pay yourself a wage, your time does not show up on the restaurant's books.) If you could be earning $15 per hour working full-time at a local factory, the opportunity cost of your time helping to run the restaurant is $600 per week (40 hours × $15). In analyzing total cost, it is important to include both direct out-of-pocket costs *and* opportunity costs.

SHORT-RUN VERSUS LONG-RUN DECISIONS

The decisions made by a firm—how much to produce, how to produce it, and what inputs to demand—all take time into account. If a firm decides that it wants to double or triple its output, it may need time to arrange financing, hire architects and contractors, and build a new plant. Planning for a major expansion can take years. In the meantime, the firm must decide how much to produce within the constraint of its existing plant. If a firm decides to get out of a particular business, it may take time to arrange an orderly exit. There may be contract obligations to fulfill, equipment to sell, and so forth. Once again, the firm must decide what to do in the meantime.

A firm's immediate response to a change in the economic environment may differ from its response over time. Consider, for example, a small restaurant with 20 tables that becomes very popular. The immediate problem is getting the most profit within the constraint of the existing restaurant. The owner might consider adding a few tables or speeding up service to squeeze in a few more customers. Some popular restaurants do not take reservations, forcing people to wait at the bar, which increases drink revenues and keeps tables full at all times. At the same time, the owner may be thinking of expanding his current facility, moving to a larger facility, or opening a second restaurant. In the future, he might buy the store next door and double his capacity. Such decisions might require him to negotiate a lease, buy new equipment, and hire more staff. It takes time to make and implement these decisions.

Because the character of immediate response differs from long-run adjustment, it is useful to define two time periods: the short run and the long run. Two assumptions define the **short run**: (1) a fixed scale (or a fixed factor of production) and (2) no entry into or exit from the industry. First, the short run is defined as that period during which existing firms have some *fixed factor of production*—that is, during which time some factor locks them into their current scale of operations. Second, new firms cannot enter, and existing firms cannot exit, an industry in the short run. Firms may curtail operations, but they are still locked into some costs, even though they may be in the process of going out of business.

Just which factor or factors of production are fixed in the short run differs from industry to industry. For a manufacturing firm, the size of the physical plant is often the greatest limitation. A factory is built with a given production rate in mind. Although that rate can be increased, output cannot increase beyond a certain limit in the short run. For a private physician, the limit may be her own capacity to see patients; the day has only so many hours. In the long run, she may invite others to join her practice and

short run *The period of time for which two conditions hold: The firm is operating under a fixed scale (fixed factor) of production, and firms can neither enter nor exit an industry.*

expand, but for now, in the short run, she *is* the firm, and her capacity is the firm's capacity. For a farmer, the fixed factor may be land. The capacity of a small farm is limited by the number of acres being cultivated.

In the **long run**, there are no fixed factors of production. Firms can plan for any output level they find desirable. They can double or triple output, for example. In addition, new firms can start up operations (enter the industry), and existing firms can go out of business (exit the industry).

No hard-and-fast rule specifies how long the short run is. The point is simply that firms make two basic kinds of decisions: those that govern the day-to-day operations of the firm and those that involve longer-term strategic planning. Sometimes major decisions can be implemented in weeks. Often, however, the process takes years.

THE BASES OF DECISIONS: MARKET PRICE OF OUTPUT, AVAILABLE TECHNOLOGY, AND INPUT PRICES

As we said earlier, a firm's three fundamental decisions are made with the objective of maximizing profits. Because profits equal total revenues minus total costs, each firm needs to know how much it costs to produce its product and how much its product can be sold for.

To know how much it costs to produce a good or service, I need to know something about the production techniques that are available and about the prices of the inputs required. To estimate how much it will cost me to operate a gas station, for instance, I need to know what equipment I need, how many workers, what kind of a building, and so forth. I also need to know the going wage rates for mechanics and unskilled laborers, the cost of gas pumps, interest rates, rents per square foot of land on high-traffic corners, and the wholesale price of gasoline. And, of course, I need to know how much I can sell gasoline and repair services for.

In the language of economics, I need to know three things:

> The Bases of Decision Making:
>
> 1. The market price of output;
> 2. The techniques of production that are available; and
> 3. The prices of inputs.
>
> Output price determines potential revenues. The techniques available tell me how much of each input I need, and input prices tell me how much they will cost. Together, the available production techniques and the prices of inputs determine costs.

The rest of this chapter and the whole next chapter focus on costs of production. We begin at the heart of the firm, with the production process itself. Faced with a set of input prices, firms must decide on the best, or optimal, method of production (Figure 7.4). The **optimal method of production** is the one that minimizes cost. With cost determined and the market price of output known, a firm will make a final judgment about the quantity of product to produce and the quantity of each input to demand.

THE PRODUCTION PROCESS

Production is the process through which inputs are combined and transformed into outputs. **Production technology** relates inputs to outputs. Specific quantities of inputs are needed to produce any given service or good. A loaf of bread requires certain amounts of water, flour, and yeast, some kneading and patting, as well as an oven and gas or electricity. A trip from downtown New York to Newark, New Jersey, can be produced with a taxicab, 45 minutes of a driver's labor, some gasoline, and so forth.

long run *That period of time for which there are no fixed factors of production. Firms can increase or decrease scale of operation, and new firms can enter and existing firms can exit the industry.*

optimal method of production *The production method that minimizes cost.*

production technology *The quantitative relationship between inputs and outputs.*

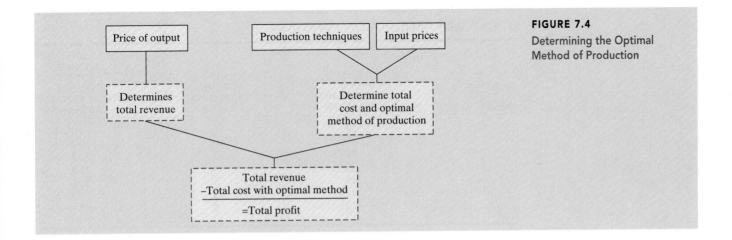

FIGURE 7.4
Determining the Optimal Method of Production

Most outputs can be produced by a number of different techniques. You can tear down an old building and clear a lot to create a park in several ways, for example. Five hundred men and women could descend upon it with sledgehammers and carry the pieces away by hand; this would be a **labor-intensive technology**. The same park could be produced by two people with a wrecking crane, a steam shovel, a backhoe, and a dump truck; this would be a **capital-intensive technology**. Similarly, different inputs can be combined to transport people from Oakland to San Francisco. The Bay Area Rapid Transit carries thousands of people simultaneously under San Francisco Bay and uses a massive amount of capital relative to labor. Cab rides to San Francisco require much more labor relative to capital; a driver is needed for every few passengers.

In choosing the most appropriate technology, firms choose the one that minimizes the cost of production. For a firm in an economy with a plentiful supply of inexpensive labor but not much capital, the optimal method of production will involve labor-intensive techniques. For example, assembly of items like running shoes is done most efficiently by hand. That is why Nike produces virtually all of its shoes in developing countries where labor costs are very low. In contrast, firms in an economy with high wages and high labor costs have an incentive to substitute away from labor and to use more capital-intensive, or labor-saving, techniques. Suburban office parks use more land and have more open space in part because land in the suburbs is more plentiful and less expensive than land in the middle of a big city.

PRODUCTION FUNCTIONS: TOTAL PRODUCT, MARGINAL PRODUCT, AND AVERAGE PRODUCT

The relationship between inputs and outputs (that is, the production technology) expressed numerically or mathematically is called a **production function** (or **total product function**). A production function shows units of total product as a function of units of inputs.

Imagine, for example, a small sandwich shop. All the sandwiches made in the shop are grilled, and the shop owns only one grill, which can accommodate only two people comfortably. As columns 1 and 2 of the production function in Table 7.2 show, one person working alone can produce only 10 sandwiches per hour. He has to answer the phone, wait on customers, keep the tables clean, and so on. The second worker can stay at the grill full time and not worry about anything except making sandwiches. Because the two workers together can produce 25 sandwiches, the second worker can produce 25 − 10 = 15 sandwiches per hour. A third person trying to use the grill produces crowding, but, with careful use of space, more sandwiches can be produced. The third worker adds 10 sandwiches per hour. Note that the added output from hiring a third

The most capital-intensive sector in the U.S. in 1994 was mining, with $692,077 worth of fixed capital for every worker. The most labor-intensive sector was construction, at only $16,682 of fixed capital for every worker. Fixed capital per worker in some other industries in 1994 was:

Finance, insurance and real estate	$310,281
Agriculture	127,310
Manufacturing	122,587
Wholesale trade	102,645
Retail trade	37,930
Services	23,798

Source: Statistical Abstract of the United States, 1996, Tables 641, 856.

labor-intensive technology
Technology that relies heavily on human labor rather than capital.

capital-intensive technology
Technology that relies heavily on capital rather than human labor.

production function or **total product function** *A numerical or mathematical expression of a relationship between inputs and outputs. It shows units of total product as a function of units of inputs.*

TABLE 7.2 PRODUCTION FUNCTION

(1) LABOR UNITS (EMPLOYEES)	(2) TOTAL PRODUCT (SANDWICHES PER HOUR)	(3) MARGINAL PRODUCT OF LABOR	(4) AVERAGE PRODUCT OF LABOR (TOTAL PRODUCT ÷ LABOR UNITS)
0	0	-	-
1	10	10	10.0
2	25	15	12.5
3	35	10	11.7
4	40	5	10.0
5	42	2	8.4
6	42	0	7.0

worker is less because of the capital constraint, *not* because the third worker is somehow less efficient or hard working. We assume that all workers are equally capable.

The fourth and fifth workers can work at the grill only while the first three are putting the pickles, onions, and wrapping on the sandwiches they have made. But then the first three must wait to get back to the grill. Worker four adds 5 sandwiches per hour to the total, and worker five adds just 2. Adding a sixth worker adds no output at all: The current maximum capacity of the shop is 42 sandwiches per hour.

Figure 7.5a graphs the total product data from Table 7.2.

marginal product *The additional output that can be produced by adding one more unit of a specific input, ceteris paribus.*

▶ **Marginal Product and the Law of Diminishing Returns**   Marginal product is the additional output that can be produced by hiring one more unit of a specific input, holding all other inputs constant. As column 3 of Table 7.2 shows, the marginal product of the

FIGURE 7.5

Production Function for Sandwiches

A *production function* is a numerical representation of the relationship between inputs and outputs. In Figure 7.5a, total product (sandwiches) is graphed as a function of labor inputs. The *marginal product* of labor is the additional output that one additional unit of labor produces. Figure 7.5b shows that the marginal product of the second unit of labor at the sandwich shop is 15 units of output. The marginal product of the fourth unit of labor is 5 units of output.

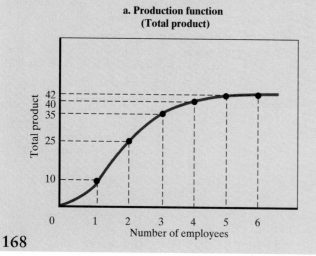

a. Production function (Total product)

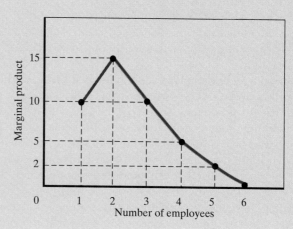

b. Marginal product of labor

first unit of labor in the sandwich shop is 10 sandwiches; the marginal product of the second is 15; the third, 10; and so forth. The marginal product of the sixth worker is 0. Figure 7.5b graphs the marginal product of labor curve from the data in Table 7.2.

The **law of diminishing returns** states that *after a certain point, when additional units of a variable input are added to fixed inputs* (in this case, the building and grill), *the marginal product of the variable input* (in this case, labor) *declines*. The British economist David Ricardo first formulated the law of diminishing returns on the basis of his observations of agriculture in nineteenth-century England. Within a given area of land, he noted, successive "doses" of labor and capital yielded smaller and smaller increases in crop output. The law of diminishing returns is true in agriculture because only so much more can be produced by farming the same land more intensely. In manufacturing, diminishing returns set in when a firm begins to strain the capacity of its existing plant.

At our sandwich shop, diminishing returns set in when the third worker is added. The marginal product of the second worker is actually higher than the first (see Figure 7.5b). The first worker takes care of the phone and the tables, which frees the second worker to concentrate exclusively on sandwich making. But from that point on, the grill gets crowded.

Diminishing returns characterize many productive activities. Consider, for example, an independent accountant who works primarily for private citizens preparing their tax returns. As he adds more and more clients, he must work later and later into the evening. An hour spent working at 1 A.M. after a long day is likely to be less productive than an hour spent working at 10 A.M. Here the fixed factor of production is the accountant himself. Ultimately, the capacity of his mind and body limit his production, much like the walls of a plant limit production in a factory.

Diminishing returns, or *diminishing marginal product*, begin to show up when more and more units of a variable input are added to a fixed input, such as scale of plant. Recall that we defined the short run as that period in which some fixed factor of production constrains the firm. It then follows that:

> Diminishing returns always apply in the short run, and in the short run every firm will face diminishing returns. This means that every firm finds it progressively more difficult to increase its output as it approaches capacity production.

> **Marginal Product versus Average Product**   **Average product** is the average amount produced by each unit of a variable factor of production. At our sandwich shop with one grill, that variable factor is labor. In Table 7.2, you saw that the first two workers together produce 25 sandwiches per hour. Their average product is therefore 12.5 (25 ÷ 2). The third worker adds only 10 sandwiches per hour to the total. These 10 sandwiches are the *marginal* product of labor. The *average product* of the first three units of labor, however, is 11.7 (the average of 10, 15, and 10). Stated in equation form, the average product of labor is the *total* product divided by total units of labor:

$$\text{Average product of labor} = \frac{\text{Total product}}{\text{Total units of labor}}$$

Average product "follows" marginal product, but it does not change as quickly. If marginal product is above average product, the average rises; if marginal product is below average product, the average falls. Suppose, for example, that you have had six exams and that your average is 86. If you score 75 on the next exam, your average score will fall, but not all the way to 75. In fact, it will fall only to 84.4. If you score a 95 instead, your average will rise to 87.3. As columns 3 and 4 of Table 7.2 show, marginal product at the sandwich shop declines continuously after the third worker is hired. Average product also decreases, but more slowly.

law of diminishing returns
When additional units of a variable input are added to fixed inputs after a certain point, the marginal product of the variable input declines.

average product *The average amount produced by each unit of a variable factor of production.*

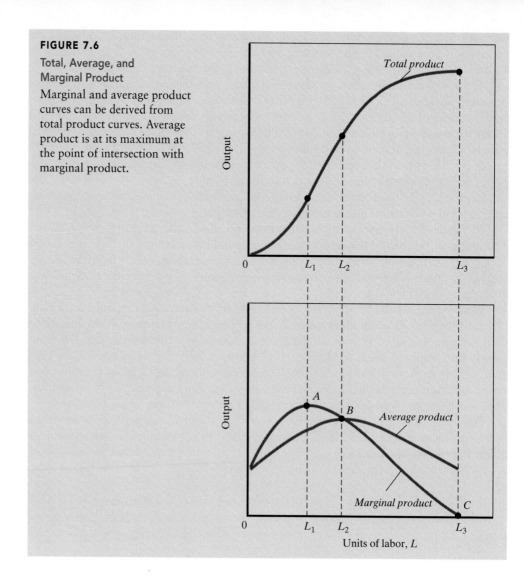

FIGURE 7.6

Total, Average, and Marginal Product

Marginal and average product curves can be derived from total product curves. Average product is at its maximum at the point of intersection with marginal product.

Figure 7.6 shows a typical production function and the marginal and average product curves derived from it. The marginal product curve is a graph of the slope of the total product curve—that is, of the production function. Average product and marginal product start out equal, as they do in Table 7.2. As marginal product climbs, the graph of average product follows it, but more slowly, up to L_1 (point A).

Notice that marginal product starts out increasing. (It did so in the sandwich shop as well.) Most production processes are designed to be run well by more than one worker. Take an assembly line, for example. To work efficiently, an assembly line needs a worker at every station; it's a cooperative process. The marginal product of the first workers is low or zero. But as workers are added, the process starts to run and marginal product rises.

At point A (L_1 units of labor), marginal product begins to fall. Because every plant has a finite capacity, efforts to increase production will always run into the limits of that capacity. At point B (L_2 units of labor), marginal product has fallen to equal the average product, which has been increasing. Between point B and point C (between L_2 and L_3 units of labor), marginal product falls below average product, and average product begins to follow it *down*. Average product is at its maximum at point B, where it is equal to marginal product.

At L_3 more labor yields no more output, and marginal product is zero—the assembly line has no more positions, the grill is jammed, and the accountant is so tired that he can't see another client.[2] (If you have trouble understanding the relationships among the three curves in Figure 7.6, review the calculations in Table 7.2 and review the appendix on graphing in chapter 1.)

PRODUCTION FUNCTIONS WITH TWO VARIABLE FACTORS OF PRODUCTION

So far we have considered production functions with only one variable factor of production. But inputs work together in production. In general, additional capital increases the productivity of labor. Because capital—buildings, machines, and so on—is of no use without people to operate it, we say that capital and labor are *complementary inputs*.

A simple example will clarify this point. Consider again the sandwich shop. If the demand for sandwiches began to exceed the capacity of the shop to produce them, the shop's owner might decide to expand capacity. This would mean purchasing more capital in the form of a new grill.

A second grill would essentially double the shop's productive capacity. The new higher capacity would mean that the sandwich shop would not run into diminishing returns as quickly. With only one grill, the third and fourth workers are less productive because the single grill gets crowded. With two grills, however, the third and fourth workers could produce 15 sandwiches per hour using the second grill. In essence, the added capital raises the *productivity* of labor (that is, the amount of output produced per worker per hour).

Just as the new grill enhances the productivity of workers in the sandwich shop, new businesses and the capital that they put in place raise the productivity of workers in countries like Malaysia, India, and Kenya.

This simple relationship lies at the heart of worries about productivity at the national and international levels. Building new, modern plants and equipment enhances a nation's productivity. Since the 1950s, for example, Japan has accumulated capital (i.e., built plant and equipment) faster than any other country in the world. The result is a very high average quantity of output per worker in Japan.

CHOICE OF TECHNOLOGY

As our sandwich shop example shows, inputs (factors of production) are complementary. Capital enhances the productivity of labor. Workers in the sandwich shop are more productive when they are not crowded on a single grill. Similarly, labor enhances the productivity of capital. When more workers are hired at a plant that is operating at 50 percent of capacity, previously idle machines suddenly become productive.

But inputs can also be substituted for one another. If labor becomes expensive, firms can adopt labor-saving technologies; that is, they can substitute capital for labor. Assembly lines can be automated by replacing human beings with machines, and capital can be substituted for land when land is scarce. (See the Global Perspective box titled "Production Technologies: Robots in the United States, Skyscrapers in Asia.") If capital becomes relatively expensive, firms can substitute labor for capital. In short, most goods and services can be produced in a number of ways, using alternative technologies. One of the key decisions that all firms must make is which technology to use.

---

[2]In theory, the total product curve could turn downward beyond L_3. This would imply that more workers would actually get in the way and that output would *fall*. If this were to happen, marginal product would actually be negative beyond L_3.

PRODUCTION TECHNOLOGIES: ROBOTS IN THE UNITED STATES, SKYSCRAPERS IN ASIA

Most products can be produced with different combinations of inputs. The choice of technique depends on the prices of land, labor, and capital, which can change over time and from location to location. The following examples illustrate the importance of technological choice.

SUBSTITUTION OF CAPITAL FOR LABOR: ROBOTICS IN MANUFACTURING

The ultimate substitution of capital for labor is robotics. Twenty-five years ago, robots were confined to the world of science fiction. Today, robots are everywhere:

> Industrial robots are hard at work in the industrial heartland, spot-welding car bodies on auto assembly lines, placing tiny parts on circuit boards in electronics factories and packing frozen hamburger patties into boxes at food-processing plants. And rather than replacing workers in droves, robots are reserved for tasks that either are ill suited to human hand and eye or are so onerous or strenuous that people don't want to do them. . . .
>
> Lower cost and greater reliability are the keys, said Steven W. Holland, a robotics specialist at General Motors. Prices today are about half what they were [15] years ago for comparable machines and reliability is four times better, he said.[a]

SUBSTITUTION OF CAPITAL FOR LAND: OFFICE TOWERS IN ASIA

As you travel into any major city in the world from a distance of 30 miles out, the density of development

CAPITAL RAISES THE PRODUCTIVITY OF LABOR SOMETIMES IN COMPLICATED WAYS, AS IN THIS OPERATING ROOM.

increases and buildings tend to get taller and taller. Building a tall building is simply the substitution of capital for land in production, and it occurs most frequently where land prices are very high. When available land is scarce and the demand for it is increasing, land prices rise and tall buildings appear. This is exactly what has been happening in Asia:

> Frenzied building in the capitals of South-East Asia has long been one of the most visible symbols of the region's spectacular economic boom. . . .
>
> [In Malaysia] growth has averaged nearly 9 percent for a decade, and buildings in the capital, Kuala Lumpur, have gone up at a rate to

match. The opening . . . of the world's tallest building added 360,000 square metres of space—more than was built in the past two years combined. . . .

Office buildings are going up at a frenetic pace in mainland Chinese cities like Beijing and Shanghai.[b]

Sources: [a]John Holusha, "Industrial Robots Make the Grade," *The New York Times,* September 7, 1994, p. D1. Copyright © 1994 by The New York Times Co. Reprinted by permission. [b]*The Economist,* April 12, 1997, p. 72.

AT 1,483 FEET, THE TALLEST BUILDING IN THE WORLD—PETRONIUS TOWERS IN KUALA LUMPUR, MALAYSIA.

For more on substitution of resources in production, see the Case and Fair Web page at http://www.prenhall.com/casefair.

TABLE 7.3 INPUTS REQUIRED TO PRODUCE 100 DIAPERS USING ALTERNATIVE TECHNOLOGIES

TECHNOLOGY	UNITS OF CAPITAL (K)	UNITS OF LABOR (L)
A	2	10
B	3	6
C	4	4
D	6	3
E	10	2

Consider the choices available to the diaper manufacturer in Table 7.3. Five different techniques of producing 100 diapers are available. Technology A is the most labor intensive, requiring 10 hours of labor and 2 units of capital to produce 100 diapers. (You can think of units of capital as machine hours.) Technology E is the most capital intensive, requiring only 2 hours of labor but 10 hours of machine time.

To choose a production technique, the firm must look to input markets to find out the current market prices of labor and capital. What is the wage rate (P_L), and what is the cost per hour of capital (P_K)?

Suppose that labor and capital are both available at a price of $1 per unit. Column 4 of Table 7.4 presents the calculations required to determine which technology is the best. The winner is technology C. Assuming that the firm's objective is to maximize profits, it will choose the least-cost technology. Using technology C, the firm can produce 100 diapers for $8. All four of the other technologies produce 100 diapers at a higher cost.

Now suppose that the wage rate (P_L) were to rise sharply, from $1 to $5. You might guess that this increase would lead the firm to substitute labor-saving capital for workers, and you'd be right. As column 5 of Table 7.4 shows, the increase in the wage rate means that technology E is now the cost-minimizing choice for the firm. Using 10 units of capital and only 2 units of labor, the firm can produce 100 diapers for $20. All other technologies are now more costly.

> Two things determine the cost of production: (1) the technologies that are available and (2) input prices. Profit-maximizing firms will choose the technology that minimizes the cost of production given current market input prices.

TABLE 7.4 COST-MINIMIZING CHOICE AMONG ALTERNATIVE TECHNOLOGIES (100 DIAPERS)

(1) TECHNOLOGY	(2) UNITS OF CAPITAL (K)	(3) UNITS OF LABOR (L)	(4) COST $= (L \times P_L) + (K \times P_K)$ IF $P_L = \$1$ $P_K = \$1$	(5) COST $= (L \times P_L) + (K \times P_K)$ IF $P_L = \$5$ $P_K = \$1$
A	2	10	$12	$52
B	3	6	$9	$33
C	4	4	$8	$24
D	6	3	$9	$21
E	10	2	$12	$20

So far, we have looked only at a *single* level of output. That is, we have determined how much it will cost to produce 100 diapers using the best available technology when $P_K = \$1$ and $P_L = \$1$ or $\$5$. But the best technique for producing 1,000 diapers or 10,000 diapers may be entirely different. The next chapter explores the relationship between cost and the level of output in some detail. One of our main objectives in that chapter will be to determine the amount that a competitive firm will choose to supply during a given time period.

SUMMARY

1. Firms vary in size and internal organization, but they all take inputs and transform them into outputs through a process called *production*.

2. In perfect competition, no single firm has any control over prices. This follows from two assumptions: (1) perfectly competitive industries are composed of many firms, each small relative to the size of the industry, and (2) each firm in a perfectly competitive industry produces *homogeneous products*.

3. The demand curve facing a competitive firm is perfectly elastic. If a single firm raises its price above the market price, it will sell nothing. Because it can sell all it produces at the market price, a firm has no incentive to reduce price.

THE BEHAVIOR OF PROFIT-MAXIMIZING FIRMS

4. Profit-maximizing firms in all industries must make three choices: (1) how much output to supply, (2) how to produce that output, and (3) how much of each input to demand.

5. Profit equals total revenue minus total cost. Total cost includes (1) out-of-pocket costs (2) a normal rate of return on capital, and (3) the opportunity cost of each factor of production.

6. A *normal rate of return* to capital is included in total cost because tying up resources in a firm's capital stock has an opportunity cost. If you start a business or buy a share of stock in a corporation, you do so because you expect to make a normal rate of return. Investors will not invest their money in a business unless they expect to make a normal rate of return.

7. A positive *profit* level occurs when a firm is earning an above-normal rate of return on capital.

8. Two assumptions define the *short run*: (1) a fixed scale or fixed factor of production and (2) no entry to or exit from

the industry. In the *long run*, firms can choose any scale of operations they want, and new firms can enter and leave the industry.

9. To make decisions, firms need to know three things: (1) the market price of their output, (2) the production techniques that are available, and (3) the prices of inputs.

THE PRODUCTION PROCESS

10. The relationship between inputs and outputs (the *production technology*) expressed numerically or mathematically is called a *production function* or *total product function*.

11. The *marginal product* of a variable input is the additional output that an added unit of that input will produce if all other inputs are held constant. According to the *law of diminishing returns*, when additional units of a variable input are added to fixed inputs after a certain point, the marginal product of the variable input will decline.

12. *Average product* is the average amount of product produced by each unit of a variable factor of production. If marginal product is above average product, the average product rises; if marginal product is below average product, the average product falls.

13. Capital and labor are at the same time complementary and substitutable inputs. Capital enhances the productivity of labor, but it can also be substituted for labor.

CHOICE OF TECHNOLOGY

14. One of the key decisions that all firms must make is which technology to use. Profit-maximizing firms will choose that combination of inputs that minimizes costs and therefore maximizes profits.

REVIEW TERMS AND CONCEPTS

PROBLEM SET

1. Assume that the graph below gives the current situation in the perfectly competitive market for raw cotton:

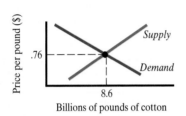

a. Graph the demand curve facing a single representative cotton farmer.

b. Explain the shape of the individual farmer's demand curve carefully. What specific assumptions lie behind its shape?

2. Suppose that in 1998 you became president of a small non-profit theater company. Your playhouse has 120 seats and a small stage. The actors have national reputations, and demand for tickets is enormous relative to the number of seats available; every performance is sold out months in advance. You are elected because you have demonstrated an ability to raise funds successfully. Describe some of the decisions that you must make in the short run. What might you consider to be your "fixed factor"? What alternative decisions might you be able to make in the long run? Explain.

3. Ted Baxter runs a small, very stable newspaper company in southern Oregon. The paper has been in business for 25 years. The total value of the firm's capital stock is $1,000,000, which Ted owns outright. This year the firm earned a total of $250,000 after out-of-pocket expenses. Without taking the opportunity cost of capital into account, this means that Ted is earning a 25 percent return on his capital. Suppose that risk-free bonds are currently paying a rate of 10 percent to those who buy them.

a. What is meant by the "opportunity cost of capital"?

b. Explain why opportunity costs are "real" costs even though they do not involve out-of-pocket expenses.

c. What is the opportunity cost of Ted's capital?

d. How much excess profit is Ted earning?

4. The following table gives total output or total product as a function of labor units used:

LABOR	TOTAL OUTPUT
0	0
1	5
2	9
3	12
4	14
5	15

a. Define diminishing returns.

b. Does the table indicate a situation of diminishing returns? Explain your answer.

5. Suppose that wimps can be produced using two different production techniques, A and B. The following table provides the total input requirements for each of five different total output levels:

TECH.	Q = 1		Q = 2		Q = 3		Q = 4		Q = 5	
	K	L	K	L	K	L	K	L	K	L
A	2	5	1	10	5	14	6	18	8	20
B	5	2	8	3	11	4	14	5	16	6

a. Assuming that the price of labor (P_L) is $1 and the price of capital (P_K) is $2, calculate the total cost of production for each of the five levels of output using the optimal (least-cost) technology at each level.

b. How many labor hours (units of labor) would be employed at each level of output? How many machine hours (units of capital)?

c. Graph total cost of production as a function of output. (Put cost on the Y axis and output, Q, on the X axis.) Again, assume that the optimal technology is used.

d. Repeat a. through c. under the assumption that the price of labor (P_L) rises from $1 to $3 while the price of capital (P_K) remains at $2.

6. A student who lives on the fourth floor of Bates Hall is assigned to a new room on the seventh floor during her junior year. She has 11 heavy boxes of books and "stuff" to move. Discuss the alternative combinations of capital and labor that might be used to make the move. How would your answer differ if the move were to a new dorm 3 miles across campus? To a new college 400 miles away?

7. Suppose that widgets can be produced using two alternative technologies that employ the following combinations of capital and labor:

		NUMBER OF WIDGETS PER HOUR					
		Q = 1		Q = 2		Q = 3	
		K	L	K	L	K	L
Technology	A	2	5	3	10	4	13
	B	5	1	8	2	10	3

a. Assume that the price of capital (P_K) is $1 per unit and the price of labor (P_L) is $1 per unit. What is the optimal (least-cost) technology for producing one widget per hour? Two widgets? Three widgets?

b. Using the optimal technology in each case, what is the cost of producing each of the three levels of output?

c. How much capital in units and how many workers (units of L) would you employ to produce one widget per hour? Two widgets? Three widgets?

d. Repeat a. through c. assuming that P_L = $1 and P_K = $2.

8. The following is a production function:

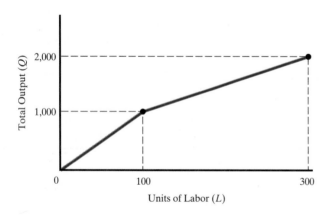

a. Draw a graph of marginal product as a function of output. (*Hint*: Marginal product is the additional number of units of output per unit of labor at each level of output.)

b. Does this graph exhibit diminishing returns?

9. During the early phases of industrialization, the number of persons engaged in agriculture usually drops sharply, even as agricultural output is growing. Given what you know about production technology and production functions, can you explain this seeming inconsistency?

10. Since the end of World War II, manufacturing firms in the United States and in Europe have been moving farther and farther outside of central cities. At the same time, firms in finance, insurance, and other parts of the service sector have been locating near the downtown areas in tall buildings. One major reason seems to be that manufacturing firms find it difficult to substitute capital for land, while service-sector firms that use office space do not.

a. What kinds of buildings represent substitution of capital for land?

b. Why do you think that manufacturing firms might find it difficult to substitute capital for land?

c. Why is it relatively easier for a law firm or an insurance company to substitute capital for land?

d. Why is the demand for land likely to be very high near the center of a city?

*e. One of the reasons for substituting capital for land near the center of a city is that land is more expensive near the center. What is true about the relative supply of land near the center of a city? (*Hint*: What is the formula for the area of a circle?)

11. The number of repairs produced by a computer repair shop depends on the number of workers as follows:

NUMBER OF WORKERS	NUMBER OF REPAIRS
	(PER WEEK)
0	0
1	8
2	20
3	35
4	45
5	52
6	57
7	60

Assume that all inputs (office space, telephone, utilities) other than labor are fixed in the short run.

a. Add two additional columns to the table, and enter the marginal product and average product for each number of workers.

b. Over what range of labor input are there increasing returns to labor? Diminishing returns to labor? Negative returns to labor?

c. Over what range of labor input is marginal product greater than average product? What is happening to average product as employment increases over this range?

d. Over what range of labor input is marginal product smaller than average product? What is happening to average product as employment increases over this range?

12. A firm can use three different production technologies, with capital and labor requirements at each level of output as follows:

DAILY OUTPUT	TECHNOLOGY 1		TECHNOLOGY 2		TECHNOLOGY 3	
	K	L	K	L	K	L
100	3	7	4	5	5	4
150	3	10	4	7	5	5
200	4	11	5	8	6	6
250	5	13	6	10	7	8

a. Suppose the firm is operating in a high-wage country, where capital cost is $100 per unit per day and labor cost is $80 per worker per day. For each level of output, which technology is the cheapest?

b. Now suppose the firm is operating in a low-wage country, where capital cost is $100 per unit per day but labor cost is only $40 per unit per day. For each level of output, which technology is the cheapest?

c. Suppose the firm moves from a high-wage to a low-wage country but that its level of output remains constant at 200 units per day. How will its total employment change?

TAKE IT TO THE NET

We invite you to visit the Case and Fair page on the Prentice Hall Web site:

http://www.prenhall.com/casefair

for this chapter's World Wide Web exercise.

APPENDIX TO CHAPTER 7

ISOQUANTS AND ISOCOSTS

This chapter has shown that the cost structure facing a firm depends on two key pieces of information: (1) input (factor) prices and (2) technology. This appendix presents a more formal analysis of technology and factor prices and their relationship to cost.

A NEW LOOK AT TECHNOLOGY: ISOQUANTS

Table 7A.1 is expanded from Table 7.3 to show the various combinations of capital (K) and labor (L) that can be used to produce three different levels of output (q). For

example, 100 units of X can be produced with 2 units of capital and 10 units of labor, or with 3 units of K and 6 units of L, or with 4 units of K and 4 units of L, and so forth. Similarly, 150 units of X can be produced with 3 units of K and 10 units of L, or with 4 units of K and 7 units of L, and so forth.

A graph that shows all the combinations of capital and labor that can be used to produce a given amount of output is called an **isoquant**. Figure 7A.1 graphs three isoquants, one each for $q_x = 50$, $q_x = 100$, and $q_x = 150$, based on the data in Table 7A.1. Notice that all the points on the graph have been connected, indicating that there are an infinite number of combinations of labor and capital that can produce each level of output. For example, 100 units of output can also be produced with 3.50 units of labor and 4.75 units of capital. (Verify that this point is on the isoquant labeled $q_x = 100$.)

Figure 7A.1 shows only three isoquants, but there are many more not shown. For example, there are separate isoquants for $q_x = 101$, $q_x = 102$, and so on. If we assume that producing fractions of a unit of output is possible, there must be an isoquant for $q_x = 134.57$, for $q_x = 124.82$, and so on. One could imagine an infinite number of isoquants in Figure 7A.1. The higher the level of output, the farther up and to the right the isoquant will lie.

TABLE 7A.1

ALTERNATIVE COMBINATIONS OF CAPITAL (K) AND LABOR (L) REQUIRED TO PRODUCE 50, 100, AND 150 UNITS OF OUTPUT

	$q_x = 50$		$q_x = 100$		$q_x = 150$	
	K	L	K	L	K	L
A	1	8	2	10	3	10
B	2	5	3	6	4	7
C	3	3	4	4	5	5
D	5	2	6	3	7	4
E	8	1	10	2	10	3

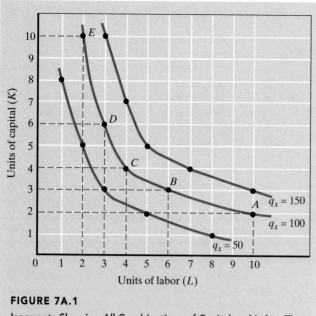

FIGURE 7A.1

Isoquants Showing All Combinations of Capital and Labor That Can Be Used to Produce 50, 100, and 150 Units of Output

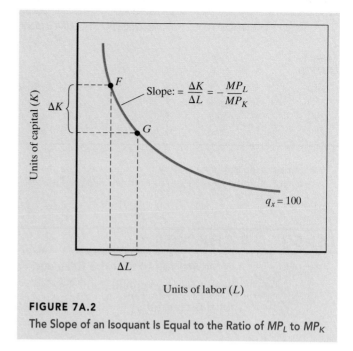

FIGURE 7A.2

The Slope of an Isoquant Is Equal to the Ratio of MP_L to MP_K

Figure 7A.2 derives the slope of an isoquant. Because points F and G are both on the $q_x = 100$ isoquant, the two points represent two different combinations of K and L that can be used to produce 100 units of output. In moving from point F to point G along the curve, less capital is employed but more labor is used. An approximation of the amount of output lost by using less capital is ΔK times the marginal product of capital (MP_K). The *marginal product of capital* is the number of units of output produced by a single marginal unit of capital. Thus, $\Delta K \cdot MP_K$ is the total output lost by using less capital.

But for output to remain constant (as it must, because F and G are on the same isoquant), the loss of output from using less capital must be exactly matched by the added output produced by using more labor. This amount can be approximated by ΔL times the marginal product of labor (MP_L). Because the two must be equal, it follows that:

$$\Delta K \cdot MP_K = -\Delta L \cdot MP_L.\text{[1]}$$

If we then divide both sides of this equation by ΔL and then by MP_K, we arrive at the following expression for the slope of the isoquant:

$$\text{Slope of isoquant: } \frac{\Delta K}{\Delta L} = -\frac{MP_L}{MP_K}$$

[1] We need to add the negative sign to ΔL because in moving from point F to point G, ΔK is a negative number and ΔL is a positive number. The minus sign is needed to balance the equation.

The ratio of MP_L to MP_K is called the **marginal rate of technical substitution**. It is the rate at which a firm can substitute capital for labor and hold output constant.

FACTOR PRICES AND INPUT COMBINATIONS: ISOCOSTS

A graph that shows all the combinations of capital and labor that are available for a given total cost is called an **isocost line**. (Recall that total cost includes opportunity costs and a normal rate of return.) Just as there are an infinite number of isoquants (one for every possible level of output), there are an infinite number of isocost lines, one for every possible level of total cost.

Figure 7A.3 shows three simple isocost lines assuming that the price of labor (P_L) is $1 per unit and the price of capital (P_K) is $1 per unit. The lowest isocost line shows all the combinations of K and L that can be purchased for $5. For example, $5 will buy five units of labor and no capital (point A), or three units of labor and two units of capital (point B), or no units of labor and five units of capital (point C).

All these points lie along a straight line. The equation of that straight line is:

$$(P_K \cdot K) + (P_L \cdot L) = TC.$$

Substituting our data for the lowest isocost line into this general equation, we get:

$$(\$1 \cdot K) + (\$1 \cdot L) = \$5, \text{ or } K + L = 5.$$

Remember that the X and Y scales are units of labor and units of capital, not dollars.

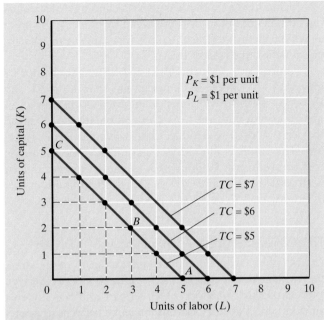

FIGURE 7A.3

Isocost Lines Showing the Combinations of Capital and Labor Available for $5, $6, and $7

An isocost line shows all the combinations of capital and labor that are available for a given total cost.

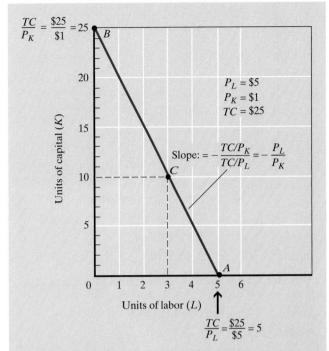

FIGURE 7A.4

Isocost Line Showing All Combinations of Capital and Labor Available for $25

One way to draw an isocost line is to determine the endpoints of that line and draw a line connecting them.

On the same graph are two additional isocosts showing the various combinations of K and L available for a total cost of $6 and $7. These are only three of an infinite number of isoquants. At any total cost, there is an isocost that shows all the combinations of K and L available for that amount.

Figure 7A.4 shows another isocost line. This isocost assumes a different set of factor prices, $P_L = \$5$ and $P_K = \$1$. The diagram shows all the combinations of K and L that can be bought for $25. One way to draw the line is to determine the endpoints. For example, if the entire $25 were spent on labor, how much labor could be purchased? The answer is, of course, 5 units ($25 divided by $5 per unit). Thus, point A, which represents 5 units of labor and no capital, is on the isocost line. Similarly, if all of the $25 were spent on capital, how much capital could be purchased? The answer is 25 units ($25 divided by $1 per unit). Thus, point B, which represents 25 units of capital and no labor, is also on the isocost line. Another point on this particular isocost is 3 units of labor and 10 units of capital, point C.

The slope of an isocost line can be calculated easily if you first find the endpoints of the line. In Figure 7A.4, we

can calculate the slope of the isocost line by taking $\Delta K / \Delta L$ between points B and A. Thus,

$$\text{Slope of isocost line: } \frac{\Delta K}{\Delta L} = -\frac{TC/P_K}{TC/P_L} = \frac{P_L}{P_K}.$$

Plugging in the endpoints from our example, we get:

$$\text{Slope of line } AB = -\frac{\$5}{\$1} = -5.$$

FINDING THE LEAST-COST TECHNOLOGY WITH ISOQUANTS AND ISOCOSTS

Figure 7A.5 superimposes the isoquant for $q_x = 50$ on the isocost lines in Figure 7A.3, which assume that $P_K = \$1$ and $P_L = \$1$. The question now becomes one of choosing among the combinations of K and L that can be used to produce 50 units of output. Recall that each point on the isoquant (labeled $q_x = 50$ in Figure 7A.5) represents a different technology—a different combination of K and L.

We assume that our firm is a competitive, profit-maximizing firm that will choose the combination that minimizes cost. Because every point on the isoquant lies on

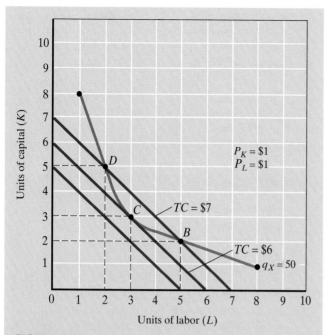

FIGURE 7A.5

Finding the Least-Cost Combination of Capital and Labor to Produce 50 Units of Output

Profit-maximizing firms will minimize costs by producing their chosen level of output with the technology represented by the point at which the isoquant is tangent to an isocost line. Here, the cost-minimizing technology—three units of capital and three units of labor—is represented by point C.

some particular isocost line, we can determine the total cost for each combination along the isoquant. For example, point D (five units of capital and two units of labor) lies along the isocost for a total cost of $7. Notice that five units of capital and two units of labor cost a total of $7. (Remember, $P_K = \$1$ and $P_L = \$1$.) But the same amount of output (50 units) can be produced at lower cost. Specifically, by using three units of labor and three units of capital (point C), total cost is reduced to $6. *No other combination of K and L along isoquant $q_x = 50$ is on a lower isocost line.* In seeking to maximize profits, then,

> The firm will choose the combination of inputs that is least costly. The least costly way to produce any given level of output is indicated by the point of tangency between an isocost line and the isoquant corresponding to that level of output.[2]

---

[2]This assumes that the isoquants are continuous and convex (bowed) toward the origin.

In Figure 7A.5, the least-cost technology of producing 50 units of output is represented by point A, the point at which the $q_x = 50$ isoquant is just tangent to (that is, just touches) the isocost line.

Figure 7A.6 adds the other two isoquants from Figure 7A.1 to Figure 7A.5. Assuming that $P_K = \$1$ and $P_L = \$1$, the firm will move along each of the three isoquants until it finds the least-cost combination of K and L that can be used to produce that particular level of output. The result is plotted in Figure 7A.7. The minimum cost of producing 50 units of X is $6; the minimum cost of producing 100 units of X is $8; and the minimum cost of producing 150 units of X is $10.

THE COST-MINIMIZING EQUILIBRIUM CONDITION

At the point where a line is just tangent to a curve, the two have the same slope. (We have already derived expressions for the slope of an isocost and the slope of an isoquant.) At each point of tangency (such as at points A, B, and C in Figure 7A.6), then, the following must be true:

$$\text{Slope of isoquant} = -\frac{MP_L}{MP_K} = \text{Slope of isocost} = -\frac{P_L}{P_K}$$

Thus:

$$\frac{MP_L}{MP_K} = \frac{P_L}{P_K}$$

Dividing both sides by P_L and multiplying both sides by MP_K, we get:

$$\frac{MP_L}{P_L} = \frac{MP_K}{P_K}$$

This is the firm's cost-minimizing equilibrium condition.

This expression makes sense if you think about what it says. The left side of the equation is the marginal product of labor divided by the price of a unit of labor. Thus, it is the product derived from the last dollar spent on labor. The right-hand side of the equation is the product derived from the last dollar spent on capital. If the product derived from the last dollar spent on labor were not equal to the product derived from the last dollar spent on capital, the firm could decrease costs by using more labor and less capital or by using more capital and less labor.

Look back to chapter 6 and see if you can find a similar expression and some similar logic in our discussion of household behavior. In fact, there is great symmetry between the theory of the firm and the theory of household behavior.

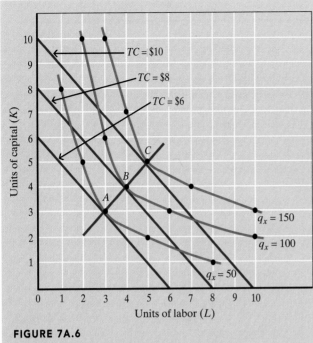

FIGURE 7A.6

Minimizing Cost of Production for $q_x = 50$, $q_x = 100$, and $q_x = 150$

Plotting a series of cost-minimizing combinations of inputs—shown in this graph as points A, B, and C—on a separate graph results in a *cost curve* like the one shown in Figure 7A.7.

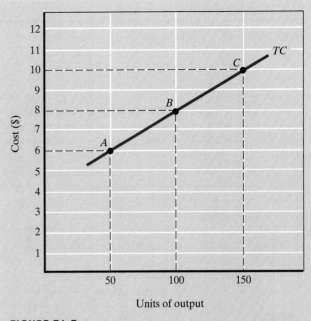

FIGURE 7A.7

A Cost Curve Shows the *Minimum* Cost of Producing Each Level of Output

SUMMARY

1. An *isoquant* is a graph that shows all the combinations of capital and labor that can be used to produce a given amount of output. The slope of an isoquant is equal to $-MP_L/MP_K$. The ratio of MP_L to MP_K is the *marginal rate of technical substitution*. It is the rate at which a firm can substitute capital for labor and hold output constant.

2. An *isocost line* is a graph that shows all the combinations of capital and labor that are available for a given total cost. The slope of an isocost line is equal to $-P_L/P_K$.

3. The least-cost method of producing a given amount of output is found graphically at the point at which an isocost line is just tangent to (that is, just touches) the isoquant corresponding to that level of production. The firm's cost-minimizing equilibrium condition is $MP_L/P_L = MP_K/P_K$.

REVIEW TERMS AND CONCEPTS

isocost line A graph that shows all the combinations of capital and labor available for a given total cost. 178

isoquant A graph that shows all the combinations of capital and labor that can be used to produce a given amount of output. 177

marginal rate of technical substitution The rate at which a firm can substitute capital for labor and hold output constant. 178

1. Slope of isoquant: $\dfrac{\Delta K}{\Delta L} = -\dfrac{MP_L}{MP_K}$

2. Slope of isocost line:
$$\frac{\Delta K}{\Delta L} = -\frac{TC/P_K}{TC/P_L} = -\frac{P_L}{P_K}$$

PROBLEM SET

1. Assume that $MP_L = 5$ and $MP_K = 10$. Assume also that $P_L = \$2$ and $P_K = \$5$. This implies that the firm should substitute labor for capital. Explain why.

2. In the isoquant/isocost diagram (Figure 1), suppose that the firm is producing 1,000 units of output at point A using 100 units of labor and 200 units of capital. As an outside consultant, what actions would you suggest to management to improve profits? What would you recommend if the firm were operating at point B, using 100 units of capital and 200 units of labor?

3. Using the information from the isoquant/isocost diagram (Figure 2), and assuming that $P_L = P_K = \$2$, complete Table 1.

FIGURE 1

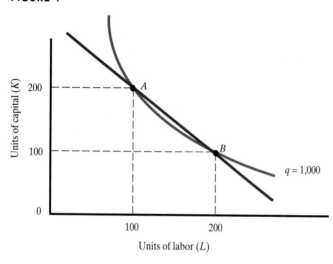

FIGURE 2

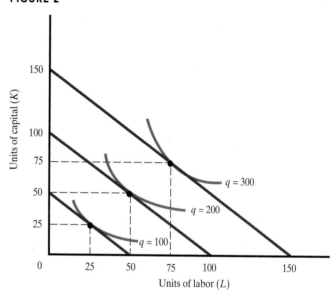

TABLE 1

OUTPUT UNITS	TOTAL COST OF OUTPUT	UNITS OF LABOR DEMANDED	UNITS OF CAPITAL DEMANDED
100			
200			
300			

SHORT-RUN COSTS
AND OUTPUT DECISIONS

THIS CHAPTER continues our examination of the decisions that firms make in their quest for profits. You have seen that firms in perfectly competitive industries make three specific decisions (Figure 8.1). These decisions are:

1. How much output to supply;
2. How to produce that output (that is, which production technique/ technology to use); and
3. What quantity of each input to demand.

Remember though that *all* types of firms make these decisions, not just those in perfectly competitive industries. We continue to use perfectly competitive firms as a teaching device, but much of the material in this chapter applies to firms in noncompetitive industries as well.

We have assumed so far that firms are in business to earn profits and that they make choices to maximize those profits. (Remember that *profit* is the difference between revenues and costs.) Because firms in perfectly competitive markets are price-takers in both input and output markets, many decisions depend upon prices over which firms have no control. Like households, firms also face market constraints.

In the last chapter, we focused on the production process. This chapter focuses on the *costs* of production. To calculate costs, a firm must know two things: the quantity and combination of inputs it needs to produce its product and how much those inputs cost. (Don't forget that economic costs include a normal return to capital—the opportunity cost of capital.)

Take a moment and look back at the circular flow diagram, Figure 7.1. There you can see exactly where we are in our study of the competitive market system. The goal of this chapter is to look behind the supply curve in output markets. It is important to understand, however, that producing output implies demanding inputs at the same time. You can also see in Figure 7.1 two of the information sources that firms use in their output supply and input demand decisions: Firms look to *output markets* for the price of output and to *input markets* for the prices of capital and labor.

FIGURE 8.1
Decisions Facing Firms

DECISIONS are based on	*INFORMATION*
1. The quantity of output to *supply*	1. The price of output
2. How to produce that output (which technique to use)	2. Techniques of production available*
3. The quantity of each input to *demand*	3. The price of inputs*
	*determines production costs

COSTS IN THE SHORT RUN

Our emphasis in this chapter is on costs *in the short run only*. Recall that the short run is that period during which two conditions hold: (1) Existing firms face limits imposed by some fixed factor of production, and (2) new firms cannot enter, and existing firms cannot exit, an industry.

In the short run, all firms (competitive and noncompetitive) have costs that they must bear regardless of their output. In fact, some costs must be paid even if the firm stops producing (that is, even if output is zero). These kinds of costs are called **fixed costs**, and firms can do nothing in the short run to avoid them or to change them. In the long run, a firm has no fixed costs, because it can expand, contract, or exit the industry.

Firms do have certain costs in the short run that depend on the level of output they have chosen. These kinds of costs are called **variable costs**. Fixed costs and variable costs together make up **total costs**:

$$TC = TFC + TVC$$

where *TC* denotes total costs, *TFC* denotes total fixed costs, and *TVC* denotes total variable costs. We will return to this equation after discussing fixed costs and variable costs in detail.

FIXED COSTS

In discussing fixed costs, we must distinguish between total fixed costs and average fixed costs.

▶ **Total Fixed Cost (TFC)** Total fixed cost is sometimes called *overhead*. If you operate a factory, you must heat the building to keep the pipes from freezing in the winter. Even if no production is taking place, you may have to keep the roof from leaking, pay a guard to protect the building from vandals, and make payments on a long-term lease. There may also be insurance premiums, taxes, and city fees to pay, as well as contract obligations to workers.

Fixed costs represent a larger portion of total costs for some firms than for others. Electric companies, for instance, maintain generating plants, thousands of miles of distribution wires, poles, transformers, and so forth. Usually, such plants are financed by issuing bonds to the public (that is, by borrowing). The interest that must be paid on these bonds represents a substantial part of the utilities' operating cost and is a fixed cost in the short run, no matter how much (if any) electricity they are producing.

For the purposes of our discussion in this chapter, we will assume that firms use only two inputs: labor and capital.[1] Recall that capital yields services over time in the

fixed cost *Any cost that does not depend on the firm's level of output. These costs are incurred even if the firm is producing nothing. There are no fixed costs in the long run.*

variable cost *A cost that depends on the level of production chosen.*

total cost (TC) *Fixed costs plus variable costs.*

---

[1]Although this may seem unrealistic, virtually everything that we will say about firms using these two factors can easily be generalized to firms that use many factors of production.

production of other goods and services. It is the plant and equipment of a manufacturing firm; the computers, desks, chairs, doors, and walls of a law office; and the boat that Bill and Colleen built on their desert island. It is sometimes assumed that capital is a fixed input in the short run and that labor is the only variable input. To be a bit more realistic, however, we will assume that capital has both a fixed *and* a variable component. After all, some capital can be purchased in the short run.

Consider a small consulting firm that employs several economists, research assistants, and secretaries. It rents space in an office building and has a five-year lease. The rent on the office space can be thought of as a fixed cost in the short run. The monthly electric and heating bills are also essentially fixed (although the amounts may vary slightly from month to month). So are the salaries of the basic administrative staff. Payments on some capital equipment—a large copying machine and the main word processing system, for instance—can also be thought of as fixed.

The same firm also has costs that vary with output. When there is a lot of work, the firm hires more employees at both the professional and research assistant level. The capital used by the consulting firm may also vary, even in the short run. Payments on the computer system do not change, but the firm may rent additional computer time when necessary. It can buy additional personal computers, network terminals, or databases quickly, if need be. It must pay for the copy machine, but the machine costs more when it is running than when it is not.

Total fixed costs (*TFC*) are those costs that do not change with output, even if output is zero. Column 2 of Table 8.1 presents data on the fixed costs of a hypothetical firm. Fixed costs are $1,000 at all levels of output (*q*). Figure 8.2a shows total fixed costs as a function of output. Because *TFC* does not change with output, the graph is simply a straight horizontal line at $1,000. The important thing to remember here is that:

> Firms have no control over fixed costs in the short run. For this reason, fixed costs are sometimes called **sunk costs**.

> ▶ **Average Fixed Cost (AFC)** Average fixed cost (*AFC*) is total fixed cost (*TFC*) divided by the number of units of output (*q*):

$$AFC = \frac{TFC}{q}$$

For example, if the firm in Figure 8.2 produced three units of output, average fixed costs would be $333 ($1,000 divided by three). If the same firm produced five units of output, average fixed cost would be $200 ($1,000 divided by five). *Average fixed cost falls as output rises*, because the same total is being spread over, or divided by, a larger number of units (see column 3 of Table 8.1). This phenomenon is sometimes called **spreading overhead**.

Graphs of average fixed cost, like that in Figure 8.2b (which presents the average fixed cost data from Table 8.1), are downward-sloping curves. Notice that *AFC* approaches zero as the quantity of output increases. If output were 100,000 units, average fixed cost would equal only one cent per unit in our example ($1,000 ÷ 100,000 = $.01). *AFC* never actually reaches zero.

VARIABLE COSTS

> ▶ **Total Variable Cost (TVC)** Total variable cost (*TVC*) is the sum of those costs that vary with the level of output in the short run. To produce more output, a firm uses more inputs. The cost of additional output depends directly on the additional inputs that are required and how much they cost.

TABLE 8.1

SHORT-RUN FIXED COST (TOTAL AND AVERAGE) OF A HYPOTHETICAL FIRM

(1) q	(2) TFC	(3) AFC (TFC/q)
0	$1,000	$ —
1	1,000	1,000
2	1,000	500
3	1,000	333
4	1,000	250
5	1,000	200

total fixed costs (TFC) or overhead *The total of all costs that do not change with output, even if output is zero.*

sunk costs *Another name for fixed costs in the short run because firms have no choice but to pay them.*

average fixed cost (AFC) *Total fixed cost divided by the number of units of output; a per-unit measure of fixed costs.*

spreading overhead *The process of dividing total fixed costs by more units of output. Average fixed cost declines as quantity rises.*

total variable cost (TVC) *The total of all costs that vary with output in the short run.*

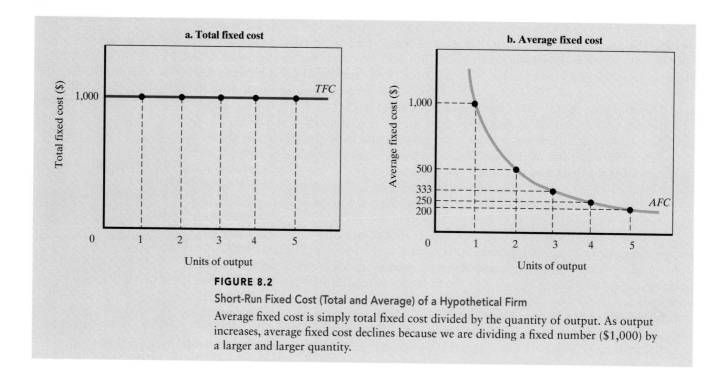

FIGURE 8.2

Short-Run Fixed Cost (Total and Average) of a Hypothetical Firm

Average fixed cost is simply total fixed cost divided by the quantity of output. As output increases, average fixed cost declines because we are dividing a fixed number ($1,000) by a larger and larger quantity.

FAST FACTS

A car's fixed costs are relatively high and variable costs are relatively low. A $15,000 Ford financed over 5 years at 10% interest means $318.71 monthly loan payments, whether you drive it or not. Add insurance of $100 a month, and fixed costs are $418 per month. If the car gets 20 miles per gallon and uses unleaded regular gas costing $1.25 per gallon, variable cost is only 6.25 cents per mile (ignoring wear and tear).

total variable cost curve *A graph that shows the relationship between total variable cost and the level of a firm's output.*

As you saw in chapter 7, input requirements are determined by technology. Firms generally have a number of production techniques available to them, and the option they choose is assumed to be the one that produces the desired level of output at the least cost. To find out which technology involves the least cost, a firm must compare the total variable costs of producing that level of output using different production techniques.

This is as true of small businesses as it is of large manufacturing firms. Suppose, for example, that you are a small farmer. A certain amount of work has to be done to plant and harvest your 120 acres. You might hire four farmhands and divide up the tasks, or you might buy several pieces of complex farm machinery (capital) and do the work single-handedly. Clearly, your final choice depends on a number of things. What machinery is available? What does it do? Will it work on small fields such as yours? How much will it cost to buy each piece of equipment? What wage will you have to pay farmhands? How many will you need to get the job done? If machinery is expensive and labor is cheap, you will probably choose the labor-intensive technology. If farm labor is expensive and the local farm equipment dealer is going out of business, you might get a good deal on some machinery and choose the capital-intensive method.

Having compared the costs of alternative production techniques, the firm may be influenced in its choice by the current scale of its operation. Remember, in the short run a firm is locked into a *fixed* scale of operations. A firm currently producing on a small scale may find that a labor-intensive technique is the least costly, whether or not labor is comparatively expensive. The same firm producing on a larger scale might find a capital-intensive technique less costly.

The **total variable cost curve** is a graph that shows the relationship between total variable cost and the level of a firm's output (*q*). At any given level of output, total variable cost depends on (1) the techniques of production that are available and (2) the prices of the inputs required by each technology. To examine this relationship in more detail, let us look at some hypothetical production figures.

TABLE 8.2 DERIVATION OF TOTAL VARIABLE COST SCHEDULE FROM TECHNOLOGY AND FACTOR PRICES

PRODUCE	USING TECHNIQUE	UNITS OF INPUT REQUIRED (PRODUCTION FUNCTION) K	L	TOTAL VARIABLE COST ASSUMING $P_K = \$2$, $P_L = \$1$ $TVC = (K \times P_K) + (L \times P_L)$
1 unit of output	A	4	4	$(4 \times \$2) + (4 \times \$1) = \$12$
	B	2	6	$(2 \times \$2) + (6 \times \$1) = \boxed{\$10}$
2 units of output	A	7	6	$(7 \times \$2) + (6 \times \$1) = \$20$
	B	4	10	$(4 \times \$2) + (10 \times \$1) = \boxed{\$18}$
3 units of output	A	9	6	$(9 \times \$2) + (6 \times \$1) = \boxed{\$24}$
	B	6	14	$(6 \times \$2) + (14 \times \$1) = \$26$

Table 8.2 presents an analysis that might lie behind three points on a typical firm's total variable cost curve. In this case, there are two production techniques available, A and B, one somewhat more capital intensive than the other. We will assume that the price of labor is $1 per unit and the price of capital is $2 per unit. For the purposes of this example, we focus on *variable capital*—that is, on capital that can be changed in the short run. In practice, some capital (such as buildings and large, specialized machines) is fixed in the short run. In our example, we will use K to denote variable capital. Remember, however, that the firm has other capital, capital that is fixed in the short run.

Analysis reveals that to produce one unit of output, the labor-intensive technique is least costly. Technique A requires four units of both capital and labor, which would cost a total of $12. Technique B requires six units of labor but only two units of capital for a total cost of only $10. To maximize profits, the firm would use technique B to produce one unit. The total variable cost of producing one unit of output would thus be $10.

The relatively labor-intensive technique B is also the best method of production for two units of output. Using B, the firm can produce two units for $18. If the firm decides to produce three units of output, however, technique A is the cheaper. Using the least-cost technology (A), the total variable cost of production is $24. The firm will use nine units of capital at $2 each and six units of labor at $1 each.

Figure 8.3 graphs the relationship between variable costs and output based on the data in Table 8.2, assuming the firm chooses, for each output, the least-cost technology.

> The total variable cost curve embodies information about both factor, or input, prices and technology. It shows the cost of production using the best available technique at each output level, given current factor prices.

▶ **Marginal Cost (MC)** The most important of all cost concepts is that of **marginal cost** (MC), the increase in total cost that results from the production of one more unit of output. Let us say, for example, that a firm is producing 1,000 units of output per period and decides to raise its rate of output to 1,001. Producing the extra unit raises costs, and the increase (that is, the cost of producing the 1,001st unit) is the marginal cost. Focusing on the "margin" is one way of looking at variable costs: Marginal costs reflect changes in variable costs because they vary when output changes. Fixed costs do not change when output changes.

Table 8.3 shows how marginal cost is derived from total variable cost by simple subtraction. The total variable cost of producing the first unit of output is $10. Raising

marginal cost (MC) *The increase in total cost that results from producing one more unit of output. Marginal costs reflect changes in variable costs.*

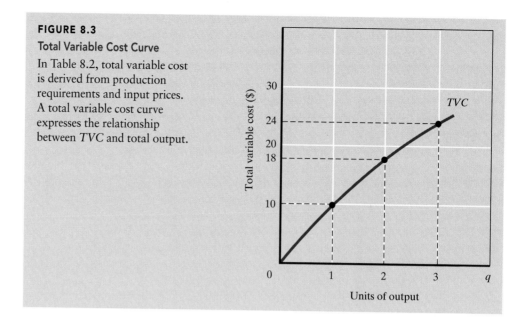

FIGURE 8.3

Total Variable Cost Curve

In Table 8.2, total variable cost is derived from production requirements and input prices. A total variable cost curve expresses the relationship between *TVC* and total output.

TABLE 8.3

DERIVATION OF MARGINAL COST FROM TOTAL VARIABLE COST

UNITS OF OUTPUT	TOTAL VARIABLE COSTS ($)	MARGINAL COSTS ($)
0	0	0
1	10	10
2	18	8
3	24	6

production from one unit to two units increases total variable cost from $10 to $18; the difference is the marginal cost of the second unit, or $8. Raising output from two to three units increases total variable cost from $18 to $24. The marginal cost of the third unit, therefore, is $6.

It is important to think for a moment about the nature of marginal cost. Specifically, marginal cost is the cost of the added inputs, or resources, needed to produce one additional unit of output. Look back at Table 8.2, and think about the additional capital and labor needed to go from one unit to two units. Producing one unit of output with technique *B* requires two units of capital and six units of labor; producing two units of output using the same technique requires four units of capital and 10 units of labor. Thus, the second unit requires two *additional* units of capital and four *additional* units of labor. What then is the added, or marginal, cost of the second unit? Two units of capital cost $2 each ($4 total) and four units of labor cost $1 each (another $4), for a total marginal cost of $8, which is exactly the number we derived in Table 8.3.

While the easiest way to derive marginal cost is to look at total variable cost and subtract, don't lose sight of the fact that when a firm increases its output level, it hires or demands more inputs. *Marginal cost* measures the *additional* cost of inputs required to produce each successive unit of output.

➤ **The Shape of the Marginal Cost Curve in the Short Run** The assumption of a fixed factor of production in the short run means that a firm is stuck at its current scale of operation (in our example, the size of the plant). As a firm tries to increase its output, it will eventually find itself trapped by that scale. Thus, our definition of the short run also implies that *marginal cost eventually rises with output*. The firm can hire more labor and use more materials—that is, it can add variable inputs—but diminishing returns eventually set in.

Recall the sandwich shop, with one grill and too many workers trying to prepare sandwiches on it, from chapter 7. With a fixed grill capacity, more laborers could

AN INDEPENDENT ACCOUNTANT
PREPARING TAX RETURNS FOR
HIS CLIENTS FACES DIMINISHING
RETURNS AS HE GETS TIRED AND
BECOMES LESS EFFECTIVE.

make more sandwiches, but the marginal product of each successive cook declined as more people tried to use the grill. If each additional unit of labor adds less and less to total output, *it follows that it requires more labor to produce each additional unit of output.* Thus, each additional unit of output costs more to produce. In other words, *diminishing returns, or decreasing marginal product, implies increasing marginal cost* (Figure 8.4).

Recall too the accountant who helps people file their tax returns. He has an office in his home and works alone. His fixed factor of production is that there are only 24 hours in a day and he has only so much stamina. In the long run, he may decide to hire and train an associate, but in the meantime (the short run) he has to decide how much to produce, and that decision is constrained by his current scale of operations. The biggest component of the accountant's cost is time. When he works, he gives up leisure and other things that he could do with his time. With more and more clients, he works later and later into the night. As he does so, he becomes less and less productive, and his hours become more and more valuable for sleep and relaxation. In other words, the marginal cost of doing each successive tax return rises.

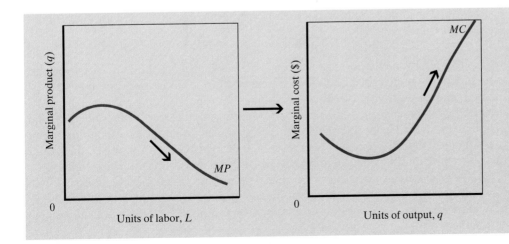

FIGURE 8.4

Declining Marginal Product Implies That Marginal Cost Will Eventually Rise with Output

In the short run, every firm is constrained by some fixed factor of production. A fixed factor implies diminishing returns (declining marginal product) and a limited capacity to produce. As that limit is approached, marginal costs rise.

189

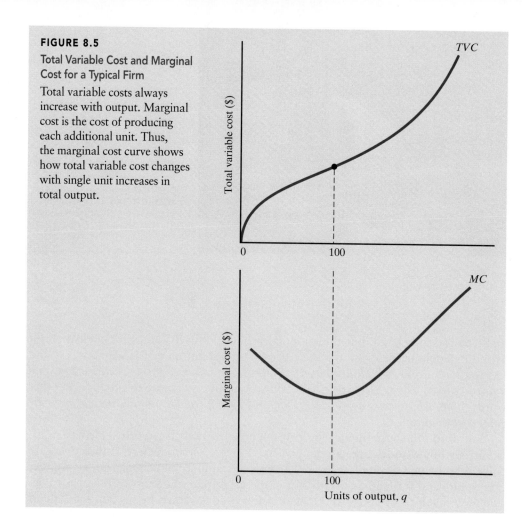

FIGURE 8.5

Total Variable Cost and Marginal Cost for a Typical Firm

Total variable costs always increase with output. Marginal cost is the cost of producing each additional unit. Thus, the marginal cost curve shows how total variable cost changes with single unit increases in total output.

To reiterate:

> In the short run, every firm is constrained by some fixed input that (1) leads to diminishing returns to variable inputs and (2) limits its capacity to produce. As a firm approaches that capacity, it becomes increasingly costly to produce successively higher levels of output. Marginal costs ultimately increase with output in the short run.

➤ **Graphing Total Variable Costs and Marginal Costs** Figure 8.5 shows the total variable cost curve and the marginal cost curve of a typical firm. Notice first that the shape of the marginal cost curve is consistent with short-run diminishing returns. At first *MC* declines, but eventually the fixed factor of production begins to constrain the firm, and marginal cost rises. Up to 100 units of output, producing each successive unit of output costs slightly less than producing the one before. Beyond 100 units, however, the cost of each successive unit is greater than the one before. (Remember the sandwich shop.)

Clearly, more output costs more than less output. Total variable costs (*TVC*), therefore, *always increase* when output increases. Even though the cost of each additional unit changes, *total* variable cost rises when output rises. Thus the *total* variable cost curve always has a positive slope.

TABLE 8.4 SHORT-RUN COSTS OF A HYPOTHETICAL FIRM

(1) q	(2) TVC	(3) MC (Δ TVC)	(4) AVC (TVC/q)	(5) TFC	(6) TC (TVC + TFC)	(7) AFC (TFC/q)	(8) ATC (TC/q or AFC + AVC)
0	$0	$—	$—	$1,000	$1,000	$ —	$ —
1	10	10	10	1,000	1,010	1,000	1,010
2	18	8	9	1,000	1,018	500	509
3	24	6	8	1,000	1,024	333	341
4	32	8	8	1,000	1,032	250	258
5	42	10	8.4	1,000	1,042	200	208.4
—	—	—	—	—	—	—	—
—	—	—	—	—	—	—	—
500	8,000	20	16	1,000	9,000	2	18

You might think of the total variable cost curve as a staircase. Each step takes you out along the quantity axis by a single unit, and the height of each step is the increase in total variable cost. As you climb the stairs, you are always going up, but the steps have different heights. At first, the stairway is steep, but as you climb, the steps get smaller (marginal cost declines). The 100th stair is the smallest. As you continue to walk out beyond 100 units, the steps begin to get larger; the staircase gets steeper (marginal cost increases).

Remember that the slope of a line is equal to the change in the units measured on the Y axis divided by the change in the units measured on the X axis. The slope of a total variable cost curve is thus the change in total variable cost divided by the change in output ($\Delta TVC/\Delta q$). Because marginal cost is by definition the change in total variable cost resulting from an increase in output of one unit ($\Delta q = 1$), *marginal cost actually is the slope of the total variable cost curve:*

$$\text{Slope of } TVC = \frac{\Delta TVC}{\Delta q} = \frac{\Delta TVC}{1} = \Delta TVC = MC.$$

Notice that up to 100 units, marginal cost decreases and the variable cost curve becomes flatter. The slope of the total variable cost curve is declining—that is, total variable cost increases, but at a *decreasing rate*. Beyond 100 units of output, marginal cost increases and the total variable cost curve gets steeper—total variable costs continue to increase, but at an *increasing rate*.

➤ **Average Variable Cost (AVC)** A more complete picture of the costs of a hypothetical firm appears in Table 8.4. Column 2 shows total variable costs—derived from information on input prices and technology. Column 3 derives marginal cost by simple subtraction. For example, raising output from three units to four units increases variable costs from $24 to $32, making the marginal cost of the fourth unit $8 ($32 − $24). The marginal cost of the fifth unit is $10, the difference between $32 (*TVC*) for four units and $42 (*TVC*) for five units.

Average variable cost (AVC) is total variable cost divided by the number of units of output (*q*):

average variable cost (AVC)
Total variable cost divided by the number of units of output.

$$AVC = \frac{TVC}{q}$$

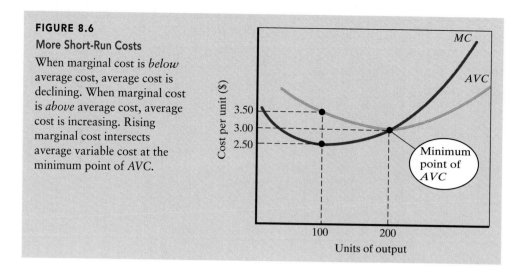

FIGURE 8.6

More Short-Run Costs

When marginal cost is *below* average cost, average cost is declining. When marginal cost is *above* average cost, average cost is increasing. Rising marginal cost intersects average variable cost at the minimum point of *AVC*.

In Table 8.4, we calculate *AVC* in column 4 by dividing the numbers in column 2 (*TVC*) by the numbers in column 1 (*q*). For example, if the total variable cost of producing five units of output is $42, then the average variable cost is $42 ÷ 5, or $8.40.

> Marginal cost is the cost of *one additional unit*. Average variable cost is the average variable cost per unit of *all the units* being produced.

▶ **Graphing Average Variable Costs and Marginal Costs** The relationship between average variable cost and marginal cost can be illustrated graphically. When marginal cost is *below* average, average variable cost declines toward it. When marginal cost is *above* average variable cost, average variable cost increases toward it.

Figure 8.6 duplicates the lower diagram for a typical firm in Figure 8.5 but adds average variable cost. As the graph shows, average variable cost *follows* marginal cost, but lags behind.

As we move from left to right, we are looking at higher and higher levels of output per period. As we increase production, marginal cost—which at low levels of production is above $3.50 per unit—falls as coordination and cooperation begin to play a role. At 100 units of output, marginal cost has fallen to $2.50. Notice that average variable cost falls as well, but not as rapidly as marginal cost.

After 100 units of output, we begin to see diminishing returns. Marginal cost begins to increase as higher and higher levels of output are produced. But notice that average cost is still falling until 200 units because marginal cost remains below it. At 100 units of output, marginal cost is $2.50 per unit but the *average* variable cost of production is $3.50. Thus even though marginal cost is rising after 100 units, it is still pulling the average of $3.50 downward.

At 200 units, however, marginal cost has risen to $3.00 and average cost has fallen to $3.00; marginal and average costs are equal. At this point marginal cost continues to rise with higher output. But from 200 units upward, *MC* is *above* *AVC*, and thus exerts an *upward* pull on the average variable cost curve. At levels of output below 200 units, marginal cost is below average variable cost, and average variable cost decreases as output increases. At levels of output above 200 units, *MC* is above *AVC*, and *AVC* increases as output increases.

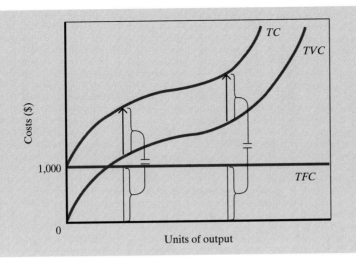

FIGURE 8.7

Total Cost = Total Fixed Cost + Total Variable Cost

Adding *TFC* to *TVC* means adding the same amount of total fixed cost to every level of total variable cost. Thus, the total cost curve has the same shape as the total variable cost curve; it is simply higher by an amount equal to *TFC*.

If you follow this logic you will see that:

> Marginal cost intersects average variable cost at the lowest, or minimum, point of *AVC*.

An example using test scores should help you to understand the relationship between *MC* and *AVC*. Consider the following sequence of test scores: 95, 85, 92, 88. The average of these four is 90. Suppose you get an 80 on your fifth test. This score will drag down your average to 88. Now suppose that you get an 85 on your sixth test. This score is higher than 80, but it's still *below* your 88 average. As a result, your average continues to fall (from 88 to 87.5), even though your marginal test score rose. But if instead of an 85 you get an 89—just one point over your average—you've turned your average around; it is now rising.

TOTAL COSTS

We are now ready to complete the cost picture by adding total fixed costs to total variable costs. Recall that

$$TC = TFC + TVC$$

Total cost is graphed in Figure 8.7, where the same vertical distance (equal to *TFC*, which is constant) is simply added to *TVC* at every level of output. In Table 8.4, column 6 adds the total fixed cost of $1,000 to total variable cost to arrive at total cost.

▶ **Average Total Cost (ATC)**   Average total cost (*ATC*) is total cost divided by the number of units of output (*q*):

average total cost (ATC) *Total cost divided by the number of units of output.*

$$ATC = \frac{TC}{q}$$

Column 8 in Table 8.4 shows the result of dividing the costs in column 6 by the quantities in column 1. For example, at five units of output, *total* cost is $1,042; *average* total cost is $1,042 ÷ 5, or $208.40. The average total cost of producing 500 units of output is only $18—that is, $9,000 ÷ 500.

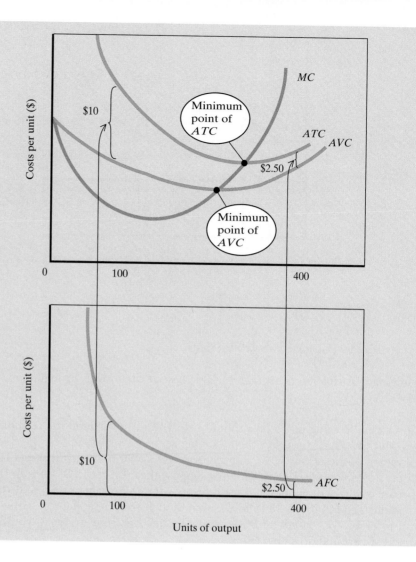

Another, more revealing, way of deriving average total cost is to add average fixed cost and average variable cost together:

$$ATC = AFC + AVC$$

For example, column 8 in Table 8.4 is the sum of column 4 (*AVC*) and column 7 (*AFC*).

Figure 8.8 derives average total cost graphically for a typical firm. The bottom part of the figure graphs average fixed cost. At 100 units of output, average fixed cost is $TFC/q = \$1,000 \div 100 = \$10$. At 400 units of output, $AFC = \$1,000 \div 400 = \$2.50$. The top part of Figure 8.8 shows the declining *AFC* added to *AVC* at each level of output. Because *AFC* gets smaller and smaller, *ATC* gets closer and closer to *AVC* as output increases, but the two lines never meet.

▶ **The Relationship Between Average Total Cost and Marginal Cost** The relationship between average *total* cost and marginal cost is exactly the same as the relationship between average *variable* cost and marginal cost. The average total cost curve follows the marginal cost curve, but lags behind because it is an average over all units of output. The average total cost curve lags behind the marginal cost curve even more than the average variable cost curve does, because the cost of each added unit of production is now averaged not only with the variable cost of all previous units produced, but with fixed costs as well.

Fixed costs equal $1,000 and are incurred even when the output level is zero. Thus, the first unit of output in the example in Table 8.4 costs $10 in variable cost to produce. The second unit costs only $8 in variable cost to produce. The total cost of two units is $1,018; average total cost of the two is ($1,010 + $8)/2, or $509. The marginal cost of the third unit is only $6. The total cost of three units is thus $1,024, or $1,018 + $6, and the average total cost of three units is ($1,010 + $8 + $6)/3, or $341.

As you saw with the test scores example, marginal cost is what drives changes in average total cost:

> If marginal cost is *below* average total cost, average total cost will *decline* toward marginal cost. If marginal cost is *above* average total cost, average total cost will *increase*. As a result, marginal cost intersects average *total* cost at *ATC*'s minimum point, for the same reason that it intersects the average *variable* cost curve at its minimum point.

SHORT-RUN COSTS: A REVIEW

Let us now pause to review what we learned about the behavior of firms. We know that firms make three basic choices: how much product or output to produce or supply, how to produce that output, and how much of each input to demand in order to produce what they intend to supply. We assume that these choices are made to maximize profits. Profits are equal to the difference between a firm's revenue from the sale of its product and the costs of producing that product: profit = total revenue minus total cost.

So far, we have looked only at costs, but costs are only one part of the profit equation. To complete the picture, we must turn to the output market and see how these costs compare with the price that a product commands in the market. Before we do so, however, it is important to consolidate what we have said about costs.

Before a firm does anything else, it needs to know the different methods that it can use to produce its product. The technologies available determine the combinations of inputs that are needed to produce each level of output. Firms choose the technique that produces the desired level of output at least cost. The cost curves that result from the analysis of all this information show the cost of producing each level of output using the best available technology.

Remember that so far we have talked only about short-run costs. The curves we have drawn are therefore *short-run cost curves*. The shape of these curves is determined in large measure by the assumptions that we make about the short run, especially the assumption that some fixed factor of production leads to diminishing returns. Given this assumption, marginal costs eventually rise, and average cost curves are likely to be U-shaped.

After gaining a complete knowledge of how to produce a product and how much it will cost to produce it at each level of output, the firm turns to the market to find out what it can sell its product for. It is to the output market that we now turn our attention.

OUTPUT DECISIONS: REVENUES, COSTS, AND PROFIT MAXIMIZATION

To calculate potential profits, firms must combine their cost analyses with information on potential revenues from sales. After all, if a firm can't sell its product for more than the cost of production, it won't be in business long. In contrast, if the market gives the firm a price that is significantly greater than the cost it incurs to produce a unit of

Because perfectly competitive firms are very small relative to the market, they have no control over price. A firm can sell all it wants at the market price but would sell nothing if it charged a higher price. Thus, the demand curve facing a perfectly competitive firm is simply a horizontal line at the market equilibrium price, P^*.

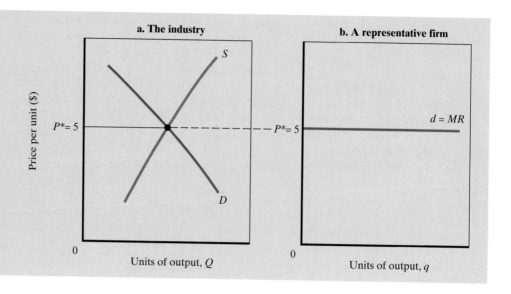

a. The industry

b. A representative firm

The best example of a competitive industry—each firm is small relative to the market and products are homogeneous—is agriculture. In 1995, there were over 2 million farms in the United States; the average had 469 acres. That same year, 2.2 billion bushels of wheat were produced, yielding 36 bushels per acre. A farm of 2,000 acres would have produced 72,000 bushels, or 3/1,000 of 1% of total output.

its product, the firm may have an incentive to expand output. Large profits might also attract new competitors to the market.

Let us now examine in detail how a firm goes about determining how much output to produce. For the sake of simplicity, we will continue to examine the decisions of a perfectly competitive firm. A perfectly competitive industry has many firms that are small relative to the size of the market, and the output of one firm is identical to the output of its competitors. In such an environment, product price is determined by the interaction of many suppliers and many demanders.

Figure 8.9 shows a typical firm in a perfectly competitive industry. Price is determined in the market at $P^* = \$5$. The individual firm can charge any price that it wants for its product, but if it charges above $5, the quantity demanded falls to zero, and the firm won't sell anything. The firm could also sell its product for less than $5, but there is no reason to do so.

> In the short run, a competitive firm faces a demand curve that is simply a horizontal line at the market equilibrium price. In other words, competitive firms face perfectly elastic demand in the short run.

In Figure 8.9, market equilibrium price is $P^* = \$5$ and the firm's perfectly elastic demand curve is labeled d.

TOTAL REVENUE (*TR*) AND MARGINAL REVENUE (*MR*)

total revenue (TR) *The total amount that a firm takes in from the sale of its product: The price per unit times the quantity of output the firm decides to produce (P × q).*

Profit is the difference between total revenue and total cost. **Total revenue** is the total amount that a firm takes in from the sale of its product. A perfectly competitive firm sells each unit of product for the same price, regardless of the output level it has chosen. Therefore, total revenue is simply the price per unit times the quantity of output that the firm decides to produce:

$$\text{Total revenue} = \text{Price} \times \text{Quantity}$$

$$TR = P \times q$$

Marginal revenue (MR) is the added revenue that a firm takes in when it increases output by one additional unit. If a firm producing 10,521 units of output per month increases that output to 10,522 units per month, it will take in an additional amount of revenue each month. The revenue associated with the 10,522nd unit is simply the amount that the firm sells that one unit for. Thus, for a competitive firm, marginal revenue is simply equal to the current market price of each additional unit sold. In Figure 8.9, for example, the market price is $5. Thus, if the representative firm raises its output from 10,521 units to 10,522 units, its revenue will increase by $5.

marginal revenue (MR) *The additional revenue that a firm takes in when it increases output by one additional unit. In perfect competition, P = MR.*

A firm's *marginal revenue curve* shows how much revenue the firm will gain by raising output by one unit at every level of output. The *marginal revenue curve and the demand curve facing a competitive firm are identical.* The horizontal line in Figure 8.9b can be thought of as both the demand curve facing the firm and its marginal revenue curve:

$$P^* = d = MR$$

COMPARING COSTS AND REVENUES TO MAXIMIZE PROFIT

The discussion in the next few paragraphs conveys one of the most important concepts in all of microeconomics. As we pursue our analysis, remember that we are working under two assumptions: (1) that the industry we are examining is perfectly competitive and (2) that firms choose the level of output that yields the maximum total profit.

➤ **The Profit-Maximizing Level of Output** Look carefully at the diagrams in Figure 8.10. Once again we have the whole market, or industry, on the left and a single, typical small firm on the right. And again the current market price is P^*.

First, the firm observes market price (Figure 8.10a) and knows that it can sell all that it wants to for $P^* = \$5$ per unit. Next, it must decide how much to produce. It might seem reasonable to pick the output level where marginal cost is at its minimum point—in this case, at an output of 100 units. Here the difference between marginal revenue, $5, and marginal cost, $2.50, is the greatest.

But remember that a firm wants to maximize the difference between *total* revenue and *total* cost, not the difference between *marginal* revenue and *marginal* cost. The fact that marginal revenue is greater than marginal cost actually indicates that profit is *not* being maximized! Think about the 101st unit. Adding that single unit to production each period adds $5 to revenues but adds only about $2.50 to cost. Profits each period would be higher by about $2.50. Thus, the optimal (profit-maximizing) level of output is clearly higher than 100 units.

Now look at an output level of 250 units. Here, once again, raising output increases profit. The revenue gained from producing the 251st unit (marginal revenue) is still $5, and the cost of the 251st unit (marginal cost) is only about $4.

> As long as marginal revenue is greater than marginal cost, even though the difference between the two is getting smaller, added output means added profit. Whenever marginal revenue exceeds marginal cost, the revenue gained by increasing output by one unit per period exceeds the cost incurred by doing so.

This logic leads us to 300 units of output. At 300 units, marginal cost has risen to $5. At 300 units of output, $P^* = MR = MC = \$5$.

Notice that if the firm were to produce *more* than 300 units, marginal cost rises above marginal revenue. At 340 units of output, for example, the cost of the 341st unit is about $5.70 while that added unit of output still brings in only $5 in

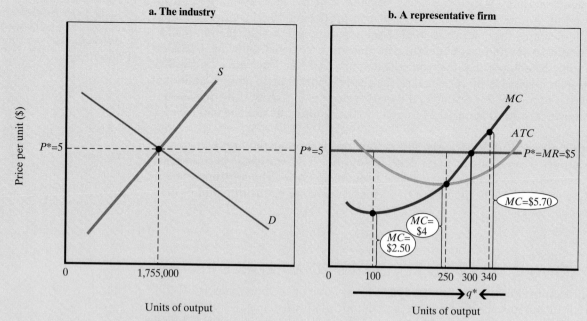

FIGURE 8.10

The Profit-Maximizing Level of Output for a Perfectly Competitive Firm

If price is above marginal cost, as it is at 100 and 250 units of output, profits can be increased by raising output; each additional unit increases revenues by more than it costs to produce the additional output. Beyond $q^* = 300$, however, added output will reduce profits. At 340 units of output, an additional unit of output costs more to produce than it will bring in revenue when sold on the market. Profit-maximizing output is thus q^*, the point at which $P^* = MC$.

revenue, thus reducing profit. It simply does not pay to increase output above the point where marginal cost rises above marginal revenue because such increases will *reduce* profit.

> The profit-maximizing perfectly competitive firm will produce up to the point where the price of its output is just equal to short-run marginal cost—the level of output at which $P^* = MC$.[2]

Thus, in Figure 8.10, the profit-maximizing level of output, q^*, is 300 units.

Keep in mind, though, that all types of firms (not just those in perfectly competitive industries) are profit maximizers. Thus,

> The profit-maximizing output level for *all* firms is the output level where $MR = MC$.

---

[2]To be very precise, it is possible for price to be equal to marginal cost at two points, one where marginal cost is declining and another where marginal cost is increasing (see graph to the left). Profit is maximized where marginal cost crosses price on its way up (q_2). The marginal costs of the first few units of production are high, because at such a low level of output the firm is not using its plant very efficiently. It would never make sense to produce at these low levels. In fact, to stop at the first point where $P = MC$ (q_1) would be to *minimize* profits. Can you figure out why?

TABLE 8.5   PROFIT ANALYSIS FOR A SIMPLE FIRM

(1)	(2)	(3)	(4)	(5)	(6) TR	(7) TC	(8) PROFIT
q	TFC	TVC	MC	P = MR	(P × q)	(TFC + TVC)	(TR − TC)
0	$10	$ 0	$—	$15	$ 0	$10	$ − 10
1	10	10	10	15	15	20	− 5
2	10	15	5	15	30	25	5
3	10	20	5	15	45	30	15
4	10	30	10	15	60	40	20
5	10	50	20	15	75	60	15
6	10	80	30	15	90	90	0

In perfect competition, however, $MR = P$, as shown above. Hence, for perfectly competitive firms we can rewrite our profit-maximizing condition as $P = MC$.

Important note: The key idea here is that firms will produce as long as marginal revenue exceeds *marginal cost.* If marginal cost rises smoothly, as it does in Figure 8.10, then the profit-maximizing condition is that MR (or P) *exactly equals* MC. But if marginal cost moves up in increments—as it does in the following numerical example—marginal revenue or price may never exactly equal marginal cost. The key idea still holds!

▶ **A Numerical Example**   Table 8.5 presents some data for another hypothetical firm. Let's assume that the market has set a $15 unit price for the firm's product. Total revenue in column 6 is the simple product of $P \times q$ (the numbers in column 1 times $15). The table derives total, marginal, and average costs exactly as Table 8.4 did. Here, however, we have included revenues, and we can calculate the profit, which is shown in column 8.

Column 8 shows that a profit-maximizing firm would choose to produce four units of output. At this level, profits are $20. At all other output levels, they are lower. Now let's see if "marginal" reasoning leads us to the same conclusion.

First, should the firm produce at all? If it produces nothing, it suffers losses equal to $10. If it increases output to one unit, marginal revenue is $15 (remember that it sells each unit for $15), and marginal cost is $10. Thus, it gains $5, reducing its loss from $10 each period to $5.

Should the firm increase output to two units? The marginal revenue from the second unit is again $15, but the marginal cost is only $5. Thus, by producing the second unit, the firm gains $10 ($15 − $5) and turns a $5 loss into a $5 profit. The third unit adds $10 to profits. Again, marginal revenue is $15 and marginal cost is $5, an increase in profit of $10, for a total profit of $15.

The fourth unit offers still more profit. Price is still above marginal cost, which means that producing that fourth unit will increase profits. Price, or marginal revenue, is $15, and marginal cost is just $10. Thus, the fourth unit adds $5 to profit. At unit number five, however, diminishing returns push marginal cost up above price. The marginal revenue from producing the fifth unit is $15, while marginal cost is now $20. As a result, profit per period drops by $5, to $15 per period. Clearly, the firm will not produce the fifth unit.

The profit-maximizing level of output is thus four units. The firm produces as long as price (marginal revenue) is greater than marginal cost. For an in-depth example of profit maximization see the Application box titled "Case Study in Marginal Analysis: An Ice-Cream Parlor."

CASE STUDY IN MARGINAL ANALYSIS: AN ICE CREAM PARLOR

The following is a description of the decisions made in 1997 by the owner of a small ice-cream parlor in Ohio. After being in business for one year, this entrepreneur had to ask herself, should I stay in business?

The cost figures on which she based her decisions are presented below. These numbers are real, but they do not include one important item: the managerial labor provided by the owner. In her calculations, the entrepreneur did not include a wage for herself, but we will assume an opportunity cost of $30,000 per year ($2,500 per month).

FIXED COSTS

The fixed components of the store's monthly costs include the following:

Rent (1,150 square feet)....	$2,012.50
Electricity..............	325.00
Interest on loan	737.50
Maintenance	295.00
Telephone..............	65.00
Total	$3,435.00

Not all of the items on this list are strictly fixed, however. Electricity costs, for example, would be slightly higher if the store produced more ice cream and stayed open longer, but the added cost would be minimal.

VARIABLE COSTS

The ice-cream store's variable costs include two components: (1) behind-the-counter labor costs, and (2) the cost of making ice cream. The store employs high school students at a wage of $5.15 per hour. Including the employer's share of the *social security tax*, the gross cost of each hour of labor is $5.54 per hour. There are two employees working in the store at all times. The full cost of producing ice cream is $3.27 per gallon. Each gallon contains approximately 12 servings. Customers can add toppings free of charge, and the average cost of the toppings taken by a customer is about $.05:

Gross labor costs.........	$5.54/hour
Costs of producing one gallon of ice cream (12 servings per gallon)	$3.27
Average cost of added toppings per serving	$ .05

REVENUES

The store sells ice-cream cones, sundaes, and floats. The average price of a purchase at the store is $1.45. The store is open 8 hours per day, 26 days a month and serves an average of 240 customers per day:

Average purchase	$1.45
Days open per month	26
Average number of customers per day	240

From the information given above, it is possible to calculate the store's average monthly profit. Total revenue is equal to 240 customers × $1.45 per

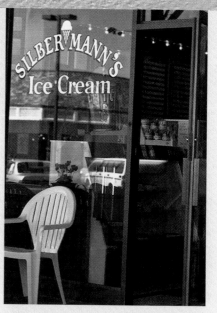

MARGINAL ANALYSIS IS AS IMPORTANT TO THE OWNER OF A SMALL ICE CREAM STORE AS IT IS TO THE MANAGERS OF MILLION-DOLLAR OPERATIONS.

customer × 26 open days in an average month: $TR = \$9,048$ per month.

PROFITS

The store sells 240 servings per day. Because there are 12 servings of ice cream per gallon, the store uses exactly 20 gallons per day (240 servings divided by 12). Total costs are $3.27 × 20, or $65.40, per day for ice cream and $12 per day for toppings (240 × $.05). The cost of variable labor is $5.54 × 8

THE SHORT-RUN SUPPLY CURVE

Consider how the typical firm shown in Figure 8.10 would behave in response to an increase in price. In Figure 8.11a, assume that something causes demand to increase (shift to the right), driving price from $5 to $6 and finally to $7. When price is $5, a profit-maximizing firm will choose output level 300 in Figure 8.11b. To produce any less, or to raise output above that level, would lead to a lower level of profit. At $6 the hours × 2 workers, or $88.64 per day. Total variable costs are therefore $166.04 ($65.40 + $12.00 + $88.64) per day. The store is open 26 days a month, so the total variable cost per month is $4,317.04.

Adding fixed costs of $3,435 to variable costs of $4,317.04, we get total cost of operation of $7,752.04 per month. Thus, the firm is averaging a profit of $1,295.96 per month ($9,048 − 7,752.04). *But this is not an "economic profit" because we haven't accounted for the opportunity cost of the owner's time and efforts.* In fact, when we factor in an implicit wage of $2,500 per month for the owner, we see that the store is suffering *losses of $1,204.04 per month* ($1,295.96 − $2,500).

Total Revenue (*TR*) $9,048.00
Total Fixed Cost (*TFC*) 3,435.00
+Total Variable Cost (*TVC*). . 4,317.04
Total Costs (*TC*). 7,752.04

Total Profit (*TR* − *TC*). 1,295.96
Adjustment for Implicit
   Wage. 2,500.00
Economic Profit   − 1,204.04

Should the entrepreneur stay in business? If she wants to make $2,500 per month and she thinks that nothing about her business will change, she must shut down in the long run. But two things keep her going: (1) a decision to stay open longer and (2) hope for more customers in the future.

OPENING LONGER HOURS: MARGINAL COSTS AND MARGINAL REVENUES

The store's normal hours of operation are noon until 8 P.M. On an experimental basis, the owner extends its hours until 11 P.M. for one month. The following table shows the average number of additional customers for each of the added hours:

Hour	Customers
8–9 P.M.	41
9–10 P.M.	20
10–11 P.M.	8

Assuming that the late customers spend an average of $1.45, we can calculate the marginal revenue and the marginal cost of staying open longer. The marginal cost of one serving of ice cream is

$3.27 divided by 12 = $0.27 + .05 (for topping) = $0.32. (See table below.)

Marginal analysis tells us that the store should stay open for two additional hours. Each day that the store stays open from 8 to 9 P.M. it will make an added profit of $59.45 − $24.20, or $35.25. Staying open from 9 to 10 P.M. adds $29.00 − $17.48, or $11.52, to profit. Staying open the third hour, however, *decreases* profits because the marginal revenue generated by staying open from 10 to 11 P.M. is less than the marginal cost. The entrepreneur decides to stay open for two additional hours per day. This adds $46.77 ($35.25 + 11.52) to profits each day, a total of $1,216.02 per month.

By adding the two hours, the store turns an economic loss of $1,204.04 per month into a small ($11.98) profit after accounting for the owner's implicit wage of $2,500 per month.

The owner decided to stay in business. She now serves over 350 customers per day, and the price of a dish of ice cream has risen to $2.50 while costs have not changed very much. In 1998, she cleared a profit of nearly $10,000 per month!

HOUR	MARGINAL REVENUE (MR)	MARGINAL COST (MC)		ADDED PROFIT PER HOUR (MR − MC)
8–9 P.M.	$1.45 × 41 = $59.45	Ice Cream: $0.32 × 41 = Labor: 2 × $5.54 = Total	$13.12 11.08 $24.20	$35.25
9–10 P.M.	$1.45 × 20 = $29.00	Ice Cream: $0.32 × 20 = Labor: 2 × $5.54 = Total	$ 6.40 11.08 $17.48	$11.52
10–11 P.M.	$1.45 × 8 = $11.60	Ice Cream: $0.32 × 8 = Labor: 2 × $5.54 = Total	$ 2.56 11.08 $13.64	$−2.04

For more on marginal analysis, see the Case and Fair Web at
http://www.prenhall.com/casefair.

same firm would increase output to 350, but it would stop there. Similarly, at $7, the firm would raise output to 400 units of output.

The *MC* curve in Figure 8.11b relates price and quantity supplied. At any market price, the marginal cost curve shows the output level that maximizes profit. A curve that shows how much output a profit-maximizing firm will produce at every price also fits the definition of a supply curve. (Review chapter 4 if this point is not clear to you.) It, therefore, follows that:

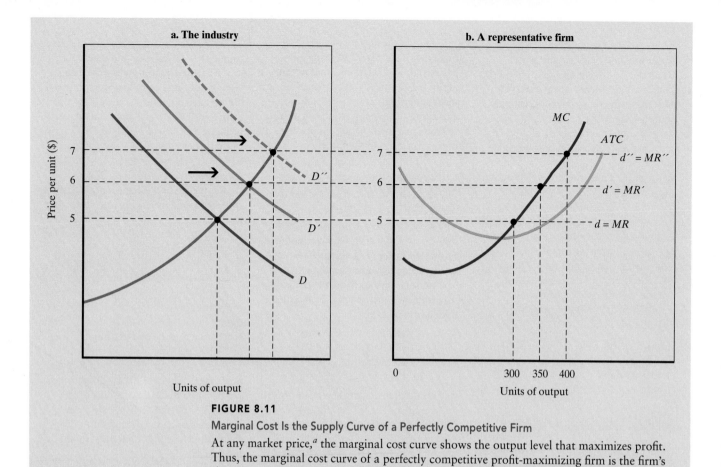

FIGURE 8.11

Marginal Cost Is the Supply Curve of a Perfectly Competitive Firm

At any market price,[a] the marginal cost curve shows the output level that maximizes profit. Thus, the marginal cost curve of a perfectly competitive profit-maximizing firm is the firm's short-run supply curve.

---

[a]*This is true except when price is so low that it pays a firm to shut down—a point that will be discussed in chapter 9.*

> The marginal cost curve of a competitive firm is the firm's short-run supply curve.

But as you will see, one very important exception exists to this general rule: There is some price level below which the firm will shut down its operations and simply bear losses equal to fixed costs even if price is above marginal cost. This important point is discussed in chapter 9.

LOOKING AHEAD

At the beginning of this chapter we set out to combine information on technology, factor prices, and output prices to understand the supply curve of a competitive firm. We have now accomplished that goal.

Because marginal cost is such an important concept in microeconomics, you should carefully review any sections of this chapter that were unclear to you. Above all, keep in mind that the *marginal cost curve* carries information about both *input prices* and *technology*. The firm looks to output markets for information on potential revenues, and the current market price defines the firm's marginal revenue curve. The point where price (which is equal to marginal revenue in perfect competition) is just equal to marginal cost is the perfectly competitive firm's profit-maximizing level of output. Thus, with one important exception, the marginal cost curve *is* the perfectly competitive firm's supply curve in the short run.

In the next chapter, we turn to the long run. What happens when firms are free to choose their scale of operations without being limited by a fixed factor of production? Without diminishing returns that set in as a result of a fixed scale of production, what determines the shape of cost curves? What happens when new firms can enter industries in which profits are being earned? How do industries adjust when losses are being incurred? How does the structure of an industry evolve over time?

SUMMARY

1. Profit-maximizing firms make decisions in order to maximize profit (total revenue minus total cost).

2. To calculate production costs, firms must know two things: (1) the quantity and combination of inputs they need to produce their product, and (2) how much those inputs cost.

COSTS IN THE SHORT RUN

3. *Fixed costs* are costs that do not change with a firm's output. In the short run, firms cannot avoid them or change them, even if production is zero.

4. *Variable costs* are those costs that depend on the level of output chosen. Fixed costs plus variable costs equal *total costs* $(TC = TFC + TVC)$.

5. *Average fixed cost* (AFC) is total fixed cost divided by the quantity of output. As output rises, average fixed cost declines steadily because the same total is being spread over a larger and larger quantity of output. This phenomenon is called *spreading overhead*.

6. Numerous combinations of inputs can be used to produce a given level of output. *Total variable cost* (TVC) is the sum of all costs that vary with output in the short run.

7. *Marginal cost* (MC) is the increase in total cost that results from the production of one more unit of output. If a firm is producing 1,000 units, the additional cost of increasing output to 1,001 units is marginal cost. Marginal cost measures the cost of the additional inputs required to produce each successive unit of output. Because fixed costs do not change when output changes, marginal costs reflect changes in variable costs.

8. In the short run, a firm is limited by a fixed factor of production, or a fixed scale of plant. As a firm increases output, it will eventually find itself trapped by that scale. Because of the fixed scale, marginal cost eventually rises with output.

9. Marginal cost is the slope of the total variable cost curve. The total variable cost curve always has a positive slope,

because total costs always rise with output. But increasing marginal cost means that total costs ultimately rise at an increasing rate.

10. *Average variable cost* (AVC) is equal to total variable cost divided by the quantity of output.

11. When marginal cost is above average variable cost, average variable cost is *increasing*. When marginal cost is below average variable cost, average variable cost is *declining*. Marginal cost intersects average variable cost at AVC's minimum point.

12. *Average total cost* (ATC) is equal to total cost divided by the quantity of output. It is also equal to the sum of average fixed cost and average variable cost.

13. If marginal cost is below average total cost, average total cost will decline toward marginal cost. If marginal cost is above average total cost, average total cost will increase. Marginal cost intersects average total cost at ATC's minimum point.

OUTPUT DECISIONS: REVENUES, COSTS, AND PROFIT MAXIMIZATION

14. A perfectly competitive firm faces a demand curve that is a horizontal line (in other words, perfectly elastic demand).

15. *Total revenue* (TR) is simply price times the quantity of output that a firm decides to produce and sell. *Marginal revenue* (MR) is the additional revenue that a firm takes in when it increases output by one unit.

16. For a perfectly competitive firm, marginal revenue is equal to the current market price of its product.

17. A profit-maximizing firm in a perfectly competitive industry will produce up to the point at which the price of its output is just equal to short-run marginal cost: $P = MC$. The more general profit-maximizing formula is $MR = MC$ ($P = MR$ in perfect competition). The marginal cost curve of a perfectly competitive firm is the firm's short-run supply curve, with one exception (discussed in chapter 9).

REVIEW TERMS AND CONCEPTS

1. $TC = TFC + TVC$

2. $AFC = TFC/q$

3. slope of $TVC = MC$

4. $AVC = TVC/q$

5. $ATC = TC/q = AFC + AVC$

6. $TR = P \times q$

7. Profit-maximizing level of output for all firms: $MR = MC$

8. Profit-maximizing level of output for perfectly competitive firms: $P = MC$

PROBLEM SET

1. The following table gives capital and labor requirements for 10 different levels of production:

q	K	L
0	0	0
1	2	5
2	4	9
3	6	12
4	8	15
5	10	19
6	12	24
7	14	30
8	16	37
9	18	45
10	20	54

a. Assuming that the price of labor (P_L) is $5 per unit and the price of capital (P_K) is $10 per unit, compute and graph the total variable cost curve, the marginal cost curve, and the average variable cost curve for the firm.

b. Do the curves have the shapes that you might expect? Explain.

c. Using the numbers here, explain the relationship between marginal cost and average variable cost.

d. Using the numbers here, explain the meaning of "marginal cost" in terms of additional inputs needed to produce a marginal unit of output.

e. If output price was $57, how many units of output would the firm produce? Explain.

2. Do you agree or disagree with each of the following statements? Explain your reasons.

a. If marginal cost is rising, average cost must also be rising.

b. A profit-maximizing firm must minimize cost. Thus firms will always produce the level of output at which average total cost is minimized.

c. Average fixed cost does not change as output changes.

3. A firm's cost curves are given by the following table:

Q	TC	TFC	TVC	AVC	ATC	MC
0	$100	$100				
1	130	100				
2	150	100				
3	160	100				
4	172	100				
5	185	100				
6	210	100				
7	240	100				
8	280	100				
9	330	100				
10	390	100				

a. Complete the table.

b. Graph AVC, ATC, and MC on the same graph. What is the relationship between the MC curve and ATC? Between MC and AVC?

c. Suppose that market price is $30. How much will the firm produce in the short run? How much are total profits?

d. Suppose that market price is $50. How much will the firm produce in the short run? What are total profits?

e. Suppose that market price is $10. How much would the firm produce in the short run? What are total profits?

4. A 1998 Berkeley graduate inherited her mother's printing company. The capital stock of the firm consists of three machines of various vintages, all in excellent condition. All machines can be running at the same time:

	COST OF PRINTING AND BINDING PER BOOK	MAXIMUM TOTAL CAPACITY PER MONTH
Machine 1	$1.00	100 books
Machine 2	$2.00	200 books
Machine 3	$3.00	500 books

a. Assume that "cost of printing and binding per book" includes *all* labor and materials, including the owner's own wages. Assume further that Mom signed a long-term contract (50 years) with a service company to keep the machines in good repair for a fixed fee of $100 per month.
 (1) Derive the firm's marginal cost curve.
 (2) Derive the firm's total cost curve.

b. At a price of $2.50, how many books would the company produce? What would total revenues be? Total costs? Total profits?

5. The following curve is a production function for a firm that uses just one variable factor of production, labor. It shows total output, or product, for every level of inputs:
 a. Derive and graph the marginal product curve.
 b. Suppose that the wage rate is $4. Derive and graph the firm's marginal cost curve.
 c. If output sells for $6, what is the profit-maximizing level of output? How much labor will the firm hire?

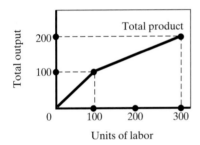

6. Elena and Emmanuel live on the Black Sea in Bulgaria and own a small fishing boat. A crew of four is required to take the boat out fishing. The current wage paid to the four crew members is a total of 5,000 levs per day (a lev is the Bulgarian unit of currency). Assume that the cost of operating and maintaining the boat is 1,000 levs per day when fishing, and zero otherwise. The following schedule gives the appropriate catch for each period during the year:

PERIOD	CATCH PER DAY
Prime fishing: 180 days	100 kilograms
Month 7: 30 days	80 kilograms
Month 8: 30 days	60 kilograms
Rest of the year	40 kilograms

The price of fish in Bulgaria is no longer regulated by the government, and is now determined in competitive markets.

Suppose that the price has been stable all year at 80 levs per kilogram.
 a. What is the marginal product of a day's worth of fishing during prime fishing season? During month 7? During month 8?
 b. What is the marginal cost of a kilogram of fish during prime fishing season? During month 7? During month 8? During the rest of the year?
 c. If you were Elena and Emmanuel, how many months per year would you hire the crew and go out fishing? Explain your answer using marginal logic.

7. For each of the following businesses, what is the likely fixed factor of production that defines the short run?
 a. a 160-acre potato farm
 b. a Chinese restaurant
 c. a dentist in private practice
 d. a car dealership
 e. a bank

8. A producer of hard disk drives for notebook computers currently has a factory with two disk-pressing machines, which it cannot change in the short run. Each of the machines costs $100 per day (the opportunity cost of the funds used to buy them). Each hired worker costs $50 per day. The relationship between output and the number of workers is as follows:

Q	L	TFC	TVC	TC	AFC	AVC	ATC	MC
0	0							
1	10							
2	15							
3	18							
4	22							
5	28							
6	36							
7	48							

a. Fill in the columns for total fixed cost (*TFC*), total variable cost (*TVC*), total cost (*TC*), average fixed cost (*AFC*), average variable cost (*AVC*), average total cost (*ATC*), and marginal cost (*MC*).
 b. Verify that the two alternative methods of figuring *ATC* (*TC/q* and *AVC* + *AFC*) give the same answer (except for rounding).
 c. Over what range of output are there decreasing marginal costs? Increasing marginal costs? Increasing returns to labor? Diminishing returns to labor?
 d. At which level of output is *AVC* minimized? At which level is *ATC* minimized?
 e. Suppose this firm operates in a perfectly competitive output market and can sell as many disk drives as it wants for $410 each. In the short run, what is the profit-maximizing level of output for this firm?
 f. Does the profit-maximizing output level you found above minimize average total costs? If not, how could the firm be maximizing profits if it is not minimizing costs?

*9. Why do newspaper boxes use a simple technology that allows occasional cheaters to remove more than one newspaper, while soft-drink machines use a more complicated technology to ensure that each customer gets only one drink? (*Hint:* There are at least two explanations for this phenomenon. One involves the concept of marginal cost; the other relies on the concept of marginal utility.)

TAKE IT TO THE NET

We invite you to visit the Case and Fair page on the Prentice Hall Web site:

http://www.prenhall.com/casefair

for this chapter's World Wide Web exercise.

Chapter 9

COSTS AND OUTPUT DECISIONS IN THE LONG RUN

THE LAST TWO CHAPTERS discussed the behavior of profit-maximizing competitive firms in the short run. Recall that all firms must make three fundamental decisions: (1) how much output to produce or supply, (2) how to produce that output, and (3) how much of each input to demand.

Firms use information on input prices, output prices, and technology to make the decisions that will lead to the most profit. Because profits equal revenues minus costs, firms must know how much their products will sell for and how much production will cost, using the most efficient technology.

In chapter 8 we saw how cost curves can be derived from production functions and input prices. Once a firm has a clear picture of its short-run costs, the price at which it sells its output determines the quantity of output that will maximize profit. Specifically, a profit-maximizing perfectly competitive firm will supply output up to the point that price (marginal revenue) equals marginal cost. The marginal cost curve of such a firm is thus the same as its supply curve.

In this chapter, we turn from the short run to the long run. The condition in which firms find themselves in the short run (Are they making profits? Are they incurring losses?) determines what is likely to happen in the long run. Remember that output (supply) decisions in the long run are less constrained than in the short run, for two reasons. First, in the long run, the firm has no fixed factor of production that confines its production to a given scale. Second, firms are free to enter industries in order to seek profits and to leave industries in order to avoid losses.

The long run has important implications for the shape of cost curves. As we saw, in the short run a fixed factor of production eventually causes marginal cost to increase along with output. This is not the case in the long run, however. With no fixed scale, the shapes of cost curves become more complex and less easy to generalize about. The shapes of long-run cost curves have important implications for the way an industry's structure is likely to evolve over time.

We begin our discussion of the long run by looking at firms in three short-run circumstances: (1) firms earning economic profits, (2) firms suffering economic losses but continuing to operate to reduce or minimize those losses, and (3) firms that decide to shut down and bear losses just equal to fixed costs. We then examine how these firms will alter their decisions in response to these short-run conditions.

Although we continue to focus on perfectly competitive firms, it should be stressed that *all* firms are subject to the spectrum of short-run profit or loss situations, regardless of market structure. Assuming perfect competition allows us to simplify our analysis and provides us with a strong background for understanding the discussions of imperfectly competitive behavior in later chapters.

SHORT-RUN CONDITIONS AND LONG-RUN DIRECTIONS

Before beginning our examination of firm behavior, let us review the concept of profit. Recall that a normal rate of return is included in the definition of total cost (see chapter 7). A *normal rate of return* is a rate that is just sufficient to keep current investors interested in the industry. Because we define *profit* as total revenue minus total cost and because total cost includes a normal rate of return, our concept of profit takes into account the opportunity cost of capital. If a firm is earning an above-normal rate of return, it has a positive profit level, but otherwise not. When there are positive profits in an industry, new investors are likely to be attracted to the industry.

When we say that a firm is suffering a *loss*, we mean that it is earning a rate of return that is below normal. Such a firm may be suffering a loss as an accountant would measure it, or it may simply be earning at a very low (that is, below normal) rate. Investors are not going to be attracted to an industry in which there are losses. A firm that is **breaking even,** or earning a zero level of profit, is one that is earning exactly a normal rate of return. New investors are not attracted, but current ones are not running away either.

With these distinctions in mind, then, we can say that for any firm one of three conditions holds at any given moment: (1) The firm is making positive profits, (2) the firm is suffering losses, or (3) the firm is just breaking even. Profitable firms will want to maximize their profits in the short run, while firms suffering losses will want to minimize those losses in the short run.

breaking even *The situation in which a firm is earning exactly a normal rate of return.*

MAXIMIZING PROFITS

The best way to understand the behavior of a firm that is currently earning profits is by way of example.

▶ **Example: The Blue Velvet Car Wash** When a firm earns revenues in excess of costs (including a normal rate of return), it is earning positive profits. Let us take as an example the Blue Velvet Car Wash. Suppose that investors have put up $500,000 to construct a building and purchase all the equipment required to wash cars. Let's also suppose that investors expect to earn a minimum return of 10 percent on their investment. If the money to set up the business had been borrowed from the bank instead, the car wash owners would have paid a 10 percent interest rate. In either case, total cost must include $50,000 per year (10 percent of $500,000).

The car wash is open 50 weeks per year and is capable of washing up to 800 cars per week. Whether it is open and operating or not, the car wash has fixed costs. Those costs include $1,000 per week to investors (that is, the $50,000 per year normal return to investors) and $1,000 per week in other fixed costs (a basic maintenance contract on the equipment, insurance, and so forth).

When the car wash is operating, there are also variable costs. Workers must be paid, and materials such as soap and wax must be purchased. The wage bill is $1,000 per week. Materials, electricity, and so forth run $600 at full capacity. If the car wash is not in operation, there are no variable costs. Table 9.1 summarizes the costs of the Blue Velvet Car Wash.

This car wash business is quite competitive. There are many car washes of equal quality in the area, and they offer their service at $5. If Blue Velvet wants customers, it cannot charge a price above $5. (Recall the perfectly elastic demand curve facing perfectly competitive firms; review chapter 8 if necessary.) If we assume that Blue Velvet washes 800 cars each week, it takes in revenues of $4,000 from operating (800 cars × $5). Is this total revenue enough to make a positive profit?

The answer is yes. Revenues of $4,000 are sufficient to cover both fixed costs of $2,000 and variable costs of $1,600, leaving a positive profit of $400 per week.

▶ **Graphic Presentation** Figure 9.1 graphs the performance of a firm that is earning positive profits in the short run. Figure 9.1a illustrates the industry, or the market, and Figure 9.1b illustrates a representative firm. At present, the market is clearing at a price of $5. Thus, we assume that the individual firm can sell all it wants at a price of $P^* = \$5$, but that it is constrained by its capacity. Its marginal cost curve rises in the short run because of a fixed factor. You already know that a perfectly competitive profit-maximizing firm produces up to the point that price equals marginal cost. As long as price (marginal revenue) exceeds marginal cost, firms can push up profits by

TABLE 9.1

BLUE VELVET CAR WASH WEEKLY COSTS

TOTAL FIXED COSTS (*TFC*):	
1. Normal return to investors	$1,000
2. Other fixed costs (maintenance contract, insurance, etc.)	1,000
	$2,000
TOTAL VARIABLE COSTS (*TVC*) (800 WASHES):	
1. Labor	$1,000
2. Materials	600
	$1,600
TOTAL COSTS (*TC* = *TFC* + *TVC*):	$3,600
Total Revenue (*TR*) at *P* = $5 (800 × $5)	$4,000
Profit (*TR* − *TC*)	$400

FIGURE 9.1

Firm Earning Positive Profits in the Short Run

A profit-maximizing perfectly competitive firm will produce up to the point where $P^* = MC$. Profits are the difference between total revenue and total costs. At $q^* = 300$, total revenue is $5 \times 300 = \$1,500$, total cost is $\$4.20 \times 300 = \$1,260$; and total profit = $\$1,500 - \$1,260 = \$240$.

a. The industry

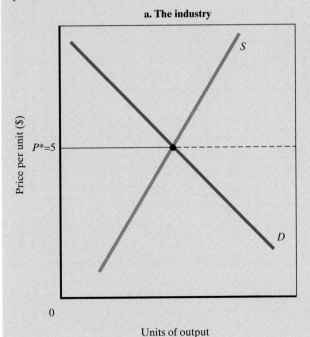

b. A representative firm

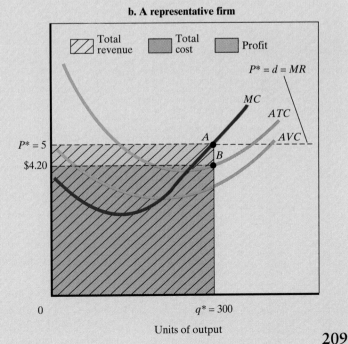

209

A BUSINESS LIKE THIS CAR WASH WILL OPERATE IN THE SHORT RUN IF AND ONLY IF REVENUES ARE SUFFICIENT TO COVER VARIABLE COSTS.

increasing short-run output. The firm in the diagram, then, will supply $q^* = 300$ units of output (point A, where $P = MC$).

Both revenues and costs are shown graphically. *Total revenue* (*TR*) is simply the product of price and quantity: $P^* \times q^* = \$5 \times 300 = \$1,500$. On the diagram, total revenue is equal to the area of the rectangle P^*Aq^*0. (The area of a rectangle is equal to its length times its width.) At output q^*, average total cost is $4.20 (point B). Numerically, it is equal to the length of line segment q^*B. Because average total cost is derived by dividing total cost by q, we can get back to total cost by *multiplying* average total cost by q. That is,

$$ATC = \frac{TC}{q}$$

and

$$TC = ATC \times q.$$

Total cost (*TC*), then, is $4.20 \times 300 = \$1,260$, the area shaded blue in the diagram. *Profit* is simply the difference between total revenue (*TR*) and total cost (*TC*), or $240. This is the area that is shaded pink in the diagram. This firm is earning positive profits.

A firm that is earning positive profits in the short run and expects to continue doing so has an incentive to expand its scale of operation in the long run. Those profits also give new firms an incentive to enter and compete in the market.

MINIMIZING LOSSES

A firm that is not earning positive profits or breaking even is suffering a loss. Firms suffering losses fall into two categories: (1) those that find it advantageous to shut down operations immediately and bear losses equal to fixed costs, and (2) those that continue to operate in the short run to minimize their losses. The most important thing to remember here is that firms cannot exit the industry in the short run. The firm can shut down, but it cannot get rid of its fixed costs by going out of business. Fixed costs must be paid in the short run no matter what the firm does.

Whether a firm suffering losses decides to produce or not to produce in the short run depends on the advantages and disadvantages of continuing production. If a firm shuts down, it earns no revenues and has no variable costs to bear. If it continues to produce, it both earns revenues and incurs variable costs. Because a firm must bear fixed costs *whether or not* it shuts down, its decision depends *solely on whether revenues from operating are sufficient to cover variable costs*. **Operating profit (or loss)** (sometimes called **net operating revenue**) is defined as total revenue (*TR*) minus total variable cost (*TVC*). In general:

operating profit (or loss) or **net operating revenue**
Total revenue minus total variable cost (TR − TVC).

- If revenues exceed variable costs, operating profit is positive and can be used to offset fixed costs and reduce losses, and it will pay the firm to keep operating.
- If revenues are smaller than variable costs, the firm suffers operating losses that push total losses above fixed costs. In this case, the firm can minimize its losses by shutting down.

➤ **Producing at a Loss to Offset Fixed Costs: The Blue Velvet Revisited**   Suppose that competitive pressure pushes the price per wash down to $3. Total revenues for Blue Velvet would fall to $2,400 per week (800 cars × $3). If variable costs remained at $1,600, total costs would be $3,600 ($1,600 + $2,000 fixed costs), a figure higher than total revenues. The firm would then be suffering losses of $3,600 − $2,400 = $1,200.

In the long run, Blue Velvet may want to go out of business, but in the short run it is stuck, and it must decide what to do.

TABLE 9.2 — A FIRM WILL OPERATE IF TOTAL REVENUE COVERS TOTAL VARIABLE COST

CASE 1: SHUT DOWN		CASE 2: OPERATE AT PRICE = $3	
Total Revenue (q = 0):	$0	Total Revenue ($3 × 800):	$2,400
Fixed costs	$2,000	Fixed costs	$2,000
Variable costs	+ 0	Variable costs	+1,600
Total costs	$2,000	Total costs	$3,600
Profit/Loss (TR − TC):	− $2,000	Operating Profit/Loss (TR − TVC):	$800
		Total Profit/Loss (TR − TC):	− $1,200

The car wash has two options: operate or shut down. If it shuts down, it has no variable costs, but it also earns no revenues, and its losses will be equal to its fixed costs of $2,000 (Table 9.2, Case 1). If it decides to stay open (Table 9.2, Case 2), it will make operating profits. Revenues will be $2,400, more than sufficient to cover variable costs of $1,600. By operating, the firm gains $800 per week operating profits that it can use to offset its fixed costs. By operating, then, the firm reduces its losses from $2,000 to $1,200.

▶ **Graphic Presentation**   Figure 9.2 graphs a firm suffering losses. The market price, set by the forces of supply and demand, is $P^* = \$3.50$. If the firm decides to operate, it will do best by producing up to the point where price (marginal revenue) is equal to marginal cost—in this case, at an output of $q^* = 225$ units.

Once again, total revenue (TR) is simply the product of price and quantity $(P^* \times q^*) = \$3.50 \times 225 = \$787.50$, or the area of rectangle P^*Aq^*0. Average total cost at $q^* = 225$ is $4.10, and it is equal to the length of q^*B. Total cost is the product of average total cost and q^* $(ATC \times q^*)$, or $\$4.10 \times 225 = \$922.50$. Because total cost is greater than total revenue, the firm is suffering losses of $135, shown on the graph by the gray shaded rectangle.

Operating profit—the difference between total revenue and total *variable* cost—can also be identified. On the graph, total revenue (as we said) is $787.50. *Average variable cost* at q^* is the length of q^*E. Total variable cost is the product of average variable cost and q^* and is therefore equal to $\$3.10 \times 225 = \$697.50$. Profit on operation is thus $787.50 − $697.50 = $90, the area of the pink shaded rectangle.

Remember that average total cost is equal to average fixed cost plus average variable cost. This means that at every level of output average fixed cost is the difference between average total and average variable cost:

$$ATC = AFC + AVC$$

or

$$AFC = ATC - AVC = \$4.10 - \$3.10 = \$1.00$$

In Figure 9.2, therefore, average fixed cost is equal to the length of BE (the difference between ATC and AVC at q^*, or $1.00). Because total fixed cost is simply average fixed cost $1.00 times $q^* = \$225$, total fixed cost is equal to $225, the entire gray and pink shaded rectangle. Thus, if the firm had shut down, its losses would be equal to $225. By operating, the firm earns an operating profit equal to the pink shaded area ($90) covering some fixed costs and reducing losses to the gray shaded area ($135).

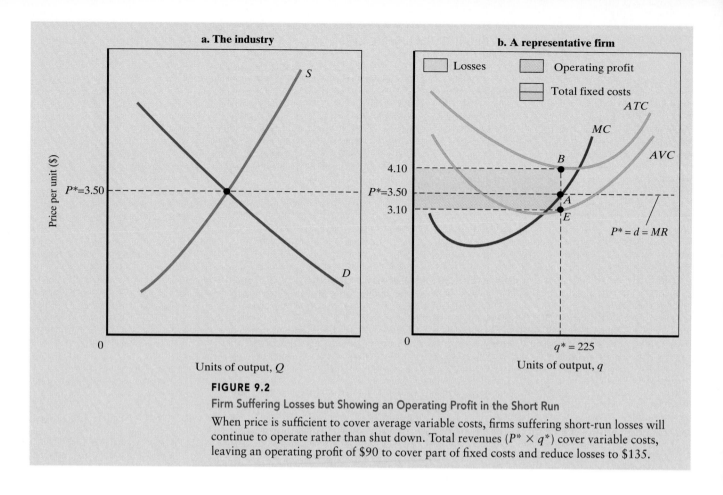

a. The industry

S

$P^*=3.50$

D

Price per unit ($)

0

Units of output, Q

b. A representative firm

Losses   Operating profit

Total fixed costs

ATC

MC

AVC

4.10 ---- B

$P^*=3.50$ ---- A

3.10 ----
E

$P^* = d = MR$

0

$q^* = 225$

Units of output, q

FIGURE 9.2

Firm Suffering Losses but Showing an Operating Profit in the Short Run

When price is sufficient to cover average variable costs, firms suffering short-run losses will continue to operate rather than shut down. Total revenues ($P^* \times q^*$) cover variable costs, leaving an operating profit of $90 to cover part of fixed costs and reduce losses to $135.

If we think only in averages, it seems logical that a firm in this position will continue to operate:

> As long as price (which is equal to average revenue per unit) is sufficient to cover average variable costs, the firm stands to gain by operating rather than by shutting down.

➤ **Shutting Down to Minimize Loss**   When revenues are insufficient to cover even variable costs, firms suffering losses find it advantageous to shut down, even in the short run.

Suppose, for example, that competition and the availability of sophisticated new machinery pushed the price of a car wash all the way down to $1.50. Washing 800 cars per week would then yield revenues of only $1,200 (Table 9.3). With variable costs at $1,600, operating would mean losing an additional $400 *over and above* fixed costs of $2,000. This means that total losses would amount to $2,400. Clearly, a profit-maximizing/loss-minimizing car wash would reduce its losses from $2,400 to $2,000 by shutting down, even in the short run.

> Any time that price (average revenue) is below the minimum point on the average variable cost curve, total revenue will be less than total variable cost, and operating profit will be negative—that is, there will be a loss on operation. In other words, when price is below all points on the average variable cost curve, the firm will suffer operating losses at any possible output level the firm could choose. When this is the case, the firm will stop producing and bear losses equal to fixed costs. This is

| TABLE 9.3 | A FIRM WILL SHUT DOWN IF TOTAL REVENUE IS LESS THAN TOTAL VARIABLE COST |

CASE 1: SHUT DOWN		CASE 2: OPERATE AT PRICE = $1.50	
Total Revenue (q = 0):	$0	Total Revenue ($1.50 × 800):	$1,200
Fixed costs	$2,000	Fixed costs	$2,000
Variable costs	+ 0	Variable costs	+1,600
Total costs	$2,000	Total costs	$3,600
Profit/Loss (*TR* − *TC*):	−$2,000	Operating Profit/Loss (*TR* − *TVC*):	−$400
		Total Profit/Loss (*TR* − *TC*):	−$2,400

why the bottom of the average variable cost curve is called the **shut-down point**. At all prices above it, the *MC* curve shows the profit-maximizing level of output. At all prices below it, optimal short-run output is zero.

We can now refine our earlier statement that a perfectly competitive firm's marginal cost curve is actually its short-run supply curve. Recall that a profit-maximizing perfectly competitive firm will produce up to the point at which $P = MC$. As we have just seen, though, a firm will shut down when P is less than the minimum point on the *AVC* curve. Also recall that the marginal cost curve intersects the *AVC* curve at *AVC*'s lowest point. It therefore follows that:

The short-run supply curve of a competitive firm is that portion of its marginal cost curve that lies above its average variable cost curve (Figure 9.3).

THE SHORT-RUN INDUSTRY SUPPLY CURVE

Supply in a competitive industry is simply the sum of the quantity supplied by the individual firms in the industry at each price level. The **short-run industry supply curve** is the sum of the individual firm supply curves—that is, the marginal cost curves (above

shut-down point *The lowest point on the average variable cost curve. When price falls below the minimum point on AVC, total revenue is insufficient to cover variable costs and the firm will shut down and bear losses equal to fixed costs.*

short-run industry supply curve *The sum of marginal cost curves (above AVC) of all the firms in an industry.*

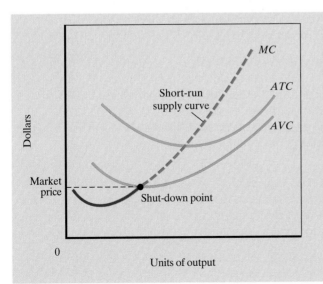

FIGURE 9.3

Short-Run Supply Curve of a Perfectly Competitive Firm

At prices below average variable cost, it pays a firm to shut down rather than to continue operating. Thus, the short-run supply curve of a competitive firm is the part of its marginal cost curve that lies *above* its average variable cost curve.

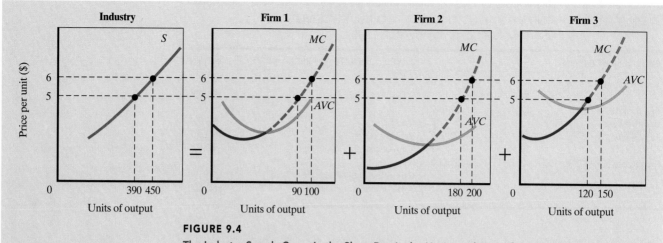

FIGURE 9.4

The Industry Supply Curve in the Short Run Is the Horizontal Sum of the Marginal Cost Curves (above *AVC*) of All the Firms in an Industry

If there are only three firms in the industry, the industry supply curve is simply the sum of all the products supplied by the three firms at each price. For example, at $6, firm 1 supplies 100 units, firm 2 supplies 200 units, and firm 3 supplies 150 units, for a total industry supply of 450.

AVC) of all the firms in the industry. Because quantities are being added (that is, because we are finding the total quantity supplied in the industry at each price level), the curves are added horizontally.

Figure 9.4 shows the supply curve for an industry with just three firms.[1] At a price of $6, firm 1 produces 100 units, the output where *P = MC*. Firm 2 produces 200 units, and firm 3 produces 150 units. The total amount supplied on the market at a price of $6 is thus 450 (100 + 200 + 150). At a price of $5, firm 1 produces 90 units, firm 2 produces 180 units, and firm 3 produces 120 units. At a price of $5, the industry thus supplies 390 units (90 + 180 + 120).

Two things can cause the industry supply curve to shift. In the short run, the industry supply curve shifts if something—an increase in the price of some input, for instance—shifts the marginal cost curves of all the individual firms simultaneously. For example, when the cost of producing components of home computers decreased, the marginal cost curves of all computer manufacturers shifted downward. Such a shift amounted to the same thing as an outward shift in their supply curves. Each firm was willing to supply more computers at each price level because computers were now cheaper to produce.

In the long run, an increase or decrease in the number of firms—and, therefore, in the number of individual firms' supply curves—shifts the total industry supply curve. If new firms enter the industry, the industry supply curve moves to the right; if firms exit the industry, the industry supply curve moves to the left.

We return to shifts in industry supply curves and discuss them further when we take up long-run adjustments later in this chapter.

LONG-RUN DIRECTIONS: A REVIEW

Table 9.4 summarizes the different circumstances that perfectly competitive firms may face as they plan for the long run. Profit-making firms will produce up to the point where price and marginal cost are equal in the short run. If there are positive profits, in

[1]Perfectly competitive industries are assumed to have many firms. Many is, of course, more than three. We use three firms here simply for the purposes of illustration.

TABLE 9.4 PROFITS, LOSSES, AND PERFECTLY COMPETITIVE FIRMS' DECISIONS IN THE LONG AND SHORT RUN

	SHORT-RUN CONDITION	SHORT-RUN DECISION	LONG-RUN DECISION
Profits		$P = MC$: operate	Expand: new firms enter
Losses	1. With operating profit ($TR \geq TVC$)	$P = MC$: operate (losses < fixed costs)	Contract: firms exit
	2. With operating losses ($TR < TVC$)	Shut down: losses = fixed costs	Contract: firms exit

the long run there is an incentive for firms to expand their scales of plant and for new firms to enter the industry.

Firms suffering losses will produce if, and only if, revenues are sufficient to cover variable costs. If a firm can earn a profit on operations, it can reduce the losses it would suffer if it shut down. Such firms, like profitable firms, will also produce up to the point where $P = MC$. If firms suffering losses cannot cover variable costs by operating, they will shut down and bear losses equal to fixed costs. Whether or not a firm that is suffering losses decides to shut down in the short run, it has an incentive to contract in the long run. The simple fact is that when firms are suffering losses, they will generally exit the industry in the long run.

In the short run, a firm's decision about how much to produce depends on the market price of its product and the shapes of its cost curves. Remember that the short-run cost curves show costs that are determined by the *current* scale of plant. In the long run, however, firms have to choose among many *potential* scales of plant.

The long-run decisions of individual firms depend on what their costs are likely to be at different scales of operation. Just as firms have to analyze different technologies to arrive at a cost structure in the short run, they must also compare their costs at different scales of plant to arrive at long-run costs. Perhaps a larger scale of operations will reduce production costs and provide an even greater incentive for a profit-making firm to expand. Or perhaps large firms will run into problems that constrain growth. The analysis of long-run possibilities is even more complex than the short-run analysis, because more things are variable—scale of plant is not fixed, for example, and there are no fixed costs because firms can exit their industry in the long run. In theory, firms may choose *any* scale of operation, and so they must analyze many possible options.

Now let us turn to an analysis of cost curves in the long run.

LONG-RUN COSTS: ECONOMIES AND DISECONOMIES OF SCALE

The shapes of short-run cost curves follow directly from the assumption of a fixed factor of production. As output increases beyond a certain point, the fixed factor (which we usually think of as fixed scale of plant) causes diminishing returns to other factors and thus increasing marginal costs. In the long run, however, there is no fixed factor of production. Firms can choose any scale of production. They can double or triple output or go out of business completely.

The shape of a firm's *long-run* average cost curve depends on how costs vary with scale of operations. For some firms, increased scale, or size, reduces costs. For others, increased scale leads to inefficiency and waste. When an increase in a firm's scale of production leads to lower average costs, we say that there are **increasing returns to scale,** or **economies of scale.** When average costs do not change with the scale of production, we say that there are **constant returns to scale.** Finally, when an increase in a firm's scale of production leads to higher average costs, we say that there are **decreasing returns to scale,** or **diseconomies of scale.** Because these economies of scale all are found within the individual firm, they are considered *internal* economies of scale. In the appendix to this chapter, we talk about *external* economies of scale, which describe economies or diseconomies of scale on an industrywide basis.

INCREASING RETURNS TO SCALE

Technically, the phrase *increasing returns to scale* refers to the relationship between inputs and outputs. When we say that a production function exhibits increasing returns, we mean that a given percentage increase in inputs leads to a *larger* percentage increase in the production of output. For example, if a firm doubled or tripled inputs, it would more than double or triple output.

When firms can count on fixed input prices—that is, when the prices of inputs do not change with output levels—increasing returns to scale also means that as output rises, average cost of production falls. The term *economies of scale* refers directly to this reduction in cost per unit of output that follows from larger-scale production.

▶ **The Sources of Economies of Scale** Most of the economies of scale that immediately come to mind are technological in nature. Automobile production, for example, would be much more costly per unit if a firm were to produce 100 cars per year by hand. Early in this century, Henry Ford introduced standardized production techniques that increased output volume, reduced costs per car, and made the automobile available to almost everyone.

Some economies of scale result not from technology but from sheer size. Very large companies, for instance, can buy inputs in volume at discounted prices. Large firms may also produce some of their own inputs at considerable savings. And they can certainly save in transport costs when they ship items in bulk.

Economies of scale can be seen all around us. A bus that carries 100 people between Vancouver and Seattle uses less labor, capital, and gasoline than 100 people driving 100 different automobiles. The cost per passenger (average cost) is lower on the bus. Roommates who share an apartment are taking advantage of economies of scale. Costs per person for heat, electricity, and space are lower when an apartment is shared than if each person rented a separate apartment.

▶ **Example: Economies of Scale in Egg Production** Nowhere are economies of scale more visible than in agriculture. Consider the following example. A few years ago a major agribusiness moved into a small Ohio town and set up a huge egg-producing operation. The new firm, Chicken Little Egg Farms Inc., is completely mechanized. Complex machines feed the chickens and collect and box the eggs. Large refrigerated trucks transport the eggs all over the state daily. In the same town, some small farmers still own fewer than 200 chickens. These farmers collect the eggs, feed the chickens, clean the coops by hand, and deliver the eggs to county markets.

Table 9.5 presents some hypothetical cost data for Homer Jones's small operation and for Chicken Little Inc. Jones has his operation working well. He has several hundred chickens and spends about 15 hours per week feeding, collecting, delivering, and so forth. In the rest of his time he raises soybeans. We can value Jones's time at $8 per hour, because that is the wage he could earn working at a local manufacturing plant. When we add up all Jones's costs, including a rough estimate of the land and capital costs attributable to egg production, we arrive at $177 per week. Total production on the Jones farm runs about 200 dozen, or 2,400, eggs per week, which means that Jones's average cost comes out to $.074 per egg.

TABLE 9.5

TABLE 9.5   WEEKLY COSTS SHOWING ECONOMIES OF SCALE IN EGG PRODUCTION

JONES FARM	TOTAL WEEKLY COSTS
15 hours of labor (implicit value $8 per hour)	$120
Feed, other variable costs	25
Transport costs	15
Land and capital costs attributable to egg production	17
	$177
Total output	2,400 eggs
Average cost	$.074 per egg

CHICKEN LITTLE EGG FARMS INC.	TOTAL WEEKLY COSTS
Labor	$5,128
Feed, other variable costs	4,115
Transport Costs	2,431
Land and capital costs	19,230
	$30,904
Total output	1,600,000 eggs
Average cost	$.019 per egg

The costs of Chicken Little Inc. are much higher in total; weekly costs run over $30,000. A much higher percentage of costs are capital costs—the firm uses lots of sophisticated machinery that cost millions to put in place. Total output is 1.6 million eggs per week, and the product is shipped all over the Midwest. The comparatively huge scale of plant has driven average production costs all the way down to $.019 per egg.

While these numbers are hypothetical, you can see why small farmers in the United States are finding it difficult to compete with large-scale agribusiness concerns that can realize significant economies of scale. For more on this topic, see the Application Box titled "Why Small Farmers Have Trouble Competing: Economies of Scale in Agriculture and Hog Raising."

▶ **Graphic Presentation**   A firm's **long-run average cost curve (*LRAC*)** shows the different scales on which it can choose to operate in the long run. In other words, a firm's *LRAC* curve traces out the position of all its possible short-run curves, each corresponding to a different scale. At any time, the existing scale of plant determines the position and shape of the firm's short-run cost curves. But the firm must consider in its long-run strategic planning whether to build a plant of a *different* scale. The long-run average cost curve simply shows the positions of the different sets of short-run curves among which the firm must choose. The long-run average cost curve is the "envelope" of a series of short-run curves; it "wraps around" the set of all possible short-run curves like an envelope. (Later in this chapter, the Issues and Debates titled "The Long-Run Average Cost Curve: Flat or U-Shaped?" describes the debate on how the *LRAC* is constructed.)

Figure 9.5 shows short-run and long-run average cost curves for a firm that realizes economies of scale up to about 100,000 units of production and roughly constant returns to scale after that. The diagram shows three potential scales of operation, each with its own set of short-run cost curves. Each point on the *LRAC* curve represents the minimum cost at which the associated output level can be produced.

Once the firm chooses a scale on which to produce, it becomes locked into one set of cost curves in the short run. If the firm were to settle on Scale 1, it would not realize the major cost advantages of producing on a larger scale. By roughly doubling its scale of operations from 50,000 to 100,000 units (Scale 2), the firm reduces average costs per unit significantly.

long-run average cost curve (*LRAC*) *A graph that shows the different scales on which a firm can choose to operate in the long run.*

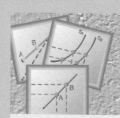

WHY SMALL FARMERS HAVE TROUBLE COMPETING: ECONOMIES OF SCALE IN AGRICULTURE AND HOG RAISING

Economies of scale, or increasing returns to scale, exist when larger firms have lower average costs than smaller firms. If economies of scale exist in agriculture, one would expect the average size of farms to increase over time as smaller operations find themselves unable to compete. Indeed, over the past 21 years, the number of farms in the United States has dropped by 18 percent and average farm size has increased by 12 percent:

AS A RESULT OF ECONOMIES OF SCALE IN AGRICULTURE, FAMILY-OWNED FARMS ARE INCREASINGLY BEING REPLACED BY LARGE-SCALE AGRIBUSINESSES. ECONOMIES OF SCALE ARE NOT ONLY PRESENT IN SUGAR BEET AND OTHER PRODUCE FARMING (LEFT), BUT ALSO IN HOG AND OTHER LIVESTOCK FARMING (RIGHT).

YEAR	NUMBER OF FARMS	AVERAGE SIZE (ACRES)
1975	2,521	420
1980	2,440	426
1985	2,293	441
1990	2,146	460
1996	2,063	469

Numerous studies have found evidence of scale economies in farming. In a recent article in the *Journal of Economic History*, Nancy Virts found that large-scale tenant plantations in the post–Civil War South had cost advantages over smaller plantations. In another article in the *American Journal of Agricultural Economics*, Stephen Cooke found that between 1974 and 1983 very large corn producers (500–1,000 acres) were 4 to 8 percent more cost-efficient than large producers (300–460 acres) and 8 to 15 percent more cost-efficient than medium-sized producers (175–290 acres).[a]

In 1994, the U.S. hog industry felt the presence of scale economies dramatically, as large-scale production techniques were introduced into the industry. With production increasing, prices fell sharply:

Hog prices were gutted yesterday as a record slaughter rate underscored the ongoing supply glut.

December live hogs plunged 70 cents to $32.70 per hundredweight.

The Agriculture Department said late Friday that 2.055 million hogs were slaughtered last week. It was the highest weekly slaughter on record. . . . The huge slaughter rate was no surprise, said Chuck Levitt, senior analyst with Alaron Trading

Corp. The expanded capacity of huge commercial hog-producing operations are resulting in more supply, he explained. These mega-producers operate at a lower average cost than the traditional small-and-medium sized farmers, and so can more easily survive the price slump.[b]

Sources: [a]Nancy Virts, "The Efficiency of Southern Tenant Plantations, 1900–1945," *Journal of Economic History* 51(2), June 1991, 385–395; Stephen Cooke, "Cost Efficiency in U.S. Corn Production," *American Journal of Agricultural Economics* 71(4), November 1989, 1003–1010; [b]Quote from: Donald Gold, "Hogs Fall to New 14-Year Low; Analysts Cite Relentless Supply," *Investor's Business Daily*, November 8, 1994, p. B7.

For more on economies of scale, see the Case and Fair Web page at http://www.prenhall.com/casefair.

Figure 9.5 shows that at every moment firms face two different cost constraints. In the long run, firms can change their scale of operation, and costs may be different as a result. But at any *given* moment, a particular scale of operation exists, constraining the firm's capacity to produce in the short run. That is why we see both short- and long-run curves in the same diagram.

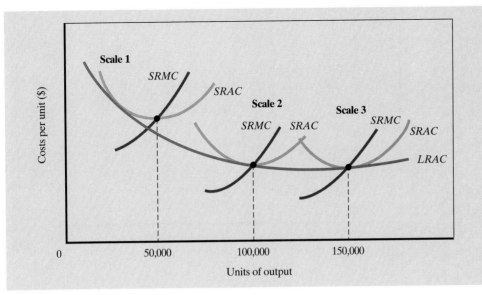

FIGURE 9.5

A Firm Exhibiting Economies of Scale
The long-run average cost curve of a firm shows the different scales on which the firm can choose to operate in the long run. Each scale of operation defines a different short run. Here we see a firm exhibiting economies of scale; moving from Scale 1 to Scale 3 reduces average cost.

CONSTANT RETURNS TO SCALE

Technically, the term *constant returns* means that the quantitative relationship between input and output stays constant, or the same, when output is increased. If a firm doubles inputs, it doubles output; if it triples inputs, it triples output; and so forth. Furthermore, if input prices are fixed, constant returns implies that average cost of production does not change with scale. In other words, constant returns to scale means that the firm's long-run average cost curve remains flat.

The firm in Figure 9.5 exhibits roughly constant returns to scale between Scale 2 and Scale 3. The average cost of production is about the same in each. If the firm exhibited constant returns at levels above 150,000 units of output, the *LRAC* would continue as a flat, straight line.

Economists have studied cost data extensively over the years to estimate the extent to which economies of scale exist. Evidence suggests that in most industries firms don't have to be gigantic to realize cost savings from scale economies. For example, automobile production is accomplished in thousands of separate assembly operations, each with its own economies of scale. Perhaps the best example of efficient production on a small scale is the manufacturing sector in Taiwan. Taiwan has enjoyed very rapid growth based on manufacturing firms that employ fewer than 100 workers!

One simple argument supports the empirical result that most industries seem to exhibit constant returns to scale (a flat *LRAC*) after some level of output. Competition always pushes firms to adopt the least-cost technology and scale. If cost advantages result with larger-scale operations, the firms that shift to that scale will drive the smaller, less efficient firms out of business. A firm that wants to grow when it has reached its "optimal" size can do so by building another identical plant. It thus seems logical to conclude that most firms face constant returns to scale *as long as* they can replicate their existing plants. Thus, when you look at developed industries, you can expect to see firms of different sizes operating with similar costs. These firms produce using roughly the same scale of plant, but larger firms simply have more plants.

DECREASING RETURNS TO SCALE

When average cost increases with scale of production, a firm faces *decreasing returns to scale*, or *diseconomies of scale*. The most often cited example of a diseconomy of scale is bureaucratic inefficiency. As size increases beyond a certain point, operations tend to become more difficult to manage. You can easily imagine what happens when a firm

FIGURE 9.6

A Firm Exhibiting Economies
and Diseconomies of Scale

Economies of scale push
this firm's costs down
to q^*. Beyond q^*, the firm
experiences diseconomies
of scale; q^* is the level of
production at lowest average
cost, using optimal scale.

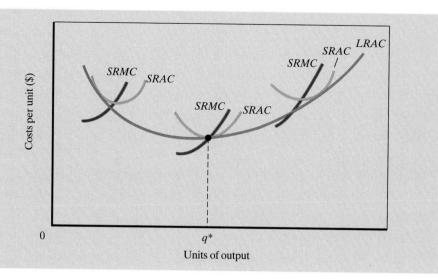

grows top-heavy with managers who have accumulated seniority and high salaries. The coordination function is more complex for larger firms than for smaller ones, and the chances that it will break down are greater.

A large firm is also more likely than a small firm to find itself facing problems with organized labor. Unions can demand higher wages and more benefits, go on strike, force firms to incur legal expenses, and take other actions that increase production costs. (This does not mean that unions are "bad," but rather that their activities often increase costs.)

Figure 9.6 describes a firm that exhibits both economies of scale and diseconomies of scale. Average costs decrease with scale of plant up to q^* and increase with scale after that. This long-run average cost curve looks very much like the short-run average cost curves we have examined in the last two chapters. But do not confuse the two:

> All short-run average cost curves are U-shaped, because we assume a fixed scale of plant that constrains production and drives marginal cost upward as a result of diminishing returns. In the long run, we make no such assumption; rather, we assume that scale of plant can be changed.

Thus, the same firm can face diminishing returns—a short-run concept—and still have a long-run cost curve that exhibits economies of scale.

The shape of a firm's long-run average cost curve depends on how costs react to changes in scale. Some firms do see economies of scale, and their long-run average cost curves slope downward. Most firms seem to have flat long-run average cost curves. Still others encounter diseconomies, and their long-run average costs slope upward.

It is important to note that economic efficiency requires taking advantage of economies of scale (if they exist) and avoiding diseconomies of scale. The **optimal scale of plant** is the one that minimizes average cost. In fact, as we will see next, competition forces firms to use the optimal scale.

optimal scale of plant
The scale of plant that minimizes average cost.

LONG-RUN ADJUSTMENTS TO SHORT-RUN CONDITIONS

We began this chapter by discussing the different short-run positions in which firms may find themselves. Firms can be operating at a profit or suffering economic losses; they can be shut down or producing. The industry is not in equilibrium if firms have an incentive to enter or exit in the long run. Thus, when firms are earning economic profits (profits

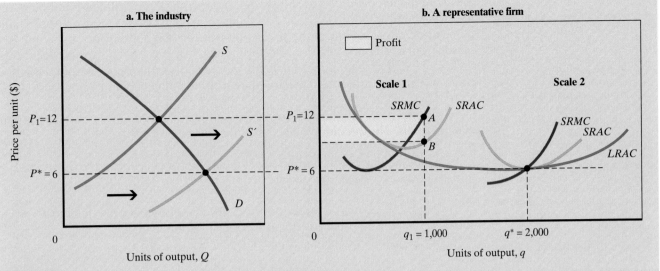

FIGURE 9.7

Firms Expand in the Long Run When Increasing Returns to Scale Are Available

When economies of scale can be realized, firms have an incentive to expand. Thus firms will be pushed by competition to produce at their optimal scales. Price will be driven to the minimum point on the *LRAC* curve.

above normal) or are suffering economic losses (profits below normal, or negative), the industry is not at an equilibrium, and firms will change their behavior. What they are likely to do depends in part on costs in the long run. This is why we have spent a good deal of time discussing economies and diseconomies of scale.

We can now put these two ideas together and discuss the actual long-run adjustments that are likely to take place in response to short-run profits and losses.

SHORT-RUN PROFITS: EXPANSION TO EQUILIBRIUM

We begin our analysis of long-run adjustments with a perfectly competitive industry in which firms are earning positive profits. We assume that all firms in the industry are producing with the same technology of production, and that each firm has a long-run average cost curve that is U-shaped. A U-shaped long-run average cost curve implies that there are some economies of scale to be realized in the industry, and that all firms ultimately begin to run into diseconomies at some scale of operation.

Figure 9.7 shows a representative perfectly competitive firm initially producing at Scale 1. Market price is $P_1 = \$12$, and individual firms are enjoying economic profits. Total revenue at our representative firm, which is producing 1,000 units of output per period, exceeds total cost. Our firm's profit per period is equal to the shaded pink rectangle. (Make sure you understand why the pink rectangle represents profits. Remember that perfectly competitive firms maximize profit by producing at $P = MC$—in Figure 9.7, at point A.)

At this point, our representative firm has not realized all the economies of scale available to it. By expanding to Scale 2, it will reduce average costs significantly, and it will increase profits unless price drops. As long as firms are enjoying profits and economies of scale exist, firms will expand. Thus, we assume that the firm in Figure 9.7 shifts to Scale 2.

At the same time, the existence of positive profits will attract new entrants to the industry. Both the entrance of new firms and the expansion of existing firms have the same effect on the short-run industry supply curve (Figure 9.7a). Both cause

the short-run supply curve to shift to the right, from S to S'. Because the short-run industry supply curve is the sum of all the marginal cost curves (above the minimum point of AVC) of all the firms in the industry, it will shift to the right, for two reasons. First, because all firms in the industry are expanding to a larger scale, their individual short-run marginal cost curves shift to the right. Second, with new firms entering the industry, there are more firms and thus more marginal cost curves to add up.

As capital flows into the industry, the supply curve in Figure 9.7a shifts to the right and price falls. The question is, where will the process stop? In general:

> Firms will continue to expand as long as there are economies of scale to be realized, and new firms will continue to enter as long as positive profits are being earned.

In Figure 9.7a, final equilibrium is achieved only when price falls to $P^* = \$6$ and firms have exhausted all the economies of scale available in the industry. At $P^* = \$6$, no profits are being earned and none can be earned by changing the level of output.

Look carefully at the final equilibrium in Figure 9.7. Each firm will choose the scale of plant that produces its product at minimum long-run average cost. Competition drives firms to adopt not just the most efficient technology in the *short* run, but also the most efficient scale of operation in the *long* run.

> In the long run, equilibrium price (P^*) is equal to long-run average cost, short-run marginal cost, and short-run average cost. Profits are driven to zero:
>
> $$P^* = SRMC = SRAC = LRAC,$$
>
> where $SRMC$ denotes short-run marginal cost, $SRAC$ denotes short-run average cost, and $LRAC$ denotes long-run average cost. No other price is an equilibrium. Any price above P^* means that there are profits to be made in the industry, and new firms will continue to enter. Any price below P^* means that firms are suffering losses, and firms will exit the industry. Only at P^* will profits be just equal to zero, and only at P^* will the industry be in equilibrium.

SHORT-RUN LOSSES: CONTRACTION TO EQUILIBRIUM

Firms that suffer short-run losses have an incentive to leave the industry in the long run, but cannot do so in the short run. As we have seen, some firms incurring losses will choose to shut down and bear losses equal to fixed costs. Others will continue to produce in the short run in an effort to minimize their losses.

Figure 9.8 depicts a firm that will continue to produce $q_1 = 1,000$ units of output in the short run, despite its losses. (We are assuming here that the firm is earning losses that are smaller than the firm's fixed costs.) With losses, the long-run picture will change. Firms have an incentive to get out of the industry. As they exit, the industry's short-run supply curve shifts to the left. As it shifts, the equilibrium price rises, from $8 to $9.

Once again the question is: How long will this adjustment process continue? In general:

> As long as losses are being sustained in an industry, firms will shut down and leave the industry, thus reducing supply—shifting the supply curve to the left. As this happens, price rises. This gradual price rise reduces losses for firms remaining in the industry until those losses are ultimately eliminated.

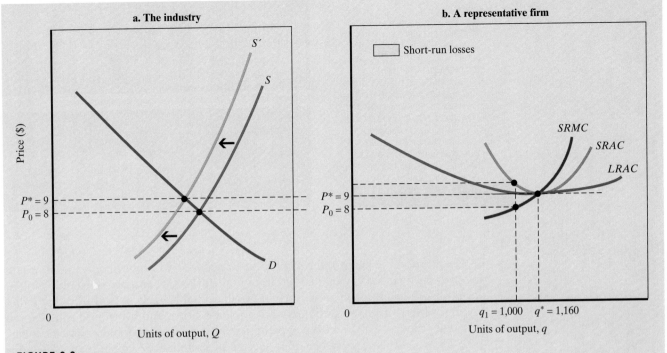

a. The industry

b. A representative firm

FIGURE 9.8

Long-Run Contraction and Exit in an Industry Suffering Short-Run Losses

When firms in an industry suffer losses, there is an incentive for them to exit. As firms exit, the supply curve shifts from S to S', driving price up to P^*. As price rises, losses are gradually eliminated and the industry returns to equilibrium.

In Figure 9.8, equilibrium occurs when price rises to $P^* = \$9$. At that point, remaining firms will maximize profits by producing $q^* = 1,160$ units of output. Price is just sufficient to cover average costs, and economic profits and losses are zero.

> Whether we begin with an industry in which firms are earning profits or suffering losses, the final long-run competitive equilibrium condition is the same:
>
> $$P^* = SRMC = SRAC = LRAC,$$
>
> and profits are zero. At this point, individual firms are operating at the most efficient scale of plant—that is, at the minimum point on their $LRAC$ curve.

THE LONG-RUN ADJUSTMENT MECHANISM: INVESTMENT FLOWS TOWARD PROFIT OPPORTUNITIES

The central idea in our discussion of entry, exit, expansion, and contraction is this:

> In efficient markets, investment capital flows toward profit opportunities. The actual process is complex and varies from industry to industry.

We talked about efficient markets in chapter 1. In efficient markets, profit opportunities are quickly eliminated as they develop. To illustrate this point, we described driving up to a toll booth and suggested that shorter-than-average lines are quickly eliminated as cars shift into them. So, too, are profits in competitive industries eliminated as new competing firms move into open slots, or perceived opportunities, in the industry.

WHEN FIRMS IN AN INDUSTRY ARE MAKING POSITIVE PROFITS, CAPITAL IS LIKELY TO FLOW INTO THAT INDUSTRY. ENTREPRENEURS START NEW FIRMS, AND FIRMS PRODUCING ENTIRELY DIFFERENT PRODUCTS MAY JOIN THE COMPETITION. THE SUCCESS OF SNAPPLE'S LINE OF NATURAL TEAS AND JUICES HAS INSPIRED A SLEW OF IMITATORS TO COMPETE IN THE NONCARBONATED SOFT DRINK INDUSTRY.

In practice, the entry and exit of firms in response to profit opportunities usually involves the financial capital market. In capital markets, people are constantly looking for profits. When firms in an industry do well, capital is likely to flow into that industry in a variety of forms. Entrepreneurs start new firms, and firms producing entirely different products may join the competition in order to break into new markets. It happens all around us. The tremendous success of premium ice-cream makers Ben and Jerry's and Häagen-Dazs spawned dozens of competitors. In one Massachusetts town of 35,000, a small ice-cream store opened to rave reviews, long lines, and high prices and positive profits. Within a year there were four new ice cream/yogurt stores, no lines, and lower prices. Magic? No: just the natural functioning of competition.

long-run competitive equilibrium *When P = SRMC = SRAC = LRAC and profits are zero.*

When there is promise of positive profits, investments are made and output expands. When firms end up suffering losses, firms contract, and some go out of business. It can take quite a while, however, for an industry to achieve **long-run competitive equilibrium**, the point at which $P = SRMC = SRAC = LRAC$ and profits are zero. In fact, because costs and tastes are in a constant state of flux, very few industries ever really get there. The economy is always changing. There are always some firms making profits and some firms suffering losses.

This, then, is a story about tendencies:

> Investment, in the form of new firms and expanding old firms, will, over time, tend to favor those industries in which profits are being made. And, over time, industries in which firms are suffering losses will gradually contract from disinvestment.

In 1996, the United States had 71,811 business failures. In July of 1997, F. W. Woolworth announced it would close all 400 of its remaining five and dime stores in the face of mounting operating losses after 117 years of operation.

Sources: Economic Report of the President, 1998, Table B96; New York Times, July 18, 1997.

OUTPUT MARKETS: A FINAL WORD

In the last four chapters, we have been building a model of a simple market system under the assumption of perfect competition. Let us provide just one more example to review the actual response of a competitive system to a change in consumer preferences.

Over the past two decades, Americans have developed a taste for wine in general and for California wines in particular. We know that household demand is constrained by income, wealth, and prices, and that income is (at least in part) determined by the choices that households make. Within these constraints, households choose, and, increasingly, they choose—or demand—wine. The demand curve for wine has shifted to the right, causing excess demand followed by an increase in price.

With higher prices, wine producers find themselves earning positive profits. *This increase in price and consequent rise in profits is the basic signal that leads to a reallocation of society's resources.* In the short run, wine producers are constrained

THE LONG-RUN AVERAGE COST CURVE: FLAT OR U-SHAPED?

The long-run average cost curve has been a source of controversy in economics for many years. A long-run average cost curve was first drawn as the "envelope" of a series of short-run curves in a classic article written by Jacob Viner in 1931.[a] In preparing that article, Viner gave his draftsman the task of drawing the long-run curve through the minimum points of all the short-run average cost curves.

In a supplementary note written in 1950, Viner commented:

> ... the error in Chart IV is left uncorrected so that future teachers and students may share the pleasure of many of their predecessors of pointing out that if I had known what an envelope was, I would not have given my excellent draftsman the technically impossible and economically inappropriate task of drawing an AC curve which would pass through the lowest cost points of all the AC curves yet not rise above any AC curve at any point. ...[b]

While this story is an interesting part of the lore of economics, a more recent debate concentrates on the economic content of this controversy. In 1986, Professor Herbert Simon of Carnegie-Mellon University stated bluntly:

> I think the textbooks are a scandal ... the most widely used textbooks use the old long-run and short-run cost curves to illustrate the theory of the firm. ... [the U-shaped long-run cost curve] postulated that in the long run the size of the firm would increase to a scale associated with the minimum cost on the long-run curve. It was supposed to predict something about the size distribution of firms in the industry. It doesn't do that and there are other problems. Most serious is the fact that most empirical studies show the firm's cost curves not to be U-shaped, but in fact to slope down to the right

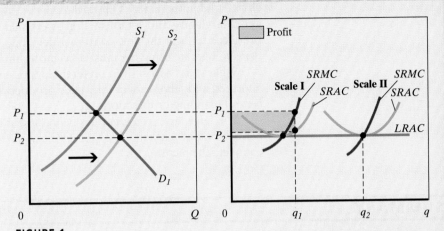

FIGURE 1

Long-Run Expansion in an Industry with Constant Returns to Scale

and then level off, without a clearly defined minimum point.[c]

Professor Simon makes an important point. Suppose that we were to redraw Figure 9.7b with a flat long-run average cost curve. Figure 1 shows a firm earning short-run profits using Scale I, but there are no economies of scale to be realized.

Despite the lack of economies of scale, expansion of such an industry would likely take place in much the same way as we have described. First, existing firms have an incentive to expand because they are making profits. At current prices, a firm that doubles its scale would earn twice the profits even if cost did not fall with expansion. Of course, as long as profits persist, new firms have an incentive to enter the industry. Both events will shift the short-run industry supply curve to the right, from S_1 to S_2 and price will fall, from P_1 to P_2. Expansion and entry will stop only when price has fallen to LRAC. Only then will profits be eliminated. At equilibrium, $P = SRMC = SRAC = LRAC$.

This model does not predict the final firm size or the structure of the industry. When the long-run AC curve is U-shaped, firms stop expanding at the minimum

point on LRAC because further expansion means higher costs. Thus, optimal firm size is determined technologically. If the LRAC curve is flat, however, small firms and large firms have identical average costs.

If this is true, and it seems to be in many industries, the structure of the industry in the long run will depend on whether existing firms expand faster than new firms enter. If new firms enter quickly in response to profit opportunities, the industry will end up with large numbers of small firms. But if existing firms expand more rapidly than new firms enter, the industry may end up with only a few very large firms. There is thus an element of randomness in the way industries expand. In fact, most industries contain some large firms and some small firms, which is exactly what Simon's flat LRAC model predicts.

[a]Jacob Viner, "Cost Curves and Supply Curves," *Zeitschrift fur Nationalokonomie*, vol. III (1–1931), 23–46.

[b]George J. Stigler and Kenneth E. Boulding, eds., *AEA Readings in Price Theory*, vol. VI (Chicago: Richard D. Irwin, 1952), p. 227.

[c]Interview with Herbert A. Simon. "The Failure of Armchair Economics," *Challenge*, November–December, 1986, pp. 23–24.

 For more on long-run and short-run average cost curves, see the Case and Fair Web page at http://www.prenhall.com/casefair.

by their current scales of operation. California has only a limited number of vineyards and only a limited amount of vat capacity, for example.

In the long run, however, we would expect to see resources flow in to compete for these profits, and this is exactly what happens. New firms enter the wine-producing business. New vines are planted and new vats and production equipment are purchased and put in place. Vineyard owners move into new states—Rhode Island, Texas, and Maryland—and established growers increase production. Overall, more wine is produced to meet the new consumer demand. At the same time, competition is forcing firms to operate using the most efficient technology available.

What starts as a shift in preferences thus ends up as a shift in resources. Land is reallocated and labor moves into wine production. All this is accomplished without any central planning or direction.

You have now seen what lies behind the demand curves and supply curves in competitive output markets. The next two chapters take up competitive *input* markets and complete the picture.

SUMMARY

1. For any firm, one of three conditions holds at any given moment: (1) The firm is earning positive profits, (2) the firm is suffering losses, or (3) the firm is just breaking even—that is, earning a normal rate of return and thus zero profits.

SHORT-RUN CONDITIONS AND LONG-RUN DIRECTIONS

2. A firm that is earning positive profits in the short run and expects to continue doing so has an incentive to expand in the long run. Profits also provide an incentive for new firms to enter the industry.

3. In the short run, firms suffering losses are stuck in the industry. They can shut down operations ($q = 0$), but they must still bear fixed costs. In the long run, firms suffering losses can exit the industry.

4. A firm's decision about whether to shut down in the short run depends solely on whether its revenues from operating are sufficient to cover its variable costs. If revenues exceed variable costs, the *operating profits* can be used to pay some fixed costs and thus reduce losses.

5. Any time that price is below the minimum point on the average variable cost curve, total revenue will be less than total variable cost, operating profit will be negative, and the firm will shut down. The minimum point on the average variable cost curve (which is also the point where marginal cost and average variable cost intersect) is called the *shut-down point*. At all prices above the shut-down point, the *MC* curve shows the profit-maximizing level of output. At all prices below it, optimal short-run output is zero.

6. The *short-run supply curve* of a firm in a perfectly competitive industry is the portion of its marginal cost curve that lies above its average variable cost curve.

7. Two things can cause the industry supply curve to shift: (1) in the short run, anything that causes marginal costs to change across the industry, such as an increase in the price of a particular input, and (2) in the long run, entry or exit of firms.

LONG-RUN COSTS: ECONOMIES AND DISECONOMIES OF SCALE

8. When an increase in a firm's scale of production leads to lower average costs, the firm exhibits *increasing returns to scale*, or *economies of scale*. When average costs do not change with the scale of production, the firm exhibits *constant returns to scale*. When an increase in a firm's scale of production leads to higher average costs, the firm exhibits *diseconomies of scale*.

9. A firm's *long-run average cost curve* (LRAC) shows the costs associated with different scales on which it can choose to operate in the long run.

LONG-RUN ADJUSTMENTS TO SHORT-RUN CONDITIONS

10. When short-run profits exist in an industry, firms will enter and existing firms will expand. These events shift the industry supply curve to the right. When this happens, price falls and ultimately profits are eliminated.

11. When short-run losses are suffered in an industry, some firms exit and some firms reduce scale. These events shift the industry supply curve to the left, raising price and eliminating losses.

12. *Long-run competitive equilibrium* is reached when $P = SRMC = SRAC = LRAC$ and profits are zero.

13. In efficient markets investment capital flows toward profit opportunities.

REVIEW TERMS AND CONCEPTS

breaking even, 208

constant returns to scale, 216

decreasing returns to scale, or diseconomies of scale, 216

increasing returns to scale, or economies of scale, 216

long-run average cost curve (*LRAC*), 217

long-run competitive equilibrium, 224

operating profit (or loss) or net operating revenue, 210

optimal scale of plant, 220

short-run industry supply curve, 213

shut-down point, 213

Long-run competitive equilibrium:
$$P = SRMC = SRAC = LRAC$$

PROBLEM SET

1. Explain why it is possible that a firm with a production function that exhibits increasing returns to scale can run into diminishing returns at the same time.

2. Which of the following industries do you think are likely to exhibit large economies of scale? Explain why in each case.
   a. Home building
   b. Electric power generation
   c. Vegetable farming
   d. Software development
   e. Aircraft manufacturing
   f. Higher education
   g. Accounting services

3. For Cases A through F below, would you (1) operate or shut down in the short run, and (2) expand your plant or exit the industry in the long run?

	A	B	C	D	E	F
Total revenue	1,500	2,000	2,000	5,000	5,000	5,000
Total cost	1,500	1,500	2,500	6,000	7,000	4,000
Total fixed cost	500	500	200	1,500	1,500	1,500

4. Do you agree or disagree with the following statements? Explain why in a sentence or two.
   a. A firm will never sell its product for less than it costs to produce it.
   b. If the short-run marginal cost curve is U-shaped, the long-run average cost curve is likely to be U-shaped as well.

5. The Smythe chicken farm outside of Little Rock, Arkansas, produces 25,000 chickens per month. Total cost of production at the Smythe farm is $28,000. Down the road are two other farms. The Faubus Farm produces 55,000 chickens a month and total cost is $50,050. Mega Farm produces 100,000 chickens per month at a total cost of $91,000. These data suggest that there are significant economies of scale in chicken production. Do you agree or disagree with this statement? Explain your answer.

6. Indicate whether you agree or disagree with each of the following statements. Briefly explain your answers.
   a. Firms that exhibit constant returns to scale have U-shaped long-run average cost curves.
   b. Firms minimize costs. Thus, a firm earning short-run profits will choose to produce at the minimum point on its average total cost function.
   c. The supply curve of a competitive firm in the short run is its marginal cost curve above average total cost.
   d. A firm suffering losses in the short run will continue to operate as long as total revenue will at least cover fixed cost.

7. You are given the following cost data:

Q	TFC	TVC
0	12	0
1	12	5
2	12	9
3	12	14
4	12	20
5	12	28
6	12	38

If the price of output is $7, how many units of output will this firm produce? What is the total revenue? What is the total cost? Will the firm operate or shut down in the short run? The long run? Briefly explain your answers.

8. The following cost data are given for a small pushcart business. The business was started by partners Ann and Sue, who purchased a new pushcart with $20,000 of their own money. The pushcart is located at the Denver airport and is used to sell leather belts. Each year Ann and Sue sell 3,000 belts for $10 each. The belts cost them $5 each from their supplier. Staffing the cart 12 hours a day costs them $14,000 in wages per year. If the normal rate of return is 10 percent, how much profit are Ann and Sue making?

9. The following problem traces the relationship between firm decisions, market supply, and market equilibrium in a perfectly competitive market.

a. Complete the following table for a single firm in the short run:

OUTPUT	TFC	TVC	TC	AVC	ATC	MC
0	$300	$0	___	___	___	
1	___	$100	___	___	___	___
2	___	$150	___	___	___	___
3	___	$210	___	___	___	___
4	___	$290	___	___	___	___
5	___	$400	___	___	___	___
6	___	$540	___	___	___	___
7	___	$720	___	___	___	___
8	___	$950	___	___	___	___
9	___	$1,240	___	___	___	___
10	___	$1,600	___	___	___	___

b. Using the information in the table, fill in the following supply schedule for this individual firm under perfect competition, and indicate profit (positive or negative) at each output level. (*Hint:* At each hypothetical price, what is the *MR* of producing one more unit of output? Combine this with the *MC* of another unit to figure out the quantity supplied.)

PRICE	QUANTITY SUPPLIED	PROFIT
$50	___	___
$70	___	___
$100	___	___
$130	___	___
$170	___	___
$220	___	___
$280	___	___
$350	___	___

c. Now suppose there are 100 firms in this industry, all with identical cost schedules. Fill in the market quantity supplied at each price in this market:

PRICE	MARKET QUANTITY SUPPLIED	MARKET QUANTITY DEMANDED
$50	___	1,000
$70	___	900
$100	___	800
$130	___	700
$170	___	600
$220	___	500
$280	___	400
$350	___	300

d. Fill in the blanks: From the market supply and demand schedules in c., the equilibrium market price for this good is _____ and the equilibrium market quantity is _____. Each firm will produce a quantity of _____ and earn a _____ (profit/loss) equal to _____.

e. In d., your answers characterize the short-run equilibrium in this market. Do they characterize the long-run equilibrium as well? If yes, explain why. If no, explain why not (i.e., what would happen in the long run to change the equilibrium, and why?).

*10. Assume that you are hired as an analyst at a major New York consulting firm. Your first assignment is to do an industry analysis of the tribble industry. After extensive research and two all-nighters, you have obtained the following information.

- *Long-run costs:*
  Capital costs: $5 per unit of output
  Labor costs: $2 per unit of output

- No economies or diseconomies of scale.

- Industry currently earning a normal return to capital (profit is zero).

- The industry is perfectly competitive. Each firm produces the same amount of output, and there are 100 firms.

- *Total industry output:* 1.2 million tribbles

Demand for tribbles is expected to grow rapidly over the next few years to a level twice as high as it is now, but (due to short-run diminishing returns) each of the 100 existing firms is likely to be producing only 50 percent more.

a. Sketch the long-run cost curve of a representative firm.

b. Show the current conditions by drawing two diagrams, one showing the industry and one showing a representative firm.

c. Sketch the increase in demand and show how the industry is likely to respond in the short run and in the long run.

*11. Consider Adam, a baker of apple pies. To make one pie, Adam uses one hour of labor and one pound of apples. He bakes the pies in an oven that he leases for $100 per day. A (short-run) contract requires him to pay the lease even if he bakes no pies. The hourly wage that Adam pays is $5, and each pound of apples costs $2. Assume that Adam has only one oven available, and that he can bake a maximum of 50 apple pies in one day.

a. What are Adam's fixed costs (per day)? Variable costs? Total costs? (Express these as a function of q, the number of apple pies.)

b. Determine and graph average variable cost, average fixed cost, average total cost, and marginal cost.

c. Suppose that the market for apple pies is perfectly competitive. Adam can therefore sell all the pies he wants in one day for $8 each. How many apple pies should Adam produce per day in the short run? What will his profits or losses be?

d. At a price of $8, how many pies (per day) should Adam produce in the long run? Explain your answer.

e. What is the minimum price necessary for Adam to operate in the short run? In the long run?

TAKE IT TO THE NET

We invite you to visit the Case and Fair page on the Prentice Hall Web site:

http://www.prenhall.com/casefair

for this chapter's World Wide Web exercise.

APPENDIX TO CHAPTER 9

EXTERNAL ECONOMIES AND DISECONOMIES AND THE LONG-RUN INDUSTRY SUPPLY CURVE

Sometimes average costs increase or decrease with the size of the industry, in addition to responding to changes in the size of the firm itself. When long-run average costs decrease as a result of industry growth, we say that there are **external economies**. When average costs increase as a result of industry growth, we say that there are **external diseconomies**. (Remember the distinction between internal and external economies: *Internal* economies of scale are found within firms, while *external* economies occur on an industrywide basis.)

In 1997 and 1998, for example, one of the fastest growing sectors in the U.S. economy was the biotechnology industry. Among many other things, biotech firms produce genetically engineered plants (such as a frost-resistant strawberry and broccoli that tastes like a Twinkie) and complex drugs using bioengineered organisms.

Most biotechnology firms are located in one of four areas in the United States: Boston, southern New Jersey, North Carolina, and California. Locating near one another can produce potential external economies. As the industry grows, local schools (private and public) may begin to train students for jobs in the industry, reducing training expenses for the firms. In addition, people in the industry have easy access to and learn from one another. As an industry grows, suppliers can save money shipping to one location rather than fifteen. Just as the computer producers of a generation earlier found concentration of location to bring big cost advantages, so too the biotech industry is likely to reap significant cost advantages as the industry grows and matures.

While the biotechnology industry is one in which external economies are a possibility, the construction industry is one in which external *diseconomies* exist. Recent decades have seen several construction booms during which the construction industry expanded. One of the biggest expansions took place between 1975 and 1979; another occurred between 1992 and 1994. Of course, expansion affects the price of lumber and lumber products. Increases in construction activity cause the demand for lumber products to rise, and this price increase causes the cost of construction to shift upward for all construction firms.

Table 9A.1 shows one indicator of construction activity: new housing permits issued. In 1992 and 1993, the industry grew very rapidly. In 1991, an average of 79,500 new housing permits were issued each month. By 1994, the figure was up nearly 40 percent to 111,000. This growth was accompanied by a very rapid increase in lumber prices as demand for lumber products ballooned. From 1991 to 1993, the price of lumber products increased about 43 percent, while prices in general increased only about 6 percent.

In the construction industry, a change in the scale of any individual firm's operations has no impact on the price of lumber, because no one firm has any control over the price. The increase in costs in the early 1990s resulted in part from expansion of the *industry* that led to an external diseconomy.

THE LONG-RUN INDUSTRY SUPPLY CURVE

Recall that long-run competitive equilibrium is achieved when entering firms responding to profits or exiting firms fleeing from losses drive price to a level that just covers long-run average costs. Profits are zero, and $P = LRAC = SRAC = SRMC$. At this point, individual firms are operating at the most efficient scale of plant—that is, at the minimum point on their $LRAC$ curve.

As we saw in the text, long-run equilibrium is not easily achieved. But even if a firm or an industry does achieve long-run equilibrium, it will not remain at that point indefinitely. Economies are dynamic. As population and the

TABLE 9A.1 CONSTRUCTION ACTIVITY AND THE PRICE OF LUMBER PRODUCTS, 1991–1994

YEAR	MONTHLY AVERAGE, NEW HOUSING PERMITS	PERCENTAGE INCREASE OVER THE PREVIOUS YEAR	PERCENTAGE CHANGE IN THE PRICE OF LUMBER PRODUCTS	PERCENTAGE CHANGE IN CONSUMER PRICES
1991	79,500	—	—	—
1992	92,167	+15.9	+14.7	+3.0
1993	100,917	+9.5	+24.6	+3.0
1994	111,000	+10.0	NA	+2.1

Sources: Federal Reserve Bank of Boston, *New England Economic Indicators,* July, 1994, p. 21; *Statistical Abstract of the United States,* 1994, Tables 754, 755.

stock of capital grow, and as preferences and technology change, some sectors will expand and some will contract. How do industries adjust to long-term changes? The answer depends on both internal and external factors.

The extent of *internal* economies (or diseconomies) determines the shape of a firm's long-run average cost curve (*LRAC*). If a firm changes its scale and either expands or contracts, its average costs will increase, decrease, or stay the same *along* the *LRAC* curve. Recall that the *LRAC* curve shows the relationship between a firm's output (*q*) and average total cost (*ATC*). A firm enjoying internal economies will see costs decreasing as it expands its scale; a firm facing internal diseconomies will see costs increasing as it expands its scale.

But external economies and diseconomies have nothing to do with the size of *individual* firms in a competitive market. Because individual firms in perfectly competitive industries are very small relative to the market, other firms are affected only minimally when an individual firm changes its output or scale of operation. *External* economies and diseconomies arise from industry expansions; that is, they arise when many firms increase their output simultaneously or when new firms enter an industry. If industry expansion causes costs to increase (external diseconomies), the *LRAC* curves facing individual firms shift upward; costs increase regardless of the level of output finally chosen by the firm. Similarly, if industry expansion causes costs to decrease (external economies), the *LRAC* curves facing individual firms shift downward; costs decrease at all potential levels of output.

An example of an expanding industry facing external economies is illustrated in Figure 9A.1. Initially, the industry and the representative firm are in long-run competitive equilibrium at the price P_1 determined by the intersection of the initial demand curve D_1 and the initial supply curve S_1. P_1 is the long-run equilibrium

price; it intersects the initial long-run average cost curve ($LRAC_1$) at its minimum point. At this point, economic profits are zero.

Let us assume that as time passes, demand increases—that is, the demand curve shifts to the right from D_1 to D_2. This increase in demand will push price all the way to P_2. Without drawing the short-run cost curves, we know that economic profits now exist and that firms are likely to enter the industry to compete for them. In the absence of external economies or diseconomies, firms would enter the industry, shifting the supply curve to the right and driving price back to the bottom of the long-run average cost curve, where profits are zero. But the industry in Figure 9A.1 enjoys external economies. As firms enter and the industry expands, costs decrease. And as the supply curve shifts to the right from S_1 toward S_2, the long-run average cost curve shifts downward to $LRAC_2$. Thus, to reach the new long-run equilibrium level of price and output, the supply curve must shift all the way to S_2. Only when the supply curve reaches S_2 is price driven down to the new equilibrium price of P_3, the minimum point on the *new* long-run average cost curve.

Presumably, further expansion would lead to even greater savings because the industry encounters external economies. The dashed line in Figure 9A.1a, which traces out price and total output over time as the industry expands, is called the **long-run industry supply curve (*LRIS*)**. When an industry enjoys external economies, its long-run supply curve slopes down. Such an industry is called a **decreasing-cost industry**.

In Figure 9.A.2, we derive the long-run industry supply curve for an industry that faces external *diseconomies*. (These were suffered in the construction industry, you will recall, when increased house-building activity drove up lumber prices.) As demand expands from D_1 to D_2, price is driven up from P_1 to P_2. In response to the resulting higher profits, firms enter, shifting the short-run supply schedule

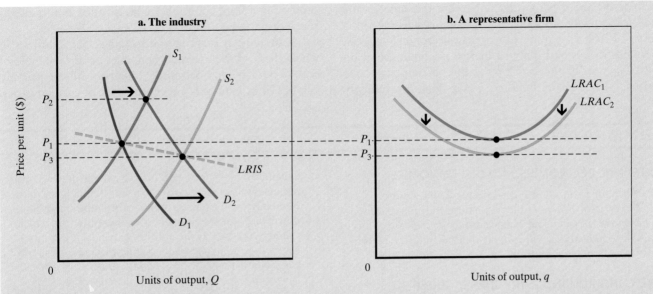

FIGURE 9A.1

A Decreasing-Cost Industry: External Economies

In a decreasing-cost industry, average cost declines as the industry expands. As demand expands from D_1 to D_2, price rises from P_1 to P_2. As new firms enter and existing firms expand, supply shifts from S_1 to S_2, driving price down. If costs decline as a result of the expansion to $LRAC_2$, the final price will be below P_1 at P_3. The long-run industry supply curve (*LRIS*) slopes downward in a decreasing-cost industry.

FIGURE 9A.2

An Increasing-Cost Industry: External Diseconomies

In an increasing-cost industry, average cost increases as the industry expands. As demand shifts from D_1 to D_2, price rises from P_1 to P_2. As new firms enter and existing firms expand output, supply shifts from S_1 to S_2, driving price down. If long-run average costs rise as a result to $LRAC_2$, the final price will be P_3. The long-run industry supply curve (*LRIS*) slopes up in an increasing-cost industry.

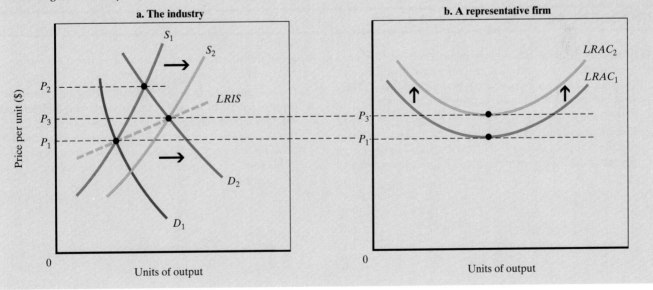

to the right and driving price down. But this time, as the industry expands, the long-run average cost curve shifts up to $LRAC_2$ as a result of external diseconomies. Now, price has to fall back only to P_3 (the minimum point on $LRAC_2$), not all the way to P_1, to eliminate economic profits. This type of industry, whose long-run industry supply curve slopes up to the right, is called an **increasing-cost industry**.

It should not surprise you to know that industries in which there are no external economies or diseconomies of scale have flat, or horizontal, long-run industry supply curves. These industries are called **constant-cost industries**.

SUMMARY

EXTERNAL ECONOMIES AND DISECONOMIES

1. When long-run average costs decrease as a result of industry growth, we say that the industry exhibits *external economies*. When long-run average costs increase as a result of industry growth, we say that the industry exhibits *external diseconomies*.

THE LONG-RUN INDUSTRY SUPPLY CURVE

2. The *long-run industry supply curve (LRIS)* is a graph that traces out price and total output over time as an industry expands. A *decreasing-cost industry* is one in which average costs fall as the industry expands. It exhibits external economies, and its long-run industry supply curve slopes downward. An *increasing-cost industry* is one in which average costs rise as the industry expands. It exhibits external diseconomies, and its long-run industry supply curve slopes upward. A *constant-cost industry* is one that shows no external economies or diseconomies as the industry grows. Its long-run industry supply curve is horizontal, or flat.

REVIEW TERMS AND CONCEPTS

constant-cost industry An industry that shows no economies or diseconomies of scale as the industry grows. Such industries have flat, or horizontal, long-run supply curves. 232

decreasing-cost industry An industry that realizes external economies—that is, average costs decrease as the industry grows. The long-run supply curve for such an industry has a negative slope. 230

external economies and **diseconomies** When industry growth results in a decrease of long-run average costs, there are *external economies*; when industry growth results in an increase of long-run average costs, there are *external diseconomies*. 229

increasing-cost industry An industry that encounters external diseconomies—that is, average costs increase as the industry grows. The long-run supply curve for such an industry has a positive slope. 232

long-run industry supply curve (LRIS) A graph that traces out price and total output over time as an industry expands. 230

PROBLEM SET

1. In deriving the short-run industry supply curve (the sum of firms' marginal cost curves), we assumed that input prices are constant because competitive firms are price-takers. This same assumption holds in the derivation of the long-run industry supply curve. Do you agree or disagree? Explain.

2. Consider an industry that exhibits external diseconomies of scale. Suppose that over the next 10 years, demand for that industry's product increases rapidly. Describe in detail the adjustments likely to follow. Use diagrams in your answer.

3. A representative firm producing cloth is earning a short-run profit at a price of $10 per yard. Draw a supply and demand diagram showing equilibrium at this price. Assuming that the industry is a constant-cost industry, use the diagram to show the long-term adjustment of the industry as demand grows over time. Explain the adjustment mechanism.

Chapter 10

INPUT DEMAND:
THE LABOR AND
LAND MARKETS

AS WE HAVE SEEN, all business firms must make three decisions: (1) how much to produce and supply in output markets; (2) how to produce that output (that is, which technology to use), and (3) how much of each input to demand. So far, our discussion of firm behavior has focused on the first two questions. In chapters 7 through 9, we explained how profit-maximizing firms choose among alternative technologies and decide how much to supply in output markets.

We now turn to the behavior of firms in perfectly competitive *input* markets, going behind input demand curves in much the same way that we went behind output supply curves in the previous two chapters. When we look behind input demand curves, we discover the exact same set of decisions that we saw when we analyzed output supply curves. In a very real sense, we have already talked about everything covered in this chapter. It is the *perspective* that is new.

The three main inputs are labor, land, and capital. Transactions in the labor and land markets are fairly straightforward. In the labor market, households sell labor directly to firms in exchange for wages. In the land market, landowners sell or rent land directly to others. The capital market is more complex. To buy a capital asset—a machine, for example—a firm must use funds that it obtains from households. The firm must then pay interest to the households for the use of the funds. In a sense, then, households supply capital, just as they supply labor. This chapter discusses input markets in general, while the next chapter focuses on the capital market in some detail.

INPUT MARKETS: BASIC CONCEPTS

Before we begin our discussion of input markets, it will be helpful to establish some basic concepts: derived demand, complementary and substitutable inputs, diminishing returns, and marginal revenue product.

▶ **Demand for Inputs: A *Derived* Demand** A firm cannot make a profit unless there is a demand for its product. Households must be willing to pay

233

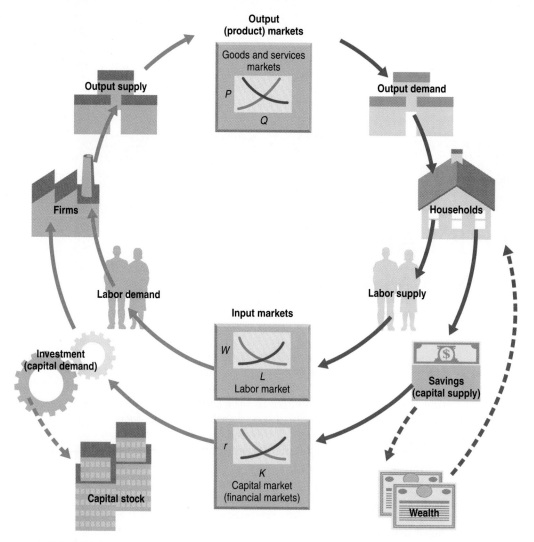

FIGURE 10.1

Firm and Household Decisions

Firms and households interact in both input and output markets. This chapter highlights firm choices in input markets.

for the firm's output. The quantity of output that a firm produces (in both the long run and the short run) thus depends on the value placed by the market on the firm's product. This means that demand for inputs depends on the demand for outputs. In other words, input demand is **derived** from output demand.

The value attached to a product and the inputs needed to produce that product define the input's productivity. Formally, the **productivity of an input** is the amount of output produced per unit of that input. When a large amount of output is produced per unit of an input, the input is said to be *highly productive*. When only a small amount of output is produced per unit of the input, the input is said to exhibit *low productivity*.

Inputs are demanded by a firm if and only if households demand the good or service produced by that firm.

derived demand *The demand for resources (inputs) that is dependent on the demand for the outputs those resources can be used to produce.*

productivity of an input *The amounts of output produced per unit of that input.*

PART TWO
*Microeconomics:
Consumers and Firms*

Prices in competitive input markets depend on firms' demand for inputs, households' supply of inputs, and the interaction between the two. In the labor market, for example, households must decide whether to work and how much to work. In chapter 6 we saw that the opportunity cost of working for a wage is either leisure or the value derived from unpaid labor—working in the garden, for instance, or raising children. In general, firms will demand workers as long as the value of what those workers produce exceeds what they must be paid. Households will supply labor as long as the wage they receive exceeds the value of leisure or the value that they derive from nonpaid work.

▶ **Inputs: Complementary and Substitutable** Inputs can be *complementary* or *substitutable*. Two inputs used together may enhance, or complement, each other. For example, a new machine is useless without someone to run it. But machines can also be substituted for labor, or—less often perhaps—labor can be substituted for machines.

All this means that a firm's input demands are tightly linked to one another. An increase or decrease in wages naturally causes the demand for labor to change, but it may also have an effect on the demand for capital or land. If we are to understand the demand for inputs, therefore, we must understand the connections among labor, capital, and land.

▶ **Diminishing Returns** Recall that the short run is the period during which some fixed factor of production limits a firm's capacity to expand. Under these conditions, the firm that decides to increase output will eventually encounter diminishing returns. Stated more formally, a fixed scale of plant means that the marginal product of variable inputs eventually declines.

Recall also that **marginal product of labor (MP_L)** is the additional output produced if a firm hires one additional unit of labor. For example, if a firm pays for 400 hours of labor per week—10 workers working 40 hours each—and asks one worker to stay an extra hour, the product of the 401st hour is the marginal product of labor for that firm.

In chapter 7, we talked at some length about declining marginal product at a sandwich shop. The first two columns of Table 10.1 reproduce some of the production data from that shop. You may remember that the shop has only one grill, at which only two or three people can work comfortably. In this example, the grill is the fixed factor of production in the short run. Labor is the variable factor. The first worker can produce 10 sandwiches per hour, and the second can produce 15 (see column 3 of Table 10.1). The second worker can produce more because the first is busy answering the phone and taking care of customers, as well as making sandwiches. After the second worker, however, marginal product declines. The third worker adds only 10 sandwiches per hour, because

marginal product of labor (MP_L) *The additional output produced by one additional unit of labor.*

TABLE 10.1 MARGINAL REVENUE PRODUCT PER HOUR OF LABOR IN SANDWICH PRODUCTION (ONE GRILL)

(1) TOTAL LABOR UNITS (EMPLOYEES)	(2) TOTAL PRODUCT (SANDWICHES PER HOUR)	(3) MARGINAL PRODUCT OF LABOR (MP_L) (SANDWICHES PER HOUR)	(4) PRICE (P_X) (VALUE ADDED PER SANDWICH)*	(5) MARGINAL REVENUE PRODUCT ($MP_L \times P_X$) (PER HOUR)
0	0	—	—	—
1	10	10	$.50	$5.00
2	25	15	.50	7.50
3	35	10	.50	5.00
4	40	5	.50	2.50
5	42	2	.50	1.00
6	42	0	.50	0

*The "price" is essentially profit per sandwich; see discussion in text.

the grill gets crowded. The fourth worker can squeeze in quickly while the others are serving or wrapping, but adds only 5 additional sandwiches each hour, and so forth.[1]

In this case, the grill's capacity ultimately limits output. To see how the firm might make a rational choice about how many workers to hire, we need to know more about the value of the firm's product and the cost of labor.

> **Marginal Revenue Product**   The **marginal revenue product** (*MRP*) of a variable input is the additional revenue a firm earns by employing one additional unit of that input, *ceteris paribus*. If labor is the variable factor, for example, hiring an additional unit will lead to added output (the *marginal product* of labor). The sale of that added output will yield revenue. *Marginal revenue product* is the revenue produced by selling the good or service that is produced by the marginal unit of labor. In a competitive firm, marginal revenue product is the value of a factor's marginal product.

Using labor as our variable factor, we can state this proposition more formally by saying that if MP_L is the marginal product of labor and P_X is the price of output, then the marginal revenue product of labor is:

$$MRP_L = MP_L \times P_X$$

When calculating marginal revenue product, we need to be precise about what is being produced. A sandwich shop, to be sure, sells sandwiches, but it does not produce the bread, meat, cheese, mustard, and mayo that go into the sandwiches. What the shop is producing is "sandwich cooking and assembly services." The shop is "adding value" to the meat, bread, and other ingredients by preparing and putting them all together in ready-to-eat form. With this in mind, let's assume that each finished sandwich in our shop sells for $.50 over and above the costs of its ingredients. Thus, the *price of the service* the shop is selling is $.50 per sandwich, and the only variable cost of providing that service is that of the labor used to put the sandwiches together. Thus, if X is the product of our shop, $P_X = \$.50$.

Table 10.1, column 5, calculates the marginal revenue product of each worker if the shop charges $.50 per sandwich over and above the costs of its ingredients. The first worker produces 10 sandwiches per hour which, at $0.50 each, generates revenues of $5 per hour. The addition of a second worker yields $7.50 an hour in revenues. After the second worker, diminishing returns drive MRP_L down. The marginal revenue product of the third worker is $5 per hour; for the fourth worker, only $2.50, and so forth.

Figure 10.2 graphs the data from Table 10.1. Notice that the marginal revenue product curve has the same downward slope as the marginal product curve, but that *MRP* is measured in dollars, not units of output. The *MRP* curve shows the dollar value of labor's marginal product.

LABOR MARKETS

Let's begin our discussion of input markets simply, by discussing a firm that uses only one variable factor of production.

A FIRM USING ONLY ONE VARIABLE FACTOR OF PRODUCTION: LABOR

Demand for an input depends on that input's marginal revenue product and its unit cost, or price. The price of labor, for example, is the wage determined in the labor market. (At this point we are continuing to assume that the sandwich shop uses only one

marginal revenue product (*MRP*) *The additional revenue a firm earns by employing one additional unit of input,* ceteris paribus.

---

[1]As we said in chapter 7, we assume that all workers are equally skilled and motivated. The third worker is no less hard working or skilled than the first two. Rather, the grill is getting crowded. Put another way, the capital constraint is binding.

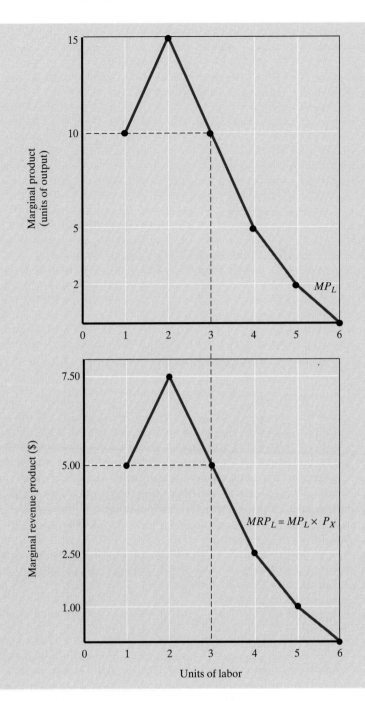

The marginal revenue product
of labor is the price of output,
P_X, times the marginal product
of labor, MP_L.

MP_L

$MRP_L = MP_L \times P_X$

Units of labor

variable factor of production—labor. Remember that competitive firms are price-takers
in both output and input markets. Such firms can hire all the labor they want to hire as
long as they pay the market wage.) We can think of the hourly wage at the sandwich
shop, then, as the marginal cost of a unit of labor.

A profit-maximizing firm will add inputs—in the case of labor, it will hire
workers—as long as the marginal revenue product of that input exceeds its
market price.

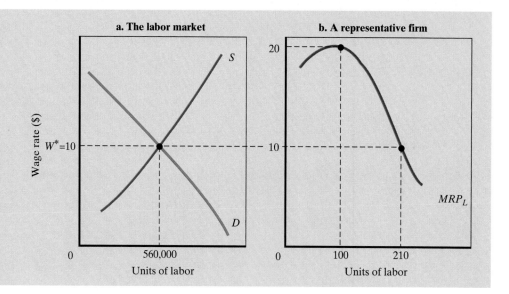

FIGURE 10.3

Marginal Revenue Product and Factor Demand for a Firm Using One Variable Input (Labor)

A competitive firm using only one variable factor of production will use that factor as long as its marginal revenue product exceeds its unit cost. A perfectly competitive firm will hire labor as long as MRP_L is greater than the going wage, W^*. The hypothetical firm will demand 210 units of labor.

Look again at the figures for the sandwich shop in Table 10.1, column 5. Now suppose that the going wage for sandwich makers is $4 per hour. A profit-maximizing firm would hire three workers. The first worker would yield $5 per hour in revenues and the second would yield $7.50, but they each would cost only $4 per hour. The third worker would bring in $5 per hour, but still cost only $4 in marginal wages. The marginal product of the fourth worker, however, would not bring in enough revenue ($2.50) to pay his salary. Total profit is thus maximized by hiring three workers.

Figure 10.3 presents this same concept graphically. The labor market appears in Figure 10.3a; Figure 10.3b shows a single firm that employs workers. This firm, incidentally, does not represent just the firms in a single industry. Because firms in many different industries demand labor, the representative firm in Figure 10.3b represents any firm in any industry that uses labor.

The firm faces a market wage rate of $10. We can think of this as the marginal cost of a unit of labor. (Note that we are now discussing the margin in units of *labor*; in previous chapters, we talked about marginal units of *output*.) Given a wage of $10, how much labor would the firm demand?

One might think that 100 units would be hired, the point at which the difference between marginal revenue product and wage rate is greatest. But the firm is interested in maximizing *total* profit, not *marginal* profit. Hiring the 101st unit of labor generates $20 in revenue at a cost of only $10. Because MRP_L is greater than the cost of the input required to produce it, hiring one more unit of labor adds to profit. This will continue to be true as long as MRP_L remains above $10, which is all the way to 210 units. At that point, the wage rate is equal to the marginal revenue product of labor, or

$$W^* = MRP_L = 10.$$

The firm will not demand labor beyond 210 units, because the cost of hiring the 211th unit of labor would be greater than the value of what that unit produces. (Recall that the fourth sandwich maker can produce only an extra $2.50 an hour in sandwiches, while his salary is $4 per hour.)

Thus the curve in Figure 10.3b tells us how much labor a firm that uses only one variable factor of production will hire at each potential market wage rate. If the market wage falls, the quantity of labor demanded will rise. If the market wage rises, the

FAST FACTS

AVERAGE HOURLY EARNINGS: PRIVATE NONFARM PAYROLLS IN THE UNITED STATES

1960	$2.09
1970	$3.23
1980	$6.66
1990	$10.01
1997[a]	$12.22

[a]Figure for June.

Source: Bureau of Labor Statistics.

quantity of labor demanded will fall. This description should sound familiar to you—it is, in fact, the description of a demand curve. Therefore we can now say that:

> When a firm uses only one variable factor of production, that factor's marginal revenue product curve is the firm's demand curve for that factor in the short run.

For another example of the relevance of marginal revenue product, see the Application box titled "Millionaire Baseball Players and Their Marginal Revenue Product."

► **Comparing Marginal Revenue and Marginal Cost to Maximize Profits** In chapter 8, we saw that a competitive firm's marginal cost curve is the same as its supply curve. That is, at any output price, the marginal cost curve determines how much output a profit-maximizing firm will produce. We came to this conclusion by comparing the marginal revenue that a firm would earn by producing one more unit of output with the marginal cost of producing that unit of output.

There is no difference between the reasoning in chapter 8 and the reasoning in this chapter. The only difference is that what is being measured at the margin has changed. In chapter 8, the firm was comparing the marginal revenues and costs of producing *another unit of output*. Here, the firm is comparing the marginal revenues and costs of employing *another unit of input*. To see this similarity, look at Figure 10.4. If the only variable factor of production is labor, the condition $W^* = MRP_L$ is the same condition as $P = MC$. The two statements say exactly the same thing.

In both cases, the firm is comparing the cost of production with potential revenues from the sale of product *at the margin*. In chapter 8, the firm compared the price of output (P, which is equal to MR in perfect competition) directly with cost of production (MC), where cost was derived from information on factor prices and technology. (Review the derivation of cost curves in chapter 8 if this is unclear.) Here, information on output price and technology is contained in the marginal revenue product curve, which is compared with information on input price to determine the optimal level of input to demand.

The assumption of one variable factor of production makes the trade-off facing firms easy to see. Figure 10.5 shows that in essence firms weigh the value of labor as reflected in the market wage against the value of the product of labor as reflected in the price of output:

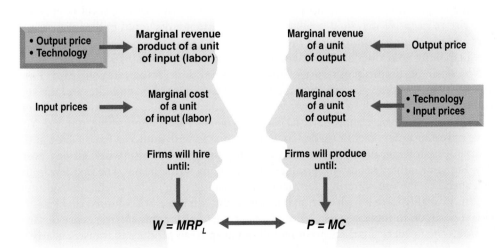

FIGURE 10.4
The Two Profit-Maximizing Conditions Are Simply Two Views of the Same Choice Process

FIGURE 10.5

The Trade-Off Facing Firms

Firms weigh the cost of labor as reflected in wage rates against the value of labor's marginal product. Assume that labor is the only variable factor of production. Then, if society values a good more than it costs firms to hire the workers to produce that good, the good will be produced.

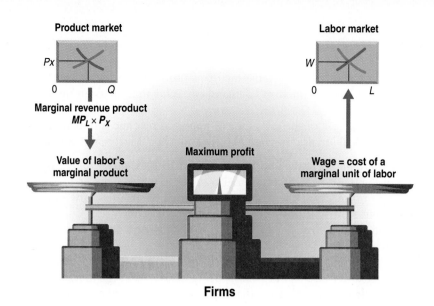

Product market

Px

0   Q

Marginal revenue product
$MP_L \times P_X$

Value of labor's marginal product

Maximum profit

Labor market

W

0   L

Wage = cost of a marginal unit of labor

Firms

Assuming that labor is the only variable input, if society values a good more than it costs firms to hire the workers to produce that good, the good will be produced. In general, the same logic also holds for more than one input. Firms weigh the value of outputs as reflected in output price against the value of inputs as reflected in marginal costs.

➤ **Deriving Input Demands** For the small sandwich shop, calculating the marginal product of a variable input (labor) and marginal revenue product was easy. Although it may be more complex, the decision process is essentially the same both for big corporations and for small proprietorships.

When an airline hires more flight attendants, for example, it increases the quality of its service to attract more passengers and thus sell more of its product. In deciding how many to hire, the airline must figure out how much new revenue the added flight attendants are likely to generate relative to their wages.

At the sandwich shop, diminishing returns set in at a certain point. The same holds true for an airplane. Once a sufficient number of attendants are on a plane, additional attendants add little to the quality of service, and beyond a certain level might even give rise to negative marginal product. Too many attendants could bother the passengers and make it difficult to get to the restrooms.

In making your own decisions, you too compare marginal gains with input costs in the presence of diminishing returns. Suppose you grow vegetables in your yard. First, you save money at the grocery store. Second, you can plant what you like, and the vegetables taste better fresh from the garden. Third, you simply like to work in the garden.

Like the sandwich shop and the airline, you also face diminishing returns. You have only 625 square feet of garden to work with, and with land as a fixed factor in the short run, your marginal product will certainly decline. You can work all day every day, but your limited space will produce only so many string beans. The first few hours you spend each week watering, fertilizing, and dealing with major weed and bug infestations probably have a high marginal product. But after five or six hours, there is little else you can do to increase yield. Diminishing returns also apply to your sense of satisfaction. The farmers' markets are now full of cheap fresh produce that tastes nearly as good as yours. And once you have been out in the garden for a few hours, the hot sun and hard work start to lose their charm.

MILLIONAIRE BASEBALL PLAYERS AND THEIR MARGINAL REVENUE PRODUCT

Consider the following article, which appeared in the *New York Times* on February 21, 1997:

BONDS SIGNS HUGE EXTENSION

Barry Bonds agreed to a two-year, $22.9 million contract extension yesterday with the San Francisco Giants that gives the three-time National League most valuable player the highest average salary in the majors.

The extension, which will begin in 1999, also includes a third year at the Giants' option.

That could ensure the left fielder's services through the year 2001.

"With today's announcement, I'm happy to say that baseball's best player will be wearing a San Francisco Giants uniform into the 21st century," said Giants General Manager Brian Sabean.

Bonds' average salary of $11.45 million bests the average of $11 million a year that Belle will receive with the White Sox.[a]

How in the world could anyone be worth $11.45 million per year? Why would owners be willing to pay millions of dollars a year to a single player? As we've seen in this chapter, profit-maximizing employers will hire workers only as long as their marginal revenue product (MRP_L) is greater than or equal to their wage. Could it then be possible that Barry Bonds is "worth it"?

Gerald W. Scully, Professor of Management at the University of Texas at Dallas, has made a statistical estimate of the contribution that ballplayers made to the revenues of their teams during the 1980s. The results may surprise you:

[In 1984] . . . an extra victory was worth $195,653. Now consider the effect on revenues of adding a hitter like Andre Dawson, the National League MVP of 1987, or a pitcher like Roger Clemens, the Cy Young Award winner in the American League in 1986. Dawson had a slugging average of .568 over 621 at bats. Chicago had a team slugging average of .432 over 5,583 at bats. Dawson contributed 11.1 percent of the at-bats and 0.063 of the team's slugging average. Given the relationship between slugging average and wins, those 63 points were conservatively worth 11 games. The marginal revenue [product] of those 11 games was about $2.2 million. Roger Clemens posted a 24–4 record in Boston in 1986. Assuming that Clemens was the source of the margin of victory in those net 20 games, his performance was worth $3.9 million [in 1986] . . . By such economic standards such players are not overpaid.[b]

DO YOU THINK BARRY BONDS' MARGINAL REVENUE PRODUCT IS GREATER THAN $11.5 MILLION PER YEAR?

Sources: [a]Murray Chass, "Bond Signs Huge Extension," *The New York Times*, February 21, 1997, p. B21. Copyright © 1997 by The New York Times Co. Reprinted by permission. [b]Gerald W. Scully, *The Business of Major League Baseball* (Chicago: University of Chicago Press, 1989), pp. 155–156.

For more on professional athletes and their salaries, see the Case and Fair Web page at http://www.prenhall.com/casefair.

Although your gardening does not involve a salary (unlike the sandwich shop and the airline, which pay out wages), the labor you supply has a value that must be weighed. When the returns diminish beyond a certain point, you must weigh the value of additional gardening time against leisure and the other options available to you.

Less labor is likely to be employed as the cost of labor rises. If the competitive labor market pushed the daily wage to $6 per hour, the sandwich shop would hire only two workers instead of three (see Table 10.1). If you suddenly became very busy at school, your time would become more valuable, and you would probably devote fewer hours to gardening.

OPTIONAL MATERIAL

A FIRM EMPLOYING TWO VARIABLE FACTORS OF PRODUCTION IN THE SHORT AND LONG RUN

When a firm employs more than one variable factor of production, the analysis of input demand becomes more complicated, but the principles stay the same. We shall now consider a firm that employs variable capital (K) and labor (L) inputs, and thus faces factor prices P_K and P_L.[2] (Recall that *capital* refers to plant, equipment, and inventory used in production. We assume that some portion of the firm's capital stock is fixed in the short run, but that some of it is variable—for example, some machinery and equipment can be installed quickly.) Our analysis can be applied to any two factors of production and can easily be generalized to three or more. It can also be applied to the long run, when all factors of production are variable.

You have seen that inputs can be complementary or substitutable. Land, labor, and capital are used *together* to produce outputs. The worker who uses a shovel digs a bigger hole than one with no shovel. Add a steam shovel and that worker becomes even more productive. When an expanding firm adds to its stock of capital, it raises the productivity of its labor, and vice versa. Thus, each factor complements the other. At the same time, though, land, labor, and capital can also be *substituted* for one another. If labor becomes expensive, some labor-saving technology (robotics, for example) may take its place.

In firms employing just one variable factor of production, a change in the price of that factor affects only the demand for the factor itself. When more than one factor can vary, however, we must consider the impact of a change in one factor price on the demand for other factors as well.

> ▶ **Substitution and Output Effects of a Change in Factor Price**   Table 10.2 presents data on a hypothetical firm that employs variable capital and labor. Suppose that the firm faces a choice between two available technologies of production—technique A, which is capital intensive, and technique B, which is labor intensive. When the market price of labor is $1 per unit and the market price of capital is $1 per unit, the labor-intensive method of producing output is less costly. Each unit costs only $13 to produce using technique B, while the unit cost of production using technique A is $15. If the price of labor rises to $2, however, technique B is no longer less costly. Labor has become more expensive relative to capital. The unit cost rises to $23 for labor-intensive technique B, but to only $20 for capital-intensive technique A.

Table 10.3 shows the impact of such an increase in the price of labor on both capital and labor demand when a firm produces 100 units of output. When each input factor costs $1 per unit, the firm chooses technique B and demands 300 units of capital and 1,000 units of labor. Total variable cost is $1,300. An increase in the price of labor

---

TABLE 10.2   RESPONSE OF A FIRM TO AN INCREASING WAGE RATE

TECHNOLOGY	INPUT REQUIREMENTS PER UNIT OF OUTPUT K	L	UNIT COST IF $P_L = \$1$ $P_K = \$1$ $(P_L \times L) + (P_K \times K)$	UNIT COST IF $P_L = \$2$ $P_K = \$1$ $(P_L \times L) + (P_K \times K)$
A (capital intensive)	10	5	$15	$20
B (labor intensive)	3	10	$13	$23

---

[2]The price of labor, P_L, is the same as the wage rate, W. We will often use the term P_L instead of W to stress the symmetry between labor and capital.

TABLE 10.3 THE SUBSTITUTION EFFECT OF AN INCREASE IN WAGES ON A FIRM PRODUCING 100 UNITS OF OUTPUT

	TO PRODUCE 100 UNITS OF OUTPUT:		
	TOTAL CAPITAL DEMANDED	TOTAL LABOR DEMANDED	TOTAL VARIABLE COST
When P_L = $1, P_K = $1, firm uses technology B.	300	1,000	$1,300
When P_L = $2, P_K = $1, firm uses technology A.	1,000	500	$2,000

to $2 causes the firm to switch from technique *B* to technique *A*. In doing so, it *substitutes* capital for labor. The amount of labor demanded drops from 1,000 to 500 units. The amount of capital demanded increases from 300 to 1,000 units, while total variable cost increases to $2,000.

The tendency of firms to substitute away from a factor whose relative price has risen and toward a factor whose relative price has fallen is called the **factor substitution effect**. The factor substitution effect is part of the reason that *input demand curves slope downward*. When an input, or factor of production, becomes less expensive, firms tend to substitute it for other factors and thus buy *more* of it. When a particular input becomes more expensive, firms tend to substitute other factors and buy *less* of it.

The firm described in Tables 10.2 and 10.3 continued to produce 100 units of output after the wage rate doubled. An *increase* in the price of a production factor, however, also means an increase in the costs of production. Notice that total variable cost increased from $1,300 to $2,000. When a firm faces higher costs, it is likely to produce less in the short run. When a firm decides to cut output, its demand for all factors declines—including, of course, the factor whose price increased in the first place. This is called the **output effect of a factor price increase**.

A *decrease* in the price of a factor of production, in contrast, means lower costs of production. If their output price remains unchanged, firms will increase output. This, in turn, means that demand for all factors of production will increase. This is the **output effect of a factor price decrease**.

The output effect helps explain why input demand curves slope downward. Output effects and factor substitution effects work in the same direction. Consider, for example, a decline in the wage rate. Lower wages mean that a firm will substitute labor for capital and other inputs. Stated somewhat differently, the factor substitution effect leads to an increase in the quantity of labor demanded. Lower wages mean lower costs, and lower costs lead to more output. This increase in output means that the firm will hire more of all factors of production, including labor itself. This is the output effect of a factor price decrease. Notice that both effects lead to an increase in the demand for labor when the wage rate falls.

MANY LABOR MARKETS

Although Figure 10.1 depicts "*the* labor market," many labor markets exist. There is a market for baseball players, for carpenters, for chemists, for college professors, and for unskilled workers. Still other markets exist for taxi drivers, assembly line workers, secretaries, and corporate executives. Each market has a set of skills associated with it and a supply of people with the requisite skills.

factor substitution effect
The tendency of firms to substitute away from a factor whose price has risen and toward a factor whose price has fallen.

If labor markets are competitive, the wages in those markets are determined by the interaction of supply and demand. As we have seen, firms will hire workers only as long as the value of their product exceeds the relevant market wage. This is true in all competitive labor markets.

LAND MARKETS

Unlike labor and capital, land has a special feature that we have not yet considered: It is in strictly fixed (perfectly inelastic) supply in total. The only real questions about land thus center around how much it is worth and to what use it will be put.

Because land is fixed in supply, we say that its price is **demand determined**. In other words, the price of land is determined exclusively by what households and firms are willing to pay for it. The return to any factor of production in fixed supply is called a **pure rent**.

demand determined price
The price of a good that is in fixed supply; it is determined exclusively by what firms and households are willing to pay for the good.

pure rent *The return to any factor of production that is in fixed supply.*

Thinking of the price of land as demand determined can be confusing because all land is not the same. Some land is clearly more valuable than other land. What lies behind these differences? As with any other factor of production, land will presumably be sold or rented to the user who is willing to pay the most for it. The value of land to a potential user may depend upon the characteristics of the land itself or upon its location. For example, more fertile land should produce more farm products per acre and thus command a higher price than less fertile land. A piece of property located at the intersection of two highways may be of great value as a site for a gas station because of the amount of traffic that passes the intersection daily.

A numerical example may help to clarify our discussion. Consider the potential uses of a corner lot in a suburb of Kansas City. Alan wants to build a clothing store on the lot. He anticipates that he can earn economic profits of $10,000 per year there because of the land's excellent location. Bella, another person interested in buying the corner lot, believes that she can earn $35,000 per year in economic profit if she builds a drugstore there. Clearly, Bella will be able to outbid Alan, and the landowner will sell (or rent) to the highest bidder.

Because location is often the key to profits, landowners are frequently able to "squeeze" their renters. One of the most popular locations in the Boston area, for example, is Harvard Square. There are dozens of restaurants in and around the square, and most of them are full most of the time. Despite this seeming success, most Harvard Square restaurant owners are not getting rich. Why? Because they must pay very high rents on the location of their restaurants. A substantial portion of each restaurant's revenues goes to rent the land that (by virtue of its scarcity) is the key to unlocking those same revenues.

Although Figure 10.6 shows that the supply of land is perfectly inelastic (a vertical line), the supply of land in a *given use* may not be perfectly inelastic or fixed. Think, for example, about farmland and land available for housing developments. As a city's population grows, housing developers find themselves willing to pay more and more for land. As land becomes more valuable for development, some farmers sell out, and the supply of land available for development increases. This analysis would lead us to draw an upward-sloping supply curve (not a perfectly inelastic supply curve) for land in the land-for-development category.

Nonetheless, our major point—that land earns a pure rent—is still valid:

The supply of land of a *given quality* at a *given location* is truly fixed in supply. Its value is determined exclusively by the amount that the highest bidder is willing to pay for it. Because land cannot be reproduced, supply is perfectly inelastic.

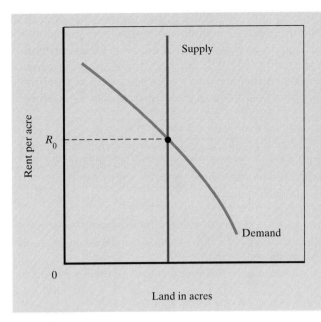

FIGURE 10.6

The Rent on Land Is Demand Determined

Because land in general (and each parcel in particular) is in fixed supply, its price is demand determined. Graphically, a fixed supply is represented by a vertical, perfectly inelastic, supply curve. Rent, R_0, depends exclusively on demand—what people are willing to pay.

RENT AND THE VALUE OF OUTPUT PRODUCED ON LAND

Because the price of land is demand determined, rent depends on what the potential users of the land are willing to pay for it. As we've seen, land will end up being used by whoever is willing to pay the most for it. But what determines willingness to pay? Let us now connect our discussion of land markets with our earlier discussions of factor markets in general.

As our example of two potential users bidding for a plot of land shows, the bids depend on the land's potential for profit. Alan's plan would generate $10,000 a year; Bella's would generate $35,000 a year. But these profits do not just materialize. Rather, they come from producing and selling an output that is valuable to households. Land in a popular downtown location is expensive because of what can be produced on it. Note that land is needed as an input into the production of nearly all goods and services. A restaurant located next to a popular theater can charge a premium price because it has a relatively captive clientele. Clearly, the restaurant must produce a quality product to stay in business, but the location alone provides a substantial profit opportunity.

THE DEMAND FOR LAND IS A DERIVED DEMAND. AGRICULTURAL OR EVEN DESERT LAND WILL BE DEVELOPED WHEN THERE IS A DEMAND FOR HOUSING, BECAUSE LAND IS A KEY INPUT USED IN THE PRODUCTION OF HOUSING.

It should come as no surprise that the demand for land follows the same rules as the demand for inputs in general. A profit-maximizing firm will employ an additional factor of production as long as its marginal revenue product exceeds its market price. For example, a profit-maximizing firm will hire labor as long as the revenue earned from selling labor's product is sufficient to cover the cost of hiring additional labor—which for perfectly competitive firms equals the wage rate. The same thing is true for land:

> A firm will pay for and use land as long as the revenue earned from selling the product produced on that land is sufficient to cover the price of the land. Stated in equation form, the firm will use land up to the point at which $MRP_A = P_A$, where A is land (acres).

Just as the demand curve for labor reflects the value of labor's product as determined in output markets, so the demand for land depends on the value of land's product in output markets. The profitability of the restaurant located next to the theater results from the fact that the meals produced there command a price in the marketplace.

The allocation of a given plot of land among competing uses thus depends on the trade-off between competing products that can be produced there. Agricultural land becomes developed when its value in producing housing or manufactured goods, or providing space for a mini mall, exceeds its value in producing crops. A corner lot in Kansas City becomes the site of a drugstore rather than a clothing store because the people in that neighborhood have a greater need for a drugstore.

One final word about land: Because land cannot be moved physically, the value of any one parcel depends to a large extent upon the uses to which adjoining parcels are put. A factory belching acrid smoke will probably reduce the value of adjoining land, while a new highway that increases accessibility may enhance it.

OPTIONAL MATERIAL
The Firm's Profit-Maximization Condition in Input Markets

Thus far we have discussed the labor and land markets in some detail. Although we will put off a detailed discussion of capital until the next chapter, it is now possible to generalize about competitive demand for factors of production. Every firm has an incentive to use variable inputs as long as the revenue generated by those inputs covers the costs of those inputs at the margin. More formally, firms will employ each input up to the point that its price equals its marginal revenue product. This condition holds for all factors at all levels of output:

Profit-Maximizing Condition for the Perfectly Competitive Firm:	$P_L = MRP_L = (MP_L \times P_X)$ $P_K = MRP_K = (MP_K \times P_X)$ $P_A = MRP_A = (MP_A \times P_X)$

where L is labor, K is capital, A is land (acres), X is output, and P_X is the price of that output.

When all these conditions are met, the firm will be using the optimal, or least costly, combination of inputs. If all these conditions hold at the same time, it is possible to rewrite them in another way:

$$\frac{MP_L}{P_L} = \frac{MP_K}{P_K} = \frac{MP_A}{P_A} = \frac{1}{P_X}$$

Your intuition tells you much the same thing that these equations do: The marginal product of the last dollar spent on labor must be equal to the marginal product of the last dollar spent on capital, which must be equal to the marginal product of the last dollar spent on land, and so forth. If this were not the case, the firm could produce more with less and reduce cost. Suppose, for example, that $MP_L/P_L > MP_K/P_K$. In this situation, the firm can produce more output by shifting dollars out of capital and into labor.

Hiring more labor drives down the marginal product of labor, and using less capital increases the marginal product of capital. This means that the ratios come back to equality as the firm shifts out of capital and into labor.

So far we have used very general terms to discuss the nature of input demand by firms in competitive markets, where input prices and output prices are taken as given. The most important point here is that demand for a factor depends on the value that the market places on its marginal product.[3] The rest of this chapter explores the forces that determine the shapes and positions of input demand curves.

INPUT DEMAND CURVES

When we discussed supply and demand in chapter 5, we spent a good deal of time talking about the factors that influence the responsiveness, or elasticity, of output demand curves. We have not yet talked about *input* demand curves in any detail, however, and we now need to say more about what lies behind them.

SHIFTS IN FACTOR DEMAND CURVES

Factor (input) demand curves are derived from information on technology (that is, production functions) and output price (see Figure 10.4). A change in the demand for outputs, a change in the quantity of complementary or substitutable inputs, changes in the prices of other inputs, and technological change all can cause factor demand curves to shift. These shifts in demand are important because they directly affect the allocation of resources among alternative uses, as well as the level and distribution of income.

▶ **The Demand for Outputs** A firm will demand an input as long as its marginal revenue product exceeds its market price. Marginal revenue product, which in perfect competition is equal to a factor's marginal product times the price of output, is the value of the factor's marginal product:

$$MRP_L = MP_L \times P_X.$$

The amount that a firm is willing to pay for a factor of production, then, depends directly on the value of the things that the firm produces. It follows that:

If product demand increases, product price will rise and marginal revenue product (factor demand) will increase—the *MRP* curve will shift to the right. If product demand declines, product price will fall and marginal revenue product (factor demand) will decrease—the *MRP* curve will shift to the left.

Go back and raise the price of sandwiches from $.50 to $1 in the sandwich shop example examined in Table 10.1 to see that this is so.

To the extent that any input is used intensively in the production of some product, changes in the demand for that product cause factor demand curves to shift and the prices of those inputs to change. Land prices are a good example. Thirty-five years ago, the area in Manhattan along the west side of Central park from about 80th Street north was a run-down neighborhood full of abandoned houses. The value of land

FAST FACTS

"There is a rapidly growing literature in economics dealing with the increase in earnings inequality over the last few decades. . . . This literature reaches virtually unanimous agreement that during the 1980's relative demand increased for workers at the high end of the skill distribution and thus caused their wages to rise."

Source: George E. Johnson, "Changes in Earnings Inequality: The Role of Demand Shifts," *Journal of Economic Perspectives,* Spring 1997, p. 41.

[3]If you worked through the appendix to chapter 7, you saw this same condition derived graphically from an isocost/isoquant diagram. Note: $MP_L/P_L = MP_K/P_K \rightarrow MP_L/MP_K = P_L/P_K$.

there was virtually zero. During the mid-1980s, increased demand for housing caused rents to hit record levels. Some single-room apartments, for example, rented for as much as $1,400 per month.

With the higher price of output (rent), input prices increased substantially. Small buildings on 80th Street and Central Park West sold for well over a million dollars, and the value of the land figures very importantly in these building prices. In essence, a shift in demand for an output (housing in the area) pushed up the marginal revenue product of land from zero to very high levels.

► **The Quantity of Complementary and Substitutable Inputs** In our discussion thus far, we have kept coming back to the fact that factors of production complement one another. The productivity of, and thus the demand for, any one factor of production depends upon the quality and quantity of the other factors with which it works.

The effect of capital accumulation on wages is one of the most important themes in all of economics. In general:

> The production and use of capital enhances the productivity of labor, and normally increases the demand for labor and drives up wages.

Take as an example transportation. In a poor country like Bangladesh, one person with an ox cart can move a small load over bad roads very slowly. By contrast, the stock of capital used by workers in the transportation industry in the United States is enormous. A truck driver in the United States works with a substantial amount of capital. The typical 18-wheel tractor trailer, for example, is a piece of capital worth over $100,000. The roads themselves are capital that was put in place by the government. The amount of material that a single driver can now move between distant points in a short time is staggering relative to what it was just 25 years ago.

► **The Prices of Other Inputs** When a firm has a choice among alternative technologies, the choice it makes depends to some extent on relative input prices. You saw in Tables 10.2 and 10.3 that an increase in the price of labor substantially increased the demand for capital as the firm switched to a more capital-intensive production technique.

During the 1970s, the large increase in energy prices relative to prices of other factors of production had a number of effects on the demand for those other inputs. Insulation of new buildings, installation of more efficient heating plants, and similar efforts substantially raised the demand for capital as capital was substituted for energy in production. But it has also been argued that the energy crisis led to an increase in demand for labor. If capital and energy are complementary inputs—that is, if technologies that are capital intensive are also energy intensive—the argument goes, the higher energy prices tended to push firms away from capital-intensive techniques and toward more labor-intensive techniques.[4] A new highly automated technique, for example, might need fewer workers, but it would also require a vast amount of electricity to operate. High electricity prices could lead a firm to reject the new techniques and stick with an old, more labor-intensive, method of production.

► **Technological Change** Closely related to the impact of capital accumulation on factor demand is the potential impact of **technological change**—that is, the introduction of new methods of production or new products. New technologies usually introduce ways to produce outputs with fewer inputs by increasing the productivity of existing inputs or by raising marginal products. Because marginal revenue product reflects productivity, increases in productivity directly shift input demand curves. If the marginal product of labor rises, for example, the demand for labor shifts to the right (increases).

technological change
The introduction of new methods of production or new products intended to increase the productivity of existing inputs or to raise marginal products.

[4]This argument was made in a series of papers by Professor Dale Jorgenson of Harvard University.

Technological change can and does have a powerful influence on factor demands. As new products and new techniques of production are born, so are demands for new inputs and new skills. As old products become obsolete, so too do the labor skills and other inputs needed to produce them.

RESOURCE ALLOCATION AND THE MIX OF OUTPUT IN COMPETITIVE MARKETS

We now have a complete, but simplified, picture of household and firm decision making. We have also examined some of the basic forces that determine the allocation of resources and the mix of output in perfectly competitive markets.

In this competitive environment, profit-maximizing firms make three fundamental decisions: (1) how much to produce and supply in output markets, (2) how to produce (which technology to use), and (3) how much of each input to demand. Chapters 7 to 9 looked at these three decisions from the perspective of the output market. We derived the supply curve of a competitive firm in the short run and discussed output market adjustment in the long run. Deriving cost curves, we learned, involves evaluating and choosing among alternative technologies. Finally, we saw how a firm's decision about how much product to supply in output markets implicitly determines input demands. Input demands, we argued, are also derived demands. That is, they are ultimately linked to the demand for output.

To show the connection between output and input markets, this chapter took these same three decisions and examined them from the perspective of input markets. Firms hire up to the point at which each input's marginal revenue product is equal to its price.

➤ **The Distribution of Income**   In the last few chapters, we have been focusing primarily on the firm. But throughout our study of microeconomics, we have also been building a theory that explains the distribution of income among households. We can now put the pieces of this puzzle together.

As we saw in this chapter, income is earned by households as payment for the factors of production that household members supply in input markets. Workers receive wages in exchange for their labor, owners of capital receive profits and interest in exchange for supplying capital (saving), and landowners receive rents in exchange for the use of their land. The incomes of workers depend on the wage rates determined in the market. The incomes of capital owners depend on the market price of capital (the amount households are paid for the use of their savings). And the incomes of landowners depend on the rental values of their land.

If markets are competitive, the equilibrium price of each input is equal to its marginal revenue product ($W = MRP_L$, and so forth). In other words, at equilibrium, each factor ends up receiving rewards determined by its productivity as measured by marginal revenue product. This is referred to as the **marginal productivity theory of income distribution.** We will turn to a more complete analysis of income distribution in chapter 17.

marginal productivity theory of income distribution
At equilibrium, all factors of production end up receiving rewards determined by their productivity as measured by marginal revenue product.

LOOKING AHEAD

We have now completed our discussion of competitive labor and land markets. (More on the labor market and labor unions can be found in chapter 19.) The next chapter takes up the complexity of what we have been loosely calling the "capital market." There we discuss the relationship between the market for physical capital and financial capital markets, and look at some of the ways that firms make investment decisions. Once we examine the nature of overall competitive equilibrium in chapter 12, we can finally begin relaxing some of the assumptions that have restricted the scope of our inquiry—most importantly, the assumption of perfect competition in input and output markets.

SUMMARY

1. The exact same set of decisions that lies behind output supply curves also lies behind input demand curves. It is only the perspective that is different.

INPUT MARKETS: BASIC CONCEPTS

2. Demand for inputs depends on demand for the outputs that they produce; input demand is thus a *derived demand*. *Productivity* is a measure of the amount of output produced per unit of input.

3. In general, firms will demand workers as long as the value of what those workers produce exceeds what they must be paid. Households will supply labor as long as the wage exceeds the value of leisure or the value that they derive from nonpaid work.

4. Inputs are at the same time *complementary* and *substitutable*.

5. In the short run, some factor of production is fixed. This means that all firms encounter diminishing returns in the short run. Stated somewhat differently, diminishing returns means that all firms encounter declining marginal product in the short run.

6. The *marginal revenue product* (MRP) of a variable input is the additional revenue a firm earns by employing one additional unit of the input, *ceteris paribus*. MRP is equal to the input's marginal product times the price of output.

LABOR MARKETS

7. Demand for an input depends on that input's marginal revenue product. Profit-maximizing perfectly competitive firms will buy an input (e.g., hire labor) up to the point where the input's marginal revenue product equals its price. For a firm employing only one variable factor of production, the *MRP* curve is the firm's demand curve for that factor in the short run.

8. For a perfectly competitive firm employing one variable factor of production, labor, the condition $W = MRP_L$, is exactly the same as the condition $P = MC$. Firms weigh the value of outputs as reflected in output price against the value of inputs as reflected in marginal costs.

9. When a firm employs two variable factors of production, a change in factor price has both a *factor substitution effect* and an *output effect*.

10. A wage increase may lead a firm to substitute capital for labor and thus cause the quantity demanded of labor to decline. This is the *factor substitution effect of the wage increase*.

11. A wage increase increases cost, and higher cost may lead to lower output and less demand for all inputs, including labor. This is the *output effect of the wage increase*. The effect is the opposite for a wage decrease.

LAND MARKETS

12. Because land is in strictly fixed supply, its price is *demand determined*—that is, its price is determined exclusively by what households and firms are willing to pay for it. The return to any factor of production in fixed supply is called a *pure rent*. A firm will pay for and use land as long as the revenue earned from selling the product produced on that land is sufficient to cover the price of the land. The firm will use land up to the point at which $MRP_A = P_A$, where A is land (acres).

THE FIRM'S PROFIT-MAXIMIZING CONDITION IN INPUT MARKETS

13. Every firm has an incentive to use variable inputs as long as the revenue generated by those inputs covers the costs of those inputs at the margin. Therefore, firms will employ each input up to the point that its price equals its marginal revenue product. This profit-maximizing condition holds for all factors at all levels of output.

INPUT DEMAND CURVES

14. A shift in a firm's demand curve for a factor of production can be influenced by the demand for the firm's product, the quantity of complementary and substitutable inputs, the prices of other inputs, and changes in technology.

RESOURCE ALLOCATION AND THE MIX OF OUTPUT IN COMPETITIVE MARKETS

15. Because the price of a factor at equilibrium in competitive markets is equal to its marginal revenue product, the distribution of income among households depends in part on the relative productivity of factors. This is the *marginal productivity theory of income distribution*.

REVIEW TERMS AND CONCEPTS

demand determined price, 244
derived demand, 234
factor substitution effect, 243
marginal product of labor (MP_L), 235
marginal productivity theory of income distribution, 249

marginal revenue product (MRP), 236
output effect of a factor price increase/decrease, 243
productivity of an input, 234
pure rent, 244
technological change, 248

Equations:
$MRP_L = MP_L \times P_X$
$W^* = MRP_L$

PROBLEM SET

1. Assume that a firm that manufactures widgets can produce them with one of three processes, used alone or in combination. The following table indicates the amounts of capital and labor required by each of the three processes to produce one widget.

	UNITS OF LABOR	UNITS OF CAPITAL
Process 1	4	1
Process 2	2	2
Process 3	1	3

a. Assuming that capital costs $3 per unit and labor costs $1 per unit, which process will be employed?

b. Plot the three points on the firm's *TVC* curve corresponding to $q = 10$, $q = 30$, and $q = 50$.

c. At each of the three output levels, how much K and L will be demanded?

d. Repeat parts a. through c., assuming the price of capital is $3 per unit and that the price of labor has risen to $4 per unit.

2. The following schedule shows the technology of production at the Delicious Apple Orchard for 1998:

WORKERS	TOTAL BUSHELS OF APPLES PER DAY
0	0
1	40
2	70
3	90
4	100
5	105
6	102

If apples sell for $2 per bushel and workers can be hired in a competitive labor market for $30 per day, how many workers should be hired? What if workers unionized and the wage rose to $50? (*Hint:* Create marginal product and marginal revenue product columns for the table.) Explain your answers clearly.

3. The following graph is the production function for a firm using only one variable factor of production, labor:

a. Graph the marginal product of labor for the firm as a function of the number of labor units hired.

b. Assuming that the price of output, P_X, is equal to $6, graph the firm's marginal revenue product schedule as a function of the number of labor units hired.

c. If the current equilibrium wage rate is $4 per hour, how many hours of labor would you hire? How much output will you produce?

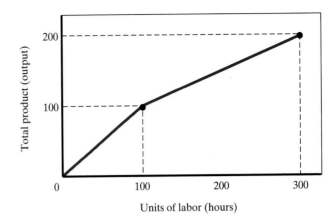

4. Describe how each of the following events would affect (1) the demand for construction workers and (2) construction wages in Portland, Oregon. Illustrate with supply and demand curves:

a. A sharp increase in interest rates on new-home mortgages reduces the demand for new houses substantially.

b. The economy of the area booms. Office rents rise, creating demand for new office space.

c. A change in the tax laws in 1997 made real estate developments more profitable. As a result, three major developers start planning to build major shopping centers.

5. The demand for land is a derived demand. Think of a popular location near your school. What determines the demand for land in that area? What outputs are sold by businesses located there? Discuss the relationship between land prices and the prices of those products.

6. Many states provide firms with an "investment tax credit" that effectively reduces the price of capital. In theory, these credits are designed to stimulate new investment and thus create jobs. Critics have argued that if there are strong factor substitution effects, these subsidies could actually *reduce* employment in the state. Explain their arguments.

7. Doug's farm in Idaho has four major fields that he uses to grow potatoes. The productivity of each field is given below:

	ANNUAL YIELD, HUNDREDS OF POUNDS
Field 1	10,000
Field 2	8,000
Field 3	5,000
Field 4	3,000

Assume that each field is the same size and that the variable costs of farming are $25,000 per year per field. The variable costs cover labor and machinery time, which is rented. Doug must decide each year how many fields to plant. In 1995, potato farmers received $6.35 per 100 pounds. How many fields did Doug plant? Explain. By 1998, the price of potatoes had fallen to $4.50 per 100 pounds. How will this price decrease change Doug's decision? How will it affect his demand for labor? How will it affect the value of Doug's land?

8. In 1997, *Business Week* reported that one of the highest paid executives in the United States was Frank Lanza of Lockheed Martin, the aircraft builder. That year, Lanza's compensation was over $50 million! Can you use the concepts of derived demand and marginal revenue product to justify such an enormous figure?

9. Assume that you are living in a house with two other people and that the house has a big lawn that has to be mowed. One of your roommates, who hates to work outdoors, suggests hiring a neighbor's daughter to mow the grass for $40 per week rather than sharing the work and doing it yourselves. How would you go about deciding who will mow the lawn? What factors would you raise in deciding? What are the trade-offs here?

10. Consider the following information for a T-shirt manufacturing firm that can sell as many T-shirts as it wants for $3 per shirt:

NUMBER OF WORKERS	NUMBER OF SHIRTS PRODUCED PER DAY	MP_L	TR	MRP_L
0	0	___	___	___
1	30	___	___	___
2	80	___	___	___
3	110	___	___	___
4	135	___	___	___
5	___	20	___	___
6	170	___	___	___
7	___	___	___	30
8	___	___	___	15

a. Fill in all the blanks in the table.

b. Verify that MRP_L for this firm can be calculated in two ways: (1) the change in TR from adding another worker and (2) MP_L times the price of output.

c. If this firm must pay a wage rate of $40 per worker per day, how many workers should it hire? Briefly, why?

d. Suppose the wage rate rises to $50 per worker. How many workers should be hired now? Why?

e. Suppose the firm adopts a new technology that doubles output at each level of employment and that the price of shirts remains at $3. What is the effect of this new technology on MP_L? MRP_L? At a wage of $50, how many workers should the firm hire now?

*11. For a given firm, $MRP_L = 50, and $MRP_K = 100, while $P_L = 10 and $P_K = 20.

a. Is the firm maximizing profits? Why or why not?

b. Can you identify a specific action that would increase this firm's profits?

TAKE IT TO THE NET

We invite you to visit the Case and Fair page on the Prentice Hall Web site:

http://www.prenhall.com/casefair

for this chapter's World Wide Web exercise.

Chapter 11

INPUT DEMAND:
THE CAPITAL MARKET AND THE INVESTMENT DECISION

WE SAW IN CHAPTER 10 that perfectly competitive firms hire factors of production (inputs) up to the point at which each factor's marginal revenue product is equal to that factor's price. The three main factors of production are land, labor, and capital. We also saw that factor prices are determined by the interaction of supply and demand in the factor markets. The wage rate is determined in the labor market, the price of land is determined in the land market, and the price of capital is determined in the capital market.

In chapter 10, we explored the labor and land markets in some detail. In this chapter we consider the capital market more fully. Transactions between households and firms in the labor and land markets are direct. In the labor market, households offer their labor directly to firms in exchange for wages. In the land market, landowners rent or sell their land directly to firms in exchange for rent or an agreed-upon price. In the capital market, though, households often *indirectly* supply the financial resources necessary for firms to purchase capital. When households save and add funds to their bank accounts, for example, firms can borrow these funds from the bank to finance their capital purchases.

Earlier, in chapter 9, we discussed the incentives new firms have to enter industries in which profit opportunities exist and the incentives that existing firms have to leave industries in which they are suffering losses. We also described the conditions under which existing firms have an incentive either to expand or to reduce their scales of operation. That chapter was in a preliminary way describing the process of capital allocation. When new firms enter an industry or an existing firm expands, someone pays to put capital (plant, equipment, and inventory) in place. Because the future is uncertain, capital investment decisions always involve risk. In market capitalist systems, the decision to put capital to use in a particular enterprise is made by private citizens putting their savings at risk in search of private gain. This chapter describes the set of institutions through which such transactions take place.

CAPITAL, INVESTMENT, AND DEPRECIATION

Before we proceed with our analysis of the capital market, we need to review some basic economic principles and introduce some related concepts.

CAPITAL

One of the most important concepts in all of economics is the concept of **capital**.

> Capital goods are those goods produced by the economic system that are used as inputs to produce other goods and services in the future. Capital goods thus yield valuable productive services over time.

capital *Those goods produced by the economic system that are used as inputs to produce other goods and services in the future.*

▶ **Tangible Capital**   When we think of capital, we generally think of the physical, material capital employed by business firms. The major categories of **physical**, or **tangible**, **capital** are (1) nonresidential structures (office buildings, power plants, factories, shopping centers, warehouses, and docks, for example); (2) durable equipment (machines, trucks, sandwich grills, automobiles, and so on); (3) residential structures; and (4) inventories of inputs and outputs that firms have in stock.

physical or **tangible, capital** *Material things used as inputs in the production of future goods and services. The major categories of physical capital are nonresidential structures, durable equipment, residential structures, and inventories.*

Most firms need tangible capital, along with labor and land, to produce their products. A restaurant's capital requirements include a kitchen, ovens and grills, tables and chairs, silverware, dishes, and light fixtures. These items must be purchased up front and maintained if the restaurant is to function properly. A manufacturing firm must have a plant, specialized machinery, trucks, and inventories of parts. A winery needs casks, vats, piping, temperature-control equipment, and cooking and bottling machinery.

The capital stock of a retail drugstore is made up mostly of inventories. Drugstores do not produce the aspirin, vitamins, and toothbrushes that they sell. Instead, they buy those things from manufacturers and put them on display. The product actually produced and sold by a drugstore is convenience. Like any other product, convenience is produced with labor and capital in the form of a store with lots of products, or inventory, displayed on the sales floor and kept in storerooms. The inventories of inputs and outputs that manufacturing firms maintain are also capital. To function smoothly and meet the demands of buyers, for example, the Ford Motor Company maintains inventories of both auto parts (tires, windshields, etc.) and completed cars.

An apartment building is also capital. Produced by the economic system, it yields valuable services over time, and it is used as an input to produce housing services, which are rented out.

▶ **Social Capital: Infrastructure**   Some physical or tangible capital is owned by the public rather than by private firms. **Social capital**, sometimes called **infrastructure**, is capital that provides services to the public. Most social capital takes the form of public works like highways, roads, bridges, mass transit systems, and sewer and water systems. Police stations, fire stations, city halls, courthouses, and police cars all are forms of social capital that are used as inputs to produce the services that government provides.

social capital, or infrastructure *Capital that provides services to the public. Most social capital takes the form of public works (roads and bridges) and public services (police and fire protection).*

All firms use some forms of social capital in producing their outputs. Recent economic research has shown that a country's infrastructure plays a very important role in helping private firms produce their products efficiently. When public capital is not properly cared for—for example, when roads deteriorate or when airports are not modernized to accommodate increasing traffic—private firms that depend on efficient transportation networks suffer. In his economic plan presented to the Congress in early 1993, President Clinton proposed increasing government spending on infrastructure—road and bridge repair, the development of a high-speed rail network, and several other transportation projects. Congress cut most of the proposed spending to save money in 1993. The debate will no doubt continue as the twenty-first century begins.

> **Intangible Capital** Not all capital is physical. Some things that are intangible (non-material) satisfy every part of our definition of capital. When a business firm invests in advertising to establish a brand name, it is producing a form of **intangible capital** called goodwill. This goodwill yields valuable services to the firm over time.

When a firm establishes a training program for employees, it is investing in its workers' skills. One can think of such an investment as the production of an intangible form of capital called **human capital**. It is produced with labor (instructors) and capital (classrooms, computers, projectors, and books). Human capital in the form of new or augmented skills is an input—it will yield valuable productive services for the firm in the future.

When research produces valuable results, such as a new production process that reduces costs or a new formula that creates a new product, the new technology itself can be considered capital. Furthermore, even ideas can be patented and the rights to them can be sold.

> **The Time Dimension** The most important dimension of capital is the fact that it exists through time. Labor services are used at the time they are provided. Households consume services and nondurable goods[1] almost immediately after purchase. But capital exists now and into the future. Therefore,

> The value of capital is only as great as the value of the services it will render over time.[2]

> **Measuring Capital** Labor is measured in hours, and land is measured in square feet or acres. But because capital comes in so many forms, it is virtually impossible to measure it directly in physical terms. The indirect measure generally used is *current market value*. The measure of a firm's **capital stock** is the current market value of its plant, equipment, inventories, and intangible assets. Using value as a measuring stick, business managers, accountants, and economists can, in a sense, add buildings, barges, and bulldozers into a measure of total capital.

Capital is measured as a *stock* value. That is, it is measured at a point in time. The capital stock of the XYZ Corporation on July 31, 1998, is $3,453,231. Or at the beginning of 1996, the gross nonresidential fixed capital stock (buildings and equipment) of all private industries (including farms) in the United States was $8.0 trillion, including $4.9 trillion in structures and $3.1 trillion in equipment.[3]

Although it is measured in terms of money, or value, it is very important to think of the actual capital stock itself:

> When we speak of capital, we refer not to money or to financial assets such as bonds or stocks, but rather to the firm's physical plant, equipment, inventory, and intangible assets.

intangible capital *Nonmaterial things that contribute to the output of future goods and services.*

human capital *A form of intangible capital that includes the skills and other knowledge that workers have or acquire through education and training and that yields valuable services to a firm over time.*

capital stock *For a single firm, the current market value of the firm's plant, equipment, inventories, and intangible assets.*

---

[1]Consumer goods are generally divided into two categories: durables and nondurables. Technically, *durable goods* are goods expected to last for more than one year. *Nondurable goods* are goods expected to last less than one year.

[2]Conceptually, consumer durable goods, such as automobiles, washing machines, and the like, are capital. They are produced, they yield services over time, and households use them as inputs to produce services such as transportation and clean laundry.

[3]U.S. Department of Commerce, Bureau of Economic Analysis, *Survey of Current Business*, May, 1997. The total capital stock was over $22.5 trillion.

INVESTMENT AND DEPRECIATION

Recall the difference between stock and flow measures discussed in earlier chapters. *Stock measures* are valued at a particular point in time, while *flow measures* are valued over a period of time. The easiest way to think of the difference between a stock and a flow is to think about a tub of water. The volume of water in the tub is measured at a point in time and is a stock. The amount of water that flows into the tub *per hour* and the amount of water that evaporates out of the tub *per day* are flow measures. Flow measures have meaning only when the time dimension is added. Clearly, water flowing into the tub at a rate of five gallons per hour is very different from a rate of five gallons per year.

Capital stocks are affected over time by two flows: investment and depreciation. When a firm produces or puts in place new capital—a new piece of equipment, for example—it has invested. **Investment** is a flow that increases the stock of capital. Because it has a time dimension, we speak of investment per period (by the month, quarter, or year).

investment *New capital additions to a firm's capital stock. Although capital is measured at a given point in time (a stock), investment is measured over a period of time (a flow). The flow of investment increases the capital stock.*

As you proceed, be careful to keep in mind that the term *investing* is *not* used in economics to describe the act of buying a share of stock or a bond. Although people commonly use the term this way ("I invested in some Union Carbide stock" or "he invested in Treasury bonds"), the term *investment* when used correctly refers *only to an increase in capital.*

Table 11.1 presents data on private investment in the United States economy in 1997. About half of the total was new durable equipment. Almost all the rest was investment in structures, both residential (apartment buildings, condominiums, houses, and so forth) and nonresidential (factories, shopping malls, and so forth). Inventory investment was small.

depreciation *The decline in an asset's economic value over time.*

Depreciation is the decline in an asset's (resource's) economic value over time. If you have ever owned a car, you are aware that its resale value falls with age. Suppose you bought a new Pontiac in 1998 for $20,500 and you decide to sell it two years and 25,000 miles later. Checking the newspaper and talking to several dealers, you find out that, given its condition and the mileage, you can expect to get $12,000 for it. It has depreciated $8,500 ($20,500 − $12,000). Table 11.1 shows that in 1997 private depreciation in the U.S. economy was $716.8 billion.

A capital asset can depreciate because it wears out physically or because it becomes obsolete. Take, for example, a computer control system in a factory. If a new, technologically superior system does the same job for half the price, the old system may be replaced even if it still functions well. The Pontiac depreciated because of wear and tear *and* because new models had become available.

TABLE 11.1 PRIVATE INVESTMENT IN THE U.S. ECONOMY, 1997

	BILLIONS OF CURRENT DOLLARS	AS A PERCENTAGE OF TOTAL GROSS INVESTMENT	AS A PERCENTAGE OF GDP
Nonresidential structures	229.9	18.5	2.8
Durable equipment	615.5	49.6	7.6
Inventories	68.3	5.5	0.8
Residential structures	327.2	26.4	4.0
Total gross private investment	1,240.9	100.0	15.2
−Depreciation	−716.8	−57.8	− 8.9
Net investment =	524.1	42.2	6.3
(gross investment minus depreciation)			

Source: U.S. Department of Commerce, Bureau of Economic Analysis.

THE CAPITAL MARKET

Where does capital come from? How and why is it produced? How much and what kinds of capital are produced? Who pays for it? These questions are answered in the complex set of institutions in which households supply their savings to firms that demand funds in order to buy capital goods. Collectively, these institutions are called the **capital market**.

Although governments and households make some capital investment decisions, most decisions to produce new capital goods—that is, to invest—are made by firms. However, a firm cannot invest unless it has the funds to do so. Although firms can invest in many ways, it is always the case that:

> The funds that firms use to buy capital goods come, directly or indirectly, from households. When a household decides not to consume a portion of its income, it saves. Investment by firms is the *demand for capital*. Saving by households is the *supply of capital*. Various financial institutions facilitate the transfer of households' savings to firms that use them for capital investment.

Let us use a simple example to see how the system works. Suppose that some firm wants to purchase a machine that costs $1,000 and that some household decides at the same time to save $1,000 from its income. Figure 11.1 shows one way that the household's decision to save might connect with the firm's decision to invest.

Either directly or through a financial intermediary (such as a bank), the household agrees to loan its savings to the firm. In exchange, the firm contracts to pay the household interest at some agreed-upon rate each period. If the household lends directly to the firm, the firm gives the household a **bond**, which is nothing more than a contract promising to repay the loan at some specific time in the future. The bond also specifies the flow of interest to be paid in the meantime.

The new saving adds to the household's stock of wealth. The household's *net worth* has increased by the $1,000, which it holds in the form of a bond.[4] The bond

capital market *The market in which households supply their savings to firms that demand funds in order to buy capital goods.*

bond *A contract between a borrower and a lender, in which the borrower agrees to pay the loan at some time in the future, along with interest payments along the way.*

FIGURE 11.1

$1,000 in Savings Becomes $1,000 of Investment

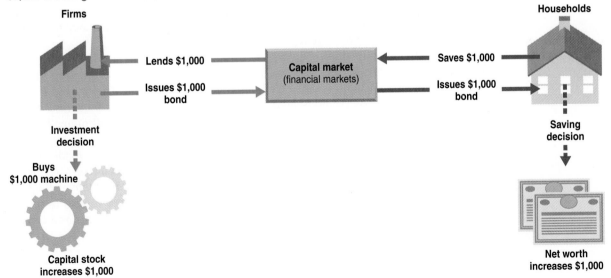

---

[4]Note that it is the *act of saving* that increases the household's wealth, not the act of buying the bond. Buying the bond simply transforms one financial asset (money) into another (a bond). The household could simply have held on to the money.

represents the firm's promise to repay the $1,000 at some future date with interest. The firm uses the $1,000 to buy a new $1,000 machine, which it adds to its capital stock. In essence, the household has supplied the capital demanded by the firm. It's almost as if the household bought the machine and rented it to the firm for an annual fee. Presumably, this investment will generate added revenues that will facilitate the payment of interest to the household.

> In general, projects are undertaken as long as the revenues likely to be realized from the investment are sufficient to cover the interest payments to the household.

Sometimes the transfer of household savings through the capital market into investment occurs without a financial intermediary. Recall from chapter 4 that an *entrepreneur* is one who organizes, manages, and assumes the risk of a new firm. When an entrepreneur starts a new business by buying capital with his own savings, he is both demanding capital and supplying the resources (i.e., his savings) needed to purchase that capital. No third party is involved in the transaction. Most investment, however, is accomplished with the help of financial intermediaries (third parties such as banks, insurance companies, and pension funds) that stand between the supplier (saver) and the demander (investing firm). The part of the capital market in which savers and investors interact through intermediaries is often called the **financial capital market**.

financial capital market *The part of the capital market in which savers and investors interact through intermediaries.*

CAPITAL INCOME: INTEREST AND PROFITS

It should now be clear to you how capital markets fit into the circular flow: They facilitate the movement of household savings into the most productive investment projects. When households allow their savings to be used to purchase capital, they receive payments, and these payments (along with wages and salaries) are part of household incomes. Income that is earned on savings that have been put to use through financial capital markets is called **capital income**. Capital income is received by households in many forms, the two most important of which are *interest* and *profits*.

capital income *Income earned on savings that have been put to use through financial capital markets.*

interest *The payments made for the use of money.*

> **Interest** The most common form of capital income received by households is interest. In simplest terms, **interest** is the payment made for the use of money. Banks pay interest to depositors, whose deposits are loaned out to businesses or individuals who want to make investments.[5] Banks also *charge* interest to those who borrow money. Corporations pay interest to households that buy their bonds. The government borrows money by issuing bonds, and the buyers of those bonds receive interest payments.

The *interest rate* is almost always expressed as an annual rate. It is the annual interest payment expressed as a percentage of the loan or deposit. For example, a $1,000 bond (representing a $1,000 loan from a household to a firm) that carries a fixed 10 percent interest rate will pay the household $100 per year ($1,000 × .10) in interest. A savings account that carries a 5 percent annual interest rate will pay $50 annually on a balance of $1,000.

The interest rate is usually agreed to at the time a loan or deposit is made. Sometimes borrowers and lenders agree to adjust periodically the level of interest payments depending on market conditions. These types of loans are called *adjustable* or *floating rate loans.* (*Fixed-rate loans* are loans in which the interest rate never varies.) In recent years there have even been adjustable rates of interest on savings accounts and certificates of deposit.

---

[5]Although we are focusing on investment by businesses, households can and do make investments also. The most important form of household investment is the construction of a new house, usually financed by borrowing in the form of a mortgage. A household may also borrow to finance the purchase of an existing house, but when it does so, no new investment is taking place.

A loan's interest rate depends on a number of factors. A loan that involves more risk will generally pay a higher interest rate than a loan with less risk. Similarly, firms that are considered bad credit risks will pay higher interest rates than firms with good credit ratings. You have probably heard radio or TV advertisements by finance companies offering to loan money to borrowers "regardless of credit history." This means that they will loan to people or businesses that pose a relatively high risk of *defaulting*, or not paying off the loan. What they do not tell you is that the interest rate will be quite high!

It is generally agreed that the safest borrower is the U.S. government, even though its debt is now over $5 trillion and continues to rise. With the "full faith and credit" of the U.S. government pledged to buyers of U.S. Treasury bonds and bills, most people believe that there is little risk that the government will not repay its loans. For this reason, the U.S. government can borrow money at a lower interest rate than any other borrower.

> **Profits** We saw in chapter 3 that corporate profits after tax are divided into two categories: dividends (after-tax profits distributed to shareholders) and retained earnings (after-tax profits retained by the corporation). These profits are *accounting profits*, and this concept of profit is not the same as the one we introduced in chapter 7 and have been using ever since. Recall that our definition of profit is total revenue minus total cost, where total cost includes the normal rate of return on capital. We defined profit in this way because true economic cost includes the opportunity cost of capital.

profit *The excess of revenues over cost in a given period.*

Suppose, for example, that I decide to open a candy store that requires an initial investment of $100,000. Clearly, if I borrow the $100,000 from a bank, I am not making a profit until I cover the interest payments on my loan. Even if I use my own savings or raise the funds I need by selling shares in my business, I am not making a profit until I cover the opportunity cost of using those funds to start my business. Because I always have the option of lending my funds at the current market interest rate, I earn a profit only when my total revenue is large enough to cover my total cost, including the forgone interest revenue I could make from lending my funds at the current market interest rate.

As another example, suppose that the Kauai Lamp Company was started in 1998, and that 100 percent of the $1 million needed to start up the company (to buy the plant and equipment) was raised by selling shares of stock. Now suppose that the company earns $200,000 per year, all of which is paid out to shareholders. Because $200,000 is 20 percent of the company's total capital stock, the shareholders are earning a rate of return of 20 percent. But only part of the $200,000 is profit. If the market interest rate is 11 percent, then 11 percent of $1 million ($110,000) is part of the cost of capital. The shareholders are only earning a profit of $90,000 given our definition of profit.

> **Functions of Interest and Profit** Capital income serves several functions. First, interest may function as an incentive to postpone gratification. When you save, you pass up the chance to buy things that you want right now. One view of interest holds that it is the reward for postponing consumption.

Second, profit serves as a reward for innovation and risk taking. Every year *Fortune* magazine publishes the names of the richest people in the United States, and virtually every major fortune listed there is traceable to the founding of some business enterprise that "made it big." In recent years, big winners have included retail stores (Sam Walton of Wal-Mart), high-tech companies (David Packard of Hewlett-Packard and Bill Gates of Microsoft), and sports equipment companies (Philip Knight of Nike).

SOME ENTREPRENEURS DO VERY WELL. DAVE THOMAS OF WENDY'S GOT RICH SELLING HAMBURGERS AND CHICKEN SANDWICHES TO PEOPLE.

Many argue that rewards for innovation and risk taking are the essence of the U.S. free enterprise system. Innovation is at the core of economic growth and progress. More efficient production techniques mean that the resources saved can be used to produce new things. There is another side to this story, however: Critics of the free enterprise system claim that such large rewards are not justified and that accumulations of great wealth and power are not in society's best interests.

FINANCIAL MARKETS IN ACTION

When a firm issues a fixed-interest-rate bond, it borrows funds and pays interest at an agreed-upon rate to the person or institution that buys the bond. Many other mechanisms, four of which are illustrated in Figure 11.2, also channel household savings into investment projects. The Global Perspective box titled "Rural Credit in Bangladesh and Indonesia" offers additional examples.

➤ **Case A: Business Loans**   As I look around my home town, I see several ice cream stores doing very well, but I think that I can make better ice cream than they do. To go into the business, I need capital: ice cream-making equipment, tables, chairs, freezers, signs, and a store. Because I put up my house as collateral, I am not a big risk, and the bank grants me a loan at a fairly reasonable interest rate. Banks have these funds to lend only because households deposit their savings there.

➤ **Case B: Venture Capital**   A scientist at a leading university develops an inexpensive method of producing a very important family of virus-fighting drugs, using microorganisms created through gene splicing. The business could very well fail within 12 months, but if it succeeds, the potential for profit is huge.

Our scientist goes to a *venture capital fund* for financing. Such funds take household savings and put them into high-risk ventures in exchange for a share of the profits if the new businesses succeed. By investing in many different projects, the funds reduce the risk of going broke. Once again, household funds make it possible for firms to undertake investments. If a venture succeeds, those owning shares in the venture capital fund receive substantial profits.

➤ **Case C: Retained Earnings**   General Motors Corporation decides that it wants to build a new assembly plant in Tennessee, and it discovers that it has enough funds to pay for the new facility. The new investment is thus paid for through internal funds, or *retained earnings*.

The result is exactly the same as if the firm had gone to households via some financial intermediary and borrowed the funds. If GM uses its profits to buy new capital, it does so only with the shareholders' implicit consent. When a firm takes its own profit and uses it to buy capital assets instead of paying it out to its shareholders, the total value of the firm goes up, as does the value of the shares held by stockholders. As in our other examples, GM's capital stock increases, and so does the net worth of households.

When a household owns a share of stock that *appreciates*, or increases in value, the appreciation is part of the household's income. Unless the household sells the stock and consumes the gain, that gain is part of saving. In essence, when a firm retains earnings for investment purposes, it is actually saving on behalf of its shareholders.

➤ **Case D: The Stock Market** A former high-ranking government official decides to start a new peanut processing business in Atlanta, and he also decides to raise the funds needed by issuing shares of stock. Households buy the shares with income that they decide not to spend. In exchange, they are entitled to a share of the peanut firm's profits.

The shares of stock become part of households' net worth. The proceeds from stock sales are used to buy plant equipment and inventory. Savings flow into investment, and the firm's capital stock goes up by the same amount as household net worth.

CAPITAL ACCUMULATION AND ALLOCATION

You can see from the preceding examples that various, and sometimes complex, connections between households and firms facilitate the movement of saving into productive investment. The methods may differ, but the results are the same.

Think again about Colleen and Bill, whom we discussed in chapter 2. They found themselves alone on a deserted island. They had to make choices about how to allocate

RURAL CREDIT IN BANGLADESH AND INDONESIA

In the mid-1990s, Congress debated a plan submitted by President Clinton to establish a $382 million government fund to expand lending in poor central city and rural areas, where commercial banks find it too risky to lend. The idea was based on a successful rural credit institution in Bangladesh called the Grameen ("Village") Bank.

The Grameen Bank was founded in 1977 by a U.S.-trained economist named Mohammed Yunus. The project was supported by the Bangladesh Bank and seven other government-owned commercial banks. Within four years, the Grameen Bank had extended its operations to 433 villages. By 1995, it had loaned money to 1.6 million people in 32,000 villages. The average loan is about $100 and the maximum loan is $1,200. A small farmer might borrow money to buy a cow, or a fisherman might borrow to buy materials for a fishing net. The most amazing thing about the Grameen Bank is that 96 percent of its loans have been paid back in full.

One of the bank's interesting innovations is that it lends to groups. Loans are made to groups of five people of roughly equal socioeconomic status. These groups elect their own leaders and discipline is maintained through peer pressure. The groups must meet weekly and make weekly installment payments:

Lending to small groups formed by potential borrowers who are collectively responsible for repayment serves several purposes. Small groups . . . generate a sense of belonging and a clear perception that each individual's performance is crucial to the group's overall success or failure. Motivated group members tend to monitor their more lax peers, for no group member can receive further credit until the entire group's debts are repaid.[a]

Grameen Bank's function is exactly the same as the function of Citibank, the stock market, and other financial intermediaries: to collect household saving and make it available to businesses, which pay a fee to use it for the purchase or creation of capital.

A number of small funds supported by foundations have opened in the United States on the Grameen model. Most seem to have very low default rates on loans to very small enterprises in rural or central city areas. But to date, the scale is nothing like it is in Bangladesh.

An institution similar to the Grameen Bank is the Unit Desa ("Village Unit") of the Bank Rakyat Indonesia, which supplies credit and collects saving in rural Indonesia. A recent report describes two typical loans.

One loan of 1.2 million rupiah (about $700) was made to a couple to buy a grinding and milling machine to be used for grinding coffee and milling corn and rice. Before taking the loan, the family was making a living in petty trading. After the loan, the family operated a processing service for the surrounding area and had three full-time employees outside the immediate family. It paid the loan back in full.

THE GRAMEEN BANK OF BANGLADESH MAKES SMALL LOANS TO VILLAGE-CENTERED GROUPS. MOST OF THE BANK'S CLIENTS HAVE BEEN FISHERMEN OR FARMERS. TO DATE, 96 PERCENT OF THE BANK'S LOANS HAVE BEEN REPAID IN FULL. THE FARMER HERE IS HARVESTING JUTE.

Another loan of 3 million rupiah (about $1,800) was made to two partners to buy a steam furnace for a bean-curd processing factory. At the time the loan was made, the factory employed four workers and supplied about fifteen bean-curd peddlers a day. With the steam processor, the output of the factory doubled and four additional full-time workers were hired.[b]

Sources: [a]Jacob Yaron, "Successful Rural Finance Institutions," *Finance and Development*, March 1994, p. 34; [b]Richard Patton and Jay Rosengard, *Progress with Profits: The Development of Rural Banking in Indonesia* (Cambridge, MA: Harvard Institute for International Development, 1990).

For more on international capital markets, see the Case and Fair Web page at **http://www.prenhall.com/casefair.**

available resources, including their time. By spending long hours working on a house or a boat, Colleen and Bill are saving and investing. First, they are using resources that could be used to produce more immediate rewards—they could gather more food or simply lie in the sun and relax. Second, they are applying those resources to the production of capital and capital accumulation.

Industrialized or agrarian, small or large, simple or complex, all societies exist through time and must allocate resources over time. In simple societies, investment and saving decisions are made by the same people. However:

> In modern industrial societies, investment decisions (capital production decisions) are made primarily by firms. Households decide how much to save, and in the long run saving limits or constrains the amount of investment that firms can undertake. The capital market exists to direct savings into profitable investment projects.

THE DEMAND FOR NEW CAPITAL AND THE INVESTMENT DECISION

We saw in chapter 9 that firms have an incentive to expand in industries that earn positive profits (that is, a rate of return above normal) and in industries in which economies of scale lead to lower average costs at higher levels of output. We also saw that positive profits in an industry stimulate the entry of new firms. The expansion of existing firms and the creation of new firms both involve investment in new capital.

Even when there are no profits in an industry, firms must still do some investing. First, equipment wears out and must be replaced if the firm is to stay in business. Second, firms are constantly changing. A new technology may become available, sales patterns may shift, or the firm may expand or contract its product line.

With these points in mind, we now turn to a discussion of the investment decision process within the individual firm. In the end we will see (just as we did in chapter 10) that a perfectly competitive firm invests in capital up to the point at which the marginal revenue product of capital is equal to the price of capital. (Because we based much of our discussion in chapter 10 on the assumption of perfect competition, it makes sense to continue doing so here. Keep in mind, though, that much of what we say here also applies to firms that are not perfectly competitive.)

FORMING EXPECTATIONS

We have already said that the most important dimension of capital is time. Capital produces useful services over *some period of time*. In building an office tower, a developer makes an investment that will be around for decades. In deciding where to build a branch plant, a manufacturing firm commits a large amount of resources to purchase capital that will be in place for a long time.

It is important to remember, though, that capital goods do not begin to yield benefits until they are *used*. Often the decision to build a building or purchase a piece of equipment must be made years before the actual project is completed. While the acquisition of a small business computer may take only days, the planning process for downtown development projects in big U.S. cities has been known to take decades.

▶ **The Expected Benefits of Investments** Decision makers must have expectations about what is going to happen in the future. A new plant will be very valuable—that is, it will produce much profit—if the market for a firm's product grows and the price of that product remains high. The same plant will be worth little if the economy goes into a slump or consumers grow tired of the firm's product. An office tower may turn out to be an excellent investment, but not if many new office buildings go up at the same time, flooding the office space market, pushing up the vacancy rate, and driving down rents. It follows, then, that:

> The investment process requires that the potential investor evaluate the expected flow of future productive services that an investment project will yield.

Remember that households, business firms, and governments all undertake investments. A household must evaluate the future services that a new roof will yield. A firm must evaluate the flow of future revenues that a new plant will generate. Governments must estimate how much benefit society will derive from a new bridge or a war memorial.

An official of the General Electric Corporation once described the difficulty involved in making such predictions. GE subscribes to a number of different economic forecasting services. In the early 1980s, those services provided the firm with 10-year predictions of new housing construction that ranged from a low of 400,000 new units per year to a high of 4 million new units per year. Because General Electric sells millions of household appliances to contractors building new houses, condominiums, and apartments, the forecast was critical. If GE decided that the high number was more accurate, it would need to spend literally billions of dollars on new plant and equipment to prepare for the extra demand. If GE decided that the low number was more accurate, it would need to begin closing several of its larger plants and disinvesting. In fact, GE took the middle road. It assumed that housing production would be between 1.5 and 2 million units—which, in fact, it turned out to be.

General Electric is not an exception. All firms must rely on forecasts to make sensible investment and production decisions, but forecasting is an inexact science because so much depends on events that cannot be foreseen.

➤ **The Expected Costs of Investments** The benefits of any investment project take the form of future profits. These profits must be forecast. But costs must also be evaluated. Like households, firms have access to financial markets, both as borrowers and as lenders. If a firm borrows, it must *pay* interest over time. If it lends, it will *earn* interest. If the firm borrows to finance a project, the interest on the loan is part of the cost of the project.

Even if a project is financed with the firm's own funds, rather than by borrowing, there is an opportunity cost involved. A thousand dollars put into a capital investment project will generate an expected flow of future profit; the same $1,000 put into the financial market (in essence, loaned to another firm) will yield a flow of interest payments. The project will not be undertaken unless it is expected to yield more than the market interest rate. The cost of an investment project may thus be direct or indirect because:

> The ability to lend at the market rate of interest means that there is an *opportunity cost* associated with every investment project. The evaluation process thus involves not only estimating future benefits, but also comparing them with the possible alternative uses of the funds required to undertake the project. At a minimum, those funds could earn interest in financial markets.

COMPARING COSTS AND EXPECTED RETURN

Once expectations have been formed, firms must quantify them—that is, they must assign some dollars-and-cents value to them. One way to quantify expectations is to calculate an **expected rate of return** on the investment project. For example, if a new computer network that costs $400,000 is likely to save $100,000 per year in data processing costs forever after, the expected rate of return on that investment is 25 percent per year. Each year the firm will save $100,000 as a result of the $400,000 investment. The expected rate of return will be less than 25 percent if the computer network wears out or becomes obsolete after a while and the cost savings cease. In short:

> The expected rate of return on an investment project depends on the price of the investment, the expected length of time the project provides additional cost savings or revenue, and the expected amount of revenue attributable each year to the project.

expected rate of return *The annual rate of return that a firm expects to obtain through a capital investment.*

TABLE 11.2 POTENTIAL INVESTMENT PROJECTS AND EXPECTED RATES OF RETURN FOR A HYPOTHETICAL FIRM, BASED ON FORECASTS OF FUTURE PROFITS ATTRIBUTABLE TO THE INVESTMENT

PROJECT	(1) TOTAL INVESTMENT (DOLLARS)	(2) EXPECTED RATE OF RETURN (PERCENT)
A. New computer network	400,000	25
B. New branch plant	2,600,000	20
C. Sales office in another state	1,500,000	15
D. New automated billing system	100,000	12
E. Ten new delivery trucks	400,000	10
F. Advertising campaign	1,000,000	7
G. Employee cafeteria	100,000	5

Table 11.2 presents a menu of investment choices and expected rates of return that face a hypothetical firm. Because expected rates of return are based on forecasts of future profits attributable to the investments, any change in expectations would change all the numbers in column 2.

Figure 11.3 graphs the total amount of investment in millions of dollars that the firm would undertake at various interest rates. If the interest rate were 24 percent, the firm would fund only Project A, the new computer network. It can borrow at 24 percent and invest in a computer that is expected to yield 25 percent. At 24 percent, then, the firm's total investment is $400,000. The first vertical orange line in Figure 11.3 shows that at any interest rate above 20 percent and below 25 percent, only $400,000 worth of investment (that is, Project A) will be undertaken.

If the interest rate were 18 percent, the firm would fund Projects A and B, and its total investment would rise to $3 million ($400,000 + $2,600,000). If the firm could

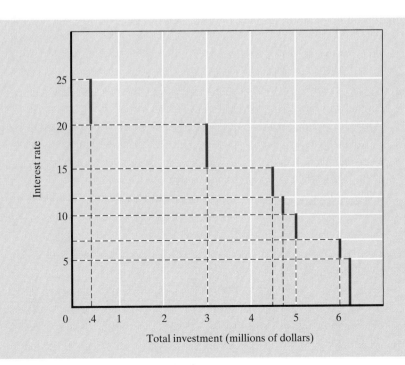

FIGURE 11.3

Total Investment as a Function of the Market Interest Rate

The demand for new capital depends on the interest rate. When the interest rate is low, firms are more likely to invest in new plant and equipment than when the interest rate is high. This is because the interest rate determines the direct cost (interest on a loan) or the opportunity cost (alternative investment) of each project.

borrow at 18 percent, the flow of additional profits generated by the new computer and the new plant would more than cover the costs of borrowing, but none of the other projects would be justified. The rates of return on Projects A and B (25 percent and 20 percent, respectively) both exceed the 18 percent interest rate. Only if the interest rate fell below 5 percent would the firm fund all seven investment projects.

The investment schedule in Table 11.2 and its graphic depiction in Figure 11.3 describe the firm's demand for new capital, expressed as a function of the market interest rate. If we add the total investment undertaken by *all* firms at every interest rate, we arrive at the demand for new capital in the economy as a whole. In other words, the market demand curve for new capital is simply the sum of all the individual demand curves for new capital in the economy (Figure 11.4). In a sense, the investment demand schedule is a ranking of all the investment opportunities in the economy in order of expected yield.

> Only those investment projects in the economy that are expected to yield a rate of return higher than the market interest rate will be funded. At lower market interest rates, more investment projects are undertaken.

The most important thing to remember about the investment demand curve is that its shape and position depend critically on the *expectations* of those making the investment decisions. Because many influences affect these expectations, they are usually volatile and subject to frequent change. Thus, while lower interest rates tend to stimulate investment, and higher interest rates tend to slow it, many other hard-to-measure and hard-to-predict factors also affect the level of investment spending. These might include government policy changes, election results, global affairs, inflation, and changes in currency exchange rates.

▶ **The Expected Rate of Return and the Marginal Revenue Product of Capital** The concept of the expected rate of return on investment projects is analogous to the concept of the marginal revenue product of capital (MRP_K). Recall that we defined an input's marginal revenue product as the additional revenue a firm earns by employing one additional unit of that input, *ceteris paribus*. Also recall our earlier discussion of labor demand in a sandwich shop in chapter 7. If an additional worker can produce 15 sandwiches in one hour (the marginal product of labor: $MP_L = 15$) and each sandwich brings in $.50 (the price of

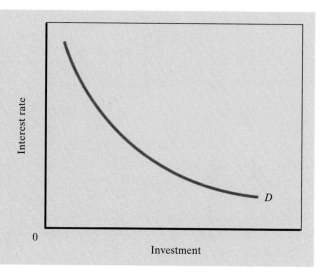

FIGURE 11.4

Investment Demand

Lower interest rates are likely to stimulate investment in the economy as a whole, while higher interest rates are likely to slow investment.

the service produced by the sandwich shop: $P_X = \$.50$), the marginal revenue product of labor is equal to $7.50 ($MRP_L = MP_L \times P_X = 15 \times \$.50 = \$7.50$).

Now think carefully about the return to an additional unit of new capital (the marginal revenue product of capital). Suppose that the rate of return on an investment in a new machine is 15 percent. This means that the investment project yields the same return as a bond yielding 15 percent. If the current interest rate is less than 15 percent, the investment project will be undertaken because:

> A perfectly competitive profit-maximizing firm will keep investing in new capital up to the point at which the expected rate of return is equal to the interest rate. This is analogous to saying that the firm will continue investing up to the point at which the marginal revenue product of capital is equal to the price of capital, or $MRP_K = P_K$, which is what we learned in chapter 10.

A FINAL WORD ON CAPITAL

The concept of capital is one of the central ideas in economics. Capital is produced by the economic system itself. Capital generates services over time, and it is used as an input in the production of goods and services.

The enormous productivity of modern industrial societies is due in part to the tremendous amount of capital that they have accumulated over the years. It may surprise you to know that the average worker in the United States works with about $75,000 worth of capital. There is no question that the economic success of modern Japan has resulted first and foremost from the very high rates of investment that began in that country after World War II and have continued for nearly 60 years.

The bulk of this chapter described the institutions and processes that determine the amount and types of capital produced in a market economy. Existing firms in search of increased profits, potential new entrants to the markets, and entrepreneurs with new ideas all are continuously evaluating potential investment projects. At the same time, households are saving. Each year households save some portion of their after-tax incomes. This new saving becomes part of their net worth, and they want to earn a return on it. Each year a good portion of the saving finds its way into the hands of firms that use it to buy new capital goods.

Between households and firms is the financial capital market. Millions of people participate in financial markets every day. There are literally thousands of financial managers, pension funds, mutual funds, brokerage houses, options traders, and banks whose sole purpose is to earn the highest possible rate of return on people's saving.

Brokers, bankers, and financial managers are continuously scanning the financial horizons for profitable investments. What businesses are doing well? What businesses are doing poorly? Should we lend to an expanding firm? All the analysis done by financial managers seeking to earn a high yield for clients, by managers of firms seeking to earn high profits for their stockholders, and by entrepreneurs seeking profits from innovation serves to channel capital into its most productive uses. Within firms, the evaluation of individual investment projects involves forecasting costs and benefits and valuing streams of potential income that will be earned only in future years.

We have now completed our discussion of competitive input and output markets. We have looked at household and firm choices in output markets, labor markets, land markets, and capital markets.

We now turn to a discussion of the allocative process that we have described. How do all the parts of the economy fit together? Is the result good or bad? Can we improve on it? All this is the subject of chapter 12.

SUMMARY

CAPITAL, INVESTMENT, AND DEPRECIATION

1. In market capitalist systems, the decision to put capital to use in a particular enterprise is made by private citizens putting their savings at risk in search of private gain. The set of institutions through which such transactions occur is called the *capital market*.

2. *Capital goods* are those goods produced by the economic system that are used as inputs to produce other goods and services in the future. Capital goods thus yield valuable productive services over time.

3. The major categories of *physical*, or *tangible*, *capital* are nonresidential structures, durable equipment, residential structures, and inventories. *Social capital* (or *infrastructure*) is capital that provides services to the public. *Intangible* (*nonmaterial*) *capital* includes *human capital* and goodwill.

4. The most important dimension of capital is that it exists through time. Therefore, its value is only as great as the value of the services it will render over time.

5. The most common measure of a firm's *capital stock* is the current market value of its plant, equipment, inventories, and intangible assets. However, in thinking about capital it is important to think of the actual capital stock rather than its simple monetary value.

6. In economics, the term *investment* refers to the creation of new capital, not to the purchase of a share of stock or a bond. Investment is a flow that increases the capital stock.

7. *Depreciation* is the decline in an asset's economic value over time. A capital asset can depreciate because it wears out physically or because it becomes obsolete.

THE CAPITAL MARKET

8. Income that is earned on savings that have been put to use through *financial capital markets* is called *capital income*. The two most important forms of capital income are *interest* and *profits*. Interest is the fee paid by a borrower to a lender. Interest rewards households for postponing gratification, and profit rewards entrepreneurs for innovation and risk taking.

9. In modern industrial societies, investment decisions (capital production decisions) are made primarily by firms. Households decide how much to save, and in the long run, saving limits the amount of investment that firms can undertake. The capital market exists to direct savings into profitable investment projects.

THE DEMAND FOR NEW CAPITAL AND THE INVESTMENT DECISION

10. Before investing, investors must evaluate the expected flow of future productive services that an investment project will yield.

11. The availability of interest to lenders means that there is an opportunity cost associated with every investment project. This cost must be weighed against the stream of earnings that a project is expected to yield.

12. A firm will decide whether to undertake an investment project by comparing costs with expected returns. The *expected rate of return* on an investment project depends on the price of the investment, the expected length of time the project provides additional cost savings or revenue, and the expected amount of revenue attributable each year to the project.

13. The investment demand curve shows the demand for capital in the economy as a function of the market interest rate. Only those investment projects that are expected to yield a rate of return higher than the market interest rate will be funded. Lower interest rates should stimulate investment.

14. A perfectly competitive profit-maximizing firm will keep investing in new capital up to the point at which the expected rate of return is equal to the interest rate. This is equivalent to saying that the firm will continue investing up to the point at which the marginal revenue product of capital is equal to the price of capital, or $MRP_K = P_K$.

REVIEW TERMS AND CONCEPTS

PROBLEM SET

1. Which of the following are capital, and which are not? Explain your answers.
   - **a.** A video poker game machine at a local bar that takes quarters
   - **b.** A $10 bill
   - **c.** A college education
   - **d.** The Golden Gate Bridge
   - **e.** The shirts on the rack in Sears
   - **f.** A government bond
   - **g.** The Empire State Building
   - **h.** A savings account
   - **i.** The Washington Monument
   - **j.** A Honda plant in Marysville, Ohio

2. You and 99 other partners are offered the chance to buy a gas station. Each partner would put up $10,000. The revenues from the operation of the station have been steady at $420,000 per year for several years and are projected to remain steady into the future. The costs (not including opportunity costs) of operating the station (including maintenance and repair, depreciation, salaries, and so forth) have also been steady at $360,000 per year. Currently five-year Treasury Bills are yielding 7.5 percent interest. Would you go in on the deal?

3. In August 1997, the Prudential Insurance Company of America put the Prudential Center, the largest commercial complex in Boston (including a 52-story office tower), up for sale. If you were a real estate investment company considering bidding on the complex, what would you want to know first? What specific factors would you need to form expectations about? What information would you need to help form those expectations?

4. The board of directors of the Quando Company in Singapore was presented with the following list of investment projects for implementation in 1998:

PROJECT	TOTAL COST SINGAPORE DOLLARS	ESTIMATED RATE OF RETURN
Factory in Kuala Lumpur	17,356,400	13%
Factory in Bangkok	15,964,200	15
A new company aircraft	10,000,000	12
A factory outlet store	3,500,000	18
A new computer network	2,000,000	20
A cafeteria for workers	1,534,000	7

Sketch total investment as a function of the interest rate (with the interest rate on the Y axis). Currently, the interest rate in Singapore is 8 percent. How much investment would you recommend to Quando's board?

5. During 1994 and 1995, the U. S. central bank (the Federal Reserve Bank) took action to increase interest rates. How might this action affect the future productive capacity of the economy?

6. During the second quarter of 1997, the Molson Beer Company of Canada earned $18,700,000 (Canadian). Molson is a corporation whose shares are owned by the public. Some of Molson's profits are paid to owners, some go to the Canadian government, and some are retained for investment. Explain.

7. Give at least three examples of how savings can be channeled into productive investment. Why is investment so important for an economy? What do you sacrifice when you invest today?

8. From a newspaper like the *Wall Street Journal*, from the business section of your local daily, or from the Internet, look up the prime interest rate, the corporate bond rate, and the interest rate on 10-year U.S. government bonds today. List some of the reasons these three rates are different.

9. Explain what we mean when we say that "households supply capital and firms demand capital."

10. Suppose that I decide to start a small business. To raise start-up funds, I sell 1,000 shares of stock for $100 each. For the next five years, I take in annual revenues of $50,000. My total annual costs of operating the business are $20,000. If all of my earnings are paid out as dividends to shareholders, how much of my total annual earnings can be considered profit? Assume that the current interest rate is 10 percent.

11. Describe the capital stock of your college or university. How would you go about measuring its value? Has your school made any major investments in recent years? If so, describe them. What does your school hope to gain from these investments?

12. "Lower interest rates are discouraging to households, and they are likely to invest less." Do you agree or disagree with this statement? Explain your answer.

TAKE IT TO THE NET

We invite you to visit the Case and Fair page on the Prentice Hall Web site:

http://www.prenhall.com/casefair

for this chapter's World Wide Web exercise.

APPENDIX TO CHAPTER 11

CALCULATING PRESENT VALUE

We have seen in this chapter that a firm's major goal in making investment decisions is to evaluate revenue streams that will not materialize until the future. One way for the firm to decide whether or not to undertake an investment project is to compare the expected rate of return from the investment with the current interest rate available in the financial market. We discussed this procedure in the text. The purpose of this appendix is to present an alternative method of evaluating future revenue streams through present-value analysis.

PRESENT VALUE

Consider the expected flow of profits from the investment shown in Table 11A.1. If such a project cost $1,200 to put in place, would the firm undertake it? At first glance, you might answer yes. After all, the total flow of profit is $1,600. But this flow of profit is fully realized only after five years have passed. The same $1,200 could be put into a money market account, where it would earn interest and perhaps produce a higher yield than if it were invested in the project. You can easily see that the desirability of the investment project will depend on the interest rate that is available in the market.

One way of thinking about interest is to say that it *allows us to buy and sell claims to future dollars*. Future dollars have prices in the present. That is, a contract for $1 to be delivered in 1 year, 2 years, or 10 years can be purchased today. How? By simply depositing a certain amount in an interest-bearing certificate or account. Using the *present prices* of future dollars gives us a way to compare present costs with values that will be realized in the future. This method allows us to evaluate investment projects that will yield benefits into the future.

It is not difficult to figure the "price" today of $1 to be delivered in one year. You must now pay an amount (X) such that when you get X back in one year with interest you will have $1. If r is the interest rate available in the

market, r times X, or rX, is the amount of interest that X will earn for you in one year. Thus, at the end of a year you will have $X + rX$, or $X(1 + r)$, and you want this to be equal to $1. Solving for X algebraically:

$$\$1 = X(1 + r), \text{ so } X = \frac{\$1}{1 + r}$$

We say that X is the **present value (PV)**, or **present discounted value**, of $1 one year from now. Actually, X is the current market price of $1 to be delivered in one year: It is the amount you have to put aside now if you want to end up with $1 a year from now.

Now let's go more than one year into the future and consider more than a single dollar. For example, what is the present value of a claim on $100 in two years? Using the same logic as above, let X be the present value, or current market price, of $100 payable in two years. Thus, X plus the interest it would earn compounded for two years is equal to $100.[1] After one year, you would have $X + rX$, or $X(1 + r)$. After two years, you would have this amount plus another year's interest on the whole amount:

$$X(1 + r) + r[X(1 + r)]$$
$$\text{or}$$
$$X(1 + r)(1 + r), \text{ which is } X(1 + r)^2$$

Again solving algebraically for X:

$$\$100 = X(1 + r)^2, \text{ so } X = \frac{\$100}{(1 + r)^2}$$

If the market interest rate were 10 percent, or .10, then the present value of $100 in two years would be

$$X = \frac{\$100}{(1.1)^2} = \$82.64.$$

If you put $82.64 in a certificate earning 10 percent per year, you would earn $8.26 in interest after one year, giving you $90.90. Interest in the second year would be $9.09, leaving you with $100 at the end of two years.

In general, the present value (PV), or present discounted value, of R dollars t years from now is

$$PV = \frac{R}{(1 + r)^t}$$

TABLE 11A.1 EXPECTED PROFITS FROM A $1,200 INVESTMENT PROJECT

Year 1	$100
Year 2	100
Year 3	400
Year 4	500
Year 5	500
All later years	0
Total	1,600

---

[1]Thus far, all our examples have involved *simple interest*—interest that is computed on principal alone, not on principal plus interest. In the real world, however, many loans involve *compound interest*—interest that is computed on the basis of principal plus interest. If you deposit funds into an interest-compounding account at a bank and do not withdraw the interest payments as they are added to your account, you will earn interest on your previously earned interest.

Table 11A.2 calculates the present value of the income stream in Table 11A.1 at an interest rate of 10 percent. The total present value turns out to be $1,126.06. This tells the firm that it can simply go to the financial market today and buy a contract that pays $100 one year from now, another that pays $100 two years from now, still another that pays $400 three years from now, and so forth, all for the low price of $1,126.06. To put this another way, it could lend out or deposit $1,126.06 in an account paying a 10 percent interest rate, withdraw $100 next year, withdraw $100 in the following year, take another $400 at the end of three years, and so forth. When it takes its last $500 at the end of the fifth year, the account will be empty—the balance in the account will be exactly zero. Thus, *at current market interest rates*, the firm has exactly duplicated the income stream that the investment project would have yielded for a total present price of $1,126.06. Why then would it pay out $1,200 to undertake this investment? The answer, of course, is that it would not.

We can restate the point this way:

> If the present value of the income stream associated with an investment is less than the full cost of the investment project, the investment should not be undertaken.

It is important to remember here that we are discussing the *demand for new capital*. Business firms must evaluate potential investments in order to decide whether they are worth undertaking. This involves predicting the flow of potential future profits arising from each project and comparing those future profits with the return available in the financial market at the current interest rate. The present-value method allows firms to calculate how much it would *cost today* to purchase a contract for the exact same flow of earnings in the financial market.

LOWER INTEREST RATES, HIGHER PRESENT VALUES

Now suppose that interest rates fall from 10 percent to 5 percent. With a lower interest rate, the firm will have to *pay more* now to purchase the same number of future dollars. Take, for example, the present value of $100 in two years. You saw that if the firm puts aside $82.64 at 10 percent interest, it will have $100 in two years—at a 10 percent interest rate, the present discounted value, or current market price, of $100 in two years is $82.64. But $82.64 put aside at a 5 percent interest rate would generate only $4.13 in interest in the first year and $4.34 in the second year, for a total balance of $91.11 after two years. In order to get $100 in two years, the firm needs to put aside more than $82.64 now. Solving for X as we did before,

$$X = \frac{\$100}{(1+r)^2} = \frac{\$100}{(1.05)^2} = \$90.70.$$

When the interest rate falls from 10 percent to 5 percent, the present value of $100 in two years rises by $8.06 ($90.70 − $82.64).

Table 11A.3 recalculates the present value of the full stream at the lower interest rate; it shows that a decrease in the interest rate from 10 percent to 5 percent causes the total present value to rise to $1,334.59. Because the investment project will yield the same stream of earnings for a present price of only $1,200, it is now a better deal than the financial markets. Under these conditions, a profit-maximizing firm will make the investment. As discussed in the chapter, a lower interest rate leads to more investment.

The basic rule is:

> If the present value of an expected stream of earnings from an investment exceeds the cost of the investment necessary to undertake it, then the investment should be undertaken. But if the present value of an

TABLE 11A.2 CALCULATION OF TOTAL PRESENT VALUE OF A HYPOTHETICAL INVESTMENT PROJECT
(ASSUMING r = 10 PERCENT)

END OF . . .	(R)	DIVIDED BY $(1 + r)^t$ =	PRESENT VALUE ($)
Year 1	100	(1.1)	90.91
Year 2	100	(1.1)²	82.65
Year 3	400	(1.1)³	300.53
Year 4	500	(1.1)⁴	341.51
Year 5	500	(1.1)⁵	310.46
Total present value:			1,126.06

TABLE 11A.3 CALCULATION OF TOTAL PRESENT VALUE OF A HYPOTHETICAL INVESTMENT PROJECT
(ASSUMING r = 5 PERCENT)

END OF . . .	(R)	DIVIDED BY $(1 + r)^t$ =	PRESENT VALUE ($)
Year 1	100	(1.05)	95.24
Year 2	100	(1.05)²	90.70
Year 3	400	(1.05)³	345.54
Year 4	500	(1.05)⁴	411.35
Year 5	500	(1.05)⁵	391.76
Total present value:			1,334.59

expected stream of earnings falls short of the cost of the investment, then the financial market can generate the same stream of income for a smaller initial investment, and the investment should not be undertaken.

SUMMARY

1. The present value (PV) of R dollars to be paid t years in the future is the amount you need to pay today, at current interest rates, to ensure that you end up with R dollars t years from now. It is the current market value of receiving R dollars in t years.

2. If the present value of the income stream associated with an investment is less than the full cost of the investment project, the investment project should not be undertaken. If the present value of an expected stream of income exceeds the cost of the investment necessary to undertake it, then the investment should be undertaken.

REVIEW TERMS AND CONCEPTS

present value (PV), or present discounted value The present discounted value of R dollars to be paid t years in the future is the amount you need to pay today, at current interest rates, to ensure that you end up with R dollars t years from now. It is the current market value of receiving R dollars in t years. 270

$$PV = \frac{R}{(1 + r)^t}$$

PROBLEM SET

1. Your Uncle Joe has just died and left $10,000 payable to you when you turn 30 years old. You are now 20. Currently, the annual rate of interest one can obtain by buying 10-year bonds is 6.5 percent. Your brother offers you $6,000 cash right now to sign over your inheritance. Would you do it?

2. A special task force has determined that the present discounted value of the benefits from a bridge project comes to $23,786,000. The total construction cost of the bridge is $25,000,000. This implies that the bridge should be built. Do you agree with this conclusion? Explain your answer. What impact could a substantial decline in interest rates have on your answer?

3. Calculate the present value of the income streams A–E, in Table 1, at an 8 percent interest rate and again at a 10 percent rate.

   Suppose that the investment behind the flow of income in E is a machine that cost $1,235 at the beginning of year 1. Would you buy the machine if the interest rate were 8 percent? If the interest rate were 10 percent?

4. Determine what someone should be willing to pay for each of the following bonds when the market interest rate for borrowing and lending is 5 percent.
   a. A bond that promises to pay $3,000 in a lump-sum payment after 1 year.

   b. A bond that promises to pay $3,000 in a lump-sum payment after 2 years.
   c. A bond that promises to pay $1,000 per year for 3 years.

5. What should someone be willing to pay for each of the bonds in question 4 if the interest rate is 10 percent?

6. Based on your answers to questions 4 and 5, state whether each of the following is true or false:
   a. Ceteris paribus, the price of a bond increases when the interest rate increases.
   b. Ceteris paribus, the price of a bond increases when any given amount of money is received sooner rather than later.

TABLE 1

END OF YEAR	A	B	C	D	E
1	$80	$80	$100	$100	$500
2	80	80	100	100	300
3	80	80	1,100	100	400
4	80	80	0	100	300
5	1,080	80	0	100	0
6	0	80	0	1,100	0
7	0	1,080	0	0	0

Gᴇɴᴇʀᴀʟ ᴇǫᴜɪʟɪʙʀɪᴜᴍ AND THE EFFICIENCY OF PERFECT COMPETITION

IN THE LAST SEVEN CHAPTERS, we have built a model of a simple perfectly competitive economy. Our discussion has revolved around the two fundamental decision-making units, *households* and *firms*, which interact in two basic market arenas, *input markets* and *output markets*. (Look again at the circular flow diagram, shown in Figure 12.1.) By limiting our discussion to perfectly competitive firms, we have been able to examine how the basic decision-making units interact in the two basic market arenas.

Households make constrained choices in both input and output markets. In chapters 4 and 5 we discussed an individual household demand curve for a single good or service. Then in chapter 6 we went behind the demand curve and saw how income, wealth, and prices define the budget constraints within which households exercise their tastes and preferences. We soon discovered, however, that we cannot look at household decisions in output markets without thinking about the decisions made simultaneously in input markets. Household income, for example, depends on choices made in input markets: whether to work, how much to work, what skills to acquire, and so forth. Input market choices are constrained by such factors as current wage rates, the availability of jobs, and interest rates.

Firms are the primary producing units in a market economy. Profit-maximizing firms, to which we have limited our discussion, earn their profits by selling products and services for more than it costs to produce them. With firms, as with households, output markets and input markets cannot be analyzed separately. All firms make three specific decisions simultaneously: (1) how much output to supply, (2) how to produce that output (that is, which technology to use) and (3) how much of each input to demand.

In chapters 7 to 9, we explored these three decisions from the viewpoint of output markets. We saw that the portion of the marginal cost curve that lies above a firm's average variable cost curve is the supply curve of a perfectly competitive firm in the short run. Implicit in the marginal cost curve is a choice of technology and a set of input demands. In chapters 10 and 11, we looked at the perfectly competitive firm's three basic decisions from the viewpoint of input markets.

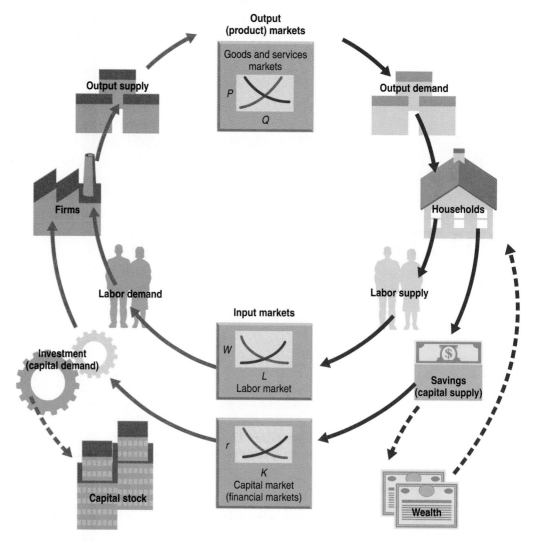

FIGURE 12.1

Firm and Household Decisions

Firms and households interact in both input and output markets.

Output and input markets are connected because firms and households make simultaneous choices in both arenas. But there are other connections among markets as well. Firms buy in both capital and labor markets, for example, and they can substitute capital for labor and vice versa. A change in the price of one factor can easily change the demand for other factors. Buying more *capital*, for instance, usually changes the marginal revenue product of *labor* and shifts the labor demand curve. Similarly, a change in the price of a single good or service usually affects household demand for other goods and services, as when a price decrease makes one good more attractive than other close substitutes. The same change also makes households better off when they find that the same amount of income will buy more. Such additional "real income" can be spent on any of the other goods and services that the household buys.

The point here is simple:

Input and output markets cannot be considered separately or as if they operated independently. While it is important to understand the decisions of individual firms and households and the functioning of individual markets, we now need to "add it all up," to look at the operation of the system as a whole.

You have seen the concept of equilibrium applied both to markets and to individual decision-making units. In individual markets, supply and demand determine an equilibrium price. Perfectly competitive firms are in short-run equilibrium when price and marginal cost are equal ($P = MC$). In the long run, however, equilibrium in a competitive market is achieved only when economic profits are eliminated. Households are in equilibrium when they have equated the marginal utility per dollar spent on each good to the marginal utility per dollar spent on all other goods. This process of examining the equilibrium conditions in individual markets and for individual households and firms separately is called **partial equilibrium analysis**.

A **general equilibrium** exists when all markets in an economy are in simultaneous equilibrium. An event that disturbs the equilibrium in one market may disturb the equilibrium in many other markets as well. The ultimate impact of the event depends on the way *all* markets adjust to it. Thus, partial equilibrium analysis, which looks at adjustments in one isolated market, may be misleading.

Thinking in terms of a general equilibrium leads to some important questions. Is it possible for all households and firms and all markets to be in equilibrium simultaneously? Are the equilibrium conditions that we have discussed separately compatible with one another? Why is an event that disturbs an equilibrium in one market likely to disturb many others simultaneously?

In talking about general equilibrium, the first concept we explore in this chapter, we continue our exercise in *positive economics*—that is, we seek to understand how systems operate without making value judgments about outcomes. Later in the chapter, we turn from positive economics to *normative economics* as we begin to judge the economic system. Are its results good or bad? Can we make them better?

In judging the performance of any economic system, you will recall, it is essential first to establish specific criteria to judge by. In this chapter, we use two such criteria: *efficiency* and *equity* (fairness). First we demonstrate that the allocation of resources is **efficient**—that is, the system produces what people want and does so at the least possible cost—if all the assumptions that we have made thus far hold. When we begin to relax some of our assumptions, however, it will become apparent that free markets may *not* be efficient. Several sources of inefficiency naturally occur within an unregulated market system. In the final part of this chapter, we introduce the potential role of government in correcting market inefficiencies and achieving fairness.

partial equilibrium analysis *The process of examining the equilibrium conditions in individual markets and for households and firms separately.*

general equilibrium *The condition that exists when all markets in an economy are in simultaneous equilibrium.*

efficiency *The condition in which the economy is producing what people want at least possible cost.*

GENERAL EQUILIBRIUM ANALYSIS

Two examples will help us illustrate some of the insights that we can gain when we move from partial to general equilibrium analysis. In this section, we will consider the impact on the economy of (1) a major technological advance and (2) a shift in consumer preferences. This chapter's Global Perspective box, "Growth and Change in Global Markets," provides some other examples. As you read, remember that we are looking for the connections between markets, particularly between input and output markets.

A TECHNOLOGICAL ADVANCE: THE ELECTRONIC CALCULATOR

Students working in quantitative fields of study in the late 1960s, and even as late as the early 1970s, recall classrooms filled with noisy mechanical calculators. At that time, a calculator weighed about 40 pounds and was only able to add, subtract, multiply, and divide. These machines had no memories, and they took 20 to 25 seconds to do one multiplication problem.

Different sectors and different regions of the U.S. economy are constantly experiencing different rates of growth and change. So, too, are different countries around the world growing and changing in different ways. The following four clips from the *New York Times* describe some of these changes. All four illustrate important links between markets. They show how changes in product demand, for example, can have impacts on labor and capital markets, and how labor and capital markets can affect product markets.

1. An expanding sector demands labor, attracting workers from other sectors and driving up wages.

   In Kentucky, new auto plants—particularly Toyota's sprawling factory in Georgetown . . . —have attracted networks of parts suppliers in recent years, offering thousands of new jobs at $10 an hour or more. They have hired many people who have shifted to the new factory work from lower-paying jobs in construction and tobacco fields.[a]

2. Increasing corporate profits in Japan translate into higher incomes and bonuses, fueling demand for products in Japan:

   Goldman, Sachs & Company estimates that for the fiscal year ending in March, corporate profits [in Japan] will rise 24 percent on a gain in sales of only six-tenths of 1 percent.

   Rising profits should translate into higher wages and bonuses,

helping fuel the [Japanese] recovery, said Jesper Koll, head of research in Japan for J. P. Morgan.[b]

3. Demand for Japanese autos contributes to demand for palladium, which interacts with supply problems, potentially raising the cost of producing electronic goods.

   Palladium prices soared yesterday as Western industries grew increasingly desperate for supplies amid questions about the financial health of the world's largest single supplier. Deliveries of new supplies have been at a standstill since December amid labor troubles and political infighting in Russia, where the Norilsk Nickel mine produces two-thirds of world inventories.

   Palladium is used in electronics and computers and is particularly important to the Japanese automobile sector.[c]

4. Interest rates increase in the capital market, decreasing the demand for new and existing housing. (That is, fewer people look to buy existing homes and the number of new housing projects decreases.) Lower housing demand hurts inputs and complementary products like lumber and carpets:

   "We're very concerned about what is going to happen to housing," [one analyst said]. "As interest rates go up, housing will be caught. My forecast is housing will slow, and this will hit our lumber, furniture and carpet industries."[d]

PALLADIUM MINED IN RUSSIA IS USED IN THE PRODUCTION OF ELECTRONICS. WHEN THE SUPPLY WAS RECENTLY SHUT DOWN BY LABOR PROBLEMS, IT ULTIMATELY HAD IMPACTS ALL THE WAY TO THE JAPANESE AUTO INDUSTRY.

Sources: [a]Louis Uchitelle, "U.S. Job Machine Absorbing Fresh Workers," *The New York Times*, July 10, 1997, p. 1; [b]Andrew Pollack, "Japan Is Struggling to Get Back on Track," *The New York Times*, Jan. 3, 1995, p. C10; [c]"Prices for Palladium Surge Amid Problems on Supplies," *The New York Times*, May 20, 1997, p. D17; [d]Edward Gargan, "Southeast's Lure: Jobs, Jobs, Jobs," *The New York Times*, Jan. 3, 1995, p. C6. © 1995, 1997 by The New York Times Co. Reprinted by permission.

 For more examples of general equilibrium analysis, see the Case and Fair Web page at **http://www.prenhall.com/casefair.**

Major corporations had rooms full of accountants with such calculators on their desks, and the sound when 30 or 40 of them were running was deafening. During the 1950s and 1960s, most firms had these machines, but few people had a calculator in their homes because the cost of a single machine was several hundred dollars. Some high schools had calculators for accounting classes, but most schoolchildren in the United States had never seen one.

In the 1960s, Wang Laboratories developed an electronic calculator. Bigger than a modern personal computer, it had several keyboards attached to a single main processor. It could add, subtract, multiply, and divide, but it also had a memory. Its main virtue was speed and quiet. It did calculations instantaneously without any noise. The Wang machine sold for around $1,500.

The beginning of the 1970s saw rapid developments in the industry. First, calculators shrank in size. The Bomar Corporation made one of the earliest hand calculators, the Bomar Brain. These early versions could do nothing more than add, subtract, multiply, and divide, they had no memories, and they still sold for several hundred dollars. Then, in the early 1970s, a number of technological breakthroughs made it possible to mass produce very small electronic circuits (silicon chips). These circuits in turn made calculators very inexpensive to produce, and it is here that we begin our general equilibrium story. Costs in the calculator industry shifted downward dramatically (Figure 12.2b). As costs fell, profits increased. Attracted by economic profits, new firms rapidly entered the market. Instead of one or two firms producing state-of-the-art machines, dozens of firms began cranking them out by the thousands. As a result, the industry supply curve shifted out to the right, driving down prices toward the new lower costs (see Figure 12.2a).

As the price of electronic calculators fell, the market for the old mechanical calculators died a quiet death. With no more demand for their product, producers found themselves suffering losses and got out of the business. As the price of electronic calculators kept falling, thousands of people who had never had a calculator began to buy them. By 1973, calculators were available at discount appliance stores for $60 to $70, and by 1975, 18.1 million were produced annually and sold at an average price of $62. The average price fell to under $30 and sales hit 30.9 million by 1983. You can now buy a basic calculator for less than $5, or get one free with a magazine subscription.

FIGURE 12.2

Cost-Saving Technological Change in the Calculator Industry

The 1970s and 1980s brought major technological changes to the calculator industry. In 1975, 18.1 million calculators were sold at an average price of $62. As technology made it possible to produce at lower costs, cost curves shifted downward. As new firms entered the industry and existing firms expanded, output rose and market price dropped. In 1983, 30.9 million calculators were produced and sold at an average price of $30.

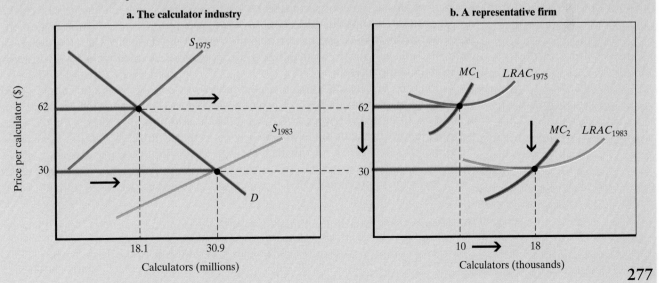

In 1987, 33.8 million calculators were produced.[1] In 1990, the Commerce Department stopped counting!

The rapid decline in the cost of producing calculators led to a rapid expansion of supply and a decline in price. (See Figure 12.2a.) The lower prices increased the quantity demanded to such an extent that most U.S. homes now have at least one calculator, and thousands of people walk around with calculators in their pockets.

This is only a partial equilibrium story, however. The events we have described also had effects on many other markets. In other words, they disturbed the general equilibrium. When mechanical calculators became obsolete, many people who had over the years developed the skills required to produce and repair those complex machines found themselves unemployed. At the same time, demand boomed for workers in the production, distribution, and sales of the new electronic calculators. The new technology thus caused a reallocation of labor across the labor market.

Capital was also reallocated. New firms invested in the plant and equipment needed to produce electronic calculators. Old capital owned by the firms that previously made mechanical calculators became obsolete and depreciated, and it ended up on the scrap heap. The mechanical calculators themselves, once an integral part of the capital stocks of accounting firms, banks, and so forth, were scrapped and replaced by the cheaper, more efficient new models.[2]

When a new billion-dollar industry suddenly appears, it earns billions of dollars in revenues that might have been spent on other things. Even though the effects of this success on any one other industry were probably small, general equilibrium analysis tells us that in the absence of the new industry and the demand for its product, households will demand other goods and services, and other industries will produce more. In this case, society has benefited a great deal. Everyone can now buy a very useful product at a low price. The new calculators have raised the productivity of certain kinds of labor and reduced costs in many industries.

> A significant—if not sweeping—technological change in a single industry affects many markets. Households face a different structure of prices and must adjust their consumption of many products. Labor reacts to new skill requirements and is reallocated across markets. Capital is also reallocated.

A SHIFT IN CONSUMER PREFERENCES: THE WINE INDUSTRY IN THE 1970s

For a more formal view of the general equilibrium effects of a change in one market on other markets, consider an economy with just two sectors, X and Y. For purposes of our discussion, let us say that the wine business in the United States is industry X and everything else is industry Y. Let us also assume that the wine industry is perfectly competitive.

During the 1970s, U.S. consumer preferences in alcoholic beverages shifted significantly in favor of wine. Table 12.1 provides some data. Domestic wine production increased by 74 percent between 1965 and 1980. In addition, in 1980 the United States imported more than nine times as much wine as it had in 1965. Overall demand increased 86.6 percent. Part of this increase was due to increased population, part was probably due to a change in the age distribution of the population, and part was due to a simple change in preferences. Per capita consumption of wine rose 53 percent.

---

[1]U.S. Department of Commerce, Bureau of the Census, *Statistical Abstract of the United States, 1983/1984, 1990, 1992.* Compiled from reports of associations and manufacturers.

[2]In recent years, of course, the electronic calculator has increasingly been replaced by the personal computer. In 1997, more than 90 million personal computers were in use in the United States (up from 2 million in 1981). More than 13 million new PCs are now being produced each year.

TABLE 12.1 PRODUCTION AND CONSUMPTION OF WINE IN THE UNITED STATES, 1965–1980

YEAR	U.S. PRODUCTION (MILLIONS OF GALLONS)	IMPORTS (MILLIONS OF GALLONS)	TOTAL (MILLIONS OF GALLONS)	CONSUMPTION PER CAPITA (GALLONS)
1965	565	10	575	1.32
1970	713	22	735	1.52
1975	782	40	822	1.96
1980	983	91	1073	2.02
Percent change, 1965–1980	+ 74.0	+ 810.0	+ 86.6	+ 53.0

Source: U.S. Department of Commerce, Bureau of the Census, *Statistical Abstract of the United States*, 1985, Table 1364, p. 765.

Figure 12.3 shows the initial equilibrium in sectors X and Y. We assume that both sectors are initially in long-run competitive equilibrium. Total output in sector X is Q_X^0, the product is selling for a price of P_X^0, and each firm in the industry produces up to where P_X^0 is equal to marginal cost—q_X^0. At that point, price is just equal to average cost, and economic profits are zero. The same condition holds initially in sector Y. The market is in zero profit equilibrium at a price of P_Y^0.

Now assume that a change in consumer preferences (or in the age distribution of the population, or in something else) shifts the demand for X out to the right from D_X^0 to D_X^1. That shift drives price up to P_X^1. If households decide to buy more X, without an increase in income they must buy *less* of something else. Because everything else is represented by Y in this example, the demand for Y must decline, and the demand curve for Y shifts to the left, from D_Y^0 to D_Y^1.

With the shift in demand for X, price rises to P_X^1 and profit-maximizing firms immediately increase output to q_X^1, (the point where $P_X^1 = MC_X$). But now there are positive profits in X. With the downward shift of demand in Y, price falls to P_Y^1. Firms in sector Y cut back to q_Y^1 (the point where $P_Y^1 = MC_Y$), and the lower price causes firms producing Y to suffer losses.

In the short run, adjustment is simple. Firms in both industries are constrained by their current scales of plant. Firms can neither enter nor exit their respective industries. Each firm in industry X raises output somewhat, from q_X^0 to q_X^1. Firms in industry Y cut back from q_Y^0 to q_Y^1.

In response to the existence of profit in sector X, the capital market begins to take notice. In chapter 9 we saw that new firms are likely to enter an industry in which there are profits to be earned. Financial analysts see the profits as a signal of future healthy growth, and entrepreneurs may become interested in moving into the industry.

Adding all this together, we would expect to see investment begin to favor sector X. This is indeed the case: Capital begins to flow into sector X. As new firms enter, the short-run supply curve in the industry shifts to the right and continues to do so until all profits are eliminated. In the top left diagram in Figure 12.3, the supply curve shifts out from S_X^0 to S_X^1, a shift that drives the price back down to P_X^0.

We would also expect to see a movement out of sector Y because of losses. Some firms will exit the industry. In the bottom left diagram in Figure 12.3, the supply curve shifts back from S_Y^0 to S_Y^1, a shift that drives the price back up to P_Y^0. At this point all losses are eliminated.

Note that a new general equilibrium is not reached until equilibrium is reestablished in all markets. If costs of production remain unchanged, as they do in Figure 12.3, this equilibrium occurs at the initial product prices, but with more resources and production in X and fewer in Y. In contrast, if an expansion in X drives up the prices of resources used specifically in X, the cost curves in X will shift upward and the final, post-expansion,

FAST FACTS

As economies grow and develop, some sectors expand, others contract. As income rises, the agricultural sector shrinks and the service sector grows:

Percent of National Output, 1995

Economies, Income	A	I	S
Lower	25%	38%	35%
Middle	11	35	52
High	2	32	66
World	5	33	63

A = agriculture
I = industry
S = services

Source: World Bank, *World Development Report,* 1997, Table 12.

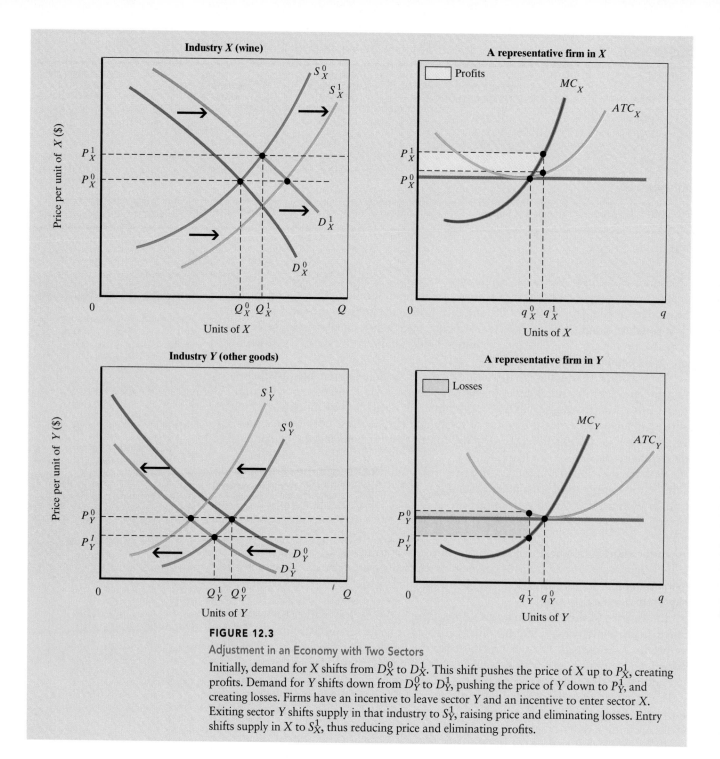

FIGURE 12.3

Adjustment in an Economy with Two Sectors

Initially, demand for X shifts from D_X^0 to D_X^1. This shift pushes the price of X up to P_X^1, creating profits. Demand for Y shifts down from D_Y^0 to D_Y^1, pushing the price of Y down to P_Y^1, and creating losses. Firms have an incentive to leave sector Y and an incentive to enter sector X. Exiting sector Y shifts supply in that industry to S_Y^1, raising price and eliminating losses. Entry shifts supply in X to S_X^1, thus reducing price and eliminating profits.

zero-profit equilibrium will occur at a higher price. Such an industry is called an *increasing-cost industry*.

Wine production is in fact an increasing-cost industry. Wine production is relatively "land intensive," and good wine is produced only from good land where the climate is right for grapes. Table 12.2 shows the number of vineyards and total acreage in grape production in 1974 and 1982. Between those years, over 10,000 new grape producers started up operations in the United States. In California alone, 150,000 additional acres were

TABLE 12.2 LAND IN GRAPE PRODUCTION IN THE UNITED STATES AND IN CALIFORNIA ALONE, 1974 AND 1982

	NUMBER OF VINEYARDS	NUMBER OF ACRES
United States		
1974	14,208	712,804
1982	24,982	874,996
Percent change	+ 75.8	+ 22.8
California		
1974	8,333	607,011
1982	10,481	756,720
Percent change	+ 25.8	+ 24.7

Source: U.S. Department of Commerce, Bureau of the Census, *Census of Agriculture* (1974 and 1982), 1, part 51.

planted with grape vines. Thus, the expansion in the wine business affected the land market: Land prices in the good wine-growing regions increased, which increased costs in the wine industry. This means that the new equilibrium price of wine after the demand shift was higher than before, contrary to the non-increasing cost case shown in Figure 12.3.[3]

FORMAL PROOF OF A GENERAL COMPETITIVE EQUILIBRIUM

Economic theorists have struggled with the question of whether a set of prices that equates supply and demand in all markets simultaneously can actually exist when there are literally thousands and thousands of markets. If such a set of prices were not possible, the result could be continuous cycles of expansion, contraction, and instability.

The nineteenth-century French economist Leon Walras struggled with the problem, but he could never provide a formal proof. Using advanced mathematical tools, economists Kenneth Arrow and Gerard Debreu and mathematicians John von Neumann and Abraham Wald have now shown the existence of at least one set of prices that *will* clear all markets in a large system simultaneously.

ALLOCATIVE EFFICIENCY AND COMPETITIVE EQUILIBRIUM

Chapters 4 through 11 built a complete model of a simple, perfectly competitive economic system. But recall that in chapters 4 and 5 we made a number of important assumptions. We assumed that both output markets and input markets are perfectly competitive—that is, that no individual household or firm is large enough relative to the market to have any control over price. In other words, we assumed that firms and households are *price-takers*.

We also assumed that households have perfect information on product quality and on all prices available, and that firms have perfect knowledge of technologies and input prices. Finally, we said that decision makers in a competitive system always consider all the costs and benefits of their decisions, that there are no "external" costs.

If all these assumptions hold, the economy will produce an efficient allocation of resources. As we relax these assumptions one by one, however, you will discover that the allocation of resources is no longer efficient and that a number of sources of inefficiency occur naturally.

---

[3]To complete the story of the U.S. wine industry: The decade of the 1980s was one of decline. Between 1980 and the end of the decade, domestic wine production dropped to 611 million gallons, a 38 percent decrease from the 1980 figure. This decline caused many producers to suffer losses and many went out of business.

PARETO EFFICIENCY

In chapter 1 we introduced several specific criteria used by economists to judge the performance of economic systems and to evaluate alternative economic policies. These criteria are (1) efficiency, (2) equity, (3) growth, and (4) stability. In chapter 1 you also learned that an *efficient* economy is one that produces the things that people want at least cost. The idea behind the efficiency criterion is that the economic system exists to serve the wants and needs of the people. If resources can be somehow reallocated to make the people "better off," then they should be. We want to use the resources at our disposal to produce maximum well-being. The trick is defining "maximum well-being."

For many years, social philosophers wrestled with the problem of "aggregation." When we say "maximum well-being" we mean maximum *for society*. Societies are made up of many people, however, and the problem has always been how to maximize satisfaction, or well-being, for all members of society. What has emerged is the now widely accepted concept of *allocative efficiency*, first developed by the Italian economist Vilfredo Pareto in the nineteenth century. Pareto's very precise definition of efficiency is often referred to as **Pareto efficiency** or **Pareto optimality**.

Pareto efficiency or **Pareto optimality** *A condition in which no change is possible that will make some members of society better off without making some other members of society worse off.*

Specifically, a change is said to be efficient if it makes some members of society better off without making other members of society worse off. An efficient, or *Pareto optimal*, system is one in which no such changes are possible. An example of a change that makes some people better off and nobody worse off is a simple voluntary exchange. I have apples; you have nuts. I like nuts; you like apples. We trade. We both gain, and no one loses.

For such a definition to have any real meaning, we must answer two questions: (1) What do we mean by "better off"? and (2) How do we account for changes that make some people better off and others worse off?

The answer to the first question is simple. People themselves decide what "better off" and "worse off" mean. I am the only one who knows whether I'm better off after a change. If you and I exchange one item for another because I like what you have and you like what I have, we both "reveal" that we are better off after the exchange because we agreed to it voluntarily. If everyone in the neighborhood wants a park and they all contribute to a fund to build one, they have consciously changed the allocation of resources, and they all are better off for it.

The answer to the second question is more complex. Nearly every change that one can imagine leaves some people better off and some people worse off. If some gain and some lose as the result of a change, and it can be demonstrated that the value of the gains exceeds the value of the losses, then the change is said to be *potentially efficient*. In practice, however, the distinction between a *potential* and an *actual* efficient change is often ignored, and all such changes are simply called *efficient*.

▶ **Example: Budget Cuts in Massachusetts**   Several years ago, in an effort to reduce state spending, the budget of the Massachusetts Registry of Motor Vehicles was cut substantially. This meant, among other things, a sharp reduction in the number of clerks in each office. Almost immediately Massachusetts residents found themselves waiting in line for hours when they had to register their automobiles or get their driver's licenses.

Clearly, drivers and car owners began paying a price: standing in line, which uses time and energy that could otherwise be used more productively. But before we can make sensible efficiency judgments, we must be able to measure, or at least approximate, the value of both the gains and the losses produced by the budget cut. To approximate the losses to car owners and drivers, we might ask how much people would be willing to pay to avoid standing in those long lines.

One office estimated that 500 people stood in line every day for about one hour each. If each person were willing to pay just $2 to avoid standing in line, the damage incurred would be $1,000 (500 × $2) per day. If the registry were open 250 days per year, the reduction in labor force at that office alone would create a cost to car owners, conservatively estimated, of $250,000 (250 × $1,000) per year.

Estimates also showed that taxpayers in Massachusetts saved about $80,000 per year by having fewer clerks at that office. If the clerks were reinstated, there would be some gains and some losses. Car owners and drivers would gain, and taxpayers would lose. But because we can show that the value of the gains would substantially exceed the value of the losses, it can be argued that reinstating the clerks would be an efficient change. Note that the only *net* losers would be those taxpayers who don't own a car and don't hold driver's licenses.[4]

THE EFFICIENCY OF PERFECT COMPETITION

In chapter 2 we discussed the "economic problem" of dividing up scarce resources among alternative uses. We also discussed the three basic questions that all societies must answer, and we set out to explain how these three questions are answered in a competitive economy:

> The
> Three
> Basic
> Questions

1. *What will be produced?* What determines the final mix of output?
2. *How will it be produced?* How do capital, labor, and land get divided up among firms? In other words, what is the allocation of resources among producers?
3. *Who will get what is produced?* What determines which households get how much? What is the distribution of output among consuming households?

The following discussion of efficiency uses these three questions and their answers to prove informally that perfect competition is efficient. To demonstrate that the perfectly competitive system leads to an efficient, or Pareto optimal, allocation of resources, we need to show that no changes are possible that will make some people better off without making others worse off. Specifically, we will show that under perfect competition (1) resources are allocated among firms efficiently, (2) final products are distributed among households efficiently, and (3) the system produces the things that people want.

> **Efficient Allocation of Resources Among Firms** The simple definition of efficiency holds that firms must produce their products using the best available—that is, lowest cost—technology. Clearly, if more output could be produced with the same amount of inputs, it would be possible to make some people better off without making others worse off.

The perfectly competitive model we have been using rests on several assumptions that assure us that resources in such a system would indeed be efficiently allocated among firms. Most important of these is the assumption that individual firms maximize profits. To maximize profit, a firm must minimize the cost of producing its chosen level of output. With a full knowledge of existing technologies, firms will choose the technology that produces the output they want at least cost.

There is more to this story than meets the eye, however. Inputs must be allocated *across* firms in the best possible way. If we find that it is possible, for example, to take capital from firm A and swap it for labor from firm B and produce more product in both firms, then the original allocation was inefficient. Recall our example from chapter 2. Farmers in Ohio and Kansas both produce wheat and corn. The climate and soil in most of Kansas are best suited to wheat production; the climate and soil in Ohio are best

TO DETERMINE WHETHER IT IS EFFICIENT TO HIRE ADDITIONAL CLERKS AT THE DMV, THE COST MUST BE WEIGHED AGAINST THE VALUE OF PEOPLE'S TIME SPENT WAITING IN LONG LINES!

[4]But, you might ask, aren't there other gainers and losers? What about the clerks themselves? In analysis like this, it is usually assumed that the citizens who pay lower taxes now spend their added income on other things. The producers of those other things need to expand to meet the new demand, and they hire more labor. Thus, a contraction of 100 jobs in the public sector will open up 100 jobs in the private sector. If the economy is fully employed, the transfer of labor to the private sector is assumed to create no net gains or losses to the workers themselves.

suited to corn production. Clearly, Kansas should produce most of the wheat and Ohio should produce most of the corn. A law that forces Kansas land into corn production and Ohio land into wheat production would result in less of both—an inefficient allocation of resources. But if markets are free and open, Kansas farmers will naturally find a higher return by planting wheat, and Ohio farmers will find a higher return in corn. The free market, then, should lead to an efficient allocation of resources among firms.

The same argument can be made more general. Misallocation of resources among firms is unlikely as long as every single firm faces the same set of prices and trade-offs in input markets. Recall from chapter 10 that perfectly competitive firms will hire additional factors of production as long as their marginal revenue product exceeds their market price. As long as all firms have access to the *same* factor markets and the *same* factor prices, the last unit of a factor hired will produce the same value in each firm. Certainly firms will use different technologies and factor combinations, but at the margin, no single profit-maximizing firm can get more value out of a factor than that factor's current market price. For example, if workers can be hired in the labor market at a wage of $6.50, *all* firms will hire workers as long as the marginal revenue product produced by the marginal worker (labor's marginal revenue product—MRP_L) remains above $6.50. *No* firms will hire labor beyond the point at which MRP_L falls below $6.50. Thus, at equilibrium, additional workers are not worth more than $6.50 to any firm, and switching labor from one firm to another will not produce output of any greater value to society. Each firm has hired the profit-maximizing amount of labor. In short:

> The assumptions that factor markets are competitive and open, that all firms pay the same prices for inputs, and that all firms maximize profits lead to the conclusion that the allocation of resources among firms is efficient.

> ▶ **Efficient Distribution of Outputs Among Households**   Even if the system is producing the right things, and is doing so efficiently, these things still have to get to the right people. Just as open, competitive factor markets ensure that firms don't end up with the wrong inputs, open, competitive output markets ensure that households don't end up with the wrong goods and services.

Within the constraints imposed by income and wealth, households are free to choose among all the goods and services available in output markets. A household will buy a good as long as that good generates utility, or subjective value, greater than its market price. Utility value is revealed in market behavior. You don't go out and buy something unless you are willing to pay *at least* the market price.

Remember that the value you place on any one good depends on what you must give up to have that good. The trade-offs available to you depend on your budget constraint. The trade-offs that are desirable depend on your preferences. If you buy a $400 CD player for your dorm room, you may be giving up a trip home. If I buy it, I may be giving up four new tires for my car. But we've both revealed that the CD player is worth at least as much to us as all the other things that $400 can buy. As long as we are free to choose among all the things that $400 can buy, we will not end up with the wrong things; it's not possible to find a trade that will make us both better off.

> We all know that people have different tastes and preferences, and that they will buy very different things in very different combinations. But as long as everyone shops freely in the same markets, no redistribution of final outputs among people will make them better off. If you and I buy in the same markets and pay the same prices, and I buy what I want and you buy what you want, neither of us can possibly end up with the wrong combination of things. But free and open markets are essential to this result.

> **Producing What People Want: The Efficient Mix of Output** It does no good to produce things efficiently or to distribute them efficiently if the system produces the wrong things. Will competitive markets produce the things that people want?

If the system is producing the wrong mix of output, we should be able to show that producing more of one good and less of another will make people better off. To show that perfectly competitive markets are efficient, then, we must demonstrate that no such changes in the final mix of output are possible.

The condition that ensures that the right things are produced is $P = MC$. That is, in both the long run and the short run, a perfectly competitive firm will produce at the point where the price of its output is equal to the marginal cost of production. The logic is this: When a firm weighs price and marginal cost, it weighs the value of its product to society *at the margin* against the value of the things that could otherwise be produced with the same resources. Figure 12.4 summarizes this logic.

The argument is quite straightforward. *First, price reflects households' willingness to pay.* By purchasing a product, individual households reveal that it is worth at least as much as the other things that the same money could buy. Thus, current price reflects the value that households place on a good.

Second, marginal cost reflects the opportunity cost of the resources needed to produce a good. If a firm producing X hires a worker, it must pay the market wage. That wage must be sufficient to attract that worker out of leisure or away from firms producing other products. The same argument holds for capital and land.

Thus, if the price of a good ends up greater than marginal cost, producing more of it will generate benefits to households in excess of opportunity costs, and society gains. Similarly, if the price of a good ends up below marginal cost, resources are being used to produce something that households value less than opportunity costs. Producing less of it creates gains to society.[5]

> Society will produce the efficient mix of output if all firms equate price and marginal cost.

FIGURE 12.4

The Key Efficiency Condition: Price Equals Marginal Cost

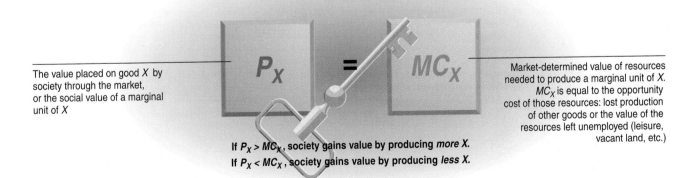

The value placed on good X by society through the market, or the social value of a marginal unit of X

$$P_X = MC_X$$

Market-determined value of resources needed to produce a marginal unit of X. MC_X is equal to the opportunity cost of those resources: lost production of other goods or the value of the resources left unemployed (leisure, vacant land, etc.)

If $P_X > MC_X$, society gains value by producing *more X*.
If $P_X < MC_X$, society gains value by producing *less X*.

---

[5]It is important to understand that firms do not act *consciously* to balance social costs and benefits. In fact, the usual assumption is that firms are self-interested, private profit-maximizers. It just works out that in perfectly competitive markets, when firms are weighing private benefits against private costs, they are actually (perhaps without knowing it) weighing the benefits and costs to society as well.

Figure 12.5 shows how a simple competitive market system leads individual households and firms to make efficient choices in input and output markets. For simplicity, the figure assumes only one factor of production, labor. Households weigh the market wage against the value of leisure and time spent in unpaid household production. But the wage is a measure of labor's potential product because firms weigh labor cost (wages) against the value of the product produced, and hire up to the point at which $W = MRP_L$. Households use wages to buy market-produced goods. Thus, households implicitly weigh the value of market-produced goods against the value of leisure and household production.

When a firm's scale is balanced, it is earning maximum profit; when a household's scale is balanced, it is maximizing utility. Under these conditions, no changes can improve social welfare.

PERFECT COMPETITION VERSUS REAL MARKETS

So far, we have built a model of a perfectly competitive market system that produces an efficient allocation of resources, an efficient mix of output, and an efficient distribution of output. But the perfectly competitive model is built on a set of assumptions, all of which must hold for our conclusions to be fully valid. We have assumed that all firms and households are price-takers in input and output markets, that firms and households have perfect information, and that all firms maximize profits.

But these assumptions do not always hold in real-world markets. When this is the case, the conclusion that free, unregulated markets will produce an efficient outcome breaks down. The remainder of this chapter discusses some inefficiencies that occur naturally in markets and some of the strengths, as well as the weaknesses, of the market mechanism. We also discuss the usefulness of the competitive model for understanding the real economy.

FIGURE 12.5

Efficiency in Perfect Competition Follows from a Weighing of Values by Both Households and Firms

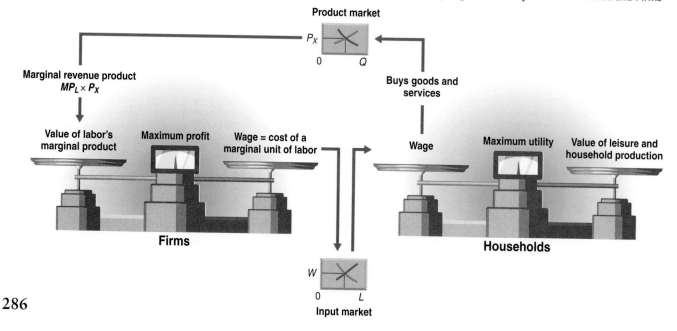

THE SOURCES OF MARKET FAILURE

In suggesting some of the problems encountered in real markets and some of the possible solutions to these problems, the rest of this chapter previews the next part of this book, which focuses on the economics of market failure and the potential role of government in the economy.

Market failure occurs when resources are misallocated, or allocated inefficiently. The result is waste or lost value. In this section, we briefly describe four important sources of market failure: (1) *imperfect market structure*, or noncompetitive behavior, (2) the existence of *public goods*, (3) the presence of *external costs and benefits*, and (4) *imperfect information*. Each condition results from the failure of one of the assumptions basic to the perfectly competitive model, and each is discussed in more detail in later chapters. Each also points to a potential role for government in the economy. The desirability and extent of actual government involvement in the economy are hotly debated subjects.

market failure *Occurs when resources are misallocated, or allocated inefficiently. The result is waste or lost value.*

IMPERFECT MARKETS

Until now we have operated on the assumption that the number of buyers and sellers in each market is large. When each buyer and each seller is only one of a great many in the market, no individual buyer or seller can independently influence price. Thus, all economic decision makers are by virtue of their relatively small size forced to take input prices and output prices as given. When this assumption does not hold—that is, when single firms have some control over price and potential competition—the result is **imperfect competition** and an inefficient allocation of resources.

A Kansas wheat farmer is probably a "price-taker," but Microsoft and Chrysler Corporation most certainly are not. Many firms in many industries do have some control over price. The degree of control that is possible depends on the character of competition in the industry itself.

An industry that comprises just one firm producing a product for which there are no close substitutes is called a **monopoly**. Although a monopoly has no other firms to compete with, it is still constrained by market demand. To be successful, the firm still has to produce something that people want. Essentially, a monopoly must choose both price and quantity of output simultaneously because the amount that it will be able to sell depends on the price it sets. If the price is too high, it will sell nothing. Presumably a monopolist sets price in order to maximize profit. That price is generally significantly above average costs, and such a firm usually earns economic profits.

In competition, economic profits will attract the entry of new firms into the industry. A rational monopolist who is not restrained by the government does everything possible to block any such entry in order to preserve economic profits in the long run. As a result, society loses the benefits of more product and lower prices. A number of barriers to entry can be raised. Sometimes a monopoly is actually licensed by government, and entry into its market is prohibited by law. Taiwan has only one beer company; many areas in the United States have only one local telephone company. Ownership of a natural resource can also be the source of monopoly power. If I buy up all the coal mines in the United States and I persuade Congress to restrict coal imports, no one can enter the coal industry and compete with me.

Between monopoly and perfect competition are a number of other imperfectly competitive market structures. *Oligopolistic industries* are made up of a small number of firms, each with a degree of price-setting power. *Monopolistically competitive industries* are made up of a large number of firms that acquire price-setting power by differentiating their products or by establishing a brand name. Only General Mills can produce Wheaties, for example, and only Miles Laboratories can produce Alka-Seltzer.

imperfect competition *An industry in which single firms have some control over price and competition. Imperfectly competitive industries give rise to an inefficient allocation of resources.*

monopoly *An industry composed of only one firm that produces a product for which there are no close substitutes and in which significant barriers exist to prevent new firms from entering the industry.*

> In all imperfectly competitive industries, output is lower—the product is under-produced—and price is higher than it would be under perfect competition. The equilibrium condition $P = MC$ does not hold, and the system does not produce the most efficient product mix.

In the United States, many forms of noncompetitive behavior are illegal. A firm that attempts to monopolize an industry or conspires with other firms to reduce competition risks serious penalties. The most famous recent antitrust case ended in 1982 with the break-up of the American Telephone and Telegraph Company. The case was originally filed in 1974 by the Justice Department, which charged that AT&T had used its power to freeze out competition in the long-distance and equipment markets. This sort of behavior, the Justice Department argued, prevents society from enjoying the benefits of free competition. Recently, three industries once thought to be "natural monopolies" are shifting away from government regulation toward becoming fully competitive industries: local telephone service, electricity, and natural gas. (All of this is discussed in much more detail in chapters 13, 14, and 15.)

PUBLIC GOODS

public goods, or **social goods**
Goods or services that bestow collective benefits on members of society. Generally, no one can be excluded from enjoying their benefits. The classic example is national defense.

A second major source of inefficiency lies in the fact that private producers simply do not find it in their best interest to produce everything that members of society want. More specifically, there is a whole class of goods called **public goods,** or **social goods,** that will be underproduced or not produced at all in a completely unregulated market economy.[6]

Public goods are goods or services that bestow collective benefits on society; they are, in a sense, collectively consumed. The classic example is national defense, but there are countless others—police protection, preservation of wilderness lands, and public health, to name a few. These things are "produced" using land, labor, and capital just like any other good. Some public goods, such as national defense, benefit the whole nation. Others, such as clean air, may be limited to smaller areas—the air may be clean in a Kansas town but dirty in a Southern California city.

private goods *Products produced by firms for sale to individual households.*

Public goods are consumed by everyone, not just by those who pay for them. Once the good is produced, no one can be excluded from enjoying its benefits. Producers of **private goods,** like hamburgers, can make a profit because they don't hand over the product to you until you pay for it. Chapters 4 through 11 centered on the production of private goods.

If the provision of public goods were left to private, profit-seeking producers with no power to force payment, a serious problem would arise. Suppose, for example, that I value some public good, X. If there were a functioning market for X, I would be willing to pay for it. But suppose that I am asked to contribute voluntarily to the production of X. Should I contribute? Perhaps I should on moral grounds, but not on the basis of pure self-interest.

At least two problems can get in the way. First, because I cannot be excluded from using X for not paying, I get the good whether I pay or not. Why should I pay if I don't have to? Second, because public goods that provide collective benefits to large numbers of people are expensive to produce, any one person's contribution is not likely to make much difference to the amount of the good ultimately produced. Would the national defense suffer, for example, if you didn't pay your share of the bill? Probably not. Thus, nothing happens if you don't pay. The output of the good doesn't change much, and you get it whether you pay or not.

[6]While they are normally referred to as public *goods,* many of the things we are talking about are *services.*

A CLASSIC EXAMPLE OF A
PUBLIC GOOD IS A PARK
SUCH AS CENTRAL PARK IN
MANHATTAN PRODUCING
COLLECTIVE BENEFITS FOR
NEW YORKERS AND TOURISTS.

Private provision of public goods fails. A completely laissez-faire market system will not produce everything that all members of a society might want. Citizens must band together to ensure that desired public goods are produced, and this is generally accomplished through government spending financed by taxes.

Public goods are the subject of chapter 16.

EXTERNALITIES

A third major source of inefficiency is the existence of external costs and benefits. An **externality** is a cost or benefit imposed or bestowed on an individual or group that is outside, or external to, the transaction—in other words, something that affects a third party. In a city, external costs are pervasive. The classic example is pollution, but there are thousands of others, such as noise, congestion, and painting your house a color that the neighbors think is ugly.

Not all externalities are negative, however. For example, housing investment may yield benefits for neighbors. A farm located near a city provides residents in the area with nice views, fresher air, and a less congested environment.

Externalities are a problem only if decision makers do not take them into account. The logic of efficiency presented earlier in this chapter required that firms weigh social benefits against social costs. If a firm in a competitive environment produces a good, it is because the value of that good to society exceeds the social cost of producing it—this is the logic of $P = MC$. If social costs or benefits are overlooked or left out of the calculations, inefficient decisions result.

The market itself has no automatic mechanism that provides decision makers an incentive to consider external effects. Through government, however, society has established over the years a number of different institutions for dealing with externalities. Tort law, for example, is a body of legal rules that deal with third-party effects. Under certain circumstances, those who impose costs are held strictly liable for them. In other circumstances, liability is assessed only if the cost results from "negligent" behavior. Tort law deals with small problems as well as larger ones. If a neighbor sprays her lawn with a powerful chemical and kills your prize shrub, you can take her to court and force her to pay for it. Huge damages were caused when a large oil tanker ran aground in Japan in 1997. Most damage claims resulting from the accident will be settled in court.

The effects of externalities can be enormous. For years, companies piled chemical wastes indiscriminately into dump sites near water supplies and residential areas. In some locations, those wastes seeped into the ground and contaminated the drinking water. In response to the evidence that smoking damages not only the smoker but others as well, governments have increased prohibitions against smoking on airplanes and in public places.

externality *A cost or benefit resulting from some activity or transaction that is imposed or bestowed upon parties outside the activity or transaction.*

FAST FACTS

The classic example of an externality is air pollution. Here are measures of air quality for some selected cities:

City	Pollution Level*
Calcutta	393
Beijing	370
Jakarta	271
Teheran	261
Accra	137
Kuala Lumpur	119
Bangkok	105
Sao Paulo	98
Helsinki	81
New York City	61
Frankfurt	42
Brussels	22

*Annual mean micrograms of suspended particulates per cubic meter of air.

Source: World Bank, *World Development Indicators, 1997,* Table 3.8.

In 1997, attorneys general for a majority of states approved a tentative agreement with the tobacco industry to pay billions of dollars in damage claims to avoid pending lawsuits filed on behalf of citizens damaged by smoking or breathing secondhand smoke.

For years, economists have suggested that a carefully designed set of taxes and subsidies could help to "internalize" external effects. For example, if a paper mill that pollutes the air and waterways is taxed in proportion to the damage caused by that pollution, it would consider those costs in its decisions.

Sometimes, interaction among and between parties can lead to the proper consideration of externality without government involvement. If someone plays her radio loudly on the fourth floor of your dormitory, that person imposes an externality on the other residents of the building. The residents, however, can get together and negotiate a set of mutually acceptable rules to govern radio playing.

> The market does not always force consideration of all the costs and benefits of decisions. Yet for an economy to achieve an efficient allocation of resources, all costs and benefits must be weighed.

We discuss externalities in detail in chapter 16.

IMPERFECT INFORMATION

imperfect information *The absence of full knowledge regarding product characteristics, available prices, and so forth.*

The fourth major source of inefficiency is **imperfect information** on the part of buyers and sellers:

> The conclusion that markets work efficiently rests heavily on the assumption that consumers and producers have full knowledge of product characteristics, available prices, and so forth. The absence of full information can lead to transactions that are ultimately disadvantageous.

Some products are so complex that consumers find it difficult to judge the potential benefits and costs of purchase. Buyers of life insurance have a very difficult time sorting out the terms of the more complex policies and determining the true "price" of the product. Consumers of almost any service that requires expertise, such as plumbing or medical care, have a hard time evaluating what is needed, much less how well it is done. It is difficult for a used car buyer to find out the true "quality" of the cars in Big Jim's Car Emporium.

Some forms of misinformation can be corrected with simple rules such as truth-in-advertising regulations. In some cases, the government provides information to citizens; job banks and consumer information services exist for this purpose. In some industries, such as medical care, there is no clear-cut solution to the problem of noninformation or misinformation. We discuss all these topics in detail in chapter 16.

EVALUATING THE MARKET MECHANISM

Is the market system good or bad? Should the government be involved in the economy, or should it leave the allocation of resources to the free market? So far, our information is mixed and incomplete. To the extent that the perfectly competitive model reflects the way markets really operate, there seem to be some clear advantages to the market system. But when we relax the assumptions and expand our discussion to include noncompetitive behavior, public goods, externalities, and the possibility of imperfect information, we see at least a potential role for government.

The market system does seem to provide most participants with the incentive to weigh costs and benefits and to operate efficiently. Firms can make profits only if a demand for their products exists. If there are no externalities, or if such costs or benefits

To get a feel for the range of government involvement from country to country, the following shows total central government expenditure as a percent of gross domestic product for 11 nations:

Country	Central Government Spending as % of GDP, 1995
Italy	49.9%
France	46.8
Czech Republic	45.0
Brazil	39.0
Germany	33.9
Australia	29.1
United States	22.9
Ghana	20.6
Indonesia	16.2
Mexico	14.3
Thailand	10.5

Source: World Bank, *World Development Report, 1997,* Table 14.

are properly internalized, firms *will* weigh social benefits and costs in their production decisions. Under these circumstances, the profit motive should provide competitive firms with an incentive to minimize cost and to produce their products using the most efficient technologies. Likewise, competitive input markets should provide households with the incentive to weigh the value of their time against the social value of what they can produce in the labor force.

But markets are far from perfect. Freely functioning markets in the real world do not always produce an efficient allocation of resources, and this provides a potential role for government in the economy. Many have called for government involvement in the economy to correct for market failure—that is, to help markets function more efficiently. As you will see, however, many feel that government involvement in the economy creates more inefficiency than it cures.

In addition, we have thus far discussed only the criterion of efficiency, and economic systems and economic policies must be judged by many other criteria, not the least of which is *equity*, or fairness. Indeed, some contend that the outcome of any free market is ultimately unfair, because some become rich while others remain very poor.

Part 3, which follows, explores the issue of market imperfections and government involvement in the economy in greater depth.

SUMMARY

GENERAL EQUILIBRIUM ANALYSIS

1. Both firms and households make simultaneous choices in both input and output markets. For example, input prices determine output costs and affect firms' output supply decisions. Wages in the labor market affect labor supply decisions, income, and ultimately how much output households can and do purchase.

2. A *general equilibrium* exists when all markets in an economy are in simultaneous equilibrium. An event that disturbs the equilibrium in one market may disturb the equilibrium in many other markets as well. *Partial equilibrium* analysis can be misleading, because it looks only at adjustments in one isolated market.

ALLOCATIVE EFFICIENCY AND COMPETITIVE EQUILIBRIUM

3. An *efficient* economy is one that produces the goods and services that people want at least possible cost. A change is said to be efficient if it makes some members of society better off without making others worse off. An efficient, or *Pareto optimal*, system is one in which no such changes are possible.

4. If a change makes some people better off and some people worse off, but it can be shown that the value of the gains exceeds the value of the losses, the change is said to be *potentially efficient*, or simply *efficient*.

5. If all the assumptions of perfect competition hold, the result is an efficient, or Pareto optimal, allocation of resources. To prove this statement, it is necessary to show that resources are allocated efficiently among firms, that final products are

distributed efficiently among households, and that the system produces what people want.

6. The assumptions that factor markets are competitive and open, that all firms pay the same prices for inputs, and that all firms maximize profits lead to the conclusion that the allocation of resources among firms is efficient.

7. People have different tastes and preferences, and they buy very different things in very different combinations. But as long as everyone shops freely in the same markets, no redistribution of outputs among people will make them better off. This leads to the conclusion that final products are distributed efficiently among households.

8. Because perfectly competitive firms will produce as long as the price of their product is greater than the marginal cost of production, they will continue to produce as long as a gain for society is possible. The market thus guarantees that the right things are produced. In other words, the perfectly competitive system produces what people want.

THE SOURCES OF MARKET FAILURE

9. When the assumptions of perfect competition do not hold, the conclusion that free, unregulated markets will produce an efficient allocation of resources breaks down.

10. An imperfectly competitive industry is one in which single firms have some control over price and competition. Forms of *imperfect competition* include monopoly, monopolistic competition, and oligopoly. In all imperfectly competitive industries, output is lower and price is higher than it would be in competition. Imperfect competition is a major source of market inefficiency.

11. *Public*, or *social*, *goods* bestow collective benefits on members of society. Because the benefits of social goods are collective, people cannot in most cases be excluded from enjoying them. Thus, private firms usually do not find it profitable to produce public goods. The need for public goods is thus another source of inefficiency.

12. An *externality* is a cost or benefit that is imposed or bestowed on an individual or group that is outside, or external to, the transaction. If such social costs or benefits are overlooked, the decisions of households or firms are likely to be wrong or inefficient.

13. Market efficiency depends on the assumption that buyers have perfect information on product quality and price and that firms have perfect information on input quality and price. *Imperfect information* can lead to wrong choices and inefficiency.

EVALUATING THE MARKET MECHANISM

14. Sources of market failure—such as imperfect markets, social goods, externalities, and imperfect information—are considered by many to justify the existence of government and governmental policies that seek to redistribute costs and income on the basis of efficiency, equity, or both.

REVIEW TERMS AND CONCEPTS

efficiency, 275
externality, 289
general equilibrium, 275
imperfect competition, 287
imperfect information, 290
market failure, 287

monopoly, 287
Pareto efficiency, or Pareto optimality, 282
partial equilibrium analysis, 275
private goods, 288
public goods, or social goods, 288

Key efficiency condition in perfect competition: $P_X = MC_X$

PROBLEM SET

1. During the 1990s, cellular telephones became very popular. At the same time new technology made them less expensive to produce. Assuming the technological advance caused cost curves to shift downward at the same time that demand was shifting to the right, draw a diagram or diagrams to show what will happen in the short and long run.

2. In 1997, retailing giant Montgomery Ward went out of business, and the retailing industry seemed in turmoil. The advent of home shopping via cable television and the World Wide Web, and the rise of "big box" warehouse stores like Sam's Club and B. J.'s, have cut deeply into the profits of smaller stores and more traditional department stores. Review the discussion of the wine industry in this chapter. Using the same two-sector framework, discuss the economics of expansion in part of the retail sector and contraction in another part of the retail sector. Assuming the new stores and venues provide less service and employ fewer workers, describe the impact on the labor market.

3. A medium-sized bakery has just opened in Slovakia. A loaf of bread is currently selling for 14 koruna (the Slovakian currency) over and above the cost of intermediate goods (flour, etc.). Assuming that labor is the only variable factor of production, the following table gives the production function for bread:

WORKERS	LOAVES OF BREAD
0	0
1	15
2	30
3	42
4	52
5	60
6	66
7	70

a. Suppose that the current wage rate in Slovakia is 119 koruna per hour. How many workers will the bakery employ?

b. Suppose that the economy of Slovakia begins to grow, incomes rise, and the price of a loaf of bread is pushed up to 20 koruna. Assuming no increase in the price of labor, how many workers will the bakery hire?

c. An increase in the demand for labor pushes up wages to 125 koruna per hour. What impact will this increase in cost have on employment and output in the bakery at the 20-koruna price of bread?

d. If all firms behaved like our bakery, would the allocation of resources in Slovakia be efficient? Explain your answer.

4. Country A has soil that is suited to corn production and yields 135 bushels per acre. Country B has soil that is not suited for corn and yields only 45 bushels per acre. Country A has soil that is not suited for soybean production and yields 15 bushels per acre. Country B has soil that is suited for soybeans and yields 35 bushels per acre. In 1997, there was no trade between A and B because of high taxes, and both countries together produced huge quantities of corn and soybeans. In 1998, taxes were eliminated because of a new trade agreement. What is likely to happen? Can you justify the trade agreement on the basis of Pareto efficiency? Why or why not?

5. Do you agree or disagree with each of the following statements? Explain your answer.
   a. "Housing is a public good and should be produced by the public sector because private markets will fail to produce it efficiently."
   b. "Monopoly power is inefficient, because large firms will produce too much product, dumping it on the market at artificially low prices."
   c. "Medical care is an example of a potentially inefficient market because consumers do not have perfect information about the product."

6. Which of the following are examples of Pareto efficient changes? Explain your answers.
   a. Cindy trades her laptop computer to Bob for his old car.
   b. Competition is introduced into the electric industry and electricity rates drop. A study shows that benefits to consumers are larger than the lost monopoly profits.
   c. A high tax on wool sweaters deters buyers. The tax is repealed.
   d. A federal government agency is reformed and costs are cut 23 percent with no loss of service quality.

7. A major source of chicken feed in the United States is anchovies, small fish that can be scooped up out of the ocean at low cost. Every seven years, the anchovies disappear to spawn, and producers must turn to grain, which is more expensive, to feed their chickens. What is likely to happen to the cost of chicken when the anchovies disappear? What are substitutes for chicken? How are the markets for these substitutes affected? Name some complements to chicken. How are the markets for these complements affected? How might the allocation of farmland be changed as a result of the anchovies' disappearance?

8. Suppose two passengers both end up with a reservation for the last seat on a train from San Francisco to Los Angeles. Two alternatives are proposed:

   a. Toss a coin.
   b. Sell the ticket to the highest bidder.
   Compare the two from the standpoint of efficiency and equity.

9. Assume that there are two sectors in an economy: goods (G) and services (S). Both sectors are perfectly competitive, with large numbers of firms and constant returns to scale. As income rises, households spend a larger portion of their incomes on S and a smaller portion on G. Using supply and demand curves for both sectors and a diagram showing a representative firm in each sector, explain what would happen to output and prices in the short run and the long run in response to an increase in income. (Assume that the increase in income causes demand for G to shift left and demand for S to shift right.) In the long run what would happen to employment in the goods sector? In the service sector? (*Hint:* See Figure 12.3.)

10. Which of the following are actual Pareto efficient changes? Explain briefly.
    a. You buy 3 oranges for $1 from a street vendor.
    b. You are near death from thirst in the desert, and must pay a passing vagabond $10,000 for a glass of water.
    c. A mugger steals your wallet.
    d. You take a taxi ride in downtown Manhattan during rush hour.

11. Each instance below is an example of one of the four types of market failure discussed in this chapter. In each case identify the type of market failure, and defend your choice briefly.
    a. An auto repair shop convinces you that you need a $2,000 valve job, when all you really need is an oil change.
    b. Everyone in a neighborhood would benefit if an empty lot were turned into a park, but no entrepreneur will come forward to finance the transformation.
    c. Someone who lives in an apartment building buys a Wayne Newton album, then blasts it on full volume at 3 A.M.
    d. The only two airlines flying direct between St. Louis and Atlanta make an agreement to raise their prices.

12. Two factories in the same town hire workers with exactly the same skills. Union agreements require factory A to pay its workers $10 per hour, while factory B must pay $6 per hour. Each factory hires the profit-maximizing number of workers. Is the allocation of labor between these two factories efficient? Explain why or why not.

TAKE IT TO THE NET

We invite you to visit the Case and Fair page on the Prentice Hall Web site:

http://www.prenhall.com/casefair

for this chapter's World Wide Web exercise.

THE FARMING INDUSTRY IN NEW ENGLAND: CAN IT SURVIVE?

The farming industry is affected by economic factors that determine prices, output, profits and losses, and the number and size of firms. Some of these factors have affected the relative importance of farming across different regions in the United States. For example, individuals today who fly to some Midwestern cities can observe a landscape dominated by farming. In contrast, air travelers to any New England city might not see even one farm as they approach their destination.

The New England farming industry has changed greatly over the past 150 years. Between 1850 and 1880, the number of farms and total farm acreage increased by about 24 percent and 17 percent, respectively (see Table 1). Since 1880, the number of farms, total farm acreage, and farmland as a percentage of total land decreased significantly. By 1990, the average size of farms, as measured by average acreage per farm, was nearly 60 percent larger than between 1850 and 1940.

A number of factors contributed to the early decline of farming in New England. First, the development of railroads and refrigeration reduced the cost of importing food from other regions where climates were more favorable to agricultural production. Second, new and improved farming equipment and other technological advances created economies of scale favoring large farms. Both factors created advantages for large-scale farming in the Midwest while adversely affecting the farming industry in New England.

More recent developments have contributed further to the decline of farming in New England. As per capita income rose, the increased demand for nonfood items caused increases in commercial development. This growth in commercial development and increased demand for housing have caused relatively high land values in New England; consequently, this increased demand for land for nonfarm uses has caused New England land to have relatively higher priced farmland. "While the average U.S. farm was valued at $832 per acre (including buildings) in 1995, the average value in New England ranged from $1,245 in Maine to $6,947 in Rhode Island" (Katz, 1997, p. 14).

These relatively higher land prices create three problems for New England farmers: (1) Greater pressure exists for farming to generate the necessary revenues to keep land in agriculture. (2) Although agricultural land is generally taxed at a lower rate than other land, the average property tax per acre of farmland in New England is higher than the average for the United States—$6 per acre nationally versus, for example, $11 per acre in Maine and $57 per acre in Rhode Island. (3) Higher land prices also make it relatively more expensive for New England farms to expand.

Changes in the availability of labor and other farm inputs have also affected the industry. Increases in city wages relative to wages paid in rural areas have caused better-educated workers to go to the cities, reducing the number of workers available to farmers and causing farm wages, all else fixed, to be higher than they otherwise would be. Furthermore, as the number of New England farms has declined, some suppliers of other farm inputs (e.g., fertilizer and seed) have left the region. This reduction in the supply of nonlabor inputs raised the cost of farming. It's understandable that New England farmers over time have become increasingly uncertain about their industry. Farmers uncertain about their economic future may not, for example, purchase new equipment or even properly maintain their existing equipment.

TABLE 1

Farming in New England

YEAR	NUMBER OF FARMS	FARM ACREAGE	AVERAGE ACREAGE PER FARM	FARM LAND AS PERCENTAGE OF TOTAL LAND
1850	167,700	18,367,000	110	46
1880	207,200	21,484,000	104	53
1940	135,200	13,371,000	99	33
1960	56,900	9,316,000	164	23
1970	28,600	5,600,000	196	14
1990	28,900	4,621,000	160	11

Note: Data from Katz (1997).

All these developments have caused a large number of farms to close, as reflected in the data in the table. The remaining farms have made changes to survive. Some farms now specialize in perishable items and goods that are costly to transport (e.g., milk, cranberries, and Christmas trees). Given the increase in income and the subsequent increase in the demand for gourmet foods (in addition to changing preferences toward organic foods), some farms now produce a variety of specialty goods (e.g., shiitake mushrooms).

Despite the negative effects of relatively high city wages on farming, some farming households have taken advantage of these wages, supplementing their farm income with income earned in other occupations. Higher land values have also allowed some farmers to sell part of their land to subsidize their farming. And some farmers have attempted to create a link between farming and tourism through such programs as working farms.

The decline in the number of farms and the amount of land allocated to farming has created concerns not just for farmers but for environmentalists, policy makers, and residents. Some view the preservation of farming and farmland as a means of protecting an environmental resource. Furthermore, the preservation of farmland ensures

that a portion of the landscape can be maintained as open space. Still others place great value on both the cultural heritage of farming and on the "aesthetics" of the New England farm.

A number of policies have been implemented to protect both farming and farmland. (1) Farmland generally receives tax breaks compared with residential and other commercial properties. (2) Federal and state governments have set aside funds to purchase development rights of farmland. (3) Price supports and subsidies have been used to maintain farming income. (4) Some towns, for example in Maine, have placed a moratorium on building new homes and have loosened development restrictions in town centers to redirect business activity. Before implementing any of these policies, however, policy makers must ask whether their goal is to preserve farming or farmland. If the goal is to preserve farming as an economic activity, "only working farms will do" (Katz, 1997, p. 17).

Questions for Analytical Thinking

1. Assume that the market for food is perfectly competitive. Using the supply and demand graph for the food industry and the *ATC, AVC, MC,* and *MR* graph

for the representative New England farm (i.e., firm), graphically illustrate and explain what effect the development of refrigeration and railroads had on the price of food and, therefore, on the profits of New England farms.

2. The development of new farming equipment and other technological innovations placed a premium on large farms.
   a. Explain how these developments might have affected the cost structure of farming in the United States.
   b. When many of these developments occurred, it was difficult or impossible, given the landscape, for farmers in New England to increase the size of their farms. Based on this information, what effect do you think the development of new farming equipment and other technological innovations had on the profits of New England farms? Explain.

3. Explain how the relatively higher property taxes in New England affect the competitiveness of New England farms. In particular, explain what effect, if any, these relatively higher property taxes have on the average total cost and average variable cost rates on farmland in New England and consequently on the profitability of New England

farms. Finally, do you think any individuals in New England might oppose a policy that reduces tax rates on farmland in New England? Explain.

4. There have been several widely publicized cases where contaminated food was sold to the public (e.g., strawberries in 1996 and processed hamburger in 1997). As the public becomes more concerned about the quality of the food supply, how might this affect the viability of New England farms? Explain.

5. "... if our end is preserving farming, as an economic activity and as the site of a long legacy of social and cultural traditions, then only working farms will do" (Katz, 1997, p. 17). What do you think this statement means? Explain.

Sources: Clarke Canfield, "Kennebunk: New Rules Steer Village Growth," *Special Report: Suburban Sprawl, Portland Press Herald,* July 7, 1997; Clarke Canfield, "Dayton: Small Town's 'Been Found'," *Special Report: Suburban Sprawl, Portland Press Herald,* July 7, 1997; Jane Katz, "Farming in the Shadow of Suburbia," *Regional Review,* Federal Reserve Bank of Boston, Spring 1997, Vol. 7, No. 1, pp. 12–17; Letters: "On the Farm," *Regional Review,* Federal Reserve Bank of Boston, Summer 1997, Vol. 7, No. 2, p. 4; Peter Pochna and Clarke Canfield, "The Pattern of Growth in Southern Maine Has Its Costs," *Special Report: Suburban Sprawl, Maine Sunday Telegram,* July 6, 1997.

Chapter

13

MONOPOLY

IN CHAPTERS 6 THROUGH 12, we built a model of a perfectly competitive economy. To do so, we needed to make some assumptions. In chapter 12 we began to see what happens when we relax them.

A number of assumptions, you will recall, underlie the logic of perfect competition. One is that a large number of firms and households interact in each output market. Another is that firms in a given market produce undifferentiated, or homogeneous, products. Together, these two conditions limit firms' choices. With many firms in each market, no single firm has any control over market prices. Single firms may decide how much to produce and how to produce, but the market determines output price. The assumption that new firms are free to enter industries and to compete for profits led us to conclude that opportunities for economic profit are eliminated in the long run as competition drives price to a level equal to the average cost of production.

In the next two chapters, we explore the implications of relaxing these assumptions. In this chapter, we focus on the case of a single firm in an industry—a monopoly.

IMPERFECT COMPETITION AND MARKET POWER: CORE CONCEPTS

A market, or industry, in which individual firms have some control over the price of their output is **imperfectly competitive**. All firms in an imperfectly competitive market have one thing in common: They exercise **market power,** the ability to raise price without losing all demand for their product. Imperfect competition and market power are major sources of inefficiency.

Imperfect competition does not mean that *no* competition exists in the market. In some imperfectly competitive markets competition occurs in *more* arenas than in perfectly competitive markets. Firms can differentiate their products, advertise, improve quality, market aggressively, cut prices, and so forth.

For a firm to exercise control over the price of its product, it must be able to *limit competition* by erecting barriers to entry. If your firm produces T-shirts, and if other firms can enter freely into the industry and produce exactly the same T-shirts that you produce, the result will be the outcome that

imperfectly competitive industry *An industry in which single firms have some control over the price of their output.*

market power *An imperfectly competitive firm's ability to raise price without losing all demand for its product.*

you would expect in a perfectly competitive industry: The supply will increase, the price of T-shirts will be driven down to their average cost, and economic profits will be eliminated.

But note that T-shirts having the official National Basketball Association team logo are more expensive than generic T-shirts. If your firm can prevent other firms from producing exactly the same product, or if it can prevent other firms from entering the market, then it has a chance of preserving its economic profits. Only the NBA's licensees are allowed to use the official logo.

DEFINING INDUSTRY BOUNDARIES

A *monopoly*, you will recall, is an industry with a single firm in which the entry of new firms is blocked. An *oligopoly* is an industry in which there is a small number of firms, each large enough to have an impact on the market price of its outputs. Firms that differentiate their products in industries that have many producers and free entry are called *monopolistic competitors* (review Figure 3.1). But where do we set the boundary of an industry? Although Procter & Gamble is the only firm that can produce Ivory, there are many other brands of soap. In general:

> The ease with which consumers can substitute for a product limits the extent to which a monopolist can exercise market power. The more broadly a market is defined, the more difficult it becomes to find substitutes.

Consider hamburger. A firm that produces Brand X hamburger faces stiff competition from other hamburger sellers, even though it is the only producer of Brand X. The Brand X firm has little market power because near-perfect substitutes for its hamburger are available. But if a firm were the *only* producer of hamburger (or, better yet, the only producer of beef), it would have more market power, because fewer (or no) alternatives would be available. When fewer substitutes exist, a monopolist has more power to raise price because demand for its product is less elastic, as Figure 13.1 shows. A monopolist that produces all the food in an economy would exercise enormous market power because there are no substitutes at all for food as a category.

To be meaningful, therefore, our definition of a monopolistic industry must be more precise. We define **pure monopoly** as an industry with a single firm (1) that produces a product for which there are *no close substitutes* and (2) in which significant barriers to entry prevent other firms from entering the industry to compete for profits.

BARRIERS TO ENTRY

Firms that already have market power can maintain that power either by preventing other firms from producing an exact duplicate of their product or by preventing firms from entering the industry. A number of **barriers to entry** can be erected.

> **Government Franchises** Many firms are monopolies by virtue of government directive. Although the industry was largely deregulated in 1996, local telephone-operating companies, for example, are still granted exclusive licenses by most states to provide "local exchange service." State governments also grant electric companies the sole right to supply power within given areas. The usual defense of this kind of monopoly power by **government franchise** is that it is more efficient for a single firm to produce the particular product (usually a service) than for many firms to produce the same product. If very large economies of scale are possible, it makes no sense to have many small firms producing the same thing at much higher costs. (We discuss these so-called "natural monopolies" later in this chapter.)

Public utility commissions in each state watch over electric companies and locally operating telephone companies. One of government's responsibilities is to regulate the prices charged by these utilities to ensure that they don't abuse their monopoly power.

pure monopoly *An industry with a single firm that produces a product for which there are no close substitutes and in which significant barriers to entry prevent other firms from entering the industry to compete for profits.*

barrier to entry *Something that prevents new firms from entering and competing in imperfectly competitive industries.*

government franchise *A monopoly by virtue of government directive.*

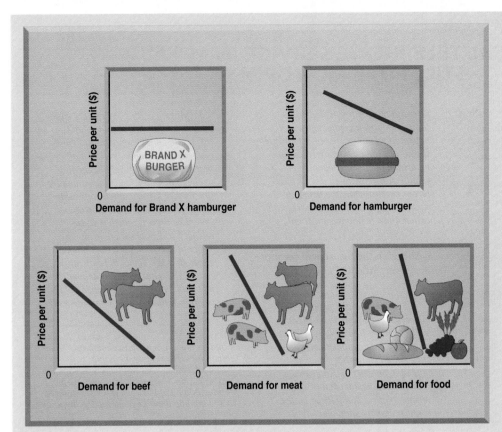

FIGURE 13.1

The Boundary of a Market and Elasticity

We can define an industry as broadly or as narrowly as we like. The more broadly we define the industry, the fewer substitutes there are, and the less elastic demand for that industry's product is likely to be. A monopoly is an industry with one firm that produces a product for which there are *no close substitutes*. The producer of Brand X hamburger cannot properly be called a monopolist because this producer has no control over market price and there are many substitutes for Brand X hamburger.

Fairness, or equity, is another frequently cited defense of government-regulated monopoly. Technological progress in the telecommunications industry has reduced the advantages that come from size, for example, but some states are clearly not ready to open local exchange service to competition. The reason is that most state governments want to ensure that everyone has access to a telephone at affordable rates. In most states, private households are provided with telephone service at a price below the cost of producing it; local telephone companies earn the bulk of their profits from business users, who are charged a price above cost. Deregulating local service, it is argued, would mean higher telephone bills for households, a change that many would consider "unfair."

Large economies of scale and equity are not the only justifications that governments give for granting monopoly licenses, however. Sometimes government wants to maintain control of an industry, and a monopoly is easier to control than a competitive industry. Iowa, Maine, New Hampshire, and Ohio, for example, permit liquor to be sold only through state-controlled and -managed liquor stores. However, when large economies of scale do not exist in an industry, or when equity is not a concern, the arguments in favor of government-run monopolies are much weaker. One argument is that the state wants to prevent private parties from encouraging and profiting from "sin." Another is that government monopolies are a convenient source of revenues. How can anyone criticize the state-licensed, implicit taxation of drinking or gambling?

➤ **Patents** Another legal barrier that prevents entry into an industry is a **patent**, which grants exclusive use of the patented product or process to the inventor. Patents are issued in the United States under authority of Article I, Section 8, of the Constitution, which gives Congress the power to "promote the progress of science and the useful

patent *A barrier to entry that grants exclusive use of the patented product or process to the inventor.*

LOCAL TELEPHONE SERVICE IN 1997: STILL PURE MONOPOLY

One of the last truly "pure" monopolies in the United States is local telephone service. In nearly all states, the law restricts consumers to a single monopoly provider. This may be changing. In 1996, the Congress passed the Telecommunications Act, which contained a provision requiring states to open up local service to competition. These provisions, however, were struck down by the U.S. Court of Appeals for the 8th Circuit on July 18, 1997:

> An appeals court struck down key elements of the Federal Communications Commission's rules for opening local telephone markets to competition yesterday, adding yet another obstacle to the already rocky landscape of telecommunications regulation.
>
> The Federal appeals court ruling could further slow the

introduction of unbridled competition—and the lower prices expected to result from that competition—in the nation's telecommunications business, because it would allow states to develop different mechanisms for bringing new companies into the market rather than following uniform F.C.C. guidelines.[a]

Although the future will see more competition, little had changed by 1997:

> Sixteen months after the Government opened the $100 billion local phone market to no-holds-barred competition, a new study has found that fewer than half of 1 percent of Americans receive their residential phone service from a competitor to the monopoly provider.

Moreover, the most likely rivals to the local monopolies—AT&T, MCI, and other long-distance carriers—are entering the residential market only grudgingly, according to the study, which was compiled by the Yankee Group, a telecommunications research firm in Boston.

The report, which is to be released today, is sure to stoke the anger of consumer advocates who argue that the Telecommunications Act of 1996 has failed to deliver on its central promise of fostering competition in the local phone business.[b]

---

[a]Seth Schiesel, "Court Sets Back F.C.C. Efforts to Open Local Phone Markets," *The New York Times*, July 19, 1997, p. 1.
[b]Mark Landler, "Monopolies Still Rule the Local Phone Markets," *The New York Times*, May 22, 1997, p. D1. Copyright © 1997 by The New York Times Co. Reprinted by permission.

For more on monopolies, see the Case and Fair Web page at
http://www.prenhall.com/casefair.

---

arts, by securing for limited times to authors and inventors the exclusive right to their respective writings and discoveries." Patent protection in the United States is currently granted for a period of 20 years.

Patents provide an incentive for invention and innovation. New products and new processes are developed through research undertaken by individual inventors and by firms. Research requires resources and time, which have opportunity costs. Without the protection that a patent provides, the results of research would become available to the general public very quickly. If research did not lead to expanded profits, very little research would be done. On the negative side, though, patents do serve as a barrier to competition, and they do slow down the benefits of research flowing through the market to consumers.

The expiration of patents after a given number of years represents an attempt to balance the benefits of firms and the benefits of households: On the one hand, it is important to stimulate invention and innovation; on the other hand, invention and innovation do society no good unless their benefits eventually flow to the public.[1]

In recent years, public attention has been focused on the high price of health care. One of the first problems faced by the Clinton administration was how to deal with

---

[1]Another alternative is *licensing*. With licensing, the new technology is used by all producers, and the inventor splits the benefits with consumers. Because forcing the non-patent-holding producers to use an inefficient technology results in waste, some analysts have proposed adding mandatory licensing to the current patent system.

THE DeBeers Company of South Africa controls about 80 percent of the market for uncut diamonds. Yet, DeBeers' decades-old monopoly is being threatened by a recent spate of prospectors digging for diamonds in the Angolan Cuango River.

health care costs. One factor contributing to these costs is the very high price of many prescription drugs. Equipped with newly developed tools of bioengineering, the pharmaceutical industry has been granted thousands of patents for new drugs. When a new drug for treating a disease is developed, the patent holder can charge a very high price for it. The drug companies argue that these rewards are justified by high research and development costs; others say these profits are the result of a monopoly protected by the patent system.

➤ **Economies of Scale and Other Cost Advantages** Some products can be produced efficiently only in big, expensive production facilities. For example, the Federal Trade Commission has estimated that an oil refinery large enough to achieve maximum-scale economies in the production of gasoline would cost more than $500 million to build. A small entrepreneur is not going to jump into the refining business in search of economic profit! The need to raise an initial investment of half a billion dollars is compounded by the riskiness of the business. Hence, large capital requirements are often a barrier to entry.

Sometimes large economies of scale are not production related. Breakfast cereal can be produced efficiently on a very small scale, for example; large-scale production does not reduce costs. But to compete, a new firm would need an advertising campaign costing millions of dollars. The large front-end investment requirement in the presence of risk is likely to deter would-be entrants to the cereal market.

➤ **Ownership of a Scarce Factor of Production** You can't enter the diamond-producing business unless you own a diamond mine. There are not many diamond mines in the world, and most are already owned by a single firm, the DeBeers Company of South Africa. Once, the Aluminum Company of America (now Alcoa) owned or controlled virtually 100 percent of the bauxite deposits in the world and until the 1940s monopolized the production and distribution of aluminum. Obviously, if production requires a particular input, and one firm owns the entire supply of that input, that firm will control the industry. Ownership alone is a barrier to entry!

PRICE: THE FOURTH DECISION VARIABLE

To review: A firm has market power when it has some control over the price of its product—raising the price of its product without losing all demand. The exercise of market power requires that the firm be able to limit competition in some way. It does this either by erecting barriers to the entry of new firms or by preventing other firms from producing the same product.

Regardless of the source of market power, output price is not taken as given by the firm. Rather,

> Price is a decision variable for imperfectly competitive firms. Firms with market power must decide not only (1) how much to produce, (2) how to produce it, and (3) how much to demand in each input market (see Figure 7.3), but also (4) *what price to charge for their output.*

This does not mean that "market power" allows a firm to charge any price it likes. The market demand curve constrains the behavior even of a pure monopolist. To sell its product successfully, a firm must produce something that people want and sell it at a price they are willing to pay.

PRICE AND OUTPUT DECISIONS IN PURE MONOPOLY MARKETS

To analyze monopoly behavior, we make two assumptions: (1) that entry to the market is blocked, and (2) that firms act to maximize profits.

Initially, we also assume that our pure monopolist buys in competitive input markets. Even though the firm is the only one producing for its product market, it is only one among many firms buying factors of production in input markets. The local telephone company must hire labor like any other firm. To attract workers it must pay the market wage; to buy fiber-optic cable, it must pay the going price. In these input markets the monopolistic firm is a price-taker.

On the cost side of the profit equation, then, a pure monopolist does not differ one bit from a perfect competitor. Both choose the technology that minimizes the cost of production. The cost curve of each represents the minimum cost of producing each level of output. The difference arises on the revenue, or demand, side of the equation, where we begin our analysis.

DEMAND IN MONOPOLY MARKETS

A competitive firm, you will recall, faces a fixed, market-determined price, and we assume it can sell all it wants to sell at that price; it is constrained only by its current capacity in the short run. The demand curve facing a competitive firm is thus a horizontal line (Figure 13.2). Raising the price of its product means losing all demand, because perfect substitutes are available. The competitive firm has no incentive to charge a lower price either.

Because a competitive firm can charge only one price, regardless of the output level chosen, its *marginal revenue*—the additional revenue that it earns by raising output by one unit—is simply the price of the output, or $P^* = \$5$ in Figure 13.2. Remember that marginal revenue is important because a profit-maximizing firm will increase output as long as marginal revenue exceeds marginal cost.

The most important distinction between competition and monopoly is that:

> With one firm in a monopoly market, there is no distinction between the firm and the industry. In a monopoly, the firm *is* the industry. The market demand curve is the demand curve facing the firm, and the total quantity supplied in the market is what the firm decides to produce.

To proceed, we need a few more assumptions. First, we assume that a monopolistic firm cannot price discriminate. It sells its product to all demanders at the same price. (*Price discrimination* means selling to different consumers or groups of consumers at different prices.)

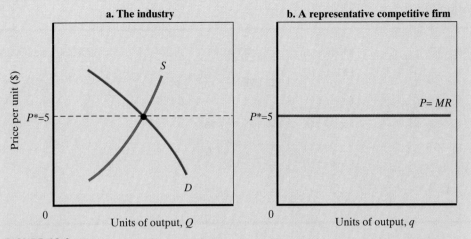

a. The industry

b. A representative competitive firm

FIGURE 13.2

The Demand Curve Facing a Perfectly Competitive Firm Is Perfectly Elastic; in a Monopoly, the Market Demand Curve Is the Demand Curve Facing the Firm

Perfectly competitive firms are price-takers; they are small relative to the size of the market and thus cannot influence market price. The implication is that the demand curve facing a perfectly competitive firm is perfectly elastic. If the firm raises its price, it sells nothing, and there is no reason for the firm to lower its price if it can sell all it wants at $P^* = \$5$. In a monopoly, the firm *is* the industry. Thus the market demand curve is the demand curve facing the monopoly, and the total quantity supplied in the market is what the monopoly decides to produce.

We also assume that the monopoly faces a known demand curve. That is, we assume that the firm has enough information to predict how households will react to different prices. (Many firms use statistical methods to estimate the elasticity of demand for their products. Other firms may use less formal methods, including trial and error, sometimes called "price searching." All firms with market power must have some sense of how consumers are likely to react to various prices.) Knowing the demand curve it faces, the firm must *simultaneously* choose both the quantity of output to supply and the price of that output. Once the firm chooses a price, the market determines how much will be sold. Stated somewhat differently, the monopoly chooses the point on the market demand curve where it wants to be.

➤ **Marginal Revenue and Market Demand** Just like a competitor, a profit-maximizing monopolist will continue to produce output as long as marginal revenue exceeds marginal cost. Because the market demand curve is the demand curve for a monopoly, a monopolistic firm faces a downward-sloping demand curve.

Consider the hypothetical demand schedule in Table 13.1. Column 3 lists the total revenue that the monopoly would take in at different levels of output. If it were to produce one unit, that unit would sell for $10, and total revenue would be $10. Two units would sell for $9 each, in which case total revenue would be $18. As column 4 shows, marginal revenue from the second unit would be $8 ($18 minus $10). Notice that the marginal revenue from increasing output from one unit to two units ($8) is *less* than the price of the second unit ($9).

Now consider what happens when the firm considers setting production at four units rather than three. The fourth unit would sell for $7, but because the firm can't price discriminate, it must sell *all four* units for $7 each. Had the firm chosen to produce only three units, it could have sold those three units for $8 each. Thus, offsetting the revenue gain of $7 is a revenue loss of $3—that is, $1 for each of the three units that would have sold at the higher price. The marginal revenue of the fourth unit is

TABLE 13.1 MARGINAL REVENUE FACING A MONOPOLIST

(1) QUANTITY	(2) PRICE	(3) TOTAL REVENUE	(4) MARGINAL REVENUE
0	$11	$ 0	$—
1	10	10	10
2	9	18	8
3	8	24	6
4	7	28	4
5	6	30	2
6	5	30	0
7	4	28	−2
8	3	24	−4
9	2	18	−6
10	1	10	−8

$7 minus $3, or $4, which is considerably below the price of $7. (Remember, unlike a monopoly, a perfectly competitive firm does not have to charge a lower price to sell more; thus $P = MR$ in competition.)

> For a monopolist, an increase in output involves not just producing more and selling it, but also reducing the price of its output in order to sell it.

Marginal revenue can also be derived simply by looking at the change in total revenue. At three units of output, total revenue is $24; at four units of output, total revenue is $28. Marginal revenue is the difference, or $4.

Moving from six to seven units of output actually reduces total revenue for the firm. At seven units, marginal revenue is negative. Although it is true that the seventh unit will sell for a positive price ($4), the firm must sell all seven units for $4 each (for a total revenue of $28). If output had been restricted to six units, each would have sold for $5. Thus, offsetting the revenue gain of $4 is a revenue loss of $6—that is, $1 for each of the six units that the firm would have sold at the higher price. Increasing output from

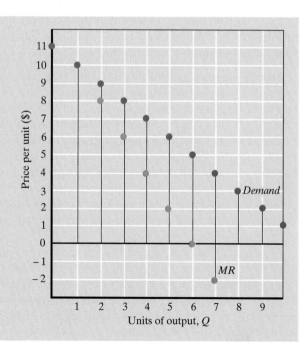

FIGURE 13.3

Marginal Revenue Curve Facing a Monopolist

At every level of output except one unit, a monopolist's marginal revenue is below price. This is because (1) we assume that the monopolist must sell all its product at a single price (no price discrimination), and (2) to raise output and sell it, the firm must lower the price it charges. Selling the additional output will raise revenue, but this increase is offset somewhat by the lower price charged for all units sold. Therefore, the increase in revenue from increasing output by one (the marginal revenue) is less than price.

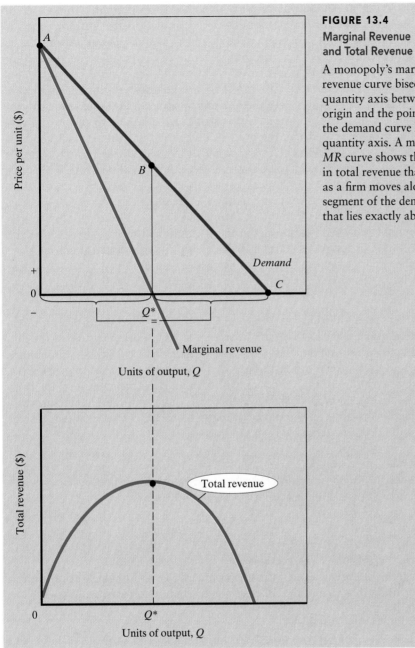

FIGURE 13.4

**Marginal Revenue
and Total Revenue**

A monopoly's marginal
revenue curve bisects the
quantity axis between the
origin and the point where
the demand curve hits the
quantity axis. A monopoly's
MR curve shows the change
in total revenue that results
as a firm moves along the
segment of the demand curve
that lies exactly above it.

six to seven units actually decreases revenue by $2. Figure 13.3 graphs the marginal revenue schedule derived in Table 13.1. Notice that at every level of output except one unit, marginal revenue is *below* price. Marginal revenue turns from positive to negative after six units of output. When the demand curve is a straight line, the marginal revenue curve bisects the quantity axis between the origin and the point where the demand curve hits the quantity axis (Figure 13.4).

Look carefully at Figure 13.4. What you can see in the diagram is that:

A monopoly's marginal revenue curve shows the change in total revenue that results as a firm moves along the segment of the demand curve that lies directly above it.

Consider starting at an output of zero units per period in the top panel of Figure 13.4. At zero units, of course, total revenue (shown in the bottom panel) is zero because nothing is sold. To begin selling, the firm must lower the product's price. Marginal revenue is positive, and total revenue begins to increase. To sell increasing quantities of the good, the firm must lower its price more and more. As output increases between zero and Q^* and the firm moves down its demand curve from point A to point B, marginal revenue remains positive and total revenue continues to increase. The quantity of output (Q) is rising, which tends to push total revenue $(P \times Q)$ *up*. At the same time, the price of output (P) is falling, which tends to push total revenue $(P \times Q)$ *down*. Up to point B, the effect of increasing Q dominates the effect of falling P, and total revenue rises: Marginal revenue is positive (above the quantity axis).[2]

But what happens as we move further along the quantity axis above Q^*—that is, further down the demand curve from point B toward point C? We are still lowering P to sell more output, but above (to the right of) Q^*, marginal revenue is negative and total revenue in the bottom panel starts to fall. Beyond Q^*, the effect of cutting price on total revenue is larger than the effect of increasing quantity. As a result, total revenue $(P \times Q)$ falls. At point C, revenue once again is at zero, this time because price has dropped to zero![3]

► **The Monopolist's Profit-Maximizing Price and Output** We have spent much time in defining and explaining marginal revenue because it is an important factor in the monopolist's choice of profit-maximizing price and output. Figure 13.5 superimposes a demand curve and the marginal revenue curve derived from it over a set of cost curves. In determining price and output, a monopolistic firm must go through the same basic decision process that a competitive firm goes through. Any profit-maximizing firm will raise its production as long as the added revenue from the increase outweighs the added cost. In more specific terms, we can say that:

> All firms, including monopolies, raise output as long as marginal revenue is greater than marginal cost. Any positive difference between marginal revenue and marginal cost can be thought of as marginal profit.

The optimal price/output combination for the monopolist in Figure 13.5 is $P_m = \$4.00$ and $Q_m = 4,000$ units, the quantity at which the marginal revenue curve and the marginal cost curve intersect. At any output below 4,000, marginal revenue is greater than marginal cost. At any output above 4,000, increasing output would reduce profits, because marginal cost exceeds marginal revenue. This leads us to conclude that:

> The profit-maximizing level of output for a monopolist is the one at which marginal revenue equals marginal cost: $MR = MC$.

Because marginal revenue for a monopoly lies below the demand curve, the final price chosen by the monopolist will be above marginal cost ($P_m = \$4.00$ is greater than $MC = \$1.50$). At 4,000 units of output, price will be fixed at $4 (point A on the

---

[2]Recall from chapter 5 that if the percentage change in Q is greater than the percentage change in P as you move along a demand curve, the absolute value of elasticity of demand is greater than 1. Thus, as we move along the demand curve in Figure 13.4 between point A and point B, demand is *elastic*.

[3]Beyond Q^*, between points B and C on the demand curve in Figure 13.4, the decline in price must be bigger in percentage terms than the increase in quantity. Thus the absolute value of elasticity beyond point B is less than 1: Demand is inelastic. At point B, marginal revenue is zero; the decrease in P exactly offsets the increase in Q, and elasticity is unitary or equal to -1.

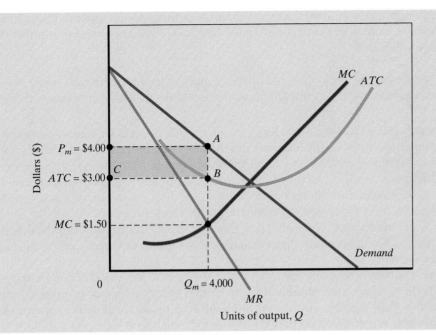

FIGURE 13.5
Price and Output Choice for a
Profit-Maximizing Monopolist

A profit-maximizing
monopolist will raise output
as long as marginal revenue
exceeds marginal cost.
Maximum profit is at an
output of 4,000 units per
period and a price of $4.
Above 4,000 units of output,
marginal cost is greater than
marginal revenue; increasing
output beyond 4,000 units
would reduce profit.

demand curve), and total revenue will be $P_m \times Q_m = \$4 \times 4,000 = \$16,000$ (area $P_m A Q_m 0$). Total cost is the product of average total cost and units of output, $\$3 \times 4,000 = \$12,000$ (area $CBQ_m 0$). Total profit is the difference between total revenue and total cost, $\$16,000 - \$12,000 = \$4,000$. In Figure 13.5, total profit is the area of the pink rectangle $P_m ABC$.

Among competitive firms, the presence of positive profits provides an incentive for new firms to enter the industry, thus shifting supply to the right, driving down price, and eliminating profits. Remember, however, that for monopolies we assume that barriers to entry have been erected and that profits are protected.

➤ **The Absence of a Supply Curve in Monopoly** In perfect competition, the supply curve of a firm in the short run is the same as the portion of the firm's marginal cost curve that lies above the average variable cost curve. As the price of the good produced by the firm changes, the perfectly competitive firm simply moves up or down its marginal cost curve in choosing how much output to produce.

As you can see, however, Figure 13.5 contains nothing that we can point to and call a supply curve. The amount of output that a monopolist produces depends on its marginal cost curve *and* on the shape of the demand curve that it faces. In other words, the amount of output that a monopolist supplies is not independent of the shape of the demand curve.

> A monopoly firm has no supply curve that is independent of the demand curve for its product.

To see why, consider what a firm's supply curve means. A supply curve shows the quantity of output the firm is willing to supply at each price. If we ask a monopolist how much output she is willing to supply at a given price, the monopolist will say her supply behavior depends not just on marginal cost but also on the marginal revenue associated with that price. To know what that marginal revenue would be, the monopolist must know what her demand curve looks like.

In sum: In perfect competition, we can draw a firm's supply curve without knowing anything more than the firm's marginal cost curve. The situation for a monopolist is more complicated:

> A monopolist sets both price and quantity, and the amount of output that it supplies depends on both its marginal cost curve and the demand curve that it faces.

➤ **Monopoly in the Long and Short Run** In our analysis of perfectly competitive markets we distinguished between the long run and the short run. In the short run, all firms face some fixed factor of production, and no entry into or exit from the industry is possible. The assumption of a fixed factor of production is the primary reason that marginal cost increases with output in the short run. That is, the short-run marginal cost curve of a typical competitive firm slopes upward and to the right because of the limitations imposed by the fixed factor. In the long run, however, firms can enter and exit the industry. Long-run equilibrium is established when the entry and exit of firms drives profits in the industry to zero.

The distinction between the long and short runs is less important in monopoly markets. In the short run, monopolists are limited by a fixed factor of production, as competitive firms are. The cost curves in Figure 13.5 reflect the diminishing returns to the monopoly's fixed factor of production (for example, plant size).

What will happen to the monopoly in the long run? If the monopoly is earning positive profits (a rate of return above the normal rate of return to capital), nothing will happen. In competition, positive profits lead to expansion and entry, but in monopoly, entry is blocked. In addition, because we assume that the monopoly is a profit-maximizing firm, it will operate at the most efficient scale of production, and it will neither expand nor contract in the long run. Thus, Figure 13.5 will not change in the long run.

It is possible for a monopoly to find itself suffering losses (a rate of return below the normal rate). A monopoly that finds itself unable to cover total costs is illustrated in Figure 13.6. The best that the firm can do is produce $Q_m = 10,000$ units of output (the point at which $MR = MC$) and charge $P_m = \$4$ for its output (point E on the

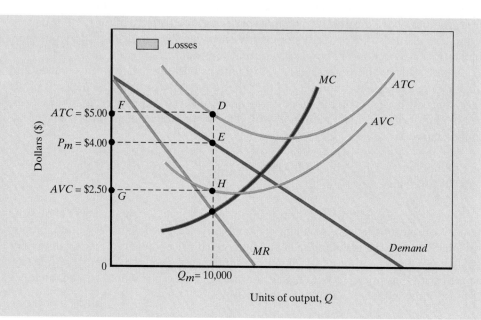

FIGURE 13.6

Price and Output Choice for a Monopolist Suffering Losses in the Short Run

It is possible for a profit-maximizing monopolist to suffer short-run losses. At 10,000 units of output (the point at which $MR = MC$), total revenue is sufficient to cover variable cost but not to cover total cost. Thus, the firm will operate in the short run but go out of business in the long run.

demand curve). But at 10,000 units of output per period, total revenue of $40,000 ($P_m \times Q_m$, where $P_m = \$4$ and $Q_m = 10,000$), which is equal to the area P_mEQ_m0, is not sufficient to cover total costs of $50,000 ($ATC \times Q_m$, where $ATC = \$5$ and $Q_m = 10,000$), which is equal to the area FDQ_m0. The firm thus suffers losses equal to $10,000, the shaded area (rectangle $FDEP_m$). Notice, however, that total revenue is sufficient to cover the level of *variable* costs, which equals $25,000 ($AVC \times Q_m$, where $AVC = \$2.50$ and $Q_m = 10,000$). Thus, operating in the short run generates a profit on operation (total revenue minus total variable costs is greater than zero) that can be used to cover some of the firm's short-run fixed costs. The basis of the monopolist's decision is thus exactly the same as that for a competitive firm:

> If a firm can reduce its losses by operating in the short run, it will do so.

Similarly, in the long run, a firm that cannot generate enough revenue to cover total costs will go out of business, whether it is competitive or monopolistic. Because the demand curve in Figure 13.6 lies completely below the average total cost curve, the monopoly will go out of business in the long run, and its product will not be produced because it is simply not worth the cost of production to buyers.

PERFECT COMPETITION AND MONOPOLY COMPARED

One way to understand monopoly is to compare equilibrium output and price in a perfectly competitive industry with the output and price that would be chosen if the same industry were organized as a monopoly. To make this comparison meaningful, let us exclude from consideration any technological advantage that a single large firm might enjoy.

We begin our comparison with a competitive industry made up of a large number of firms operating with a production technology that exhibits constant returns to scale in the long run. (Recall that *constant returns to scale* means that average cost is the same whether the firm operates one large plant or many small plants.) Figure 13.7 shows a perfectly competitive industry at long-run equilibrium, a condition in which price is equal to long-run average costs and in which there are no profits.

Now suppose that the industry were to fall under the control of a single private monopolist. The monopolist now owns one firm with many plants. But technology has not changed; only the location of decision-making power has. To analyze the monopolist's decisions, we must derive the consolidated cost curves now facing the monopoly.

The marginal cost curve of the new monopoly will simply be the horizontal sum of the marginal cost curves of the smaller firms, which are now branches of the larger firm. That is, to get the large firm's MC curve, at each level of MC we add together the output quantities from each separate plant. To understand why, consider this simple example. Suppose that there is perfect competition and that the industry is made up of just two small firms, A and B, each with upward-sloping marginal cost curves. Suppose that for firm A, $MC = \$5$ at an output of 10,000 units and for firm B, $MC = \$5$ at an output of 20,000 units. If these firms were merged, what would the marginal cost of the 30,000th unit of output per period be? The answer is $5, because the new larger firm would produce 10,000 units in plant A and 20,000 in plant B. This means that the marginal cost curve of the new firm is *exactly the same curve* as the supply curve in the industry when it was competitively organized. (Recall from chapter 9 that the industry supply curve in a perfectly competitive industry is the sum of the marginal cost curves [above average variable cost] of all the individual firms in that industry.)[4]

---

[4]The same logic will show that the average cost curve of the consolidated firm is simply the sum of the average cost curves of the individual plants.

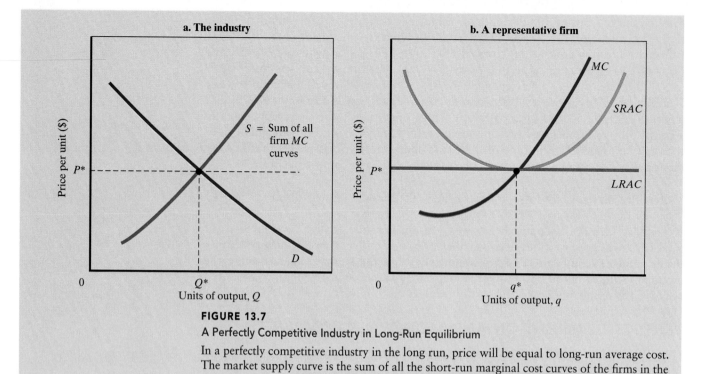

a. The industry

Price per unit ($)

$P*$

S = Sum of all firm MC curves

D

0     $Q*$

Units of output, Q

b. A representative firm

Price per unit ($)

$P*$

MC

$SRAC$

$LRAC$

0     $q*$

Units of output, q

FIGURE 13.7

A Perfectly Competitive Industry in Long-Run Equilibrium

In a perfectly competitive industry in the long run, price will be equal to long-run average cost. The market supply curve is the sum of all the short-run marginal cost curves of the firms in the industry. Here we assume that firms are using a technology that exhibits constant returns to scale: $LRAC$ is flat. Big firms enjoy no cost advantage.

Figure 13.8 illustrates the cost curve, marginal revenue curve, and demand curve of the consolidated monopoly industry. If the industry were competitively organized, total industry output would have been Q_c = 4,000 and price would have been P_c = $3. These price and output decisions are determined by the intersection of the competitive supply curve, S_c, and the market demand curve.

No longer faced with a price that it cannot influence, however, the monopolist can choose any price/quantity combination along the demand curve. The output level that maximizes profits to the monopolist is Q_m = 2,500—the point at which marginal revenue intersects marginal cost. Output will be priced at P_m = $4. To increase output beyond 2,500 units or to charge a price below $4 (which represents the amount consumers are willing to pay) would reduce profit. The result:

> Relative to a competitively organized industry, a monopolist restricts output, charges higher prices, and earns positive profits.

And remember, all we did was to transfer decision-making power from the individual small firms to a consolidated owner. The new firm gains nothing at all technologically from being big.

collusion *The act of working with other producers in an effort to limit competition and increase joint profits.*

COLLUSION AND MONOPOLY COMPARED

Suppose now that the industry just discussed did not become a monopoly. Instead, suppose the individual firm owners simply decide to work together in an effort to limit competition and increase joint profits, a behavior called **collusion**. In this

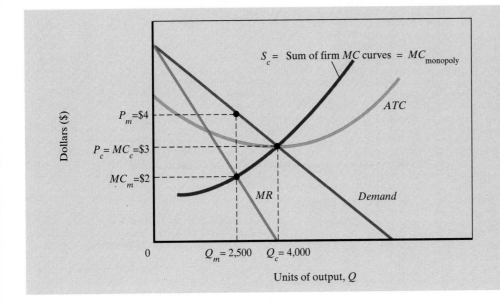

In the newly organized monopoly, the marginal cost curve is exactly the same as the supply curve that represented the behavior of all the independent firms when the industry was organized competitively. Quantity produced by the monopoly will be less than the competitive level of output, and the monopoly price will be higher than the price under perfect competition.

case, the outcome would be exactly the same as the outcome of a monopoly in the industry. Firms certainly have an incentive to collude. When they act independently, they compete away whatever profits they can find. But, as we saw in Figure 13.8, when price increases to $4 across the industry, the monopolistic firm earns positive profits.

Despite the fact that collusion is illegal, it has taken place in some industries. In one significant case in the 1960s, a number of executives of well-known electrical equipment manufacturers were successfully prosecuted for meeting secretly to fix prices and divide up markets. In January 1987, a judge moved to end a pricing agreement among milk producers in New York City that had existed since the 1930s. As a result, the wholesale price of milk dropped between $.30 and $.71 per gallon in one week! More recently, illegal price fixing was discovered among Italian bread bakeries in New York. (See the Application box later in this chapter titled "Rent-Seeking Behavior in the Italian Bread Market.")

THE SOCIAL COSTS OF MONOPOLY

So far we have seen that a monopoly produces less output and charges a higher price than a competitively organized industry, if no large economies of scale exist for the monopoly. You are probably thinking at this point that producing less and charging more to earn positive profits is not likely to be in the best interests of consumers, and you are right.

INEFFICIENCY AND CONSUMER LOSS

In chapter 12, we argued that price must equal marginal cost ($P = MC$) for markets to produce what people want. This argument rests on two propositions: (1) that price provides a good approximation of the social value of a unit of output, and (2) that marginal cost, in the absence of externalities (costs or benefits to external parties not weighed by firms), provides a good approximation of the product's social opportunity cost. In pure monopoly, price ends up above product's marginal cost.

FIGURE 13.9

Welfare Loss from Monopoly
A demand curve shows the
amounts that people are willing
to pay at each potential level of
output. Thus the demand curve
can be used to approximate
the benefits to the consumer
of raising output above 2,000
units. *MC* reflects the marginal
cost of the resources needed.
The triangle *ABC* roughly
measures the net social gain
of moving from 2,000 units
to 4,000 units (or the loss
that results when monopoly
decreases output from 4,000
units to 2,000 units).

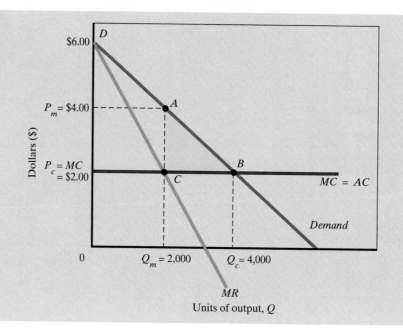

When this happens, the firm is underproducing from society's point of view; society
would be better off if the firm produced more and charged a lower price. We can,
therefore, conclude that:

Monopoly leads to an inefficient mix of output.

A slightly simplified version of the monopoly diagram appears in Figure 13.9,
which shows how we might make a rough estimate of the size of the loss to social welfare that arises from monopoly. (For clarity we will ignore the short-run cost curves
and assume constant returns to scale in the long run.) Under competitive conditions,
firms would produce output up to $Q_c = 4{,}000$ units, and price would ultimately settle
at $P_c = \$2$, equal to long-run average cost. Any price above \$2 will mean positive profits, which would be eliminated by the entry of new competing firms in the long run.
(You should remember all this from chapter 9.)

A monopoly firm in the same industry, however, would produce only $Q_m = 2{,}000$
units per period and charge a price of $P_m = \$4$, because $MR = MC$ at $Q_m = 2{,}000$
units. The monopoly would make a profit equal to total revenue minus total cost,
or $P_m \times Q_m$ minus $AC \times Q_m$. Profit to the monopoly is thus equal to the area
$P_m ACP_c$, or \$4,000. ([\$4 × 2,000] − [\$2 × 2,000] = \$8,000 − \$4,000 = \$4,000.
Remember $P_c = AC$ in this example.)

Now consider the gains and losses associated with increasing price from \$2 to
\$4 and cutting output from 4,000 units to 2,000 units. As you might guess, the win-
ner will be the monopolist and the loser will be the consumer, but let us see how it
works out.

At $P_c = \$2$, the price under perfect competition, there are no profits. Consumers
are paying a price of \$2, but the demand curve shows that many are willing to pay
more than that. For example, a substantial number of people would pay \$4 or more.
Those people willing to pay more than \$2 are receiving what we earlier called a *con-
sumer surplus*. The demand curve shows approximately how much households are

RENT-SEEKING BEHAVIOR IN THE ITALIAN BREAD MARKET

Rent-seeking behavior refers to actions taken by households or firms to create and protect positive profits. The following article from the *New York Times* speaks for itself:

For years, law-enforcement officials heard complaints about a small group of unscrupulous bakers trying to corner the Italian-bread market in much of New York City. Using threats of violence, the authorities were told, the cartel controlled the distribution of fresh Italian bread to small grocery stores in Brooklyn and Staten Island, inflating prices and eliminating competition.

But investigators found that bakers and store owners were reluctant to cooperate. The only way to get to the heart of the Italian-bread racket, they decided, was to open a bakery themselves.

So a team of a half dozen undercover detectives opened a storefront at 327 West 11th Street in Greenwich Village in early 1993 and called it Louis Basile's. Wearing bakers' whites, they pretended to bake several dozen loaves of bread each day, taking turns getting up at 3 A.M. to drive to New Jersey to buy the real stuff, and wrapping the loaves in the customized white paper sleeves that are the signature of authentic, fresh Italian bread.

It was not long after the investigators began trying to sell the bread to neighborhood grocery stores in Manhattan and Brooklyn that they heard from the Association of Independent Bakers and Distributors of Italian Bread. Over

drinks at the White Horse Tavern on Hudson Street, investigators say, a detective posing as a baker was told by two members of the association that violence could come to Basile's and its employees if they did not play by association rules.

The rules involved fixed prices for bread and a system of distribution that forced a store to buy from a single baker, said the Manhattan District Attorney, Robert M. Morgenthau. . . .

Daniel J. Castleman, head of investigations in Mr. Morgenthau's office, said association members included about 50 bakeries that supplied Italian bread to over 1,000 small grocery stores and delicatessens in the city.

Mr. Castleman said the office was unable to estimate what percentage of the city's bread sales were affected by the association's practices, in part because sales in large supermarkets were not involved. But he said the association controlled virtually all of Staten Island and most neighborhoods in Brooklyn where Italian bread was popular and was expanding into Manhattan, Queens and Westchester and Nassau counties . . .

As an example of the association's activity, Mr. Morgenthau cited a decision in 1990 to raise the retail price of bread from 75 to 85 cents. Five cents of the increase went to the bakers and the other five was divided between the bread deliverers and the store owners, he said.

"Because the association had a lock on the market, consumers had

AS A RESULT OF RENT-SEEKING BEHAVIOR, THE PRICE OF A LOAF OF ITALIAN BREAD IN NEW YORK CITY WAS RAISED TEN CENTS AND HELD AT THAT LEVEL. THAT 1990 PRICE INCREASE COST CONSUMERS MILLIONS OF DOLLARS.

no choice but to pay the increase," Mr. Morgenthau said. . . .

While Mr. Morgenthau said he could not estimate how much the association and its members profited from illegal operations, Mr. Castleman said the 1990 price increase cost consumers millions of dollars.[a]

Source: [a]Seth Faison, "Price-Fixing Plan Is Charged in New York Italian Bakeries," *The New York Times*, July 14, 1994, p. A1. Copyright © 1994 by The New York Times Co. Reprinted by permission.

For more on rent-seeking behavior, see the Case and Fair Web page at http://www.prenhall.com/casefair.

willing to pay at each level of output, and thus the area of triangle DBP_c gives us a rough measure of the "consumer surplus" being enjoyed by households when the price is \$2. Consumers willing to pay exactly \$4 get a surplus equal to \$2. Those who place the highest value on this good—that is, those who are willing to pay the most (\$6)—get a surplus equal to DP_c or \$4.

Now the industry is reorganized as a monopoly that cuts output to 2,000 units and raises price to $4. The big winner is the monopolist, who ends up earning profits equal to $4,000.

The big losers are the consumers. Their "surplus" now shrinks from the area of triangle DBP_c to the area of triangle DAP_m. Part of that loss (which is equal to DBP_c minus DAP_m, or the area P_mABP_c) is covered by the monopolist's gain of P_mACP_c, but not all of it. The loss to consumers exceeds the gain to the monopoly by the area of triangle ABC (P_mABP_c minus P_mACP_c), which roughly measures the net loss in social welfare associated with monopoly power in this industry. Because the area of a triangle is half its base times its height, the welfare loss is $1/2 \times 2,000 \times \$2 = \$2,000$. If we could push price back down to the competitive level and increase output to 4,000 units, consumers would gain more than the monopolist would lose, and the gain in social welfare would approximate the area of ABC, or $2,000.

In this example, the presence of a monopoly also causes an important change in the distribution of real income. In Figure 13.9, area P_mACP_c is profit of $4,000 flowing every period to the monopolist. If price were pushed down to $2 by competition or regulation, those profits would pass to consumers in the form of lower prices. Society may value this resource transfer on equity grounds in addition to efficiency grounds.

Of course, monopolies may have social costs that do not show up on these diagrams. Monopolies, which are protected from competition by barriers to entry, do not face the same pressures to cut costs and to innovate as competitive firms do. A competitive firm that does not use the most efficient technology will be driven out of business by firms that do. One of the significant arguments against tariffs and quotas to protect such industries as automobiles and steel from foreign competition is that protection removes the incentive to be efficient and competitive.

RENT-SEEKING BEHAVIOR

In recent years, economists have encountered another serious worry. While triangle ABC in Figure 13.9 represents a real net loss to society, part of rectangle P_mACP_c (the $4,000 monopoly profit) may also end up lost. To understand why we need to think about the incentives facing potential monopolists.

The area of rectangle P_mACP_c shows positive profits. If entry into the market were free and competition were open, these profits would eventually be competed to zero. Owners of businesses earning profits have an incentive to prevent this from happening. In fact, the diagram shows exactly how much they would be willing to pay to prevent it. A rational owner of a competitive firm would be willing to pay any amount less than the entire rectangle. Any portion of profits left over after expenses is better than zero, which would be the case if free competition eliminated all profits.

There are many things that a potential monopolist can do to protect his or her profits. One obvious approach is to push the government to impose restrictions on competition. A classic example is the behavior of taxicab drivers, organizations in New York and other large cities. To operate a cab legally in New York City, you need a license. The city tightly controls the number of licenses available. If entry into the taxi business were open, competition would hold down cab fares to the cost of operating cabs. But cab drivers have become a powerful lobbying force and have muscled the city into restricting the number of licenses issued. This restriction keeps fares high and preserves monopoly profits.

There are countless other examples. The steel industry and the automobile industry spend large sums lobbying Congress for tariff protection.[5] Some experts claim that

[5] A tariff is a tax on imports designed to give a price advantage to domestic producers.

both the establishment of the now-defunct Civil Aeronautics Board in 1937 to control competition in the airline industry and the extensive regulation of trucking by the Federal Trade Commission prior to deregulation in the 1970s came about partly through industry efforts to restrict competition and preserve profits.

This kind of behavior, in which households or firms take action to preserve positive profits, is called **rent-seeking behavior**.[6] Recall from chapter 10 that rent is the return to a factor of production in strictly limited supply. Rent-seeking behavior has two important implications.

First, it consumes resources. Lobbying and building barriers to entry are not costless activities. Lobbyists' wages, expenses of the regulatory bureaucracy, and the like must be paid. Periodically faced with the prospect that the city of New York will issue new taxi licenses, cab owners and drivers have become so well organized that they can bring the city to a standstill with a strike or even a limited job action. Indeed, positive profits may be completely consumed through rent-seeking behavior that produces nothing of social value; all it does is help to preserve the current distribution of income.

Second, the frequency of rent-seeking behavior leads us to another view of government. So far we have considered only the role that government might play in helping to achieve an efficient allocation of resources in the face of market failure—in this case, failures that arise from imperfect market structure. Later in this chapter and chapter 15 we survey the measures government might take to ensure that resources are efficiently allocated when monopoly power arises. But the idea of rent-seeking behavior introduces the notion of **government failure**, in which the government becomes the tool of the rent seeker, and the allocation of resources is made even less efficient than before.

This idea of government failure is at the center of **public choice theory**, which holds that governments are made up of people, just as business firms are. These people—politicians and bureaucrats—can be expected to act in their own self-interest, just as owners of firms do. We turn to the economics of public choice in chapter 16.

REMEDIES FOR MONOPOLY

Monopoly power is not in the public interest, and numerous antimonopoly laws have been enacted. The most significant, the Sherman Act, was passed in 1890. As we will see in chapter 15, the government has taken two approaches to limiting monopoly power: (1) breaking up the monopoly into a number of smaller competing firms (restructuring the industry), and (2) allowing the firm to operate as a monopoly, but under strict regulations. One way the government can control monopoly is by setting the price of its output at competitive levels.

Under some, albeit unusual, circumstances, breaking up a monopoly would *not* be in the public interest. Some monopolies may be better left intact. It is to these "natural monopolies" that we now turn our attention.

NATURAL MONOPOLY

In comparing monopoly and competition, we assumed there were constant returns to scale. When this is the case, there is no technological reason to have big firms instead of small firms. In some industries, however, there are technological economies of scale so large that it makes sense to have just one firm. Examples are rare, but public

rent-seeking behavior *Actions taken by households or firms to preserve positive profits.*

government failure *Occurs when the government becomes the tool of the rent seeker and the allocation of resources is made even less efficient by the intervention of government.*

public choice theory *An economic theory that the public officials who set economic policies and regulate the players act in their own self-interest, just as firms do.*

---

[6]The term *rent-seeking behavior* was coined by Anne Krueger in an article published in 1974. Much of the theory dates to earlier work by Gordon Tullock. See Anne O. Krueger, "The Political Economy of the Rent-Seeking Society," *American Economic Review* 64(1974) 291–303; and J. Buchanan, R. Tollison, and G. Tullock (eds.), *Toward a Theory of the Rent-Seeking Society* (College Station, TX: Texas A & M University Press, 1980).

FIGURE 13.10

A Natural Monopoly

A natural monopoly is a firm in which the most efficient scale is very large. Here average cost declines until a single firm is producing nearly the entire amount demanded in the market. With one firm producing 500,000 units, average cost is $1 per unit. With five firms each producing 100,000 units, average cost is $5 per unit.

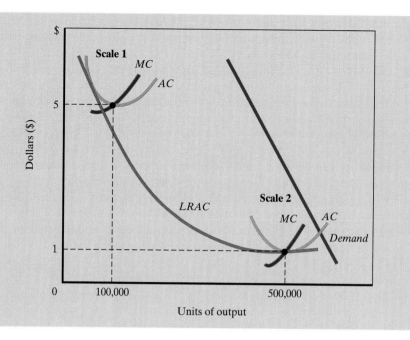

natural monopoly *An industry that realizes such large economies of scale in producing its product that single-firm production of that good or service is most efficient.*

utilities—the electric company or the local telephone company, for example—are among them. A firm that realizes such large economies of scale is called a **natural monopoly**.

Although Figure 13.10 presents an exaggerated picture, it does serve to illustrate our point. One large-scale plant (Scale 2) can produce 500,000 units of output at an average unit cost of $1. If the industry were restructured into five firms, each producing on a smaller scale (Scale 1), the industry could produce the same amount, but average unit cost would be five times as high ($5). Consumers thus see a considerable gain when economies of scale are realized.

The critical point here is that:

> Economies of scale must be realized at a scale that is close to total demand in the market.

Notice in Figure 13.10 that the long-run average cost curve continues to decline almost until it hits the market demand curve. If at a price of $1 market demand is 5 *million* units of output, there would be no reason to have only one firm in the industry. Ten firms could each produce 500,000 units, and each could reap the full benefits of the available economies of scale.

DO NATURAL MONOPOLIES STILL EXIST?

The classic examples of natural monopolies over the years have been public utilities: the telephone company, the electric company, and the gas company. The basic idea was that huge fixed costs to develop transmission lines and distribution pipes meant large economies of scale. It also made no sense to have five electric companies all running wires down every street.

Until very recently, state governments have allowed public utility companies to exist as monopolies subject to tight regulation of prices. Today everything is changing. The long-distance telephone service market has been fiercely competitive since AT&T was broken up by the courts in 1982. Even local telephone service is moving toward competition, albeit slowly (see the Application box, "Local Telephone Service in 1997").

Electricity and natural gas are not far behind. California is the first state to allow utility consumers to buy electricity from any supplier; the new regulations take effect in 1998. New York, New Jersey, Pennsylvania, Massachusetts, and New Hampshire are close behind. The trick is to force local utilities to allow low-cost suppliers to transmit power over their lines for a fee.

Although the trend is clearly away from regulation and toward competition, regulatory commissions are still firmly in control of most state utility markets. We will return to the subject of regulating natural monopolies in chapter 15.

OPTIONAL MATERIAL

MARKET POWER IN INPUT MARKETS: MONOPSONY

Up to this point, we have been talking about market power in terms of output, or product, markets. Even monopolies, we assumed, were price-takers in input markets. But it is also possible for a firm to exercise control over prices in input markets. Consider a firm that is the *only buyer* in a market, the company that hires labor in a "company town." A market with one buyer is called a **monopsony**.[7]

We have said that competitive firms are price-takers in input markets as well as output markets. The wage rate, for example, is set by the supply and demand that result when many firms demand labor and many households supply it. An individual competitive firm takes an externally determined wage rate as a given and will demand an input as long as the marginal revenue product of that input exceeds its price. The marginal revenue product of labor, for example, is the added revenue that the firm earns by hiring one additional unit of labor. The unit of labor produces some product—its marginal product—which, when sold, brings in revenue. In making input decisions, the competitive firm compares the marginal gains from hiring each unit of labor (that is, what the product of that unit sells for) against the "marginal cost" of that unit (that is, the wage rate). (If this sounds unfamiliar, you might want to review chapter 10.)

When a firm hires labor competitively, it hires all the labor it needs at the current market wage. But suppose that the firm is the *only* buyer of laborers with some particular skill. This means that the firm now faces a market supply curve rather than a market-determined equilibrium wage. The wage rate thus becomes a decision variable for the firm. If the market supply curve of labor slopes upward, and the monopsony firm needs more labor, it must offer a higher wage to get that labor. The marginal cost of an additional unit of labor is no longer just equal to the wage rate. This leads us to the concept of **marginal factor cost** (**MFC**), the additional cost of using one additional unit of a factor of production at the margin.

Using the supply schedule in Table 13.2, suppose that the monopsony firm wants to increase its use of labor from three units to four. The fourth unit of labor will work for a wage of $8 per hour, but because our firm cannot price discriminate, it must pay all workers the higher wage. When the monopsony employed three workers, it had to pay them only $6 per hour each. When the fourth unit of labor is added, those three will each earn an additional $2 per hour. The total cost of increasing labor from three to four units, therefore, is the $8 that goes to the fourth worker plus the $2 to each of the other three. The marginal factor cost is thus $14. In other words, increasing the

monopsony *A market in which there is only one buyer for a good or service.*

marginal factor cost (MFC) *The additional cost of using one more unit of a given factor of production.*

---

[7]The terms *monopoly* and *monopsony* both derive from Greek root words. In both cases *mon(o)* means "sole" or "single." "Monopoly" adds a form of the Greek verb *polein*, "to sell." "Monopsony" adds a form of the Greek verb *opsonein*, "to buy food."

TABLE 13.2   DERIVING MARGINAL FACTOR COST
FOR A MONOPSONIST

(1) UNITS OF LABOR SUPPLIED	(2) WAGE	(3) TOTAL FACTOR COST (TFC)	(4) MARGINAL FACTOR COST (MFC)
0	$ 0	$—	$—
1	2	2	—
2	4	8	6
3	6	18	10
4	8	32	14
5	10	50	18
6	12	72	22
7	14	98	26

use of labor by one unit will cost the firm $14. The marginal factor cost is higher than the wage rate at every level of labor demand except one worker, because the higher wage needed to attract any additional labor supply goes to all workers, not just to the marginal worker.

Figure 13.11 shows a typical marginal factor cost schedule that is above the labor supply schedule facing a monopsonist in a labor market. It is superimposed on the firm's marginal revenue product of labor schedule. Using our now-familiar marginal logic, we can conclude that:

> A profit-maximizing firm hires labor as long as its marginal revenue product exceeds its marginal factor cost. Therefore, the profit-maximizing amount of labor for the monopsonist occurs at the point where $MRP_L = MFC$.

FIGURE 13.11

A Monopsonist Will Hold Wages below Marginal Revenue Product and Hire Less Labor than a Perfect Competitor

For a monopsonist, the marginal cost of hiring one additional unit of labor is higher than the wage rate, because the firm must increase the wage of all workers to attract the new worker into the labor force. The monopsonist will hire only up to 400,000 hours of labor and pay a wage of $8 per hour.

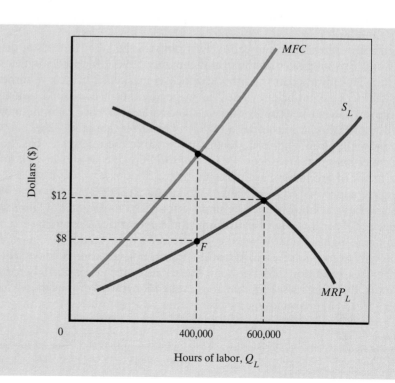

Note that this condition is true for all firms, not just monopsonists. In perfectly competitive labor markets, the wage equals the marginal factor cost. Thus the profit-maximizing amount of labor for a perfectly competitive firm can be written as $MRP_L = W$, which is what we learned in chapter 10.

The monopsonist in Figure 13.11 would hire labor up to 400,000 hours (the point at which MFC and MRP_L intersect) and thus set a wage equal to $8 per hour (point F on the supply curve). In competition, the wage would be $12 per hour, the point at which quantity supplied and quantity demanded (marginal revenue product) are equal, and 600,000 hours of labor would be hired. (Review chapter 10 if this reasoning is unclear to you.) Thus, much like a monopolist who curtails production and charges a price above the level set by competition, a monopsonist cuts back on the hours of labor hired and pays a wage below the level set by competition.

As you saw in chapter 12, the condition $W = MRP_L$ ensures that households supply, and that firms hire, the efficient amount of labor. This condition implies that the market wage facing households and affecting their labor-supply behavior reflects the value of the product of labor. With monopsony, the wage rate is held considerably below MRP_L at competitive equilibrium. Because marginal revenue product is the value of labor's product, keeping the wage lower keeps people out of the workforce who would otherwise be producing output that has a value to society. Thus, monopsony is inefficient.

IMPERFECT MARKETS: A REVIEW AND A LOOK AHEAD

A firm has *market power* when it exercises some control over the price of its output or the prices of the inputs that it uses. The extreme case of a firm with market power is the pure monopolist. In pure monopoly, a single firm produces a product for which there are no close substitutes in an industry in which all new competitors are barred from entry.

Our focus in this chapter on pure monopoly (which occurs rarely) has served a number of purposes. First, the monopoly model describes a number of industries quite well. Second, the monopoly case illustrates the observation that imperfect competition leads to an inefficient allocation of resources. Finally, the analysis of pure monopoly offers insights into the more commonly encountered market models of monopolistic competition and oligopoly, which we discussed briefly in this chapter and will discuss in detail in the next chapter.

SUMMARY

1. A number of assumptions underlie the logic of pure competition. Among them: (1) A large number of firms and households are interacting in each market; (2) firms in a given market produce undifferentiated, or homogeneous, products; and (3) new firms are free to enter industries and to compete for profits. The first two imply that firms have no control over input prices or output prices; the third implies that opportunities for positive profit are eliminated in the long run.

IMPERFECT COMPETITION AND MARKET POWER: CORE CONCEPTS

2. A market in which individual firms have some control over price is imperfectly competitive. Such firms exercise *market power*. The three forms of *imperfect competition* are monopoly, oligopoly, and monopolistic competition.

3. A *pure monopoly* is an industry with a single firm that produces a product for which there are no close substitutes and in which there are significant *barriers to entry*.

4. There are many barriers to entry, including government franchises and licenses, patents, economies of scale, and ownership of scarce factors of production.

5. Market power means that firms must make four decisions instead of three: (1) how much to produce, (2) how to produce it, (3) how much to demand in each input market, and (4) *what price to charge for their output*.

6. Market power does not imply that a monopolist can charge any price it wants. Monopolies are constrained by market demand. They can sell only what people will buy and only at a price that people are willing to pay.

PRICE AND OUTPUT DECISIONS IN PURE MONOPOLY MARKETS

7. In perfect competition, many firms supply homogeneous products. With only one firm in a monopoly market, however, there is no distinction between the firm and the industry—the firm *is* the industry. The market demand curve is thus the firm's demand curve, and the total quantity supplied in the market is what the monopoly firm decides to produce.

8. For a monopolist, an increase in output involves not just producing more and selling it but also reducing the price of its output in order to sell it. Thus marginal revenue, to a monopolist, is not equal to product price, as it is in competition. Rather, marginal revenue is lower than price because to raise output one unit *and to be able to sell* that one unit, the firm must lower the price it charges to all buyers.

9. A profit-maximizing monopolist will produce up to the point at which marginal revenue is equal to marginal cost ($MR = MC$).

10. Monopolies have no identifiable supply curves. They simply choose a point on the market demand curve. That is, they choose a price and quantity to produce, which depend on both marginal cost and the shape of the demand curve.

11. In the short run, monopolists are limited by a fixed factor of production, just as competitive firms are. Monopolies that do not generate enough revenue to cover costs will go out of business in the long run.

12. Compared to a competitively organized industry, a monopolist restricts output, charges higher prices, and earns positive profits. Because MR always lies below the demand curve for a monopoly, monopolists will always charge a price higher than MC (the price that would be set by perfect competition).

THE SOCIAL COSTS OF MONOPOLY

13. When firms price above marginal cost, the result is an inefficient mix of output. The decrease in consumer surplus is larger than the monopolist's profit, thus causing a net loss in social welfare.

14. Actions that firms take to preserve positive profits, such as lobbying for restrictions on competition, are called rent seeking. *Rent-seeking behavior* consumes resources and adds to social cost, thus reducing social welfare even further.

NATURAL MONOPOLY

15. When a firm exhibits economies of scale so large that average costs continuously decline with output, it may be efficient to have only one firm in an industry. Such an industry is called a *natural monopoly*.

(OPTIONAL) MARKET POWER IN INPUT MARKETS: MONOPSONY

16. A market with only one buyer is a *monopsony*. The problems of firms that exercise market power in input markets are similar to the problems of monopoly.

17. *Marginal factor cost* is the additional cost of using one more unit of a given factor of production. A profit-maximizing firm will hire labor as long as its marginal revenue product exceeds its marginal factor cost.

REVIEW TERMS AND CONCEPTS

barrier to entry, 298
collusion, 310
government failure, 315
government franchise, 298
imperfectly competitive industry, 297

marginal factor cost (*MFC*), 317
market power, 297
monopsony, 317
natural monopoly, 316

patent, 299
public choice theory, 315
pure monopoly, 298
rent-seeking behavior, 315

PROBLEM SET

1. Do you agree or disagree with each of the following statements? Explain your reasoning.
   a. For a monopoly, price is equal to marginal revenue because a monopoly has the power to control price.
   b. A natural monopoly will produce at an efficient level of output if its price is simply set by the regulatory agency at marginal cost.
   c. Because a monopoly is the only firm in an industry, it can charge virtually any price for its product.

2. Explain why the marginal revenue curve facing a competitive firm differs from the marginal revenue curve facing a monopolist.

3. Assume that the potato chip industry in the Northwest in 1997 was competitively structured and in long-run competitive equilibrium; firms were earning a normal rate of return. In 1998 two smart lawyers quietly bought up all the firms and began operations as a monopoly called "Wonks." To operate efficiently, Wonks hired a management consulting firm, which estimated long-run costs and demand. These results are presented in the following figure:

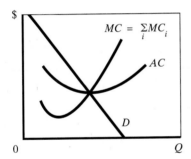

(ΣMC_i = the horizontal sum of the marginal cost curves of the individual branches/firms)
   a. Indicate 1997 output and price on the diagram.
   b. Assuming that the monopolist is a profit-maximizer, indicate on the graph total revenue, total cost, and total profit after the consolidation.
   c. Compare the perfectly competitive outcome with the monopoly outcome.
   d. In 1998, an old buddy from law school files a complaint with the antitrust division of the Justice Department claiming that Wonks has monopolized the potato chip industry. Justice concurs and prepares a civil suit. Suppose you work in the White House and the president asks you to prepare a brief memo (two or three paragraphs) outlining the issues. In your response, be sure to include
      1. the economic justification for action
      2. a proposal to achieve an efficient market outcome.

4. Willy's Widgets, a monopoly, faces the following demand schedule (sales in widgets per month):

Price	$20	$30	$40	$50	$60	$70	$80	$90	$100
Quantity demanded	40	35	30	25	20	15	10	5	0

Calculate marginal revenue over each interval in the schedule (for example, between $q = 40$ and $q = 35$). Recall that marginal revenue is the added revenue from an additional *unit* of production/sales and assume that MR is constant within each interval.

If marginal cost is constant at $20 and fixed cost is $100, what is the profit-maximizing level of output? (Choose one of the specific levels of output from the schedule.) What is the level of profit? Explain your answer using marginal cost and marginal revenue.

Repeat the exercise for $MC = \$40$.

5. The following diagram shows the cost structure of a monopoly firm as well as market demand. Identify on the graph and calculate the following:
   a. profit-maximizing output level
   b. profit-maximizing price
   c. total revenue
   d. total cost
   e. total profit or loss

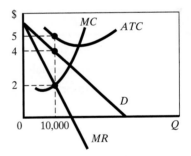

6. Consider the following monopoly that produces paperback books:

Fixed costs = $1,000
Marginal cost = $1 (and is constant).

   a. Draw the average total cost curve and the marginal cost curve on the same graph.
   b. Assume that all households have the same demand schedule, given by the following relationship:

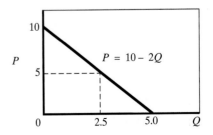

$$P = 10 - 2Q$$

If there are 400 households in the economy, draw the market demand curve and the marginal revenue schedule facing the monopolist.

c. What is the monopolist's profit-maximizing output? What is the monopolist's price?

d. What is the "efficient price," assuming no externalities?

e. Suppose that the government "imposed" the efficient price by setting a ceiling on price at the efficient level. What is the long-run output of the monopoly?

f. Can you suggest an alternative approach for achieving an efficient outcome?

*7. Consider the following labor supply schedule and production data:

LABOR SUPPLY		PRODUCTIVITY	
WAGE RATE	QUANTITY OF LABOR SUPPLIED	UNITS OF LABOR	MARGINAL REVENUE PRODUCT OF LABOR
4	1	1	$10
5	2	2	9
6	3	3	8
7	4	4	7
8	5	5	6
9	6	6	5
10	7	7	4

a. Calculate marginal factor cost at each level of labor supply.

b. If the firm whose marginal revenue product schedule is given is a monopsonist, how much labor will be demanded? What wage will be paid? Explain your answer.

c. If the *MRP* schedule of labor were the industry demand schedule in a competitive industry, what would the wage rate be? How many units of labor would be employed?

TAKE IT TO THE NET

We invite you to visit the Case and Fair page on the Prentice Hall Web site:

http://www.prenhall.com/casefair

for this chapter's World Wide Web exercise.

MONOPOLISTIC
COMPETITION
AND OLIGOPOLY

WE HAVE NOW EXAMINED TWO "pure" market structures. At one extreme is *perfect competition*, a market structure in which many firms, each small relative to the size of the market, produce undifferentiated products and have no market power at all. Each competitive firm takes price as given and faces a perfectly elastic demand for its product. At the other extreme is *pure monopoly*, a market structure in which only one firm is the industry. The monopoly holds the power to set price and is protected against competition by barriers to entry. Its market power would be complete if it did not face the discipline of the market demand curve. Even a monopoly, however, must produce a product that people want and are willing to pay for.

Most industries in the United States fall somewhere between these two extremes. In this chapter, we focus on two types of industries in which firms exercise some market power but at the same time face competition. One type, *monopolistic competition*, differs from perfect competition only in that firms can differentiate their products. Entry to a monopolistically competitive industry is free, and each industry is made up of many firms.

The other type, *oligopoly*, is a broad category that covers many kinds of firm behavior and industry structure. An oligopoly is an industry comprising a small number of competitors; each firm in an oligopoly is large enough to have some control over market price, but beyond that the character of competition varies greatly from industry to industry. An oligopoly may have two firms or twenty, and those firms may produce differentiated or undifferentiated products.

MONOPOLISTIC COMPETITION

A **monopolistically competitive industry** has the following characteristics:

1. a large number of firms;
2. no barriers to entry;
3. product differentiation.

monopolistic competition
A common form of industry (market) structure in the United States, characterized by a large number of firms, none of which can influence market price by virtue of size alone. Some degree of market power is achieved by firms producing differentiated products. New firms can enter and established firms can exit such an industry with ease.

TABLE 14.1 PERCENTAGE OF VALUE OF SHIPMENTS ACCOUNTED FOR BY THE LARGEST FIRMS IN SELECTED INDUSTRIES, 1987

SIC#	INDUSTRY DESIGNATION	FOUR LARGEST FIRMS	EIGHT LARGEST FIRMS	TWENTY LARGEST FIRMS	NUMBER OF FIRMS
3792	Travel trailers and campers	41	57	72	270
3942	Dolls	34	47	67	204
2521	Wood office furniture	26	34	51	611
2731	Book publishing	23	38	62	2504
2391	Curtains and draperies	22	32	48	1004
2092	Fresh or frozen seafood	19	28	47	600
3564	Blowers and fans	14	22	41	518
2335	Woman's dresses	11	17	30	3943
3089	Misc. plastic products	5	8	13	7605

Source: U.S. Department of Commerce, Bureau of the Census, 1992 Census of Manufacturers, *Concentration Ratios in Manufacturing*. Subject Series MC92-S-2, 1997.

While pure monopoly and perfect competition are rare, monopolistic competition is common in the United States, for example, in the restaurant business. The San Francisco Yellow Pages devote 26 pages to listing over 1,500 different restaurants in the area. Each produces a slightly different product and attempts to distinguish itself in consumers' minds. Entry to the market is certainly not blocked. One location near Union Square saw five different restaurants start up and go out of business in five years. Although many restaurants fail, small ones can compete and survive because there are no economies of scale in the restaurant business.

The feature that distinguishes monopolistic competition from monopoly and oligopoly is that firms that are monopolistic competitors cannot influence market price by virtue of their size. No one restaurant is big enough to affect the market price of a prime rib dinner, even though all restaurants can control their *own* prices. Rather, firms gain control over price in monopolistic competition by *differentiating* their products. You make it in the restaurant business by producing a product that people want that others are not producing and/or by establishing a reputation for good food and good service. By producing a unique product or establishing a particular reputation, a firm becomes, in a sense, a "monopolist"—that is, no one else can produce the exact same good.

The feature that distinguishes monopolistic competition from pure monopoly is that good substitutes are available in a monopolistically competitive industry. With 1,500 restaurants in the San Francisco area, there are dozens of good Italian, Chinese, and French restaurants. San Francisco's Chinatown, for example, has about 50 small Chinese restaurants, with over a dozen packed on a single street. The menus are nearly identical, and they all charge virtually the same prices. At the other end of the spectrum are restaurants, with established names and prices far above the cost of production, that are always booked. That is the goal of every restaurateur who ever put a stockpot on the range.

Table 14.1 presents some data on nine national manufacturing industries that have the characteristics of monopolistic competition.[1] Each of these industries includes

---

[1]The data are tabulated and reported by Standard Industrial Classification, or SIC, codes. This classification system for industries has been developed over a period of years and is administered by the Department of Commerce. The system operates in such a way that industry definitions become progressively narrower, and thus industry descriptions become more specific, with successive additions of digits. There are 20 *major groups* (SIC 20: food and kindred products), 150 *groups* (SIC 20 1: meat products), 450 *industries* (SIC 201 1: meat-packing plants), 1,500 *product classes* (SIC 2011 2: bacon), and 13,000 *products* that add two more digits to make up a seven-digit code. The Census Bureau compiles its numbers from data collected in the Census of Manufacturers, done every five years. The data from the 1997 census will not be released for a few years.

hundreds of individual firms, some larger than others, but all small relative to the industry. The top four firms in book publishing, for example, account for 23 percent of total shipments. The top 20 firms account for 62 percent of the market, while the market's remaining 38 percent is split among almost 2,500 separate firms.

> Firms in a monopolistically competitive industry are small relative to the total market. New firms can enter the industry in pursuit of profit, and relatively good substitutes for the firms' products are available. Firms in monopolistically competitive industries try to achieve a degree of market power by differentiating their products—by producing something new, different, or better, or by creating a unique identity in the minds of consumers.

To discuss the behavior of such firms, we begin with a few words about advertising and product differentiation.

PRODUCT DIFFERENTIATION, ADVERTISING, AND SOCIAL WELFARE

Monopolistically competitive firms achieve whatever degree of market power they command through **product differentiation**. To be chosen over competitors, products must have distinct positive identities in consumers' minds. This differentiation is often accomplished through advertising.

In 1995 firms spent over $156 billion on advertising, as Table 14.2 shows. You couldn't get through life (and probably not a day) without hearing "Coke is it." Advertising reaches us through every medium of communication. Table 14.3 shows national network television advertising expenditures by major industrial category. The automobile industry leads the pack with expenditures of nearly $1.7 billion in television advertising in 1994. In 1997, 30 seconds of prime commercial advertising time during Super Bowl XXXI between Green Bay and New England cost $1.3 million. A 30-second spot on the last episode of *Cheers* in 1993 and during NBC's showing of *Jurassic Park* in 1995 each cost $650,000.

The effects of product differentiation in general and advertising in particular on the allocation of resources have been hotly debated for years. Advocates claim that these forces give the market system its vitality and power. Critics argue that they cause waste and inefficiency. Before we proceed to the models of monopolistic competition and oligopoly, let's look at this debate.

> **The Case for Product Differentiation and Advertising** The big advantage of product competition is that it provides us with the variety inherent in a steady stream of new products while ensuring the quality of those products. A modern economy can satisfy a tremendous variety of tastes and preferences. A walk through several neighborhoods of a big city, or an hour in a modern department store or mall, should convince you that human wants are infinite—well, nearly—in their variety.

Free and open competition with differentiated products is the only way to satisfy all of us. Think of the variety of music we listen to—bluegrass, heavy metal, country, folk, rap, classical, grunge. Business firms engage in constant market research to satisfy these wants. What do consumers want? What colors? What cuts? What sizes? The only firms that succeed are the ones that answer these questions correctly and thereby satisfy an existing demand.

In recent years, quite a few of us have taken up the sport of running. The market has responded in a big way. Now there are numerous running magazines; hundreds of orthotic shoes designed specifically for runners with particular running styles; running suits of every color, cloth, and style; weights for the hands, ankles, and shoe laces; tiny radios to slip into your sweatbands; and so forth. Even physicians have differentiated their products: Sports medicine clinics have diets for runners, therapies for runners,

TABLE 14.2

TOTAL ADVERTISING EXPENDITURES IN 1995

	DOLLARS (BILLIONS)
Newspapers	36.8
Television	36.7
Direct mail	32.6
Other	20.3
Yellow Pages	10.3
Radio	11.5
Magazines	8.6
Total	156.8

Source: McCann Erickson, Inc., Reported in U.S. Bureau of the Census, *Statistical Abstract of the United States,* 1996, p. 574.

product differentiation *A strategy that firms use to achieve market power. Accomplished by producing products that have distinct positive identities in consumers' minds.*

TABLE 14.3

EXPENDITURES FOR TELEVISION NETWORK ADVERTISING IN 1994

	DOLLARS (MILLIONS)
Automobiles	1,696
Food and food products	1,429
Toiletries and toilet goods	1,095
Proprietary medicines	988
Restaurants and drive-ins	839
Consumer services	916
Soft drinks and confectionery	679
Laundry soap, cleansers, polishes	280
Beer and wine	341
All other industries	11,893

Source: Television Bureau of Advertising, Inc. (New York). Reported in U.S. Bureau of the Census, *Statistical Abstract of the United States,* 1996, p. 575.

THERE ARE RUNNING SHOES FOR
SERIOUS RUNNERS, RUNNING
SHOES FOR NOT-SO-SERIOUS
RUNNERS, SHOES FOR WALKERS,
EVEN WALKING SHOES THAT
LOOK LIKE RUNNING SHOES FOR
WALKERS. THERE ARE ALL KINDS
OF SHOES TO FIT ALL KINDS OF
FEET AND SATISFY PEOPLE WHO
HAVE THOSE FEET. THIS IS WHAT
PRODUCT DIFFERENTIATION AND
ADVERTISING ARE ALL ABOUT.

and doctors specializing in shin splints or Morton's toe. There is even a running shoe with a small computer built into the heel to monitor a runner's time, distance, and calories expended!

The products that satisfy a real demand survive. The market shows no mercy to products no one wants. They sit on store shelves, are sold at heavily discounted prices or not at all, and eventually disappear. Firms making products that don't sell go out of business, the victims of an economic Darwinism in which only the products that can thrive in a competitive environment survive.

The standard of living rises when the technology of production improves—that is, when we learn to produce more with fewer resources. But the standard of living also rises when we have product *innovation*, when new and better products come on the market. Think of all the things today that didn't exist 10 or 15 years ago: compact disc players, microwave ovens, VCRs, mountain bikes, and personal computers.

Variety is also important to us psychologically. The astonishing range of products available exists not just because your tastes differ from mine. Human beings get bored easily. We grow tired of things, and diminishing marginal utility sets in. I don't go only to French restaurants; it's nice to eat Greek or Chinese food once in a while too. To satisfy many people with different preferences that change over time, the market must be free to respond with new products.

People who visit planned economies always comment on the lack of variety. Before the Berlin Wall came down in 1989 and East and West Germany were reunited in 1990, those allowed passed from colorful and exciting West Berlin into dull and gray

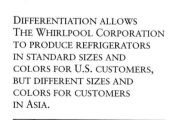

DIFFERENTIATION ALLOWS
THE WHIRLPOOL CORPORATION
TO PRODUCE REFRIGERATORS
IN STANDARD SIZES AND
COLORS FOR U.S. CUSTOMERS,
BUT DIFFERENT SIZES AND
COLORS FOR CUSTOMERS
IN ASIA.

East Berlin; variety seemed to vanish. As the Wall came down, thousands of Germans from the East descended on the department stores of the West. Visitors to China since the economic reforms of the mid-1980s claim that the biggest visible sign of change is the increase in the selection of products available to the population.

Proponents of product differentiation also argue that it leads to efficiency. If my product is of higher quality than my competition's, my product will sell more and my firm will do better. If I can produce something of high quality more cheaply—that is, more efficiently—than my competition can, I will force them to do likewise or go out of business. Creating a brand name through advertising also helps to ensure quality. Firms that have spent millions to establish a brand name or a reputation for quality have something of value to protect.

For product differentiation to be successful, consumers must know about product quality and availability. In perfect competition, where all products are alike, we assume that consumers have perfect information; without it, the market fails to produce an efficient allocation of resources. Complete information is even more important when we allow for product differentiation. How do consumers get this information? Through advertising, at least in part. The basic function of advertising, according to its proponents, is to assist consumers in making informed, rational choices.

Supporters of product differentiation and advertising also claim that these techniques promote competition. New products can compete with old, established brands only if they can get their messages through to consumers. When consumers are informed about a wide variety of potential substitutes, they can more effectively resist the power of monopolies.

> The advocates of free and open competition believe that differentiated products and advertising give the market system its vitality and are the basis of its power. They are the only ways to begin to satisfy the enormous range of tastes and preferences in a modern economy. Product differentiation also helps to ensure high quality and efficient production, and advertising provides consumers with the valuable information on product availability, quality, and price that they need to make efficient choices in the marketplace.

➤ **The Case Against Product Differentiation and Advertising** Product differentiation and advertising waste society's scarce resources, argue critics. They say enormous sums of money are spent to create minute, meaningless differences among products.

Drugs, both prescription and nonprescription, are an example. Companies spend millions of dollars to "hype" brand-name drugs that contain exactly the same compounds as those available under their generic names. The antibiotics erythromycin and erythrocin have the same ingredients, yet the latter is half as expensive. Aspirin is aspirin, yet we pay twice the price for an advertised brand, because the manufacturer has convinced us that there is a tangible—or intangible—difference.

Do we really need 50 different kinds of soap, all of whose prices are inflated substantially by the cost of advertising? For a firm producing a differentiated product, advertising is part of the everyday cost of doing business; its price is built into the average cost curve and thus into the price of the product in the short run and the long run. Thus, consumers pay to finance advertising.

In a way, advertising and product differentiation turn the market system completely around. An economic system is supposed to meet the needs and satisfy the desires of members of society. Advertising is intended to change people's preferences and to create wants that otherwise would not have existed. From the advertiser's viewpoint, people exist to satisfy the needs of the economy.[2]

---

[2]This point was made by John Kenneth Galbraith in *The Affluent Society* (Boston: Houghton Mifflin, 1958).

Critics also argue that the information content of advertising is minimal at best and deliberately deceptive at worst. It is meant to change our minds, to persuade us, and to create brand "images." Try to determine how much real information there is in the next 10 advertisements you see on television. To the extent that no information is conveyed, critics argue, advertising creates no real value, and thus a substantial portion of the $157 billion worth of resources that we devote to advertising is wasted.

Competitive advertising can also easily turn into unproductive warfare. Suppose there are five firms in an industry and one firm begins to advertise heavily. To survive, the others respond in kind. If one firm drops out of the race, it will certainly lose out. Advertising of this sort may not increase demand for the product or improve profitability for the industry. Instead, it is often a "zero sum game"—a game in which the sum of the gains equals the sum of the losses.

Advertising may reduce competition by creating a barrier to the entry of new firms into an industry. One famous case study taught at the Harvard Business School calculates the cost of entering the breakfast cereal market. To be successful, a potential entrant would have to start with millions of dollars in an extensive advertising campaign to establish a brand name recognized by consumers. Entry to the breakfast cereal game is not completely blocked, but such financial requirements make it much more difficult.

Finally, some argue that advertising by its very nature imposes a cost on society. We are continuously bombarded by bothersome jingles and obtrusive images. Driving home from work, we pass 50 billboards and listen to 15 minutes of news and 20 minutes of advertising on the radio. When we get home, we throw away 10 pieces of unsolicited junk mail, glance at a magazine containing 50 pages of writing and 75 pages of advertisements, and perhaps watch a television show that is interrupted every 5 minutes for a "message."

> The bottom line, critics of product differentiation and advertising argue, is waste and inefficiency. Enormous sums are spent to create minute, meaningless, and possibly nonexistent differences among products. Advertising raises the cost of products and frequently contains very little information. Often, it is merely an annoyance. Product differentiation and advertising have turned the system upside down: People exist to satisfy the needs of the economy, not vice versa. Advertising can lead to unproductive warfare and may serve as a barrier to entry, thus reducing real competition.

➤ **No Right Answer**   You will see over and over as you study economics that many questions have no right answers. There are strong arguments on both sides of the advertising debate, and even the empirical evidence leads to conflicting conclusions. Some studies show that advertising leads to concentration and positive profits; others, that advertising improves the functioning of the market.[3]

PRICE AND OUTPUT DETERMINATION IN MONOPOLISTIC COMPETITION

Recall that monopolistically competitive industries are made up of a large number of firms, each small relative to the size of the total market. Thus, no one firm can affect market price by virtue of its size alone. Firms do differentiate their products, however. By doing so, they gain some control over price.

➤ **Product Differentiation and Demand Elasticity**   Purely competitive firms face a perfectly elastic demand for their product: All firms in a perfectly competitive industry produce exactly the same product. If Firm A tried to raise price, buyers would go elsewhere

---

[3]The most widely quoted study showing that advertising restricts competition is William S. Comoner and Thomas A. Wilson, *Advertising and Market Power* (Cambridge, MA: Harvard University Press, 1974). As one example of the opposing argument, see John M. Scheidell, *Advertising, Prices, and Consumer Reaction: A Dynamic Analysis* (Washington, DC: American Enterprise Institute, 1978).

The following are among the largest manufacturing industries, in terms of number of firms in the industry.

Industry	Number of Firms
Commercial printing	28,485
Industrial machinery	22,596
Logging	12,985
Wood kitchen cabinets	4,303
Women's dresses	3,943
Ready mixed concrete	3,249

Source: Census of Manufacturing, 1992, "Concentration Ratios in Manufacturing," Subject Series MC92-S-2, released 1997.

and Firm A would sell nothing. When a firm can distinguish its product from all others in the minds of consumers, as we assume it can under monopolistic competition, it probably can raise price without losing all demand. Figure 14.1 shows how product differentiation might make demand somewhat less elastic for a hypothetical firm.

A monopoly is an industry with a single firm that produces a good for which there are no close substitutes. A monopolistically competitive firm is like a monopoly in that it is the only producer of its unique product. Only one firm can produce Cheerios or Wheat Thins or Johnson's Baby Shampoo or Oreo cookies. But unlike the product in a monopoly market, the product of a monopolistically competitive firm has many close substitutes competing for the consumer's favor.

> Although the demand curve faced by a monopolistic competitor is likely to be less elastic than the demand curve faced by a perfectly competitive firm, it is likely to be more elastic than the demand curve faced by a monopoly.

➤ **Price/Output Determination in the Short Run** Under conditions of monopolistic competition, a profit-maximizing firm behaves much like a monopolist in the short run. First, marginal revenue is not equal to price, because the monopolistically competitive firm has some control over output price. Like a monopolistic firm, a monopolistically competitive firm must lower price to increase output and sell it. The monopolistic

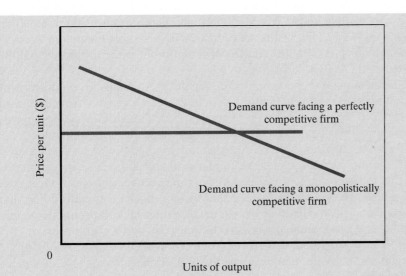

Demand curve facing a perfectly competitive firm

Demand curve facing a monopolistically competitive firm

FIGURE 14.1

Product Differentiation Reduces the Elasticity of Demand Facing a Firm

The demand curve faced by a monopolistic competitor is likely to be less elastic than the demand curve faced by a perfectly competitive firm, but more elastic than the demand curve faced by a monopolist because close substitutes for the products of a monopolistic competitor are available.

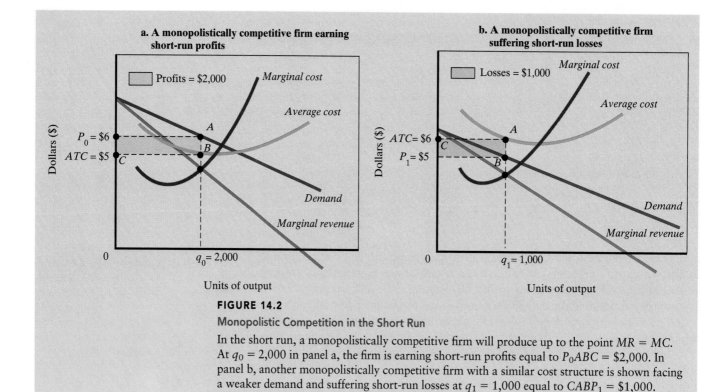

a. A monopolistically competitive firm earning short-run profits

Profits = $2,000

Marginal cost

Average cost

$P_0 = \$6$

$ATC = \$5$

A

B

C

Demand

Marginal revenue

Dollars ($)

0

$q_0 = 2,000$

Units of output

b. A monopolistically competitive firm suffering short-run losses

Losses = $1,000

Marginal cost

Average cost

$ATC = \$6$

$P_1 = \$5$

C

A

B

Demand

Marginal revenue

Dollars ($)

0

$q_1 = 1,000$

Units of output

FIGURE 14.2

Monopolistic Competition in the Short Run

In the short run, a monopolistically competitive firm will produce up to the point $MR = MC$. At $q_0 = 2,000$ in panel a, the firm is earning short-run profits equal to $P_0ABC = \$2,000$. In panel b, another monopolistically competitive firm with a similar cost structure is shown facing a weaker demand and suffering short-run losses at $q_1 = 1,000$ equal to $CABP_1 = \$1,000$.

competitor's marginal revenue curve thus lies *below* its demand curve, intersecting the quantity axis midway between the origin and the point at which the demand curve intersects it. (If necessary, review chapter 13 to get a grip on this idea.)

The firm chooses that output-price combination that maximizes profit.

> To maximize profit, the monopolistically competitive firm will increase production until the marginal revenue from increasing output and selling it no longer exceeds the marginal cost of producing it. This occurs at the point at which marginal revenue equals marginal cost: $MR = MC$.

In Figure 14.2a, the profit-maximizing output is $q_0 = 2,000$, where marginal revenue equals marginal cost. To sell 2,000 units, the firm must charge $6. Total revenue is $P_0 \times q_0 = \$12,000$, or the area of P_0Aq_00. Total cost is equal to average total cost times q_0, which is $10,000, or CBq_00. Total profit is the difference, $2,000 (the pink shaded area P_0ABC).

Nothing guarantees that a firm in a monopolistically competitive industry will earn positive profits in the short run. Figure 14.2b shows what happens when a firm with similar cost curves faces a weaker market demand. Even though the firm does have some control over price, market demand is insufficient to make the firm profitable.

As in pure competition, such a firm minimizes its losses by producing up to the point where marginal revenue is equal to marginal cost. Of course, as in competition, the price that the firm charges must be sufficient to cover variable costs. Otherwise, the firm will shut down and suffer losses equal to total fixed costs, rather than increase losses by producing more. In other words, the firm must make a profit on operation. In Figure 14.2b, the loss-minimizing level of output is $q_1 = 1,000$ at a price of $5. Total revenue is $P_1 \times q_1 = \$5,000$, or P_1Bq_10. Total cost is $ATC \times q_1 = \$6,000$, or CAq_10. Because total cost is greater than revenue, the firm suffers a loss of $1,000, equal to the gray shaded area, $CABP_1$.

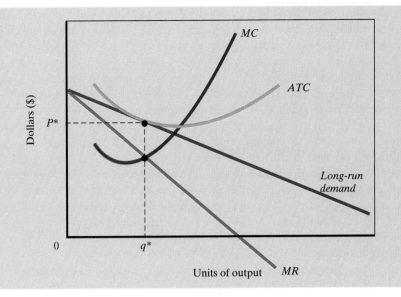

FIGURE 14.3

Monopolistically Competitive Firm at Long-Run Equilibrium

As new firms enter a monopolistically competitive industry in search of profits, the demand curves of profit-making existing firms begin to shift to the left, pushing marginal revenue with them as consumers switch to the new close substitutes. This process continues until profits are eliminated, which occurs for a firm when its demand curve is just tangent to its average cost curve.

➤ **Price/Output Determination in the Long Run** In analyzing monopolistic competition, we assume entry and exit are free in the long run. Firms can enter an industry when there are profits to be made, and firms suffering losses can go out of business. But entry into an industry of this sort is somewhat different from entry into pure competition, because products are differentiated in monopolistic competition. A firm that enters a monopolistically competitive industry is producing a close substitute for the good in question, *but not the same good.*

Let us begin with a firm earning positive profits in the short run. Those profits provide an incentive for new firms to enter the industry. The new firms compete by offering close substitutes, driving down the demand for the product of the firm that was earning profits. If several restaurants seem to be doing well in a particular location, others may start up and attract business from them.

New firms will continue to enter the market until profits are eliminated. As the new firms enter, the demand curve facing each old firm begins to shift to the left, pushing the marginal revenue curve along with it. (Review chapter 13 if you are unsure why.) This shift continues until profits are eliminated, which occurs when the demand curve slips down to the average total cost curve. Graphically, this is the point at which the demand curve and the average total cost curve are tangent (the point at which they just touch and have the same slope). Figure 14.3 shows a monopolistically competitive industry in long-run equilibrium. At q^* and P^*, price and average total cost are equal, so there are no profits or losses.

Look carefully at this tangency, which in Figure 14.3 is at output level q^*. The tangency occurs at the profit-maximizing level of output. At this point, marginal cost is equal to marginal revenue. At any level of output other than q^*, *ATC* lies above the demand curve. This means that at any other level of output, *ATC* is greater than the price that the firm can charge. (Recall that the demand curve shows the price that can be charged at every level of output.) Hence, price equals average cost at q^* and profits equal zero.

This equilibrium must occur at the point at which the demand curve is *just tangent* to the average total cost curve. If the demand curve cut across the average cost curve, intersecting it at two points, the demand curve would be *above* the average cost curve at some levels of output. Producing at those levels of output would mean positive profits. Positive profits would attract entrants, shifting the market demand curve to the left and lowering profits. If the demand curve were always *below* the average cost curve, all levels of output would produce losses for the firm. This would cause firms to exit the industry, shifting the market demand curve to the right and increasing profits (or reducing losses) for those firms still in the industry.

> The firm's demand curve must end up tangent to its average total cost curve for profits to equal zero. This is the condition for long-run equilibrium in a monopolistically competitive industry.

Even if some monopolistically competitive firms start with losses, the long-run equilibrium will be zero profits for all firms remaining in the industry. (Look back at Figure 14.2b, which shows a firm suffering losses.) Suppose many restaurants open in a small area, for example. In Columbus, Ohio, near the intersection of I-270 and Fishinger Road, there are a dozen or so "quick dinner" restaurants crowded into a small area. Given so many restaurants, it seems likely that there will be a "shake-out" sometime in the near future—that is, one or more of the restaurants suffering losses will decide to drop out.

When this happens, the firms remaining in the industry will get a larger share of the total business, and their demand curves will shift to the right. Firms will continue to drop out and thus the demand curves of the remaining firms will continue to shift until all losses are eliminated. Thus, we end up with the same long-run equilibrium as when we started out with firms earning positive profits. At equilibrium, demand is tangent to average total cost, and there are no profits or losses.

ECONOMIC EFFICIENCY AND RESOURCE ALLOCATION

We have already noted some of the similarities between monopolistic competition and pure competition. Because entry is free and economic profits are eliminated in the long run, we might conclude that the result of monopolistic competition is efficient. There are two problems, however.

First, once a firm achieves any degree of market power by differentiating its product (as is the case in monopolistic competition), its profit-maximizing strategy is to hold down production and charge a price above marginal cost, as you saw in Figures 14.2 and 14.3. Remember from chapter 12 that price is the value that society places on a good, and marginal cost is the value that society places on the resources needed to produce that good. By holding production down and price above marginal cost, monopolistically competitive firms prevent the efficient use of resources. More product could be produced at a resource cost below the value that consumers place on the product.

Second, as Figure 14.3 shows, the final equilibrium in a monopolistically competitive firm is necessarily to the left of the low point on its average total cost curve. That means a typical firm in a monopolistically competitive industry will not realize all the economies of scale available. (In pure competition, you will recall, firms are pushed to the bottom of their long-run average cost curves, and the result is an efficient allocation of resources.)

Suppose a number of firms enter an industry and build plants on the basis of initially profitable positions. But as more and more firms compete for those profits, individual firms find themselves with smaller and smaller market shares, and they end up eventually with "excess capacity." The firm in Figure 14.3 is not fully using its existing capacity because competition drove its demand curve to the left. In monopolistic competition we end up with many firms, each producing a slightly different product at a scale that is less than optimal. Would it not be more efficient to have a smaller number of firms, each producing on a slightly larger scale?

The costs of less-than-optimal production, however, need to be balanced against the gains that can accrue from aggressive competition among products. If product differentiation leads to the introduction of new products, improvements in old products, and greater variety, then an important gain in economic welfare may counteract (and perhaps outweigh) the loss of efficiency from pricing above marginal cost or not fully realizing all economies of scale.

Most industries that comfortably fit the model of monopolistic competition are very competitive. Price competition coexists with product competition, and firms do not earn incredible profits. Nor do they violate any of the antitrust laws that we discuss in detail in the next chapter.

Monopolistically competitive firms have not been a subject of great concern among economic policy makers. Their behavior appears to be sufficiently controlled by competitive forces, and no serious attempt has been made to regulate or control them.

OLIGOPOLY

An **oligopoly** is an industry dominated by a few firms that, by virtue of their individual sizes, are large enough to influence the market price. Oligopolies exist in many forms. In some oligopoly markets, products are differentiated—the classic example is the automobile industry. In others, products are nearly homogeneous. In primary copper production, for example, only eight firms produce virtually all the basic metal. Some oligopolies have a very small number of firms, each large enough to influence price—only five firms are involved in cellulosic manmade fibers (a $1.8 billion industry), for example. Others have many firms, of which only a few control market price—four firms control 86 percent of the market for electrical lamps, but 76 firms compete in the industry.

An industry that has a relatively small number of firms that dominate the market is called a *concentrated industry*. Oligopolies are concentrated industries. Table 14.4 contains some data on 10 industries that are relatively concentrated. Although the largest firms account for most of the output in each of these industries, some seem to support a large number of smaller firms.

The complex interdependence that usually exists among firms in these industries makes oligopoly difficult to analyze. The behavior of any one firm depends on the reactions it expects of all the others in the industry. Because individual firms make so many decisions—how much output to produce, what price to charge, how much to advertise, whether and when to introduce new product lines, and so forth—industrial strategies are usually complex and difficult to generalize about.

oligopoly *A form of industry (market) structure characterized by a few dominant firms. Products may be homogeneous or differentiated. The behavior of any one firm in an oligopoly depends to a great extent on the behavior of others.*

TABLE 14.4 PERCENTAGE OF VALUE OF SHIPMENTS ACCOUNTED FOR BY THE LARGEST FIRMS IN HIGH-CONCENTRATION INDUSTRIES, 1987

SIC#	INDUSTRY DESIGNATION	FOUR LARGEST FIRMS	EIGHT LARGEST FIRMS	NUMBER OF FIRMS
2823	Cellulosic manmade fiber	98	100	5
3331	Primary copper	98	99	11
3633	Household laundry equipment	94	99	10
2111	Cigarettes	93	100	8
2082	Malt beverages (beer)	90	98	160
3641	Electric lamp bulbs	86	94	76
2043	Cereal breakfast foods	85	98	42
3711	Motor vehicles	84	91	398
3482	Small arms ammunition	84	95	55
3632	Household refrigerators and freezers	82	98	52

Source: U.S. Department of Commerce, Bureau of the Census, 1992 Census of Manufacturers, *Concentration Ratios in Manufacturing.* Subject Series MC 92-S-2, 1997.

OLIGOPOLY MODELS

Because many different types of oligopolies exist, a number of different oligopoly models have been developed. The following provides a sample of the alternative approaches to the behavior (or conduct) of oligopolistic firms. As you will see, all kinds of oligopoly have one thing in common:

> The behavior of any given oligopolistic firm depends on the behavior of the other firms in the industry comprising the oligopoly.

> **The Collusion Model** In chapter 13, we examined what happens when a perfectly competitive industry falls under the control of a single profit-maximizing firm. In that analysis, we assumed neither technological nor cost advantages to having one firm rather than many. We saw that when many competing firms act independently, they produce more, charge a lower price, and earn less profit than they would have if they had acted as a single unit. If these firms get together and agree to cut production and increase price—that is, if firms can agree *not* to price compete—they will have a bigger total-profit pie to carve up. When a group of profit-maximizing oligopolists colludes on price and output, the result is exactly the same as it would be if a monopolist controlled the entire industry.

> The colluding oligopoly will face market demand and produce only up to the point at which marginal revenue and marginal cost are equal ($MR = MC$), and price will be set above marginal cost.

Review "Collusion and Monopoly Compared" in chapter 13 if you are not sure why.

A group of firms that gets together and makes price and output decisions jointly is called a **cartel**. Perhaps the most familiar example of a cartel today is the Organization of Petroleum Exporting Countries (OPEC). As early as 1970, the OPEC cartel began to cut petroleum production. Its decisions in this matter led to a 400 percent increase in the price of crude oil on world markets during 1973 and 1974.

Price fixing is not controlled internationally, but it is illegal in the United States. Nonetheless, the incentive to fix prices can be irresistible, and industries are caught in the act from time to time. One famous case in the 1950s involved explicit agreements among a number of electrical equipment manufacturers. In that case, 12 people from five companies met secretly on a number of occasions and agreed to set prices and split up contracts and profits. The scheme involved rotating the winning bids among the firms. Ultimately the scheme was exposed, and the participants were tried, convicted, and sent to jail.

For a cartel to work, a number of conditions must be present. First, demand for the cartel's product must be inelastic. If many substitutes are readily available, the cartel's price increases may become self-defeating as buyers switch to substitutes. Second, the members of the cartel must play by the rules. If a cartel is holding up prices by restricting output, there is a big incentive for members to cheat by increasing output. Breaking ranks can mean very large profits!

Collusion occurs when price- and quantity-fixing agreements are explicit. **Tacit collusion** occurs when firms end up fixing price without a specific agreement, or when such agreements are implicit. A small number of firms with market power may fall into the practice of setting similar prices or following the lead of one firm without ever meeting or setting down formal agreements.

> **The Cournot Model** Perhaps the oldest model of oligopoly behavior was put forward by Augustin Cournot almost 150 years ago. The **Cournot model** is based on three assumptions: (1) there are just two firms in an industry—a *duoploy*; (2) each firm takes the output of the other as given; and (3) both firms maximize profits.

cartel *A group of firms that gets together and makes joint price and output decisions to maximize joint profits.*

tacit collusion *Collusion occurs when price- and quantity-fixing agreements among producers are explicit. Tacit collusion occurs when such agreements are implicit.*

Cournot model *A model of a two-firm industry (duopoly) in which a series of output-adjustment decisions leads to a final level of output between the output that would prevail if the market were organized competitively and the output that would be set by a monopoly.*

The story begins with a new firm producing nothing and the existing firm producing everything. The existing firm takes the market demand curve as its own, acting like a monopolist. When the new firm starts operating, it assumes that the existing firm will continue to produce the same level of output and charge the same price as before. The market demand of the new firm, then, is market demand less the amount that the existing firm is currently selling. In essence, the new firm assumes that its demand curve is everything on the market demand curve below the price charged by the older firm.

When the new firm starts operation, the existing firm discovers that its demand has eroded because some output is now sold by the new firm. The old firm now assumes that the new firm's output will remain constant, subtracts the new firm's demand from market demand, and produces a new, lower level of output. But that throws the ball back to the new firm, which now finds that the competition is producing *less*.

These adjustments get smaller and smaller, with the new firm raising output in small steps and the older firm lowering output in small steps until the two firms split the market and charge the same price. Like the collusion model:

> The Cournot model of oligopoly results in a quantity of output somewhere between output that would prevail if the market were organized competitively and output that would be set by a monopoly.

Although the Cournot model illustrates the interdependence of decisions in oligopoly, its assumptions about strategic reactions are quite naive. The two firms in the model react only after the fact and never anticipate the competition's moves.

► **The Kinked Demand Curve Model**   Another common model of oligopolistic behavior assumes that firms believe that rivals will follow if they *cut* prices but not if they *raise* prices. This **kinked demand curve model** assumes that the elasticity of demand in response to an increase in price is different from the elasticity of demand in response to a price cut. The result is a "kink" in the demand for a single firm's product.

You can see some of these reactions in the demand curve in Figure 14.4. If the initial price of Firm B's product is P^*, raising its price above P^* would cause Firm B to face an elastic demand curve if its rivals did not also raise their prices (segment d_1 of the demand curve). That is, in response to the price increase, demand for Firm B's

kinked demand curve model
A model of oligopoly in which the demand curve facing each individual firm has a "kink" in it. The kink follows from the assumption that competitive firms will follow if a single firm cuts price but will not follow if a single firm raises price.

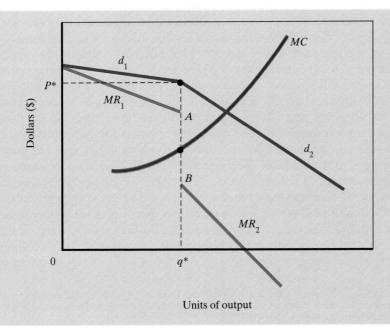

FIGURE 14.4

A Kinked Demand Curve Oligopoly Model

The kinked demand model assumes that competing firms follow price cuts but not price increases. Thus, if Firm B increases its price, the competition will not, and quantity demanded of Firm B's product will fall off quickly. But if Firm B cuts price, other firms will also cut price and the price cut will not gain as much quantity demanded for Firm B as it would if other firms did not follow. At prices above P^* demand is relatively elastic. Below P^* demand is less elastic.

335

product would fall off quickly. The reaction to a price *decrease* would not be as great, however, because rivals would decrease price too. Firm B would lose some of its market share by increasing price, but it would not gain a larger share by decreasing price (segment d_2 of the demand curve).

Recall the very important point that a firm's marginal revenue curve reflects the changes in demand occurring along the demand curve *directly above it*. (Review the derivation of the marginal revenue curve in chapter 13 if this is not fresh in your mind.) This being the case, MR_1 reflects the changes in P and q along demand curve segment d_1. MR_2 reflects changes in P and q along demand curve segment d_2. Because the demand curve is discontinuous at q^*, the marginal revenue curve is also discontinuous, jumping from point A all the way down to point B.

As always, profit-maximizing firms will produce as long as marginal revenue is greater than marginal cost. If, as in Figure 14.4, the marginal cost curve passes through q^* at any point between A and B, the optimal price is P^* and the optimal output is q^*. To the left of q^*, marginal revenue is greater than marginal cost. To maximize profits, then, the firm should increase output. To the right of q^*, marginal cost is greater than marginal revenue—the firm should decrease output.

Notice that this model predicts that price in oligopolistic industries is likely to be more stable than costs. In Figure 14.4, the marginal cost curve can shift up or down by a substantial amount before it becomes advantageous for the firm to change price at all. A number of attempts have been made to test whether oligopolistic prices are indeed more stable than costs. While the results do not support the hypothesis of stable prices, the evidence is far from conclusive.[4]

The kinked demand curve model has been criticized because (1) it fails to explain why price is at P^* to begin with, and (2) the assumption that competing firms will follow price cuts but not price increases is overly simple—real-world oligopolistic pricing strategies are much more complex.

> ▶ **The Price-Leadership Model**   In another form of oligopoly, one firm dominates an industry and all the smaller firms follow the leader's pricing policy—hence **price leadership**. If the dominant firm knows the smaller firms will follow its lead, it will derive its own demand curve simply by subtracting from total market demand the amount of demand that the smaller firms will satisfy at each potential price.

price leadership *A form of oligopoly in which one dominant firm sets prices and all the smaller firms in the industry follow its pricing policy.*

The price-leadership model assumes (1) that the industry is made up of one large firm and a number of smaller, competitive firms; (2) that the dominant firm maximizes profit subject to the constraint of market demand *and* subject to the behavior of the smaller, competitive firms; (3) that the dominant firm allows the smaller firms to sell all they want at the price the leader has set. The difference between the quantity demanded in the market and the amount supplied by the smaller firms is the amount that the dominant firm will produce.

The result has the quantity demanded in the market split between the smaller firms and the dominant firm. This result is based entirely on the dominant firm's market power. The only constraint facing a monopoly firm, you will recall, is the behavior of demanders—that is, the market demand curve. In this case, however, the presence of smaller firms acts to constrain the dominant firm's power. If we were to assume that the smaller firms were out of the way, the dominant firm would face the market demand curve on its own. This means the dominant firm has a clear incentive to push the smaller firms out of the industry. One way is to lower the price until all of the smaller firms go out of business and then raise the price once the market has been monopolized. The practice of a large, powerful firm driving smaller firms out of the market by temporarily selling at an artificially low price is called *predatory pricing*. As we will see in the next chapter, such

[4]See, for example, Julian Simon, "A Further Test of the Kinky Oligopoly Demand Curve," *American Economic Review* (December 1969); and George Stigler, "The Kinky Oligopoly Demand Curve and Rigid Prices," *Journal of Political Economy* 55 (1947).

behavior, common during the nineteenth century in the United States, became illegal with the passage of antimonopoly legislation around the turn of the century.

> As in the other oligopoly models, an oligopoly with a dominant price leader will produce a level of output between the output that would prevail under competition and the output that a monopolist would choose in the same industry. It will also set a price between the monopoly price and the competitive price. Some competition is usually more efficient than none at all.

> **Game Theory** The firms in Cournot's model do not anticipate the moves of the competition. Yet in choosing strategies in an oligopolistic market, real-world firms can and do try to guess what the opposition will do in response.

In 1944, John von Neumann and Oskar Morgenstern published a path-breaking work in which they analyzed a set of problems, or *games*, in which two or more people or organizations pursue their own interests and in which no one of them can dictate the outcome.[5] During the last few years, game theory has become an increasingly popular field of study and a fertile area for research. The notions of game theory have been applied to analyses of firm behavior, politics, international relations, and foreign policy. In 1994 the Nobel Prize in Economic Science was awarded jointly to three early game theorists: John F. Nash of Princeton, John C. Harsanyi of Berkeley, and Reinhard Selten of the University of Bonn.

Game theory goes something like this: In all conflict situations, and thus all games, there are decision makers (or players), rules of the game, and payoffs (or prizes). Players choose strategies without knowing with certainty what strategy the opposition will use. At the same time, though, some information that indicates how their opposition may be "leaning" may be available to the players.

Figure 14.5 illustrates what is called a payoff matrix for a very simple game. Each of two firms, A and B, must decide whether to mount an expensive advertising campaign. If neither firm decides to advertise, each will earn a profit of $50,000. But if one firm advertises and the other does not, the firm that does will increase its profit by 50 percent (to $75,000), while driving the competition into the loss column. If both firms decide to advertise, they will each earn profits of $10,000. They may generate a bit more demand by advertising, but that demand is completely wiped out by the expense of the advertising itself.

Long distance giants AT&T, MCI, and Sprint dominate the market for long-distance telephone service. They react strategically toward each other as a classic oligopoly. On June 30, 1997, AT&T announced a price reduction of 5% for day and evening calls and 15% for night and weekend calls. MCI immediately matched AT&T's cuts. On the following day, Sprint was still deliberating how to respond.

Source: Mark Landler, "AT&T Long-Distance Rates Cut and MCI Joins in Move," *The New York Times*, July 1, 1997, p. D2.

game theory *Analyzes oligopolistic behavior as a complex series of strategic moves and reactive countermoves among rival firms. In game theory, firms are assumed to anticipate rival reactions.*

FIGURE 14.5
Payoff Matrix for Advertising Game

A's STRATEGY	B's STRATEGY	
	Don't advertise	Advertise
Don't advertise	A's profit = $50,000 B's profit = $50,000	A's loss = $25,000 B's profit = $75,000
Advertise	A's profit = $75,000 B's loss = $25,000	A's profit = $10,000 B's profit = $10,000

[5]See J. von Neumann and O. Morgenstern, *Theory of Games and Economic Behavior* (Princeton, NJ: Princeton University Press, 1944).

If Firms A and B could collude (and we assume that they cannot), their optimal strategy would be to agree not to advertise. That solution maximizes the joint profits to both firms. If neither firm advertises, joint profits are $100,000. If both firms advertise, joint profits are only $20,000. If only one of the firms advertises, joint profits are $75,000 − $25,000 = $50,000.

The strategy that Firm A will actually choose depends on the information available concerning B's likely strategy. In this case, it is possible to predict behavior. Consider A's choice of strategy. Regardless of what B does, it pays A to advertise. If B does not advertise, A makes $25,000 more by advertising than by not advertising. Thus, A will advertise. If B does advertise, A must advertise to avoid a loss. The same logic holds for B. Regardless of the strategy pursued by A, it pays B to advertise. A **dominant strategy** is one that is best no matter what the opposition does. In this game, both players have a dominant strategy, and it is likely that both will advertise.

dominant strategy *In game theory, a strategy that is best no matter what the opposition does.*

The result of the game in Figure 14.5 is an example of what is called a prisoners' dilemma. The term comes from a game in which two prisoners (call them Ginger and Rocky) are accused of robbing the local 7-11 together, but the evidence is shaky. If both confess, they each get five years in prison for armed robbery. If neither confesses, they get convicted of a lesser charge, shoplifting, and get one year in prison each. The problem is that the district attorney has offered each of them a deal independently. If Ginger confesses and Rocky doesn't, Ginger goes free and Rocky gets seven years. If Rocky confesses and Ginger doesn't, Rocky goes free and Ginger gets seven years. The payoff matrix for the prisoners' dilemma is given in Figure 14.6.

Looking carefully at the payoffs, you may notice that both Ginger and Rocky have dominant strategies: to confess. That is, Ginger is better off confessing regardless of what Rocky does, and Rocky is better off confessing regardless of what Ginger does. The likely outcome is thus that both will confess, even though they would be better off if they both kept their mouths shut!

Is there any way out of this dilemma? There may be under circumstances in which the game is played over and over. Look back at Figure 14.5. The best outcome for both firms is for neither to advertise. Suppose Firm A decided not to advertise for one period to see how Firm B would respond. If Firm B continued to advertise, A would have to resume advertising to survive. But suppose B's strategy was to play tit for tat. That is, suppose that B decided to simply match A's strategy. In this case, both firms might—with no explicit collusion—end up not advertising after A figures out what B is doing. (For an example of the prisoners' dilemma at work in the airline industry, see the Application box titled "A Prisoners' Dilemma, Price Fixing, and the U.S. Airlines.")

There are many games in which one player does not have a dominant strategy but in which the outcome is predictable. Consider the game in Figure 14.7a in which C

FIGURE 14.6
The Prisoners' Dilemma

GINGER	ROCKY	
	Don't confess	Confess
Don't confess	Ginger: 1 year Rocky: 1 year	Ginger: 7 years Rocky: free
Confess	Ginger: free Rocky: 7 years	Ginger: 5 years Rocky: 5 years

FIGURE 14.7

Payoff Matrixes for Left/Right–Top/Bottom Strategies

a. Original Game

	D's STRATEGY	
C's STRATEGY	**Left**	**Right**
Top	C wins $100 D wins $0	C wins $100 D wins $100
Bottom	C loses $100 D wins $0	C wins $200 D wins $100

b. New Game

	D's STRATEGY	
C's STRATEGY	**Left**	**Right**
Top	C wins $100 D wins $0	C wins $100 D wins $100
Bottom	C loses $10,000 D wins $0	C wins $200 D wins $100

does not have a dominant strategy. If D plays the left strategy, C will play the top strategy. If D plays the right strategy, C will play the bottom strategy. But what strategy will D choose to play? If C knows the options, she will see that D has a dominant strategy and is likely to play it. D does better playing the right-hand strategy regardless of what C does; he can guarantee himself a $100 win by choosing right and is guaranteed to win nothing by playing left. Because D's behavior is predictable (he will play the right-hand strategy), C will play bottom. When all players are playing their best strategy *given* what their competitors are doing, the result is called a **Nash equilibrium.**

Now suppose that the game in Figure 14.7a were changed. Suppose that all the payoffs are the same except that if D chooses left and C chooses bottom, C loses $10,000 (Figure 14.7b). While D still has a dominant strategy (playing right), C now stands to lose a great deal by choosing bottom on the off chance that D chooses left instead. When uncertainty and risk are introduced, the game changes. C is likely to play top and guarantee herself a $100 profit rather than to risk losing $10,000 to win $200, even if there is just a small chance of D's choosing left. A **maximin strategy** is one chosen by a player to maximize the minimum gain that it can earn. In essence, one who plays a maximin strategy assumes that the opposition will play the strategy that does the most damage.

When game theory first appeared in the late 1940s, it seemed that it would in time be able to explain the behavior of oligopolistic firms in great detail. However, when we move from two potential strategies to three or four, and particularly when we move to more than two players, the number of potential outcomes and the properties of the strategy pairings become enormously complex. As a result, it becomes very difficult to predict the strategy (or the combination of strategies) that a firm might choose in any given circumstance.

In the end, game theory leaves us with a greater understanding of the problem of oligopoly but with an incomplete and inconclusive set of propositions about the likely behavior of oligopolistic firms. Some very interesting conclusions emerge about a fairly small number of specific game circumstances, but game theory doesn't provide much help with an industry of five firms, each simultaneously choosing product, pricing, output, and advertising strategies.

About all we are left with is the certainty of interdependence:

> The strategy that an oligopolistic firm chooses is likely to depend on that firm's perception of competing firms' likely responses.

➤ **Contestable Markets** Before we discuss the performance of oligopolies, we should note one relatively new theory of behavior that has limited applications but some important implications for understanding imperfectly competitive market behavior.

A market is **perfectly contestable** if entry to it *and* exit from it are costless. That is, a market is perfectly contestable if a firm can move into it in search of profits but lose

Nash equilibrium *In game theory, the result of all players playing their best strategy given what their competitors are doing.*

maximin strategy *In game theory, a strategy chosen to maximize the minimum gain that can be earned.*

perfectly contestable market *A market in which entry and exit are costless.*

A PRISONERS' DILEMMA, PRICE FIXING, AND THE U.S. AIRLINES

During the years 1990, 1991, and 1992 the U.S. airline industry lost a combined total of just under $10 billion. These losses were incurred despite the move to more fuel-efficient airplanes, falling fuel prices in 1991 and 1992, more passengers, and longer average trips. What explains the industry's disastrous performance?

Some economists have argued that part of the explanation may lie in game theory. Consider the following simple game (all numbers are in millions): Suppose United and American are competing for a lucrative route between the coasts. Each may choose independently to cut price or charge a high price. The profits from the route depend on the strategies chosen by both firms and are given in the four boxes.

Notice that if the game is played a single time, each firm has a dominant strategy. That is, AA will choose to cut fares regardless of what UA does and UA will choose to cut fares regardless of what AA does. The outcome is that each loses $100 million. If somehow both were to charge a high price, UA would earn $100 million and AA would earn $120 million. This is a classic prisoners' dilemma. That is, both firms would benefit if they could get together and agree to charge a higher price. But if they are not allowed to collude, they both end up suffering losses.

		United Airlines (UA)	
		Price High	Cut Fares
American Airlines (AA)	Price High	UA's profit = $100 AA's profit = $120	UA's profit = $140 AA's profit = −$200
	Cut Fares	UA's profit = −$200 AA's profit = $150	UA's profit = −$100 AA's profit = −$100

Recall from the text that one solution to the prisoners' dilemma might be to try a "tit for tat" strategy in repeated trials in the hopes of signaling the opposition that if it charges a high price you will too. This is exactly what the airlines attempted to do to solve their problem. But the behavior was noticed by passenger groups and state attorneys general, who immediately sued the airlines for price fixing.

The following excerpt from the *New York Times* describes part of the settlement made by the airlines:

Major airlines agreed to pay $40 million in discounts to state and local governments to settle a price-fixing lawsuit, a group of 10 state attorneys general said yesterday.

The airlines settled a separate class-action suit last year brought by passengers by agreeing to pay out $458 million in discounts. The airlines earlier this year resolved a Federal antitrust suit by agreeing not to announce price changes in advance . . .

The price-fixing claims centered on an airline practice of announcing price changes in advance through the reservation systems. If competitors did not go along with the price change, it could be rescinded before it was to take effect.[a]

Source: [a] Associated Press, "Suit Settled by Airlines," *The New York Times*, October 12, 1994, p. D8. Copyright © 1994 by The New York Times Co. Reprinted by permission.

For more on game theory, see the Case and Fair Web page at
http://www.prenhall.com/casefair.

nothing if it fails. To be part of a perfectly contestable market, a firm must have capital that is both mobile and easily transferable from one market to another.

Take, for example, a small airline that can move its capital stock from one market to another with little cost. Provincetown Boston Airlines (PBA) flies between Boston, Martha's Vineyard, Nantucket, and Cape Cod during the summer months. During the winter, the same planes are used in Florida, where they fly up and down that state's west coast between Naples, Fort Meyers, Tampa, and other cities. A similar situation may occur when a new industrial complex is built at a fairly remote site and a number of trucking companies offer their services. Because the trucking companies' capital stock is mobile, they can move their trucks somewhere else at no great cost if business is not profitable.

Because entry is cheap, participants in a contestable market are continuously faced with competition or the threat of it. Even if there are only a few firms competing, the openness of the market forces all of them to produce efficiently or be driven out of business. This threat of competition remains high because new firms face little risk in going after a new market. If things don't work out in a crowded market, they don't lose their investment. They can simply transfer their capital to a different place or different use.

> In contestable markets, even large oligopolistic firms end up behaving like perfectly competitive firms. Prices are pushed to long-run average cost by competition, and positive profits do not persist.

➤ **Summary**   Oligopoly is a market structure that is consistent with a variety of behaviors.

> The only necessary condition of oligopoly is that firms are large enough to have some control over price. Oligopolies are concentrated industries. At one extreme is the cartel, in which a few firms get together and jointly maximize profits—in essence, acting as a monopolist. At the other extreme, the firms within the oligopoly vigorously compete for small contestable markets by moving capital quickly in response to observed profits. In between are a number of alternative models, all of which stress the interdependence of oligopolistic firms.

OLIGOPOLY AND ECONOMIC PERFORMANCE

How well do oligopolies perform? Should they be regulated or changed? Are they efficient, or do they lead to an inefficient use of resources? On balance, are they good or bad?

With the exception of the contestable-markets model, all the models of oligopoly we have examined lead us to conclude that concentration in a market leads to pricing above marginal cost and output below the efficient level. When price is above marginal cost at equilibrium, consumers are paying more for the good than it costs to produce that good in terms of products forgone in other industries. To increase output would be to create value that exceeds the social cost of the good, but profit-maximizing oligopolists have an incentive not to increase output.

Entry barriers in many oligopolistic industries also prevent new capital and other resources from responding to profit signals. Under competitive conditions or in contestable markets, positive profits would attract new firms and thus increase production. But this does not happen in most oligopolistic industries. The problem is most severe when entry barriers exist and firms explicitly or tacitly collude. The results of collusion are identical to the results of a monopoly. Firms jointly maximize profits by fixing prices at a high level and splitting up the profits.

Product differentiation under oligopoly presents us with the same dilemma that we encountered in monopolistic competition. On the one hand, vigorous product competition among oligopolistic competitors produces variety and leads to innovation in response to the wide variety of consumer tastes and preferences. It can thus be argued that vigorous product competition is efficient. On the other hand, product differentiation may lead to waste and inefficiency. Product differentiation accomplished through advertising may have nothing to do with product quality, and advertising itself may have little or no information content. If it serves as an entry barrier that blocks competition, product differentiation can cause the market allocation mechanism to fail.

Oligopolistic, or concentrated, industries are likely to be inefficient for several reasons. First, profit-maximizing oligopolists are likely to price above marginal cost. When price is above marginal cost, there is underproduction from society's point of view—in other words, society could get more for less, but it doesn't. Second, strategic behavior can lead to outcomes that are not in society's best interest. Specifically, strategically competitive firms can force themselves into deadlocks that waste resources. Finally, to the extent that oligopolies differentiate their products and advertise, there is the promise of new and exciting products. At the same time, however, there remains a real danger of waste and inefficiency.

INDUSTRIAL CONCENTRATION AND TECHNOLOGICAL CHANGE

One of the major sources of economic growth and progress throughout history has been technological advance. Innovation, both in methods of production and in the creation of new and better products, is one of the engines of economic progress. Much innovation starts with research and development efforts undertaken by firms in search of profit.

Several economists, notably Joseph Schumpeter and John Kenneth Galbraith, argued in works now considered classics that industrial concentration actually increases the rate of technological advance. As Schumpeter put it in 1942:

> As soon as we . . . inquire into the individual items in which progress was most conspicuous, the trail leads not to the doors of those firms that work under conditions of comparatively free competition but precisely to the doors of the large concerns . . . and a shocking suspicion dawns upon us that big business may have had more to do with creating that standard of life than keeping it down.[6]

This caused the economics profession to pause and take stock of its theories. The conventional wisdom had been that concentration and barriers to entry insulate firms from competition and lead to sluggish performance and slow growth.

The evidence regarding where innovation comes from is mixed. Certainly, most small businesses do not engage in research and development, and most large firms do. When R&D expenditures are considered as a percentage of sales, firms in industries with high concentration ratios spend more on research and development than firms in industries with low concentration ratios.

Oligopolistic companies such as AT&T have done a great deal of research. AT&T's Bell Laboratories (now a new separate company called Lucent Technologies) has probably done more important research over the last several decades than any other organization in the country. It has been estimated that Bell Labs conducted 10 percent of *all* the basic industrial research in the United States during the 1970s. IBM, which despite its recent problems set the industry standard in personal computers, has certainly introduced as much new technology to the computer industry as any other firm.

However, the "high-tech revolution" grew out of many tiny start-up operations. Companies such as Apple Computers, Lotus Development Corporation, and Intel barely existed only a generation ago. The new biotechnology firms that are just beginning to work miracles with genetic engineering are still tiny operations that started with research done by individual scientists in university laboratories.

[6]A. Schumpeter, *Capitalism, Socialism, and Democracy* (New York: Harper, 1942); and J. K. Galbraith, *American Capitalism* (Boston: Houghton Mifflin, 1952).

As with the debate about product differentiation and advertising, significant ambiguity on this subject remains. Indeed, there may be no right answer. Technological change seems to come in fits and starts, sometimes from small firms and sometimes from large ones.

A ROLE FOR GOVERNMENT?

Certainly there is much to guard against in the behavior of large, concentrated industries. Barriers to entry, large size, and product differentiation all lead to market power and to potential inefficiency. Barriers to entry and collusive behavior stop the market from working toward an efficient allocation of resources.

For several reasons, however, economists no longer attack industry concentration with the same fervor they once did. First, the theory of contestable markets shows that even firms in highly concentrated industries can be pushed to produce efficiently under certain market circumstances. Second, the benefits of product differentiation and product competition are real, at least in part. After all, a constant stream of new products and new variations of old products does come to the market almost daily. Third, the effects of concentration on the rate of research and development spending are, at worst, mixed. It is certainly true that large firms do a substantial amount of the total research in the United States. Finally, in some industries, substantial economies of scale simply preclude a completely competitive structure.

In addition to the debate over the desirability of industrial concentration, there is a never-ending debate regarding the role of government in regulating markets. One view is that high levels of concentration lead to inefficiency and that government should act to improve the allocation of resources—to help the market work more efficiently. This logic has been used to justify the laws and other regulations aimed at moderating noncompetitive behavior.

An opposing view holds that the clearest examples of effective barriers to entry are those actually created by government. This view holds that government regulation in past years has been ultimately anticompetitive and has made the allocation of resources less efficient than it would have been with no government involvement. Recall from chapter 13 that those who earn positive profits have an incentive to spend resources to protect themselves and their profits from competitors. This *rent-seeking* behavior may include using the power of government.

Complicating the debate further is international competition. Increasingly, firms are faced with competition from foreign firms in domestic markets at the same time that they are competing with other multinational firms for a share of foreign markets. We live in a truly global economy today. Thus, firms that dominate a domestic market may be fierce competitors in the international arena. This has implications for the proper role of government. Some contend that instead of breaking up AT&T, the government should have allowed it to be a bigger, stronger international competitor. We will return to this debate in the next chapter.

SUMMARY

MONOPOLISTIC COMPETITION

1. A monopolistically competitive industry has the following structural characteristics: (1) a large number of firms, (2) no barriers to entry, and (3) *product differentiation*. Relatively good substitutes for a monopolistic competitor's products are available. Monopolistic competitors try to achieve a degree of market power by differentiating their products.

2. Advocates of free and open competition believe that differentiated products and advertising give the market system its vitality and are the basis of its power. Critics argue that product differentiation and advertising are wasteful and inefficient.

3. By differentiating their products, firms hope to be able to raise price without losing all demand. The demand curve facing a monopolistic competitor is less elastic than the demand curve faced by a perfectly competitive firm but more elastic than the demand curve faced by a monopoly.

4. To maximize profit in the short run, a monopolistically competitive firm will produce as long as the marginal revenue from increasing output and selling it exceeds the marginal cost of producing it. This occurs at the point at which $MR = MC$.

5. When firms enter a monopolistically competitive industry, they introduce close substitutes for the goods being produced. This attracts demand away from the firms already in the industry. Demand faced by each firm shifts left, and profits are ultimately eliminated in the long run. This long-run equilibrium occurs at the point where the demand curve is just tangent to the average total cost curve.

6. Monopolistically competitive firms end up pricing above marginal cost. This is inefficient, as is the fact that monopolistically competitive firms will not realize all economies of scale available.

OLIGOPOLY

7. An *oligopoly* is an industry dominated by a few firms that, by virtue of their individual sizes, are large enough to influence market price. The behavior of a single oligopolistic firm depends on the reactions it expects of all the other firms in the industry. Industrial strategies usually are very complicated and difficult to generalize about.

8. When firms collude, either explicitly or tacitly, they jointly maximize profits by charging an agreed-upon price or by setting output limits and splitting profits. The result is exactly the same as it would be if one firm monopolized the industry: The firm will produce up to the point at which $MR = MC$, and price will be set above marginal cost.

9. The *Cournot model* of oligopoly is based on three assumptions: (1) that there are just two firms in an industry—a situation called *duopoly*; (2) that each firm takes the output of the other as a given; and (3) that both firms maximize profits. The model holds that a series of output-adjustment decisions in the duopoly leads to a final level of output between that which would prevail under perfect competition and that which would be set by a monopoly.

10. A firm faces a kinked demand curve if competitors follow price cuts but fail to respond to price increases. The *kinked demand curve* model predicts that in oligopolistic industries price is likely to be more stable than costs.

11. The *price-leadership* model of oligopoly leads to a result similar but not identical to the collusion model. In this organization, the dominant firm in the industry sets a price and allows competing firms to supply all they want at that price. An oligopoly with a dominant price leader will produce a level of output between what would prevail under competition and what a monopolist would choose in the same industry. It will also set a price between the monopoly price and the competitive price.

12. *Game theory* analyzes the behavior of firms as if their behavior were a series of strategic moves and countermoves. It helps us understand the problem of oligopoly but leaves us with an incomplete and inconclusive set of propositions about the likely behavior of individual oligopolistic firms.

13. A market is *perfectly contestable* if entry to it and exit from it are costless—that is, if a firm can move into a market in search of profits but lose nothing if it fails. Firms in such industries must have mobile capital. In contestable markets, even large oligopolistic firms end up behaving like perfect competitors: Prices are pushed to long-run average cost by competition, and positive profits do not persist.

14. The behavior of oligopolistic firms is likely to lead to an inefficient allocation of resources.

REVIEW TERMS AND CONCEPTS

cartel, 334
Cournot model, 334
dominant strategy, 338
game theory, 337
kinked demand curve model, 335

maximin strategy, 339
monopolistic competition, 323
Nash equilibrium, 339
oligopoly, 333

perfectly contestable market, 339
price leadership, 336
product differentiation, 325
tacit collusion, 334

PROBLEM SET

1. Which of the following industries would you classify as an oligopoly? Which would you classify as monopolistically competitive? Explain your answer. If you are not sure, what information do you need to know to decide?

a. athletic shoes
b. rock bands
c. watches
d. aircraft
e. ice cream

2. All over the world in 1998, people were singing. In Japan, Karaoke bars drew millions of patrons who wanted to sing popular songs accompanied by recorded videos and a prompter lighting up the words. In Taiwan, literally tens of thousands of Karaoke (KTV) establishments exist where groups of people can go into small private rooms and sing to each other while being prompted on a video screen. Each establishment is a bit different from the next. Some are up-scale and expensive; others are less expensive, have a smaller selection of songs to choose from, and are not as well maintained. Ten years ago the industry did not exist.
   a. Into what industry category does the Taiwanese Karaoke business seem to fall?
   b. The first Karaoke establishments in Taiwan made lots of money. What do you think has happened to the price of admission and the profits of most KTV establishments in recent years? Use a graph to explain your answer.

3. For each of the following state whether you agree or disagree. Explain your answer carefully.
   a. Successful product differentiation has the effect of increasing the elasticity of demand facing a monopolistically competitive firm.
   b. Long-run equilibrium in a monopolistically competitive industry is virtually identical to long-run equilibrium in monopoly.
   c. In monopolistically competitive industries, firms are able to exert market power (control prices) by virtue of their size relative to the market.

4. Write a brief essay explaining each statement:
   a. "A dominant firm price leader in an oligopolistic industry may actually function as a monopolistically competitive firm in the face of international competition in *world* markets."
   b. "The Beatles were once a monopolistically competitive firm that became a monopolist."

5. Which of the following markets are likely to be perfectly contestable? Explain your answers.
   a. Shipbuilding
   b. Trucking
   c. Housecleaning services
   d. Wine production

6. The matrix in Figure 1 shows payoffs based on the strategies chosen by two firms. If they collude and hold prices at $10, each will earn profits of $5 million. If A cheats on the agreement, lowering its price, but B does not, A will get 75 percent of the business and earn profits of $8 million and B will lose $2 million. Similarly, if B cheats and A does not, B will earn $8 million and A will lose $2 million. If both cut prices, they will end up with $2 million each in profits.

   Which strategy minimizes the maximum potential loss for A? For B? If you were A, which strategy would you choose? Why? If A cheats, what will B do? If B cheats, what will A do? What is the most likely outcome of such a game? Explain.

7. Assume that you are in the business of building houses. You have analyzed the market carefully, and you know that at a price of $120,000 you will sell 800 houses per year. In addition, you know that at any price above $120,000 no one will buy your houses because the government provides equal quality houses to anyone who wants one at $120,000. You also know that for every $20,000 you lower your price, you will be able to sell an additional 200 units. For example, at a price of $100,000 you can sell 1,000 houses, at a price of $80,000 you can sell 1,200 houses, and so forth.
   a. Sketch the demand curve facing your firm.
   b. Sketch the effective marginal revenue curve facing your firm.
   c. If the marginal cost of building a house is $100,000, how many will you build, and what price will you charge? What if *MC* = $85,000?

8. Examine the short-run graph in Figure 2 for a monopolistically competitive firm.
   a. What is the profit-maximizing level of output?
   b. What price will be charged in the short run?
   c. How much is short-run total revenue? Total cost? Total profit?
   d. Describe what will happen to this firm in the long run.

9. Write a position paper on industrial concentration for a new president. Is this a problem in the United States? What are some of the possible advantages and disadvantages of government actions against concentrated industries?

10. The payoff matrixes in Figure 3 show the payoffs for two games. The payoffs are given in parentheses. The figure on the left refers to the payoff to A, the figure on the right to the payoff to B. Hence (2, 25) means a $2 payoff to A and a $25 payoff to B.
    a. Is there a dominant strategy in each game for each player?

FIGURE 1

	B's STRATEGY	
	STAND BY AGREEMENT	CHEAT
STAND BY AGREEMENT	A's profit = $5 million B's profit = $5 million	A's profit = −$2 million B's profit = $8 million
CHEAT	A's profit = $8 million B's profit = −$2 million	A's profit = $2 million B's profit = $2 million

A's STRATEGY

b. If Game 1 were repeated a large number of times, and you were A and you could change your strategy, what might you do?

c. Which strategy would you play in Game 2? Why?

FIGURE 2

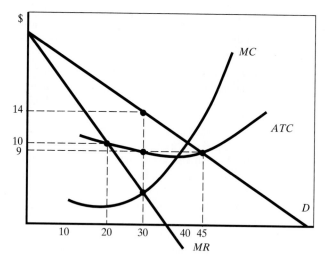

FIGURE 3

GAME 1: PRICING

		FIRM B	
		PRICE HIGH	PRICE LOW
FIRM A	PRICE HIGH	(15, 15)	(2, 25)
	PRICE LOW	(25, 2)	(5, 5)

GAME 2: CHICKEN

		BOB (B)	
		SWERVE	DON'T SWERVE
ANN (A)	SWERVE	(5, 5)	(3, 10)
	DON'T SWERVE	(10, 3)	(−10, −10)

TAKE IT TO THE NET

We invite you to visit the Case and Fair page on the Prentice Hall Web site:

http://www.prenhall.com/casefair

for this chapter's World Wide Web exercise.

Chapter 15

ANTITRUST POLICY
AND REGULATION

IF ALL THE ASSUMPTIONS of perfect competition hold, the allocation of resources in an economy is efficient—the system produces the goods and services that people want, and produces them at lowest cost. No reshuffling of resources or output can improve the welfare of some without reducing the welfare of others. This was the message of chapter 12.

As we began to relax some of the assumptions of perfect competition, we found several sources of market failure. Chapters 13 and 14 examined the first of these, *imperfect markets*. Firms that are able to achieve some degree of control over their products' price are likely to end up charging more than the socially optimal price and producing less than the socially optimal output. Thus far we have looked carefully at three imperfect market structures that tend to be inefficient: monopoly, monopolistic competition, and oligopoly.

When unregulated markets fail to produce efficiently, governments can and do act to improve the allocation of resources. However, government actions can also lead to a less efficient allocation of resources. This chapter discusses in some detail the history and theory of government involvement in imperfectly competitive markets.

THE DEVELOPMENT OF ANTITRUST LAW

Historically, governments in market economies have assumed two basic and seemingly contradictory roles with respect to imperfectly competitive industries: (1) They *promote* competition and restrict market power, primarily through antitrust laws, and (2) they *restrict* competition by regulating industries.

HISTORICAL BACKGROUND

The period immediately following the Civil War was one of rapid growth and change in the United States. As migrants headed to the open spaces, population swelled in the West as well as in the East. Railroads were built between all major cities, and in 1869 a golden spike driven at Promontory Point, Utah, completed the transcontinental railroad line linking the East with California. Between 1864 and 1874, what was already a substantial rail network doubled in size. At the same time, factories sprang up to accommodate new methods of production. Between 1870 and 1913, the economy grew faster than at any other time in U.S. history.

Before the Civil War, most firms had been small and their markets local. The high cost of horse-drawn and water transportation limited access to local markets, and production technologies were efficient only on a small scale. But the railroads opened up the nation, and firms began to compete for national markets. Many of the new technologies exhibited economies of scale; real advantages to size in some industries soon became apparent.

Communications technology also changed. In 1877 an inventor offered to sell Western Union, for $100,000, a patent on a new method of sending information over wires. Alexander Graham Bell's asking price was too high for Western Union, and it turned down the offer. Within 10 years, telephone lines operated by Bell companies crisscrossed the country, linking city after city.[1]

As all of these forces drew the United States together, the character of the economy changed. Small firms selling to local markets were replaced by large firms selling to regional and national markets. With size came power, and with power came hunger for more power. Competition was fierce and often brutal.

The successful exercise of power meant driving competition out of business and controlling markets, and for many firms these became explicit goals. Thousands of smaller firms were gobbled up by big ones. Cartels fixed prices and controlled output. Price cutting to drive competitors out of business was common. In this climate, the **trust** flourished. Under these arrangements, shareholders of independent firms agreed to give up their stock in exchange for trust certificates that entitled them to a share of the trust's common profits. A group of trustees then operated the trust as a monopoly, controlling output and setting price.

It wasn't long before people saw that something was wrong with the system that had emerged. Small independent farmers facing large powerful railroads, monopsonistic buyers, and declining agricultural prices began to organize. Formed in 1867, the National Grange became a strong pressure group on behalf of farmers against the

trust *An arrangement in which shareholders of independent firms agree to give up their stock in exchange for trust certificates that entitle them to a share of the trust's common profits. A group of trustees then operates the trust as a monopoly, controlling output and setting price.*

THE EARLY DAYS OF ANTITRUST ENFORCEMENT, 1881. UNCLE SAM BREAKING THE GOULD-VANDERBILT MONOPOLY—NOTICE THE BAGS OF MONEY UNDER THE DESK!

[1]See Gerald Brock, *The Telecommunications Industry* (Cambridge, Mass.: Harvard University Press, 1980).

power of big business. At the same time, life for the laboring classes in the cities and in factory towns was grim, with child labor, long hours, meager wages, and crowded housing in slums.

"Big business" was held responsible, and its image was probably best captured in cartoons of grotesquely fat men with big cigars and diamond stickpins crushing workers and farmers underfoot. Perhaps the best known and most vilified of these "robber barons" was Jay Gould, who made a fortune manipulating railroad stocks and trying to monopolize the railroad business. In 1881 Gould controlled more miles of railroad track than any other individual or group. While recent research shows that Gould may not have been as evil as most history books portray him, there is no question that he wielded enormous power.

LANDMARK ANTITRUST LEGISLATION

Even though public sentiment increasingly favored reform, faith in the market and in private enterprise also remained strong. In response to public pressure, Congress began to formulate antitrust legislation. In 1887, it created the **Interstate Commerce Commission (ICC)** to oversee and correct abuses in the railroad industry; in 1890, it passed the **Sherman Act**, which declared monopoly and trade restraints illegal. To control monopoly power in general, the Sherman Act turned not to regulation and public enterprise but rather to competition and the market.

▶ **The Sherman Act of 1890**   The real substance of the Sherman Act is contained in two short sections:

> *Section 1.* Every contract, combination in the form of trust or otherwise, or conspiracy, in restraint of trade or commerce among the several States, or with foreign nations, is hereby declared to be illegal. . . .

> *Section 2.* Every person who shall monopolize, or attempt to monopolize, or combine or conspire with any other person or persons, to monopolize any part of the trade or commerce among the several States, or with foreign nations, shall be deemed guilty of a misdemeanor, and, on conviction thereof, shall be punished by fine not exceeding five thousand dollars, or by imprisonment not exceeding one year, or by both said punishments, in the discretion of the court.

The biggest problem with the Sherman Act lay in its interpretation. Its language seemed to declare monopolistic structure, as well as certain kinds of monopolistic conduct, to be illegal. But it was unclear what specific acts were to be considered "restraints of trade." Competition itself can act as a restraint.

When a statute is unclear, it usually falls to the courts to provide clarification. Unfortunately, the courts only added to the confusion in the early years of antitrust legislation and enforcement. In 1911 two major antitrust cases were brought before the Supreme Court. The two companies involved, Standard Oil and American Tobacco, seemed to epitomize the textbook definition of monopoly, and both appeared to exhibit the structure and the conduct outlawed by the Sherman Act. Standard Oil controlled about 91 percent of the refining industry, and although the exact figure is still disputed, the American Tobacco Trust probably controlled between 75 percent and 90 percent of the market for all tobacco products except cigars. Both companies had used tough tactics to swallow up competition or to drive it out of business. Not surprisingly, the Supreme Court found both firms guilty of violating Sections 1 and 2 of the Sherman Act and ordered their dissolution.[2]

Interstate Commerce Commission (ICC) *A federal regulatory group created by Congress in 1887 to oversee and correct abuses in the railroad industry.*

Sherman Act *Passed by Congress in 1890, the act declared every contract or conspiracy to restrain trade among states or nations illegal and declared any attempt at monopoly, successful or not, a misdemeanor. Interpretation of which specific behaviors were illegal fell to the courts.*

STANDARD OIL CONTROLLED ABOUT 91 PERCENT OF THE REFINING INDUSTRY IN 1911.

---

[2]*United States v. Standard Oil Co. of New Jersey*, 221 U.S. 1(1911): *United States v. American Tobacco Co.*, 221 U.S. 106(1911).

The court made clear, however, that the Sherman Act did not outlaw every action that seemed to restrain trade, only those that were "unreasonable." In enunciating this **rule of reason**, the court seemed to say that structure alone was not a criterion for unreasonableness. Thus it was possible for a near-monopoly not to violate the Sherman Act as long as it had won its market using "reasonable" tactics.

Subsequent court cases confirmed that a firm could be convicted of violating the Sherman Act only if it had exhibited *unreasonable conduct*. Between 1911 and 1920, cases were brought against Eastman Kodak, International Harvester, United Shoe Machinery, and United States Steel. The first three controlled overwhelming shares of their respective markets and the fourth controlled 60 percent of the country's capacity to produce steel. But all four cases were dismissed on the grounds that these companies had shown no evidence of "unreasonable conduct."

The enunciation of the rule of reason did little to clarify the language of the Sherman Act, and just what explicit acts the courts would deem "unreasonable" remained a mystery. The original supporters of the act were upset by the lack of enforcement; business simply wanted to know the rules of the game. In response, Congress went back to the drawing board in 1914 and passed the Clayton Act and the Federal Trade Commission Act.

> ➤ **The Clayton Act and the Federal Trade Commission, 1914** Designed both to strengthen the Sherman Act and to clarify the rule of reason, the **Clayton Act** of 1914 outlawed a number of specific practices. First, it made *tying contracts* illegal. Such contracts force a customer to buy one product to obtain another. Second, it limited mergers that would "substantially lessen competition or tend to create a monopoly." Third, it banned *price discrimination*—charging different customers different prices for reasons other than changes in cost or matching competitors' prices.

The **Federal Trade Commission (FTC)**, created by Congress in 1914, was established to investigate "the organization, business conduct, practices, and management" of companies that engage in interstate commerce. At the same time, the act establishing the Commission added another vaguely worded prohibition to the books: "Unfair methods of competition in commerce are hereby declared unlawful." The determination of what constituted "unfair" behavior was left up to the Commission. The FTC was also given the power to issue "cease-and-desist orders" where it found behavior in violation of the law.

Nonetheless, the legislation of 1914 retained the focus on *conduct*, and thus the rule of reason remained central to all antitrust action in the courts.

> ➤ **The Alcoa Case, 1945** The history of antitrust law has been an ongoing struggle between the rule of reason and various actions and outcomes that the courts have declared *per se* (intrinsic) violations of antitrust law. For example, a **per se rule** against price fixing evolved over a number of years until 1926, when the Supreme Court held unequivocally that price fixing violates Section 1 of the Sherman Act whether the resulting price is reasonable or not.

Prior to 1945, most antitrust law enforcement continued to focus on *conduct*. In most cases, the rule of reason determined whether the conduct was or was not illegal. Even though United States Steel grew large enough to dominate the market for iron and steel, for example, it did not coerce its remaining rivals or conspire to fix prices, and thus it did not engage in unreasonable conduct. As the court said, "The law does not make *mere size* [italics added] an offense or the existence of unexerted power an offense." In short, the courts decreed, it was not illegal to be a benevolent monopoly.

This was the basic position of the courts until 1945, when the rule of reason was challenged in a different way in the landmark Alcoa case.[3] The United States charged

---

³*United States v. Aluminum Co. of America*, 148 F. 2nd 416 (1945).

rule of reason *The criterion introduced by the Supreme Court in 1911 to determine whether a particular action was illegal ("unreasonable") or legal ("reasonable") within the terms of the Sherman Act.*

Clayton Act *Passed by Congress in 1914 to strengthen the Sherman Act and clarify the rule of reason, the act outlawed specific monopolistic behaviors such as tying contracts, price discrimination, and unlimited mergers.*

Federal Trade Commission (FTC) *A federal regulatory group created by Congress in 1914 to investigate the structure and behavior of firms engaging in interstate commerce, to determine what constitutes unlawful "unfair" behavior, and to issue cease-and-desist orders to those found in violation of antitrust law.*

per se rule *A rule enunciated by the courts declaring a particular action or outcome to be a per se (intrinsic) violation of antitrust law, whether the result is reasonable or not.*

the Aluminum Company of America (Alcoa) with violating Section 2 of the Sherman Act by monopolizing the market for newly refined aluminum. At the time, Alcoa controlled 90 percent of the raw aluminum market.

The court did not hold that any specific behavior, or conduct, by which Alcoa achieved its monopoly position was in itself illegal. It said, in fact, that Alcoa had used "normal, prudent, but not predatory business practices. . . . These included building capacity well ahead of demand." Rather, it was the *structure* of the market itself that led Judge Learned Hand to order the dissolution of Alcoa:

> No monopolist monopolizes unconscious of what he is doing. So here "Alcoa" meant to keep, and did keep, that complete and exclusive hold upon the ingot market with which it started. That was to "monopolize" that market, however innocently it otherwise proceeded.

One other case is worth a brief note here, because it extended the Sherman Act as it was interpreted in the Alcoa case to cover an oligopoly that was acting like a monopoly. In 1946 the United States brought suit against the three largest domestic cigarette producers. The court found no specific evidence of collusion, but did find that the firms had acted *as if* they were taking account of each other's behavior in setting prices. The case, in essence, extended the law to include tacit collusion as well as explicit conspiracy.[4]

➤ **Other Legislation** Several other pieces of legislation designed to deal with specific problem areas followed the Clayton Act. In 1921 the **Willis-Graham Act** formally exempted telephone mergers from antitrust review. The telephone industry was one of the very few industries that the government essentially declared a natural monopoly and decided to regulate rather than dissolve.

The **Wheeler-Lea Act** of 1938 extended the language of the Federal Trade Commission Act to include "deceptive" as well as "unfair" methods of competition. The act thus gave the FTC the power to deal with false and deceptive advertising and the sale of harmful products.

The **Celler-Kefauver Act** of 1950 extended the government's authority to ban mergers. The original Clayton Act could block only *horizontal mergers* (mergers in which firms producing the same product join together). The Celler-Kefauver Act extended the

Willis-Graham Act (1921)
Declared the telephone industry a natural monopoly and exempted telephone mergers from review.

Wheeler-Lea Act (1938)
Extended the language of the Federal Trade Commission Act to include "deceptive" as well as "unfair" methods of competition.

Celler-Kefauver Act (1950)
Extended the government's authority to ban vertical and conglomerate mergers.

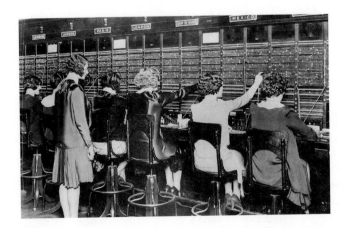

THE GOVERNMENT DECLARED THE TELEPHONE INDUSTRY A NATURAL MONOPOLY BACK IN THE 1920s.

---

[4]See William H. Nicholls, "The Tobacco Case of 1946," *American Economic Review* (May 1949), p. 296. Also *American Tobacco Co. et al. v. United States*, 328 U.S. 781 (1946). In the *American Tobacco* case, fines totaling $255,000 were levied against the tobacco companies and their executives, but no structural remedies were applied. There is little evidence that the behavior of these companies changed after the fines were paid.

government's power to block *vertical mergers* (mergers of firms at various stages in a production process—movie-making companies, movie-distribution companies, and theater chains, for example) and *conglomerate mergers* (mergers of firms producing unrelated products). In all cases, however, the fact that the merger would substantially lessen competition had to be established.

The most recent significant piece of antitrust legislation is the **Hart-Scott-Rodino Antitrust Procedural Improvements Act** of 1980. Many large firms, such as law firms and accounting firms, are not corporations and prior to 1980 were not subject to the antitrust laws. The Hart-Scott-Rodino Act extended the antitrust laws to proprietorships and partnerships. In addition, the act requires that all proposed mergers between firms be reported to the Justice Department.

REGULATION OF MERGERS

The Clayton Act of 1914 had given government the authority to limit mergers that might "substantially lessen competition in an industry." The Celler-Kefauver Act of 1950 enabled the Justice Department to monitor and enforce these provisions. (For a recent Justice Department move against a proposed merger, see Issues and Debates box, "Justice Department Halts Merger of Office Depot and Staples in 1997.")

In 1968 the Justice Department issued its first guidelines designed to reduce uncertainty about the mergers it would find acceptable. The 1968 guidelines were strict. For example, if the largest four firms in an industry controlled 75 percent or more of a market, an acquiring firm with a 15 percent market share would be challenged if it wanted to acquire a firm that controlled as little as an additional 1 percent of the market.

In 1982 the Antitrust Division, in keeping with President Reagan's hands-off policy toward big business, issued a new set of far more lenient guidelines. Revised in 1984, they remain in place today. The 1982/1984 standards are based on a measure of market structure called the **Herfindahl-Hirschman Index (HHI)**. The HHI is calculated by expressing the market share of each firm in the industry as a percentage, squaring these figures, and adding. For example, in an industry in which two firms each control 50 percent of the market, the index is

$$50^2 + 50^2 = 2,500 + 2,500 = 5,000.$$

For an industry in which four firms each control 25 percent of the market, the index is

$$25^2 + 25^2 + 25^2 + 25^2 = 625 + 625 + 625 + 625 = 2,500.$$

Table 15.1 shows HHI calculations for several hypothetical industries. The Justice Department's courses of action, summarized in Figure 15.1, are as follows:

If the Herfindahl-Hirschman Index is less than 1,000, the industry is considered unconcentrated, and any proposed merger will go unchallenged by the Justice

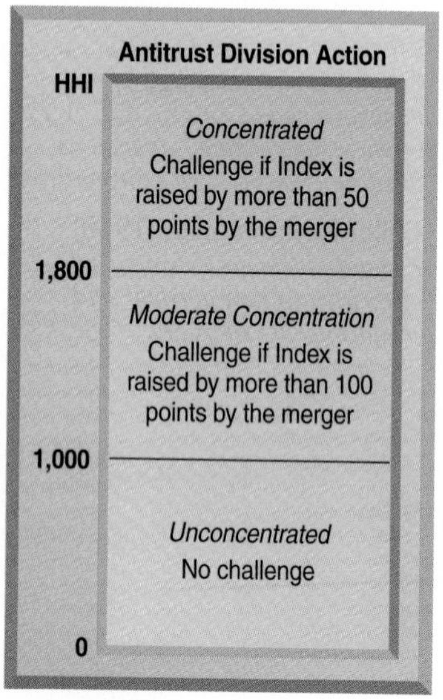

Hart-Scott-Rodino Act *The 1980 antitrust legislation that extended the antitrust laws to proprietorships and partnerships and requires that all proposed mergers be reported to the Department of Justice.*

Herfindahl-Hirschman Index (HHI) *A mathematical calculation that uses market share figures to determine whether or not a proposed merger will be challenged by the government.*

FIGURE 15.1

Department of Justice Merger Guidelines (revised 1984)

Note: See Phillip Areeda, *Antitrust Analysis*, 3rd ed. 1986 supplement (Boston: Little Brown, 1986), p. 185.

TABLE 15.1 CALCULATION OF A SIMPLE HERFINDAHL-HIRSCHMAN INDEX FOR FOUR HYPOTHETICAL INDUSTRIES, EACH WITH NO MORE THAN FOUR FIRMS

		PERCENTAGE SHARE OF:			HERFINDAHL-HIRSCHMAN INDEX
	FIRM 1	FIRM 2	FIRM 3	FIRM 4	
Industry A	50	50	—	—	$50^2 + 50^2 = 5,000$
Industry B	80	10	10	—	$80^2 + 10^2 + 10^2 = 6,600$
Industry C	25	25	25	25	$25^2 + 25^2 + 25^2 + 25^2 = 2,500$
Industry D	40	20	20	20	$40^2 + 20^2 + 20^2 + 20^2 = 2,800$

JUSTICE DEPARTMENT HALTS MERGER
OF OFFICE DEPOT AND STAPLES IN 1997

In one of the most widely publicized cases in recent history, the Antitrust Division of the Department of Justice fought the merger of two huge office supply store chains, Staples and Office Depot. On June 30, 1997, a federal district judge issued a restraining order supporting the position of the Justice Department:

ANTITRUST OFFICIALS ARGUE AGAINST OFFICE SUPPLY DEAL: STAPLES AND OFFICE DEPOT DEFEND MERGER

> Government antitrust officials said today that internal company documents demonstrated that a merger of the office supply giants **Staples Inc.** and **Office Depot Inc.** would allow the new company to raise prices with impunity in dozens of markets across the United States.
>
> George S. Cary, deputy director of the F.T.C.'s antitrust bureau, said that internal pricing studies by Staples showed that the office supply chain charged significantly more for identical goods in markets where it had no competition from either of the other two office supply superstore chains, Office Depot and **Office Max Inc.**[a]

OFFICE DEPOT AND STAPLES MERGER HALTED: JUDGE'S RULING APPEARS TO DOOM AGREEMENT

> Executives of the office supply giants **Staples Inc.** and **Office Depot Inc.** said today that their proposed merger was almost certainly dead after a Federal judge issued an order temporarily blocking the $4 billion combination.
>
> Company officials said they were stunned and disappointed by the decision of Judge Thomas F. Hogan of the United States District Court for the District of Columbia, who ruled that the proposed merger would drastically reduce competition in the office products business.
>
> The judge accepted the Government's contention that office supply superstores constitute a unique market segment and that allowing two of the three major competitors in the field to combine would permit the new company, with more than 1,100 stores and $11 billion in annual sales, to raise prices with impunity. . . .

> The decision was a major victory for Federal Trade Commission antitrust lawyers, who brought the case this spring despite sharp conflict within the agency over the wisdom of challenging the merger. The Government's assertion that the Staples–Office Depot combination would give the company near-monopoly pricing power was controversial in antitrust circles because the company would control only 6 percent to 8 percent of the overall office products market.[b]

Sources: [a]John M. Broder, "Antitrust Officials Argue Against Office Supply Deal," *The New York Times*, May 20, 1997, p. D2; [b]John M. Broder, "Office Depot and Staples Merger Halted," *The New York Times*, July 1, 1997, p. D1. Copyright © 1997 by The New York Times Co. Reprinted by permission.

For more on antitrust and regulation, see the Case and Fair Web page at
http://www.prenhall.com/casefair.

Department. If the index is between 1,000 and 1,800, the department will challenge any merger that would increase the index by over 100 points. Herfindahl indexes above 1,800 mean that the industry is considered concentrated already, and the Justice Department will challenge any merger that pushes the index up more than 50 points.

CHAPTER FIFTEEN
*Antitrust Policy
and Regulation*

Some industries with high Herfindahl Indexes include:

Industry	H-H Index
Breakfast cereal	2,253
Chips and snacks	2,710
Primary copper	2,827
Electric lamps	2,702
Batteries	2,929
Photographic equipment	2,408

Source: U.S. Dept. of Commerce, Economics and Statistics Administration, 1997.

In 1982 two breweries, Pabst and Heileman, proposed a merger. At the time, the Herfindahl index in the beer industry was about 1772. Before the merger, each firm had about 7.5 percent of the market. Thus, after a merger, the new firm would have a combined share of 15 percent. The merger would thus raise the index by 112.5:

$$(15^2) - (7.5^2 + 7.5^2) = 225 - 112.5 = 112.5$$

$$\underbrace{}_{Post\text{-}merger} \underbrace{}_{Pre\text{-}merger}$$

Because the merger increased the index by more than 100 points, it was challenged by the Justice Department.

In 1984 the same two companies reapplied to the Justice Department for permission to merge. This time Pabst agreed to sell four of its brands—accounting for over one third of its total production—and one brewery to a third party. The sale was sufficient to bring the merger within the guidelines, and the Antitrust Division dropped its objections. But the merger never took place. Heileman was bought by an Australian company and in 1991 went bankrupt.

In 1992 the Department of Justice and the FTC issued joint Horizontal Merger Guidelines updating and expanding the 1984 guidelines. The most interesting part of the new provisions is that the government will examine each potential merger to determine if it enhances the firms' power to engage in "coordinated interaction" with other firms in the industry. The guidelines define "coordinated interaction" as:

> actions by a group of firms that are profitable for each of them only as the result of the accommodating reactions of others. This behavior includes tacit or express collusion, and may or may not be lawful in and of itself.[5]

Clearly, the new guidelines show the increased influence of game theory models of non-cooperative collusion (see chapter 14).

THE ENFORCEMENT OF ANTITRUST LAW

With this brief history of the antitrust laws, we turn to antitrust enforcement.

INITIATING ANTITRUST ACTIONS

Two different administrative bodies have the responsibility for initiating actions on behalf of the U.S. government against individuals or companies thought to be in violation of the antitrust laws. These agencies are the Antitrust Division of the Justice Department and the Federal Trade Commission. In addition, private citizens can initiate antitrust actions.

---

[5]U.S. Department of Justice, Federal Trade Commission, *Horizontal Merger Guidelines*, 1992, p. 34.

➤ **Government Actions: The Antitrust Division and the FTC** The 1914 legislation that established the FTC, and the Wheeler-Lea Act that followed, gave the FTC broad powers to forbid "unfair and deceptive" conduct. The FTC is composed of five members appointed by the president and confirmed by the Senate for terms of seven years. A large staff of lawyers and economists investigates and prosecutes offenders. The FTC can issue cease-and-desist orders to offenders, but such orders carry no criminal or civil penalties for past damages or monetary fines. In essence, the FTC exists to prevent *further* unlawful action, and in practice most FTC proceedings end in formal agreements rather than in cease-and-desist orders.

The FTC has also established a set of trade regulation rules that make clear what practices it deems unfair and subject to action. One such rule, for example, states that a service station that fails to display octane ratings clearly on gas pumps is guilty of an "unfair or deceptive act or practice." These rules simplify the process of adjudication by making the standards of conduct clear.

Along with the **Antitrust Division of the Department of Justice**, the FTC initiates actions against those who violate antitrust law. The power to impose penalties and remedies formally rests with the courts, but the Antitrust Division decides which cases to prosecute. All cases involving criminal complaints against individuals or companies originate in the Antitrust Division, but it is fairly small. Its resources are limited, and the vigor with which it pursues antitrust violators changes with the views of the president and the attorney general.

➤ **Private Actions** Antitrust cases may also be brought to the courts by private citizens. Since 1914, private persons have been empowered to bring suits as long as they can clearly demonstrate a significant injury or threat of injury. Much like the old rule of reason, however, the law is vague about what constitutes a "significant injury or threat." The original suit against AT&T that ended in the divestiture in 1982 was brought by a private company, MCI.

SANCTIONS AND REMEDIES

The courts are empowered to impose a number of remedies if they find that antitrust law has been violated. Certain civil and criminal penalties can be exacted for past wrongs, and other measures can prevent future wrongs. Specifically, the courts can "(1) forbid the continuation of illegal acts, (2) force the defendant to dispose of the fruits of his or her wrong, and (3) restore competitive conditions":

> In fashioning effective relief, the courts have considerable discretion in their choice of remedy. Antitrust decrees have, for example, ordered defendants to dispose of subsidiary companies; to create a company with appropriate assets and personnel to compete effectively with defendant; to make patents, trademarks and trade secrets or know-how available to competitors at reasonable royalties or even without any royalties; to provide goods and services to all who wish to buy; to revise the terms on which defendant buys or sells; and to cancel, shorten or modify outstanding agreements with competitors, suppliers or customers.[6]

➤ **Consent Decrees** Between 75 percent and 80 percent of all government-initiated civil suits are settled with the signing of a consent decree. **Consent decrees** are formal agreements between the prosecuting government and the defendants that must be approved by the courts. Such decrees can be signed before, during, or after a trial. Because antitrust cases are long and expensive to litigate, both parties benefit if settlement comes early. A recent case involving allegations of price-fixing by Ivy League

Antitrust Division (of the Department of Justice) *One of two federal agencies empowered to act against those in violation of antitrust laws. It initiates action against those who violate antitrust laws and decides which cases to prosecute and against whom to bring criminal charges.*

consent decrees *Formal agreements on remedies between all the parties to an antitrust case that must be approved by the courts. Consent decrees can be signed before, during, or after a trial.*

---

[6]Phillip Areeda, *Antitrust Analysis: Problems, Text and Cases*, 3rd ed. (Boston: Little, Brown, 1986), p. 61.

colleges was settled before trial when eight of the nine schools involved signed a consent decree.

Consent decrees have encompassed a variety of agreements. A company may agree to give up a patent that is serving as a barrier to effective competition, for example, or it may agree to be broken up into separate competing companies, as in the AT&T case (described in detail later in this chapter).

The most celebrated recent consent decree involved Microsoft, which the Justice Department accused of using its dominance in operating-system software to gain market power in other areas. (Virtually all IBM and IBM-compatible personal computers use Microsoft DOS or Windows as their main operating system.) In July 1994, the Justice Department reached a tentative agreement with Microsoft and did not move to file a formal complaint. Under the consent decree, Microsoft agreed to give computer manufacturers more freedom to install software from other software companies. In 1997, Microsoft found itself charged with violating the terms of the consent decree and was back in court. A partial agreement was struck with the Justice Department in January 1998 (see Applications box, "An Unlawful Monopoly?").

➤ **Criminal Actions**   In 1955 and again in 1974, the sanctions for violating the Sherman Act were changed. The original act held that violations were misdemeanors and made no distinction between individuals and corporations. Today the penalties are considerably more severe:

> Every person who shall make any contract or engage in any combination or conspiracy hereby declared to be illegal shall be deemed guilty of a *felony*, and on conviction thereof, shall be punished by a fine not exceeding *one million dollars* if a corporation, or, if any other person, *one hundred thousand dollars* or by imprisonment not exceeding three years, or by both said punishments, in the discretion of the court.[7]

The practice of the Antitrust Division has been to limit criminal proceedings to outrageous violations, where intent to violate is clear. In 1961, for example, seven prominent executives of major U.S. corporations that produced electrical equipment were found guilty of flagrantly violating well-established laws. They had secretly met and agreed to fix prices. All seven received 30-day jail sentences. (For two recent price-fixing cases, see Issues and Debates box, "Price-Fixing Allegations in 1997.")

➤ **Treble Damages**   Any person or private company that sustains injury or financial loss because of an antitrust violation can recover damages from the guilty party over and above any fines levied. The award made by the court must be three times the actual damages (*treble damages*):

> [A]ny person injured in his business or property by reason of anything forbidden in the antitrust laws. . . .shall recover threefold the damages by him sustained, and the cost of suit, including a reasonable attorney's fee.[8]

This provision, of course, provides a powerful incentive for private parties to invoke the antitrust laws.

EXEMPTIONS FROM ANTITRUST STATUTES

The antitrust laws specifically exempt several industries. As noted, the Willis-Graham Act of 1921 declared the telephone industry a natural monopoly and exempted telephone mergers from review. Over the years, Congress and the courts have added others to the list. Today this list includes, but is not limited to, lobbying organizations, labor unions, sports organizations, and regulated industries.

FAST FACTS

In October 1996, Archer Daniels Midland Company, one of the country's most influential corporations, pleaded guilty to criminal price-fixing charges and was fined $100 million. That fine is by far the largest ever obtained by the Justice Department in a price-fixing case. The charge was that Archer Daniels conspired to fix the prices of lysine, a feed additive, and citric acid, used in a number of food products.

[7]26 Stat. 209 (1890), as amended 15 U.S.C.A. 1–7 (1980). Changes to the statute are italicized in the text.
[8]See Areeda, *Antitrust Analysis*.

AN UNLAWFUL MONOPOLY?

In October 1997, the Justice Department filed charges against computer software giant Microsoft. The following is an excerpt from the Justice Department petition to the U.S. District Court:

AN 'UNLAWFUL MONOPOLY'

Microsoft is the world's largest and most powerful personal computer software producer. Through its Windows operating system products, it possesses a monopoly in the market for operating-system software for Intel-compatible personal computers and from this monopoly enjoys a corporate profit rate and market capitalization that are among the highest of any major American company.

Microsoft unlawfully maintained its monopoly by using *exclusionary and anticompetitive contracts to market its PC operating system software. To stop this conduct, the United States sued Microsoft in July 1994. . . . Microsoft settled that lawsuit by consenting to [a] final judgment which prohibits Microsoft from imposing various anti-competitive terms in its contracts with PC original-equipment manufacturers (OEMs) that pre-install Microsoft's operating-system software products on the computers they sell.*

Conditioning its Windows licenses on licensing Internet Explorer is precisely the sort of improper use of Microsoft's market power to protect and extend its monopoly that this court's final judgment sought to prevent and which it expressly prohibits. [This] *constitutes a clear and serious violation of the terms and purpose of the final judgment. . . .*

In December 1997, a U.S. District Court ordered Microsoft to stop forcing computer makers to install its browser, Internet Explorer, as a condition of licensing Windows 95. For a month Microsoft held out, but on January 22, 1998, Microsoft and the Justice Department reached an agreement. Under the agreement computer makers could obtain Windows 95 with Internet Explorer disabled or with its icon removed. While all the issues were not settled, the war was on hold.

Source: U.S. Department of Justice (Web site), November 11, 1997.

For more on this subject, see the Case and Fair Web page at
http://www.prenhall.com/casefair.

➤ **Lobbying** A monopoly would be willing to pay most of its monopoly profits to protect itself from competition. (Recall rent-seeking behavior in chapter 13.) One of the activities that monopolies could spend these profits on is lobbying for exemption from the antitrust laws. In the mid-1960s, Congress decided that representatives of any industry group can join together for purposes of lobbying Congress. Lobbying is protected under the *Noerr-Pennington Doctrine*, named after the court cases in which it was first enunciated.[9]

➤ **Labor Unions** Although the Sherman Act was originally used to fight the power of labor unions, the Clayton Act specifically exempted collective bargaining agreements from antitrust actions.

➤ **Sports Organizations** The issue of monopoly power versus competition in sports, both college and professional, is extremely complex and has been the subject of countless court cases. Players have argued, with some success, that the sports leagues enjoy monopoly power and that they have conspired against the players to hold down salaries. Similarly, entry into professional baseball, basketball, and football leagues is effectively barred. I can't simply hire a team, build a stadium, and start competing in

---

[9]*Eastern Railroad Presidents Conference v. Noerr Motor Freight, Inc.*, 365 U.S. 127 (1961); and *United Mine Workers of America v. Pennington*, 381 U.S. 637 (1965).

PRICE-FIXING ALLEGATIONS IN 1997

Two price-fixing cases hit the newspapers in 1997. One involved a complicated bid-rigging scheme in the art market; the other involved toilet tissue.

TOP ART DEALERS ARE SUBPOENAED IN POSSIBLE PRICE-RIGGING SCHEME

United States Justice Department investigators have subpoenaed truckloads of financial documents from more than a dozen prominent Manhattan art dealers and from Sotheby's and Christie's, the world's largest auction houses, in what appears to be a wide-ranging antitrust investigation. . . .

It has long been rumored in the art world that some dealers try to buy on the cheap, by forming rings of dealers who agree to refrain from bidding against one another. The practice, called "bid pooling" or "bid rigging" inhibits prices from reaching their fair value at auction. Then the dealers resell the work at an exaggerated

profit. Such collusive behavior is prohibited as an illegal restraint of trade under the Sherman Antitrust Act. Penalties for violations can include substantial fines and imprisonment of up to three years. . . .

Under the practice, a ring of dealers chooses a single dealer to bid on an object. The dealers then hold a private auction among themselves.

They often split the profit among themselves that arises out of the difference between the low price paid by the individual dealer and the higher price paid at the private auction.[a]

PAPER MAKERS FACING PRICE-FIXING SUIT

The nation's leading producers of toilet tissue and other sanitary paper products were accused of price fixing today in a suit by the State of Florida.

The Florida Attorney General, Bob Butterworth, says the cost of

wood pulp has fallen 18 percent since 1989, while the cost of commercial sanitary paper has soared 41 percent. . . .

The complaint seeks civil penalties of $1 million against each of the 10 for violation of Florida's antitrust statute. It also seeks $10,000 for each violation of Florida's Deceptive and Unfair Trade Practices Act. It was filed in a Federal court in Gainesville, Fla.

The court action accuses the companies of "conspiring to fix the prices of sanitary paper products sold to schools, hospitals, prisons, hotels, restaurants, factories and other large-scale purchasers."[b]

Sources: [a]Carol Vogel, "Top Art Dealers Are Subpoenaed in Possible Price-Rigging Scheme," *The New York Times,* June 3, 1997, p. 1; [b]"Paper Makers Facing Price-Fixing Suit," *The New York Times,* May 14, 1997, p. D5. Copyright © 1997 by The New York Times Co. Reprinted by permission.

For more on antitrust and price fixing, see the Case and Fair Web page at http://www.prenhall.com/casefair.

---

one of the existing leagues. These issues were very much on the public's mind during the U.S. baseball strike of 1994 to 1995.

Congress has specifically allowed the mergers of the American Football League with the National Football League and the National Basketball Association with the American Basketball Association despite the fact that the amount of competition was substantially decreased by the two mergers. While debate continues about whether the sports exemption is in the public interest, it is clear that sports associations enjoy considerable protection from the antitrust statutes in their dealings with players, owners, and potential competitors.

ANTITRUST POLICY IN EUROPE AND JAPAN

The nations of the European Union and Japan have also instituted antitrust policy, though these countries' laws are much more lenient. The basis of competition policy in the European Union is contained in Articles 85 and 86 of the 1957 Treaty of Rome. Article 85 deals with the joint exercise of market power and outlaws price-fixing and agreements to limit production or share markets. A second part of Article 85, however, provides for exemptions from these rules in the case of any agreement "which contributes to improving production or distribution of goods or to promoting technical or economic progress, while allowing consumers a fair share of the resulting benefit . . ."[10] This provision provides the enforcement authority great latitude in interpreting agreements. No such clause exists in U.S. antitrust laws.

Article 86 of the Treaty of Rome deals with anticompetitive behavior on the part of single firms. Among other things it outlaws predatory pricing, tying contracts, and unfair trade practices.

Enforcement of the EU's antitrust laws is handled by a Directorate General of the European Union Commission. Under the Treaty, the Commission is empowered to levy fines and to declare contracts null and void. Since 1989, the Commission has also had the power to regulate mergers.

Japan has had an antitrust policy since 1947, when it passed the Antimonopoly Law. The law prohibits "private monopolization, unreasonable restraint of trade and unfair business practices, by preventing the excessive concentration of economic power."[11] In its basic provisions, the law appears to be similar to the corresponding laws of the United States and the European Union.

But in practice, Japanese antitrust policy has been very different. The Japanese Fair Trade Commission (JFTC), empowered to enforce the Antimonopoly Law in Japan, operates in a society very suspicious of unfettered competition and within a centralized and hierarchical government that has traditionally played a substantial role in protecting and promoting specific industries. The specific goals of the Ministry of Trade and Industry (MITI) include promotion of large-scale industry and strategic mergers to help industries compete internationally. In addition, Japanese law specifically allows legal cartels during periods of hard times. The number of legal cartels in Japan peaked at over 1,000 during the mid-1960s, but has dropped steadily since.

While many investigations are conducted by the JFTC, few end up with charges being filed, and fines are rare. When criminal charges were filed in November 1991 against a cartel of wrapping paper manufacturers, it was only the second set of such charges ever filed in Japan.[12]

THE ANTITRUST ENFORCEMENT DEBATE

Should the Antitrust Division be more aggressive in prosecuting antitrust violators? Just what level of enforcement activity should we settle for? Critics of business who favor more enforcement argue that the Antitrust Division does not have the resources to enforce the law.[13] Others argue that while some level of enforcement activity is useful, the Antitrust Division is overly aggressive and should be scaled back. Administration and enforcement of the law are costly, and laws and penalties neither can nor do stop all undesirable behavior.

The break-up of AT&T in 1982 brought this debate into the public arena. Some people believe that the outcome of the AT&T case has been a disaster, that it has torn apart the greatest telephone company in the world and has made consumers worse off. In fact, local telephone rates have risen substantially since 1982. Others argue that the outcome of the case has been an enormous success and we are just beginning to see the fruits of intense competition in the form of new and better products and services. They

---

[10]Stephen Martin, *Industrial Economics* (New York: Macmillan, 1994), p. 55.

[11]Ibid., p. 61.

[12]Ibid., p. 191.

[13]For fiscal year 1995, the budget of the Antitrust Division was about $75 million per year. Staffing was 398 full-time employees that year, down from over 600 in 1990. (See *Budget of the United States, Fiscal Year 1995.*)

say the rise in local rates is due to the gradual elimination of an inefficient subsidy to local rate payers that regulators had, over the years, unwisely built into long-distance rates. They also say long-distance rates have fallen sharply.

The issues raised by this debate require further discussion. In the sections that follow we review the economic logic behind the antitrust laws before turning to a discussion of recent criticism leveled at enforcement practices.

THE CASE FOR ANTITRUST ENFORCEMENT

In a sense, the first part of this book—particularly chapters 13 and 14—has already made the case for antitrust laws. As you have seen, competition has many potential benefits. It drives firms to produce at least cost and provides an incentive to introduce new, efficient production techniques and new products. Thus, the argument goes, the government should step in when anticompetitive behavior or monopoly power threatens to rob society of the benefits of open competition.

The antitrust laws do more than condemn monopoly; they also restrict certain specific kinds of conduct, whether the industry is monopolistic or not. Most of the specific practices outlawed by the antitrust laws can result in serious social costs and waste of society's scarce resources. Thus, it is easy to build an economic case for governmental enforcement of prohibitions against unfair and deceptive practices, price-fixing, collusion, and price discrimination.

> **Unfair or Deceptive Practices**   For a market economy to work, consumers must have valid information on product availability, quality, and price. The variety and complexity of modern life forces the average consumer to consider many products that cannot be fully understood or personally evaluated. Medical care, financial services, insurance, drugs, food products, consumer electronics, and products in other areas are so complicated and specialized that the consumer may be misinformed about them, if not deliberately deceived. In such cases, it may be reasonable for the government to act on behalf of consumers to prevent unfair and deceptive acts or practices. (We discuss this in chapter 16.)

> **Price-Fixing and Collusion**   Firms can use price-fixing and collusion to protect themselves from competition. Both practices allow firms that would otherwise compete to act together as a monopoly and reap monopoly profits. Competitive markets drive product prices close to the cost of production, and in the long run competitive firms will earn only normal profits. If a monopolist were to gain control of an industry, it would clearly be in his or her interest to cut output, raise price, and do everything possible to prevent competition. If firms were permitted to set prices jointly or collude to restrict output and share the market, they would act just like a monopoly, and consumers would lose. Consumers would pay more for the same product than they would pay under competition, and less of the product would be produced. (In chapter 13 you learned how the size of this net loss to society from the monopolization of an industry is calculated.)

price discrimination *Occurs when a firm charges different buyers different prices for the same product. Such strategies are illegal if they drive out competition.*

> **Price Discrimination**   Under the Clayton Act, **price discrimination** that tends to lessen competition is illegal. Suppose several companies buy rolled steel to make filing cabinets. The largest producer, by virtue of its size and bargaining power, may be able to obtain a very low price from the steel producers, a price not justified by cost savings due to large volume. The bargaining power gives the large producer an advantage over its smaller competitors. This can lead to monopoly power in the long run.

Not all forms of price discrimination are inefficient. *Third degree price discrimination*, dividing consumers into identifiable groups and charging them different prices, goes on all around us. Airlines, druggists, movie theaters, public transportation systems, and telephone companies all charge different prices for children, senior citizens,

PART THREE
*Market Imperfections
and Government*

students, military personnel, and other identifiable groups. Professional journals charge individuals and institutions (libraries) very different subscription fees. Rental car companies offer discounts to members of AAA, frequent fliers, and employees of certain businesses.

For third degree price discrimination to work, resales must be prevented. Otherwise, the differences in price would be arbitraged. *Arbitrage* occurs when someone buys a good at one price and immediately sells it to someone else at a higher price. Many firms have devised methods to minimize arbitrage possibilities. This is easily accomplished for services, which must be sold directly to the person consuming them, but difficult for goods, which can be resold easily.

Assuming that resale cannot occur, is third degree price discrimination inefficient? There is no easy answer. Suppose Frank and Sarah both like widgets. Frank is willing to pay $3 for a widget, but the price is $5. Clearly, Frank will not buy. Sarah is able to buy widgets for $1 each. She is willing to pay $2 for a widget. The optimal solution, from society's point of view, is for Sarah to buy a widget for $1 and then sell it to Frank for $3. But this cannot happen if resale is prevented! Because exchange is blocked, it is likely that society will end up with the wrong distribution of output. Also, when a firm charges more than one price for its product, it is clearly not selling at least some of its product at marginal cost. (Remember: one of the conditions for allocative efficiency is $P = MC$.)

Whether third degree price discrimination is in society's best interest depends on the alternative market solution. If the alternative is that the firm will sell all of its product at a single, high, monopoly price, then price discrimination may be preferable. If a firm with market power can expand its output beyond the amount that it would sell at a single fixed price by selling more to certain groups at lower prices, the result will be more efficient and more socially desirable.

➤ **Highly Concentrated Industries**   Arguments in favor of antitrust action against firms in highly concentrated industries on the basis of industry structure alone are more difficult to make. In theory, a monopoly can be just as efficient as a competitive industry if it does not exercise its power and if it continues to minimize costs and to innovate as if it had rivals. Those who favor antitrust action on the basis of structure alone argue, however, that such behavior is extremely unlikely.

Between 1911 and 1945, the courts and the Antitrust Division were stuck with the rule of reason. Under this rule, months of testimony were often necessary to demonstrate "unreasonable conduct," if it could be demonstrated at all. In the Alcoa decision, Judge Hand essentially said "enough is enough." When a firm controls 90 percent of a clearly defined market, an illegal monopoly exists, he decided, and there is no such thing as a benevolent monopoly.

➤ **The Antitrust Laws as a Deterrent**   Because we can only speculate about what would have happened without them, we cannot say whether the antitrust laws have "worked" or not. Some decisions have clearly produced the desired results. The Standard Oil decision, for example, gave us several regional oil companies that came to compete vigorously in the refining business. And clear evidence indicates that price-fixing complaints tend to lower prices.

But you cannot measure the success of the speed limit laws by looking only at the behavior of those who get speeding tickets; you must also look at how fast most people drive. Proponents of antitrust enforcement argue that the real gains of such a policy lie in the cases that never make it to court, because antitrust laws and rules serve as a significant deterrent. Without such laws, they argue, the temptation to fix prices, collude, and engage in deceptive advertising would be irresistible. If no prohibitions existed, can anyone doubt that firms would merge, dominate markets, and exploit monopoly power? As you saw in chapters 13 and 14, the profit incentive for firms to do all these things is compelling.

THE CASE AGAINST ANTITRUST ENFORCEMENT

In recent years, antitrust laws have come under increasing criticism. While few complain about the laws that make certain kinds of conduct illegal, there is growing concern about remedies aimed at concentrated industries that seem to be performing fairly well. Several themes recur in this recent criticism.

▶ **Regulations as the Penalty for Success?** Critics of regulation contend that the Antitrust Division and the FTC are not concerned with inefficient firms that have not done well; rather, they are interested only in the firms that, in a sense, have done *too well*. If a company produces a better mousetrap and comes to dominate an industry, the government nails it for being a monopoly!

One example of regulation as the "penalty for success" occurred in the early 1960s. Extensive research led the General Motors Corporation to come up with improvements in the design of intracity buses. Those improvements were patented, and as a result GM came to dominate the market for intracity buses.

After a long antitrust battle, the court issued a consent decree forcing GM to give up its patents to the competition. In addition, any further design improvements that GM made through research and development would likewise have to be made available to its competitors. The result was that GM stopped developing new and better buses, and travelers ended up with worse buses than they might have had.

Many people made the same argument about the divestiture of AT&T in 1982: We had a well-managed and enormously successful private company—the best telephone company in the world. No one argued that AT&T had done anything wrong or unethical. Rather, the argument was that competition might lead to an even better result—new products, better service, and lower rates. But, the critics cried, the key word was "might." And, they added, resorting to familiar and compelling logic, "If it's not broken, don't fix it!"

▶ **The Need for Big, Strong Companies to Face Global Competition** For most of its history, the United States did not have to worry much about global competition. Today everyone knows the names Toyota, Volvo, Sony, and many others. Giant corporations in the Far East and Europe are filling U.S. markets with sophisticated products and masterful marketing techniques.

It is said that the old theory of competitive markets doesn't work when one country's industries face competition from foreign companies whose governments aid and abet their activities. The Japanese government, for example, does everything in its power to help its giant firms penetrate foreign markets and grow, while the United States government forces U.S. megafirms to defend themselves in court against antitrust judgments.

Cooperation among firms (a major joint research effort, for example), if allowed, might help U.S. industries fight foreign competition. But firms in concentrated industries are unlikely to participate in joint ventures for fear of antitrust action.

▶ **Negative Effects on Research, Development, and Growth** The Schumpeterian hypothesis (chapter 14) is the foundation for the argument that large firms can devote significant resources to research and development activities, while lower levels of industrial concentration lead to less R&D. But the evidence is mixed. Larger firms are more likely to have research staffs than smaller firms, but the number of patents procured and the number of important developments over the years do not seem to show any systematic correlation with firm size.[14] Nonetheless, this may not be true in all industries:

[14] See Richard Caves, *American Industry: Structure, Conduct, Performance*, 7th ed. (Englewood Cliffs, N.J.: Prentice Hall, 1992).

Lucent Technologies
Bell Labs Innovations

AFTER DIVESTITURE, BELL LABS EVOLVED INTO LUCENT TECHNOLOGIES. IT CONTINUES TO DEVELOP NEW APPLICATIONS OF TECHNOLOGY AT A RAPID PACE.

After the Alcoa case in 1945, Kaiser, Reynolds, and several other new firms entered the aluminum industry: A study examined technical progress [before and after the Alcoa case] and concluded that the reduction in seller concentration was responsible at least in part for increased progressiveness . . . . the existence of several producers has led to competitive marketing, increasing the pressures to develop new alloys and new uses for aluminum, including many consumer products such as foil. Reduced concentration seems to have provided a significant competitive stimulus to innovation.[15]

Conflicting evidence comes from the telecommunications industry. Before its breakup, for example, AT&T maintained an enormous research facility called Bell Laboratories. Founded in 1925, at its peak it had 17 research centers in nine states and employed thousands of scientists and engineers. We can safely say that no single research program was responsible for more important technological breakthroughs, including the transistor, the solar battery, and the laser. Yet research and new product development are proceeding at an amazing rate in the new companies that were broken off from AT&T in 1982 and in those that are springing up around it. Today Bell Labs is a thriving separate firm called Lucent Technologies.

➤ **Efficient Capital Flows and Relatively Contestable Markets** Another argument against vigorous antitrust enforcement is that barriers to entry are not as formidable as they once were. Capital markets have become more efficient; investors are always looking for profitable ventures and are now able to mobilize the huge sums necessary to enter almost any industry if there are profits to be earned. The efficiency of capital markets serves to make more and more markets contestable. Critics of antitrust enforcement argue that both actual entry and the threat of new entry make market power less of a problem.

➤ **Distrust of Government** Even if it can be shown that antitrust enforcement is a good idea in theory, many people simply do not want to put more power in the hands of government. They feel that government intervention creates more problems than it solves. Bureaucracy is slow and wasteful, the argument goes, and the people in a particular industry clearly know more about what they do than those government employees charged with regulating that industry.

---

[15]Ibid.

THE POLICY MAKERS' DILEMMA

One of the lessons that we hope you will take from this course (and from your entire college education) is that complicated questions have no simple answers. There are strong arguments for government involvement in the economy. Unchecked monopoly power, collusion, and price-fixing can be enormously expensive to a society. It is also easy to show that competition provides incentives for efficient production, innovation, and a healthy economy.

It is equally clear, unfortunately, that enforcement of the antitrust laws has imposed costs on society. Successful companies have paid a price for their success. Some, such as GM, have been forced to give back markets that they won through vigorous competition. Antitrust activities may also have played a part in reducing the United States' ability to compete for international markets.

> The role of policy makers is to understand the arguments, weigh the evidence, and proceed accordingly. While policy decisions must be made without knowledge of the outcome, enlightened uncertainty is better than ignorance.

REGULATION

At the beginning of this chapter we said that the government plays two basic roles that seem contradictory: (1) It *promotes* competition and restricts market power, primarily through antitrust laws and other acts of Congress, and (2) it *restricts* competition by simultaneously regulating and protecting certain industries. So far, we have looked exclusively at the way the government protects competition. Now we turn to government activities that end up protecting monopoly power.

The government regulates many areas of the economy that have nothing to do with market structure. Some of these areas (environmental protection, for example) are discussed in later chapters. In the section that follows, however, we examine only the regulation of natural monopolies.

REGULATION OF NATURAL MONOPOLY

In chapter 13 we introduced you to some of the ways the market fails when market power is unrestrained. Firms that can control price and bar the entry of new firms overprice and underproduce relative to what is best for society. Solutions to this problem are possible, at least in theory. One is to restructure the industry to make it more competitive. A second is to impose some sort of price regulation—a price ceiling at marginal cost, for example. Another is public or government ownership and operation.

The antitrust laws that we examined in this chapter are based on the proposition that competition, not regulation or public ownership, is the best way to achieve efficiency in an economy. Although the courts exercise great discretion, everything they do—from requiring firms to give up patents to breaking firms up into smaller competing units—aims at stimulating competition. Nonetheless, it has always been understood that not all markets can be, or should be, competitively structured. Most important among these exceptions are firms or industries that can take advantage of very large economies of scale—the natural monopolies mentioned earlier in this chapter and described in chapter 13.

Figure 15.2 illustrates a natural monopoly. Notice that average total cost is still declining when the demand curve intersects it. To break such a firm into smaller pieces, each producing some fraction of total demand, would mean that each of the small firms would have to produce at a much higher average cost. (All of this

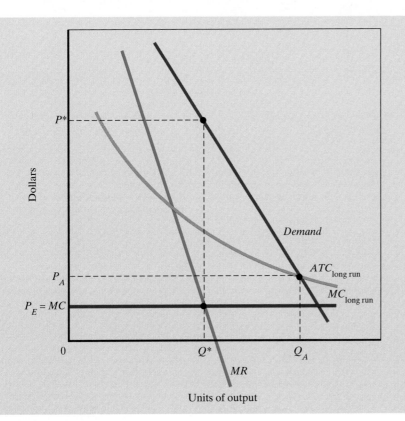

FIGURE 15.2

Regulating a Natural Monopoly

A natural monopoly exists when a firm exhibits very large economies of scale. Here long-run average costs facing the firm continue to decline with output even when a single firm is producing all the output demanded in the market. With no regulation, the firm would produce at Q^* and price at P^*. Regulating price to be equal to marginal cost, P_E, would be efficient but would result in losses. Setting price at P_A means that average cost is covered and that investors earn a normal rate of return.

is implied by the existence of large economies of scale. If this is not clear to you, review chapter 13.)

Most natural monopolies have very high fixed costs and low marginal costs. An oft-cited example has been the local electric company. Building a power generation plant and putting up poles and wires is costly. Once they are in place, the cost of generating and distributing one additional kilowatt of electricity is low. Part of the reasoning behind the protection of such industries is that having more than one firm undertake the very large initial investment is a waste of resources. (As you see in the Issues and Debates box, "Congress Deregulates Electricity in 1998; Congress Ponders a Wider Deregulation," electricity is becoming a competitive market.)

One solution to the natural monopoly problem is to let the firm continue to exist as a monopoly but to regulate the price of its product and its rate of return. If the natural monopoly in Figure 15.2 went unregulated, it would produce Q^* units of output (the point at which $MR = MC$) and charge price P^*, far above marginal costs. But imposing a simple price ceiling at $P = MC$ would not work, because at that price marginal cost is below average total cost, and the firm could not make even a zero profit. Remember that price is equal to average *revenue,* and if average revenue is less than average total cost, total revenue will be less than total cost. This implies a loss.

Theory suggests three options for regulation: (1) Set the *efficient price* ($P = MC$) and provide a subsidy out of general government revenues to the monopoly; (2) set price equal to average cost (P_A), which would allow firms to charge a price that covers all costs, including a normal return on invested capital; or (3) impose a fee on each user of the monopoly's product—a basic service charge as a lump sum and a price for usage equal to marginal cost. The last two options both require that some regulatory commission set the firm's rate of return.

CALIFORNIA DEREGULATES ELECTRICITY IN 1998; CONGRESS PONDERS A WIDER DEREGULATION

CALIFORNIA TO LET SMALL CUSTOMERS PICK THEIR POWER SUPPLIERS IN '98

California regulators said yesterday that they would speed up a plan to allow utility customers to buy electricity from any supplier of their choosing by 1998.

The decision by the California Public Utilities Commission is expected to put pressure on a number of states, including New York, New Jersey, Pennsylvania, Massachusetts and New Hampshire, that are also in the process of deregulating their utility markets.[a]

SIDES SQUARE OFF ON DECONTROLLING ELECTRICITY SALES

A high-stakes battle is unfolding in Congress and across the country over legislation to give consumers the same choice in buying electricity that they now have in choosing airlines and long-distance telephone companies.

At stake is the restructuring of the electric power industry, an enterprise worth $200 billion a year that has been tightly regulated since Franklin D. Roosevelt was President. . . .

The legislation's proponents, led by large manufacturers, argue that increasing competition could slash the electricity bills of homeowners, retailers, schools and farmers, as well as manufacturers, by 15 percent to 50 percent.

Since the 1930's, electric utilities have been a collection of monopolies regulated by the states they serve. Utilities have been protected from competition and guaranteed rates that yield a profit. As a result, electricity prices vary widely from state to state, with customers in the Pacific Northwest paying, in some cases, one-third the rates of consumers in the Northeast.

Congress deregulated the wholesale electricity market in 1992; last year, the Federal Energy Regulatory Commission expanded the authority of utilities and some municipalities to bargain for the cheapest power supplier. Under this arrangement, utilities and other power producers buy and sell electricity and send it to one another over existing transmission lines. . . .

The proposed bills would deregulate only the power-generating part of the industry. Transmission and distribution would remain monopolies, with companies charging one another fees to ship electricity over their lines.[b]

Sources: [a]Eric Schmitt, "Sides Square Off on Decontrolling Electricity Sales," *The New York Times*, April 14, 1997, p. 1; [b]Agis Salpukas, "California to Let Small Customers Pick Their Power Suppliers in '98," *The New York Times*, May 7, 1997, p. D1. Copyright © 1997 by The New York Times Co. Reprinted by permission.

For more on deregulation, see the Case and Fair Web page at
http://www.prenhall.com/casefair.

> ➤ **Public Ownership versus Privatization**   A fourth solution to the natural monopoly problem is public (or government) ownership and operation of business. Many U.S. and foreign cities operate their own public utilities. The railroad systems of many countries are run by the government, often quite efficiently. France, for example, operates one of the most efficient and innovative railroads in the world.

Despite some successful examples of public ownership, however, the prevailing opinion seems to be that the government should stay out of a particular business if the private sector can do the job. One popular trend of the 1980s and 1990s has been **privatization**, or the transfer of government businesses to the private sector. Japan sold the Japan National Railway to the public, and Britain and France have sold stock in state-owned banks, energy companies, and telecommunications firms. U.S. states and localities have privatized garbage collection, recycling services, fire fighting, prisons, and even water treatment facilities. In 1988, a special commission appointed by President Reagan recommended the privatization of air traffic control operations, public housing, and mail services.

Why the rush to privatize? The logic is simple. The incentive to be efficient is greater when one's own money is at risk. Those opposed to privatization argue that natural monopoly must be regulated or nationalized because private companies do not

privatization *The transfer of government business to the private sector.*

always act in the public interest. They also say government does a creditable job of running its businesses: More than 70 percent of people receiving government services say that they are satisfied.

THE PROBLEMS OF REGULATION

The theory of natural monopoly sounds simple: Regulatory commissions set prices that allow regulated monopolies to earn a normal rate of return. A number of problems are inherent in regulation, however, and these will probably always perplex the regulator to some degree.

▸ **Gathering and Analyzing the Necessary Data**   Regulation requires analyzing lots of information. The first problem is calculating the base—presumably some measure of the "value" of the firm's capital investment—on which a fair return should be allowed. Debate over the value of a public utility can go on and on.

The regulatory commission must also analyze costs. Should all costs be allowed in setting price? Which costs are reasonable? Public utility commissions (PUCs) have developed methods for analyzing all the information necessary, but analysis is a difficult process, subject to differences of opinion and to error.

Furthermore, the political process that attends rate regulation is time-consuming and cumbersome. Public utility commissions are impaneled to act in the "public interest." The public must be consulted in public hearings and open sessions. And the final decisions made by PUCs can be reviewed in the courts.

▸ **Lack of Incentives to Be Efficient**   Because the return to a regulated natural monopoly is set by a commission, the monopoly may lack the incentive to use efficient production techniques. For example, if a regulatory commission fixes the return by setting a rate expressed as a percentage of the utility's assets, the dollar amount of profit depends only on the total value of those assets. Thus, firms may actually have an incentive to overinvest in capital if the allowed return exceeds the cost of capital. This tendency is called the **Averch-Johnson effect**, after the scholars who noted the proclivity of regulated firms to build more capital capacity than they need.[16]

▸ **Excessive Nonprice Competition**   Regulated monopolies generally do not have a problem with nonprice competition, because they don't have competition. In regulated

Averch-Johnson effect
The tendency for regulated monopolies to build more capital than they need. Usually occurs when allowed rates of return are set by a regulatory agency at some percent of fixed capital stocks.

FAST FACTS

A recent article by economist Clifford Winston estimates the societal benefits of deregulation:

Industry	Range of Estimate (Billions of 1990 Dollars)
Airlines	$13.7–$19.7
Railroads	$10.4–$12.9
Trucking	$10.6
Telecommunications	$.7–$1.6
Cable television	$.4–$1.3

Source: Clifford Winston, "Economic Deregulation: Days of Reckoning for Microeconomists," *Journal of Economic Literature*, September 1993, p. 1263.

---

[16]Harvey Averch and Leland Johnson, "Behavior of the Firm under Regulatory Constraint," *American Economic Review* LII (December 1962), 1052–1069.

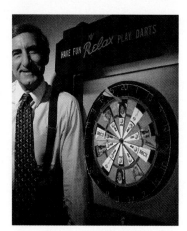

TECHNOLOGICAL CHANGE HAS MADE POSSIBLE THE DEREGULATION OF TELEPHONE SERVICE. ONE OF THE GREAT RIVALRIES OF THE 1990s IS BETWEEN AT&T AND MCI, WHICH FILED THE ORIGINAL ANTITRUST COMPLAINT AGAINST AT&T. OF THE TOP 10 ADVERTISERS IN 1994, AT&T WAS FIRST, SPENDING MORE THAN $511 MILLION ON ADVERTISING; EIGHTH WAS MCI, SPENDING $243 MILLION FOR ADVERTISING.

industries where several firms compete directly with each other while being required to charge the same price, however, product differentiation can become excessive.

The marketing zeal of the airlines in the early 1970s is a good example. Airlines offered frequent flights, designer-painted planes, a choice of five menus, free carpet slippers, and other frills hard to imagine today, in an effort to increase ticket sales. As a result of deregulation, competition now drives airlines to produce the service that people want at least cost and lower price.

THE HISTORY OF REGULATION

The Bell Telephone Company behaved like a textbook monopoly until some of its patents expired in 1894. After 1894, increasing competition in the telecommunications industry led Bell to argue *for* regulation. Worried about both antitrust actions and new competition, Bell argued that it was a natural monopoly. It made little sense, it said, to have two or more sets of telephone lines down the same road. Around the same time, many other industries put forth similar arguments.

In response to these types of arguments, many states set up public utility commissions in the early years of this century. Pro-regulation sentiment reached its peak in 1907, when seven states established new regulatory bodies. Mergers between firms in the telecommunications market were finally exempted from antitrust review by the Willis-Graham Act of 1921. By that time, telephone companies were strictly regulated in all states.

By the last part of the 1970s and the early 1980s, the feeling had grown that the government was regulating industries that were not really natural monopolies. In some cases, the arguments for regulation had eroded with technological advances in industries such as telecommunications and electricity. In other cases, the industries had not been natural monopolies to begin with. As a result, there has been a movement toward deregulation, and the mandates of various regulatory agencies are gradually changing.

The authority of the oldest regulatory agency granted nationwide powers, the *Interstate Commerce Commission* (ICC), expanded for a time to include interstate trucking as well as railroads. Today, its control over truckers' services and rates is essentially gone, and only those railroads that exhibit "market dominance" remain under its direct control. Trucking deregulation began in 1978; by 1983, competition had pushed the real price of truckload shipments down by 25 percent.

The airlines were once tightly regulated by the *Civil Aeronautics Board* (CAB), which controlled routes and fares for all interstate carriers. Today the CAB is out of business, and there is no lack of competition in the airline industry. In fact, when cutthroat competition during 1992 and 1993 kept airfares below costs, the airlines lost billions of dollars—prompting many to call for reregulation of the industry.

The *Federal Energy Regulatory Commission* once regulated the price of natural gas that travels through interstate pipelines. It also fixed the wholesale rates for electricity transmitted interstate. In 1978 Congress began gradually deregulating the price of natural gas, which is now set competitively.

The *Federal Communications Commission* regulates interstate telephone and telegraph rates and services. Regulation of local operating companies remains the responsibility of state-run public utility commissions. Clearly an industry in transition, telecommunications is likely to see much less regulation in the future.

Technological change has made it possible—and necessary—for long-distance telephone service to become competitive. This was signaled when a new company, MCI, filed a private action against AT&T, arguing that AT&T used its monopoly in local service areas and in the manufacture of equipment to monopolize the long-distance market. In 1982 AT&T reached a settlement in which it agreed to separate its long-distance service and equipment manufacturing business from its local operating companies.

More recently, the Congress and the states have been deregulating with fervor. In 1996, the Congress mandated that local connection service be opened up to competition. Although a court decision in 1997 slowed down the process, it won't be long before we can choose from a number of competing providers for local service.

Even electricity, once the classic example of a natural monopoly, is scheduled for deregulation beginning in 1998. Once again, it won't be long before we will be flooded with phone calls and mail from competing electricity providers.

THE CASE FOR DEREGULATION

Clearly, there must be a strong rationale behind the extensive deregulation that has occurred in recent years. Those who favor deregulation make two basic arguments. First, because few real natural monopolies exist anymore, there is rarely a reason for government regulation on the basis of market structure. Second, many (if not most) instances of government regulation have succeeded in reducing competition in industries where competition might be beneficial.

Be aware that this chapter does not discuss *all* forms of government regulation. In later chapters, we examine other kinds of government involvement in the economy, including environmental protection, occupational health and safety, and food and drug regulation. Here we are talking simply about government regulation of firms allowed to operate essentially as monopolies on the grounds that economies of scale make antitrust enforcement impractical.

Those who contend that the government has stifled potentially beneficial competition argue that most examples of real barriers to entry are barriers *created* by governments. We have already talked about regulation in the taxicab, telephone, and airline industries. None could be called a natural monopoly, yet all are, or were, highly regulated.

Most of these examples are consistent with the theory of rent-seeking behavior discussed in chapter 13. Recall that basic argument: If a firm finds that it is possible to earn positive profits and to protect those profits by preventing competition, it will expend resources to do so. These expenditures may include lobbying for regulatory protection. AT&T decided in 1905 that regulation was a better fate than all-out competition, so it actually sought regulation. Similarly, the trucking industry favored continued regulation, as did most of the airlines, when deregulation of each of those industries was first proposed.

Be careful not to confuse the criticisms of regulation with the criticisms of antitrust enforcement. While both call for less government, the logic behind the two arguments is quite different:

> Antitrust enforcement is undertaken to *promote* competition. In a way, it is the opposite of market regulation, which nearly always *restricts* competition.

SUMMARY

THE DEVELOPMENT OF ANTITRUST LAW

1. Governments have assumed two roles with respect to imperfectly competitive industries: (1) They *promote* competition and restrict market power, primarily through antitrust

laws and other congressional acts, and (2) they *restrict* competition by regulating industries.

2. Congress created the *Interstate Commerce Commission* in 1887 to regulate the railroads and in 1890 passed the

Sherman Act, which declared monopoly and trade restraints illegal. In 1911, the Supreme Court enunciated the *rule of reason*, which implied that monopolistic structure alone was not a criterion for antitrust enforcement.

3. In 1914 Congress passed the *Clayton Act*, which was designed to strengthen the Sherman Act and to clarify exactly what specific forms of conduct were "unreasonable" restraints of trade. In the same year, the *Federal Trade Commission* was established and given broad powers to investigate and regulate unfair methods of competition. Subsequent legislation extended the government's power to limit mergers that might substantially lessen competition in an industry. Currently the Justice Department uses the *Herfindahl-Hirschman Index* to determine whether or not it will challenge a proposed merger.

THE ENFORCEMENT OF ANTITRUST LAW

4. Responsibility for the enforcement of the antitrust laws rests primarily with the *Antitrust Division* of the Justice Department and the Federal Trade Commission. Antitrust complaints may also be brought to the courts by private citizens.

5. The courts are empowered to impose a number of remedies if they find that antitrust law has been violated. These include civil and criminal penalties, *consent decrees* that specifically forbid future illegal acts, and treble damages.

6. The antitrust laws specifically exempt certain groups. These groups include lobbying organizations, labor unions, sports organizations, and regulated industries.

THE ANTITRUST ENFORCEMENT DEBATE

7. The case for government intervention in imperfectly competitive industries is well established: Unchecked monopoly power, price discrimination, collusion, and price-fixing can be enormously expensive to society. Proponents of antitrust

enforcement say the real gains are in the cases that never make it to court because the antitrust rules and laws serve as a significant deterrent. Without such laws, the temptation to fix prices, collude, and engage in deceptive advertising would be irresistible.

8. The basic arguments against antitrust enforcement are that it penalizes success, that the United States needs strong companies to face foreign competition, that antitrust actions may reduce basic research and development, and that most markets are reasonably competitive.

REGULATION

9. When an industry demonstrates large economies of scale, it may be efficient to have only one large firm in that industry—a natural monopoly. If a single-firm industry is protected on the grounds that it is a natural monopoly, it must be regulated to prevent exploitation of its monopoly power.

10. In past years, the government has been involved in regulating industries that are not natural monopolies. In the last decade a number of these industries (including trucking, airlines, and telecommunications) have been totally or partially deregulated.

11. There are problems with regulation. First, it is difficult to collect and analyze all the data necessary to regulate an industry. Second, firms guaranteed a certain rate of return lack incentives to be efficient. This may give rise to the *Averch-Johnson effect*, in which a monopoly tends to build more capital than it needs. Finally, regulation may give rise to excessive nonprice competition.

12. The proper role of government in the world of business is hard to define. Doing nothing about noncompetitive industries inevitably results in significant social losses. The antitrust laws have strengths and weaknesses, but most economists feel they deter behavior that might cost society too much. Where large economies of scale make it logical to preserve monopoly structure in an industry, regulation is the only reasonable course of action.

REVIEW TERMS AND CONCEPTS

Antitrust Division (of the Department of Justice), 355
Averch-Johnson effect, 366
Celler-Kefauver Act, 351
Clayton Act, 350
consent decree, 355
Federal Trade Commission (FTC), 350

Hart-Scott-Rodino Act, 352
Herfindahl-Hirschman Index (HHI), 352
Interstate Commerce Commission (ICC), 349
per se rule, 350
price discrimination, 360

privatization, 366
rule of reason, 350
Sherman Act, 349
trust, 348
Wheeler-Lea Act, 351
Willis-Graham Act, 351

PROBLEM SET

1. Deregulation of electricity markets was scheduled to begin with great fanfare in California in 1998. What have been the results to date? Do consumers have a choice of companies from which to buy electricity today? Is there any evidence of price-cutting in response to the new competitive environment? (*Hint:* At the library do a search of the catalog of a major newspaper like the *New York Times* or the *Los Angeles Times* or a search on the World Wide Web.)

2. The diagram shows marginal cost, average total cost, and market demand for a large natural monopoly. On the diagram indicate the following:
   a. Unregulated profit-maximizing price.
   b. Total revenue, total cost, and profit at the price in a.
   c. The efficient price.
   d. Total revenue, total cost, and profit at the price in c.
   e. The price at which demand is satisfied and the firm is allowed to earn a "normal rate of return."

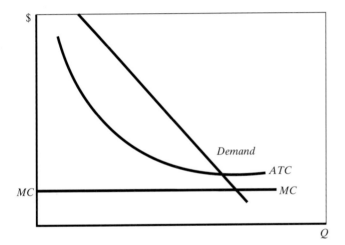

3. In an attempt to settle the strike that threatened the 1995 baseball season, the Congress threatened to revoke major league baseball's antitrust exemption. Write a brief essay either supporting or rejecting the exemption on behalf of major league baseball fans. Be sure to use economic logic in your essay.

4. What was the rule of reason enunciated by the courts in 1911? What problems did the courts encounter in implementing it? In what ways did the Clayton Act help to clarify its meaning?

5. With the Alcoa case, the position of the courts changed dramatically. What principle was changed by Judge Hand's opinion in that case? List the advantages and disadvantages of the structural approach to antitrust enforcement introduced by the Alcoa decision.

6. Suppose the glump industry were made up of five firms each controlling 15 percent of the market, and five firms each controlling 5 percent of the market. If two firms that each control 15 percent of the market in this industry proposed merging, would the merger be challenged by the Justice Department under the 1982/1984 guidelines? Explain your answer. (*Hint:* Calculate the HHI.)

7. Perhaps the strongest advocate of reforming the U.S. antitrust laws is Professor Robert H. Bork. He argues there is little justification for interfering with the natural operation of a free-market system. Sometimes called "economic Darwinism," Bork's philosophy is that monopoly or market power are of little concern because they "will be eroded if not based on superior efficiency." Write a brief essay either supporting or challenging Professor Bork's position. (For elaboration, see Robert Bork, *The Antitrust Paradox*, New York: Basic Books, 1978.)

8. Deregulation of local telephone service was mandated by the Congress in 1996. However, by the beginning of 1998, most people were still able to get local services only from a single company. How much progress has been made in opening up the market for local connection services to competition since? (*Hint:* Do a newspaper search or a search on the Web.)

9. As head of the New Hampshire Public Utility Commission, you must make a recommendation concerning electric rates in the town of Nashua, where power is provided by a private electric company that enjoys a monopoly. Currently the price of electricity is regulated at $0.105 per kilowatt hour (kwh). Total usage is 89.3 million kwh. Assume that variable costs amount to $0.048 per kwh, fixed costs of maintaining the power plant total $1.5 million annually, and demand elasticity is zero. The commission has established that a fair return on invested capital to the owners of the electric company is 10 percent. If total invested capital in the plant was $45 million, would you recommend a rate hike or a cut? By how much?

10. What potential problems do you see with Justice Department decisions based on the Herfindahl-Hirschman Index? For example, should the "market share" referred to in computing the HHI be national share or regional share? How useful do you think the HHI would be in the case of a merger between two multiproduct firms?

11. Explain why restructuring fails as a remedy in the case of a natural monopoly. Illustrate your answer with a graph. What alternatives are there to restructuring in the case of a natural monopoly?

12. Explain, using graphs, why restructuring a monopoly into a number of competing firms is likely to lead to a more efficient allocation of resources.

13. What arguments favor continued regulation of local operating companies in the telecommunications industry? What arguments favor complete deregulation of that industry?

TAKE IT TO THE NET

We invite you to visit the Case and Fair page on the Prentice Hall Web site:

http://www.prenhall.com/casefair

for this chapter's World Wide Web exercise.

Chapter 16

EXTERNALITIES, PUBLIC GOODS, IMPERFECT INFORMATION, AND SOCIAL CHOICE

IN CHAPTERS 6 THROUGH 12, we built a complete model of a perfectly competitive economy under a set of assumptions. By chapter 12, we had demonstrated that the allocation of resources under perfect competition is efficient, and we began to relax some of the assumptions on which the competitive model is based. We introduced the idea of **market failure**, and in chapters 13 and 14 we talked about three kinds of imperfect markets: monopoly, oligopoly, and monopolistic competition. In chapter 15 we discussed some of the ways government has responded to the inefficiencies of imperfect markets and to the development of market power.

As we continue our examination of market failure, we look first at *externalities* as a source of inefficiency. Often when we engage in transactions or make economic decisions, second or third parties suffer consequences that decision makers have no incentive to consider. For example, for many years manufacturing firms and power plants had no reason to worry about the impact of smoke from their operations on the quality of the air we breathe. Now we know that air pollution—an externality—harms people.

Next, we consider a second type of market failure that involves products private firms find unprofitable to produce even if members of society want them. These products are called *public goods* or *social goods*. Public goods yield collective benefits, and in most societies, governments produce them or arrange to provide them. The process of choosing what social goods to produce is very different from the process of private choice.

A third source of market failure is *imperfect information*. In chapters 6 through 12, we assumed that households and firms make choices in the presence of perfect information—that households know all that there is to know about product availability, quality, and price and that firms know all there is to know about factor availability, quality, and price. When information is imperfect, a misallocation of resources may result.

market failure *Occurs when resources are misallocated or allocated inefficiently.*

Finally, while the existence of public goods, externalities, and imperfect information are examples of market failure, it is not necessarily true that government involvement will always improve matters. Just as markets can fail, so too can governments. When we look at the incentives facing government decision makers, we find several reasons behind government failure.

EXTERNALITIES AND ENVIRONMENTAL ECONOMICS

externality *A cost or benefit resulting from some activity or transaction that is imposed or bestowed upon parties outside the activity or transaction. Sometimes called* spillovers *or* neighborhood effects.

An **externality** exists when the actions or decisions of one person or group impose a cost or bestow a benefit on second or third parties. Externalities are sometimes called *spillovers* or *neighborhood effects*. Inefficient decisions result when decision makers fail to consider social costs and benefits.

The presence of externalities is a significant phenomenon in modern life. Examples are everywhere: Air, water, land, sight, and sound pollution; traffic congestion; automobile accidents; abandoned housing; nuclear accidents; and secondhand cigarette smoke are only a few. The study of externalities is a major concern of *environmental economics*.

The opening of Eastern Europe in 1989 and 1990 revealed that environmental externalities are not limited to free-market economies. Part of the logic of a planned economy is that when economic decisions are made socially (by the government, presumably acting on behalf of the people) rather than privately, planners can and will take all costs—private and social—into account. This has not been the case, however. When East and West Germany were reunited and the borders of Europe were opened, we saw the disastrous condition of the environment in virtually all of Eastern Europe. (See Figure 16.1 and the Global Perspective box "Transitional Economies and Environmental Issues.")

As societies become more urbanized, externalities become more important: When we live closer together, our actions are more likely to affect others.

FIGURE 16.1

Environmental Problems in Eastern Europe

Source: Marlise Simons, "East Europe Sniffs Freedom's Air and Gasps," *The New York Times*, Nov. 3, 1994, p. A1. Copyright © 1994 by The New York Times Co. Reprinted by permission.

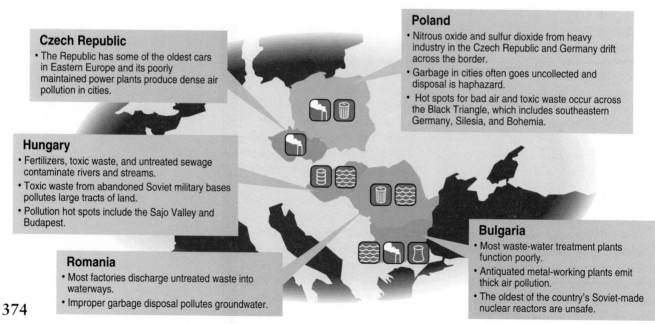

Czech Republic
• The Republic has some of the oldest cars in Eastern Europe and its poorly maintained power plants produce dense air pollution in cities.

Poland
• Nitrous oxide and sulfur dioxide from heavy industry in the Czech Republic and Germany drift across the border.
• Garbage in cities often goes uncollected and disposal is haphazard.
• Hot spots for bad air and toxic waste occur across the Black Triangle, which includes southeastern Germany, Silesia, and Bohemia.

Hungary
• Fertilizers, toxic waste, and untreated sewage contaminate rivers and streams.
• Toxic waste from abandoned Soviet military bases pollutes large tracts of land.
• Pollution hot spots include the Sajo Valley and Budapest.

Romania
• Most factories discharge untreated waste into waterways.
• Improper garbage disposal pollutes groundwater.

Bulgaria
• Most waste-water treatment plants function poorly.
• Antiquated metal-working plants emit thick air pollution.
• The oldest of the country's Soviet-made nuclear reactors are unsafe.

TRANSITIONAL ECONOMIES AND ENVIRONMENTAL ISSUES

In theory, socialist economies are supposed to pay attention to externalities and social costs better than free-market economies, where private firms must often be prodded to consider external effects. The radical changes that have taken place in Eastern Europe over the last few years certainly challenge this once-conventional wisdom, as the following excerpt describes:

PRAGUE— . . . . almost five years after the collapse of Communism, the region's environment continues to decay. Chemical works, smelters, coal mines and power plants are still infusing air and water with waste far surpassing international standards and causing severe health problems. Toxic dumps go on poisoning ground water and cities keep on spewing their raw sewage into rivers.

What's more, capitalism is bringing its own problems—more traffic pollution, less public transport, more plastic foam, more clashes between environmentalists and the peddlers of consumerism.

There have been some gains. Factory emissions have dropped, perversely the result of a sputtering economy in which many plants

have closed or slowed production. But the enormous task of installing filters, scrubbers and treatment plants has barely begun. And energy still comes largely from highly polluting brown coal . . .

In theory, Communism with its strict central planning had more power than free-wheeling capitalism to avoid or prevent damaging nature. Yet, with its squandering of raw materials and energy, the economic artifice made in Moscow produced exceptional levels of pollution that maimed the lives of many of its citizens.

In the end, it was this poisoning that provided a rare platform for challenging the state when other forms of protest were not tolerated. The environmental devastation became a powerful catalyst as citizens' groups formed throughout the East, spurring broader protests before the fall of Communism. Almost inevitably, in 1989, the new leaders had to commit themselves to an urgent clean-up. . . .

On the cold and high plateaus where the German, Czech and Polish borders meet and tree stumps look as if ravaged by fire, foresters have been planting new and hardy seedlings. Yet

POLLUTION HAS BEEN A PROBLEM IN EASTERN EUROPE FOR DECADES, BUT ONLY SINCE THE FALL OF COMMUNISM HAVE SUCH PROBLEMS COME TO THE WORLD'S ATTENTION.

few young firs are surviving. In the valleys below, a phalanx of power plants and industries driven by brown coal are still spewing sulfur and soot, as they have done for more than three decades. This region, dubbed the Black Triangle, is one of the world's biggest makers of acid rain.[a]

Source: [a]Marlise Simons, "East Europe Sniffs Freedom's Air and Gasps," *The New York Times*, Nov. 3, 1994, p. A1. Copyright © 1994 by The New York Times Co. Reprinted by permission.

For more on economies and the environment, see the Case and Fair Web page at
http://www.prenhall.com/casefair.

MARGINAL SOCIAL COST AND MARGINAL-COST PRICING

Profit-maximizing perfectly competitive firms will produce output up to the point at which price is equal to marginal cost ($P = MC$). Let us take a moment here to review why this is essential to the proposition that competitive markets produce what people want—an efficient mix of output.

When a firm weighs price and marginal cost and no externalities exist, it is weighing the full benefits to society of additional production against the full costs to society of that production. Those who benefit from the production of a product are the people or households who end up consuming it. The price of a product is a good measure of what an additional unit of that product is "worth," because those who value it more highly already buy it. People who value it less than the current price are not buying it. If marginal cost includes all costs—that is, all costs *to society*—of producing a marginal unit of a good, then additional production is efficient, provided that P is greater than MC. Up to the point where $P = MC$, each unit of production yields benefits in excess of cost.

Consider a firm in the business of producing laundry detergent. As long as the price per unit that consumers pay for that detergent exceeds the cost of the resources needed to produce one marginal unit of it, the firm will continue to produce. Producing up to the point where $P = MC$ is efficient, because for every unit of detergent produced, consumers derive benefits that exceed the cost of the resources needed to produce it. Producing at a point where $MC > P$ is inefficient, because marginal cost will rise above the unit price of the detergent. For every unit produced beyond the level at which $P = MC$, society uses up resources that have a value in excess of the benefits that consumers place on detergent. Figure 16.2a shows a firm and an industry in which no externalities exist.

But suppose that the production of the firm's product imposes external costs on society as well. If it does not factor those additional costs into its decisions, the firm is likely to overproduce. In Figure 16.2b, a certain measure of external costs is added to the firm's marginal cost curve. We see these external costs in the diagram, but the firm is ignoring them. The curve labeled *MSC*, **marginal social cost**, is the sum of the marginal costs of producing the product plus the correctly measured damage costs imposed in the process of production.

If the firm does not have to pay for these damage costs, it will produce exactly the same level of output ($q*$) as before, and price ($P*$) will continue to reflect only the costs that the firm actually pays to produce its product. The firms in this industry will continue to produce, and consumers will continue to consume their product, but the market price takes into account only part of the full cost of producing the good. At equilibrium ($q*$), marginal social costs are considerably greater than *price*. (Recall that *price* is a measure of the full value to consumers of a unit of the product at the margin.)

Say our detergent plant freely dumps untreated toxic waste into a river. The waste imposes specific costs on people who live downstream: It kills the fish in the river, it makes the river ugly to look at and rotten to smell, and it destroys the river for recreational use. There may also be health hazards, depending on what chemicals the firm is dumping. Obviously, the plant's product provides certain benefits. Its soap is valuable to consumers, who are willing and able to pay for it. The firm employs people and capital, and its revenues are sufficient to cover all costs. The issue is how the *net benefits* produced by the plant compare with the damage that it does. You don't need an economic model to know that *someone* should consider the costs of those damages.

> ▶ **Acid Rain and the Clean Air Act** Acid rain is an excellent example of an externality and the issues and conflicts in dealing with externalities. Manufacturing firms and power plants in the Midwest burn coal with a high sulfur content. When the smoke from those plants mixes with moisture in the atmosphere, the result is a dilute acid that is windblown north to Canada and east to New York and New England, where it falls to earth in the rain. The subject of a major conflict between the U.S. and Canadian governments and between industry and environmental groups, this acid rain is imposing enormous costs where it falls. Estimates of damage from fish kills, building deterioration, and deforestation range into the billions of dollars.

Decision makers at the manufacturing firms and public utilities using high-sulfur coal should weigh these costs, of course. But there is another side to this story. Burning cheap coal and not worrying about the acid rain that may be falling on someone else means jobs and cheap power for residents of the Midwest. Forcing coal-burning plants to pay for past damages from acid rain or even requiring them to begin weighing the costs that they are presently imposing will undoubtedly raise electricity prices and production costs in the Midwest.[1] Some firms will be driven out of business and some jobs will be lost. However, if the electricity and other products produced in the Midwest are worth the full costs imposed by acid rain, plants would not shut down; consumers

marginal social cost (MSC) *The total cost to society of producing an additional unit of a good or service. MSC is equal to the sum of the marginal costs of producing the product and the correctly measured damage costs involved in the process of production.*

[1]Look at Figure 16.2. If the firm is suddenly forced to pay the full cost of production, it will reduce output. The gains from this output reduction are greater than the value of the goods given up because marginal social cost is above price.

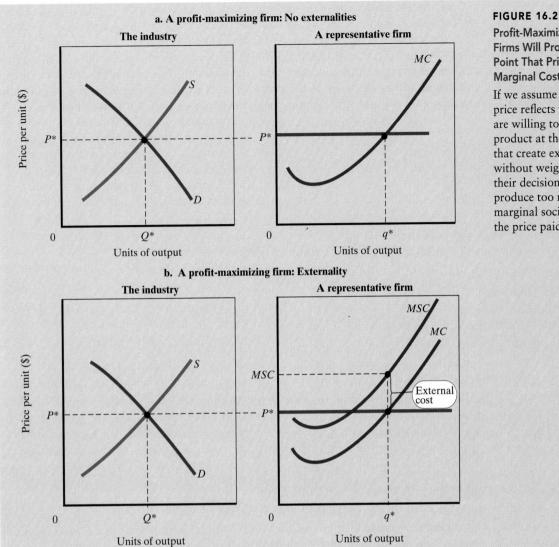

a. A profit-maximizing firm: No externalities

The industry

Price per unit ($)

S

P^*

D

0   Q^*

Units of output

A representative firm

MC

P^*

0   q^*

Units of output

b. A profit-maximizing firm: Externality

The industry

Price per unit ($)

S

P^*

D

0   Q^*

Units of output

A representative firm

MSC

MC

MSC

P^*

External cost

0   q^*

Units of output

FIGURE 16.2

Profit-Maximizing Competitive Firms Will Produce up to the Point That Price Equals Marginal Cost ($P = MC$)

If we assume that the current price reflects what consumers are willing to pay for a product at the margin, firms that create external costs without weighing them in their decisions are likely to produce too much. At q^*, marginal social cost exceeds the price paid by consumers.

would pay higher prices. If those goods are not worth the full cost, they should not be produced, at least not in current quantities or using current production methods.

The case of acid rain highlights the fact that efficiency analysis ignores the *distribution* of gains and losses. That is, to establish efficiency we need only to demonstrate that the total value of the gains exceeds the total value of the losses. If Midwestern producers and the consumers of their products were forced to pay an amount equal to the damages they cause, the gains from reduced damage in the East and in Canada would be at least as great as costs in the Midwest. The beneficiaries of forcing Midwestern firms to consider these costs would be the households and firms in the East and in Canada. After many years of debate, Congress passed and President Bush signed the Clean Air Act of 1990. Included in the law are strict emissions standards aimed, in part, at controlling the production and distribution of acid rain. An interesting provision of the Clean Air Act is its use of "tradable pollution rights," which we discuss later in this chapter.

Another part of the 1990 act allows states to petition the EPA for relief if they can establish a source of polluted air. In 1997 a group of Northeastern states did exactly that, pointing the finger at Midwest power plants. (See Issues and Debates box, "Smoggy Summer of 1997 Causes Pressure from Northeastern States.")

➤ **Other Externalities**   Other examples of external effects are all around us. When I drive my car into the center of the city at rush hour, I contribute to the congestion and impose costs (in the form of lost time and auto emissions) on others. One focus of a 1992 world environmental conference called the Earth Summit was the possibility of worldwide climate warming as a result of "greenhouse emissions" (like carbon dioxide) from industrial plants and automobiles. While potential costs are high, great uncertainty, both in the scientific evidence and in the magnitude of the potential costs, surrounds the issue.

Secondhand cigarette smoke has become a matter of public concern. In December 1994, a judge in Florida ruled that nonsmokers could bring a class-action suit based on the health consequences of passive smoke. Smoking has been banned on domestic air carriers, and many states have passed laws severely restricting smoking in public places.

In 1997, the big tobacco firms initialed a tentative agreement to pay over $350 billion to compensate those harmed by smoke and to reimburse states for smoking-related medical expenses paid under the Medicaid program. (See box, "The 1997 Tobacco Settlement.")

Despite these problems, not all externalities are negative: an abandoned house in an urban neighborhood that is restored and occupied makes the neighborhood better and adds value to the neighbors' homes.

PRIVATE CHOICES AND EXTERNAL EFFECTS

To help us understand externalities, let us use a simple two-person example. Harry lives in a dormitory at a big public college in the Southwest, where he is a first-year student. When he graduated from high school, his family gave him an expensive stereo system. Unfortunately, the walls of Harry's dorm are made of quarter-inch sheetrock over three-inch aluminum studs. You can hear people sleeping four rooms away. Harry likes bluegrass music of the "twangy" kind. Because of a hearing loss after an accident on the Fourth of July some years ago, he often does not notice the volume of his music.

Jake, who lives next door to Harry, isn't much of a music lover, but when he does listen, it's Brahms and occasionally Mozart. So Harry's music bothers Jake.

Let's assume there are no further external costs or benefits to anyone other than Harry and Jake. Figure 16.3 diagrams the decision process that the two dorm residents face. The downward-sloping curve labeled *MB* represents the value of the marginal benefits that Harry derives from listening to his music. Of course, Harry doesn't sit down to draw this curve, any more than anyone else (other than an economics student) sits down to draw actual demand curves. Curves like this are simply abstract representations of the way people behave. But if you think about it, such a curve must exist. To ask how much an hour of listening to music is worth to you is to ask how much you would be willing to pay to have it.

NONSMOKERS ARE NOT MERELY GRIMACING FROM SECONDHAND SMOKE. SUFFERING HEALTH CONSEQUENCES OF PASSIVE SMOKING, THEY ARE BRINGING CLASS-ACTION SUITS AGAINST TOBACCO COMPANIES.

SMOGGY SUMMER OF 1997 CAUSES PRESSURE FROM NORTHEASTERN STATES

The Clean Air Act of 1990 imposed limits on the amount of pollution but leaves discretion to the states over how to comply. In July 1997, the Environmental Protection Agency set new, tougher standards for ozone and fine particulates, but states were given a long time to comply.

Under the Clean Air Act, states or local governments are allowed to petition the EPA if they can identify a specific source or group of sources that are unlawfully impairing the air quality downwind. The Northeastern states did exactly that in the smoggy summer of 1997:

NORTHEAST STATES PRESSURING E.P.A. TO MOVE ON SMOG

As the Northeast suffers through one of the worst smog seasons of the decade, most state governments in the region are about to petition the Environmental Protection Agency to crack down on Midwestern utilities, where much of the pollution originates.

Maine, Massachusetts, New York and several other

"downwind" states have agreed to a common legal strategy that will press the Federal agency to act aggressively on the problem of wind-borne smog that crosses state lines and contributes to unhealthful air in New York City and across the Northeast.

The petitions, brought under the Clean Air Act, will ask the agency to impose strict new emissions limits on specific sources of pollution, especially on coal-fired electric utility plants in states like Ohio, where pollution from power plants is not so tightly regulated as in the Northeast.

To bolster their case, the Northeasterners have devised a new way of reminding the public just how bad the smog is day to day, using computerized weather maps that were shown on some television stations beginning today. Just as meteorologists have long been able to show their viewers snow moving in from the Great Lakes, they will now be able to offer graphic displays of smog creeping across the Northeastern states.

The environmental agency, which in July set a new, stricter national air quality standard for ozone, the principal ingredient of smog, was already planning on its own to encourage Midwestern states to do more to control utility emissions as a way of meeting that standard.

Under the Clean Air Act, however, a given state ordinarily chooses its own methods of meeting Federal standards; it may, for example, choose to focus on emissions from automobiles, motorized farm equipment or manufacturing plants rather than from utilities. So the Northeastern states hope to use the petition process to emphasize the pollution from the utilities, an approach that, state officials of the region say, could lead to controls on the electric plants as much as five years sooner than otherwise.[a]

Source: [a]John H. Cushman Jr., "Northeast States Pressuring E.P.A. to Move on Smog," *The New York Times*, August 8, 1997, p. 1. Copyright © 1997 by The New York Times Co. Reprinted by permission.

For more on internalizing externalities, see the Case and Fair Web page at **http://www.prenhall.com/casefair.**

Start at $0.01 and raise the "price" slowly in your mind. Presumably, you must stop at some point; where you stop depends on your taste for music and your income.

You can think, then, about the benefits Harry derives from listening to bluegrass as the maximum amount of money that he would be willing to pay to listen to his music for an hour. For the first hour, say, the figure for *MB* is $0.50. We assume diminishing marginal utility, of course. The more hours Harry listens, the lower the additional benefits from each successive hour. As the diagram shows, the *MB* curve falls below $0.05 per hour after eight hours of listening.

We call the costs that Harry must pay for each additional hour of listening to music **marginal private costs,** labeled *MPC* in Figure 16.3. These include the cost of electricity and so forth. These costs are constant at $0.05 per hour.

Then there is Jake. Although Harry's music doesn't poison Jake, give him lung cancer, or even cause him to lose money, it damages him nonetheless: He gets a headache, loses sleep, and can't concentrate on his work. Jake is harmed, and it is possible (at least conceptually) to measure that harm in terms of the maximum amount that he would be

marginal private cost (MPC)
The amount that a consumer pays to consume an additional unit of a particular good.

CHAPTER SIXTEEN
Externalities, Public Goods, Information

379

THE 1997 TOBACCO SETTLEMENT

On June 20, 1997, the tobacco industry and attorneys general of 40 states announced an agreement to end decades of antitobacco litigation. The settlement took months of intensive negotiations. It essentially eliminated class action suits against the tobacco companies as well as all currently pending state law suits. In exchange, the tobacco companies agreed to pay $368.5 billion over 25 years. The money would go to reimburse states for the cost of treating tobacco-related illnesses, to compensate smokers who win individual lawsuits against the tobacco companies, and to pay for public education and health programs. The companies also agreed to curtail advertising of cigarettes, especially to teenagers. It would mean the demise of Joe Camel and the Marlboro Man and the end of tobacco billboards and tobacco's sponsorship of sporting events. It also set goals for the reduction of teenage smoking.

To be implemented, the agreement needed legislation from the Congress, which also required the president's signature. In July 1997 the president set up an interagency task force to examine the proposed settlement and to make recommendations. By September, opponents and proponents of the agreement were locked in a bitter struggle for the votes of legislators.

One of the interesting issues to economists is who will pay. The answer: Smokers will pay through higher cigarette prices. Because the ultimate users are the ones benefiting from the use of the product, they should bear the full cost of using the product, including *external costs*. As a result, while cigarette smoking will not cease, the quantity of cigarettes demanded will fall.

. . . NEVERTHELESS, DEMAND FOR CIGARETTES REMAINS INELASTIC.

But how far? While estimates of the price elasticity of demand for cigarettes vary, virtually all suggest that demand is inelastic—that is, between 0 and −1. Three separate well-respected studies put the figure at around −0.4. This implies that a 10 percent rise in cigarette prices would cause a decline in cigarette smoking of about 4 percent. For teenagers, strapped for cash, the figure is likely somewhat higher. While analysts also differ on the size of the price increase likely required to pay for the settlement, most seem to peg it around $.70 per pack. Using $1.90 as the average price in 1997, that represents a 36 percent increase. Using an elasticity of −0.4, smoking should decline by about 15 percent.

Is that enough? It's not clear. One of the terms of the agreement is to reduce teenage smoking by 58 percent by the year 2001. Clearly, price alone will not do the trick.

The day the agreement was announced, the price of stocks in the biggest tobacco companies went up!

Stock prices reflect the expected future profits of the tobacco companies as well as the uncertainty resulting from the unknown liabilities that could come from future lawsuits. The uncertainty was reduced, but could tobacco profits rise after the settlement even with the $368 billion payout? The answer is yes.

There are several reasons. First, recall that demand is inelastic, and a price increase increases total revenue when demand is inelastic (see chapter 5). Second, because the $368 billion is paid out over 25 years, its "present value" (see chapter 11 appendix) is much lower. One estimate puts the true cost in 1997 dollars at $194.5 billion; that is, if the tobacco companies put $194.5 billion in corporate bonds today, it would have enough including interest to pay the full $368 billion over the next 25 years. Third, the tobacco firms will be spared the costs of countless future lawsuits. Although the settlement seems like a lot, shareholders seem to expect that profits will rise.

For more on internalizing externalities, see the Case and Fair Web page at
http://www.prenhall.com/casefair.

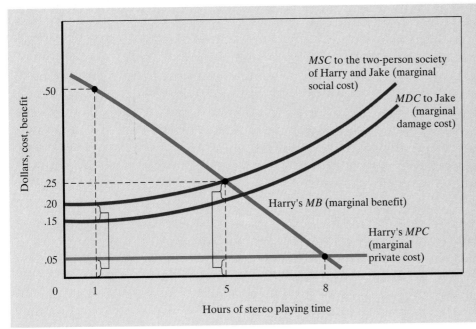

FIGURE 16.3

Externalities in a College Dormitory

The marginal benefits to Harry exceed the marginal costs he must bear to play his stereo for a period of up to eight hours. But when the stereo is playing, a cost is being imposed on Jake. When we add the costs borne by Harry to the damage costs imposed on Jake we get the full cost of the stereo to the two-person society made up of Harry and Jake. Playing the stereo more than five hours is inefficient because the benefits to Harry are less than the social cost for every hour above five. If Harry considers only his private costs, he will play the stereo for too long a time from society's point of view.

willing to pay to avoid it. The damage, or cost, imposed on Jake is represented in Figure 16.3 by the curve labeled *MDC*. Formally, **marginal damage cost (MDC)** is the additional harm done by increasing the level of an externality-producing activity by one unit. Assuming Jake would be willing to pay some amount of money to avoid the music, it is reasonable to assume the amount increases each successive hour. His headache gets worse with each additional hour forced to listen to bluegrass.

In the simple society of Jake and Harry, it's easy to add up social benefits and costs. At every level of output (stereo playing time), total social cost is the sum of the private costs borne by Harry and the damage costs borne by Jake. In Figure 16.3, *MPC* (constant at $.05 per hour) is added to *MDC* to get *MSC*.

Consider now what would happen if Harry simply ignored Jake.[2] If Harry decides to play the stereo, Jake will be damaged. As long as Harry gains more in personal benefits from an additional hour of listening to music than he incurs in costs, the stereo will stay on. He will play it for eight hours (the point where Harry's $MB = MPC$). This result is inefficient; for every hour of play beyond five, the marginal social cost borne by society (in this case, a society made up of Harry and Jake) exceeds the benefits to Harry (that is, $MSC >$ Harry's MB).

It is generally true, then, that:

> When economic decisions ignore external costs, whether those costs are borne by one person or by society, those decisions are likely to be inefficient.

We will return to Harry and Jake to see how they deal with their problem. First, we need to discuss the general problem of correcting for externalities.

INTERNALIZING EXTERNALITIES

A number of mechanisms are available to provide decision makers with incentives to weigh the external costs and benefits of their decisions, a process called *internalization*. In some cases, externalities are internalized through bargaining and negotiation without

marginal damage cost (MDC)
The additional harm done by increasing the level of an externality-producing activity by one unit. If producing product X pollutes the water in a river, MDC is the additional cost imposed by the added pollution that results from increasing output by one unit of X per period.

---

[2]It may actually be easier for people to ignore the social costs imposed by their actions when those costs fall on large numbers of other people whom they do not have to look in the eye or whom they do not know personally. For the moment, however, we assume that Harry takes no account of Jake.

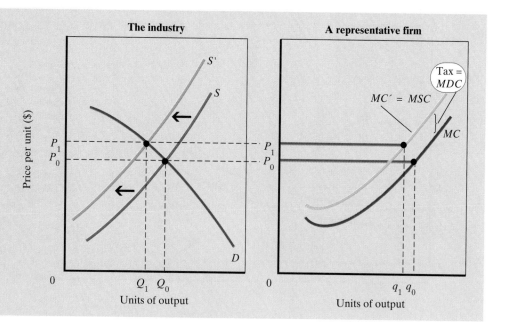

FIGURE 16.4

Tax Imposed on a Firm Equal to Marginal Damage Cost

If a per unit tax exactly equal to marginal damage costs is imposed on a firm, the firm will weigh the tax, and thus the damage costs, in its decisions. At the new equilibrium price, P_1, consumers will be paying an amount sufficient to cover full resource costs as well as the cost of damage imposed. The efficient level of output for the firm is q_1.

government involvement. In other cases, private bargains fail and the only alternative may be government action of some kind.

Five approaches have been taken to solving the problem of externalities: (1) government-imposed taxes and subsidies, (2) private bargaining and negotiation, (3) legal rules and procedures, (4) the sale or auctioning of rights to impose externalities, and (5) direct government regulation. While each is best suited for a different set of circumstances, all five provide decision makers with an incentive to weigh the external effects of their decisions.

➤ **Taxes and Subsidies**   Traditionally, economists have advocated marginal taxes and subsidies as a direct way of forcing firms to consider external costs or benefits. When a firm imposes an external social cost, the reasoning goes, a per unit tax should be imposed equal to the damages of each successive unit of output produced by the firm—the tax should be *exactly equal* to marginal damage costs.[3]

Figure 16.4 repeats the diagram that appears as Figure 16.2b, but this time the damage costs are paid by the firm in the form of a per-unit tax (that is, the tax = MDC). The firm now faces a marginal cost curve that is the same as the marginal social cost curve (MC' = MSC). Remember that the industry supply curve is the sum of the marginal cost curves of the individual firms. This means that as a result of the tax the industry supply curve shifts back to the left, driving up price from P_0 to P_1. The efficient level of output is q_1, where P = MC'. (Recall our general equilibrium analysis from chapter 12.)

Because a profit-maximizing firm equates price with marginal cost, the new price to consumers covers both the resource costs of producing the product and the damage costs. The consumer-decision process is once again efficient at the margin, because marginal social benefit as reflected in market price is equal to the full marginal cost of the product.

Measuring Damages   The biggest problem with this approach is that damages must be estimated in financial terms. For the detergent plant polluting the nearby river to be properly taxed, the government must evaluate the damages done to residents downstream in money terms. This is difficult, but not impossible. When legal remedies are

---

[3]As we discuss later in this chapter, damage costs are difficult to measure. It is often assumed that they are proportional to the volume of pollutants discharged into the air or water. Instead of taxes, governments often impose *effluent charges*, which make the cost to polluters proportional to the amount of pollution caused. We will use "tax" to refer to both taxes and effluent charges.

pursued, judges are forced to make such estimates as they decide on compensation to be paid. Surveys of "willingness to pay," studies of property values in affected versus non-affected areas, and sometimes the market value of recreational activities can provide basic data.

The monetary value of damages to health and loss of life is, naturally, much more difficult to estimate, and any measurement of such losses is controversial. But even here, policy makers frequently make judgments that implicitly set values on life and health. Tens of thousands of deaths and millions of serious injuries result from traffic accidents in the United States every year, yet Americans are unwilling to give up driving or to reduce the speed limit to 40 miles per hour—the costs of either course of action would be too high. In response to public demand, Congress in 1987 passed legislation to allow states to increase the speed limit to 65 miles per hour on rural parts of interstate highways. If most Americans are willing to increase the risk of death in exchange for shorter driving times, the value we place on life clearly has its limits.

Be sure to realize that taxing externality-producing activities may not eliminate damages. Taxes on these activities are not designed to eliminate externalities; they are simply meant to force decision makers to consider the full costs of their decisions. Even if we assume that a tax correctly measures all the damage done, the decision maker may find it advantageous to continue causing the damage. The detergent manufacturer may find it most profitable to pay the tax and go on polluting the river. It can continue to pollute because the revenues from selling its product are sufficient to cover the cost of resources used *and to compensate the damaged parties fully.* In such a case, producing the product in spite of the pollution is "worth it" to society. It would be inefficient for the firm to stop polluting. Only if damage costs were very high would it make sense to stop. Thus, you can see the importance of proper measurement of damage costs.

Reducing Damages to an Efficient Level Taxes also provide firms with an incentive to use the most efficient technology for dealing with damage. If a tax reflects true damages, and if it is reduced when damages are reduced, firms may choose to avoid or reduce the tax by using a different technology that causes less damage. Suppose our soap manufacturer is taxed $10,000 per month for polluting the river. If the soap plant can ship its waste to a disposal site elsewhere at a cost of $7,000 per month and thereby avoid the tax, it will do so. If a plant belching sulfides into the air can install "smoke scrubbers" that eliminate emissions for an amount less than the tax imposed for polluting the air, it will do so.

The Incentive to Take Care and to Avoid Harm You should understand that all externalities involve at least two parties and that it is not always clear which party is "causing" the damage. Take our friends Harry and Jake. Harry enjoys music; Jake enjoys quiet. If Harry plays his music, he imposes a cost on Jake. If Jake can force Harry to stop listening to music, he imposes a cost on Harry.

Often, the best solution to an externality problem may not involve stopping the externality-generating activity. Suppose Jake and Harry's dormitory has a third resident, Pete. Pete hates silence and loves bluegrass music. The resident adviser on Harry's floor arranges for Pete and Jake to switch rooms. What was once an external cost has been transformed into an external benefit. Everyone is better off. Harry and Pete get to listen to music, and Jake gets his silence.

Sometimes, the most efficient solution to an externality problem is for the damaged party to avoid the damage. But if full compensation is paid by the damager, damaged parties may have no incentive to do so. Consider a laundry located next to the exhaust fans from the kitchen of a Chinese restaurant. Suppose damages run to $1,000 per month because the laundry must use special air filters in its dryers so that the clothes will not smell of Szechuan spices. The laundry looks around and finds a perfectly good alternative location away from the restaurant that rents for only $500 per month above its current rent. Without any compensation from the Chinese restaurant, the laundry will move and the total damage will be the $500 per month extra rent that it must pay. But if the restaurant compensates the laundry for damages of $1,000 a month, why should the laundry move? Under these conditions, a move is unlikely, even though it would be efficient.

Subsidizing External Benefits   Sometimes activities or decisions generate external benefits instead of costs, as in the case of Harry and Pete. Real estate investment provides another example. Investors who revitalize a downtown area—an old theater district in a big city, for example—provide benefits to many people, both in the city and in surrounding areas.

Activities that provide such external social benefits may be subsidized at the margin to give decision makers an incentive to consider them. Just as ignoring social costs can lead to inefficient decisions, so too can ignoring social benefits. Government subsidies for housing and other development, either directly through specific expenditure programs or indirectly through tax exemptions, have been justified on such grounds.

▶ **Bargaining and Negotiation**   In a notable article written in 1960, Ronald Coase pointed out that the government need not be involved in every case of externality.[4] Coase argued that private bargains and negotiations are likely to lead to an efficient solution in many social damage cases without any government involvement at all. This argument is referred to as the **Coase theorem.**

Coase theorem *Under certain conditions, when externalities are present, private parties can arrive at the efficient solution without government involvement.*

For Coase's solution to work, three conditions must be satisfied. First, the basic rights at issue must be clearly understood. Either Harry has the right to play his stereo or Jake has the right to silence. These rights will probably be spelled out in dorm rules. Second, there must be no impediments to bargaining. Parties must be willing and able to discuss the issues openly and without cost. Third, only a few people can be involved. Serious problems can develop when one of the parties to a bargain is a large group of people, such as all the residents of a large town.

For the sake of our example, let us say that all three of these conditions hold for Harry and Jake and that no room swap with someone like Pete is possible. The dorm rules establish basic rights in this case by specifying that during certain hours of the day, Harry has the right to play his stereo as loudly as he pleases. Returning to Figure 16.3 and our earlier discussion, suppose that under the rules Harry is free to choose any number of music-playing hours between zero and eight.

Because Harry is under no legal constraint to pay any attention to Jake's wishes, you might be tempted to think that he will ignore Jake and play his stereo for eight hours. (Recall that up to eight hours, the marginal benefits to Harry exceed the marginal costs that he must pay.) However, Jake is willing to pay Harry to play his stereo fewer than eight hours. For the first hour of play, the marginal damage to Jake is $0.15, so Jake would be willing to pay Harry $0.15 in the first hour to have Harry turn off his stereo. The opportunity cost to Harry of playing the first hour is thus $0.15 plus the (constant) marginal private cost of $0.05, or $0.20. Because the marginal gain to Harry in the first hour is $0.50, Harry would not accept the bribe. Likewise, for hours two through five the marginal benefit to Harry exceeds the bribe that Jake would be willing to pay plus the marginal private cost.

After five hours, however, Jake is willing to pay $0.25 per hour to have Harry turn off his stereo. This means that the opportunity cost to Harry is $0.30. But after five hours the marginal benefit to Harry of another hour of listening to his stereo falls below $0.25. Harry will thus accept the bribe not to listen to his music in the sixth hour. Similarly, a bribe of $0.25 per hour is sufficient to have Harry not play the stereo in the seventh and eighth hours, and Jake would be willing to pay such a bribe. Five hours is the efficient amount of playing time. More hours or fewer hours reduces net total benefits to Harry and Jake.

---

[4]See Ronald Coase, "The Problem of Social Cost," *Journal of Law and Economics* (1960).

Coase also pointed out that bargaining will bring the contending parties to the right solution regardless of where rights are initially assigned. For example, suppose that the dorm rules state that Jake has the right to silence. This being the case, Jake can go to the dorm administrators and have them enforce the rule. Now when Harry plays the stereo and Jake asks him to turn it off, Harry must comply.

Now the tables are turned. Accepting the dorm rules (as he must), Harry knocks on Jake's door. Jake's damages from the first hour are only $0.15. This means that if he were compensated by more than $0.15, he would allow the music to be played. Now the stage is set for bargaining. Harry gets $0.45 in net benefit from the first hour of playing the stereo ($0.50 minus private cost of $0.05). Thus, he is willing to pay up to $0.45 for the privilege. If there are no impediments to bargaining, money will change hands. Harry will pay Jake some amount between $0.15 and $0.45 and, just as before, the stereo will continue to play. Jake has, in effect, sold his right to have silence to Harry. As before, bargaining between the two parties will lead to five hours of stereo playing. At exactly five hours, Jake will stop taking compensation and tell Harry to turn the stereo off. (Look again at Figure 16.3 to see that this is true.)

In both cases the offer of compensation might be made in some form other than cash. Jake may offer Harry goodwill, a favor or two, or the use of his Harley Davidson for an hour.

Coase's critics are quick to point out that the conditions required for bargaining to produce the efficient result are not always present. The biggest problem with Coase's system is also a common problem. Very often one party to a bargain is a large group of people, and our reasoning may be subject to a fallacy of composition.

Suppose a power company in Pittsburgh is polluting the air. The damaged parties are the 100,000 people who live near the plant. Let's assume the plant has the right to pollute. The Coase theorem predicts that the people who are damaged by the smoke will get together and offer a bribe (as Jake offered a bribe to Harry). If the bribe is sufficient to induce the power plant to stop polluting or reduce the pollutants with air scrubbers, then it will accept the bribe and cut down on the pollution. If it is not, the pollution will continue, but the firm will have weighed all the costs (just as Harry did when he continued to play the stereo) and the result will be efficient.

But not everyone will contribute to the bribe fund. First, each contribution is so small relative to the whole that no single contribution makes much of a difference. Making a contribution may seem unimportant or unnecessary to some. Second, everyone gets to breathe the cleaner air, whether he or she contributes to the bribe or not. Many people will not participate simply because they are not compelled to, and the private bargain breaks down—the bribe that the group comes up with will be less than the full damages unless everyone participates. (We discuss these two problems—the "drop-in-the-bucket" and the "free-rider"—later in this chapter.) When the number of damaged parties is large, government taxes or regulation may be the only avenue to a remedy.

> **Legal Rules and Procedures** For bargaining to result in an efficient outcome, the initial assignment of rights must be clear to both parties. When rights are established by law, more often than not some mechanism to protect those rights is also built into the law. In some cases where a nuisance exists, for example, there may be injunctive remedies. In such cases, the victim can go to court and ask for an **injunction** that forbids the damage-producing behavior from continuing. If the dorm rules specifically give Jake the right to silence, Jake's getting the resident adviser to speak to Harry is something like getting an injunction.

Injunctive remedies are irrelevant when the damage has already been done. Consider accidents. If your leg has already been broken as the result of an automobile accident, enjoining the driver of the other car from drinking and driving won't work—it's too late. In these cases, rights must be protected by **liability rules**, rules that require A to compensate B for damages imposed. In theory, such rules are designed to do exactly the same thing that taxing a polluter is designed to do: provide decision makers with

injunction *A court order forbidding the continuation of behavior that leads to damages.*

liability rules *Laws that require A to compensate B for damages imposed.*

an incentive to weigh all the consequences, actual and potential, of their decisions. Just as taxes do not stop all pollution, liability rules do not stop all accidents.

However, the threat of liability actions does induce people to take more care than they might otherwise. Product liability is a good example. If a person is damaged in some way because a product is defective, the producing company is in most cases held liable for the damages, even if the company took reasonable care in producing the product. Producers have a powerful incentive to be careful. If consumers know they will be generously compensated for any damages, however, they may not have as powerful an incentive to be careful when using the product.

➤ **Selling or Auctioning Pollution Rights** We have already established that not all externality-generating activities should be banned. Around the world, the private automobile has become the clearest example of an externality-generating activity whose benefits (many believe) outweigh its costs.

Many externalities are imposed when we drive our cars. First, congestion is an externality. Even though the marginal "harm" imposed by any one driver is small, the sum total is a serious cost to all who spend hours in traffic jams. Second, most of the air pollution in the United States comes from automobiles. The problem is most evident in Los Angeles, where smog loaded with harmful emissions (mostly from cars) blankets the city virtually every day. Finally, driving increases the likelihood of accidents, raising insurance costs to all.

While we do not ignore these costs from the standpoint of public policy, we certainly have not banned driving. This is also true for many other forms of pollution. In many cases we have consciously opted to allow ocean dumping, river pollution, and air pollution within limits.

The right to impose environmental externalities is beneficial to the parties causing the damage. In a sense, the right to dump in a river or pollute the air or the ocean is a resource. Thinking of the privilege to dump in this way suggests an alternative mechanism for controlling pollution: selling or auctioning the pollution rights to the highest bidder. The Clean Air Act of 1990 takes this approach by limiting the quantity of emissions from the nation's power plants. To minimize the initial cost of compliance and to distribute the burden fairly, each plant is issued tradable pollution rights. These rights can be sold at auction to those plants whose costs of compliance are highest.

Another example of selling externality rights is in Singapore, where the right to buy a car is auctioned each year. Despite very high taxes and the need for permits to drive in downtown areas, the roads in Singapore have become congested. The government decided to limit the number of new cars on the road because the external costs

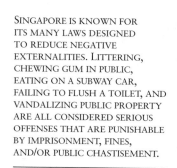

SINGAPORE IS KNOWN FOR ITS MANY LAWS DESIGNED TO REDUCE NEGATIVE EXTERNALITIES. LITTERING, CHEWING GUM IN PUBLIC, EATING ON A SUBWAY CAR, FAILING TO FLUSH A TOILET, AND VANDALIZING PUBLIC PROPERTY ARE ALL CONSIDERED SERIOUS OFFENSES THAT ARE PUNISHABLE BY IMPRISONMENT, FINES, AND/OR PUBLIC CHASTISEMENT.

associated with them (congestion and pollution) have become very high. With these limits imposed, the decision was made to distribute car-ownership rights to those who place the highest value on them. It seems likely that taxi drivers, trucking companies, bus lines, and traveling salespeople will buy the licenses; families who drive for convenience instead of taking public transportation will find them too expensive.

Congestion and pollution are not the only externalities that Singapore takes seriously. In 1994, the fine for littering was $625, for failing to flush a public toilet $94, and for eating on a subway $312. In addition, 514 people were convicted in 1992 of illegally smoking in public.

▶ **Direct Regulation of Externalities**   Taxes, subsidies, legal rules, and public auction are all methods of indirect regulation designed to induce firms and households to weigh the social costs of their actions against their benefits. The actual size of the external cost/benefit depends on the reaction of households and firms to the incentives provided by the taxes, subsidies, and rules.

For obvious reasons, many externalities are too important to be regulated indirectly. Dumping cancer-causing chemicals into the ground near a public water supply is simply illegal, and those who do it can be prosecuted and sent to jail.

Direct regulation of externalities takes place at the federal, state, and local level. The Environmental Protection Agency is a federal agency established by an act of Congress in 1970. Since the 1960s, Congress has passed lots of legislation that set specific standards for permissible discharges into the air and water. Every state has a division or department charged with regulating activities that are likely to harm the environment. Most airports in the United States have landing patterns and hours that are regulated by local governments to minimize noise.

Many criminal penalties and sanctions for violating environmental regulations are like the taxes imposed on polluters. Not all violations and crimes are stopped, but violators and criminals face "costs." For the outcome to be efficient, the penalties they expect to pay should reflect the damage their actions impose on society.

PUBLIC (SOCIAL) GOODS

Another source of market failure lies in **public goods**, often called **social**, or **collective**, **goods**. Public goods are defined by two closely related characteristics: They are nonrival in consumption and/or their benefits are nonexcludable. As we will see, these goods represent a market failure because they have characteristics that make it difficult for the private sector to produce them profitably:

> In an unregulated market economy with no government to see that they are produced, public goods would at best be produced in insufficient quantity and at worst not produced at all.

public goods (social or **collective goods)** *Goods that are nonrival in consumption and/or their benefits are nonexcludable.*

THE CHARACTERISTICS OF PUBLIC GOODS

A good is **nonrival in consumption** when A's consumption of it does not interfere with B's consumption of it. This means that the benefits of the goods are collective—they accrue to everyone. National defense, for instance, benefits us all. The fact that I am protected in no way detracts from the fact that you are protected; every citizen is protected just as much as every other citizen. If the air is cleaned up, my breathing that air does not interfere with your breathing it, nor (under ordinary circumstances) is that air used up as more people breathe it. Private goods in contrast are *rival in consumption*. If I eat a hamburger, you cannot eat it too.

Goods can sometimes generate collective benefits and still be rival in consumption. This happens when crowding occurs. A park or a pool can accommodate many people

nonrival in consumption *A characteristic of public goods: One person's enjoyment of the benefits of a public good does not interfere with another's consumption of it.*

nonexcludable *A characteristic of most public goods: Once a good is produced, no one can be excluded from enjoying its benefits.*

at the same time, generating collective benefits for everyone. But when too many people crowd in on a hot day, they begin to interfere with each other's enjoyment.

Most public goods are also **nonexcludable**. Once the good is produced, people cannot be excluded for any reason from enjoying its benefits. Once a national defense system is established, it protects everyone.

For a private profit-making firm to produce a good and make a profit, it must be able to withhold that good from those who do not pay. McDonald's can make money selling chicken sandwiches only because you don't get the chicken sandwich unless you pay for it first. If payment were voluntary, McDonald's would not be in business for long.

Consider an entrepreneur who decides to offer better police protection to the city of Metropolis. Careful (and we assume correct) market research reveals that the citizens of Metropolis want high-quality protection and are willing to pay for it. Not everyone is willing to pay the same amount. Some can afford more, others less, and people have different preferences and different feelings about risk. Our entrepreneur hires a sales force and begins to sell his service. Soon, he encounters a problem. Because his is a private company, payment is voluntary. He can't force anyone to pay. Payment for a hamburger is voluntary too, but a hamburger can be withheld for nonpayment. The good that our new firm is selling, however, is by nature a public good.

As a potential consumer of a public good, I face a dilemma. I want more police protection, and, let's say, I'm even willing to pay $50 a month for it. But nothing is contingent upon my payment. First, if the good is produced, the crime rate falls and all residents benefit. I get that benefit whether I pay for it or not. I get a free ride! And that is why this dilemma is called the **free-rider problem**. Second, my payment is very small relative to the amount that must be collected to provide the service. Thus, the amount of police protection actually produced will not be significantly affected by the amount that I contribute, or whether I contribute at all. This is the **drop-in-the-bucket problem**.

free-rider problem *A problem intrinsic to public goods: Because people can enjoy the benefits of public goods whether they pay for them or not, they are usually unwilling to pay for them.*

drop-in-the-bucket problem *A problem intrinsic to public goods: The good or service is usually so costly that its provision generally does not depend on whether or not any single person pays.*

> A consumer acting in his or her own self-interest has no incentive to contribute voluntarily to the production of public goods. Some will feel a moral responsibility or social pressure to contribute, and those people indeed may do so. But the economic incentive is missing, and most people do not find room in their budgets for many voluntary payments.

INCOME DISTRIBUTION AS A PUBLIC GOOD?

In the next chapter, we add the issues of justice and equity to the matters of economic efficiency that we are considering here. There we explain that the government may wish to change the distribution of income that results from the operation of the unregulated market on the grounds that the distribution is not fair. Before we do so, we need to note that some economists have argued for redistribution of income on grounds that it generates public benefits.

For example, let us say that many members of U.S. society want to eliminate hunger in the United States. Suppose you are willing to give $200 per year in exchange for the knowledge that people are not going to bed hungry. Many private charities in the United States use the money they raise to feed the poor. If you want to contribute, you can do so privately, through charity. So why do we need government involvement?

To answer this, we must consider the benefits of eliminating hunger. First, it generates collective psychological benefits; simply knowing that people are not starving helps us sleep better. Second, eliminating hunger may reduce disease, and this has lots of beneficial effects. People who are fit and strong are more likely to stay in school and to get and keep jobs. This reduces welfare claims and contributes positively to the economy. If people are less likely to get sick, insurance premiums for everyone will go down. Robberies may decline because fewer people are desperate for money. This means that all of us are less likely to be victims of crime, now and in the future.

These are goals that members of society may want to achieve. But just as there is no economic incentive to contribute voluntarily to national defense, so there is no economic incentive to contribute to private causes. If hunger is eliminated, you benefit whether you contributed or not—the free-rider problem! At the same time, poverty is a huge problem and your contribution cannot possibly have any influence on the amount of national hunger—the drop-in-the-bucket problem! The goals of income redistribution may be more like national defense than like a chicken sandwich from McDonald's.

> If we accept the idea that redistributing income generates a public good, private endeavors may fail to do what we want them to do, and government involvement may be called for.

PUBLIC PROVISION OF PUBLIC GOODS

All societies, past and present, have had to face the problem of providing public goods. When members of society get together to form a government, they do so to provide themselves with goods and services that will not be provided if they act separately. Like any other good or service, a body of laws (or system of justice) is produced with labor, capital, and other inputs. Law and the courts yield social benefits, and they must be set up and administered by some sort of collective, cooperative effort.

Notice that we are talking about public *provision*, not public *production*. Once the government decides what service it wants to provide, it often contracts with the private sector to produce the good. Much of the material for national defense is produced by private defense contractors. Highways, government offices, data processing services, and so forth are usually produced by private firms.

One of the immediate problems of public provision is that it frequently leads to public dissatisfaction. It is easy to be angry at government. Part, but certainly not all, of the reason for this dissatisfaction lies in the nature of the goods that government provides. Firms that produce or sell private goods post a price—we can choose to buy any quantity we want, or we can walk away without any. It makes no sense to get mad at a shoe store, because no one can force you to shop there.

You cannot shop for collectively beneficial public goods. When it comes to national defense, the government must choose one and only one kind and quantity of (collective) output to produce. Because none of us can choose how much should be spent or on what, we are all dissatisfied. Even if the government does its job with reasonable efficiency, at any given time about half of us think that we have too much national defense and about half of us think that we have too little.

In 1993, the Congress passed and the president signed the Brady bill. It included $3.4 billion over 5 years to put 50,000 additional police officers on the streets and imposed a 5-day waiting period for purchase of a handgun. The legislation aimed to lower the crime rate and produce a public good. In fact, the FBI's Crime Index dropped 1% in 1994 and another 1% in 1995; violent crime decreased in both years by 3%. In 1996, the Crime Index dropped 3% overall and violent crime decreased by 7%. Many feel the drop was at least in part the result of a growing economy.

OPTIMAL PROVISION OF PUBLIC GOODS

In the early 1950s, Paul Samuelson demonstrated that there exists an *optimal*, or *most efficient*, level of output for every public good.[5] The discussion of the Samuelson solution that follows leads us straight to the thorny problem of how societies, as opposed to individuals, make choices.

➤ **Samuelson's Theory** An efficient economy produces what people want. Private producers, whether competitors or monopolists, are constrained by the market demand for their products. If they can't sell their products for more than it costs to produce them, they are out of business. But because private goods permit exclusion, firms can withhold their products until households pay. Buying a product at a posted price reveals that it is "worth" at least that amount to you and to everyone who buys it.

---

[5]Paul A. Samuelson, "Diagrammatic Exposition of a Theory of Public Expenditure," *Review of Economics and Statistics* XXXVII (1955).

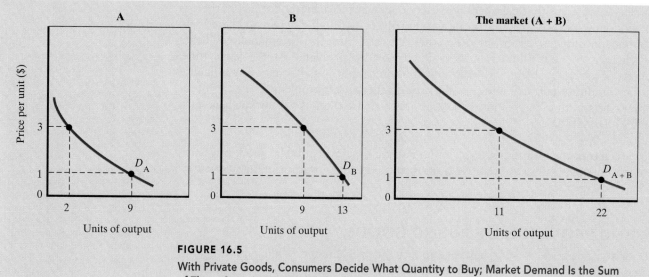

FIGURE 16.5

With Private Goods, Consumers Decide What Quantity to Buy; Market Demand Is the Sum of Those Quantities at Each Price

At a price of $3, A buys 2 units and B buys 9 for a total of 11. At a price of $1, A buys 9 units and B buys 13 for a total of 22. We all buy the quantity of each private good that we want. Market demand is the horizontal sum of all individual demand curves.

Market demand for a private good is the sum of the quantities that each household decides to buy (as measured on the horizontal axis). The diagrams in Figure 16.5 review the derivation of a market demand curve. Assume society consists of two people, A and B. At a price of $1, A demands 9 units of the private good and B demands 13. Market demand at a price of $1 is 22 units. If price were to rise to $3, A's demand would drop to 2 units and B's would drop to 9 units; market demand at a price of $3 is 2 + 9 = 11 units. The point is that:

> The price mechanism forces people to reveal what they want, and it forces firms to produce only what people are willing to pay for, but it works this way only because exclusion is possible.

People's preferences and demands for public goods are conceptually no different than their preferences and demands for private goods. You may want fire protection and be willing to pay for it in the same way you want to listen to a CD. To demonstrate that an efficient level of production exists, Samuelson assumes we know people's preferences. Figure 16.6 shows demand curves for buyers A and B. If the public good were available in the private market at a price of $6, A would buy X_1 units. Or, put another way, A is willing to pay $6 per unit to obtain X_1 units of the public good. B is willing to pay only $3 per unit to obtain X_1 units of the public good.

Remember: Public goods are nonrival and/or nonexcludable—benefits accrue simultaneously to everyone. One, and only one, quantity can be produced, and that is the amount that everyone gets. If X_1 units are produced, A gets X_1 and B gets X_1. If X_2 units are produced, A gets X_2 and B gets X_2.

To arrive at market demand for public goods, then, we do not sum quantities. Rather, *we add up the amounts that individual households are willing to pay for each potential level of output.* In Figure 16.6, A is willing to pay $6 per unit for X_1 units and B is willing to pay $3 per unit for X_1 units. Thus, if society consists only of A and B, society is willing to pay $9 per unit for X_1 units of public good X. For X_2 units of output, society is willing to pay a total of $4 per unit.

PART THREE
*Market Imperfections
and Government*

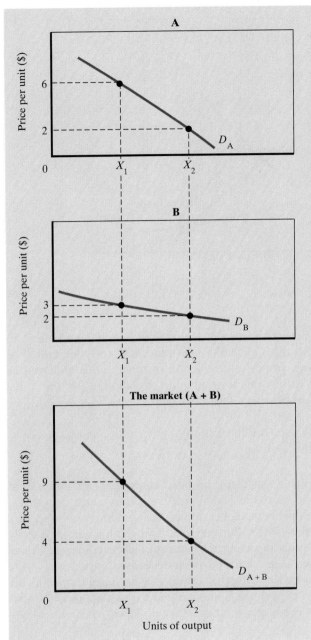

FIGURE 16.6

With Public Goods, There Is Only *One* Level of Output, and Consumers Are Willing to Pay Different Amounts for Each Level

A is willing to pay $6 per unit for X_1 units of the public good. B is willing to pay only $3 for X_1 units. Society—in this case A and B—is willing to pay a total of $9 for X_1 units of the good. Because only one level of output can be chosen for a public good, we must add A's contribution to B's to determine market demand. This means adding demand curves vertically.

For private goods, market demand is the horizontal sum of individual demand curves—we add the different *quantities* that households consume (as measured on the *horizontal* axis). For public goods, market demand is the vertical sum of individual demand curves—we add the different *amounts* that households are willing to pay to obtain each level of output (as measured on the *vertical* axis).

Samuelson argued that once we know how much society is willing to pay for a public good, we need only compare that amount to the cost of its production. Figure 16.7 reproduces A's and B's demand curves and the total demand curve for the public good. As long as society (in this case, A and B) is willing to pay more than the marginal cost of production, the good should be produced. If A is willing to pay $6 per unit of public good and B is willing to pay $3 per unit, society is willing to pay $9.

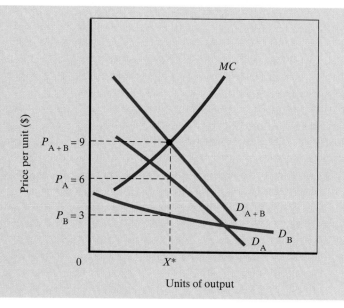

FIGURE 16.7

Optimal Production of a Public Good

Optimal production of a public good means producing as long as society's total willingness to pay per unit ($D_{A + B}$) is greater than the marginal cost of producing the good.

optimal level of provision for public goods *The level at which resources are drawn from the production of other goods and services only to the extent that people want the public good and are willing to pay for it. At this level, society's willingness to pay per unit is equal to the marginal cost of producing the good.*

The efficient level of output here is X^* units. If at that level A is charged a fee of $6 per unit of X produced and B is charged a fee of $3 per unit of X, everyone should be happy. Resources are being drawn from the production of other goods and services only to the extent that people want the public good and are willing to pay for it. We have arrived at the **optimal level of provision for public goods.**

> At the optimal level, society's total willingness to pay per unit is equal to the marginal cost of producing the good.

▶ **The Problems of Optimal Provision**   One major problem exists, however. To produce the optimal amount of each public good, the government must know something that it cannot possibly know—everyone's preferences. Because exclusion is impossible, nothing forces households to reveal their preferences. Furthermore, if we ask households directly about their willingness to pay, we run up against the same problem encountered by our protection-services salesman above. If my actual payment depends on my answer, I have an incentive to hide my true feelings. Knowing that I cannot be excluded from enjoying the benefits of the good and that my payment is not likely to have an appreciable influence on the level of output finally produced, what incentive do I have to tell the truth—or to contribute?

How does society decide which public goods to provide? We assume that members of society want certain public goods. Private producers in the market cannot make a profit by producing these goods, and the government cannot obtain enough information to measure society's demands accurately. No two societies have dealt with this dilemma in the same way. In some countries, dictators simply decide for the people. In others, representative political bodies speak for the people's preferences. In still others, people vote directly. None of these solutions works perfectly. We will return to the problem of social choice at the end of the chapter.

LOCAL PROVISION OF PUBLIC GOODS: TIEBOUT HYPOTHESIS

In 1956 Charles Tiebout made this point: To the extent that local governments are responsible for providing public goods, an efficient market-choice mechanism may exist. Consider a set of towns that are identical except for police protection. Towns that choose to spend a lot of money on police are likely to have a lower crime rate. A lower crime rate will attract households who are risk averse and are willing to pay higher taxes for lower risk of being a crime victim. Those who are willing to bear greater risk may choose to live in the low-tax/high-crime towns. Also, if some town is very efficient at crime prevention, it will attract residents—given that each town has limited space, property values will be bid up in this town. The higher home price in this town is the "price" of the lower crime rate.

According to the **Tiebout hypothesis**, an efficient mix of public goods is produced when local prices (in the form of taxes or higher housing costs) come to reflect consumer preferences just as they do in the market for private goods. What is different in the Tiebout world is that people exercise consumer sovereignty not by "buying" different combinations of goods in a market, but by "voting with their feet" (choosing among bundles of public goods and tax rates produced by different towns and participating in local government).

Tiebout hypothesis *An efficient mix of public goods is produced when local land/housing prices and taxes come to reflect consumer preferences just as they do in the market for private goods.*

IMPERFECT INFORMATION

In chapters 6 through 12, we assumed households and firms have complete information on products and inputs. To make informed choices among goods and services available in the market, households must have full information on product quality, availability, and price. To make sound judgments about what inputs to use, firms must have full information on input availability, quality, and price.

The absence of full information can cause households and firms to make mistakes. A voluntary exchange is almost always evidence that both parties benefit. Thus most voluntary exchanges are efficient. But in the presence of imperfect information, not all exchanges are efficient. An obvious example is fraud. Frank sells a bottle of colored water to Ed claiming it will grow hair on Ed's bald head. Had Ed known what was really in the bottle, he would not have purchased it.

Firms as well as consumers can be the victims of incomplete or inaccurate information. Recall that a profit-maximizing competitive firm will hire workers as long as the marginal revenue product of labor (MRP_L) is greater than the wage rate. But how can a firm judge the *productivity* of a potential hire? Also, suppose that a worker steals from the firm. Clearly, the cost of employing that worker is greater than just the wage that he or she is paid.

ADVERSE SELECTION

The problem of **adverse selection** can occur when a buyer or seller enters an exchange with another party who has more information. Suppose there are only two types of workers: lazy workers and hard workers. Each worker knows which she is, but employers cannot tell. If there is only one wage rate, lazy workers will be overpaid relative to their productivity and hard workers will be underpaid. Recall that workers weigh the value of leisure and nonmarket production against the wage in deciding whether to enter the labor force. Because hard workers will end up underpaid relative to their productivity, fewer hard workers than is optimal will be attracted into the labor force. Similarly, because lazy workers are overpaid relative to their productivity, more of them will be attracted into the labor force than is optimal. Hence, the market has selected among workers adversely.

adverse selection *Can occur when a buyer or seller enters into an exchange with another party who has more information.*

The classic case of adverse selection is the used car market. Suppose owners (potential sellers) of used cars have all the information about the real quality of their cars. Suppose further that half of all used cars are "lemons" (bad cars) and that half are "cherries" (good cars), and consumers (potential used-car buyers) are willing to pay $6,000 for a cherry but only $2,000 for a lemon.

If half the cars for sale were lemons and half were cherries, the market price of a car would be about $4,000, and consumers would have a 50–50 chance of getting a lemon. But there is an adverse selection problem because of unequal information: Used car *sellers* know whether they have a lemon or a cherry while used car *buyers* do not. Lemon owners know they are making out like bandits by selling at $4,000, while cherry owners know they are not getting what their car is really worth. Thus, more lemon owners are attracted into selling their cars than are cherry owners.

Over time, buyers come to understand that the probability of getting a lemon is greater than the probability of getting a cherry, and the price of used cars drops. This makes matters worse because it provides even less incentive for cherry owners to sell their cars. This process will continue until only lemons are left in the market. Once again, the unequal information leads to an adverse selection.[6]

Adverse selection is also a problem in insurance markets. Insurance companies insure people against risks like health problems or accidents. Individuals know more about their own health than anyone else, even with required medical exams. If medical insurance rates are set at the same level for everyone, then medical insurance is a better deal for those who are unhealthy than for those who are healthy and likely never to have a claim. This means more unhealthy people will buy insurance, which forces insurance companies to raise premiums. As with used cars, fewer healthy people and more unhealthy people will end up with insurance.

MORAL HAZARD

moral hazard *Arises when one party to a contract passes the cost of his or her behavior on to the other party to the contract.*

Another information problem that arises in insurance markets is *moral hazard*. Often, people enter into contracts in which the result of the contract, at least in part, depends on one of the parties' future behavior. A **moral hazard** problem arises when one party to a contract passes the cost of his or her behavior on to the other party to the contract. For example, accident insurance policies are contracts that agree to pay for repairs to your car if it is damaged in an accident. Whether you have an accident or not in part depends on whether you drive cautiously. Similarly, apartment leases may specify that the landlord perform routine maintenance around the apartment. If you punch the wall every time you get angry, your landlord ultimately pays the repair bill.

Such contracts can lead to inefficient behavior. The problem is like the externality problem in which firms and households have no incentive to consider the full costs of their behavior. If my car is fully insured against theft, why should I lock it? If visits to the dentist are free under my dental insurance plan, why not get my teeth cleaned six times a year?

Like adverse selection, the moral hazard problem is an information problem. Contracting parties cannot always determine the future behavior of the person with whom they are contracting. If all future behavior could be predicted, contracts could be written to try to eliminate undesirable behavior. Sometimes this is possible. Life insurance companies do not pay off in the case of suicide. Fire insurance companies will not write a policy unless you have smoke detectors. If you cause unreasonable damage to an apartment, your landlord can retain your security deposit.

> It is impossible to know everything about behavior and intentions. If a contract absolves one party of the consequences of his or her action, and people act in their own self-interest, the result is inefficient.

MARKET SOLUTIONS

Imperfect information violates one of the assumptions of perfect competition, but not all information problems are market failures. In fact, information is itself valuable, and there is an incentive for competitive producers to produce it. As with any other good, there is an efficient quantity of information production.

Often, information is produced by consumers and producers themselves. The information-gathering process is called *market search*. When we go shopping for a "good buy" or for the "right" sweater, we are collecting the information that we need

[6]This discussion is based on a classic article by George Akerlof, "The Market for 'Lemons': Quality, Uncertainty, and the Market Mechanism," *Quarterly Journal of Economics* 84 (August 1970), 488–500.

to make an informed choice. Just as products are produced as long as the marginal benefit from additional output exceeds the marginal cost of production, consumers have an incentive to continue searching out information until the expected marginal benefit from an additional hour of search is equal to the cost of that additional hour. After I've looked in 11 different stores that sell sweaters, I know a great deal about the quality and prices available. Continuing to look takes up valuable time and effort that could be used doing other things. In shopping for a house or a car, I may spend much more time and effort searching out information than I might for a sweater, because the potential benefits (or losses) are much greater.

Firms also spend time and resources searching for information. Potential employers ask for letters of reference, resumes, and interviews before offering employment. Market research helps firms respond to consumer preferences. It should come as no surprise to you that the general rule is:

> Like consumers, profit-maximizing firms will gather information as long as the marginal benefits from continued search are greater than the marginal costs.

Many firms produce information for consumers and businesses. *Consumer Reports* is a magazine that tests consumer products and sells the results in the form of a periodical. Credit bureaus keep track of people's credit histories and sell credit reports to firms who need them to evaluate potential credit customers. "Head-hunting" firms collect information and search out applicants for jobs.

Because the market handles many information problems efficiently, we don't need to assume perfect information to arrive at an efficient allocation of resources. However, some information problems are not handled well by the market.

GOVERNMENT SOLUTIONS

Information is essentially a public good. If a set of test results on the safety of various products is produced, my having access to that information in no way reduces the value of that information to others. In other words, information is nonrival in consumption. When information is very costly for individuals to collect and disperse, it may be cheaper for government to produce it once for everybody.

In many cases, the government has set up special administrative agencies to ensure that accurate information reaches the public. As we noted in chapter 15, Congress established the Federal Trade Commission in 1914 specifically to deal with unfair and deceptive trade practices. The FTC regulates advertising, sets standards for disclosure of contents, and so forth. The Consumer Product Safety Commission sets standards of safety for potentially unsafe products. The Food and Drug Administration regulates the content of foods and drugs permitted on the market. It is illegal to sell a drug that has not been demonstrated to be effective. Many state governments have passed "lemon laws" that grant car buyers certain rights in case they end up with a troublesome car.

SOCIAL CHOICE

One view of government, or the public sector, holds that it exists to provide things that "society wants." A society is a collection of individuals, and each has a unique set of preferences. Defining what society wants, therefore, becomes a problem of **social choice**—of somehow adding up, or aggregating, individual preferences.

It is also important to understand that government is made up of individuals—politicians and government workers—whose *own* objectives in part determine what government does. To understand government, we must understand the incentives facing politicians and public servants, as well as the difficulties of aggregating the preferences of the members of a society.

social choice *The problem of deciding what society wants. The process of adding up individual preferences to make a choice for society as a whole.*

FIGURE 16.8

Preferences of Three Top University Officials

VP1 prefers A to B and B to C. VP2 prefers B to C and C to A. The Dean prefers C to A and A to B.

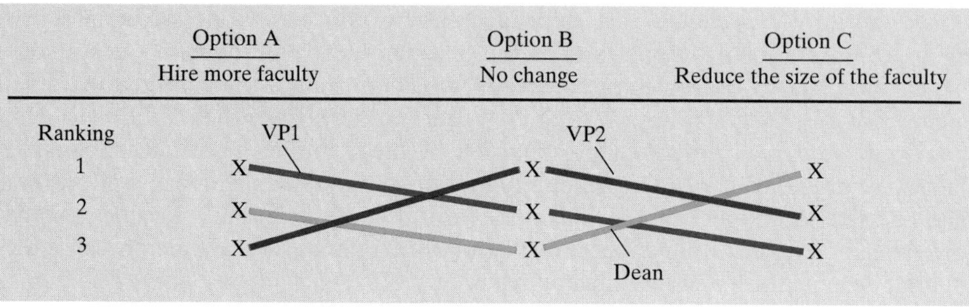

		Option A Hire more faculty	Option B No change	Option C Reduce the size of the faculty
Ranking		VP1	VP2	
1		X	X	X
2		X	X	X
3		X	X	X
			Dean	

THE VOTING PARADOX

Democratic societies use ballot procedures to determine aggregate preferences and to make the social decisions that follow from them. If all votes could be unanimous, efficient decisions would be guaranteed. Unfortunately, unanimity is virtually impossible to achieve when hundreds of millions of people, each with his or her own different preferences, are involved.

The most common social decision-making mechanism is majority rule—but it is not perfect. In 1951, Kenneth Arrow proved the **impossibility theorem**[7]—that it is impossible to devise a voting scheme that respects individual preferences and gives consistent, nonarbitrary results.

One example of a seemingly irrational result emerging from majority-rule voting is the voting paradox. Suppose that, faced with a decision about the future of the institution, the president of a major university opts to let her three top administrators vote on the following options: Should the university (A) increase the number of students and hire more faculty, (B) maintain the current size of the faculty and student body, or (C) cut back on faculty and reduce the student body? Figure 16.8 represents the preferences of the three administrators diagrammatically.

The vice president for finance (VP1) wants growth. He prefers A to B and B to C. The vice president for development (VP2), however, doesn't want to rock the boat. She prefers maintaining the current size of the institution, option B, to either of the others. If the status quo is out of the question, she would prefer option C. The dean believes in change; he wants to shake the place up, and he doesn't care whether that means increase or decrease. He prefers C to A and A to B.

Table 16.1 shows the results of the vote. When the three vote on A versus B, they vote in favor of A—to increase the size of the university rather than keep it the same size. VP1 and the dean outvote VP2. Voting on B and C produces a victory for option B; two of the three would rather hold the line than decrease the size of the institution. After two votes we have the result that A (increase) is preferred to B (no change) and that B (no change) is preferred to C (decrease).

The problem arises when we then have the three vote on A against C. Both VP2 and the dean vote for C, giving it the victory; C is actually preferred to A. But if A beats B, and B beats C, how can C beat A? The results are inconsistent.

The **voting paradox** illustrates several points. Most important is that when preferences for public goods differ across individuals, any system for adding up, or aggregating, those preferences can lead to inconsistencies. In addition, it illustrates just how much influence the person who sets the agenda has. If a vote had been taken on A and C first, the first two votes might never have occurred. This is why rules committees in both houses of Congress have enormous power; they establish the rules under which, as well as the order in which, legislation will be considered.

Another problem with majority-rule voting is that it leads to logrolling. **Logrolling** occurs when representatives trade votes—D helps get a majority in favor of E's program,

impossibility theorem *A proposition demonstrated by Kenneth Arrow showing that no system of aggregating individual preferences into social decisions will always yield consistent, nonarbitrary results.*

voting paradox *A simple demonstration of how majority-rule voting can lead to seemingly contradictory and inconsistent results. A commonly cited illustration of the kind of inconsistency described in the impossibility theorem.*

logrolling *Occurs when congressional representatives trade votes, agreeing to help each other get certain pieces of legislation passed.*

[7]Kenneth Arrow, *Social Choice and Individual Values* (New York: John Wiley, 1951).

TABLE 16.1 RESULTS OF VOTING ON UNIVERSITY'S PLANS: THE VOTING PARADOX

VOTE	VP1	VP2	DEAN	RESULT*
	VOTES OF:			
A versus B	A	B	A	A wins: A > B
B versus C	B	B	C	B wins: B > C
C versus A	A	C	C	C wins: C > A

*A > B is read "A is preferred to B."

and in exchange E helps D get a majority on her program. It is not clear whether any bill could get through any legislature without logrolling. Neither is it clear whether logrolling is, on balance, a good thing or a bad thing from the standpoint of efficiency. On the one hand, a program that benefits one region or group of people might generate enormous net social gains, but because the group of beneficiaries is fairly small, it will not command a majority of delegates. If another bill that is likely to generate large benefits to another area is also awaiting a vote, a trade of support between the two sponsors of the bills should result in the passage of two good pieces of efficient legislation. On the other hand, logrolling can also turn out unjustified, inefficient, "pork barrel" legislation.

A number of other problems also follow from voting as a mechanism for public choice. For one, voters do not have much of an incentive to become well informed. When you go out to buy a car or, on a smaller scale, a CD player, you are the one who suffers the full consequences of a bad choice. Similarly, you are the beneficiary of the gains from a good choice. Not so in voting. Although many of us feel that we have a civic responsibility to vote, no one really believes that his or her vote will actually determine the outcome of an election. The time and effort it takes just to get to the polls is enough to deter many people. Becoming informed involves even more costs, and it is not surprising that many people do not do it.

Beyond the fact that a single vote is not likely to be decisive is the fact that the costs and benefits of wise and unwise social choices are widely shared. If the congressman that I elect makes a bad mistake and wastes a billion dollars, I bear only a small fraction of that cost. Even though the sums involved are large in aggregate, individual voters find little incentive to become informed.

Two additional problems with voting are that choices are almost always limited to *bundles* of publicly provided goods, and we vote infrequently. Many of us vote for Republicans or Democrats. We vote for president only every four years. We elect senators for six-year terms. In private markets, we can look at each item separately and decide how much of each we want. We also can shop daily. In the public sector, though, we vote for a platform or a party that takes a particular position on a whole range of issues. In the public sector it is very difficult, or impossible, for voters to unbundle issues.

There is, of course, a reason why bundling occurs in the sphere of public choice. It is difficult enough to convince people to go to the polls once a year. If we voted separately on every appropriation bill, we would spend our lives at the polls. This is one reason for representative democracy. We elect officials who we hope will become informed and represent our interests and preferences.

GOVERNMENT INEFFICIENCY

Recent work in economics has focused not just on the government as an extension of individual preferences but also on government officials as people with their own agendas and objectives. That is, government officials are assumed to maximize their own utility, not the social good. To understand the way government functions, we need to look less at the preferences of individual members of society and more at the incentive structures that exist around public officials.

Officials we seem to worry about are the people who run government agencies—the Social Security Administration, the Department of Housing and Urban Development, and state registries of motor vehicles, for example. What incentive do these people have to produce a good product and to be efficient? Might such incentives be lacking?

In the private sector, where firms compete for profits, only efficient firms producing goods that consumers will buy survive. If a firm is inefficient—if it is producing at a higher-than-necessary cost—the market will drive it out of business. This is not necessarily so in the public sector. If a government bureau is producing a necessary service, or one mandated by law, it does not need to worry about customers. No matter how bad the service is at the registry of motor vehicles, everyone with a car must buy its product!

The efficiency of a government agency's internal structure depends on the way incentives facing workers and agency heads are structured. If the budget allocation of an agency is based on the last period's spending alone, for example, agency heads have a clear incentive to spend more money, however inefficiently. This point is not lost on government officials, who have experimented with many ways of rewarding agency heads and employees for cost-saving suggestions.

But critics say such efforts to reward productivity and punish inefficiency are rarely successful. It is difficult to punish, let alone dismiss, a government employee. Elected officials are subject to recall, but it usually takes gross negligence to rouse voters into instituting such a measure. And elected officials are rarely associated with problems of bureaucratic mismanagement, which they decry daily.

Critics of "the bureaucracy" argue that no set of internal incentives can ever match the discipline of the market, and they point to studies of private versus public garbage collection, airline operations, fire protection, mail service, and so forth, all of which suggest significantly lower costs in the private sector. One theme of the Reagan and Bush administrations was "privatization." If the private sector can possibly provide a service, it is likely to do so more efficiently—so the public sector should allow the private sector to take over.

One concern regarding wholesale privatization is the potential effect it may have on distribution. Late in his administration, President Reagan suggested that the federal government sell its entire stock of public housing to the private sector. But would the private sector continue to provide housing to poor people? The worry is that it would not, because it may not be profitable to do so.

Like voters, public officials suffer from a lack of incentive to become fully informed and to make tough choices. Consider an elected official. If the real objective of an elected official is to get reelected, then his or her real incentive must be to provide visible goods for his or her constituency while hiding the costs or spreading them thin. Self-interest may easily lead to poor decisions and public irresponsibility.

RENT-SEEKING REVISITED

Another problem with public choice is that special-interest groups can and do spend resources to influence the legislative process. As we said before, individual voters have little incentive to become well informed and to participate fully in the legislative process. But favor-seeking special-interest groups have a great deal of incentive to participate in political decision making. We saw in chapter 13 that a monopolist would be willing to pay to prevent competition from eroding its economic profits. Many—if not all—industries lobby for favorable treatment, softer regulation, or antitrust exemption. This, as you recall, is *rent-seeking*.

Rent-seeking extends far beyond those industries that lobby for government help in preserving monopoly powers. Any group that benefits from a government policy has an incentive to use its resources to lobby for that policy. Farmers lobby for farm subsidies, oil producers lobby for oil import taxes, and the American Association of Retired Persons lobbies against cuts in Social Security.

In the absence of well-informed and active voters, special-interest groups assume an important and perhaps a critical role. But there is another side to this story. Some have argued that favorable legislation is, in effect, for sale in the marketplace. Those willing and able to pay the most are more successful in accomplishing their goals than those with fewer resources.

> Theory may suggest that unregulated markets fail to produce an efficient allocation of resources. But this should not lead you to the conclusion that government involvement necessarily leads to efficiency. There are reasons to believe that government attempts to produce the right goods and services in the right quantities efficiently may fail.

GOVERNMENT AND THE MARKET

There is no question that government must be involved in both the provision of public goods and the control of externalities. While the argument is less clear-cut, a strong case can also be made for government actions to increase the flow of information. No society has ever existed in which citizens did not get together to protect themselves from the abuses of an unrestrained market and to provide for themselves certain goods and services that the market did not provide. The question is not *whether* we need government involvement. The question is *how much* and *what kind* of government involvement we should have.

Critics of government involvement correctly say the existence of an "optimal" level of public-goods production does not guarantee that governments will achieve it. It is easy to show that governments will generally fail to achieve the most efficient level. Nor is there any reason to believe that governments are capable of achieving the "correct" amount of control over externalities or dispersing the proper information to all who need it. Markets may fail to produce an efficient allocation of resources, but governments can fail for a number of reasons.

1. Measurement of social damages and benefits is difficult and imprecise. For example, estimates of the costs of acid rain range from practically nothing to incalculably high amounts.
2. There is no precise mechanism through which citizens' preferences for public goods can be correctly determined. All voting systems lead to inconsistent results. Samuelson's optimal solution works only if each individual in a society pays in accordance with his or her own preferences. Because this is impossible under our system, we all must be taxed to pay for the mix of public goods that the imperfect voting mechanism provides us.
3. Because government agencies are not subject to the discipline of the market, we have little reason to expect they will be efficient producers. The amount of waste, corruption, and inefficiency in government is a hotly debated issue. Although government is not subjected to the discipline of the market, it must submit to the discipline of the press, tight budgets, and the opinion of the voters.
4. Both elected and appointed officials have needs and preferences of their own, and it is naive to expect them to act selflessly for the good of society (even if they know what would be best for society). Bureaucrats in the Department of Defense, for example, have a clear incentive to increase the size of their budgets, and elected officials rely heavily on those same bureaucrats for information.

Just as critics of government involvement concede that the market fails to achieve full efficiency, defenders of government must acknowledge government's failures. Defenders of government involvement respond that we get closer to an efficient allocation of resources by trying to control externalities and by doing our best to produce the public goods (including information) that people want with the imperfect tools we have than we would by leaving everything to the market.

SUMMARY

EXTERNALITIES AND ENVIRONMENTAL ECONOMICS

1. Often when we engage in transactions or make economic decisions, second or third parties suffer consequences that decision makers have no incentive to consider. These are called *externalities*. A classic example of an external cost is pollution.

2. When external costs are not considered in economic decisions, we may engage in activities or produce products that are not "worth it." When external benefits are not considered, we may fail to do things that are indeed "worth it." The result is an inefficient allocation of resources.

3. A number of alternative mechanisms have been used to control externalities: (1) government-imposed taxes and subsidies, (2) private bargaining and negotiation, (3) legal remedies such as *injunctions* and *liability rules*, (4) the sale or auctioning of rights to impose externalities, and (5) direct regulation.

PUBLIC (SOCIAL) GOODS

4. In a free market, certain goods and services that people want will not be produced in adequate amounts. These *public goods* have characteristics that make it difficult or impossible for the private sector to produce them profitably.

5. Public goods are *nonrival in consumption* (their benefits fall collectively on members of society or on groups of members), and/or their benefits are *nonexcludable* (it is generally impossible to exclude people who have not paid from enjoying the benefits of public goods). An example of a public good is national defense.

6. One of the problems of public provision is that it leads to public dissatisfaction. We can choose any quantity of private goods that we want, or we can walk away without buying any. When it comes to public goods such as national defense, the government must choose one and only one kind and quantity of (collective) output to produce.

7. Theoretically, there exists an *optimal level of provision* for each public good. At this level, society's willingness to pay per unit equals the marginal cost of producing the good. To discover such a level we would need to know the preferences of each individual citizen.

8. According to the *Tiebout hypothesis*, an efficient mix of public goods is produced when local land/housing prices and taxes come to reflect consumer preferences just as they do in the market for private goods.

IMPERFECT INFORMATION

9. Choices made in the presence of imperfect information may not be efficient. In the face of incomplete information, consumers and firms may encounter the problem of *adverse selection*. When buyers or sellers enter into market exchanges with other parties who have more information, low-quality goods are exchanged in greater numbers than high-quality goods. *Moral hazard* arises when one party to a contract passes the cost of his or her behavior on to the other party to the contract. If a contract absolves one party of the consequences of his or her actions, and people act in their own self-interest, the result is inefficient.

10. In many cases, the market provides solutions to information problems. Profit-maximizing firms will continue to gather information as long as the marginal benefits from continued search are greater than the marginal costs. Consumers will do the same: More time is afforded to the information search for larger decisions. In other cases, government must be called on to collect and disperse information to the public.

SOCIAL CHOICE

11. Because we can't know everyone's preferences about public goods, we are forced to rely on imperfect *social choice* mechanisms, such as majority rule.

12. The theory that free markets do not achieve an efficient allocation of resources should not lead us to conclude that government involvement necessarily leads to efficiency. Governments also fail.

GOVERNMENT AND THE MARKET

13. Defenders of government involvement in the economy acknowledge its failures but believe we get closer to an efficient allocation of resources with government than without it. By trying to control externalities and by doing our best to provide the public goods that society wants, we do better than we would if we left everything to the market.

REVIEW TERMS AND CONCEPTS

adverse selection, 393
Coase theorem, 384
drop-in-the-bucket problem, 388
externality, 374
free-rider problem, 388
impossibility theorem, 396
injunction, 385
liability rules, 385

logrolling, 396
marginal damage cost (*MDC*), 381
marginal private cost (*MPC*), 379
marginal social cost (*MSC*), 376
market failure, 373
moral hazard, 394
nonexcludable, 388

nonrival in consumption, 387
optimal level of provision for public goods, 392
public goods (social or collective goods), 387
social choice, 395
Tiebout hypothesis, 393
voting paradox, 396

PROBLEM SET

1. "If government imposes on the firms in a polluting industry penalties (taxes) that exceed the actual value of the damages done by the pollution, the result is an inefficient and unfair imposition of costs on those firms and on the consumers of their products." Discuss. Use a diagram to show how consumers are harmed.

2. The November election of 1994 saw incumbents lose in record numbers, and Republicans took control of both houses of the Congress for the first time in 40 years. Voters were clearly not happy with what they saw happening in Washington. Three economic theories may help explain their anger:
   a. *Public goods theory:* Because public goods are collective, the government is constrained to pick a single level of output for all of us. National defense is an example. The government must pick one level of defense expenditure, and some of us will think it's too much, some will think it's too little, and no one is happy.
   b. *Problems of social choice:* It is simply impossible to choose collectively in a rational way that satisfies voters/consumers of public goods.
   c. *Public choice and public officials:* Once elected or appointed, public officials tend to act in accordance with their own preferences and not out of concern for the public.
      Briefly explain each theory and how it may be a source of voter anger. Which of the three do you find the most persuasive?

3. Two areas of great concern to government in recent years have been education and health care. Using the concepts of public goods and imperfect information, write a brief essay justifying or criticizing government involvement in these two areas.

4. It has been argued that the following are examples of "mixed goods." They are essentially private but partly public. For each, describe the private and public components and discuss briefly why the government should or should not be involved in their provision.

a. Elementary and secondary education
b. Higher education
c. Medical care
d. Air traffic control

5. A paper factory dumps polluting chemicals into the Snake River. Thousands of citizens live along the river, and they bring suit claiming damages. You are asked by the judge to testify at the trial as an impartial expert. The court is considering four possible solutions, and you are asked to comment on the potential efficiency and equity of each. Your testimony should be brief.
   a. Deny the merits of the case and simply affirm the polluter's right to dump. The parties will achieve the optimal solution without government.
   b. Find in favor of the plaintiff. The polluters will be held liable for damages and must fully compensate citizens for all past and future damages imposed.
   c. Order an immediate end to the dumping. No damages awarded.
   d. Refer the matter to the Environmental Protection Agency, which will impose a tax on the factory equal to the marginal damage costs. Proceeds will not be paid to the damaged parties.

6. Explain why you agree or disagree with each of the following statements:
   a. The government should be involved in providing housing for the poor because housing is a "public good."
   b. From the standpoint of economic efficiency, an unregulated market economy tends to overproduce public goods.

7. Society is made up of two individuals whose demands for public good X are given in Figure 1. Assuming that the public good can be produced at a constant marginal cost of $6, what is the optimal level of output? How much would you charge A? B?

8. Government involvement in general scientific research has been justified on the grounds that advances in knowledge are public goods—once produced, information can be

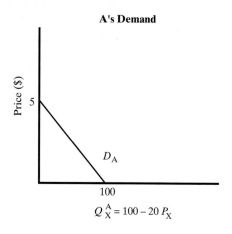

A's Demand

Price ($)

5

D_A

100

$$Q^A_X = 100 - 20\,P_X$$

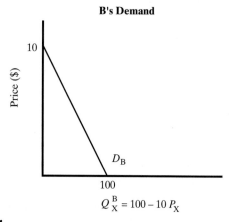

B's Demand

Price ($)

10

D_B

100

$$Q^B_X = 100 - 10\,P_X$$

FIGURE 1

shared at virtually no cost. A new production technology in an industry could be made available to all firms, reducing costs of production, driving down price, and benefiting the public. The patent system, however, allows private producers of "new knowledge" to exclude others from enjoying the benefits of that knowledge. Inventors would have little incentive to produce new knowledge if there were no possibility of profiting from their inventions. If one company holds exclusive rights to an advanced production process, it

produces at lower cost but can use the exclusion to acquire monopoly power and hold price up.

 a. On balance, is the patent system a good or a bad thing?
 b. Is government involvement in scientific research a good idea? Discuss.

9. "The Coase theorem implies that we never need to worry about regulating externalities because the private individuals involved will reach the efficient outcome through negotiations." Is this statement true or false? Justify your answer and use examples.

10. Explain how imperfect information problems such as adverse selection or moral hazard might affect the following markets or situations:
 a. Workers applying for disability benefits from a company
 b. The market for used computers
 c. The market for customized telephone systems for college offices and dorms
 d. The market for automobile collision insurance

11. Assume that your economics class has 100 people in it. Next week your professor asks you to bring $20 to class. You will be asked to split the $20 between two investments, A and B. A is a riskless asset with a zero rate of return. Every dollar that you put into A will be returned to you at the end of class. B is a pooled investment with a 50 percent rate of return. Every dollar invested in this pool will be matched by $.50 by your professor. The money in the investment pool, including the 50 percent bonus, will then be divided *equally among ALL members of the class.* In other words, your share of the Asset B investment pool depends only on the total amount invested in the pool, and not in any way on how much you invested in Asset B. The professor has pledged to keep your personal investment split a secret, and the class is not allowed to collude. How much would you invest in A and how much in B? Explain your reasoning. Have you learned anything about the public goods problem?

12. The Issues & Debates box in this chapter entitled "The 1997 Tobacco Settlement" discusses the 1997 agreement between the attorneys general of 40 states and the big tobacco companies. What has happened since? Did Congress approve? Have there been court rulings? You might search the Web or scan the newspapers to prepare your answer.

TAKE IT TO THE NET

We invite you to visit the Case and Fair page on the Prentice Hall Web site:
http://www.prenhall.com/casefair
for this chapter's World Wide Web exercise.

INCOME DISTRIBUTION AND POVERTY

WHAT ROLE SHOULD GOVERNMENT play in the economy? Thus far, we have focused only on actions the government might be called upon to take to improve market efficiency. But even if we achieved markets that are perfectly efficient, would the result be fair? We now turn to the question of **equity,** or fairness.

Somehow, the goods and services produced in every society get distributed among its citizens. Some citizens end up with mansions in Palm Beach, ski trips to Gstaad, and Maseratis; others end up without enough to eat and live in shacks. This chapter focuses on distribution. Why do some people get more than others? What are the sources of inequality? Should the government change the distribution generated by the market?

▶ **The Utility Possibilities Frontier** Ideally, in discussing distribution, we should talk not about the distribution of things but about the distribution of well-being. In the nineteenth century, philosophers used the concept of *utility* as a measure of well-being. As they saw it, people make choices among goods and services on the basis of the utility those goods and services yield. People act to maximize utility. If you prefer a night at the symphony to a rock concert, it is because you expect to get more utility from the symphony. If we extend this thinking, we might argue that if household A gets more total utility than household B, A is better off than B.

Utility is not directly observable or measurable. But thinking about it as if it were can help us understand some of the ideas that underlie debates about distribution. Suppose society consisted of two people, I and J. Next suppose that the line *PP'* in Figure 17.1 represents all the combinations of I's utility and J's utility that are possible, given the resources and technology available in their society. (This is an extension of the production possibilities frontier in chapter 2.)

Any point inside *PP'*, or the **utility possibilities frontier,** is inefficient because both I and J could be better off. *A* is one such point. *B* is one of many possible points along *PP'* that society should prefer to *A*, because both members are better off at *B* than they are at *A*.

While point *B* is preferable to point *A* from everyone's point of view, how does point *B* compare with point *C*? Both *B* and *C* are efficient; I cannot be made better off without making J worse off, and vice versa. All the

equity *Fairness.*

utility possibilities frontier
A graphical representation of a two-person world that shows all points at which A's utility can be increased only if B's utility is decreased.

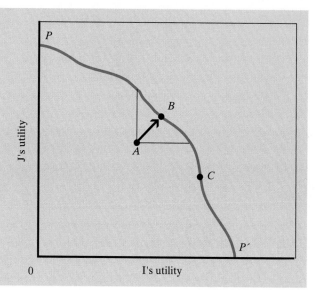

FIGURE 17.1

Utility Possibilities Frontier

If society were made up of two people, I and J, and all of the assumptions of perfect competition held, the market system would lead to some point along PP'. Every point along PP' is efficient; it is impossible to make I better off without making J worse off, and vice versa. But which point is best? Is B better than C?

points along PP' are efficient, but they may not be equally desirable. If all the assumptions of competitive market theory held, the market system would lead to one of the points along PP'. The actual point reached would depend upon I's and J's initial endowments of wealth, skills, and so forth.

In practice, however, the market solution leaves some people out. The rewards of a market system are linked to productivity, and some people in every society are simply not capable of being very productive or have not had the opportunity to become more productive. All societies make some provision for the very poor. Most often, public expenditures on behalf of the poor are financed with taxes collected from the rest of society. Society makes a judgment that those who are better off should give up some of their rewards so that those at the bottom can have more than the market system would allocate to them. In a democratic state, such redistribution is presumably undertaken because a majority of the members of that society think it is fair, or just.

Early economists drew analogies between social choices among alternative outcomes and consumer choices among alternative outcomes. A consumer chooses on the basis of his or her own unique utility function, or measure of his or her own well-being; a society, they said, chooses on the basis of a social welfare function that embodies the society's ethics.

Such theoretical discussions of fairness and equity focus on the distribution and redistribution of utility. But because utility is neither observable nor measurable, most discussions of social policy center on the *distribution of income* or the *distribution of wealth* as indirect measures of well-being. It is important that you remember throughout this chapter, however, that income and wealth are imperfect measures of well-being. Someone with a profound love of the outdoors may choose to work in a national park for a low wage rather than a consulting firm in a big city for a high wage. The choice reveals that she is better off, even though her measured income is lower. As another example, think about five people with $1 each. Now suppose that one of those people has a magnificent voice, and that the other four give up their dollars to hear her sing. The exchange leads to inequality of measured wealth—the singer has $5 and no one else has any, but all are better off than they were before.

Although income and wealth are imperfect measures of utility, they have no observable substitutes and are therefore the measures we use throughout this chapter. First, we review the factors that determine the distribution of income in a market setting. Second, we look at the data on income distribution, wealth distribution, and poverty in the United States. Third, we talk briefly about some theories of economic justice. Finally, we describe a number of current redistributional programs, including public assistance (or welfare), food stamps, Medicaid, and public housing.

THE SOURCES OF HOUSEHOLD INCOME

Why do some people and some families have more income than others? Before we turn to data on the distribution of income, let us review what we already know about the sources of inequality:

> Households derive their incomes from three basic sources: (1) from wages or salaries received in exchange for labor; (2) from property (that is, capital, land, and so forth); and (3) from government.

WAGES AND SALARIES

About 60 percent of personal income in the United States in 1997 was received in the form of wages and salaries. Hundreds of different wage rates are paid to employees for their labor in thousands of different labor markets. As you saw in chapter 10, competitive market theory predicts that all factors of production (including labor) are paid a return equal to their marginal revenue product—the market value of what they produce at the margin. There are reasons why one type of labor might be more productive than another and why some households have higher incomes than others.

> **Required Skills, Human Capital, and Working Conditions** Some people are born with attributes that translate into valuable skills. Patrick Ewing, David Robinson, and Shaquille O'Neal are great basketball players, partly because they happen to be over seven feet tall. They didn't decide to go out and invest in height; they were born with the right genes. Some people have perfect pitch and beautiful voices; others are tone deaf. Some people have quick mathematical minds; others cannot add two and two.

The rewards of a skill that is in limited supply depend on the demand for that skill. Men's professional basketball is extremely popular, and the top NBA players make millions of dollars per year. There are some great women basketball players, too, but because women's professional basketball has not become popular in the United States, these women's skills go comparatively unrewarded. In tennis, however, people want to see women play, and women therefore earn prize money similar to the money earned by men.

Some people with rare skills can make enormous salaries in a free market economy. Luciano Pavarotti has a voice that millions of people are willing to pay to hear in person and on tapes and CDs. Garth Brooks sells a million copies of every album he makes. Before Pablo Picasso died, he could sell small sketches for vast sums of money. Were they worth it? They were worth exactly what the highest bidder was willing to pay.

Not all skills are inborn. Some people have invested in training and schooling to improve their knowledge and skills, and therein lies another source of inequality in wages. When we go to school, we are investing in **human capital** that we expect to yield dividends, partly in the form of higher wages, later on. Human capital is also produced through on-the-job training. People learn their jobs and acquire "firm-specific" skills when they are on the job. Thus, in most occupations there is a reward for experience. Pay scale often reflects numbers of years on the job, and those with more experience earn higher wages than those in similar jobs with less experience.

Some jobs are more desirable than others. Entry-level positions in "glamour" industries such as publishing and television tend to be low-paying. Because talented people are willing to take entry-level jobs in these industries at salaries below what they could earn in other occupations, there must be other, nonwage rewards. It may be that

THE OWNER OF THIS SIMPLE SKETCH BY PICASSO PROBABLY PAID A LOT OF MONEY FOR IT. A LOT!

human capital *The stock of knowledge, skills, and talents that people possess; it can be inborn or acquired through education and training.*

ACCORDING TO EXPERTS, THE ALASKAN FISHING INDUSTRY FACES THE MOST DANGEROUS WORKING CONDITIONS IN THE COUNTRY. FOR THIS REASON, ALASKAN FISHERMEN ARE PAID COMPENSATING DIFFERENTIALS THAT RAISE THEIR AVERAGE WAGE HIGH ABOVE THE AVERAGE WAGE OF THE U.S. GENERAL POPULATION.

compensating differentials
Differences in wages that result from differences in working conditions. Risky jobs usually pay higher wages; highly desirable jobs usually pay lower wages.

the job itself is more personally rewarding, or that a low-paying apprenticeship is the only way to acquire the human capital necessary to advance. In contrast, less desirable jobs often pay wages that include **compensating differentials**. Of two jobs requiring roughly equal levels of experience and skills that compete for the same workers, the job with the poorer working conditions usually has to pay a slightly higher wage to attract workers away from the job with the better working conditions.

Compensating differentials are also required when a job is very dangerous. Those who take great risks are usually rewarded with high wages. High-beam workers on skyscrapers and bridges command premium wages. Firefighters in cities that have many old, run-down buildings are usually paid more than those in relatively tranquil rural or suburban areas.

➤ **Multiple Household Incomes** Another source of wage inequality among households lies in the fact that many households have more than one earner in the labor force. Second, and even third, incomes are becoming more the rule than the exception for U.S. families. In 1960 about 37 percent of women over the age of 16 were in the labor force. By 1978 the figure had increased to over 50 percent, and it continued to climb slowly but steadily to a level of nearly 60 percent by 1997. (Women's wages, however, are not on average as high as men's wages. See the Issues and Debates box, "A Rising Gap Between Men's and Women's Wages in 1997.")

Comparing two-earner and one-earner households highlights another problem of using money income as a measure of well-being. Consider a family of four with both parents working and an identical family with only one wage earner. The two-earner family will have a significantly higher money income, but the comparison ignores the value of what the non-wage-earning spouse produces. When one parent stays home, he or she normally provides services that would otherwise have to be purchased. The children are cared for, the house is maintained, food may be grown in the garden. When both parents work, there are expenses for day care, housecleaning, yard work, home repairs, and so forth.

When one parent stays home voluntarily, that family has revealed that it values the home-produced services more than the income it would otherwise earn. It is better off than it would be if both parents were working, even though it has a lower money income. Again, this means that we must exercise caution when discussing the fairness of the distribution of money income.

➤ **Unemployment** Before turning to property income, we need to mention another cause of inequality in the United States that is the subject of much discussion in macroeconomics: *unemployment*.

People earn wages only when they have jobs. In recent years, the United States has been through two severe recessions (economic downturns). In 1975, the unemployment

A RISING GAP BETWEEN MEN'S AND WOMEN'S WAGES IN 1997

The Department of Labor released data in 1997 that showed the gap between the median weekly wages of men and women is widening:

WAGE DIFFERENCE BETWEEN WOMEN AND MEN WIDENS

After nearly two decades in which the wage gap between men and women was steadily narrowing, it is now widening again, piquing confusion and concern among economists and women's groups alike.

According to the Bureau of Labor Statistics, the median weekly earnings of full-time working women are just under 75 percent of the men's median, down from 77 percent four years ago.

There are two views about why these differences exist. One view holds that most wage differentials can be attributed to choices women make about what jobs to take, how many hours to work, and when to enter and leave the labor force. The argument is that labor markets are efficient and that wages reflect productivity. Women earn lower wages because they have chosen to enter occupations that require little training and have low productivity, or because they avoid dangerous occupations and seek those that allow free movement into and out of the labor force.

This view also argues that the gap between women's and men's wages will close when women obtain the same amount of training as men, when they enter the same professions, and when they remain on the job without taking time off to raise families.

The second view holds that women's choices are not free and that wage differentials cannot be explained by differences in productivity. This view maintains that women are channeled into certain occupations by custom, tradition, and discrimination

FIGURE 1

Figure: Bar chart titled with y-axis "Percentage" (0 to 80) and x-axis "Year" showing three bars: 1978 ≈ 61, 1993 ≈ 78, 1997* ≈ 75.

*Second-quarter figures.

Source: Bureau of Labor Statistics.

ALTHOUGH MEN AND WOMEN NOW WORK SIDE BY SIDE IN MOST INDUSTRIES, ON AVERAGE, WOMEN STILL EARN SIGNIFICANTLY LESS THAN MEN.

and that wages in those occupations are kept artificially low. It is argued that jobs requiring similar skills, contributing similar amounts to employer earnings, and having similar working conditions are likely to be paid low wages when they are traditionally filled by women.

In 1963, Congress passed the Equal Pay Act, which prohibited unequal pay for equal work. The current move is to require equal pay for comparable work. A large number of states, including California, Iowa, Minnesota, Montana, Oregon, and Washington, have passed comparable worth laws for state employees. In the mid-1970s Australia adopted such a plan nationwide. As a result, base pay for women rose from 65 percent of men's to 94 percent between 1970 and 1980.

Critics of the comparable worth approach argue that such laws will end up hurting women. Raising wages above their equilibrium levels, it is argued, will cause employers to hire fewer women. Those who end up with jobs will earn higher wages, but some will be left out. There is

mixed evidence on this score from the Australian experience. One study found that pay equalization slowed the growth of women's employment by one third and increased women's unemployment by half a percentage point. Other studies found virtually no effect.[a]

The recent decrease may be the result of a strong economy and changes in the welfare laws (see the Issues and Debates box "Major Welfare Reform Takes Effect in 1997" in this chapter).

"Not-married women with children have had an enormous increase in employment, which coincides with the dropping welfare caseloads," said June O'Neill, the Republican-appointed head of the Congressional Budget Office. "These are the least skilled people entering the workforce, and that would have a downward pull on median wages."[a]

Source: [a]Tamar Lewin, "Wage Difference Between Men and Women Widens," The New York Times, Sept. 15, 1997, p. 1. Copyright © 1997 by The New York Times Co. Reprinted by permission.

For more on wages and salaries and comparable worth, see the Case and Fair Web page at
http://www.prenhall.com/casefair.

rate hit 9 percent, and over 8 million people were unable to find work; in 1982, the unemployment rate was nearly 11 percent, and over 12 million were jobless. More recently, the recovery from the milder recession of 1990 to 1991 was slow at first. By late 1997 the number of unemployed dropped below 6.6 million (an unemployment rate of 4.8 percent).

Unemployment hurts primarily those who are laid off, and thus its costs are narrowly distributed. For some workers, the costs of unemployment are lowered by unemployment compensation benefits paid out of a fund accumulated with receipts from a tax on payrolls.

INCOME FROM PROPERTY

property income *Income from the ownership of real property and financial holdings. It takes the form of profits, interest, dividends, and rents.*

Another source of income inequality is that some people have **property income**—from the ownership of real property and financial holdings—while many others do not. Some people own a great deal of wealth, and some have no assets at all. Overall, about 25 percent of personal income in the United States in 1997 came from ownership of property.

> The amount of property income that a household earns depends upon (1) how much property it owns and (2) what kinds of assets it owns. Such income generally takes the form of profits, interest, dividends, and rents.

Households come to own assets through saving and through inheritance. Many of today's large fortunes were inherited from previous generations. The Rockefellers, the Kennedys, and the Fords, to name a few, still have large holdings of property originally accumulated by previous generations. Thousands of families receive smaller inheritances each year from their parents. (Under 1997 tax laws, $600,000 can pass from one generation to another free of estate taxes.) Most families receive little through inheritance; most of their wealth or property comes from saving.

Often fortunes accumulate in a single generation when a business becomes successful. The late Sam Walton built a personal fortune estimated at over $23 billion on a chain of retail stores including Wal-Mart. *Fortune* magazine estimates that Bill Gates, founder and chief executive officer of Microsoft, is worth over $35 billion. Masatoshi Ito made $5 billion running a supermarket chain in Japan.

INCOME FROM THE GOVERNMENT: TRANSFER PAYMENTS

transfer payments *Payments by government to people who do not supply goods or services in exchange.*

About 16 percent of personal income in 1997 came from governments in the form of **transfer payments**. Transfer payments are payments made by government to people who do not supply goods or services in exchange. Some, but not all, transfer payments are made to people with low incomes, precisely because they have low incomes. Transfer payments thus reduce the amount of inequality in the distribution of income.

Not all transfer income goes to the poor. The biggest single transfer program at the federal level is Social Security.

> Transfer programs are by and large designed to provide income to those in need. They are part of the government's attempts to offset some of the problems of inequality and poverty.

THE DISTRIBUTION OF INCOME

economic income *The amount of money a household can spend during a given period without increasing or decreasing its net assets. Wages, salaries, dividends, interest income, transfer payments, rents, and so forth are sources of economic income.*

Despite the many problems with using income as a measure of well-being, it is useful to know something about how income is actually distributed. Before we examine these data, we should pin down precisely what the data represent.

Economic income is defined as the amount of money a household can spend during a given period without increasing or decreasing its net assets. Economic income

TABLE 17.1 DISTRIBUTION OF TOTAL INCOME AND COMPONENTS
IN THE UNITED STATES, 1997 (PERCENTAGES)

HOUSEHOLDS	TOTAL INCOME	WAGES AND SALARIES	PROPERTY INCOME	TRANSFER INCOME
Bottom fifth	6.0	5.7	1.0	27.6
Second fifth	9.1	11.9	4.0	26.1
Third fifth	14.7	19.9	8.4	18.7
Fourth fifth	23.6	27.3	16.4	13.9
Top fifth	46.6	35.2	70.2	13.7
Top 1 percent	10.0	3.2	29.7	1.5

Source: Brookings Merge File and authors' estimates.

includes anything that enhances your ability to spend—wages, salaries, dividends, interest received, proprietors' income, transfer payments, rents, and so forth. If you own an asset (such as a share of stock) that increases in value, that gain is part of your income, whether you sell the asset to "realize" the gain or not. Normally, we speak of "before-tax" income, with taxes considered a use of income.

INCOME INEQUALITY IN THE UNITED STATES

Table 17.1 presents some estimates of the distribution of several income components and of total income for households in 1997. The measure of income used to calculate these figures is very broad; it includes both taxable and nontaxable items, as well as estimates of realized capital gains. It does not include unrealized capital gains, and so it is not a complete measure of economic income.

The data are presented by "quintiles," that is, the total number of households is first ranked by income and then split into five groups of equal size. In 1997 the top quintile earned nearly 50 percent of total income, while the bottom quintile earned just 6 percent. The top 1 percent (which is part of the top quintile) earned more than the bottom 20 percent.

Wage and salary income (that is, labor income) was more evenly distributed than total income. The top 1 percent earned only 3.2 percent, and the middle groups earned a larger share. The combined middle three quintiles, or 60 percent of the total, received 59 percent of wages and salaries, compared with only 47 percent of all income.

Income from property is more unevenly distributed than wages and salaries. Property income comes from owning things: Land earns rent, stocks earn dividends and appreciate in value, bonds and deposit accounts earn interest, owners of small businesses earn profits, and so forth. The top 20 percent of households earned over 70 percent of property income, and the top 1 percent earned almost 30 percent.

Transfer payments include social security benefits, unemployment compensation, and welfare payments, as well as an estimate of nonmonetary transfers from the government to households—food stamps and Medicaid and Medicare program benefits, for example. Transfers flow to low-income households, but not solely to them. Social security benefits, for example, which account for about half of all transfer payments, flow to everyone who participated in the system for the requisite number of years and who has reached the required age, regardless of income. Nonetheless, transfers represent a much more important income component at the bottom of the distribution than at the top. Although not shown in Table 17.1, transfers account for more than 80 percent of the income of the bottom 10 percent of households, but only about 3 percent of income among the top 10 percent of households.

TABLE 17.2 DISTRIBUTION OF MONEY INCOME OF U.S. FAMILIES BY QUINTILES, 1947–1994 (PERCENTAGES)

	1947	1960	1972	1980	1984	1994
Bottom fifth	5.0	4.8	5.4	5.2	4.7	4.2
Second fifth	11.8	12.2	11.9	11.5	11.0	10.0
Third fifth	17.0	17.8	17.5	17.5	17.0	15.7
Fourth fifth	23.1	24.0	23.9	24.3	24.4	23.3
Top fifth	43.0	41.3	41.4	41.5	42.9	46.9
Top 5 percent	17.2	15.9	15.9	15.3	16.0	20.1

Source: Statistical Abstract of the United States, various editions; Dept. of Commerce, HHES Division.

money income *The measure of income used by the Census Bureau. Because it excludes noncash transfer payments and capital gains income, it is less inclusive than "economic income."*

▶ **Changes in the Distribution of Income**   Table 17.2 presents the distribution of money income among U.S. families[1] at a number of points in time. **Money income**, the measure used by the Census Bureau in its surveys and publications, is slightly less complete than the income measure used in the calculations in Table 17.1. It does not include noncash transfer benefits, for example, nor does it include capital gains.

As you can see, income distribution in the United States has remained stable over a long time. Between the end of World War II and 1980, there was a slight move toward equality: The share of income going to both the top 5 percent and the top 20 percent declined, while the share going to the bottom 20 percent increased slightly. Between 1980 and 1994, however, the trend reversed, with the top fifth gaining share and the bottom four fifths losing share.

Lorenz Curve *A widely used graph of the distribution of income, with cumulative percentage of families plotted along the horizontal axis and cumulative percentage of income plotted along the vertical axis.*

▶ **The Lorenz Curve and the Gini Coefficient**   The distribution of income can be graphed in several ways. The most widely used graph is the **Lorenz Curve**, shown in Figure 17.2. Plotted along the horizontal axis is the percentage of families, and along the vertical axis is the cumulative percentage of income. The curve shown here represents the year 1994, using data from Table 17.2.

During that year, the bottom 20 percent of families earned only 4.2 percent of total money income. The bottom 40 percent earned 14.2 percent (4.2 percent plus 10.0 percent), and so forth. If income were distributed equally—that is, if the bottom 20 percent earned 20 percent of the income, the bottom 40 percent earned 40 percent of the income, and so forth—the Lorenz Curve would be a 45-degree line between zero and 100 percent. More unequal distributions produce Lorenz Curves that are farther from the 45-degree line.

Gini coefficient *A commonly used measure of inequality of income derived from a Lorenz Curve. It can range from zero to a maximum of 1.*

The **Gini coefficient** is a measure of the degree of inequality in a distribution. It is the ratio of the shaded area in Figure 17.2 to the total triangular area below and to the right of the diagonal line 0A.

If income is equally distributed, there is no shaded area (because the Lorenz Curve and the 45-degree line are the same), and the Gini coefficient is zero. The Lorenz Curves for distributions with more inequality are farther down to the right, their shaded areas are larger, and their Gini coefficients are higher. The maximum Gini coefficient is 1. As the Lorenz Curve shifts down to the right, the shaded area becomes a larger portion of the total triangular area below 0A. If one family earned

[1]The term *family* excludes unmarried individuals living alone and groups of people living together who are not related by blood, marriage, or adoption. In the United States in 1992, there were a total of 99 million households—69 million family households and 30 million nonfamily households.

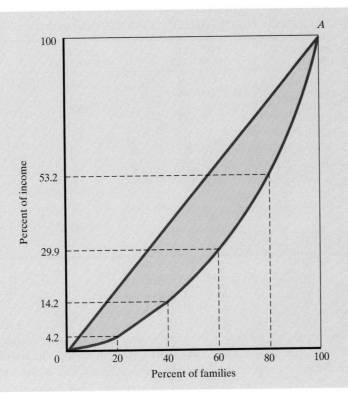

FIGURE 17.2

Lorenz Curve for the United States, 1994

The Lorenz Curve is the most common way of presenting income distribution graphically. The larger the shaded area, the more unequal the distribution. If distribution were equal, the Lorenz Curve would be the 45-degree line 0A.

all the income (with no one else receiving anything), the shaded area and the triangle would be the same, and the ratio would equal 1.

> **Differences Between African American Households, White Households, and Single-Person Households**   So far we have been looking at income distribution among all families. But looking just at families without differentiating them in any way hides some needed distinctions. First, income distribution differs significantly between African American and Hispanic families and white families. Second, many people do not belong to a family—they may be unmarried living alone or they may be part of a group of unrelated people living together.

Table 17.3 presents data on the distribution of money income for different types of households. The differences between the groupings are dramatic. Over 25 percent of African American households, but only 13.5 percent of white households, have annual incomes below $10,000. At the upper end, 32 percent of white households, but only 17 percent of African American households, have incomes above $50,000.

The category of single-person households includes the elderly living alone, college students, and single people in apartments. While it is hard to generalize about such a mixed bag, the income distribution of this group differs from that of other households in notable ways. Nearly a third of one-person households have incomes below $10,000, and only 8.6 percent have incomes over $50,000, compared with 30 percent of all households.

The income difference between multi-person households and single-person households is in part due to the fact that many households contain more than one earner. Of the 69.3 million families in the United States in 1994, 53.9 million had a husband and wife present and 35.1 million had at least two earners.[2]

---

[2]*Statistical Abstract of the United States, 1996,* Table 723.

TABLE 17.3 **DISTRIBUTION OF MONEY INCOME OF HOUSEHOLDS, 1995** (PERCENTAGES)

	ALL HOUSEHOLDS	AFRICAN AMERICAN HOUSEHOLDS	WHITE HOUSEHOLDS	HISPANIC HOUSEHOLDS	ONE-PERSON HOUSEHOLDS
0–10,000	13.5	26.3	11.7	20.5	30.3
10–15,000	9.1	11.5	8.7	12.2	16.5
15–25,000	16.7	18.9	16.4	20.4	21.5
25–35,000	14.2	12.8	14.4	14.9	13.1
35–50,000	16.3	13.3	16.7	14.4	10.0
50–75,000	16.5	10.8	17.3	10.9	5.6
75,000 +	13.7	6.3	14.6	6.7	3.0
Total	100.0	100.0	100.0	100.0	100.0

Note: Totals may not add to 100 due to rounding.

Source: Statistical Abstract of the United States, 1996, Table 711.

FAST FACTS

The Labor Department recently released a survey of living standards of poor and nonpoor households. The following gives some results:

	N	P
Own home	78%	41%
Own car	97%	77%
Have phone	97%	77%
Two or more people/room	4%	19%
Violent crimes/ 1,000 people	26	54
No health insurance	13%	29%

N = Nonpoor Households

P = Poor Households

Source: Department of Labor, Bureau of Labor Statistics, Monthly Labor Review.

poverty line The officially established income level that distinguishes the poor from the nonpoor. It is set at three times the cost of the Department of Agriculture's minimum food budget.

POVERTY

Most of the government's concern with income distribution and redistribution has focused on poverty. *Poverty* is a very complicated word to define. In simplest terms, it means the condition of people who have very low incomes. The dictionary defines the term simply as "lack of money or material possessions." But how low does your income have to be before you are classified as poor?

▶ **The Problem of Definition** Philosophers and social policy makers have long debated the meaning of "poverty." One school of thought argues that poverty should be measured by determining how much it costs to buy the "basic necessities of life." For many years, the Bureau of Labor Statistics published "family budget" data designed to track the cost of specific "bundles" of food, clothing, and shelter that were supposed to represent the minimum standard of living.

Critics argue that defining bundles of necessities is a hopeless task. While it might be possible to define a minimally adequate diet, what is a "minimum" housing unit? Is a car a necessity? What about medical care? In reality, low-income families end up using what income they have in an enormous variety of ways.

Some say poverty is culturally defined and is therefore a relative concept, not an absolute one. Poverty in Bangladesh is very different from poverty in the United States. Even within the United States, urban poverty is very different from rural poverty. If poverty is a relative concept, the definition of it might change significantly as a society accumulates wealth and achieves higher living standards.

Although it is difficult to define precisely, the word *poverty* is one that we all understand intuitively to some degree. It conveys images of run-down, overcrowded, rat-infested housing, homeless people, untreated illness, and so forth. But it is also a word that we have been forced to define formally for purposes of keeping statistics and administering public programs.

▶ **The Official Poverty Line** In the early 1960s, the U.S. government established an official poverty line. Because poor families tend to spend about one-third of their incomes on food:

The official **poverty line** has been set at a figure that is simply three times the cost of the Department of Agriculture's minimum food budget.

Each year the Department of Agriculture sets out a nutritionally sound minimum food bundle. For example, a week's food for a woman between 20 and 34 years old includes 4 eggs; 1¼ pounds of meat, fish, or poultry; 3 pounds of potatoes; 12 ounces of dark green or yellow vegetables; 3 pounds of other vegetables; and 8 ounces of fat or oil. In 1994, the department estimated that such a bundle would cost about $97.06 per week for a family of four people. Multiply that times 52 weeks for a total of $5,047 per year; triple that, and you have a poverty line for a family of four set at $15,141.

▶ **Poverty in the United States Since 1960**   In 1962 Michael Harrington published *The Other America: Poverty in the United States*, a book that woke the American people to the problem of poverty and stimulated the government to declare a "war on poverty" in 1964. In 1960 official figures had put the number of the poor in the United States at just under 40 million, or 22 percent of the total population. In his book, Harrington argued that the number had reached over 50 million.

By the late 1960s the number living below the official poverty line had declined to about 25 million, where it stayed for over a decade. Between 1978 and 1983, the number of poor jumped nearly 45 percent, from 24.5 million to 35.3 million, the highest number since 1964. The figure stood at 38.1 million in 1995. As a percentage of the total population, the poor accounted for between 11 percent and 12.6 percent of the population throughout the 1970s. That figure increased sharply to 15.2 percent between 1979 and 1983. From 1983 to 1989 the rate dropped to 12.8 percent, rising back to 14.5 percent in 1995.

While the official 1995 figures put the poverty rate at 14.5 percent of the population, they do not show that some groups in society experience more poverty than others. Table 17.4 shows the official poverty count for 1964 and 1995 by demographic group. One of the problems with the official count is that it considers only money income as defined by the census and is therefore somewhat inflated. Many federal programs designed to help people out of poverty include noncash benefits (sometimes called *in-kind benefits*) such as food stamps, public housing, and so forth. If added to income, these benefits would reduce the number of those officially designated as below the poverty line. The right-hand column in Table 17.4 shows how many would be classified as poor if noncash benefits were taken into account.

The poverty rate among African Americans is nearly three times as high as the poverty rate among whites. Even after noncash benefits are counted, more than one

TABLE 17.4   PERCENTAGE OF PERSONS IN POVERTY BY DEMOGRAPHIC GROUP, 1964–1995

	OFFICIAL MEASURE 1964	OFFICIAL MEASURE 1995	ADJUSTED FOR IN-KIND TRANSFERS AT MARKET VALUE, 1995*
All	19.0	14.5	9.8
White	14.9	11.7	8.0
African American	49.6	30.6	20.0
Hispanic	NA	30.7	20.0
Female householder— no husband present	45.9	38.6	NA
Elderly (65 +)	28.5	11.7	NA
Children under 18	20.7	21.2	NA

*Note: *Includes food, housing, and medical benefits.*

Source: Statistical Abstract of the United States, 1996, Tables 730, 734, 736, 740.

in five African Americans lives in poverty. In addition, the same proportion of Hispanics as African Americans had incomes below the poverty line after in-kind transfers in 1995.

The group with the highest incidence of poverty in 1995 was women living in households with no husband present. In 1964, 45.9 percent of such women lived in poverty. By 1995 the figure was still 38.6 percent. During the 1980s there was increasing concern about the "feminization of poverty," a concern that continues today.

Poverty rates among the elderly have been reduced considerably over the last few decades, dropping from 28.5 percent in 1964 to 11.7 percent in 1995. Certainly social security, supplemental security income, and Medicare have played a role in reducing poverty among the elderly.

The only category for which poverty rates have increased since 1964 is that of children. In 1964, 20.7 percent of all children under 18 lived in poverty; by 1995, the figure had risen to 21.2 percent, more than one in five!

THE DISTRIBUTION OF WEALTH

Data on the distribution of wealth are not as readily available as data on the distribution of income. Periodically, however, the government conducts a detailed survey of the holdings that make up wealth. Some of the results of this survey for 1995 are presented in Table 17.5. The top 10 percent of families ranked by income control 72.5 percent of all the nation's assets.

Clearly, the distribution of wealth is much more unequal than the distribution of income. Part of the reason is that wealth is passed from generation to generation and accumulates. Large fortunes also accumulate when small businesses become successful large businesses. Some argue that an unequal distribution of wealth is the natural and inevitable consequence of risk taking in a market economy: It provides the incentive necessary to motivate entrepreneurs and investors. Others believe that too much inequality can undermine democracy and lead to social conflict. Many of the arguments for and against income redistribution, discussed in the next section, apply equally well to wealth redistribution.

THE REDISTRIBUTION DEBATE

Debates about the role of government in correcting for inequity in the distribution of income revolve around philosophical and practical issues. *Philosophical* issues deal with the "ideal." What should the distribution of income be if we could give it any shape we desired? What is "fair"? What is "just"? *Practical* issues deal with what is, and what is not, possible. Suppose we wanted zero poverty. How much would it cost, and what would we sacrifice? When we take wealth or income away from higher-income people and give it to lower-income people, do we destroy incentives? What are the effects of this kind of redistribution?

Policy makers must deal with both kinds of issues, but it seems logical to confront the philosophical issues first. If you do not know where you want to go, you cannot talk very well about how to get there or how much it costs. You may find that you do not want to go anywhere at all. Many respected economists and philosophers argue quite convincingly that the government should *not* redistribute income.

ARGUMENTS AGAINST REDISTRIBUTION

Those who argue against government redistribution believe that the market, when left to operate on its own, is fair. This argument rests on the proposition that "one is entitled to the fruits of one's efforts."[3] Remember that if market theory is correct, rewards

TABLE 17.5

PERCENT OF ASSETS HELD BY FAMILIES, 1995

	TOP 10 PERCENT
Stocks	70.5
Bonds	90.9
Business assets	86.9
Principal residence*	33.4
Other real estate	71.9
Total assets**	72.5

*Owner-occupied housing.

**Note: Checking, savings, certificates of deposit, IRAs, Keogh plans, stocks, bonds, businesses, real estate, automobiles.

Source: Authors' tabulations based on User Tapes, 1995 Survey of Consumer Finances.

[3]Powerful support for this notion of "entitlement" can be found in the works of the seventeenth-century English philosophers Thomas Hobbes and John Locke.

paid in the market are linked to productivity. In other words, labor and capital are paid in accordance with the value of what they produce.

This view also holds that property income—income from land or capital—is no less justified than labor income. All factors of production have marginal products. Capital owners receive profits or interest because the capital they own is productive.

The argument against redistribution also rests on the principles behind "freedom of contract" and the protection of property rights. When I agree either to sell my labor or to commit my capital to use, I do so freely. In return I contract to receive payment, which becomes my "property." When a government taxes me and gives my income to someone else, that action violates these two basic rights.

The more common arguments against redistribution are not philosophical. Rather, they point to more practical problems. First, it is said that taxation and transfer programs interfere with the basic incentives provided by the market. Taxing higher-income people reduces their incentive to work, save, and invest. Taxing the "winners" of the economic game also discourages risk taking. Furthermore, providing transfers to those at the bottom reduces their incentive to work as well. All of this leads to a reduction in total output that is the "cost" of redistribution.

Another practical argument against redistribution is that it does not work. Some critics see the rise in the poverty rate during the early 1980s and again in the early 1990s as an indication that antipoverty programs simply drain money without really helping the poor out of poverty. Whether or not these programs actually help people out of poverty, the charge of bureaucratic inefficiency in administration always exists. Social programs must be administered by people who must be paid. The Department of Health and Human Services employs over 120,000 people to run the social security system, process Medicaid claims, and so forth. Some degree of waste and inefficiency is inevitable in any sizable bureaucracy.

ARGUMENTS IN FAVOR OF REDISTRIBUTION

The argument most often used in favor of redistribution is that a society as wealthy as the United States has a moral obligation to provide all its members with the necessities of life. The Constitution does carry a guarantee of the "right to life." In declaring war on poverty in 1964, President Lyndon Johnson put it this way:

> There will always be some Americans who are better off than others. But it need not follow that the "poor are always with us". . . . It is high time to redouble and to concentrate our efforts to eliminate poverty. . . . We know what must be done and this nation of abundance can surely afford to do it.[4]

Many people, often through no fault of their own, find themselves left out. Some are born with mental or physical problems that severely limit their ability to "produce." Then, there are children. Even if some parents can be held accountable for their low incomes, do we want to punish innocent children for the faults of their parents and thus perpetuate the cycle of poverty? The elderly, without redistribution of income, would have to rely exclusively on savings to survive once they retire, and many conditions can lead to inadequate savings. Should the victims of bad luck be doomed to inevitable poverty? Illness is perhaps the best example. The accumulated savings of very few can withstand the drain of extraordinary hospital and doctors' bills and the exorbitant cost of nursing home care.

Proponents of redistribution refute "practical" arguments against it by pointing to studies that show little negative effect on the incentives of those who benefit from transfer programs. For many—children, the elderly, the mentally ill—incentives are irrelevant, they say, and providing a basic income to most of the unemployed does not

---

[4]*Economic Report of the President*, 1964.

discourage them from working when they have the opportunity to do so.[5] We now turn briefly to several more formal arguments.

➤ **Utilitarian Justice**   First put forth by the Englishmen Jeremy Bentham and John Stuart Mill in the late eighteenth and early nineteenth centuries, the essence of the utilitarian argument in favor of redistribution is that "a dollar in the hand of a rich person is worth less than a dollar in the hand of a poor person." The rich spend their marginal dollars on luxury goods. It is easy to spend over $100 per person for a meal in a good restaurant in New York or Los Angeles. The poor spend their marginal dollars on necessities—food, clothing, and medical care. If the marginal utility of income declines as income rises, the value of a dollar's worth of luxury goods is worth less than a dollar's worth of necessity. Thus, redistributing from the rich to the poor increases total utility. To put this notion of **utilitarian justice** in everyday language: Through income redistribution, the rich sacrifice a little and the poor gain a lot.

The utilitarian position is not without problems. People have very different tastes and preferences. Who is to say that you value a dollar more or less than I do? Because utility is unobservable and unmeasurable, comparisons between individuals cannot be easily made. Nonetheless, many people find the basic logic of the utilitarians persuasive.

➤ **Social Contract Theory—Rawlsian Justice**   The work of Harvard philosopher John Rawls has generated a great deal of recent discussion, both within the discipline of economics and between economists and philosophers.[6] In the tradition of Hobbes, Locke, and Rousseau, Rawls argues that, as members of society, we have a contract with one another. In the theoretical world that Rawls imagines, an original *social contract* is drawn up, and all parties agree to it without knowledge of who they are or who they will be in society. This condition is called the "original position" or the "state of nature." With no vested interests to protect, members of society are able to make disinterested choices.

As we approach the contract, everyone has a chance to end up very rich or homeless. On the assumption that we are all "risk averse," Rawls believes that people will attach great importance to the position of the least fortunate members of society because anyone could end up there. **Rawlsian justice**, then, is argued from the assumption of risk aversion. Rawls concludes that any contract emerging from the original position would call for an income distribution that would "maximize the well-being of the worst-off member of society."

Any society bound by such a contract would allow for inequality, but only if that inequality had the effect of improving the lot of the very poor. If inequality provides an incentive for people to work hard and innovate, for example, those inequalities should be tolerated as long as some of the benefits go to those at the bottom.

➤ **The Works of Karl Marx**   For decades, a rivalry existed between the United States and the Soviet Union. At the heart of this rivalry was a fundamental philosophical difference of opinion about how economic systems work and how they should be managed. At the center of the debate were the writings of Karl Marx.

Marx did not write very much about socialism or communism. His major work, *Das Kapital* (published in the nineteenth century), was a three-volume analysis and critique of the capitalist system that he saw at work in the world around him. We know what Marx thought was wrong with capitalism, but he was not very clear about what would replace it. In one essay, late in his life, he wrote, "from each according to his ability, to each according to his needs,"[7] but he was not specific about the applications of this principle.

utilitarian justice *The idea that "a dollar in the hand of a rich person is worth less than a dollar in the hand of a poor person." If the marginal utility of income declines with income, transferring income from the rich to the poor will increase total utility.*

Rawlsian justice *A theory of distributional justice that concludes that the social contract emerging from the "original position" would call for an income distribution that would maximize the well-being of the worst-off member of society.*

---

[5]For a discussion of the empirical evidence on the effects of transfer programs and taxation on incentives, see chapter 19.

[6]See John Rawls, *A Theory of Justice* (Cambridge, Mass.: Harvard University Press, 1972).

[7]Karl Marx, "Critique of the Gotha Program" (May 1875), in *The Marx-Engels Reader*, ed. Robert Tucker (New York: W. W. Norton), p. 388.

Marx's view of capital income does have important implications for income distribution. In the preceding chapters, we discussed profit as a return to a productive factor: Capital, like labor, is productive and has a marginal product. But, Marx attributed all value to labor and none to capital. According to Marx's **labor theory of value**, the value of any commodity depends only on the amount of labor needed to produce it. The owners of capital are able to extract profit, or "surplus value," because labor creates more value in a day than it is paid for. Like any other good, labor power is worth only what it takes to "produce" it. In simple words, this means that under capitalism labor is paid a subsistence wage.

Marx saw profit as an illegitimate expropriation by capitalists of the fruits of labor's efforts. It follows, then, that Marxians see the property income component of income distribution as the primary source of inequality in the United States today. Without capital income, the distribution of income would be much more equal. (Refer again to Table 17.1.)

Despite the fact that the Soviet Union no longer exists, Marxism remains a powerful force in the world. China, Vietnam, Cuba, and a number of other countries remain Communist, and many believe that the Marxian critique of capitalism was correct even though one version of an alternative has failed.

▶ **Income Distribution as a Public Good**   Those who argue that the unfettered market produces a just income distribution do not believe private charity should be forbidden. Voluntary redistribution does not involve any violation of property rights by the state.

In chapter 16, however, you saw there may be a problem with private charity. Suppose people really do want to end the hunger problem. As they write out their checks to charity, they encounter the classic public-goods problem. First, there are free riders. If hunger and starvation are eliminated, the benefits—even the merely psychological benefits—flow to everyone, whether they contributed or not. Second, any contribution is a drop in the bucket. One individual contribution is so small that it can have no real effect.

With private charity, as with national defense, nothing depends upon whether I pay or not. Thus, private charity may fail for the same reason that the private sector is likely to fail to produce national defense and other public goods. People will find it in their interest not to contribute. Thus, we turn to government to provide things we want that will not be provided adequately if we act separately—in this case, help for the poor and hungry.

REDISTRIBUTION PROGRAMS AND POLICIES

The role of government in changing the *distribution of income* is hotly debated. The debate involves not only what government programs are appropriate to fight poverty but the character of the tax system as well. Unfortunately, the quality of the public debate on the subject is low. Usually it consists of a series of claims and counterclaims about what social programs do to incentives rather than a serious inquiry into what our distributional goal should be.

In this section, we talk about the tools of redistributional policy in the United States. As we do so, you will have a chance to assess for yourself some of the evidence about their effects.

FINANCING REDISTRIBUTION PROGRAMS: TAXES

Redistribution always involves those who end up with less and those who end up with more. Because redistributional programs are financed by tax dollars, it is important to know who the donors and recipients are—who pays the taxes and who receives the benefits of those taxes.

labor theory of value *Stated most simply, the theory that the value of a commodity depends only on the amount of labor required to produce it.*

The mainstay of the U.S. tax system is the individual income tax, authorized in 1913 by the Sixteenth Amendment to the Constitution. The income tax is *progressive*—those with higher incomes pay a higher percentage of their incomes in taxes. Even though the tax is subject to many exemptions, deductions, and so forth that allow some taxpayers to reduce their tax burdens, all studies of the income tax show that its burden as a percentage of income rises as income rises.

With the passage of the Tax Reform Act of 1986, Congress initiated a major change in income tax rates and regulations. The reforms were to simplify the tax and make it easier for people to comply with and harder to avoid. In addition, the act reduced the number of tax brackets and the overall progressivity of the rates. The largest reduction was in the top rate, cut from 50 percent to 28 percent in 1986. It also substantially reduced the tax burdens of those at the very bottom by increasing the amount of income one can earn before paying any tax at all.

In 1993, President Clinton signed into law a tax bill that increased the top rate to 36 percent for families with taxable incomes over $140,000 and individuals with taxable incomes over $115,000. In addition, families with incomes of over $250,000 paid a surtax (a tax rate on a tax rate) of 10 percent, bringing the marginal rate for those families to 39.6 percent. Families with low incomes will receive grants and credits under the plan. In 1998, the brackets were adjusted somewhat, but overall the new tax system is substantially more progressive.

The individual income tax is only one tax among many. More important to the individual is the *overall* burden of taxation, including all federal, state, and local taxes. Most studies of the effect of taxes on the distribution of income, both before and after the Tax Reform Act, have concluded that the overall burden is roughly proportional. In other words:

> Everyone pays about the same percentage of his or her income in total taxes.

Table 17.6 presents an estimate of effective tax rates paid in 1995 by families that have been ranked by income. While some progressivity is visible, it is very slight. The bottom 20 percent of the income earners pay 34 percent of their total incomes in tax. The top 1 percent pay 37.6 percent. We can conclude from these data that the tax side of the equation produces very little change in the distribution of income.

EXPENDITURE PROGRAMS

Some programs designed to redistribute income or to aid the poor provide cash income to recipients. Others provide benefits in the form of health care, subsidized housing, or food stamps. Still others provide training or help workers find jobs.

➤ **Social Security** By far the largest income redistribution program in the United States is social security. The **social security system** is really three programs financed through separate trust funds. The *Old Age and Survivors Insurance program (OASI)*, the largest of the three, pays cash benefits to retired workers, their survivors, and their dependents. The *Disability Insurance program (DI)* pays cash benefits to disabled workers and their dependents. The third, *Health Insurance (HI)* or Medicare, provides medical benefits to workers covered by OASI and DI and the railroad retirement program. The social security system has been credited with substantially reducing poverty among the elderly.

Most workers in the United States must participate in the social security system. For many years, federal employees and employees belonging to certain state and municipal retirement systems were not required to participate, but federal employees are now being brought into the system. Today well over 90 percent of all workers in the United States contribute to social security.

TABLE 17.6

EFFECTIVE RATES OF FEDERAL, STATE, AND LOCAL TAXES, 1995
(TAXES AS A PERCENTAGE OF TOTAL INCOME)

Bottom 20%	34.0%
Second 20%	31.3
Third 20%	32.4
Fourth 20%	32.8
Top 20%	34.4
Top 10%	35.2
Top 5%	35.9
Top 1%	37.6

Source: Authors' estimate, Brookings Merge File, Congressional Budget Office, 1997.

social security system *The federal system of social insurance programs. It includes three separate programs that are financed through separate trust funds: the Old Age and Survivors Insurance program (OASI), the Disability Insurance program (DI), and the Health Insurance program (HI, or Medicare).*

Participants and their employers are required to pay a *payroll tax* to the *Federal Insurance Corporation Association (FICA)* to finance the social security system. The tax in 1997 was 7.65 percent paid by employers and 7.65 percent paid by employees on wages up to $65,400. Self-employed people assume the entire FICA burden themselves.

You are entitled to social security benefits if you participate in the system for 10 years. Benefits are paid monthly to you after you retire or, if you die, to your survivors. A complicated formula based on your average salary while you were paying into the system determines your benefit level. Those who earned more receive a higher level of benefits. But there are maximum and minimum monthly benefits. By and large, low-salaried workers get more out of the system than they paid into it while they were working. High-salaried workers usually get out of the system considerably less than they put in.

The social security system is self-financing, but it is different from funded retirement systems. In a *funded system*, deposits (by the employer, the employee, or both) are made to an account in the employee's name. Those funds are invested and earn interest or dividends that accumulate until retirement, when they are withdrawn. Funded retirement plans operate very much like a savings plan that you might set up independently except that you cannot touch the contents until you retire.

In the U.S. social security system, the tax receipts from today's workers are used to pay benefits to retired and disabled workers and their dependents today. Currently, the system is collecting more than it is paying out, and the excess is accumulating in the trust funds. This is necessary to keep the system solvent, because after the year 2010 there will be a large increase in the number of retirees and a relative decline in the number of workers. These demographic changes are the result of a high birth rate between 1946 and 1964—the so-called "baby boom." At the beginning of 1996, 26.7 million retired persons received social security benefits and 5.9 million received disability payments.

► **Public Assistance** Next to social security, the biggest cash transfer program in the United States is **public assistance**, more commonly called **welfare**. Aimed specifically at the poor, welfare falls into two major categories.

Most welfare is paid in the form of *Temporary Assistance for needy families*. Benefit levels are set by the states, and they vary widely. In 1996 the maximum monthly payment to a one-parent family of three was $120 per month in Mississippi, $650 per month in Vermont, and $923 per month in Alaska; the average monthly payment in the United States was $377. To participate, a family must have very low income and virtually no assets. In 1995 there were 13.6 million recipients of AFDC (Aid to Families with Dependent Children) in the United States, of whom just under 70 percent were children. Those adults who find jobs and enter the labor force lose benefits quickly as their incomes rise. This loss of benefits acts as a tax on beneficiaries, and some argue that it discourages welfare recipients from seeking jobs.

A second category of welfare payments is *general assistance*, which goes to the very poor regardless of family circumstances. In 1992 there were about 980,000 general assistance recipients.

No topics raise passions more than welfare and welfare reform. The issue has been a focal point of "liberal/conservative" name calling for more than three decades. In 1996, the Congress passed and President Clinton signed a major overhaul of the welfare system in the United States. The name of the program was changed to Temporary Assistance for Needy Families from its former name, Aid to Families with Dependent Children, as of July 1997. The key change mandated that states limit most recipients to no more than 5 years of benefits over a lifetime. Some argue that the result will be a disaster, with some families left with nothing. Others argue that the previous system led to dependency and that there was no incentive to work.

The new legislation provided funds for added services to parents with young children, but leaves a great deal of discretion in states' hands. Only time will tell how it

public assistance, or **welfare**
Government transfer programs that provide cash benefits to (1) families with dependent children whose incomes and assets fall below a very low level and (2) the very poor regardless of whether or not they have children.

Between January 1993 and January 1997, the number of individuals receiving welfare benefits fell by 20%, or 2.75 million recipients—the largest decline in over 50 years. A recent study estimated that 44% of the decline was due to an improving economy and 31% was due to reforms enacted by various states (see Issues and Debates box, "Major Welfare Reform Takes Effect in 1997").

Source: Phillip B. Levine and Diane Whitmore, "Explaining the Decline in Welfare Receipt, 1993–1997," Council of Economic Advisors Technical Report, May 9, 1997.

turns out. We will return to the debate over welfare and work effort in chapter 19. (For a more complete discussion see the Issues and Debates box, "Major Welfare Reform Takes Effect in 1997.")

➤ **Supplemental Security Income**   The *Supplemental Security Income program (SSI)* is a federal program that was set up under the Social Security Administration in 1974. The program is financed out of general revenues. That is, there is no trust fund, nor are there any earmarked taxes from which SSI benefits are paid out.

SSI is designed to take care of the elderly who end up very poor and have no, or very low, social security entitlement. In 1995, 6.5 million people received SSI payments, about half of whom also received some social security benefits. As with welfare, qualified recipients must have very low incomes and virtually no assets.

➤ **Unemployment Compensation**   In 1997, governments paid out over $24 billion in benefits to unemployed workers. The money to finance this benefit comes from taxes paid by employers into special funds. Companies that hire and fire frequently pay a higher tax rate, while companies with relatively stable employment levels pay a lower tax rate. Tax and benefit levels are determined by the states, within certain federal guidelines.

Workers who qualify for **unemployment compensation** begin to receive benefit checks soon after they are laid off. These checks continue for a period specified by the state. Most unemployment benefits continue for 20 weeks. In times of recession the benefit period is often extended on a state-by-state basis. The average unemployed worker receives only about 36 percent of his or her normal wages, and not all workers are covered. To qualify for benefits, an unemployed person must have worked recently for a covered employer for a specified time for a given amount of wages. Recipients must also demonstrate willingness and ability to seek and accept suitable employment. Although 9 of 10 employed persons are covered by unemployment insurance paid for by employers, only 36 percent of the unemployed received benefits in 1995.

Unemployment benefits are not aimed at the poor alone, although many of the unemployed are poor. Unemployment benefits are paid regardless of a person's income from other sources and regardless of assets.

➤ **Medicaid and Medicare**   The largest in-kind transfer programs in the United States are Medicare and Medicaid. The **Medicaid** program provides health and hospitalization benefits to people with low incomes. Although the program is administered by the states, about 57 percent of the cost is borne by the federal government. In 1994 about 35.1 million people received benefits; in 1997, total payments were $185 billion and rising.

Medicare, which is run by the Social Security Administration, is a health insurance program for the aged and certain disabled persons. Most U.S. citizens over age 65 receive Medicare hospital insurance coverage regardless of their income. In addition, they may elect to enroll in a supplementary medical insurance program under Medicare by paying a premium. Medicare pays only a part of total hospital expenses. When their hospital stay is longer than 60 days, for example, patients are responsible for $130 per day.

In 1997, over 38 million aged and disabled were covered by Medicare. Benefit payments are expected to reach $200 billion by 1998. Medicare has become a political football in Washington in recent years. Projections using conservative assumptions suggest that in 2005 total annual outlays will reach $263 billion and that the Medicare fund will be $375 billion in the red. As the baby boom generation reaches retirement after 2010, the current system is clearly unsustainable. This will be "the" issue in the 2000 presidential election.

➤ **Food Stamps**   The Food Stamp program is an antipoverty program fully funded out of general federal tax revenues, with states bearing 50 percent of the program's administrative costs. **Food stamps** are vouchers that have a face value greater than their cost and that can be used to purchase food at grocery stores. The amount by which the face

unemployment compensation
A state government transfer program that pays cash benefits for a certain period of time to laid-off workers who have worked for a specified period of time for a covered employer.

Medicaid and **Medicare**
In-kind government transfer programs that provide health and hospitalization benefits: Medicare to the aged and their survivors and to certain of the disabled, regardless of income, and Medicaid to people with low incomes.

food stamps *Vouchers that have a face value greater than their cost and that can be used to purchase food at grocery stores.*

PART THREE
Market Imperfections and Government

MAJOR WELFARE REFORM
TAKES EFFECT IN 1997

In 1996, the Congress passed and the president signed a sweeping and controversial package of reforms to the welfare system in the United States. The legislation gave much more freedom to states to design innovative programs to get people off the welfare rolls and back into the workforce. The new legislation took effect on July 1, 1997.

U.S. WELFARE SYSTEM DIES AS STATE PROGRAMS EMERGE

The nation's 62-year-old welfare system, condemned last year by Federal law, will formally die on Tuesday, and a season of state legislative debate has brought new clarity to the decentralized system rising in its place.

If the emerging programs share a unifying theme, it can be summarized in a word: work. States are demanding that recipients find it faster, keep it longer and perform it as a condition of aid. Most states regard even a low-paying, dead-end job as preferable to the education and training programs they offered in the past. And recipients who break the rules are facing penalties of unprecedented severity.

But the hard edge also has a softer side. Operating on the assumption that work requires support, many states are investing in work-related services. Near-record increases for child care head the list,

but states are also spending more on transportation, job placement and programs that let working recipients keep more of their benefits even while earning paychecks.

• • •

Though the new system has often been described as a cut, it will provide states with about $2 billion more this year than they otherwise would have had, according to a rough estimate by the House Ways and Means Committee. That is because Washington now sends the states fixed payments based on the welfare population of earlier years, even though the rolls are plummeting.

The Government is also giving states an additional $600 million this year for child care. Added together, the new Federal money represents an increase of about 16 percent, or an additional $650 for every family in the program.

The program, which used to be called Aid to Families with Dependent Children, serves about four million adults, most of them single mothers, and more than seven million children. As of Tuesday, it takes on a new name to stress a new ethos of time limits and work rules: Temporary Assistance for Needy Families.

The combination of freedom, money and new expectations has produced a moment of dizzying

change. Wisconsin is essentially abolishing cash aid, substituting a giant work program that will stretch from the sprawling ghettos of Milwaukee to the Minnesota border. Oregon is putting its hopes in intensified casework; Texas in private contractors. Illinois has put up $100 million of state money to offer child care to all low-income workers, whether they have been on welfare or not. New Jersey has created a $3.7 million transportation fund, to get poor people to far-away jobs.

• • •

As of Tuesday, states must start limiting most recipients to no more than five years of benefits in a lifetime. But a survey by the National Governors Association found at least 20 states imposing shorter limits on all or part of their caseload.

Texas has the shortest limit, of 12 months for those deemed most able to work. Tennessee has a limit of 18 consecutive months, and in Connecticut the limit is 21 months. Ten states, from Massachusetts to Oregon, have two-year limits, but the details vary widely.[a]

Source: [a]Jason DeParle, "U.S. Welfare System Dies as State Programs Emerge," *The New York Times*, June 30, 1997, p. 1. Copyright © 1997 by The New York Times Co. Reprinted by permission.

For more on welfare reform, see the Case and Fair Web page at
http://www.prenhall.com/casefair.

value of the stamps exceeds their cost depends on income and family size. Only low-income families and single persons are eligible to receive food stamps.

It is generally acknowledged that a thriving black market in food stamps exists. Families that want or need cash can sell their food stamps to people who will buy them for less than face value but more than the original recipient paid for them.

In 1995 there were 26.6 million participants in the Food Stamp program, up from 20 million in 1990. The total cost of the program in 1995 was $27.9 billion.

▶ **Housing Programs** Over the years, the federal government and state governments have administered many different housing programs designed to improve the quality of housing for low-income people. The biggest is the Public Housing program, financed

CHAPTER SEVENTEEN
Income Distribution and Poverty

421

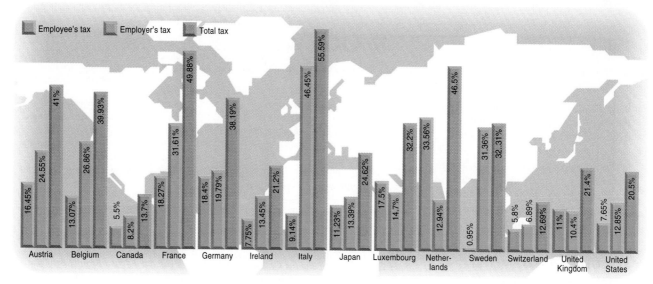

FIGURE 17.3

Employer-Employee Payroll Tax Rates for Social Security Programs, by Country, 1993

Note: "Social security programs" is defined as the total of (1) old-age, disability, and survivors' insurance, (2) public health or sickness insurance, (3) workers' compensation, (4) unemployment insurance, and (5) family allowance programs.

Source: U.S. Social Security Administration, Office of Research and Statistics, *Social Security Programs Throughout the World*, biannual.

by the federal government but administered by local public housing authorities. Public housing tenants pay rents equal to no more than 30 percent of their incomes. In many cases, this means they pay zero. The largest housing program, called "Section 8," provides housing assistance payments to tenants and slightly above-market rent guarantees to participating landlords.

In 1996 there were 32.5 million rental housing units in the United States, of which 1.3 million were in public housing projects. Another 3.5 million received a government rent subsidy.

➤ **International Comparisons**   Many U.S. employers and employees complain about the taxes they pay to fund the country's social security programs. In 1993, 7.65 percent of a U.S. worker's paycheck and 12.85 percent of an employer's total payroll (a grand total of 20.5 percent) was used to fund programs for old-age, disability, and survivors' insurance; public health or sickness insurance; workers' compensation; unemployment insurance; and family allowance programs.

Figure 17.3 shows that the taxes U.S. businesses and workers pay to support social security programs are among the lowest in the world. In France, workers and employers pay a total of 49.88 percent, and in Italy they pay a total of 55.59 percent.

HOW EFFECTIVE ARE ANTIPOVERTY PROGRAMS?

The number of persons officially classified as poor dropped sharply during the 1960s and early 1970s. Between 1978 and 1983, however, the number of poor increased nearly 45 percent. After falling back between 1983 and 1989, the figure hit 39.3 million in 1994, the highest total since 1964. (The figure fell slightly to 38.1 million in 1995.) This increase is at the center of a great debate over the effectiveness of antipoverty programs.

Some say economic growth is the best way to cure poverty. Poverty programs are expensive and must be paid for with tax revenues. The high rates of taxation to support these programs, critics say, have eroded the incentive to work, save, and invest, slowing the rate of economic growth, and the rise in poverty is evidence that antipoverty programs do not work.

The opposite view is that poverty would be much more widespread without antipoverty programs. Poverty has increased not because of *increasing* programs but because the "real" level of transfer payments has actually *fallen* significantly. In other words, transfer payments have not kept up with rising prices.

Despite the anti-big-government rhetoric of recent years, most of what the government did to change the distribution of income 15 years ago it still does today. The volume of redistribution is less, but most major programs have remained largely intact. Many still argue we do too little. Poverty rates remain higher today than 20 years ago, and the number of homeless people continues to increase.

GOVERNMENT OR THE MARKET? A REVIEW

Part two (chapters 6 to 12) introduced you to the behavior of households and firms in input and output markets. You learned that if all the assumptions of perfect competition held in the real world, the outcome would be perfectly efficient.

But as we began to relax the assumptions of perfect competition in part three (chapters 13 to 17), we began to see a potential role for government in the economy. Some firms acquire market power and tend to underproduce and overprice. Unregulated markets give private decision makers no incentives to weigh the social costs of externalities. Goods that provide collective benefits may not be produced in sufficient quantities without government involvement. And, as we saw in this chapter, the final distribution of well-being determined by the free market may not be considered equitable by society.

Remember, however, that government is not a cure for all economic woes. There is no guarantee that public sector involvement will improve matters. Many argue that government involvement may bring about even more inequity and inefficiency because bureaucrats are often driven by self-interest, not public interest.

You now have a strong foundation in microeconomic theory. Part four of this book—chapters 18 to 20—presents several topics in applied economics: public finance, labor economics, urban economics, the economics of crime, the economics of health care reform, and the economics of immigration. These chapters are meant to provide you with an overview of how the discipline addresses some of the most pressing problems of our time. They also represent a preview of what you will encounter in more advanced courses in economics.

SUMMARY

1. Even if all markets were perfectly efficient, the result might not be fair. Even in relatively free market economies, governments redistribute income and wealth, usually in the name of fairness, or *equity*.

2. Because utility is neither directly observable nor measurable, most policy discussions deal with the distributions of income and wealth as imperfect substitutes for the concept of "the distribution of well-being."

THE SOURCES OF HOUSEHOLD INCOME

3. Households derive their incomes from three basic sources: (1) from wages or salaries received in exchange for labor

(about 61 percent); (2) from property such as capital and land (about 23 percent); and (3) from government (about 16 percent).

4. Differences in wage and salary incomes across households result from differences in the characteristics of workers (skills, training, education, experience, and so on) and from differences in jobs (dangerous, exciting, glamorous, difficult, and so forth). Household income also varies with the number of household members in the labor force, and it can decline sharply if members become unemployed.

5. The amount of property income that a household earns depends on the amount and kinds of property it owns. Transfer income from governments flows substantially, but not exclusively, to lower-income households. Except for social security, transfer payments are by and large designed to provide income to those in need.

THE DISTRIBUTION OF INCOME

6. The 20 percent of families at the top of the income distribution received 50.1 percent of the total income in the United States in 1995, while the bottom 20 percent earned just 3.1 percent. Income distribution in the United States has remained basically stable over a long period of time.

7. The Lorenz Curve is a commonly used graphic device for describing the distribution of income. The **Gini coefficient** is an index of income inequality that ranges from zero for perfect equality to 1 for total inequality.

8. Poverty is very difficult to define. Nonetheless, the official poverty line in the United States is fixed at three times the cost of the Department of Agriculture's minimum food budget. In 1994 the poverty line for a family of four was $15,141.

9. Between 1960 and 1970, the number of people officially classified as poor fell from 40 million to 25 million. That number did not change much between 1970 and 1978. Between 1978 and 1983, the number of poor people increased by nearly 45 percent to 35.3 million. In 1995 the figure was 38.1 million.

10. Data on the distribution of wealth are not as readily available as data on the distribution of income. The distribution of wealth in the United States is more unequal than the distribution of income. The wealthiest 10 percent of households own 72.5 percent of all household assets.

THE REDISTRIBUTION DEBATE

11. The basic philosophical argument against government redistribution rests on the proposition that one is entitled to the fruits of one's efforts. It also rests on the principles of freedom of contract and protection of property rights. More common arguments focus on the negative effects of redistribution on incentives to work, save, and invest.

12. The basic philosophical argument in favor of redistribution is that a society as rich as the United States has a moral obligation to provide all its members with the basic necessities of life. More formal arguments can be found in the works of the utilitarians, Rawls, and Marx.

REDISTRIBUTION PROGRAMS AND POLICIES

13. In the United States, redistribution is accomplished through taxation and through a number of government transfer programs. The largest of these are social security, public assistance, supplemental security, unemployment compensation, Medicare and Medicaid, food stamps, and various housing subsidy programs, including public housing.

14. The increase in poverty during the 1980s and 1990s is at the center of a great debate over the effectiveness of antipoverty programs. One view holds that the best way to cure poverty is with economic growth. Poverty programs are expensive and must be paid for with tax revenues. The high rates of taxation required to support these programs have eroded the incentive to work, save, and invest, thus slowing the rate of economic growth. In addition, the rise in poverty is cited as evidence that antipoverty programs do not work. The opposite view holds that without antipoverty programs, poverty would be much worse.

REVIEW TERMS AND CONCEPTS

compensating differentials, 406
economic income, 408
equity, 403
food stamps, 420
Gini coefficient, 410
human capital, 405
labor theory of value, 417

Lorenz Curve, 410
Medicaid and Medicare, 420
money income, 410
poverty line, 412
property income, 408
public assistance, or welfare, 419

Rawlsian justice, 416
social security system, 418
transfer payments, 408
unemployment compensation, 420
utilitarian justice, 416
utility possibilities frontier, 403

PROBLEM SET

1. The median annual income of women fell as a percentage of the same figure for men in 1997 (see Issues and Debates box, "A Rising Gap between Men's and Women's Wages in 1997," in this chapter). Overall, the figure stood at 74.8 percent. But it is larger for older workers. For example, for full-time workers between the ages of 25 and 29 the ratio of women's median to men's was 82.4 percent. The same figure for workers between 40 and 44 was 62 percent and for workers between 60 and 64 it fell to 57.4 percent. What explanations can you offer for this pattern?

2. In 1993, President Bill Clinton proposed, and the U.S. Congress passed, a number of measures to increase the progressivity of the U.S. individual income tax, including tax relief at the bottom of the income scale and an increase in the top bracket's rate from 28 percent to 39.6 percent. What are the arguments in favor of such a policy? What are some of the possible consequences of such a policy? In retrospect, were the Clinton proposals a good idea?

3. Using the data in the following table, create two graphs. The first graph should plot the Lorenz Curves for African American families and white families. The second graph should plot the Lorenz Curve for the 1980 "all" data and the Lorenz Curve for the 1995 "all" data.

   In each graph, which has the higher Gini coefficient? How do you interpret the result?

| | PERCENT OF INCOME | | | |
	AFRICAN AMERICAN	WHITE	1995 ALL	1980 ALL
Lower fifth	3.2	4.6	4.2	5.1
Second fifth	8.5	10.3	10.0	11.6
Third fifth	15.1	15.8	15.7	17.5
Fourth fifth	24.7	23.0	23.3	24.3
Highest fifth	48.7	46.3	46.9	41.6

4. Between 1993 and 1997, the welfare rolls in the United States fell by 20 percent. What explanations can you offer for this rather dramatic drop?

5. Economists call education "an investment in human capital." Define capital. In what sense is education capital?

Investments are undertaken in order to earn a rate of return. Describe the return to an investment in a college education. How would you go about measuring it? How would you decide if it is good enough to warrant the investment?

6. Below is a list of establishment categories and average weekly earnings for nonsupervisory employees in a recent year. Using the concepts of "human capital" and "compensating differentials," explain why they might be expected to differ in the ways that they do:

Computer programming	$724.85
Heavy construction firms	535.29
Logging firms	447.02
Gas stations	218.13
Car washes	161.19

7. During the mid-1980s, house values and rents rose sharply in California and in the northeastern United States. Homeowners, who have higher incomes on average than renters, benefit from house-price increases and are protected from housing-cost increases. Renters experience rising rents and falling standards of living if incomes do not keep up with housing-cost increases. Using the *Statistical Abstract of the United States*, look up residential rent, home prices, and income levels for your area. What has happened in the last 10 years? Do you think the performance of the housing market in recent years has increased or decreased inequality in your area?

8. New Ph.D.'s in economics entering the job market find that academic jobs (jobs teaching at colleges and universities) pay about 30 percent less than nonacademic jobs such as working at a bank or a consulting firm. Those who take academic jobs are clearly worse off than those who take nonacademic jobs. Do you agree? Explain your answer.

9. Should welfare benefits be higher in California and New York than they are in Mississippi? Defend your answer.

10. Poverty among the elderly has been sharply reduced in the last quarter century. How has this been accomplished?

11. "Income inequality is evidence that our economic system is working well, not poorly." What arguments might this speaker use to support his opinion of income redistribution policies? How might he respond when racial or sexual disparities are brought to his attention?

TAKE IT TO THE NET

We invite you to visit the Case and Fair page on the Prentice Hall Web site:
http://www.prenhall.com/casefair
for this chapter's World Wide Web exercise.

WAGE INEQUALITY IN THE UNITED STATES

The distribution of wages in the United States has changed significantly since the 1970s. For example, the gap has widened between the earnings of high-wage workers and low-wage workers. This increased wage inequality has resulted in a number of debates about its causes and implications. Individuals concerned about the costs of rising wage inequality point to similar increases in the poverty rate during the period. They say the increased crime, homelessness, and other social- and health-related costs are caused by the reduction in earnings of low-wage workers. Others argue, "the widening inequality in earnings and the buoyant demand for skilled workers also indirectly encourages greater growth in the economy by increasing the incentives for young people to invest in themselves" [a](Becker, 1997, p. 66).

Several methods are used to measure changes in the distribution of wages in addition to measuring changes in the distributions of household income, wealth, and consumption. When measuring wage inequality, economists examine the ratios of the wages of individuals at different points on the distribution of wages. The ratio of the wages of a worker at the 90th percentile of the distribution (that is, 90 percent of all workers earn less than this worker) to the wages of a worker at the tenth percentile of the distribution (that is, 10 percent of all workers earn less than this worker) is called the "90 to 10" ratio. Similarly defined 90 to 50 and 50 to 10 wage ratios can also be calculated to provide additional information about the distribution of wages. This should become clear as we consider actual data.

The 90 to 10 ratio for male workers in 1979 was 3.7, indicating that the wages of the worker at the 90th percentile were 3.7 times greater than the wages of a worker at the 10th percentile. By 1995, this ratio had risen to 4.8, an increase of approximately 30 percent. This increase in the 90 to 10 ratio indicates that wage inequality has increased. The 90 to 10 ratio of female workers also increased between 1979 and 1995 from 2.6 to 4.1.

In addition to studying how the distribution of wages, measured at particular points along the distribution, changes over time, economists examine wage inequality of workers with different observable traits (for example, race, gender, education, and experience). A comparison of the wages of college graduates with the wages of high school graduates indicates that a "college premium" exists. This college premium, declining during the 1970s, increased throughout the 1980s and continued to increase in the early 1990s. A comparison of the wages of experienced workers with the wages of recent entrants to the labor market indicates that the "experience premium" has also increased over time.

Of particular concern to policy makers and economists is the rising gap between the wages of less-skilled workers (for example, high school graduates) and the wages of more-skilled workers (for example, college graduates). To study possible causes of this increasing wage gap, assume the wages of less-skilled labor and more-skilled labor are determined in separate markets. Specifically, the

supply and demand for less-skilled labor determines both the wage and employment of less-skilled workers. Likewise, the supply and demand for more-skilled labor determines the wage and employment of more-skilled workers (Figure 1). The possible causes of the increase in wage inequality include demand-side determinants of wages, supply-side determinants of wages, and institutional determinants of wages.

Three demand factors are believed to affect wage inequality.

1. Many argue the most important is recent changes in technology (like the increased use of personal computers) that have placed a premium on more-skilled labor. A change in technology that raises the productivity of more-skilled labor and has little or no effect on the productivity of less-skilled labor is called skill-biased technological change. As skill-biased technological change occurs, firms respond by increasing the demand for more-skilled labor and reducing the demand for less-skilled labor.
2. Changes in international trade have contributed to the increased wage inequality. For example, because import industries employ relatively less-skilled labor, U.S. firms faced with greater competition respond by decreasing both output and the demand for less-skilled labor. Furthermore, some U.S. firms have opted to move some of their production processes to locations outside the United States to take advantage of lower wages in foreign labor markets.
3. Changes in the relative demand for certain types of goods may have caused a decline in the relative demand for less-skilled labor. An example is the shift of jobs from the manufacturing sector to the service sector.

Several supply factors may also have contributed to the recent increase in wage inequality.

1. Increased immigration may have resulted in an increase in the supply of less-skilled workers, causing a relative decline in their wages.
2. Increases in the cost of higher education might have limited increases in the supply of more-skilled workers.
3. Increased labor force participation of women could have caused an increase in wage inequality, because during this period women generally have had less experience.

Two institutional factors could have contributed to the increase in wage inequality.

1. The existence of a minimum wage causes the distribution of wages to be less dispersed than it otherwise would be because the minimum wage (a price floor) prevents wages from falling below a given level. From 1981 to 1990, the minimum wage was $3.35 per hour. Because of increases in the overall price level in the United States, the real value of the minimum wage fell during this period. Reductions in the real value of the minimum wage would, therefore, allow the real value of wages at the bottom of the wage distribution to fall.
2. The degree of unionization in the labor market can affect the distribution of wages; unions are more frequently found in the less-skilled labor market. Specifically, the existence of unions generally causes wages to be less dispersed in unionized sectors. During the 1980s, we have observed a decline in unionization rates. This decline in unionization would cause an increase in the dispersion of wages (that is, increased wage inequality).

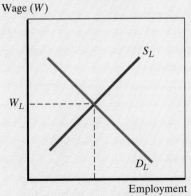

Less-skilled labor market

Wage (W)

S_L

W_L

D_L

Employment

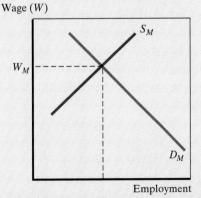

More-skilled labor market

Wage (W)

S_M

W_M

D_M

Employment

FIGURE 1

Note: S_L, D_L, and W_L represent the supply, demand, and wage for less-skilled labor. S_M, D_M, and W_M represent the supply, demand, and wage for more-skilled labor.

427

A number of policies have been proposed to reduce wage inequality —increases in the minimum wage (as were recently enacted in 1996 and 1997), expanded loan programs to college students, government-funded training programs, and import restrictions, among others. There remains debate about the causes of this increased wage inequality and about policies to allay it, but most economists and policy makers agree that a better-educated workforce will do much to reduce the recent growth in wage inequality in the United States.

Questions for Analytical Thinking

1. Suppose the U.S. Congress increases the funds in the federal loan program to college students. Explain what effect this might have on the supply of less-skilled and more-skilled labor. Based on your analysis, what effect would this increased funding have on the wage gap? Explain.

2. a. During the 1980s, college enrollment rates increased while the college premium also increased. What do these two observations suggest must have happened to the supply and demand for more-skilled labor during this period? Explain.
   b. Explain how increases in the college premium, all else fixed, might affect future college enrollment rates. Based on your analysis, why do you think some economists argue that increases in the wage gap may be offset by future labor supply decisions? Explain.

3. Becker[b] (1997, p. 65) notes that "when greater [wage] inequality is due to higher rates of return on human capital and other investments in knowledge, it can be an engine that drives an economy toward more rapid economic growth." What do you think Becker means by this? Explain.

4. Assume the distribution of income has experienced the same changes that the distribution of wages did between 1979 and 1995. Based on the changes in the 90–10 ratios for males and females, explain what happened to the shape of the Lorenz curve in the United States between 1979 and 1995.

5. There is tremendous debate about how to improve the quality of the U.S. public school system (for example, school vouchers). Explain how an improved public school system might affect wage inequality.

6. In addition to the distribution of wages, assume that policy makers are also concerned about the distribution of income. First, using the supply and demand curves for less-skilled labor, explain what effect an increase in the minimum wage, all else fixed, will have on wage inequality. Second, because policy makers are also concerned about the distribution of income, why might it be important to take into account the employment effects of an increase in the minimum wage? Explain.

[a]Gary Becker, "Maybe the Earnings Gap Isn't Such a Bad Thing," in *The Economics of Life* (New York: McGraw Hill, 1997); [b]Gary Becker, "Maybe the Earnings Gap Isn't Such a Bad Thing," in *The Economics of Life* (New York: McGraw Hill, 1997).

Sources: Nicole M. Fortin and Thomas Lemieux, "Institutional Changes and Rising Wage Inequality: Is There a Linkage," *Journal of Economic Perspectives*, Spring 1997, Vol. 11, No. 2, pp. 75–96; Peter Gottschalk, "Inequality, Income Growth, and Mobility: The Basic Facts," *Journal of Economic Perspectives*, Spring 1997, Vol. 11, No. 2, pp. 21–40; George E. Johnson, "Changes in Earnings Inequality: The Role of Demand Shifts," *Journal of Economic Perspectives*, Spring 1997, Vol. 11, No. 2, pp. 41–54; Robert H. Topel, "Factor Proportions and Relative Wages: The Supply-Side Determinants of Wage Inequality," *Journal of Economic Perspectives*, Spring 1997, Vol. 11, No. 2, pp. 55–74; Robert Valletta, "Rising Wage Inequality in the U.S.," *Economic Letter*, Federal Reserve Bank of San Francisco, Number 97–25, September 5, 1997; John C. Weicher, "The Rich and the Poor: Demographics of the U.S. Wealth Distribution," *Review*, Federal Reserve Bank of St. Louis, July/August 1997, Vol. 79, No. 4, pp. 25–38; *Economic Report of the President* (Washington, D.C.: U.S. Government Printing Office, 1997).

Chapter

18

PUBLIC FINANCE:
THE ECONOMICS
OF TAXATION

AN INTRODUCTORY COURSE IN ECONOMICS

has several goals, one of which is to introduce theory about how economies work. The first 17 chapters contain what amounts to the core of microeconomic theory.

Another purpose is to survey the major subfields of the discipline. In chapter 1 we briefly described a number of these subfields. This chapter is the first of several that expand on those brief descriptions. Because the discipline is so varied, we cannot survey all the areas of economic inquiry. So we limit our discussion to five of the most debated economic issues today: public finance (chapter 18), labor economics (chapter 19), and the economics of crime, immigration, and health-care reform (chapter 20).

THE ECONOMICS OF TAXATION

The five chapters in part three analyzed the potential role of government in the economy. Together, those chapters discuss much of the field of *public economics*. From there, it is an easy transition to *public finance*, which begins our survey of applied economics. No matter what functions we end up assigning to government, to do anything at all government must first raise revenues. The primary vehicle that the government uses to finance itself is taxation.[1]

> Taxes may be imposed on transactions, institutions, property, meals, and other things, but in the final analysis they are paid by individuals or households.

---

[1]Before we proceed, you may want to review the discussion of the public sector in chapter 3. There we describe the basic sources of revenue for federal, state, and local governments, as well as the things those revenues are spent on. You will often hear the taxing and spending policies of federal or state governments referred to as "fiscal policies." The word *fiscal* comes from *fisc*, another word for a government treasury.

TAXES: BASIC CONCEPTS

To begin our analysis of the U.S. tax system, we need to clarify some terms. There are many kinds of taxes, and tax analysts use a specific language to describe them. Every tax has two parts: a *base* and a *rate structure*. The **tax base** is the measure or value upon which the tax is levied. In the United States, taxes are levied on a variety of bases, including income, sales, property, and corporate profits. The **tax rate structure** determines the portion of the tax base that must be paid in taxes. A tax rate of 25 percent on income, for example, means that I pay a tax equal to 25 percent of my income.

tax base *The measure or value upon which a tax is levied.*

tax rate structure *The percentage of a tax base that must be paid in taxes—25% of income, for example.*

▶ **Taxes on Stocks versus Taxes on Flows** Tax bases may be either stock measures or flow measures. The local property tax is a tax on the value of residential, commercial, or industrial property. For instance, homeowners are taxed on the current assessed value of their homes. Current value is a stock variable—it is measured or estimated at a point in time.

Other taxes are levied on flows. (Review chapter 4 if the difference between stock and flow variables is unclear.) Income is a flow. Most people are paid weekly, biweekly, or monthly, and they have taxes deducted from every paycheck. Retail sales take place continuously, and a retail sales tax takes a portion of that flow.

▶ **Proportional, Progressive, and Regressive Taxes** All taxes are ultimately paid out of income. A tax whose burden is a constant proportion of income for all households is a **proportional tax**. A tax of 20 percent on all forms of income, with no deductions or exclusions, is a proportional tax.

proportional tax *A tax whose burden is the same proportion of income for all households.*

progressive tax *A tax whose burden, expressed as a percentage of income, increases as income increases.*

A tax that exacts a higher proportion of income from higher-income households than from lower-income households is a **progressive tax**. Because its rate structure increases with income, the U.S. individual income tax is a progressive tax. Under current law, a family with a taxable income of $30,000 would pay a tax of 15 percent, while a family with an income of $100,000 would pay about 23 percent.

regressive tax *A tax whose burden, expressed as a percentage of income, falls as income increases.*

A tax that exacts a lower proportion of income from higher-income families than from lower-income families is a **regressive tax**. *Excise taxes* (taxes on specific commodities) are regressive. The retail sales tax is also a regressive tax. Suppose the retail sales tax in your state is 5 percent. You might assume it is a proportional tax because everyone pays 5 percent. But all people do not spend the same fraction of their income on taxable goods and services. In fact, higher-income households save a larger fraction of their incomes. Even though they spend more on more expensive things and may pay more taxes in *dollars* than lower-income families, they end up paying a smaller *proportion* of their incomes in sales tax.

Table 18.1 shows this principle at work in three families. The lowest-income family saves 20 percent of its $10,000 income, leaving $8,000 for consumption. With a 5 percent sales tax, the household pays $400, or 4 percent of total income, in tax. The $50,000 family saves 50 percent of its income, or $25,000, leaving $25,000 for consumption. With the 5 percent sales tax, the household pays $1,250, only 2.5 percent of its total income, in tax.

▶ **Marginal versus Average Tax Rates** When discussing a specific tax or taxes in general, we should distinguish between average tax rates and marginal tax rates. Your *average tax rate* is the total amount of tax you pay divided by your total income. If you earned a total income of $15,000 and paid income taxes of $1,500, your average income tax rate would be 10 percent ($1,500 divided by $15,000). If you paid $3,000 in taxes, your average rate would be 20 percent ($3,000 divided by $15,000).

Your *marginal tax rate* is the tax rate you pay on any additional income you earn. If you take a part-time job and pay an additional $280 in tax on the extra $1,000 you've earned, your marginal tax rate is 28 percent ($280 divided by $1,000).

Marginal and average tax rates are usually different. The U.S. individual income tax shows how and why marginal tax rates can differ. Each year, you must file a tax

TABLE 18.1 THE BURDEN OF A HYPOTHETICAL 5% SALES TAX IMPOSED ON THREE HOUSEHOLDS WITH DIFFERENT INCOMES

HOUSEHOLD	INCOME	SAVING RATE, %	SAVING	CONSUMPTION	5% TAX ON CONSUMPTION	TAX AS A % OF INCOME
A	$ 10,000	20	$ 2,000	$ 8,000	$ 400	4.0
B	20,000	40	8,000	12,000	600	3.0
C	50,000	50	25,000	25,000	1,250	2.5

return with the Internal Revenue Service on or before April 15. On that form you first figure out the total tax you are responsible for paying. Next, you determine how much was withheld from your income and sent to the IRS by your employer. If too much was withheld, you get a refund; if not enough, you have to write a check to the government for the difference.

In figuring out the total amount of tax you must pay, you first add up all your income. You are then allowed to subtract certain items from it. Among the things that virtually all taxpayers can subtract are the *personal exemption* and the *standard deduction*.[2] After everything is subtracted, you are left with *taxable income*. Taxable income is then subject to a set of marginal rates that rise with income. Table 18.2 presents the marginal individual income tax rates for 1997.

Suppose you are a single taxpayer who earned $80,000 in 1997. During 1997 you had tax withheld by your employer. By April 15, 1998, you must file a return to see if your employer withheld too much or too little. Rushing to meet the deadline, you must do the following calculations, which are summarized in Table 18.3.

First, you take your total income, $80,000, and subtract the personal exemption ($2,650) and the standard deduction ($4,150), leaving "Taxable Income" of $73,200. To figure the tax, three separate calculations are involved.[3] The first $24,650 is taxed at 15 percent (see Table 8.2). The tax on this amount is simply .15 × $24,650, or $3,697.50.

The second "slice" of income, between $24,650 and $59,750, is taxed at 28 percent. The difference between $59,750 and $24,650 is $35,100. The tax on this amount is .28 × $35,100 or $9,828.00. Finally, taxable income over $59,750 but less than $124,650 is taxed at 31 percent. Because taxable income is $73,200, the excess is simply $73,200 − $59,750 or $13,450. The tax on this amount is .31 × $13,450 or $4,169.50. Thus, total tax due is $3,397.50 + $9,828.00 + $4,169.50 = $17,695.00. You now check to see if the amount withheld by your employer was too little or too much. If you paid too much, you get a refund; if you did not pay enough, you must send Uncle Sam a check for the shortfall by April 15!

You can now see the difference between average and marginal tax rates. Your average rate in 1997 was $17,695 as a percentage of $80,000, or 22.1 percent. But note

TABLE 18.2

INDIVIDUAL INCOME TAX RATES, 1997

MARRIED COUPLES FILING JOINTLY TAXABLE INCOME	TAX RATE
$0–$41,200	15%
$41,200–$99,600	28%
$99,600–$151,750	31%
$151,700–$271,500	36%
Over $271,500	39.6%

SINGLE TAXPAYERS TAXABLE INCOME	TAX RATE
$0–$24,650	15%
$24,650–$59,750	28%
$59,750–$124,650	31%
$124,650–$271,500	36%
Over $271,500	39.6%

Source: Internal Revenue Service.

---

[2]Deductions and exemptions have no definition other than that they are amounts that you are allowed to subtract from income before figuring your tax. In 1997, a single taxpayer could subtract a *personal exemption* of $2,650. A married couple could subtract twice that amount plus $2,650 for every dependent child in the family. If your parents claim you as a dependent, you cannot claim an exemption for yourself when you file as an individual. Taxpayers in 1997 were also permitted to subtract either a *standard deduction* of $4,150 ($6,900 for a married couple) or itemized deductions if they exceeded $4,150. Expenditures that can be itemized and deducted include extraordinary medical expenses, state and local income and property taxes, mortgage interest paid, and charitable contributions. The standard deduction is larger for those who are over 65 and/or blind.

[3]Taxpayers do not have to do these calculations. Rather, filers simply look up the tax due for their particular income level in the tax table that accompanies their tax form package.

TABLE 18.3 TAX CALCULATIONS FOR A SINGLE TAXPAYER
WHO EARNED $80,000 IN 1997

Total income	$80,000
− Personal exemption	2,650
− Standard deduction	4,150
= Taxable income	$73,200

Tax Calculation

$0–24,650 taxed at 15% → ($24,650) × .15 =	$3,697.50
$59,750 − $24,650 taxed at 28% → ($59,750 − $24,650) × .28 = $35,100 × .28 =	$9,828.00
income above $59,750 taxed at 31% → (73,200 − $59,750) × .31 = $13,450 × .31 =	$4,169.50
Total tax = $17,695.00	$17,695.00
Average tax rate = $17,695/$80,000 =	22.1%
Marginal tax rate =	31%

that any *additional* income that you might have earned up to $124,650 would be taxed at 31 percent because it is simply more income over $59,750.

> Marginal tax rates influence behavior. Decisions about how much to work depend on how much of the added income you get to take home. Similarly, a firm's decision about how much to invest depends in part on the additional, or marginal, profits that the investment project would yield after tax.

TAX EQUITY

One of the criteria for evaluating the economy that we defined in chapter 1 (and returned to in chapter 17) was fairness, or *equity*. Everyone agrees that tax burdens should be distributed fairly, that all of us should pay our "fair share" of taxes, but there is endless debate about what constitutes a fair tax system.

One theory of fairness is called the **benefits-received principle**. Dating back to the eighteenth-century economist Adam Smith and earlier writers, the benefits-received principle holds that taxpayers should contribute to government according to the benefits they derive from public expenditures. This principle ties the tax side of the fiscal equation to the expenditure side. For example, the owners and users of cars pay gasoline and automotive excise taxes, which are paid into the Federal Highway Trust Fund to build and maintain the federal highway system. The beneficiaries of public highways are thus taxed in rough proportion to their use of those highways.

The difficulty with applying the benefits principle is that the bulk of public expenditures are for public goods—national defense, for example. The benefits of public goods fall collectively on all members of society, and there is no way to determine what value individual taxpayers receive from them.

A different principle, and one that has dominated the formulation of tax policy in the United States for decades, is the **ability-to-pay principle**. This principle holds that taxpayers should bear tax burdens in line with their ability to pay. Here the tax side of the fiscal equation is viewed separately from the expenditure side. Under this system, the problem of attributing the benefits of public expenditures to specific taxpayers or groups of taxpayers is avoided.

> **Horizontal and Vertical Equity** If we accept the idea that ability to pay should be the basis for the distribution of tax burdens, two principles follow. First, the principle of *horizontal equity* holds that those with equal ability to pay should bear equal

benefits-received principle
A theory of fairness holding that taxpayers should contribute to government (in the form of taxes) in proportion to the benefits that they receive from public expenditures.

ability-to-pay principle *A theory of taxation holding that citizens should bear tax burdens in line with their ability to pay taxes.*

tax burdens. Second, the principle of *vertical equity* holds that those with greater ability to pay should pay more.

Although these notions seem appealing, we must have answers to two interdependent questions before they can be meaningful. First, how is ability to pay measured? What is the "best" tax base? Second, if A has a greater ability to pay than B, *how much* more should A contribute?

WHAT IS THE "BEST" TAX BASE?

The three leading candidates for best tax base are *income, consumption*, and *wealth*. Before we consider each as a basis for taxation, let us see what they mean.

Income—to be precise, *economic income*—is anything that enhances your ability to command resources. The technical definition of economic income is the value of what you consume plus any change in the value of what you own:

Economic Income = Consumption + Change in Net Worth

This broad definition includes many items not counted by the Internal Revenue Service and some items the Census Bureau does not include in its definition of "money income." Economic income includes all money receipts, whether from employment, profits, or transfers from the government. It also includes the value of benefits not received in money form, such as medical benefits, employer retirement contributions, paid country club memberships, and so forth. Increases or decreases in the value of stocks or bonds, whether or not they are "realized" through sale, are part of economic income. For income tax purposes, capital gains count as income only when they are realized, but for purposes of defining economic income, all increases in asset values count, whether they are realized or not.

A few other items that we do not usually think of as income are included in a comprehensive definition of income. If I own my house outright and live in it rent free, income flows from my house just as interest flows from a bond or profit from a share of stock. By owning the house, I enjoy valuable housing benefits that I would otherwise have to pay rent for. I am my own landlord and I am, in essence, earning my own rent. Other components of economic income include any gifts and bequests received and food grown at home.

In economic terms, income is income, regardless of source and use.

Consumption is the total value of things that a household consumes in a given period.

Wealth, or *net worth*, is the value of all the things you own after your liabilities are subtracted. If you were to sell off today everything of value you own—stocks, bonds, houses, cars, and so forth—at their current market prices and pay off all your debts—loans, mortgages, and so forth—you would end up with your net worth.

Net worth = Assets − Liabilities

Remember, income and consumption are *flow* measures. We speak of income per month or per year. Wealth and net worth are *stock* measures at a point in time.

For years, conventional wisdom among economists held that income was the best measure of ability to pay taxes. Many who feel that consumption is a better measure have recently challenged that assumption. The following arguments are not just arguments about fairness and ability to pay; they are also arguments about the best base for taxation.

Remember as you proceed that the issue is which *base* is the best base, not which *tax* is the best tax or whether taxes ought to be progressive or regressive. While sales taxes are regressive, it is possible to have a personal consumption tax that is progressive. Under such a system, individuals would report their income as they do now, but all documented saving would be deductible. The difference between income and saving is a measure of personal consumption that could be taxed with progressive rates.

➤ **Consumption as the Best Tax Base**   The view favoring consumption as the best tax base dates back at least to the seventeenth-century English philosopher Thomas Hobbes, who argued that people should pay taxes in accordance with "what they actually take out of the common pot, not what they leave in." The standard of living, the argument goes, depends not on income but on how much income is spent. If we want to redistribute well-being, therefore, the tax base should be consumption, because consumption is the best measure of well-being.

A second argument with a distinguished history dates back to work done by Irving Fisher in the early part of this century. Fisher and many others have argued that a tax on income discourages saving by taxing savings twice. A story told originally by Fisher illustrates this theory nicely.[4]

Suppose Alex builds a house for Frank. Alex is paid $10,000 and given an orchard containing 100 apple trees. Alex spends the $10,000 today, but he saves the orchard, and presumably he will consume or sell the fruit it bears every year in the future. At year's end the state levies a 10 percent tax on Alex's total income, which includes the $10,000 and the orchard. First, the government takes 10 percent of the $10,000, which is 10 percent of Alex's consumption. Second, it takes 10 percent of the orchard—10 trees—which is 10 percent of Alex's saving. If this is all the government did, there would be no double taxation of saving. If, however, the income tax is also levied in the following year, Alex will be taxed on the income generated by the 90 trees that he still owns. If the income tax is levied in the year after that, Alex will again be taxed on the income generated by his orchard, and so on. The income tax is thus taxing Alex's saving more than once. To tax the orchard fairly, the system should take 10 percent of the trees *or* 10 percent of the fruit going forward . . . *but not both*! To avoid the double taxation of saving, either the original saving of 100 trees should not be taxed or the income generated from the after-tax number of trees (90) should not be taxed.

The same logic can be applied to cash saving. Suppose the income tax rate is 25 percent and you earn $20,000. Out of the $20,000 you consume $16,000 and save $4,000. At the end of the year, you owe the government 25 percent of your total income, or $5,000. You can think of this as a tax of 25 percent on consumption ($4,000) and 25 percent on savings ($1,000). Why, then, do we say that the income tax is a double tax on saving? To see why you have to think about the $4,000 that is saved.

If you save $4,000, you will no doubt put it to some use. Safe possibilities include putting it in an interest-bearing account or buying a bond with it. If you do either, you will earn interest that you can consume in future years. In fact, when we save and earn interest we are spreading some of our present earnings over future years of consumption. Just as the orchard yields future fruit, so the bond yields future interest, which is considered income in the year it is earned and is taxed as such. The only way you can earn that future interest income is if you leave your money tied up in the bond or the account. You can consume the $4,000 today or you can have the future flow of interest; you can't have both. Yet both are taxed!

ALEX'S ORCHARD.

[4]Irving Fisher and Herbert Fisher, *Constructive Income Taxation: A Proposal for Reform* (New York: Harper, 1942), ch. 8, p. 56.

It is also inefficient. As you will see later, a tax that distorts economic choices creates *excess burdens*. By double taxing saving, an income tax distorts the choice between consumption and saving, which is really the choice between present consumption and future consumption. Double taxing also tends to reduce the saving rate and the rate of investment—and ultimately the rate of economic growth.

▶ **Income as the Best Tax Base** Your ability to pay is your ability to command resources, and many argue that your income is the best measure of your capacity to command resources today. According to proponents of income as a tax base, you should be taxed not on what you actually draw out of the common pot, but rather on the basis of your *ability* to draw from that pot. In other words, your decision to save or consume is no different from your decision to buy apples, to go out for dinner, or to give money to your mother. It is your *income* that enables you to do all these things, and it is income that should be taxed, regardless of its sources and regardless of how you use it. Saving is just another use of income.

If income is the best measure of ability to pay, the double taxation argument doesn't hold water. An income tax taxes savings twice only if consumption is the measure used to gauge a person's ability to pay. It does not do so if income is the measure used. Acquisition of the orchard enhances your ability to pay today; a bountiful crop of fruit enhances your ability to pay when it is produced. Interest income is no different from any other form of income; it too enhances your ability to pay. Taxing both is thus fair.

▶ **Wealth as the Best Tax Base** Still others argue that the real power to command resources comes not from any single year's income but from accumulated wealth. Aggregate net worth in the United States is many times larger than aggregate income.

If two people have identical annual incomes of $10,000, but one also has an accumulated net worth of $1 million, is it reasonable to argue that these two people have the same ability to pay, or that they should pay equal taxes? Most people would answer no. Those who favor income taxation, however, argue that net wealth comes from after-tax income that has been saved. An income tax taxes consumption and saving correctly, they say. To subsequently take part of what has been saved would be an unfair second hit—*real* double taxation.

▶ **No Simple Answer** Before the 1970s, most tax economists favored a comprehensive income base. Today, many economists favor a comprehensive personal consumption tax. Part of the reason for the increasing popularity of consumption taxes is a growing concern with the low saving rate in the United States. Since 1978 there has been concern with productivity growth, and many point to the inadequacy of saving as the culprit. As we saw in earlier chapters, household saving provides resources for firms to invest in capital that raises the productivity of labor.

The issue of consumption versus income arose in 1995 following the Republican takeover of the Congress. In January, the Congress set up a special commission to review the possibility of shifting to a consumption base as an alternative to the income tax. Many favor shifting to a comprehensive *value-added tax* (or *VAT*). The VAT is essentially a national sales tax.[5] Most European countries rely very heavily on value-added taxes. The average VAT rate among members of the European Union is 17 percent.

In October 1997, Representatives Dick Armey of Texas and W. J. Tauzin of Louisiana went on a national tour to drum up support for their versions of a completely new tax code. Armey favored a simple flat wage tax/business tax that would be

FAST FACTS

The U.S. individual income tax is really a hybrid between an income tax and a consumption tax because a good deal of saving escapes taxation. The contributions made by employers to pension funds are not taxed, nor are any profits under $500,000 made when a person sells his or her principal residence. There are also provisions that allow most taxpayers to make deposits to special retirement accounts and to deduct the amount deposited from their taxable income.

---

[5]A standard value-added tax (VAT) would be collected from all firms at the same rate based on the value that a firm adds to the product during the production process, hence the term *value-added*. For example, an automobile maker would not be taxed on the cost of tires, because tires would have already been taxed at the tire manufacturing firm.

very much like a VAT. Tauzin favored a national sales tax to substitute for the personal and corporate income taxes.

Opposition to the VAT focuses on its inherent regressivity. Recall, a personal consumption tax could be progressive, but a transaction-based sales tax or VAT is regressive. European countries reduce regressivity by exempting food, housing, and clothing. It can be argued that the U.S. individual income tax already exempts much of saving because employer contributions to pension plans and increases in accumulated equity in private homes are not taxed. Opponents of a new VAT also worry that a huge new revenue source might tempt the government to raise taxes.

TAX INCIDENCE: WHO PAYS?

When a government levies a tax, it writes a law assigning responsibility for payment to specific people or specific organizations. To understand a tax, we must look beyond those named in the law as the initial taxpayers.

First, remember the principle of tax analysis: The burden of a tax is ultimately borne by individuals or households; institutions have no real taxpaying capacity. Second, the burden of a tax is not always borne by those initially responsible for paying it. Directly or indirectly, tax burdens are often *shifted* to others. When we speak of the **incidence of a tax**, we are referring to the ultimate distribution of its burden.

The simultaneous reactions of many households and/or firms to the presence of a tax may cause relative prices to change, and price changes affect households' well-being. Households may feel the impact of a tax on the sources side or on the uses side of the income equation. (We use the term *income equation* because the amount of income from all *sources* must be exactly equal to the amount of income allocated to all *uses*—including saving—in a given period.) On the **sources side**, a household is hurt if the net wages or profits that it receives fall; on the **uses side**, a household is hurt if the prices of the things that it buys rise. If your wages remain the same but the price of every item that you buy doubles, you are in the same position you would have been in if your wages had been cut by 50 percent and prices hadn't changed. In short:

> The imposition of a tax or a change in a tax can change behavior. Changes in behavior can affect supply and demand in markets and cause prices to change. When prices change in input or output markets, some households are made better off and some are made worse off. These final changes determine the ultimate burden of the tax.

Tax shifting takes place when households can alter their behavior and do something to avoid paying a tax. This is easily accomplished when only certain items are singled out for taxation. Suppose a heavy tax were levied on bananas. Initially the tax would make the price of bananas much higher, but there are many potential substitutes for bananas. Consumers can avoid the tax by not buying bananas, and that is what many will do. But, as demand drops, the market price of bananas falls and banana growers lose money. The tax shifts from consumers to the growers, at least in the short run.

A tax such as the retail sales tax, which is levied at the same rate on *all* consumer goods, is harder to avoid. The only thing consumers can do to avoid such a tax is to consume less of everything. If consumers do, saving will increase, but otherwise there are few opportunities for tax avoidance and therefore for tax shifting.

> Broad-based taxes are less likely to be shifted and more likely to "stick" where they are levied than "partial taxes" are.

---

tax incidence *The ultimate distribution of tax's burden.*

sources side/uses side *The impact of a tax may be felt on one or the other or on both sides of the income equation. A tax may cause net income to fall (damage on the sources side), or it may cause prices of goods and services to rise so that income buys less (damage on the uses side).*

tax shifting *Occurs when households can alter their behavior and do something to avoid paying a tax.*

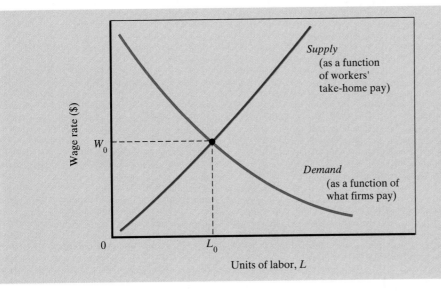

FIGURE 18.1

Equilibrium in a Competitive
Labor Market—No Taxes

With no taxes on wages, the
wage that firms pay is the
same as the wage that workers
take home. At a wage of W_0,
the quantity of labor supplied
and the quantity of labor demanded are equal.

In the figure: *Supply* (as a function of workers' take-home pay); *Demand* (as a function of what firms pay); W_0; L_0; Wage rate ($\$$); Units of labor, L

THE INCIDENCE OF PAYROLL TAXES

In 1997 nearly 40 percent of federal revenues came from social insurance taxes, also called "payroll taxes." The revenues from payroll taxes go to support social security, unemployment compensation, and other health and disability benefits for workers. (These are discussed in chapter 17.) Some of these taxes are levied on employers as a percentage of payroll, and some are levied on workers as a percentage of wages or salaries earned.

To analyze the payroll tax, let us take a tax of $\$T$ per unit of labor levied on employers and sketch the reactions likely to follow. When the tax is first levied, firms find that the price of labor is higher. Before the tax was levied, they paid $\$W$ per hour; after, they must pay $\$W + \$T$. Firms may react in two ways. First, they may substitute capital for the now-more-expensive labor. Second, higher costs and lower profits may lead to a cut in production. Both reactions mean a lower demand for labor. Lower demand for labor reduces wages, and part of the tax is thus passed on (or *shifted to*) the workers, who end up earning less. The extent to which the tax is shifted to workers depends on how workers react to the lower wages.

We can develop a more formal analysis of this situation with a picture of the market before the tax is levied. Figure 18.1 shows equilibrium in a hypothetical labor market with no payroll tax. Before we proceed, we should review the factors that determine the shapes of the supply and demand curves.

▶ **Labor Supply and Labor Demand Curves in Perfect Competition: A Review** Recall that the demand for labor in competitive markets depends on its productivity. As you saw in chapter 10, a competitive, profit-maximizing firm will hire labor up to the point at which the market wage is equal to labor's marginal revenue product. The shape of the demand curve for labor shows how responsive *firms* are to changes in wages.

Recall from chapter 6 that household behavior and, thus, the shape of the labor supply curve depend on the relative strengths of income and substitution effects. The labor supply curve represents the reaction of workers to changes in the wage rate. Household behavior depends on the *after-tax* wage that they actually take home per hour of work. In contrast, labor demand is a function of the full amount that firms must pay per unit of labor, an amount that may include a tax if it is levied directly on payroll, as it is in our

FIGURE 18.2

Incidence of a Per Unit Payroll Tax in a Competitive Labor Market

With a tax on firms of $\$T$ per unit of labor hired, the market will adjust, shifting the tax partially to workers. When the tax is levied, firms must first pay $W_0 + T$. This reduces labor demand to L_d. The result is excess supply, which pushes wages down to W_1 and passes some of the burden of the tax on to workers.

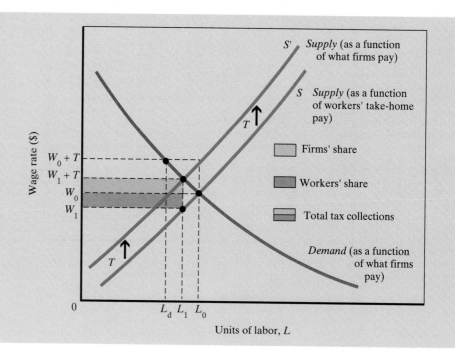

example. Such a tax, when present, drives a "wedge" between the price of labor that firms face and take-home wages.

> ### Imposing a Payroll Tax: Who Pays?

In Figure 18.1, there were no taxes, and the wage firms paid was the same as the wage workers took home. At a wage of W_0, quantity of labor supplied and quantity of labor demanded were equal, and the labor market was in equilibrium.[6]

But suppose employers must pay a tax of $\$T$ per unit of labor. Figure 18.2 shows a new supply curve that is parallel to the old supply curve but above it by a distance, T. The new curve, S', shows labor supply as a function of what firms pay. Regardless of how the ultimate burden of the tax is shared, there is a difference between what firms pay and what workers take home.

If the initial wage is W_0 per hour, firms will face a price of $W_0 + T$ per unit of labor immediately after the tax is levied. Workers still receive only W_0, however. The higher wage rate—that is, the higher price of labor that firms now face—reduces the quantity of labor demanded from L_0 to L_d, and the firms lay off workers. Workers initially still receive W_0, so that amount of labor supplied does not change, and the result is an excess supply of labor equal to $(L_0 - L_d)$.

The excess supply applies downward pressure to the market wage, and wages fall, shifting some of the tax burden onto workers. The issue is: How far will wages fall? Figure 18.2 shows that a new equilibrium is achieved at W_1, with firms paying $W_1 + T$. When workers take home W_1, they will supply L_1 units of labor; if firms must pay $W_1 + T$, they will demand L_1 units of labor, and the market clears.

---

[6]Although the supply curve has a positive slope, that slope implies nothing about the actual shape of the labor supply curve in the United States. Empirical estimates of supply elasticities are treated more fully in chapter 19.

In this case, then, the burden of the payroll tax is shared by employers and employees. Initially, firms paid W_0; after the tax, they pay $W_1 + T$. Initially, workers received W_0; after the tax, they end up with the lower wage W_1. Total tax collections by the government are equal to $T \times L_1$; geometrically, they are equal to the entire shaded area in Figure 18.2. The workers' share of the tax burden is the lower portion, $(W_0 - W_1) \times L_1$. The firms' share is the upper portion, $[(W_1 + T) - W_0] \times L_1$.

The relative sizes of the firms' share and the workers' share of the total tax burden depend on the shapes of the demand and supply curves. Look at Figure 18.2 and try to imagine what would happen to the size of the worker's shaded rectangle if the supply curve became steeper (more vertical). A more vertical supply curve means that the quantity of labor supplied is relatively inelastic—it does not change very much when net wages change. A more vertical supply curve would mean that the lower shaded rectangle (the workers' share) would be larger and the upper shaded rectangle (the firms' share) would be smaller. A more elastic (horizontal) supply curve would mean that the lower shaded rectangle (workers' share) would be smaller and the upper shaded rectangle (firms' share) would be larger.

> Workers bear the bulk of the burden of a payroll tax if labor supply is relatively inelastic, and firms bear the bulk of the burden of a payroll tax if labor supply is relatively elastic.

Empirical studies of labor supply behavior in the United States suggest that for most of the work force, the elasticity of labor supply is close to zero. Therefore:

> Most of the payroll tax in the United States is probably borne by workers.

The result would be exactly the same if the tax were initially levied on workers rather than on firms. Go back to the equilibrium in Figure 18.2, with wages at W_0. But now assume the tax of T per hour is levied on workers rather than firms. The burden will end up being shared by firms and workers in the *exact same proportions*. Initially, take-home wages will fall to $W_0 - T$. Workers will supply less labor, creating excess demand and pushing market wages up. That shifts part of the burden back to employers. The "story" is different, but the result is the same.

Table 18.4 presents an estimate of the incidence of payroll taxes (social security taxes) in the United States in 1994. This estimate assumes that both the employers' share and employees' share of the payroll taxes are ultimately *borne by employees*.

The payroll tax is regressive for two reasons. First, in 1994 most of the tax (6.2 percent of total wage and salary income levied on both employers and employees) did not apply to wages and salaries above $62,200. The remainder of the total 7.65 percent tax—1.45 percent—applied to all wage and salary income. Second, wages and salaries fall as a percentage of total income as we move up the income scale. Those with higher incomes earn a larger portion of their incomes from profits, dividends, rents, and so forth, and these kinds of income are not subject to the payroll tax.

Some economists dispute the conclusion that the payroll tax is borne entirely by wage earners. Even if labor supply is inelastic, some wages are set in the process of collective bargaining between unions and large firms. If the payroll tax results in a higher gross wage in the bargaining process, firms may find themselves faced with higher costs. Higher costs either reduce profits to owners or are passed on to consumers in the form of higher product prices.

But as you will see in chapter 19, a smaller and smaller portion of the labor force is unionized. In spite of arguments to the contrary, then, to the extent that markets are competitive, the burden of the payroll tax does fall heavily on employees.

TABLE 18.4

ESTIMATED INCIDENCE OF PAYROLL TAXES IN THE UNITED STATES IN 1994

POPULATION RANKED BY INCOME	TAX AS A % OF TOTAL INCOME
Bottom 20%	7.6
Second 20%	9.8
Third 20%	10.7
Fourth 20%	11.2
Top 20%	8.0
Top 10%	6.7
Top 5%	5.3
Top 1%	3.0

Source: Congressional Budget Office, 1997.

THE INCIDENCE OF CORPORATE PROFITS TAXES

Another tax that requires careful analysis is the corporate profits tax that is levied by the federal government, as well as by most states. The *corporate profits tax* or *corporation income tax*, is a tax on the profits of firms that are organized as corporations. The owners of partnerships and proprietorships do not pay this tax; rather, they report their firms' income directly on their individual income tax returns.

We can think of the corporate tax as a tax on *capital income*, or profits, in one sector of the economy. For simplicity we assume there are only two sectors of the economy, corporate and noncorporate, and only two factors of production, labor and capital. Owners of capital receive profits, and workers (labor) are paid a wage.

Like the payroll tax, the corporate tax may affect households on the sources or the uses side of the income equation. The tax may affect profits earned by owners of capital, wages earned by workers, or prices of corporate and noncorporate products. Once again, the key question is how large these changes are likely to be.

When first imposed, the corporate profits tax initially reduces net (after-tax) profits in the corporate sector. Assuming the economy was in long-run equilibrium before the tax was levied, firms in both the corporate and noncorporate sectors were earning a *normal rate of return;* there was no reason to expect higher profits in one sector than in the other. Suddenly, firms in the corporate sector become significantly less profitable as a result of the tax. (In 1998, for example, the tax rate applicable to most corporations was 35 percent.)

In response to these lower profits, capital investment begins to favor the nontaxed sector because after-tax profits are higher there. Firms in the taxed sector contract in size or (in some cases) go out of business, while firms in the nontaxed sector expand and new firms enter its various industries. As this happens, the flow of capital from the taxed to the nontaxed sector reduces the profit rate in the nontaxed sector: More competition springs up, and product prices are driven down. Some of the tax burden shifts to capital income earners in the noncorporate sector, who end up earning lower profits.

As capital flows out of the corporate sector in response to lower after-tax profits, the profit rate in that sector rises somewhat because fewer firms means less supply, which means higher prices, and so forth. Presumably, capital will continue to favor the nontaxed sector until the after-tax profit rates in the two sectors are equal. Even though the tax is imposed on just one sector, it eventually depresses after-tax profits in all sectors equally.

Under these circumstances, the products of corporations will probably become more expensive and products of proprietorships and partnerships will probably become less expensive. But because almost everyone buys both corporate and noncorporate products, these *excise effects* (that is, effects on the prices of products) are likely to have a minimal impact on the distribution of the tax burden; in essence, the price increases in the corporate sector and the price decreases in the noncorporate sector cancel each other out.

Finally, what effect does the imposition of a corporate income tax have on labor? Wages could actually rise or fall, but the effect is not likely to be large. Taxed firms will have an incentive to substitute labor for capital because capital income is now taxed. This could benefit labor by driving up wages. In addition, the contracting sector will use less labor *and* capital, but if the taxed sector is the capital-intensive corporate sector, the bulk of the effect will be felt by capital; its price will fall more than the price of labor.

> **The Burden of the Corporate Tax** The ultimate burden of the corporate tax appears to depend on several factors: the relative capital/labor intensity of the two sectors, the ease with which capital and labor can be substituted in the two sectors, and elasticities of demand for the products of each sector. In 1962 Arnold Harberger of the University of Chicago analyzed this and concluded:

Owners of corporations, proprietorships, and partnerships all bear the burden of the corporate tax in rough proportion to profits, even though it is directly levied only on corporations.

He also found that wage effects of the corporate tax were small and that excise effects, as we just noted, probably cancel each other out.[7]

Although most economists accept Harberger's view of the corporate tax, there are arguments against it. For example, a profits tax on a monopoly firm earning above-normal profits is *not* shifted to other sectors unless the tax drives profits below the competitive level.

You might be tempted to conclude that because monopolists can control market price, they will simply pass on the profits tax in higher prices to consumers of monopoly products. But theory predicts just the opposite: that the tax burden will remain with the monopolist.

Remember that monopolists are constrained by market demand. That is, they choose the combination of price and output that is consistent with market demand and that maximizes profit. If a proportion of that profit is taxed, the choice of price and quantity will not change. Why not? Quite simply, if you behave so as to maximize profit, and then I come and take half of your profit, you maximize your half by maximizing the whole, which is exactly what you would do in the absence of the tax. Thus, your price and output do not change, the tax is not shifted, and you end up paying the tax. In the long run, capital will not leave the taxed monopoly sector, as it did in the competitive case. Even with the tax, the monopolist is earning higher profits than are possible elsewhere.

The great debate about whom the corporate tax hurts illustrates the advantage of broad-based direct taxes over narrow-based indirect taxes. Because it is levied on an institution, the corporate tax is indirect, and therefore it is always shifted. Furthermore, it taxes only one factor (capital) in only one part of the economy (the corporate sector). The income tax, in contrast, taxes all forms of income in all sectors of the economy, and it is virtually impossible to shift. It is difficult to argue that a tax is a good tax if we can't be sure who ultimately ends up paying it.

Table 18.5 presents an estimate of the actual incidence of the U.S. corporation income tax in 1994.[8] The burden of the corporate income tax is clearly progressive, because profits and capital income make up a much bigger part of the incomes of high-income households.

THE OVERALL INCIDENCE OF TAXES IN THE UNITED STATES: EMPIRICAL EVIDENCE

Many researchers have done complete analyses under varying assumptions about tax incidence, and in most cases their results are similar:

State and local taxes (with sales taxes playing a big role) seem as a group to be mildly regressive. Federal taxes, dominated by the individual income tax but increasingly affected by the regressive payroll tax, are mildly progressive. The overall system is mildly progressive.

Data on international income tax rates and incidence can be found in chapter 3.

[7]Arnold Harberger, "The Incidence of the Corporate Income Tax," *Journal of Political Economy*, Vol. LXX (June 1962).

[8]These figures assume that all of the burden falls on capital income. None of the burden is assumed to fall on consumers or wage earners.

TABLE 18.5

ESTIMATED BURDEN OF THE U.S. CORPORATION INCOME TAX IN 1994

POPULATION RANKED BY INCOME	CORPORATE TAX BURDEN AS A % OF TOTAL INCOME
Bottom 20%	0.5
Second 20%	1.0
Third 20%	1.4
Fourth 20%	1.5
Top 20%	4.6
Top 10%	5.8
Top 5%	7.2
Top 1%	9.7

Source: Congressional Budget Office, 1997.

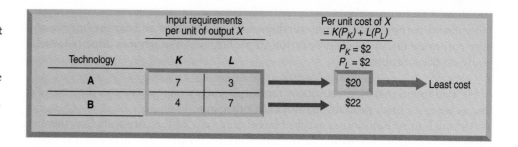

FIGURE 18.3

Firms Choose the Technology that Minimizes the Cost of Production

If the industry is competitive, long-run equilibrium price will be $20 per unit of X. If 1,000 units of X are sold, consumers will pay a total of $20,000 for X.

Technology	Input requirements per unit of output X		Per unit cost of X = $K(P_K) + L(P_L)$ $P_K = \$2$ $P_L = \$2$
	K	**L**	
A	7	3	$20 → Least cost
B	4	7	$22

EXCESS BURDENS AND THE PRINCIPLE OF NEUTRALITY

You have seen that when households and firms make decisions in the presence of a tax that differ from those they would make in its absence, the burden of the tax can be shifted from those for whom it was originally intended. Now we can take the same logic one step further:

> When taxes distort economic decisions, they impose burdens on society that in aggregate exceed the revenue collected by the government.

excess burden *The amount by which the burden of a tax exceeds the total revenue collected. Also called* dead weight losses.

The amount by which the burden of a tax exceeds the revenue collected by the government is called the **excess burden** of the tax. The *total burden* of a tax is the sum of the revenue collected from the tax and the excess burden created by the tax. Because excess burdens are a form of waste, or lost value, tax policy should be written to minimize them. (Excess burdens are also called *dead weight losses*.)

The size of the excess burden imposed by a tax depends on the extent to which economic decisions are distorted. The general principle that emerges from the analysis of excess burdens is the **principle of neutrality**.

principle of neutrality *All else equal, taxes that are neutral with respect to economic decisions (that is, taxes that do not distort economic decisions) are generally preferable to taxes that distort economic decisions. Taxes that are not neutral impose excess burdens.*

> *Ceteris paribus* or all else equal,[9] a tax that is neutral with respect to economic decisions is preferred to one that distorts economic decisions.

In practice, all taxes change behavior and distort economic choices. A product-specific excise tax raises the price of the taxed item, and people can avoid the tax by buying substitutes. An income tax distorts the choice between present and future consumption and between work and leisure. The corporate tax influences investment and production decisions—investment is diverted away from the corporate sector, and firms may be induced to substitute labor for capital.

HOW DO EXCESS BURDENS ARISE?

The idea that a tax can impose an extra cost, or excess burden, by distorting choices can be illustrated by example. Consider a competitive industry that produces an output, X, using the technology shown in Figure 18.3. Using technology A, firms can produce one unit of output with seven units of capital (K) and three units of labor (L). Using technology B, the production of one unit of output requires four units of capital and seven units of labor. A is thus the more capital-intensive technology.

---

[9]The phrase *ceteris paribus* (all else equal) is important. In judging the merits of a tax or a change in tax policy, the degree of neutrality is only one criterion among many, and it often comes into conflict with others. For example, tax A may impose a larger excess burden than tax B, but society may deem A more equitable.

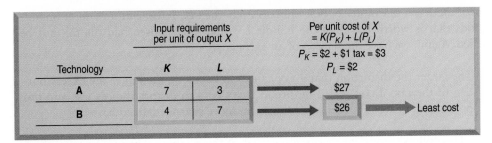

FIGURE 18.4

Imposition of a Tax on Capital Distorts the Choice of Technology

If the industry is competitive, price will be $26 per unit of X when a tax of $1 per unit of capital is imposed. If technology B is used, and if we assume that total sales remain at 1,000 units, total tax collections will be 1,000 × 4 × $1 = $4,000. But consumers will pay a total of $26,000 for the good—$6,000 more than before the tax. Thus, there is an excess burden of $2,000.

If we assume labor and capital each cost $2 per unit, it costs $20 to produce each unit of output with technology A and $22 with technology B. Firms will choose technology A. Because we assume competition, output price will be driven to cost of production, and the price of output will in the long run be driven to $20 per unit.

Now let us narrow our focus to the distortion of technology choice that is brought about by the imposition of a tax. Assume demand for the good in question is perfectly inelastic at 1,000 units of output. That is, regardless of price, households will buy 1,000 units of product. A price of $20 per unit means consumers pay a total of $20,000 for 1,000 units of X.

Now suppose the government levies a tax of 50 percent on capital. This has the effect of raising the price of capital, P_K, to $3. Figure 18.4 shows what would happen to unit cost of production after the tax is imposed. With capital now more expensive, the firm switches to the more labor-intensive technology B. With the tax in place, X can be produced at a unit cost of $27 per unit using technology A but for $26 per unit using technology B.

If demand is inelastic, buyers continue to buy 1,000 units of X regardless of its price. (We shall ignore any distortions of consumer choices that might result from the imposition of the tax.) Recall that the tax is 50 percent, or $1 per unit of capital used. Because it takes four units of capital to produce each unit of output, firms—which are now using technology B—will pay a total tax to the government of $4 per unit of output produced. With 1,000 units of output produced and sold, total tax collections amount to $4,000.

But if you look carefully, you will see that the burden of the tax exceeds $4,000. After the tax, consumers will be paying $26 per unit for the good. Twenty-six dollars is now the unit cost of producing the good using the best available technology in the presence of the capital tax. Consumers will pay $26,000 for 1,000 units of the good. This represents an increase of $6,000 over the previous total of $20,000. The revenue raised from the tax is $4,000, but its total burden is $6,000. There is an *excess burden* of $2,000.

How did this excess burden arise? Look back at Figure 18.3. You can see that technology B is less efficient than technology A (unit costs of production are $2 higher per unit using technology B). But the tax on capital has caused firms to switch to this less efficient, labor-intensive mode of production. The result is a waste of $2 per unit of output. The total burden of the tax is equal to the revenue collected plus the loss due to the wasteful choice of technology, and the excess burden is $2 per unit times 1,000 units, or $2,000.

The same principle holds for taxes that distort consumption decisions. Suppose that I prefer to consume bundle X to bundle Y when there is no tax but choose bundle Y

The only tax that has no excess burden is the lump sum tax, where the tax you pay does not depend on your behavior or your income or your wealth. Everyone pays the same amount; there is no way to avoid the tax. In 1990, the government of Prime Minister Margaret Thatcher of Great Britain replaced the local property tax with a tax that was very similar to a lump sum tax. Such a tax is highly regressive, and the perceived unfairness of it led her successor, John Major, to call for its repeal in 1991.

when there is a tax in place. Not only do I pay the tax, I also end up with a bundle of goods that is worth less than the bundle I would have chosen had the tax not been levied. Again, we have the burden of an extra cost.

> The larger the distortion that a tax causes in behavior, the larger the excess burden of the tax. Taxes levied on broad bases tend to distort choices less and impose smaller excess burdens than taxes on more sharply defined bases.

This follows from our discussion earlier in this chapter: The more partial the tax, the easier it is to avoid. An important part of the logic behind the tax reforms of 1986 was that broader bases and lower rates reduce the distorting effects of the tax system and minimize excess burdens.[10] For a full discussion of more recent proposals, see this chapter's Issues and Debates box, "The Taxpayer Relief Act of 1997."

THE PRINCIPLE OF SECOND BEST

Now that we have established the connection between taxes that distort decisions and excess burdens, we can add more complexity to our earlier discussions. Although it may seem that distorting taxes always create excess burdens, this is not necessarily the case. A distorting tax is sometimes desirable when other distortions already exist in the economy. This is called the **principle of second best**.

> At least two kinds of circumstances favor nonneutral (that is, distorting) taxes: the presence of externalities and the presence of other distorting taxes.

We already examined externalities at some length in chapter 16. If some activity by a firm or household imposes costs on society that are not considered by decision makers, then firms and households are likely to make economically inefficient choices. Pollution is the classic example of an externality, but there are thousands of others. An efficient allocation of resources can be restored if a tax is imposed on the externality-generating activity that is exactly equal to the value of the damages caused by it. Such a tax forces the decision maker to consider the full economic cost of the decision.

Because taxing for externalities changes decisions that would otherwise be made, it does in a sense "distort" economic decisions. But its purpose is to force decision makers to consider real costs that they would otherwise ignore. In the case of pollution, for example, the distortion caused by a tax is desirable. Instead of causing an excess burden, it results in an efficiency gain. (Review chapter 16 if this is not clear.)

A distorting tax can also improve economic welfare when there are other taxes present that already distort decisions. Suppose there were only three goods, *X, Y,* and *Z,* and a 5 percent excise tax on *Y* and *Z.* The taxes on *Y* and *Z* distort consumer decisions away from those goods and toward *X.* Imposing a similar tax on *X* reduces the distortion of the existing system of taxes. When consumers face equal taxes on all goods, they cannot avoid the tax by changing what they buy. The distortion caused by imposing a tax on *X* corrects for a pre-existing distortion—the taxes on *Y* and *Z.*

Let's return to the example described earlier in Figures 18.3 and 18.4. Imposing the tax of 50 percent on the use of capital generated revenues of $4,000 but imposed a burden of $6,000 on consumers. A distortion now exists. But what would happen if the government now imposed an additional tax of 50 percent, or $1 per unit, on labor? Such a tax would push our firm back toward the more efficient technology A.

principle of second best
The fact that a tax distorts an economic decision does not always imply that such a tax imposes an excess burden. If previously existing distortions exist, such a tax may actually improve efficiency.

[10]Charles McClure, "Rationale Underlying the Treasury Proposals," *Economic Consequences of Tax Simplification,* Federal Reserve Bank of Boston (1986).

THE TAXPAYER RELIEF ACT OF 1997

On August 5, 1997, President Clinton signed into law two bills passed by the Congress the previous week: *The Taxpayer Relief Act of 1997* and *The Balanced Budget Act of 1997*. The two acts were the result of two years of heavy negotiations between the Democratic White House and a Republican Congress. The tax changes focused on education, saving, and capital gains. No changes were made to the basic rate structures of either the corporation income tax or the individual income tax.

CHILD TAX CREDIT

Beginning in tax year 1998 (returns filed in 1999), parents will be able to claim a "tax credit" for every child in the family. The amount of the credit is $400 in 1998 and it increases to $500 in 1999 and subsequent years. The credit is simply an amount subtracted from a taxpayer's tax bill at the end of the year.

EDUCATION CREDIT

Also beginning in tax year 1998, taxpayers will be able to claim another credit of up to $1,500 for payments made for tuition and fees (not books) paid to qualifying colleges, universities, and technical schools. The student can be the taxpayer, a spouse, or a dependent. The student must be enrolled at least half time for one term to claim the credit.

EDUCATIONAL INDIVIDUAL RETIREMENT ACCOUNT

In addition to the two credits, taxpayers are encouraged to save for tuition expenses by depositing money into designated accounts called "education IRAs." Up to $500 per year may be contributed to an account for each beneficiary. Earnings on the account are tax free until withdrawal, and withdrawals are not taxed as long as they are used for the payment of tuition and fees at a qualified institution. Again, this started in 1998.

DEDUCTION FOR INTEREST ON EDUCATION LOANS

Taxpayers who itemize their deductions will be allowed to deduct interest on educational loans. A limit of $2,500 will be phased in between 1998 and 2001.

NEW BACKLOADED RETIREMENT ACCOUNTS

The Taxpayer Relief Act introduces a new vehicle for retirement saving. Like the Education IRA, contributions are not deductible, but income earned on the account, like interest, is not taxable; neither are distributions from the account as long as the taxpayer is over 59-1/2 years old and uses the account to finance the purchase of a first home, or is disabled.

NEW CAPITAL GAINS TAX RATE

When you sell a share of stock or any other asset for more than you paid for it, the difference is a "capital gain." Under the law prior to the 1997 act, capital gains were treated as income, but the maximum rate applied to them was 28 percent. Under the new law, the maximum rate on capital gains was reduced to 20 percent. In addition, any gains on the sale of a principal residence under $500,000 for a married couple ($250,000 for a single person) are tax free.

NEW EXEMPTION LIMIT FOR ESTATE TAXES

Under the old law, when a person died and left his or her property to others, the federal government imposed a tax on amounts over $600,000. Between 1998 and 2006, the tax-free part will be raised to $1 million.

The bills also contain provisions for $24 billion in added spending for children's health care and added 15 cents a pack to tobacco taxes.

For more on taxpayer relief, see the Case and Fair web page at **http://www.prenhall.com/casefair.**

In fact, the labor tax will generate a total revenue of $6,000, but the burden it imposes on consumers would be only $4,000. (It is a good idea for you to work these figures out yourself.)

➤ **Optimal Taxation**   The idea that taxes work together to affect behavior has led tax theorists to search for optimal taxation systems. Knowing how people will respond to taxes would allow us to design a system that would minimize the overall excess burden. For example, if we know the elasticity of demand for all traded goods, we can devise an optimal system of excise taxes that are heaviest on those goods with relatively inelastic demands and lightest on those goods with relatively elastic demands.

FIGURE 18.5

The Excess Burden of a Distorting Excise Tax

A tax that alters economic decisions imposes a burden that exceeds the amount of taxes collected. An excise tax that raises the price of a good above marginal cost drives some consumers to buy less desirable substitutes, reducing consumer surplus.

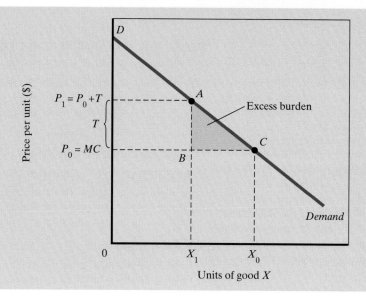

Of course, it is impossible to collect all the information required to implement the optimal tax systems that have been suggested. This point brings us full circle, and we end up where we started, with the *principle of neutrality*: All else equal, taxes that are neutral with respect to economic decisions are generally preferable to taxes that distort economic decisions. Taxes that are not neutral impose excess burdens.

OPTIONAL MATERIAL

MEASURING EXCESS BURDENS

It is possible to measure the size of excess burdens if we know something about how people respond to price changes. Look at the demand curve in Figure 18.5. The product originally sold for a price, P_0, equal to marginal cost (which, for simplicity, we assume is constant). Recall, when input prices are determined in competitive markets, marginal cost reflects the real value of the resources used in producing the product.

To measure the total burden of the tax we need to recall the notion of consumer surplus from chapter 6. At any price, some people pay less for a product than it is worth to them. All we reveal when we buy a product is that it is worth *at least* the price being charged. For example, if only one unit of product X were auctioned, someone would pay a price close to D in Figure 18.5. By paying only P_0, that person received a "surplus" equal to $(D - P_0)$. (For a review of consumer surplus and how it is measured, see chapter 6.)

Consider what happens when an excise tax raises the price of X from P_0 to $P_1 = P_0 + T$, where T is the tax per unit of X. First, the government collects revenue. The amount of revenue collected is equal to T times the number of units of X purchased (X_1). You can see that $T \times X_1$ is equal to the area of rectangle P_1ABP_0. Second, because consumers must now pay a price of P_1, the consumer surplus generated in the market is reduced from the area of triangle DCP_0 to the area of the smaller triangle DAP_1. The excess burden is equal to the original (pre-tax) consumer surplus *minus* the after-tax surplus *minus* the total taxes collected by the government.

In other words, the original value of consumer surplus (triangle DCP_0) has been broken up into three parts: the area of triangle DAP_1 that is still consumer surplus; the area of rectangle P_1ABP_0 that is tax revenue collected by the government; and the area

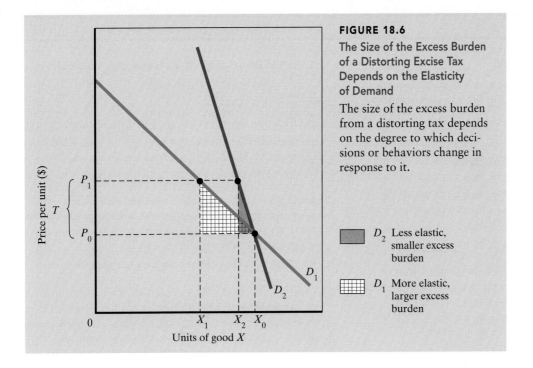

FIGURE 18.6

The Size of the Excess Burden of a Distorting Excise Tax Depends on the Elasticity of Demand

The size of the excess burden from a distorting tax depends on the degree to which decisions or behaviors change in response to it.

D_2 Less elastic, smaller excess burden

D_1 More elastic, larger excess burden

of triangle ACB that is lost. Thus, the area ACB is an approximate measure of the excess burden of the tax. The total burden of the tax is the sum of the revenue collected and the excess burden: the area of P_1ACP_0.

EXCESS BURDENS AND THE DEGREE OF DISTORTION

The size of the excess burden that results from a decision-distorting tax depends on the degree to which decisions change in response to that tax. In the case of an excise tax, consumer behavior is reflected in elasticity of demand:

> The more elastic the demand curve, the greater is the distortion caused by any given tax rate.

Figure 18.6 shows how the size of the consumer response determines the size of the excess burden. At price P_0, the quantity demanded by consumers is X_0. Now suppose that the government imposes a tax of $\$T$ per unit of X. The two demand curves (D_1 and D_2) illustrate two possible responses by consumers. The change in quantity demanded along D_1 (from X_0 to X_1) is greater than the change in quantity demanded along D_2 (from X_0 to X_2). In other words, the response of consumers illustrated by D_1 is more elastic than the response of consumers along D_2.

The excess burdens that would result from the tax under the two assumptions about demand elasticity are approximately equal to the areas of the shaded triangles in Figure 18.6. As you can see, where demand is more responsive (more elastic), the excess burden is larger.

If demand were perfectly inelastic, no distortion would occur, and there would be no excess burden. The tax would simply transfer part of the surplus being earned by consumers to the government. That is why some economists favor uniform land taxes over other taxes. Because land is in perfectly inelastic supply, a uniform tax on all land uses distorts economic decisions less than taxes levied on other factors of production that are in variable supply.

SUMMARY

THE ECONOMICS OF TAXATION

1. Public finance is one of the major subfields of applied economics. A major interest within this subfield is the economics of taxation.

2. Taxes are ultimately paid by people. Taxes may be imposed on transactions, institutions, property, and all kinds of other things, but in the final analysis, taxes are paid by individuals or households.

3. The *base* of a tax is the measure or value upon which the tax is levied. The *rate structure* of a tax determines the portion of the base that must be paid in tax.

4. A tax whose burden is a constant proportion of income for all households is a *proportional tax*. A tax that exacts a higher proportion of income from higher-income households is a *progressive tax*. A tax that exacts a lower proportion of income from higher-income households is a *regressive tax*. In the United States, income taxes are progressive, and sales and excise taxes are regressive.

5. Your average tax rate is the total amount of tax you paid divided by your total income. Your marginal tax rate is the tax rate that you pay on any additional income that you've earned. Marginal tax rates have the most influence on behavior.

6. There is much disagreement over what constitutes a fair tax system. One theory contends that people should bear tax burdens in proportion to the benefits that they receive from government expenditures. This is the *benefits-received principle*. Another contends that people should bear tax burdens in line with their ability to pay. This *ability-to-pay principle* has dominated U.S. tax policy.

7. The three leading candidates for best tax base are income, consumption, and wealth.

TAX INCIDENCE: WHO PAYS?

8. As a result of behavioral changes and market adjustments, tax burdens are often not borne by those initially responsible for paying them. When we speak of the *incidence of a tax*, we are referring to the ultimate distribution of its burden.

9. Taxes change behavior, and changes in behavior can affect supply and demand in markets, causing prices to change. When prices change in input markets or in output markets, some people may be made better off and some worse off. These final changes determine the ultimate burden of a tax.

10. *Tax shifting* occurs when households can alter their behavior and do something to avoid paying a tax. In general, broad-based taxes are less likely to be shifted and more likely to stick where they are levied than partial taxes are.

11. When labor supply is more elastic, firms bear the bulk of a tax imposed on labor. When labor supply is more inelastic, workers bear the bulk of the tax burden. Because the elasticity of labor supply in the United States is close to zero, most economists conclude that most of the payroll tax in the United States is probably borne by workers.

12. The payroll tax is regressive for two reasons. First, in 1994 most of the tax (6.2 percent of total income levied on both employers and employees) did not apply to wages and salaries above $62,200. The remainder of the total 7.65 percent—only 1.45 percent—applied to all wage and salary income. Second, wages and salaries fall as a percentage of total income as we move up the income scale. Those with higher incomes earn a larger portion of their incomes from profits, dividends, rents, and so forth, and these kinds of income are not subject to the payroll tax.

13. The ultimate burden of the corporate tax appears to depend on several factors. One generally accepted study shows that the owners of corporations, proprietorships, and partnerships all bear the burden of the corporate tax in rough proportion to profits, even though it is directly levied only on corporations; that wage effects are small; and that excise effects are roughly neutral. However, there is still much debate about whom the corporate tax "hurts." The burden of the corporate tax is progressive, because profits and capital income make up a much bigger part of the incomes of high-income households.

14. Under a reasonable set of assumptions about tax shifting, state and local taxes seem as a group to be mildly regressive. Federal taxes, dominated by the individual income tax but increasingly affected by the regressive payroll tax, are mildly progressive. The overall system is mildly progressive.

EXCESS BURDENS AND THE PRINCIPLE OF NEUTRALITY

15. When taxes distort economic decisions, they impose burdens that in aggregate exceed the revenue collected by the government. The amount by which the burden of a tax exceeds the revenue collected by the government is called the *excess burden*. The size of excess burdens depends on the degree to which economic decisions are changed by the tax. The *principle of neutrality* holds that the most efficient taxes are broad-based taxes that do not distort economic decisions.

16. The *principle of second best* holds that a tax that distorts economic decisions does not necessarily impose an excess burden. If previously existing distortions or externalities exist, such a tax may actually improve efficiency.

(OPTIONAL) MEASURING EXCESS BURDENS

17. The excess burden imposed by a tax is equal to the pre-tax consumer surplus minus the after-tax consumer surplus minus the total taxes collected by the government. The more elastic the demand curve, the greater is the distortion caused by any given tax rate.

REVIEW TERMS AND CONCEPTS

ability-to-pay principle, 432
benefits-received principle, 432
excess burden, 442
principle of neutrality, 442
principle of second best, 444

progressive tax, 430
proportional tax, 430
regressive tax, 430
sources side/uses side, 436

tax base, 430
tax incidence, 436
tax rate structure, 430
tax shifting, 436

PROBLEM SET

1. Representative Dick Armey in 1998 argued for shifting the country's main revenue system from an income tax to a national sales tax or a value-added tax. Would you favor such a shift? What are the arguments for and against it?

2. Suppose that in 1999 Congress passed and the president signed a new simple income tax with a flat rate of 25 percent on all of income over $25,000 (no tax on the first $25,000). Assume that the tax is imposed on every individual separately. For each of the following total income levels calculate taxes due and compute the average tax rate. Plot the average tax rate on a graph with income along the horizontal axis. Is the tax proportional, progressive, or regressive? Explain why.
   a. $25,000
   b. $35,000
   c. $45,000
   d. $60,000
   e. $80,000
   f. $100,000

3. Using the tax brackets and rates for 1998 in Tables 18.2 and 18.3, compute the total tax for each of the following. In each case calculate average and marginal tax rates. Assume in each case that the taxpayer chooses the standard deduction.
   a. A single taxpayer earning $35,000
   b. A married couple with two dependent children earning $50,000
   c. A single taxpayer earning $90,000
   d. A married couple with two dependent children earning $110,000

4. A number of specific tax provisions passed the Congress and were enacted into law in 1997. Assume that you were a prospective candidate for Congress in 1998. Write a brief essay describing the changes and explaining why they are good or bad.

5. A citizens' group in the Pacific Northwest has the following statement in its charter:

   "Our goal is to ensure that large, powerful corporations pay their fair share of taxes in this country."

To implement this goal, the group has recommended and lobbied for an increase in the corporation income tax and a reduction in the individual income tax. Would you support such a petition? Explain your logic.

6. "Taxes imposed on necessities that have low demand elasticities impose large excess burdens because consumers can't avoid buying them." Do you agree or disagree? Explain.

7. For each of the following, do you agree or disagree? Why?
   a. "Economic theory predicts unequivocally that a payroll tax reduction will increase the supply of labor."
   b. "Corporation income taxes levied on a monopolist are likely to be regressive, because the monopoly can pass on their burden to consumers."
   c. "All nonneutral taxes are undesirable."

8. In calculating total faculty compensation, the administration of Doughnut University includes payroll taxes (social security taxes) paid as a *benefit* to faculty. After all, those tax payments are earning future entitlements for the faculty under social security. However, the American Association of University Professors has argued that, far from being a benefit, the employer's contribution is simply a tax and that its burden actually falls on the faculty, even though it is paid by the university. Discuss both sides of this debate.

9. Developing countries rarely have sophisticated income tax schemes like that in the United States. The primary means of raising revenues in many developing countries is through commodity taxes. What problems do you see with taxing particular goods in these countries? (*Hint:* Think about elasticities of demand.)

10. Suppose a special tax were introduced that used the value of one's automobile as the tax base. Each person would pay taxes equal to 10 percent of the value of his or her car. Would the tax be proportional, regressive, or progressive? What assumptions do you make in answering this question? What distortions do you think would appear in the economy if such a tax were introduced?

11. You are given the following information on a proposed "restaurant meals tax" in the Republic of Olympus.

Olympus collects no other specific excise taxes, and all other government revenues come from a neutral lump-sum tax. (A lump-sum tax is a tax of a fixed sum paid by all people, regardless of their circumstances.) Assume further that the burden of the tax is fully borne by consumers.

Now consider the following data:

- Meals consumed before the tax: 12 million
- Meals consumed after the tax: 10 million
- Average price per meal: $15 (not including the tax)
- Tax rate: 10 percent

Estimate the size of the excess burden of the tax. What is the excess burden as a percentage of revenues collected from the tax?

TAKE IT TO THE NET

 We invite you to visit the Case and Fair page on the Prentice Hall Web site:
http://www.prenhall.com/casefair
for this chapter's World Wide Web exercise.

Chapter 19

THE ECONOMICS OF LABOR MARKETS AND LABOR UNIONS

IN 1998, OVER 130 MILLION PEOPLE in the United States' civilian labor force of 137 million held jobs. Somehow 130 million people sorted themselves into thousands of different occupations and jobs, performing an array of tasks in exchange for wages that range from a few dollars an hour to millions of dollars a year. Some have little or no formal education; others have invested many years and thousands of dollars in education and training. Some work only part time; others hold more than one job. Some large employers hire hundreds of people each year into well-defined jobs. Small firms may hire only one or two people every few years for loosely defined jobs. And, many people work for themselves.

This chapter addresses questions like: How do people and jobs get matched? How are wage rates determined? Under what circumstances do people get trained? When do firms hire? What happens when people lose their jobs? These questions are answered in what we refer to collectively as "the labor market," but in fact there are many labor markets. There is a market for professional basketball players, a market for lawyers, a market for carpenters, and a market for unskilled workers. Each market operates under a different set of rules and through a different set of institutions, but the basic forces that drive all of them are the same.

The importance of the labor market to the economy should not be underestimated. Indeed, perhaps the most dramatic of all the changes currently under way in the republics of the former Soviet Union and Eastern Europe is the introduction of a labor market. Under the central planning systems that dominated Eastern Europe before 1989, national planning agencies determined the economies' staffing needs. Training programs were then designed to meet those needs, and people were channeled through the training programs into jobs. The introduction of a labor market into these systems means that the responsibility for finding a job is left to workers and the responsibility for finding workers is left to firms. Firms can exercise choice in hiring and firing. Presumably, employment and advancement in the Eastern European economies will begin to depend more on productivity.

Earlier chapters have touched on the economics of labor markets: chapter 6, decisions that lie behind the labor supply curve; chapter 10, factors that determine the demand for labor; and chapter 17, reasons for the inequality of wages. After a quick review, this chapter discusses the workings of labor markets in a more systematic fashion.

In the final part of the chapter, we take up labor unions. Labor unions have existed for about 200 years, and their effects are the subject of considerable controversy. Do unions succeed in raising wages? Do they create unemployment? What is their impact on productivity? Almost everyone has a strong opinion about unions. Some say they are responsible for many of our economic woes; others believe that they are the only hope for economic justice.

COMPETITIVE LABOR MARKETS: A REVIEW

A brief review of a few key concepts is in order before we begin to examine the theory of labor markets. (You may also wish to review chapter 10 at this point.)

▶ **Marginal Revenue Product and the Demand for Labor**   Remember that firms make several decisions simultaneously: They decide how much to produce, they choose among alternative techniques of production, and they decide how much of each input to demand. If they have market power, they also decide what price to charge. In making these decisions, they use information from product output markets, from input markets, and from their knowledge of technology.

You need to understand the concept of marginal revenue product (MRP) to understand the demand for labor. The **marginal revenue product of labor (MRP_L)** is the additional revenue that a firm would take in by hiring one additional unit of labor, *ceteris paribus*. Because labor is presumed to be productive, hiring more yields more product. The product produced by one marginal unit of labor is called the *marginal physical product of labor* or simply *marginal product of labor*. To be turned into revenue, that product must be sold. Product prices are determined in output markets, and purely competitive firms take them as given. For perfectly competitive firms the added revenue from hiring one more unit of labor is the marginal product of labor (MP_L) *times the price of output*: $MP_L \times P_X$.[1]

Figure 19.1 graphs a firm's decision to hire in a competitive labor market. The market-determined wage rate is W^*. The firm can hire all the labor it wants at that wage. We can think of W^* as the marginal cost of a unit of labor. Firms will hire as long as the marginal gains in revenue from hiring additional units of labor (MRP_L) equal or exceed W^*. When labor is the only variable input, the MRP curve is the firm's demand curve for labor. When more than one factor of production can vary, the demand curve is more complicated but essentially the same. (This is explained in chapter 10.)

> Demand for labor depends on what labor can produce and how much its product sells for in output markets. The *physical* product of labor is technologically determined. Given the state of the technology, machinery, and other equipment available, and the level of effort required to produce something, there is a limit to what one unit of labor can produce. The *revenue* product of labor depends on the market value of its product; if no one wants to buy a product, that product has no market value.

---

marginal revenue product of labor (MRP_L) *The additional revenue that a firm will take in by hiring one additional unit of labor,* ceteris paribus. *For perfectly competitive firms, the marginal revenue product of labor is equal to the marginal physical product of labor times the price of output.*

---

[1]For firms in imperfect markets where output is set by the firm, marginal revenue is equal to marginal physical product times marginal revenue—$MRP_L = MP_L \times MR$. MRP_L is still the revenue gained by hiring an added unit of labor.

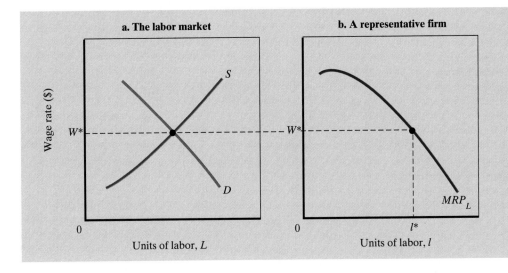

a. The labor market

b. A representative firm

FIGURE 19.1

Demand for Labor in Competitive Markets Depends on Labor's Productivity

Competitive firms will hire labor as long as marginal revenue product of labor ($MRP_L = MP_L \times P_X$) equals or exceeds the market wage, W^*. When labor is the only variable factor of production, the marginal revenue product curve is the demand curve for labor.

▶ **The Supply of Labor** Households supply labor. In any labor market, the supply of labor depends on some factors households control and some they do not.

First, each household member must decide whether to work. In this regard, households face a trade-off. Working yields a wage as well as some nonpecuniary rewards and/or costs—you may like your working environment and derive satisfaction from being creative or productive, or you may hate your job because it is dull or dangerous. The opportunity cost of working is either the value of what can be produced using the same time *or* the value of leisure. If you are not in the labor force working for a wage, you can paint your house, raise children, or sleep in the sun.

Beyond this basic decision to work or not, there is a more complicated set of choices and constraints. Not everyone can supply labor in every market. A 110-pound man would probably not offer his services to the National Football League as a football player. A carpenter with no medical training would be breaking the law if she sold herself as a surgeon. Each market requires its own set of skills that workers are either born with or must acquire.

▶ **Human Capital** The stock of knowledge, skills, and talents that human beings possess by nature or through education and training is called **human capital**. When people who have special skills or knowledge earn higher wages, a part of their wage can be thought of as a return on human capital.

Both households and firms invest in human capital. The principal form of human capital investment financed mainly by households is education. When parents send their children to school, they are investing in human capital that they hope will pay dividends later. The principal form of human capital investment financed primarily by firms is **on-the-job training**. Presumably, training workers raises their productivity and yields dividends to the firms that provide training.

Governments also invest in human capital. Federal and state governments have sponsored and subsidized numerous training programs over the years. Local governments are responsible for public elementary and secondary education, state governments have built excellent state university systems, and the federal government provides billions of dollars in student financial aid. Some argue that public health expenditures are also essentially human capital investment. A healthy labor force is a prerequisite for a productive labor force. (This argument was used by those favoring comprehensive health-care reform during the Clinton administration.)

human capital *The stock of knowledge, skills, and talents that people possess; it can be inborn or acquired through education and training.*

on-the-job training *The principal form of human capital investment financed primarily by firms.*

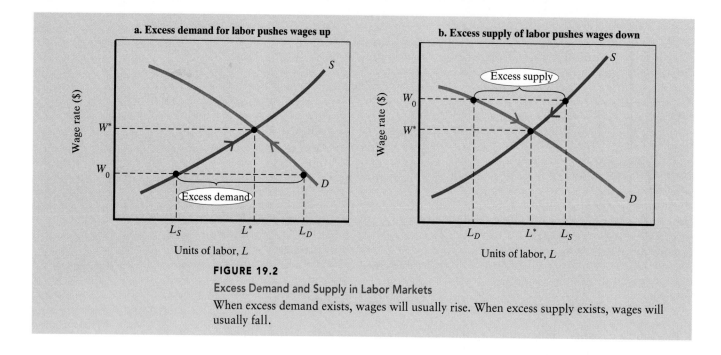

FIGURE 19.2

Excess Demand and Supply in Labor Markets

When excess demand exists, wages will usually rise. When excess supply exists, wages will usually fall.

➤ **The Equilibrium Wage**   Wage rates in competitive markets are determined by supply and demand:

> If quantity of labor demanded exceeds quantity of labor supplied, wages should rise until the quantity demanded and the quantity supplied are equal. The resulting higher wages should reduce the quantity of labor demanded and increase the quantity of labor supplied.

Figure 19.2a shows excess demand for labor; as you see, the initial wage of W_0 rises until the market clears at W^*. When an excess supply of labor exists, we expect to see market wages fall. At W_0 in Figure 19.2b, quantity supplied exceeds quantity demanded; this creates a downward pressure on wages. If wages fall, quantity demanded will increase and quantity supplied will fall until equilibrium is restored at W^*.

Disequilibria sometimes persist, however. Minimum wage laws may prevent wages from falling in response to a surplus. Union contracts may hold wages above the equilibrium level. Even in competitive markets, some prices are slow to adjust in response to surpluses.

THE LABOR MARKET IN ACTION

So far we have discussed the labor market only in the abstract. A better way to grasp the basic economic logic of labor markets is to work through a number of concrete examples of the theory as it applies in everyday decisions.

➤ **Investing in Human Capital: Should I Go to School?**   Cathy graduated from Liberty State College with an associate degree two years ago. Currently she works as a technical assistant in a small firm that trains people to work with personal computers. She likes the job, but feels trapped; there isn't any room to move up in the company without more training. She makes $7.50 per hour.

A technical school located near Cathy's home is offering a one-year program leading to a certificate of proficiency in two computer languages. With this training, which would move her up a notch in the labor market, she is eligible for a job paying $9.50

FIGURE 19.3
Analysis of a Decision to Attend
a Training Program for One Year

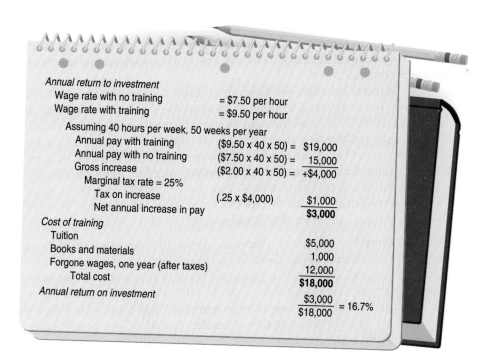

Annual return to investment		
Wage rate with no training	= $7.50 per hour	
Wage rate with training	= $9.50 per hour	
Assuming 40 hours per week, 50 weeks per year		
Annual pay with training	($9.50 x 40 x 50) =	$19,000
Annual pay with no training	($7.50 x 40 x 50) =	15,000
Gross increase	($2.00 x 40 x 50) =	+$4,000
Marginal tax rate = 25%		
Tax on increase	(.25 x $4,000)	$1,000
Net annual increase in pay		**$3,000**
Cost of training		
Tuition		$5,000
Books and materials		1,000
Forgone wages, one year (after taxes)		12,000
Total cost		**$18,000**
Annual return on investment		$\frac{\$3,000}{\$18,000}$ = 16.7%

per hour. But tuition at the school is $5,000, and students must attend full time. If going to school full time for a year means Cathy must give up her job, she will incur an opportunity cost of $12,000 in take-home pay ($15,000 less taxes of $3,000) in addition to the $5,000 tuition. If the books and materials that she needs for the program cost $1,000, the full cost of a year's training is $18,000. Cathy must decide if the investment is worth making.

Cathy is considering an investment in human capital. The training will increase her productivity and her future wages. Figure 19.3 shows some simple calculations. If we assume Cathy works 40 hours per week and 50 weeks per year, her gross wages will increase by $4,000 each year when she graduates from school. To determine the *net* return, we must remember to subtract taxes. At her income level, the marginal tax rate (the rate applicable to marginal dollars of income) is about 25 percent.[2] This figure includes social security (7.65 percent), federal income taxes (15 percent), and a city income tax (2.5 percent). (There are no state income taxes in her state.) After taxes, Cathy's income will be $3,000 a year higher if she gets the training.

If we assume that these flows will continue into the future—that is, they will stay the same in "real," or inflation-adjusted, dollars—then Cathy's investment will yield 16.7 percent ($3,000 ÷ $18,000) per year in real terms. Whether this is a "good" return depends on the market. In 1998, long-term savings bonds yielded only about 6.5 percent before taking inflation into account. Cathy's expected return is certainly better than that on a savings account, which pays only about 3 or 4 percent.

But there is much more to Cathy's situation than this. For one, we have counted only costs and benefits measured in actual dollars. When people make decisions, they usually add other costs and benefits into their calculations. Some people hate school and can't stand to study; this adds to the cost of the investment. At school, however, students might make valuable contacts, and they can use the school's placement service to get job interviews. And the higher-paying job might offer intangible psychological rewards and nicer people to work with. All of these benefits would add to the yield of the investment.

According to the College Board's Annual Survey of Colleges, undergraduates at 4-year institutions paid 5% more in 1997–1998 than they did the previous year, while at 2-year institutions they paid between 2% and 4% more. Since 1980, college costs have risen dramatically. At the same time the "college wage premium," the difference between the wages of those with a college education and those with a high school diploma, rose from 45% in 1980 to 80% in the early 1990s.

See Robert H. Topel, "Factor Proportions and Relative Wages," *Journal of Economic Perspectives,* Spring 1997.

---

[2]Notice that Cathy's *average tax rate* is only 20 percent. She is currently paying a total of $3,000 in taxes on an income of $15,000. What matters when we calculate her gains from the new job at the margin is her *marginal tax rate,* which is 25 percent. (Review chapter 18 if you are unsure why.)

Often these "utility" gains and losses dominate the pecuniary costs and benefits. Someone might decide to pursue a Ph.D. in classics even if the probability of landing a good faculty position in the field was very low. The yield on such an investment would lie entirely in psychological rewards.

Taxes and financial aid affect the yields of different courses of action and also influence decisions. For example, a $5,000 scholarship would reduce the cost of Cathy's investment to $13,000. This raises the yield on the investment to 23 percent ($3,000 ÷ $13,000) and might well tip the balance in favor of school.

A cut in taxes would have the conflicting effects of increasing the cost of the training while increasing the net benefits. Cathy would sacrifice more take-home pay (higher forgone earnings) to attend school, but she would get to keep more of the $4,000 annual wage increase in the foreseeable future. The net effect will probably be to increase the return on an investment made now.

▶ **What Does McDonald's Pay?** At two locations about 40 minutes apart, McDonald's hires workers at very different wage rates. At one franchise, a small sign on the counter reads "Help wanted, full or part time." You ask about a job, and find that only one part-time opening is available, and that the wage rate offered is the minimum wage, $5.15 per hour. At the other location, a large sign says "Full-time or part-time positions available, day or night shifts, excellent benefits and $8.50 per hour." There are six positions available at this location.

Why would one restaurant pay wages nearly twice as high as an identical restaurant with identical jobs in the same metropolitan area? Simply because the franchise owner has no applicants—thus no workers—at lower wages. Even at the higher wage rates, it's difficult keeping positions filled.

The two restaurants are buying labor in different labor markets. If people could get from one point to another at no cost, such wage differences would disappear. But there are costs. Neither restaurant is accessible by public transportation. To take a job at one, you must live nearby or have a car. Fast food restaurants like McDonald's draw much of their labor from the supply of high school students who want to work part time; most don't have cars. The high-wage franchise is on a major highway at some distance from local high schools and residential areas; the low-wage franchise is in the center of town.

There are probably other factors that affect the available labor supplies at the two locations as well. Suppose the average income of the four towns surrounding the high-wage franchise is 50 percent higher than the average income of the four towns surrounding the low-wage franchise. To the extent that the labor supply is made up of students, parents' income may have an effect. Higher-income families may spend some of their money buying leisure for their children, while lower-income families expect older children to contribute to the family income. This example illustrates three points:

> First, labor supply depends on a number of factors, including wage rates, nonlabor income, and wealth. Second, individual firms have very little control over the market wage; firms are forced to pay the wage determined by the market. Finally, because people cannot get from one place to another free of charge, and because most people do not reside at their work places—as capital does—there is an important spatial dimension to labor markets.

Different supply and demand conditions can and do prevail at different locations. This is true across regions as well as within cities. Labor markets in different regions of the country are very different.

▶ **The Importance of Individual Preferences** David was a highly paid young lawyer with a Chicago law firm. Three years ago he made partner, and his share of the firm's earnings last year was over $150,000. This year he resigned, sold his condominium, and moved to Jackson, Wyoming, where he bought a small restaurant and a cabin near the Grand Teton National Park. The best he can hope to earn from the restaurant is about $20,000 per year, and that is optimistic!

Were David's decisions irrational? If we calculate the monetary gains and losses, as we did for Cathy, we can see that David is giving up a great deal. But economic theory in no way suggests that such decisions are irrational. David made his decision to accept a lower income in exchange for things from which he derives utility. The hectic life of a big city may have been a significant cost to him. The beauty of Wyoming and the climate may be invaluable benefits. He may like to ski, or he might simply have wanted to buy more leisure time.

> Preferences play a very important role in the decisions we make about labor supply and in the decisions we make about what to consume.

There are 130 million jobholders in the United States. Every one of them has a unique set of talents and preferences. Every one of them has made a different set of decisions about investing in human capital. Some go to college and some do not. Some stay in high school and some do not. Those differences help to explain the way people end up being sorted across jobs.

> **A Word of Caution** Do not assume that individual preferences and choices makes generalization about labor market behavior impossible. An enormous amount of empirical work has documented that labor behaves in predictable ways in response to incentives. The manager of the McDonald's in the high-wage area got the desired response by raising wages, not by lowering them. People with high nonwage incomes supply less labor than people with low nonwage incomes.

The fact that labor responds to incentives is important for public policy. One of the central themes behind the economic policies pursued during the 1980s was that workers would respond to tax cuts (and therefore higher after-tax wages) by supplying more labor and working harder.

LABOR MARKETS AND PUBLIC POLICY

The government influences the operation of the labor market in a variety of ways. This section examines several current public policy issues that affect the labor market. Specifically, we examine the effects of minimum wage legislation, tax policy, welfare programs, and unemployment insurance.

THE MINIMUM WAGE CONTROVERSY

One strategy for reducing poverty that has been used for almost 100 years in many countries is the **minimum wage**. A minimum wage is the lowest wage firms are permitted to pay workers. The first minimum wage law was adopted in New Zealand in 1894. The United States adopted a national minimum wage with the passage of the Fair Labor Standards Act of 1938, although many individual states had laws on the books much earlier. Since September 1, 1997, the federal minimum wage has been $5.15 per hour.

In recent years, the minimum wage has come under increasing attack. Opponents argue that minimum wage legislation interferes with the smooth functioning of the labor market and creates unemployment. Proponents argue that it has been successful in raising the wages of the poorest workers and alleviating poverty without creating much unemployment.

These arguments can best be understood with a simple supply and demand diagram. Figure 19.4 shows hypothetical demand and supply curves for unskilled labor. The equilibrium wage rate is $4.30. At that wage, the quantity of unskilled labor supplied and the quantity of unskilled labor demanded are equal. Now suppose that a law

minimum wage *The lowest wage that firms are permitted to pay workers.*

FIGURE 19.4

Effect of Minimum Wage Legislation

If the equilibrium wage in the market for unskilled labor is below the legislated minimum wage, the result is likely to be unemployment. The higher wage will attract new entrants to the labor force (quantity supplied will increase from L^* to L_S), but firms will hire fewer workers (quantity demanded will drop from L^* to L_D).

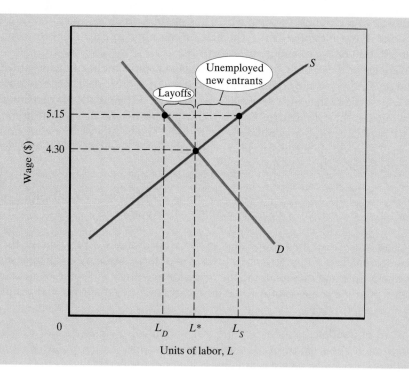

is passed setting a minimum wage of $5.15. At that wage rate, the quantity of labor supplied increases from the equilibrium level, L^*, to L_S. At the same time, the higher wage reduces the quantity of labor demanded by firms, from L^*, to L_D. As a result, firms lay off $L^* - L_D$ workers.

It is true that those workers who remain on payrolls receive higher wages. With the minimum wage in effect, unskilled workers receive $5.15 per hour instead of $4.30. But is it worth it? Some gain while others (including those who had been employed at the equilibrium wage) suffer unemployment.

A very high unemployment rate among teenage workers is cited as evidence that the unemployment problem caused by the minimum wage is significant. In August 1997, while the overall unemployment rate was 4.9 percent, the unemployment rate for teenagers (16 to 19 years) was 16.4 percent. For African American teenagers, it was over 28 percent. Proponents of the minimum wage say such data are irrelevant, that the demand for unskilled labor is relatively inelastic with respect to the wage rate, and that a small part of the unemployment problem is due to the minimum wage.

Between 1981 and 1990, proponents and opponents were locked in a political battle. Although the minimum wage remained on the books, it was not changed between 1981 and 1990 although prices rose nearly 40 percent during that period. In 1981 the minimum wage was $3.35 per hour. Adjusting for the increased cost of living, $3.35 in 1990 was enough to buy the same quantity of goods and services that $2.41 bought in 1981. Some of this erosion in purchasing power was restored when the minimum wage was raised to $4.25 in 1991, and again to $5.15 on September 1, 1997. (For more details, see the Issues and Debates box titled "The Debate Continues: The Minimum Wage in 1998.")

TAXES AND LABOR SUPPLY

One of the beliefs of the Reagan administration (which took office in 1981), echoed in the language of the Republican congressional majority in 1995, is that high rates of taxation are at the root of the economic problems faced by the United States. High tax

THE DEBATE CONTINUES:
THE MINIMUM WAGE IN 1998

In his State of the Union message to Congress in 1995, President Clinton asked for an increase in the minimum wage from $4.25 per hour to $5.15 per hour. After a battle, Congress agreed. The $5.15 minimum wage finally became effective September 1, 1997.

Under current law, the minimum wage applies to all but the smallest businesses. The new law also allows firms to hire employees under the age of 20 for an "Opportunity Wage" of $4.25 per hour during their first 90 days on the job.

Those who oppose the minimum-wage increase generally oppose the idea of a legislated minimum wage, preferring to let the market determine wage rates. They claim increasing the minimum wage will lead to unemployment; firms that cannot afford to pay more will lay off workers.

The evidence on the extent to which the minimum wage causes jobs

to be lost is changing. Professor Finis Welch at Texas A&M and two colleagues estimated that each 10 percent increase in the minimum wage produces job losses of about 1 percent of all minimum-wage workers, or about 60,000 workers in total.

But other studies find little or no effect on the number of jobs lost when the minimum wage increases. Two studies by David Card of Princeton and one by Larry Katz of Harvard and Alan Krueger, chief economist at the U.S. Department of Labor, find that an increase in the minimum wage has virtually no effect at all on unemployment.

Sources: Donald Deere and Finis Welch, "Minimum Wages and Employment," and David Card and Alan Krueger, "Estimating the Impact of Minimum Wages on Employment," both papers presented at the Annual Meeting of the American Economic Association, Washington, DC, January 8, 1995.

IN THE PAST, MANY NATIONAL CHAINS PAID THEIR EMPLOYEES THE MINIMUM OR NEAR MINIMUM WAGE. INCREASINGLY, MANY ARE FINDING THEY MUST PAY MORE THAN THAT TO ATTRACT AND RETAIN STAFF.

 For more on the minimum wage, see the Case and Fair Web page at http://www.prenhall.com/casefair.

rates reduce the incentive to work, save, and invest, it is said. If tax rates were to go down (increasing take-home pay), it is argued, more people would go to work, people already working would work harder, and more investment and capital formation would take place. All of this would expand the supply of goods and services.

These principles were embodied in the Economic Recovery Tax Act passed by Congress in 1981. This act cut individual income tax rates across the board and substantially reduced the burden of taxes on corporations. The same argument underlay the continuing tax reform debates that climaxed in the substantial changes to the tax code enacted in 1986. The president's reform proposals in May of 1985 enunciated the logic of this thinking explicitly: "By taxing workers' earnings at excessively high rates. . . [the current system]. . . discourages work. . . . and prevents workers from reaching their full potential."[3]

The tax cuts proposed for individuals and families were designed to increase the supply of labor. But economic theory shows that tax cuts could increase *or decrease* labor supply. Nobody disagrees that reducing taxes on income increases the "net wage." The issue is: What is the impact of higher net wages on the supply of labor?

[3]"The President's Tax Proposals to the Congress for Fairness, Growth, and Simplicity" (May 1985).

Income and Substitution Effects of Taxes on Labor Supply   As you recall from chapter 6, higher wages have both a substitution effect and an income effect. Higher net wages increase the price of leisure. Increasing the price, or opportunity cost, of leisure leads to additional work effort as people find an incentive to substitute other goods, bought with income from working, for leisure. This is the **substitution effect of higher wages**. But higher net wages also make people better off. By working the same number of hours, workers can earn more income. That added income can be spent on any combination of goods, including leisure. Because I have a higher income, I may decide to consume more leisure; the result is that I actually work less. This is the **income effect of higher wages**.

> The income and substitution effects of higher wages work in opposite directions. If the income effect is larger than the substitution effect, higher net wages will actually reduce the supply of labor.

► **Wages and Elasticity of Labor Supply**   Studies have attempted to measure the effect of changes in net wages on labor supply. One survey looked at 28 studies of the behavior of adult males and 22 studies of the behavior of adult females.

Twenty of the 28 studies of men's labor-force behavior found that the overall elasticity of labor supply with respect to wages is negative but small. A negative wage elasticity means that an increase in wages actually reduces labor supply. Thus, the supply of labor curve for adult males seems to bend back (Figure 6.11b). The negative income effect is therefore larger than the positive substitution effect. All but two of the studies reported positive substitution effects and negative income effects.

Table 19.1 summarizes the results of the general survey. The overall average of wage elasticities for men is −.06. In other words, a net wage increase of 10 percent would reduce the supply of male labor by 0.6 percent. The tax cuts of the 1980s probably had a tiny negative effect on the supply of adult male labor.

The evidence shows the opposite effect for women. Of the 22 studies, all but two found a positive overall wage elasticity. This suggests that for women, the substitution effect of a wage increase is greater than the income effect. The average of all 22 studies is +.94. In other words, an increase in net wages of 10 percent would increase the supply of adult female labor by a full 9.4 percent. All but one study of women found a negative income effect, while all the studies that reported substitution elasticities found them to be positive.

The tax reforms of 1986 were designed to have a maximum effect on the labor supply by cutting marginal rates but expanding the tax base at the same time. (Recall from chapter 18 that the income tax base is the amount of income that is subject to taxation.) Such a change in the tax system makes leisure more expensive relative to other goods, but it does not provide households with more income to buy leisure. There is a substitution effect but no income effect to counteract it.

---

substitution effect of higher wages *Consuming an additional hour of leisure means sacrificing the wages that would be earned by working. When the wage rate rises, leisure becomes more expensive, and households may "buy" less of it. This means working more.*

income effect of higher wages *When wages rise, people are better off. If leisure is a normal good, they may decide to consume more of it and to work less.*

TABLE 19.1   SURVEY OF LABOR SUPPLY ELASTICITY STUDIES

	TOTAL WAGE ELASTICITY	INCOME ELASTICITY	SUBSTITUTION ELASTICITY
Men (28 studies)	− .06	− .16	+ .12
Women (22 studies)	+ .94	− .17	+ .80
Overall median	+ .10	− .15	+ .25

Source: Ingemar Hansson and Charles Stuart, "Tax Revenue and the Marginal Cost of Public Funds," *Journal of Public Economics* (August 1985).

One of the first agenda items in the Republicans' "Contract with America," put forth during the congressional elections in 1994, was a major reduction in the marginal tax rates for all taxpayers. When a major tax bill was finally passed, the Taxpayer Relief Act of 1997 contained provisions to encourage saving and to subsidize education, but marginal tax rates on labor income were not changed.

WELFARE AND LABOR SUPPLY

There has always been some worry that, by providing a "guaranteed" minimum standard of living, welfare programs available to those at the bottom of the income distribution give potential workers a disincentive to enter the labor force and go to work. Are such worries justified?

When we examined the incentive effects of taxes (chapter 18), we discovered that income and substitution effects work in opposite directions. Imposing a tax reduces income. If people think of leisure as a good, they will buy less of it and will instead tend to work more when a tax is imposed. But it is also true that imposing a tax or increasing marginal tax rates reduces the opportunity cost, or price, of leisure. With leisure less expensive at the margin, people will tend to buy more of it and work less. Because the two effects counteract each other, theory cannot tell us whether taxes will increase or decrease the supply of labor.

Unlike taxes, however,

> Income maintenance programs produce income and substitution effects that work in the same direction. Theory predicts that both effects will reduce work effort and labor supply. Nearly all income maintenance programs are targeted to households with low incomes. Because households with higher incomes are ineligible, households that increase their incomes by working will lose some or all of their income maintenance benefits. The system, then, imposes an *implicit tax* on income from labor earned by those who are eligible for welfare.

Because of income-tested programs, such as food stamps and public housing, this implicit tax on earnings can be high. If you earn $3,000 and lose $2,000 worth of benefits, your implicit tax rate would be 66 percent. For some people, the loss of benefits has been estimated at over 100 percent of marginal income earned.

When we think of loss of benefits as an implicit tax, we conclude that income and substitution effects do not offset each other with an income maintenance program. Labor supply is likely to be lower in the presence of the program. Income maintenance programs provide income, some of which is "spent" on leisure. Withdrawing benefits as income rises also reduces the opportunity cost of leisure. Suppose that for every dollar of income I earn, I lose $0.50 in benefits. If the hourly wage available is $4.00, then consuming an extra hour of leisure would cost me only $2.00 ($4.00 × 0.50); I give up $4.00 in income but retain $2.00 in benefits. Thus, the substitution effect also leads to a decrease in labor supply.

Policy makers must try to determine how much of a reduction in labor supply actually results from the programs that exist today. A review of modern studies estimates overall labor supply is 4.8 percent lower than it would be if all transfer programs were eliminated.[4] A paper by two Harvard professors who later served as senior officials in the Clinton administration concludes:

> There are undoubtedly some reductions in labor supply by female family heads induced by the current program. But, studies suggest that AFDC [Aid to Families

---

[4]Sheldon Danziger, Robert Haveman, and Robert Plotnick, "How Income Transfer Programs Affect Work, Savings and the Income Distribution: A Critical Review," *Journal of Economic Literature* (September 1981).

with Dependent Children] has had a modest effect in reducing work. Welfare mothers do not seem to be very sensitive to work incentives. Most recently, changes have been made in the AFDC program which essentially eliminate all work incentives. After four months, benefits are reduced at least one dollar for each dollar the woman earns over $30. Yet there apparently has been little change in the work of single mothers.[5]

This is an important conclusion. Budget cuts in the early 1980s did indeed increase the rate at which benefits are withdrawn from welfare recipients. As a result, effective implicit tax rates are very high, in many cases over 100 percent. If millions of people continue to work in spite of such a large disincentive (and they do), there must be significant nonpecuniary rewards associated with holding a job.

One of the hottest political buttons of recent times has been welfare reform. On July 1, 1997, a new federal welfare system was born as the result of new legislation passed by the Congress and signed by President Clinton in 1996. The new legislation was targeted on the incentive to work. The old Aid to Families with Dependent Children (AFDC) was changed to "*Temporary* Assistance for Needy Families." Under the new law, states are given much more freedom to run the program as they see fit. All states are required to limit welfare to no more than 5 years of benefits over a lifetime. Many are cutting recipients off much sooner than that. States are also insisting on work as a condition of aid. To ease the pain, states are being provided through federal grants with additional aid to help with child care and medical costs for the working poor.

By 1998, welfare rolls had fallen to record low levels; it remains unclear how much of the decline was due to the strong economy and how much was due to stricter rules. (For more details, see the Issues and Debates box titled "Welfare Reform Takes Effect in 1997," in chapter 17.)

MATCHING JOBS AND WORKERS: JOB SEARCH

The flow of workers into and out of the labor force is continuous. Some enter school, some graduate, others are promoted. As the population ages, some retire. Some people quit jobs, some are fired, and some take leaves or drop out of the labor force temporarily. At the same time, some firms expand and must hire new workers, changes in technology generate needs for new skills and make others obsolete, and some firms fall on hard times and must lay people off.

This constant flux results in a continuous process of sorting available workers among available jobs. New entrants into the labor force expend time and effort searching for the best possible jobs; firms send recruiters to schools or raid competing firms, often bringing in candidates from long distances. But no matter how well these systems work:

> The distribution of skills and abilities among the available workforce never corresponds exactly to the skills and abilities currently in demand.

A newspaper may be full of available job listings while the headlines lament high unemployment rates! In the fall of 1997, when 6.7 million people were unemployed, the classified ads carried pages and pages of available jobs. Skills and abilities of available job seekers often do not match firms' needs. Moreover, the location of jobs (labor demand) does not always correspond to the location of job seekers.

A person entering the labor force for the first time or considering a job change must carefully sift through the set of jobs that might be available given his or her skills, experience, ability, and location. People, even those without highly specialized skills, might

[5]David Ellwood and Lawrence Summers, "Poverty in America: Is Welfare the Answer or the Problem?" National Bureau of Economic Research, working paper 1171 (October 1985).

have hundreds of possibilities open to them. The problem is finding out about them. Job searching is a process of gathering data. By making phone calls, applying, being rejected, or perhaps even turning down job offers, job hunters find out what is available and what they can expect. The **job search** is an extended process of information gathering.

To be counted as unemployed by the Bureau of Labor Statistics, you must be looking for a job. If you stop looking, you are no longer considered a part of the labor force and no longer technically "unemployed." This is why full-time homemakers and students are not counted as unemployed. Because workers without jobs who are seeking work are unemployed, the efficiency of the search process can have a significant impact on the amount of measured unemployment.

Thinking about the job search as an information-gathering process is revealing. We all want the best available job, the one that matches our abilities and aspirations and pays the highest possible wage. For many people, there are readily available jobs that are not desirable; every college graduate could get a job working the counter at Burger Baby's, but most have higher expectations.

> Job hunting by an individual should continue as long as the expected gains from continuing the search exceed the costs of doing so.

The opportunity costs of search are those things that are lost by continuing the search, the most important of which are *forgone earnings* and *time*. Other costs include transportation, dressing for interviews, paper, postage, and telephone bills. The potential benefits from continued search depend on the job seeker's expectations. As the person gathers more and more information, expectations should become more and more accurate.

The government can affect the search process. Consider the unemployment insurance program. Being laid off or spending an extended period of time unemployed—that is, actively looking for a job—can be devastating. During periods of high unemployment, suicide rates increase, the crime rate increases, and other indicators of "pain" appear in the economy. To alleviate some of this pain, the United States has an unemployment compensation system that pays benefits to workers who lose their jobs. Although rules are set state by state, most states pay benefits for 20 weeks. In 1992 and 1993, Congress authorized extended benefits in a number of states that experienced severe economic problems.

Unemployment benefits reduce the cost of job search, and some researchers have argued that this results in inefficiency. Until recently, unemployment benefits were not taxable, and for some people benefits make up as much as 80 percent of lost after-tax wages. With the costs of looking for a job reduced in this fashion, people have an incentive to prolong the process. Prolonged job search drains tax revenues, artificially increases the unemployment rate, and keeps productive workers off the job—another example of a trade-off between efficiency and equity.

WAGE AND INCOME DIFFERENTIALS

The labor market is made up of many separate, but often closely related, markets where a general sorting process is always going on. As a result, different occupational groups end up earning different wages, and the distribution of income reflects these differences. Wages differ across jobs for two basic reasons: differences in jobs and differences in workers.

Some jobs are more desirable. Some jobs, as in coal mining or heavy construction, involve higher levels of risk. *Ceteris paribus*, jobs that are more desirable and less risky tend to pay less than jobs that are less desirable and more risky. These wage differences are called **compensating differentials**.

In competitive markets, equilibrium wages are equal to the productivity of the marginal worker. And the product of a highly skilled machine operator is worth more than the product of an unskilled laborer. An unskilled laborer working on a routine set

job search *The process of gathering information about job availability and job characteristics.*

compensating differentials *Differences in wages that result from differences in working conditions. Risky jobs usually pay higher wages, and highly desirable jobs usually pay lower wages.*

of tasks adds little to the final value of a product compared to the value added by a skilled machinist working with complex capital equipment. Workers who supply their labor in markets that demand unusual or highly developed skills can expect to earn higher wages, *ceteris paribus*.

But wages are determined by the forces of supply *and* demand. At most major American universities, you must have a Ph.D. to be appointed to the humanities faculty. The training and skills required are high. But because there are few positions relative to the number of qualified applicants, wages for humanities professors have remained low. In contrast, many elementary and high school systems have difficulty filling open positions, particularly in math and science. As a result, teachers' salaries have increased significantly in recent years.

LABOR MARKET DISCRIMINATION, CROWDING, INEFFICIENCY

labor market discrimination
Occurs when one group of workers receives inferior treatment from employers because of some characteristic irrelevant to job performance.

Labor market discrimination occurs when one group of workers receives inferior treatment from employers because of some characteristic irrelevant to job performance. Inferior treatment may involve being systematically barred from certain occupations, receiving lower wages, or inability to win promotion or obtain training.

Suppose women (the same argument can be made for African Americans and other minorities) were systematically barred from a number of occupations. Let's call the occupations reserved for men (or whites) sector X, and the rest of the economy sector Y. Because women (or African Americans) are excluded from X, the supply of labor in sector X is reduced, and wages are higher than they would otherwise be. At the same time, women (African Americans) must *crowd* into the occupations reserved for them. Such crowding increases the supply of labor in sector Y and pushes wages down. Occupational segregation resulting from discrimination causes a wage differential if the number of restricted jobs is significant.

But there is more to the story than wage differentials. Occupational discrimination also results in a net loss of welfare in the economy. To understand this you need to recall that the demand for labor depends on the productivity of that labor. When extra workers are crowded into sector Y, wages fall. Because wages are lower, more workers will be hired. (Recall that workers will be hired as long as the value of their product at the margin exceeds the going wage.) With more workers working at a lower wage, the marginal product of workers in Y will end up lower than it otherwise would be.

The opposite occurs in sector X. With fewer workers supplying their labor in the reserved sector, wages remain high. The marginal product of workers in X remains high. What would happen if we transferred one worker at a time from sector Y to sector X? If we assume the discrimination was unrelated to job qualifications, workers will be moving from a sector in which their productivity was low at the margin to a sector where it is high. The value of the product gained in sector X is greater than the value of the product lost in sector Y. There is a net gain in value. *Ending discrimination should increase national income.*

> If workers vary in their talents in ways unrelated to gender or race, rules or behaviors that force one group into specific occupations are clearly inefficient.

Critics of discrimination theory argue that competition should put an end to discrimination rather quickly. If women (or African Americans, or any other group that is discriminated against) were more productive than the current wage would suggest, some firms would hire them into the restricted occupations, driving those who persist in their discrimination out of business.

Those who defend the discrimination and crowding theory rejoin that the pure-competition scenario is naive and unrealistic. They argue that the link between productivity and wages is difficult to establish, and that those in positions of power (often white men) have both the incentive and the ability to maintain discriminatory practices over long periods of time.

A lively and emotional debate among labor economists that has ended up in the courts in recent years is the controversy over *comparable worth*. The basic argument is that women are systematically paid less than men for work of equal, or at least comparable, value. This controversy is discussed in chapter 17.

LABOR UNIONS

Thus far we have focused on the behavior of firms and workers in competitive labor markets. There's more to this story, however. For many years, a substantial number of workers have been and still are employed under contracts negotiated between their employers and their labor unions. In 1996 just over 16 million workers—about 14.5 percent of all wage and salary workers in the United States—belonged to unions. The bargaining between firms' representatives and workers' unions does not necessarily produce the same outcome as the operation of an unregulated, competitive labor market.

Nearly all eligible workers in industries such as automobiles, mining, and steel belong to unions. But workers in other industries (most significantly, the high-tech industries) have not been unionized. While unions are still a major force in the economy and in U.S. society, they do not enjoy the influence and power they once did. Union membership has fallen a lot as a percentage of all those employed. In absolute numbers, union membership is about the same as it was in 1954, but the number of jobs has nearly doubled. In 1954 nearly 35 percent of workers were in unions. Since 1960, the figure has declined in every year but two, and now stands at its lowest level since 1937.

We begin with a brief history of the labor movement in the United States. We then turn to economic theory and an analysis of the potential effects of an organized labor force on the economy. Finally, we present some issues and controversies concerning what is known about the actual effects of unions.

THE LABOR MOVEMENT: A BRIEF HISTORY

Some scholars have associated unions with the medieval craft guilds, but there are differences between the two. Guild members were master craftsmen who owned capital and often employed workers. Unions first appeared in Great Britain and the United States in the late eighteenth and early nineteenth centuries as associations of workers with similar skills.

At that time, individual workers had no control over the conditions of their working lives; political and economic power was concentrated in the hands of wealthy business owners. However, workers found strength in uniting. From the start, union objectives have been higher wages and improved working conditions.

Employers resisted, using the law, coercion, and brute force in an effort to stop union organizing and activity. Union members were fired, workers were forced to sign **yellow-dog contracts** in which they promised not to join a union, and companies hired strikebreakers, thugs, and gunmen to intimidate organizers. Without laws on their side, the unions had no hope of success. Because changes in existing law and passage of new law follow only from political power, that power became a union goal, and politics remains at the heart of the labor movement today.

One of the earliest successful labor organizations was the **Knights of Labor,** founded in 1869. The Knights, which included both skilled and unskilled workers, attempted to organize all workers into one union. After it successfully struck the Wabash railroad owned by "robber baron" Jay Gould in 1885, its popularity and power grew dramatically. In 1886 the Knights had 700,000 members.

The decline of the Knights of Labor came quickly. Although allegations of its association with the 1886 Haymarket bombing in Chicago that killed seven policemen

yellow-dog contracts *Contracts in which workers agree not to join unions.*

Knights of Labor *One of the earliest successful labor organizations in the United States, it recruited both skilled and unskilled laborers. Founded in 1869, the power of the Knights declined after the Chicago Haymarket bombing in 1886.*

were false, the strike against Gould was gradually broken, and the Knights' radical positions on social issues cost them public support. In the end, a lack of unanimity, as well as the rapid inflow of unskilled immigrants, weakened the union's economic power, and the organization gradually disintegrated.

> **The American Federation of Labor** Founded in 1881, the **American Federation of Labor (AFL)** was meant to be a practical, nonideological movement. While its goal was to improve the lot of skilled workers, it fully accepted the existing social *and economic* system.[6]

The AFL was led for many years by Samuel Gompers, a cigar maker elected its president in 1886, serving in that capacity until his death in 1924. Made up of independent organizations, each was given exclusive jurisdiction over its particular craft or area. Between 1900 and the beginning of World War I, its membership grew from half a million to 2 million, doubling to nearly 4 million by 1920.

During the 1920s, the labor movement stagnated. A major antiunion offensive by employers, widespread antilabor sentiments, conservative U.S. presidents, and hostile courts all contributed to a significant drop in union membership. Gompers died in 1924, and the AFL was left without strong leadership.

> **The Depression and the New Deal** The Great Depression began in 1929, and with it a new start for unions. In 1932 Congress passed the *Norris-LaGuardia Act*, which banned court-ordered injunctions to prevent strikes. Franklin Roosevelt was elected president in 1932, and pro-labor legislation was part of his "New Deal" (the Roosevelt prescription for economic recovery).

The most important piece of New Deal labor legislation came in 1935. The *Wagner Act*, also called the *National Labor Relations Act*, guaranteed workers the right to join unions. It also required management to engage in **collective bargaining** if a majority of its employees so desired. To enforce the law, the act set up the **National Labor Relations Board (NLRB)**. In 1938 the Fair Labor Standards Act established the "minimum wage" at $0.25 an hour. By 1997, the minimum wage had risen to $5.15 an hour.

> **The Congress of Industrial Organizations** The AFL was an association of craft unions representing skilled workers. Prior to the 1930s, no real attempt had been made to organize the growing numbers of semiskilled workers in mass production industries, such as steel and automobiles.

John L. Lewis, president of the United Mine Workers, and a number of other unions within the AFL independently tried to organize the steel, automobile, rubber, and chemical industries. In 1935, when the AFL decided not to endorse his plan, Lewis founded the Committee for Industrial Organization, which later became the **Congress of Industrial Organizations (CIO)**. The AFL subsequently expelled the unions involved in the rebellion. The new competition between the AFL and the CIO led to organization drives that pushed total union membership up rapidly in the late 1930s and early 1940s. By the end of World War II in 1945, union membership had risen to nearly 15 million, over 35 percent of all workers.

Not surprisingly, the rapid rise in union power triggered some reaction. The *Smith-Connally Act* of 1943 and the *Taft-Hartley Act* of 1947 introduced new government controls over unions. Any strike that was deemed to "imperil the national health or safety" could be suspended by the courts through an injunction for an 80-day "cooling off period." President Reagan used such an injunction to stop a railroad strike in 1986.

---

[6]Many critics of the capitalist system find the fact that this principle has characterized the American labor movement from the beginning an anathema. The Marxist critique of capitalism argues that workers will inevitably be exploited to the point that they rise up and overthrow the capitalist system, replacing it with a socialist or Communist state. To Marxists, the labor union is the instrument of revolt. In Western Europe, union ideology has always been much closer to that envisioned by Marx than in the United States. For example, the United States has never seen a more committed anti-Communist than George Meany, who served as president of the AFL-CIO for many years.

American Federation of Labor (AFL) *Founded in 1881, the AFL was successfully led by Samuel Gompers from 1886 until 1924. A practical, nonideological union, the AFL existed as a "confederation" of individual craft unions representing skilled workers, each with an independent organization and an exclusive jurisdiction. Now merged with the CIO, the AFL maintains a preeminent position among unions today.*

collective bargaining *The process by which union leaders bargain with management as the representatives of all union employees.*

National Labor Relations Board (NLRB) *A watchdog board established by the Wagner Act in 1935. Its duties include ensuring that all workers are guaranteed the right to join unions and that firm managers participate fairly in collective bargaining if so requested by a majority of their employees.*

Congress of Industrial Organizations (CIO) *Founded by John L. Lewis, president of the United Mine Workers, after the AFL rejected his plan to organize the steel, rubber, automobile, and chemical industries in 1935. The CIO was the first union to organize semiskilled laborers in the mass production industries. After 20 years of independence, it merged with the AFL in 1955.*

PART FOUR
Current Microeconomic Issues

The Taft-Hartley Act also gave states the right to pass "right-to-work" laws. Such laws, currently enforced in 21 states, ban union shop agreements requiring workers to join unions. Right-to-work laws have seriously hampered union organizing in the states that have them.

➤ **The Merger of the AFL and the CIO**   The AFL and CIO coexisted independently for 20 years until they merged in 1955 under the leadership of two men who would dominate the movement for many years, Walter Reuther and George Meany. In 1968 Reuther's United Automobile Workers left the AFL-CIO and joined the International Brotherhood of Teamsters, the truck drivers' union that the AFL-CIO had earlier expelled for corrupt practices.

➤ **Recent History and Continued Decline**   The 1980s were not kind to the labor movement. First, in 1981 President Reagan "broke" a national strike of air traffic controllers. Public employees do not have the same right to strike as workers in other industries, and when Reagan fired 11,400 controllers, the controllers' union went bankrupt. The traveling public had been greatly inconvenienced by the strike, and the union did not receive a great deal of public sympathy.

Second, the labor movement moved decisively in 1984 to throw all its political muscle behind the Democratic presidential candidate, Walter Mondale. Partly because of intense early union organizing, Mondale received the nomination but was later overwhelmingly defeated by Ronald Reagan. Many people felt Mondale was too closely associated with unions at a time when they were falling from favor with the voting public. Mondale's overwhelming defeat certainly contributed to the difficulties faced by union organizers.

Third, international competition for U.S. markets as well as for markets around the world has increased tremendously in recent years. The U.S. steel and automobile industries, for example, have found themselves losing markets rapidly to Japanese and European producers. Fear of foreign competition has weighed in powerfully on the side of firms when contracts come up for negotiation. In the last few years, major unions, including the United Automobile Workers, have signed contracts calling for major *reductions* in wages to make various industries more competitive. Unions in other countries have made similar concessions; for more details, see the Global Perspective "Labor Unions Around the World."

Perhaps one measure of the declining power of unions is the fall in the number of major work stoppages. The Department of Labor defines a "major" work stoppage as one involving over 1,000 workers. During the early 1950s, over 400 stoppages were recorded every year. From 1974 through 1979, the average was 274 per year. Since 1982, no year has seen more than 100. In 1995, the number of major stoppages hit an all-time low of 31; there were 37 in 1996.

In 1997, the union movement got a boost from a highly visible strike by the Brotherhood of Teamsters against United Parcel Service that won major concessions in the form of higher wages and an agreement to turn 10,000 part-time jobs into full-time jobs. The strike, which ended on August 19th, virtually shut down the package delivery system in the United States and was supported by a majority of Americans in public opinion polls.

Unfortunately for the union movement, the end of 1997 and 1998 found the Teamsters embroiled in a bitter battle involving charges of corruption between Ron Carey, whose election as Teamster president was nullified by the courts, and his rival, James Hoffa Jr.

ECONOMIC EFFECTS OF LABOR UNIONS

One way to analyze union power is to think of a union as a monopolistic seller of labor in a market. If there were many buyers, the union would be similar to a pure monopolist selling in output markets: The union would restrict the supply of labor and charge

FAST FACTS

In 1996, there were 16.3 million union workers in the United States. This represented 14.5 percent of total wage and salary employment. Nearly three-fifths of the total (9.4 million) were in private industry, where they constituted 10.2 percent of wage and salary employment. The remaining 6.9 million union members were in government jobs (federal, state, and local), where they accounted for nearly 38 percent of wage and salary jobs.

Source: U.S. Department of Labor Release, January 31, 1997.

LABOR UNIONS AROUND THE WORLD

THE STRENGTH OF LABOR UNIONS VARIES FROM COUNTRY TO COUNTRY. IN THE UNITED STATES, LABOR UNION MEMBERSHIP HAS BEEN DECLINING SINCE THE 1950S. HOWEVER, IN OTHER NATIONS, SUCH AS POLAND AND THE CZECH REPUBLIC, UNIONS HAVE BEEN AN IMPORTANT SOURCE OF SOCIAL CHANGE. HERE, CZECH COAL MINERS DEMONSTRATE LOYALTY TO THEIR UNION.

Union membership in the United States has been on the decline since peaking at over 35 percent of employed workers during the 1950s. But union membership has not been declining in other parts of the world. Membership is steady or growing in many countries, including Canada, Denmark, Sweden, and Germany. Union membership is the highest in Sweden and Denmark, where only 1 in 10 workers is *not* in a union.

The roles and functions of labor unions differ from country to country. In the United States, labor unions negotiate contracts and bargain on workers' behalf. Although U.S. unions have historically supported Democratic candidates, their goals are basically economic, not political. As the 1994–1995 baseball strike and the 1997 UPS strike showed, the relationship between unions and firms in the United States tends to be adversarial, sometimes violent. Normally, industries rather than individual firms are unionized. The government's role is limited to ensuring that firms and unions "play by the rules." The National Labor Relations Board oversees collective bargaining to make sure it is fair.

In other countries, the government is much more involved in unions, and firms and unions cooperate to a much greater extent. Often, union goals are political as well as economic. For example, in the United Kingdom, where almost half of all wage and salary workers are union members, the unions are officially affiliated with the *Labor Party* and are actively involved in all aspects of politics.

In Japan, unions and firms are highly cooperative. Large companies like Toyota and Hitachi have what are called *enterprise unions*. Each enterprise union represents only one company's workers, so its loyalty is not divided among different companies. The Japanese tradition

of lifelong employment goes some way toward explaining the relationships that exist between firms and unions and their cooperative focus on firms' long-term prosperity.

The system of labor relations in Germany is called *industrial democracy*. German law requires all corporations to involve workers in the decision-making process. *Works councils* are made up of managers and workers who are jointly responsible for work rules and many operational decisions. In addition, between one-third and one-half of all boards of directors of German corporations have worker representatives as members, a system known as *codetermination*. Bargaining in Germany is done across industries and, as in Japan, a spirit of cooperation exists between workers and managers.

In Sweden and in Denmark, almost all workers belong to unions. Unions are

actually involved in setting wage levels nationally. In Sweden, unions are represented on many governmental commissions, where they represent workers.

Unfortunately, there are signs that the labor relations systems in both Germany and Japan are in danger. Recent recessions in both countries have put pressure on employment practices and are eroding the traditionally close cooperation between management and workers. In Germany, high labor costs and the economic costs of reunification are forcing companies to drive a harder bargain with unions. And in Japan, a closer look at lifetime employment policies shows that they have always been restricted to the largest companies, apply only to men, and end at age 55. Moreover, in recent years companies that have had such policies have been scaling them back.

For more on labor unions, see the Case and Fair Web page at
http://www.prenhall.com/casefair.

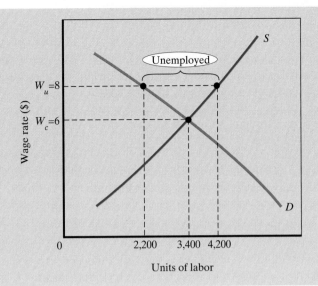

FIGURE 19.5

A Competitive Labor Market and a Monopoly Union

If the union imposes a wage of $8, demand for labor will be limited to 2,200 workers. But there will be a labor supply of 4,200 workers. Thus, many will not be able to find jobs. But if union membership is 2,200, all the unemployed would be nonunion workers.

a wage rate above the competitive equilibrium wage rate. But wages may not be the only concern of unions. Other objectives might include keeping all of their members employed or improving working conditions.

▶ **Unions as Monopolies** Let us assume only union members can be hired in some market. And suppose, as an initial condition, union membership is less than the number of workers that would be employed if the market were competitively organized and that the union's objective is to maximize its members' wages and keep them all employed. In Figure 19.5, if there were 2,200 union members, the union would set a wage of $8, corresponding to the relevant point on the demand curve for labor. This is above the competitive wage rate, $6. At $8, 4,200 laborers are working or available for work, but firms will hire only 2,200 of them. There would be an excess supply of workers, or unemployment, in this market equal to the difference between 4,200 and 2,200 (= 2,000), but the unemployed would all be nonunion workers.

For the $8 wage to hold, the union would have to restrict membership, because increasing the number of union members would also mean decreasing the wages that union members receive. (This is implied by the downward-sloping demand curve.) Restriction of union membership is common. Some unions refuse to admit new members; others have long apprenticeship programs that must be completed before a worker is admitted. Unions have also been accused of using racial and gender barriers to restrict membership.

> Union power in a competitive labor market is likely to be inefficient. Pushing up wages reduces labor demand and can cause unemployment and restrictions on union membership.

You can see the trade-off in Figure 19.5. If wages were set lower than $8, more workers would be employed. If union membership were greater than 2,200, the leadership would have to make a tough decision. They could get more members into jobs, but only by accepting a lower wage for everyone or by somehow increasing demand for their members' services.

Over the years, unions have shown great concern for keeping members in jobs. The preferred route has been to increase demand for workers rather than to take pay

featherbedding *The common union practice of preserving jobs even when it is inefficient to do so.*

cuts. Unions have used many techniques for shifting the demand curve to the right. Union contracts now include provisions for job security, especially for those with seniority. Some contracts have clauses that preserve jobs even when it is inefficient to do so. The often-cited example of this widely used and widely criticized policy, called **featherbedding**, involves the coal shovelers that trains had to carry for years after they were all powered by diesel engines rather than by coal.

Unions have sought protective trade measures such as tariffs (taxes on imports) and quotas to prevent foreign producers from cutting into the demand for domestic, union-made goods. Parking your new Toyota in the parking lot of a General Motors plant in Detroit would certainly not make you popular with your fellow union members. Some unions advertise union-produced products. The International Ladies Garment Workers for many years has run an ad accompanied by a popular jingle that tells you to "look for the union label."

> **Empirical Evidence: Do Unions Raise Wages?**   The answer is yes:

> An overwhelming number of studies using very different sets of data and techniques have found that unions have succeeded in raising wages.

A study by H. Gregg Lewis surveyed the existing literature in 1963 and found that unions succeeded in increasing wages by 10 to 15 percent.[7]

Modern cross-sectional studies using statistical techniques to control for characteristics of union and nonunion workers found that unions have succeeded in increasing wages by 20 to 30 percent.[8] In 1996, the median weekly earnings of union members were $615, whereas the median weekly earnings of those not represented by unions were $462, 25 percent lower.[9]

OPTIONAL MATERIAL

UNION POWER VERSUS MONOPSONY POWER

In chapter 13, we examined *monopsony*, a market structure in which there is just one buyer. To maximize profits, a single buyer of labor—a monopsonist—that could control part of the labor market would lower wages and hire fewer workers.

In competitive markets, firms can hire all the labor they need at the market-determined wage rate. Because every firm in competition is small relative to the market, no single firm has any control over the wage rate. A profit-maximizing competitive firm will hire labor as long as the marginal revenue product of labor (MRP_L) is equal to or greater than the market wage rate; the equilibrium condition for a competitive firm is $W = MRP_L$. In competition, the market demand curve is the sum of all the marginal revenue product curves of all the firms demanding labor.

In Figure 19.6, the market demand curve for labor is the sum of all firms' MRP_L curves. The equilibrium market wage rate is determined by the interaction of competitive demanders and the supply of labor—the S curve. If the market were organized competitively, the equilibrium wage rate would be W_c.

But suppose instead of many firms demanding labor, there is only one firm demanding labor (a *monopsonist*). This changes our analysis. Under competition, firms can hire all the labor they want at the market wage. But now the large firm faces the

---

[7]H. Greg Lewis, *Unionism and Relative Wages* (Chicago: University of Chicago Press, 1963).

[8]See Richard Freeman and James Medoff, *What Do Unions Do?* (New York: Basic Books, 1984), ch. 2, "The Union Wage Effect."

[9]U.S. Department of Labor Release, January 31, 1997.

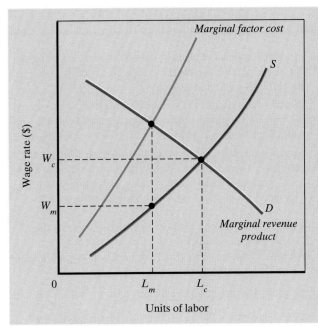

FIGURE 19.6

A Profit-Maximizing Monopsonist
A profit-maximizing monopsonist would pay a wage, W_m, below the competitive level, W_c.

market labor supply curve. This means that the more labor the firm decides to hire, the higher the wage the firm must pay. At lower wages, less labor is supplied.

The curve in Figure 19.6 called the *marginal factor cost* curve for labor (MFC_L) (see chapter 13 for a review) represents the added cost of hiring an additional unit of labor. The supply of labor curve (S) shows the wage that must be paid to attract each level of labor supply. Marginal factor cost at every level of output is *higher* than the wage because to attract added workers at the margin, the wage paid to *all* workers must be raised. Suppose that at a wage of $5, six units of labor are supplied, and that at a wage of $6, seven units of labor are supplied. Hiring six units of labor costs $30 (6 units × $5), while hiring seven units of labor costs $42 (7 units × $6). The marginal factor cost of the seventh unit of labor is thus $12 ($42 − $30), which is higher than the $6 wage rate.

A profit-maximizing firm that is the only buyer of labor in a market (our monopsonist) will hire labor as long as the marginal revenue product of labor (MRP_L) equals or exceeds the marginal factor cost (MFC_L). In Figure 19.6, the optimal quantity of labor is L_m (the point at which $MRP_L = MFC_L$), and the wage paid to workers is W_m (the lowest wage required to attract L_m units of labor). In essence, monopsony power leads to lower wages and fewer jobs than would be the case under competitive conditions.

When a monopsonist faces a monopolistic *seller* of labor such as a union, the story is different. The union tries to impose a wage rate above the going wage, W_c. The monopsonist wants to pay a wage below W_c. The result depends on the relative bargaining strengths of the union and the firm. In a sense, the union exists to resist and exercise *countervailing power* on the buying side of the labor market. Indeed, many of the most highly unionized markets are in concentrated monopsonist-like industries such as steel and automobiles.

Although union power in a competitive market is likely to be inefficient, unions may actually drive wages closer to their efficient levels in markets where the buying side is highly concentrated.

SUMMARY

COMPETITIVE LABOR MARKETS: A REVIEW

1. Demand for labor in competitive markets depends on labor's productivity. Firms will hire labor as long as the *marginal revenue product* equals or exceeds the market wage. The marginal revenue product of labor depends on the market value of its product; if no one wants to buy a product, that product has no market value.

2. Households supply labor. The supply of labor depends on some factors that households control and some that they do not. The alternatives to working for a wage are working for no pay or enjoying one's leisure. Labor supply decisions depend to a large extent on preferences for work and leisure.

3. The stock of knowledge, skills, and talents that human beings possess by nature or through education and training is called *human capital*. The principal form of human capital investment financed primarily by households is education. The principal form of human capital investment financed primarily by firms is *on-the-job training*. Governments invest heavily in human capital.

4. Wages in competitive markets are determined by supply and demand. When excess supply exists in a labor market, we can usually expect to see wages fall, but sometimes disequilibria persist.

THE LABOR MARKET IN ACTION

5. Labor supply depends on a number of factors, including wage rates, tax rates, nonlabor income, and wealth. Individual firms have very little control over the market wage; firms are forced to pay the wage that is determined by the market. Because people cannot get from one point to another free of charge and because most people do not reside at their workplaces—as capital does—there is an important spatial dimension to labor markets.

6. Personal preferences play a big role in the decisions households make about labor supply and about what to consume.

LABOR MARKETS AND PUBLIC POLICY

7. The *minimum wage* is the lowest wage that firms are permitted to pay workers by law. Opponents argue that minimum wage legislation interferes with the smooth functioning of the labor market and creates unemployment. Proponents argue that the minimum wage has been successful in raising the wages of the poorest workers and alleviating poverty without creating much unemployment. The current minimum wage is $5.15 per hour.

9. Unlike taxes, income maintenance programs produce income and substitution effects that work in the same direction. Both effects will reduce work effort and labor supply. Because households on welfare lose some or all of their benefits by working, the system imposes an implicit tax on any income that those households earn.

10. The distribution of skills and abilities among the available workforce never corresponds exactly to the skills and abilities currently in demand.

11. *Job searching* is a process of gathering data. In theory, job hunting should continue as long as the expected gains from continuing to search exceed the costs of doing so.

12. Unemployment benefits reduce the cost of the job search. Some have argued that this results in inefficiency. Until recently, unemployment benefits were not taxable, and for some people they make up as much as 80 percent of lost after-tax wages. With the costs of looking for a job reduced in this fashion, people have an incentive to prolong the process. Prolonged job search drains tax revenues, artificially increases the unemployment rate, and keeps productive workers off the job.

WAGE AND INCOME DIFFERENTIALS

13. *Ceteris paribus*, jobs that are more desirable and less risky tend to pay less than jobs that are less desirable and more risky. These wage differences are called *compensating differentials*.

14. *Labor market discrimination* occurs when one group of workers receives inferior treatment from employers because of some characteristic irrelevant to job performance. Inferior treatment may involve being systematically barred from certain occupations, receiving lower wages, or being unable to win promotion or obtain training. If workers vary in their talents in ways unrelated to gender or race, rules or behaviors that force one group into specific occupations are inefficient.

LABOR UNIONS

15. Although unions are still a major force in the economy and in U.S. society, they do not enjoy the power or the influence they once did. As a percentage of those employed, union membership now stands at its lowest level since 1937. The decline of unionism has been attributed to politics, antiunion sentiment in both the business community and the general public, and increased foreign and domestic competition.

16. Union power in a competitive labor market is likely to be inefficient. Pushing up wages reduces labor demand and can cause unemployment and restrictions on union membership.

17. An overwhelming number of studies have found that unions have succeeded in raising wages. Modern cross-sectional studies find that unions have raised wages by 20 percent to 30 percent.

(OPTIONAL) UNION VERSUS MONOPSONY POWER

18. Although union power in a competitive labor market is likely to be inefficient, unions may actually drive wages closer to their efficient levels in markets where the buying side is highly concentrated.

REVIEW TERMS AND CONCEPTS

American Federation of Labor (AFL), 466

collective bargaining, 466

compensating differentials, 463

Congress of Industrial Organizations (CIO), 466

featherbedding, 470

human capital, 453

income effect of higher wages, 460

job search, 463

Knights of Labor, 465

labor market discrimination, 464

marginal revenue product of labor (MRP_L), 452

minimum wage, 457

National Labor Relations Board (NLRB), 466

on-the-job training, 453

substitution effect of higher wages, 460

yellow-dog contracts, 465

PROBLEM SET

1. In September 1997, the minimum wage increased to $5.15 per hour. At the same time, the average hourly earnings of workers on nonfarm payrolls was over $12.25. Opponents of the minimum wage argue that the increase is likely to increase unemployment. If the minimum wage is *below* the average wage, how could the increase lead to unemployment?

2. Liza was working two jobs in 1998. She was a receptionist during the day making $10 per hour. In the evening she was a waitress at Molly's Pub where she made $17 an hour including tips. In June, her grandfather died and left her $400,000. She decided to cut back her waitressing job to two nights a week. Can you say how much of her decrease in hours worked is due to an income effect? A substitution effect?

3. In August 1997, the Bureau of Labor Statistics reported that the number of persons classified as employed (working for a wage) increased by 96,000 to 129,804,000. At the same time the unemployment rate increased from 4.8 percent to 4.9 percent as 94,000 additional people were classified as unemployed. How could the unemployment rate rise when the number of employed actually increased?

4. Draw a diagram to illustrate each situation:
   a. A labor supply curve for a group of households for whom the income effect of a wage increase is stronger than the substitution effect.
   b. The effect of a general increase in the productivity of labor (an overall rise in the marginal product of labor).
   c. The effect of a union contract that succeeds in raising wage rates above the competitive equilibrium.
   d. The effect of a minimum wage above equilibrium in a competitive labor market.

5. Jane is considering returning to school to get an MBA. She currently makes $30,000 and pays $9,000 in taxes (30 percent). Tuition at the school of her choice is $15,000 per year, and the program requires two years to complete. She must attend full time and would receive no financial aid.
   a. What is the total monetary cost of an MBA?

   b. What other information might you need to get a better picture of the full cost of acquiring an MBA? (*Hint:* What about summers?)
   c. If the degree raises Jane's expected after-tax wage by $5,000 per year in real terms for a long time, what is the rate of return on investment in an MBA? What if the increase were $15,000?
   d. To make a final decision, what other factors might Jane want to consider?

6. Some people have suggested that the Department of Labor should establish a computerized national and regional job bank to provide people with listings of available jobs. Is this a good idea, or is it an unwarranted intrusion of the government into the private sector? Explain your answer.

7. In 1997, a major welfare reform program went into effect, transferring a great deal of power from the federal government to the states. The law required states to limit benefits to 5 years over a recipient's lifetime and did provide some additional funds for day care and added medical benefits for the working poor. Write a brief essay describing the pros and cons of the reform. Be sure to include a discussion of labor supply effects.

8. Explain how the functioning of income-tested programs such as welfare acts as a tax on the poor that can have an effect on their work effort.

9. Explain how the 1993 extension of unemployment insurance benefits could actually lead to unemployment. If evidence were found to support this claim, should we repeal the extension or abandon the unemployment compensation system? Explain.

10. In many developing countries, the government sector pays a higher wage for workers than the private sector does. This has been criticized on the grounds that it creates unemployment as people queue for government jobs in the cities rather than stay in the countryside working for market-determined wages. Using supply and demand curves, show how this situation could lead to higher wages and less employment in the private sector job market.

*11. The American Brotherhood of Widget Makers has 15,000 members. Today all are employed at $15 per hour. The union is considering a push to raise wages by $1.50 per hour. A union economist says evidence for the industry suggests a labor demand elasticity of −1. What is the potential cost of a new wage contract that accepts the 10 percent hike? What further contract provisions might you suggest to reduce or eliminate these potential losses?

12. What factors are important in determining a person's wages? Connect these factors to explanations of why some groups (e.g., women, African Americans, teenagers) earn less than others.

TAKE IT TO THE NET

We invite you to visit the Case and Fair page on the Prentice Hall Web site:

http://www.prenhall.com/casefair

for this chapter's World Wide Web exercise.

Chapter 20

CURRENT TOPICS

IN APPLIED MICROECONOMICS: HEALTH CARE, IMMIGRATION, AND URBAN PROBLEMS

THIS CHAPTER DISCUSSES THREE TOPICS in applied microeconomics. Health care and immigration are on the front burner of domestic politics. Urban economics and the economics of urban problems will fill a hole in the microeconomic theory you have studied thus far. We have talked about many decisions that firms and households make—what to produce, how to produce, what to consume, how much labor to supply—but we have not yet examined firm and household decisions about *where to produce* and *where to live*. The rise of cities and the concentrations of urban populations are the direct consequences of firms' and households' location decisions.

THE ECONOMICS OF HEALTH-CARE REFORM

No issue looms larger in U.S. politics than health-care reform. When elected in 1992, President Clinton listed health reform as his number-one priority. In October of 1993, he sent to Congress a 1,342-page bill that sought to restructure completely the nation's health-care system. But by the end of 1994, the 103rd Congress declared the Clinton health-reform proposal dead, even though it had come closer to making meaningful reforms than any previous Congress had. In 1998, worries about the Medicare program for the elderly were a central theme in the congressional election.

Why has health-care reform become a focal point in the United States? What is it about the market for health-care services that calls for government involvement? What proposals have been put forth to change the way health-care services are delivered and to whom they are delivered? In this section, we address these and other questions, applying the logic of economics to the market for health care.[1]

HEALTH CARE IN THE UNITED STATES: THE BASIC FACTS

Three facts about health care seem to generate the most concern among those who advocate reform. First, health care is very expensive and is getting more expensive by the day. In 1994, total health-care expenditures in the United States topped $1 trillion, about 14.5 percent of GDP. As a percentage of GDP, the United States spends twice as much on health care as the average developed country. No other country spends more than 10 percent of its GDP on health care. Yet the United States insures a much smaller fraction of its population than do most other industrial countries and ranks poorly on indicators of health outcomes like life expectancy and infant mortality. U.S. per capita spending on health—approximately $3,600 in 1995—is expected to rise to over $5,000 by the year 2000, and total health-care spending is expected to reach 18 percent of GDP by the year 2005. As Figure 20.1 shows, U.S. per capita spending on health care is the highest in the world. The figure for the United States is more than 50 percent higher than any other country's rate of spending.

Second, in 1996 approximately 42 million Americans, or 15.6 percent of the population, had no health insurance, and the number was growing. Many find they cannot change jobs or leave welfare for fear of losing health benefits.

Third, the government spent nearly $460 billion on health and health-related programs including Medicaid (medical payments for the very poor) and Medicare (medical payments for the elderly). The public sector accounted for nearly half of the nation's medical care expenditures. Not only is this total enormous, but it is the fastest growing item in the federal budget. Projections show that the cost of medical-care programs will grow by nearly 10 percent annually over the foreseeable future, creating enormous budget problems at all levels of government.

SHOULD GOVERNMENT BE INVOLVED?

Should the government be involved in the market for health-care services? If so, what role should it play? Other sectors of the economy are large and growing rapidly too, but no one is calling for government to "fix" things. The entertainment industry (music, CDs, concerts, theme parks, and so forth) is consuming a larger and larger share of U.S. spending, but it has not stimulated much public outcry.

The market for health-care services is like any other market in the economy in that most people obtain their health services from the private sector. Basically, health care is a **private good**. People can be excluded from its benefits if they do not pay, and the primary beneficiary of services provided is the patient herself. Most physicians are in private practice or work for private hospitals or health maintenance organizations (HMOs), many of which are in business to make a profit. For the most part, health-care costs are determined in markets by the interaction of supply and demand. Just as in any other market, labor costs (such as physicians' salaries) and capital costs interact with technology to determine costs of production, and willingness and ability to pay play a role in determining demand.

However, a number of characteristics of the market for health-care services suggest a role for government. First, asymmetric (imperfect) information, fee-for-service reimbursement, externalities, and imperfect market structure all suggest that the market

private good *A product produced by firms for sale to individual households. People can be excluded from the benefits of a private good if they do not pay for it.*

[1]This discussion owes much to a symposium on health-care reform published in the *Journal of Economic Perspectives*, Volume 8, Number 3, Summer 1994, especially "A Guide to Health Care Reform," by David Cutler. In addition, *The Economic Report of the President, 1993*, contains an excellent summary of the arguments for reform.

FIGURE 20.1

Per Capita Health Spending
for Selected Countries, 1995

Source: OECD Health Data 1997.

may well be operating inefficiently.[2] Second, the fact that many citizens are without coverage is thought by many to be inequitable.

▶ **Asymmetric Information**   For markets to be efficient, buyers must have complete information on product quality and price. Yet the health-care market is characterized by **asymmetric information**, a situation in which the participants in an economic transaction have different information about the transaction. Most of us know little about medicine. It takes years of education and on-the-job-training to become a licensed physician. In addition, the practice of medicine has become increasingly specialized, and the gap between a doctor's knowledge and his patient's knowledge has increased. Virtually all the information on product quality and price rests with the supplier—essentially, with the physician. In a private office, in a hospital, or in a health maintenance organization, the services we "buy" are chosen for us by the person who supplies them to us! Clearly, when suppliers control the information needed to make effective demand decisions, the opportunity for abuse and waste exists. One recent study documents that a substantial number of expensive medical procedures carried out were inappropriate or of limited value.[3]

Asymmetric information may also result in the problem of **adverse selection**, discussed in chapter 16. Adverse selection happens when insurance buyers know more about their health than the insurer. Suppose there are only two types of people: sick people and well people. If insurers could not tell the difference, they would charge the average cost of providing health-care coverage. By doing so, they would charge the sick much less than the expected costs of their coverage. The sick would be more likely to buy health insurance, while some of the well would buy no insurance. Because a larger percentage of the insured will be the sick, premiums would rise, further discouraging the well from buying insurance. This would continue until only the sick are insured at very high prices—not an ideal situation. Thus asymmetric information may lead to a need for government involvement.

▶ **Fee-For-Service Reimbursement**   If health care meant going to the doctor's office a couple of times a year, we would not worry about having insurance. But most people

asymmetric information *A situation in which the participants in an economic transaction have different information about the transaction.*

adverse selection *An imperfect-information problem that can occur when a buyer or seller enters into an exchange with another party who has more information.*

---

[2]For a review of externalities and imperfect information, see chapter 16. For a review of efficiency and imperfect market structure, see chapter 12.

[3]*Economic Report of the President, 1994*, Chart 4.5.

FIGURE 20.2

Health Insurance Coverage
in the United States, 1996

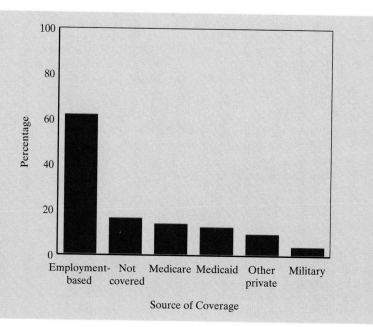

*NOTE: The figures add to more
than 100 percent because many
people are covered by two or
more plans.*

Source: U.S. Bureau of the
Census, Housing and Household
Economic Statistics Division,
September 1997.

know that the costs of a serious illness can be catastrophic. Spending a week in a hospital and having a serious operation can cost well over $100,000. A normal childbirth with only a single day in the hospital costs several thousand dollars. Even a high-income family without health insurance could end up bankrupt if a family member sustained a serious head injury in an accident.

So, the majority of the U.S. population is covered by health insurance. As Figure 20.2 shows, 61 percent of the population are covered by a plan to which their employer contributes, 9 percent pay for their own private health insurance, and about 28 percent are insured by the government through Medicare, Medicaid, and other programs. About 15 percent of the U.S. population are uninsured.

Coverage by insurance leads to a number of problems. First, full coverage creates a **moral hazard** problem. If patients do not bear the costs of health care, they have an incentive to overuse medical services. Even though most insurance policies carry a **deductible** (an annual out-of-pocket expenditure that an insurance policyholder must make before the plan makes any reimbursement) and a **copayment** (a fixed amount of money that an insured person pays for each visit to a doctor's office), consumers of health services pay far less than the cost of providing the service, and most insurance policies demand no payment at all from the patient after a fairly low maximum contribution has been made.

Second, the method of reimbursement employed by most insurance companies may lead health-care providers to oversupply their services. Traditionally, health-care providers are reimbursed on a **fee-for-service** basis. As long as the price paid by the insurer is greater than the marginal cost of production, providers have an incentive to oversupply. This makes the problem of asymmetric information more serious. Suppliers have not only all the information needed to make an informed choice about what services a patient needs, but also a big incentive to oversupply.

In addition, the fact that those who get very sick are very costly to insurance companies has led most insurance providers to use experience rating. **Experience rating** means charging individuals or groups of individuals premiums linked to their current state of health or to the probability that they will become sick. Insurance companies, which are in business to make money, will not insure people at all if certain preexisting conditions (such as heart disease, cancer, or AIDS) exist when the application is filed. Because most injuries and illnesses do not result from the behavior of the insured,

moral hazard *Arises when one party to a contract passes the cost of his or her behavior on to the other party to the contract.*

deductible *An annual out-of-pocket expenditure that an insurance policy holder must make before the insurance plan makes any reimbursement.*

copayment *A fixed amount of money that an insured person pays for each visit to a doctor's office.*

fee-for-service reimbursement *A program in which insurance companies reimburse health-care providers for the services they've rendered.*

experience rating *The insurance-company practice of charging individuals or groups of individuals premiums that are linked to their current state of health or to the probability that they will become sick.*

experience rating does not for the most part improve the efficiency of health care. In a sense, experience rating defeats the purpose of insurance—to spread risk so that no single household faces the full cost of an illness.

► **Externalities** As we saw in chapter 16, an *externality* exists when the actions or decisions of one person or group impose a cost or bestow a benefit on some second or third parties. The result is usually inefficient. The most often-used example is pollution. One way of "internalizing" externalities is to tax activities that generate public harms and to subsidize activities that generate public benefits.

Health care may generate positive externalities. The public health is improved when individuals receive immunizations and communicable diseases are treated in a timely fashion. Poor health may lead to negative externalities. Poor health leads to lower productivity, and lower productivity leads to lower wages. Poverty, welfare dependency, and homelessness may all be linked to some extent to health.

Certainly the current structure of governmental assistance to the very poor and lack of insurance coverage for the near-poor combine to reduce the incentive to work and may lead some to stay on welfare to avoid losing their health benefits. Higher welfare payments impose an external cost on taxpayers.

► **Imperfect Structure and Market Power** Drug and biotechnology companies spend millions on research and development to create drugs and discover procedures that will cure diseases and save lives. Their incentive is provided by the patent system, which protects the producers of new drugs, equipment, and procedures for up to 20 years. This monopoly power has led to unbelievably high prices for some patented prescription drugs and equipment.

As we discussed in chapter 13, there are two sides to this story. A patent system is necessary to provide the private sector with an incentive to engage in research and development. However, should patent protection be decreased or eliminated when the product of research is a life-saving drug that can be produced at a low cost? Many have called for more funds for publicly sponsored research where the results would be available as a public good.

Another example of imperfect market structure can be found in the labor market. Since 1910, the American Medical Association (AMA) has controlled the system of medical education in the United States. Some argue that by limiting the number of trained physicians, the AMA has been able to keep the average physician's salary high. In addition, the AMA has lobbied very hard to block the entry of potential substitutes for physicians' services, including nurses and chiropractors.

► **Equity** Although a number of inefficiencies are associated with providing health-care services in the United States, what seems to generate the most concern is an equity issue. In 1996, 42 million Americans had no health insurance. What makes this issue cross the political spectrum is that it is not the very poor who are not covered. Welfare recipients and others who are very poor are covered under Medicaid. Rather, it is the near-poor, the working poor, and middle-income families who work for firms that do not provide health coverage. Government-funded coverage to these people would not provide them with an incentive to work less, and no one can claim that they are uncovered because of laziness.

Many view health care as a right that all citizens should have regardless of ability to pay. Several of the theories of redistribution we discussed in chapter 17 lend support to the idea of government involvement in providing universal coverage. Voters may well understand that health care produces positive externalities and support programs out of self-interest. And those who subscribe to the idea of Rawlsian justice would argue that a just set of rules, determined by members of society before they know the circumstances that their life will lead them to, would declare a set of basic entitlements for all that would include medical care.

THE CAUSES OF THE HIGH COST OF MEDICAL CARE

Before turning to potential solutions and reform proposals, we need to summarize what we know and do not know about the causes of the high cost of health care in the United States.

At the outset we must realize that high cost is not necessarily a bad thing. For example, if the only reasons for higher costs were that (1) the average age of the U.S. population is increasing and health-care costs for the elderly are higher, and (2) modern technology has produced excellent new tools for diagnosis and treatment that are very expensive (for example, CAT scan and MRI machines), there would be little need for intervention. But most analysts believe inefficiency and waste play a large role.

Among the biggest sources of inefficiency—asymmetric information, the moral hazard problem, fee-for-service reimbursement, externalities, and imperfect market structure—exactly what percentage of the high cost of care results directly from these problems is hard to estimate. But most analysts say it is substantial.

Although the aging of the population and the introduction of Medicare (mandatory tax-financed health insurance for the elderly) have raised costs, three facts point in other directions. First, the leading edge of the baby boom generation is only now approaching 50 years of age, not yet into the "costly" years. Second, as Table 20.1 shows, many other countries have populations that are significantly older on average than that of the United States. The United States ranks at the low end of the group of developed countries in the percentage of population over the age of 65. Third, costs jumped when Medicare was introduced, but they have continued to rise very rapidly despite a reduction in the percentage of those covered and no major changes in the age distribution of the population.

There is no question that improved technology—which has been reflected in new kinds of expensive equipment, treatments, and procedures such as organ transplants—accounts for some of the increased costs, but there is little empirical evidence on precisely how much. Because only one-third of the increase in costs reflects higher expenses of hospital care, and technology accounts for only a portion of hospital-care costs, we must look to other factors for explanation.

Often cited as a factor is the high cost of malpractice lawsuits. Doctors who make mistakes are often sued, and juries have made huge damage awards to the victims. The result is expensive malpractice insurance premiums for physicians, hospitals, and other providers. Here there is some evidence because we can measure the total direct cost of malpractice, which turns out to be only about 1 percent of total health-care spending. But direct costs may be only part of the story. Because of the threat of malpractice suits, physicians may practice defensive medicine. **Defensive medicine** is the practice of ordering tests, procedures, or treatments that are not cost-effective for the patient but protect the doctor from the possibility of being sued later. A recent study estimates the cost of such additional procedures and tests at around 3 percent of total health-care spending.[4]

> Although an aging population, increasing malpractice insurance costs, and advancing technology all play some role in explaining higher health-care costs, the bulk of the problem lies in asymmetric information, moral hazard, and inefficient reimbursement methods. Much, however, remains to be explained.

REFORM PROPOSALS

A number of reforms have been offered to solve the growing problems of U.S. health care. The Clinton plan, presented to Congress in 1993 and rejected in 1994, contained most of the following proposals; many can be expected to resurface as the debate continues. This is by no means a comprehensive list of all reform proposals.

TABLE 20.1

POPULATION OVER 65 AS A PERCENTAGE OF TOTAL POPULATION FOR SELECTED COUNTRIES, 2000

Italy	17.5
United Kingdom	15.9
France	16.4
Germany	16.5
Spain	16.4
Portugal	15.1
Japan	16.5
The Netherlands	14.1
United States	12.7
Canada	12.8

Source: U.S. Bureau of the Census, International Data Base.

defensive medicine *Ordering medical tests, procedures, or treatments that are not cost-effective to protect oneself from being sued for malpractice later on.*

[4]See Cutler, "A Guide to Health Care Reform."

> **Encourage Managed Care** Managed care providers offer complete and comprehensive medical care plans, including physical examinations, general physician visits, specialists, and hospitalization. The most common form of managed care plan is the **health maintenance organization**, or **HMO**, a health-care plan that provides comprehensive medical services for employees and their families at a flat fee. The big advantage of managed care is that payment is received on a per capita basis rather than a fee-for-service basis. The provider gets paid one fee regardless of the actual expenses incurred on each patient's behalf. Another managed care system gaining popularity is the **preferred provider organization (PPO)**. In a PPO, an employer or insurance company establishes a network of doctors and hospitals to provide a broad set of medical services for a flat fee per participant. In return for the lower fee, the doctors and hospitals who join the PPO network expect to receive a larger volume of patients. HMOs and PPOs give the provider an incentive to order cost-effective tests and procedures and not to oversupply. (See Issues and Debates box, "The Market for Health Care Responds to Rising Costs.") The Clinton plan provided incentives for consumers to choose such plans by making the alternatives more expensive. Although managed care has many supporters, its detractors raise two main objections: It limits patients' choice of physician and may provide an incentive for health-care providers to hold back on some necessary tests or procedures that otherwise would have been done.

> **Require Community Rating** We have already discussed the problems associated with experience rating. By denying coverage to those with preexisting conditions and charging those in high-risk categories exorbitant premiums, little is gained in terms of efficiency because most people do not choose to be sick or to be in high-risk categories. Most reform proposals, including the Clinton plan that didn't make it through Congress, require **community rating**, a system in which insurance providers must accept all applicants and charge premiums based only on age, location, and perhaps some elements of behavior such as smoking. Everyone in each category would be charged the same premium regardless of health condition. A big benefit of such a system would be increased job mobility.

> **Finance Reform** One controversial feature of the Clinton plan was the **employer mandate**. Under this provision, all employers would be required to provide insurance for all employees and to pay on average 80 percent of the community-rated premiums. Employer contributions would be capped at 7.9 percent of payroll, and small firms (fewer than 75 employees) and firms with low average wages (below $24,000) would receive subsidies to keep the cost below 3.5 percent of payroll.

Critics argue employer mandates will hurt small business and result in job losses. Advocates point to over half of the U.S. population currently covered by employer-sponsored health care and they say small business would receive a subsidy. But the most convincing argument to economists who support employer mandates is this: Even though firms pay for government health-care insurance through payroll taxes and for private health insurance through benefit programs, these costs are actually passed on to wage and salary workers over time in the form of lower wages and salaries in the labor market! Workers ultimately bear the burden of most health-care costs anyway.[5] So, the costs of an employer mandate would in the long run be passed through to workers in the form of lower wages.

Under the Clinton plan, the self-employed would have been responsible for their own coverage, but their premiums would have been based on income level.

> **Premium Caps** The most controversial part of the Clinton plan among economists was its cap on premiums. Specifically, real per capita premiums were not to increase by more than 1.5 percent annually through 1996. This would have been reduced by 0.5 percent each year to zero in 1999. The purpose was to ensure that the presumed

health maintenance organization (HMO) *A health-care plan that provides comprehensive medical services for employees and their families at a flat fee.*

preferred provider organization (PPO) *A managed health-care plan in which an employer or insurance company establishes a network of doctors and hospitals to provide a broad set of medical services for a flat fee per participant. In return for the lower fee, the doctors and hospital who join the PPO network expect to receive a larger volume of patients.*

community rating *A system in which insurance providers must accept all applicants and charge premiums based only on age, location, and perhaps some elements of behavior (such as smoking).*

employer mandate *A system of health-care insurance provision in which all employers are required to provide health insurance and to pay on average 80 percent of the community-rated premiums.*

FAST FACTS

Medicaid and Medicare financed 36.1% of all personal health care expenditures in 1995. Medicare funded $184 billion in benefits for the nearly 37.5 million aged and disabled people enrolled in the program, 61% for the hospital care and 22% for physicians' services.

Source: Health Care Financing Administration, release January 27, 1997.

---

[5]We showed how the burden of payroll taxes paid by firms can be shifted to workers in chapter 18.

THE MARKET FOR HEALTH CARE RESPONDS TO RISING COSTS

On January 27, 1997, Health and Human Services Secretary Donna Shalala released the latest available figures on U.S. national health expenditures. Although health-care costs have not stopped rising, the rate of increase has slowed: growth in the nation's health-care spending decelerated sharply from double-digit rates of the late 1980s and early 1990s to 6.6 percent in 1993, 5.1 percent in 1994, and 5.5 percent in 1995. The lower growth rates in 1994 and 1995 were the lowest in more than three decades.

At the root of the slowdown was an even more significant slowdown in the growth of *private* spending, which increased only 2.9 percent in 1995. Interestingly, the market seems to be moving in the direction of at least one of the proposed reforms without government involvement.

In the two years that Congress wrangled over health care before quashing proposals for fundamental change, private market forces were acting on their own to transform the country's medical system dramatically.

Indeed, cost cutting, intensive competition and the growing role of large profit seeking corporations

in health care escalated some of the very trends that many members of Congress said they most opposed, like limitations on the choice of doctors. Among the milestones American health care reached without fanfare during 1993 and 1994 were these:

■ **A MAJORITY** *of privately insured Americans were enrolled in managed-care plans that limit choice of doctors and treatments. Sixty-five percent of workers at medium and large companies were in such plans by 1994.*

■ **FOR-PROFIT** *health maintenance organizations grew so fast that they overtook nonprofit H.M.O.'s as the dominant force in managed care. Today the majority of all people enrolled in H.M.O.'s, the most common and stringent form of managed care, are in plans run by for-profit companies.*

■ **AT LEAST** *three-fourths of all doctors signed contracts, covering at least some of their patients, to cut their fees and accept oversight of their medical decisions. Among doctors who work in group practices, the share of such managed-care contracts was 89 percent by*

1993, up sharply from 56 percent the year before.

Run for decades more like a collection of cottage industries than a system that now accounts for one-seventh of the economy, medical care is increasingly the domain of big business, offering a rich new playing field for Wall Street. Mergers and acquisitions of hospitals; clinics; doctor groups with their patient lists; medical laboratories, and other patient-care services, have totaled $20 billion this year, up from just $6 billion in 1992. Combined with the $22 billion in pharmaceutical deals, health care mergers surpassed in value those of any other industry for 1994, according to the Securities Data Company, a research firm in Newark.

But this restructuring has done nothing to ease the plight of the uninsured, whose numbers keep climbing, and it is also raising profound new questions about how quality care and medical ethics can be guarded.[a]

Source: [a]Erik Eckholm, "While Congress Remains Silent, Health Care Transforms Itself," *The New York Times*, December 18, 1994, p. 1. Copyright © 1994 by The New York Times Co. Reprinted by permission.

For more on health care and the economy, see the Case and Fair Web page at
http://www.prenhall.com/casefair.

efficiency and cost savings from managed care and reduced fee-for-service reimbursement would be realized. Economists do not like the inefficiency that comes with artificially imposed restrictions on price movements.

THE ECONOMICS OF IMMIGRATION

Few topics have received as much play in the press in recent years as immigration. And few topics elicit as much emotional response. In December 1994, voters in California approved by a 3-to-2 margin Proposition 187, a highly controversial referendum that prevents illegal immigrants from receiving state education, welfare, and nonemergency medical benefits. In 1995, Governor Lawton Chiles of Florida declared a statewide emergency and demanded a stop to the tens of thousands of Cubans flooding into Florida. President Clinton responded by sending the Coast Guard to intercept them and take them to a detention camp at Guantanamo Naval Base in Cuba. Later, some were sent to Panama and some were allowed to enter the United States. The recent exodus of Cubans provoked memories of the 1981 Mariel boat lift, as a result of which over 125,000 refugees arrived in Florida. Many were criminals who still are in U.S. prisons.

What impact does immigration have on a country's economy? All bad, as many would have us believe? One element of the agreement among the members of the European Union is the abolition of border controls to encourage the free flow of labor among member countries in response to wage differentials and economic conditions. The relaxation of immigration rules in Europe was done to encourage economic growth and prosperity.

A BRIEF HISTORY OF IMMIGRATION INTO THE UNITED STATES

Immigration into the United States has come in irregular waves. The first "Great Migration" occurred between 1880 and 1924, when 25.8 million immigrants entered the country, a figure that represented more than 40 percent of the period's total population increase. During the 1920s, however, Congress established a national-origins quota system that limited the annual flow from the Eastern Hemisphere countries to 150,000. Under the new laws, visas were issued in proportion to the ethnic composition of the United States in 1920. The result was that 60 percent of the visas went to German and British immigrants. The flow of immigrants slowed to a trickle during the 1930s but has been expanding ever since. At present, immigration is approaching 800,000 per year. Many of today's immigrants are illegal. Studies indicate that during the late 1980s between 2 million and 3 million people were illegally residing in the United States and 200,000 to 300,000 new illegals were arriving each year. Though the Border Patrol intercepts and returns about 1.3 million illegals per year, many illegal immigrants enter legally through customs and simply remain in the country.

In 1986 the Congress enacted the **Immigration Reform and Control Act**, which granted amnesty to about 3 million illegals and imposed a set of strong employer sanctions designed to slow the flow of immigrants into the United States. The **Immigration Act of 1990** increased the number of legal immigrants allowed in each year by 150,000.

Prior to 1960, the largest single group of immigrants into the United States came from Europe. Between 1960 and 1990 the largest group of immigrants came from the Americas, especially Mexico, Canada, and Cuba. Beginning in 1970, the number of immigrants from Asia began to grow rapidly. Table 20.2 shows the number of foreign-born persons from the top 10 countries of origin in 1997.

MANY AGRICULTURAL FIRMS IN TEXAS AND CALIFORNIA RELY ON IMMIGRATION FROM MEXICO, CENTRAL AMERICA, AND SOUTH AMERICA TO SUPPLY THEM WITH LABOR DURING THE PEAK GROWING SEASON. HOWEVER, DOES IMMIGRATION REDUCE DOMESTIC WAGES AND INCREASE UNEMPLOYMENT NATIONALLY? THE EVIDENCE IS MIXED.

Immigration Reform and Control Act (1986) *Granted amnesty to about 3 million illegal aliens and imposed a strong set of employer sanctions designed to slow the flow of immigrants into the United States.*

Immigration Act of 1990 *Increased the number of legal immigrants allowed into the United States each year by 150,000.*

TABLE 20.2 FOREIGN BORN POPULATION OF THE UNITED STATES BY COUNTRY OF ORIGIN: 1997

RANK	COUNTRY OF ORIGIN	NUMBER (THOUSANDS)	PERCENT OF TOTAL
1	Mexico	7,017	27.2
2	Philippines	1,132	4.4
3	China and Hong Kong	1,107	4.3
4	Cuba	913	3.5
5	Vietnam	770	3.0
6	India	748	2.9
7	Dominican Republic	632	2.5
8	El Salvador	607	2.4
9	Great Britain	606	2.4
10	Korea	591	2.3
	Elsewhere	11,655	45.2

Source: U.S. Department of Justice Immigration and Naturalization Service.

ECONOMIC ARGUMENTS FOR FREE IMMIGRATION

Should a country permit completely free immigration into its borders? The argument for free immigration is that it increases world output. Labor flows across borders in response to wage differentials. Consider Mexico and the United States. Low-wage workers in Mexico migrate to the United States because wages are higher in the United States. If markets are basically competitive, wages reflect the workers' productivity. In other words, because the United States has more capital and uses more advanced technology than Mexico, the productivity of low-wage workers is higher in the United States than in Mexico. The same labor produces more total output after immigration, and world output rises.[6]

Now consider France and Italy. If a labor shortage develops in France because the demand for French wine increases, French wages will rise and attract workers from other European countries. If at the same time the demand for leather goods produced in Italy drops, Italian wages will fall, and Italian workers will move to France, where their productivity is higher.

The argument for the free movement of labor among nations is exactly the same as the argument for the free movement of labor among the sectors of the domestic economy. Suppose an economy produces only two goods, X and Y. If demand for good X picks up, the demand for labor used to produce X rises as the marginal revenue product of labor employed in the production of X increases. Labor will move out of the production of good Y if and only if its productivity is higher in X in terms of the value of output. This movement ensures efficiency. Recall the simple definition that an efficient economy produces what people want at least cost.

Those who favor a looser policy believe immigrants do not displace U.S. workers but rather take jobs that Americans do not want. Immigrants serve as domestics and low-wage farm workers producing things that the United States needs. In addition, the U.S. economy has absorbed wave after wave of immigrants while maintaining virtually full employment. Almost all U.S. citizens except Native Americans have relatively recent ancestors who were immigrants.

THE ARGUMENT AGAINST FREE IMMIGRATION

No economist disputes the idea that the distribution of income is likely to change among countries and among groups within each country in response to immigration. Assuming that immigrants are low-wage workers, equilibrium wages in the market for low-skill labor will rise in the country of origin and fall in the country of destination. In addition, the return to capital will rise in the destination country, pushing up profits, while capital income will fall in the country of origin.

The argument for free immigration assumes all workers get jobs. However, the popular impression is certainly that immigrants (who usually work for very low wages) take jobs away from low-income Americans and drive up unemployment rates. And, many believe immigrants often end up on welfare rolls and become a burden to taxpayers. Opponents also point to crime in ethnic neighborhoods and rivalries among ethnic groups as evidence of further costs to society.

THE EVIDENCE: THE NET COSTS OF IMMIGRATION

To determine whether the benefits of immigration outweigh its costs, we must ask: To what extent does immigration reduce domestic wages and increase unemployment? Recent studies found metropolitan areas that have greater numbers of immigrants seem to have only slightly lower wages and only slightly higher unemployment rates.[7]

---

[6]For a review of how the labor market works, see chapters 10 and 19.

[7]See George Borjas, "The Economics of Immigration," *Journal of Economic Literature*, December, 1994, for a review of the literature.

A study by David Card of Princeton University looks at wages and employment opportunities in the Miami area during and after the Mariel boat lift in 1981. Almost overnight, about 125,000 Cubans arrived and increased the labor force in Miami by over 7 percent. Card looked at trends in wages and unemployment among Miami workers between 1980 and 1985 and found virtually no effect. The data he examined mirrored the experience of workers in Los Angeles, Houston, Atlanta, and similar cities that were not hit by the same shock.[8]

A more recent study by Borjas, Freeman, and Katz takes issue with much of the work done to date. They argue that immigrants do not stay in the cities at which they arrive, but move within the United States in response to job opportunities and wage differentials. They say the effects of immigration on wages and unemployment must be analyzed at the national level, not at the city level. Their study points to the large decline in the wages of high-school dropouts relative to workers with more education during the 1980s. Their results suggest a third of the drop in the relative wages of high-school dropouts can be attributed to lower-skilled immigrants.[9]

On the issue of immigration's effects on government costs, mixed evidence also exists. It is clear earlier generations of immigrants have had a positive effect on both the economy as a whole and on government budgets specifically. Studies of early immigrants' wage patterns show that their wages on average exceed native workers' wages after 15 years. First-generation immigrants as a group might be paying more in taxes than they collect in means-tested benefits such as welfare.

But the data show that over time there has been a steep drop in the level of education, experience, and skills among immigrants. At the same time, participation in welfare programs among immigrants has jumped sharply. Borjas estimates that in 1990, immigrant households in the United States contributed between $7.6 billion and $10.1 billion in tax revenues while collecting $23.8 billion in benefits from means-tested programs.[10]

IS IMMIGRATION BAD OR GOOD?

Immigration is another economic issue in which no right answer clearly emerges. The evidence on the effects of immigration is mixed; theory gives us arguments on both sides of the issue. Only time will tell whether the recent wave of immigrants will assimilate as well as past waves. Meanwhile, immigration will remain a "hot button" issue politically, and the United States will be called upon to make some decisions about the treatment of recent immigrants.

URBAN ECONOMICS AND THE ECONOMICS OF URBAN PROBLEMS

Since chapter 4, we have been discussing the economic decisions made by individual firms and households: how much to produce, what to produce, which technology to use, how much of each input to demand, what to consume, and how much to save. But we have not yet touched on one equally important decision—*where to locate*. Every household must live somewhere, and every firm must locate its facilities. Our world has been shaped by the collective location decisions of millions of households and firms. The collection of factories, office buildings, roads, houses, apartment buildings, stores, museums, and schools that we know as a city exists because people once decided those things needed to be close together.

FAST FACTS

Over 21% of immigrants admitted in 1996 intended to live in either New York City or Los Angeles. The majority were female (54%) and their median age was 28, with 54% below the age of 30. Persons aged 65 or older were just 5% of all immigrants. The leading occupations among the 25,000 immigrants reporting a professional or technical occupation in 1996 were nurses (4,154) and engineers (4,135).

Source: U.S. Department of Justice, Immigration and Naturalization Service, "Characteristics of Legal Immigrants," September 26, 1997.

---

[8]David Card, "The Impact of the Mariel Boat Lift on the Miami Labor Market," *Industrial and Labor Relations Review*, January 1990, pp. 245–257.

[9]George Borjas, Richard Freeman, and Lawrence Katz, "On the Labor Market Effects of Immigration and Trade," in *Immigration and the Work Force: Economic Consequences for the United States and Source Areas*, eds. George Borjas and Richard Freeman (Chicago: University of Chicago Press, 1992).

[10]Ibid.

Location decisions are similar to other decisions made by firms and households. For households, location decisions depend on preferences, incomes, and relative prices. A graduate of Florida State University who decides to look for a job in Atlanta may like the Atlanta area, but her decision is also likely to be influenced by factors such as job opportunities, wage rates, and the cost of living. For firms, decisions depend on potential revenues, costs, and profits. Digital Equipment Corporation opened a production facility in Ireland because it seemed profitable to do so. Honda opened a large plant in Ohio for the same reason.

THE LOCATION OF BUSINESS FIRMS

No topic is of greater concern for state governors than employment, and employment in a state or a region depends upon location decisions made by business firms. Just as presidents rise and fall with the national economy, governors rise and fall with their states' economies. Most states have development departments responsible for attracting new firms and encouraging established firms to stay and expand. Within the last dozen years, many states have established tax reform commissions. Top on the agenda of practically every one of them has been a study of the impact of state taxes on industrial location decisions.

Business location decisions are complicated. The easiest way to see how complicated they are is to look at the profit function of a single firm. *Profits* are the difference between total revenue and total cost of production:

$$\text{Profit} = TR - TC = P \times q - (P_1 X_1 + P_2 X_2 + \cdots + P_n X_n).$$

Total revenue (TR) is the price of output times the quantity of output sold ($P \times q$). *Total cost* (TC) is the total cost of all the inputs required. In the equation, we have n inputs, which include labor, capital, land, transport costs, and so forth. P_1 is the price of the first input, X_1 is the quantity of the first input used, and so forth.

Before we introduced the question of location to our analysis of profit-maximizing firms, we assumed that each firm knew the price of output, the price of each input required, and the technologies of production available. That information was used to pick one profit-maximizing level of output. Adding the location question brings with it a complication:

> Every variable in a profit function may change from location to location.

When a firm shops around for a location, it must think about the price it can charge, the amount it might sell, the costs of transportation, wage rates, rent levels, the taxes it must pay, and so forth *at every possible location*. Once these factors are calculated, the firm will presumably pick the location where its profit will be highest.

> **The Profit Equation: Locational Variation in Revenues** Revenues depend on demand, but, more specifically, they depend on price (P) and how much the firm can sell (q). A gas station located on a deserted country road would not sell much gasoline. A store that sells deep-sea fishing equipment exclusively would probably not last long in Nebraska. Many firms comfortably located along major state and U.S. highways found themselves in deep trouble when the interstate highway system diverted traffic away from them.

> **The Profit Equation: Locational Variation in Costs** Some costs vary from location to location, some do not. For many firms, the cost of transporting inputs to the point of production and outputs to the point of sale make up a large component of final cost. Transport costs depend on what needs to be transported where!

Consider automobiles: Components must be produced, then assembled, and the final product must be shipped to dealers all over the world. Many of an automobile's component parts are produced from steel and aluminum. Moving iron ore, bauxite, and coal to the sites of aluminum and steel production, transporting the raw materials to production facilities, moving finished parts to assembly plants, and shipping assembled automobiles to dealers is an enormously complex set of tasks. The costs of all these tasks depend on the sites of ore sources, production facilities, assembly plants, and dealers.

Wage rates also vary across the country. The highest average wages are in the Pacific Northwest and in the north central industrial states of Michigan, Ohio, Indiana, and Iowa. The lowest-priced labor is in the deep South and in northern New England.

The cost of capital to a firm depends to a great extent on the cost of financing. Neither the cost of borrowing nor the cost of raising funds through bond or stock offerings varies significantly across cities and regions, because the banking industry is highly integrated. If interest rates in Phoenix increase, Phoenix banks can obtain funds from outside the region, or firms themselves may turn directly to credit markets outside the area.

➤ **Location and Public Policy** As we already noted, public officials seek to influence firms' locational choices. Both tax and expenditure policies have been designed to encourage businesses. Several years ago, New York State included in its corporate franchise tax provisions designed to promote the expansion of firms within the state. The "jobs-incentive-credit" program, for example, reduced a firm's taxes if it expanded its employment in the state by a minimum of 1 percent during the year. More recently, the federal government has designated a number of "enterprise zones" in which locating firms receive special tax treatment.

Some states and cities negotiate property tax rates with new firms, offering juicy abatements and other perquisites. Others build access roads or new freeway interchanges that benefit new firms. During the 1960s, when urban renewal was seen as the salvation of run-down inner cities, city governments paid for most of the land and site-improvement costs before development began.

For years, economists have debated whether state tax and expenditure policies have a significant effect on business location decisions. The evidence is mixed. Those who find no effect argue that state and local taxes represent a very small portion of total costs for most firms, and that tax rates vary less across states than most people think. When decision makers are asked in surveys about the factors that played a key role in their location decisions, taxes and other special incentives do not score high. Many statistical studies have found that state and local taxes and expenditure policies are insignificant in location decision. The factors that do seem to play a role include the availability of a trained labor force, wage rates, and transport costs. But the view that state taxes and expenditures have little or no effect on location decisions is not universally held by economists. Other studies have found statistical evidence that site choice *is* sensitive to tax rates. Others point to specific examples of firms that claim to have been influenced by tax incentives.

There is another side to this story. The fact that firms may react either positively or negatively to differences in tax rates and state spending policies forces state officials to be more responsible. Interstate tax competition, some economists argue, forces public officials to look long and hard at potentially wasteful tax and expenditure policies.

THE LOCATION OF HOUSEHOLDS

Everyone needs a place to live. And at least one person in almost every household is employed. This means residential locations depend a lot on workplace locations. Because of the costs associated with getting from home to work and back, the tendency is for households to cluster around areas of high employment.

➤ **Monocentric City Models** The earliest models constructed to analyze residential location assumed all employment was located at the center of the city and households bid against each other for the locations most accessible to the central city.

These models argued that those who end up living close to the center city bear lower transportation costs because their commute is shorter. This desirability of location is reflected in bids for land. But as people relocate from the center, their transportation costs increase. Location therefore becomes less desirable and bids for housing fall. An equilibrium can exist only where the land prices just offset the lower transport costs closer to the center. If, at current land prices, a household on the periphery could increase its welfare by moving closer to the center, it would bid the closer land away from its current occupant.

With higher land prices at the center, theory predicts we will find substitution of capital for land. High-rise apartment buildings do appear most frequently in downtown areas, while garden apartments and single-family homes are usually found farther out. Despite the simplicity of the assumptions, these **monocentric**, or "single-center," **models** that assume central employment are a good way to gain an understanding of residential location.

But job location is not the only factor that affects residential location decisions. Housing is an enormously complicated "product." It has many different dimensions, and people have different preferences, which also shift over time. Some families have a taste for space; others feel lost in it. Some love urban living; others are afraid of crime. Some want to be near water; others prefer mountains. Many people never leave their hometowns; others can't wait to get away. Some people have high incomes and others are poor. This heterogeneity of tastes and incomes is reflected in the diversity of the housing stock in the United States—from huge, single-family country estates to million-dollar downtown condominiums, from small urban apartments to rural shacks.

▶ **Discrimination in the Housing Market** Bidding for accessible locations tells only a small part of the residential location story. Census data reveal that African Americans and white Americans still live, by and large, in separate neighborhoods, both in urban and rural parts of the country. The South has many rural African Americans, and there is virtually complete segregation in its small towns. In the North, African Americans tend to live in the cities. While more mixed neighborhoods exist today than existed 20 years ago, they are few and far between.

Many theories to explain why these groups tend to live apart from each other have been offered. African Americans earn lower average incomes than whites. However, income differences explain only a small fraction of actual segregation. The hypothesis that African Americans live separately by choice and do not want to live in predominantly white neighborhoods is not supported by evidence. Ample evidence does support a third hypothesis, however—that African Americans are denied equal access to the housing market through discrimination.

Racial discrimination in the housing market has been documented in many forms. Until recent years, many property deeds carried provisions that restricted an owner's ability to sell to African Americans. These **racial covenants** were enforceable until the 1950s, when the courts found them unconstitutional. Even with such agreements declared illegal, homeowners and real estate agents in all-white neighborhoods often do everything possible to prevent selling or renting to African Americans or to those who belong to ethnic groups that form the underclass of a given region.

During the 1950s and 1960s, many African Americans moved from the rural South to the urban North. When they arrived, they found their access to the housing market limited. Certain neighborhoods were designated for their occupancy, and few were able to buy or rent elsewhere. As demand for housing increased in the designated areas, prices rose. Dozens of studies during the 1960s and early 1970s documented the existence of **ghetto premiums**. African Americans were paying more to live in the ghetto than whites of comparable means were paying to live in virtually identical housing in white neighborhoods.

Ghetto premiums seemed to disappear during the 1970s, probably more because African Americans stopped moving to the city in great waves than because discrimination had ended. A number of studies have shown that racial and ethnic discrimination in housing continues to be widespread today, despite decades of efforts to stop it. One

monocentric models *Models of residential location that assume central employment. As people move farther from the center, their costs of commuting increase. Equilibrium in the housing market exists only where land prices just offset the lower transport costs closer to the center.*

racial covenants *Provisions spelled out in property deeds that prohibit sale of that property to members of specific racial or ethnic groups.*

ghetto premiums *Evidence suggests that during the 1960s and 1970s housing in sections of U.S. cities inhabited predominantly by African Americans was more expensive than comparable housing in white neighborhoods. The price difference came to be called a ghetto premium.*

study using matched pairs of "auditors," one from each group, revealed that African Americans seeking apartments are invited to inspect 36.3 percent fewer units than their white counterparts.[11]

> ### The Filtering Process and Housing for the Poor
Most poor people today live in old housing once occupied by higher-income people, housing that has declined in quality and value. Virtually all unsubsidized new housing in the United States is built for those at the upper- and middle-income levels. As rich people buy the new homes, their old homes become available to those in lower-income brackets.

As housing "filters" down the income-distribution ladder, it depreciates. The cheapest housing, the housing available to poor people, is often housing that is the oldest or has depreciated the fastest from lack of upkeep. Housing subsidies and tax advantages offered to middle- and upper-income households and to new construction are often justified on the grounds that such programs speed up the **filtering** process. If the filtering chain works faster than the rate at which the older housing stock deteriorates, everyone will end up in better housing.

The central parts of cities are usually the oldest parts. Because the oldest housing falls to the poorest people, low-income housing has in many places become concentrated in the inner city.

For years, rent control in major U.S. cities has been a way of providing affordable housing. Rent control remains a controversial issue; the Application "Affordable Housing and Rent Control" discusses the debate in more detail.

filtering *The process whereby the newest and best housing goes to the wealthy, whose former housing passes down to those of middle income, whose former housing passes down to those of low income. Thus housing "filters" down the income-distribution ladder.*

THE ECONOMICS OF URBAN DECLINE AND RECOVERY

Many large U.S. cities endured a host of troubles during the 1960s and 1970s. Firms began moving to the suburbs, creating unemployment in the central cities. Buildings were abandoned. Crime rates rose. City governments found themselves with a declining tax base at the same time that the demand for public services was increasing. Many cities faced serious fiscal crises; many lost their bond ratings and came close to defaulting on their debts.

> ### The Sources of Urban Decline
Urban decline results directly from lack of investment. In one sense, a city is a huge agglomeration of capital: factories, houses, office buildings, warehouses, government buildings, roads, water and sewer systems, bridges, and so forth. Some is private capital, and some is public capital. But all capital depreciates, and unless it is maintained, repaired, and periodically replaced, it deteriorates.

Abandoned housing is housing that has not been maintained. Roofs need to be replaced every 10 years or so, walls must be painted, and plumbing and heating systems need to be repaired and replaced. When owners stop investing, deterioration accelerates, and the building succumbs to the scrap dealer and the rats.

Social capital decays when governments do not continuously invest in maintaining it. In many cities, water systems, sewer systems, roads and bridges, and transit systems are in a bad state of repair. Maintaining public capital is staggering. The New York City subway system, which carries over 1 billion passengers per year, consists of more than 231 miles of track, 461 stations, and 6,700 cars. The New York City water system contains 6,150 miles of main water lines, 95 percent of which is made of old cast iron pipe of various ages, strengths, and sizes. Anyone who has driven in New York knows what the streets are like. One 1979 estimate put the costs of needed replacement and repair to New York's streets, water systems, and subways at nearly $12 billion,[12] undoubtedly much higher now.

urban decline *The deterioration of the private and social capital stock of a city that results from the lack of investment by both private and public sectors.*

---

[11]See John Yinger, "Measuring Racial Discrimination with Fair Housing Audits: Caught in the Act," *American Economic Review,* December 1986.

[12]David Grossman, *The Future of New York City's Capital Plant* (Washington, D.C.: The Urban Institute, 1979).

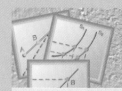

AFFORDABLE HOUSING AND RENT CONTROL

Several U.S. cities have confronted the problem of affordable housing by passing *rent control laws*, which impose a price ceiling on the monthly rent that landlords can charge. Although these laws have been almost universally criticized by economists, they remain in force in many cities, including New York.

One of the most bitterly contested legislative battles over rent regulation occurred in the New York State Legislature in 1997. Just hours after the law that regulated rents on more than 70,000 apartments in New York City expired on June 15, a compromise between rent control advocates and opponents was reached. The compromise preserved rent control, but it allowed landlords to raise rents by 20 percent whenever a vacancy occurred; it decontrolled units that rent for more than $2,000 per month or that were occupied by tenants earning more than $175,000 annually; and it limited a tenant's ability to pass on controlled units to relatives.

The argument against rent control is illustrated in Figure 1. The quantity of housing services is measured along the horizontal axis; monthly rent per unit is measured along the vertical axis. Without rent control, the market is in equilibrium at a rent of R^*. At that price, Q^* units of housing services are supplied and the same number of units (Q^*) of housing services are demanded.

The imposition of a ceiling on rents ($\bar{R}$ in Figure 1) causes excess demand as the quantity of housing services demanded increases (from Q^* to Q_D) and the quantity supplied decreases (from Q^* to Q_S). The lower rents, critics argue, reduce landlords' incentives to maintain their property and to invest in new units. And even if new units are not subject to rent control (as in New York City), detractors claim, the existence of rent control deters would-be developers from building new units for fear of being subject to control later. Far from increasing the supply of affordable housing, rent control *reduces* the stock of affordable housing. Furthermore, because the occupancy of rent-controlled units is not limited to the poor, rent control laws

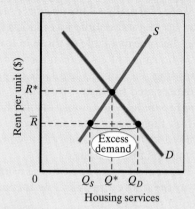

FIGURE 1

may end up providing a subsidy to upper-income households.

But there is another side to this story. Those who favor rent control argue that it brings about a transfer from landlords to tenants, and that such laws do not change the behavior of landlords very much. Because state and federal budgets for direct housing subsidies are limited, many see rent control as the only alternative to increased homelessness.

For more on the economics of housing and rent control, see the Case and Fair Web page at
http://www.prenhall.com/casefair.

Urban economists point to a number of factors that explain the lack of investment in social capital during the last quarter century. Since the end of World War II, firms have been gradually moving out of the central cities and into the suburban ring. Improvement in both transportation and communications technology has made the suburbs a more attractive location. Of course, people wanted to be close to their jobs, so they began to move out of the cities toward the new suburban business centers. As a result, suburban housing investment boomed, while inner-city housing began to decay. Then, during the 1950s and 1960s, poor rural African Americans moved to northern cities in record numbers. Discrimination limited their housing choices, and they became concentrated in central cities. Because very little low-income family housing, subsidized or unsubsidized, is located in the suburbs of America, the urban poor have had little choice but to live in central cities.

All of this had a devastating effect on city budgets. First, the tax base declined because business firms were moving to the suburbs. Inner-city housing filtered down the depreciation ladder, property values decreased, and some properties fell off the tax rolls altogether. Second, the expenditures required to run city government increased. Old, poorly maintained buildings are more likely to catch fire, increasing the need for fire protection.

Because crime rates are higher in poor areas than in high-income areas, more police and courts are needed. In addition, poor and homeless people need more social services.

With the squeeze on city budgets, it is not surprising that the social capital stock in many cities is inadequately maintained. Roads, water systems, and government buildings are all in various states of disrepair.

▶ **The Property Tax Problem** Property tax policies, with local responsibility for public services, education, and a substantial portion of the social welfare system, have led to increasing segregation by income and have exacerbated urban decay.

Local government has always been responsible for elementary and secondary education and for most local public services, such as police and fire protection. Nationally, about three-quarters of all local tax receipts come from the *property tax*, a proportional tax on the assessed value of all property. This can have important implications for the economic development of localities.

Consider two towns, A and B. A is the older town with depreciating housing occupied by lower-income people. Because more of A's population is poor, social welfare expenditures and the need for social services will be high. These needed services put added pressure on the tax system. If property *values* are lower in A, the tax *rates* required to support the higher level of service may be extraordinary.

Suppose the average house in A is valued at $30,000 and the average house in B is valued at $120,000. Citizens of both towns have an average of one school-age child per household. A property tax rate of 2 percent in town A would yield enough to finance $600 per student per year, while the same rate in town B would yield $2,400 per student per year. In many U.S. cities, suburban school districts boast much lower tax rates *and* higher expenditures for education.[13]

The higher tax rate *and* lower quality of education and public services in cities put added pressure on those who can afford it to move to the suburbs. The increased income segregation that results further exacerbates the problem of decline.

THE PROBLEMS OF CRIME

It is estimated that the economic cost of crime in the United States was over $500 billion in 1997, including the costs of police, courts, prisons, private protection, stolen goods, damage, injury, and death. Of the 13.5 million reported crimes in the United States in 1996, 88 percent took place in metropolitan areas. That same year 19,645 people, more than 10 percent of whom were under 18 years of age, were murdered. The economics of urban areas includes the economics of crime!

▶ **Crime as "Rational Behavior"** One economic way to view criminal activity is as a negative externality; consider the incentives facing criminals and potential victims. A crime may be committed when the expected gains exceed the expected costs. A thief will break into a house if and only if the stolen property is expected to be worth more than the "expected cost" of the break-in. In this sense, breaking into the house might be considered "rational behavior."

In most cases of criminal activity, outcomes are uncertain. A robber who breaks into a house doesn't know for sure what he will find and what it will be worth. By choosing a house in a wealthy neighborhood, he increases the likelihood of finding valuable goods that can be resold. He is also not sure whether he will be caught, and if caught whether he will be convicted. For example, thieves who prowl rich neighborhoods are more likely to find high-tech alarm systems, and wealthy towns may have better police forces. The greater probability of a good heist can be offset by a greater probability of being caught.

---

[13] The system of financing education using local property tax revenues has been challenged in the courts on numerous occasions. The best-known cases were *Serrano v. Priest* in the California Supreme Court in 1971 and the *San Antonio Independent School District v. Rodriguez*, which went to the U.S. Supreme Court in 1972. In 1987 the same issue was raised in New Jersey when Camden, a relatively poor, declining city, brought suit against the state, pointing to nearby Cherry Hill, where property tax rates were lower and school expenditures higher.

From society's point of view, those who impose external costs should have an incentive to consider those costs in their decisions. To force firms to internalize the costs of pollution, for example, a government can impose a tax equal to the marginal damage costs. In the case of a crime, the "expected" penalty should equal the social cost of the crime. For crimes like double parking, the penalties are minor. For armed robbery, the penalties are more severe.

Just as criminals weigh the cost of getting caught against the potential value of their crime, potential victims weigh the costs of becoming a victim against the costs of risk avoidance. Rich people who live in accessible city neighborhoods usually have expensive alarm systems because the likelihood of being robbed is high. People who live in small towns, where most people know each other, rarely have alarms. When you decide to go to the theater in a rough part of town, you weigh the potential costs of being a victim against the benefits of seeing the show. Law enforcement, paid for by tax dollars, also has a cost. Police officers, courts, and prisons all are expensive. The job of an efficient government is to fund criminal justice activities as long as their marginal social benefit in the form of reduced crime is greater than their marginal cost.

Research indicates that criminal behavior can be explained using this logic. It is a well-established fact, for example, that higher unemployment rates during economic downturns cause crime rates to rise. Why? Because the expected costs (including opportunity costs) of crime are very low and the expected benefits are high to a poor unemployed person. If the potential gain from selling drugs is great and the likelihood of being caught is low, the result is a lot of drug dealing.

Is it surprising that a lot of crimes take place in high-density urban areas? No. Most cities have low-income residents and high levels of unemployment. Courts are crowded, as are prisons, and apprehension and conviction rates are low. In addition, the city's high density means many opportunities for crime and a better chance of escaping into the crowd.

According to a recent Roper College Track poll, U.S. college students see crime as the number-two issue facing the country today. This concern is reflected in the larger society. It is not surprising that crime has become a major topic of debate in recent political campaigns. Most candidates propose two types of policy to reduce crime. The first would increase the probability of catching criminals, because a higher probability of being caught increases criminals' "expected penalty." With no chance of being caught, the expected penalty is zero. Hire more police officers and train them better, install alarm systems, do wiretaps, and so forth, the argument goes, and more criminals will be caught. When apprehension rates rise, crime rates will decrease because criminals will fear being caught more than they do now.

The second type of policy calls for increasing the penalties for criminal activity. This is the reason behind mandatory jail terms for those who commit certain crimes. People behind bars cannot commit crimes, and the fear of being in jail for long periods may deter people.

> **"Irrational" Crime** Not all criminal activity is rational. Crimes of passion, domestic violence, murder, and rape are often acts committed in a moment of rage or despair, rather than conscious rational acts. A very large number of assaults and murders are committed by spouses and friends of the victim.

Needless to say, such crimes are not committed after a rational weighing of expected costs and benefits. Many criminals regret their crimes at the moment they are committed. This has led many to advocate strict gun-control laws to minimize the probability that a person in a fit of rage would find himself or herself with easy access to weapons.

The economic analysis of legal rules and institutions is fast becoming a well-developed field of study. We have hardly scratched the surface of what economics has to offer in analyzing criminal behavior.

SUMMARY

THE ECONOMICS OF HEALTH-CARE REFORM

1. No issue looms larger in U.S. politics than health-care reform: health care is expensive and getting more expensive. 15 percent of the U.S. population has no health insurance, health-care expenditures make up an increasing portion of the federal budget.

2. Efficiency- and equity-related factors appear to favor government involvement in providing health-care services. *Asymmetric information* and *fee-for-service reimbursement* programs give health-care providers an incentive to oversupply expensive services. Oversupply is inefficient from society's point of view, and poor health can be considered a negative externality that imposes costs on society. Market power allows companies to charge high prices for drugs and technology they've developed—prices the working poor and the uninsured cannot afford. Many believe health care should be provided to all, regardless of ability to pay.

3. An aging population, increasing malpractice insurance costs, and advancing technology all play roles in high health-care costs, but the problem lies in asymmetric information, moral hazard, and inefficient reimbursement methods.

4. Proposals offered to solve the growing problems of the U.S. health-care sector include: (1) managed care programs, such as *health maintenance organizations (HMOs)* and *preferred provider organizations (PPOs)*, (2) *community rating systems*, in which insurance providers must accept all applications and charge premiums based only on age, location, and some elements of behavior, (3) *employer mandates*, which would require all employers to provide insurance for all employees, and (4) caps on insurance premiums.

THE ECONOMICS OF IMMIGRATION

5. Immigration into the United States has come in irregular waves since the "Great Migration" of 1880 to 1924. Today, legal immigration is about 800,000 per year.

6. Those who argue for free immigration say that it increases world output and that the United States has absorbed many waves of immigrants while maintaining virtually full employment. Those against free immigration believe immigrants take jobs away from low-income Americans and end up on welfare. The economic literature shows mixed results. Some studies find that immigration has no effect on wage rates; other studies indicate that recent immigrants collect more in means-tested benefits than they provide in tax revenue.

URBAN ECONOMICS AND THE ECONOMICS OF URBAN PROBLEMS

7. The world has been shaped by the location decisions of millions of households and firms. For firms, location decisions depend on potential revenues, costs, and profits, which are likely to be different at every potential location. Public officials have sought for decades to influence firms' locational choices. For households, location decisions depend on preferences, incomes, and relative prices.

8. *Monocentric city models* assume that as people move farther from the center city, their costs of commuting increase. Thus residential land closest to the center of the city is likely to be the most expensive, with land values decreasing farther and farther from the center. Equilibrium in the housing market exists only when land prices just offset the lower transport costs closer to the center.

9. African Americans and white Americans still live, by and large, in separate neighborhoods, in part because discrimination has denied African Americans equal access to the housing market.

10. Most poor people today live in old housing, once occupied by higher-income people, that has declined in quality and value. Virtually all unsubsidized new housing is built for upper- and middle-income. As rich people buy the new homes, their old homes *filter* down to lower-income people.

11. Many large U.S. cities experienced decline and decay during the 1960s and 1970s. *Urban decline* results directly from lack of investment, both public and private. Housing stocks have deteriorated, businesses have moved to the suburbs, and social capital—bridges, roads, and transit systems—have fallen into disrepair. Property tax policies, together with local responsibility for public services, education, and a substantial portion of the social welfare system, have exacerbated urban decay.

12. Efforts to reduce rational crime focus on (1) policies that increase the probability of catching criminals, and (2) policies that increase the penalties for criminal activity.

REVIEW TERMS AND CONCEPTS

PROBLEM SET

1. Medicare reform is an increasingly hot topic in politics. How did the debate unfold during the 1998 congressional campaign? What are the reasons for concern? What solutions have been offered by the various candidates? To find the answers you may want to search the Web or an index to a major newspaper.

2. What is the likely effect of each of the following on health-care costs? Explain your answers briefly.
   a. A shift from fee-for-service reimbursement to a fixed fee per member in group plans.
   b. Universal coverage with community rating.
   c. An increase in copayments by patients in HMOs.

3. The Issues and Debates box in this chapter documents the rise in the use of managed care providers of health services. What sets a managed care plan apart from other providers? Why do you suppose that managed care providers arose naturally in the marketplace in 1994 to 1995? What are the disadvantages of managed care?

4. What is the current status of Proposition 187, the immigration law passed in 1994 in California? Has it been challenged in the courts? If so, what was the decision? Do you agree or disagree with the basic aims of Proposition 187? Why?

5. In the early 1980s the Mariel boat lift brought 120,000 Cubans to Miami. This represented a 7 percent increase in the workforce of the Miami metropolitan area. However, work by David Card found no impact on employment or wages in Miami. How can you explain this finding? Does your answer depend on whether you think of a metropolitan area as a closed economy or an open economy? Does Card's research mean that immigration has no impact on wages?

6. Recently retired from academic life, Emily is considering opening a gas station. Her research suggests the following:

	LOCATION A	LOCATION B
Expected annual sales	1 million gallons	2 million gallons
Price of lot	$250,000	$1,000,000

Gasoline sells for $1.10 per gallon at all locations (there is only one grade of gasoline).

Gasoline can be purchased from wholesalers for $1 per gallon. It would cost $300,000 to build a gasoline station, regardless of location.

Annual costs of running a station are $50,000, regardless of how much gasoline is sold—this includes maintenance and full upkeep on the building.

The interest rate is 10 percent.

Emily is considering locations A and B. Each is a one-acre lot. Would you advise Emily to go into business? If so, where should she locate?

7. The largest single federal housing subsidy is the provision of the individual income tax that allows homeowners to deduct property taxes and mortgage interest payments from their income for tax purposes. Describe in detail how a subsidy that accrues almost exclusively to middle- and upper-income families might raise the quality of housing occupied by lower-income families. (*Hint:* Recall the filtering process.) What specific assumptions would one have to make to predict such a result?

8. H. Ross Perot, in his unsuccessful run for the presidency, proposed a 50-cent-per-gallon gasoline tax. If gasoline prices remained high for a long time, in what ways might you expect a stiff gasoline tax to affect the spatial arrangement of households and firms?

9. Some cities in the United States have experienced renewed development in their central business districts. High-rise office buildings were built at a record pace in the early 1980s in some older U.S. cities that had earlier experienced decline. That growth has been denounced by some community leaders on the grounds that the benefits do not accrue to city residents, but rather to suburban residents. Make a list of all the benefits and costs you can think of that might result from a modern office tower in an older city. What groups benefit? What groups lose out? Be sure to include some discussion of the housing market.

10. What externalities, both positive and negative, are most frequently encountered by city dwellers? By suburb dwellers?

11. Some people point to an improving economy and the aging of the baby boom generation as the reasons for a decreasing crime rate between 1992 and 1998. Others point to an increasingly harsh judicial climate. How does the aging of the baby boom generation tend to influence the crime rate? Using the model of "rational crime" in the chapter, explain how stricter law enforcement with harsh penalties and an improving economy might affect the costs and benefits of crime.

TAKE IT TO THE NET

We invite you to visit the Case and Fair page on the Prentice Hall Web site:

http://www.prenhall.com/casefair

for this chapter's World Wide Web exercise.

LABOR MARKET DISCRIMINATION AND PROFESSIONAL SPORTS

On April 15, 1947, Jackie Robinson became the first African American player in major league baseball. Robinson opened the door for other African American and Latin American players who had previously been barred from participation in the major leagues. Five decades after his first appearance in a Brooklyn Dodger uniform, African Americans have experienced significant economic gains as many racial barriers have fallen. Despite these well-documented gains, the effects of race and ethnicity on economic outcomes remain an issue of concern for policy makers and an area of research for economists.

Economists generally define labor market discrimination as "unequal treatment (for example, on the basis of race, gender, or age) of equally productive workers." To test whether discrimination exists, economists must first construct measures of productivity. In many occupations, however, objective measures of worker productivity are difficult to obtain. For this reason some economists have studied discrimination in professional sports. In baseball, for example, a number of easily obtained and "precise measures of productivity" exist. Once the effects of worker productivity have been taken into account, economists can estimate the effects of race and ethnicity on economic outcomes. If we find that race and/or ethnicity have a significant effect on economic outcomes, we can conclude that discrimination exists.

There are three possible sources of discrimination.

1. Employer discrimination can, for example, explain the existence of major league baseball's color line prior to 1947.

2. Co-workers can also be a source of discrimination. For example, some white workers might require a higher wage to work with minorities. One Brooklyn Dodger player asked to be traded when Jackie Robinson joined the team, and players on at least one competing team threatened to strike if Robinson played against them.

3. Customers can be a source of discrimination. For example, some white fans might prefer to attend games (i.e., purchase the product) in which a greater number of white players participate.

Labor market discrimination can take on several forms.

Salary discrimination is unequal pay to equally productive workers. To estimate the effects of race and ethnicity on players' salaries, economists first develop a salary equation where a player's salary is, for example, an increasing function of the player's productivity. Researchers then estimate whether the salary functions are affected by the player's race or ethnicity. In cases where race and ethnicity negatively affect player salaries, the difference in the salaries of equally productive white and, for example, African American players represents an estimate of the salary discrimination.

Hiring discrimination would occur if, for example, African American players must achieve higher performance levels to be hired or promoted from, say, the minor leagues to the major leagues.

Positional discrimination (or, equivalently, positional segregation) would occur when African Americans are underrepresented at particular playing positions on the fields.

A number of studies have examined whether these different sources and different forms of discrimination exist. While there is evidence of some salary discrimination against African American and Latin American baseball players in the 1960s and 1970s, there is no evidence of salary discrimination in the more recent 1980s and 1990s.

In contrast to baseball, there is evidence of salary discrimination against African American players in the National Basketball Association during the 1980s. The estimated negative effects of a professional basketball player's race in these salary equations suggest that the salary of an African American player was 11 percent to 25 percent less than that of an equally productive white player.

There is also some evidence of hiring discrimination and positional segregation in professional sports. In hockey, during the 1982 to 1984 seasons French-Canadians needed to achieve higher levels of performance to be chosen as high in the amateur draft as did English-Canadians. Researchers have also observed that African Americans are underrepresented at, for example, the pitcher and catcher positions in baseball and at the quarterback, kicker, and linebacker positions in football (during the 1960s and 1970s). And despite the very recent increases in the number of African Americans and Latin Americans in managerial positions, there remains concern that barriers to entry continue to exist for minorities. Former National Football League coach Bill Walsh argues that "those with the most influence have not necessarily been actively addressing the social undercurrent. I do not believe that any present owner is consciously racist. . . . But the core problem remains at the head coaching level."

Analysis of the effects of race and ethnicity on attendance at games and on team revenues indicates that customer discrimination also exists. In the 1960s, there was evidence that the presence of African American players had a negative effect on major league baseball teams' revenues. These negative effects no longer existed by the end of the 1970s. In basketball, a different picture emerges in the 1980s. There is evidence that African American players had a negative effect on fan attendance and that the racial composition of the team's geographic area affected the racial composition of the team during the 1980 to 1986 seasons. And finally, analysis of the market for baseball cards indicates that the player's race or ethnicity affects the price a card collector is willing to pay for that card.

Questions for Analytical Thinking

1. The average salary of African American players in the National Basketball Association (NBA) is higher than the average salary of white players in the NBA. To what extent does this difference in average salaries suggest that player race no longer affects player salaries in professional basketball? Explain.

2. Suppose you were asked to examine whether salary discrimination based on gender exists among faculty members at your college or university.
   a. Explain what type of information you would need to conduct such a study.
   b. What difficulties might you encounter in attempting to measure the productivity of faculty members? Explain.
   c. How might any difficulties you describe in part b hinder your ability to examine the existence of salary discrimination by gender? Explain.

3. A number of recent studies have examined whether racial discrimination exists in mortgage lending by banks. Discuss what type of information you would need to examine whether the race of loan applicants affects the lending behavior of banks.

4. A recent study indicates that a baseball player's race or ethnicity can negatively affect whether some members of the Baseball Writers' Association of America—the electors—vote for that player's induction into the National Baseball Hall of Fame. If this is true, how might the racial or ethnic biases of these writers represent an additional source of discrimination? Explain.

Sources: Torben Andersen and Sumner J. La Croix, "Customer Racial Discrimination in Major League Baseball," *Economic Inquiry*, October 1991, Vol. 29, pp. 665–677; Lynn Browne and Geoffrey Tootell, "Mortgage Lending in Boston—A Response to the Critics," *New England Economic Review*, Federal Reserve Bank of Boston, September/October 1995, pp. 53–78; David W. Findlay and Clifford E. Reid, "Voting Behavior, Discrimination and the National Baseball Hall of Fame," *Economic Inquiry*, Vol. 35, July 1997, pp. 562–578; Lawrence Kahn, "Discrimination in Professional Sports: A Survey of the Literature," *Industrial and Labor Relations Review*, April 1991, Vol. 44, No. 3, pp. 395–418; Clark Nardinelli and Curtis Simon, "Customer Racial Discrimination in the Market for Memorabilia: The Case of Baseball," *Quarterly Journal of Economics*, August 1990, Vol. 105, pp. 575–595; Bill Walsh, "Reaching Across the N.F.L. 'Color Line,'" *New York Times*, January 23, 1998.

MACROECONOMICS

PART FIVE

CONCEPTS AND PROBLEMS IN MACROECONOMICS

INTRODUCTION TO MACROECONOMICS

WE NOW BEGIN OUR STUDY of macroeconomics. We glimpsed the differences between microeconomics and macroeconomics in chapter 1. **Microeconomics** examines the functioning of individual industries and the behavior of individual decision-making units, typically business firms and households. With a few assumptions about how these units behave (firms maximize profits, households maximize utility), we can derive useful conclusions about how markets work, how resources are allocated, and so forth.

Macroeconomics, instead of focusing on the factors that influence the production of particular products and the behavior of individual industries, focuses on the determinants of total national output. Macroeconomics studies not household income but *national* income, not individual prices but the *overall* price level. It does not analyze the demand for labor in the automobile industry but rather total employment in the economy.

Both microeconomics and macroeconomics are concerned with the decisions of households and firms. Microeconomics deals with individual decisions, macroeconomics deals with the sum of these individual decisions. *Aggregate* is used in macroeconomics to refer to sums. When we speak of **aggregate behavior,** we mean the behavior of all households and firms together. We also speak of aggregate consumption and aggregate investment, which refer to total consumption and total investment in the economy.

Because microeconomists and macroeconomists look at the economy from different perspectives, you might expect they will reach somewhat different conclusions about the way the economy behaves. This is true to some extent. Microeconomists generally conclude that markets work well. They see prices as flexible, adjusting to maintain equality between quantity supplied and quantity demanded. Macroeconomists, however, observe that important prices in the economy—for example, the wage rate (or price of labor)—often seem "sticky." **Sticky prices** are prices that do not always adjust rapidly to maintain equality between quantity supplied and quantity demanded. Microeconomists do not expect to see the quantity of apples supplied exceeding the quantity of apples demanded, because the price of apples is not sticky. But macroeconomists—who analyze aggregate behavior—examine periods of high unemployment, where the quantity of labor

microeconomics *Deals with the functioning of individual industries and the behavior of individual decision-making units—business firms and households.*

macroeconomics *Deals with the economy as a whole. Macroeconomics focuses on the determinants of total national income, deals with aggregates such as aggregate consumption and investment, and looks at the overall level of prices rather than individual prices.*

aggregate behavior *The behavior of all households and firms together.*

sticky prices *Prices that do not always adjust rapidly to maintain equality between quantity supplied and quantity demanded.*

497

supplied appears to exceed the quantity of labor demanded. At such times, it appears that wage rates do not adjust fast enough to equate the quantity of labor supplied and the quantity of labor demanded.

Until recently, macroeconomists tended to be relatively uninterested in reconciling their analyses with the postulates and conclusions of microeconomic theory. The new trend among macroeconomists, however, is to try to make macroeconomic analysis consistent with microeconomic postulates—that is, with the idea that firms and households make their decisions along the lines suggested by microeconomic theory. If prices do not appear to adjust to equate the quantity supplied and the quantity demanded, for example, macroeconomists now look for solid microeconomic reasons why not. One of the aims of this book is to explain the **microeconomic foundations of macroeconomics**.

microeconomic foundations of macroeconomics *The microeconomic principles underlying macroeconomic analysis.*

THE ROOTS OF MACROECONOMICS

THE GREAT DEPRESSION

Great Depression *The period of severe economic contraction and high unemployment that began in 1929 and continued throughout the 1930s.*

Economic events of the 1930s, the decade of the **Great Depression**, spurred a great deal of thinking about macroeconomic issues. The 1920s had been prosperous years for the U.S. economy. Virtually everyone who wanted a job could get one, incomes rose substantially, and prices were stable. Beginning in late 1929, things took a sudden turn for the worse. In 1929, 1.5 million people were unemployed. By 1933, that had increased to 13 million out of a labor force of 51 million. In 1929, the United States produced $103 billion worth of new goods and services; by 1933, production had fallen to $55 billion, a drop of nearly 50 percent. In October of 1929, when stock prices collapsed on Wall Street, billions of dollars of personal wealth were lost. Unemployment remained above 14 percent of the labor force until 1940.

➤ **Classical Models** Before the Great Depression, economists applied microeconomic models, sometimes referred to as "classical models," to economy-wide problems. (The word *macroeconomics* was not invented until after World War II.) For example, classical supply and demand analysis assumed that an excess supply of labor would drive down wages to a new equilibrium level; as a result, unemployment would not persist.

In other words, classical economists believed that *recessions* (downturns in the economy) were self-correcting. As output falls and the demand for labor shifts to the left, the argument went, the wage rate will decline, thereby raising the quantity of labor demanded by firms who would want to hire more workers at the new lower wage rate. (Graph this movement along the new demand curve yourself.)

But, during the Great Depression unemployment levels remained very high for nearly 10 years. In large measure, the failure of simple classical models[1] to explain the prolonged existence of high unemployment provided the impetus for the development of macroeconomics. It is not surprising that what we now call macroeconomics was born in the 1930s.

➤ **The Keynesian Revolution** One of the most important works in the history of economics, *The General Theory of Employment, Interest and Money*, by John Maynard Keynes, was published in 1936. Building on what was already understood about markets and their behavior, Keynes set out to construct a theory that would explain the confusing economic events of his time.

[1]Classical models are also sometimes known as "market clearing" models because they emphasize that prices and wages adjust to ensure that markets always clear—that is, that the quantity supplied is equal to the quantity demanded.

Much of macroeconomics has roots in Keynes's work. According to Keynes, it is not prices and wages that determine the level of employment, as classical models had suggested, but rather the level of aggregate demand for goods and services. Keynes believed governments could intervene in the economy and affect the level of output and employment. The government's role during periods when private demand is low, Keynes argued, is to stimulate aggregate demand and, by so doing, to lift the economy out of recession. (See Application box, "The Great Depression and John Maynard Keynes.")

RECENT MACROECONOMIC HISTORY

After World War II, and especially in the 1950s, Keynes's views began to gain increasing influence over both professional economists and government policy makers. Governments came to believe they could intervene in their economies to attain specific employment and output goals, and they began to use their powers to tax and spend, as well as their ability to affect interest rates and the money supply, for the explicit purpose of controlling the economy's ups and downs. This view of government policy became firmly established in the United States with the passage of the Employment Act of 1946. This act established the President's Council of Economic Advisors, a group of economists who advise the president on economic issues. It also committed the federal government to intervening in the economy to prevent large declines in output and employment.

➤ **Fine Tuning in the 1960s** The notion that the government could, and should, act to stabilize the macroeconomy reached the height of its popularity in the 1960s. During these years, Walter Heller, the chairman of the Council of Economic Advisors under both President Kennedy and President Johnson, alluded to **fine tuning** as the government's role in regulating inflation and unemployment. During the 1960s, many economists believed the government could use the tools available to manipulate unemployment and inflation levels fairly precisely.

fine tuning *The phrase used by Walter Heller to refer to the government's role in regulating inflation and unemployment.*

➤ **Disillusionment Since the 1970s** Since 1970, the U.S. economy has been through a series of wide fluctuations in employment, output, and inflation. In 1974 to 1975 and again in 1980 to 1982, the United States experienced severe recessions. While not as catastrophic as the Great Depression of the 1930s, these recessions left millions without jobs and resulted in billions of dollars of lost output and income. In 1974 to 1975 and again in 1979 to 1981, the United States saw very high rates of inflation. The U.S. economy also experienced a moderate recession in 1990 to 1991 and very slow growth for about two years after the recession. (We discuss these events in more detail in later chapters.)

Moreover, the 1970s witnessed the birth of **stagflation** (stagnation + inflation). Stagflation occurs when the overall price level rises rapidly (inflation) during periods of recession or high and persistent unemployment (stagnation). Until the 1970s, rapidly rising prices had been observed only in periods when the economy was prospering and unemployment was low (or at least declining). The problem of stagflation was vexing, both for macroeconomic theorists and for policy makers concerned with the health of the economy.

It was clear by 1975 that the macroeconomy was more difficult to control than either Heller's words or textbook theory had led economists to believe. The events of the 1970s and afterward have had an important influence on macroeconomic theory. Much of the faith in the simple Keynesian model and the "conventional wisdom" of the 1960s has been lost. New ways of understanding the behavior of the macroeconomy have been proposed, but as yet there is no consensus as to which explanation is best. It is precisely this flux in macroeconomics, the sense that the discipline is wide open and that many of the most important issues have yet to be resolved, that makes it so exciting to study.

stagflation *Occurs when the overall price level rises rapidly (inflation) during periods of recession or high and persistent unemployment (stagnation).*

THE GREAT DEPRESSION AND JOHN MAYNARD KEYNES

Much of the framework of modern macroeconomics comes from the works of John Maynard Keynes, whose *General Theory of Employment, Interest and Money* was published in 1936. The following excerpt by Robert L. Heilbroner provides some insights into Keynes's life and work.

> By 1933 the nation was virtually prostrate. On street corners, in homes, in Hoovervilles (communities of makeshift shacks), 14 million unemployed sat, haunting the land . . . .
>
> It was the unemployment that was hardest to bear. The jobless millions were like an embolism in the nation's vital circulation; and while their indisputable existence argued more forcibly than any text that something was wrong with the system, the economists wrung their hands and racked their brains . . . . but could offer neither diagnosis nor remedy. Unemployment—this kind of unemployment—was simply not listed among the possible ills of the system: it was absurd, impossible,

> unreasonable, and paradoxical. But it was there.
>
> It would seem logical that the man who would seek to solve this impossible paradox of not enough production existing side by side with men fruitlessly seeking work would be a Left-winger, an economist with strong sympathies for the proletariat, an angry man. Nothing could be further from the fact. The man who tackled it was almost a dilettante with nothing like a chip on his shoulder. The simple truth was that his talents inclined in every direction. He had, for example, written a most recondite book on mathematical probability, a book that Bertrand Russell had declared "impossible to praise too highly"; then he had gone on to match his skill in abstruse logic with a flair for making money—he accumulated a fortune of £500,000 by way of the most treacherous of all roads to riches: dealing in international currencies and commodities. More impressive yet, he had written his mathematics treatise on the side, as it were, while engaged

JOHN MAYNARD KEYNES.

in Government service, and he piled up his private wealth by applying himself for only half an hour a day while still abed.

> But this is only a sample of his many-sidedness. He was an economist, of course—a Cambridge don with all the dignity and erudition

MACROECONOMIC CONCERNS

Three of the major concerns of macroeconomics are *inflation*, *output growth*, and *unemployment*. Government policy makers would like to have low inflation, high output growth, and low unemployment. They may not be able to achieve these goals, but the goals themselves are clear. (The effectiveness of government policies is the subject of later chapters.)

One troublesome fact should be kept in mind throughout this discussion:

> Almost all macroeconomic events are interrelated—making progress on one front often means making conditions worse on another.

For example, some economists believe the only way to cure inflation is to put the economy into a recession (increasing unemployment and lowering output). Not all the good things we want may be compatible with each other, alas. Macroeconomics is rife with trade-offs! One aim of the following chapters is to explore and explain the nature of these trade-offs.

THE GREAT DEPRESSION PERSISTED LONG AFTER THE STOCK MARKET CRASH IN 1929.

that go with such an appointment. . . . He managed to be simultaneously the darling of the Bloomsbury set, the cluster of Britain's most avant-garde intellectual brilliants, and also the chairman of a life insurance company, a niche in life rarely noted for its intellectual abandon. He was a pillar of stability in delicate matters of international diplomacy, but his official correctness did not prevent

him from acquiring a knowledge of other European politicians that included their . . . neuroses and financial prejudices . . . . He ran a theater, and he came to be a Director of the Bank of England. He knew Roosevelt and Churchill and also Bernard Shaw and Pablo Picasso. . . .

His name was John Maynard Keynes, an old British name (pronounced to rhyme with "rains")

that could be traced back to one William de Cahagnes and 1066. Keynes was a traditionalist; he liked to think that greatness ran in families, and it is true that his own father was John Neville Keynes, an illustrious enough economist in his own right. But it took more than the ordinary gifts of heritage to account for the son; it was as if the talents that would have sufficed half a dozen men were by happy accident crowded into one person.

By a coincidence he was born in 1883, in the very year that Karl Marx passed away. But the two economists who thus touched each other in time, although each was to exert the profoundest influence on the philosophy of the capitalist system, could hardly have differed from one another more. Marx was bitter, at bay, heavy and disappointed; as we know, he was the draftsman of Capitalism Doomed. Keynes loved life and sailed through it buoyant, at ease, and consummately successful to become the architect of Capitalism Viable.[a]

Source: [a]Reprinted with the permission of Simon & Schuster from *The Worldly Philosophers* by Robert L. Heilbroner. Copyright © 1953, 1961, 1967, 1972, 1980, 1986 by Robert L. Heilbroner. Also reprinted with permission of Penguin Books Limited, U.K.

 For more on John Maynard Keynes, Keynesian economics, and the Great Depression, see the Case and Fair Web page at http://www.prenhall.com/casefair.

INFLATION

Inflation is an increase in the overall price level. The reduction of inflation has long been a goal of government policy. Especially problematic are **hyperinflations**, or periods of very rapid increases in the overall price level.

Most Americans are unaware of what life is like under very high inflation. In some countries people are accustomed to prices rising by the day, by the hour, or even by the minute. During the hyperinflation in Bolivia in 1984 and 1985, the price of one egg rose from 3,000 pesos to 10,000 pesos in one week. In 1985, three bottles of aspirin sold for the same price as a luxury car had sold for in 1982. At the same time, the problem of handling money became a burden. Banks stopped counting deposits—a $500 deposit was equivalent to about 32 million pesos, and it just did not make sense to count a huge sack full of bills. Bolivia's currency, printed in West Germany and England, was the country's third biggest import in 1984, surpassed only by wheat and mining equipment.

Skyrocketing prices in Bolivia are a small part of the story. When inflation approaches rates of 2,000 percent per year, the economy, and the whole organization, of a country begin to break down. Workers may go on strike to demand wage increases in

inflation *An increase in the overall price level.*

hyperinflation *A period of very rapid increases in the overall price level.*

CHAPTER TWENTY-ONE
Introduction to Macroeconomics

501

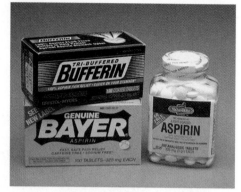

WITH THE MONEY YOU NEEDED TO BUY A LUXURY CAR SUCH AS THIS ONE IN 1982, YOU COULD BUY NO MORE THAN THREE BOTTLES OF HEADACHE PAINKILLER IN 1985—HYPERINFLATION IN BOLIVIA.

business cycle *The cycle of short-term ups and downs in the economy.*

aggregate output *The total quantity of goods and services produced in an economy in a given period.*

recession *A period during which aggregate output declines. Conventionally, a period in which aggregate output declines for two consecutive quarters.*

depression *A prolonged and deep recession.*

line with the high inflation rate, firms find it almost impossible to secure credit, and the economy grinds to a halt. Fortunately, hyperinflations usually end very abruptly. In a few months, Bolivia went from having the highest inflation rate in the world to one of the lowest inflation rates in the Western Hemisphere.

Hyperinflations are rare. Nonetheless, economists have devoted much effort to identifying the costs and consequences of even moderate inflation. Who gains from inflation? Who loses? What costs does inflation impose on society? How severe are they? What causes inflation? What is the best way to stop it? We will focus on some of these questions in chapters 23 and 29 where we will see that inflation is a major issue in macroeconomics.

OUTPUT GROWTH

Rather than grow at an even rate at all times, economies tend to experience short-term ups and downs in their performance. The technical name for these ups and downs is the **business cycle**. The main measure of how an economy is doing is **aggregate output,** the total quantity of goods and services produced in the economy in a given period. When less is produced (in other words, when aggregate output decreases), there are fewer goods and services to go around, and the average standard of living declines. When firms cut back on production, they also lay off workers, increasing the rate of unemployment.

Recessions are periods during which aggregate output declines. It has become conventional to classify an economic downturn as a "recession" when aggregate output declines for two consecutive quarters. A prolonged and deep recession is called a **depression,** although economists do not agree on when a recession becomes a depression. Since the beginning of the twentieth century, the United States has experienced one depression (during the 1930s), three severe recessions (1946, 1974 to 1975, and 1980 to 1982), and a number of less severe, shorter recessions (1954, 1958, 1970, and 1990 to 1991). Other countries have also experienced recessions in the twentieth century, some roughly coinciding with U.S. recessions, some not. In 1994, while the U.S. recovery was under way, Japan was still in a recession.

Devising explanations for and predicting the business cycle, macroeconomics tries to address: Why does the economy fluctuate so much? Why at times does it not seem to respond to the simple forces of supply and demand?

There is more to output than its up-and-down movements during business cycles. The size of the growth rate of output over a long period (longer, say, than the typical length of a business cycle) is also of concern to macroeconomists and policy makers. If the growth rate of output is greater than the growth rate of the population, there is a growing amount of goods and services produced per person. So, on average, people are becoming better off. Policy makers are thus concerned not only with smoothing fluctuations in output during a business cycle but also with policies that might increase the long-run growth rate. Long-run growth issues are taken up in chapters 23 and 24.

UNEMPLOYMENT

You cannot listen to the news or read a newspaper without noticing that data on the unemployment rate are released each month. The **unemployment rate**—the percentage of the labor force unemployed—is a key indicator of the economy's health. Because the unemployment rate is usually closely related to the economy's aggregate output, announcements of each month's new figure are followed with great interest by economists, politicians, and policy makers.

Although macroeconomists are interested in learning why the unemployment rate has risen or fallen in a given period, they also try to answer a more basic question: Why is there any unemployment at all? We do not expect to see zero unemployment. At any time, some firms may go bankrupt due to competition from rivals, bad management, or bad luck. Employees of such firms typically are not able to find new jobs immediately, and while they are looking for work, they will be unemployed. Also, workers entering the labor market for the first time may require a few weeks, or months, to find a job.

If we base our analysis on supply and demand, as we have in all our discussions so far, we would expect conditions to change in response to the existence of unemployed workers. Specifically, when there is unemployment beyond some minimum amount, there is an excess supply of workers—at the going wage rates, there are people who want to work who cannot find work. In microeconomic theory, the response to excess supply is a decrease in the price of the commodity in question and therefore an increase in the quantity demanded, a reduction in the quantity supplied, and the restoration of equilibrium. With the quantity supplied equal to the quantity demanded, the market clears.

The existence of unemployment seems to imply that the aggregate labor market is not in equilibrium—that something prevents the quantity supplied and the quantity demanded from equating. But why do labor markets not clear when other markets do? Or is it that labor markets are clearing and the unemployment data are reflecting something different? The implications of the unemployment data, a major puzzle in macroeconomics, are the focus of chapters 23 and 30.

GOVERNMENT IN THE MACROECONOMY

Much of our discussion of macroeconomics concerns the potential role of government in influencing the economy. There are three kinds of policy that the government has used to influence the macroeconomy:

Government policies for influencing the macroeconomy	1. fiscal policy 2. monetary policy 3. growth or supply-side policies

▶ **Fiscal Policy** One way the federal government affects the economy is through its tax and expenditure decisions, or **fiscal policy**. The federal government collects taxes from households and firms and spends these funds on items ranging from missiles to parks to social security payments to interstate highways. Both the magnitude and composition of these taxes and expenditures have a major effect on the economy.

One of Keynes's main ideas in the 1930s was that fiscal policy could and should be used to stabilize the level of output and employment. Specifically, Keynes believed the government should cut taxes and/or raise spending—called *expansionary fiscal policies*—to get the economy out of a slump. Conversely, he held that the government should raise taxes and/or cut spending—called *contractionary fiscal policies*—to bring the economy out of an inflation.

FAST FACTS

Unemployment rates vary from country to country. In 1997, 4.9% of the workforce in the United States was unemployed; the figure was 3.4% in Japan, 5.3% in Great Britain, 8.6% in Australia, 11.7% in Germany, 12.4% in Italy, and 20.8% in Spain. Unemployment is difficult to measure in the emerging economies.

Source: The Economist, October 11–17, 1997.

fiscal policy *Government policies regarding taxes and expenditures.*

GRAFFITI SCULPTURE? NO, IT'S WHAT REMAINS OF THE BERLIN WALL, WHICH HAD SEPARATED THE TWO HALVES OF BERLIN BETWEEN 1961 AND 1989, WHEN THE WALL WAS DISMANTLED. SINCE THEN, THE REUNIFIED GERMANY HAS FACED MANY ECONOMIC CHALLENGES. MACROECONOMICS STUDIES NOT ONLY WHAT HAS HAPPENED IN GERMANY SINCE 1989, BUT ALSO HOW ECONOMIC EVENTS IN GERMANY AFFECT THE REST OF THE WORLD.

monetary policy *The tools used by the Federal Reserve to control the money supply.*

➤ **Monetary Policy**   Taxes and spending are not the only variables the government controls. Through the Federal Reserve, the nation's central bank,[2] the government can determine the quantity of money in the economy. The effects and proper role of **monetary policy** are among the most hotly debated subjects in macroeconomics. Most economists agree that the quantity of money supplied affects the overall price level, interest rates and exchange rates, the unemployment rate, and the level of output. The main controversies arise regarding how monetary policy manifests itself and exactly how large its effects are.

➤ **Growth Policies**   Many economists are skeptical about the government's ability to regulate the business cycle with any degree of precision using monetary and fiscal policy. Their view is that the focus of government policy should be to stimulate aggregate supply—to stimulate the potential growth of aggregate output and income. A host of policies have been aimed at increasing the rate of growth. Many of these are targeted at specific markets and are largely discussed in microeconomics. One major worry of macroeconomists is that government borrowing to finance excesses of spending over tax collections (the "deficit") is sopping up saving that would otherwise flow to businesses to be used for investment in capital. Another focus of pro-growth government policies has been the tax system. A major goal of tax reforms in 1981 and 1986 was to increase the incentive to work, save, and invest by lowering tax rates. In addition, the Taxpayer Relief Act of 1997 included a number of pro-growth measures that we will discuss later. These are sometimes referred to as **supply-side policies**. (See Application box, "Shift of Focus Toward Growth During the 1990s.")

supply-side policies *Government policies that focus on aggregate supply and increasing production rather than stimulating aggregate demand.*

THE COMPONENTS OF THE MACROECONOMY

Macroeconomics focuses on four groups: *households* and *firms* (the private sector), the *government* (the public sector), and the *rest of the world* (the international sector). We provided data on each in chapter 3. These four groups interact in a variety of ways, many involving either the receipt or payment of income.

THE CIRCULAR FLOW DIAGRAM

A useful way of seeing the economic interactions among the four sectors in the economy is a **circular flow** diagram, which shows the income received and payments made by each. A simple circular flow diagram is pictured in Figure 21.1.

circular flow *A diagram showing the income received and payments made by each sector of the economy.*

[2]The Federal Reserve is a quasi-independent agency, and it does not always do what the president or Congress wants it to do. Nevertheless, because it is part of the government rather than part of the private sector, we consider it in this section.

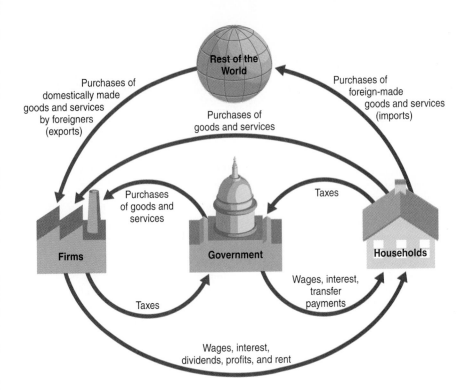

FIGURE 21.1

The Circular Flow of Payments

Households receive income from firms and the government, purchase goods and services from firms, and pay taxes to the government. They also purchase foreign-made goods and services (imports). Firms receive payments from households and the government for goods and services; they pay wages, dividends, interest, and rents to households, and taxes to the government. The government receives taxes from both firms and households, pays both firms and households for goods and services—including wages to government workers—and pays interest and transfers to households. Finally, people in other countries purchase goods and services produced domestically (exports). *Note:* Though not shown in this diagram, firms and governments also purchase imports.

Let's walk through the circular flow step by step. Households work for firms and the government, and they receive wages for their work. Our diagram shows a flow of wages *into* the household sector as payment for those services. Households also receive interest on corporate and government bonds and dividends from firms. Many households receive other payments from the government, such as social security benefits, veterans' benefits, and welfare payments. Economists call these kinds of payments from the government (for which the recipients do not supply goods, services, or labor) **transfer payments**. Together, all these receipts make up the total income received by the households.

Households spend by buying goods and services from firms and by paying taxes to the government. These items make up the total amount paid out by the households. The difference between the total receipts and the total payments of the households is the amount that the households save or dissave.[3] If households receive more than they spend, they *save* during the period. If they receive less than they spend, they *dissave*. A household can dissave by using up some of its previous savings or by borrowing. In the circular flow diagram, household spending is shown as a flow *out* of the household sector.

Firms sell goods and services to households and the government. These sales earn revenue, which shows up in the circular flow diagram as a flow *into* the firm sector. Firms pay wages, interest, and dividends to households, and they pay taxes to the government. These payments are shown flowing *out* of the firm sector.

The government collects taxes from households and firms. The government also makes payments. It buys goods and services from firms, pays wages and interest to households, and makes transfer payments to households. If the government's revenue is less than its payments, the government is dissaving.

Finally, households spend some of their income on *imports*—goods and services produced in the rest of the world. Similarly, people in foreign countries purchase *exports*—goods and services produced by domestic firms and sold to other countries.

transfer payments *Cash payments made by the government to people who do not supply goods, services, or labor in exchange for these payments. They include social security benefits, veterans' benefits, and welfare payments.*

---

[3]Saving by households is sometimes termed a "leakage" from the circular flow because it withdraws income, or current purchasing power, from the system.

SHIFT OF FOCUS TOWARD GROWTH DURING THE 1990s

The recession of 1990 to 1991 ended during the second quarter of 1991. Between 1991 and 1998 the U.S. economy experienced a period of relative stability—low inflation; and the lowest rates of unemployment in 25 years. This led policy makers to focus more attention on the growth of output/income. You can see the focus in the following excerpts from the *1997 Economic Report of the President*:

> The sources of economic growth can be grouped under three headings: increases in physical capital, improvements in human capital, and increases in the overall efficiency of the economy—the amount of output per unit of input. The Administration's economic agenda is based on strengthening each of these three pillars of economic growth.

INCREASING PHYSICAL CAPITAL

The first pillar of economic growth is increases in physical capital, which enables workers to produce more goods and services. Because it reduces the government's borrowing, deficit reduction will remain the key to how much of national saving is available for private investment in physical capital.

IMPROVING HUMAN CAPITAL

The second pillar of economic growth is improvements in what economists call human capital: the knowledge, experience, and skills of the workforce. As the economy has changed, the demands imposed on the brainpower of the American workforce have increased enormously. . . . the President has set ambitious goals for the Nation's education system: every 8-year-old should be able to read, every 12-year-old should be able to log onto the Internet, every 18-year-old should be able to go to college, and every classroom and library in America should be linked to the Internet.

An array of policies, current and proposed, are directed toward achieving these goals.

RESEARCH AND DEVELOPMENT

The third pillar of growth is greater economic efficiency—learning to produce more output with fewer inputs. Additions to the Nation's technological arsenal through research and development are an important contributor to efficiency: private industry invests over $100 billion in research and

development each year. This is a huge sum, but it may not be enough: history and economic theory suggest that, left to their own devices, private firms will not invest sufficiently in improving technology, because they themselves do not realize the full benefit therefrom.

INCREASING COMPETITION

Improving the efficiency of the economy is not just a matter of improving technology. How the economy is organized plays just as important a role in creating incentives for firms to use their capital and labor as efficiently as possible. If the market economy is to deliver on its promise of growth and prosperity, markets have to be competitive, because it is competition that drives firms to be efficient and innovative.

EXPANDING TRADE

The third source of increasing efficiency in the economy is more-open markets abroad. Like the freeing up of domestic markets, opening of foreign markets shifts resources into relatively more productive areas.

For more on economic growth, see the Case and Fair Web page at
http://www.prenhall.com/casefair.

One lesson of the circular flow diagram is that everyone's expenditure is someone else's receipt. If you buy a personal computer from IBM, you make a payment to IBM and IBM receives revenue. If IBM pays taxes to the government, it has made a payment and the government has received revenue.

> Everyone's expenditures go somewhere. It is impossible to sell something without there being a buyer, and it is impossible to make a payment without there being a recipient. Every transaction must have two sides.

THE THREE MARKET ARENAS

Another way of looking at the ways households, firms, the government, and the rest of the world relate to each other is to consider the markets in which they interact, as depicted in Figure 21.2.

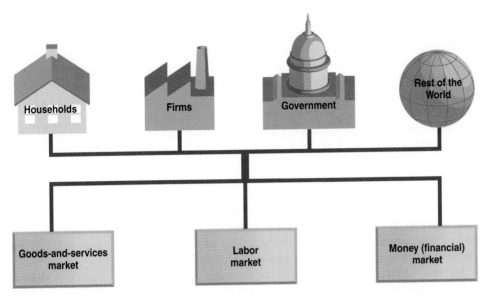

FIGURE 21.2

The Three Basic Markets
Households, firms, the
government, and the rest
of the world all interact in
the goods-and-services, labor,
and money markets.

The three	1. goods-and-services market
market	2. labor market
arenas	3. money (financial) market

➤ **Goods-and-Services Market**   Households and the government purchase goods and services from firms in the *goods-and-services market*. In this market, firms also purchase goods and services from each other. For example, Levi Strauss buys denim from other firms to make its blue jeans. In addition, firms buy capital goods from other firms. If General Motors needs new robots on its assembly lines, it will probably buy them from another firm rather than make them itself.

Firms *supply* to the goods-and-services market. Households, the government, and firms *demand* from this market. Finally, the rest of the world both buys from and sells to the goods-and-services market. As we mentioned in chapter 3, the United States now imports hundreds of billions of dollars worth of automobiles, VCRs, oil, and other goods. At the same time, the United States exports hundreds of billions of dollars worth of computers, airplanes, and agricultural goods.

➤ **Labor Market**   Interaction in the *labor market* takes place when firms and the government purchase labor from households. In this market, households *supply* labor, and firms and the government *demand* labor. In the U.S. economy, firms are the largest demanders of labor, although the government is also a substantial employer. The total supply of labor in the economy depends on the sum of decisions made by households. Individuals must decide whether to enter the labor force (whether to look for a job at all) and how many hours to work.

Labor is also supplied to and demanded from the rest of the world. In recent years, the labor market has become an international market. For example, vegetable and fruit farmers in California would find it very difficult to bring their product to market if it were not for the labor of migrant farm workers from Mexico. For years, Turkey has provided Germany with "guest workers" who are willing to take low-paying jobs that more prosperous German workers avoid.

➤ **Money Market**   In the *money market*—sometimes called the *financial market*—households purchase stocks and bonds from firms. Households *supply* funds to this market in the expectation of earning income in the form of dividends on stocks and interest on bonds. Households also *demand* (borrow) funds from this market to finance various purchases. Firms borrow to build new facilities in the hope of earning more in the future. The government borrows by issuing bonds. The rest of the world both borrows from and lends to the money market; every morning there are reports on TV and radio about the Japanese and British stock markets. Much of the borrowing and lending of households, firms, the government, and the international sector is coordinated by financial institutions—commercial banks, savings and loan associations, insurance companies, and the like. These institutions take deposits from one group and lend them to others.

When a firm, a household, or the government borrows to finance a purchase, it has an obligation to pay that loan back, usually at some specified time in the future. Most loans also involve payment of interest as a fee for the use of the borrowed funds. When a loan is made, the borrower nearly always signs a "promise to repay," or *promissory note*, and gives it to the lender. When the federal government borrows, it issues "promises" called **Treasury bonds, notes,** or **bills** in exchange for money. Corporations issue **corporate bonds**. A corporate bond might state, for example, "General Electric Corporation agrees to pay $5,000 to the holder of this bond on January 1, 2001, and interest thereon at 8.3 percent annually until that time."

Instead of issuing bonds to raise funds, firms can also issue shares of stock. A **share of stock** is a financial instrument that gives the holder a share in the firm's ownership and therefore the right to share in the firm's profits. If the firm does well, the value of the stock increases, and the stockholder receives a *capital gain*[4] on the initial purchase. In addition, the stock may pay **dividends**—that is, the firm may return some of its profits directly to its stockholders, rather than retain them to buy capital. If the firm does poorly, so does the stockholder. The capital value of the stock may fall, and dividends may not be paid.

Stocks and bonds are simply contracts, or agreements, between parties. I agree to loan you a certain amount, and you agree to repay me this amount plus something extra at some future date. Or I agree to buy part ownership in your firm, and you agree to give me a share of the firm's future profits.

A critical variable in the money market is the *interest rate*. Although we sometimes talk as if there were only one interest rate, there is never just one interest rate at any time. Rather, the interest rate on a given loan reflects the length of the loan and the perceived risk to the lender. A business that is just getting started will have to pay a higher rate than will General Motors. A 30-year mortgage has a different interest rate than a 90-day loan. Nevertheless, interest rates tend to move up and down together, and their movement reflects general conditions in the financial market. (We discuss interest rates in later chapters.)

THE METHODOLOGY OF MACROECONOMICS

Macroeconomists build models based on theories, and they test their models using data. In this sense, the methodology of macroeconomics is similar to the methodology of microeconomics.

CONNECTIONS TO MICROECONOMICS

How do macroeconomists try to explain aggregate behavior? One way assumes that the same factors that affect individual behavior also affect aggregate behavior. For example, we know from microeconomics that an individual's wage rate should affect her consumption habits and the amount of labor she is willing to supply. If we were to apply this microeconomic hypothesis to the aggregate data, we would say that the average wage rate in the economy should affect total consumption and total labor supply (which seems to be true).

Treasury bonds, notes, and **bills** *Promissory notes issued by the federal government when it borrows money.*

corporate bonds *Promissory notes issued by corporations when they borrow money.*

shares of stock *Financial instruments that give to the holder a share in the firm's ownership and therefore the right to share in the firm's profits.*

dividends *The portion of a corporation's profits that the firm pays out each period to its shareholders.*

---

[4]A *capital gain* occurs whenever the value of an asset increases. If you bought a stock for $1,000 and it is now worth $1,500, you have earned a capital gain of $500. A capital gain is "realized" when you sell the asset. Until you sell, the capital gain is *accrued* but not *realized*.

The reason for looking to microeconomics for help in explaining macroeconomic events is simple:

> Macroeconomic behavior is the sum of all the microeconomic decisions made by individual households and firms. If the movements of macroeconomic aggregates, such as total output or total employment, reflect decisions made by individual firms and households, we cannot understand the former without some knowledge of the factors that influence the latter.

Consider unemployment. The unemployment rate is the number of people unemployed as a fraction of the labor force. To be classified as "in the labor force," a person must either have a job or be seeking one actively. To understand aggregate unemployment, we need to understand individual household behavior in the labor market. Why do people choose to enter the labor force? Under what circumstances will they drop out? Why does unemployment exist even when the economy seems to be doing very well? A knowledge of microeconomic behavior is the logical starting point for macroeconomic analysis.

AGGREGATE DEMAND AND AGGREGATE SUPPLY

A major theme through the next few chapters is the behavior of aggregate demand and aggregate supply. **Aggregate demand** is the total demand for goods and services. **Aggregate supply** is the total supply of goods and services.

Figure 21.3 shows *aggregate demand* and *aggregate supply* curves. Measured on the horizontal axis is aggregate output. Measured on the vertical axis is the *overall price level*, not the price of a particular good or service—very important to keep it in mind. The economy is in equilibrium at the point at which these curves intersect.

As you will discover, aggregate demand and supply curves are much more complicated than the simple demand and supply curves we described in chapters 4 and 5. The simple logic of supply, demand, and equilibrium in individual markets does not explain what is depicted in Figure 21.3. It will take the entire next chapter for us to describe what is meant by "aggregate output" and the "overall price level." Furthermore, although we will look to the behavior of households and firms in individual markets for clues about how to analyze aggregate behavior, there are important differences when we move from the individual to the aggregate level.

aggregate demand *The total demand for goods and services in an economy.*

aggregate supply *The total supply of goods and services in an economy.*

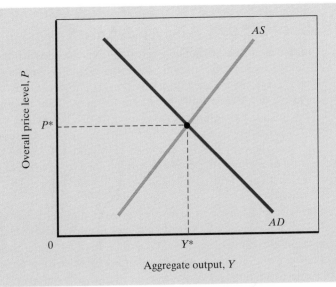

FIGURE 21.3

The Aggregate Demand and Aggregate Supply Curves

A major theme in macroeconomics is the behavior of aggregate demand and aggregate supply. The logic behind the aggregate demand and aggregate supply curves is much more complex than the logic underlying the simple demand and supply curves described in chapters 4 and 5.

Consider, for example, *demand*, one of the most important concepts in economics. When the price of a specific good increases, perhaps the most important determinant of consumer response is the availability of other goods that can be substituted for the good whose price has increased. Part of the reason that an increase in the price of airline tickets causes a decline in the quantity of airline tickets demanded is that a higher price relative to other goods means that the opportunity cost of buying a ticket is higher: The sacrifice required in terms of other goods and services has increased. But when the overall price level changes, there may be no changes at all in relative prices. When analyzing the behavior of aggregate demand, the availability of substitutes is irrelevant.

Microeconomics teaches us that, *ceteris paribus*, the quantity demanded of a good falls when its price rises and rises when its price falls. (This is the microeconomic law of demand.) In other words, individual demand curves and market demand curves slope downward to the right. The reason the *aggregate* demand curve in Figure 21.3 slopes downward to the right is complex. As we will see later, the downward slope of the aggregate demand curve is related to what goes on in the money (financial) market.

The aggregate supply curve is very different from the supply curve of an individual firm or market. A firm's supply curve is derived under the assumption that all its input prices are fixed. In other words, the firm's input prices are assumed to remain unchanged as the price of the firm's output changes. When we derived Clarence Brown's soybean supply schedule in chapter 4, we took his input prices as fixed. A change in an input price leads to a shift in Brown's supply curve, not a movement along it. If we are examining changes in the overall price level, however, *all* prices are changing (including input prices), so the aggregate supply curve cannot be based on the assumption of fixed input prices. We will see that the aggregate supply curve is a source of controversy in macroeconomics.

Because of the complexity of the aggregate demand and aggregate supply curves, we will need to build our analysis piece by piece. In chapter 22, we discuss the methods of measuring economic activity and aggregate output. In chapter 23, we describe the key macroeconomic problems of business cycles, inflation, and unemployment. Chapters 24 through 29 present the material we need to understand the equilibrium levels of aggregate output and the overall price level. In these chapters, we discuss the behavior of households, firms, and the government in both the goods-and-services market and the money market. Chapter 30 brings the labor market into the picture. Later chapters elaborate on this material and discuss a number of macroeconomic policy issues.

THE U.S. ECONOMY IN THE TWENTIETH CENTURY: TRENDS AND CYCLES

As we said, most macroeconomic variables go through ups and downs over time, and the economy as a whole experiences periods of prosperity and periods of recession. The trend of the U.S. economy in the twentieth century, however, has been toward prosperity. One measure of an economy's prosperity is the amount of goods and services that it produces during a year, or its gross domestic product (GDP, the subject of the next chapter). An economy is said to grow from one year to another if GDP is larger in the second year than in the first. Between 1900 and 1997, the U.S. economy grew at an average rate of 3.4 percent per year. During those years the economy was on average 3.4 percent richer each year than it had been the year before. This is the economy's "long-run" growth rate.

Remember that we are discussing the average growth rate here. The economy did not actually grow by 3.4 percent every year. In some years, growth was less than 3 percent, and in some years growth was negative (GDP fell). In other years, the growth rate was greater than 3.4 percent. So, we need to distinguish between *long-term*, or *secular*, *trends* in economic performance and *short-term*, or *cyclical*, *variations*.

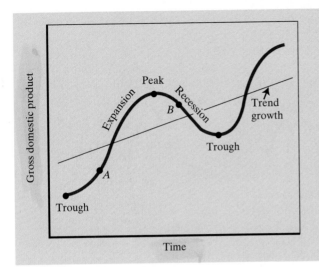

FIGURE 21.4

A Typical Business Cycle

In this business cycle, the economy is expanding as it moves through point *A* from the trough to the peak. When the economy moves from a peak down to a trough, through point *B*, the economy is in recession.

EXPANSION AND CONTRACTION: THE BUSINESS CYCLE

Macroeconomics is concerned both with long-run trends—Why has the U.S. economy done so well over the past 100 years while Great Britain's has done rather poorly?—and with short-run fluctuations in economic performance—Why did the world experience a severe recession in the early 1980s? Most of this part of the text focuses on short-run fluctuations, known as the *business cycle*, because they are somewhat better understood. A typical business cycle is illustrated in Figure 21.4.

Because the U.S. economy on average grows over time, the business cycle in Figure 21.4 shows a positive trend—the *peak* (the highest point) of a new business cycle is higher than the peak of the previous cycle. The period from a *trough*, or bottom of the cycle, to a peak is called an **expansion** or a **boom**. During an expansion, output and employment grow. The period from a peak to a trough is called a **contraction, recession,** or **slump,** when output and employment fall.

In judging whether an economy is expanding or contracting, note the difference between the level of economic activity and its rate of change. If the economy has just left a trough (point *A* in Figure 21.4), it will be growing (rate of change is positive), but its level of output will still be low. If the economy has just started to decline from a peak (point *B*), it will be contracting (rate of change is negative), but its level of output will still be high.

The business cycle in Figure 21.4 is symmetric, which means the length of an expansion is the same as the length of a contraction. All business cycles are not symmetric, however. It is possible, for example, for the expansion phase to be longer than the contraction phase. When contraction comes, it may be fast and sharp, while expansion may be slow and gradual. Moreover, the economy is not nearly as regular as the business cycle in Figure 21.4 indicates. While there are ups and downs in the economy, they tend to be erratic.

What do actual business cycles in the United States look like? See Figure 21.5, where the percentage deviation of U.S. GDP around its trend is plotted for 1900 to 1997. Although many business cycles have occurred in the last nine decades, each has been unique. The economy is not so simple that it has regular cycles.

The periods of the Great Depression and World War II are the low and high points of Figure 21.5, although other large contractions and expansions have taken place. Note the expansion in the 1960s and the recessions at the beginning of the 1980s and 1990s. Some of the cycles have been long, some have been very short. Note also that GDP actually increased between 1933 and 1937, even though at its peak in 1937 GDP was still quite low. The economy did not really come out of the Depression until the defense buildup prior to the start of World War II.

expansion or **boom** *The period in the business cycle from a trough up to a peak, during which output and employment rise.*

contraction, recession, or **slump** *The period in the business cycle from a peak down to a trough, during which output and employment fall.*

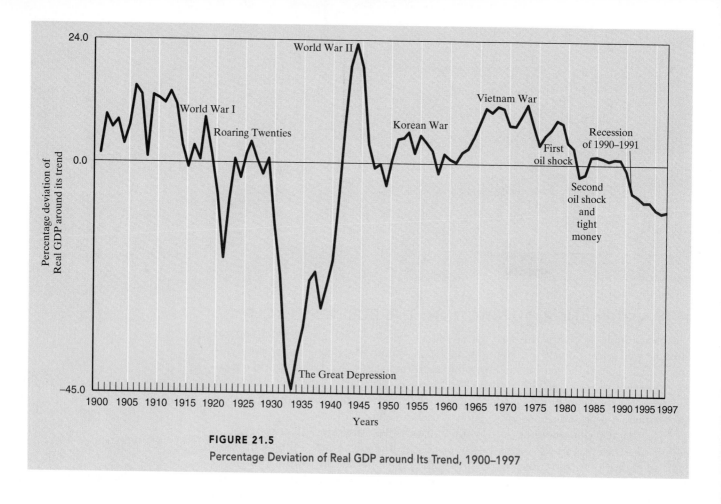

FIGURE 21.5

Percentage Deviation of Real GDP around Its Trend, 1900–1997

THE U.S. ECONOMY SINCE 1970

Since 1970, the U.S. economy has seen three recessions and large fluctuations in the rate of inflation. By analyzing how the various parts of the economy behaved during these hectic times, we can learn a lot about macroeconomic behavior. The following chapters concentrate on these years.

Figures 21.6, 21.7, and 21.8 show the behavior of three key variables during the period since 1970: GDP, the unemployment rate, and the rate of inflation. These graphs are based on quarterly data (data compiled for each quarter of the year) rather than on annual data. The first quarter of a year consists of January, February, and March; the second quarter consists of April, May, and June; and so on. The Roman numerals I, II, III, and IV denote the four quarters. (For example, "1972 III" refers to the third quarter, or summer, of 1972.)

Figure 21.6 plots GDP for the period 1970 I to 1997 IV. In the following chapters we will look at three recessionary periods within this period: 1974 I to 1975 IV, 1980 II to 1983 I, and 1990 III to 1991 I. These periods make useful reference points when we examine how other variables behave during the three periods.[5]

One concern of macroeconomics is unemployment. Unemployment generally rises during recessions and falls during expansions. This can be seen in Figure 21.7, which plots the unemployment rate for the period 1970 I to 1997 IV. Note that unemployment

[5]As Figure 21.6 shows, GDP rose in the middle of 1981 before falling again in the last quarter of 1981. Given this fact, one possibility would be to treat the 1980 II to 1983 I period as if it included two separate recessionary periods: 1980 II to 1981 I and 1981 IV to 1983 I. Because the expansion in 1981 was so short-lived, however, we have chosen not to separate the period into two parts.

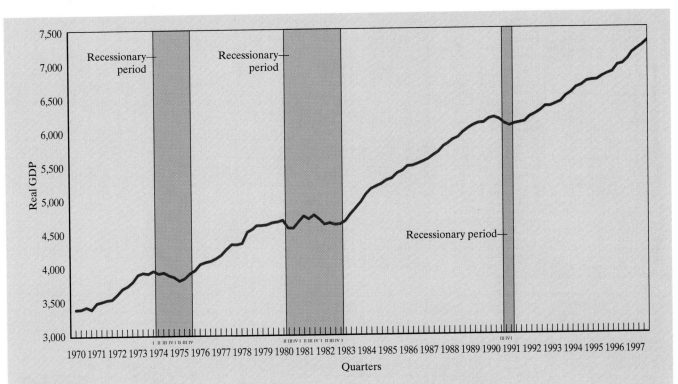

FIGURE 21.6

Real GDP, 1970 I to 1997 IV

Real GDP in the United States since 1970 has risen overall, but there have been three recessionary periods: 1974 I to 1975 IV, 1980 II to 1983 I, and 1990 III to 1991 I.

FIGURE 21.7

Unemployment Rate, 1970 I to 1997 IV

The U.S. unemployment rate since 1970 shows wide variations. The three recessionary reference periods show increases in the unemployment rate.

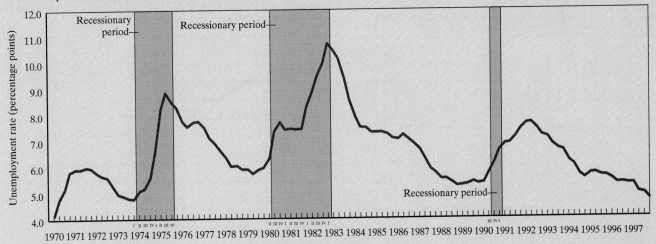

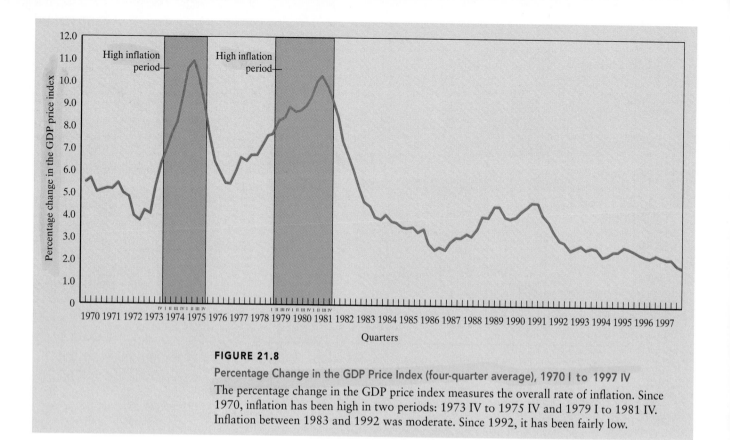

FIGURE 21.8

Percentage Change in the GDP Price Index (four-quarter average), 1970 I to 1997 IV

The percentage change in the GDP price index measures the overall rate of inflation. Since 1970, inflation has been high in two periods: 1973 IV to 1975 IV and 1979 I to 1981 IV. Inflation between 1983 and 1992 was moderate. Since 1992, it has been fairly low.

rose in all three recessions. In the 1974 to 1975 recession, the unemployment rate reached a maximum of 8.8 percent in the second quarter of 1975. During the 1980 to 1982 recession, it reached a maximum of 10.7 percent in the fourth quarter of 1982. The unemployment rate continued to rise after the 1990 to 1991 recession and reached a peak of 7.6 percent in 1992 III. By the end of 1994 the unemployment rate had fallen to 5.6 percent, and by the end of 1997 it had fallen further to 4.7 percent.

Macroeconomics is also concerned with the inflation rate. A measure of the overall price level is the GDP price index, an economy-wide price index. (The construction of the GDP price index is discussed in the next chapter. It is an index of prices of all domestically produced goods in the economy.) The percentage change in the GDP price index provides one measure of the overall rate of inflation. Figure 21.8 plots the percentage change in the GDP price index for the 1970 I to 1997 IV period.[6] For reference purposes, we have picked two periods within this time as showing particularly high inflation: 1973 IV to 1975 IV and 1979 I to 1981 IV. In the first period, the inflation rate peaked at 10.9 percent in the first quarter of 1975. In the second period, it peaked at 10.3 percent in the first quarter of 1981. Since 1983, the rate of inflation has been quite low by the standards of the 1970s. In the fourth quarter of 1997 it was only 1.8 percent.

Macroeconomics tries to explain the behavior of and the connections among variables such as GDP, the unemployment rate, and the GDP price index. When you can understand the movements shown in Figures 21.6, 21.7, and 21.8, you will have come a long way in understanding how the economy works.

[6]The percentage change in Figure 21.8 is the percentage change over four quarters. For example, the value for 1970 I is the percentage change from 1969 I, the value for 1970 II is the percentage change from 1969 II, and so on.

SUMMARY

1. *Microeconomics* examines the functioning of individual industries and the behavior of individual decision-making units. *Macroeconomics* is concerned with the sum, or aggregate, of these individual decisions—the consumption of *all* households in the economy, the amount of labor supplied and demanded by *all* individuals and firms, the total amount of *all* goods and services produced.

THE ROOTS OF MACROECONOMICS

2. Macroeconomics was born out of the effort to explain the *Great Depression* of the 1930s. Since that time, the discipline has evolved, concerning itself with new issues as the problems facing the economy have changed. Through the late 1960s, it was believed that the government could "fine tune" the economy to keep it running on an even keel at all times. The poor economic performance of the 1970s, however, showed that *fine tuning* does not always work.

MACROECONOMIC CONCERNS

3. The three topics of primary concern to macroeconomists are increases in the overall price level, or *inflation*; the growth rate of aggregate output; and the level of unemployment.

GOVERNMENT IN THE MACROECONOMY

4. Among the tools that governments have available to them for influencing the macroeconomy are *fiscal policy* (decisions on taxes and government spending); *monetary policy* (control of the money supply); and *growth or supply-side policies* (policies that focus on increasing the long-run growth rate).

THE COMPONENTS OF THE MACROECONOMY

5. The *circular flow* diagram shows the flow of income received and payments made by the three sectors of the economy—private, public, and international. Everybody's expenditure is someone else's receipt—every transaction must have two sides.

6. Another way of looking at how households, firms, the government, and the international sector relate is to consider the markets in which they interact: the goods-and-services market, labor market, and money (financial) market.

THE METHODOLOGY OF MACROECONOMICS

7. Because macroeconomic behavior is the sum of all the microeconomic decisions made by individual households and firms, we cannot possibly understand the former without some knowledge of the factors that influence the latter. The movements of macroeconomic aggregates reflect decisions made by individual firms and households.

8. A major theme in macroeconomics is the behavior of *aggregate demand* and *aggregate supply*. The logic underlying the aggregate demand and supply curves is more complex than the logic underlying individual market demand and supply curves.

THE U.S. ECONOMY IN THE TWENTIETH CENTURY: TRENDS AND CYCLES

9. Macroeconomics is concerned with both long-run trends and the short-run fluctuations that are part of the *business cycle*. Since 1970, the U.S. economy has seen three *recessions* and large fluctuations in the rate of *inflation*.

REVIEW TERMS AND CONCEPTS

aggregate behavior, 497
aggregate demand, 509
aggregate output, 502
aggregate supply, 509
business cycle, 502
circular flow, 504
contraction, recession, or slump, 511
corporate bonds, 508
depression, 502
dividends, 508

expansion or boom, 511
fine tuning, 499
fiscal policy, 503
Great Depression, 498
hyperinflation, 501
inflation, 501
macroeconomics, 497
microeconomic foundations
  of macroeconomics, 498
microeconomics, 497

monetary policy, 504
recession, 502
shares of stock, 508
stagflation, 499
sticky prices, 497
supply-side policy, 504
transfer payments, 505
Treasury bonds, notes, bills, 508
unemployment rate, 503

PROBLEM SET

1. Define inflation. Assume that you live in a simple economy in which only three goods are produced and traded: fish, fruit, and meat. Suppose that on January 1, 1998, fish sold for $2.50 per pound, meat was $3.00 per pound, and fruit was $1.50 per pound. At the end of the year, you discover that the catch was low and that fish prices had increased to $5.00 per pound, but fruit prices stayed at $1.50 and meat prices had actually fallen to $2.00. Can you say what happened to the overall "price level"? How might you construct a measure of the "change in the price level"? What additional information might you need to construct your measure?

2. Define unemployment. Should everyone who does not hold a job be considered "unemployed?" To help with your answer, draw a supply and demand diagram depicting the labor market. What is measured along the demand curve? What factors determine the quantity of labor demanded during a given period? What is measured along the labor supply curve? What factors determine the quantity of labor supplied by households during a given period? What is the opportunity cost of holding a job?

3. During 1997, the chairman of the Board of Governors of the Federal Reserve System voiced his concern that the unemployment rate, which was below 5 percent, was getting too low. Because employment is certainly a major concern of macroeconomic policy, and because job *creation* is considered a major goal, what is Mr. Greenspan's concern? What other goal(s) of macro policy might be affected by very low rates of unemployment?

4. The economy was the number one issue during the 1992 presidential campaign. Most people believed that the economy was in recession. However, a careful look at the data shows that GDP stopped falling and began growing in the spring of 1991. In other words, the recession ended a full year and a half before the election. What was it about the economy that led the public to perceive things as so bad?

5. During 1995, the U.S. economy continued to recover from the recession of the early 1990s. However, different regions of the economy were growing at very different rates. The recession hit hardest in California and the Northeast, and the recovery was late in coming in those regions. California and Connecticut had very slow job growth right through 1994.

   Describe the economy of your state. What is the most recently reported unemployment rate? How has the number of payroll jobs changed over the last three months? The last year? How does your state's performance compare to the U.S. economy's performance over the last year? What explanations have been offered in the press? How accurate are these?

6. Explain briefly how macroeconomics is different from microeconomics. How can macroeconomists use microeconomic theory to guide them in their work, and why might they wish to do so?

7. During 1993, when the economy was growing very slowly, President Clinton recommended a series of spending cuts and tax increases designed to reduce the deficit. These were passed by Congress in the Omnibus Budget Reconciliation Act of 1993. Some who opposed the bill argue that the United States was pursuing a "contractionary fiscal policy" at precisely the wrong time. Explain their logic.

8. Many of the expansionary periods during the twentieth century have occurred during wars. Why do you think this is true?

9. In the 1940s, you could buy a soda for 5¢, eat dinner at a restaurant for less than a dollar, and purchase a house for $10,000. From this statement, it follows that consumers today are worse off than consumers in the 1940s. Comment.

*10. During 1994 and 1995, the Federal Reserve became increasingly concerned with inflation. As the economy grew at a more and more rapid rate, the Fed acted to raise interest rates sharply. For example, the interest rate that home buyers had to pay on 30-year fixed-rate mortgages jumped from 7 percent to over 9 percent. This policy was designed to slow the rate of spending growth in the economy. How might higher interest rates be expected to slow the rate of spending growth? Give some examples.

TAKE IT TO THE NET

We invite you to visit the Case and Fair page on the Prentice Hall Web site:
http://www.prenhall.com/casefair
for this chapter's World Wide Web exercise.

MEASURING NATIONAL OUTPUT AND NATIONAL INCOME

MACROECONOMICS RELIES ON DATA, much of it collected by the government. To study the economy, we need data on total output, total income, total consumption, and the like. One source of these data are the **national income and product accounts,** which describe the components of national income in the economy.

The national income and product accounts do more than convey data about the performance of the economy. They also provide a conceptual framework that macroeconomists use to think about how the pieces of the economy fit together. When an economist thinks about the macroeconomy, the categories and vocabulary he or she uses come from the national income and product accounts.

The national income and product accounts can be compared to the mechanical or wiring diagrams for an automobile engine. The diagrams do not explain how an engine works—they identify the key parts of an engine and show how they are connected. Trying to understand the macroeconomy without understanding national income accounting is like trying to fix an engine without a mechanical diagram and with no names for the engine parts.

GROSS DOMESTIC PRODUCT

The key concept in the national income and product accounts is **gross domestic product,** or **GDP.**

> GDP is the total market value of a country's output. It is the market value of all *final goods* and services produced within a given period of time by factors of production located within a country.

U.S. GDP for 1997—the value of all the output produced by factors of production in the United States in 1997—was $8,079.9 billion.

national income and product accounts *Data collected and published by the government describing the various components of national income and output in the economy.*

gross domestic product (GDP) *The total market value of all final goods and services produced within a given period by factors of production located within a country.*

FINAL GOODS AND SERVICES

final goods and services
Goods and services produced for final use.

intermediate goods *Goods that are produced by one firm for use in further processing by another firm.*

value added *The difference between the value of goods as they leave a stage of production and the cost of the goods as they entered that stage.*

Goods and services produced refers to **final goods and services**. Many goods are **intermediate goods**—they are produced by one firm for use in further processing by another firm. Tires sold to automobile manufacturers are intermediate goods. The value of intermediate goods is not counted in GDP.

Why aren't intermediate goods counted in GDP? Suppose that in producing a car GM pays $100 to Goodyear for tires. GM uses these tires (among other components) to assemble a car, which it sells for $12,000. The value of the car (including its tires) is $12,000, not $12,000 + $100. The final price of the car already reflects the value of all its components. To count in GDP both the value of the tires sold to the automobile manufacturers and the value of the automobiles sold to the consumers would result in double counting.

Double counting can also be avoided by counting only the value added to a product by each firm in its production process. The **value added** during some stage of production is the difference between the value of goods as they leave that stage of production and the cost of the goods as they entered that stage. Value added is illustrated in Table 22.1. The four stages of the production of a gallon of gasoline are (1) oil drilling, (2) refining, (3) shipping, and (4) retail sale. In the first stage, value added is the value of sales. In the second stage, the refiner purchases the oil from the driller, refines it into gasoline, and sells it to the shipper. The refiner pays the driller $0.50 per gallon and charges the shipper $0.65. The value added by the refiner is thus $0.15 per gallon. The shipper then sells the gasoline to retailers for $0.80. The value added in the third stage of production is $0.15. Finally, the retailer sells the gasoline to consumers for $1.00. The value added at the fourth stage is $0.20, and the total value added in the production process is $1.00, the same as the value of sales at the retail level. Adding the total values of sales at each stage of production ($0.50 + $0.65 + $0.80 + $1.00 = $2.95) would significantly overestimate the value of the gallon of gasoline.

> In calculating GDP, we can either sum up the value added at each stage of production or we can take the value of final sales. We do not use the value of total sales in an economy to measure how much output has been produced.

EXCLUSION OF USED GOODS AND PAPER TRANSACTIONS

GDP is concerned only with new, or current, production. Old output is not counted in current GDP because it was already counted back at the time it was produced. It would be double counting to count sales of used goods in current GDP. If someone sells a used

TIRES TAKEN FROM THAT PILE AND MOUNTED ON THE WHEELS OF THE NEW CAR BEFORE IT IS SOLD ARE CONSIDERED INTERMEDIATE GOODS TO THE AUTO PRODUCER. TIRES FROM THAT PILE TO REPLACE TIRES ON YOUR OLD CAR ARE CONSIDERED FINAL GOODS.

TABLE 22.1 **VALUE ADDED IN THE PRODUCTION OF A GALLON OF GASOLINE** (HYPOTHETICAL NUMBERS)

STAGE OF PRODUCTION	VALUE OF SALES	VALUE ADDED
(1) Oil drilling	$0.50	$0.50
(2) Refining	0.65	0.15
(3) Shipping	0.80	0.15
(4) Retail sale	1.00	0.20
Total value added		$1.00

car to you, the transaction is not counted in GDP, because no new production has taken place. Similarly, a house is counted in GDP only at the time it is built, not each time it is resold. In short:

> GDP ignores all transactions in which money or goods change hands but in which no new goods and services are produced.

Sales of stocks and bonds are not counted in GDP. These sales are exchanges of paper assets and do not correspond to current production. But what if I sell the stock or bond for more than I originally paid for it? Profits from the stock or bond market have nothing to do with current production, so they are not counted in GDP. However, if I pay a fee to a broker for selling a stock of mine to someone else, this fee is counted in GDP, because the broker is performing a service for me. This service is part of current production. Be careful to distinguish between exchanges of stocks and bonds for money (or for other stocks and bonds), which do not involve current production, and fees for performing such exchanges, which do.

EXCLUSION OF OUTPUT PRODUCED ABROAD BY DOMESTICALLY OWNED FACTORS OF PRODUCTION

> GDP is the value of output produced by factors of production *located within a country.*

The three basic factors of production are land, labor, and capital. The labor of U.S. citizens counts as a domestically owned factor of production for the United States. The output produced by U.S. citizens abroad (for example, U.S. citizens working for a foreign company) is *not* counted in U.S. GDP because the output is not produced within the United States. Likewise, profits earned abroad by U.S. companies are not counted in U.S. GDP. However, the output produced by foreigners working in the United States is counted in U.S. GDP because the output is produced within the United States. Also, profits earned in the United States by foreign-owned companies are counted in U.S. GDP.

It is sometimes useful to have a measure of the output produced by factors of production owned by a country's citizens regardless of where the output is produced. This measure is called **gross national product,** or **GNP.** For most countries, including the United States, the difference between GDP and GNP is small.[1] In 1997 GNP for

gross national product (GNP)
The total market value of all final goods and services produced within a given period by factors of production owned by a country's citizens, regardless of where the output is produced.

---

[1]In a few countries, however, there is a large difference between GDP and GNP. For instance, the tiny country of Lesotho (surrounded entirely by South Africa) has an extremely poor and rudimentary domestic economy. Most residents of Lesotho earn their living by working in the mines and industries of neighboring South Africa. These payments from abroad are not counted in GDP, although they are part of GNP. According to the International Financial Statistics published by the International Monetary Fund, Lesotho's GNP exceeded its GDP by 72 percent in a recent year.

THIS SUBURU PLANT IN LAFAYETTE, INDIANA, IS OWNED BY A JAPANESE FIRM, THOUGH MOST OF THE PLANT'S WORKERS ARE U.S. CITIZENS. ALL OF THE PLANT'S OUTPUT IS INCLUDED IN U.S. GDP, BUT ONLY PART OF IT IS INCLUDED IN U.S. GNP. THE WAGES PAID TO U.S. WORKERS ARE PART OF GNP, WHEREAS THE PLANT'S PROFITS ARE NOT. THE PLANT'S PROFITS ARE PART OF JAPANESE GNP.

the United States was $8,060.1 billion, which is close to the $8,079.9 billion value for U.S. GDP.

The distinction between GDP and GNP can be tricky. Consider the Honda plant in Marysville, Ohio. The plant is owned by the Honda Corporation, a Japanese firm, but most of the workers employed at the plant are U.S. workers. Although all of the output of the plant is included in U.S. GDP, only part of it is included in U.S. GNP. The wages paid to U.S. workers are part of U.S. GNP, while the profits from the plant are not. The profits from the plant are counted in Japanese GNP because this is output produced by Japanese-owned factors of production (Japanese capital in this case). The profits, however, are not counted in Japanese GDP because they were not earned in Japan.

The centrality of GDP as a working concept cannot be overestimated. Just as an individual firm needs to evaluate the success or failure of its operations each year, so the economy as a whole needs to assess itself. GDP, as a measure of the total production of an economy, provides us with a country's economic report card.

CALCULATING GDP

expenditure approach *A method of computing GDP that measures the amount spent on all final goods during a given period.*

income approach *A method of computing GDP that measures the income—wages, rents, interest, and profits—received by all factors of production in producing final goods.*

GDP can be computed in two ways. One is to add up the amount spent on all final goods during a given period. This is the **expenditure approach** to calculating GDP. The other is to add up the income—wages, rents, interest, and profits—received by all factors of production in producing final goods. This is the **income approach** to calculating GDP. These two methods lead to the same value for GDP for the reason we discussed in the previous chapter: *Every payment (expenditure) by a buyer is at the same time a receipt (income) for the seller.* We can measure either income received or expenditures made, and we will end up with the same total output.

Suppose the economy is made up of just one firm and the firm's total output this year sells for $1 million. Because the total amount spent on output this year is $1 million, this year's GDP is $1 million. Remember: The expenditure approach calculates GDP on the basis of total expenditures for final goods and services in the economy.

But *every one* of the million dollars of GDP is either paid to someone or remains with the owners of the firm as profit. Using the income approach, we add up the wages paid to employees of the firm, the interest paid to those who lent money to the firm, and the rents paid to those who leased land, buildings, or equipment to the firm. What is left over is profit, which is, of course, income to the owners of the firm. If we add up the incomes of all the factors of production, including profits to the owners, we get a GDP of $1 million.

THE EXPENDITURE APPROACH

Recall from chapter 21 the four main groups in the economy: households, firms, the government, and the rest of the world. There are also four main categories of expenditure:

> **Expenditure Categories:**
>
> - Consumption (*C*)—household spending on consumer goods.
> - Investment (*I*)—spending by firms and households on new capital: plant, equipment, inventory, and new residential structures.
> - Government consumption and investment (*G*).
> - Net exports (*EX* − *IM*)—net spending by the rest of the world, or exports (*EX*) minus imports (*IM*).

The expenditure approach calculates GDP by adding together these four components of spending. In equation form:

$$\text{GDP} = C + I + G + (EX - IM)$$

U.S. GDP was $8,079.9 billion in 1997. The four components of the expenditure approach are shown in Table 22.2, along with their various categories.

▶ **Consumption (C)**   A large part of GDP consists of **personal consumption expenditures** (*C*). Table 22.2 shows that in 1997 the amount of personal consumption expenditures accounted for 67.9 percent of GDP. These are expenditures by consumers on goods and services.

There are three main categories of consumer expenditures: durable goods, nondurable goods, and services. **Durable goods,** such as automobiles, furniture, and household appliances, last a relatively long time. **Nondurable goods,** such as food, clothing, gasoline, and cigarettes, are used up fairly quickly. Payments for **services**—those things that we buy that do not involve the production of physical items—include expenditures for doctors, lawyers, and educational institutions. As Table 22.2 shows, in 1997 durable goods expenditures accounted for 8.2 percent of GDP, nondurables for 19.7 percent, and services for 40.0 percent.

personal consumption expenditures (C) *A major component of GDP: expenditures by consumers on goods and services.*

durable goods *Goods that last a relatively long time, such as cars and household appliances.*

nondurable goods *Goods that are used up fairly quickly, such as food and clothing.*

services *The things we buy that do not involve the production of physical things, such as legal and medical services and education.*

TABLE 22.2   COMPONENTS OF GDP, 1997: THE EXPENDITURE APPROACH

	BILLIONS OF DOLLARS	PERCENTAGE OF GDP
Total Gross Domestic Product	8,079.9	100.0
Personal Consumption Expenditures (C)	5,485.8	67.9
Durable goods	659.3	8.2
Nondurable goods	1,592.0	19.7
Services	3,234.5	40.0
Gross Private Domestic Investment (I)	1,242.5	15.4
Nonresidential	846.9	10.5
Residential	327.2	4.0
Change in business inventories	68.4	0.8
Government Consumption and Gross Investment (G)	1,452.7	18.0
Federal	523.8	6.5
State and local	928.9	11.5
Net Exports (EX − IM)	−101.1	−1.3
Exports (*EX*)	957.1	11.8
Imports (*IM*)	1,058.1	13.1

Note: Numbers may not add exactly because of rounding.

Source: U.S. Department of Commerce, Bureau of Economic Analysis.

> ▶ **Investment (I)** *Investment,* as we use it in economics, refers to the purchase of new capital—housing, plants, equipment, and inventory. The economic use of the term is in contrast to its everyday use, where *investment* often refers to purchases of common stocks, bonds, or mutual funds ("He *invested* in some 8 percent corporate bonds"). Two subjects that have generated much interest lately, foreign investment in the United States and U.S. investment abroad, are discussed in the Global Perspective "Foreign Investment in the United States and U.S. Investment Abroad."

Total investment in capital by the private sector is called **gross private investment** (**I**). Expenditures by firms for machines, tools, plants, and so forth make up **nonresidential investment.**[2] Because these are goods that firms buy for their own final use, they are part of "final sales" and counted in GDP. Expenditures for new houses and apartment buildings constitute **residential investment.** The third component of gross private investment, the **change in business inventories,** is the amount by which firms' inventories change during a period. Business inventories can be looked at as the goods that firms produce now but intend to sell later. In 1997, gross private investment accounted for 15.4 percent of GDP. Of this, 10.5 percent was nonresidential investment, 4.0 percent was residential investment, and 0.8 percent was change in business inventories.

Change in Business Inventories   It is sometimes confusing to students that inventories are counted as capital and that changes in inventory are counted as investment. But conceptually it makes some sense. The inventory a firm owns has a value, and it serves a purpose, or provides a service, to the firm. That it has value is obvious. Think of the inventory of a new car dealer or of a clothing store, or stocks of newly produced but unsold computers awaiting shipment. All these have value.

But what *service* does inventory provide? Firms keep stocks of inventory for a number of reasons. One is to meet unforeseen demand. Firms are never sure how much they will sell from period to period. Sales go up and down. To maintain the goodwill of their customers, firms need to be able to respond to unforeseen increases in sales. The only way to do that is with inventory.

Some firms use inventory to provide direct services to customers—the main function of a retail store. A grocery store provides a service—convenience. The store itself doesn't produce any food at all. It simply assembles a wide variety of items and puts them on display so consumers with varying tastes can come and shop in one place for what they want. The same is true for a clothing or hardware store. To provide their services, such stores need light fixtures, counters, cash registers, buildings, and lots of inventory.

Capital stocks are made up of plant, equipment, and inventory; inventory accumulations are part of the change in capital stocks, or investment.

Remember: GDP is not the market value of total final *sales* during a period—it is the market value of total *production.* The relationship between total production and total sales is this: Total production (GDP) equals final sales of domestic goods plus the change in business inventories:

$$\text{GDP} = \text{Final sales} + \text{Change in business inventories.}$$

In 1997, production exceeded sales by $68.4 billion. Inventories at the end of 1997 were $68.4 billion *more* than they were at the beginning of 1997.

 Gross Investment versus Net Investment   During the process of production, capital (especially machinery and equipment) produced in previous periods gradually wears out. GDP does not give us a true picture of the real production of an economy. GDP

---

gross private investment (I)
Total investment in capital—that is, the purchase of new housing, plants, equipment, and inventory by the private (or nongovernment) sector.

nonresidential investment
Expenditures by firms for machines, tools, plants, and so on.

residential investment
Expenditures by households and firms on new houses and apartment buildings.

change in business inventories
The amount by which firms' inventories change during a period. Inventories are the goods that firms produce now but intend to sell later.

---

[2]The distinction between what is considered investment and what is considered consumption is sometimes fairly arbitrary. A firm's purchase of a car or a truck is counted as investment, but a household's purchase of a car or a truck is counted as consumption of durable goods. In general, expenditures by firms for items that last longer than a year are counted as investment expenditures. Expenditures for items that last less than a year are seen as purchases of intermediate goods.

FOREIGN INVESTMENT IN THE UNITED STATES AND U.S. INVESTMENT ABROAD

In recent years, much concern has been expressed over the fact that many U.S. assets have been sold to foreign investors. For example, Japanese investors have bought hotels, banks, movie companies, and office towers and have invested in factories, colleges, and retail stores in the United States. In 1990, a Japanese firm bought Rockefeller Center in New York City.

Should the United States be worried about profits earned on these investments leaving the country? How much of the United States' capital stock is owned by foreign investors? How much of the capital stock of the rest of the world does the United States own?

As Table 1 shows, total foreign direct investment in the United States did indeed increase dramatically during the 1980s, jumping from $54.5 billion in 1979 to $630.0 billion in 1996. Japan's holdings of U.S. capital assets increased from $3.5 billion at the end of 1979 to $118.1 billion at the end of 1996. That's about $34 in 1996 for every dollar in 1979.

Japan was the second-largest foreign owner of U.S. assets in 1996, behind number one Great Britain. In 1996, Japan owned 18.7 percent of all foreign-owned assets in the United States, while Great Britain owned 22.6 percent. The Dutch came in third at 11.7 percent.

Table 2 presents data on U.S. ownership of capital assets abroad. Currently, about four-fifths of U.S. foreign holdings are in developed countries, with Europe accounting for about 50 percent. The remaining one-fifth of U.S. foreign holdings are located in developing countries, mostly in Latin America. Investment by U.S. multinational firms in developing countries has been very controversial, with some arguing that these companies exert political pressure on host governments. The most famous case of this type involved the alleged

participation of IT&T in a military coup in Chile in the early 1970s.

At the beginning of the 1980s, the United States owned nearly 3.5 times as much capital in foreign countries as foreigners owned in the United States. By 1996, however, foreign direct invest-

ment in the United States was about 80 percent of U.S. direct investment abroad. Interestingly, in spite of the dramatic increases during the 1980s, foreign holdings of U.S. capital assets represented only 2.7 percent of total U.S. fixed capital in 1996.

TABLE 1 FOREIGN DIRECT INVESTMENT IN THE UNITED STATES (TOTAL HOLDINGS AT YEAR'S END, 1979 AND 1996)

	1979		1996	
	BILLIONS OF DOLLARS	PERCENT OF TOTAL	BILLIONS OF DOLLARS	PERCENT OF TOTAL
Country				
Canada	7.2	13.2	53.8	8.5
Europe	37.4	68.6	410.4	65.1
U. K.	9.8	18.0	142.6	22.6
Netherlands	NA	NA	73.8	11.7
Japan	3.5	6.4	118.1	18.7
Other	6.4	11.7	47.7	7.7
Total	54.5	100.0	630.0	100.0
Percent of total U.S. fixed capital	0.6	—	2.7	—

Note: NA = not available.
Sources: Survey of Current Business, August 1981 and August 1997.

TABLE 2 U.S. DIRECT INVESTMENT IN FOREIGN COUNTRIES (TOTAL HOLDINGS AT YEAR'S END, 1979 AND 1996)

	1979		1996	
	BILLIONS OF DOLLARS	PERCENT OF TOTAL	BILLIONS OF DOLLARS	PERCENT OF TOTAL
Country				
Developed countries	138.6	74.2	631.6	79.3
Europe	82.6	44.2	399.6	50.2
Canada	40.2	21.5	91.6	11.5
Developing countries	44.5	23.8	160.5	20.2
Latin America	35.1	18.8	144.2	18.1
Other	3.6	1.9	4.4	0.6
Total	186.8	100.0	796.5	100.0

Sources: Survey of Current Business, August 1981 and August 1997.

For more on investment and GDP, see the Case and Fair Web page at
http://www.prenhall.com/casefair.

includes newly produced capital goods but does not take account of capital goods "consumed" in the production process.

Capital assets decline in value over time. The amount an asset's value falls each period is called its **depreciation**.[3] A personal computer purchased by a business today may be expected to have a useful life of four years before becoming worn out or obsolete. Over that period, the computer steadily depreciates.

What is the relationship between gross private investment (I) and depreciation? **Gross investment** is the total value of all newly produced capital goods (plant, equipment, housing, and inventory) produced in a given period. It takes no account of the fact that some capital wears out and must be replaced. **Net investment** is equal to gross investment minus depreciation. Net investment is a measure of how much the stock of capital *changes* during a period. If net investment is positive, the capital stock has increased; if net investment is negative, the capital stock has decreased. Put another way, the capital stock at the end of a period is equal to the capital stock that existed at the beginning of the period plus net investment:

$$\text{Capital}_{\text{end of period}} = \text{Capital}_{\text{beginning of period}} + \text{Net investment}$$

> **Government Consumption and Investment (G)**   Government consumption and investment (G) include expenditures by federal, state, and local governments for final goods (bombs, pencils, school buildings) and services (military salaries, congressional salaries, school teachers' salaries). Some of these expenditures are counted as government consumption and some are counted as government gross investment. Government transfer payments (social security benefits, veterans' disability stipends, etc.) are not included in G because these transfers are not purchases of anything currently produced. The payments are not made in exchange for any goods or services. Because interest payments on the government debt are also counted as transfers, they are also excluded from GDP on the grounds that they are not payments for current goods or services.

As Table 22.2 shows, government consumption and investment accounted for $1,452.7 billion, or 18.0 percent of U.S. GDP, in 1997. Federal government consumption and investment in 1997 accounted for 6.5 percent of GDP, and state and local government consumption and investment accounted for 11.5 percent.

> **Net Exports (EX − IM)**   The value of **net exports** (*EX − IM*) is the difference between *exports* (sales to foreigners of U.S.-produced goods and services) and *imports* (U.S. purchases of goods and services from abroad). This figure can be positive or negative. In 1997, the United States exported less than it imported, so the level of net exports was negative (−$101.1 billion). Before 1976, the United States had generally been a net exporter—exports exceeded imports, so the net export figure was positive.

The reason for including net exports in the definition of GDP is simple. Consumption, investment, and government spending (C, I, and G) include expenditures on goods produced both domestically and by foreigners. Therefore, $C + I + G$ overstates domestic production because it contains expenditures on foreign-produced goods—that is, imports (IM), which have to be subtracted out of GDP to obtain the correct figure. At the same time, $C + I + G$ understates domestic production because some of what a nation produces is sold abroad and therefore not included in C, I, or G—exports (EX) have to be added in. If a U.S. firm produces computers and sells them in Germany, the computers are part of U.S. production and should be counted as part of U.S. GDP.

depreciation *The amount by which an asset's value falls in a given period.*

gross investment *The total value of all newly produced capital goods (plant, equipment, housing, and inventory) produced in a given period.*

net investment *Gross investment minus depreciation.*

government consumption and investment (G) *Expenditures by federal, state, and local governments for final goods and services.*

net exports (EX − IM) *The difference between exports (sales to foreigners of U.S.-produced goods and services) and imports (U.S. purchases of goods and services from abroad). The figure can be positive or negative.*

---

[3]This is the formal definition of economic depreciation. Because depreciation is difficult to measure precisely, accounting rules allow firms to use shortcut methods to approximate the amount of depreciation that they incur each period. To complicate matters even more, the U.S. tax laws allow firms to deduct depreciation for tax purposes under a different set of rules.

TABLE 22.3 COMPONENTS OF GDP, 1997: THE INCOME APPROACH

	BILLIONS OF DOLLARS	PERCENTAGE OF GDP
Gross Domestic Product	8,079.9	100.0
National Income	6,649.7	82.3
Compensation of employees	4,703.6	58.2
Proprietors' income	544.5	6.7
Corporate profits	805.0	10.0
Net interest	448.7	5.6
Rental income	147.9	1.8
Depreciation	867.9	10.7
Indirect Taxes Minus Subsidies	542.5	6.7
Net Factor Payments to the Rest of the World	19.8	0.2

Source: See Table 22.2.

THE INCOME APPROACH

Table 22.3 presents the income approach to calculating GDP, which looks at GDP in terms of who receives it as income, not who purchases it.

The income approach to GDP breaks down GDP into four components: national income, depreciation, indirect taxes minus subsidies, and net factor payments to the rest of the world:

> GDP = National income + Depreciation + (Indirect taxes − Subsidies)
>   + Net factor payments to the rest of the world.

As we examine each, keep in mind that total expenditures always equal total income.

▶ **National Income** **National income** is the total income earned by factors of production owned by a country's citizens. Table 22.3 shows that national income is the sum of five items: (1) compensation of employees, (2) proprietors' income, (3) corporate profits, (4) net interest, and (5) rental income. **Compensation of employees,** the largest of the five items by far, includes wages and salaries paid to households by firms and by the government, as well as various supplements to wages and salaries such as contributions that employers make to social insurance and private pension funds. **Proprietors' income** is the income of unincorporated businesses, and **corporate profits** are the income of corporate businesses. **Net interest** is the interest paid by business. (Interest paid by households and by the government is not counted in GDP because it is not assumed to flow from the production of goods and services.) **Rental income,** a minor item, is the income received by property owners in the form of rent.

▶ **Depreciation** Recall from our discussion of net versus gross investment that when capital assets wear out or become obsolete, they decline in value. The measure of that decrease in value is called depreciation. This depreciation is a part of GDP in the income approach.

It may seem odd that we must *add* depreciation to national income when we calculate GDP by the income approach. But remember that we want a measure of *all* income, including income that results from the replacement of existing plant and equipment. Because national income does not include depreciation,[4] to get to total

national income *The total income earned by the factors of production owned by a country's citizens.*

compensation of employees *Includes wages, salaries, and various supplements—employer contributions to social insurance and pension funds, for example— paid to households by firms and by the government.*

proprietors' income *The income of unincorporated businesses.*

corporate profits *The income of corporate businesses.*

net interest *The interest paid by business.*

rental income *The income received by property owners in the form of rent.*

---

[4]National income does not include depreciation because depreciation has been subtracted from corporations' total revenue in computing the value of corporate profits, and the value of corporate profits is what is used in computing national income.

income (gross domestic product) we need to add depreciation. In 1997, depreciation accounted for $867.9 billion, or 10.7 percent of U.S. GDP.

> **Indirect Taxes Minus Subsidies** In calculating final sales on the expenditures side, **indirect taxes**—sales taxes, customs duties, and license fees, for example—are included. These taxes must be accounted for on the income side.

To clarify this, suppose the sales tax is 7 percent and a firm sells 100,000 jelly beans for $100 plus tax. The total sales price is $107—the value of output recorded in the expenditure approach to calculating GDP. Of this $107, $7 goes to pay the tax to the government, some goes to pay wages to the workers in the jelly bean factory, and some goes to pay interest. The rest is the firm's profits plus depreciation.

To have the income and expenditure sides match, the sales tax must be recorded on the income side. If it were not included as part of income, then the basic rule that everyone's expenditure is someone else's income would be violated. Indirect taxes are an expenditure of the households or firms who buy things, but they are not income of firms that sell the products. (Thinking along these lines, indirect taxes can be considered income of the government.) We must add indirect taxes on the income side to make things balance.

Subsidies are payments made by the government for which it receives no goods or services in return. These subsidies are subtracted from national income to get GDP. (Remember: GDP is indirect taxes *minus* subsidies.) For example, farmers receive substantial subsidies from the government. Subsidy payments to farmers are income to farm proprietors and are thus part of national income, but they do not come from the sale of agricultural products, so are not part of GDP. To balance the expenditure side with the income side, these subsidies must be subtracted on the income side.[5]

> **Net Factor Payments to the Rest of the World** **Net factor payments to the rest of the world** equal the payments of factor income (income to the factors of production) to the rest of the world *minus* the receipts of factor income from the rest of the world. This item is added for the following reason. National income is defined as the income of factors of production *owned* by the country. GDP, however, is output produced by factors of production located *within* the country. In other words, national income includes some income that should not be counted in GDP—namely, the income a country's citizens earn abroad—and this income must be subtracted. In addition, national income does not include some income that is counted in GDP—namely, the foreigners' income in the country whose GDP we are calculating—and this income must be added. Table 22.3 shows that the value of net factor payments to the rest of the world was positive in 1997 ($19.8 billion). This means that U.S. payments of factor income to the rest of the world exceeded U.S. receipts of factor income from the rest of the world in 1997.

As you can see in Table 22.3, U.S. GDP as calculated by the income approach was $8,079.9 billion in 1997—the same amount that we calculated using the expenditure approach.

FROM GDP TO DISPOSABLE PERSONAL INCOME

Although GDP is the most important item in national income accounting, other concepts are also useful to know. Some are presented in Table 22.4. The top of the table shows how GNP is calculated from GDP. Remember that a country's GDP is total

---

indirect taxes *Taxes like sales taxes, customs duties, and license fees.*

subsidies *Payments made by the government for which it receives no goods or services in return.*

net factor payments to the rest of the world *Payments of factor income to the rest of the world minus the receipt of factor income from the rest of the world.*

---

[5]In Table 22.3, two other items are included in the value for indirect taxes minus subsidies: business transfer payments and the statistical discrepancy. Business transfer payments are deducted from corporate profits, and so they need to be added to income. The statistical discrepancy adjusts for errors in the data collection.

TABLE 22.4 GDP, GNP, NNP, NATIONAL INCOME, PERSONAL INCOME, AND DISPOSABLE PERSONAL INCOME, 1997

	DOLLARS (BILLIONS)
GDP	8,079.9
Plus: Receipts of factor income from the rest of the world	+262.2
Less: Payments of factor income to the rest of the world	−282.0
Equals: **GNP**	8,060.1
Less: Depreciation	−867.9
Equals: **Net national product (NNP)**	7,192.2
Less: Indirect taxes minus subsidies	−542.5
Equals: **National income**	6,649.7
Less: Corporate profits minus dividends	−484.7
Less: Social insurance payments	−732.1
Plus: Personal interest income received from the government and consumers	+319.9
Plus: Transfer payments to persons	+1,121.2
Equals: **Personal income**	6,873.9
Less: Personal taxes	−988.7
Equals: **Disposable personal income**	5,885.2

Source: See Table 22.2.

production by factors of production located within that country, while its GNP is total production by factors of production owned by that country. If we take U.S. GDP, add to it factor income earned by U.S. citizens from the rest of the world (receipts of factor income from the rest of the world), and subtract from it factor income earned in the United States by foreigners (payments of factor income to the rest of the world), we get GNP.

From GNP, we can calculate net national product (NNP). Recall that the expenditure approach to GDP includes gross investment as one of the components of GDP (and of GNP). Gross domestic product does not account for the fact that some of the nation's capital stock is used up in the process of producing the nation's product. **Net national product (NNP)** is gross national product minus depreciation. In a sense, it is a nation's total product minus (or "net of") what is required to maintain the value of its capital stock. Because GDP does not take into account any depreciation of the capital stock that may have occurred, NNP is sometimes a better measure of how the economy is doing than is GDP.

To calculate national income, we subtract indirect taxes minus subsidies from NNP (subtract indirect business taxes and add subsidies). We subtract indirect taxes because they are included in NNP but do not represent payments to factors of production and are not part of national income. We add subsidies because they are payments to factors of production but are not included in NNP.

Personal income is the total income of households. To calculate personal income from national income, two items are subtracted: (1) corporate profits minus dividends, and (2) social insurance payments. Both need explanation. First, some corporate profits are paid to households in the form of dividends, and dividends are part of personal income. The profits that remain after dividends are paid—corporate profits minus dividends—are not paid to households as income. Therefore, corporate profits minus dividends must be subtracted from national income when computing personal income. Second, social insurance payments are payments made to the government, some by firms and some by employees. Because these payments are not received by households, they must be subtracted from national income when computing personal income.

net national product (NNP) *Gross national product minus depreciation; a nation's total product minus what is required to maintain the value of its capital stock.*

personal income *The total income of households. Equals (national income) minus (corporate profits minus dividends) minus (social insurance payments) plus (interest income received from the government and households) plus (transfer payments to households). The income received by households after paying social insurance taxes but before paying personal income taxes.*

TABLE 22.5 DISPOSABLE PERSONAL INCOME AND PERSONAL SAVING, 1997

	DOLLARS (BILLIONS)
Disposable personal income	5,885.2
Less:	
Personal consumption expenditures	−5,485.8
Interest paid by consumers to business	−154.8
Personal transfer payments to foreigners	−17.9
Equals: Personal saving	226.7
Personal saving as a percentage of disposable personal income:	3.9%

Source: See Table 22.2.

Two items must be added to national income to calculate personal income: (1) personal interest income received from the government and consumers, and (2) transfer payments to persons. As we have pointed out, interest payments made by the government and consumers (households) are not counted in GDP and not reflected in national income figures.[6] But these payments are income received by households, so they must be added to national income when computing personal income.[7] Similarly, transfer payments to persons are not counted in GDP because they do not represent the production of any goods or services. But social security checks and other cash benefits are income received by households and must also be added to national income when computing personal income.

Personal income is the income received by households before paying personal income taxes but after paying social insurance contributions. The amount of income that households have to spend or save is called **disposable personal income**, or **after-tax income**. It is equal to personal income minus personal taxes.

Because disposable personal income is the amount of income that households can spend or save, it is an important income concept. Table 22.5 shows there are three categories of spending: (1) personal consumption expenditures, (2) interest paid by consumers to business, and (3) personal transfer payments to foreigners. The amount of disposable personal income left after total personal spending is **personal saving**. If your monthly disposable income is $500 and you spend $450, you have $50 left at the end of the month. Your personal saving is $50 for the month. Your personal saving level can be negative: If you earn $500 and spend $600 during the month, you have *dissaved* $100. To spend $100 more than you earn, you will either have to borrow the $100 from someone, take the $100 from your savings account, or sell an asset you own.

The **personal saving rate** is the percentage of disposable personal income saved, an important indicator of household behavior. A low saving rate means households are spending a large amount of their income. A high saving rate means households are

disposable personal income or **after-tax income** *Personal income minus personal income taxes. The amount that households have to spend or save.*

personal saving *The amount of disposable income that is left after total personal spending in a given period.*

personal saving rate *The percentage of disposable personal income that is saved. If the personal saving rate is low, households are spending a large amount relative to their incomes; if it is high, households are spending cautiously.*

---

[6]Interest payments on government bonds are not included in national income, while interest payments on bonds of private firms are, because government debt is assumed to be the result of activities, such as past wars, that do not add to current production. In contrast, it is presumed that firms sell bonds to finance investment that does add to current production. Interest payments by households are not included in national income because they are not considered to add to current production.

[7]Households can pay and receive interest. As a group, households receive more interest than they pay.

cautious in their spending. As Table 22.5 shows, the U.S. personal saving rate in 1997 was 3.9 percent. Saving rates tend to rise during recessionary periods, when consumers become anxious about their future, and fall during boom times, as pent-up spending demand gets released.

NOMINAL VERSUS REAL GDP

So far, we have looked at GDP measured in **current dollars**, or the current prices we pay for things. When a variable is measured in current dollars, it is described in *nominal terms*. **Nominal GDP** is GDP measured in current dollars—all components of GDP valued at their current prices.

In many applications of macroeconomics, nominal GDP is not a very desirable measure of production. Why? Assume there is only one good—say, pizza. In each year 1 and 2, 100 units (slices) of pizza were produced. Production thus remained the same for year 1 and year 2. But suppose the price of pizza increased from $1.00 per slice in year 1 to $1.10 per slice in year 2. Nominal GDP in year 1 is $100 (100 units × $1.00 per unit), and nominal GDP in year 2 is $110 (100 units × $1.10 per unit). Nominal GDP has increased by $10, even though no more slices of pizza were produced. If we use nominal GDP to measure growth, we can be misled into thinking production has grown when all that has really happened is a rise in the price level.

If there were only one good in the economy—like pizza—it would be easy to measure production and compare one year's value to another's. We would add up all the pizza slices produced each year. In the example, production is 100 in both years. If the number of slices had increased to 105 in year 2, we would say production increased by five slices between year 1 and year 2, which is a 5 percent increase. But, alas, there is more than one good in the economy.

At the end of 1995, the Bureau of Economic Analysis (BEA) of the U.S. Department of Commerce—which produces the national income and product accounts—changed the procedure to adjust nominal GDP for price changes. The new procedure has some advantages over the older one, as we will see. To the extent that this change leads to improved measures of GDP, it can have significant and positive effects on policy decisions. The decisions of both monetary policy makers and fiscal policy makers are influenced by GDP growth, and improved measures of growth should lead to better decisions.

As you read the following, keep in mind that the job of adjusting nominal GDP to account for price changes is not easy. Even in an economy of just apples and oranges, it would not be obvious how to add up apples and oranges to get an overall measure of output. The BEA's task is to add up thousands of goods, each of whose price is changing over time.

In the following, we will use the concept of a **weight**, either price weights or quantity weights. What is a weight? It is easiest to define the term by an example. Suppose in your economics course there is a final exam and two other tests. If the final exam counts for one half of the grade and the other two tests for one fourth each, the "weights" are one half, one fourth, and one fourth. If instead the final exam counts for 80 percent of the grade and the other two tests for 10 percent each, the weights are .8, .1, and .1. The more important an item is in a group, the larger its weight.

CALCULATING REAL GDP

Nominal GDP adjusted for price changes is called *real GDP*. All of the main issues involved in computing real GDP can be discussed using a simple three-good economy and two years. Table 22.6 presents all the data that we will need. The table presents

current dollars *The current prices that one pays for goods and services.*

nominal GDP *Gross domestic product measured in current dollars.*

weight *The importance attached to an item within a group of items.*

TABLE 22.6 A THREE-GOOD ECONOMY

	(1) PRODUCTION YEAR 1 Q_1	(2) PRODUCTION YEAR 2 Q_2	(3) PRICE PER UNIT YEAR 1 P_1	(4) PRICE PER UNIT YEAR 2 P_2	(5) GDP IN YEAR 1 IN YEAR 1 PRICES $P_1 \times Q_1$	(6) GDP IN YEAR 2 IN YEAR 1 PRICES $P_1 \times Q_2$	(7) GDP IN YEAR 1 IN YEAR 2 PRICES $P_2 \times Q_1$	(8) GDP IN YEAR 2 IN YEAR 2 PRICES $P_2 \times Q_2$
Good A	6	11	$.50	$.40	$3.00	$5.50	$2.40	$4.40
Good B	7	4	$.30	$1.00	$2.10	$1.20	$7.00	$4.00
Good C	10	12	$.70	$.90	$7.00	$8.40	$9.00	$10.80
Total					$12.10 Nominal GDP in year 1	$15.10	$18.40	$19.20 Nominal GDP in year 2

base-year *The year chosen for the weights in a fixed-weight procedure.*

fixed-weight procedure *A procedure that uses weights from a given base year.*

price and quantity data for two years and three goods. The goods are labeled *A, B,* and *C,* and the years are labeled 1 and 2. *P* denotes price, and *Q* denotes quantity.

The first thing to note from Table 22.6 is that *nominal output*—in current dollars—in year 1 for good *A* is the price of good *A* in year 1 ($.50) times the number of units of good *A* produced in year 1 (6), which is $3.00. Similarly, nominal output in year 1 is $7 \times \$.30 = \$2.10$ for good *B* and $10 \times \$.70 = \$7.00$ for good *C.* The sum of these three amounts, $12.10 in column 5, is nominal GDP in year 1 in this simple economy. Nominal GDP in year 2—calculated by using year 2's quantities and year 2's prices—is $19.20 (column 8). Nominal GDP has risen from $12.10 in year 1 to $19.20 in year 2, an increase of 58.7 percent.[8]

You can see that the price of each good changed between year 1 and year 2—the price of good *A* fell (from $.50 to $.40) and the prices of goods *B* and *C* rose (*B* from $.30 to $1.00; *C* from $.70 to $.90). Some of the change in nominal GDP between years 1 and 2 is due to price changes and not production changes. How much can we attribute to price changes and how much to production changes? Here, things get tricky. The BEA's old procedure was to pick a **base year** and use the prices in that base year as weights to calculate real GDP. This is a **fixed-weight procedure** because the weights used, which are the prices, are the same for all years—namely, the prices that prevailed in the base year.

Let us use the fixed-weight procedure and year 1 as the base year, which means using year 1 prices as the weights. Then in Table 22.6, real GDP in year 1 is $12.10 (column 5), and real GDP in year 2 is $15.10 (column 6). Note that both columns use year 1 prices, and that nominal and real GDP are the same in year 1 because year 1 is the base year. Real GDP has increased from $12.10 to $15.10, an increase of 24.8 percent.

Let's now use the fixed-weight procedure and year 2 as the base year, which means using year 2 prices as the weights. In Table 22.6, real GDP in year 1 is $18.40 (column 7), and real GDP in year 2 is $19.20 (column 8). Note, both columns use year 2 prices, and nominal and real GDP are the same in year 2 because year 2 is the base year. Real GDP has increased from $18.40 to $19.20, an increase of 4.3 percent.

This example shows that growth rates can be sensitive to the choice of the base year—24.8 percent using year 1 prices as weights and 4.3 percent using year 2 prices as weights. The old BEA procedure simply picked one year as the base year and did all the

[8]The percentage change is calculated as $[(19.20 - 12.10)/12.10] \times 100 = .587 \times 100 = 58.7$ percent.

calculations using the prices in that year as weights. The new procedure made two important changes. The first (using the current example) was to "split the difference" between 24.8 percent and 4.3 percent. What does "splitting the difference" mean? One way would be to take the average of the two numbers, which is 14.55 percent. What the BEA did was to take the *geometric* average, which for the current example is 14.09 percent.[9] These two averages (14.55 percent and 14.09 percent) are quite close, and the use of either would give similar results. The point here is not that the geometric average was used, but that the first change was to split the difference using some average. Note that this new procedure requires two "base" years, because 24.8 percent was computed using year 1 prices as weights and 4.3 percent was computed using year 2 prices as weights.

The second BEA change was to use years 1 and 2 as the base years when computing the percentage change between years 1 and 2, then use years 2 and 3 as the base years when computing the percentage change between years 2 and 3, and so on. The two base years change as the calculations move through time. The series of percentage changes computed in this way is taken to be the series of growth rates of real GDP, and so in this way nominal GDP is adjusted for price changes. To make sure you understand this, review the calculations in Table 22.6; all the data you need to see what is going on are in this table.

CALCULATING THE GDP PRICE INDEX

We now switch gears from real GDP, a quantity measure, to the GDP price index, a price measure. One of economic policy makers' goals is to keep changes in the overall price level small. For this reason policy makers need not only good measures of how real output is changing but also good measures of how the overall price level is changing. The GDP price index is one measure of the overall price level. We can use the data in Table 22.6 to show how the GDP price index is computed by the BEA.

In Table 22.6, the price of good *A* fell from $.50 in year 1 to $.40 in year 2; the price of good *B* rose from $.30 to $1.00; and the price of good *C* rose from $.70 to $.90. If we were interested only in how individual prices change, this is all the information we would need. But if we are interested in how the overall price *level* changes, we need to weight the individual prices in some way. The obvious weights to use are the quantities produced, but which quantities—year 1's or year 2's? The same issues arise here for the quantity weights as for the price weights in computing real GDP.

Let's first use the fixed-weight procedure and year 1 as the base year, which means using year 1 quantities as the weights. Then in Table 22.6, the "bundle" price in year 1 is $12.10 (column 5), and the bundle price in year 2 is $18.40 (column 7). Both columns use year 1 quantities. The bundle price has increased from $12.10 to $18.40, an increase of 52.1 percent.

Next use the fixed-weight procedure and year 2 as the base year, which means using year 2 quantities as the weights. Then the bundle price in year 1 is $15.10 (column 6), and the bundle price in year 2 is $19.20 (column 8). Both columns use year 2 quantities. The bundle price has increased from $15.10 to $19.20, an increase of 27.2 percent.

This example shows that overall price increases can be sensitive to the choice of the base year—52.1 percent using year 1 quantities as weights and 27.2 percent using year 2 quantities as weights. Again, the old BEA procedure simply picked one year as the base year and did all the calculations using the quantities in the base year as weights. The new procedure first splits the difference between 52.1 percent and 27.2 percent by taking the geometric average, which is 39.1 percent. Second, it uses years 1 and 2 as the base years when computing the percentage change between years 1 and 2, years 2 and 3

---

[9]The geometric average is computed as the square root of 124.8 × 104.3, which is 114.09, or 14.09 percent.

as the base years when computing the percentage change between years 2 and 3, and so on. The series of percentage changes computed in this way is taken to be the series of percentage changes in the GDP price index, that is, a series of inflation rates of the overall price level.

THE PROBLEMS OF FIXED WEIGHTS

To see why the BEA switched to the new procedure, let's consider a number of problems with using fixed price weights to compute real GDP. First, 1987 price weights, the last price weights the BEA used before it changed procedures, are not likely to be very accurate for, say, the 1950s. Many structural changes have taken place in the U.S. economy in the last 30 to 40 years, and it seems unlikely that 1987 prices are good weights to use for the 1950s.

Another problem is that the use of fixed price weights does not account for the responses in the economy to supply shifts. Say bad weather leads to a lower production of oranges in year 2. In a simple supply and demand diagram for oranges, this corresponds to a shift of the supply curve to the left, which leads to an increase in the price of oranges and a decrease in the quantity demanded. As consumers move up the demand curve, they are substituting away from oranges. If technical advances in year 2 result in cheaper ways of producing computers, the result is a shift of the computer supply curve to the right, which leads to a decrease in the price of computers and an increase in the quantity demanded. Consumers are substituting toward computers. (You should be able to draw supply-and-demand diagrams for both these cases.) Table 22.6 shows this tendency. The quantity of good *A* rose between years 1 and 2 and the price decreased (the computer case), whereas the quantity of good *B* fell and the price increased (the orange case). The computer supply curve has been shifting to the right over time, due primarily to technical advances. The result has been large decreases in the price of computers and large increases in the quantity demanded.

To see why these responses pose a problem for the use of fixed price weights, consider the data in Table 22.6. Because the price of good *A* was higher in year 1, the increase in production of good *A* is weighted more if we use year 1 as the base year than if we used year 2 as the base year. Also, because the price of good *B* was lower in year 1, the decrease in production of good *B* is weighted less if we use year 1 as the base year. These effects make the overall change in real GDP larger if we use year 1 price weights than if we use year 2 price weights. Using year 1 price weights ignores the kinds of substitution responses discussed in the previous paragraph and leads to what many feel are too-large estimates of real GDP changes. In the past, the BEA tended to move the base year forward about every five years, resulting in the past estimates of real GDP growth being revised downward. It is undesirable to have past growth estimates change simply because of the change to a new base year. (The last change in the base year was from 1982 to 1987.) The new BEA procedure avoids many of these fixed-weight problems.

Similar problems arise when using fixed-quantity weights to compute price indexes. For example, the fixed-weight procedure ignores the substitution away from goods whose prices are increasing and toward goods whose prices are decreasing or increasing less rapidly. The procedure tends to overestimate the increase in the overall price level. As discussed in the next chapter, there are still many price indexes that are computed using fixed weights. The GDP price index differs because it does not use fixed weights. It is also a price index for all the goods and services produced in the economy. Other price indexes cover fewer goods and services.

It should finally be stressed that there is no "right" way of computing real GDP. The economy consists of many goods, each with its own price, and there is no exact way of adding together the production of the different goods. We can say that the BEA's new procedure for computing real GDP avoids the problems associated with the use of fixed weights, and it seems to be an improvement over the old procedure.

LIMITATIONS OF THE GDP CONCEPT

We generally think of increases in GDP as good. Increasing GDP (or preventing its decrease) is usually considered one of the chief goals of the government's macroeconomic policy. Because some serious problems arise when we try to use GDP as a measure of happiness or well-being, we now point out some of the limitations of the GDP concept as a measure of welfare.

GDP AND SOCIAL WELFARE

If crime levels went down, society would be better off, but a decrease in crime is not an increase in output and is not reflected in GDP. Neither is an increase in leisure time. Yet, to the extent that households desire extra leisure time (rather than having it forced on them by a lack of jobs in the economy), an increase in leisure is also an increase in social welfare. Furthermore, some increases in social welfare are associated with a *decrease* in GDP. An increase in leisure during a time of full employment, for example, leads to a decrease in GDP because less time is spent on producing output.

Most nonmarket and domestic activities, such as housework and child care, are not counted in GDP even though they amount to real production. However, if I decide to send my children to day care or hire someone to clean my house or to drive my car for me, GDP increases. The salaries of day-care staff, cleaning people, and chauffeurs are counted in GDP, but the time I spend doing the same things is not counted. A mere change of institutional arrangements, even though no more output is being produced, can show up as a change in GDP.

Furthermore, GDP seldom reflects losses or social ills. GDP accounting rules do not adjust for production that pollutes the environment. The more production there is, the larger is GDP, regardless of how much pollution results in the process.

GDP also has nothing to say about the distribution of output among individuals in a society. It does not distinguish, for example, between the case in which most output goes to a few people and the case in which output is evenly divided among all people. We cannot use GDP to measure the effects of redistributive policies (which take income from some people and give income to others). Such policies have no direct impact on GDP. GDP is also neutral about the kinds of goods an economy produces. Symphony performances, handguns, cigarettes, professional football games, Bibles, soda pop, milk, economics textbooks, and comic books all get counted.

In spite of these limitations, GDP is a highly useful measure of economic activity and well-being. If you doubt this, answer this simple question: Would you rather live in the United States of 200 years ago, when rivers were less polluted and crime rates were probably lower, or in the United States of today? Most people say they prefer the present. Even with all the "negatives," GDP per person and the average standard of living are much higher today than 200 years ago.

THE UNDERGROUND ECONOMY

Many transactions are missed in the calculation of GDP, even though in principle they should be counted. Most illegal transactions are missed unless they are "laundered" into legitimate business. Income that is earned but not reported as income for tax

TABLE 22.7

PER CAPITA GNP FOR SELECTED COUNTRIES, 1995

COUNTRY	U.S. DOLLARS
Switzerland	40,630
Japan	39,640
Norway	31,250
Denmark	29,890
Germany	27,510
United States	26,980
Austria	26,890
France	24,990
Sweden	23,750
Finland	20,580
Canada	19,380
Australia	18,720
United Kingdom	18,700
Israel	15,920
Spain	13,580
Portugal	9,740
Greece	8,210
Chile	4,160
Mexico	3,320
Botswana	3,020
Turkey	2,780
Jamaica	1,510
Jordan	1,510
Philippines	1,050
Indonesia	980
Bolivia	800
Egypt	790
Mali	250
Mozambique	80

Source: The World Bank Atlas, 1997.

underground economy *The part of the economy in which transactions take place and in which income is generated that is unreported and therefore not counted in GDP.*

per capita GDP or **GNP** *A country's GDP or GNP divided by its population.*

IN SOME COUNTRIES, THE ONLY WAY TO PURCHASE CONSUMER GOODS MAY BE THROUGH THE UNDERGROUND MARKET.

purposes is usually missed, although some adjustments are made in the GDP calculations to take misreported income into account. The part of the economy that should be counted in GDP but is not is sometimes called the **underground economy**.

Tax evasion is usually thought to be the major incentive for people to participate in the underground economy. Studies estimate the size of the U.S. underground economy ranging from 5 percent to 30 percent of GDP,[10] comparable to the size of the underground economy in most European countries and probably much smaller than the size of the underground economy in the Eastern European countries. Estimates of Italy's underground economy range from 10 percent to 35 percent of Italian GDP. At the lower end of the scale, estimates for Switzerland range from 3 percent to 5 percent.

Why should we care about the underground economy? To the extent that GDP reflects only a part of economic activity rather than a complete measure of what the economy produces, it is misleading. Unemployment rates, for example, may be lower than officially measured if people work in the underground economy without reporting this fact to the government. Also, if the size of the underground economy varies between countries—as it does—we can be misled when we compare GDP between countries. For example, Italy's GDP would be much higher if we considered its underground sector as part of the economy, while Switzerland's GDP would change very little.

PER CAPITA GDP/GNP

GDP and GNP are sometimes measured in per capita terms. **Per capita GDP or GNP** is a country's GDP or GNP divided by its population. It is a better measure of well-being for the average person than is total GDP or GNP. Table 22.7 lists the per capita GNP of various countries for 1995. Switzerland has the highest per capita GNP, followed by Japan and Norway. U.S. per capita GNP was $26,980. Mozambique was estimated to have a per capita GNP of only $80 in 1995.

PART FIVE
Concepts and Problems in Macroeconomics

[10]See, for example, Edgar L. Feige, "Defining and Estimating Underground and Informal Economies: The New Industrial Economic Approach," *World Development* 19(7) (1990); and "The Underground Economy in the United States," Occasional Paper No. 2, U.S. Department of Labor, September 1992.

LOOKING AHEAD

This chapter has introduced many key variables that macroeconomists are interested in, including GDP and its components. There is much more to be learned about the data that macroeconomists use. In the next chapter, we will discuss the data on employment, unemployment, and the labor force, and in chapters 26 and 27, we will discuss the data on money and interest rates. Finally, in chapter 36, we will discuss in more detail the data on the relationship between the United States and the rest of the world.

SUMMARY

1. One source of data on the key variables in the macroeconomy are the national income and product accounts. These accounts provide a conceptual framework that macroeconomists use to think about how the pieces of the economy fit together.

GROSS DOMESTIC PRODUCT

2. *Gross domestic product (GDP)* is the key concept in national income accounting. GDP is the total market value of all final goods and services produced within a given period by factors of production located within a country. GDP excludes intermediate goods. To include goods both when they are purchased as inputs and when they are sold as final products would be double counting and an overstatement of the value of production.

3. GDP excludes all transactions in which money or goods change hands but in which no new goods and services are produced. GDP includes the income of foreigners working in the United States and the profits that foreign companies earn in the United States. GDP excludes the income of U.S. citizens working abroad and profits earned by U.S. companies in foreign countries.

4. *Gross national product (GNP)* is the market value of all final goods and services produced during a given period by factors of production owned by a country's citizens.

CALCULATING GDP

5. The *expenditure approach* to GDP adds up the amount spent on all final goods and services during a given period. The four main categories of expenditures are *personal consumption expenditures (C), gross private domestic investment (I), government consumption and investment (G),* and *net exports (EX − IM)*. The sum of these equals GDP.

6. The three main components of personal consumption expenditures (C) are *durable goods, nondurable goods,* and *services.*

7. *Gross private domestic investment (I)* is the total investment made by the private sector in a given period. There are three kinds of investment: *nonresidential investment, residential investment,* and *changes in business inventories.* Gross investment does not take *depreciation*—the decrease in the value of assets—into account. *Net investment* is equal to gross investment minus depreciation.

8. Government consumption and investment (G) include expenditures by state, federal, and local governments for final goods and services. The value of *net exports (EX − IM)* equals the differences between exports (sales to foreigners of U.S.-produced goods and services) and imports (U.S. purchases of goods and services from abroad).

9. Because every payment (expenditure) by a buyer is a receipt (income) for the seller, GDP can be computed in terms of who receives it as income—the *income approach* to calculating gross domestic product. The GDP equation using the income approach is GDP = National income + Depreciation + (Indirect taxes − Subsidies) + Net factor payments to the rest of the world.

FROM GDP TO DISPOSABLE PERSONAL INCOME

10. GNP minus depreciation is *net national product (NNP). National income* is the total amount earned by the factors of production in the economy; it is equal to NNP less indirect taxes minus subsidies. *Personal income* is the total income of households. *Disposable personal income* is what households have to spend or save after paying their taxes. The *personal saving rate* is the percentage of disposable personal income saved rather than spent.

NOMINAL VERSUS REAL GDP

11. GDP measured in current dollars (the current prices that one pays for goods) is *nominal GDP.* If we use nominal GDP to measure growth, we can be misled into thinking that production has grown when all that has happened is a

rise in the price level, or inflation. A better measure of production is *real GDP*, which is nominal GDP adjusted for prices changes.

12. The GDP price index is a measure of the overall price level.

LIMITATIONS OF THE GDP CONCEPT

13. We generally think of increases in GDP as good, but some problems arise when we try to use GDP as a measure of happiness or well-being. The peculiarities of GDP accounting mean that institutional changes can change the value of GDP even if real production has not changed. GDP ignores most social ills, such as pollution. Furthermore, GDP tells us nothing about what kinds of goods are being produced or how income is distributed across the population. GDP also ignores many transactions of the underground economy.

14. *Per capita GDP or GNP* is a country's GDP or GNP divided by its population. Per capita GDP or GNP is a better measure of well-being for the average person than is total GDP or GNP.

REVIEW TERMS AND CONCEPTS

base year, 530

change in business inventories, 522

compensation of employees, 525

corporate profits, 525

current dollars, 529

depreciation, 524

disposable personal income, or after-tax, income, 528

durable goods, 521

expenditure approach, 520

final goods and services, 518

fixed-weight procedure, 530

government consumption and investment (*G*), 524

gross domestic product (*GDP*), 517

gross investment, 524

gross national product (*GNP*), 519

gross private investment (*I*), 522

income approach, 520

indirect taxes, 526

intermediate goods, 518

national income, 525

national income and product accounts, 517

net exports (*EX − IM*), 524

net factor payments to the rest of the world, 526

net interest, 525

net investment, 524

net national product (*NNP*), 527

nominal GDP, 529

nondurable goods, 521

nonresidential investment, 522

per capita GDP or GNP, 534

personal consumption expenditures (*C*), 521

personal income, 527

personal saving, 528

personal saving rate, 528

proprietors' income, 525

rental income, 525

residential investment, 522

services, 521

subsidies, 526

underground economy, 534

value added, 518

weight, 529

Expenditure approach to GDP: $GDP = C + I + G + (EX - IM)$

$GDP = $ Final sales $+$ GDP $-$ Change in business inventories

Net investment $=$ Capital end of period $-$ Capital beginning of period

Income approach to GDP: $GDP = $ National income $+$ Depreciation $+$ (Indirect taxes $-$ Subsidies) $+$ Net factor payments to the rest of the world

PROBLEM SET

1. From the table for this problem, calculate the following:
   a. Gross private investment
   b. Net exports
   c. Gross domestic product
   d. Gross national product
   e. Net national product
   f. National income
   g. Personal income
   h. Disposable income

Transfer payments	*pg 527*	15
Subsidies		5
Social insurance payments		35
Depreciation		50
Receipts of factor income from the rest of the world		4
Government consumption and investment		75
Imports		50
Payments of factor income to the rest of the world		5
Personal interest income from government and households		35
Indirect taxes		20
Exports		60
Net private domestic investment		100
Personal taxes		60
Corporate profits		45
Personal consumption expenditures		250
Dividends		4

2. How do we know that calculating GDP by the expenditure approach yields the same answer as calculating GDP by the income approach?

3. Why do we bother to construct real GDP if we already know nominal GDP?

4. What are some of the problems using fixed weights to compute real GDP and the GDP price index? How does the BEA's approach attempt to solve these problems?

5. Explain what double counting is and discuss why GDP is not equal to total sales.

6. The following table gives some figures from a forecast of real GDP and population done by a well-known consulting firm in 1997. According to the forecast, approximately how much price inflation will there be between 1998 and 1999? What is per capita GDP projected to be in 1998? 1999? Compute the forecast rate of change in real GDP and per capita real GDP between 1998 and 1999.

Real GDP 1998 (billions)	$7,282.7
Real GDP 1999 (billions)	$7,457.1
Population 1998 (millions)	270.3
Population 1999 (millions)	272.6

7. In 1997, in Swaziland and Lesotho, countries in Africa, GNP was substantially bigger than GDP. Locate the two countries on a map of Africa. Given their location, can you explain why this might be the case?

8. During 1997, real GDP in Germany rose about 2.9 percent. During the same period, retail sales in Germany rose only about 1.1 percent in real terms. What are some possible explanations for retail sales to consumers growing more slowly than GDP? (*Hint:* Think of the composition of GDP using the expenditure approach.)

9. Which of the following transactions would not be counted in GDP? Explain your answers.
   a. General Motors issues new shares of stock to finance the construction of a plant.
   b. General Motors builds a new plant.
   c. Company A successfully launches a hostile takeover of Company B, in which it purchases all the assets of Company B.
   d. Your grandmother wins $10 million in the lottery.
   e. You buy a new copy of this textbook.
   f. You buy a used copy of this textbook.
   g. The government pays out social security benefits.
   h. A public utility installs new antipollution equipment in its smokestacks.
   i. Luigi's Pizza buys 30 pounds of mozzarella cheese, holds it in inventory for one month, and then uses it to make pizza, which it sells.
   j. You spend the weekend cleaning your apartment.
   k. A drug dealer sells $500 worth of illegal drugs.

10. If you buy a new car, the entire purchase is counted as consumption in the year in which you make the transaction. Explain briefly why this is in one sense an "error" in national income accounting. (*Hint:* How is the purchase of a car different from the purchase of a pizza?) How might you correct this error?

11. Explain why imports are subtracted in the expenditure approach to calculating GDP.

12. GDP calculations do not directly include the economic costs of environmental damage (for example, global warming, acid rain). Do you think these costs should be included in GDP? Why or why not? How could GDP be amended to include environmental damage costs?

TAKE IT TO THE NET

 We invite you to visit the Case and Fair page on the Prentice Hall Web site:

http://www.prenhall.com/casefair

for this chapter's World Wide Web exercise.

Chapter 23

MACROECONOMIC CONCERNS: UNEMPLOYMENT, INFLATION, AND GROWTH

SOMETIME DURING 1990, total employment in the United States stopped growing and began to decline. In May, total employment hit 119.9 million. By October, more than 500,000 people had lost their jobs, and by March 1991, more than 1.5 million people had lost their jobs. At the same time, after nearly eight years of steady growth, real output declined in the third and fourth quarters of 1990 and the first quarter of 1991. For many, this recession was a curiosity, something in the news. After all, 118.5 million out of 120 million workers still had jobs. But for the workers who lost their jobs, the pain was real:

> Standing in the unemployment line today, a cross section of Americans from a beautician to a film editor to a sales manager to a corporate vice president, voiced a shared sense of insecurity about the future as jobs disappear and companies close. They said their hunt for work had taken on new urgency as they watched the economy worsen and opportunities dry up. Gathered at an unemployment office in west Los Angeles, they listened with a very personal concern to the news that the unemployment rate in California had climbed today to its highest point in four years.
>
> "The hardest thing is to see how panicked people are," said Bill Williams, a part owner of a small marketing company in Huntington Beach that recently went out of business. "Right now I don't have a dime. I'm worried about buying things like sugar. I'm close to losing my home."[1]

---

[1]Seth Mydans, "For Jobless, Era of Plenty Fades to Fear," *The New York Times*, December 8, 1990, p. 1.

Twelve years earlier, the United States had wrestled with high inflation. Prices *increased* an average of 11.3 percent in 1979 and 13.5 percent in 1980. As President Jimmy Carter noted in a report to Congress in January 1980:

> It is my strong conviction that inflation remains the nation's number one economic problem. Energy and housing prices are still moving up rapidly, adding directly to inflation and continuing to threaten a new price-wage spiral in the rest of the economy. Our immediate objective must be to prevent the spread of double-digit price increases from oil to the rest of the economy. . . . Halting the spread of inflation is not enough, however. We must take steps to reduce it.[2]

These "twin evils" of unemployment and inflation are concerns of macroeconomists. In this chapter we explore these concerns, describing the periodic ups and downs in the economy that we call the business cycle. Later chapters focus on the likely causes of business cycles and some of the things that government may do to prevent or minimize the damage they create. First, we need to know more about what the business cycle is. What are recessions and depressions? Who is hurt by them? What are the consequences of inflation? Who benefits and who loses when the price level rises rapidly? Why should policy makers in Washington be concerned about the business cycle?

Also, as mentioned in chapter 21, macroeconomists are concerned about the size of the long-run growth rate of output. What factors influence the long-run growth rate? Why do some countries grow faster than others? Can policy makers influence the growth rate? We briefly consider long-run growth issues in this chapter and then return to them in chapter 34.

RECESSIONS, DEPRESSIONS, UNEMPLOYMENT

recession *Roughly, a period in which real GDP declines for at least two consecutive quarters. Marked by falling output and rising unemployment.*

Recall that a **recession** is roughly a period in which real GDP declines for at least two consecutive quarters. Also recall that real GDP is a measure of the actual output of goods and services in the economy during a given period. When real GDP falls, less is being produced. When less output is produced, fewer inputs are used, employment declines, the unemployment rate rises, and a smaller percentage of the capital stock at our disposal is utilized (more plants and equipment are running at less than full capacity). When real output falls, real income declines.

depression *A prolonged and deep recession. The precise definitions of prolonged and deep are debatable.*

A **depression** is a prolonged and deep recession, although there is disagreement over how severe and how prolonged a recession must be to be called a depression. Nearly everyone agrees the U.S. economy experienced a depression between 1929 and the late 1930s. The most severe recession since the 1930s took place between 1980 and 1982.

In Figure 21.6, we divided the period since 1970 into three "recessionary" periods, 1974 to 1975, 1980 to 1982, and 1990 to 1991. Table 23.1 summarizes some of the differences between the recession of 1980 to 1982 and the early part of the Great Depression. Between 1929 and 1933, real GDP declined by 27 percent. In other words, in 1933 the United States produced 27 percent less than in 1929. While only 3.2 percent of the labor force was unemployed in 1929, 25.2 percent was unemployed in 1933. By contrast, between 1980 and 1982 real GDP declined by just 0.2 percent. The unemployment rate rose from 5.8 percent in 1979 to 9.7 percent in 1982. *Capacity utilization rates*, which show the percentage of factory capacity being used in production, are not available for the 1930s, so we have no point of comparison. However, Table 23.1 shows capacity utilization fell from 85.2 percent in 1979 to 72.1 percent in 1982. Although the recession in the early 1980s was severe, it did not come close to the severity of the Great Depression.

---

[2]Jimmy Carter, *Economic Report of the President*, transmitted to Congress, January 1980.

TABLE 23.1 REAL GDP AND UNEMPLOYMENT RATES, 1929–1933 AND 1980–1982

THE EARLY PART OF THE GREAT DEPRESSION, 1929–1933

	PERCENTAGE CHANGE IN REAL GDP	UNEMPLOYMENT RATE	NUMBER OF UNEMPLOYED (MILLIONS)
1929		3.2	1.5
1930	−9.0	8.9	4.3
1931	−6.3	16.3	8.0
1932	−13.3	24.1	12.1
1933	−1.2	25.2	12.8

Note: Percentage fall in real GDP between 1929 and 1933 was 27.0 percent.

THE RECESSION OF 1980–1982

	PERCENTAGE CHANGE IN REAL GDP	UNEMPLOYMENT RATE	NUMBER OF UNEMPLOYED (MILLIONS)	CAPACITY UTILIZATION (PERCENTAGE)
1979		5.8	6.1	85.2
1980	−0.3	7.1	7.6	80.9
1981	2.3	7.6	8.3	79.9
1982	−2.1	9.7	10.7	72.1

Note: Percentage fall in real GDP between 1979 and 1982 was 0.2 percent.

Sources: *Historical Statistics of the United States* and U.S. Department of Commerce, Bureau of Economic Analysis.

DEFINING AND MEASURING UNEMPLOYMENT

The most frequently discussed symptom of a recession is unemployment. In September of 1982, the United States' unemployment rate was over 10 percent for the first time since the 1930s. But although unemployment is widely discussed, most people are unaware of what unemployment statistics mean or how they are derived.

The unemployment statistics released to the press on the first Friday of each month are based on a survey of households conducted by the Bureau of Labor Statistics (BLS), a branch of the Department of Labor. Each month the BLS draws a sample of 65,000 households and completes interviews with all but about 2,500 of them. Each interviewed household answers questions regarding the work activity of household members 16 years of age or older during the calendar week that contains the twelfth of the month. (The survey is conducted in the week that follows the week that contains the twelfth of the month.)

If a household member 16 years of age or older worked one hour or more as a paid employee, either for someone else or in his own business or farm, he is classified as **employed**. A household member is also considered employed if he worked 15 hours or more without pay in a family enterprise. Finally, a household member is counted as employed if she held a job from which she was temporarily absent due to illness, bad weather, vacation, labor-management disputes, or personal reasons, whether she was paid or not.

Those who are not employed fall into one of two categories: (1) unemployed or (2) not in the labor force. To be considered **unemployed**, a person must be available for work and have made specific efforts to find work during the previous four weeks.

employed *Any person 16 years old or older (1) who works for pay, either for someone else or in his or her own business for one or more hours per week, (2) who works without pay for 15 or more hours per week in a family enterprise, or (3) who has a job but has been temporarily absent, with or without pay.*

unemployed *A person 16 years old or older who is not working, is available for work, and has made specific efforts to find work during the previous four weeks.*

not in the labor force *People who are not looking for work, either because they do not want a job or because they have given up looking.*

labor force *The number of people employed plus the number of unemployed.*

Persons not looking for work, either because they do not want a job or have given up looking, are classified as **not in the labor force**. People not in the labor force include full-time students, retirees, individuals in institutions, and those staying home to take care of children or elderly parents.

The total **labor force** in the economy is the number of people employed plus the number of unemployed:

$$\text{Labor force} = \text{Employed} + \text{Unemployed}$$

The total population 16 years of age or older is equal to the number of people in the labor force plus the number not in the labor force:

$$\text{Population} = \text{Labor force} + \text{Not in labor force}$$

unemployment rate *The ratio of the number of people unemployed to the total number of people in the labor force.*

With these numbers, several ratios can be calculated. The **unemployment rate** is the ratio of the number of people unemployed to the total number of people in the labor force:

$$\text{Unemployment rate} = \frac{\text{Unemployed}}{\text{Employed} + \text{Unemployed}}$$

In January 1998, the labor force contained 137.5 million people, 131.1 million of whom were employed and 6.4 million of whom were unemployed and looking for work. The unemployment rate was 4.7 percent:

$$\frac{6.4}{131.1 + 6.4} = 4.7\%$$

labor-force participation rate *The ratio of the labor force to the total population 16 years old or older.*

The ratio of the labor force to the population 16 years old or over is called the **labor-force participation rate**:

$$\text{Labor-force participation rate} = \frac{\text{Labor force}}{\text{Population}}$$

Table 23.2 shows the relationship among these numbers for selected years since 1953. The year 1982 shows the effects of the recession. Although the unemployment rate has gone up and down, the labor-force participation rate has grown steadily since 1953. Most of this increase is due to the growth in the participation rate of women between the ages of 25 and 54.

Column 3 in Table 23.2 shows how many new workers the U.S. economy has absorbed in recent years. The number of employed workers increased by about 38 million between 1953 and 1982 and by about 30 million between 1982 and 1997.

COMPONENTS OF THE UNEMPLOYMENT RATE

The unemployment rate by itself conveys a limited amount of information. To understand the level of unemployment better, we must look at unemployment rates across groups of people, regions, and industries.

▶ **Unemployment Rates for Different Demographic Groups** There are big differences in rates of unemployment across demographic groups. Table 23.3 shows the unemployment rate for November 1982—the worst month of the recession in 1982—and for January 1998, broken down by race, sex, and age. In November 1982, when the overall unemployment rate hit 10.8 percent, the rate for whites was 9.6 percent while the rate for African Americans was more than twice that—20.2 percent.

TABLE 23.2 EMPLOYED, UNEMPLOYED, AND THE LABOR FORCE, 1953–1997

	(1) POPULATION 16 YEARS OLD OR OVER (MILLIONS)	(2) LABOR FORCE (MILLIONS)	(3) EMPLOYED (MILLIONS)	(4) UNEMPLOYED (MILLIONS)	(5) LABOR-FORCE PARTICIPATION RATE	(6) UNEMPLOYMENT RATE
1953	107.1	63.0	61.2	1.8	58.9	2.9
1960	117.2	69.6	65.8	3.9	59.4	5.5
1970	137.1	82.8	78.7	4.1	60.4	4.9
1980	167.7	106.9	99.3	7.6	63.8	7.1
1982	172.3	110.2	99.5	10.7	64.0	9.7
1990	189.2	125.8	118.8	7.0	66.5	5.6
1997	203.1	136.3	129.6	6.7	67.1	4.9

Note: Figures are civilian only (military excluded).

Source: Economic Report of the President, 1998, p. 322.

During the recession in 1982, men fared worse than women. In November 1982, 9.0 percent of white men 20 years and over, but only 8.1 percent of white women 20 years and over, were unemployed. For African Americans, 19.3 percent of men 20 years and over and 16.5 percent of women 20 years and over were unemployed. Teenagers between 16 and 19 years of age fared worst. African American men between 16 and 19 experienced an unemployment rate of 52.4 percent in November 1982. The figure was nearly as high (46.3 percent) for African American women in the same age bracket.

Although the rates were much lower for all groups in January 1998, the pattern was similar. The highest unemployment rates were for African American teenagers— 31.8 percent for men and 28.5 percent for women.

The main point of Table 23.3 is that an unemployment rate of 4.7 percent does not mean every group in society has a 4.7 percent unemployment rate.

> There are large differences in unemployment rates across demographic groups.

> **Unemployment Rates in States and Regions** Unemployment rates vary by geographical location. For a variety of reasons, not all states and regions have the same level of unemployment. States and regions have different combinations of industries, which do not all grow and decline at the same time and at the same rate. And, the labor force is not completely mobile—workers often cannot or do not want to pack up and move to take advantage of job opportunities in other parts of the country.

The last 20 years have seen remarkable changes in the relative prosperity of regions, particularly in the Northeast and the oil-rich Southwest. During the early 1970s, the Northeast (New England in particular) was hit by a serious decline in its industrial base. Textile mills, leather goods plants, and furniture factories closed in the face of foreign competition or moved south to states with lower wages. During the recession of 1975, Massachusetts and Michigan had very high unemployment rates (11.2 percent and 12.5 percent respectively). Riding the crest of rising oil prices, Texas had one of the lowest unemployment rates at that time (5.6 percent) (Table 23.4).

During the recession of 1982, Texas continued to do well. And Massachusetts took a sharp turn for the better. The unemployment rate in Massachusetts went from

TABLE 23.3

UNEMPLOYMENT RATES BY DEMOGRAPHIC GROUP, 1982 AND 1998

		NOV. 1982	JAN. 1998
Total		10.8	4.7
White		9.6	4.0
Men	20+ Yrs.	9.0	3.3
	16–19 Yrs.	22.7	14.2
Women	20+ Yrs.	8.1	3.7
	16–19 Yrs.	19.7	8.8
African American		20.2	9.3
Men	20+ Yrs.	19.3	7.9
	16–19 Yrs.	52.4	31.8
Women	20+ Yrs.	16.5	8.0
	16–19 Yrs.	46.3	28.5

Source: U.S. Department of Labor, Bureau of Labor Statistics.

TABLE 23.4

REGIONAL DIFFERENCES IN UNEMPLOYMENT, 1975, 1982, AND 1991

	1975	1982	1991
U.S. avg.	8.5	9.7	6.7
Cal.	9.9	9.9	7.5
Fla.	10.7	8.2	7.3
Ill.	7.1	11.3	7.1
Mass.	11.2	7.9	9.0
Mich.	12.5	15.5	9.2
N.J.	10.2	9.0	6.6
N.Y.	9.5	8.6	7.2
N.C.	8.6	9.0	5.8
Ohio	9.1	12.5	6.4
Tex.	5.6	6.9	6.6

Sources: Statistical Abstract of the United States, various editions.

discouraged-worker effect
The decline in the measured unemployment rate that results when people who want to work but cannot find jobs grow discouraged and stop looking, thus dropping out of the ranks of the unemployed and the labor force.

TABLE 23.5

UNEMPLOYMENT IN DIFFERENT INDUSTRIES, 1998

	JANUARY 1998
Mining	4.0
Construction	7.9
Manufacturing	3.9
Durable goods	3.4
Nondurable goods	4.5
Transportation and public utilities	3.8
Wholesale and retail trade	5.9
Finance	2.6
Services	4.3
Agriculture	10.6
Government	2.4
National average	4.7

Source: U.S. Department of Labor, Bureau of Labor Statistics.

nearly three points above the national average during the 1975 recession to nearly two points below during the 1982 recession.

By 1987, things had changed. Although not shown in Table 23.4, Massachusetts had one of the lowest unemployment rates in the country in 1987 (an amazing 2.8 percent) and Texas (at 8.5 percent) had one of the highest. In Massachusetts, high-tech firms such as Wang Laboratories and Digital Equipment, two firms that employed a total of over 100,000 people, had grown dramatically. In contrast, the fall in crude oil prices from over $30 per barrel to under $15 per barrel in the early 1980s forced the oil-based economy of Texas into a deep and prolonged recession. Then, in 1991, Massachusetts experienced yet another reversal with an unemployment rate of 9 percent.

The economy of Michigan is heavily tied to the fortunes of the automobile industry. During the recession of 1982, Michigan had the highest unemployment rate in the country at 15.5 percent. Not only did the automobile industry suffer from the decline in the U.S. economy, it also faced stiff foreign competition, primarily from Japan. Michigan also suffered in 1991, with an unemployment rate of 9.2 percent.

> The national unemployment rate does not tell the whole story. A low national rate of unemployment does not mean that the entire nation is growing and producing at the same rate.

▶ **Unemployment Rates in Different Industries** Unemployment rates also differ from industry to industry. Table 23.5 shows that in January 1998 the unemployment rate in the construction industry was 3.2 percentage points higher than the national average. The three lowest unemployment rates were for government (2.4 percent), finance (2.6 percent), and durable goods manufacturing (3.4 percent).

▶ **Discouraged-Worker Effects** Remember: People who stop looking for work are classified as having dropped out of the labor force rather than as being unemployed. During recessions people may become discouraged about finding a job and stop looking. This lowers the unemployment rate, because those no longer looking for work are no longer counted as unemployed.

To demonstrate how this **discouraged-worker effect** lowers the unemployment rate, suppose there are 10 million unemployed out of a labor force of 100 million. This means an unemployment rate of 10/100 = .10, or 10 percent. If 1 million of these 10 million unemployed people stop looking for work and drop out of the labor force, there would be 9 million unemployed out of a labor force of 99 million. The unemployment rate would then drop to 9/99 = .091, or 9.1 percent.

The Bureau of Labor Statistics survey provides some evidence on the size of the discouraged-worker effect. Respondents who indicate that they have stopped searching for work are asked why they stopped. If the respondent cites inability to find employment as the sole reason for not searching, that person might be classified as a discouraged worker.

The number of discouraged workers seems to hover around 1 percent of the size of the labor force in normal times. During the 1980 to 1982 recession, the number of discouraged workers increased steadily to a peak of 1.5 percent. By the end of the first quarter of 1991, the recession of 1990 to 1991 had produced 997,000 discouraged workers.[3] Some economists argue that adding the number of discouraged workers to the number who are now classified as unemployed gives a better picture of the unemployment situation.

▶ **The Duration of Unemployment** The unemployment rate measures unemployment at a given point in time. It tells us nothing about how long the average unemployed worker is out of work.

---
[3]*The New York Times*, April 6, 1991, p. 1.

Table 23.6 shows that during recessionary periods the average duration of unemployment rises. Between 1979 and 1983, the average duration of unemployment rose from 10.8 weeks to 20 weeks. The slow growth following the 1990 to 1991 recession resulted in an increase in duration of unemployment to 17.7 weeks in 1992 and to 18.8 weeks in 1994. By 1997 average duration was down to 15.8 weeks.

THE COSTS OF UNEMPLOYMENT

In the Employment Act of 1946, the Congress declared it was the

> continuing policy and responsibility of the federal government to use all practicable means. . . . to promote maximum employment, production, and purchasing power.

In 1978, Congress passed the Full Employment and Balanced Growth Act, commonly referred to as the *Humphrey-Hawkins Act*, which formally established a specific unemployment target of 4 percent.

Why should full employment be a policy objective of the federal government? What costs does unemployment impose on society?

▶ **Some Unemployment Is Inevitable** Before we discuss the costs of unemployment, we must realize that some unemployment is simply part of the natural workings of the labor market. Remember: to be classified as unemployed, a person must be looking for a job. Every year, thousands of people enter the labor force for the first time. Some have dropped out of high school, some are high school or college graduates, and still others are finishing graduate programs. At the same time, new firms are starting up and others are expanding and creating new jobs, while other firms are contracting or going out of business.

At any moment, there is a set of job seekers and a set of jobs that must be matched with one another. It is important that the right people end up in the right jobs. The right job for a person will depend on that person's skills, her preferences regarding work environment (large firm or small, formal or informal), where she lives, and her willingness to commute. At the same time, firms want workers who can meet the requirements of the job and grow with the company.

To make a good match, workers must acquire information on job availability, wage rates, location, and work environment. Firms must acquire information on worker availability and skills. Information-gathering consumes time and resources. The search may involve travel, interviewing, preparation of a résumé, telephone calls, and hours going through the newspaper. But to the extent that these efforts lead to a better match of workers and jobs, they are well spent. As long as the gains to firms and workers exceed the costs of search, the result is efficient.

▶ **Frictional and Structural Unemployment** When the BLS does its survey about work activity during the week containing the twelfth of each month, it interviews many people who are involved in the normal search for work. Some are either entering the labor force or switching jobs. This unemployment is both natural and beneficial for the economy.

The portion of unemployment due to the normal working of the labor market is called **frictional unemployment**. The frictional unemployment rate can never be zero. It may, however, change over time. As jobs become more and more differentiated and the number of required skills increases, matching skills and jobs becomes more complex, and the frictional unemployment rate may rise.

The concept of frictional unemployment is somewhat abstract because it is hard to know what "the normal working of the labor market" means. The industrial structure of the U.S. economy is continually changing. Manufacturing, for instance, has yielded part of its share of total employment to services and to finance, insurance, and real estate. Within the manufacturing sector, the steel and textiles industries have contracted sharply, while high-technology sectors, such as electronic components, have expanded.

TABLE 23.6

AVERAGE DURATION OF UNEMPLOYMENT, 1979–1997

	WEEKS
1979	10.8
1980	11.9
1981	13.7
1982	15.6
1983	20.0
1984	18.2
1985	15.6
1986	15.0
1987	14.5
1988	13.5
1989	11.9
1990	12.0
1991	13.7
1992	17.7
1993	18.0
1994	18.8
1995	16.6
1996	16.7
1997	15.8

Sources: U.S. Department of Labor, Bureau of Labor Statistics.

frictional unemployment
The portion of unemployment that is due to the normal working of the labor market; used to denote short-run job/skill matching problems.

Although the unemployment that arises from such structural shifts could be classified as frictional, it is usually called **structural unemployment**. The term *frictional unemployment* is used to denote short-run job/skill matching problems, problems that last a few weeks. *Structural unemployment* denotes longer-run adjustment problems—those that tend to last for years.

Although structural unemployment is expected in a dynamic economy, it is painful to the workers who experience it. In some ways, those who lose their jobs because their skills are obsolete are the ones who experience the greatest pain. The fact that structural unemployment is natural and inevitable does not mean it costs society nothing.

Economists sometimes use the phrase **natural rate of unemployment** to refer to unemployment that occurs as a normal part of the functioning of the economy. This concept is also somewhat vague, because "natural" is not a precise word. It is probably best to think of the natural rate as the sum of the frictional rate and the structural rate. Estimates of the natural rate range from 4 percent to 7 percent, but most labor market analysts assume that it lies somewhere in the 5 percent to 6 percent range.

➤ **Cyclical Unemployment and Lost Output** Although some unemployment is "natural," there are times when the unemployment rate seems to be above the natural rate. In 1979, the unemployment rate was 5.8 percent, but it did not fall below 6 percent again until 1987, eight years later. In the meantime, the United States experienced a major recession, during which the unemployment rate rose substantially. The increase in unemployment that occurs during recessions and depressions is called **cyclical unemployment**.

In one sense, an increase in unemployment during a recession is simply a manifestation of a more fundamental problem. The basic problem is that firms are producing less. Remember that a recession entails a decline in real GDP, or real output. When firms cut back and produce less, they employ fewer workers and less capital. Thus, the first and most direct cost of a recession is the loss of real goods and services that otherwise would have been produced.

Never was the loss of output more dramatic than during the Great Depression. In Table 23.1 you saw that real output fell about 30 percent between 1929 and 1933. It is, of course, the real output of the economy that matters most—the food we eat, the medical care we get, the cars we drive, the movies we watch, the new houses that are built, the pots we cook in, and the education we receive. When output falls by 30 percent, life changes for a lot of people.

During the recession of 1980 to 1982, the growth rate of real GDP was on average zero. In Table 23.1, had real GDP grown at 3 percent each year from 1979, the total growth in output in the 1980 to 1982 period would have been about 9 percent instead of the 0 percent that actually occurred. This is a substantial loss of output.

➤ **Social Consequences** The costs of recessions and depressions are neither evenly distributed across the population nor easily quantifiable. The social consequences of the Depression of the 1930s are perhaps the hardest to comprehend. Most people alive today did not live through the Great Depression and can only read about it in books or hear stories told by parents and grandparents. Few emerged from this period unscathed. At the bottom were the poor and the fully unemployed, about 25 percent of the labor force. But even those who kept their jobs found themselves working part time. Many people lost all or part of their savings as the stock market crashed and thousands of banks failed.

Congressional committees heard story after story. In Cincinnati, where the labor force totaled about 200,000, 48,000 were wholly unemployed, 40,000 more were on short time, and relief payments to the needy averaged $7 to $8 per week:

> Relief is given to a family one week and then they are pushed off for a week in the hope that somehow or other the breadwinner may find some kind of work. . . .

We are paying no rent at all. That, of course, is a very difficult problem because we are continually having evictions, and social workers . . . are hard put to find places for people whose furniture has been put out on the street.[4]

From Birmingham, Alabama, in 1932:

. . . we have about 108,000 wage and salary workers in my district. Of that number, it is my belief that not exceeding 8000 have their normal incomes. At least 25,000 men are altogether without work. Some of them have not had a stroke of work for more than 12 months. Perhaps 60,000 or 70,000 are working from one to five days a week, and practically all have had serious cuts in wages and many of them do not average over $1.50 per day.[5]

Economic hardship accompanied the recent recessions as well. Between 1979 and 1983, the number of people officially classified as living in poverty in the United States rose from 26.1 million (11.7 percent of the population) to 35.5 million (15.3 percent). In addition to economic hardship, prolonged unemployment may also bring with it social and personal ills: anxiety, depression, a deterioration of physical and psychological health, drug abuse (including alcoholism), and suicide. There is also some evidence that the number of welfare recipients rises and falls with unemployment. See the Issues and Debates box "Unemployment and Welfare: 1991 to 1997."

THE BENEFITS OF RECESSIONS

Do recessions have any benefits? Yes: Recessions are likely to slow the rate of inflation. We saw in Figure 21.8 two serious inflationary periods since 1970: 1974 to 1975 and 1979 to 1981. Each was followed by a recession during which the rate of inflation decreased. As Table 23.7 shows, inflation fell from a 1974 rate of 11.0 percent to 5.8 percent in 1976. In 1983, the inflation rate also fell, to 3.2 percent, from a 1980 rate of 13.5 percent.

It appears recessions do help to counteract inflation, but more analysis is needed before we can understand why (see chapter 29). The point here is:

Recessions may help to reduce inflation.

Some argue recessions may increase efficiency by driving the least efficient firms in the economy out of business and forcing surviving firms to trim waste and manage their resources better. As we will discuss in chapter 36, a recession leads to a decrease in the demand for imports, which improves a nation's balance of payments—that is, its record of trade with other countries.

INFLATION

Ups in the business cycle often, but not always, seem to encourage inflation. Table 23.8 shows the rate of inflation during the three most recent periods of expansion. The inflation rate rose from 3.2 percent to 11.0 percent from 1972 to 1974. The trend in inflation was also upward from 1976 to 1980. The sustained growth that began in 1983, however, did not seem to bring rapid inflation.

Why is inflation a problem? If you understand that wages and salaries, as well as other forms of income, increase along with prices during periods of inflation, you will see this question is more subtle than you might think. If my income doubles and the prices of the things I buy double, am I any worse off? I can buy exactly the same things

TABLE 23.7

INFLATION RATES, 1974–1976 AND 1980–1983

RECESSION BEGINS	INFLATION RATE
→ 1974	11.0
1975	9.1
1976	5.8
→ 1980	13.5
1981	10.3
1982	6.2
1983	3.2

Source: See Table 23.9.

TABLE 23.8

INFLATION DURING THREE EXPANSIONS

	INFLATION RATE
1972	3.2
1973	6.2
1974	11.0
1976	5.8
1977	6.5
1978	7.6
1979	11.3
1980	13.5
1984	4.3
1985	3.6
1986	1.9
1987	3.6
1988	4.1
1989	4.8

Source: See Table 23.9.

---

[4]U.S. Senate Hearings before a subcommittee of the Committee of Manufacturers, 72nd Congress, first session (1931), p. 239. Cited in Lester Chandler, *America's Greatest Depression, 1929–1941* (New York: Harper and Row, 1970), p. 43.

[5]Senate Hearings, in Lester Chandler, *America's Greatest Depression*, p. 43.

In the spring of 1991 the U.S. economy began to grow following a brief recession. In 1992, civilian employment totaled 118.5 million, and the unemployment rate stood at 7.5 percent, with 9.6 million looking for work. During the next six years, the economy expanded and unemployment declined.

By August of 1997, the economy had added 18 million jobs, real GDP had expanded over 17 percent, and the number of unemployed was down to 6.7 million, or 4.9 percent of the labor force.

At the same time, there was a steady decline in the number of persons receiving welfare benefits. Although there is much debate about the causes of the decline in welfare, no one doubts that it is partly the result of the strong economy. A 1997 paper written by economists Phillip Levine and Diane Whitmore at the Council of Economic Advisers tries to sort out the link.

The pattern of association between the number of welfare recipients and the number of unemployed is not new and it can be seen in Figure 1.

The authors conclude:

From January 1993 to January 1997, the number of individuals receiving welfare fell by 20 percent, or 2.75 million recipients—the largest decline in over 50 years. Three explanations for this decline are (1) economic growth, which created 12 million new jobs over the period, (2) Federal waivers, which allowed 43 states to experiment with

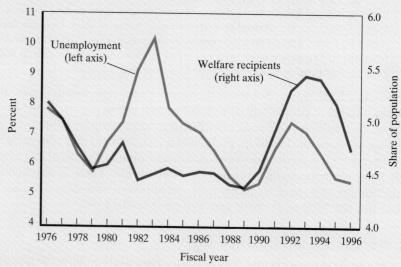

FIGURE 1

Unemployment Rate and Rate of Welfare Receipt[a]

innovative ideas to help reduce welfare dependency, and (3) other policies affecting work-related incentives, including the 1990 and 1993 expansions of the Earned Income Tax Credit (EITC) and the recent rise in federal and state spending on child care. Over 40 percent of the decline resulted from a falling unemployment rate associated with the economic expansion and almost one-third from statewide welfare reform waivers (Figure 2).[b]

Sources: [a]Phillip Levine and Diane Whitmore, "Explaining the Decline in Welfare Receipt," Council of Economic Advisers, May 9, 1997; [b]Ibid; [c]Ibid.

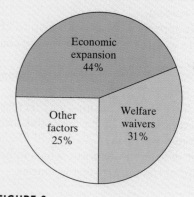

FIGURE 2

Reasons for the Decline in Welfare Caseloads, 1993 to 1996[c]

For more on unemployment and welfare, see the Case and Fair Web page at
http://www.prenhall.com/casefair.

that I bought yesterday, so to the extent that my well-being depends on what I am able to buy, the answer is no.

However, incomes and prices do not all increase at the same rate during inflations. For some people, income increases faster than prices; for others, prices increase faster. Some people benefit from inflations, others are hurt.

The remainder of this chapter focuses on the problem of inflation: its measurement, its costs, and the gains and losses experienced during inflationary periods.

DEFINING INFLATION

What is inflation? Not all price increases constitute inflation. Prices of individual goods and services are determined in many ways. In competitive markets, the interaction of many buyers and many sellers—the operation of supply and demand—determines prices. In imperfectly competitive markets, prices are determined by producers' decisions. (This is the core of microeconomic theory.)

In any economy, prices are continuously changing as markets adjust to changing conditions. Lack of rain may dry up corn and wheat fields, reducing supply and pushing up the price of agricultural products. At the same time, high levels of production by oil producers may be driving down the price of oil and petroleum products. Simultaneously, the United Auto Workers may be negotiating a contract with the Ford Motor Company that raises (or lowers) wage rates.

When the price of one good rises, that price increase may or may not be part of a larger inflation. Remember: **inflation** is an increase in the overall price level. It happens when many prices increase simultaneously. We measure inflation by looking at a large number of goods and services and calculating the average increase in their prices during some period of time. **Deflation** is a decrease in the overall price level. It occurs when many prices decrease simultaneously.

It is useful to distinguish between a *one-time* increase in the overall price level and an increase in the overall price level that continues over time. For example, the overall price level could rise 10 percent in a single month and stop rising, or it could increase steadily over some years. Economists often use *inflation* to refer only to increases in the price level that continue over some significant period. We will refer to such periods as periods of **sustained inflation**.

inflation *An increase in the overall price level.*

deflation *A decrease in the overall price level.*

sustained inflation *An increase in the overall price level that continues over a significant period.*

PRICE INDEXES

Price indexes are used to measure overall price levels. We discussed how these indexes are constructed in the previous chapter. The price index that pertains to all goods and services in the economy is the *GDP price index*. As we saw in chapter 22, the BEA does not use fixed weights to construct the GDP price index. Most other price indexes are constructed using fixed weights.

The most popular fixed-weight price index is the **consumer price index (CPI)**. The CPI was first constructed during World War I as a basis for adjusting shipbuilders' wages, which the government controlled during the war. Currently, the CPI is computed by the Bureau of Labor Statistics each month, using a bundle of goods meant to represent the "market basket" purchased monthly by the typical urban consumer. The quantities of each good in the bundle that are used for the weights are based on extensive surveys of consumers.

Table 23.9 shows values of the CPI since 1950. The percentage changes in the table are calculated using the index. (The base period for this index is three years, 1982 to 1984, rather than the more usual one year.) For example, from 1970 to 1971 the CPI increased from 38.8 to 40.5. The percentage change is simply $[(40.5 - 38.8)/38.8] \times 100$, which is 4.4 percent.

Remember from the previous chapter that a fixed-weight price index like the CPI does not account for consumers' substitution away from high-priced goods.

consumer price index (CPI) *A price index computed each month by the Bureau of Labor Statistics using a bundle that is meant to represent the "market basket" purchased monthly by the typical urban consumer.*

Changes in the CPI somewhat overstate changes in the cost of living.

For further discussion of the CPI, see the Issues and Debates box "Controversy Over the CPI—1997."

Other popular price indexes are **producer price indexes (PPIs)**, once called *wholesale price indexes*. These are indexes of prices that producers receive for products at all stages in the production process, not just the final stage. The indexes are calculated

producer price indexes (PPIs) *Measures of prices that producers receive for products at all stages in the production process.*

TABLE 23.9 THE CPI, 1950–1997

YEAR	% Δ IN THE CPI	CPI	YEAR	% Δ IN THE CPI	CPI
1950	1.3	24.1	1974	11.0	49.3
1951	7.9	26.0	1975	9.1	53.8
1952	1.9	26.5	1976	5.8	56.9
1953	0.8	26.7	1977	6.5	60.6
1954	0.7	26.9	1978	7.6	65.2
1955	−0.4	26.8	1979	11.3	72.6
1956	1.5	27.2	1980	13.5	82.4
1957	3.3	28.1	1981	10.3	90.9
1958	2.8	28.9	1982	6.2	96.5
1959	0.7	29.1	1983	3.2	99.6
1960	1.7	29.6	1984	4.3	103.9
1961	1.0	29.9	1985	3.6	107.6
1962	1.0	30.2	1986	1.9	109.6
1963	1.3	30.6	1987	3.6	113.6
1964	1.3	31.0	1988	4.1	118.3
1965	1.6	31.5	1989	4.8	124.0
1966	2.9	32.4	1990	5.4	130.7
1967	3.1	33.4	1991	4.2	136.2
1968	4.2	34.8	1992	3.0	140.3
1969	5.5	36.7	1993	3.0	144.5
1970	5.7	38.8	1994	2.6	148.2
1971	4.4	40.5	1995	2.8	152.4
1972	3.2	41.8	1996	3.0	156.9
1973	6.2	44.4	1997	2.3	160.5

Sources: U.S. Department of Labor, Bureau of Labor Statistics.

separately for various stages in the production process. The three main categories are *finished goods, intermediate materials,* and *crude materials,* although there are subcategories within each of these categories.

One advantage of some of the producer price indexes is that they detect price increases early in the production process. Because their movements sometimes foreshadow future changes in consumer prices, they are considered to be leading indicators of future consumer prices.

THE COSTS OF INFLATION

If you asked most people why inflation is "bad," they would tell you that it lowers the overall standard of living by making goods and services more expensive. That is, it cuts into people's purchasing power. People are fond of recalling the days when a bottle of Coca-Cola cost a dime and a hamburger cost a quarter. Just think what we could buy today if prices had not changed!

What people usually do not think about is what their incomes were in the "good old days." The fact that the cost of a Coke has increased from 10¢ to 50¢ does not mean anything in real terms if people who once earned $5,000 now earn $25,000. Why? The reason is simple:

People's income from wages and salaries, profits, interest and rent increases during inflations. The wage rate is the price of labor, rent is the price of land, and so on. During inflations, most prices—including input prices—tend to rise together, and input prices determine both the incomes of workers and the incomes of owners of capital and land.

CONTROVERSY OVER THE CPI—1997

One function of the Consumer Price Index (CPI) is to adjust programs like social security for changes in the cost of living. For years, the accuracy and appropriateness of the CPI as a measure of the cost of living has been debated. The following excerpt from the 1997 *Economic Report of the President* describes the controversy:

> Many researchers have argued that the CPI overstates increases in the cost of living. Much of this research comes from the Bureau of Labor Statistics (BLS), which produces the CPI. This research has identified several possible sources of bias; the degree of consensus on the importance of each varies.

SUBSTITUTION BIAS

The CPI prices a fixed market basket of commodities. Shares of these commodities in the basket are based on spending patterns observed in a base period. But consumers do not buy the same basket of goods from year to year. When the prices of some goods rise more quickly than those of other goods, consumers often substitute away from those that have become relatively expensive and toward others that have become relatively cheap. Increases in the CPI measure how much additional income a typical consumer would need to buy the base-period market basket at the new prices. In contrast, a true cost-of-living index would measure how much more income a consumer needs to maintain the same level of economic well-being, taking into account the ability

to substitute among goods. By ignoring substitution, the CPI overstates increases in the cost of living.

QUALITY ADJUSTMENT

Measuring inflation properly requires distinguishing between changes in the underlying price and changes in quality. The BLS measures quality changes when it can. Some are easy to measure, for example when bakers double the size of their chocolate chip cookies. Others are more difficult but straightforward: for example, optional automobile equipment that later becomes standard, such as air bags or antilock brakes, can be quality-adjusted by its price when it was sold as an option. Quality adjustments generally have a significant effect on price increases as measured by the CPI.

NEW PRODUCTS

New products, such as air conditioners in the 1950s or videocassette recorders in the 1980s, usually decline sharply in price during the first years they are available for sale. But these products are not usually included in the CPI basket until years after their introduction, and so the CPI never records their initial price declines.

OUTLET SUBSTITUTION

Over time, consumers may change their shopping patterns, shifting from high-priced to low-priced outlets, where the quality of service is often lower. Current methods assume that all of the difference in

price between high- and low-priced outlets reflects differences in the quality of service. To the extent this assumption is not appropriate, current methods overlook one source of price decline.

An advisory commission appointed by the Senate Finance Committee has estimated that the current CPI overstates inflation by 1.1 percentage points per year. Their estimate of bias is the sum of the following parts:

SOURCE OF BIAS	ESTIMATE OF BIAS (PERCENTAGE POINTS)
Substitution	
Upper level (between-category)	0.15
Lower level (within-category)	.25
New products and quality change	.60
Switching to new outlets	.10
Total	1.1
Plausible range	.8–1.6

Others, including Bureau of Labor Statistics commissioner Katherine Abraham, strongly dispute the results of the commission's study. They claim that the bias is significant but much smaller, closer to 0.4 percent in total.

Source: *Economic Report of the President, 1997, pp. 67–71.*

For more on the consumer price index, see the Case and Fair Web page at **http://www.prenhall.com/casefair.**

➤ **Inflation Changes the Distribution of Income** Whether you gain or lose during a period of inflation depends on whether your income rises faster or slower than the prices of the things you buy. The group most often mentioned when the impact of inflation is discussed is people living on fixed incomes. If your income is fixed and prices rise, your ability to purchase goods and services falls proportionately. But who are the fixed-income earners?

Most people think of the elderly. Many retired workers living on private pensions receive monthly checks that will never increase. Many pension plans, however, pay benefits that are *indexed* to inflation. The benefits these plans provide automatically increase when the general price level rises. If prices rise 10 percent, benefits also rise 10 percent. The biggest source of income for the elderly is social security. These benefits are fully indexed; when prices rise (that is, when the CPI rises) by 5 percent, social security benefits also increase by 5 percent.

The poor have not fared so well. Welfare benefits, which are not indexed, have not kept pace with the price level over the last two decades. Benefits to families with dependent children under the AFDC program declined 33 percent in real terms between 1970 and 1988. In five states—Idaho, Illinois, Kentucky, New Jersey, and Texas—the average benefits fell by more than 50 percent in real terms.[6]

▶ **Effects on Debtors and Creditors**   It is also commonly believed that debtors benefit at the expense of creditors during an inflation. Certainly, if I loan you $100 to be paid back in a year, and prices increase 10 percent in the meantime, I get back 10 percent less in real terms than what I loaned you.

But suppose we had both anticipated prices would rise 10 percent. I would have taken this into consideration in the deal that I made with you. I would charge you an interest rate high enough to cover the decrease in value due to the anticipated inflation. If we agree on a 15 percent interest rate, then you must pay me $115 at the end of a year. The difference between the interest rate on a loan and the inflation rate is referred to as the **real interest rate**. In our deal, I will earn a real interest rate of 5 percent. By charging a 15 percent interest rate, I have taken into account the anticipated 10 percent inflation rate. In this sense, I am not hurt by the inflation—I keep pace with inflation and earn a profit on my money, too—despite the fact that I am a creditor.

On the other hand, an unanticipated inflation—an inflation that takes people by surprise—can hurt creditors. If the actual inflation rate during the period of my loan to you turns out to be 20 percent, then I as a creditor will be hurt. I charged you 15 percent interest, expecting to get a 5 percent real rate of return, when I needed to charge you 25 percent to get the same 5 percent real rate of return. Because inflation turned out to be higher than expected, I got a negative real return of 5 percent.

> Inflation that is higher than expected benefits debtors; inflation that is lower than expected benefits creditors.

▶ **Administrative Costs and Inefficiencies**   There are costs associated even with anticipated inflation. One is the administrative cost associated with simply keeping up. During the rapid inflation in Israel in the early 1980s, a telephone hotline was set up to give the hourly price index! Store owners have to recalculate and re-post prices frequently, and this takes time that could be used more efficiently.

More frequent banking transactions may be required. For example, interest rates tend to rise with anticipated inflation. When interest rates are high, the opportunity costs of holding cash outside of banks is high. People therefore hold less cash and need to stop at the bank more often. (We discuss this in more detail in the next part of this book.) In addition, if people are not fully informed, or if they do not understand what is happening to prices in general, they may make mistakes in their business dealings. These mistakes can lead to a misallocation of resources.

▶ **Increased Risk and Slower Economic Growth**   When unanticipated inflation occurs regularly, the degree of risk associated with investments in the economy increases.

real interest rate *The difference between the interest rate on a loan and the inflation rate.*

[6]Alicia H. Munnell, "The Current Status of Our Social Welfare System," Federal Reserve Bank of Boston, monograph (1987).

Increases in uncertainty may make investors reluctant to invest in capital and to make long-term commitments. Because the level of investment falls, the prospects for long-term economic growth are lessened.

INFLATION: PUBLIC ENEMY NUMBER ONE?

Economists have debated the seriousness of the costs of inflation for decades. Some, like Alan Blinder, say "inflation, like every teenager, is grossly misunderstood, and this gross misunderstanding blows the political importance of inflation out of all proportion to its economic importance."[7] Others, like Phillip Cagan and Robert Lipsey, argue "it was once thought that the economy would in time make all the necessary adjustments [to inflation], but many of them are proving to be very difficult. . . . for financial institutions and markets, the effects of inflation have been extremely unsettling."[8]

No matter what the real economic cost of inflation, people don't like it. It makes us uneasy and unhappy. In 1974, President Ford verbalized some of this discomfort when he said "our inflation, our public enemy number one, will unless whipped destroy our country, our homes, our liberties, our property, and finally our national pride, as surely as any well-armed wartime enemy."[9] In this belief, our elected leaders have vigorously pursued policies designed to stop inflation. This brings us to where we started. If, as we suggested earlier, the recessions of 1974 to 1975 and 1980 to 1982 were the price we had to pay to stop inflation, stopping inflation is costly.

GLOBAL UNEMPLOYMENT AND INFLATION

Unemployment and inflation are not just concerns of the United States. Other countries at times experience high unemployment or high inflation (or both). The Great Depression of the 1930s was a worldwide phenomenon, and most countries experienced high rates of inflation in the 1970s after the OPEC oil price increases.

The highest rates of inflation in 1997 among countries where we have data were in Bulgaria, Congo, and Rumania. Very high rates of inflation are seen in the other transition economies of Eastern Europe and in developing countries, particularly in Latin America. At the same time, Europe was struggling with high unemployment. Unemployment figures for developing countries are difficult to obtain and hard to interpret. (See Table 23.10.)

OUTPUT GROWTH

It was pointed out in chapter 21 that the average growth rate of output in the U.S. economy since 1900 has been about 3.4 percent per year. Some years are better than others, but on average the rate is 3.4 percent. The key question in the area of economics called "growth theory" is: What determines this rate? Why 3.4 percent and not 2 percent or 4 percent? This question is the subject of chapter 34, but a few points can be made now.

First, machines (capital) and workers (labor) are needed to produce output. Other things being equal, the more capital and labor there is in a country the more output can be produced. Second, machines differ in their efficiency and workers differ in their skills. Other things being equal, the more efficient the capital is, the more output can be produced per unit of capital, and the more skilled labor is, the more output can be produced per worker.

A country's growth rate of output thus depends on (1) how fast its capital stock is growing, (2) how fast the average efficiency of the capital stock is growing, (3) how

TABLE 23.10

INFLATION AND UNEMPLOYMENT IN 1997

COUNTRY	RATE OF INFLATION
Bulgaria	1,268%
Congo	544%
Rumania	175%
Turkey	90%
Venezuela	39%
Mexico	19%
Colombia	18%
Hungary	18%

COUNTRY	RATE OF UNEMPLOYMENT
Spain	20.8%
Belgium	14.1%
France	12.5%
Italy	12.4%
Germany	11.7%
Canada	9.0%

Source: The Economist, October 11, 1997.

---

[7]Alan Blinder, *Hard Heads, Soft Hearts: Tough-Minded Economics for a Just Society* (Reading, Mass.: Addison-Wesley, 1987).

[8]Phillip Cagan and Robert Lipsey, "The Financial Effects of Inflation," National Bureau of Economic Research (Cambridge, Mass.: General Series #103, 1978), pp. 67–68.

[9]U.S. President, Weekly Compilation of Presidential Documents, vol. 10, no. 41, p 1247. Cited in Blinder, *Hard Heads*.

fast the number of workers (labor force) is growing, and (4) how fast the average skill level of the labor force is growing. Let's take each of these four in turn.

We saw in chapter 22 that the capital stock increases when net investment is positive, that is, when the number of new machines produced (gross investment) exceeds the number of machines that wear out (depreciation). Positive net investment values are thus good for output growth because this means that the capital stock is increasing, which allows more output to be produced.

If machines are getting more efficient over time, there is "technical progress." An example of technical progress: Each year personal computers get faster and more efficient. Because the more efficient capital is, the more output can be produced per unit of capital, technical progress increases the growth rate of output.

The labor force of a country can increase either because the population is growing or because there is an increase in labor force participation (the number of workers as a fraction of the total population). Ignoring possible unemployment problems, the faster the growth rate of the labor force, the greater will be the growth rate of output.

Finally, if workers are becoming more skilled over time, this will increase output growth, because on average workers are becoming more efficient. Workers can acquire skills through education and on-the-job training. A worker's skills are sometimes called "human capital." As with physical capital, the more human capital there is, the more output will be produced. Output growth depends in part on the growth of human capital.

Three of the main focuses of growth theory are investment, technical progress, and human capital. A related concern is "productivity," defined as output per worker. If output is growing at 3 percent and the labor force is growing at 1 percent (due, say, to population growth), then productivity is growing at 2 percent. Positive net investment, positive technical progress, and an increase in human capital per worker all contribute to an increase in productivity, because all three lead to an increase in output per worker. We will have more to say about this in chapter 34.

LOOKING AHEAD

This ends our introduction to the basic concepts and problems of macroeconomics. The first chapter of this part introduced the field, the second discussed the measurement of national product and national income, and this chapter discussed three of the macroeconomy's major concerns—unemployment, inflation, and growth.

Thus far, we have said nothing about what *determines* the level of national output, the number of employed and unemployed workers, and the rate of inflation in an economy. The following chapters provide the background in macroeconomic theory you need to understand *how* the macroeconomy functions. With this knowledge, you will be able to understand how the government can influence the economy through its taxing, spending, and monetary policies.

SUMMARY

RECESSIONS, DEPRESSIONS, AND UNEMPLOYMENT

1. A *recession* is a period in which real GDP declines for at least two consecutive quarters. When less output is produced, employment declines, the unemployment rate rises, and a smaller percentage of the capital stock is used. When real output falls, real income declines.

2. A *depression* is a prolonged and deep recession, although there is disagreement over how severe and how prolonged a recession must be to be called a depression.

3. The *unemployment rate* is the ratio of the number of unemployed people to the number of people in the labor force. To be considered unemployed and in the labor force, a person must be looking for work.

4. Big differences in rates of unemployment exist across demographic groups, regions, and industries. African Americans, for example, experience much higher unemployment rates than whites.

5. A person who decides to stop looking for work is considered to have dropped out of the labor force and is no longer classified as unemployed. People who stop looking because they are discouraged about finding a job are sometimes called *discouraged workers*.

6. Some unemployment is inevitable. Because new workers are continually entering the labor force, because industries and firms are continuously expanding and contracting, and because people switch jobs, there is a constant process of job search as workers and firms try to match the best people to the available jobs. This unemployment is both natural and beneficial for the economy.

7. The unemployment that occurs because of short-run job/skill matching problems is called *frictional unemployment*. The unemployment that occurs because of longer-run structural changes in the economy is called *structural unemployment*. The *natural rate of unemployment* is the sum of the frictional rate and the structural rate. The increase in unemployment that occurs during recessions and depressions is called *cyclical unemployment*.

8. The major costs associated with recessions and unemployment are decreased real output, the damage done to the people who are unemployed, and lost output in the future. Benefits of recessions are that they may help to reduce inflation, increase efficiency, and improve a nation's balance of payments.

INFLATION

9. An *inflation* is an increase in the overall price level. It happens when many prices increase simultaneously. Inflation is measured by calculating the average increase in the prices of a large number of goods during some period of time. A *deflation* is a decrease in the overall price level. A *sustained inflation* is an increase in the overall price level that continues over a significant period of time.

10. A number of different indexes are used to measure the overall price level. Among them are the *GDP price index, consumer price index (CPI),* and *producer price indexes (PPIs)*.

11. Whether a person gains or loses during a period of inflation depends on whether his or her income rises faster or slower than the prices of the things he or she buys. The elderly are more insulated from inflation than most people think, because social security benefits and many pensions are indexed to inflation. Welfare benefits, which are not indexed to inflation, have not kept pace with inflation since 1970.

12. Inflation that is higher than expected benefits debtors, and inflation that is lower than expected benefits creditors.

GLOBAL UNEMPLOYMENT RATES AND INFLATION

13. Unemployment rates and rates of inflation differ markedly across time and countries and can reach quite high levels at times.

OUTPUT GROWTH

14. Output growth depends on (1) the growth rate of the capital stock, (2) technical progress, (3) the growth rate of the labor force, and (4) the growth rate of human capital per worker.

REVIEW TERMS AND CONCEPTS

consumer price index (CPI), 549
cyclical unemployment, 546
deflation, 549
depression, 540
discouraged-worker effect, 544
employed, 541
frictional unemployment, 545
inflation, 549
labor force, 542
labor-force participation rate, 542
natural rate of unemployment, 546
not in the labor force, 542

producer price indexes (PPIs), 549
real interest rate, 552
recession, 540
structural unemployment, 546

sustained inflation, 549
unemployed, 541
unemployment rate, 542

1. Labor force = Employed + Unemployed

2. Population = Labor force + Not in labor force

3. Unemployment rate = $\dfrac{\text{Unemployed}}{\text{Employed} + \text{Unemployed}}$

4. Labor-force participation rate = $\dfrac{\text{Labor force}}{\text{Population}}$

PROBLEM SET

1. Between July and August of 1997, total employment in the U.S. economy grew from 129,708,000 to 129,804,000, an increase of 96,000. At the same time, the unemployment rate rose from 4.8 percent to 4.9 percent.
   a. How can unemployment rise when the number employed is also rising?
   b. If 6,677,000 were unemployed, calculate approximately how large the labor force was in August.

2. In August 1997, economists were saying that the U.S. economy was close to full employment even though the unemployment rate was 4.9 percent. How can they make this assertion?

3. Using Table 23.2, calculate the changes in the unemployment rate and the labor-force participation rate that would occur if one million unemployed persons dropped out of the labor force in 1997.

4. "When an inefficient firm or a firm producing a product that people no longer want goes out of business, people are unemployed, but that's part of the normal process of economic growth and development; the unemployment is part of the natural rate and need not concern policy makers." Discuss this and its relevance to the economy today.

5. What is the unemployment rate in your state today? What was it in 1970, 1975, and 1982? How has your state done relative to the national average? Do you know, or can you determine, why?

6. Suppose that all wages, salaries, welfare benefits, and other sources of income were indexed to inflation. Would inflation still be considered a problem? Why or why not?

7. a. What do the CPI and the PPI measure? Why do we need all these price indexes? (Think about what purpose you would use each one for.)

   b. Consider an economy with two goods, gum and lemon drops. Suppose that, between year 1 and year 2, there is a downward shift in the supply schedule for gum and an upward shift in the supply schedule for lemon drops. Explain why the CPI for this two-good economy would overstate the increase in the cost of living.

8. Consider the following statements:
   a. "More people are employed in Tappania now than at any time in the past 50 years."
   b. "The unemployment rate in Tappania is higher now than it has been in 50 years."
   Can both of these statements be true at the same time? Explain.

9. Policy makers talk about the "capacity" of the economy to grow. What specifically is meant by the "capacity" of the economy? How might capacity be measured? In what ways is capacity limited by labor constraints? Capital constraints? What are the consequences if demand in the economy exceeds capacity? What signs would you look for?

10. What was the rate of growth in real GDP during the most recent quarter? You can find the answer in publications such as the *Survey of Current Business*, *The Economist*, or *Businessweek*. Has growth been increasing or decreasing? What policies might you suggest for increasing the economy's potential long-run rate of growth?

11. Suppose the stock of capital and the workforce are both increasing at 3 percent annually in the country of Wholand. At the same time, real output is growing at 6 percent. How is that possible in the short run? In the long run?

TAKE IT TO THE NET

We invite you to visit the Case and Fair page on the Prentice Hall Web site:

http://www.prenhall.com/casefair

for this chapter's World Wide Web exercise.

CRIMINAL BUSINESS CYCLES

Macroeconomic historians will look back on the decade of the 1990s as one of the most remarkable in the post–World War II era. By the end of 1997 the U.S. economy experienced 81 months of uninterrupted growth—nearly twice the post–World War II average for peacetime expansions. If the current expansion persists through the end of 1998, as most economists expect it will, this business cycle boom will be the longest peacetime expansion on record.[1] During the final quarter of 1997 the unemployment rate in the United States had fallen to its lowest level in 24 years and inflation was at its lowest level in 30 years. And it appeared likely that Bill Clinton would be the first president since Lyndon Johnson to witness a budget surplus during his term in office. Coincidentally, as President Clinton noted in his 1998 State of the Union Address, serious crime in the United States has declined for a record five consecutive years.

Economic expansions of this sort have many political and social benefits. Economists and political scientists have shown that the chances of an incumbent president being re-elected increase significantly if the economy is doing well. In fact, economists and political scientists refer to the *political business cycle* to express politicians' attempts to use fiscal or monetary policy to affect the outcome of an election.

To an economist, President Kennedy's "rising tide lifts all boats" means an expanding economy translates into higher living standards, improvements in the distribution of income across classes, and lower poverty rates. All of these factors contribute to the stylized fact that crime rates tend to fall when the economy is booming, or what might be casually referred to as a *criminal business cycle!*

The idea that crime and economic conditions might be related is not new. In the sixteenth century, Sir Thomas More asked, "What can they then else do but steal. . . ?" when he expressed concern for tenant farmers who were being moved off the land by English landlords and thereby deprived of their livelihood.

More recently, academic studies have established a positive link between employment and crime, especially among young males. A 1994 study sampled a cohort of young men living in Philadelphia between their tenth and eighteenth birthdays and found that working and attending school significantly decreased the probability of committing criminal acts.

However, other studies have found that the link between labor market conditions and crime rates is not so simple and in fact breaks down completely during some periods and for certain types of crime.

Because many factors contribute to crime, it's difficult to measure the precise impact of employment, income, and education on different types of criminal behavior. However, it makes sense that for some segments of the population desperate economic conditions can lead to desperate acts.

For some cities the recent economic boom has coincided with some considerable reductions in crime. For example, employment growth in Boston has averaged about 1 percent from 1991 to 1996, while crime has fallen by 28 percent. In Dallas the story is even more dramatic. Employment growth has averaged nearly 3 percent since 1991, whereas crime has fallen by over 35 percent. (See Figure 1.)

Researchers in California found that the factor most contributing to a city's gang violence was the unemployment rate. In communities where unemployment ran highest (between 14 percent and 16 percent), the murder rate was almost 15 times greater than in communities where the unemployment rate was between 4 percent and 7 percent.

Questions for Analytical Thinking

1. In New York City, employment has been growing at an annual rate of about 1 percent since 1994, yet the unemployment rate rose 2 full percentage points from the fourth quarter of 1994 to the second quarter of 1997. Why might both the unemployment rate and the number of persons employed increase in an expanding economy?

2. Find data for your state or city on recent employment patterns and crime rates. Visit the FBI Internet site at *http://www.fbi.gov* for crime statistics for your area and the Bureau of Labor Statistics Internet site at *http://www.bls.gov* for employment statistics.

3. What impact might an increase in the minimum wage, like that passed by Congress in 1995, have on crime rates?

4. Some regions of the country, like Detroit, have actually experienced an increase in crime and

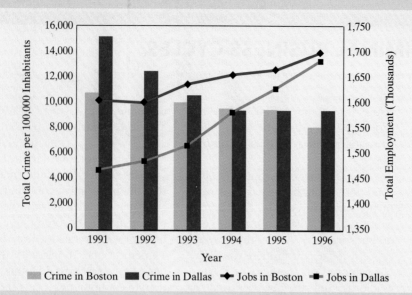

FIGURE 1

More Jobs, Less Crime

unemployment during the current expansion. What factors might explain this?

[1] Business cycle troughs and peaks are dated by the National Bureau of Economic Research. The NBER's dating of modern-day business cycles begins with a trough in December 1854. According to the NBER, the longest period of uninterrupted U.S. economic growth coincided with the Vietnam War during the 106 months of February 1961 through December 1969.

Sources: Jason Bram, David Brauer, and Elizabeth Miranda, "New York City's Unemployment Picture," *Current Issues in Economics and Finance,* December 1997, Vol. 3, No. 14, Federal Reserve Bank of New York; Chester Britt, "Crime and Unemployment in the United States, 1958–1990: A Time Series Analysis," *American Journal of Economics and Sociology,* January 1994, Vol. 53, No. 1, pp. 99–109; Bill Clinton, President of the United States, *1998 State of the Union Address,* available on-line at: *http://www.white-house.gov/WH/SOTU98/address.html*; David Dickinson, "Criminal Benefits; Unemployment and Crime," *New Statesman & Society* (UK), January 14, 1994, Vol. 7, No. 285, p. 20; Richard B. Freeman, "Why Do So Many Young American Men Commit Crimes and What Might We Do About It?" *Journal of Economic Perspectives,* Winter 1996, Vol. 10, No. 1, pp. 25–42; Ann Dryden Witte and Helen Tauchen, "Work and Crime: An Exploration Using Panel Data," *NBER Working Paper 4794,* July 1994; Tadashi Yamada, Tetsuji Yamada, and Johan M. Kang, "Crime Rates Versus Labor Market Conditions: Theory and Time Series Evidence," *NBER Working Paper 3801,* August 1991.

Chapter

24

AGGREGATE EXPENDITURE AND EQUILIBRIUM OUTPUT

WE NOW BEGIN OUR DISCUSSION of macroeconomic theory. We know how to calculate GDP, but what factors *determine* it? We know how to define and measure inflation and unemployment, but what circumstances *cause* inflation and unemployment? And what, if anything, can government do to reduce unemployment and inflation?

Analyzing the various components of the macroeconomy is a complex undertaking. The level of GDP, the overall price level, and the level of employment—three chief concerns of macroeconomists—are influenced by events in three broadly defined "markets": goods-and-services markets, financial (money) markets, and labor markets. We will explore each market, as well as the links between them, in more detail in the chapters that follow.

► **Macroeconomic Markets** Figure 24.1 presents the plan of the next seven chapters, which form the core of macroeconomic theory. In chapters 24 and 25, we describe the market for goods and services, often called the *goods market*. In chapter 24, we explain several basic concepts and show how the equilibrium level of national income is determined in a simple economy with no government and no imports or exports. In chapter 25, we provide a more complete picture of the economy by adding government purchases, taxes, and net exports to the analysis.

In chapters 26 and 27, we focus on the *money market*. Chapter 26 introduces the money market and the banking system and discusses the way the U.S. central bank (the Federal Reserve) controls the money supply. Chapter 27 analyzes the demand for money and the way interest rates are determined. Chapter 28 then examines the relationship between the goods market and the money market. Chapter 29 explores the aggregate demand and supply curves first mentioned in chapter 21. Chapter 29 also analyzes how the overall price level is determined, as well as the relationship between output and the price level. Finally, chapter 30 discusses the supply of and demand for labor and the functioning of the *labor market* in

559

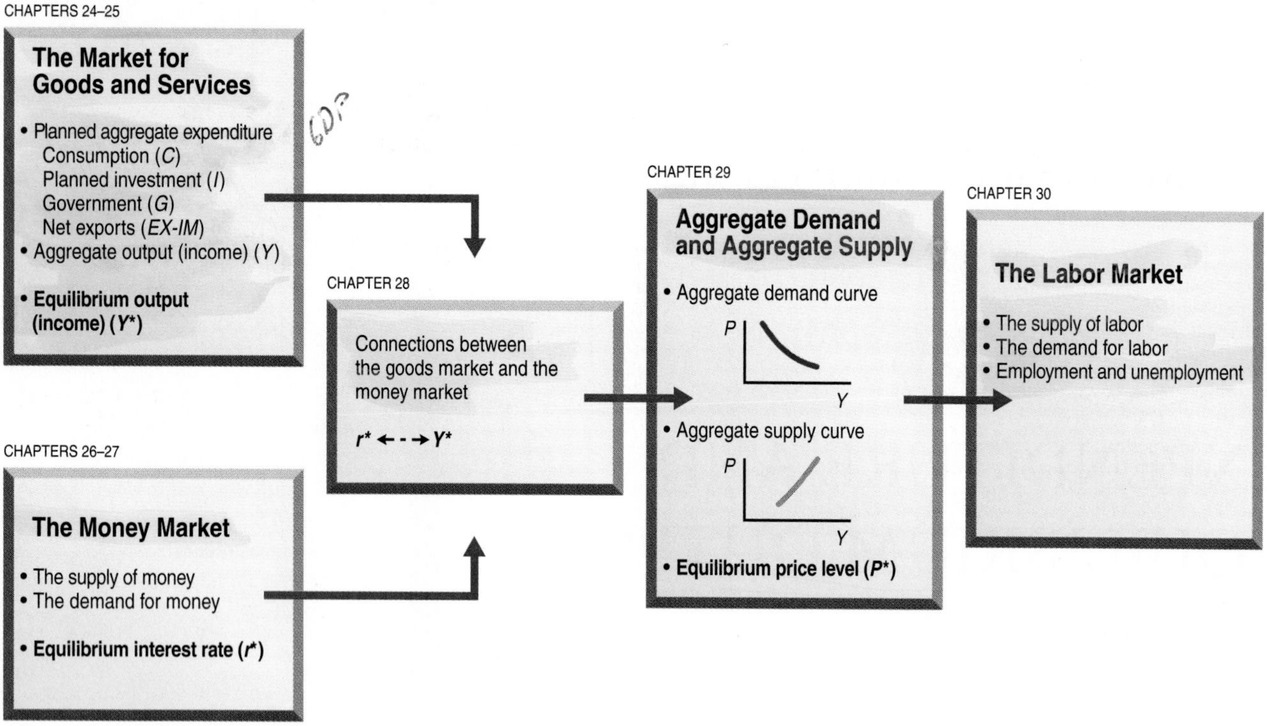

The Market for Goods and Services

- Planned aggregate expenditure
  Consumption (*C*)
  Planned investment (*I*)
  Government (*G*)
  Net exports (*EX-IM*)
- Aggregate output (income) (*Y*)

- **Equilibrium output (income) (*Y**)**

GDP?

CHAPTER 28

Connections between the goods market and the money market

$r^* \leftarrow - \rightarrow Y^*$

CHAPTER 29

Aggregate Demand and Aggregate Supply

- Aggregate demand curve

  P

  Y

- Aggregate supply curve

  P

  Y

- **Equilibrium price level (*P**)**

CHAPTER 30

The Labor Market

- The supply of labor
- The demand for labor
- Employment and unemployment

CHAPTERS 26–27

The Money Market

- The supply of money
- The demand for money

- **Equilibrium interest rate (*r**)**

FIGURE 24.1

Understanding Markets in the Macroeconomy

the macroeconomy. This material is essential to an understanding of employment and unemployment.[1]

Before we begin our discussion of aggregate output and aggregate income, we need to stress that production, consumption, and the other activities that we will be discussing in this and the following chapters are ongoing activities. Nonetheless, it is helpful to think about these activities as if they took place in a series of *production periods*. During each period, some output is produced, income is generated, and spending takes place. At the end of each period we can examine the results. Was everything that was produced in the economy sold? What percentage of income was spent? What percentage was saved? Is output (income) likely to rise or fall in the next period? The answers to these questions help us to keep track of the economy's performance.

AGGREGATE OUTPUT AND AGGREGATE INCOME (*Y*)

Each period, firms produce some aggregate quantity of goods and services, which we refer to as *aggregate output* (*Y*). In chapter 22, we introduced real gross domestic product as a measure of the quantity of output produced in the economy, *Y*. Output includes the production of services, consumer goods, and investment goods. It is important to think of these as components of "real" output.

We have already seen that GDP (*Y*) can be calculated in terms of either income or expenditures. Because every dollar of expenditure is received by someone as income, we

---

[1]Throughout chapters 24 to 30, we provide examples and policy applications relevant to our discussion in each chapter. In chapter 31, we use everything we know about the three broadly defined markets to analyze such macroeconomic topics as stabilization policy and the federal budget deficit.

can compute total GDP (Y) either by adding up the total spent on all final goods during a period *or* by adding up all the income—wages, rents, interest, and profits—received by all the factors of production.

We will use the variable Y to refer to both **aggregate output** and **aggregate income** because they are the same seen from two different points of view. When output increases, additional income is generated. More workers may be hired and paid; workers may put in, and be paid for, more hours; and owners may earn more profits. When output is cut, income falls, workers may be laid off or work fewer hours (and be paid less), and profits may fall.

> In any given period, there is an exact equality between aggregate output (production) and aggregate income. You should be reminded of this fact whenever you encounter the combined term **aggregate output (income)**.

Aggregate output can also be looked on as the aggregate quantity supplied, because it is the amount that firms are supplying (producing) during the period. In the discussions that follow, we use the phrase *aggregate output (income)*, rather than *aggregate quantity supplied*, but keep in mind that the two are equivalent. Also remember that "aggregate output" means "real GDP."

▶ **Think in Real Terms** From the outset you must think in "real terms." For example, when we talk about output (Y), we mean real output, not nominal output. Although we discussed in chapter 22 that the calculation of real GDP is complicated, you can ignore these complications in the following analysis. To help make things easier to read, we will frequently use dollar values for Y, but do not confuse Y with nominal output. The main point is to think of Y as being in real terms—the quantities of goods and services produced, not the dollars circulating in the economy.

INCOME, CONSUMPTION, AND SAVING (Y, C, AND S)

Each period (weeks, months, years, etc.), households receive some aggregate amount of income (Y). We begin our analysis in a simple world with no government and a "closed" economy, that is, no imports and no exports. In such a world, a household can do two, and only two, things with its income: It can buy goods and services—that is, it can *consume*—or it can save. The part of its income that a household does not consume in a given period is called **saving** (Figure 24.2). Total household saving in the economy (S) is by definition equal to income minus consumption (C):

$$\text{Saving} \equiv \text{Income} - \text{Consumption}$$
$$S \equiv Y - C$$

aggregate output *The total quantity of goods and services produced (or supplied) in an economy in a given period.*

aggregate income *The total income received by all factors of production in a given period.*

aggregate output (income) (Y) *A combined term used to remind you of the exact equality between aggregate output and aggregate income.*

saving (S) *The part of its income that a household does not consume in a given period. Distinguished from savings, which is the current stock of accumulated saving.*

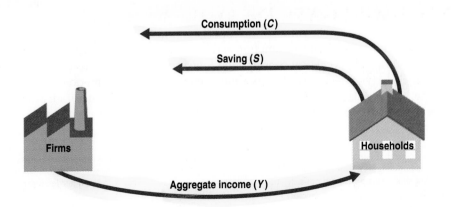

FIGURE 24.2

Saving ≡ Aggregate Income − Consumption

All income is either spent on consumption or saved in an economy in which there are no taxes. Thus, $S \equiv Y - C$.

The triple equal sign means this is an **identity,** or something that is always true. You will encounter several identities in this chapter; be sure to commit them to memory.

Remember: Saving does *not* refer to the total savings accumulated over time. Saving (without the final *s*) refers to the portion of a *single period's* income that is not spent in that period. Saving (*S*) is the amount added to *accumulated savings* in any given period. *Saving* is a flow variable; *savings* is a stock variable. (Review chapter 4 if you are unsure of the difference between stock and flow variables.)

EXPLAINING SPENDING BEHAVIOR

So far, we have said nothing about behavior. We have not described the consumption and saving behavior of households, nor have we speculated about how much aggregate output firms will decide to produce in a given period. Rather, we have only a framework and a set of definitions to work with.

But macroeconomics, you will recall, is the study of behavior. To understand the functioning of the macroeconomy, we must understand the behavior of households and firms. In our simple economy in which there is no government, there are two types of spending behavior: spending by households, or *consumption*, and spending by firms, or *investment*.

➤ **Household Consumption and Saving** How do households decide how much to consume? In any given period, the amount of aggregate consumption in the economy depends on a number of factors, including:

Some Determinants of Aggregate Consumption:	1. Household income
	2. Household wealth
	3. Interest rates
	4. Households' expectations about the future

These factors work together to determine the spending and saving behavior of households, both individually and in the aggregate. No surprise! Households with higher income and higher wealth are likely to spend more than households with less income and less wealth. Lower interest rates reduce the cost of borrowing, so lower interest rates are likely to stimulate spending. (Higher interest rates increase the cost of borrowing and are likely to decrease spending.) Finally, positive expectations about the future are likely to increase current spending, while uncertainty about the future is likely to decrease current spending. In 1990, for example, households began consuming less partly because of their uncertainty about the outcome of the Persian Gulf conflict.

While all these factors are important, we will concentrate for now on the relationship between income and consumption.[2] In *The General Theory*, Keynes argued that the amount of consumption undertaken by a household is directly related to its income:

The higher your income is, the higher your consumption is likely to be. People with more income tend to consume more than people with less income.

The relationship between consumption and income is called a **consumption function.** Figure 24.3 shows a hypothetical consumption function for an individual household. The curve is labeled $c(y)$, which is read "c as a function of y," or "consumption as a function of income." There are several things you should notice about the curve. First, it has a positive slope. In other words, as y increases, so does c. Second, the curve intersects the

---

[2]The assumption that consumption is dependent solely on income is, of course, overly simplistic. Nonetheless, many important insights about how the economy works can be obtained through this simplification. In chapter 32, we relax this assumption and consider the behavior of households and firms in the macroeconomy in more detail.

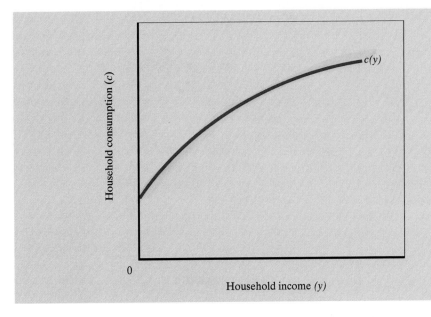

FIGURE 24.3

A Consumption Function for a Household

A consumption function for an individual household shows the level of consumption at each level of household income.

c axis above zero. This means that even at an income of zero, consumption is positive. Even if a household found itself with a zero income, it still must consume to survive. It would borrow or live off its savings, but its consumption could not be zero.

Keep in mind that Figure 24.3 shows the relationship between consumption and income for an individual household. But also remember that macroeconomics is concerned with aggregate consumption. Specifically, macroeconomists want to know how *aggregate* consumption (the total consumption of all households) is likely to respond to changes in *aggregate* income. If all individual households increase their consumption as income increases, and we assume that they do, it is reasonable to assume that a positive relationship exists between aggregate consumption (*C*) and aggregate income (*Y*).

For simplicity, assume that points of aggregate consumption, when plotted against aggregate income, lie along a straight line, as in Figure 24.4. Because the aggregate consumption function is a straight line, we can write the following equation to describe it:

$$C = a + bY$$

Y is aggregate output (income), *C* is aggregate consumption, and *a* is the point at which the consumption function intersects the *C* axis—a constant. The letter *b* is the slope of the line, in this case $\Delta C/\Delta Y$ (because consumption [*C*] is measured on the

UNCERTAINTY ABOUT THE FUTURE TENDS TO DECREASE CURRENT SPENDING, AS IT DID DURING THE PERSIAN GULF WAR IN 1990.

FIGURE 24.4

An Aggregate Consumption Function

The consumption function shows the level of consumption at every level of income. The upward slope indicates that higher levels of income lead to higher levels of consumption spending.

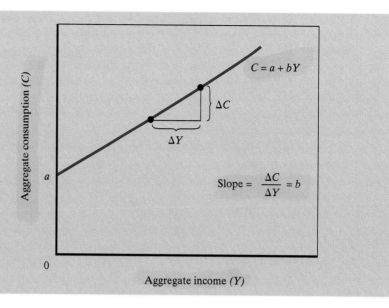

vertical axis, and income [Y] is measured on the horizontal axis).[3] Every time income increases (say by ΔY), consumption increases by b times ΔY. Thus, $\Delta C = b \times \Delta Y$ and $\Delta C / \Delta Y = b$.

Suppose the slope of the line in Figure 24.4 were .75 (that is, $b = .75$). An increase in income (ΔY) of $100 would increase consumption by $b\Delta Y = .75 \times \$100$, or $75.

The **marginal propensity to consume (MPC)** is the fraction of a change in income that is consumed. In the consumption function here, b is the MPC. An MPC of .75 means consumption changes by .75 of the change in income. The slope of the consumption function is the MPC.

marginal propensity to consume (MPC) *That fraction of a change in income that is consumed, or spent.*

marginal propensity to save (MPS) *That fraction of a change in income that is saved.*

$$\text{Marginal propensity to consume} \equiv \text{Slope of consumption function} \equiv \frac{\Delta C}{\Delta Y}$$

There are only two places income can go: consumption or saving. If $0.75 of a $1.00 increase in income goes to consumption, $0.25 must go to saving. If income decreases by $1.00, consumption will decrease by $0.75 and saving will decrease by $0.25. The **marginal propensity to save (MPS)** is the fraction of a change in income that is saved: $\Delta S / \Delta Y$, where ΔS is the change in saving. Because everything not consumed is saved, the MPC and the MPS must add up to one.

$$MPC + MPS \equiv 1$$

Because the MPC and the MPS are important concepts, it may help to review their definitions.

The marginal propensity to consume (MPC) is the fraction of an increase in income that is consumed (or the fraction of a decrease in income that comes out of consumption). The marginal propensity to save (MPS) is the fraction of an increase in income that is saved (or the fraction of a decrease in income that comes out of saving).

In recent years the average propensity to save (APS) seems to be falling in the United States. The following are Department of Commerce figures for personal saving as a percentage of per capita real (1992 dollars) disposable (after-tax) income in the United States:

Year	Real Disposable Income per Capita	Savings Rate
1970	$12,022	8.4%
1980	14,813	8.2
1990	17,941	5.0
1996	19,242	5.3

[3]The Greek letter Δ (delta) means "change in." For example, ΔY (read "delta Y") means the "change in income." If income (Y) in 1995 is $100 and income in 1996 is $110, then ΔY for this period is $110 − $100 = $10. For a review of the concept of slope, see the appendix to chapter 1.

TABLE 24.1 CONSUMPTION SCHEDULE DERIVED FROM THE EQUATION $C = 100 + .75Y$

AGGREGATE INCOME, Y (BILLIONS OF DOLLARS)	AGGREGATE CONSUMPTION, C (BILLIONS OF DOLLARS)
0	100
80	160
100	175
200	250
400	400
600	550
800	700
1,000	850

Because C is aggregate consumption and Y is aggregate income, it follows that the *MPC* is *society's* marginal propensity to consume out of national income and that the *MPS* is *society's* marginal propensity to save out of national income.

➤ **Numerical Example** The numerical examples used in the rest of this chapter are based on the following consumption function:

$$C = \underbrace{100}_{a} + \underbrace{.75}_{b}Y$$

This equation is simply an extension of the generic $C = a + bY$ consumption function we have been discussing. At a national income of zero, consumption is $100 billion ($a$). As income rises, so does consumption. We will assume that for every $100 billion increase in income (ΔY), consumption rises by $75 billion ($\Delta C$). This means that the slope of the consumption function (b) is equal to $\Delta C/\Delta Y$, or $75 billion/$100 billion = .75. The marginal propensity to consume out of national income is therefore .75; the marginal propensity to save is .25. Some numbers derived from this consumption function appear in Table 24.1 and are graphed in Figure 24.5.

Now consider saving. We already know $Y \equiv C + S$, income equals consumption plus saving. Once we know how much consumption will result from a given level of income, we know how much saving there will be. Recall that saving is everything that is not consumed.

$$S \equiv Y - C$$

From the numbers in Table 24.1, we can easily derive the saving schedule in Table 24.2. At an income of $200 billion, consumption is $250 billion; saving is thus a negative $50 billion ($S \equiv Y - C = \$200$ billion $- \$250$ billion $= -\$50$ billion). At an aggregate income of $400 billion, consumption is exactly $400 billion, and saving is zero. At $800 billion in income, saving is a positive $100 billion.

These numbers are graphed as a saving function in Figure 24.6. The 45° line—the solid black line in the top graph—provides a convenient way of comparing C and Y. (All the points along a 45° line are points at which the value on the horizontal axis equals the value on the vertical axis. Thus, the 45° line in Figure 24.6 represents all the points at which aggregate income equals aggregate consumption.) Where the consumption function is *above* the 45° line, consumption exceeds income, and saving is negative. Where the consumption function *crosses* the 45° line, consumption is equal to income, and saving is zero. Where the consumption function is *below* the 45° line, consumption is less than income, and saving is positive. Note that the slope of the saving function is $\Delta S/\Delta Y$, which is equal to the marginal propensity to save (*MPS*).

FIGURE 24.5

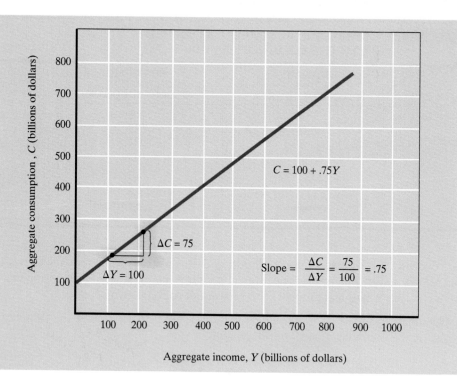

An Aggregate Consumption Function Derived from the Equation $C = 100 + .75Y$

In this simple consumption function, consumption is $100 billion at an income of zero. As income rises, so does consumption. For every $100 billion increase in income, consumption rises by $75 billion. The slope of the line is .75.

The consumption function and the saving function are mirror images of one another. No information appears in one that does not also appear in the other. These functions tell us how households in the aggregate will divide income between consumption spending and saving at every possible income level. In other words, they embody aggregate household behavior.

PLANNED INVESTMENT (*I*)

Consumption, as we've seen, is the spending by households on goods and services. But what kind of spending do firms engage in? The answer is *investment*.

▶ **What Is Investment?**   Let's begin with a brief review of terms and concepts. In everyday language, we use *investment* to refer to what we do with our savings: "I invested in

TABLE 24.2   DERIVING A SAVING SCHEDULE FROM
A CONSUMPTION SCHEDULE

Y AGGREGATE INCOME (BILLIONS OF DOLLARS)	−	*C* AGGREGATE CONSUMPTION (BILLIONS OF DOLLARS)	=	*S* AGGREGATE SAVING (BILLIONS OF DOLLARS)
0		100		−100
80		160		−80
100		175		−75
200		250		−50
400		400		0
600		550		50
800		700		100
1,000		850		150

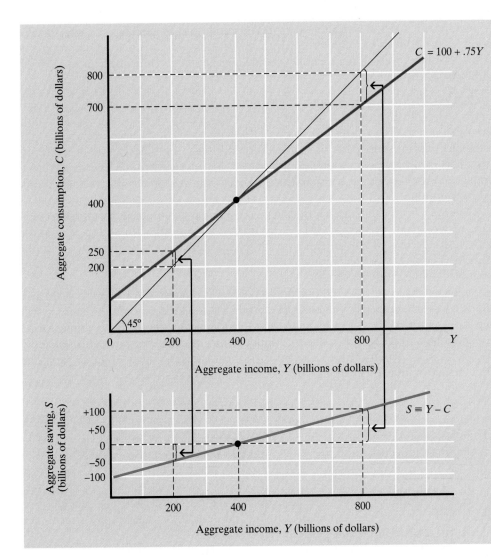

FIGURE 24.6

Deriving a Saving Function from a Consumption Function Because $S \equiv Y - C$, it is easy to derive a saving function from a consumption function. A 45° line drawn from the origin can be used as a convenient tool to compare consumption and income graphically. At $Y = 200$, consumption is 250. The 45° line shows us that consumption is larger than income by 50. Thus $S \equiv Y - C = -50$. At $Y = 800$, consumption is less than income by 100. Thus, $S = 100$ when $Y = 800$.

a mutual fund and some IBM stock." In the language of economics, however, *investment* always refers to the creation of capital stock. To an economist, an investment is something that is used to create value in the future.

You must not confuse the two uses of the term. When a firm builds a new plant or adds new machinery to its current stock, it is investing. A restaurant owner who buys tables, chairs, cooking equipment, and silverware is investing. When a college builds a new sports center, it is investing. From now on, we use **investment** only to refer to purchases by firms of new buildings and equipment and inventories, all of which add to firms' capital stocks.

Recall that inventories are part of the capital stock. When firms add to their inventories, they are investing—they are buying something that creates value in the future. Most of the capital stock of a clothing store consists of its inventories of unsold clothes in its warehouses and on its racks and display shelves. The service provided by a grocery or department store is the convenience of having a large variety of commodities in inventory available for purchase at a single location.

Manufacturing firms generally have two kinds of inventories: *inputs* and *final products*. General Motors has stocks of tires, rolled steel, engine blocks, valve covers, and thousands of other things in inventory, all waiting to be used in producing new cars. In addition, GM has an inventory of finished automobiles awaiting shipment.

investment *Purchases by firms of new buildings and equipment and additions to inventories, all of which add to firms' capital stock.*

Investment is a flow variable—it represents additions to capital stock in a specific period. A firm's decision on how much to invest each period is determined by many factors. For now, we will focus simply on the effects that given investment levels have on the rest of the economy.

> **Actual versus Planned Investment** One of the most important insights of macroeconomics is deceptively simple: A firm may not always end up investing the exact amount that it planned to. The reason is that a firm does not have complete control over its investment decision; some parts of that decision are made by other actors in the economy. (This is not true of consumption, however. Because we assume households have complete control over their consumption, planned consumption is always equal to actual consumption.)

Generally, firms can choose how much new plant and equipment they wish to purchase in any given period. If GM wants to buy a new robot to stamp fenders or McDonald's decides to buy an extra french-fry machine, it can usually do so without difficulty. There is, however, another component of investment over which firms have less control—inventory investment.

Suppose GM expects to sell one million cars this quarter and has inventories at a level it considers proper. If the company produces and sells one million cars, it will keep its inventories just where they are now (at the desired level). Now suppose GM produces one million cars, but due to a sudden shift of consumer interest it sells only 900,000 cars. By definition, GM's inventories of cars must go up by 100,000 cars. The firm's **change in inventory** is equal to production minus sales. The point here is:

change in inventory *Production minus sales.*

One component of investment—inventory change—is partly determined by how much households decide to buy, which is not under the complete control of firms. If households do not buy as much as firms expect them to, inventories will be higher than expected, and firms will have made an inventory investment that they did not plan to make.

Because involuntary inventory adjustments are neither desired nor planned, we need to distinguish between actual investment and **desired, or planned, investment.** We will use I to refer to desired or planned investment only. In other words, I will refer to planned purchases of plant and equipment and planned inventory changes. **Actual investment,** in contrast, is the *actual* amount of investment that takes place. If actual inventory investment turns out to be higher than firms planned, then actual investment is greater than I, planned investment.

desired, or planned, investment *Those additions to capital stock and inventory that are planned by firms.*

actual investment *The actual amount of investment that takes place; it includes items such as unplanned changes in inventories.*

For the purposes of this chapter, we will take the amount of investment that firms plan to make each period (I) as fixed at some given level. We assume this level does not vary with income. In the example that follows, we will assume that $I = \$25$ billion, regardless of income. As Figure 24.7 shows, this means the planned investment function is a horizontal line.

PLANNED AGGREGATE EXPENDITURE (AE)

We define total **planned aggregate expenditure (AE)** in the economy to be consumption (C) plus planned investment (I):[4]

planned aggregate expenditure (AE) *The total amount the economy plans to spend in a given period. Equal to consumption plus planned investment:* AE ≡ C + I.

$$\text{Planned aggregate expenditure} \equiv \text{Consumption} + \text{Planned investment}$$
$$AE \equiv C + I$$

[4]In practice, planned aggregate expenditure also includes government spending (G) and net exports ($EX - IM$): $AE \equiv C + I + G + (EX - IM)$. In this chapter we are assuming that G and ($EX - IM$) are zero. This assumption is relaxed in the next chapter.

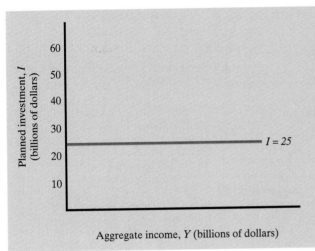

FIGURE 24.7

The Planned Investment Function

For the time being, we will assume that planned investment is fixed. It does not change when income changes, so its graph is just a horizontal line.

AE is the total amount that the economy plans to spend in a given period. We will now use the concept of planned aggregate expenditure to discuss the economy's equilibrium level of output.

EQUILIBRIUM AGGREGATE OUTPUT (INCOME)

Thus far, we have described the behavior of firms and households. We now discuss the nature of equilibrium and explain how the economy achieves equilibrium.

A number of definitions of *equilibrium* are used in economics. They all refer to the idea that at equilibrium, there is no tendency for change. In microeconomics, equilibrium is said to exist in a particular market (say, the market for bananas) at the price for which the quantity demanded is equal to the quantity supplied. At this point, both suppliers and demanders are satisfied. The equilibrium price of a good is the price at which suppliers want to furnish the amount that demanders want to buy.

In macroeconomics, we define **equilibrium** in the goods market as that point at which planned aggregate expenditure is equal to aggregate output.

> Aggregate output $\equiv Y$
> Planned aggregate expenditure $\equiv AE \equiv C + I$
> Equilibrium: $Y = AE$, or $Y = C + I$

equilibrium *Occurs when there is no tendency for change. In the macroeconomic goods market, equilibrium occurs when planned aggregate expenditure is equal to aggregate output.*

This definition of equilibrium can hold if, and only if, planned investment and actual investment are equal. (Remember: we are assuming there is no unplanned consumption.) To understand why, consider Y not equal to AE. First, suppose aggregate output is greater than planned aggregate expenditure:

$$Y > C + I$$
Aggregate output > Planned aggregate expenditure

When output is greater than planned spending, there is unplanned inventory investment. Firms planned to sell more of their goods than they sold, and the difference shows up as an unplanned increase in inventories.

Next, suppose planned aggregate expenditure is greater than aggregate output:

$$C + I > Y$$
Planned aggregate expenditure > Aggregate output

When planned spending exceeds output, firms have sold more than they planned to. Inventory investment is smaller than planned. Planned and actual investment are not

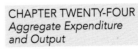

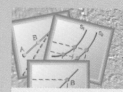

INVENTORIES ACCUMULATING IN 1997: WORRIES ABOUT DECLINING OUTPUT

When GDP data for the second quarter of 1997 were released by the Department of Commerce in August of that year, inventories of unsold goods were up substantially. The following article from the *New York Times* describes the worry:

Largely ignored in the latest blizzard of economic figures was one indicator that is notoriously hard to interpret but that by autumn could be on every investor's lips. Inventories.

After rising a hefty $64 billion in the January-to-March quarter, the Commerce Department initially estimated that inventories

jumped another $67 billion during the spring.

The sum "will be upped to about $95 billion, which would be a record rate of inventory accumulation" for a quarter, said Bruce Steinberg, chief economist at Merrill Lynch. And this, he contended, has "crucial negative implications" for the economy for the rest of 1997.

The theory is straightforward. When goods pile up excessively on store shelves—and in warehouses and factory yards—this costly situation must be redressed sooner or later. This, by ripple effect, means production is cut back and economic growth sags—or even disappears.

Often, a huge stockpile "eventually sows the seeds of a slowdown," said Richard D. Rippe, senior economist at Prudential Securities.

In practice, though, it is often difficult to tell to what extent mounting inventories reflect a retrenchment by consumers or justified confidence by companies that they will be able to sell larger volumes of goods.[a]

Source: [a]Robert D. Hershey Jr., "As Inventories Rise Will There Be a Ripple Effect?" *The New York Times,* August 17, 1997, p. F4. Copyright © 1997 by The New York Times Co. Reprinted by permission.

 For more on aggregate output and aggregate expenditures, see the Case and Fair Web page at http://www.prenhall.com/casefair.

---

equal. Only when output is exactly matched by planned spending will there be no unplanned inventory investment.

> Equilibrium in the goods market is achieved only when aggregate output (Y) and planned aggregate expenditure ($C + I$) are equal, or when actual and planned investment are equal.

Table 24.3 derives a planned aggregate expenditure schedule and shows the point of equilibrium for our numerical example. (Remember, all our calculations are based on $C = 100 + .75Y$.) To determine planned aggregate expenditure, we add consumption spending (C) to planned investment spending (I) at every level of income. Glancing down columns 1 and 4, we see one, and only one, level at which aggregate output and planned aggregate expenditure are equal: $Y = 500$.

Figure 24.8 illustrates the same equilibrium graphically. Figure 24.8a adds planned investment, constant at $25 billion, to consumption at every level of income. Because planned investment is a constant, the planned aggregate expenditure function is simply the consumption function displaced vertically by that constant amount. Figure 24.8b plots the planned aggregate expenditure function with the 45° line. The 45° line, which represents all points on the graph where the variables on the horizontal and vertical axes are equal, allows us to compare measurements along the two axes. The planned aggregate expenditure function crosses the 45° line at a single point, where $Y = $500 billion.[5] At that point, $Y = C + I$.

Now let's look at some other levels of aggregate output (income). First, consider $Y = $800 billion. Is this an equilibrium output? Clearly not. At $Y = $800 billion, planned aggregate expenditure is $725 billion. (See Table 24.3.) This amount is less than

---

[5]The point at which the two lines cross is sometimes called the *Keynesian cross.*

TABLE 24.3 DERIVING THE PLANNED AGGREGATE EXPENDITURE SCHEDULE AND FINDING EQUILIBRIUM (ALL FIGURES IN BILLIONS OF DOLLARS)
THE FIGURES IN COLUMN 2 ARE BASED ON THE EQUATION $C = 100 + .75Y$.

(1) AGGREGATE OUTPUT (INCOME) (Y)	(2) AGGREGATE CONSUMPTION (C)	(3) PLANNED INVESTMENT (I)	(4) PLANNED AGGREGATE EXPENDITURE (AE) C + I	(5) UNPLANNED INVENTORY CHANGE Y − (C + I)	(6) EQUILIBRIUM? (Y = AE?)
100	175	25	200	−100	No
200	250	25	275	−75	No
400	400	25	425	−25	No
500	475	25	500	0	Yes
600	550	25	575	+25	No
800	700	25	725	+75	No
1,000	850	25	875	+125	No

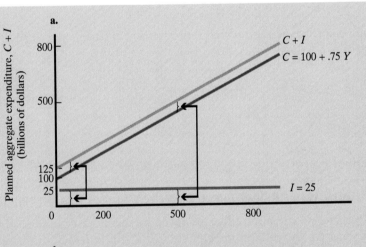

FIGURE 24.8

Equilibrium Aggregate Output

Equilibrium occurs when planned aggregate expenditure and aggregate output are equal. Planned aggregate expenditure is the sum of consumption spending and planned investment spending.

571

aggregate output, which is $800 billion. Because output is greater than planned spending, the difference ends up in inventory as unplanned inventory investment. In this case, unplanned inventory investment is $75 billion.

Next, consider $Y = \$200$ billion. Is this an equilibrium output? No. At $Y = \$200$ billion, planned aggregate expenditure is $275 billion. Planned spending (AE) is greater than output (Y), and there is unplanned inventory disinvestment of $75 billion.

At $Y = \$200$ billion and $Y = 800$ billion, planned investment and actual investment are unequal. There is unplanned investment, and the system is out of balance. Only at $Y = \$500$ billion, where planned aggregate expenditure and aggregate output are equal, will planned investment equal actual investment.

Finally, let us find the equilibrium level of output (income) algebraically. Recall that we know the following:

$$(1)\ Y = C + I \qquad \text{(equilibrium)}$$
$$(2)\ C = 100 + .75Y \qquad \text{(consumption function)}$$
$$(3)\ I = 25 \qquad \text{(planned investment)}$$

Substituting (2) and (3) into (1) we get

$$Y = \underbrace{100 + .75Y}_{C} + \underbrace{25.}_{I}$$

There is only one value of Y for which this statement is true, and we can find it by rearranging terms:

$$Y - .75Y = 100 + 25$$
$$Y - .75Y = 125$$
$$.25Y = 125$$
$$Y = \frac{125}{.25} = 500$$

The equilibrium level of output is 500, as seen in Table 24.3 and Figure 24.8.

THE SAVING/INVESTMENT APPROACH TO EQUILIBRIUM

Because aggregate income must either be saved or spent, by definition, $Y \equiv C + S$—which is an identity. The equilibrium condition is $Y = C + I$—but this is not an identity because it does not hold when we are out of equilibrium.[6] Substituting $C + S$ for Y in the equilibrium condition, we can write:

> Saving/investment approach to equilibrium: $C + S = C + I$
> Because we can subtract C from both sides of this equation, we are left with $S = I$. Thus, only when planned investment equals saving will there be equilibrium.

This saving/investment approach to equilibrium stands to reason intuitively if we recall two things: (1) Output and income are equal, and (2) saving is income that is not spent. Because it is not spent, saving is like a leakage out of the spending stream. Only if that leakage is counterbalanced by some other component of planned spending can the resulting planned aggregate expenditure equal aggregate output. This other component is planned investment (I).

This counterbalancing effect can be seen in Figure 24.9. Aggregate income flows into households, and consumption and saving flow out. The diagram shows saving flowing from households into the financial market. Firms use this saving to finance investment

[6]It would be an identity if I included unplanned inventory accumulations—in other words, if I were actual investment rather than planned investment.

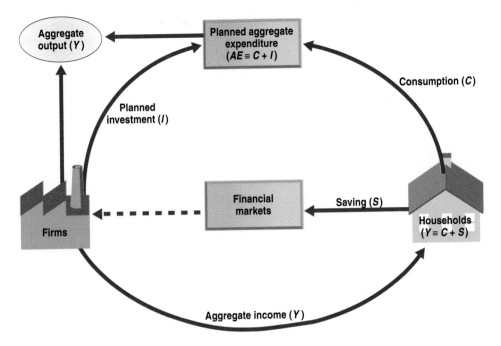

FIGURE 24.9

Planned Aggregate
Expenditure and Aggregate
Output (Income)

Saving is a leakage out of the
spending stream. If planned
investment is exactly equal to
saving, then planned aggregate
expenditure is exactly equal
to aggregate output, and there
is equilibrium.

projects. If the planned investment of firms equals the saving of households, then planned aggregate expenditure ($AE \equiv C + I$) equals aggregate output (income) (Y), and there is equilibrium: The *leakage* out of the spending stream—saving—is matched by an equal *injection* of planned investment spending into the spending stream. For this reason, the saving/investment approach to equilibrium is also called the *leakages/injections approach* to equilibrium.

Figure 24.10 reproduces the saving schedule derived in Figure 24.6 and the horizontal investment function from Figure 24.7. Notice that $S = I$ at one, and only one, level of aggregate output, $Y = 500$. At $Y = 500$, $C = 475$ and $I = 25$. In other words, $Y = C + I$, and therefore equilibrium exists.

ADJUSTMENT TO EQUILIBRIUM

We have defined equilibrium and learned how to find it, but we have said nothing about how firms might react to *disequilibrium*. Let's consider the actions firms might take when planned aggregate expenditure exceeds aggregate output (income).

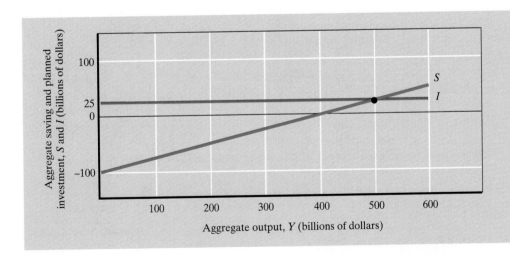

FIGURE 24.10

The $S = I$ Approach to
Equilibrium

Aggregate output will be equal
to planned aggregate expenditure only when saving equals
planned investment ($S = I$).
Saving and planned investment are equal at $Y = 500$.

We already know the only way firms can sell more than they produce is by selling some inventory. This means that when planned aggregate expenditure exceeds aggregate output, unplanned inventory reductions have occurred. It seems reasonable to assume firms will respond to unplanned inventory reductions by increasing output. If firms increase output, income must also increase (output and income are two ways of measuring the same thing). As General Motors builds more cars it hires more workers (or pays its existing workforce for working more hours), buys more steel, uses more electricity, and so on. These purchases by GM represent income for the producers of labor, steel, electricity, and so on. If GM (and all other firms) try to keep their inventories intact by increasing production, they will generate more income in the economy as a whole. This will lead to more consumption. Remember, when income rises, consumption also rises.

> The adjustment process will continue as long as output (income) is below planned aggregate expenditure. If firms react to unplanned inventory reductions by increasing output, an economy with planned spending greater than output will adjust to equilibrium, with Y higher than before. If planned spending is less than output, there will be unplanned increases in inventories. In this case, firms will respond by reducing output. As output falls, income falls, consumption falls, and so forth, until equilibrium is restored, with Y lower than before.

As Figure 24.8 shows, at any level of output above $Y = 500$, such as $Y = 800$, output will fall until it reaches equilibrium at $Y = 500$, and at any level of output below $Y = 500$, such as $Y = 200$, output will rise until it reaches equilibrium at $Y = 500$.[7]

THE MULTIPLIER

Now that we know how the equilibrium value of income is determined, we ask: How does the equilibrium level of output change when planned investment changes? If there is a sudden change in planned investment, how will output respond, if it responds at all? As we will see, the change in equilibrium output is *greater* than the initial change in planned investment. Output changes by a multiple of the change in planned investment. So, this multiple is called the **multiplier**!

multiplier *The ratio of the change in the equilibrium level of output to a change in some autonomous variable.*

autonomous variable *A variable that is assumed not to depend on the state of the economy—that is, it is taken as given.*

The multiplier is defined as the ratio of the change in the equilibrium level of output to a change in some autonomous variable. A variable is **autonomous** when it is assumed not to depend on the state of the economy—that is, it is taken as given. In this chapter, we consider planned investment to be autonomous. This simplifies our analysis and provides a foundation for later discussions.

With planned investment as given, we can ask how much the equilibrium level of output changes when planned investment changes. Remember that we are not trying here to explain *why* planned investment changes; we are simply asking how much the equilibrium level of output changes when (for whatever reason) planned investment changes. (Beginning in chapter 28, we will no longer take planned investment as given and will explain how planned investment is determined.)

Consider a sustained increase in planned investment of $25 billion—that is, suppose I increases from $25 billion to $50 billion and stays at $50 billion. If equilibrium

---

[7]In discussing simple supply and demand equilibrium in chapters 4 and 5, we saw that when quantity supplied exceeds quantity demanded, the price falls and the quantity supplied declines. Similarly, when quantity demanded exceeds quantity supplied, the price rises and the quantity supplied increases. In the analysis here we are ignoring potential changes in prices or in the price level and focusing on changes in the level of real output (income). Later, after we have introduced money and the price level into the analysis, prices will be very important. At this stage, however, only aggregate output (income) (Y) adjusts when aggregate expenditure exceeds aggregate output (with inventory falling) or when aggregate output exceeds aggregate expenditure (with inventory rising).

existed at I = \$25 billion, an increase in planned investment of \$25 billion will cause a disequilibrium, with planned aggregate expenditure greater than aggregate output by \$25 billion. Firms immediately see unplanned reductions in their inventories, and, as a result, they begin to increase output.

Let's say the increase in planned investment comes from an anticipated increase in travel that leads airlines to purchase more airplanes, car rental companies to increase purchases of automobiles, and bus companies to purchase more buses (all capital goods). The firms experiencing unplanned inventory declines will be automobile manufacturers, bus producers, and aircraft producers—General Motors, Ford, McDonnell Douglas, Boeing, and so forth. In response to declining inventories of planes, buses, and cars, these firms will increase output.

Now suppose these firms raise output by the full \$25 billion increase in planned investment. Does this restore equilibrium? No, because when output goes up, people earn more income and a part of that income will be spent. This increases planned aggregate expenditure even further. In other words, an increase in I also leads indirectly to an increase in C. To produce more airplanes, Boeing has to hire more workers or ask its existing employees to work more hours. It also must buy more engines from General Electric, more tires from Goodyear, and so forth. Owners of these firms will earn more profits, produce more, hire more workers, and pay out more in wages and salaries.

> This added income does not vanish into thin air. It is paid to households that spend some of it and save the rest. The added production leads to added income, which leads to added consumption spending.

If planned investment (I) goes up by \$25 billion initially *and is sustained at this higher level*, an increase of output of \$25 billion will *not* restore equilibrium, because it generates even more consumption spending (C). People buy more consumer goods. There are unplanned reductions of inventories of basic consumption items—washing machines, food, clothing, and so forth—and this prompts other firms to increase output. The cycle starts all over again.[8]

Clearly, output and income can rise by significantly more than the initial increase in planned investment. But how much? How large is the multiplier? This is answered graphically in Figure 24.11. Assume the economy is in equilibrium at point A, where equilibrium output is 500. The increase in I of 25 shifts the $AE \equiv C + I$ curve up by 25, because I is higher by 25 at every level of income. The new equilibrium occurs at point B, where the equilibrium level of output is 600. Like point A, point B is on the 45° line and is an equilibrium value. Output (Y) has increased by 100 (600 − 500), or four times the initial increase in planned investment of 25, between point A and point B. The multiplier in this example is 4. At point B, aggregate spending is also

---

[8]Figure 24.9 can help you understand the multiplier effect. Note in the figure how an increase in planned investment makes its way through the circular flow. Initially, aggregate output is at equilibrium with $Y = C + I$. That is, every period, aggregate output is produced by firms, and every period, planned aggregate expenditure is just sufficient to take all those goods and services off the market.

Now note what happens when planned investment spending increases and is sustained at a higher level. Firms experience unplanned declines in inventories and they increase output; more real output is produced in subsequent periods. But the added output means more income; thus we see added income flowing to households. This means more spending. Households spend some portion of their added income (equal to the added income times the MPC) on consumer goods.

The higher consumption spending means that even if firms responded fully to the increase in investment spending in the first round, the economy is still out of equilibrium. Follow the added spending back over to firms in Figure 24.9 and you can see that with higher consumption, planned aggregate expenditure will be greater. Firms again see an unplanned decline in inventories and they respond by increasing the output of consumer goods. This sets off yet another round of income and expenditure increases: Output rises, and income rises as a result, thus increasing consumption. Higher consumption leads to yet another disequilibrium, inventories fall, and output (income) rises again.

FIGURE 24.11

The Multiplier as Seen
in the Planned Aggregate
Expenditure Diagram

At point A, the economy is in
equilibrium at $Y = 500$. When
I increases by 25, planned
aggregate expenditure is initially
greater than aggregate output.
As output rises in response,
additional consumption is
generated, pushing equilibrium
output up by a multiple of the
initial increase in I. The new
equilibrium is found at point B,
where $Y = 600$. Equilibrium
output has increased by 100
$(600 - 500)$, or *four times* the
amount of the increase in
planned investment.

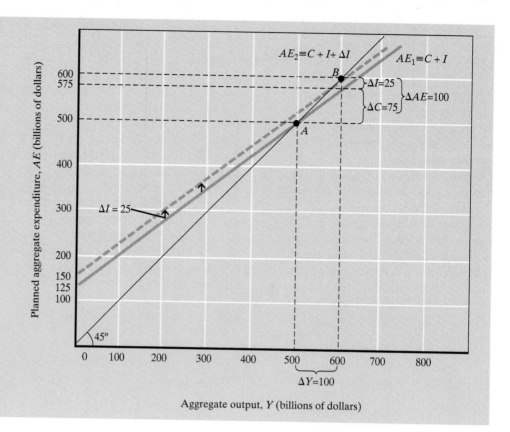

higher by 100. If 25 of this additional 100 is investment (I), as we know it is, the remaining 75 is added consumption (C). From point A to point B then, $\Delta Y = 100$, $\Delta I = 25$, and $\Delta C = 75$.

Why doesn't the multiplier process go on forever? Because only a fraction of the increase in income is consumed in each round. Successive increases in income become smaller and smaller in each round of the multiplier process until equilibrium is restored.

The size of the multiplier depends on the slope of the planned aggregate expenditure line. The steeper the slope of this line, the greater the change in output for a given change in investment. When planned investment is fixed, as in our example, the slope of the $AE \equiv C + I$ line is just the marginal propensity to consume $(\Delta C/\Delta Y)$. The greater the MPC, the greater the multiplier. This should not be surprising. A large MPC means that consumption increases a lot when income increases. The more consumption changes, the more output has to change to achieve equilibrium.

▶ **The Multiplier Equation**   Is there a way to determine the size of the multiplier without using graphic analysis? Yes, there is.

Assume that the market is in equilibrium at an income level of $Y = 500$. Now suppose planned investment (I), and thus planned aggregate expenditure (AE), increases and remains higher by $25 billion. Planned aggregate expenditure is greater than output, there is an unplanned inventory reduction, and firms respond by increasing output (income) (Y). This leads to a second round of increases, and so on.

What will restore equilibrium? Look at Figure 24.10 and recall: planned aggregate expenditure $(AE \equiv C + I)$ is not equal to aggregate output (Y) unless $S = I$; the leakage of saving must exactly match the injection of planned investment spending for the economy to be in equilibrium. Recall also, we assumed that planned investment jumps to a new higher level and stays there; it is a *sustained* increase of $25 billion in planned investment spending. As income rises, consumption rises and so does saving. Our $S = I$ approach to equilibrium leads us to conclude:

> Equilibrium will be restored only when saving has increased by exactly the amount of the initial increase in I.

Otherwise, I will continue to be greater than S, and $C + I$ will continue to be greater than Y. (The $S = I$ approach to equilibrium leads to an interesting paradox in the macroeconomy. See Issues and Debates, "The Paradox of Thrift.")

It is possible to figure how much Y must increase in response to the additional planned investment before equilibrium will be restored. Y will rise, pulling S up with it until the change in saving is exactly equal to the change in planned investment—that is, until S is again equal to I at its new higher level. Because added saving is a *fraction* of added income (the MPS), the increase in *income* required to restore equilibrium must be *a multiple* of the increase in planned investment.

Recall that the marginal propensity to save (MPS) is the fraction of a change in income that is saved. It is defined as the change in S (ΔS) over the change in income (ΔY):

$$MPS \equiv \frac{\Delta S}{\Delta Y}$$

Because ΔS must be equal to ΔI for equilibrium to be restored, we can substitute ΔI for ΔS and solve:

$$MPS = \frac{\Delta I}{\Delta Y}. \text{ Therefore, } \Delta Y = \Delta I \times \frac{1}{MPS}.$$

As you can see, the change in equilibrium income (ΔY) is equal to the initial change in planned investment (ΔI) times $1/MPS$. The multiplier is $1/MPS$:

$$\text{Multiplier} \equiv \frac{1}{MPS}$$

Because $MPS + MPC \equiv 1$, $MPS \equiv 1 - MPC$. It follows that the multiplier is equal to:

$$\text{Multiplier} \equiv \frac{1}{1 - MPC}$$

In our example, the MPC is .75, so the MPS must equal $1 - .75$, or .25. Thus, the multiplier is 1 divided by .25, or 4. The change in the equilibrium level of Y is $4 \times \$25$ billion, or \$100 billion.[9] Also note that the same analysis holds when planned investment falls. If planned investment falls by a certain amount and is sustained at this lower level, output will fall by a multiple of the reduction in I. As the initial shock is felt and firms cut output, they lay people off. The result: Income, and subsequently consumption, falls.

> ### The Size of the Multiplier in the Real World
In considering the size of the multiplier, it is important to realize that the multiplier we derived in this chapter is based on a *very* simplified picture of the economy. First, we have assumed that planned investment is fixed and does not respond to changes in the economy. Second, we have thus far ignored the role of government, financial markets, and the rest of the world in the macroeconomy. For these reasons, it would be a mistake to move on from this chapter thinking that national income can be increased by \$100 billion simply by increasing planned investment spending by \$25 billion.

---

[9]The multiplier can also be derived algebraically, as the appendix to this chapter demonstrates.

THE PARADOX OF THRIFT

An interesting paradox can arise when households attempt to increase their saving. What happens if households become concerned about the future and want to save more today to be prepared for hard times tomorrow? If households increase their planned saving, the saving schedule in Figure 1 shifts upward, from S to S'. The plan to save more is a plan to consume less, and the resulting drop in spending leads to a drop in income. Income drops by a multiple of the initial shift in the saving schedule. Before the increase in saving, equilibrium exists at point A, where S = I and Y = $500 billion. Increased saving shifts the equilibrium to point B, the point at which S' = I. New equilibrium output is $300 billion—a $200 billion decrease (ΔY) from the initial equilibrium.

By consuming less, households have actually *caused* the hard times about which they were apprehensive. Worse, the new equilibrium finds saving at the same level as it was before consumption dropped ($25 billion). In their attempt to save more, households have caused a contraction in output, and thus in income. They end up consuming less, but they have not saved any more.

It should be clear why saving at the new equilibrium is equal to saving at the old equilibrium. Equilibrium requires that saving equal planned investment, and because planned investment is unchanged, saving must remain unchanged for equilibrium to exist. This paradox shows that the interactions among sectors in the economy can be of crucial importance.

The **paradox of thrift** is "paradoxical" because it contradicts the widely held belief that "a penny saved is a

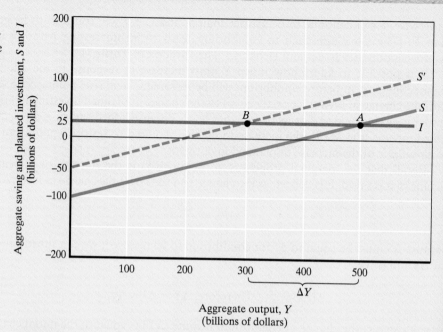

FIGURE 1

The Paradox of Thrift

An increase in planned saving from S to S' causes equilibrium output to decrease from $500 billion to $300 billion. The decreased consumption that accompanies increased saving leads to a contraction of the economy and to a reduction of income. But at the new equilibrium, saving is the same as it was at the initial equilibrium. Increased efforts to save have caused a drop in income but no overall change in saving.

penny earned." This may be true for an individual, but when society as a whole saves more, the result is a drop in income but no increased saving.

Does the paradox of thrift always hold? Recall our assumption that planned investment is fixed. Let us drop this assumption for a moment. If the extra saving that households want to do to ward off hard times is channeled

into additional investment through financial markets, there is a shift up in the I schedule. The paradox could then be averted. If investment increases, a new equilibrium can be achieved at a higher level of saving and income. This result, however, depends critically on the existence of a channel through which additional household saving finances additional investment.

For more on saving, investment, and the multiplier, see the Case and Fair Web page at
http://www.prenhall.com/casefair.

As we relax these assumptions in the following chapters, you will see that most of what we add to make our analysis more realistic has the effect of *reducing* the size of the multiplier. For example:

1. The appendix to chapter 25 shows that when tax payments depend on income (as they do in the real world), the size of the multiplier is reduced. As the economy expands, tax payments increase and act as a drag on the economy. The multiplier effect is smaller.
2. As you will see in chapter 28, planned investment (I) is not fixed; rather, it depends on the interest rate in the economy. This too has the effect of reducing the size of the multiplier.
3. Thus far we have not discussed how the overall price level is determined in the economy. When we do in chapter 29, we will see that part of an expansion of the economy is likely to take the form of an increase in the price level rather than an increase in output. When this happens, the size of the multiplier is reduced.
4. We introduce the role of imports and exports in chapter 25 and treat them in chapter 36. In these chapters, you will see that the multiplier effect on domestic production will be reduced if some domestic spending leaks into foreign markets.

These juicy tidbits give you something to look forward to as you proceed through the rest of this book. For now, however, it is enough to point out that:

> In reality, the size of the multiplier is about 1.4. That is, a sustained increase in autonomous spending of $10 billion into the U.S. economy can be expected to raise real GDP over time by about $14 billion.

This is a far cry from the value of 4.0 that we used in this chapter.

▶ **The Multiplier in Action: Recovering From the Great Depression** The Great Depression began in 1930 and lasted nearly a decade. Real output in 1938 was lower than real output in 1929, and the unemployment rate never fell below 14 percent of the labor force between 1930 and 1940. How did the economy get "stuck" at such a low level of income and a high level of unemployment? The Keynesian model that we analyzed in this chapter can help us answer this question.

If firms do not wish to undertake much investment (I is low) or if consumers decide to increase their saving and cut back on consumption, then planned spending will be low. Firms do not want to produce more because, with many workers unemployed, households do not have the income to buy the extra output that firms might produce. And households, who would purchase more if they had more income, cannot find jobs that would enable them to earn additional income. The economy is caught in a vicious circle.

How might such a cycle be broken? One way is for planned aggregate expenditure to increase, increasing aggregate output via the multiplier effect. This increase in *AE* may occur naturally, or it may be caused by a change in government policy.

In the late 1930s, for example, the economy experienced a surge of both residential and nonresidential investment. Between 1935 and 1940, total investment spending (in real terms) increased 64 percent and residential investment more than doubled. There can be no doubt that this increased investment had a multiplier effect. In just five years, employment in the construction industry increased by more than 400,000, employment in manufacturing industries jumped by more than 1 million, and total employment grew by more than 5 million. As more workers were employed, more income was generated, and some of this added income was spent on consumption goods. Inventories declined and firms began to expand output. Between 1935 and 1940, real output (income) increased by more than one third and the unemployment rate dropped from 20.3 percent to 14.6 percent.

But 14.6 percent is a very high rate of unemployment; the Depression was not yet over. Between 1940 and 1943 the Depression ended, with the unemployment rate dropping to 1.9 percent in 1943. This recovery was triggered by the mobilization for World War II and the significant increase in government purchases of goods and services, which rose from $14 billion in 1940 to $88.6 billion in 1943. In the next chapter, we will explore this *government spending multiplier*, and you'll see how the government can help stimulate the economy by increasing its spending.

LOOKING AHEAD: THE GOVERNMENT AND INTERNATIONAL SECTORS

In this chapter, we took the first step in understanding how the economy works. We described the behavior of two sectors (household and firm) and discussed how equilibrium is achieved in the market for goods and services. In the next chapter, we will relax some of the assumptions we have made and take into account the roles of government spending and net exports in the economy. This will give us a more realistic picture of how our economy works.

SUMMARY

AGGREGATE OUTPUT AND AGGREGATE INCOME (Y)

1. Each period, firms produce an aggregate quantity of goods and services called *aggregate output* (Y). Because every dollar of expenditure is received by someone as income, aggregate output and aggregate income are the same thing.

2. The total amount of aggregate consumption that takes place in any given period of time depends on factors such as household income, household wealth, interest rates, and households' expectations about the future.

3. If taxes are zero, households do only two things with their income: They can either spend on consumption or save. C refers to aggregate consumption by households. S refers to aggregate saving by households. By definition, saving equals income minus consumption: $S \equiv Y - C$.

4. The higher someone's income is, the higher his or her consumption is likely to be. This is also true for the economy as a whole: There is a positive relationship between aggregate consumption (C) and aggregate income (Y).

5. The *marginal propensity to consume* (MPC) is the fraction of a change in income that is consumed, or spent. The *marginal propensity to save* (MPS) is the fraction of a change in income that is saved. Because all income must be either saved or spent, $MPS + MPC \equiv 1$.

6. The primary form of spending that firms engage in is investment. Strictly speaking, *investment* refers to the purchase by firms of new buildings and equipment and additions to inventories, all of which add to firms' capital stock.

7. *Actual investment* can differ from planned investment because changes in firms' inventories are part of actual investment and inventory changes are not under the complete control of firms. Inventory changes are partly determined by how much households decide to buy. I refers to planned investment only.

EQUILIBRIUM AGGREGATE OUTPUT (INCOME)

8. In an economy in which government spending and net exports are zero, *planned aggregate expenditure* (AE) equals consumption plus planned investment: $AE \equiv C + I$. *Equilibrium* in the goods market is achieved when planned aggregate expenditure equals aggregate output: $C + I = Y$. This holds if, and only if, planned investment and actual investment are equal.

9. Because aggregate income must be saved or spent, the equilibrium condition $Y = C + I$ can be rewritten as $C + S = C + I$, or $S = I$. Only when planned investment equals saving will there be equilibrium. This approach to equilibrium is the *saving/investment approach* to equilibrium or the *leakages/injections approach* to equilibrium.

10. When planned aggregate expenditure exceeds aggregate output (*income*), there is an unplanned fall in inventories. Firms will increase output. This increased output leads to increased income and even more consumption. This process will continue as long as output (income) is below planned aggregate expenditure. If firms react to unplanned inventory reductions by increasing output, an economy with planned spending greater than output will adjust to equilibrium, with Y higher than before.

11. Equilibrium output changes by a multiple of the change in planned investment or any other autonomous variable. The multiplier is $1/MPS$.

12. When households increase their planned saving, income decreases and saving does not change. Saving does not increase because in equilibrium saving must equal planned investment and planned investment is fixed. If planned investment also increased, this *paradox of thrift* could be averted and a new equilibrium could be achieved at a higher level of saving and income. This result depends on the existence of a channel through which additional household saving finances additional investment.

REVIEW TERMS AND CONCEPTS

actual investment, 568
aggregate income, 561
aggregate output, 561
aggregate output (income) (Y), 561
autonomous variable, 574
change in inventory, 568

consumption function, 562
desired, or planned, investment (I), 568
equilibrium, 569
identity, 562
investment, 567
marginal propensity to consume (MPC), 564

marginal propensity to save (MPS), 564
multiplier, 574
paradox of thrift, 578
planned aggregate expenditure (AE), 568
saving (S), 561

1. $S \equiv Y - C$
2. $MPC \equiv$ slope of consumption function $\equiv \dfrac{\Delta C}{\Delta Y}$
3. $MPC + MPS \equiv 1$
4. $AE \equiv C + I$
5. Equilibrium condition: $Y = AE$ or $Y = C + I$
6. Saving/investment approach to equilibrium: $S = I$
7. Multiplier $\equiv \dfrac{1}{MPS} \equiv \dfrac{1}{1 - MPC}$

PROBLEM SET

1. Briefly define the following terms and explain the relationship between them:

   MPC . . . . Multiplier
   Actual investment . . . . Planned investment
   Aggregate expenditure . . . . Real GDP
   Aggregate output . . . . Aggregate income

2. Crack econometricians in the Republic of Yuck estimate the following:

   Real GNP (Y) . . . . 200 billion Yuck dollars
   Planned investment
   spending . . . . 75 billion Yuck dollars

   Yuck is a simple economy with no government, no taxes, and no imports or exports. Yuckers (citizens of Yuck) are creatures of habit. They have a rule that everyone saves exactly 25 percent of income. Assume that planned investment is fixed and remains at 75 billion Yuck dollars.

   You are asked by the business editor of the *Weird Harold*, the local newspaper, to predict the economic events of the next few months. Using the data given, can you make a forecast? What is likely to happen to inventories? What is likely to happen to the level of real GDP? Is the economy at an equilibrium? When will things stop changing?

3. The following questions refer to this table:

AGGREGATE OUTPUT/INCOME	CONSUMPTION	PLANNED INVESTMENT
2,000	2,100	300
2,500	2,500	300
3,000	2,900	300
3,500	3,300	300
4,000	3,700	300
4,500	4,100	300
5,000	4,500	300
5,500	4,900	300

   a. At each level of output, calculate saving. At each level of output, calculate unplanned investment (inventory change). What is likely to happen to aggregate output if the economy were producing at each of the levels indicated? What is the equilibrium level of output?

   b. Over each range of income (2,000 to 2,500, 2,500 to 3,000, and so on), calculate the marginal propensity to consume. Calculate the marginal propensity to save. What is the multiplier?

c. Assuming there is no change in the level of the *MPC* and the *MPS*, and planned investment jumps by 200 and is sustained at that higher level, recompute the table. What is the new equilibrium level of *Y*? Is this consistent with what you compute using the multiplier?

4. Explain the multiplier intuitively. Why is it that an increase in planned investment of $100 raises equilibrium output by more than $100? Why is the effect on equilibrium output finite? How do we know that the multiplier is 1/*MPS*?

5. Explain how planned investment can differ from actual investment.

6. You are given the following data regarding Freedonia, a legendary country:

(1) Consumption function: $C = 200 + 0.8Y$
(2) Investment function: $I = 100$
(3) $AE \equiv C + I$
(4) $AE = Y$

a. What is the marginal propensity to consume in Freedonia? The marginal propensity to save?

b. Graph equations (3) and (4) and solve for equilibrium income.

c. Suppose equation (2) were changed to

(2′) $I = 110$.

What is the new equilibrium level of income? By how much does the $10 increase in planned investment change equilibrium income? What is the value of the multiplier?

d. Calculate the saving function for Freedonia. Plot this saving function on a graph with equation (2). Explain why the equilibrium income in this graph must be the same as in part b.

7. If I decide to save an extra dollar, my saving goes up by that amount. But if everyone decides to save an extra dollar, income falls and saving does not rise. Explain.

8. You learned earlier that expenditures and income should always be equal. In this chapter, you've learned that *AE* and aggregate output (income) can be different. Is there an inconsistency here?

TAKE IT TO THE NET

We invite you to visit the Case and Fair page on the Prentice Hall Web site:

http://www.prenhall.com/casefair

for this chapter's World Wide Web exercise.

APPENDIX TO CHAPTER 24

DERIVING THE MULTIPLIER ALGEBRAICALLY

In addition to deriving the multiplier using the simple substitution we used in the chapter, we can also derive the formula for the multiplier by using simple algebra.

Recall that our consumption function is

$$C = a + bY$$

where *b* is the marginal propensity to consume. In equilibrium,

$$Y = C + I$$

Now we solve these two equations for *Y* in terms of *I*. Substituting the first equation into the second, we get

$$Y = \underbrace{a + bY}_{C} + I$$

This equation can be rearranged to yield

$$Y - bY = a + I$$
$$Y(1 - b) = a + I$$

We can then solve for *Y* in terms of *I* by dividing through by $(1 - b)$:

$$Y = (a + I)\left(\frac{1}{1 - b}\right)$$

Now look carefully at this expression and think about increasing *I* by some amount, ΔI, with *a* held constant. If *I* increases by ΔI, income will increase by

$$\Delta Y = \Delta I \times \frac{1}{1 - b}$$

Because $b \equiv MPC$, the expression becomes

$$\Delta Y = \Delta I \times \frac{1}{1 - MPC}$$

The multiplier is

$$\frac{1}{1 - MPC}$$

Finally, because $MPS + MPC \equiv 1$, *MPS* is equal to $1 - MPC$, making the alternative expression for the multiplier 1/*MPS*, just as we saw in this chapter.

Chapter 25

THE GOVERNMENT AND FISCAL POLICY

NOTHING IN MACROECONOMICS or microeconomics arouses as much controversy as the role of government in the economy.

In microeconomics, the active presence of government in regulating competition, providing roads and education, and redistributing income is applauded by those who believe a free market simply does not work well if left to its own devices. Opponents of government intervention say it is the government, not the market, that performs badly. They say bureaucracy and inefficiency could be eliminated or reduced if the government played a smaller role in the economy.

In macroeconomics, the debate over what the government can and should do has a similar flavor, although the issues are somewhat different. At one end of the spectrum are the Keynesians and their intellectual descendants, who believe that the macroeconomy is likely to fluctuate too much if left on its own and that the government should smoothe out fluctuations in the business cycle. These ideas can be traced to Keynes's analysis in *The General Theory*, which suggests that governments can use their taxing and spending powers to increase aggregate expenditure (and thereby stimulate aggregate output) in recessions or depressions. At the other end are those who claim that government spending is incapable of stabilizing the economy, or worse, destabilizing and harmful.

Perhaps the one thing most people can agree on is that, like it or not, governments are important actors in the economies of virtually all countries. For this alone, it is worth our while to analyze the way government influences the functioning of the macroeconomy.

While the government has a variety of powers—including regulating firms' entry into and exit from an industry, setting standards for product quality, setting minimum wage levels, and regulating the disclosure of information—in macroeconomics we study a government with general, but limited, powers. Specifically, government can affect the macroeconomy through two policy channels: fiscal policy and monetary policy. **Fiscal policy**, the focus of this chapter, refers to the government's spending and taxing behavior—in other words, its budget policy.[1] Fiscal policy is generally divided into three categories: (1) policies regarding government purchases of goods

fiscal policy *The government's spending and taxing policies.*

---

[1]The word *fiscal* comes from the root *fisc*, which refers to the "treasury" of a government.

monetary policy *The behavior of the Federal Reserve regarding the nation's money supply.*

and services, (2) policies regarding taxes, and (3) policies regarding transfer payments (such as unemployment compensation, social security benefits, welfare payments, and veterans' benefits) to households. **Monetary policy**, in the next two chapters, refers to the behavior of the nation's central bank, the Federal Reserve, regarding the nation's money supply.

GOVERNMENT IN THE ECONOMY

Given the scope and power of local, state, and federal governments, there are some matters over which they exert great control and some matters beyond their control. We need to distinguish between variables that a government controls directly and variables that are a consequence of government decisions *combined with the state of the economy.*

For example, tax rates are controlled by the government. By law, Congress has the authority to decide who and what should be taxed and at what rate. Tax *revenue*, on the other hand, is not subject to complete control by the government. Revenue from the personal income tax system depends both on personal tax rates (which Congress sets) *and* on the income of the household sector (which depends on many factors not under direct government control, such as how much households decide to work). Revenue from the corporate profits tax depends both on corporate profits tax rates and on the size of corporate profits. The government controls corporate tax rates but not the size of corporate profits.

Government expenditures also depends both on government decisions and on the state of the economy. For example, in the United States the unemployment insurance program pays benefits to unemployed people. When the economy goes into a recession, the number of unemployed workers increases and so does the level of government unemployment insurance payments.

Because taxes and expenditures often go up or down in response to changes in the economy rather than as the result of deliberate decisions by policy makers, we will occasionally use **discretionary fiscal policy** to refer to changes in taxes or spending that are the result of deliberate changes in government policy.

discretionary fiscal policy *Changes in taxes or spending that are the result of deliberate changes in government policy.*

GOVERNMENT PURCHASES (G), NET TAXES (T), AND DISPOSABLE INCOME (Y_d)

In the previous chapter, we explored the equilibrium level of national output for a simple economy—no taxes, no government spending, and no exports—to provide a general idea of how the macroeconomy operates.

To get more realistic, we need to consider an economy in which government is an active participant. There are no countries in the world without a government. We begin by adding the government sector into the simple economy in chapter 24.

To keep things simple, we will combine two government activities—the collection of taxes and the payment of transfer payments—into a category we call **net taxes** (T). Specifically, net taxes are equal to the tax payments made to the government by firms and households minus transfer payments made to households by the government. The other variable we will consider is government purchases of goods and services (G).

net taxes (T) *Taxes paid by firms and households to the government minus transfer payments made to households by the government.*

Our earlier discussions of household consumption did not take taxes into account. We assumed that all the income generated in the economy was spent or saved by households. When we take into account the role of government, as Figure 25.1 does, we see that as income (Y) flows toward households, the government takes income from households in the form of net taxes (T). The income that ultimately gets to households is called **disposable, or after-tax, income** (Y_d):

disposable, or **after-tax, income (Y_d)** *Total income minus net taxes:* $Y - T$.

$$\text{Disposable income} \equiv \text{Total income} - \text{Net taxes}$$
$$Y_d \equiv Y - T$$

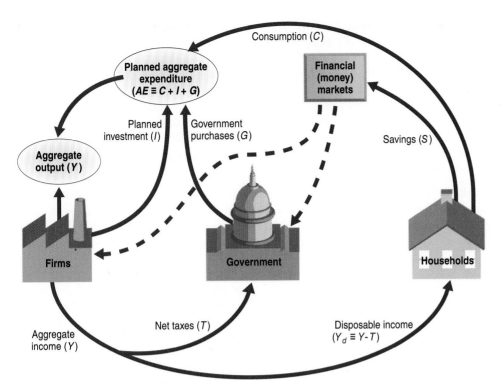

Y_d excludes taxes paid by households and includes transfer payments made to households by the government. For now we are assuming that T does not depend on Y—that is, net taxes do not depend on income. This assumption is relaxed in appendix B to this chapter. Taxes that do not depend on income are sometimes called *lump-sum taxes*.

As Figure 25.1 shows, the disposable income (Y_d) of households must end up either as consumption (C) or saving (S). Thus,

$$Y_d \equiv C + S$$

This equation is an identity—something that is always true.

Because disposable income is aggregate income (Y) minus net taxes (T), we can write another identity:

$$Y - T \equiv C + S$$

Adding T to both sides:

$$Y \equiv C + S + T$$

This identity says aggregate income gets cut into three pieces. Government takes a slice (net taxes, T), and then households divide the rest between consumption (C) and saving (S).

Because governments spend money on goods and services, we need to expand our definition of planned aggregate expenditure. Planned aggregate expenditure (AE) is the sum of consumption spending by households (C), planned investment by business firms (I), *and* government purchases of goods and services (G):[2]

$$AE \equiv C + I + G$$

---

[2]We are still assuming that net exports ($EX - IM$) are zero. In practice, $AE \equiv C + I + G + (EX - IM)$. We bring net export into the analysis at the end of this chapter.

budget deficit *The difference between what a government spends and what it collects in taxes in a given period: G − T.*

In May 1997 the president and Congress agreed to a budget plan that would reduce the U.S. budget deficit to zero by 2002. The plan involved tax cuts and spending reductions. Little did they know that by the fall of 1997, the budget would be very nearly balanced (*G = T*) because of the strong economy. A strong economy means higher incomes and higher corporate profits and, thus, higher tax revenues.

A government's **budget deficit** is the difference between what it spends (*G*) and what it collects in taxes (*T*) in a given period:

$$\text{Budget deficit} \equiv G - T$$

If *G* exceeds *T*, the government must borrow from the public to finance the deficit. It does so by selling Treasury bonds and bills (more on this later). In this case, a part of household saving (*S*) goes to the government. The dashed lines in Figure 25.1 mean that some *S* goes to firms to finance investment projects and some goes to the government to finance its deficit.[3]

▶ **Adding Taxes to the Consumption Function**   In chapter 24, we examined the consumption behavior of households and noted that aggregate consumption (*C*) depends on aggregate income (*Y*): In general, the higher aggregate income is, the higher is aggregate consumption. For the sake of illustration, we used a specific linear consumption function:

$$C = a + bY$$

where *a* is the amount of consumption that would take place if national income were zero and *b* is the marginal propensity to consume.

We need to modify this consumption function because we have added government to the economy. With taxes a part of the picture, it makes sense to assume that disposable income (Y_d), rather than before-tax income (*Y*), determines consumption behavior. If you earn a million dollars, but have to pay \$950,000 in taxes, you have no more disposable income than someone who earns only \$50,000 but pays no taxes. What you have available for spending on current consumption is your disposable income, not your before-tax income.

To modify our aggregate consumption function to incorporate disposable income rather than before-tax income, instead of $C = a + bY$, we write

$$C = a + bY_d$$

or

$$C = a + b(Y - T)$$

Our consumption function now has consumption depending on disposable income rather than on before-tax income.

▶ **Investment**   What about investment? The government can affect investment behavior through its tax treatment of depreciation and other tax policies. Investment may also vary with economic conditions and interest rates, as we will see later. For our present purposes, we continue to assume that planned investment (*I*) is fixed.

EQUILIBRIUM OUTPUT: $Y = C + I + G$

We know from chapter 24 that equilibrium occurs where $Y = AE$—that is, where aggregate output equals planned aggregate expenditure. Remember: Planned aggregate expenditure in an economy with a government is $AE \equiv C + I + G$, so the equilibrium condition is:

$$\text{Equilibrium condition: } Y = C + I + G$$

The equilibrium analysis in chapter 24 holds here also. If output (*Y*) exceeds planned aggregate expenditure ($C + I + G$), there will be an unplanned increase in

---

[3]Although it is almost unheard of these days, governments do sometimes run budget surpluses. A *surplus* occurs when net taxes are greater than government purchases of goods and services. A surplus is simply a negative deficit.

TABLE 25.1 FINDING EQUILIBRIUM FOR $I = 100$, $G = 100$, AND $T = 100$
(ALL FIGURES IN BILLIONS OF DOLLARS)

(1) OUTPUT (INCOME) Y	(2) NET TAXES T	(3) DISPOSABLE INCOME $Y_d \equiv Y - T$	(4) CONSUMPTION SPENDING $(C = 100 + .75\,Y_d)$	(5) SAVING S $(Y_d - C)$	(6) PLANNED INVESTMENT SPENDING I	(7) GOVERNMENT PURCHASES G	(8) PLANNED AGGREGATE EXPENDITURE $C + I + G$	(9) UNPLANNED INVENTORY CHANGE $Y - (C + I + G)$	(10) ADJUST-MENT TO DISEQUILI-BRIUM
300	100	200	250	−50	100	100	450	−150	Output↑
500	100	400	400	0	100	100	600	−100	Output↑
700	100	600	550	50	100	100	750	−50	Output↑
900	100	800	700	100	100	100	900	0	Equilibrium
1,100	100	1,000	850	150	100	100	1,050	+50	Output↓
1,300	100	1,200	1,000	200	100	100	1,200	+100	Output↓
1,500	100	1,400	1,150	250	100	100	1,350	+150	Output↓

inventories—actual investment will exceed planned investment. Conversely, if $C + I + G$ exceeds Y, there will be an unplanned decrease in inventories.

An example will illustrate the government's effect on the macroeconomy and the equilibrium condition. First, our consumption function, $C = 100 + .75Y$ before we introduced the government sector, now becomes

$$C = 100 + .75Y_d$$

or

$$C = 100 + .75\,(Y - T)$$

Second, we assume that the government is currently purchasing $100 billion of goods and services and collecting net taxes (T) of $100 billion.[4] In other words, the government is running a balanced budget, financing all of its spending with taxes. Third, we assume that planned investment (I) is $100 billion.

Table 25.1 calculates planned aggregate expenditure at several levels of disposable income. For example, at $Y = 500$, disposable income is $Y - T$, or 400.[5] Therefore, $C = 100 + .75(400) = 400$. Assuming that I is fixed at 100, and assuming that G is fixed at 100, planned aggregate expenditure is 600 ($C + I + G = 400 + 100 + 100$). Because output ($Y$) is only 500, planned spending is greater than output by 100. As a result, there is an unplanned inventory decrease of 100, giving firms an incentive to raise output. Thus, output of 500 is below equilibrium.

If $Y = 1,300$, then $Y_d = 1,200$, $C = 1,000$, and planned aggregate expenditure is 1,200. Here, planned spending is *less* than output, there will be an unplanned inventory increase of 100, and firms have an incentive to cut back output. Thus, output of 1,300 is above equilibrium. Only when output is 900 are output and planned aggregate expenditure equal, and only at $Y = 900$ does equilibrium exist.

In Figure 25.2, we derive the same equilibrium level of output graphically. First, the consumption function is drawn, taking into account net taxes of 100. The old function was $C = 100 + .75Y$. The new function is $C = 100 + .75(Y - T)$ or $C = 100 + .75(Y - 100)$, rewritten as $C = 100 + .75Y - 75$, or $C = 25 + .75Y$. For example, consumption at an income of zero is 25 ($C = 25 + .75Y = 25 + .75(0) = 25$). The marginal propensity to consume has not changed—we assume it remains .75. Note that the consumption function in Figure 25.2 plots the points in columns 1 and 4 of Table 25.1.

---

[4]As we pointed out earlier, the government does not have complete control over tax revenues and transfer payments. We ignore this problem here, however, and set tax revenues minus transfers at a fixed amount. Things will become more realistic later in this chapter and in appendix B.

[5]For the rest of this discussion, we will understand but not state that figures are in billions of dollars.

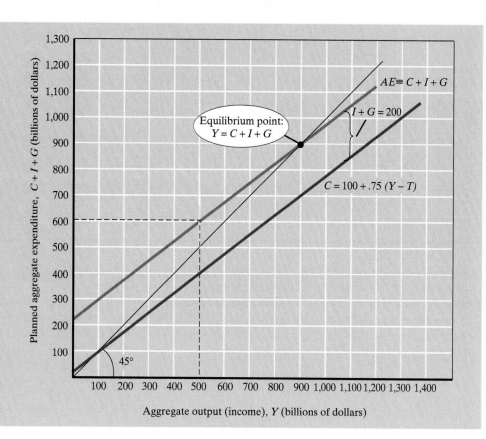

FIGURE 25.2

Finding Equilibrium Output/Income Graphically

Because G and I are both fixed at 100, the aggregate expenditure function is the new consumption function displaced upward by $I + G = 200$. Equilibrium occurs at $Y = C + I + G = 900$.

Equilibrium point:
$Y = C + I + G$

$AE \equiv C + I + G$

$I + G = 200$

$C = 100 + .75\ (Y - T)$

45°

Planned aggregate expenditure, $C + I + G$ (billions of dollars)

Aggregate output (income), Y (billions of dollars)

Planned aggregate expenditure, recall, adds planned investment to consumption. But now, in addition to 100 in investment, we have government purchases of 100. Because I and G are constant at 100 each at all levels of income, we add $I + G = 200$ to consumption at every level of income. The result is the new AE curve. This curve is just a plot of the points in columns 1 and 8 of Table 25.1. The 45° line helps us find the equilibrium level of real output, which, we already know, is 900. If you examine any level of output above or below 900, you will find disequilibrium. Look, for example, at $Y = 500$ on the graph. At this level, planned aggregate expenditure is 600, but output is only 500. Inventories will fall below what was planned, and firms will have an incentive to increase output.

➤ **The Leakages/Injections Approach to Equilibrium**   As in the last chapter, we can also examine equilibrium using the leakages/injections approach. Look at the circular flow of income in Figure 25.1. The government takes out net taxes (T) from the flow of income—a leakage—and households save (S) some of their income—also a leakage from the flow of income. The planned spending injections are government purchases (G) and planned investment (I). If leakages ($S + T$) equal planned injections ($I + G$), there is equilibrium:

Leakages/injections approach to equilibrium: $S + T = I + G$

To derive this, we know that in equilibrium, aggregate output (income) (Y) equals planned aggregate expenditure (AE). By definition, AE equals $C + I + G$, and by definition Y equals $C + S + T$. Therefore, at equilibrium

$$C + S + T = C + I + G$$

Subtracting C from both sides leaves

$$S + T = I + G$$

Note that equilibrium does *not* require that $G = T$ (a balanced government budget) or that $S = I$. It is only necessary that the sum of S and T equals the sum of I and G.

Column 5 of Table 25.1 calculates aggregate saving by subtracting consumption from disposal income at every level of disposable income ($S \equiv Y_d - C$). Because I and G are fixed, $I + G$ equals 200 at every level of income. The table shows that $S + T$ equals 200 only at $Y = 900$. Thus, the equilibrium level of output (income) is 900, the same answer we arrived at through numerical and graphical analysis.

FISCAL POLICY AT WORK: MULTIPLIER EFFECTS

You can see from Figure 25.2 that if the government were able to change the levels of either G or T, it would be able to change the equilibrium level of output (income). At this point, we are assuming that the government controls G and T.

THE GOVERNMENT SPENDING MULTIPLIER

Suppose you are the chief economic adviser to the president and the economy is sitting at the equilibrium output pictured in Figure 25.2. Output and income are being produced at a rate of $900 billion per year, and the government is currently buying $100 billion worth of goods and services each year and is financing them with $100 billion in taxes. The budget is balanced. In addition, the private sector is investing (producing capital goods) at a rate of $100 billion per year.

The president calls you into the Oval Office and says, "Unemployment is too high. We need to lower unemployment by increasing output and income." After some research, you determine that an acceptable unemployment rate could be achieved only if aggregate output increases to $1,100 billion.

You now need to determine: How can the government use taxing and spending policy—fiscal policy—to increase the equilibrium level of national output? Suppose that the president has let it be known that taxes must remain at present levels—the Congress just passed a major tax reform package—so adjusting T is out of the question for several years. That leaves you with G. Your only option is to increase government spending while holding taxes constant.

To increase spending without raising taxes (which provides the government with revenue to spend), the government must borrow. When G is bigger than T, the government runs a deficit, and the difference between G and T must be borrowed. For the moment we will ignore the possible effect of the deficit and focus only on the effect of a higher G with T constant.

Meanwhile, the president is awaiting your answer. How much of an increase in spending would be required to generate a $200 billion increase in the equilibrium level of output, pushing it from $900 billion up to $1,100 billion and reducing unemployment to the president's acceptable level?

You might be tempted to say that because we need to increase income by 200 (1,100 − 900), we should increase government spending by the same amount—but what would happen? The increased government spending will throw the economy out of equilibrium. Because G is a component of aggregate spending, planned aggregate expenditure will increase by 200. Planned spending will be greater than output, inventories will be lower than planned, and firms will have an incentive to increase output. Suppose output rises by the desired 200. You might think, "We increased spending by 200 and output by 200, so equilibrium is restored."

There is more to the story than this. The moment output rises, the economy is generating more income. This was the desired effect: the creation of more employment. The newly employed workers are also consumers and some of their income gets spent. With higher consumption spending, planned spending will be greater than output,

FAST FACTS

The Taxpayer Relief Act of 1997 was passed by the Congress and signed by the president in August 1997. The act reduced taxes effective in 1997. While the act scaled back government spending in the long run, many cuts do not take effect until after the year 2000. In 1998 and 1999, government spending is expected to rise and tax revenues are expected to fall, increasing the deficit.

Source: Congressional Budget Office, 1997.

inventories will be lower than planned, and firms will raise output, and thus raise income, again. This time firms are responding to the new consumption spending. Already, total income is over 1,100.

This story should sound familiar. It is the multiplier in action. Although this time it is government spending (G) that is changed rather than planned investment (I), the effect is the same as the multiplier effect we described in chapter 24. An increase in government spending has the same impact on the equilibrium level of output and income as an increase in planned investment. A dollar of extra spending from either G or I is identical with respect to its impact on equilibrium output. The equation for the government spending multiplier is the same as the equation for the multiplier for a change in planned investment.[6]

$$\text{Government spending multiplier} \equiv \frac{1}{MPS}$$

government spending multiplier *The ratio of the change in the equilibrium level of output to a change in government spending.*

Formally, the **government spending multiplier** is defined as the ratio of the change in the equilibrium level of output to a change in government spending. This is the same definition we used in the previous chapter, but now the autonomous variable is government spending rather than planned investment.

Remember that we were thinking of increasing government spending (G) by 200. We can use the multiplier analysis to see what the new equilibrium level of Y would be for an increase in G of 200. The multiplier in our example is 4. (Because b—the MPC—is .75, the MPS must be $1 - .75 = .25$. And $1/.25 = 4$). Thus, Y will increase by 800 (4×200). Because the initial level of Y was 900, the new equilibrium level of Y is $900 + 800 = 1,700$ when G is increased by 200.

The level of 1,700 is much larger than the level of 1,100 that we calculated as necessary to lower unemployment to the desired level. Let's back up, then. If we want Y to increase by 200 and if the multiplier is 4, we need G to increase by only $200/4 = 50$. If G changes by 50, the equilibrium level of Y will change by 200, and the new value of Y will be 1,100 ($900 + 200$), as desired.

Looking at Table 25.2, we can check our answer to be sure that it is an equilibrium. Look first at the old equilibrium of 900. When government purchases (G) were 100, aggregate output (income) was equal to planned aggregate expenditure ($AE \equiv C + I + G$) at $Y = 900$. But now G has increased to 150. At $Y = 900$, $(C + I + G)$ is greater than Y, there's an unplanned fall in inventories, and output will rise. But by how much? The multiplier told us that equilibrium income would rise by four times the 50 change in G. Y should rise by $4 \times 50 = 200$, from 900 to 1,100 before equilibrium is restored. Let's check. If $Y = 1,100$, then consumption is $C = 100 + .75 Y_d = 100 + .75(1,000) = 850$. Because I equals 100 and G now equals 100 (the original level of G) + 50 (the additional G brought about by the fiscal policy change) = 150, then $C + I + G = 850 + 100 + 150 = 1,100$. $Y = AE$, and the economy is in equilibrium.

The graphic solution to the president's problem is presented in Figure 25.3. A 50 increase in G shifts the planned aggregate expenditure function up by 50. The new equilibrium income occurs where the new AE line (AE_2) crosses the 45° line, at $Y = 1,100$.

THE TAX MULTIPLIER

Remember that fiscal policy comprises policies regarding government spending *and* policies regarding taxation. To see what effect a change in tax policy has on the economy, imagine the following. You are still chief economic adviser to the president, but now you are instructed to devise a plan to reduce unemployment to an acceptable level *without* increasing the level of government spending. In your plan, instead of increasing

[6]We derive the government spending multiplier algebraically in appendix A to this chapter.

TABLE 25.2 FINDING EQUILIBRIUM AFTER A $50 BILLION GOVERNMENT SPENDING INCREASE
(ALL FIGURES IN BILLIONS OF DOLLARS; G HAS INCREASED FROM 100 IN TABLE 10.1 TO 150 HERE)

(1) OUTPUT (INCOME) Y	(2) NET TAXES T	(3) DISPOSABLE INCOME $Y_d \equiv Y - T$	(4) CONSUMPTION SPENDING $(C = 100 + .75 \, Y_d)$	(5) SAVING S $(Y_d - C)$	(6) PLANNED INVESTMENT SPENDING I	(7) GOVERNMENT PURCHASES G	(8) PLANNED AGGREGATE EXPENDITURE $C + I + G$	(9) UNPLANNED INVENTORY CHANGE $Y - (C + I + G)$	(10) ADJUSTMENT TO DISEQUILIBRIUM
300	100	200	250	−50	100	150	500	−200	Output↑
500	100	400	400	0	100	150	650	−150	Output↑
700	100	600	550	50	100	150	800	−100	Output↑
900	100	800	700	100	100	150	950	−50	Output↑
1,100	100	1,000	850	150	100	150	1,100	0	Equilibrium
1,300	100	1,200	1,000	200	100	150	1,250	+50	Output↓

government spending (G), you decide to cut taxes and maintain the current level of spending. A tax cut increases disposable income, which is likely to lead to added consumption spending. (Remember our general rule that increased income leads to increased consumption.) Would the decrease in taxes affect aggregate output (income) the same as an increase in G?

Clearly, a decrease in taxes would increase income. The government spends no less than it did before the tax cut, and households find they have a larger after-tax, or disposable, income than they had before. This leads to an increase in consumption. Planned aggregate expenditure will increase, which will lead to inventories being lower than planned, which will lead to a rise in output. When output rises, more workers will be employed and more income will be generated, causing a second-round increase in consumption, and so on. Thus, income will increase by a multiple of the decrease in taxes. But there is a wrinkle!

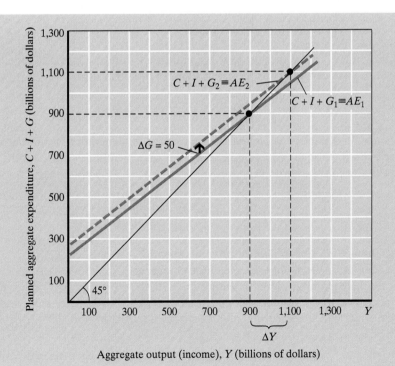

FIGURE 25.3

The Government Spending Multiplier

Increasing government spending by 50 shifts the AE function up by 50. As Y rises in response, additional consumption is generated. Overall, the equilibrium level of Y increases by 200, from 900 to 1,100.

591

> The multiplier for a change in taxes is *not the same* as the multiplier for a change in government spending.

tax multiplier *The ratio of change in the equilibrium level of output to a change in taxes.*

Why does the **tax multiplier**—the ratio of change in the equilibrium level of output to a change in taxes—differ from the spending multiplier? To answer this, we need to compare the ways in which a tax cut and a spending increase work their way through the economy.

Look at Figure 25.1. When the government increases spending, there is an immediate and direct impact on the economy's *total* spending. Because G is a component of planned aggregate expenditure, an increase in G leads to a dollar-for-dollar increase in planned aggregate expenditure. When taxes are cut, there is no direct impact on spending. Taxes enter the picture only because they have an effect on the household's disposable income, which influences household's consumption (which is part of total spending). As Figure 25.1 shows, the tax cut flows through households before affecting aggregate expenditure.

Let's assume the government decides to cut taxes by $1. By how much would spending increase? We already know the answer. The marginal propensity to consume tells us how much consumption spending changes when disposable income changes. In the example running through this chapter, the marginal propensity to consume out of disposable income is .75. This means that if households' after-tax incomes rise by $1, they will increase their consumption not by the full $1, but by only $0.75.[7]

To summarize: When government spending increases by $1, planned aggregate expenditure increases initially by the full amount of the rise in G, or $1. When taxes are cut, however, the initial increase in planned aggregate expenditure is only the MPC times the change in taxes. Because the initial increase in planned aggregate expenditure is smaller for a tax cut than for a government spending increase, the final effect on the equilibrium level of income will be smaller.

We figure the size of the tax multiplier in the same way we derived the multiplier for an increase in investment and an increase in government purchases. The final change in the equilibrium level of output (income) (Y) is:

$$\Delta Y = (\text{initial increase in aggregate expenditure}) \times \left(\frac{1}{MPS}\right)$$

Because the initial change in aggregate expenditure caused by a tax change of ΔT is $(-\Delta T \times MPC)$, we can solve for the tax multiplier by substitution:

$$\Delta Y = (-\Delta T \times MPC) \times \left(\frac{1}{MPS}\right) = -\Delta T \times \left(\frac{MPC}{MPS}\right)$$

Because a tax cut will cause an *increase* in consumption expenditures and output and a tax increase will cause a *reduction* in consumption expenditures and output, the tax multiplier is a negative multiplier:

$$\text{Tax multiplier} \equiv -\left(\frac{MPC}{MPS}\right)$$

We derive the tax multiplier algebraically in appendix A to this chapter.

If the MPC is .75, as in our example, the multiplier is $-.75/.25 = -3$. A tax cut of 100 will increase the equilibrium level of output by $-100 \times -3 = 300$. This is very different than the effect of our government spending multiplier of 4. Under these same conditions, a 100 increase in G will increase the equilibrium level of output by 400 (100×4).

FAST FACTS

During the fall of 1997, real GDP in Japan had contracted at an annual rate of 11.2 percent—its biggest decline in 23 years! During the previous few years, Japan had been increasing taxes to balance the budget. The *New York Times* reported, "economists said that today's figures could prompt the Government to abandon its fiscal austerity program and perhaps even cut corporate taxes, a move that has been encouraged by a number of Government ministries."

Source: Sheryl WuDunn, "Japan's Economy Shrinks by 11.2% Annual Rate," *The New York Times*, September 12, 1997, p. C1.

---

[7]What happens to the other $.25? Remember that whatever households do not consume is, by definition, saved. The other $.25 thus gets allocated to saving.

THE BALANCED-BUDGET MULTIPLIER

We have now discussed (1) changing government spending with no change in taxes, and (2) changing taxes with no change in government spending. But what if government spending and taxes are increased by the same amount? That is, what if the government decides to pay for its extra spending by increasing taxes by the same amount? The government's budget deficit would not change, because the increase in expenditures would be matched by an increase in tax income.

You might think in this case that equal increases in government spending and taxes have no effect on equilibrium income. After all, the extra government spending equals the extra amount of tax revenues collected by the government. But this is not so. Take, for example, a government spending increase of $40 billion. We know from the preceding analysis that an increase in G of 40, with taxes (T) held constant, should increase the equilibrium level of income by 40 × the government spending multiplier. The multiplier is $1/MPS$ or $1/.25 = 4$. The equilibrium level of income should rise by 160 (40 × 4).

Now suppose that instead of keeping tax revenues constant, we finance the 40 increase in government spending with an equal increase in taxes, so as to maintain a balanced budget. What happens to aggregate spending as a result of both the rise in G and the rise in T? There are two initial effects. First, government spending rises by 40. This effect is direct, immediate, and positive. But now the government also collects 40 more in taxes. The tax increase has a *negative* impact on overall spending in the economy, but it does not fully offset the increase in government spending.

The final impact of a tax increase on aggregate expenditure depends on how households respond to it. The only thing we know about household behavior so far is that households spend 75 percent of their added income and save 25 percent. We know that when disposable income falls, both consumption and saving are reduced. A tax *increase* of 40 reduces disposable income by 40, and that means consumption falls by 40 × MPC. Because $MPC = .75$, consumption falls by 30 (40 × .75).

The net result in the beginning is that government spending rises by 40 and consumption spending falls by 30. Aggregate expenditure increases by 10 right after the simultaneous balanced-budget increases in G and T.

So, a balanced-budget increase in G and T will raise output. But by how much? How large is this **balanced-budget multiplier**? The answer may surprise you:

> Balanced-budget multiplier ≡ 1

balanced-budget multiplier
The ratio of change in the equilibrium level of output to a change in government spending where the change in government spending is balanced by a change in taxes so as not to create any deficit. The balanced-budget multiplier is equal to one: The change in Y resulting from the change in G and the equal change in T is exactly the same size as the initial change in G or T itself.

Let's combine what we know about the tax multiplier and the government spending multiplier to explain this. To find the final effect of a simultaneous increase in government spending and increase in net taxes, we need to add the multiplier effects of the two. The government spending multiplier is $1/MPS$. The tax multiplier is $-MPC/MPS$. Their sum is $(1/MPS) + (-MPC/MPS) \equiv (1 - MPC)/MPS$. Because $MPC + MPS \equiv 1$, then $1 - MPC \equiv MPS$. This means $(1 - MPC)/MPS \equiv MPS/MPS \equiv 1$.[8]

Back to our example. Using the government spending multiplier, we saw that a 40 increase in G would *raise* output at equilibrium by 160 (40 × the government spending multiplier of 4). Using the tax multiplier, we know that a 40 tax hike will *reduce* the equilibrium level of output by 120 (40 × the tax multiplier, -3). The net effect is 160 minus 120, or 40. It should be clear, then, that the effect on equilibrium Y is equal to the balanced increase in G and T. In other words, the net increase in the equilibrium level of Y resulting from the change in G and the change in T is exactly the size of the initial change in G or T itself.

If the president wanted to raise Y by 200 without increasing the deficit, a simultaneous increase in G and T of 200 would do it. To see why, look at the numbers in

---

[8]We also derive the balanced-budget multiplier in appendix A to this chapter.

TABLE 25.3 FINDING EQUILIBRIUM AFTER A $200-BILLION BALANCED-BUDGET INCREASE IN G AND T (ALL FIGURES IN BILLIONS OF DOLLARS; BOTH G AND T HAVE INCREASED FROM 100 IN TABLE 25.1 TO 300 HERE.)

(1) OUTPUT (INCOME) Y	(2) NET TAXES T	(3) DISPOSABLE INCOME $Y_d \equiv Y - T$	(4) CONSUMPTION SPENDING ($C = 100 + .75\,Y_d$)	(5) PLANNED INVESTMENT SPENDING I	(6) GOVERNMENT PURCHASES G	(7) PLANNED AGGREGATE EXPENDITURE $C + I + G$	(8) UNPLANNED INVENTORY CHANGE $Y - (C + I + G)$	(9) ADJUST-MENT TO DISEQUI-LIBRIUM
500	300	200	250	100	300	650	−150	Output↑
700	300	400	400	100	300	800	−100	Output↑
900	300	600	550	100	300	950	−50	Output↑
1,100	300	800	700	100	300	1,100	0	Equilibrium
1,300	300	1,000	850	100	300	1,250	+50	Output↓
1,500	300	1,200	1,000	100	300	1,400	+100	Output↓

Table 25.3. In Table 25.1, we saw an equilibrium level of output at 900. With both G and T up by 200, the new equilibrium is 1,100—higher by 200. At no other level of Y do we find $(C + I + G) = Y$.

> An increase in government spending has a direct initial effect on planned aggregate expenditure; a tax increase does not. The initial effect of the tax increase is that households cut consumption by the *MPC* times the change in taxes. This change in consumption is less than the change in taxes, because the *MPC* is less than 1. The positive stimulus from the government spending increase is thus greater than the negative stimulus from the tax increase. The net effect is that the balanced-budget multiplier is 1.

Table 25.4 summarizes everything we have said about fiscal policy multipliers. If anything is still unclear, review the relevant discussions in this chapter.

➤ **A Warning** Although we have added government, the story we have told about the multiplier is still incomplete and oversimplified. For example, we have been treating net taxes (T) as a lump-sum, fixed amount, whereas in practice, taxes depend on income. Appendix B to this chapter shows that the size of the multiplier is reduced when we make the more realistic assumption that taxes depend on income.

TABLE 25.4 SUMMARY OF FISCAL POLICY MULTIPLIERS

	POLICY STIMULUS	MULTIPLIER	FINAL IMPACT ON EQUILIBRIUM Y
Government-spending multiplier	Increase or decrease in the level of government purchases: ΔG	$\dfrac{1}{MPS}$	$\Delta G \cdot \dfrac{1}{MPS}$
Tax multiplier	Increase or decrease in the level of net taxes: ΔT	$\dfrac{-MPC}{MPS}$	$\Delta T \cdot \dfrac{-MPC}{MPS}$
Balanced-budget multiplier	Simultaneous balanced-budget increase or decrease in the level of government purchases and net taxes: $\Delta G = \Delta T$	1	ΔG

We continue to add more realism to our analysis in the next section and in the chapters that follow. (See the Application box "Fiscal Policy during the Recessions of 1974–1975, 1980–1982, and 1990–1991" for a discussion of the government's use of fiscal policy during the last three recessions.)

ADDING THE INTERNATIONAL SECTOR

In chapter 21, we noted that the U.S. economy does not operate in a vacuum. Rather, it influences and is influenced by the rest of the world. But we have not yet taken into account the role of imports and exports in the macroeconomy.

Opening the economy to foreign trade adds a fourth component to planned aggregate expenditure—exports of goods and services, or EX. Exports are foreign purchases of goods and services produced in the United States. Opening the economy to the rest of the world also means that U.S. consumers and businesses have greater choice because they can buy foreign-produced goods and services (imports, or IM) in addition to domestically produced goods and services.

We can think of imports (IM) as a leakage from the circular flow and exports (EX) as an injection into the circular flow. (Review Figure 21.1.) With imports and exports, the equilibrium condition for the economy is:

> Open-economy equilibrium: $Y = C + I + G + (EX - IM)$

The quantity ($EX - IM$) is referred to as **net exports**.

Increases or decreases in net exports can throw the economy out of equilibrium and cause national income to change. For example, a large decrease in exports, *ceteris paribus*, would mean a drop in spending on domestically produced goods and services. The result would be an unplanned rise in inventories and a fall in output. Furthermore, if some domestic spending leaks into foreign markets (imports), the multiplier effect on domestic production will be reduced.

We discuss the international sector and its effects on the macroeconomy in detail in chapter 36. For now, we continue to use $Y = C + I + G$ as the basis of our analysis to keep our discussions clear and concise. Keep in mind that the international sector is an important player in the macroeconomy.

net exports *An economy's total exports* (EX) *minus its total imports* (IM).

THE FEDERAL BUDGET, DEFICIT, AND DEBT

Because fiscal policy is the manipulation of items in the federal budget, we need to consider those aspects of the budget relevant to our study of macroeconomics. The **federal budget** is an enormously complicated document, up to thousands of pages each year. It lists in detail all the things the government plans to spend money on and all the sources of government revenues for the coming year. It is the product of a complex interplay of social, political, and economic forces.

"The budget" is really three different budgets. First, it is a *political document* that dispenses favors to certain groups or regions (the elderly benefit from social security, farmers from agricultural price supports, students from federal loan programs, and so on) and places burdens (taxes) on others. Second, it is a *reflection of goals* the government wants to achieve. For example, in addition to assisting farmers, agricultural price supports are meant to preserve the "family farm." Tax breaks for corporations engaging in research and development of new products are meant to encourage research. Finally, the budget may be an *embodiment of some beliefs about how (if at all) the government should manage the macroeconomy*. The macroeconomic aspects of the budget are only a part of a more complicated story, a story that may be of more concern to political scientists than to economists.

federal budget *The budget of the federal government.*

FISCAL POLICY DURING THE RECESSIONS OF 1974–1975, 1980–1982, AND 1990–1991

As we've seen, the government can stimulate a sluggish economy by increasing government expenditures (*G*) and cutting taxes (*T*). Such policies have the effect of increasing aggregate expenditure (demand) and increasing equilibrium output (income). You might expect the government to increase *G* and/or cut *T* whenever the economy is in a recession.

Yet, the government has taken very different actions to deal with the three recessions that the U.S. economy has experienced since 1970. The last time the president and Congress consciously used fiscal policy to fight a recession was in 1975, during the administration of President Gerald Ford. The following from the *Economic Report of the President, 1976* suggests the policy succeeded in accomplishing its goals:

> *During the first part of 1975 the economy moved rapidly through the final stages of the most severe recession of the postwar period. Real gross national product (GNP) fell at an annual rate of 9.2 percent in the first quarter and then began to increase. . . .*
>
> *Economic policy shifted early in the year to counter the decline in output. The President proposed a $16-billion tax reduction in the State of the Union message in January and the Congress enacted a $21-billion net reduction in March. Because of these tax cuts, and associated one-time social security payments, real disposable personal income rose sharply in the second quarter. . . .*
>
> *GNP rose sharply in the second half of the year; and by the end of the year the initial phase of a recovery was clearly evident. . . .*

AS THE ECONOMY ENTERS A RECESSION, NATIONAL OUTPUT DECREASES AND HOUSEHOLDS HAVE LESS INCOME. WITH LOWER INCOMES, PEOPLE SPEND LESS AND SOME FIRMS MAY GO OUT OF BUSINESS.

The idea of using fiscal policy to stimulate aggregate expenditure and increase output during a recession was explicitly rejected by President Reagan in the 1980s. Instead, the Reagan administration favored policies designed to stimulate the supply side (rather than the demand side) of the market. These *supply-side policies* (discussed in chapter 19) focused on cutting taxes (a fiscal policy tool) to increase incentives to work, save, and invest. Reagan believed the added labor supply and investment brought about by lower taxes would lead to an expansion of the supply of goods and services, which would reduce inflation and unemployment.

President Reagan's policy worked, partially for reasons he did not intend. There is no question that the major supply-side tax cuts enacted in 1981 with President Reagan's blessing had the effect of stimulating aggregate *demand* (spending). This outcome makes perfect sense if you remember the theory we've developed so far: Lower taxes mean higher disposable income, and higher disposable income means more consumption and ultimately greater output.

This trend against using fiscal policy to stimulate the economy continued into the 1990s. As the recession of 1990 to 1991 was beginning, Congress and President Bush passed the Omnibus Budget Reconciliation Act, which *cut* federal expenditures and *increased* taxes in an effort to reduce the federal deficit. This policy did not stimulate the economy, which remained sluggish until the end of 1992.

For more on the effects of fiscal policy, see the Case and Fair web page at
http://www.prenhall.com/casefair.

TABLE 25.5 FEDERAL GOVERNMENT RECEIPTS AND
EXPENDITURES, 1997 (BILLIONS OF DOLLARS)

	AMOUNT	PERCENTAGE OF TOTAL
Receipts		
Personal taxes	774.4	44.9
Corporate taxes	211.9	12.3
Indirect business taxes	91.3	5.3
Contributions for social insurance	645.9	37.5
Total	**1,723.4**	**100.0**
Current Expenditures		
Consumption	463.8	26.5
Transfer payments	795.5	45.4
Grants-in-aid to state and local governments	224.2	12.8
Net interest payments	230.3	13.1
Net subsidies of government enterprises	38.4	2.2
Total	**1,752.2**	**100.0**
Current Surplus (+) or deficit (−) (Receipts − Current Expenditures)	−28.8	

Source: U.S. Department of Commerce, Bureau of Economic Analysis.

THE BUDGET

A highly condensed version of the federal budget is shown in Table 25.5. (Some of this reviews material from chapter 3, but here we highlight the budget components of particular importance to macroeconomics.) In 1997, the government had total receipts of $1,723.4 billion, largely from personal income taxes ($774.4 billion) and contributions for social insurance ($645.9 billion).[9] Receipts from corporate taxes accounted for $211.9 billion, or only 12.3 percent of total receipts. Not everyone is aware of the fact that corporate taxes as a percentage of government receipts are quite small relative to personal taxes and social security taxes.

The federal government also made $1,752.2 billion in expenditures in 1997. Of this, $795.5 billion represented transfer payments (social security, military retirement benefits, and unemployment compensation).[10] Consumption ($463.8 billion) was the next largest component, followed by interest on the federal debt ($230.3 billion) and grants-in-aid to state and local governments ($224.2 billion).

THE DEFICIT

The difference between the federal government's expenditures and its receipts is the **federal deficit**. Table 25.5 shows that the federal government spent slightly more than it took in during 1997, resulting in a deficit of $28.8 billion.

The federal deficit was high from the early 1980s until 1997. You can see this in Figure 25.4, where the federal deficit as a percentage of GDP is plotted for the 1970 I to 1997 IV period. As the figure shows, the deficit has been positive throughout the entire

federal deficit *Federal government expenditures minus receipts.*

---

[9]Contributions for social insurance are employer and employee social security taxes.

[10]Remember that there is an important difference between transfer payments and government purchases of goods and services. Much of the government budget goes for things that an economist would classify as transfers (payments that are grants or gifts) rather than purchases of goods and services. It is only the latter that are included in our variable G. Transfers are counted as part of net taxes.

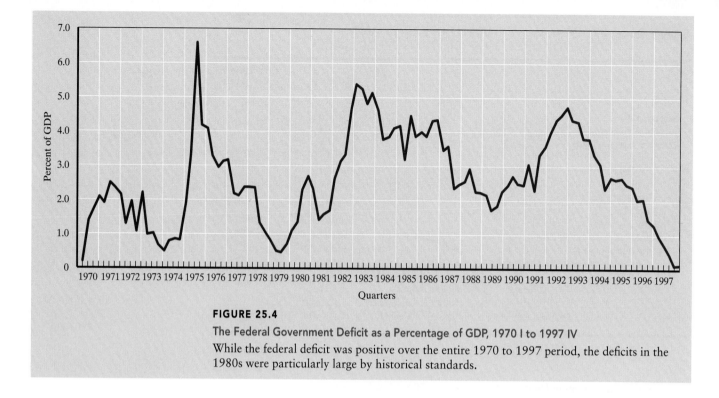

FIGURE 25.4

The Federal Government Deficit as a Percentage of GDP, 1970 I to 1997 IV

While the federal deficit was positive over the entire 1970 to 1997 period, the deficits in the 1980s were particularly large by historical standards.

period. Except for a period in the mid 1970s, the deficit was fairly low until the early 1980s, where it reached 5.4 percent of GDP in 1982 IV. It has fallen rapidly since 1992, and in 1997 IV it was only 0.1 percent of GDP.

How did such large deficits in the 1980s come about? There are several reasons. First, government purchases as a percentage of GDP rose in the early 1980s and then remained high. This increase primarily reflected the defense buildup of the Reagan years. Second, interest payments as a percentage of GDP rose substantially. Third, personal income tax rates fell as a result of the Economic Recovery Tax Act of 1981. With defense spending and interest payments rising rapidly and personal tax rates falling, it is not surprising that the deficit rose substantially during the 1980s. The government simply spent a lot more than it collected in taxes.

THE DEBT

When the government runs a deficit, it must borrow to finance it. To borrow, the federal government sells government securities to the public. It issues pieces of paper promising to pay a certain amount, with interest, in the future. In return, it receives funds from the buyers of the paper and uses these funds to pay its bills. This borrowing increases the **federal debt**, the total amount owed by the federal government. The federal debt is the total of all accumulated deficits minus surpluses over time.

Some of the securities that the government issues end up being held by the federal government itself at the Federal Reserve or in government trust funds. The term **privately held federal debt** refers only to the *privately held* debt of the U.S. government. At the end of October 1997, the federal debt was $5.4 trillion, of which $3.3 trillion was privately held.

Given the large deficits that the federal government has run up since the early 1980s, it should not be surprising that the federal debt has risen sharply from the early

federal debt *The total amount owed by the federal government.*

privately held federal debt *The privately held (non-government-owned) debt of the U.S. government.*

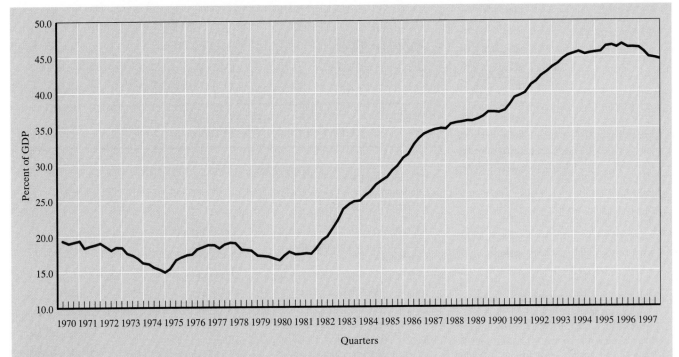

FIGURE 25.5

The Federal Government Debt as a Percentage of GDP, 1970 I to 1997 IV

The federal government debt increased dramatically in the 1980s as a result of the large deficits. The percentage has stabilized during the Clinton administrations.

1980s on. You can see this in Figure 25.5, where the privately held federal debt as a percentage of GDP is plotted for the 1970 I to 1997 IV period. The debt rose rapidly between 1982 and 1992—from 19.4 percent of GDP in 1982 I to 43.5 percent in 1992 IV. With the smaller deficits under the Clinton administration, the debt as a percentage of GDP has remained roughly constant since 1992.

One consequence of the large federal debt is that interest payments by the federal government are large. Table 25.5 shows that interest payments in 1997 were $230.3 billion, or 2.9 percent of GDP. In 1980, before the large increase in the debt, interest payments as a percentage of GDP were only 1.8 percent. Most of the federal debt is owned by U.S. citizens, and so most interest payments are simply a transfer from one group within the country (taxpayers) to another (bondholders). (See Application box, "Who Owns the Public Debt?")

THE ECONOMY'S INFLUENCE ON THE DEFICIT

▶ **Tax Revenues Depend on the State of the Economy**   Some parts of the government's budget depend on the state of the economy, over which the government has no direct control. Consider the revenue side of the budget. The government passes laws that set tax rates and tax brackets, variables the government does control. Tax revenue, on the other hand, depends on taxable income, and income depends on the state of the economy, which the government does *not* control. The government can set a personal income tax rate of 20 percent, but the revenue that the tax brings in will depend on the average income earned by households. The government will collect more revenue when average income is $40,000 than when average income is $20,000.

WHO OWNS THE PUBLIC DEBT?

At the end of October 1997, the total U.S. government debt was $5,369.7 billion, of which $3,346.6 billion was privately held. The difference between the total debt and the privately held debt—$2,023.1 billion—is the amount of the debt held by the government itself, including that held by the Federal Reserve. The Federal Reserve held $424.5 billion, and various government trust funds (such as the trust funds administered by the Social Security Administration) held the rest. Other federal trust funds that own U.S. Treasury obligations include federal employees' retirement funds, highway trust funds, the military retirement fund, and the airport and airway trust fund.

Why does the Federal Reserve hold so much of the debt? The Fed is responsible for controlling the U.S. money supply. As the economy grows, the money supply must be expanded to accommodate that growth. In December 1988, the money supply (M1) was $787.0 billion; by December 1997 it had grown to $1,076.0 billion.

The Fed expands the money supply primarily through open market operations—that is, by buying U.S. government securities in the open market. The Fed pays for these securities by writing a check or by expanding a bank's reserve account at the Fed. In either case, reserves are injected into the system. These additional reserves allow banks to lend more money, which ultimately expands the money supply. In essence, the Fed is creating money when it buys securities.

As a result, the Fed has come to own more than $424.5 billion worth of Treasury securities. The Fed uses the interest it receives on these obligations to finance its operations. It turns the excess interest back to the Treasury each year.

TABLE 1 ESTIMATED PRIVATE OWNERSHIP OF PUBLIC DEBT SECURITIES, DECEMBER 1996

	BILLIONS OF $	% OF TOTAL
Commercial banks	261.7	7.7
Individuals	356.6	10.5
Insurance companies	214.1	6.3
Money market funds	91.6	2.7
Corporations	258.5	7.6
State and local governments	363.7	10.7
Foreigners	1,131.8	33.2
Other*	733.2	21.5
Total	3,411.2	100.0

*Note: Includes savings and loans, credit unions, mutual savings banks, and pension funds.

Source: Economic Report of the President, 1998, Table B-89.

What happens to the funds held by the various government trust funds? They are used to buy Treasury securities! This makes deficit accounting a very tricky business. Table 10.5 shows that the federal government deficit as reported in the National Income and Product Accounts was $28.8 billion in 1997. However, the social security system ran a surplus of $63.7 billion that year. If we remove this surplus from the official numbers, the 1997 deficit was $92.5 billion.

Most privately held government debt is held in "public debt securities." Table 1 presents the breakdown of the private ownership of these securities in December 1996. "Private ownership" includes state and local governments. Most of the $363.7 billion owned by states and localities is held in pension funds administered by those governments for their employees. For example, many states have a teachers' retirement fund, and many of the dollars in those funds are invested in Treasury securities. These funds are not really owned by the government because each dollar in them represents an obligation of the state or local government to a retiree.

You can see from Table 1 that the private ownership of Treasury obligations is widespread. Individuals directly own $356.6 billion, or 10.5 percent of the total. Commercial banks account for 7.7 percent, insurance companies for 6.3 percent, and money market funds for 2.7 percent.

In recent years there has been some concern that the United States is relying too much on foreign countries (particularly Japan) to finance its deficits. The table shows that foreigners accounted for 33.2 percent of the total private ownership of public debt securities. This figure is up from 17.3 percent in December 1987.

For more on the public debt, see the Case and Fair web page at http://www.prenhall.com/casefair.

➤ Some Government Expenditures Depend on the State of the Economy

Some items on the expenditure side of the government budget also depend on the state of the economy. As the economy expands, unemployment falls, and the result is a decrease in unemployment benefits. Welfare payments and food stamp allotments also decrease somewhat. Some of the people who receive these benefits during bad times are able to find jobs when the state of the economy improves, and they begin earning enough income that they no longer qualify. Transfer payments tend to go down automatically during an expansion. (During a slump, transfer payments tend to increase because there are more people without jobs and more poor people generally.)

Another reason government spending is not completely controllable is that inflation often picks up when the economy is expanding. This can lead the government to spend more than it had planned to spend. Suppose the government has ordered 20 planes at $2 million each and inflation causes the actual price to be higher than expected. If the government decides to go ahead and buy the planes anyway, it will be forced to increase its spending. Finally, any change in the interest rate changes government interest payments. An increase in interest rates means that the government spends more in interest payments.

➤ Automatic Stabilizers

As the economy expands, the government's tax receipts increase. Also, transfer payments fall as the economy expands, which leads to a decrease in government expenditures. The revenue and expenditure items that change in response to changes in economic activity in such a way as to moderate changes in GDP are known as **automatic stabilizers**. As the economy expands or contracts, "automatic" changes in government revenues and expenditures take place that tend to reduce the change in, or stabilize, GDP.

automatic stabilizers *Revenue and expenditure items in the federal budget that automatically change with the state of the economy in such a way as to stabilize GDP.*

The fact that some revenues *automatically* tend to rise and some expenditures *automatically* tend to fall in an expansion means that the government surplus is larger, or the deficit is smaller, in an expansion than it otherwise would be. Suppose we wanted to assess whether a government is practicing a policy designed to increase spending and income. If we looked only at the size of the government budget deficit, we might be fooled into thinking that the government is trying to stimulate the economy when, in fact, the real source of the deficit is a slump in the economy that caused revenues to fall and transfer payments to increase.

➤ Fiscal Drag

If the economy is doing well, income will be high and so will tax revenue. Tax revenue rises with increases in income for two reasons. First, there is more income to be taxed when people are earning more. Second, as people earn more income, they move into higher tax brackets and the average tax rate that they pay increases. This

THE NATIONAL DEBT CLOCK IN NEW YORK CITY SHOWS HOW MUCH U.S. DEBT INCREASES EACH SECOND.

type of increase in tax rates is a **fiscal drag**, because the increase in average tax rates that results when people move into higher brackets acts as a "drag" on the economy. As the economy expands and income increases, the automatic tax increase mechanism built into the system goes to work. Tax rates go up, reducing the after-tax wage, and this slows down the expansion.

Before 1982, people found themselves pushed into higher tax brackets by inflation alone. Suppose my income rose 10 percent in 1981, but the price level also rose by 10 percent in that year. My income did not increase at all in real terms, but because the tax brackets were not legislated in real terms, I ended up paying more taxes. Since 1982, however, tax brackets have been indexed—that is, adjusted for inflation—and this has substantially reduced the automatic fiscal drag built into the system.

▶ **Full-Employment Budget** Because the condition of the economy affects the budget deficit so strongly, we cannot accurately judge either the intent or the success of fiscal policies just by looking at the deficit. Instead of looking simply at the size of the deficit, economists have developed an alternative way to measure how effective fiscal policy actually is. By examining what the budget would be like if the economy were producing at the full-employment level of output—the so-called **full-employment budget**—we can establish a benchmark for evaluating fiscal policy.

The distinction between the actual and full-employment deficits is important. Suppose the economy is in a slump and the deficit is $250 billion. Also suppose that if there were full employment, the deficit would fall to $75 billion. The $75 billion deficit that would remain even with full employment would be due to the structure of tax and spending programs rather than to the state of the economy. This deficit—the deficit that remains at full employment—is sometimes called the **structural deficit**. The $175 billion ($250 billion − $75 billion) part of the deficit caused by the fact the economy is in a slump is known as the **cyclical deficit**. The existence of the cyclical deficit depends on where the economy is in the business cycle, and it ceases to exist when full employment is reached. By definition, the cyclical deficit of the full-employment budget is zero.

DEBT AND DEFICITS: THE REST OF THE WORLD

The United States is not the only country in the world that has had problems with budget deficits. Table 25.6 shows the deficit and debt in 1997 as a percentage of GDP for six countries plus the United States. The table shows that Italy's government ran a deficit equal to 3.2 percent of its GDP in 1997 and had an outstanding debt equal to 116.3 percent of its GDP that year. Canada had the lowest deficit as a percentage of GDP in 1997, followed by the United States and the United Kingdom. Japan's government debt was only 18.2 percent of its GDP, but the values for the other countries were much higher. Canada was the next highest after Italy, with a debt equal to 66.5 percent of GDP in 1997.

THE MONEY MARKET AND MONETARY POLICY: A PREVIEW

We have now seen how households, firms, and the government interact in the goods market, how equilibrium output (income) is determined, and how the government uses fiscal policy to influence the economy. (We've also provided a brief introduction to the international sector's influence on aggregate expenditure and equilibrium output.) In the following two chapters we analyze the money market and monetary policy—the government's other major tool for influencing the economy.

TABLE 25.6

GOVERNMENT DEFICITS AND DEBT AS A PERCENTAGE OF NOMINAL GDP, 1997, FOR SELECTED COUNTRIES

	DEFICIT	DEBT
Canada	0.2	66.5
France	3.2	48.6
Germany	3.1	53.4
Italy	3.2	116.3
Japan	2.7	18.2
United Kingdom	2.0	47.9
United States	0.3	51.7

Source: International Monetary Fund, *World Economic Outlook*, October 1997.

SUMMARY

1. The government can affect the macroeconomy through two specific policy channels. *Fiscal policy* refers to the government's taxing and spending behavior. *Discretionary fiscal policy* refers to changes in taxes or spending that are the result of deliberate changes in government policy. *Monetary policy* refers to the behavior of the Federal Reserve regarding the nation's money supply.

GOVERNMENT IN THE ECONOMY

2. The government does not have complete control over tax revenues and certain expenditures, which are partially dictated by the state of the economy.

3. As a participant in the economy, the government makes purchases of goods and services (G), collects taxes, and makes transfer payments to households. *Net taxes* (T) is equal to the tax payments made to the government by firms and households minus transfer payments made to households by the government.

4. *Disposable*, or *after-tax*, *income* (Y_d) is equal to the amount of income received by households after taxes: $Y_d \equiv Y - T$. After-tax income determines households' consumption behavior.

5. The *budget deficit* is equal to the difference between what the government spends and what it collects in taxes: $G - T$. When G exceeds T, the government must borrow from the public to finance its deficit.

6. In an economy in which government is a participant, planned aggregate expenditure equals consumption spending by households (C) plus planned investment spending by firms (I) plus government spending on goods and services (G): $AE \equiv C + I + G$. Because the condition $Y = AE$ is necessary for the economy to be in equilibrium, it follows that $Y = C + I + G$ is the macroeconomic equilibrium condition. The economy is also in equilibrium when leakages out of the system equal injections into the system. This occurs when savings and net taxes (the leakages) equal planned investment and government purchases (the injections): $S + T = I + G$.

FISCAL POLICY AT WORK: MULTIPLIER EFFECTS

7. Fiscal policy has a multiplier effect on the economy. A change in government spending gives rise to a multiplier equal to $1/MPS$. A change in taxation brings about a multiplier equal to $-MPC/MPS$. A simultaneous equal increase or decrease in government spending and taxes has a multiplier effect of 1.

ADDING THE INTERNATIONAL SECTOR

8. Opening the economy to foreign trade adds two components to the equilibrium condition: exports (EX) and imports (IM). Exports are an injection into the circular flow; imports are a leakage from the circular flow. The equilibrium condition for the economy becomes $Y = C + I + G + (EX - IM)$ when the international sector is taken into account. The expression ($EX - IM$) is referred to as *net exports*.

THE FEDERAL BUDGET, DEFICIT, AND DEBT

9. The federal deficit was quite large in the 1980s. Reasons for the deficit include the defense buildup of the Reagan years, the high amount of interest paid on already-existing debt, and cuts in personal tax rates. With defense spending and interest payments rising rapidly and personal income tax rates falling, the government has simply been spending more than it has been collecting in taxes.

10. *Automatic stabilizers* are revenue and expenditure items in the federal budget that automatically change with the state of the economy and tend to stabilize GDP. For example, during expansions the government automatically takes in more revenue, because people are making more money that is taxed. Higher income and tax brackets also mean fewer transfer payments.

11. *Fiscal drag* is the negative effect on the economy that occurs when average tax rates increase because taxpayers have moved into higher income brackets during an expansion. These higher taxes reduce disposable income and slow down the expansion. Since 1982, tax brackets have been indexed to inflation, and this has reduced the fiscal drag built into the tax system.

12. The *full-employment budget* is an economist's construction of what the federal budget would be if the economy were producing at a full-employment level of output. The *structural deficit* is the federal deficit that remains even at full employment. *Cyclical deficits* occur when there is a downturn in the business cycle.

REVIEW TERMS AND CONCEPTS

fiscal drag, 602
fiscal policy, 583
full-employment budget, 602
government spending multiplier, 590
monetary policy, 584
net exports ($EX - IM$), 595
net taxes (T), 584
privately held federal debt, 598
structural deficit, 602
tax multiplier, 592

1. Disposable income $Y_d \equiv Y - T$
2. $AE \equiv C + I + G$
3. Government budget deficit $\equiv G - T$
4. Equilibrium in an economy with government: $Y = C + I + G$
5. Leakages/injections approach to equilibrium in an economy with government:
   $S + T = I + G$
6. Government spending multiplier $\equiv \dfrac{1}{MPS}$
7. Tax multiplier $\equiv -\dfrac{MPC}{MPS}$
8. Balanced-budget multiplier $\equiv 1$
9. Open-economy equilibrium position: $Y = C + I + G + (EX - IM)$

PROBLEM SET

1. Define *saving* and *investment*. Data for the simple closed economy of Newt show that in 1998 saving exceeded investment and the government is running a balanced budget. What is likely to happen? What would happen if the government were instead running a deficit and saving were equal to investment?

2. Crack economists in the economy of Yuk estimate the following:

Real output/income	1,000 billion Yuks
Government purchases	200 billion Yuks
Total net taxes	200 billion Yuks
Investment spending (planned)	100 billion Yuks

   Assume that Yukkers consume 75 percent of their disposable incomes and save 25 percent.
   a. You are asked by the business editor of the *Yuk Gazette* to predict the events of the next few months. Using the data given, can you make a forecast? (Assume that investment is constant.)
   b. If no changes were made, at what level of GDP (Y) would the economy of Yuk settle?
   c. Some local conservatives blame Yuk's problems on the size of the government sector. They suggest cutting government purchases by 25 billion Yuks. What effect would such cuts have on the economy? (Be specific.)

3. On July 3, 1997, the new government of Prime Minister Tony Blair in Great Britain passed its first budget in the Parliament. The top budget priority was a tax cut for business that gave British businesses the lowest tax rates of any Western industrialized country. To offset the business tax cut were a number of tax increases including higher consumption taxes and a windfall tax on profits from privatized utilities. Overall, the result was slightly higher government spending and an increase in tax revenues that exactly matched the spending increase. Would you expect such a package to increase or decrease British GDP? Explain.

4. "A $1 increase in government spending will raise equilibrium income by more than a $1 tax cut, yet both have the same impact on the budget deficit. So if we care about the budget deficit, the best way to stimulate the economy is through increases in spending, not cuts in taxes." Comment.

5. Assume that in 1998, the following prevails in the Republic of Nurd:

$Y = \$200$	$G = \$0$
$C = \$160$	$T = \$0$
$S = \$40$	
I (planned) $= \$30$	

   Assume that households consume 80 percent of their income, they save 20 percent of their income, $MPC = .8$, and $MPS = .2$. That is, $C = .8Y_d$ and $S = .2Y_d$.
   a. Is the economy of Nurd in equilibrium? What is Nurd's equilibrium level of income? What is likely to happen in the coming months if the government takes no action?
   b. If $200 is the "full employment" level of Y, what fiscal policy might the government follow if its goal is full employment?
   c. If the full-employment level of Y is $250, what fiscal policy might the government follow?
   d. Suppose $Y = \$200$, $C = \$160$, $S = \$40$, and $I = \$40$. Is Nurd's economy in equilibrium?
   e. Starting with the situation in d., suppose the government starts spending $30 each year with no taxation and continues to spend $30 every period. If I remains constant, what will happen to the equilibrium level of Nurd's domestic product (Y)? What will the new levels of C and S be?
   f. Starting with the situation in d., suppose the government starts taxing the population $30 each year without spending anything and continues to tax at that rate every period. If I remains constant, what will happen to the equilibrium level of Nurd's domestic product (Y)?

What will be the new levels of C and S? How does your answer to f. differ from your answer to e? Why?

6. Some economists claim World War II ended the Great Depression of the 1930s. The war effort was financed by borrowing massive sums of money from the public. Explain how a war could end a recession. Look at recent and back issues of the *Economic Report of the President* or the *Statistical Abstract of the United States*. How large was the federal government's debt as a percentage of GDP in 1946? How large is it today?

7. Suppose all tax collections are fixed (rather than dependent on income), and all spending and transfer programs are also fixed (in the sense that they do not depend on the state of the economy, as, for example, unemployment benefits now do). If this were the case, would there be any automatic stabilizers in the government budget? Would there be any distinction between the full-employment deficit and the actual budget deficit? Explain.

8. Answer the following:
   a. *MPS* = .4. What is the government spending multiplier?
   b. *MPC* = .9. What is the government spending multiplier?
   c. *MPS* = .5. What is the government spending multiplier?
   d. *MPC* = .75. What is the tax multiplier?
   e. *MPS* = .1. What is the tax multiplier?
   f. If the government spending multiplier is 6, what is the tax multiplier?
   g. If the tax multiplier is −2, what is the government spending multiplier?
   h. If government purchases and taxes are both increased by $100 billion simultaneously, what will the effect be on equilibrium output (income)?

9. What is the relationship between the government budget deficit and the government debt? Suppose that the United States managed to balance its budget in fiscal year 1998. Would there be any effect on the size of the debt?

TAKE IT TO THE NET

We invite you to visit the Case and Fair page on the Prentice Hall Web site:

http://www.prenhall.com/casefair

for this chapter's World Wide Web exercise.

APPENDIX A TO CHAPTER 25

DERIVING THE FISCAL POLICY MULTIPLIERS

THE GOVERNMENT SPENDING AND TAX MULTIPLIERS

In the chapter, we noted that the government spending multiplier is 1/*MPS*. (This is the same as the investment multiplier.) We can also derive the multiplier algebraically using our hypothetical consumption function:

$$C = a + b(Y - T)$$

where *b* is the marginal propensity to consume. As you know, the equilibrium condition is

$$Y = C + I + G$$

Substituting for *C*, we get

$$Y = a + b(Y - T) + I + G$$
$$Y = a + bY - bT + I + G$$

This equation can be rearranged to yield

$$Y - bY = a + I + G - bT$$
$$Y(1 - b) = a + I + G - bT$$

Now solve for *Y* by dividing through by (1 − *b*):

$$Y = \frac{1}{(1 - b)}(a + I + G - bT)$$

We see from this last equation that if *G* increases by 1 with the other determinants of *Y* (*a*, *I*, and *T*) remaining constant, *Y* increases by 1/(1 − *b*). The multiplier is, as before, simply 1/(1 − *b*), where *b* is the marginal propensity to consume. And, of course, 1 − *b* equals the marginal propensity to save, so the government spending multiplier is 1/*MPS*.

We can also derive the tax multiplier. The last equation says that when *T* increases by $1, holding *a*, *I*, and *G* constant, income decreases by *b*/(1 − *b*) dollars. The tax multiplier is −*b*/(1 − *b*), or −*MPC*/(1 − *MPC*) = −*MPC*/*MPS*. (Remember that we add the negative sign to the tax multiplier because the tax multiplier is a *negative* multiplier.)

THE BALANCED-BUDGET MULTIPLIER

It is easy to show formally that the balanced-budget multiplier = 1. When taxes and government spending are simultaneously increased by the same amount, there are two effects on planned aggregate expenditure: one positive and one negative. The initial impact of a balanced-budget increase in government spending and taxes on aggregate expenditure would be the *increase* in government purchases (ΔG) minus the *decrease* in consumption (ΔC) caused by the tax increase. The decrease in consumption brought about by the tax increase is equal to $\Delta C = \Delta T(MPC)$.

Increase in spending:	ΔG
$-$Decrease in spending:	$\Delta C = \Delta T(MPC)$
= Net increase in spending	$\Delta G - \Delta T(MPC)$

In a balanced-budget increase, $\Delta G = \Delta T$, so we can substitute:

Net initial increase in spending:
$$\Delta G - \Delta G(MPC) = \Delta G(1 - MPC).$$

Because $MPS = (1 - MPC)$, the initial increase in spending is

$$\Delta G(MPS).$$

We can now apply the expenditure multiplier $\left(\dfrac{1}{MPS}\right)$ to this net initial increase in spending:

$$\Delta Y = \Delta G\left(\frac{1}{MPS}\right) = \Delta G$$

Thus, the final total increase in the equilibrium level of Y is just equal to the initial balanced increase in G and T. That means the balanced-budget multiplier = 1.

APPENDIX B TO CHAPTER 25

THE CASE IN WHICH TAX REVENUES DEPEND ON INCOME

In this chapter, we used the simplifying assumption that the government collects taxes in a lump sum. This made our discussion of the multiplier effects somewhat easier to follow. But now suppose that the government collects taxes not solely as a lump sum that is paid regardless of income, but also partly in the form of a proportional levy against income. This is a more realistic assumption. Typically, tax collections are either based on income (as with the personal income tax) or they follow the ups and downs in the economy (as with sales taxes). Instead of setting taxes equal to some fixed amount, let's say that tax revenues depend on income. If we call the amount of net taxes collected T, we can write: $T = T_0 + tY$.

This equation contains two parts. First, we note that net taxes (T) will be equal to an amount T_0 if income (Y) is zero. Second, the tax rate (t) indicates how much net taxes change as income changes. Suppose that T_0 is equal to -200 and t is 1/3. The resulting tax function is $T = -200 + 1/3Y$, which is graphed in Figure 25A.1. Note that when income is zero, the government collects "negative net taxes," which simply means that it makes transfer payments of 200. As income rises, tax collections increase because every extra dollar of income generates $.33 in extra revenues for the government.

How do we incorporate this new tax function into our discussion? All we do is replace the old value of T (in the example in the chapter, T was set equal to 100) with

the new value, $-200 + 1/3Y$. Look first at the consumption equation. Consumption (C) still depends on disposable income, as it did before. Also, disposable income is still $Y - T$, or income minus taxes. Instead of disposable

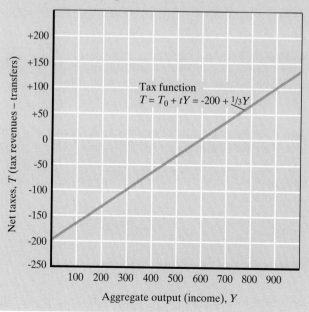

FIGURE 25A.1

The Tax Function

This graph shows net taxes (taxes minus transfer payments) as a function of aggregate income.

Net taxes, T (tax revenues − transfers)

Tax function
$T = T_0 + tY = -200 + \frac{1}{3}Y$

Aggregate output (income), Y

income equaling $Y - 100$, however, the new equation for disposable income is

$$Y_d \equiv Y - T$$

$$Y_d \equiv Y - (-200 + 1/3Y)$$

$$Y_d \equiv Y + 200 - 1/3Y$$

Because consumption still depends on after-tax income, exactly as it did before, we have

$$C = 100 + .75Y_d$$

$$C = 100 + .75(Y + 200 - 1/3Y)$$

Nothing else needs to be changed. We solve for equilibrium income exactly as before, by setting planned aggregate expenditure equal to aggregate output. Recall that planned aggregate expenditure is $C + I + G$, and aggregate output is Y. If we assume, as before, that $I = 100$ and $G = 100$, the equilibrium is

$$Y = C + I + G$$

$$Y = \underbrace{100 + .75(Y + 200 - 1/3Y)}_{C} + \underbrace{100}_{I} + \underbrace{100.}_{G}$$

This equation may look difficult to solve, but it is not. It simplifies to

$$Y = 100 + .75Y + 150 - .25Y + 100 + 100$$

$$Y = 450 + .5Y$$

$$.5Y = 450$$

This means that $Y = 450/.5 = 900$, the new equilibrium level of income.

Consider the graphic analysis of this equation as shown in Figure 25A.2, where you should note that when we make taxes a function of income (instead of a lump-sum amount), the AE function becomes *flatter* than it was before. Why? When tax collections do not depend on income, an increase in income of \$1 means disposable income also increases by a dollar. Because taxes are a constant amount, adding more income does not raise the amount of taxes paid. Disposable income therefore changes dollar-for-dollar with any change in income.

When taxes depend on income, a \$1 increase in income does not increase disposable income by a full dollar, because some of the additional dollar goes to pay extra taxes. Under the modified tax function of Figure 25A.2, an extra dollar of income will increase disposable income by only \$.67, because \$.33 of the extra dollar goes to the government in the form of taxes.

No matter how taxes are calculated, the marginal propensity to consume out of disposable (or after-tax) income is the same—each extra dollar of disposable income will increase consumption spending by \$.75. But a \$1 change in before-tax income does not have the same effect on disposable income in each case. Suppose we were to increase income by \$1. With the lump-sum tax function, disposable income would rise by \$1, and consumption would increase by the MPC times the change in Y_d, or \$.75. When taxes depend on income, disposable income would rise by only \$.67 from the \$1 increase in income,

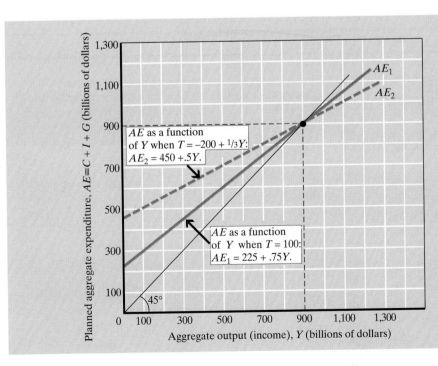

FIGURE 25A.2

Different Tax Systems

When taxes are strictly lump sum ($T = 100$) and do not depend on income, the aggregate expenditure function is steeper than when taxes depend on income.

AE as a function of Y when $T = -200 + 1/3Y$: $AE_2 = 450 + .5Y$.

AE as a function of Y when $T = 100$: $AE_1 = 225 + .75Y$.

and consumption would rise by only the *MPC* times the change in disposable income, or $.75 \times .67 = $.50$.

If a \$1 increase in income raises expenditure by \$.75 in one case, and by only \$.50 in the other, the second aggregate expenditure function must be flatter than the first.

THE GOVERNMENT SPENDING AND TAX MULTIPLIERS ALGEBRAICALLY

All this means that if taxes are a function of income, the three multipliers (investment, government spending, and tax) are less than they would be if taxes were a lump-sum amount. Using the same linear consumption function we used in chapters 23 and 24, we can derive the multiplier:

$$C = a + b(Y - T)$$

$$C = a + b(Y - T_0 - tY)$$

$$C = a + bY - bT_0 - btY$$

We know that $Y = C + I + G$. Through substitution we get:

$$Y = \underbrace{a + bY - bT_0 - btY}_{C} + I + G$$

Solving for Y:

$$Y = \frac{1}{1 - b + bt}(a + I + G - bT_0)$$

This means that a \$1 increase in G or I (holding a and T_0 constant) will increase the equilibrium level of Y by:

$$\frac{1}{1 - b + bt}$$

If $b = MPC = .75$ and $t = .20$, the spending multiplier is 2.5. (Compare this to 4, which would be the value of the spending multiplier if taxes were a lump sum—that is, if $t = 0$.)

Holding a, I, and G constant, a fixed or lump-sum tax cut (a cut in T_0) will increase the equilibrium level of income by:

$$\frac{b}{1 - b + bt}$$

Thus, if $b = MPC = .75$ and $t = .20$, the tax multiplier is -1.875. (Compare this to -3, which would be the value of the tax multiplier if taxes were a lump sum.)

SUMMARY

1. When taxes depend on income, a \$1 increase in income does not increase disposable income by a full dollar, because some of the additional dollar must go to pay extra taxes. This means that if taxes are a function of income, the three multipliers (investment, government spending, and tax) are less than they would be if taxes were a lump-sum amount.

PROBLEM SET

1. Given the following for the economy of a country:
   (1) Consumption function: $C = 85 + 0.5Y_d$
   (2) Investment function: $I = 85$
   (3) Government spending: $G = 60$
   (4) Net taxes: $T = -40 + 0.25Y$
   (5) Disposable income: $Y_d \equiv Y - T$
   (6) Equilibrium: $Y = C + I + G$.

   Solve for equilibrium income. (*Hint:* Be very careful in doing the calculations. They are not difficult, but it is easy to make careless mistakes that produce very wrong results.) How much does the government collect in net taxes when the economy is in equilibrium? What is the government's budget deficit or surplus?

Chapter 26

THE MONEY SUPPLY AND THE FEDERAL RESERVE SYSTEM

IN THE LAST TWO CHAPTERS, we explored how consumers, firms, and the government interact in the goods market. In this chapter and the next we show how money markets work in the macroeconomy. We begin with what money is and the role it plays in the U.S. economy. We then discuss the forces that determine the supply of money and show how banks create money. Finally, we discuss the workings of the nation's central bank, the Federal Reserve, and the tools at its disposal to control the money supply.

Microeconomics has little to say about money. Microeconomic theories and models are concerned primarily with *real* quantities (apples, oranges, hours of labor) and *relative* prices (the price of apples relative to the price of oranges, the price of labor relative to the prices of other goods). Most of the key ideas in microeconomics do not require that we know anything about money. As we shall see, this is not the case in macroeconomics.

AN OVERVIEW OF MONEY

You often hear people say things like "He makes a lot of money" (in other words, "He has a high income") or "She's worth a lot of money" (meaning "She is very wealthy"). It is true that your employer uses money to pay you your income, and your wealth may be accumulated in the form of money. But *money is not income, and money is not wealth*.

To see that money and income are not the same, think of a $20 bill. That bill may pass through a thousand hands in a year, yet never be used to pay anyone a salary. Suppose I get a $20 bill from an automatic teller machine, and I spend it on dinner. The restaurant puts that $20 bill in a bank in the next day's deposit. The bank gives it to a woman cashing a check the following day; she spends it at a baseball game that night. The bill has been through many hands but not as part of anyone's income.

WHAT IS MONEY?

We will soon get to a formal definition of money, but let's start out with the basic idea of what money is.

> Money is anything that is generally accepted as a medium of exchange.

Most people take the ability to obtain and use money for granted. When the whole monetary system works well, as it generally does in the United States, the basic mechanics of the system are virtually invisible. People take for granted that they can walk into any store, restaurant, boutique, or gas station and buy whatever they want, as long as they have enough green pieces of paper.

The idea that you can buy things with money is so natural and obvious that it seems absurd to mention it. But stop and ask yourself: "How is it that a shop owner is willing to part with a steak and a loaf of bread that I can eat in exchange for some pieces of paper that are intrinsically worthless?" And why, on the other hand, are there times and places where it takes a shopping cart full of money to purchase a dozen eggs? The answers to these questions lie in what money is: a means of payment, a store of value, and a unit of account.

barter *The direct exchange of goods and services for other goods and services.*

> **A Means of Payment, or Medium of Exchange** Money is vital to the working of a market economy. Imagine what life would be like without it. The alternative to a monetary economy is **barter**, people exchanging goods and services for other goods and services directly instead of exchanging via the medium of money.

How does a barter system work? Suppose you want bacon, eggs, and orange juice for breakfast. Instead of going to the store and buying these things with money, you would have to find someone who has these items and is willing to trade them. You would also have to have something the bacon seller, the orange juice purveyor, and the egg vendor want. Having pencils to trade will do you no good if the bacon, orange juice, and egg sellers do not want pencils.

A barter system requires a *double coincidence of wants* for trade to take place. That is, to effect a trade, I not only have to find someone who has what I want, but that person must also want what I have. Where the range of goods traded is small, as it is in relatively unsophisticated economies, it is not difficult to find someone to trade with, and barter is often used. In a complex society with many goods, barter exchanges involve an intolerable amount of effort. Imagine trying to find people who offer for sale all the things you buy in a typical trip to the grocery store, and who are willing to accept goods that you have to offer in exchange for their goods.

medium of exchange, or **means of payment** *What sellers generally accept and buyers generally use to pay for goods and services.*

Some agreed-upon **medium of exchange** (or, **means of payment**) neatly eliminates the double-coincidence-of-wants problem. Under a monetary system, money is exchanged for goods or services when people buy things; goods or services are exchanged for money when people sell things. No one ever has to trade goods for other goods directly. Money is a lubricant in the functioning of a market economy.

store of value *An asset that can be used to transport purchasing power from one time period to another.*

> **A Store of Value** Economists have identified other roles for money aside from its primary function as a medium of exchange. Money also serves as a **store of value**—an asset that can be used to transport purchasing power from one time period to another. If you raise chickens and at the end of the month sell them for more than you want to spend and consume immediately, you may keep some of your earnings in the form of money until the time you want to spend it.

There are many other stores of value besides money. You could have decided to hold your "surplus" earnings by buying such things as antique paintings, baseball cards, or diamonds, which you could sell later when you want to spend your earnings. Money has several advantages over these other stores of value. First, it comes in convenient denominations and is easily portable. You don't have to worry about making change for a

Renoir to buy a gallon of gasoline. Second, because money is also a means of payment, it is easily exchanged for goods at all times. (A Renoir is not easily exchanged for other goods.) These two factors compose the **liquidity property of money**. Money is easily spent, flowing out of your hands like liquid. Renoirs and ancient Aztec statues are neither convenient nor portable and are not readily accepted as a means of payment.

The main disadvantage of money as a store of value is that the value of money falls when the prices of goods and services rise. If the price of potato chips rises from $1 per bag to $2 per bag, the value of a dollar bill, in terms of potato chips, falls from one bag to half a bag. When this happens, it may be better to use potato chips (or antiques or real estate) as a store of value.

> ▶ **A Unit of Account**   Money also serves as a **unit of account**—a consistent way of quoting prices. All prices are quoted in monetary units. A textbook is quoted as costing $45, not 140 bananas or 4 videotapes, and a banana is quoted as costing 25¢, not 1.4 apples or 16 pages of a textbook.

Obviously, a standard unit of account is extremely useful when quoting prices. This function of money may have escaped your notice—what else would people quote prices in except money?

COMMODITY AND FIAT MONIES

Introductory economics textbooks are full of stories about the various items that have been used as money by various cultures—candy bars, cigarettes (in World War II prisoner-of-war camps), huge wheels of carved stone (on the island of Yap in the South Pacific), cowrie shells (in West Africa), beads (among North American Indians), cattle (in southern Africa), small green scraps of paper (in contemporary North America). The list goes on. These various kinds of money are generally divided into two groups, commodity monies and fiat money.

Commodity monies are those items used as money that also have an intrinsic value in some other use. For example, prisoners of war made purchases with cigarettes, quoted prices in terms of cigarettes, and held their wealth in the form of accumulated cigarettes. Of course, cigarettes could also be smoked—they had an alternative use apart from serving as money. Gold represents another form of commodity money. For hundreds of years gold could be used directly to buy things, but it also had other uses, ranging from jewelry to dental fillings.

By contrast, money in the United States today is mostly fiat money. **Fiat money**, sometimes called **token money**, is money that is intrinsically worthless. The actual value of a one-, ten-, or fifty-dollar bill is basically zero; what other uses are there for a small piece of paper with some green ink on it?

Why would anyone accept worthless scraps of paper as money instead of something that has some value, such as gold, cigarettes, or cattle? If your answer is "Because the paper money is backed by gold or silver," you are wrong! There was a time when dollar bills were convertible directly into gold. The government backed each dollar bill in circulation by holding a certain amount of gold in its vaults. If the price of gold were $35 per ounce, for example, the government agreed to sell one ounce of gold for 35 dollar bills. But dollar bills are no longer backed by any commodity—gold, silver, or anything else. They are exchangeable only for dimes, nickels, pennies, other dollars, and so on.

The public accepts paper money as a means of payment and a store of value because the government has taken steps to ensure that its money is accepted. The government declares its paper money to be **legal tender**. That is, the government declares that its money must be accepted in settlement of debts. It does this by fiat (hence *fiat money*). It passes laws defining certain pieces of paper printed in certain inks on certain plates to be legal tender, and that is that. Printed on every Federal Reserve note in the United States is "This note is legal tender for all debts, public and private." Often, the government can get a start on gaining acceptance for its paper money by requiring that

liquidity property of money
The property of money that makes it a good medium of exchange as well as a store of value: It is portable and readily accepted and thus easily exchanged for goods.

unit of account *A standard unit that provides a consistent way of quoting prices.*

SOME OF YAP'S STONE MONEY WHEELS ARE SO LARGE THAT THEY ARE NEVER MOVED.

commodity monies *Items used as money that also have intrinsic value in some other use.*

fiat, or **token, money** *Items designated as money that are intrinsically worthless.*

legal tender *Money that a government has required to be accepted in settlement of debts.*

it be used to pay taxes. (Note that you cannot use chickens, baseball cards, or Renoir paintings to pay your taxes, only checks or currency.)

Aside from declaring its currency legal tender, the government usually does one other thing to ensure that paper money will be accepted: It promises the public that it will not print paper money so fast that it loses its value. Expanding the supply of currency so rapidly that it loses much of its value has been a problem throughout history and is known as **currency debasement**. Debasement of the currency has been a special problem of governments that lack the strength to take the politically unpopular step of raising taxes. Printing money to be used on government expenditures of goods and services can serve as a substitute for tax increases, and weak governments have often relied on the printing press to finance their expenditures. A recent example is Bulgaria, where the inflation rate hit a record of 1,268 percent in 1997. We will discuss money and inflation at great length in later chapters.

MEASURING THE SUPPLY OF MONEY IN THE UNITED STATES

We now turn to the various kinds of money in the United States. Recall that money is used: to buy things (a means of payment); to hold wealth (a store of value); and to quote prices (a unit of account). Unfortunately, these characteristics apply to a broad range of assets in the U.S. economy. As we will see, it is not at all clear where we should draw the line and say, "Up to this is money, beyond this is something else."

To solve the problem of multiple monies, economists have given different names to different measures of money. The two most common measures of money are transactions money, also called *M1*, and broad money, also called *M2*.

▶ **M1: Transactions Money**   What should be counted as money? Clearly, coins and dollar bills, as well as higher denominations of currency, must be counted as money—they fit all the requirements. But what about checking accounts? Checks too can be used to buy things and can serve as a store of value. In fact, bankers call checking accounts *demand deposits*, because depositors have the right to go to the bank and cash in (demand) their entire checking account balances at any time. That makes your checking account balance virtually equivalent to bills in your wallet, and it should be included as part of the amount of money you hold.

If we take the value of all currency (including coins) held outside of bank vaults and add to it the value of all demand deposits, traveler's checks, and other checkable deposits, we have defined **M1**, or **transactions money**. As its name suggests, this is the money that can be directly used for transactions—to buy things.

 Currency held outside banks + Demand deposits + Traveler's checks + Other checkable deposits

A *checkable deposit* is any deposit account with a bank or other financial institution on which a check can be written. Checkable deposits include: demand deposits; *negotiable order of withdrawal (NOW) accounts*, which are like checking accounts that pay interest; and *automatic-transfer savings (ATS) accounts*, which automatically transfer funds from savings to checking (or vice versa) when the balance on one of those accounts reaches a predetermined level.

M1 on March 2, 1998, was $1,085.1 billion. M1 is a stock measure—it is measured at a point in time. It is the total amount of coins and currency outside of banks and the total dollar amount in checking accounts *on a specific day*. Until now, we have considered supply as a flow—a variable with a time dimension: the quantity of wheat supplied *per year*, the quantity of automobiles supplied to the market *per year*, and so forth. But M1 is a stock variable.

Cash remains an important part of the U.S. economy, but some people believe it is becoming a thing of the past.

currency debasement *The decrease in the value of money that occurs when its supply is increased rapidly.*

M1, or transactions money *Money that can be directly used for transactions.*

FAST FACTS

On January 1, 1999, many countries in Europe are scheduled to become part of the new European Monetary Union. The deutsche mark, franc, and lira will be exchanged for the "euro," a common European currency. Europe will become more like the United States, where 50 states share a common monetary unit. The currency will be issued by and controlled by the new European Central Bank.

➤ **M2: Broad Money**   Although *M1* is the most widely used measure of the money supply, there are others. Should savings accounts be considered money? Many of these accounts cannot be used for transactions directly, but it is easy to convert them into cash or to transfer funds from a savings account into a checking account. And what about money market accounts (which allow only a few checks per month but pay market-determined interest rates) and money market mutual funds (which sell shares and use the proceeds to purchase short-term securities)? These can be used to write checks and make purchases, although only over a certain amount.

If we add **near monies**, close substitutes for transactions money, to *M1*, we get **M2**, called **broad money** because it includes not-quite-money monies such as savings accounts, money market accounts, and other near monies.

$$\text{M2} \equiv \text{M1} + \text{Savings accounts} + \text{Money market accounts} + \text{Other near monies}$$

On March 2, 1998, *M2* was $4,114.8 billion, considerably larger than the total *M1* of $1,085.1 billion. The main advantage of looking at *M2* instead of *M1* is that *M2* is sometimes more stable. For instance, when banks introduced new forms of interest-bearing checking accounts in the early 1980s, *M1* shot up as people switched their funds from savings accounts to checking accounts. But *M2* remained fairly constant because the fall in savings account deposits and the rise in checking account balances were both part of *M2*, canceling each other out.

➤ **Beyond M2**   Because a wide variety of financial instruments bear some resemblance to money, some economists have advocated including almost all of them as part of the money supply. In recent years, for example, credit cards have come to be used extensively in exchange. Everyone who has a credit card has a credit limit—you can charge only a certain amount on your card before you have to pay it off. Usually we pay our credit card bills with a check. One of the very broad definitions of money includes the amount of available credit on credit cards (your charge limit minus what you have charged but not paid) as part of the money supply.

There are no rules for deciding what is money and what is not. This poses problems for economists and those in charge of economic policy. However, *for our purposes here, "money" will always refer to transactions money, or M1.* For simplicity, we will say that *M1* is the sum of two *general* categories: currency in circulation and deposits. Keep in mind, however, that *M1* has *four* specific components: currency held outside banks, demand deposits, travelers checks, and other checkable deposits.

THE PRIVATE BANKING SYSTEM

Most of the money in the United States today is "bank money" of one sort or another. *M1* is made up largely of checking account balances rather than currency, and currency makes up an even smaller part of *M2* and other broader definitions of money. Any understanding of money requires some knowledge of the structure of the private banking system.

Banks and other financial intermediaries borrow from individuals or firms with excess funds and lend to those who need funds. For example, commercial banks receive funds in various forms, including deposits in checking and savings accounts. They take these funds and loan them out in the form of car loans, mortgages, commercial loans, and so forth. Banks and banklike institutions are called **financial intermediaries** because they "mediate," or act as a link between people who have funds to lend and those who need to borrow.

The main types of financial intermediaries are commercial banks, followed by savings and loan associations, life insurance companies, and pension funds. Since about 1970, the legal distinctions between the different types of financial intermediaries have narrowed considerably. It used to be, for example, that checking accounts could be

A CASHLESS SOCIETY: DIFFERENT MEANINGS IN THE UNITED STATES AND RUSSIA IN 1997

When Americans talk of the "cashless" society it conjures up images of credit cards, debit cards, internet transactions, electronic bill paying, and so forth. Although about 80 percent of the 360 billion transactions in the United States each year are paid for with cash, the majority of which are under $20, the trend is toward on-line transfers via the computer and toward plastic cards.

But when the Russians talk of the cashless society, they mean there is no money. Because the majority of people still work for the government in Russia, and the government is broke, millions of workers across the country have been going without cash wages for some time. How do they survive? The firms pay people in kind and they engage in barter.

The Russian-European Center for Economic Policy, a monitoring organization sponsored by the European Union, estimated that the proportion of industrial sales in Russia settled with barter rose from about 10 percent in 1993 to 40 percent in 1996. One car company is said to pay nine-tenths of its bills with finished automobiles.

Stories about individual household transactions abound. Siberian

IN SOME PARTS OF WHAT WAS RUSSIA, "CASHLESS SOCIETY" IS LITERALLY WHAT IT SAYS—NO MONEY. WITHOUT CURRENCY, WORKERS MAY BE PAID IN WHAT THEY PRODUCE, SUCH AS THE COFFINS "PAID" TO WORKERS IN SIBERIA IN 1997.

workers in 1997 were paid in coffins; workers at a factory in Volgograd were paid in bras. In Altai, Siberia, a local theater charged two eggs for admission, and when eggs ran

out, tickets became denominated in empty bottles.

Source: "The Cashless Society," *The Economist,* March 15, 1997.

For more on cashless economies, see the Case and Fair Web page at
http://www.prenhall.com/casefair.

held only in commercial banks and that commercial banks could not pay interest on checking accounts. Savings and loan associations were prohibited from offering certain kinds of deposits and were restricted primarily to making loans for mortgages.

The Depository Institutions Deregulation and Monetary Control Act, enacted by Congress in 1980, eliminated many of the previous restrictions on the behavior of financial institutions. Many types of institutions now offer checking accounts, and interest is paid on many types of checking accounts. Savings and loan associations now make loans for many things besides home mortgages. The Sears Financial Network is one of a number of financial service firms offering, under one roof, a wide variety of services that used to be offered by separate providers such as banks, brokerage houses, insurance companies, and financial planners.

HOW BANKS CREATE MONEY

So far we have described the general way that money works and the way the supply of money is measured in the United States. But how much money is there available at a given time? Who supplies it, and how does it get supplied? We are now ready to analyze these questions in detail. In particular, we want to explore a process that many find mysterious: the way banks *create money*.

A HISTORICAL PERSPECTIVE: GOLDSMITHS

To begin to see how banks create money, consider the origins of the modern banking system. In the fifteenth and sixteenth centuries, citizens of many lands used gold as money, particularly for large transactions. Because gold is both inconvenient to carry around and susceptible to theft, people began to place their gold with goldsmiths for safekeeping. Upon receiving the gold, a goldsmith would issue a receipt to the depositor, charging him a small fee for looking after his gold. After a time, these receipts themselves, rather than the gold that they represented, began to be traded for goods. The receipts became a form of paper money, making it unnecessary to go to the goldsmith to withdraw gold for a transaction.

At this point, all the receipts issued by goldsmiths were backed 100 percent by gold. If a goldsmith had 100 ounces of gold in his safe, he would issue receipts for 100 ounces of gold, and no more. Goldsmiths functioned as warehouses where people stored gold for safekeeping. The goldsmiths found, however, that people did not come often to withdraw gold. Why should they, when paper receipts that could easily be converted to gold were "as good as gold"? (In fact, receipts were better than gold—more portable, safer from theft, and so on.) As a result, goldsmiths had a large stock of gold continuously on hand.

Because they had what amounted to "extra" gold sitting around, goldsmiths gradually realized that they could lend out some of this gold without any fear of running out of gold. Why would they do this? Because instead of just keeping their gold idly in their vaults, they earned interest on loans. Something subtle, but dramatic, happened at this point. The goldsmiths changed from mere depositories for gold into banklike institutions that had the power to create money. This transformation occurred as soon as goldsmiths began making loans. Without adding any more real gold to the system, the goldsmiths increased the amount of money in circulation by creating additional claims to gold (that is, receipts, which entitled the bearer to receive a certain number of ounces of gold on demand).[1] There were thus more claims than there were ounces of gold.

A detailed example may help to clarify this. Suppose you go to a goldsmith who is functioning only as a depository, or warehouse, and ask for a loan to buy a plot of land that costs 20 ounces of gold. Also suppose that the goldsmith has 100 ounces of gold on deposit in his safe and receipts for exactly 100 ounces of gold out to the various people who deposited the gold. If the goldsmith decides he is tired of being a mere goldsmith and wants to become a real bank, he will loan you some gold. You don't want the gold itself, of course; rather, you want a slip of paper that represents 20 ounces of gold. The goldsmith in essence "creates" money for you by giving you a receipt for 20 ounces of gold (even though his entire supply of gold already belongs to various other people).[2] When he does, there will be receipts for 120 ounces of gold in circulation instead of the 100 ounces worth of receipts before your loan, and the supply of money will have increased.

---

[1]Remember, these receipts circulated as money, and people used them to make transactions without feeling the need to cash them in—that is, to exchange them for gold itself.

[2]In return for lending you the receipt for 20 ounces of gold, the goldsmith expects to get an IOU promising to repay the amount (in gold itself or with a receipt from another goldsmith) with interest after a certain period of time.

People think the creation of money is mysterious. Far from it! The creation of money is simply an accounting procedure, among the most mundane of human endeavors. You may suspect the whole process is fundamentally unsound, or somehow dubious. After all, the banking system began when someone issued claims for gold that already belonged to someone else. Here you may be on slightly firmer ground.

Goldsmiths-turned-bankers did face certain problems. Once they started making loans, their receipts outstanding (claims on gold) were greater than the amount of gold they had in their vaults at any given moment. If the owners of the 120 ounces worth of gold receipts all presented their receipts and demanded their gold at the same time, the goldsmith would be in trouble. With only 100 ounces of gold on hand, everyone could not get his or her gold at once.

In normal times, people would be happy to hold receipts instead of real gold, and this problem would never arise. If, however, people began to worry about the goldsmith's financial safety, they might begin to have doubts about whether their receipts really were as good as gold. Knowing there were more receipts outstanding than there were ounces of gold in the goldsmith's vault, people might start to demand gold for receipts.

This situation leads to a paradox. It makes perfect sense to hold paper receipts (instead of gold) if you know you can always get gold for your paper. In normal times, goldsmiths could feel perfectly safe in loaning out more gold than they actually had in their possession. But once you (and everyone else) start to doubt the safety of the goldsmith, then you (and everyone else) would be foolish not to demand your gold back from the vault.

A **run** on a goldsmith (or in our day, a **run on a bank**) occurs when many people present their claims at the same time. These runs tend to feed on themselves. If I see you going to the goldsmith to withdraw your gold, I may become nervous and decide to withdraw my gold as well. It is the *fear* of a run that usually causes the run. Runs on a bank can be triggered by a variety of causes: rumors that an institution may have made loans to borrowers who cannot repay, wars, failures of other institutions that have borrowed money from the bank, and so on. As you will see later in this chapter, today's bankers differ from goldsmiths—today's banks are subject to a "required reserve ratio." Goldsmiths had no legal reserve requirements, although the amount that they loaned out was subject to the restriction imposed on them by their fear of running out of gold.

THE MODERN BANKING SYSTEM

To understand how the modern banking system works, you need to be familiar with some basic principles of accounting. Once you are comfortable with the way banks keep their books, the whole process of money creation will seem logical.

> **A Brief Review of Accounting** Central to accounting practices is the statement that "the books always balance." In practice, this means that if we take a snapshot of a firm—any firm, including a bank—at a particular moment in time, then by definition:

$$\text{Assets} - \text{Liabilities} \equiv \text{Net Worth, or}$$
$$\text{Assets} \equiv \text{Liabilities} + \text{Net Worth}.$$

Assets are things a firm owns that are worth something. For a bank, these assets include the bank building, its furniture, its holdings of government securities, cash in its vaults, bonds, stocks, and so forth. Most important among a bank's assets, for our purposes at least, are its *loans*. A borrower gives the bank an *IOU*, a promise to repay a certain sum of money on or by a certain date. This promise is an asset of the bank because it is worth something. The bank could (and sometimes does) sell the IOU to another bank for cash.

Other bank assets include cash on hand (sometimes called *vault cash*) and deposits with the United States' central bank—the **Federal Reserve Bank (the Fed)**. As we will

run on a bank *Occurs when many of those who have claims on a bank (deposits) present them at the same time.*

Federal Reserve System (the Fed) *The central bank of the United States.*

PART SIX
Macroeconomic Principles and Policy

FIGURE 26.1

Assets		Liabilities	
Reserves	20	100	Deposits
Loans	90	10	Net worth
Total	110	110	Total

FIGURE 26.1

T Account for a Typical Bank (millions of dollars)

The balance sheet of a bank must always balance, so that the sum of assets (reserves and loans) equals the sum of liabilities (deposits and net worth).

see later in this chapter, federal banking regulations require that banks keep a certain portion of their deposits on hand as vault cash or on deposit with the Fed.

A firm's *liabilities* are its debts—what it owes. A bank's liabilities are the promises to pay, or IOUs, that it has issued. A bank's most important liabilities are its deposits. *Deposits* are debts owed to the depositors, because when you deposit money in your account, you are in essence making a loan to the bank.

The basic rule of accounting says that if we add up a firm's assets and then subtract the total amount it owes to all those who have lent it funds, the difference is the firm's net worth. *Net worth* represents the value of the firm to its stockholders or owners. How much would you pay for a firm that owns $200,000 of diamonds and had borrowed $150,000 from a bank to pay for them? Clearly, the firm is worth $50,000—the difference between what it owns and what it owes. If the price of diamonds were to fall, bringing their value down to only $150,000, the firm would be worth nothing.

We can keep track of a bank's financial position using a simplified balance sheet called a T account. By convention, the bank's assets are listed on the left side of the T account, its liabilities and net worth on the right side. By definition, the balance sheet always balances, so that the sum of the item(s) on the left side of the T account is exactly equal to the sum of the item(s) on the right side.

The T account in Figure 26.1 shows a bank having $110 million in *assets*, of which $20 million are **reserves**, the deposits that the bank has made at the Fed, and its cash on hand (coins and currency). Reserves are an asset to the bank because it can go to the Fed and get cash for them, just the way you can go to the bank and get cash for the amount in your savings account. Our bank's other asset is its loans, worth $90 million.

reserves *The deposits that a bank has at the Federal Reserve bank plus its cash on hand.*

Why do banks hold reserves/deposits at the Fed? There are many reasons, but perhaps the most important is the legal requirement that they hold a certain percentage of their deposit liabilities as reserves. The percentage of its deposits that a bank must keep as reserves is known as the **required reserve ratio**. If the reserve ratio is 20 percent, then a bank with deposits of $100 million must hold $20 million as reserves, either as cash or as deposits at the Fed. To simplify, we will assume that banks hold all of their reserves in the form of deposits at the Fed.

required reserve ratio *The percentage of its total deposits that a bank must keep as reserves at the Federal Reserve.*

On the liabilities side of the T account, the bank has taken deposits of $100 million, so it owes this amount to its depositors. This means that the bank has a net worth of $10 million to its owners ($110 million in assets − $100 million in liabilities = $10 million net worth). The net worth of the bank is what "balances" the balance sheet. Remember:

When some item on a bank's balance sheet changes, there must be at least one other change somewhere else to maintain balance.

If a bank's reserves increase by $1, then one of the following must also be true: (1) its other assets (say, loans) decrease by $1; (2) its liabilities (deposits) increase by $1; or (3) its net worth increases by $1. Various fractional combinations of these are also possible.

➤ The Creation of Money

Like the goldsmiths, today's bankers seek to earn income by lending money out at a higher interest rate than they pay depositors for use of their money.

In modern times, the chances of a run on a bank are fairly small; and, even if there is a run, the central bank protects the private banks in various ways. Therefore:

> Banks usually make loans up to the point where they can no longer do so because of the reserve requirement restriction.

A bank's required amount of reserves is equal to the required reserve ratio times the total deposits in the bank. If a bank has deposits of $100 and the required ratio is 20 percent, the required amount of reserves is $20. The difference between a bank's actual reserves and its required reserves is its **excess reserves:**

$$\text{Excess reserves} \equiv \text{Actual reserves} - \text{Required reserves}$$

If banks make loans up to the point where they can no longer do so because of the reserve requirement restriction, this means that banks make loans up to the point where their excess reserves are zero.

To see why, note that when a bank has excess reserves, it has credit available, and it can make loans. Actually, a bank can make loans *only* if it has excess reserves. When a bank makes a loan, it creates a demand deposit for the borrower. This creation of a demand deposit causes the bank's excess reserves to fall because the extra deposits created by the loan use up some of the excess reserves the bank has on hand. An example will help.

Assume there is only one private bank in the country, the required reserve ratio is 20 percent, and the bank starts off with nothing, as shown in Panel 1 of Figure 26.2. Now suppose dollar bills are in circulation and someone deposits 100 of them in the bank. The bank deposits the $100 with the central bank, so it now has $100 in reserves, as shown in Panel 2. The bank now has assets (reserves) of $100 and liabilities (deposits) of $100. If the required reserve ratio is 20 percent, the bank has excess reserves of $80.

How much can the bank lend and still meet the reserve requirement? For the moment, let's suppose anyone who gets a loan keeps the entire proceeds in the bank or pays them to someone else who does. Nothing is withdrawn as cash. In this case, the bank can lend $400 and still meet the reserve requirement, as you can see in Panel 3. With $80 of excess reserves, the bank can have up to $400 of additional deposits. The $100 in reserves plus $400 in loans (which are made as deposits) equal $500 in deposits. With $500 in deposits and a required reserve ratio of 20 percent, the bank must have reserves of $100 (20 percent of $500)—and it does. The bank can lend no more than $400 because its reserve requirement must not exceed $100. When a bank has no excess reserves and thus can make no more loans, it is said to be *loaned up*.

Remember, the money supply (M1) equals cash in circulation plus deposits. Before the initial deposit, the money supply was $100 ($100 cash and no deposits). After the deposit and the loans, the money supply is $500 (no cash outside of bank vaults and $500 in deposits). It is clear, then, that when cash is converted into deposits, the supply of money can change.

The bank whose T accounts are presented in Figure 26.2 is allowed to make loans of $400 based on the assumption that loans that are made *stay in the bank* in the form of deposits. Now suppose I borrow from the bank to buy a personal computer, and I write a check to the computer store. If the store also deposits its money in the bank, my check merely results in a reduction in my account balance and an increase to the store's account balance within the bank. No cash has left the bank. As long as the system is closed in this way—remember that we have so far assumed that there is only one

---

excess reserves *The difference between a bank's actual reserves and its required reserves.*

FIGURE 26.2

Balance Sheets of a Bank in a Single-Bank Economy

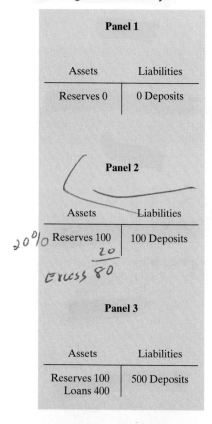

	Panel 1			**Panel 2**			**Panel 3**	
	Assets	Liabilities		Assets	Liabilities		Assets	Liabilities
Bank 1	Reserves 100	100 Deposits		Reserves 100 Loans 80	180 Deposits		Reserves 20 Loans 80	100 Deposits
Bank 2	Reserves 80	80 Deposits		Reserves 80 Loans 64	144 Deposits		Reserves 16 Loans 64	80 Deposits
Bank 3	Reserves 64	64 Deposits		Reserves 64 Loans 51.20	115.20 Deposits		Reserves 12.80 Loans 51.20	64 Deposits

Summary:	Deposits
Bank 1	100
Bank 2	80
Bank 3	64
Bank 4	51.20
⋮	⋮
Total	500.00

FIGURE 26.3

The Creation of Money: Balance Sheets of Three Banks

bank—the bank knows that it will never be called upon to release any of its $100 in reserves. It can expand its loans up to the point where its total deposits are $500.

Of course, there are many banks in the country, a situation that is depicted in Figure 26.3. As long as the banking system as a whole is closed, it is still possible for an initial deposit of $100 to result in an expansion of the money supply to $500, but more steps are involved when there is more than one bank.

To see why, assume Mary makes an initial deposit of $100 in Bank 1, and the bank deposits the entire $100 with the Fed (Panel 1 of Figure 26.3). All loans that a bank makes are withdrawn from the bank as the individual borrowers write checks to pay for merchandise. After Mary's deposit, Bank 1 can make a loan of up to $80 to Bill, because it needs to keep only $20 of its $100 deposit as reserves. (We are assuming a 20 percent required reserve ratio.) In other words, Bank 1 has $80 in excess reserves.

Bank 1's balance sheet at the moment of the loan to Bill appears in Panel 2 of Figure 26.3. Bank 1 now has loans of $80. It has credited Bill's account with the $80, so its total deposits are $180 ($80 in loans plus $100 in reserves). Bill then writes a check for $80 for a set of shock absorbers for his car. Bill wrote his check to Sam's Car Shop, and Sam deposits Bill's check in Bank 2. When the check clears, Bank 1 transfers $80 in reserves to Bank 2. Bank 1's balance sheet now looks like the top of Panel 3. Its assets include reserves of $20 and loans of $80; its liabilities are $100 in deposits. Both sides of the T account balance: The bank's reserves are 20 percent of its deposits, as required by law, and it is fully loaned up.

Now look at Bank 2. Because Bank 1 has transferred $80 in reserves to Bank 2, it now has $80 in deposits and $80 in reserves (Panel 1, Bank 2). Its reserve requirement is also 20 percent, so it has excess reserves of $64 on which it can make loans.

Now assume Bank 2 loans the $64 to Kate to pay for a textbook and Kate writes a check for $64 payable to the Manhattan College Bookstore. The final position of Bank 2, after it honors Kate's $64 check by transferring $64 in reserves to the bookstore's bank, is reserves of $16, loans of $64, and deposits of $80 (Panel 3, Bank 2).

The Manhattan College Bookstore deposits Kate's check in its account with Bank 3. Bank 3 now has excess reserves, because it has added $64 to its reserves. With a reserve ratio of 20 percent, Bank 3 can loan out $51.20 (80 percent of $64, leaving 20 percent in required reserves to back the $64 deposit).

As the process is repeated over and over, the total amount of deposits created is $500, the sum of the deposits in each of the banks. Because the banking system can be looked upon as one big bank, the outcome here for many banks is the same as the outcome in Figure 26.2 for one bank.[3]

▶ **The Money Multiplier** In practice, the banking system is not completely closed—there is some leakage out of the system. Still, the point here is:

> An increase in bank reserves leads to a greater than one-for-one increase in the money supply. Economists call the relationship between the final change in deposits and the change in reserves that caused this change the **money multiplier**. Stated somewhat differently, the money multiplier is the multiple by which deposits can increase for every dollar increase in reserves.

money multiplier *The multiple by which deposits can increase for every dollar increase in reserves; equal to one divided by the required reserve ratio.*

Do not confuse the money multiplier with the spending multipliers we discussed in the last two chapters. They are not the same thing.

In the example we just examined, reserves increased by $100 when the $100 in cash was deposited in a bank, and the amount of deposits increased by $500 ($100 from the initial deposit, $400 from the loans made by the various banks from their excess reserves). The money multiplier in this case is $500/$100 = 5. Mathematically, the money multiplier can be defined as:

$$\text{Money multiplier} \equiv \frac{1}{\text{Required reserve ratio}}$$

In the United States, the required reserve ratio varies, depending on the size of the bank and the type of deposit. For large banks and for checking deposits, the ratio is currently 10 percent, which makes the potential money multiplier 1/.10 = 10.0. This means that an increase in reserves of $1 could cause an increase in deposits of $10 if there were no leakage out of the system.

▶ **The Fed and the Money Supply** We have now seen how the private banking system creates money by making loans. However, private banks are not free to create money at will. Their ability to create money is controlled by the volume of reserves in the system, which is controlled by the Federal Reserve. The Federal Reserve, therefore, has the ultimate control over the money supply. Let's examine the structure and function of the Federal Reserve.

The Federal Reserve System

Founded in 1913 by an act of Congress (to which major reforms were added in the 1930s), the Federal Reserve is the central bank of the United States. The Fed is a complicated institution with many responsibilities, including the regulation and supervision of over 8,000 commercial banks. The organization of the Federal Reserve System is presented in Figure 26.4.

The *Board of Governors* is the most important group within the Federal Reserve System. The board consists of seven members, each appointed for 14 years by the president of the United States. The *chair* of the Federal Reserve, who is appointed by the

[3]If banks create money when they make loans, does repaying a loan "destroy" money? The answer is yes.

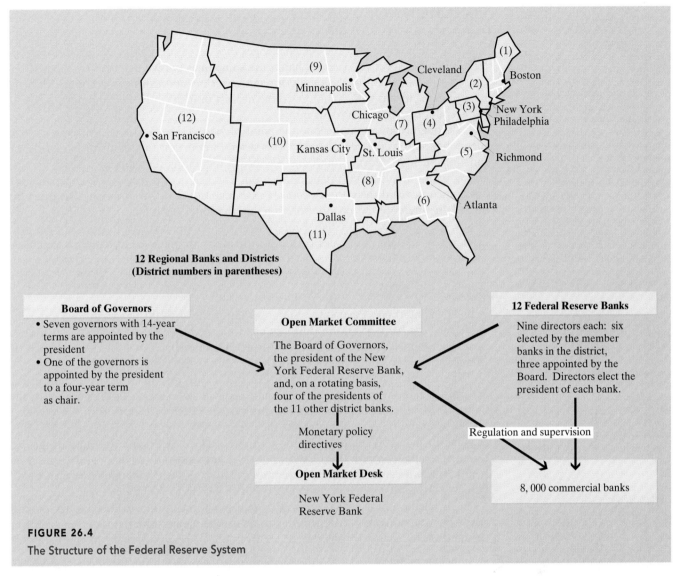

FIGURE 26.4

The Structure of the Federal Reserve System

president and whose term runs for four years, usually dominates the entire Federal Reserve System and is sometimes said to be the second most powerful person in the United States. The Fed is an independent agency in that it does not take orders from the president or from Congress.

The United States is divided into 12 Federal Reserve districts, each with its own Federal Reserve bank. These districts are indicated on the map in Figure 26.4. The district banks are like branch offices of the Federal Reserve in that they carry out the rules, regulations, and functions of the central system in their districts and report to the Board of Governors on local economic conditions.

U.S. monetary policy—the behavior of the Federal Reserve regarding the money supply—is formally set by the **Federal Open Market Committee (FOMC)**. The FOMC consists of the seven members of the Federal Reserve System's Board of Governors, the president of the New York Federal Reserve Bank, and, on a rotating basis, four of the presidents of the 11 other district banks. The FOMC sets goals regarding the money supply and interest rates, and it directs the **Open Market Desk** in the New York Federal Reserve Bank to buy and/or sell government securities. (We discuss the specifics of open market operations later in this chapter.)

Federal Open Market Committee (FOMC) *A group composed of the seven members of the Fed's Board of Governors, the president of the New York Federal Reserve Bank, and four of the other eleven district bank presidents on a rotating basis; it sets goals regarding the money supply and interest rates and directs the operation of the Open Market Desk in New York.*

Open Market Desk *The office in the New York Federal Reserve Bank from which government securities are bought and sold by the Fed.*

FUNCTIONS OF THE FED

The Fed is the central bank of the United States. (A brief discussion of the central banks of other countries, and the challenges they faced in 1998, is found in this chapter's Global Perspective.) Central banks are sometimes known as "bankers' banks" because only banks (and occasionally foreign governments) can have accounts in them. As a private citizen, you cannot go to the nearest branch of the Fed and open a checking account or apply to borrow money.

Although from a macroeconomic point of view the Fed's crucial role is to control the money supply, the Fed also performs several important functions for banks. These functions include clearing interbank payments, regulating the banking system, and assisting banks in a difficult financial position. The Fed is also responsible for managing exchange rates and the nation's foreign exchange reserves.[4] In addition, it is often involved in intercountry negotiations on international economic issues. In the early 1980s, for example, then Chair Paul Volcker played a major role in negotiations with foreign governments on issues relating to the debt problems of developing countries. More recently, Chair Alan Greenspan has been involved in discussions with European central bankers regarding the monetary problems of reuniting East and West Germany and "opening up" Eastern Europe.

 ► **Clearing Interbank Payments**   Suppose you write a $100 check, drawn on your bank, the First Bank of Fresno (FBF), to pay for tulip bulbs from Crockett Importers of Miami, Florida. Because Crockett Importers does not bank at FBF, but at Banco de Miami, how does your money get from your bank to the bank in Florida?

The answer: The Fed does it. Both FBF and Banco de Miami have accounts at the Federal Reserve. When Crockett Importers receives your check and deposits it at the Banco de Miami, the bank submits the check to the Federal Reserve, asking it to collect the funds from FBF. The Fed presents the check to FBF and is instructed to debit FBF's account for the $100 and to credit the account of Banco de Miami. Accounts at the Fed count as reserves, so FBF loses $100 in reserves and Banco de Miami gains $100 in reserves. The two banks effectively have traded ownerships of their deposits at the Federal Reserve. The *total* volume of reserves has not changed, nor has the money supply.

This function of clearing interbank payments allows banks to shift money around virtually instantaneously. All they need to do is wire the Fed and request a transfer, and the funds move at the speed of electricity from one computer account to another.

► **Other Duties of the Fed**   Besides facilitating the transfer of funds between banks, the Fed performs several other important duties. It is responsible for many of the regulations governing banking practices and standards. For example, the Federal Reserve has the authority to control mergers between banks, and it is responsible for examining banks to ensure they are financially sound and they conform to a host of government accounting regulations. And, as we saw earlier, the Fed also sets reserve requirements for all financial institutions.

One of the most important responsibilities of the Fed is to act as the **lender of last resort** for the banking system. As our discussion of goldsmiths suggested, banks are subject to the possibility of runs on their deposits. In the United States, most deposits of less than $100,000 are insured by the Federal Deposit Insurance Corporation (FDIC). Deposit insurance makes panics less likely. Because depositors know they can always get their money, even if the bank fails, they are less likely to withdraw their deposits. Not all deposits are insured, so the possibility of bank panics remains. But the Federal Reserve stands ready to provide funds to a troubled bank that cannot find any other sources of funds.

lender of last resort *One of the functions of the Fed: It provides funds to troubled banks that cannot find any other sources of funds.*

[4]*Foreign exchange reserves* are holdings of the currencies of other countries (for example, French francs) by the U.S. government. We discuss exchange rates and foreign exchange markets at length in chapter 36.

FOUR CENTRAL BANKS IN 1998

Virtually every country has a central bank run by the government. Banking systems and financial institutions differ from country to country, but the essential function of the central bank is the same in all countries: to control the supply of money and to regulate the banking system. As you will see in subsequent chapters, central banks can influence behavior and thus have an impact on the functioning of the economy. Four of the most important central banks in the world are described briefly here with a discussion of the major problem each faced in 1998.

THE UNITED STATES: THE FEDERAL RESERVE SYSTEM (NICKNAME: "THE FED")

The Fed chair in 1998 was Alan Greenspan. Greenspan was known for his strong anti-inflation views. As you will see in later chapters, excess monetary expansion can lead to inflation. Although no inflation was on the radar screens during 1997, labor markets were very tight and wage inflation was a big worry as the economy continued to expand at a healthy clip. But in October, stock markets around the world came crashing down and that took some of the wind out of the economy. Greenspan called the stock market crash a "salutatory" event.

GERMANY: THE DEUTSCHE BUNDESBANK (NICKNAME: "THE BUBA")

The biggest problem facing Germany in recent years has been the economic effects of reunification. The monetary problem was enormous. The East German currency had to be exchanged for new West German deutsche marks without creating wild inflationary swings. This was accomplished in an amazingly orderly way, and inflation remained in check. In early 1998, Bundesbank president Tietmeyer's major concern was similar to Alan Greenspan's. The economy was beginning to recover from recession and the Bundesbank's position was to hold down money supply growth to prevent inflation. In October 1997, the Bundesbank raised its key money market interest rate from 3.0 percent to 3.3 percent; it was the first move toward tightening in five years.

JAPAN: THE BANK OF JAPAN (NICKNAME: "BOJ")

The Bank of Japan faced a major problem in 1998: recession. Real GDP growth had been low for a number of years, and it was not getting any better. The banking system had been feeling great pressure from defaulted loans based on real estate and land values that had fallen sharply between 1992 and 1995. This is similar to the savings and loan crisis in the United States a few years earlier. On December 16, 1994, Mr. Yasuro Matsushita took over as governor of the Bank of Japan and has continued a policy of modest monetary expansion to try to bring Japan out of its slow growth period.

RUSSIA: THE CENTRAL BANK OF RUSSIA

The Central Bank of Russia has problems dwarfing those of Germany, the United States, and Japan. Though the list of economic woes in the New Russia was long, near the top was hyperinflation. In 1992, prices rose about 2,000 percent. By the beginning of 1995, inflation was *down* to about 15 percent per month and by the beginning of 1998 it was 15 percent per year. As the economy moved from central planning to the market, the government found it very difficult to maintain salaries and to finance a collapsing industrial structure. Ultimately it resorted to printing money to make up for the shortfall. In addition to breaking the addiction to printing money, the Central Bank has a new private banking system of over 2,000 banks that will need supervision and regulation.

For more on central banks, see the Case and Fair Web page at
http://ww.prenhall.com/casefair.

The Fed is the ideal lender of last resort for two reasons. First, providing funds to a bank that is in dire straits is risky and not likely to be very profitable, and it is hard to find private banks or other private institutions willing to do this. The Fed is a nonprofit institution whose function is to serve the overall welfare of the public. Thus, the Fed would certainly be interested in preventing catastrophic banking panics such as those that occurred in the late 1920s and the 1930s.

Second, the Fed has an essentially unlimited supply of funds with which to bail out banks facing the possibility of runs. The reason, as we shall see, is that the Fed can create reserves at will. A promise by the Fed that it will support a bank is very

TABLE 26.1 ASSETS AND LIABILITIES OF THE FEDERAL
RESERVE SYSTEM, DECEMBER 31, 1997
(millions of dollars)

ASSETS			LIABILITIES
Gold	$ 11,047	$457,469	Federal Reserve notes (outstanding)
Loans to banks	2,035		Deposits:
U.S. government securities	451,924	30,838	Bank reserves (from depository institutions)
		5,444	U.S. Treasury
All other assets	52,841	24,096	All other liabilities and net worth
Total	$517,847	$517,847	Total

Source: Federal Reserve Bulletin, March 1998.

convincing. Unlike any other lender, the Fed can never run out of money. Therefore, the explicit or implicit support of the Fed should be enough to assure depositors they are in no danger of losing their funds.

THE FED'S BALANCE SHEET

Although it is a special bank, the Federal Reserve is in some ways similar to an ordinary commercial bank. Like an ordinary bank, the Fed has a balance sheet that records its asset and liability position at any moment in time. The balance sheet for the Federal Reserve is presented in Table 26.1.

As the asset side of the balance sheet shows, the Fed owns about $11 billion of gold. *Do not think that this gold has anything to do with the supply of money.* Most of the gold was acquired during the 1930s, when it was purchased from the U.S. Treasury Department. Since 1934, the dollar has not been backed by (not convertible into) gold. You cannot take a dollar bill to the Fed to receive gold for it; all you can get for your old dollar bill is a new dollar bill.[5] Although it is unrelated to the money supply, the Fed's gold counts as an asset on its balance sheet, because it is something of value the Fed owns.

The balance sheet mentions an asset called "loans to banks." These loans are an asset of the Federal Reserve in the same way a private commercial bank's loans are among its assets. The Fed sometimes makes loans to commercial banks that are short of reserves.[6] The $2,035 billion in Table 26.1 represents these kinds of loans.

The largest of the Fed's assets by far consists of government securities: about $452 billion worth at the end of December 1997. Government securities are obligations of the federal government, such as Treasury bills and government bonds, which the Fed has purchased over the years. The way in which these bonds are acquired has important implications for the Fed's control of the money supply. (We return to this topic after our survey of the Fed's balance sheet.)

The bulk of the Fed's liabilities are Federal Reserve notes. The dollar bill you use to buy a quart of milk is clearly an asset from your point of view—it is something you own that has value. But because every financial asset is by definition a liability of some other agent in the economy, whose liability is that dollar bill? That dollar bill, and bills of all other denominations in the economy, are a liability—an IOU—of the Federal Reserve.

---

[5]The fact that the Fed is not obliged to provide gold for currency means it can never go bankrupt. When the currency was backed by gold, it would have been possible for the Fed to run out of gold if too many of its depositors came to it at the same time and asked to exchange their deposits for gold. But if depositors come to the Fed to withdraw their deposits today, all they can get are dollar bills. The dollar was convertible into gold internationally until August 15, 1971.

[6]Recall that commercial banks are required to keep a set percentage of their deposit liabilities on deposit at the Fed. If a bank suddenly finds itself short of reserves, one of its alternatives is to borrow the reserves it needs from the Fed.

They are rather strange IOUs, because all they can be redeemed for are other IOUs of exactly the same type. They are, nonetheless, classified as liabilities of the Fed.

The balance sheet shows that, like an ordinary commercial bank, the Fed has accepted deposits. These deposits are liabilities. The bulk of the Fed's deposits come from commercial banks. Remember: commercial banks are required to keep a certain share of their own deposits as deposits at the Fed. A bank's deposits at the Fed (its reserves) are an asset from the bank's point of view, and those same reserves must be a liability from the Fed's point of view.

Table 26.1 shows the Fed has accepted a small volume of deposits from the U.S. Treasury. In effect, the Fed acts as the bank for the U.S. government. When the government needs to pay for something like a new aircraft carrier, it may write out a check to the supplier of the ship drawn on its "checking account" at the Fed. Similarly, when the government receives revenues from tax collections, fines, or sales of government assets, it may deposit these funds in its account at the Fed.

HOW THE FED CONTROLS THE MONEY SUPPLY

To see how the Fed controls the supply of money in the U.S. economy we need to understand the role of reserves. As we have said, the required reserve ratio establishes a link between the reserves of the commercial banks and the deposits (money) that commercial banks are allowed to create.

The reserve requirement effectively determines how much a bank has available to lend. If the required reserve ratio is 20 percent, each $1 of reserves can support $5 in deposits. A bank that has reserves of $100,000 cannot have more than $500,000 in deposits. If it did, it would fail to meet the required reserve ratio.

If you recall that the *money supply* is equal to the sum of deposits inside banks and the currency in circulation outside of banks, you can see that reserves provide the leverage that the Fed needs to control the money supply.

> If the Fed wants to increase the supply of money, it creates more reserves, thereby freeing banks to create additional deposits by making more loans. If it wants to decrease the money supply, it reduces reserves.

Three tools are available to the Fed for changing the money supply: (1) changing the required reserve ratio; (2) changing the discount rate; and (3) open market operations.

THE REQUIRED RESERVE RATIO

The simplest way for the Fed to alter the supply of money is to change the required reserve ratio. This process is shown in Table 26.2. Let's assume the initial required reserve ratio is 20 percent.

In Panel 1, a simplified version of the Fed's balance sheet (in billions of dollars) shows that reserves are $100 billion and currency outstanding is $100 billion. The total value of the Fed's assets is $200 billion, which we assume to be all in government securities. Assuming there are no excess reserves—banks stay fully loaded up—the $100 billion in reserves supports $500 billion in deposits at the commercial banks. (Remember: The money multiplier equals 1/required reserve ratio = 1/.20 = 5. Thus, $100 billion in reserves can support $500 billion [$100 billion × 5] in deposits when the required reserve ratio is 20 percent.) The supply of money (M1, or transactions money) is therefore $600 billion: $100 billion in currency and $500 billion in (checking account) deposits at the commercial banks.

Now suppose the Fed wants to increase the supply of money to $900 billion. If it lowers the required reserve ratio from 20 percent to 12.5 percent (as in Panel 2 of Table 26.2), then the same $100 billion of reserves could support $800 billion in

TABLE 26.2 A DECREASE IN THE REQUIRED RESERVE RATIO FROM 20% TO 12.5% INCREASES THE SUPPLY OF MONEY (ALL FIGURES IN BILLIONS OF DOLLARS)

PANEL 1: REQUIRED RESERVE RATIO = 20%

Federal Reserve				Commercial Banks			
Assets			Liabilities	Assets			Liabilities
Government securities	$200	$100	Reserves	Reserves	$100	$500	Deposits
		$100	Currency	Loans	$400		

Note: Money supply (M1) = Currency + Deposits = $600.

PANEL 2: REQUIRED RESERVE RATIO = 12.5%

Federal Reserve				Commercial Banks			
Assets			Liabilities	Assets			Liabilities
Government securities	$200	$100	Reserves	Reserves	$100	$800	Deposits (+$300)
		$100	Currency	Loans (+$300)	$700		

Note: Money supply (M1) = Currency + Deposits = $900.

deposits instead of only $500 billion. In this case, the money multiplier is 1/.125, or 8. At a required reserve ratio of 12.5 percent, $100 billion in reserves can support $800 billion in deposits. The total money supply would be $800 billion in deposits plus the $100 billion in currency, for a total of $900 billion.[7]

Put another way, with the new lower reserve ratio, banks have excess reserves of $37.5 billion. At a required reserve ratio of 20 percent, they needed $100 billion in reserves to back their $500 billion in deposits. At the lower required reserve ratio of 12.5 percent, they need only $62.5 billion of reserves to back their $500 billion of deposits, so the remaining $37.5 billion of the existing $100 billion in reserves are "extra." With that $37.5 billion of excess reserves, banks can lend out more money. If we assume the system loans money and creates deposits to the *maximum* extent possible, the $37.5 billion of reserves will support an additional $300 billion of deposits ($37.5 billion × the money multiplier of 8 = $300 billion). The change in the required reserve ratio has injected an additional $300 billion into the banking system, at which point the banks will be fully loaned up and unable to increase their deposits further.

Decreases in the required reserve ratio allow banks to have more deposits with the existing volume of reserves. As banks create more deposits by making loans, the supply of money (currency + deposits) increases. The reverse is also true: If the Fed wants to restrict the supply of money, it can raise the required reserve ratio, in which case banks will find that they have insufficient reserves and must therefore reduce their deposits by "calling in" some of their loans.[8] The result is a decrease in the money supply.

---

[7]To find the maximum volume of deposits (D) that can be supported by an amount of reserves (R), divide R by the required reserve ratio. If the required reserve ratio is g, because R = gD, then D = R/g.

[8]Banks never really have to "call in" loans before they are due, to reduce the money supply. First, the Fed is almost always expanding the money supply slowly because the real economy grows steadily and, as we shall see, growth brings with it the need for more circulating money. So when we speak of "contractionary monetary policy," we mean the Fed is slowing down the rate of money growth, not reducing the money supply. Second, even if the Fed were actually to cut reserves (rather than curb their expansion), banks would no doubt be able to comply by reducing the volume of new loans they make while old ones are coming due.

For many reasons, the Fed has tended not to use changes in the reserve requirement to control the money supply. In part, this reluctance stems from the era when only some banks were members of the Federal Reserve System and, therefore, subject to reserve requirements. The Fed reasoned that if it raised the reserve requirement to contract the money supply, banks might choose to stop being members. (Because reserves pay no interest, the higher the reserve requirement, the more the penalty imposed on those banks holding reserves.) This argument no longer applies. Since the passage of the Depository Institutions Deregulation and Monetary Control Act in 1980, all depository institutions are subject to Federal Reserve requirements.

It is also true that changing the reserve requirement ratio is a crude tool. Because of lags in banks' reporting to the Fed on their reserve and deposit positions, a change in the requirement today does not affect banks for about two weeks. (However, the fact that changing the reserve requirement expands or reduces credit in every bank in the country makes it a very powerful tool when the Fed does use it.) A much better tool for controlling week-to-week changes in the money supply, as we shall see shortly, is open market operations.

THE DISCOUNT RATE

Banks may borrow from the Fed. The interest rate they pay the Fed is the **discount rate**. When banks increase their borrowing, the money supply increases.

To simplify, let's assume there is only one bank in the country and the required reserve ratio is 20 percent. The initial position of the bank and the Fed appear in Panel 1 of Table 26.3, where the money supply (currency + deposits) is $480. In Panel 2, the bank has borrowed $20 from the Fed. By using this $20 as a reserve, the bank can increase its loans by $100, from $320 to $420. (Remember: A required reserve ratio of 20 percent gives a money multiplier of 5; excess reserves of $20 allows the bank to create an additional $20 × 5, or $100, in deposits.)

discount rate *Interest rate that banks pay to the Fed to borrow from it.*

Fed's fund Rate

Bank borrowing from the Fed leads to an increase in the money supply.

TABLE 26.3 THE EFFECT ON THE MONEY SUPPLY OF COMMERCIAL BANK BORROWING FROM THE FED
(ALL FIGURES IN BILLIONS OF DOLLARS)

PANEL 1: NO COMMERCIAL BANK BORROWING FROM THE FED

Federal Reserve				Commercial Banks			
Assets		Liabilities		Assets			Liabilities
Securities	$160	$80	Reserves	Reserves	$80	$400	Deposits
		$80	Currency	Loans	$320		

Note: Money supply (M1) = Currency + Deposits = $480.

PANEL 2: COMMERCIAL BANK BORROWING $20 FROM THE FED

Federal Reserve				Commercial Banks			
Assets		Liabilities		Assets			Liabilities
Securities	$160	$100	Reserves (+$20)	Reserves (+$20)	$100	$500	Deposits (+$100)
Loans	$20	$80	Currency	Loans (+$100)	$420	$20	Amount owed to Fed (+$20)

Note: Money supply (M1) = Currency + Deposits = $580.

Banks that borrow from the Fed must eventually repay, and when they do, the money supply goes back down by exactly the amount by which it initially increased.

The Fed can influence bank borrowing through the discount rate:

> The higher the discount rate, the higher the cost of borrowing, and the less borrowing banks will want to do.

If the Fed wants to curtail the growth of the money supply, for example, it raises the discount rate and discourages banks from borrowing from it, restricting the growth of reserves (and ultimately deposits).

In practice, the Fed does not often use the discount rate to control the money supply. It does change the discount rate from time to time to keep it in line with other interest rates, but most often the discount rate follows the other rates rather than leads them.

Changing the discount rate to control the supply of money has several problems associated with it. First, although raising the discount rate does discourage borrowing by banks (and therefore reduces their ability to expand the money supply), it is never clear in advance exactly how much of an effect a change in the discount rate will have. If banks are very short of reserves, they may decide to borrow from the Fed even though the discount rate is quite high.

> The discount rate cannot be used to control the money supply with great precision, because its effects on banks' demand for reserves are uncertain.

Second, changes in the discount rate can be largely offset by movements in other interest rates. If the discount rate is set at 10 percent and the rate paid by Treasury bills is 9 percent, banks will not borrow from the Fed to purchase Treasury bills. Because they would be paying more in borrowing costs than they would be making in interest revenue, they would lose by borrowing from the Fed. If the Treasury bill rate were to rise to 11 percent, banks could profitably borrow from the Fed to purchase Treasury bills. So, a discount rate that is high enough to discourage borrowing in some circumstances may not be high enough in others.

You may wonder whether the discount rate can ever be below the rate banks charge for loans or below the rate offered on Treasury bills. If this were the case, wouldn't banks borrow enormous quantities from the Fed at the lower rate and lend at the higher rate? In practice, the discount rate is at times lower than the rate that banks charge for their loans, and yet this kind of behavior is not common. This is because the Fed places other constraints on the borrowing behavior of banks. The Fed practices **moral suasion** to discourage heavy borrowing. Because member banks know that the Fed would look disapprovingly at heavy borrowing, they do not borrow heavily, and the amount that they do borrow responds only slightly to changes in the discount rate.

moral suasion *The pressure exerted by the Fed on member banks to discourage them from borrowing heavily from the Fed.*

OPEN MARKET OPERATIONS

open market operations
The purchase and sale by the Fed of government securities in the open market; a tool used to expand or contract the amount of reserves in the system and thus the money supply.

By far the most significant of the Fed's tools for controlling the supply of money is **open market operations**. Congress has authorized the Federal Reserve to buy and sell U.S. government securities in the open market. When the Fed purchases a security, it pays for it by writing a check that, when cleared, *expands* the quantity of reserves in the system, increasing the money supply. When the Fed sells a bond, private citizens or institutions pay for it with a check that, when cleared, *reduces* the quantity of reserves in the system.

To see how open market transactions and reserve controls work, we need to review several key ideas.

> **Two Branches of Government Deal in Government Securities**   The fact that the Fed is able to buy and sell government securities—bills and bonds—may confuse students. In fact, *two* branches of government deal in financial markets for different reasons, and you must keep the two separate in your mind.

First, keep in mind that the Treasury Department is responsible for collecting taxes and paying the federal government's bills. Salary checks paid to government workers, payments to General Dynamics for a new Navy ship, social security checks to retirees, and so forth are all written on accounts maintained by the Treasury. Tax receipts collected by the Internal Revenue Service, a Treasury branch, are deposited to these accounts.

If total government spending exceeds tax receipts, the law requires the Treasury to borrow the difference. Recall that the government deficit is $(G - T)$, or government purchases minus net taxes. $(G - T)$ is the amount the Treasury must borrow each year to finance the deficit. This means:

> The Treasury *cannot* print money to finance the deficit.

The Treasury borrows by issuing bills, bonds, and notes that pay interest. These government securities, or IOUs, are sold to individuals and institutions. Often foreign countries, as well as U.S. citizens, buy them. As discussed in chapter 10, the total amount of privately held government securities is the *privately held federal debt*.

The Fed is not the Treasury. Rather, it is a quasi-independent agency authorized by Congress to buy and sell *outstanding* (preexisting) U.S. government securities on the open market. The bonds and bills initially sold by the Treasury to finance the deficit are continuously resold and traded among ordinary citizens, firms, banks, pension funds, and so forth. The Fed's participation in that trading affects the quantity of reserves in the system, as we will see.

Because the Fed owns some government securities, some of what the government owes, it owes to itself. Recall that the Federal Reserve System's largest single asset is government securities. These securities are nothing more than bills and bonds initially issued by the Treasury to finance the deficit. They were acquired by the Fed over time through direct open market purchases that the Fed made to expand the money supply as the economy expanded.

> **The Mechanics of Open Market Operations**   How do open market operations affect the money supply? Look again at Table 26.1. As you can see, most of the Fed's assets consist of the government securities we have just been talking about.

Suppose the Fed wants to decrease the supply of money. If it can reduce the volume of bank reserves on the liabilities side of its balance sheet, it will force banks in turn to reduce their own deposits (to meet the required reserve ratio). Since these deposits are part of the supply of money, the supply of money will contract.

What will happen if the Fed sells some of its holdings of government securities to the general public? The Fed's holdings of government securities must decrease, because the securities it sold will now be owned by someone else. How do the purchasers of securities pay for what they have bought? By writing checks drawn on their banks and payable to the Fed.

Let's look more carefully at how this works, with the help of Table 26.4. In Panel 1, the Fed initially has $100 billion of government securities. Its liabilities consist of $20 billion of deposits (which are the reserves of commercial banks) and $80 billion of currency. With the required reserve ratio at 20 percent, the $20 billion of reserves can support $100 billion of deposits in the commercial banks. The commercial banking system is fully loaned up. Panel 1 also shows the financial position of a private citizen, Jane Q. Public. Jane has assets of $5 billion (a large checking account deposit in the bank) and no debts, so her net worth is $5 billion.

TABLE 26.4 **OPEN MARKET OPERATIONS** (THE NUMBERS IN PARENTHESES IN PANELS 2 AND 3 SHOW THE DIFFERENCES BETWEEN THOSE PANELS AND PANEL 1. ALL FIGURES IN BILLIONS OF DOLLARS)

PANEL 1

Federal Reserve			Commercial Banks			Jane Q. Public		
Assets	Liabilities		Assets	Liabilities		Assets	Liabilities	
Securities $100	$20	Reserves	Reserves $20	$100	Deposits	Deposits $5	$0	Debts
	$80	Currency	Loans $80				$5	Net Worth

Note: Money supply (M1) = Currency + Deposits = $180.

PANEL 2

Federal Reserve			Commercial Banks			Jane Q. Public		
Assets	Liabilities		Assets	Liabilities		Assets	Liabilities	
Securities $95 (−$5)	$15 (−$5)	Reserves	Reserves $15 (−$5)	$95	Deposits	Deposits $0 (−$5)	$0	Debts
	$80	Currency	Loans $80		(−$5)	Securities $5 (+$5)	$5	Net Worth

Note: Money supply (M1) = Currency + Deposits = $175.

PANEL 3

Federal Reserve			Commercial Banks			Jane Q. PuBlic		
Assets	Liabilities		Assets	Liabilities		Assets	Liabilities	
Securities $95 (−$5)	$15 (−$5)	Reserves	Reserves $15 (−$5)	$75	Deposits	Deposits $0 (−$5)	$0	Debts
	$80	Currency	Loans $60 (−$20)		(−$25)	Securities $5 (+$5)	$5	Net Worth

Note: Money supply (M1) = Currency + Deposits = $155.

Now imagine that the Fed sells $5 billion in government securities to Jane. Jane pays for the securities by writing a check to the Fed, drawn on her bank. The Fed then reduces the reserve account of her bank by $5 billion. The balance sheets of all the participants after this transaction are shown in Panel 2. Note that the supply of money (currency plus deposits) has fallen from $180 billion to $175 billion.

This is not the end of the story. As a result of the Fed's sale of securities, the amount of reserves has fallen from $20 billion to $15 billion, while deposits have fallen from $100 billion to $95 billion. With a required reserve ratio of 20 percent, banks must have .20 × $95 billion, or $19 billion in reserves. Banks are under their required reserve ratio by $4 billion ($19 billion [the amount they should have] minus $15 billion [the amount they do have]). To comply with the federal regulations, banks must decrease their loans and their deposits.[9]

The final equilibrium position is shown in Panel 3, where commercial banks have reduced their loans by $20 billion. Notice that the change in deposits from Panel 1 to Panel 3 is $25 billion, which is five times the size of the change in reserves that the Fed brought about through its $5 billion open market sale of securities. This corresponds exactly to our earlier analysis of the money multiplier. The change

---

[9]Once again, banks never really have to call in loans. Loans and deposits would probably be reduced by slowing the rate of new lending as old loans come due and are paid off.

in money (−$25 billion) is equal to the money multiplier (5) times the change in reserves (−$5 billion).

Now consider what happens when the Fed *purchases* a government security. Suppose I hold $100 in Treasury bills, which the Fed buys from me. The Fed writes me a check for $100, and I turn in my Treasury bills. I then take the $100 check and deposit it in my local bank. This increases the reserves of my bank by $100 and begins a new episode in the money expansion story. With a reserve requirement of 20 percent, my bank can now lend out $80. If that $80 is spent and ends up back in a bank, that bank can lend $64, and so forth. (Review Figure 26.3.) The Fed can expand the money supply by buying government securities from people who own them, just the way it reduces the money supply by selling these securities.

Each business day, the Open Market Desk in the New York Federal Reserve Bank buys or sells millions of dollars' worth of securities, usually to large security dealers who act as intermediaries between the Fed and the private markets. We can sum up the effect of these open market operations this way:

- An open market *purchase* of securities by the Fed results in an increase in reserves and an *increase* in the supply of money by an amount equal to the money multiplier times the change in reserves.
- An open market *sale* of securities by the Fed results in a *decrease* in reserves and a *decrease* in the supply of money by an amount equal to the money multiplier times the change in reserves.

Open market operations are the Fed's preferred means of controlling the money supply for several reasons. First, open market operations can be used with some precision. If the Fed needs to change the money supply by just a small amount, it can buy or sell a small volume of government securities. If it wants a larger change in the money supply, it can buy or sell a larger amount. Second, open market operations are extremely flexible. If the Fed decides to reverse course, it can easily switch from buying securities to selling them. Finally, open market operations have a fairly predictable effect on the supply of money. Because banks are obliged to meet their reserve requirements, an open market sale of $100 in government securities will reduce reserves by $100, which will reduce the supply of money by $100 times the money multiplier.

Where does the Fed get the money to buy government securities when it wants to expand the money supply? The Fed creates it. In effect, it tells the bank from which it has bought a $100 security that its reserve account (deposit) at the Fed now contains $100 more than it did previously. This is where the power of the Fed, or any central bank, lies. The Fed has the ability to create money at will. In the United States, the Fed exercises this power when it creates money to buy government securities.

THE SUPPLY CURVE FOR MONEY

Thus far we know how the Fed can control the money supply by controlling the amount of reserves in the economy. If the Fed wants the quantity of money to be $1,200 billion on a given date, it can aim for this target by changing the discount rate, by changing the required reserve ratio, or by engaging in open market operations. In this sense, the supply of money is completely determined by the Fed, and the money supply curve in Figure 26.5 is a vertical line.

A vertical money supply curve says the Fed sets the money supply independent of the interest rate. A vertical money supply curve means the interest rate does not affect the Fed's decision on how much money to supply. We will see in chapter 31 that the Fed's money supply behavior is influenced by the state of the economy, but perhaps

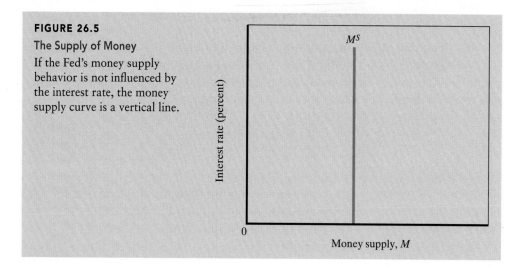

FIGURE 26.5

The Supply of Money

If the Fed's money supply behavior is not influenced by the interest rate, the money supply curve is a vertical line.

also by the interest rate. In practice, the money supply curve is not likely to be vertical. It would complicate matters at this stage of our analysis to consider Fed behavior in more detail, so we will assume for now that the money supply curve is vertical. This assumption is relaxed in chapter 31.[10]

LOOKING AHEAD

This chapter has discussed only the supply side of the money market. We have seen what money is, how banks create money by making loans, and how the Fed controls the money supply. In the next chapter we turn to the demand side of the money market. We will examine the demand for money and how the supply of and demand for money determine the equilibrium interest rate.

SUMMARY

AN OVERVIEW OF MONEY

1. Money has three distinguishing characteristics: (1) a means of payment, or medium of exchange; (2) a store of value; and (3) a unit of account. The alternative to using money is *barter*, in which goods are exchanged directly for other goods. Barter is costly and inefficient in an economy with many different kinds of goods.

2. *Commodity monies* are items used as money and also have an intrinsic value in some other use (for example, gold and cigarettes). *Fiat monies* are intrinsically worthless apart from their use as money. To ensure the acceptance of fiat monies, governments use their power to declare money *legal tender* and promise the public they will not debase the currency by expanding its supply rapidly.

3. There are various definitions of money. Currency plus demand deposits plus traveler's checks plus other checkable deposits compose M1, or *transactions money*—money that can be used directly to buy things. The addition of savings accounts and money market accounts (*near monies*) to M1 gives M2, or *broad money*.

---

[10]There is another reason the money supply curve may not be vertical. If bank borrowing from the Fed responds positively to the difference between the market interest rate and the discount rate, then as the market interest rate rises (with the discount rate fixed), banks will borrow more. We have seen that an increase in bank borrowing leads to an increase in the money supply. Therefore, the supply of money responds positively to the market interest rate, so the money supply schedule should have a positive slope. In practice this effect is fairly small, and for simplicity we will ignore it. The Fed could offset this effect completely if it raised the discount rate in line with the market interest rate.

HOW BANKS CREATE MONEY

4. The *required reserve ratio* is the percentage of a bank's deposits that must be kept as reserves at the nation's central bank, the Federal Reserve.

5. Banks create money by making loans. When a bank makes a loan to a customer, it creates a deposit in that customer's account. This deposit becomes part of the money supply. Banks can create money only when they have *excess reserves*—reserves in excess of the amount set by the required reserve ratio.

6. The *money multiplier* is the multiple by which the total supply of money can increase for every dollar increase in reserves. The money multiplier is equal to 1/required reserve ratio.

THE FEDERAL RESERVE SYSTEM

7. The Fed's most important function is controlling the nation's money supply. The Fed also performs several other functions: It clears interbank payments, is responsible for many of the regulations governing banking practices and standards, and acts as a *lender of last resort* for troubled banks that cannot find any other sources of funds. The Fed also acts as the bank for the U.S. government.

HOW THE FED CONTROLS THE MONEY SUPPLY

8. The key to understanding how the Fed controls the money supply is the role of reserves. If the Fed wants to increase the supply of money, it creates more reserves, freeing banks to create additional deposits. If it wants to decrease the money supply, it reduces reserves.

9. The Fed has three tools to control the money supply: (1) change the required reserve ratio; (2) change the *discount rate* (the interest rate member banks pay when they borrow from the Fed); or (3) engage in *open market operations* (the buying and selling of already-existing government securities). To increase the money supply, the Fed can create additional reserves by lowering the discount rate or by buying government securities, or the Fed can increase the number of deposits that can be created from a given quantity of reserves by lowering the required reserve ratio. To decrease the money supply, the Fed can reduce reserves by raising the discount rate or by selling government securities, or it can raise the required reserve ratio.

10. If the Fed's money supply behavior is not influenced by the interest rate, the supply curve for money is a vertical line.

REVIEW TERMS AND CONCEPTS

barter, 610

commodity monies, 611

currency debasement, 612

discount rate, 627

excess reserves, 618

Federal Open Market Committee (FOMC), 621

Federal Reserve System (the Fed), 616

fiat, or token, money, 611

financial intermediaries, 613

legal tender, 611

lender of last resort, 622

liquidity property of money, 611

M1, or transactions money, 612

M2, or broad money, 613

medium of exchange, or means of payment, 610

money multiplier, 620

moral suasion, 628

near monies, 613

Open Market Desk, 621

open market operations, 628

required reserve ratio, 617

reserves, 617

run on a bank, 616

store of value, 610

unit of account, 611

1. $M1 \equiv$ Currency held outside banks + Demand deposits + Traveler's checks + Other checkable deposits

2. $M2 \equiv M1$ + Savings accounts + Money market accounts + Other near monies

3. Assets $\equiv$ Liabilities + Capital (or Net Worth)

4. Excess reserves $\equiv$ Actual reserves − Required reserves

5. Money multiplier $\equiv \dfrac{1}{\text{Required reserve ratio}}$

PROBLEM SET

1. Define money. What is meant by the "store of value" function of money? What is meant by the "medium of exchange" function of money? Think of your current cash holdings and checking account balances. How much do you think you have on hand for purposes of engaging in transactions (buying stuff) on a daily basis? How much is serving as a store of value? Would the amount you hold onto as cash and in your checking account change if your local bank started paying 15 percent interest on three-month certificates of deposit? Why or why not?

2. For each of the following say whether it is an asset on the accounting books of a bank or a liability. Explain why in each case.

> Cash in the vault
> Demand deposits
> Savings deposits
> Reserves
> Loans
> Deposits at the Federal Reserve

3. If the head of the Central Bank of Japan wanted to expand the supply of money in Japan in 1999, which of the following would do it? Explain your answer.

> Increase the required reserve ratio
> Decrease the required reserve ratio
> Increase the discount rate
> Decrease the discount rate
> Buy government securities in the open market
> Sell government securities in the open market

4. In 1997, the U.S. money supply ($M1$) was $1,077 billion, broken down as follows: $396 billion in currency, $86 billion in traveler's checks, and $672 billion in checking deposits. Suppose the Fed has decided to reduce the money supply by increasing the reserve requirement from 10 percent to 11 percent. Assuming all banks were initially loaned up (had no excess reserves) and currency held outside of banks did not change, how large a change in the money supply would have resulted from the change in the reserve requirement?

5. As King of Medivalia, you are constantly strapped for funds to pay your army. Your chief economic wizard suggests the following plan: "When you collect your tax payments from your subjects, insist on being paid in gold coins. Take these gold coins, melt them down, and then remint them with an extra 10 percent of brass thrown in. You will then have 10 percent more money than you started with." What do you think of the plan? Will it work?

6. Why is $M2$ sometimes a more stable measure of money than $M1$? Explain in your own words, using the definitions of $M1$ and $M2$.

7. Do you agree or disagree with each of the following statements? Explain your answers.
   a. "When the Treasury of the United States issues bonds and sells them to the public to finance the deficit, the money supply remains unchanged because every dollar of money taken in by the Treasury goes right back into circulation through government spending. This is not true when the Fed sells bonds to the public."
   b. "The money multiplier depends on the marginal propensity to save."

*8. When the Fed adds new reserves to the system, some of these new reserves find their way out of the country into foreign banks or foreign investment funds. In addition, some portion of new reserves ends up in people's pockets and mattresses rather than in bank vaults. These "leakages" reduce the money multiplier and sometimes make it very difficult for the Fed to control the money supply precisely. Explain why this is true.

9. You are given this T account for a bank:

ASSETS		LIABILITIES	
Reserves	$500	$3,500	Deposits
Loans	3,000		

The required reserve ratio is 10 percent.
   a. How much is the bank required to hold as reserves, given its deposits of $3,500?
   b. How much are its excess reserves?
   c. By how much can the bank increase its loans?
   d. Suppose a depositor comes to the bank and withdraws $200 in cash. Show the bank's new balance sheet, assuming the bank obtains the cash by drawing down its reserves. Does the bank now hold excess reserves? Is it meeting the required reserve ratio? If not, what can it do?

10. What are the major functions of the Federal Reserve? Could any of these functions be performed by private banks, or is the central bank the only agent capable of filling these roles? Explain.

TAKE IT TO THE NET

We invite you to visit the Case and Fair page on the Prentice Hall Web site:

http://www.prenhall.com/casefair

for this chapter's World Wide Web exercise.

Chapter 27

MONEY DEMAND, THE EQUILIBRIUM INTEREST RATE, AND MONETARY POLICY

HAVING DISCUSSED THE *SUPPLY* of money in the last chapter, we now turn to the *demand* for money. One goal of this and the previous chapter is to provide a theory of how the interest rate is determined in the macroeconomy. Once we have seen how the interest rate is determined, we can turn to how the Fed affects the interest rate through **monetary policy**.

It is important that you understand exactly what the interest rate is. **Interest** is the fee a borrower pays to a lender for the use of his or her funds. Firms and the government borrow funds by issuing bonds, and they pay interest to the firms and households (the lenders) that purchase those bonds. Households and firms that have borrowed from a bank must pay interest on those loans to the bank.

The **interest rate** is the annual interest payment on a loan expressed as a percentage of the loan. A $1,000 bond (representing a $1,000 loan from a household to a firm) that pays $100 in interest per year has an interest rate of 10 percent. The interest rate is expressed as an *annual* rate. It is the amount of interest received *per year* divided by the amount of the loan.

While there are many different interest rates, we will assume that there is only one. This simplifies our analysis yet provides a valuable tool for us to understand how the parts of the macroeconomy relate to one another. Appendix A to this chapter provides more detail on the various types of interest rates.

monetary policy *The behavior of the Federal Reserve regarding the money supply.*

interest *The fee that a borrower pays to a lender for the use of his or her funds.*

interest rate *The annual interest payment on a loan expressed as a percentage of the loan. Equal to the amount of interest received per year divided by the amount of the loan.*

THE DEMAND FOR MONEY

What factors and what forces determine the demand for money are central issues in macroeconomics. As we shall see, the interest rate and the level of national income (Y) influence how much money households and firms wish to hold.

Before we proceed, we must stress one point students find troublesome. When we speak of the demand for money, we are not asking "How much cash do you wish you could have?" or "How much income would you like to earn?" or "How much wealth would you like?" (The answer to these questions is presumably "as much as possible.") Rather, we are concerned with how much of your financial assets you want to hold *in the form of money*, which does not earn interest, versus how much you want to hold in interest-bearing securities, such as bonds. We take as given the *total* amount of financial assets; our concern here is with how these assets are divided between money and interest-bearing securities.

THE TRANSACTION MOTIVE

How much money to hold involves a trade-off between the liquidity of money and the interest income offered by other kinds of assets. The main reason for holding money instead of interest-bearing assets is that money is useful for buying things. Economists call this the **transaction motive**. This rationale for holding money is at the heart of the discussion that follows.[1]

transaction motive *The main reason that people hold money— to buy things.*

➤ **Assumptions**   To keep our analysis of the demand for money clear, we need a few simplifying assumptions. First, we assume there are only two kinds of assets available to households: bonds and money. By "bonds" we mean interest-bearing securities of all kinds. By "money" we mean currency in circulation and deposits, neither of which is assumed to pay interest.[2]

Second, we assume that income for the typical household is "bunched up." It arrives once a month, at the beginning of the month. Spending, by contrast, is spread out over time; we assume that spending occurs at a completely uniform rate throughout the month—that is, that the same amount is spent each day (see Figure 27.1). The mismatch between the timing of money inflow and the timing of money outflow is sometimes called the **nonsynchronization of income and spending**.

nonsynchronization of income and spending *The mismatch between the timing of money inflow to the household and the timing of money outflow for household expenses.*

Finally, we assume that spending for the month is exactly equal to income for the month. Because we are focusing on the transactions demand for money and not on its use as a store of value, this assumption is perfectly reasonable.

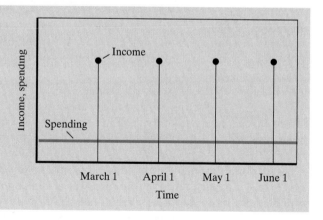

FIGURE 27.1

The Nonsynchronization of Income and Spending

Income arrives only once a month, but spending takes place continuously.

---

[1]The model that we discuss here is known in the economics profession as the Baumol/Tobin model, after the two economists who independently derived it, William Baumol of Princeton University and James Tobin of Yale University.

[2]Remember that the category "deposits" includes checking accounts. Many checking accounts pay interest. This turns out not to matter for the purposes of our discussion, however. Suppose bonds pay 10 percent interest and checking accounts pay 5 percent. (Checking accounts must pay less than bonds. Otherwise, everyone would hold all their wealth in checking accounts and none in bonds, because checking accounts are more convenient.) When it comes to choosing whether to hold bonds or money, it is the difference in the interest rates on the two that matters. People are concerned about how much extra interest they will get from holding bonds rather than money. In the example above, we could say that bonds pay 5 percent and money pays 0 percent, which makes our discussion simpler.

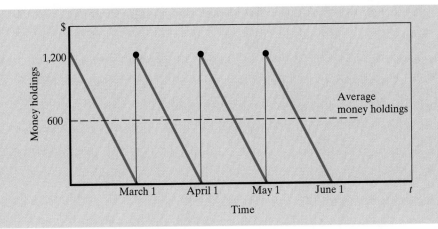

FIGURE 27.2

Jim's Monthly Checking
Account Balances: Strategy 1

Jim could decide to deposit
his entire paycheck ($1,200)
into his checking account at
the start of the month and run
his balance down to zero by
the end of the month. In this
case, his average balance
would be $600.

MONEY MANAGEMENT AND THE OPTIMAL BALANCE

Given these assumptions, how would a rational person (household) decide how much of monthly income to hold as money and how much to hold as interest-bearing bonds? Suppose Jim decides to deposit his entire paycheck in his checking account. Let's say Jim earns $1,200 per month. The pattern of Jim's bank account balance is illustrated in Figure 27.2. At the beginning of the month, Jim's balance is $1,200. As the month rolls by, Jim draws down his balance, writing checks or withdrawing cash to pay for the things he buys. At the end of the month, Jim's bank account balance is down to zero. Just in time, he receives his next month's paycheck, deposits it, and the process begins again.

One useful statistic we will need to calculate is the *average balance* in Jim's account. Jim spends his money at a constant $40 per day ($40 per day times 30 days per month = $1,200). His average balance is just his starting balance ($1,200) plus his ending balance (0) divided by 2, or ($1,200 + 0)/2 = $600. For the first half of the month Jim has more than his average of $600 on deposit, and for the second half of the month he has less than his average.

Anything wrong with Jim's strategy? Yes. If he follows the plan described, Jim is giving up interest on his funds, interest he could be earning if he held some of his funds in interest-bearing bonds instead of in his checking account. How could he manage his funds to give himself more interest?

Instead of depositing his entire paycheck in his checking account at the beginning of the month, Jim could put half his paycheck into his checking account and buy a bond with the other half. Doing this, he would run out of money in his checking account halfway through the month. At a spending rate of $40 per day, his initial deposit of $600 would last only 15 days. Jim would have to sell his bond halfway through the month and deposit the $600 from the sale of the bond in his checking account to pay his bills during the second half of the month.

Jim's money holdings (checking account balances) if he follows this strategy are shown in Figure 27.3. When he follows the buy-a-$600-bond strategy, Jim reduces the average amount of money in his checking account. Comparing the dashed green lines (old strategy) with the solid green lines (buy-$600-bond strategy), his average bank balance is exactly half of what it was with the first strategy.[3]

The buy-a-$600-bond strategy seems sensible. The object of this strategy was to keep some funds in bonds, where they could earn interest, instead of as "idle"

---

[3]Jim's average balance for the first half of the month is (starting balance + ending balance)/2, or ($600 + 0)/2 = $300. His average for the second half of the month is also $300. His average for the month as a whole is $300.

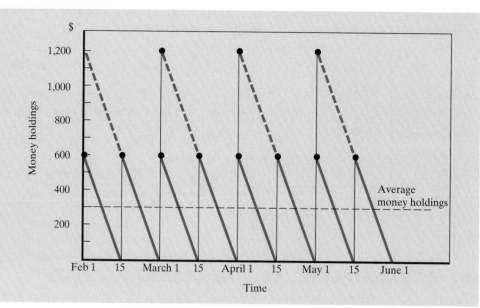

FIGURE 27.3

Jim's Monthly Checking Account Balances: Strategy 2

Jim could also choose to put one half of his paycheck into his checking account and buy a bond with the other half of his income. At mid-month, Jim would sell the bond and deposit the $600 into his checking account to pay the second half of the month's bills. Following this strategy, Jim's average money holdings would be $300.

money. But why stop there? Another possibility would be for Jim to put only $400 into his checking account on the first of the month and buy two $400 bonds. The $400 in his account will last only 10 days if he spends $40 per day, so after 10 days he must sell one of the bonds and deposit the $400 from the sale in his checking account. This will last through the 20th of the month, at which point he must sell the second bond and deposit the other $400. This strategy lowers Jim's average money holding (checking account balance) even further, reducing his money holdings to an average of only $200 per month, with correspondingly higher average holdings of interest-earning bonds.

You can imagine Jim going even further. Why not hold all wealth in the form of bonds (where it earns interest) and make transfers from bonds to money every time he makes a purchase? If selling bonds, transferring funds to checking accounts, and making trips to the bank were without cost, Jim would never hold money for more than an instant. Each time he needed to pay cash for something or write a check, he would go to the bank or call the bank, transfer the exact amount of the transaction to his checking account, and either withdraw the cash or write the check to complete the transaction. If he did this constantly, he would squeeze the most interest possible out of his funds because he would never hold assets that did not earn interest.

In practice, money management of this kind is costly. There are brokerage fees and other costs to buy or sell bonds, and time must be spent waiting in line at the bank. At the same time, it is costly to hold assets in non-interest-bearing form, because they lose potential interest revenue.

We have a trade-off problem of the type that pervades economics. Switching more often from bonds to money raises the interest revenue Jim earns (because the more times he switches, the less, on average, he has to hold in his checking account and the more he can keep in bonds), but this increases his money management costs. Less switching means more interest revenue lost (because average money holdings are higher) but lower money management costs (fewer purchases and sales of bonds, less time spent waiting in bank lines, fewer trips to the bank, and so on).

➤ **The Optimal Balance**   There is a level of average money balances that earns Jim the most profit, taking into account both the interest earned on bonds and the costs paid for switching from bonds to money. This level is his *optimal balance*.

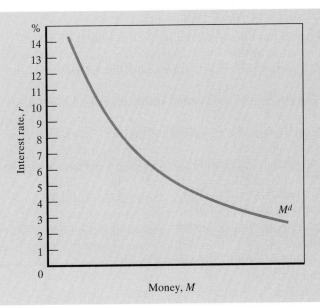

FIGURE 27.4

The Demand Curve for Money Balances

The quantity of money demanded (the amount of money households and firms wish to hold) is a function of the interest rate. Because the interest rate is the opportunity cost of holding money balances, increases in the interest rate will reduce the quantity of money that firms and households want to hold, and decreases in the interest rate will increase the quantity of money that firms and households want to hold.

How does the interest rate affect the number of switches that Jim makes and thus the average money balance he chooses to hold? It is easy to see why an increase in the interest rate lowers the optimal money balance. If the interest rate were only 2 percent, it would not be worthwhile to give up much liquidity by holding bonds instead of cash or checking balances. But if the interest rate were 30 percent, the opportunity cost of holding money instead of bonds would be quite high, and we would expect people to keep most of their funds in bonds and to spend considerable time in managing their money balances. The interest rate represents the opportunity cost of holding money (and therefore not holding bonds, which pay interest). The higher the interest rate, the higher the opportunity cost of holding money, and the less money people will want to hold. This leads us to conclude:

> When interest rates are high, people want to take advantage of the high return on bonds, so they choose to hold very little money.

Appendix B to this chapter provides a detailed example of this principle.

A demand curve for money, with the interest rate representing the "price" of money, would look like the curve labeled M^d in Figure 27.4. At higher interest rates, bonds are much more attractive than money, so people hold less money because they must make a larger sacrifice in interest for each dollar of money they hold. The curve in Figure 27.4 slopes downward, just like an ordinary demand curve for oranges or shoes. There is an inverse relationship between the interest rate and the quantity of money demanded.[4]

---

[4]The theory of money demand presented here assumes that a person knows the exact timing of her or his income and spending. In practice, both have some uncertainty attached to them. For example, some income payments may be unexpectedly delayed a few days or weeks, and some expenditures may arise unexpectedly (such as a plumbing problem). Because people know that this uncertainty exists, they may choose to hold more money than the strict transactions motive would suggest, as a precaution against unanticipated delays in income receipts or unanticipated expenses. This reason for holding money is sometimes called the *precautionary motive*.

THE SPECULATION MOTIVE

A number of theories have been offered to explain why the quantity of money households desire to hold may rise when interest rates fall, and fall when interest rates rise. One involves household expectations and the relationship of interest rates to bond values.

To understand this theory, you need to realize that the market value of most interest-bearing bonds is inversely related to the interest rate. Suppose I bought an 8 percent bond a year ago for $1,000. Now suppose the market interest rate rises to 10 percent. If I offered to sell my bond for $1,000, no one would buy it because anyone can buy a new bond and earn 10 percent in the market rather than 8 percent of my bond. But at some lower selling price, my bond becomes attractive to buyers. This is because a lower price increases the actual yield to the buyer of my bond. Suppose I sell you my bond for $500. Because the bond is paying 8 percent annually on the original $1,000 (that is, $80 per year), it is actually paying you an annual amount that comes to 16 percent of your investment in the bond ($500 × .16 = $80). If you bought that same bond from me for about $800, it would effectively pay you 10 percent interest ($800 × .10 = $80). The point here is simple:

> When market interest rates fall, bond values rise; when market interest rates rise, bond values fall.

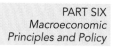

speculation motive *One reason for holding bonds instead of money: Because the market value of interest-bearing bonds is inversely related to the interest rate, investors may wish to hold bonds when interest rates are high with the hope of selling them when interest rates fall.*

Now consider my desire to hold money balances rather than bonds. If market interest rates are higher than normal, I may expect them to come down in the future. If and when interest rates fall, the bonds that I bought when they were high will increase in value. When interest rates are high, the opportunity cost of holding cash balances is high and there is a **speculation motive** for holding bonds in lieu of cash. I am "speculating" that interest rates will fall in the future.

Similarly, when market interest rates are lower than normal, I may expect them to rise in the future. Rising interest rates will bring about a decline in the value of bonds. Thus, when interest rates are low, it is a good time to be holding money and not bonds. When interest rates are low, not only is the opportunity cost of holding cash balances low, but there is also a speculative motive for holding a larger amount of money. Why should I put money into bonds now when I expect interest rates to rise in the future? (For more on the interaction between the bond market and the money market, see Application Box "The Bond Market, the Money Market, and the Speculation Motive.")

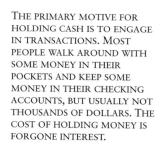

THE PRIMARY MOTIVE FOR HOLDING CASH IS TO ENGAGE IN TRANSACTIONS. MOST PEOPLE WALK AROUND WITH SOME MONEY IN THEIR POCKETS AND KEEP SOME MONEY IN THEIR CHECKING ACCOUNTS, BUT USUALLY NOT THOUSANDS OF DOLLARS. THE COST OF HOLDING MONEY IS FORGONE INTEREST.

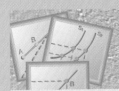

THE BOND MARKET, THE MONEY MARKET, AND THE SPECULATION MOTIVE

People are often confused when business-page headlines read "Bonds Fall, Pushing up Interest Rates" or "Bonds Rise, Driving Yields Down." Nonetheless, it is true that the current market price or value of all fixed-rate bonds, whether U.S. Treasury Bonds or German corporate bonds, fall in value when interest rates rise, and rise in value when interest rates fall.

To see why, consider Heidi, a German house painter who bought for $1,000 a 10-year German government bond with a fixed rate of 10 percent. By buying that bond, Heidi has agreed to accept a return on her money of 10 percent for 10 years. This means a check for $100 every year with a promise that her $1,000 will be returned at the end of 10 years.

Though the German government has no obligation to pay the $1,000 back before the bond matures in 10 years, Heidi may need the money before 10 years is up. To get her money back earlier, she can call a broker and sell the bond. In fact, there is a huge market for existing bonds, and existing bond prices are posted in the newspapers every day. To sell the bond, the broker has to find a buyer, and the amount that a buyer would be willing to pay depends on the current rate of interest.

Suppose Heidi wants to sell her bond two years after she purchased it. The bond still has eight years left to maturity. Assume that the Bundesbank (the German central bank) has pushed

rates for eight-year bonds to 12 percent. Someone who paid $1,000 for Heidi's bond today would be getting only $100 (10 percent) interest per year. The same person could be getting interest of $120 per year, or 12 percent, by buying a newly issued $1,000 bond. The result: Heidi's broker will not be able to sell her bond for $1,000. Instead, Heidi will have to take a loss because her bond's value has fallen.

Do bond values really fall in the real world? Absolutely. When the Federal Reserve raised U.S. interest rates in 1994, the value of outstanding bonds traded in the market fell substantially. Similarly, during Mexico's peso crises in 1995, Mexican interest rates shot up sharply, and Mexican government bonds lost a lot of their value. (U.S. holders of Mexican securities got hit even harder because the value of the peso fell too—but that's covered later in the chapter on open-market macroeconomics.)

Another way to see the same connection between the bond market and the money market is to think of a case in which the demand for bonds increases. Suppose that because of excess demand for bonds in Germany, the value of Heidi's bond goes up to $1,100. Someone who is willing to pay $1,100 for Heidi's bond *must reveal that he is willing to accept an annual yield of less than 10 percent*. After all, $100 is only 9.1 percent of $1,100. In addition, the buyer who pays $1,100 will get back only $1,000 when the bond matures.

Higher bond prices mean the interest rate bond buyers are willing to accept is lower than before! If buyers are willing to accept 9 percent on old bonds, they will accept 9 percent on new bonds.

Bond prices and interest rates are two sides of the same coin. A "rally" in the bond market means bond prices have gone up and interest rates, or bond "yields," have gone down. Similarly, when the bond market "drops," interest rates, or yields, have gone up.

These effects have important implications for money demand. Assume households choose only between holding their assets as money (which does not earn interest) or as bonds (which do earn interest). If households and firms believe interest rates are historically high and they are likely to fall, it is a *good* time to hold bonds. Why? Because a drop in rates means bond values will rise, in a sense earning bondholders a bonus. When interest rates are high and expected to fall, demand for bonds is likely to be high and money demand is likely to be low. Similarly, if people see interest rates as low and expect them to rise, it is *not* a good time to be holding bonds. Why? Because if interest rates rise, bond holders suffer losses. When interest rates are low, money demand is likely to be high and the demand for bonds is likely to be low. Thus, we have another reason for the negative relationship between interest rates and money demand. As we mentioned in the text, this is the *speculation motive* for holding money.

For more on the bond market, the money market, and the relationships between them, see the Case and Fair Web page at **http://www.prenhall.com/casefair**.

THE TOTAL DEMAND FOR MONEY

So far we have talked only about household demand for checking account balances. But the total quantity of money demanded in the economy is the sum of the demand for checking account balances *and cash* by both households *and firms*.

The trade-off for firms is the same as it was for Jim. Like households, firms must manage their money. They have payrolls to meet and purchases to make; they receive

CHAPTER TWENTY-SEVEN
*Money Demand
and Interest Rate*

cash and checks from sales; and many firms that deal with the public must make change—they need cash in the cash register. Thus, just like Jim, firms need money to engage in ordinary transactions.

But firms as well as households can hold their assets in interest-earning form. Firms manage their assets just as households do, keeping some in cash, some in their checking accounts, and some in bonds. A higher interest rate raises the opportunity cost of money for firms as well as for households and thus reduces the demand for money.

The same trade-off holds for cash. We all walk around with some money in our pockets, but not thousands of dollars, for routine transactions. We carry, on average, about what we think we will need. Why not more? Because there are costs—risks of being robbed and forgone interest.

> At any given moment, there is a demand for money—for cash and checking account balances. Although households and firms need to hold balances for everyday transactions, their demand has a limit. For both households and firms, the quantity of money demanded at any moment depends on the opportunity cost of holding money, a cost determined by the interest rate.

TRANSACTIONS VOLUME AND THE PRICE LEVEL

The money demand curve in Figure 27.4 is a function of the interest rate. There are other factors besides the interest rate that influence total desired money holdings. One is the dollar value of transactions made during a given period of time.

Suppose Jim's income were to double. Instead of making $1,200 in purchases each month, he makes $2,400 in purchases. He needs to hold more money. Why? Simple: To buy more things, he needs more money.

What is true for Jim is true for the economy as a whole. The total demand for money in the economy depends on the total dollar volume of transactions made. The total dollar volume of transactions in the economy, in turn, depends on two things: the total *number* of transactions and the average transaction *amount*. Although there are no data on the actual number of transactions in the economy, a reasonable indicator is likely to be aggregate output (income) (Y). A rise in aggregate output—real GDP—means there is more economic activity. Firms are producing and selling more output, more people are on payrolls, and household incomes are higher. In short, there are more transactions, and firms and households together will hold more money when they are engaging in more transactions. Thus, an increase in aggregate output (income) will increase the demand for money.

Figure 27.5 shows a shift of the money demand curve resulting from an increase in Y:

> For a given interest rate, a higher level of output means an increase in the *number* of transactions and more demand for money. The money demand curve shifts to the right when Y rises. Similarly, a decrease in Y means a decrease in the number of transactions and a lower demand for money. The money demand curve shifts to the left when Y falls.

The amount of money needed by firms and households to facilitate their day-to-day transactions also depends on the average *dollar amount* of each transaction. In turn, the average amount of each transaction depends on prices, or rather, on the *price level*. If all prices, including the price of labor (the wage rate) were to double, firms and households would need more money balances to carry out their day-to-day transactions—each transaction would require twice as much money. If the price of your lunch increases from $3.50 to $7.00, you will begin carrying more cash. If your

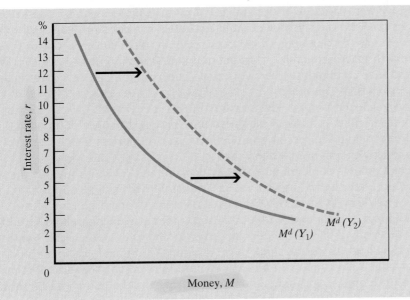

FIGURE 27.5

An Increase in Aggregate Output (Income) (Y) Will Shift the Money Demand Curve to the Right

An increase in Y means there is more economic activity. Firms are producing and selling more, and households are earning more income and buying more. There are more transactions, for which money is needed. As a result, both firms and households are likely to increase their holdings of money balances at a given interest rate.

end-of-the-month bills are twice as high as they used to be, you will keep more money in your checking account.

> Increases in the price level shift the money demand curve to the right, and decreases in the price level shift the money demand curve to the left. Even though the number of transactions may not have changed, the quantity of money needed to engage in them has.

THE DETERMINANTS OF MONEY DEMAND: REVIEW

Table 27.1 summarizes everything we have said about the demand for money. First, because the interest rate (r) is the opportunity cost of holding money balances for both firms and households: increases in the interest rate are likely to decrease the quantity of money demanded; decreases in the interest rate will increase the quantity of money demanded. Thus, the quantity of money demanded is a negative function of the interest rate.

The demand for money also depends on the dollar volume of transactions in a given period. The dollar volume of transactions depends on both aggregate output (income), Y, and the price level, P. The relationship of money demand to Y and the relationship of money demand to P are both positive. Increases in Y or in P will shift the money demand curve to the right; decreases in Y or P will shift the money demand curve to the left.

▶ **Some Common Pitfalls** We need to consider several pitfalls in thinking about money demand. First, when we spoke in earlier chapters about the demand for goods and

TABLE 27.1 DETERMINANTS OF MONEY DEMAND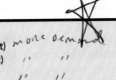

1. The interest rate: r (negative effect)
2. The dollar volume of transactions (positive effect)
   a. Aggregate output (income): Y (positive effect)
   b. The price level: P (positive effect)

services, we were speaking of demand as a *flow variable*—something measured over a period of time. If you say your demand for coffee is three cups, you need to specify whether you are talking about three cups per hour, three cups per day, or three cups per week. In macroeconomics, consumption and saving are flow variables. We consume and save continuously, but we express consumption and saving in time-period terms, such as $600 *per month*.

Money demand is *not* a flow measure. Rather it is a *stock variable*, measured at a given point in time. It answers the question: How much money do firms and households desire to hold at a specific point in time, given the current interest rate, volume of economic activity, and price level?

Second, many people think of money demand and saving as roughly the same—they are not. Say that in a given year a household had income of $50,000 and expenses of $47,000. It saved $3,000 during the year. At the beginning of the year the household had no debt and $100,000 in assets. Because the household saved $3,000 during the year, it has $103,000 in assets at the end of the year. Some of the $103,000 is held in stocks, some in bonds, some in other forms of securities, and some in money. How much the household chooses to hold in the form of money is its demand for money. Depending on the interest rate and the household's transactions, the amount of the $103,000 that it chooses to hold in the form of money could be anywhere from a few hundred dollars to many thousands. How much of its assets a household holds in the form of money is different from how much of its income it spends during the year.

Finally, recall the difference between a shift in a demand curve and a movement along the curve. The money demand curve in Figure 27.4 shows optimal money balances as a function of the interest rate *ceteris paribus*, all else equal. Changes in the interest rate cause movements *along* the curve—*changes in the quantity of money demanded*. Changes in real GDP (Y) or in the price level (P) cause shifts of the curve as shown in Figure 27.5—*changes in demand*.

THE EQUILIBRIUM INTEREST RATE

We are now in a position to consider one of the key questions in macroeconomics: How is the interest rate determined in the economy?

Financial markets (what we call the money market) work very well in the United States. Almost all financial markets clear—that is, almost all reach an equilibrium where quantity demanded equals quantity supplied. In the money market,

> The point at which the quantity of money demanded equals the quantity of money supplied determines the equilibrium interest rate in the economy.

Sounds simple, but it requires elaboration.

SUPPLY AND DEMAND IN THE MONEY MARKET

We saw in chapter 26 that the Fed controls the money supply through its manipulation of the amount of reserves in the economy. Because we are assuming that the Fed's money supply behavior does not depend on the interest rate, the money supply curve is a vertical line. (Review Figure 26.5.) In other words, we are assuming that the Fed uses its three tools (the required reserve ratio, the discount rate, and open market operations) to achieve its fixed target for the money supply.

Figure 27.6 superimposes the vertical money supply curve on the downward-sloping money demand curve. Only at interest rate r^* is the quantity of money in circulation (the money supply) equal to the quantity of money demanded. To understand why r^* is an equilibrium, we need to ask what adjustments would take place if the interest rate were not r^*.

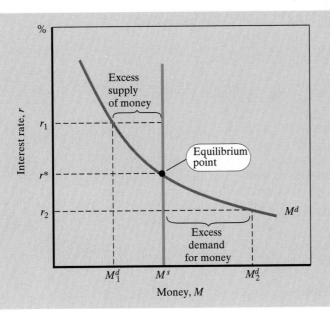

FIGURE 27.6

Adjustments in the Money Market

Equilibrium exists in the money market when the supply of money is equal to the demand for money: $M^d = M^s$. At r_1, the quantity of money supplied exceeds the quantity of money demanded, and the interest rate will fall. At r_2, the quantity demanded exceeds the quantity supplied, and the interest rate will rise. Only at r^* is equilibrium achieved.

To understand the adjustment mechanism, keep in mind that borrowing and lending is a continuous process. The Treasury sells U.S. government securities (bonds) more or less continuously to finance the deficit. When it does, it is borrowing, and must pay interest to attract bond buyers. Buyers of government bonds are, in essence, lending money to the government, just as buyers of corporate bonds are lending money to corporations that wish to finance investment projects.

Consider first r_1 in Figure 27.6. At r_1, the quantity of money demanded is M_1^d, and the quantity of money supplied exceeds the quantity of money demanded. This means there is more money in circulation than households and firms want to hold. At r_1, firms and households will attempt to reduce their money holdings by buying bonds. When there is money in circulation looking for a way to earn interest—when demand for bonds is high—those looking to borrow money by selling bonds will find that they can do so at a lower interest rate.

If the interest rate is initially high enough to create an excess supply of money, the interest rate will immediately fall, discouraging people from moving out of money and into bonds.

Now consider r_2, where the quantity of money demanded (M_2^d) exceeds the supply of money currently in circulation—households and firms do not have enough money on hand to facilitate ordinary transactions. They will try to adjust their holdings by shifting assets out of bonds and into their checking accounts. At the same time, the continuous flow of new bonds being issued must also be absorbed. The Treasury and corporations can sell bonds in an environment where people are adjusting their asset holdings to shift *out* of bonds only by offering a higher interest rate to the people who buy them.

If the interest rate is initially low enough to create an excess demand for money, the interest rate will immediately rise, discouraging people from moving out of bonds and into money.

FIGURE 27.7

The Effect of an Increase in the Supply of Money on the Interest Rate

An increase in the supply of money from M_0^s to M_1^s lowers the rate of interest from 14 percent to 7 percent.

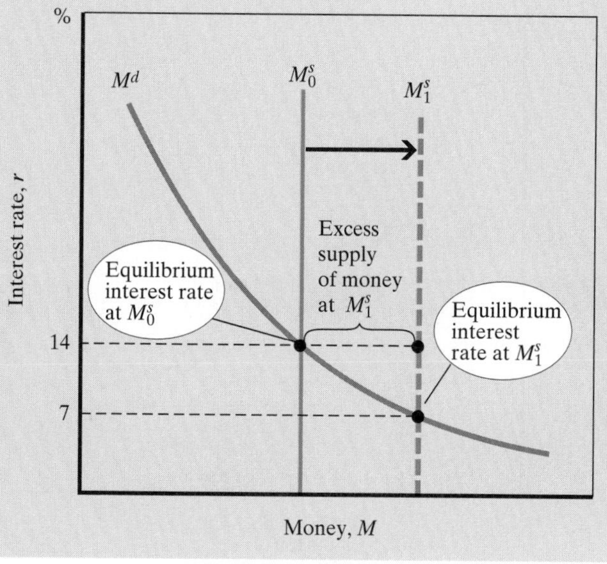

CHANGING THE MONEY SUPPLY TO AFFECT THE INTEREST RATE

With an understanding of equilibrium in the money market, we can now see how the Federal Reserve can affect the interest rate. Suppose the current interest rate is 14 percent and the Fed wants to reduce the interest rate. To do so, it would expand the money supply. Figure 27.7 shows how such an expansion would work. To expand M^s, the Fed can reduce the reserve requirement, cut the discount rate, or buy U.S. government securities on the open market. All of these practices expand the quantity of reserves in the system. Banks can make more loans, and the money supply expands. (Review chapter 26 if you are unsure why.) In Figure 27.7, the initial money supply curve, M_0^s, shifts to the right, to M_1^s.

At the 14 percent interest rate there is an excess supply of money. This immediately puts downward pressure on the interest rate as households and firms try to buy bonds with their money to earn that high interest rate. As this happens, the interest rate falls, and it will continue to fall until it reaches the new equilibrium interest rate of 7 percent. At this point, $M_1^s = M^d$, and the market is in equilibrium.

If the Fed wanted to drive the interest rate *up,* it would contract the money supply. It could do so by increasing the reserve requirement, by raising the discount rate, or by selling U.S. government securities in the open market. Whichever tool the Fed chooses, the result would be lower reserves and a lower supply of money. M_0^s in Figure 27.7 would shift to the left, and the equilibrium interest rate would rise. (As an exercise, draw a graph of this situation.)

INCREASES IN Y AND SHIFTS IN THE MONEY DEMAND CURVE

Changes in the supply of money are not the only factors that influence the equilibrium interest rate. Shifts in money demand can do the same thing.

Recall that the demand for money depends on both the interest rate and the volume of transactions. As a rough measure of the volume of transactions, we use Y, the level of aggregate output (income). Remember that the relationship between money demand and Y is positive—increases in Y mean a higher level of real economic activity. More is being produced, income is higher, and there are more transactions in the economy.

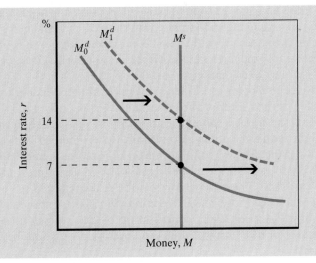

FIGURE 27.8

The Effect of an Increase in Income on the Interest Rate

An increase in aggregate output (income) shifts the money demand curve from M_0^d to M_1^d, which raises the equilibrium interest rate from 7 percent to 14 percent.

Consequently, the demand for money on the part of firms and households in aggregate is higher.

> An increase in Y shifts the money demand curve to the right.

Figure 27.8 illustrates such a shift. Y increases, causing money demand to shift from M_0^d to M_1^d. The result is an increase in the equilibrium level of the interest rate from 7 percent to 14 percent. A decrease in Y would shift M^d to the left, and the equilibrium interest rate would fall.

The money demand curve also shifts when the price level changes. If the price level rises, the money demand curve shifts to the right, because people need more money to engage in their day-to-day transactions. With the quantity of money supplied unchanged, however, the interest rate must rise to reduce the quantity of money demanded to the unchanged quantity of money supplied—a movement *along* the money demand curve.

> An increase in the price level is like an increase in Y in that both events increase the demand for money. The result is an increase in the equilibrium interest rate.

If the price level *falls*, the money demand curve shifts to the left, because people need less money for their transactions. But with the quantity of money supplied unchanged, the interest rate must fall to increase the quantity of money demanded to the unchanged quantity of money supplied.

> A decrease in the price level leads to a decrease in the equilibrium interest rate.

We explore this relationship in more detail in chapter 29.

LOOKING AHEAD: THE FED AND MONETARY POLICY

We now know that the Fed can change the interest rate by changing the quantity of money supplied. If the Fed increases the quantity of money, the interest rate falls; if it decreases the quantity of money, the interest rate rises.

But we have not yet said *why* the Fed might want to change the interest rate or what happens to the economy when the interest rate changes. We have hinted at why:

A low interest rate stimulates spending, particularly investment; a high interest rate reduces spending. By changing the interest rate the Fed can change aggregate output (income). In the next chapter, we will combine our discussions of the goods and money markets and discuss how the interest rate affects the equilibrium level of aggregate output (income) (Y) in the goods market.

The Fed's use of its power to influence events in the goods market, as well as in the money market, is the center of the government's monetary policy. When the Fed moves to contract the money supply in an effort to restrain the economy, economists call it a **tight monetary policy**. Conversely, when the Fed stimulates the economy by expanding the money supply, it has an **easy monetary policy**. The Fed moved aggressively to expand the money supply and lower interest rates in 1975, in 1982, and early in 1991. These easy money policies contributed to economic recovery from the recessions of those years. Tight money policies caused aggregate spending to decline in 1974 and 1981, contributing to the recessions of those years. During the summer of 1981, tight money helped to push some key interest rates above 20 percent!

From the end of the recession in 1991 through 1997, the U.S. economy experienced steady growth with no signs of inflation. During the spring of 1994, the Fed raised rates to slow an accelerating economy because of inflation worries. During 1995, the economy slowed down but growth resumed in 1996 and 1997. By 1997, the economy had grown so much that the Fed was worried about a labor shortage. A labor shortage could trigger inflation if wages rise. But by the end of 1997, the Fed had not acted to raise rates.

We will discuss the way in which the economy affects the Fed's behavior in chapter 31. In that chapter, we'll also discuss some of the Fed's recent policies in more detail and examine the effects of these policies on the economy.

tight monetary policy *Fed policies that contract the money supply in an effort to restrain the economy.*

easy monetary policy *Fed policies that expand the money supply in an effort to stimulate the economy.*

SUMMARY

1. *Interest* is the fee a borrower pays to a lender for the use of his or her funds. The *interest rate* is the annual interest payment on a loan expressed as a percentage of the loan; it is equal to the amount of interest received per year divided by the amount of the loan. Although there are many different interest rates in the United States, we assume there is only one interest rate in the economy. This simplifies our analysis but still provides a tool for understanding how the various parts of the macroeconomy relate to each other.

THE DEMAND FOR MONEY

2. The demand for money depends negatively on the interest rate. The higher the interest rate, the higher the opportunity cost (more interest forgone) from holding money, and the less money people will want to hold. An increase in the interest rate reduces the demand for money, and the money demand curve slopes downward.

3. The volume of transactions in the economy affects money demand. The total dollar volume of transactions depends on both the total number of transactions and the average transaction amount.

4. A reasonable measure of the number of transactions in the economy is aggregate output (income) (Y). When Y rises, there is more economic activity, more is being produced and sold, and more people are on payrolls—there are more transactions in the economy. An increase in Y causes the money demand curve to shift to the right. This follows because households and firms need more money when they are engaging in more transactions. A decrease in Y causes the money demand curve to shift left.

5. Changes in the price level affect the average dollar amount of each transaction. *Increases* in the price level will increase the demand for money (shift the money demand curve to the right) because households and firms will need more money for their expenditures. *Decreases* in the price level will decrease the demand for money (shift the money demand curve to the left).

THE EQUILIBRIUM INTEREST RATE

6. The point at which the quantity of money supplied equals the quantity of money demanded determines the equilibrium interest rate in the economy. An excess supply of

money will cause households and firms to buy more bonds, driving the interest rate down. An excess demand for money will cause households and firms to move out of bonds, driving the interest rate up.

7. The Fed can affect the equilibrium interest rate by changing the supply of money using one of its three tools—the required reserve ratio, the discount rate, or open market operations.

8. An increase in the price level is like an increase in Y in that both events cause an increase in money demand. The result

is an increase in the equilibrium interest rate. A decrease in the price level leads to reduced money demand and a decrease in the equilibrium interest rate.

9. *Tight monetary policy* refers to Fed policies that contract the money supply in an effort to restrain the economy. *Easy monetary policy* refers to Fed policies that expand the money supply in an effort to stimulate the economy. The Fed chooses between these two types of policies for different reasons at different times.

REVIEW TERMS AND CONCEPTS

easy monetary policy, 648
interest, 635
interest rate, 635

monetary policy, 635
nonsynchronization of income and
    spending, 636

speculation motive, 640
tight monetary policy, 648
transaction motive, 636

PROBLEM SET

1. During the fall of 1997, a debate was going on among the members of the Board of Governors of the Federal Reserve. One view: The economy was growing too rapidly and labor was in such short supply that wages were bound to rise, pushing up prices with them. This view argued for the Fed to make a "preemptive strike" against inflation by raising interest rates. The alternative view: The economic turmoil taking place in Asia and a downturn in the stock market in late 1997 would slow the economy enough and a preemptive strike was not needed. How explicitly does the Fed go about raising and lowering rates? In what ways would raising rates slow the economy?

2. At the beginning of 1998, interest rates in Japan were very low. However, households believed interest rates were likely to rise eventually. This implies that the quantity of money demanded in Japan at the beginning of 1998 was quite high. Using the concepts of speculative motive and transaction motive for money, explain why.

3. During the fourth quarter of 1993, real GDP in the United States grew at an annual rate of over 7 percent. During 1994, the economy continued to expand with modest inflation (Y rose at a rate of 4 percent and P increased about 3 percent). At the beginning of 1994, the prime interest rate (the interest rate that banks offer their best, least risky customers) stood at 6 percent, where it remained for over a year. By the beginning of 1995, the prime rate had increased to over 8.5 percent.
   a. Using money supply and money demand curves, show the effects of the increase in Y and P on interest rates assuming *no change* in the money supply.

   b. On a separate graph, show that the interest rate can rise even if the Federal Reserve expands the money supply as long as it does so more slowly than money demand is increasing.

4. Illustrate the following situations using supply and demand curves for money:
   a. The Fed buys bonds in the open market during a recession.
   b. During a period of rapid inflation, the Federal Reserve increases the reserve requirement.
   c. The Fed acts to hold interest rates constant during a period of high inflation.
   d. During a period of no growth in GDP and zero inflation, the Fed lowers the discount rate.
   e. During a period of rapid real growth of GDP, the Fed acts to increase the reserve requirement.

5. During a recession, interest rates may fall even if the Fed takes no action to expand the money supply. Why? Use a graph to explain.

6. During the summer of 1997, the Congress and the president agreed on a budget package to balance the federal budget. The "deal," signed into law by President Clinton in August as the Taxpayer Relief Act of 1997, contained substantial tax cuts and expenditure reductions. The tax reductions were scheduled to take effect immediately, however, while the expenditure cuts mostly come in the years 1999 to 2002. Thus, in 1998, the package was seen by economists to be mildly expansionary. If the result is an increase in the growth of real output/income, what would you expect to happen to interest rates if the Fed holds the money supply (or the rate of growth of the money supply)

constant? What would the Fed do if it wanted to raise interest rates? What if it wanted to lower interest rates? Illustrate with graphs.

7. The demand for money in a country is given by

$$M^d = 10,000 - 10,000r + Y,$$

where M^d is money demand in dollars, r is the interest rate (a 10 percent interest rate means $r = 0.1$), and Y is national income. Assume Y is initially 5,000.

a. Graph the amount of money demanded (on the horizontal axis) against the interest rate (on the vertical axis).

b. Suppose the money supply (M^s) is set by the Central Bank at $10,000. On the same graph you drew for part a., add the money supply curve. What is the equilibrium rate of interest? Explain how you arrived at your answer.

c. Suppose income rises from $Y = 5,000$ to $Y = 7,500$. What happens to the money demand curve you drew in part a? Draw the new curve, if there is one. What happens to the equilibrium interest rate if the Central Bank doesn't change the supply of money?

d. If the Central Bank wants to keep the equilibrium interest rate at the same value as it was in part b., by how much should it increase or decrease the supply of money, given the new level of national income?

e. Suppose the shift in part b. has occurred, and the money supply remains at $10,000, but there is no observed change in the interest rate. What might have happened that could explain this?

TAKE IT TO THE NET

We invite you to visit the Case and Fair page on the Prentice Hall Web site:

http://www.prenhall.com/casefair

for this chapter's World Wide Web exercise.

APPENDIX A TO CHAPTER 27

THE VARIOUS INTEREST RATES IN THE U.S. ECONOMY

Although there are many different interest rates in the economy, they tend to move up or down with one another. Here, we discuss some of their differences. We will first discuss the relationship between interest rates on securities with different *maturities*, or terms. We then discuss briefly some of the main interest rates in the U.S. economy.

THE TERM STRUCTURE OF INTEREST RATES

The *term structure of interest rates* is the relationship between the interest rates offered on securities of different maturities. The key here is understanding things like: How are these different rates related? Does a two-year security (an IOU that promises to repay principal, plus interest, after two years) pay a lower annual rate than a one-year security (an IOU to be repaid, with interest, after one year)? What happens to the rate of interest offered on one-year securities if the rate of interest on two-year securities increases?

Assume you want to invest some money for two years and at the end of the two years you want it back. Assume you want to buy government securities. For this analysis, we restrict your choices to two: (1) You can buy a two-year security today and hold it for two years, at which time you cash it in (we will assume that the interest rate on the two-year security is 9 percent per year), or (2) you can buy a one-year security today. At the end of one year, you must cash this security in; you can then buy another one-year security. At the end of the second year, you will cash in the second security. Assume the interest rate on the first one-year security is 8 percent.

Which would you prefer? Currently, you don't have enough data to answer this question. To consider choice 2 sensibly, you need to know the interest rate on the one-year security that you intend to buy in the second year. This rate will not be known until the second year. All you know now is the rate on the two-year security and the rate on the current one-year security. To decide what to do, you must form an *expectation* of the rate on the one-year security a year from now. If you expect the one-year rate (8 percent) to remain the same in the second year, you should buy the two-year security. You would earn 9 percent per year on the two-year security but only 8 percent per year on the two one-year securities. If you expect the one-year rate to rise to 12 percent a year from now, you should make the second choice. You would earn 8 percent in the first year, and you expect to earn 12 percent in the second year. The expected rate of return over the two years is about 10 percent, which is better than the 9 percent you can get on the two-year security. If you expected the one-year rate a year from now to be 10 percent, it would not matter very much which of the two choices you made. The rate of return over the two-year period would be roughly 9 percent for both choices.

We now alter the focus of our discussion to get to the topic we are really interested in—how the two-year rate is determined. Assume the one-year rate has been set by the Fed and it is 8 percent. Also assume that people expect the one-year rate a year from now to be 10 percent. What is the two-year rate? According to a theory called the *expectations theory of the term structure of interest rates*, the two-year rate is equal to the average of the current one-year rate and the one-year rate expected a year from now. In this example, the two-year rate would be 9 percent (the average of 8 percent and 10 percent).

If the two-year rate were lower than the average of the two one-year rates, people would not be indifferent as to which security they held. They would want to hold only the short-term, one-year securities. To find a buyer for a two-year security, the seller would be forced to increase the interest rate it offers on the two-year security until it is equal to the average of the current one-year rate and the expected one-year rate for next year. The interest rate on the two-year security will continue to rise until people are once again indifferent between one two-year security and two one-year securities.[1]

Let's now return to Fed behavior. We know the Fed can affect the short-term interest rate by changing the money supply. But does it also affect long-term interest rates? The answer is "somewhat." Because the two-year rate is an average of the current one-year rate and the expected one-year rate a year from now, the Fed influences the two-year rate to the extent that it influences the current one-year rate. The same holds for three-year rates and beyond. The current short-term rate is a means by which the Fed can influence longer-term rates.

In addition, Fed behavior may directly affect people's expectations of the future short-term rates, which will then affect long-term rates. If the chair of the Federal Reserve testifies before Congress that he or she is thinking about raising short-term interest rates, people's expectations of

---

[1]For longer terms, additional future rates must be averaged in. For a three-year security, for example, the expected one-year rate a year from now and the expected one-year rate two years from now are added to the current one-year rate and averaged.

higher future short-term interest rates are likely to increase. These expectations will then be reflected in current long-term interest rates.

TYPES OF INTEREST RATES

The following are some widely followed interest rates in the United States.

Three-Month Treasury Bill Rate

Government securities that mature in less than a year are called *Treasury bills*, or sometimes *T bills*. The interest rate on three-month Treasury bills is probably the most widely followed short-term interest rate.

Government Bond Rate

Government securities with terms of one year or more are called *government bonds*. There are 1-year bonds, 2-year bonds, and so on up to 30-year bonds. Bonds of different terms have different interest rates. The relationship among the interest rates on the various maturities is the term structure of interest rates that we discussed in the first part of this appendix.

Federal Funds Rate

Banks borrow not only from the Fed but also from each other. If one bank has excess reserves, it can lend some of those reserves to other banks through the federal funds market. The interest rate in this market is called the *federal funds rate*—the rate banks are charged to borrow reserves from other banks.

The federal funds market is really a desk in New York City. From all over the country, banks with excess reserves to lend and banks in need of reserves call the desk and negotiate a rate of interest. Account balances with the Fed are changed for the period of the loan without any physical movement of money.

This borrowing and lending, which takes place near the close of each working day, is generally for one day ("overnight"), so the federal funds rate is a one-day rate. It is the rate that the Fed controls most closely through its open market operations.

Commercial Paper Rate

Firms have several alternatives for raising funds. They can sell stocks, issue bonds, or borrow from a bank. Large firms can also borrow directly from the public by issuing "commercial paper," which are essentially short-term corporate IOUs that offer a designated rate of interest. The interest rate offered on commercial paper depends on the financial condition of the firm and the maturity date of the IOU.

Prime Rate

Banks charge different interest rates to different customers. You would expect to pay a higher interest rate for a car loan than General Motors would pay for a $1 million loan to finance investment. Also, you would pay more interest for an unsecured loan, a "personal" loan, than for one that was secured by some asset, such as a house or car, to be used as collateral.

The *prime rate* is a benchmark that banks often use in quoting interest rates to their customers. A very low risk corporation might be able to borrow at (or even below) the prime rate. A less well known firm might be quoted a rate of "prime plus three-fourths," which means that if the prime rate is say, 10 percent, the firm would have to pay interest of 10.75 percent. The prime rate depends on the cost of funds to the bank, it moves up and down with changes in the economy.

AAA Corporate Bond Rate

Corporations finance much of their investment by selling bonds to the public. Corporate bonds are classified by various bond dealers according to their risk. Bonds issued by General Motors are in less risk of default than bonds issued by a new, risky biotech research firm. Bonds differ from commercial paper in one important way: Bonds have a longer maturity.

Bonds are graded in much the same way students are. The highest grade is AAA, the next highest AA, and so on. The interest rate on bonds rated AAA is the *triple A corporate bond rate*, the rate that the least risky firms pay on the bonds that they issue.

PROBLEM SET

1. The following table gives three key U.S. interest rates in 1980 and again in April 1993:

	1980	1993
Three-month U.S. government bills	11.39%	2.92%
Long-term U.S. government bonds	10.81%	6.85%
Prime rate	15.26%	6.00%

Can you give an explanation for the extreme differences that you see? Specifically, comment on: (1) the fact that rates in 1980 were much higher than in 1993, and (2) the long-term rate was higher than the short-term rate in 1993 but lower in 1980.

THE DEMAND FOR MONEY: A NUMERICAL EXAMPLE

This appendix presents a numerical example showing how optimal money management behavior can be derived.

We have seen that the interest rate represents the opportunity cost of holding funds in non-interest-bearing checking accounts (as opposed to bonds, which yield interest). We have also seen that there are costs involved in switching from bonds to money. Given these costs, our objective is to determine the optimum amount of money for an individual to hold. The optimal average level of money holdings is the amount that maximizes the profits from money management. Interest is earned on average bond holdings, but the cost per switch multiplied by the number of switches must be subtracted from interest revenue to obtain the net profit from money management.

Suppose the interest rate is .05 (5 percent), it costs $2 each time a bond is sold,[1] and the proceeds from the sale are deposited in one's checking account. Suppose also that the individual's income is $1,200 and that this income is spent evenly throughout the period. This situation is depicted in the top half of Table 27B.1. The optimum value for average money holdings is the value that achieves the largest possible profit in column 6 of the table. When the interest rate is 5 percent, the optimum average money holdings are $150 (which means the individual makes three switches from bonds to money).

In the bottom half of Table 27B.1, the same calculations are performed for an interest rate of 3 percent rather than 5 percent. In this case, the optimum average money holding is $200 (which means the person/household makes two switches from bonds to money rather than three). The lower interest rate has led to an increase in the optimum average money holdings. Under the assumption that people behave optimally, the demand for money is a negative function of the interest rate: The lower the rate, the more money on average is held, and the higher the rate, the less money on average is held.

---

[1]In this example we will assume that the $2 cost does not apply to the original purchase of bonds.

TABLE 27B.1 OPTIMUM MONEY HOLDINGS

1 NUMBER OF SWITCHES[1]	2 AVERAGE MONEY HOLDINGS[2]	3 AVERAGE BOND HOLDINGS[3]	4 INTEREST EARNED[4]	5 COST OF SWITCHING[5]	6 NET PROFIT[6]
		r = 5 percent			
0	$600.00	$ 0.00	$ 0.00	$0.00	$ 0.00
1	300.00	300.00	15.00	2.00	13.00
2	200.00	400.00	20.00	4.00	16.00
3	150.00*	450.00	22.50	6.00	16.50
4	120.00	480.00	24.00	8.00	16.00

Assumptions: Interest rate *r* = 0.05. Cost of switching from bonds into money equals $2 per transaction.

		r = 3 percent			
0	$600.00	$ 0.00	$ 0.00	$0.00	$ 0.00
1	300.00	300.00	9.00	2.00	7.00
2	200.00*	400.00	12.00	4.00	8.00
3	150.00	450.00	13.50	6.00	7.50
4	120.00	480.00	14.40	8.00	6.40

Assumptions: Interest rate *r* = 0.03. Cost of switching from bonds into money equals $2 per transaction.

*Optimum money holdings.   [1]That is, the number of times you sell a bond.   [2]Calculated as 600/(col. 1 + 1).   [3]Calculated as 600 − col. 2. [4]Calculated as r × col. 3, where r is the interest rate.   [5]Calculated as t × col. 1, where t is the cost per switch ($2).   [6]Calculated as col. 4 − col. 5.

PROBLEM SET

1. Sherman Peabody earns a monthly salary of $1,500, which he receives at the beginning of each month. He spends the entire amount each month, at the rate of $50 per day. (Assume 30 days in a month.) The interest rate paid on bonds is 10 percent per month. It costs $4 every time Peabody sells a bond.

   a. Describe briefly how Mr. Peabody should decide how much money to hold.

   b. Calculate Peabody's optimal money holdings. (*Hint:* It may help to formulate a table such as the one in this appendix. You can round to the nearest $.50, and you need to consider only average money holdings of more than $100.)

   c. Suppose the interest rate rises to 15 percent. Find Peabody's optimal money holdings at this new interest rate. What would happen if the interest rate increases to 20 percent?

   d. Graph your answers to b. and c. with the interest rate on the vertical axis and the amount of money demanded on the horizontal axis. Explain why your graph slopes downward.

LOCAL CURRENCIES: A DO-IT-YOURSELF GUIDE TO MAKING MONEY

When governments finance spending by printing money, economists call it *seigniorage*. If you were to do the same thing it would be called counterfeiting, right? Not necessarily. It depends on how you do it.

In Unity, Maine, Gary Robb has been printing currency for the residents of Waldo County since 1995 using a system pioneered in Ithaca, New York, in 1991. In fact, dozens of communities around the country are experimenting with alternative currency schemes designed as a means of payment for goods and services. And it's perfectly legal! IRS and Federal Reserve officials say that there is nothing illegal about local currency, provided that it does not look like a Federal Reserve note, comes in denominations of at least $1.00, and is treated as taxable income.

There's really nothing new about local currencies. Before the Civil War, different currencies were issued by local banks. The National Bank Act of 1863 established a single currency via the charter of "national banks," which were privately owned commercial banks with the authority to create a limited amount of national bank notes. In 1914 the U.S. banking system as we now know it was established and Federal Reserve notes were introduced to end the currency confusion and facilitate transactions throughout the country.

Today, local currencies, like the Ithaca HOURS currency, function as an extension of a barter economy designed to support local businesses and nonprofit organizations and help foster a sense of community (see Figure 1).

Here's how the Ithaca HOURS system works. One Ithaca HOUR is worth $10—roughly equal to the average hourly wage in Tompkins

FIGURE 1

Ithaca HOURS Currency

Source: Courtesy Paul Glover, Ithaca HOURS.

County, New York. The currency comes in five different denominations, ranging from one-eighth of an HOUR to two HOURS, and is printed using multicolored ink on a variety of different papers, including paper made from cattail and hemp. It is protected by law from counterfeiting.

Ithaca HOURS are used to buy just about every sort of good or service, including bicycles, attorney services, groceries, movie theater tickets, eyeglasses, and chiropractic and nursing care. Over $62,000 worth of Ithaca HOURS are in circulation today. Hundreds of local merchants and service providers accept HOURS as a means of payment. There's even a local, federally charted credit union that provides interest-free HOUR loans, provides HOUR grants for new businesses, and accepts HOURS for mortgage and loan fees.

However, Ithaca HOURS have no value outside Ithaca, and businesses often take HOURS as only partial payment for a purchase, the other part in U.S. dollars, to be able to pay out-of-town suppliers. Banks and national brand chain stores generally don't accept them at all.

The supply of HOURS is overseen by an advisory board that meets regularly. Worn out HOURS are replaced and new HOURS are issued in exchange for $10 in Federal Reserve notes. A writer named Paul Glover started the system by getting 90 merchants and service providers to agree to accept Ithaca HOURS in exchange for a listing in a barter directory entitled *HOUR Town* and two Ithaca HOURS, worth $20. Every eight months, merchants and individuals listed in *HOUR Town* may apply for an additional HOUR as compensation for continued participation in the system. In this way the advisory board controls the growth in the supply of HOURS. Today over 1,500 listings make *HOUR Town* a rough equivalent of the Yellow Pages of the local phone directory.

Questions for Analytical Thinking

1. Why do you think Paul Glover set the value of an Ithaca HOUR equal to the average hourly wage in Tompkins County?

2. Does an Ithaca HOUR possess all three properties of money: unit of account; store of value; and medium of exchange? What if the Ithaca HOUR is owned by a student at Ithaca College and she takes it with her to Orlando, Florida, for spring break?

3. Why must the currency advisory board in Ithaca control the growth of the supply of Ithaca HOURS?

4. What difficulties might you confront if you tried to establish an Ithaca HOURS monetary system in your town or on your college campus?

Sources: Ellen Grahm, "Community Groups Print Local (and Legal) Currencies," *The Wall Street Journal*, June 27, 1996; Adam Corrigan, "Dealing for Hours," *Bangor Daily News*, Bangor, Maine, November 19, 1996; Lewis Solomon, *Rethinking Our Centralized Monetary System: The Case for Local Currency*, (New York: Praeger, 1996); Internet Web site: *http://www.lightlink.com/hours/ithacahours/index.html*.

Chapter
28

MONEY, THE INTEREST RATE, AND OUTPUT: ANALYSIS AND POLICY

goods market *The market in which goods and services are exchanged and in which the equilibrium level of aggregate output is determined.*

money market *The market in which financial instruments are exchanged and in which the equilibrium level of the interest rate is determined.*

IN CHAPTERS 24 and 25, we discussed the market for goods and services—the **goods market**—without mentioning money, the money market, or the interest rate. We described how the equilibrium level of aggregate output (income) (Y) is determined in the goods market. At given levels of planned investment spending (I), government spending (G), and net taxes (T), we were able to determine the equilibrium level of output in the economy.

In chapters 26 and 27, we discussed the financial market, or **money market**, barely referring to the goods market, as we explained how the equilibrium level of the interest rate is determined in the money market.

The goods market and the money market do not operate independently, however. Events in the money market affect what goes on in the goods market, and events in the goods market affect what goes on in the money market. Only by analyzing the two markets together can we determine the values of aggregate output (income) (Y) and the interest rate (r) that are consistent with the existence of equilibrium in *both* markets.

Looking at both markets simultaneously also reveals how fiscal policy affects the money market and how monetary policy affects the goods market. This is what we'll do in this chapter. By establishing how the two markets affect each other, we will show how open market purchases of government securities (which expand the money supply) affect the equilibrium level of national output and income. Similarly, we will show how fiscal policy measures (such as tax cuts) affect interest rates and investment spending.

THE LINKS BETWEEN THE GOODS MARKET AND THE MONEY MARKET

There are two key *links* between the goods market and the money market.

▶ **Link 1: Income and the Demand for Money** The first link between the goods market and the money market exists because the demand for money depends on income. As aggregate output (income) (Y) increases, the number of transactions requiring the use of money increases. (You just saw this in chapter 27.) An increase in output, with the interest rate held constant, leads to an increase in money demand.

> Income, which is determined in the goods market, has considerable influence on the demand for money in the money market.

▶ **Link 2: Planned Investment Spending and the Interest Rate**   The second link between the goods market and the money market exists because planned investment spending (I) depends on the interest rate (r). In chapters 24 and 25 we assumed that planned investment spending is fixed at a certain level, but we did so only to simplify that discussion. In practice, investment is not fixed. Rather, it depends on a number of key economic variables. One is the interest rate. The higher the interest rate, the lower the level of planned investment spending.

> The interest rate, which is determined in the money market, has significant effects on planned investment in the goods market.

INVESTMENT, THE INTEREST RATE, AND THE GOODS MARKET

It should come as no surprise that the relationship between the level of planned investment and the interest rate is negative.

> When the interest rate falls, planned investment rises.
> When the interest rate rises, planned investment falls.

To see why, recall that *investment* refers to the purchase of new capital—new machines and plants. Whether a firm decides to invest in a project depends on whether the expected profits from the project justify its costs. Usually, a big cost of an investment project is the interest cost.

Consider a firm opening a new plant, or the investment required to open a new ice-cream store. When a manufacturing firm builds a new plant, the contractor must be paid at the time the plant is built. When an entrepreneur decides to open a new ice-cream parlor, she needs freezers, tables, chairs, light fixtures, and signs. These too must be paid for when they are installed.

The money needed to carry out such projects is generally borrowed and paid back over an extended period. The real cost of an investment project depends in part on the interest rate—the cost of borrowing. When the interest rate rises, it becomes more expensive to borrow, and fewer projects are likely to be undertaken; increasing the interest rate, *ceteris paribus*, is likely to reduce the level of planned investment spending. When the interest rate falls, it becomes less costly to borrow, and more investment projects are likely to be undertaken; reducing the interest rate, *ceteris paribus*, is likely to increase the level of planned investment spending.

The relationship between the interest rate and planned investment is illustrated by the downward-sloping demand curve in Figure 28.1. The higher the interest rate, the lower the level of planned investment. At an interest rate of 3 percent, planned investment is I_0. When the interest rate rises from 3 percent to 6 percent, planned investment falls from I_0 to I_1. As the interest rate falls, however, more projects become profitable, so more investment is undertaken.

We can now use the fact that planned investment depends on the interest rate to consider how this relationship affects planned aggregate expenditure (AE). Recall that

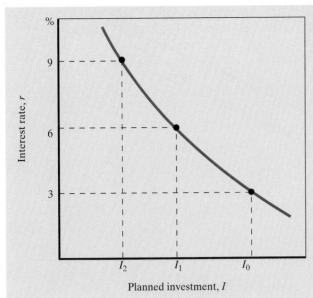

FIGURE 28.1

Planned Investment Schedule

Planned investment spending is a negative function of the interest rate.

planned aggregate expenditure is the sum of consumption, planned investment, and government purchases.[1] That is,

$$AE \equiv C + I + G$$

We now know that there are actually many possible levels of I, each corresponding to a different interest rate (as illustrated in Figure 13.1). When the interest rate changes, planned investment changes. Therefore, a change in the interest rate (r) will lead to a change in total planned spending ($C + I + G$) as well.[2]

Figure 28.2 shows what happens to planned aggregate expenditure when the interest rate rises from 3 percent to 6 percent. At the higher interest rate, planned investment is lower; planned aggregate expenditure thus shifts *downward*. Recall from chapters 24 and 25: A fall in any component of aggregate spending has an even larger (or "multiplier") effect on equilibrium income (Y). When the interest rate rises, planned investment (and planned aggregate expenditure) falls, and equilibrium output (income) falls by even more than the fall in planned investment. In Figure 28.2, equilibrium Y falls from Y_0 to Y_1 when the interest rate rises from 3 percent to 6 percent.

We can summarize the effects of a change in the interest rate on the equilibrium level of output:

The Effects of a Change in the Interest Rate:	■ A high interest rate (r) discourages planned investment (I).
	■ Planned investment is a part of planned aggregate expenditure (AE).
	■ Thus, when the interest rate rises, planned aggregate expenditure (AE) at every level of income falls.
	■ Finally, a decrease in planned aggregate expenditure lowers equilibrium output (income) (Y) by a multiple of the initial decrease in planned investment.

---

[1]As we saw in chapter 25, planned aggregate expenditure also includes net exports ($EX - IM$). The impact of adding exports and imports to our analysis is complex and will be discussed in chapter 36. For now, we are assuming that net exports are zero.

[2]When we look at the behavior of households in the macroeconomy in detail in chapter 32, you will see that consumption spending (C) is also stimulated by lower interest rates and discouraged by higher interest rates.

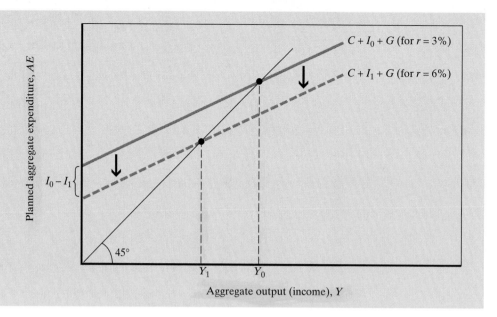

FIGURE 28.2

The Effect of an Interest Rate Increase on Planned Aggregate Expenditure

An increase in the interest rate from 3 percent to 6 percent lowers planned aggregate expenditure and thus reduces equilibrium income from Y_0 to Y_1.

Using a convenient shorthand:

$$r\uparrow \rightarrow I\downarrow \rightarrow AE\downarrow \rightarrow Y\downarrow$$

$$r\downarrow \rightarrow I\uparrow \rightarrow AE\uparrow \rightarrow Y\uparrow$$

As you see, the equilibrium level of output (Y) is not determined solely by events in the goods market, as we assumed in our earlier simplified discussions. The reason is that the money market affects the level of the interest rate, which then affects planned investment in the goods market. There is a different equilibrium level of Y for every possible level of the interest rate (r). The final level of equilibrium Y depends on what the interest rate turns out to be, which depends on events in the money market.

MONEY DEMAND, AGGREGATE OUTPUT (INCOME), AND THE MONEY MARKET

We have just seen how the interest rate—which is determined in the money market—influences the level of planned investment spending and thus the goods market. Now let's look at the other half of the story: the ways in which the goods market affects the money market.

In chapter 27, we explored the demand for money by households and firms and explained why the demand for money depends negatively on the interest rate. An increase in the interest rate raises the opportunity cost of holding non-interest-bearing money (as compared to interest-bearing bonds), encouraging people to keep more of their funds in bonds and less in checking account balances. The downward-sloping money demand curve (M^d) is shown in Figure 28.3.

We also saw in chapter 27 that the demand for money depends on the level of income in the economy. More income means more transactions, and an increased volume of transactions implies a greater demand for money. With more people earning higher incomes and buying more goods and services, more money will be demanded to meet the increased volume of transactions. An increase in income therefore shifts the money demand curve to the right. (Review Figure 27.5.)

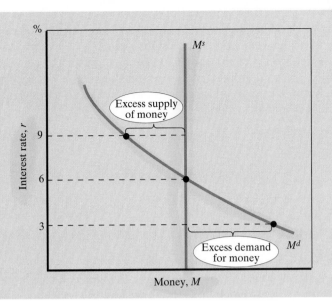

FIGURE 28.3
Equilibrium in the Money Market

If the interest rate were 9 percent, the quantity of money in circulation would exceed the amount households and firms want to hold. The excess money balances would cause the interest rate to drop as people try to shift their funds into interest-bearing bonds. At 3 percent the opposite is true. Excess demand for money balances would push interest rates up. Only at 6 percent would the actual quantity of money in circulation be equal to what the economy wants to hold in money balances.

If, as we are assuming, the Fed's choice of the amount of money to supply does not depend on the interest rate, then the money supply curve is simply a vertical line. The equilibrium interest rate is the point at which the quantity of money demanded equals the quantity of money supplied. This equilibrium is shown at a 6 percent interest rate in Figure 28.3. If the amount of money demanded by households and firms is less than the amount in circulation as determined by the Fed, as it is at an interest rate of 9 percent in Figure 28.3, the interest rate will fall. If the amount of money demanded is greater than the amount in circulation, as it is at an interest rate of 3 percent in Figure 28.3, the interest rate will rise.

Now consider what will happen to the interest rate when there is an increase in aggregate output (income) (Y). This increase in Y will cause the money demand curve to shift to the right. This is illustrated in Figure 28.4, where an increase in income from Y_0 to Y_1 has shifted the money demand curve from M_0^d to M_1^d. At the initial interest rate of 6 percent, there is now excess demand for money, and the interest rate rises from 6 percent to 9 percent.

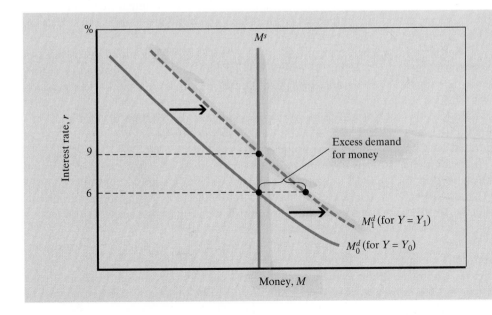

FIGURE 28.4

The Effect of an Increase in Income (Y) on the Interest Rate (r)

An increase in income from Y_0 to Y_1 shifts the M^d curve to the right. With a fixed supply of money, there is now an excess demand for money $(M^d > M^s)$ at the initial interest rate of 6 percent. This causes the interest rate to rise. At an interest rate of 9 percent the money market is again in equilibrium with $M^s = M^d$, but at a higher interest rate than before the increase in income.

The equilibrium level of the interest rate is not determined exclusively in the money market. Changes in aggregate output (income) (Y), which take place in the goods market, shift the money demand curve and cause changes in the interest rate. With a given quantity of money supplied, higher levels of Y will lead to higher equilibrium levels of r. Lower levels of Y will lead to lower equilibrium levels of r. Represented in symbols:

$$Y\uparrow \rightarrow M^d\uparrow \rightarrow r\uparrow$$

$$Y\downarrow \rightarrow M^d\downarrow \rightarrow r\downarrow$$

COMBINING THE GOODS MARKET AND THE MONEY MARKET

Now that we are aware of the links between the goods market and the money market, we can examine the two markets simultaneously. To see how the two markets interact, it will be convenient to consider the effects of changes in fiscal and monetary policy on the economy. We want to examine what happens to the equilibrium levels of aggregate output (income) (Y) and the interest rate (r) when certain key variables—notably government spending (G), net taxes (T), and the money supply (M^s)—increase or decrease.

EXPANSIONARY POLICY EFFECTS

Any government policy aimed at stimulating aggregate output (income) (Y) is said to be expansionary. An **expansionary fiscal policy** is an increase in government spending (G) or a reduction in net taxes (T) aimed at increasing aggregate output (income) (Y). An **expansionary monetary policy** is an increase in the money supply aimed at increasing aggregate output (income) (Y).

▶ **Expansionary Fiscal Policy: An Increase in Government Purchases (G) or Decrease in Net Taxes (T)**   As you know from chapter 25, government purchases (G) and net taxes (T) are the two tools of government fiscal policy. The government can stimulate the economy—that is, it can increase aggregate output (income) (Y)—either by *increasing* government purchases or by *reducing* net taxes. Though the impact of a tax cut is somewhat smaller than the impact of an increase in G, both have a multiplier effect on the equilibrium level of Y.

Consider an increase in government purchases (G) of $10 billion. This increase in expenditure causes firms' inventories to be smaller than planned. Unplanned inventory reductions stimulate production, and firms increase output (Y). But because added output means added income, some of which is subsequently spent, consumption spending (C) also increases. Again, inventories will be smaller than planned and output will rise even further. The final equilibrium level of output is higher by a multiple of the initial increase in government purchases.

This multiplier story is incomplete, however. Until this chapter, we have assumed that planned investment (I) is fixed at a certain level. But we now know that planned investment depends on the interest rate. We can now discuss what happens to the multiplier when investment varies because we now have an understanding of the money market, in which the interest rate is determined.

Return to our multiplier story at the point that firms first begin to raise output in response to an increase in government purchases. As aggregate output (income) (Y) increases, an impact is felt in the money market—the increase in income (Y) increases the demand for money (M^d). (For the moment, assume the Fed holds the quantity of

expansionary fiscal policy *An increase in government spending or a reduction in net taxes aimed at increasing aggregate output (income)* (Y).

expansionary monetary policy *An increase in the money supply aimed at increasing aggregate output (income)* (Y).

FAST FACTS

The countries with the most expansionary fiscal policy (biggest annual government deficit [G − T] as a percentage of GDP) in 1995 were Finland (9%), Greece (14.4%) and Brazil (13.3%). In 1995, Singapore ran a surplus (G < T) equal to 15% of its GDP.

Source: World Bank, *World Development Report, 1997.*

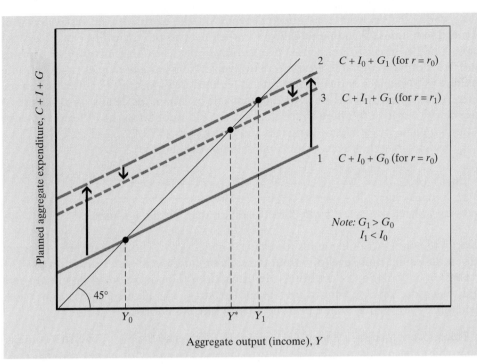

FIGURE 28.5

The Crowding-Out Effect

An increase in government spending G from G_0 to G_1 shifts the planned aggregate expenditure schedule from 1 to 2. The crowding-out effect of the decrease in planned investment (brought about by the increased interest rate) then shifts the planned aggregate expenditure schedule from 2 to 3.

money supplied [M^s] constant.) The resulting disequilibrium, with the quantity of money demanded greater than the quantity of money supplied, causes the interest rate to rise. The increase in G increases both Y and r.

The increase in r has a side effect—a higher interest rate causes planned investment spending (I) to decline. Because planned investment spending is a component of planned aggregate expenditure ($C + I + G$), the decrease in I works against the increase in G. An increase in government spending (G) increases planned aggregate expenditure and increases aggregate output, but a decrease in planned investment reduces planned aggregate expenditure and *decreases* aggregate output.

This tendency for increases in government spending to cause reductions in private investment spending is called the **crowding-out effect**. Without any expansion in the money supply to accommodate the rise in income and increased money demand, planned investment spending is partially crowded out by the higher interest rate. The extra spending created by the rise in government purchases is somewhat offset by the fall in planned investment spending. Income still rises, but the multiplier effect of the rise in G is lessened because of the higher interest rate's negative effect on planned investment.

This crowding-out effect is illustrated graphically in Figure 28.5. An increase in government purchases from G_0 to G_1 shifts the planned aggregate expenditure curve ($C + I_0 + G_0$) upward. The increase in (Y) from Y_0 to Y_1 causes the demand for money to rise, which results in a disequilibrium in the money market. The excess demand for money raises the interest rate (r) from r_0 to r_1, causing I to decrease from I_0 to I_1. The fall in I pulls the planned aggregate expenditure curve back down, which lowers the equilibrium level of income to Y^*. (Remember that equilibrium is achieved when $Y = AE$.)

Note that the size of the crowding-out effect, and the ultimate size of the government spending multiplier, depend on several things. First, we assumed the Fed did not change the quantity of money supplied. If we were to assume instead that the Fed expanded the quantity of money to accommodate the increase in G, the multiplier would be larger. In this case, the higher demand for money would be satisfied with a higher quantity of money supplied, and the interest rate would not rise. Without a higher interest rate, there would be no crowding out.

crowding-out effect *The tendency for increases in government spending to cause reductions in private investment spending.*

interest sensitivity or **insensitivity of planned investment** *The responsiveness of planned investment spending to changes in the interest rate. Interest sensitivity means that planned investment spending changes a great deal in response to changes in the interest rate; interest insensitivity means little or no change in planned investment as a result of changes in the interest rate.*

Second, the crowding-out effect depends on the **sensitivity** or **insensitivity of planned investment** spending to changes in the interest rate. Crowding out occurs because a higher interest rate reduces planned investment spending. Investment depends on factors other than the interest rate, however, and investment may at times be quite insensitive to changes in the interest rate. If planned investment does not fall when the interest rate rises, there is no crowding-out effect. For more details on one type of investment sensitive to interest-rate changes, see the Application box "Lower Interest Rates Stimulate Investment: Mortgages and Housing in 1998."

To summarize the effects of an expansionary fiscal policy:

Effects of an Expansionary Fiscal Policy:	$G\uparrow \rightarrow Y\uparrow \rightarrow M^d\uparrow \rightarrow r\uparrow \rightarrow I\downarrow$ $\rightarrow$ Y increases less than if r did not increase.

Exactly the same reasoning holds for changes in net taxes. The ultimate effect of a tax cut on the equilibrium level of output depends on how the money market reacts. The expansion of Y that a tax cut brings about will lead to an increase in the interest rate and thus a decrease in planned investment spending. The ultimate increase in Y will therefore be less than it would be if the interest rate did not rise.

▶ **Expansionary Monetary Policy: An Increase in the Money Supply** Now let's consider what will happen when the Fed decides to increase the supply of money through open market operations. At first, open market operations inject new reserves into the system and expand the quantity of money supplied (the money supply curve shifts to the right). Because the quantity of money supplied is now greater than the amount households want to hold, the equilibrium rate of interest falls. Planned investment spending (which is a component of planned aggregate expenditure) increases when the interest rate falls.

Increased planned investment spending means planned aggregate expenditure is now greater than aggregate output. Firms experience unplanned decreases in inventories, and they raise output (Y). An increase in the money supply decreases the interest rate and increases Y. However, the higher level of Y increases the demand for money (the demand for money curve shifts to the right), and this keeps the interest rate from falling as far as it otherwise would.

If you review the sequence of events that follows the monetary expansion, you can see the links between the injection of reserves by the Fed into the economy and the increase in output. First, the increase in the quantity of money supplied pushes down the interest rate. Second, the lower interest rate causes planned investment spending to rise. Third, the increased planned investment spending means higher planned aggregate expenditure, which means increased output as firms react to unplanned decreases in inventories. Fourth, the increase in output (income) leads to an increase in the demand for money (the demand for money curve shifts to the right), which means the interest rate decreases less than it would have if the demand for money had not increased.

Effects of an Expansionary Monetary Policy:	$M^s\uparrow \rightarrow r\downarrow \rightarrow I\uparrow \rightarrow Y\uparrow \rightarrow M^d\uparrow$ $\rightarrow$ r decreases less than if M^d did not increase.

The power of monetary policy to affect the goods market depends on how much of a reaction occurs at each link in this chain. Perhaps the most critical link is the link between r and I. Monetary policy can be effective *only* if I reacts to changes in r. If firms sharply increase the number of investment projects undertaken when the interest rate falls, expansionary monetary policy works well at stimulating the economy. If, however, firms are reluctant to invest even at a low interest rate, expansionary monetary policy will have limited success. In other words, the effectiveness of monetary policy depends

LOWER INTEREST RATES STIMULATE INVESTMENT: MORTGAGES AND HOUSING IN 1998

AS MORTGAGE INTEREST RATES GO DOWN, NEW HOME BUILDING PICKS UP.

One component of planned investment spending that is quite sensitive to interest rate changes is investment in housing. Home purchases are generally financed with a mortgage. A mortgage is a long-term loan. Higher mortgage rates increase the cost of buying and owning a home. Between January and December of 1994, the interest rate on 30-year fixed-rate mortgages jumped from 6.75 percent to 9.25 percent, largely as the result of an expanding economy (which was shifting the money demand curve to the right) and an increasingly resistant Fed holding the line on money supply growth. Between 1994 and 1998, rates fell with a few bumps along the way back to 6.75 percent.

Consider the effect of such a reduction in rates on the real monthly cost of a home. A potential buyer considering purchase of a $100,000 home with a 20 percent down payment faces a $658 monthly payment when mortgage rates are 9.25 percent. If interest rates fell to 6.75 percent, the same buyer would face a monthly payment of only $519. The cut in rates has the same effect as a 21 percent decrease in the price of the house!

In addition, falling mortgage rates can stimulate spending by homeowners even if they do not use the opportunity to buy a new house. How? If Sally borrowed money in 1994 to pay for a $100,000 home at 9.25 percent, she could pay off the mortgage in 1998, and "refinance" the loan and reduce her monthly payment to $494. She would

benefit from the fact that some of the loan had been paid off and that the mortgage rate was down to 6.75 percent.

The effects of falling rates are discussed in the following article from the *New York Times*:

Housing starts rose 4.8 percent in June, reversing a decline in the previous month and signaling that demand for homes could rebound as the economy enters the third quarter.

Real estate markets have been bolstered by the highest levels of consumer confidence in the economy in decades, the lowest unemployment rate in a quarter-century and historic gains in the stock market. Home builders, like economists, are optimistic about the housing industry, a survey by the National Association of Home Builders showed.

Mortgage rates have declined steadily since mid-April. The average rate on a 30-year fixed mortgage fell to 7.69 percent in June from 7.93 percent in May.

"With the fall in mortgage rates over the last few weeks, the housing sector will modestly contribute to overall economic growth" in the third quarter, said Stan Shipley, an economist at Merrill Lynch & Company in New York. Mortgage refinancings should also rise, putting more money in consumers' pockets to spend, analysts said.[a]

---

[a]"Builders Start New Homes at Faster Pace," *The New York Times*, July 18, 1997, p. C6. Copyright © 1997 by The New York Times Co. Reprinted by permission.

For more on interest rates and homebuilding, see the Case and Fair Web page at http://www.prenhall.com/casefair.

---

on the shape of the investment function. If it is nearly vertical, indicating very little responsiveness of investment to the interest rate, the middle link in this chain is weak, rendering monetary policy ineffective.

▶ **Expansionary Policy in Action: The Recessions of 1974 to 1975, 1980 to 1982, and 1990 to 1991**   The United States has experienced three recessions since 1970. In two, 1974 to

FIGURE 28.6

An expansionary fiscal policy,
like the 1975 tax cut, will
increase aggregate output
(income) and shift the money
demand curve to the right,
from M_0^d to M_1^d. If the money
supply were unchanged, the
interest rate would rise from r_0
to r_1 and planned investment
would be negatively affected.
But if the Fed were to
"accommodate" the fiscal
expansion by increasing the
money supply from M_0^s to M_1^s,
the interest rate would not rise.

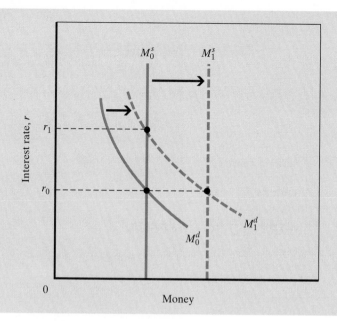

1975 and 1980 to 1982, the government engaged in tax cuts that had the effect of stimulating consumer spending (C). Because C is a component of planned aggregate expenditure, these tax cuts had the effect of increasing aggregate output (income) (Y).

Consider the recession of 1974 to 1975. The Tax Reduction Act of 1975 resulted
in a 1974 tax rebate of $8 billion that was paid to consumers in the second quarter of
1975. This rebate and other tax reductions led to increased consumer spending,
which contributed to the economic recovery that began soon after the new tax laws
went into effect.

But what about the crowding-out effect? Did the 1975 expansionary fiscal policy
drive up interest rates and crowd out private spending? In this case, no. At the same
time that Congress was cutting taxes to stimulate spending, the Fed was trying to stimulate the economy by expanding the money supply. Even though the increased output
during the expansion caused the *demand* for money to rise, the Fed was simultaneously
expanding the *supply* of money, and interest rates did not change very much. This situation is illustrated in Figure 28.6.

A similar sequence of events took place during the recession of 1980 to 1982. On
the recommendation of President Reagan, Congress passed a huge tax cut during the
summer of 1981. Like the 1975 tax cut, the 1981 tax cut led to an increase in consumer spending, which helped lift the economy out of the recession.

Recovery from the 1980 to 1982 recession was also helped along by the Fed, which
began to increase the supply of money sharply in the spring of 1982. So, even though
output and income were expanding by late 1982, thereby increasing the demand for
money, interest rates actually *declined* because the supply of money was expanding at
the same time. There was no crowding-out effect.

The recession of 1990 to 1991 began soon after Iraq's invasion of Kuwait in the
late summer of 1990. The recession was short-lived and shallow compared with the
two previous recessions. Real GDP began to rise in the second quarter of 1991. But
this recovery became known as the "jobless recovery." Because productivity increased
and large firms continued to trim payrolls even as output was expanding, the unemployment rate stayed high right into the presidential election of 1992.

President Bush debated calling for a tax cut to stimulate the economy, but concern
with the already large government deficit and pressure from the Fed convinced him to

wait. The Fed did push interest rates lower in an effort to get the economy moving. Even so, little response was evident by election time.

President Clinton called for some modest fiscal stimulus when he took office, but the Congress balked. Then, in the summer of 1993, Congress passed the Clinton deficit reduction package, which *increased* taxes and *reduced* government spending. In the meantime, monetary policy continued to be expansionary. Eventually, interest rates hit 30-year lows! For much of 1993, the three-month T-bill rate was under 3 percent for the first time since 1962, and the 30-year bond rate fell below 6 percent for the first time since the government began selling 30-year-bonds.

In late 1994, the slow-growth recovery ended and a real expansion began. To the extent that policy was responsible for the expansion, it was monetary (rather than fiscal) policy that finally got things moving.

CONTRACTIONARY POLICY EFFECTS

Any government policy that is aimed at reducing aggregate output (income) (Y) is said to be *contractionary*. Where expansionary policy is used to boost the economy, contractionary policy is used to slow the economy.

Considering that one of the four major economic goals is economic growth (chapter 1), why would the government adopt policies designed to reduce aggregate spending? As we will see in the next two chapters, one way to fight inflation is to reduce aggregate spending. When the inflation rate is high, the government may feel compelled to use its powers to contract the economy. Before we discuss the contractionary policies that the government has undertaken in recent years, we need to discuss how contractionary fiscal and monetary policy work.

▶ **Contractionary Fiscal Policy: A Decrease in Government Spending (G) or an Increase in Net Taxes (T)**   A contractionary fiscal policy is a decrease in government spending (G) or an increase in net taxes (T) aimed at decreasing aggregate output (income) (Y). The effects of this policy are the opposite of the effects of an expansionary fiscal policy.

A decrease in government purchases or an increase in net taxes leads to a decrease in aggregate output (income) (Y), a decrease in the demand for money (M^d), and a decrease in the interest rate (r). The decrease in Y that accompanies a contractionary fiscal policy is less than it would be if we did not take the money market into account because the decrease in r also causes planned investment (I) to *increase*. This increase in I offsets some of the decrease in planned aggregate expenditure brought about by the decrease in G. (This also means the multiplier effect is smaller than it would be if we did not take the money market into account.) The effects of a decrease in G, or an increase in T, can be represented as:

contractionary fiscal policy *A decrease in government spending or an increase in net taxes aimed at decreasing aggregate output (income) (Y).*

Effects of a Contractionary Fiscal Policy:	$G\downarrow$ or $T\uparrow \rightarrow Y\downarrow \rightarrow M^d\downarrow \rightarrow r\downarrow \rightarrow I\uparrow$
	▶ Y decreases less than if r did not decrease.

▶ **Contractionary Monetary Policy: A Decrease in the Money Supply**   A contractionary monetary policy is a decrease in the money supply aimed at decreasing aggregate output (income) (Y). As you recall, the level of planned investment spending is a negative function of the interest rate: The higher the interest rate, the less planned investment there will be. The less planned investment there is, the lower planned aggregate expenditure will be, and the lower the equilibrium level of output (income) (Y) will be. The lower equilibrium income results in a decrease in the demand for money, which means that the increase in the interest rate will be less than it would be if we did not take the goods market into account.

contractionary monetary policy *A decrease in the money supply aimed at decreasing aggregate output (income) (Y).*

| Effects of a Contractionary Monetary Policy: | $M^s\downarrow \rightarrow r\uparrow \rightarrow I\downarrow \rightarrow Y\downarrow \rightarrow M^d\downarrow$ |
| | r increases less than if M^d did not decrease. |

▶ **Contractionary Policy in Action: 1973 to 1974, 1979 to 1980, and 1994** The Fed has pursued strong contractionary policies twice in the last two decades: first in 1973 to 1974 and again in 1979 to 1980. In both cases, the tight monetary policies led to very high interest rates. In 1974, short-term rates exceeded 12 percent, and in 1981, some short-term rates exceeded 20 percent! These high interest rates had a negative effect on planned aggregate expenditure and contributed to the recessions that followed. The Fed's purpose in following a tight monetary policy was to slow the inflation rate. (We will see in the next chapter why a contractionary policy may bring the inflation rate down.)

In 1994, worries about inflation surfaced again as the economy began to push toward full employment. Once again, the Fed began to pull on the reins. In February, it announced the first of several increases in the discount rate and the target federal funds rate. By the end of the year, the prime rate had jumped from 6 percent to 8.5 percent. Between 1994 and 1997 the Fed made only modest changes in the discount rate.

THE MACROECONOMIC POLICY MIX

Although we've been treating fiscal and monetary policy separately, it should be clear that fiscal and monetary policy can be used simultaneously. For example, both government purchases (G) and the money supply (M^s) can be increased at the same time. We have seen that an increase in G by itself raises both Y and r, while an increase in M^s by itself raises Y but lowers r. Therefore, if the government wanted to increase Y without changing r, it could do so by increasing both G and M^s by the appropriate amounts.

policy mix *The combination of monetary and fiscal policies in use at a given time.*

Policy mix refers to the combination of monetary and fiscal policies in use at a given time. A policy mix that consists of a decrease in government spending and an increase in the money supply would favor investment spending over government spending. This is because both the increased money supply and the fall in government purchases would cause the interest rate to fall, which would lead to an increase in planned investment. The opposite is true for a mix that consists of an expansionary fiscal policy and a contractionary monetary policy. This mix favors government spending over investment spending. Such a policy will have the effect of increasing government spending and reducing the money supply. Tight money and expanded government spending would drive the interest rate up and planned investment down.

There is no rule about what constitutes the "best" policy mix or the "best" composition of output. On this, as on many other issues, economists (and others) disagree. In part, someone's preference for a certain composition of output—say, one weighted heavily toward private spending with relatively little government spending—depends on how that person stands on such issues as the proper role of government in the economy.

Table 28.1 summarizes the effects of various combinations of policies on several important macroeconomic variables. If you can explain the reasoning underlying each of the effects shown in the figure, you can be satisfied that you have a good understanding of the links between the goods market and the money market.

OTHER DETERMINANTS OF PLANNED INVESTMENT

We have assumed in this chapter that planned investment depends only on the interest rate. In reality, planned investment depends on other factors. We will discuss these factors more in chapter 32, but provide a brief description here.

TABLE 28.1 THE EFFECTS OF THE MACROECONOMIC POLICY MIX

		FISCAL	
		Expansionary ($\uparrow G$ or $\downarrow T$)	Contractionary ($\downarrow G$ or $\uparrow T$)
MONETARY	Expansionary ($\uparrow M^s$)	$Y\uparrow, r?, I?, C\uparrow$	$Y?, r\downarrow, I\uparrow, C?$
	Contractionary ($\downarrow M^s$)	$Y?, r\uparrow, I\downarrow, C?$	$Y\downarrow, r?, I?, C\downarrow$

Key:
↑: variable increases.
↓: variable decreases.
?: Forces push the variable in different directions. Without additional information, we cannot specify which way the variable moves.

➤ **Expectations and Animal Spirits** Firms' expectations about their future sales play an important role in their investment decisions. When a firm invests, it adds to its capital stock, and capital is used in the production process. If a firm expects that its sales will increase in the future, it may begin to build up its capital stock (that is, to invest) now so that it will be able to produce more in the future to meet the increased level of sales. The optimism or pessimism of entrepreneurs about the future course of the economy can have an important effect on current planned investment. Keynes used the phrase *animal spirits* to describe the feelings of entrepreneurs, and he argued that these feelings affect investment decisions.

➤ **Capital Utilization Rates** The degree of utilization of a firm's capital stock is also likely to affect planned investment. If the demand for a firm's output has been decreasing and the firm has been lowering output in response to this decline, the firm may have a low rate of capital utilization. It can be costly to get rid of capital quickly once it is in place, and firms sometimes respond to a fall in output by keeping the capital in place but utilizing it less (for example, by running machines fewer hours per day or at slower speeds). Firms tend to invest less in new capital when their capital utilization rates are low than when they are high.

➤ **Relative Labor and Capital Costs** The cost of capital (of which the interest rate is the main component) *relative* to the cost of labor can affect planned investment. If labor is expensive relative to capital (high wage rates), firms tend to substitute away from labor toward capital. They aim to hold more capital relative to labor when wage rates are high than when they are low.

The Determinants of Planned Investment:	■ The interest rate ■ Expectations of future sales ■ Capital utilization rates ■ Relative capital and labor costs

LOOKING AHEAD: THE PRICE LEVEL

Our discussion of aggregate output (income) and the interest rate in the goods market and the money market is now complete. You should now have a good understanding of how the two markets work together. However, we have not yet discussed the price level in any detail.

We cannot begin to understand the economic events of the last three decades without an understanding of the aggregate price level. The two periods of rapid increases in the price level, 1974 to 1975 and 1979 to 1981, had dramatic effects on the economy. What causes the price level to change? Are there policies that might prevent large changes in the price level or stop them once they have started? Is inflation in 1998 so low that we don't have to worry about it? Before we can answer such questions, we must understand the factors that affect the overall price level. This is the task of the next chapter. Up to this point we have taken the price level as fixed. Now it is time to relax this assumption.

SUMMARY

1. The *goods market* and the *money market* do not operate independently. Events in the money market have considerable effects on the goods market, and events in the goods market have considerable effects on the money market.

THE LINKS BETWEEN THE GOODS MARKET AND THE MONEY MARKET

2. There are two important links between the goods market and the money market: The level of real output (income) (Y), which is determined in the goods market, determines the volume of transactions each period and thus affects the demand for money in the money market; And, the interest rate (r), which is determined in the money market, affects the level of planned investment spending in the goods market.

3. There is a negative relationship between planned investment and the interest rate because the interest rate determines the cost of investment projects. When the interest rate rises, planned investment will decrease; when the interest rate falls, planned investment will increase.

4. For every value of the interest rate, there is a different level of planned investment spending and a different equilibrium level of output. The final level of equilibrium output depends on what the interest rate turns out to be, which depends on events in the money market.

5. For a given quantity of money supplied the interest rate depends on the demand for money. Money demand depends on the level of output (income). With a given money supply, then, increases and decreases in Y will affect money demand, which will affect the equilibrium interest rate.

COMBINING THE GOODS MARKET AND THE MONEY MARKET

6. An *expansionary fiscal policy* is an increase in government spending (G) or a reduction in net taxes (T) aimed at increasing aggregate output (income) (Y). An expansionary fiscal policy based on increases in government spending tends to lead to a *crowding-out effect*: Because increased government expenditures mean more transactions in the economy and thus an increased demand for money, the interest rate will rise. The decrease in planned investment spending that accompanies the higher interest rate will then partially offset the increase in aggregate expenditures brought about by the increase in G.

7. The size of the crowding-out effect, affecting the size of the government-spending multiplier, depends on two things: the assumption that the Fed does not change the quantity of money supplied and the *sensitivity* or *insensitivity of planned investment* to changes in the interest rate.

8. An *expansionary monetary policy* is an increase in the money supply aimed at increasing aggregate output (income) (Y). An increase in the money supply leads to a lower interest rate, increased planned investment, increased planned aggregate expenditure, and ultimately a higher equilibrium level of aggregate output (income) (Y). Expansionary policies have been used to lift the economy out of recessions.

9. A *contractionary fiscal policy* is a decrease in government spending or an increase in net taxes aimed at decreasing aggregate output (income) (Y). A decrease in government spending or an increase in net taxes leads to a decrease in aggregate output (income) (Y), a decrease in the demand for money, and a decrease in the interest rate. However, the decrease in Y is somewhat offset by the additional planned investment resulting from the lower interest rate.

10. A *contractionary monetary policy* is a decrease in the money supply aimed at decreasing aggregate output (income) (Y). The higher interest rate brought about by the reduced money supply causes a decrease in planned investment spending and a lower level of equilibrium output. However, the lower equilibrium level of output brings about a decrease in the demand for money, which means the increase in the interest rate will be less than it would be if we did not take the goods market into account. Contractionary policies have been used to fight inflation.

11. The *policy mix* is the combination of monetary and fiscal policies in use at a given time. There is no rule about what constitutes the best policy mix or the best composition of output. In part, one's preference for a certain composition of output depends on one's stance regarding such issues as the proper role of government in the economy.

OTHER DETERMINANTS OF PLANNED INVESTMENT

12. In addition to the interest rate, the level of planned investment in the economy also depends on expectations and animal spirits, capital utilization rates, and relative capital and labor costs.

REVIEW TERMS AND CONCEPTS

contractionary fiscal policy, 667

contractionary monetary policy, 667

crowding-out effect, 663

expansionary fiscal policy, 662

expansionary monetary policy, 662

goods market, 657

interest sensitivity or insensitivity of
planned investment, 664

money market, 657

policy mix, 668

PROBLEM SET

1. On October 9, 1997, the German central bank, the Bundesbank, surprised the world by announcing it would take action to raise interest rates. This set off a protest in Germany because unemployment is above 12 percent. What impact is an interest rate increase likely to have on the level of output?

2. During the third quarter of 1997, Japanese GDP was falling at an annual rate of over 11 percent. Many blame the big increase in Japan's taxes in the spring of 1997 designed to balance the budget. Explain how an increase in taxes with the economy growing slowly could precipitate a recession; do not skip steps in your answer. If you were head of the Japanese central bank, how would you respond? What impact would your policy have on the level of investment?

3. Some economists argue that the "animal spirits" of investors are so important in determining the level of investment in the economy that interest rates don't matter at all. Suppose that this were true—that investment in no way depends on interest rates.
   a. How would Figure 28.1 be different?
   b. What would happen to the level of planned aggregate expenditures if the interest rate changed?
   c. What would be different about the relative effectiveness of monetary and fiscal policy?

4. For each of the following, tell a story and predict the effects on the equilibrium levels of aggregate output (Y) and the interest rate (r):
   a. During the summer of 1997, the Congress passed and the president signed the *Taxpayer Relief Act of 1997*. The act contained a number of tax cuts and expenditure reductions designed to ultimately balance the budget. Many of the tax cuts took effect immediately and in 1998. The expenditure cuts were scheduled to take effect in 1999 to 2002. Assume the Fed holds M^s fixed. You may give a different answer for 1998 and for 1999 to 2002.
   b. In 1993, the Congress and the president raised taxes. At the same time, the Federal Reserve was pursuing an expansionary monetary policy.
   c. In 1990, the Perisan Gulf War led to a sharp drop in consumer confidence and a drop in consumption. Assume the Fed holds the money supply constant.

   d. The Fed attempts to increase the money supply to stimulate the economy, but plants are operating at 65 percent of their capacities and businesses are pessimistic about the future.

5. Occasionally, the Federal Reserve Open Market Committee sets a policy designed to "track" the interest rate. This means that the OMC is pursuing policies designed to keep the interest rate constant. If, in fact, the Fed were acting to counter any increases or decreases in the interest rate to keep it constant, what specific actions would you expect to see the Fed take if the following were to occur? (In answering, indicate the effects of each set of events on Y, C, S, I, M^s, M^d, and r.)
   a. There is an unexpected increase in investor confidence, leading to a sharp increase in orders for new plant and equipment.
   b. A major New York bank fails, causing a number of neurotic people (not trusting even the FDIC) to withdraw a substantial amount of cash from other banks and put it in their cookie jars.

6. Paranoia, the largest country in Central Antarctica, receives word of an imminent penguin attack. The news causes expectations about the future to be shaken. As a consequence, there is a sharp decline in investment spending plans.
   a. Explain in detail the effects of such an event on the economy of Paranoia, assuming no response on the part of the Central Bank or the Treasury (M^s, T, and G all remain constant). Be sure to discuss the adjustments in the goods market and the money market.
   b. To counter the fall in investment, the king of Paranoia calls for a proposal to increase government spending. To finance the program, the Chancellor of the Exchequer has proposed three alternative options:
      (1) Finance the expenditures with an equal increase in taxes.
      (2) Keep tax revenues constant and borrow the money from the public by issuing new government bonds.
      (3) Keep taxes constant and finance the expenditures by printing new money.

   Consider the three financing options and rank them from most expansionary to least expansionary. Explain your ranking.

7. Why might investment not respond positively to low interest rates during a recession? Why might investment not respond negatively to high interest rates during a boom?

8. In the early 1980s, the Federal Reserve was tightening the money supply to fight inflation at the same time that President Reagan was increasing defense spending and reducing taxes. What would you expect the effects of this policy mix to be?

TAKE IT TO THE NET

We invite you to visit the Case and Fair page on the Prentice Hall Web site:

http://www.prenhall.com/casefair

for this chapter's World Wide Web exercise.

APPENDIX TO CHAPTER 28

THE *IS-LM* DIAGRAM

There is a useful way of depicting graphically the determination of aggregate output (income) and the interest rate in the goods and money markets. Two curves are involved in this diagram, the *IS* curve and the *LM* curve. In this appendix, we will derive these two curves and use them to see how changes in government purchases (G) and the money supply (M^s) affect the equilibrium values of aggregate output (income) and the interest rate. The effects we describe here are the same as the effects we described in the main text; here we illustrate the effects graphically.

THE *IS* CURVE

We know that in the goods market, there is an equilibrium level of aggregate output (income) (Y) for each value of the interest rate (r). For a given value of r, we can determine the equilibrium value of Y. We also know from Figure 13.5 that the equilibrium value of Y falls when r rises and rises when r falls. There is thus a *negative* relationship between the equilibrium value of Y and r. The reason for this negative relationship is the negative relationship between planned investment and the interest rate. When the interest rate rises, planned investment (I) falls, and this decrease in I leads to a decrease in the equilibrium value of Y. The negative relationship between the equilibrium value of Y and r is shown in Figure 28A.1. This curve is called the **IS curve**.[1] Each point on the *IS* curve represents the equilibrium point in the goods market for the given interest rate.

We also know from our earlier analysis of the goods market that when government purchases (G) increase with a constant interest rate, the equilibrium value of Y increases. This means the *IS* curve shifts to the right when G increases. With the same value of r and a higher value of G, the equilibrium value of Y is larger; when G decreases, the *IS* curve shifts to the left.

THE *LM* CURVE

In the money market, there is an equilibrium value of the interest rate (r) for every value of aggregate output (income) (Y). The equilibrium value of r is determined at the point at which the quantity of money demanded equals the quantity

---

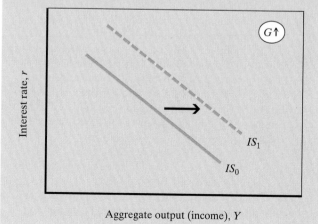

FIGURE 28A.1

The *IS* Curve

Each point on the *IS* curve corresponds to the equilibrium point in the goods market for the given interest rate. When government spending (G) increases, the *IS* curve shifts to the right, from IS_0 to IS_1.

---

[1]The letter *I* stands for investment, and the letter *S* stands for saving. *IS* refers to the fact that in equilibrium in the goods market, planned investment equals saving.

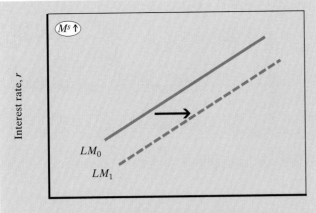

FIGURE 28A.2
The *LM* Curve
Each point on the *LM* curve corresponds to the equilibrium point in the money market for the given value of aggregate output (income). Money supply (M^s) increases shift the *LM* curve to the right, from LM_0 to LM_1.

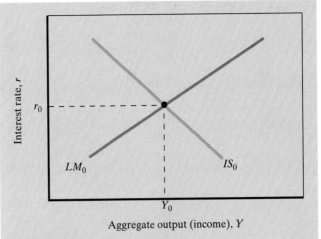

FIGURE 28A.3
The *IS-LM* Diagram
The point at which the *IS* and *LM* curves intersect corresponds to the point at which both the goods market and the money market are in equilibrium. The equilibrium values of aggregate output and the interest rate are Y_0 and r_0.

of money supplied. For a given value of *Y*, we can determine the equilibrium value of *r* in the money market. We also know from Figure 28.4 that the equilibrium value of *r* rises when *Y* rises and falls when *Y* falls—a *positive* relationship between the equilibrium value of *r* and *Y*. The reason for this positive relationship is the positive relationship between the demand for money and *Y*. When *Y* increases, the demand for money increases because more money is demanded for the increased volume of transactions in the economy. An increase in the demand for money increases the equilibrium value of *r*—thus the positive relationship between the equilibrium value of *r* and *Y*.

The positive relationship between the equilibrium value of *r* and *Y* is shown in Figure 28A.2. This curve is called the **LM curve**.[2] Each point on the **LM** curve represents equilibrium in the money market for the given value of aggregate output (income).

We also know from our analysis of the money market that when the money supply (M^s) increases with a constant level of *Y*, the equilibrium value of *r* decreases. As Figure 28A.2 shows, this means the *LM* curve shifts to the right when M^s increases. With the same value of *Y* and a higher value of M^s, the equilibrium value of *r* is lower. When M^s decreases, the *LM* curve shifts to the left.

THE *IS-LM* DIAGRAM

Figure 28A.3 shows the *IS* and *LM* curves together on one graph. The point at which the two curves intersect is the point at which equilibrium exists in *both* the goods market and the money market. There is equilibrium in the goods market because the point is on the *IS* curve, and there is equilibrium in the money market because the point is on the *LM* curve.

We now have only two tasks left. The first is to see how the equilibrium values of *Y* and *r* are affected by changes in *G*—fiscal policy. This is easy. We have just seen that an increase in *G* shifts the *IS* curve to the right. Thus, an increase in *G* leads to higher equilibrium values of *Y* and *r*. This situation is illustrated in Figure 28A.4. Conversely, a decrease in *G* leads to lower equilibrium values of *Y* and *r* because the lower level of *G* causes the *IS* curve to shift to the left. (The effects are similar for changes in net taxes, *T*.)

Our second task is to see how the equilibrium values of *Y* and *r* are affected by changes in M^s—monetary policy. This is also easy. We have just seen that an increase in M^s shifts the *LM* curve to the right. Thus, an increase in M^s leads to a higher equilibrium value of *Y* and a lower equilibrium value of *r*. This is illustrated in Figure 28A.5. Conversely, a decrease in M^s leads to a lower equilibrium value of *Y* and a higher equilibrium value of *r* because a decreased money supply causes the *LM* curve to shift to the left.

The *IS-LM* diagram is a useful way of seeing the effects of changes in monetary and fiscal policies on equilibrium

---

[2]The letter *L* stands for liquidity, a characteristic of money, and the letter *M* stands for money.

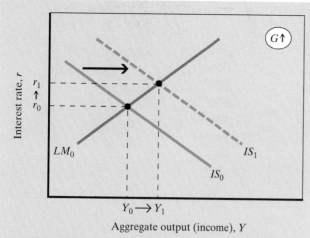

FIGURE 28A.4

An Increase in Government Purchases (G)

When G increases, the IS curve shifts to the right. This increases the equilibrium value of both Y and r.

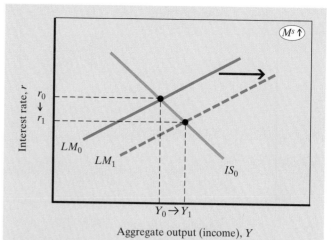

FIGURE 28A.5

An Increase in the Money Supply (M^s)

When M^s increases, the LM curve shifts to the right. This increases the equilibrium value of Y and decreases the equilibrium value of r.

aggregate output (income) and the interest rate through shifts in the two curves. Always keep in mind the economic theory that lies *behind* the two curves. Do not memorize what curve shifts when; be able to understand and explain *why* the curves shift. This means always going back to the behavior of households and firms in the goods and money markets.

It is easy to use the IS-LM diagram to see how there can be a monetary and fiscal policy mix that leads to, say, an increase in aggregate output (income) but no increase in the interest rate. If both G and M^s increase, both curves shift to the right, and the shifts can be controlled in such a way as to bring about no change in the equilibrium value of the interest rate.

SUMMARY

1. An *IS curve* illustrates the negative relationship between the equilibrium value of aggregate output (income) (Y) and the interest rate in the goods market. An *LM curve* illustrates the positive relationship between the equilibrium value of the interest rate and aggregate output (income) (Y) in the money market. The point at which the IS and LM curves intersect is the point at which equilibrium exists in both the goods market and the money market.

REVIEW TERMS AND CONCEPTS

IS curve A curve illustrating the negative relationship between the equilibrium value of aggregate output (income) (Y) and the interest rate in the goods market. 672

LM curve A curve illustrating the positive relationship between the equilibrium value of the interest rate and aggregate output (income) (Y) in the money market. 672

PROBLEM SET

1. Illustrate each of the following situations with IS/LM curves:
   a. An increase in G with the money supply held constant by the Fed.
   b. An increase in G with the Fed changing M^s by enough to keep interest rates constant.
   c. The president cuts G and increases T while the chair of the Fed expands M^s.
   d. The president increases G and holds T constant while the chair of the Fed holds M^s constant during a period of inflation.

Chapter 29

AGGREGATE DEMAND, AGGREGATE SUPPLY, AND INFLATION

ONE OF THE MOST IMPORTANT ISSUES in macroeconomics is the determination of the overall price level. Recall that inflation—an increase in the overall price level—is one of the key concerns of macroeconomists and government policy makers. Understanding the factors that affect the price level is essential to understanding macroeconomics.

In chapter 23, we discussed how inflation is measured and the costs of inflation, but made no mention of the *causes* of inflation. For simplicity, our analysis in chapters 24 through 28 took the price level as fixed. This allowed us to discuss the links between the goods market and the money market without the complication of a changing price level. Having considered how the two markets work, we are ready to take up flexible prices.

We begin by discussing the *aggregate demand curve* and the *aggregate supply curve*, introduced briefly in chapter 21. We then put the two curves together and discuss how the equilibrium price level is determined in the economy. This analysis allows us to see how the price level affects the economy and how the economy affects the price level. Finally, we consider monetary and fiscal policy effects and the causes of inflation.

THE AGGREGATE DEMAND CURVE

The place to begin our exploration of the price level is the money market. (If you have forgotten the details of how the overall price level is calculated or what it means, review chapters 22 and 23.) As we saw in Chapter 27, people's demand for money depends on income (Y), the interest rate (r), and the price level (P).

It is not hard to understand why the price level affects the demand for money. Suppose you plan to purchase one pound of chocolate, one bag of potato chips, and a Hostess Twinkie. If these items cost $2.00, $1.00, and $.50 respectively, you would need $3.50 in cash or in your checking account to make your purchases. Suppose that the price of these goods doubles. To make the same purchases, you will need $7.00.

In general, the amount of money required to make a given number of transactions depends directly and proportionately on the average price of those transactions. Doubling the price level will double the demand for money. As prices and wages rise, households will want to keep more money in their wallets and in their checking accounts, firms will need more in their cash drawers, and so forth. If prices and wages are rising at 6 percent per year, we can expect the demand for money to increase at about 6 percent per year, *ceteris paribus*.

> Money demand is a function of three variables: the interest rate (r), the level of real income (Y), and the price level (P). (Remember: Y is *real* output, or income. It measures the actual volume of output, without regard to changes in the price level.) Money demand will increase if the real level of output (income) increases, the price level increases, or the interest rate declines.

DERIVING THE AGGREGATE DEMAND CURVE

aggregate demand *The total demand for goods and services in the economy.*

Recall that **aggregate demand** is the total demand for goods and services in the economy. To derive the aggregate demand curve, we examine what happens to aggregate output (income) (Y) when the price level (P) changes. Does it increase, decrease, or remain constant when the price level increases? Our discussions of the goods market and the money market provide the tools to answer this.

The aggregate demand curve is derived assuming the fiscal policy variables [government purchases (G) and net taxes (T)] and the monetary policy variable (M^s) remain unchanged. In other words, assuming the government does not take any action to affect the economy in response to changes in the price level.

As you know, an increase in the price level increases the demand for money and shifts the money demand curve to the right, as illustrated in Figure 29.1a. At the initial interest rate of 6 percent, an increase in the price level leads to an excess demand for money. Because of the higher price level, households and firms need to hold larger

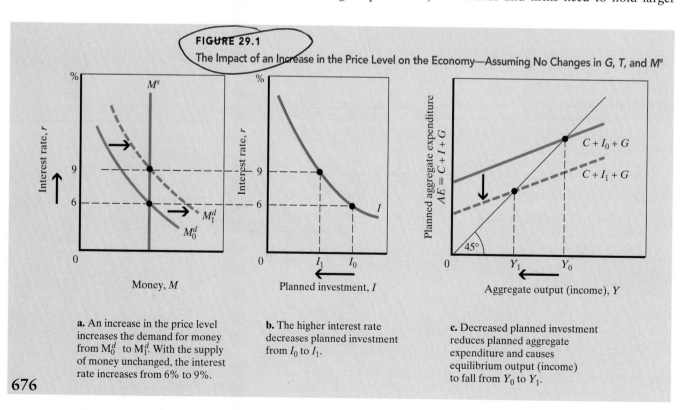

FIGURE 29.1

The Impact of an Increase in the Price Level on the Economy—Assuming No Changes in *G, T,* and *M*ˢ

a. An increase in the price level increases the demand for money from M_0^d to M_1^d. With the supply of money unchanged, the interest rate increases from 6% to 9%.

b. The higher interest rate decreases planned investment from I_0 to I_1.

c. Decreased planned investment reduces planned aggregate expenditure and causes equilibrium output (income) to fall from Y_0 to Y_1.

676

money balances than before. However, the quantity of money supplied remains the same. (Remember, we are assuming that the Fed takes no action to change the money supply.) The money market is now out of equilibrium. Equilibrium is reestablished at a higher interest rate, 9 percent.

As indicated in Figure 29.1b, with the interest rate now higher, fewer investment projects are desirable, and planned investment spending (I) falls from I_0 to I_1. Lower I means planned aggregate expenditure (AE) is lower, shown in Figure 29.1c as a downward shift of the AE curve. Lower AE means inventories are greater than planned, firms cut back on output, and Y falls from Y_0 to Y_1.

> An increase in the price level causes the level of aggregate output (income) to fall.

The situation is reversed when the price level declines. A lower price level causes money demand to fall, which leads to a lower interest rate. A lower interest rate stimulates planned investment spending, increasing planned aggregate expenditure, which leads to an increase in Y.

> A decrease in the price level causes the level of aggregate output (income) to rise.

This negative relationship between aggregate output (income) and the price level is called the **aggregate demand (AD) curve**, shown in Figure 29.2.

Each point on the aggregate demand curve represents equilibrium in both the goods market *and* the money market. We have derived the AD curve by using the analysis we did in chapter 28, in which the goods market and the money market were linked together. Therefore,

> Each pair of values of P and Y on the aggregate demand curve corresponds to a point at which both the goods market and the money market are in equilibrium.

aggregate demand (AD) curve *A curve that shows the negative relationship between aggregate output (income) and the price level. Each point on the* AD *curve is a point at which both the goods market and the money market are in equilibrium.*

THE AGGREGATE DEMAND CURVE: A WARNING

It is very important that you realize what the aggregate demand curve represents. As we pointed out in chapter 21, the aggregate demand curve is much more complex than a simple individual or market demand curve. The AD curve is *not* a market demand curve, and it is *not* the sum of all market demand curves in the economy.

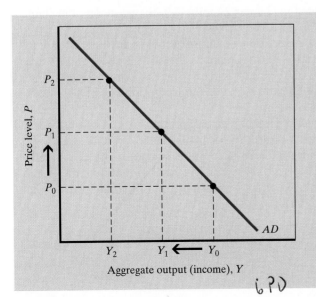

FIGURE 29.2

The Aggregate Demand (AD) Curve

At all points along the AD curve, both the goods market and the money market are in equilibrium.

To understand why, recall the logic behind a simple downward-sloping household demand curve. A demand curve shows the quantity of output demanded (by an individual household or in a single market) at every possible price, *ceteris paribus*. In drawing a simple demand curve, we are assuming that *other prices* and *income* are fixed. From these assumptions, it follows that one reason the quantity demanded of a particular good falls when its price rises is that other prices do *not* rise. The good in question therefore becomes more expensive relative to other goods, which leads households to substitute other goods for the good whose price increased. In addition, if income does not rise when the price of a good does, real income falls. This may also lead to a lower quantity demanded of the good whose price has risen.

Things are different when the *overall price level* rises. When the overall price level rises, many prices—including many wage rates (many people's income)—rise together. For this reason, we cannot use the *ceteris paribus* assumption to draw the *AD* curve. The logic that explains why a simple demand curve slopes downward fails to explain why the *AD* curve also has a negative slope.

> Aggregate demand falls when the price level increases because the higher price level causes the demand for money (M^d) to rise. With the money supply constant, the interest rate will rise to reestablish equilibrium in the money market. *It is the higher interest rate that causes aggregate output to fall.*

You do not need to understand anything about the money market to understand a simple individual or market demand curve. However, to understand what the *aggregate* demand curve represents, you must understand the interaction between the goods market and the money market. The *AD* curve in Figure 29.2 embodies everything we have learned about the goods market and the money market up to now.

> The *AD* curve is *not* the sum of all the market demand curves in the economy. It is *not* a market demand curve.

OTHER REASONS FOR A DOWNWARD-SLOPING AGGREGATE DEMAND CURVE

In addition to the effects of money supply and money demand on the interest rate, two other factors lie behind the downward slope of the *AD* curve. These are the consumption link and the real wealth effect.

▶ **The Consumption Link** We noted in chapter 24 (and will discuss in detail in chapter 32) that consumption (*C*) and planned investment (*I*) depend on the interest rate. Other things equal, consumption expenditures tend to rise when the interest rate falls and to fall when the interest rate rises—just as planned investment does. This tendency is another link between the goods market and the money market. If something happens to change the interest rate in the money market, both consumption and planned investment are affected in the goods market.

The *consumption* link provides another reason for the *AD* curve's downward slope. An increase in the price level increases the demand for money, which leads to an increase in the interest rate, which leads to a decrease in consumption (as well as planned investment), which leads to a decrease in aggregate output (income). The initial decrease in consumption (brought about by the increase in the interest rate) contributes to the overall decrease in output.

> Planned investment does not bear all the burden of providing the link from a higher interest rate to a lower level of aggregate output. Decreased consumption brought about by a higher interest rate also contributes to this effect.

▶ **The Real Wealth Effect**   We also noted in chapter 24 (and will discuss in detail in chapter 32) that consumption depends on wealth. Other things equal, the more wealth households have, the more they consume. Wealth includes holdings of money, shares of stock, bonds, and housing, among other things. If household wealth decreases, the result will be less consumption now and in the future.

The price level has an effect on some kinds of wealth. Suppose you are holding $1,000 in a checking account or in a money market fund and the price level rises by 10 percent. Your holding is now worth 10 percent less because the prices of the goods that you could buy with your $1,000 have all increased by 10 percent. The purchasing power (or "real value") of your holding has decreased by 10 percent.

An increase in the price level may also lower the real value of stocks and housing, although whether it does depends on what happens to stock prices and housing prices when the overall price level rises. If stock prices and housing prices rise by the same percentage as the overall price level, the real value of stocks and housing will remain unchanged. The point is:

> An increase in the price level lowers the real value of *some* types of wealth.

The fact that the price level lowers the real value of wealth provides another reason for the downward slope of the *AD* curve. An increase in the price level lowers the real value of wealth. This leads to a decrease in consumption, which leads to a decrease in aggregate output (income). So, there is a negative relationship between the price level and output through this **real wealth effect** or **real balance effect**.

AGGREGATE EXPENDITURE AND AGGREGATE DEMAND

Throughout our discussion of macroeconomics so far, we have referred to the total planned spending by households (C), firms (I), and the government (G) as planned aggregate expenditure. At equilibrium, planned aggregate expenditure ($AE \equiv C + I + G$) and aggregate output (Y) are equal:[1]

$$\text{Equilibrium condition: } C + I + G = Y$$

How does planned aggregate expenditure relate to aggregate demand?

> At every point along the aggregate demand curve, the aggregate quantity demanded is exactly equal to planned aggregate expenditure, $C + I + G$.

You can see this in Figures 29.1 and 29.2. When the price level rises, it is planned aggregate expenditure that decreases, moving us up the aggregate demand curve.

But the aggregate demand curve represents more than just planned aggregate expenditure. Each point on the *AD* curve represents the *particular* level of planned aggregate expenditure that is consistent with equilibrium in the goods market and money market at the given price. Notice that the variable on the horizontal axis of the aggregate demand curve in Figure 29.2 is Y. At every point along the *AD* curve, $Y = C + I + G$.

SHIFTS OF THE AGGREGATE DEMAND CURVE

The aggregate demand curve in Figure 29.2 is based on the assumption that the government policy variables G, T, and M^s are fixed. If any of these variables change, the aggregate demand curve will shift.

Consider an increase in the quantity of money supplied. If the quantity of money is expanded at any given price level, the interest rate will fall, causing planned investment

real wealth, or **real balance, effect** *The change in consumption brought about by a change in real wealth that results from a change in the price level.*

---

[1] If we include the rest of the world, the equilibrium condition is $C + I + G + (EX - IM) = Y$.

FIGURE 29.3

The Effect of an Increase in Money Supply on the *AD* Curve

FIGURE 29.3

The Effect of an Increase in Money Supply on the *AD* Curve

An increase in the money supply (M^s) causes the aggregate demand curve to shift to the right, from AD_0 to AD_1. This shift occurs because the increase in M^s lowers the interest rate, which increases planned investment (and thus planned aggregate expenditure). The final result is an increase in output at each possible price level.

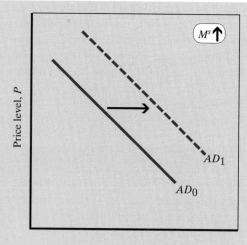

spending (and planned aggregate expenditure) to rise. The result is an increase in output at the given price level. As Figure 29.3 shows:

> An increase in the quantity of money supplied at a given price level shifts the aggregate demand curve to the right.

An increase in government purchases or a decrease in net taxes also increases aggregate output (income) at each possible price level, even though some of the increase will be crowded out if the money supply is held constant. (If you are unsure of what crowding-out is, review chapter 27.) An increase in government purchases directly increases planned aggregate expenditure, which leads to an increase in output. A decrease in net taxes results in a rise in consumption, which increases planned aggregate expenditure, which also leads to an increase in output. As Figure 29.4 shows:

> An increase in government purchases or a decrease in net taxes shifts the aggregate demand curve to the right.

FIGURE 29.4

The Effect of an Increase in Government Purchases or a Decrease in Net Taxes on the *AD* Curve

An increase in government purchases (G) or a decrease in net taxes (T) causes the aggregate demand curve to shift to the right, from AD_0 to AD_1. The increase in G increases planned aggregate expenditure, which leads to an increase in output at each possible price level. A decrease in T causes consumption to rise. The higher consumption then increases planned aggregate expenditure, which leads to an increase in output at each possible price level.

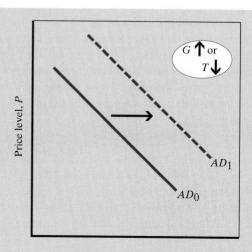

Expansionary monetary policy	Contractionary monetary policy
$M^s\uparrow \rightarrow AD$ curve shifts to the right.	$M^s\downarrow \rightarrow AD$ curve shifts to the left.
Expansionary fiscal policy	**Contractionary fiscal policy**
$G\uparrow \rightarrow AD$ curve shifts to the right.	$G\downarrow \rightarrow AD$ curve shifts to the left.
$T\downarrow \rightarrow AD$ curve shifts to the right.	$T\uparrow \rightarrow AD$ curve shifts to the left.

FIGURE 29.5
Shifts in the Aggregate Demand Curve: A Summary

The same kind of reasoning applies to decreases in the quantity of money supplied, decreases in government purchases, and increases in net taxes. All of these shift the aggregate demand curve to the left.

Figure 29.5 summarizes the ways the aggregate demand curve shifts in response to changes in M^s, G, and T. To test your understanding of the *AD* curve, go through the figure piece by piece and explain each of its components.

THE AGGREGATE SUPPLY CURVE

Aggregate supply is the total supply of goods and services in an economy. Although there is little disagreement among economists about the logic behind the aggregate demand curve, there is a great deal of disagreement about the logic behind the aggregate supply curve. There is also disagreement about its shape.

aggregate supply *The total supply of all goods and services in an economy.*

THE AGGREGATE SUPPLY CURVE: A WARNING

The **aggregate supply (*AS*) curve** shows the relationship between the aggregate quantity of output supplied by all the firms in an economy and the overall price level. To understand the aggregate supply curve, we need to understand something about the behavior of the individual firms that make up the economy.

aggregate supply (AS) curve *A graph that shows the relationship between the aggregate quantity of output supplied by all firms in an economy and the overall price level.*

It may seem logical to derive the aggregate supply curve by adding together the supply curves of all the individual firms in the economy. However, the logic behind the relationship between the overall price level in the economy and the level of aggregate output (income)—that is, the *AS* curve—is very different from the logic behind an individual firm's supply curve. The aggregate supply curve is *not* a market supply curve, and it is *not* the simple sum of all the individual supply curves in the economy. (Recall a similar warning for the aggregate demand curve.)

To understand why, recall the logic behind a simple supply curve, first introduced in chapter 4. A supply curve shows the quantity of output an individual firm would supply at each possible price *ceteris paribus*. When we draw a firm's supply curve, we assume that input prices, including wage rates, are constant. An individual firm's supply curve shows what would happen to the firm's output if the price of its output changes with *no* corresponding increase in costs. Such an assumption for an individual firm is reasonable because an individual firm is small relative to the economy as a whole. (It is unlikely that one firm raising the price of its output will lead to significant increases in input prices in the economy.) If the price of a profit-maximizing firm's output rises with *no* increase in the costs of any inputs, the firm is likely to increase output.

But what would happen if there were an increase in the overall price level? It is unrealistic to believe that costs are constant for individual firms if the overall price level is increasing, for two reasons. First, the outputs of some firms are the inputs of other firms. Therefore, if output prices rise, there will be an increase in at least some input prices. Second, it is unrealistic to assume that wage rates (an important input cost) do not rise at all when the overall price level rises. Because all input prices (including wage rates) are not constant as the overall price level changes, individual firms' supply curves *shift* as the overall price level changes, so we cannot sum them to get an aggregate supply curve.

Another reason the aggregate supply curve cannot be the sum of the supply curves of all the individual firms in the economy is that many firms (some would argue most firms) do not simply respond to prices determined in the market. Rather, they actually *set prices*. Only in perfectly competitive markets do firms simply react to prices determined by market forces. Firms in other kinds of industries (imperfectly competitive industries, to be exact) make both output *and* price decisions based on their perceptions of demand and costs. Price-setting firms do not have individual supply curves because these firms are choosing both output and price at the same time. To derive an individual supply curve, we need to imagine calling out a price to a firm and having the firm tell us how much output it will supply at that price. We cannot do this if firms are also setting prices.[2] If supply curves do not exist for imperfectly competitive firms, we certainly cannot add them together to get an aggregate supply curve!

What, then, can we say about the relationship between aggregate output and the overall price level? Because input prices change when the overall price level changes and because many firms in the economy set prices as well as output, it is clear that an "aggregate supply curve" in the traditional sense of the word *supply* does not exist. What does exist is what we might call a "price/output response" curve—a curve that traces out the price decisions and output decisions of all the markets and firms in the economy under a given set of circumstances.

What might such a curve look like?

AGGREGATE SUPPLY IN THE SHORT RUN

Many argue that the aggregate supply curve (or the "price/output response" curve) has a positive slope, at least in the short run. (We will discuss the short-run/long-run distinction in more detail later in this chapter.) In addition, many argue that at very low levels of aggregate output (for example, when the economy is in a recession), the aggregate supply curve is fairly flat, and at high levels of output (for example, when the economy is experiencing a boom), it is vertical or nearly vertical. Such a curve is shown in Figure 29.6.

To understand the shape of the *AS* curve in Figure 29.6, consider the output and price response of markets and firms to a steady increase in aggregate demand brought about by an increasingly expansionary fiscal or monetary policy. The reaction of firms to such an expansion is likely to depend on two factors: (1) how close the economy is to capacity at the time of the expansion, and (2) how rapidly input prices (such as wage rates) respond to increases in the overall price level.

▶ **Capacity Constraints** In microeconomics, "short run" describes the time in which firms' decisions are constrained by some *fixed factor of production.* A farmer is constrained in the short run by the number of acres of land on his or her farm—the amount of land owned is the fixed factor of production. Manufacturing firms' short-run production decisions are constrained by the size of their physical production facilities. In the longer run, individual firms can overcome these types of constraints by investing in greater capacity—for example, by purchasing more acreage or building a new factory.

The idea of a fixed capacity in the short run also plays a role in macroeconomics. Macroeconomists tend to focus on whether or not *individual firms* are producing at or

[2]A much more complete discussion of the output and pricing behavior of imperfectly competitive firms (monopolists, oligopolists, and monopolistic competitors) is in chapters 13 and 14. See chapter 13 for a more detailed discussion of why supply curves do not exist for imperfectly competitive firms.

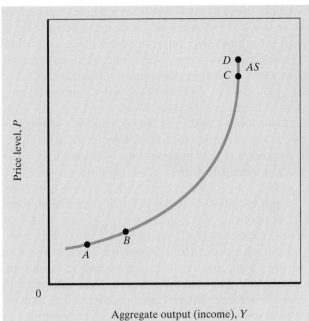

FIGURE 29.6

The Short-Run Aggregate Supply Curve

In the short run, the aggregate supply curve (the price/output response curve) has a positive slope. At low levels of aggregate output, the curve is fairly flat. As the economy approaches capacity, the curve becomes nearly vertical. At capacity, the curve is vertical.

close to full capacity. A firm is producing at full capacity if it is fully utilizing the capital and labor it has on hand. As we will discuss in detail in chapter 32, firms may at times have *excess capital* and *excess labor* on hand—amounts of capital and labor not needed to produce the current level of output. If, for example, there are costs of getting rid of capital once it is in place, a firm may choose to hold on to some of this capital, even if the economy is in a downturn and the firm has decreased its output. In this case, the firm will not be fully utilizing its capital stock. Firms may be especially likely to behave this way if they expect that the downturn will be short and that they will need the capital in the future to produce a higher level of output. Firms may have similar reasons for holding excess labor. It may be costly, both in worker morale and administrative costs, to lay off a large number of workers.

The Federal Reserve reports on the nation's "capacity utilization rate" monthly. In December of 1990, for example, during the recession of 1990 to 1991, the capacity utilization rate for manufacturing firms was 79.3 percent. This suggests about 20 percent of the nation's factory capacity was idle. During the recessions of 1974 to 1975 and 1980 to 1982, capacity utilization fell below 75 percent. At the beginning of 1998, with real output growing at a healthy pace, U.S. capacity utilization stood at 83.3 percent.

Macroeconomists also focus on whether or not the *economy as a whole* is operating at full capacity. If there is cyclical unemployment (unemployment above the frictional and structural amounts), the economy is not fully utilizing its labor force. There are people who want to work at the current wage rates who cannot find jobs.

> Even if firms are not holding excess labor and capital, the economy may be operating below its capacity if there is cyclical unemployment.

Output Levels and Price/Output Responses   At low levels of output in the economy, there is likely to be excess capacity both in individual firms and in the economy as a whole. Firms are likely to be producing at levels of output below their existing capacity constraints. That is, they are likely to be holding excess capital and labor. It is also likely that there will be cyclical unemployment in the economy as a whole in periods of low output. When this is the case, it is likely that firms will respond to an increase in demand by increasing output much more than they increase prices. Firms are below capacity, so the extra cost of producing more output is likely to be small. In addition, firms can get more labor (from the ranks of the unemployed) without much, if any, increase in wage rates.

> An increase in aggregate demand when the economy is operating at low levels of output is likely to result in an increase in output with little or no increase in the overall price level. That is, the aggregate supply (price/output response) curve is likely to be fairly flat at low levels of aggregate output.

Refer to Figure 29.6. Aggregate output is considerably higher at *B* than at *A*, but the price level at *B* is only slightly higher than it is at *A*.

If aggregate output continues to expand, things will change. As firms and the economy as a whole begin to move closer and closer to capacity, firms' response to an increase in demand is likely to change from mainly increasing output to mainly increasing prices. Why? As firms continue to increase their output, they will begin to bump into their short-run capacity constraints. In addition, unemployment will be falling as firms hire more workers to produce the increased output, so the economy as a whole will be approaching its capacity. As aggregate output rises, the prices of labor and capital (input costs) will begin to rise more rapidly, leading firms to increase their output prices.

At some level of output, it is virtually impossible for firms to expand any further. At this level, all sectors are fully utilizing their existing factories and equipment. Plants are running double shifts, and many workers are on overtime. In addition, there is little or no cyclical unemployment in the economy. At this point, firms will respond to any further increases in demand only by raising prices.

> When the economy is producing at its maximum level of output—that is, at capacity—the aggregate supply curve becomes vertical.

Between *C* and *D* in Figure 29.6, the *AS* curve is vertical. Moving from *C* to *D* results in no increase in aggregate output but a large increase in the price level.

> ### The Response of Input Prices to Changes in the Overall Price Level
Whether or not the economy is producing a level of output close to capacity, there must be some time lag between changes in input prices and changes in output prices for the aggregate supply (price/output response) curve to slope upward. If input prices changed at exactly the same rate as output prices, the *AS* curve would be vertical.

It is easy to see why. It is generally assumed that firms make decisions with the objective of maximizing profits. If all output and input prices increase 10 percent, no firm would find it advantageous to change its level of output. Why? Because the output level that maximized profits before the 10 percent increase will be the same as the level that maximizes profits after the 10 percent increase.[2] So, if input prices adjusted immediately to output prices, the aggregate supply (price/output response) curve would be vertical.

Wage rates may increase at exactly the same rate as the overall price level if the price-level increase is *fully anticipated*. If inflation were expected to be 5 percent this

---

[2]All prices going up by the same percentage is analogous to changing the monetary unit of account from, say, green dollars to red dollars, where 1.1 red dollars equals one green dollar. A change in the monetary unit of account has no effect on the firms' profit-maximizing decisions. If the nominal value of all output and input prices increases by 10 percent, then nothing *real* happens. When all nominal values go up by 10 percent, firms' decisions regarding *real* output will not change.

year, this expected increase might be built into wage and salary contracts. Most employees, however, do not receive automatic pay raises as the overall price level increases, and sometimes increases in the price level are unanticipated. Input prices—particularly wage rates—tend to lag increases in output prices for a variety of reasons. (We discuss these in chapter 30.) At least in the short run, wage rates tend to be slow to adjust to overall macroeconomic changes. It is precisely this point that has led to an important distinction between the *AS* curve in the long run and the *AS* curve in the short run.[3] We will return to this distinction shortly, but for now we will assume that the *AS* curve is shaped like the one in Figure 29.6.

SHIFTS OF THE SHORT-RUN AGGREGATE SUPPLY CURVE

Just as the aggregate demand curve can shift, so too can the aggregate supply (price/output response) curve. Recall the individual firm behavior we just considered in describing the shape of the short-run *AS* curve. Firms with the power to set prices choose the price/output combinations that maximize their profits. Firms in perfectly competitive industries choose the quantities of output to supply at given price levels. The *AS* curve traces out these price/output responses to economic conditions.

Anything that affects these individual firm decisions can shift the *AS* curve. Some of these factors include cost shocks, economic growth, stagnation, public policy, and natural disasters.

➤ **Cost Shocks** Firms' decisions are heavily influenced by costs. Some costs change at the same time the overall price level changes, some costs lag behind changes in the price level, and some may not change at all. Changes in costs that occur at the same time that the price level changes are built into the shape of the short-run *AS* curve. For example, when the price level rises, wage rates might rise by half as much in the short run. (This could happen if half of all wage contracts in the economy had cost-of-living increase clauses and half did not.) The shape of the short-run *AS* curve would reflect this response.

But sometimes cost changes occur that are *not* the result of changes in the overall price level. Example: the cost of energy. During the fall of 1990, world crude oil prices doubled from about $20 to $40 a barrel. Once it became clear the Persian Gulf War would not lead to the destruction of the Saudi Arabian oil fields, the price of crude oil on world markets fell back to below $20 per barrel. In contrast, in 1973 to 1974 and again in 1979, the price of oil increased substantially and remained at a higher level. Oil is an important input in many firms and industries, and when the price of firms' inputs rises, firms respond by raising prices and lowering output. At the aggregate level, this means an increase in the price of oil (or a similar cost increase) *shifts* the *AS* curve to the left, as in Figure 29.7a. A leftward shift of the *AS* curve means a higher price level for a given level of output.

A decrease in costs shifts the *AS* curve to the right, as in Figure 29.7b. A rightward shift of the *AS* curve means a lower price level for a given level of output.

Shifts in the *AS* curve brought about by a change in costs are referred to as **cost shocks** or **supply shocks**.

cost shock, or **supply shock**
A change in costs that shifts the aggregate supply (AS) curve.

➤ **Economic Growth** Economic growth shifts the *AS* curve to the right. Recall that the vertical part of the short-run *AS* curve represents the economy's maximum (capacity) output. This maximum output is determined by the economy's existing resources and

---

[3]Some textbooks derive the short-run aggregate supply curve by assuming *all* input prices are fixed. "Fixed input prices" means input prices do not change as the overall price level changes. This assumption is not realistic because the outputs of some firms (such as intermediate goods and capital goods) are the inputs of other firms. It is also unrealistic to assume that wage rates do not respond at all to changes in the overall price level. It is more realistic to assume that wage rates do not *fully* respond in the short run than it is to assume no response at all.

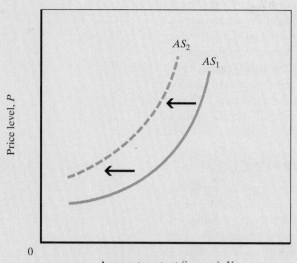

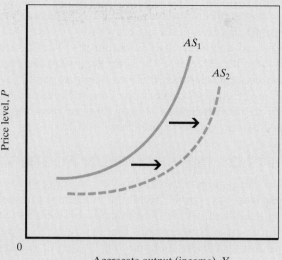

a. A decrease in aggregate supply

A leftward shift of the *AS* curve from AS_1 to AS_2 could be caused by an increase in costs (for example, an increase in wage rates or energy prices), natural disasters, economic stagnation, and the like.

b. An increase in aggregate supply

A rightward shift of the *AS* curve from AS_1 to AS_2 could be caused by a decrease in costs, economic growth, public policy that stimulates supply, and the like.

FIGURE 29.7
Shifts of the Aggregate Supply Curve

the current state of technology. If the supply of labor increases or the stock of capital grows, the *AS* curve will shift to the right. The labor force grows naturally with the population, but it can also increase for other reasons. Since the 1960s, for example, the percentage of women in the labor force has grown sharply. This increase in the supply of women workers has shifted the *AS* curve to the right.

Immigration can also shift the *AS* curve. During the 1970s, Germany, faced with a serious labor shortage, opened its borders to large numbers of "guest workers," largely from Turkey. The United States has recently experienced significant immigration, legal and illegal, from Mexico, from Central and South American countries, and from Asia. Increases in the stock of capital over time and technological advances can also shift the *AS* curve to the right. We will discuss economic growth in more detail in chapter 35.

➤ **Stagnation and Lack of Investment**   The opposite of economic growth is stagnation and decline. Over time, capital deteriorates and eventually wears out completely if it is not properly maintained. If an economy fails to invest in both public capital (sometimes called *infrastructure*) and private capital (plant and equipment) at a sufficient rate, the stock of capital will decline. If the stock of capital declines, the *AS* curve will shift to the left.

➤ **Public Policy**   Public policy can shift the *AS* curve. In the 1980s, for example, the Reagan administration put into effect a form of public policy based on supply-side economics. The idea behind these supply-side policies was to deregulate the economy and reduce taxes to increase the incentives to work, engage in entrepreneurial activity, and invest. The main purpose of these policies was to shift the *AS* curve to the right. (We discuss supply-side economics in chapter 34.)

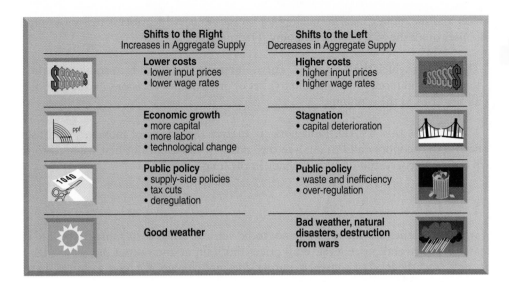

FIGURE 29.8

Factors That Shift the Aggregate Supply Curve

Shifts to the Right Increases in Aggregate Supply	Shifts to the Left Decreases in Aggregate Supply
Lower costs • lower input prices • lower wage rates	**Higher costs** • higher input prices • higher wage rates
Economic growth • more capital • more labor • technological change	**Stagnation** • capital deterioration
Public policy • supply-side policies • tax cuts • deregulation	**Public policy** • waste and inefficiency • over-regulation
Good weather	**Bad weather, natural disasters, destruction from wars**

➤ **Weather, Wars, and Natural Disasters** Changes in weather can shift the *AS* curve. A severe drought will reduce the supply of agricultural goods; the perfect mix of sun and rain will produce a bountiful harvest. If an economy is damaged by war or natural disaster, the *AS* curve will shift to the left. Whenever part of the resource base of an economy is reduced or destroyed, the *AS* curve shifts to the left.

Figure 29.8 shows some factors that might cause the *AS* curve to shift.

THE EQUILIBRIUM PRICE LEVEL

The **equilibrium price level** in the economy occurs at the point at which the *AD* curve and the *AS* curve intersect, shown in Figure 29.9, where the equilibrium price level is P_0 and the equilibrium level of aggregate output (income) is Y_0.

Figure 29.9 looks simple, but it is a powerful device for analyzing a number of macroeconomic questions. Consider first what is true at the intersection of the *AS* and *AD* curves. Each point on the *AD* curve corresponds to equilibrium in both the goods

equilibrium price level *The point at which the aggregate demand and aggregate supply curves intersect.*

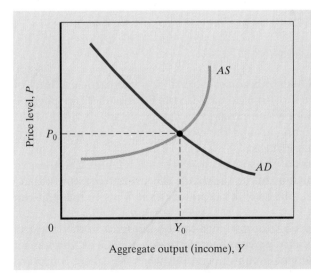

FIGURE 29.9

The Equilibrium Price Level

At each point along the *AD* curve, both the money market and the goods market are in equilibrium. Each point on the *AS* curve represents the price/output decisions of all the firms in the economy. P_0 and Y_0 correspond to equilibrium in the goods market and the money market and to a set of price/output decisions on the part of all the firms in the economy.

market and the money market. Each point on the *AS* curve represents the price/output responses of all the firms in the economy. That means:

> The point at which the *AS* and *AD* curves intersect corresponds to equilibrium in the goods and money markets and to a set of price/output decisions on the part of all the firms in the economy.

We will use this *AS/AD* framework to analyze the effects of monetary and fiscal policy on the economy and to analyze the causes of inflation. But first we need to return to the *AS* curve and discuss its shape in the long run.

THE LONG-RUN AGGREGATE SUPPLY CURVE

As we noted earlier, for the *AS* curve not to be vertical, some costs must lag behind increases in the overall price level. If all prices (both input and output prices) change at the same rate, the level of aggregate output does not change. We have assumed that in the short run at least some cost changes lag behind price level changes. But what happens in the long run?

Many economists believe costs lag behind price-level changes in the short run but ultimately move with the overall price level. For example, wage rates tend to move very closely with the price level *over time*. If the price level increases at a steady rate, inflation may come to be fully anticipated and built into most labor contracts.

If costs and the price level move in tandem in the long run, the *AS* curve is vertical. We can see why in Figure 29.10. Initially, the economy is in equilibrium at a price level of P_0 and aggregate output of Y_0 (the point at which AD_0 and AS_0 intersect). Now imagine a shift of the *AD* curve from AD_0 to AD_1. In response to this shift, both the price level and aggregate output rise in the short run, to P_1 and Y_1 respectively. But recall: the movement along the upward-sloping *AS* curve as *Y* increases from Y_0 to Y_1 assumes some costs lag behind the increase in the overall price level.

Now suppose costs fully adjust to prices in the long run. Suppose labor unions renegotiate wage contracts to catch up with the increase in prices. These kinds of cost increases, which come in later periods, cause the *AS* curve to shift to the left, from AS_0 to AS_1. If, in the final analysis, costs and prices have risen by exactly the same percentage, aggregate output will be back at Y_0 (the point at which AD_1 and AS_1 intersect).

> If wage rates and other costs fully adjust to changes in prices in the long run, then the long-run *AS* curve is vertical.

POTENTIAL GDP

Recall that even the short-run *AS* curve becomes vertical at some particular level of output. The vertical portion of the short-run *AS* curve exists because there are physical limits to the amount that an economy can produce in any given time period. At the physical limit, all plants are operating around the clock, many workers are on overtime, and there is no cyclical unemployment.

Note that the vertical portions of the short-run *AS* curves in Figure 29.10 are to the right of Y_0. If the vertical portions of the short-run *AS* curves represent "capacity," then what is the nature of Y_0, the level of output corresponding to the long-run *AS* curve?

Y_0 represents the level of aggregate output that can be *sustained* in the long run without inflation. It is sometimes called **potential output** or **potential GDP**. Output can be pushed above Y_0 under a variety of circumstances, but when it is, there is upward

potential output, or **potential GDP** *The level of aggregate output that can be sustained in the long run without inflation.*

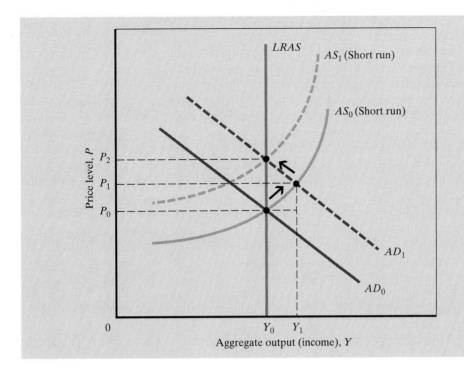

FIGURE 29.10

The Long-Run Aggregate Supply Curve

When the AD curve shifts from AD_0 to AD_1, the equilibrium price level initially rises from P_0 to P_1 and output rises from Y_0 to Y_1. Costs respond in the longer run, shifting the AS curve from AS_0 to AS_1. If costs ultimately increase by the same percentage as the price level, the quantity supplied will end up back at Y_0. Y_0 is sometimes called "potential GDP."

[handwritten note: ToTally vertical whole line moves ←]

pressure on costs. As the economy approaches short-run capacity, wage rates tend to rise as firms try to attract more people into the labor force and to induce more workers to work overtime. Rising costs shift the short-run AS curve to the left (in Figure 29.10, from AS_0 to AS_1) and drive output back to Y_0.

The underlying idea here is simple. It is possible to try to squeeze too much from an existing resource base. Labor can be overemployed. In recent years, some states experienced unemployment rates below 3 percent. When the unemployment rate is this low, there is an upward pressure on wages that ultimately constrains growth.

▶ **Short-Run Equilibrium below Potential GDP** Thus far we have argued that if the short-run aggregate supply and aggregate demand curves intersect to the right of Y_0 in Figure 29.10, wages and other input prices will rise, causing the short-run AS curve to shift left and pushing GDP back down to Y_0. Although different economists have different opinions on how to determine whether an economy is operating at or above potential GDP, there is general agreement that there is a maximum level of output (below the vertical portion of the short-run aggregate supply curve) that can be sustained without inflation.

But what about short-run equilibria that occur to the *left* of Y_0? If the short-run aggregate supply and aggregate demand curves intersect at a level of output below potential GDP, what will happen? Here again economists disagree. Those who believe the aggregate supply curve is vertical in the long run believe that when short-run equilibria exist below Y_0, GDP will tend to rise—just as GDP tends to fall when short-run equilibrium exists above Y_0. The argument is that when the economy is operating below full employment with excess capacity and high unemployment, input prices (including wages) are likely to *fall*. A decline in input prices shifts the aggregate supply curve to the *right*, causing the price level to fall and the level of real GDP to rise back to Y_0. This automatic adjustment works only if input prices fall when excess capacity and unemployment exist. We will discuss wage adjustment during periods of unemployment in detail in chapter 30.

AD, AS, AND MONETARY AND FISCAL POLICY

We are now ready to use the AS/AD framework to consider the effects of monetary and fiscal policy. We will first consider the short-run effects.

Recall that the two fiscal policy variables are government purchases (G) and net taxes (T). The monetary policy variable is the quantity of money supplied (M^s). An *expansionary* policy aims at stimulating the economy through an increase in G or M^s or a decrease in T. A *contractionary* policy aims at slowing down the economy through a decrease in G or M^s or an increase in T. We saw earlier in this chapter that an expansionary policy shifts the AD curve to the right and that a contractionary policy shifts the AD curve to the left. But how do these policies affect the equilibrium values of the price level (P) and the level of aggregate output (income)?

When considering the effects of a policy change, we must be careful to note where along the (short-run) AS curve the economy is at the time of the change. If the economy is initially on the flat portion of the AS curve, as shown by point A in Figure 29.11, then an expansionary policy, which shifts the AD curve to the right, results in a small price increase relative to the output increase: The increase in equilibrium Y (from Y_0 to Y_1) is much greater than the increase in equilibrium P (from P_0 to P_1). This is the case in which an expansionary policy works well. There is an increase in output with little increase in the price level.

If the economy is initially on the steep portion of the AS curve, as shown by point B in Figure 29.12, then an expansionary policy results in a small increase in equilibrium output (from Y_0 to Y_1) and a large increase in the equilibrium price level (from P_0 to P_1). In this case, an expansionary policy does not work well. It results in a much higher price level with little increase in output. The multiplier is therefore close to zero: Output is initially close to capacity, and attempts to increase it further lead mostly to a higher price level.

Figures 29.11 and 29.12 show it is important to know where the economy is *before* a policy change is put into effect. The economy is producing on the nearly flat part of the AS curve if most firms are producing well below capacity. When this is the case, firms will respond to an increase in demand by increasing output much more than they increase prices. If the economy is producing on the steep part of the AS curve, firms are close to capacity and will respond to an increase in demand by increasing prices much more than they increase output.

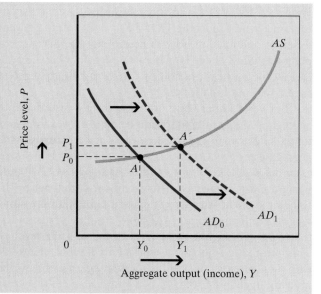

FIGURE 29.11

A Shift of the Aggregate Demand Curve When the Economy Is on the Nearly Flat Part of the AS Curve

Aggregate demand can shift to the right for a number of reasons, including an increase in the money supply, a tax cut, or an increase in government spending. If the shift occurs when the economy is on the nearly flat portion of the AS curve, the result will be an increase in output with little increase in the price level.

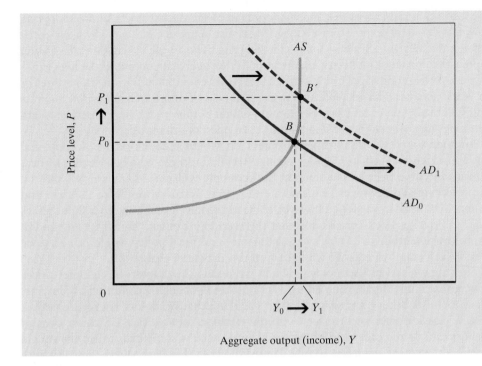

FIGURE 29.12

A Shift of the Aggregate Demand Curve When the Economy Is Operating at or Near Maximum Capacity

If a shift of aggregate demand occurs while the economy is operating near full capacity, the result will be an increase in the price level with little increase in output.

To see what happens when the economy is on the steep part of the *AS* curve, consider the effects of an increase in *G* with no change in the money supply. Why, when *G* is increased, will there be virtually no increase in *Y*? In other words, why will the expansionary fiscal policy fail to stimulate the economy? To answer this we need to go back to chapter 28 and consider what is behind the *AD* curve.

The first thing that happens when *G* increases is an unanticipated decline in firms' inventories. Because firms are very close to capacity output when the economy is on the steep part of the *AS* curve, they cannot increase their output very much. The result, as Figure 29.12 shows, is a substantial increase in the price level. The increase in the price level increases the demand for money, which (with a fixed money supply) leads to an increase in the interest rate, decreasing planned investment. *There is nearly complete crowding out of investment.* If firms are producing at capacity, prices and interest rates will continue to rise until the increase in *G* is completely matched by a decrease in planned investment and there is complete crowding out.

LONG-RUN AGGREGATE SUPPLY AND POLICY EFFECTS

We have so far been considering monetary and fiscal policy effects in the short run. Regarding the long run, it is important to realize:

> If the *AS* curve is vertical in the long run, neither monetary policy nor fiscal policy has any effect on aggregate output in the long run.

Look back at Figure 29.10. Monetary and fiscal policy shift the *AD* curve. If the long-run *AS* curve is vertical, output always comes back to Y_0. In this case, policy affects *only* the price level in the long run, and the multiplier effect of a change in government spending on aggregate output in the long run is zero. Under the same circumstances, the tax multiplier is also zero.

The conclusion that policy has no effect on aggregate output in the long run is perhaps startling. Do most economists agree that the aggregate supply curve is vertical in the long run?

Most economists agree that input prices tend to lag output prices in the short run, giving the *AS* curve some positive slope. Most also agree the *AS* curve is likely to be steeper in the long run. But how long is the long run? The longer the lag time, the greater the potential impact of monetary and fiscal policy on aggregate output. If the long run is only three to six months, policy has little chance to affect output; if the long run is three or four years, policy can have significant effects. A good deal of research in macroeconomics focuses on the length of time lags between input and output prices. In a sense, the length of the long run is one of the most important open questions in macroeconomics.

Another source of disagreement centers on whether equilibria below potential GDP, Y_0 in Figure 29.10, are self-correcting. Recall that those who believe in a vertical long-run *AS* curve believe that slack in the economy will put downward pressure on input prices (including wages), causing the short-run *AS* curve to shift to the right and pushing GDP back toward Y_0. However, some argue that wages and other input prices do *not* fall during slack periods and that the economy can get "stuck" at an equilibrium below potential GDP. In this case, monetary and fiscal policy would be necessary to restore full employment. We will return to this debate in chapter 30.

The "new classical" economics, which we discuss in chapter 34, assumes prices and wages are fully flexible and adjust very quickly to changing conditions. New classical economists believe, for example, that wage rate changes do not lag price changes. The new classical view is consistent with the existence of a vertical *AS* curve, even in the short run. At the other end of the spectrum is what is sometimes called the simple "Keynesian" view of aggregate supply. Those who hold this view believe there is a kink in the *AS* curve at capacity output, as we discuss in the Issues and Debates box "The Simple 'Keynesian' Aggregate Supply Curve."

CAUSES OF INFLATION

We now turn to inflation and use the *AS/AD* framework to consider the causes of inflation.

> **Inflation versus Sustained Inflation: A Reminder**   Before we discuss the specific causes of inflation, recall the distinction we made in chapter 23. **Inflation**, as you know, is an increase in the overall price level. Anything that shifts the *AD* curve to the right or the *AS* curve to the left causes inflation. But it is often useful to distinguish between a *one-time increase* in the price level (a one-time inflation) and an inflation that is sustained. A **sustained inflation** occurs when the overall price level continues to rise over some fairly long period of time. When we speak of a sustained inflation rate of 7 percent, for example, we generally mean that the price level has been rising at a rate of 7 percent per year over a number of years.

It is generally accepted that there are many possible causes of a one-time increase in the price level. (We discuss the main causes next.) But for the price level to continue to increase period after period, most economists believe it must be "accommodated" by an expanded money supply. This leads to the assertion that a sustained inflation, whatever the initial cause of the increase in the price level, is essentially a monetary phenomenon.

DEMAND-PULL INFLATION

Inflation initiated by an increase in aggregate demand is called **demand-pull inflation**. You can see how demand-pull inflation works by looking at Figures 29.11 and 29.12. In both, the inflation begins with a shift of the aggregate demand schedule from AD_0 to AD_1, which causes the price level to increase from P_0 to P_1. (Output also increases, from Y_0 to Y_1.) If the economy is operating on the steep portion of the *AS* curve at the time of the increase in aggregate demand, as in Figure 29.12, most of the effect will be

inflation *An increase in the overall price level.*

sustained inflation *Occurs when the overall price level continues to rise over some fairly long period of time.*

demand-pull inflation *Inflation that is initiated by an increase in aggregate demand.*

THE SIMPLE "KEYNESIAN" AGGREGATE SUPPLY CURVE

There is a great deal of disagreement regarding the shape of the AS curve. One view of the aggregate supply curve, the simple "Keynesian" view, holds that at any given moment, the economy has a clearly defined capacity, or maximum, output. This maximum output, denoted by Y_F, is defined by the existing labor force, the current capital stock, and the existing state of technology. If planned aggregate expenditure increases when the economy is producing *below* this maximum capacity, this view holds, inventories will be lower than planned and firms will increase output, but the price level will not change. Firms are operating with underutilized plants (excess capacity) and there is unemployment. Expansion does not exert any upward pressure on prices. However, if planned aggregate expenditure increases when the economy is producing near or at its maximum (Y_F), inventories will be lower than planned, but firms cannot increase their output. The result will be an increase in the price level, or inflation.

This view is illustrated in Figure 1. In the top half of the diagram, aggregate output (income) (Y) and planned aggregate expenditure $(C + I + G \equiv AE)$ are initially in equilibrium at AE_1, Y_1, and price level P_1. Now suppose a tax cut or an increase in government spending increases planned aggregate expenditure. If such an increase shifts the AE curve from AE_1 to AE_2 and the corresponding aggregate demand curve from AD_1 to AD_2, the equilibrium level of output will rise from Y_1 to Y_F. (Remember, an expansionary policy shifts the AD curve to the right.) Because we were initially producing below

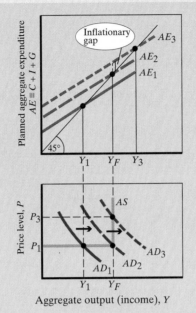

FIGURE 1

With planned aggregate expenditure of AE_1 and aggregate demand of AD_1, equilibrium output is Y_1. A shift of planned aggregate expenditure to AE_2, corresponding to a shift of the AD curve to AD_2, causes output to rise but the price level to remain at P_1. If planned aggregate expenditure and aggregate demand exceed Y_F, however, there is an inflationary gap and the price level rises to P_3.

capacity output (Y_1 is lower than Y_F), the price level will be unaffected, remaining at P_1.

But now consider what would happen if AE were to increase even further. Suppose planned aggregate expenditure were to shift from AE_2 to AE_3, with a corresponding shift of AD_2 to AD_3. If the economy were producing below capacity output, the equilibrium level of output would rise to Y_3. But the output of the economy cannot exceed the maximum output of Y_F. As inventories fall below what was planned, firms encounter a fully employed labor market and fully utilized plants. Therefore, they cannot increase their output. The result is that the aggregate supply curve becomes vertical at Y_F, and the price level is driven up to P_3.

The difference between planned aggregate expenditure and aggregate output at full capacity is sometimes referred to as an **inflationary gap**. You can see the inflationary gap in the top half of Figure 1. At Y_F (capacity output), planned aggregate expenditure (shown by AE_3) is greater than Y_F. The price level rises to P_3 until the aggregate quantity supplied and the aggregate quantity demanded are equal.

Despite the fact that the kinked aggregate supply curve provides some insights, most economists find it unrealistic. It does not seem likely that the whole economy suddenly runs into a capacity "wall" at a specific level of output. As output expands, some firms and industries will hit capacity before others.

 For more on the aggregate supply curve, see the Case and Fair Web page at
http://www.prenhall.com/casefair.

FIGURE 29.13

Cost-Push, or Supply-Side
Inflation

An increase in costs shifts the
AS curve to the left. Assuming
the government does not react
to this shift, the *AD* curve
does not shift, the price level
rises, and output falls.

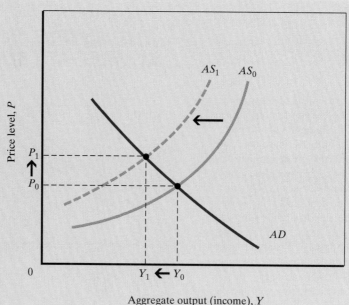

Aggregate output (income), *Y*

an increase in the price level rather than an increase in output. If the economy is operating on the flat portion of the *AS* curve, as in Figure 29.11, most of the effect will be an increase in output rather than an increase in the price level.

Remember: In the long run the initial increase in the price level will cause the *AS* curve to shift to the left as input prices (costs) respond to the increase in output prices. If the long-run *AS* curve is vertical, as depicted in Figure 29.10, the increase in costs will shift the short-run *AS* curve (AS_0) to the left to AS_1, pushing the price level even higher, to P_2. If the long-run *AS* curve is vertical, a shift in aggregate demand from AD_0 to AD_1 will result, in the long run, in *no* increase in output and a price-level increase from P_0 to P_2.

COST-PUSH, OR SUPPLY-SIDE, INFLATION

**cost-push, or supply-side,
inflation** *Inflation caused by an
increase in costs.*

Inflation can also be caused by an increase in costs, referred to as **cost-push**, or **supply-side, inflation.** Several times in the last two decades oil prices on world markets increased sharply. Because oil is used in virtually every line of business, costs increased.

An increase in costs (a cost shock) shifts the *AS* curve to the left, as Figure 29.13 shows. If we assume the government does not react to this shift in *AS* by changing fiscal or monetary policy, the *AD* curve will not shift. The supply shift will cause the equilibrium price level to rise (from P_0 to P_1) and the level of aggregate output to decline (from Y_0 to Y_1). Recall from chapter 21 that **stagflation** occurs when output is falling at the

stagflation *Occurs when output
is falling at the same time that
prices are rising.*

same time prices are rising—in other words, when the economy is experiencing both a contraction and inflation simultaneously. Figure 29.13 shows that one possible cause of stagflation is an increase in costs.

To return to monetary and fiscal policy for a moment, note from Figure 29.13 that the government could counteract the increase in costs (the cost shock) by engaging in an expansionary policy (an increase in *G* or M^s or a decrease in *T*). This would shift the *AD* curve to the right, and the new *AD* curve would intersect the new *AS* curve at a higher level of output. The problem with this policy, however, is that the intersection of the new *AS* and *AD* curves would take place at a price even higher than P_1 in Figure 29.13.

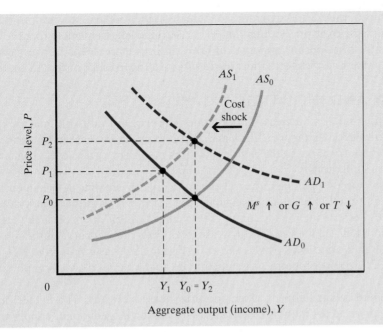

FIGURE 29.14

Cost Shocks Are Bad News for Policy Makers

A cost shock with no change in monetary or fiscal policy would shift the aggregate supply curve from AS_0 to AS_1, lower output from Y_0 to Y_1, and raise the price level from P_0 to P_1. Monetary or fiscal policy could be changed enough to have the AD curve shift from AD_0 to AD_1. This would prevent output from falling, but it would raise the price level further, to P_2.

> Cost shocks are bad news for policy makers. The only way they can counter the output loss brought about by a cost shock is by having the price level increase even more than it would without the policy action.

This situation is illustrated in Figure 29.14.

EXPECTATIONS AND INFLATION

When firms are making their price/output decisions, their *expectations* of future prices may affect their current decisions. If a firm expects that its competitors will raise their prices, in anticipation it may raise its own price.

Consider a firm that manufactures toasters. The toaster maker must decide what price to charge retail stores for its toaster. If it overestimates price and charges much more than other toaster manufacturers are charging, it will lose many customers. If it underestimates price and charges much less than other toaster makers are charging, it will gain customers but at a considerable loss in revenue per sale. The firm's *optimum price*—the price that maximizes the firm's profits—is presumably not too far from the average of its competitors' prices. If it does not know its competitors' projected prices before it sets its own price, as is often the case, it must base its price on what it expects its competitors' prices to be.

Suppose inflation has been running at about 10 percent per year. Our firm probably expects its competitors will raise their prices about 10 percent this year, so it is likely to raise the price of its own toaster by about 10 percent. This is how expectations can get "built into the system." If every firm expects every other firm to raise prices by 10 percent, every firm will raise prices by about 10 percent. Every firm ends up with the price increase it expected.

The fact that expectations can affect the price level is vexing. Expectations can lead to an inertia that makes it difficult to stop an inflationary spiral. If prices have been rising, and if people's expectations are *adaptive*—that is, if they form their expectations on the basis of past pricing behavior—then firms may continue raising prices even if demand is slowing or contracting.

In terms of the *AS/AD* diagram, an increase in inflationary expectations that causes firms to increase their prices shifts the *AS* curve to the left. Remember that the *AS* curve represents the price/output responses of firms. If firms increase their prices because of a change in inflationary expectations, the result is a leftward shift of the *AS* curve.

MONEY AND INFLATION

It is easy to see that an increase in the money supply can lead to an increase in the aggregate price level. As Figures 29.11 and 29.12 show, an increase in the money supply (M^s) shifts the *AD* curve to the right and results in a higher price level. This is simply a demand-pull inflation.

But the supply of money may also play a role in creating a sustained inflation. Consider an initial increase in government spending (*G*) with the money supply (M^s) unchanged. Because the money supply is unchanged, this is an increase in *G* that is not "accommodated" by the Fed. The increase in *G* shifts the *AD* curve to the right and results in a higher price level. This is shown in Figure 29.15 as a shift from AD_0 to AD_1. (In Figure 29.15, the economy is assumed to be operating on the vertical portion of the *AS* curve.)

Remember what happens when the price level increases. The higher price level causes the demand for money to increase. With an unchanged money supply and an increase in the quantity of money demanded, the interest rate will rise, and the result will be a decrease in planned investment (*I*) spending. The new equilibrium corresponds to higher *G*, lower *I*, a higher interest rate, and a higher price level.

Now let's take our example one step further. Suppose that the Fed is sympathetic to the expansionary fiscal policy (the increase in *G* we just discussed) and decides to expand the supply of money to keep the interest rate constant. As the higher price level pushes up the demand for money, the Fed expands the supply of money with the goal of keeping the interest rate unchanged, eliminating the crowding-out effect of a higher interest rate.

When the supply of money is expanded, the *AD* curve shifts to the right again, from AD_1 to AD_2. This shift of the *AD* curve, brought about by the increased money supply, pushes prices up even further. Higher prices in turn increase the demand for money further, which requires a further increase in the money supply, and so on.

What would happen if the Fed tried to keep the interest rate constant when the economy is operating on the steep part of the *AS* curve? The situation could lead to a **hyperinflation**, a period of very rapid increases in the price level. If no more output can be coaxed out of the economy and if planned investment is not allowed to fall (because the interest rate is kept unchanged), then it is not possible to increase *G*. As the Fed keeps pumping more and more money into the economy to keep the interest rate unchanged, the price level will keep rising.

hyperinflation *A period of very rapid increases in the price level.*

✗ SUSTAINED INFLATION AS A PURELY MONETARY PHENOMENON

Virtually all economists agree that an increase in the price level can be caused by anything that causes the *AD* curve to shift to the right or the *AS* curve to shift to the left. These include expansionary fiscal policy actions, monetary expansion, cost shocks, changes in expectations, and so forth. It is also generally agreed that for a *sustained* inflation to occur, the Federal Reserve must accommodate it. In this sense, a sustained inflation can be thought of as a purely monetary phenomenon.

This argument, first put forth by monetarists (coming in chapter 34), has gained wide acceptance. It is easy to show, as we just did, how expanding the money supply can continuously shift the *AD* curve. It is not as easy to come up with other reasons for continued shifts of the *AD* curve if the money supply is constant. One possibility is for the government to increase spending continuously without increasing taxes. But this process cannot continue forever. To finance spending without taxes, the government

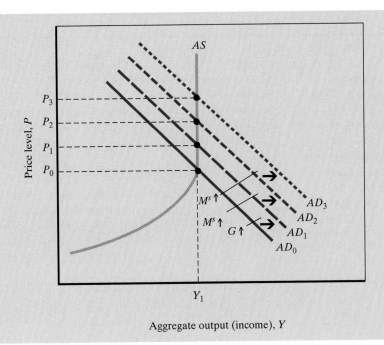

FIGURE 29.15

Sustained Inflation from an Initial Increase in G and Fed Accommodation

An increase in G with the money supply constant shifts the AD curve from AD_0 to AD_1. Although not shown in the figure, this leads to an increase in the interest rate and crowding out of planned investment. If the Fed tries to keep the interest rate unchanged by increasing the money supply, the AD curve will shift farther and farther to the right. The result is a sustained inflation, perhaps a hyperinflation.

must borrow. Without any expansion of the money supply, the interest rate will rise dramatically, making the cost of borrowing very high. But more importantly, the public must be willing to buy the government bonds that are being issued to finance the spending increases. At some point, the public may be unwilling to buy any more bonds even though the interest rate is very high.[4] At this point, the government is no longer able to increase non-tax-financed spending without the Fed's cooperation. If this is true, then a sustained inflation cannot exist without the Fed's cooperation.

In recent years, the governments of several struggling eastern European and Latin American nations have expanded their money supplies significantly. The result has been very high inflation in those countries.

LOOKING AHEAD

In chapters 24 and 25, we discussed the concept of an equilibrium level of aggregate output and income, the idea of the multiplier, and the basics of fiscal policy. Those two chapters centered on the workings of the goods market alone.

In chapters 26 and 27, we analyzed the money market by discussing the supply of money, the demand for money, the equilibrium interest rate, and the basics of monetary policy. Chapter 28 brought our analysis of the goods market together with our analysis of the money market.

In this chapter, we used everything learned so far to discuss the aggregate supply and aggregate demand curves, first mentioned in chapter 21. Using aggregate supply and aggregate demand curves, we can determine the equilibrium price level in the economy and understand some causes of inflation.

We have said little about employment, unemployment, and the functioning of the labor market in the macroeconomy. The next chapter will link everything we have done so far to this third major market arena—the labor market—and to the problem of unemployment.

---

[4]This means that the public's demand for money no longer depends on the interest rate. Even though the interest rate is very high, the public cannot be induced to have its real money balances fall any further. There is a limit regarding how much the public can be induced to have its real money balances fall.

SUMMARY

THE AGGREGATE DEMAND CURVE

1. Money demand is a function of three variables: (1) the interest rate (r); (2) the level of real income (Y); and (3) the price level (P). Money demand will increase if the real level of output (income) increases, the price level increases, or the interest rate declines.

2. At a higher price level, households and firms need to hold larger money balances. If the money supply remains the same, this increased demand for money will cause the interest rate to increase and planned investment spending to fall. As a result, planned aggregate expenditure will be lower, inventories will be greater than planned, firms will cut back on output, and Y will fall. An increase in the price level causes the level of aggregate output (income) to fall: a decrease in the price level causes the level of aggregate output (income) to rise.

3. *Aggregate demand* is the total demand for goods and services in the economy. The *aggregate demand (AD) curve* illustrates the negative relationship between aggregate output (income) and the price level. Each point on the *AD* curve is a point at which both the goods market and the money market are in equilibrium. The *AD* curve is *not* the sum of all the market demand curves in the economy.

4. At every point along the aggregate demand curve, the aggregate quantity demanded in the economy is exactly equal to planned aggregate expenditure.

5. An increase in the quantity of money supplied, an increase in government purchases, or a decrease in net taxes at a given price level shifts the aggregate demand curve to the right. A decrease in the quantity of money supplied, a decrease in government purchases, or an increase in net taxes shifts the aggregate demand curve to the left.

THE AGGREGATE SUPPLY CURVE

6. *Aggregate supply* is the total supply of goods and services in an economy. The *aggregate supply (AS) curve* shows the relationship between the aggregate quantity of output supplied by all the firms in an economy and the overall price level. The *AS* curve is *not* a market supply curve, and it is *not* the simple sum of all the individual supply curves in the economy. For this reason, it is helpful to think of the *AS* curve as a "price/output response" curve—that is, a curve that traces out the price decisions and output decisions of all the markets and firms in the economy under a given set of circumstances.

7. The shape of the short-run *AS* curve is a source of much controversy in macroeconomics. Many economists believe that at very low levels of aggregate output the *AS* curve is fairly flat, and at high levels of aggregate output the *AS* curve is vertical or nearly vertical. Thus, the *AS* curve slopes upward and becomes vertical when the economy reaches its capacity, or maximum, output.

8. Anything that affects individual firms' decisions can shift the *AS* curve. Some of these factors include cost shocks, economic growth, stagnation, public policy, and natural disasters.

THE EQUILIBRIUM PRICE LEVEL

9. The *equilibrium price level* in the economy occurs at the point at which the *AS* and *AD* curves intersect. The intersection of the *AS* and *AD* curves corresponds to equilibrium in the goods and money markets *and* to a set of price/output decisions on the part of all the firms in the economy.

THE LONG-RUN AGGREGATE SUPPLY CURVE

10. For the *AS* curve to slope upward, some input prices must lag behind increases in the overall price level. If wage rates and other costs fully adjust to changes in prices in the long run, then the long-run *AS* curve is vertical.

11. The level of aggregate output that can be sustained in the long run without inflation is called *potential output* or *potential GDP*.

AD, AS, AND MONETARY AND FISCAL POLICY

12. If the economy is initially producing on the flat portion of the *AS* curve, an expansionary policy—which shifts the *AD* curve to the right—will result in a small increase in the equilibrium price level relative to the increase in equilibrium output. If the economy is initially producing on the steep portion of the *AS* curve, an expansionary policy results in a small increase in equilibrium output and a large increase in the equilibrium price level.

13. If the *AS* curve is vertical in the long run, neither monetary nor fiscal policy has any effect on aggregate output in the long run. For this reason, the exact length of the long run is one of the most pressing questions in macroeconomics.

CAUSES OF INFLATION

14. *Inflation* is an increase in the overall price level. A *sustained inflation* occurs when the overall price level continues to rise over some fairly long period of time. Most economists believe that sustained inflations can occur only if the Fed continuously increases the money supply.

15. *Demand-pull inflation* is inflation initiated by an increase in aggregate demand. *Cost-push*, or *supply-side, inflation* is inflation initiated by an increase in costs. An increase in costs may also lead to *stagflation*—the situation in which the economy is experiencing both a contraction and inflation simultaneously.

16. Inflation can become "built into the system" as a result of expectations. If prices have been rising and people form their expectations on the basis of past pricing behavior, firms may continue raising prices even if demand is slowing or contracting.

17. When the price level increases, so too does the demand for money. If the economy is operating on the steep part of the *AS* curve and the Fed tries to keep the interest rate constant by increasing the supply of money, the result could be a hyperinflation—a period of very rapid increases in the price level.

REVIEW TERMS AND CONCEPTS

aggregate demand, 676

aggregate demand (*AD*) curve, 677

aggregate supply, 681

aggregate supply (*AS*) curve, 681

cost-push, or supply-side, inflation, 694

cost shock, or supply shock, 685

demand-pull inflation, 692

equilibrium price level, 687

hyperinflation, 696

inflation, 692

inflationary gap, 693

potential output, or potential GDP, 688

real wealth, or real balance, effect, 679

stagflation, 694

sustained inflation, 692

PROBLEM SET

1. "The aggregate demand curve slopes downward, because when the price level is lower, people can afford to buy more, and aggregate demand rises. When prices rise, people can afford to buy less, and aggregate demand falls." Is this a good explanation of the shape of the *AD* curve? Why or why not?

2. Using aggregate supply and demand curves to illustrate your points, discuss the impacts of the following events on the price level and on equilibrium GDP (*Y*) in the *short run*: *REAL INCOME*

  a. A tax cut holding government purchases constant with the economy operating at near full capacity.

  b. An increase in the money supply during a period of high unemployment and excess industrial capacity.

  c. An increase in the price of oil caused by a war in the Middle East, assuming that the Fed attempts to keep interest rates constant by accommodating inflation.

  d. The Clinton plan from early 1993: an increase in taxes and a cut in government spending, supported by a cooperative Fed acting to keep output from falling.

3. During 1997 and 1998, a debate raged over whether the United States was at or above potential GDP (see the Application box in this chapter). Some economists feared the economy was operating at a level of output above potential GDP and inflationary pressures were building. They urged the Fed to tighten monetary policy and increase interest rates to slow the economy. Others argued that a worldwide glut of cheap products was causing input prices to be lower, keeping prices from rising.

    Using aggregate supply and demand curves and other useful graphs, illustrate the following:

  a. Those pushing the Fed to act were right and prices start to rise more rapidly in 1998 and 1999. The Fed acts belatedly to slow money growth (contract the money supply), driving up interest rates and pushing the economy back to potential GDP.

  b. The worldwide glut gets worse and the result is a *falling* price level (deflation) in the United States despite expanding aggregate demand.

4. Show the effects of the following stories on the position of the aggregate demand curve. Use graphs of the money demand curve, the investment function, and aggregate expenditure function if useful. What is likely to happen to *Y*, *C*, *I*, and *r* as a result?

  a. In 1997 the Congress enacted a substantial tax cut (the Taxpayer Relief Act of 1997) that lowered taxes for many immediately. While the act contained some expenditure reductions, they did not kick in until 1999. Assume that the Fed expands the money supply to keep interest rates constant.

  b. The Federal Reserve sharply decreases the money supply to fight inflation.

5. Using aggregate supply and aggregate demand curves to illustrate, describe the effects of the following events on the price level and on equilibrium GDP in the *long run*, assuming that input prices fully adjust to output prices after some lag:

  a. An increase in the money supply above potential GDP.

  b. A decrease in government spending and in the money supply with GDP above potential GDP.

  c. Starting with the economy at potential GDP, a war in the Middle East pushes up energy prices temporarily. The Fed expands the money supply to accommodate the inflation.

6. Two separate capacity constraints are discussed in this chapter: (1) the actual physical capacity of existing plants and equipment, shown as the vertical portion of the short-run *AS* curve, and (2) potential GDP, leading to a vertical *LRAS* curve. Explain the difference between the two. Which is greater, full-capacity GDP or potential GDP? Why?

7. In country A, all wage contracts are indexed to inflation. That is, each month wages are adjusted to reflect increases in the cost of living as reflected in changes in the price level. In country B, there are no cost-of-living adjustments to wages, but the workforce is completely unionized. Unions negotiate three-year contracts. In which country is an expansionary monetary policy likely to have a larger effect on aggregate output? Explain your answer using aggregate supply and aggregate demand curves.

8. In an effort to fight inflation in 1974 and 1975, the U.S. government acted with contractionary monetary policy. Using aggregate supply and aggregate demand curves, illustrate the effects that the government expected this policy to have on aggregate output and on the price level.

The contractionary monetary policy had the effect of reducing aggregate output; the United States experienced a recession from 1974 to 1975. But although output was reduced, prices continued to increase throughout the recession. Give two alternative explanations for why prices might continue to rise even though output is falling.

TAKE IT TO THE NET

We invite you to visit the Case and Fair page on the Prentice Hall Web site:
http://www.prenhall.com/casefair
for this chapter's World Wide Web exercise.

Chapter 30

THE LABOR MARKET, UNEMPLOYMENT, AND INFLATION

IN CHAPTER 6, we stressed the three broadly defined markets in which households, firms, the government, and the rest of the world interact: (1) the *goods market*, discussed in chapters 24 and 25, (2) the *money market*, discussed in chapters 26 and 27, and (3) the *labor market*. In chapter 23 we described some features of the U.S. labor market and explained how the unemployment rate is measured. Then, in chapter 29, we considered the labor market briefly in our discussion of the aggregate supply curve. Because labor is an input, what goes on in the labor market affects the shape of the *AS* curve. If wages and other input costs lag price increases, the *AS* curve will be upward sloping; if wages and other input costs are completely flexible and rise every time prices rise by the same percentage, the *AS* curve will be vertical.

In this chapter we look further at the labor market's role in the macroeconomy. First, we consider the classical view, which holds that wages always adjust to clear the labor market. We then consider why the labor market may not always clear and why unemployment may exist. Finally, we discuss the relationship between inflation and unemployment.

> **The Labor Market: Basic Concepts** Let's review briefly what the unemployment rate measures. The **unemployment rate** is the number of people unemployed as a percentage of the labor force. To be unemployed, a person must be out of a job and actively looking for work. When a person stops looking for work, he or she is considered *out of the labor force* and is no longer counted as unemployed.

It is important to realize that even if the economy is running at or near full capacity, the unemployment rate will never be zero. The economy is dynamic. Students graduate from schools and training programs; some businesses make profits and grow, while others suffer losses and go out of business; people move in and out of the labor force and change careers. It takes time for people to find the right job and for employers to match the right worker with the jobs they have. This **frictional** and **structural unemployment** is inevitable and in many ways desirable. (Review chapter 23 if these terms are hazy to you.)

unemployment rate *The ratio of the number of people unemployed to the total number of people in the labor force.*

frictional unemployment *The portion of unemployment that is due to the normal working of the labor market; used to denote short-run job/skill matching problems.*

structural unemployment *The portion of unemployment that is due to changes in the structure of the economy that result in a significant loss of jobs in certain industries.*

In this chapter, we are concerned with **cyclical unemployment**, the increase in unemployment that occurs during recessions and depressions. When the economy contracts, the number of people unemployed and the unemployment rate rise. The United States has experienced several periods of high unemployment. During the Great Depression, the unemployment rate remained over 17 percent for nearly a decade. In December of 1982, more than 12 million people were unemployed, putting the unemployment rate at 10.8 percent.

In one sense, the reason employment falls when the economy experiences a downturn is obvious. When firms cut back on production, they need fewer workers, so people get laid off.

> Employment tends to fall when aggregate output falls and rise when aggregate output rises.

But a decline in the demand for labor does not necessarily mean that unemployment will rise. If markets work as we described in chapters 4 and 5, a decline in the demand for labor will initially create an excess supply of labor. As a result, the wage rate will fall until the quantity of labor supplied again equals the quantity of labor demanded, restoring equilibrium in the labor market. At the new lower wage rate, everyone who wants a job will have one.

If the quantity of labor demanded and the quantity of labor supplied are brought into equilibrium by rising and falling wage rates, there should be no persistent unemployment above the frictional and structural amount. This was the view held by the classical economists who preceded Keynes, and it is still the view of a number of economists today.

THE CLASSICAL VIEW OF THE LABOR MARKET

The classical view of the labor market is illustrated in Figure 30.1. Classical economists assumed the wage rate adjusts to equate the quantity of labor demanded with the quantity of labor supplied, thereby implying that unemployment does not exist. To see how this adjustment takes place, assume there is a decrease in the demand for labor that shifts the demand curve in Figure 30.1 from D_0 to D_1. This decreased demand will cause the wage rate to fall from W_0 to W^* and the amount of labor demanded to fall from L_0 to L^*. The decrease in the quantity of labor supplied is a movement along the labor supply curve.

labor supply curve *A graph that illustrates the amount of labor that households want to supply at the particular wage rate.*

Each point on the **labor supply curve** in Figure 30.1 represents the amount of labor households want to supply at the particular wage rate. Each household's decision regarding how much labor to supply is part of the overall consumer choice problem of a household.[1] Each household member looks at the market wage rate, the prices of outputs, and the value of leisure time (including the value of staying at home and working in the yard or raising children) and chooses the amount of labor to supply (if any). A household member not in the labor force has decided his or her time is more valuable in nonmarket activities.

It is easy to see why. If you choose to stay out of the labor force, it is because you (a member of society) place a higher value on the use of your time than society is currently placing on the product that you would produce if you were employed. Consider households in less-developed countries. In many, the alternative to working for a wage is subsistence farming. If the wage rate in the labor market is very low, many will choose to farm for themselves. In this case, the value of what these people produce in farming must be greater than the value that society currently places on what they would produce if they worked for a wage. If this were not true, wages would rise and more people would join the labor force.

---

[1]The household choice problem is discussed in detail in chapter 21.

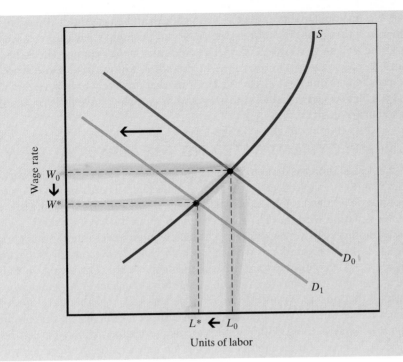

FIGURE 30.1

The Classical Labor Market

Classical economists believe that the labor market always clears. If the demand for labor shifts from D_0 to D_1, the equilibrium wage will fall from W_0 to W^*. Everyone who wants a job at W^* will have one.

Each point on the **labor demand curve** in Figure 30.1 represents the amount of labor firms want to employ at the particular wage rate. Each firm's decision about how much labor to demand is part of its overall profit-maximizing decision.[2] A firm makes a profit by selling output to households. It will hire workers if the value of its output is sufficient to justify the wage that is being paid. Thus, the amount of labor that a firm hires depends on the value of the output that workers produce.

The classical economists saw the workings of the labor market—the behavior of labor supply and labor demand—as optimal from the standpoint of both individual households and firms and from the standpoint of society. If households want more output than is currently being produced, output demand will increase, output prices will rise, the demand for labor will increase, the wage rate will rise, and more workers will be drawn into the labor force. (Some of those who preferred not to be a part of the labor force at the lower wage rate will be lured into the labor force at the higher wage rate.) At equilibrium, prices and wages reflect a trade-off between the value households place on outputs and the value of time spent in leisure and nonmarket work. At equilibrium, the people who are not working have *chosen* not to work at that market wage. There is always *full employment* in this sense. The classical economists believed the market will achieve the optimal result if left to its own devices, and there is nothing the government can do to make things better.

labor demand curve *A graph that illustrates the amount of labor that firms want to employ at the particular wage rate.*

THE CLASSICAL LABOR MARKET AND THE AS CURVE

We can now relate the classical view of the labor market to the theory of the vertical *AS* curve in chapter 29. The classical idea that wages adjust to clear the labor market is consistent with the view that wages respond quickly to price changes. Recall that the argument that the *AS* curve is vertical in the long run involves input-price adjustments. If the short-run *AS* and *AD* curves intersected above potential GDP (Y_0 in Figure 29.10), then input prices, *including wages*, would rise, shifting the *AS* curve to the left and pushing Y back down to Y_0. Similarly, if the short-run *AS* and *AD* curves intersected to

[2]The demand for inputs by firms, including the demand for labor, is discussed in chapter 25.

the left of Y_0, unemployment and excess capacity would cause input prices, *including wages*, to fall, shifting the *AS* curve to the right and pushing *Y* back up to Y_0. Also remember: if the *AS* curve is vertical, monetary and fiscal policy cannot affect the level of output and employment in the economy. It, therefore, follows that those who believe the wage rate adjusts quickly to clear the labor market are likely to believe the *AS* curve is vertical (or almost vertical) and monetary and fiscal policy have little or no effect on output and employment.

THE UNEMPLOYMENT RATE AND THE CLASSICAL VIEW

If, as the classical economists assumed, the labor market works well, how can we account for the fact that the unemployment rate at times seems high? There seem to be times when millions of people who want jobs at prevailing wage rates cannot find them. How can we reconcile this situation with the classical assumption about the labor market?

Some economists answer by arguing that the unemployment rate is not a good measure of whether the labor market is working well. We know the economy is dynamic and at any given time some industries are expanding and some are contracting. In California the construction industry contracted in the mid-1990s. Consider a carpenter who is laid off because of the industry's contraction. This person had probably developed specific skills related to the construction industry—skills not necessarily useful for jobs in other industries. If he were earning $30,000 per year as a carpenter, it may be that he could earn only $20,000 per year in another industry. He may eventually work his way back up to a salary of $30,000 in the new industry as he develops new skills, but this will take time. Will the carpenter take a job at $20,000? There are at least two reasons he may not. First, he may believe the slump in the construction industry is temporary and he will soon get his job back. Second, he may believe he can earn more than $20,000 in another industry and will continue to look for a better job.

If our carpenter decides to continue looking for a job paying more than $20,000 per year, he will be considered unemployed because he is actively looking for work. This does not necessarily mean the labor market is not working properly. The carpenter has *chosen* not to work for a wage of $20,000 per year, but if his value to any firm outside the construction industry is no more than $20,000 per year, we would not expect him to find a job paying more than $20,000. The unemployment rate as measured by the government is not necessarily an accurate indicator of whether the labor market is working properly.

If the degree to which industries are changing in the economy fluctuates over time, there will be more people like our carpenter at some times than at others. This will cause the measured unemployment rate to fluctuate. Some economists argue the measured

SOME ECONOMISTS BELIEVE UNEMPLOYMENT IS NOT A MAJOR PROBLEM. HOWEVER, THE IMAGES OF THE 1930S ARE STILL WITH US, AND MORE THAN 12 MILLION PEOPLE WERE LOOKING FOR WORK DURING THE RECESSION OF 1982.

unemployment rate may sometimes *seem* high even though the labor market is working well. The quantity of labor supplied at the current wage is equal to the quantity demanded at the current wage. The fact that there are people willing to work at a wage higher than the current wage does not mean the labor market is not working. Whenever there is an upward-sloping supply curve in a market (as is usually the case in the labor market), the quantity supplied at a price higher than the equilibrium price is always greater than the quantity supplied at the equilibrium price.

Economists who view unemployment in this way do not see it as a major problem. Yet the images of the bread lines in the 1930s are still with us, and many find it difficult to believe everything was optimal when over 12 million people were looking for work at the end of 1982. There are other views of unemployment, as we now will see.

EXPLAINING THE EXISTENCE OF UNEMPLOYMENT

If unemployment is a major macroeconomic problem—and many economists believe it is—then we need to explore some of the reasons that have been suggested for its existence. Among these are sticky wages, efficiency wage theory, imperfect information, and minimum wage laws.

STICKY WAGES

One explanation for unemployment (above and beyond normal frictional and structural unemployment) is that wages are **"sticky"** on the downward side. That is, the equilibrium wage gets stuck at a particular level and does not fall when the demand for labor falls. This is illustrated in Figure 30.2, where the equilibrium wage gets stuck at W_0 (the original wage) and does not fall to W^* when demand decreases from D_0 to D_1. The result is unemployment of the amount $L_0 - L_1$, where L_0 is the quantity of labor that households want to supply at wage rate W_0 and L_1 is the amount of labor that firms want to hire at wage rate W_0. $L_0 - L_1$ is the number of workers who would like to work at W_0 but cannot find jobs.

The sticky wage explanation of unemployment begs the question. *Why* are wages sticky, if they are, and why do wages not fall to clear the labor market during periods of

sticky wages *The downward rigidity of wages as an explanation for the existence of unemployment.*

FAST FACTS

With unemployment at a 24-year low (4.7%) late in 1997, it was not considered a big problem in the United States. If anything, there were worries about a shortage of skilled workers. In Europe, unemployment has been a chronic problem. In November 1997, unemployment was 13.4% in Belgium, 12.5% in France, 11.8% in Germany, 12.8% in Italy, and 20.8% in Spain.

Source: The Economist, November 15, 1997, p. 108.

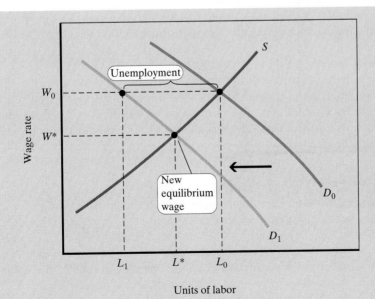

FIGURE 30.2

Sticky Wages

If wages "stick" at W_0 rather than fall to the new equilibrium wage of W^* following a shift of demand from D_0 to D_1, the result will be unemployment equal to $L_0 - L_1$.

high unemployment? Many answers have been proposed, but as yet no one answer has been agreed upon. This is one reason macroeconomics has been in a state of flux for so long. The existence of unemployment continues to be a puzzle. Although we will discuss the major theories that have been proposed to explain why wages may not clear the labor market, we can offer no conclusions. The question is still open.

> **Social, or Implicit, Contracts**   One explanation for downwardly sticky wages is that firms enter into **social, or implicit, contracts** with workers not to cut wages. It seems that extreme events—a deep recession, deregulation, or threat of bankruptcy—are necessary for firms to cut wages. Wage cuts did occur during the Great Depression, in the airline industry following deregulation of the industry in the 1980s, and recently when some U.S. manufacturing firms found themselves in danger of bankruptcy from stiff foreign competition. These are exceptions to the general rule. For reasons that may be more sociological than economic, cutting wages seems close to being a taboo.

A related argument, the **relative-wage explanation of unemployment**, holds that workers are concerned about their wages *relative* to the wages of other workers in other firms and industries and may be unwilling to accept wage cuts unless they know other workers are receiving similar cuts. Because it is difficult to reassure any one group of workers that all other workers are in the same situation, workers may resist any cut in their wages. There may be an implicit understanding between firms and workers that firms will not do anything that would make their workers worse off relative to workers in other firms.

> **Explicit Contracts**   Many workers—in particular, unionized workers—sign one- to three-year employment contracts with firms. These contracts stipulate the workers' wages for each year of the contract. Wages set in this way do not fluctuate with economic conditions, either upward or downward. If the economy slows down and firms demand fewer workers, the wage will not fall. Rather, some workers will be laid off.

Although **explicit contracts** can explain why some wages are sticky, a deeper question must also be considered. Workers and firms surely know at the time a contract is signed that unforeseen events may cause the wages set by the contract to be too high or too low. Why do firms and workers bind themselves in this way? One explanation is that negotiating wages is costly. Negotiations between unions and firms can take a considerable amount of time—time that could be spent producing output—and it would be very costly to negotiate wages weekly or monthly. Contracts are a way of bearing these costs at no more than one-, two-, or three-year intervals. There is a trade-off between the costs of locking workers and firms into contracts for long periods of time and the costs of wage negotiations. The length of contracts that minimizes negotiation costs seems to be (from what we observe in practice) between one and three years.

Some multiyear contracts adjust for unforeseen events by **cost-of-living adjustments (COLAs)** written into the contract. COLAs tie wages to changes in the cost of living: The greater the rate of inflation, the more wages are raised. COLAs thus protect workers from unexpected inflation, although many COLAs adjust wages by a smaller percentage than the percentage increase in prices.

EFFICIENCY WAGE THEORY

Another explanation for unemployment centers on the **efficiency wage theory**, which holds that the productivity of workers increases with the wage rate. If this is true, firms may have an incentive to pay wages *above* the wage at which the quantity of labor supplied is equal to the quantity of labor demanded.

An individual firm has an incentive to hire workers as long as the value of what they produce is equal to or greater than the wage rate. With no efficiency effects, the market in Figure 30.1 would produce an equilibrium wage of W^*. But suppose the

---

social, or implicit, contracts *Unspoken agreements between workers and firms that firms will not cut wages.*

relative-wage explanation of unemployment *An explanation for sticky wages (and therefore unemployment): If workers are concerned about their wages relative to other workers in other firms and industries, they may be unwilling to accept a wage cut unless they know that all other workers are receiving similar cuts.*

explicit contracts *Employment contracts that stipulate workers' wages, usually for a period of one to three years.*

cost-of-living adjustments (COLAs) *Contract provisions that tie wages to changes in the cost of living. The greater the inflation rate, the more wages are raised.*

efficiency wage theory *An explanation for unemployment that holds that the productivity of workers increases with the wage rate. If this is so, firms may have an incentive to pay wages above the market-clearing rate.*

PART SEVEN
Macroeconomic Analysis and Issues

firm could increase the productivity of all its workers by raising the wage rate above W^*. The firm's demand for labor would be no lower, but the higher wage rate would cause the quantity of labor supplied to increase. The quantity of labor supplied would exceed the quantity of labor demanded at the new higher wage—the *efficiency wage*—and the result is unemployment.

Empirical studies of labor markets have identified several potential benefits that firms receive from paying workers more than the market-clearing wage. Among them are lower turnover, improved morale, and reduced "shirking" of work.[3] But even though the efficiency wage theory predicts some unemployment, it is unlikely that the behavior it is describing accounts for much of the observed large cyclical fluctuations in unemployment over time.

IMPERFECT INFORMATION

Thus far we have been assuming that firms know exactly what wage rates they need to set to clear the labor market. They may not choose to set their wages at this level, but at least they know what the market-clearing wage is. In practice, firms may not have enough information at their disposal to know what the market-clearing wage is. In this case, firms are said to have *imperfect information*. If firms have imperfect or incomplete information, they may simply set wages wrong—wages that do not clear the labor market.

If a firm sets its wages too high, more workers will want to work for that firm than the firm wants to employ, and some potential workers will be turned away. The result is, of course, unemployment. One objection to this explanation is that it explains the existence of unemployment only in the very short run. As soon as a firm sees that it has made a mistake, why wouldn't it immediately correct its mistake and adjust its wage to the correct, market-clearing level? Why would unemployment *persist*?

If the economy were simple, it should take no more than a few months for firms to correct their mistakes. But the economy is complex. Although firms may be aware of their past mistakes and may try to correct them, new events are happening all the time. Because constant change—including a constantly changing equilibrium wage level—is characteristic of the economy, firms may find it hard to adjust wages to the market-clearing level. The labor market is not like the stock market or the market for wheat, where prices are determined in organized exchanges every day. Rather, thousands of firms are setting wages and millions of workers are responding to these wages. It may take considerable time for the market-clearing wages to be determined after they have been disturbed from an equilibrium position.

MINIMUM WAGE LAWS

Minimum wage laws explain at least a small fraction of unemployment. These laws set a floor for wage rates—a minimum hourly rate for any kind of labor. In 1998, the federal minimum wage was $5.15 per hour. If the market-clearing wage for some groups of workers is below this amount, this group will be unemployed. In Figure 30.2, if the minimum wage is W_0 and the market-clearing wage is W^*, then the number of unemployed will be $L_0 - L_1$.

Teenagers, who have relatively little job experience, are most likely to be hurt by minimum wage laws. If some teenagers can produce only $4.50 worth of output per hour, no firm would be willing to hire them at a wage of $5.15. To do so would incur a loss of $0.65 per hour. In an unregulated market, these teenagers would be able to find work at the market-clearing wage of $4.50 per hour. If the minimum wage laws prevent the wage from falling below $5.15, these workers will not be able to find jobs, and they will be unemployed.

A recent paper argues that unemployment rates in Europe are consistently higher than in the United States because European labor markets are less flexible than in the United States. Proposals to reduce unemployment go beyond increasing GDP. They include cutting jobless benefits, reducing minimum wages, and relaxing job protection laws.

See David Coe and Dennis Snower, "Policy Complementarities: The Case for Fundamental Labor Market Reform," IMF Staff Papers, Volume 44, No. 1, 1997.

minimum wage laws *Laws that set a floor for wage rates—that is, a minimum hourly rate for any kind of labor.*

Social Tool

---

[3]For a good summary, see George Akerlof and Janet Yellen, *Efficiency Wage Models of the Labor Market* (Cambridge: Cambridge University Press, 1986).

In response to this argument against the minimum wage, Congress established a subminimum wage for teenagers. The new law allows employers to hire teenagers at an "Opportunity Wage" of $4.25 for up to 90 days.

AN OPEN QUESTION

As we've seen, there are many explanations for why the labor market may not clear. The theories we have just set forth are not necessarily mutually exclusive, and there may be elements of truth in all of them. The aggregate labor market is very complicated, and there are no simple answers to why there is unemployment. Much current work in macroeconomics is concerned directly or indirectly with this question, and it is an exciting area of study. Which argument or arguments will win out in the end is an open question.

THE SHORT-RUN RELATIONSHIP BETWEEN THE UNEMPLOYMENT RATE AND INFLATION

The relationship between the unemployment rate and inflation—two of the most important variables in macroeconomics—has been the subject of much debate. We now have enough knowledge of the macroeconomy to explore this relationship.

We must begin by considering the relationship between aggregate output (income) (Y) and the unemployment rate (U). An increase in Y means firms are producing more output. To produce more output, more labor is needed in the production process. Therefore, an increase in Y leads to an increase in employment. An increase in employment means more people working (fewer people unemployed) and a lower unemployment rate. An increase in Y corresponds to a *decrease* in U. Thus U and Y are *negatively* related:[4]

> When Y rises, the unemployment rate falls, and when Y falls, the unemployment rate rises.

Next consider an upward-sloping aggregate supply (AS) curve, as shown in Figure 30.3. This curve represents the relationship between Y and the overall price level (P). The relationship is a positive one: When Y increases, P increases, and when Y decreases, P decreases.

As you will recall from the last chapter, the shape of the AS curve is determined by the behavior of firms and how they react to an increase in demand. If aggregate demand shifts to the right and the economy is operating on the nearly flat part of the AS curve—far from capacity—output will increase but the price level will not change much. However, if the economy is operating on the steep part of the AS curve—close to capacity—an increase in demand will drive up the price level, but output will be constrained by capacity and will not increase much.

Think about what will happen following an event that leads to an increase in aggregate demand. First, firms experience an unanticipated decline in inventories. They respond by increasing output (Y) and hiring workers—the unemployment rate falls. If the economy is not close to capacity, there will be little increase in the price level. But if aggregate demand continues to grow, the ability of the economy to increase output will eventually reach its limit. As aggregate demand shifts further and further to the right along the AS curve, the price level increases more and more, and output begins to reach its limit. At the point at which the AS curve becomes vertical, output cannot rise any further. If output cannot grow, the unemployment rate cannot be pushed any lower.

[4]We will see in chapter 32 that this relationship is not simple; all we need to know for now is that the two variables are negatively related.

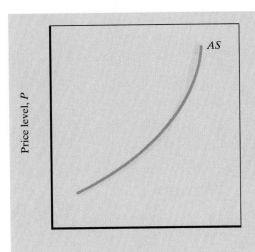

FIGURE 30.3

The Aggregate Supply Curve

The *AS* curve shows a positive relationship between the price level (*P*) and aggregate output (income) (*Y*).

There is a negative relationship between the unemployment rate and the price level. As the unemployment rate declines in response to the economy moving closer and closer to capacity output, the overall price level rises more and more, as shown in Figure 30.4.

The curve in Figure 30.4 has *not* been a major focus of attention in macroeconomics. Rather, the curve that has been extensively studied is shown in Figure 30.5, which plots the inflation rate on the vertical axis and the unemployment rate on the horizontal axis. The **inflation rate** is the percentage change in the price level, not the price level itself.

Figures 30.4 and 30.5 imply different things. Figure 30.4 says the *price level* remains the same if the unemployment rate remains unchanged. Figure 30.5 says that the *inflation rate* remains the same if the unemployment rate remains unchanged. The curve in Figure 30.5 is called the **Phillips Curve**, after A. W. Phillips, who first examined it using data for the United Kingdom. In simplest terms, the Phillips Curve is a graph showing the relationship between the inflation rate and the unemployment rate.

The rest of this chapter focuses on the Phillips Curve in Figure 30.5 because it is the macroeconomic relationship that has been studied the most. Keep in mind, however, that it is not easy to go from the *AS* curve to the Phillips Curve. We have

inflation rate *The percentage change in the price level.*

Phillips Curve *A graph showing the relationship between the inflation rate and the unemployment rate.*

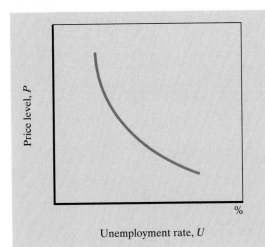

FIGURE 30.4

The Relationship between the Price Level and the Unemployment Rate

There is a negative relationship between the price level (*P*) and the unemployment rate (*U*). As the unemployment rate declines in response to the economy's moving closer and closer to capacity output, the price level rises more and more.

FIGURE 30.5

The Phillips Curve

The Phillips Curve shows the relationship between the inflation rate and the unemployment rate.

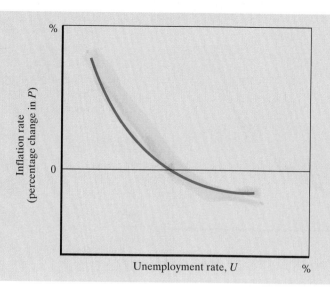

moved from graphs in which the price level is on the vertical axis (Figures 30.3 and 30.4) to a graph in which the *percentage change* in the price level is on the vertical axis (Figure 30.5). Put another way, the theory behind the Phillips Curve is somewhat different from the theory behind the *AS* curve. Fortunately, most of the insights gained from the *AS/AD* analysis regarding the behavior of the price level also apply to the behavior of the inflation rate.

THE PHILLIPS CURVE: A HISTORICAL PERSPECTIVE

In the 1950s and 1960s, there was a remarkably smooth relationship between the unemployment rate and the rate of inflation, as Figure 30.6 shows for the 1960s. As you can see, the data points fit fairly closely around a downward-sloping curve; in general,

FIGURE 30.6

Unemployment and Inflation, 1960 to 1969

During the 1960s there seemed to be an obvious trade-off between inflation and unemployment. Policy debates during the period revolved around this apparent trade-off.

Source: Table 8.9; *Economic Report of the President,* 1998, Table B-42.

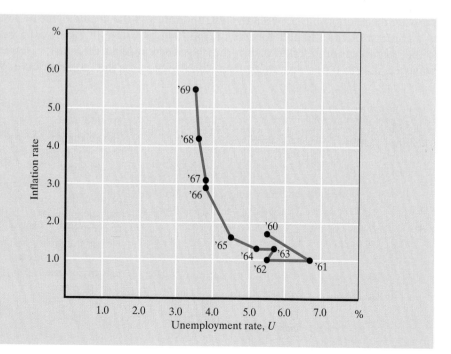

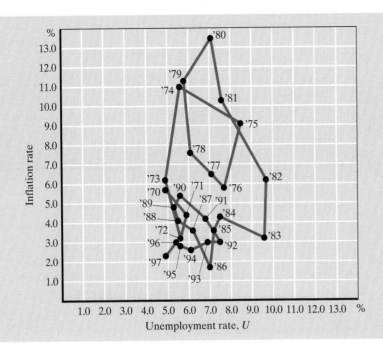

FIGURE 30.7

Unemployment and Inflation, 1970 to 1997

During the 1970s and 1980s, it became clear that the relationship between unemployment and inflation was anything but simple.

Source: Table 8.9; *Economic Report of the President,* 1998, Table B-42.

the higher the unemployment rate, the lower the rate of inflation. The Phillips Curve in Figure 30.6 shows a trade-off between inflation and unemployment. To lower the inflation rate, we must accept a higher unemployment rate, and to lower the unemployment rate, we must accept a higher rate of inflation.

Textbooks written in the 1960s and early 1970s relied on the Phillips Curve as the main explanation of inflation. Things seemed simple—inflation appeared to respond in a fairly predictable way to changes in the unemployment rate. For this reason, policy discussions in the 1960s revolved around the Phillips Curve. The role of the policy maker, it was thought, was to choose a point on the curve. Conservatives usually argued for choosing a point with a low rate of inflation and were willing to accept a higher unemployment rate in exchange for this. Liberals usually argued for accepting more inflation to keep unemployment at a low level.

Life did not turn out to be quite so simple. The Phillips Curve broke down in the 1970s and 1980s. This can be seen in Figure 30.7, which graphs the unemployment rate and inflation rate for the period from 1970 to 1997. The points in Figure 30.7 show no particular relationship between inflation and unemployment.

AS/AD ANALYSIS AND THE PHILLIPS CURVE

How can we explain the stability of the Phillips Curve in the 1950s and 1960s and the lack of stability after that? To answer, we need to return to *AS/AD* analysis.

If the *AD* curve shifts from year to year but the *AS* curve does not, the values of *P* and *Y* each year will lie along the *AS* curve (Figure 30.8a). The plot of the relationship between *P* and *Y* will be upward sloping. Correspondingly, the plot of the relationship between the unemployment rate (which decreases with increased output) and the rate of inflation will be a curve that slopes downward. In other words, we would expect to see a negative relationship between the unemployment rate and the inflation rate.

But the relationship between the unemployment rate and the inflation rate will look different if the *AS* curve shifts from year to year but the *AD* curve does not. A leftward shift of the *AS* curve will cause an *increase* in the price level (*P*) and a

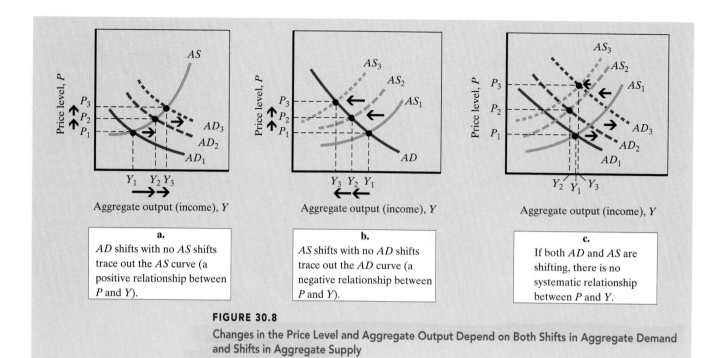

a.

AD shifts with no AS shifts trace out the AS curve (a positive relationship between P and Y).

b.

AS shifts with no AD shifts trace out the AD curve (a negative relationship between P and Y).

c.

If both AD and AS are shifting, there is no systematic relationship between P and Y.

FIGURE 30.8

Changes in the Price Level and Aggregate Output Depend on Both Shifts in Aggregate Demand and Shifts in Aggregate Supply

decrease in aggregate output (Y) (Figure 30.8b). When the AS curve shifts to the left, the economy experiences both inflation *and* an increase in the unemployment rate (because decreased output means increased unemployment). In other words, if the AS curve is shifting from year to year, we would expect to see a positive relationship between the unemployment rate and the inflation rate.

If both the AS and the AD curves are shifting simultaneously, however, there is no systematic relationship between P and Y (Figure 30.8c) and thus no systematic relationship between the unemployment rate and the inflation rate.

➤ **The Role of Import Prices**   One of the main factors that causes the AS curve to shift is the price of imports. (Remember: The AS curve shifts when input prices change, and input prices are affected by the price of imports, particularly the price of imported oil.) The price of imports is plotted in Figure 30.9 for the 1960 I to 1997 IV period. As you can see, the price of imports changed very little between 1960 and 1970. There were no large shifts in the AS curve in the 1960s due to changes in the price of imports. There were also no other large changes in input prices in the 1960s, so overall the AS curve shifted very little during the decade. The main variation in the 1960s was in aggregate demand, so the shifting AD curve traced out points along the AS curve.

Figure 30.9 also shows that the price of imports increased considerably in the 1970s. This led to large shifts in the AS curve during the decade. But the AD curve was also shifting throughout the 1970s. With both curves shifting, the data points for P and Y were scattered all over the graph, and the observed relationship between P and Y was not at all systematic.

This story about import prices and the AS and AD curves in the 1960s and 1970s carries over to the Phillips Curve. The Phillips Curve was stable in the 1960s because the primary source of variation in the economy was demand, not costs. In the 1970s both demand *and* costs were varying, so no obvious relationship between the unemployment rate and the inflation rate was apparent.

To some extent, what is remarkable about the Phillips Curve is not that it was not smooth after the 1960s but that it ever was smooth.

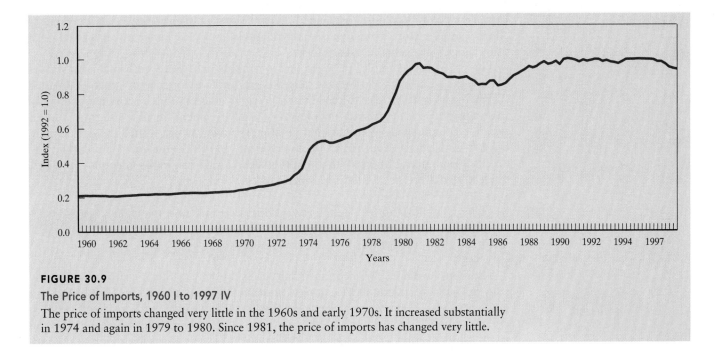

FIGURE 30.9

The Price of Imports, 1960 I to 1997 IV

The price of imports changed very little in the 1960s and early 1970s. It increased substantially in 1974 and again in 1979 to 1980. Since 1981, the price of imports has changed very little.

EXPECTATIONS AND THE PHILLIPS CURVE

Another reason the Phillips Curve is not stable concerns expectations. We saw in chapter 29 that if a firm expects other firms to raise their prices, the firm may raise the price of its own product. If all firms are behaving in this way, then prices will rise because they are expected to rise. In this sense, expectations are self-fulfilling. Similarly, if inflation is expected to be high in the future, negotiated wages are likely to be higher than if inflation is expected to be low. Wage inflation is thus affected by expectations of future price inflation. Because wages are input costs, prices rise as firms respond to the higher wage costs. Price expectations that affect wage contracts eventually affect prices themselves.

If the rate of inflation depends on expectations, then the Phillips Curve will shift as expectations change. For example, if inflationary expectations increase, the result will be an increase in the rate of inflation even though the unemployment rate may not have changed. In this case, the Phillips Curve will shift to the right. If inflationary expectations decrease, the Phillips curve will shift to the left—there will be less inflation at any given level of the unemployment rate.

It so happened that inflationary expectations were quite stable in the 1950s and 1960s. The inflation rate was moderate during most of this period, and people expected it to remain moderate. With inflationary expectations not changing very much, there were no major shifts of the Phillips Curve, which helps explain its stability during the period.

Near the end of the 1960s, inflationary expectations began to increase, primarily in response to the actual increase in inflation that was occurring because of the tight economy caused by the Vietnam War. Inflationary expectations increased even further in the 1970s as a result of large oil price increases. These changing expectations led to shifts of the Phillips Curve, which is another reason the curve was not stable during the 1970s.

IS THERE A SHORT-RUN TRADE-OFF BETWEEN INFLATION AND UNEMPLOYMENT?

Does the fact that the Phillips Curve broke down during the 1970s mean there is no trade-off between inflation and unemployment in the short run? Not at all. It simply means other things affect inflation aside from unemployment. Just as the relationship between price and quantity demanded along a standard demand curve shifts when income or other factors change, so does the relationship between unemployment and inflation change when other factors change.

In 1975, for example, inflation and unemployment were both high. As we explained earlier, this stagflation was caused partly by an increase in oil costs that shifted the aggregate supply curve to the left and partly by expectations of continued inflation that kept prices rising despite high levels of unemployment. In response to this situation, the Fed pursued a contractionary monetary policy, which shifted the AD curve to the left and led to even higher unemployment. By 1977, the rate of inflation had dropped from over 11 percent to about 6 percent. So the rise in the unemployment rate did lead to a decrease in inflation, which reflects the trade-off.

> There *is* a short-run trade-off between inflation and unemployment, but other factors besides unemployment affect inflation. Policy involves much more than simply choosing a point along a nice, smooth curve.

Back in chapter 23, we mentioned that recessions may be the price that the economy pays to eliminate inflation. We can now understand this statement better. When unemployment rises, *other things being equal*, inflation falls. We explore the trade-off between inflation and unemployment in other nations—and caution against generalizing too much—in the Global Perspective box "Inflation and Unemployment around the World, 1990 to 1992."

THE LONG-RUN *AS* CURVE, POTENTIAL GDP, AND THE NATURAL RATE OF UNEMPLOYMENT

Recall from chapter 29 that many economists believe the AS curve is vertical in the long run. In the short run, we know that some input prices (which are costs to firms) lag increases in the overall price level. If the price level rises without a full adjustment of costs, firms' profits will be higher and output will increase. In the long run, however, input prices may catch up to output price increases. If input prices rise in subsequent periods, driving up costs, the short-run aggregate supply curve will shift to the left, and aggregate output will fall.

This situation is illustrated in Figure 30.10. Assume the initial equilibrium is at the intersection of AD_0 and the long-run aggregate supply curve. Now consider a shift of the aggregate demand curve from AD_0 to AD_1. If input prices lag changes in the overall price level, aggregate output will rise from Y_0 to Y_1. (This is a movement along the short-run AS curve AS_0.) But in the longer run, input prices may catch up. For example, next year's labor contracts may make up for the fact that wage increases did not keep up with the cost of living this year. If input prices catch up in the longer run, the AS curve will shift from AS_0 to AS_1 and drive aggregate output back to Y_0. If input prices ultimately rise by exactly the same percentage as output prices, firms will produce the same level of output as they did before the increase in aggregate demand.

In chapter 29 we said Y_0 is sometimes called *potential GDP*. Aggregate output can be pushed above Y_0 in the short run. When aggregate output exceeds Y_0, however, there is upward pressure on input prices and costs. The unemployment rate is already quite low, firms are beginning to encounter the limits of their plant capacities, and so forth. At levels of aggregate output above Y_0, costs will rise, the AS curve will shift to the left, and the price level will rise. Thus potential GDP is the level of aggregate output that can be sustained in the long run without inflation.

This story is directly related to the Phillips Curve. Those who believe the AS curve is vertical in the long run at potential GDP also believe the Phillips Curve is vertical in the long run at some natural rate of unemployment. The **natural rate of unemployment** is the rate of unemployment that is consistent with the notion of a fixed long-run output

natural rate of unemployment
A concept consistent with the notion of a fixed long-run output at potential GDP. Generally considered the sum of the frictional and structural unemployment rates.

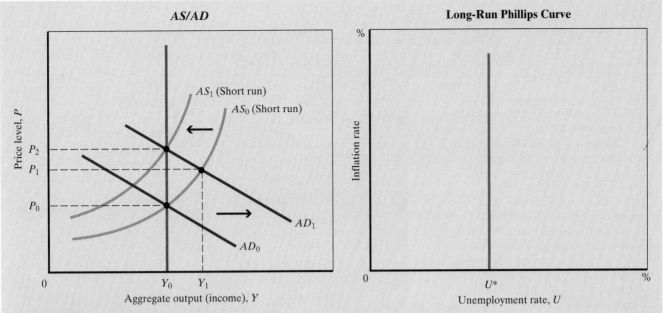

AS/AD   **Long-Run Phillips Curve**

FIGURE 30.10

The Long-Run Phillips Curve: The Natural Rate of Unemployment

If the *AS* curve is vertical in the long run, so is the Phillips Curve. In the long run, the Phillips Curve corresponds to the natural rate of unemployment—that is, the unemployment rate that is consistent with the notion of a fixed long-run output at potential GDP. U^* is the natural rate of unemployment.

at potential GDP. The logic behind the vertical Phillips Curve is that whenever the unemployment rate is pushed below the natural rate, wages begin to rise, thus pushing up costs. This leads to a *lower* level of output, which pushes the unemployment rate back up to the natural rate. At the natural rate, the economy can be considered to be at full employment.

THE NAIRU—THE NONACCELERATING INFLATION RATE OF UNEMPLOYMENT

In Figure 30.10 the long-run vertical Phillips Curve is a graph with the inflation rate on the vertical axis and the unemployment rate on the horizontal axis. The natural rate of unemployment is U^*. In the long run, according to advocates of the long-run vertical Phillips Curve, the actual unemployment rate moves to U^* because of the natural workings of the economy.

Another graph of interest is Figure 30.11, a graph with the *change in* the inflation rate on the vertical axis and the unemployment rate on the horizontal axis. Many economists believe the relationship between the change in the inflation rate and the unemployment rate is as depicted by the *PP* curve in the figure. The value of the unemployment rate where the *PP* curve crosses zero is called the **NAIRU**, the "non-accelerating inflation rate of unemployment." If the actual unemployment rate is to the left of the NAIRU, the change in the inflation rate will be positive. As depicted in the figure, at U_1 the change in the inflation rate is 1. Conversely, if the actual unemployment rate is to the right of the NAIRU, the change in the inflation rate is negative: At U_2 the change is -1.

Consider what happens if the unemployment rate decreases from the NAIRU to U_1 and stays at U_1 for many periods. Assume also that the inflation rate at the NAIRU was 2 percent. Then in the first period the inflation rate will increase from 2 percent to

NAIRU *The non-accelerating inflation rate of unemployment.*

INFLATION AND UNEMPLOYMENT AROUND THE WORLD, 1990 TO 1992

Table 1 presents unemployment and inflation figures for a number of industrial economies.

These numbers make clear that economic generalizations across countries can be hazardous, for two reasons. First, the economic events experienced by one country in a given period may be very different from the economic events experienced by another country during the same period. (For example, one country may encounter a supply shock that shifts its aggregate supply curve at the same time that another is experiencing demand-pull inflation.) Second, the trade-off between inflation and unemployment, to the extent that one exists, is determined by the institutions within the country. For example, Japan had a tradition of "lifetime" employment for male workers in the country's largest industries. Although 1992 and 1993 saw the rules beginning to change,

UNEMPLOYMENT HAS EMERGED AS A SERIOUS PROBLEM IN EUROPE IN THE 1990s. HERE, THESE WORKERS AT AN EMPLOYMENT CENTER IN GERMANY ARE HOPING TO FIND WORK.

FIGURE 30.11

The NAIRU Diagram

To the left of the NAIRU the price level is accelerating (positive changes in the inflation rate), and to the right of the NAIRU the price level is decelerating (negative changes in the inflation rate). Only when the unemployment rate is equal to the NAIRU is the price level changing at a constant rate (no change in the inflation rate).

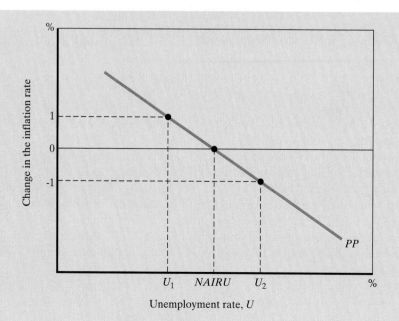

Japanese firms are still more reluctant than their U.S. counterparts to lay off workers during economic hard times. This means Japanese workers do much less "job searching" and Japan probably has a lower natural rate of unemployment than the United States. The opposite is true in the Netherlands, which has a very liberal unemployment insurance program that pays virtually 100% of lost wages to the unemployed for an extended time. Such a system is likely to lead to a higher natural rate because it makes the cost of being unemployed quite low.

A number of patterns emerge from the numbers. Seven of the 10 countries in the group experienced an increase in unemployment between 1990 and 1992. Those same seven countries experienced a simultaneous decline in inflation. Only Germany and the Netherlands saw unemployment decline, and both experienced an increase in inflation. Japan had no change in the unemployment rate. All nine countries in which the unemployment rate changed seemed to exhibit a trade-off between inflation and unemployment.

TABLE 1 UNEMPLOYMENT AND INFLATION RATES IN SELECTED COUNTRIES, 1990 TO 1992

	UNEMPLOYMENT RATE		INFLATION RATE	
	1990	1992	1990	1992
Canada	8.1	11.3 ↑	5.0	2.0 ↓
Australia	6.9	10.8 ↑	7.0	1.0 ↓
France	9.2	10.1 ↑	3.1	2.3 ↓
United Kingdom	6.8	9.6 ↑	6.4	4.3 ↓
Italy	11.4	11.6 ↑	7.6	4.5 ↓
United States	5.5	6.8 ↑	5.0	3.0 ↓
Netherlands	8.0	6.6 ↓	3.0	4.0 ↑
Sweden	1.5	4.7 ↑	11.0	2.0 ↓
Germany	6.2	5.8 ↓	3.1	4.4 ↑
Japan	2.2	2.2 -	2.2	1.6 ↓

Sources: OECD, IMF, and *Statistical Abstract of the United States*, 1994, Tables 1379, 1381.

The similarity of patterns across the seven countries experiencing higher unemployment and lower inflation demonstrates that linkages across economies do exist. All countries experienced falling commodity prices (including oil) on world markets during 1991 and 1992. In addition, countries are linked through imports and exports and through capital flows. For example, one of the reasons that the U.S. economy did not grow more quickly following the 1990 to 1991 recession was that its major trading partners (Europe and Japan) were experiencing recessions of their own and were buying less from the United States.

 For more on inflation and unemployment in other countries, see the Case and Fair Web page at http://www.prenhall.com/casefair.

3 percent. The inflation rate does not, however, just stay at the higher 3 percent value. In the next period the inflation rate will increase from 3 percent to 4 percent, and so on. The price level will be accelerating (that is, the change in the inflation rate will be positive) when the actual unemployment rate is below the NAIRU. Conversely, the price level will be decelerating (that is, the change in the inflation rate will be negative) when the actual unemployment rate is above the NAIRU.[5]

The *PP* curve in Figure 30.11 is like the *AS* curve in Figure 30.3—the same factors that shift the *AS* curve, such as cost shocks, can also shift the *PP* curve. Figure 29.8 summarizes the various factors that can cause the *AS* curve to shift, and these are also relevant for the *PP* curve. A favorable shift for the *PP* curve is to the left, because the *PP* curve crosses zero at a lower unemployment rate, which means that the NAIRU is lower. Some have argued that one possible recent source of favorable shifts is increased foreign competition, which may have kept both wage costs and other input costs down.

---

[5]The NAIRU is actually misnamed. It is the *price level* that is accelerating or decelerating, not the inflation rate, when the actual unemployment rate differs from the NAIRU. The inflation rate is not accelerating or decelerating, but simply changing by the same amount each period. The namers of the NAIRU forgot their physics.

Before about 1995, proponents of the NAIRU theory argued that the value of the NAIRU in the United States was around 6 percent. By the end of 1995 the unemployment rate declined to about 5.5 percent, and by 1997 the unemployment rate was under 5 percent. If the NAIRU were 6 percent, one should have seen a continuing increase in the inflation rate beginning about 1995. In fact, the 1995 to 1997 period saw slightly declining inflation. Not only did inflation not continually increase, it did not even increase once to a new higher value and then stay there. As the unemployment rate declined during this period, proponents of the NAIRU lowered their estimates of it, more or less in line with the actual fall in the unemployment rate. This can be justified by arguing that there have been continuing favorable shifts of the *PP* curve, such as possible increased foreign competition. Critics have argued that this procedure is close to making the NAIRU theory vacuous. Can the theory really be tested if the estimate of the NAIRU is changed whenever it is not consistent with the data? How trustworthy is the appeal to favorable shifts?

Macroeconomists are currently debating whether equations estimated under the NAIRU theory are good approximations. More time is needed before any definitive answers can be given.

LOOKING AHEAD

This chapter concludes our basic analysis of how the macroeconomy works. In the preceding seven chapters, we have examined how households and firms behave in the three market arenas—the goods market, the money market, and the labor market. We have seen how aggregate output (income), the interest rate, and the price level are determined in the economy, and we have examined the relationship between two of the most important macroeconomic variables, the inflation rate and the unemployment rate. In chapter 31, we use everything we have learned up to this point to examine a number of important policy issues.

SUMMARY

1. Because the economy is dynamic, *frictional* and *structural unemployment* are inevitable and in some ways desirable. Times of *cyclical unemployment* are of concern to macroeconomic policy makers.

2. In general, employment tends to fall when aggregate output falls and rise when aggregate output rises.

THE CLASSICAL VIEW OF THE LABOR MARKET

3. Classical economists believe the interaction of supply and demand in the labor market brings about equilibrium and that unemployment (beyond the frictional and structural amounts) does not exist.

4. The classical view of the labor market is consistent with the theory of a vertical aggregate supply curve.

EXPLAINING THE EXISTENCE OF UNEMPLOYMENT

5. Some economists argue that the unemployment rate is not an accurate indicator of whether the labor market is working properly. Unemployed people who are considered part of the labor force may be offered jobs but may be unwilling to take those jobs at the offered salaries. Some of the unemployed may have chosen not to work, but this does not mean that the labor market has malfunctioned.

6. Those who do not subscribe to the classical view of the labor market suggest several reasons why unemployment exists. Downwardly *sticky wages* may be brought about by *implicit* or *explicit contracts* not to cut wages. If the equilibrium wage rate falls but wages are prevented from falling also, the result will be unemployment.

7. *Efficiency wage theory* holds that the productivity of workers increases with the wage rate. If this is true, firms may have an incentive to pay wages above the wage at which the quantity of labor supplied is equal to the quantity of labor demanded. At all wages above the equilibrium, there will be an excess supply of labor and therefore unemployment.

8. If firms are operating with incomplete or imperfect information, they may not know what the market-clearing wage is. As a result, they may set their wages incorrectly and bring about unemployment. Because the economy is so

complex, it may take considerable time for firms to correct these mistakes.

9. *Minimum wage laws*, which set a floor for wage rates, are one factor contributing to teenagers' unemployment. If the market-clearing wage for some groups of workers is below the minimum wage, some members of this group will be unemployed.

THE SHORT-RUN RELATIONSHIP BETWEEN THE UNEMPLOYMENT RATE AND INFLATION

10. There is a negative relationship between the unemployment rate (U) and aggregate output (income) (Y): When Y rises, U falls. When Y falls, U rises.

11. The relationship between the unemployment rate and the price level is negative: As the unemployment rate declines and the economy moves closer to capacity, the price level rises more and more.

12. The *Phillips Curve* represents the relationship between the *inflation rate* and the *unemployment rate*. During the 1950s and 1960s, this relationship was stable, and there seemed to be a predictable trade-off between inflation and

unemployment. As a result of import price increases (which led to shifts in aggregate supply) and shifts in aggregate demand brought about partially by inflationary expectations, the relationship between the inflation rate and the unemployment rate was erratic in the 1970s. There *is* a short-run trade-off between inflation and unemployment, but other things besides unemployment affect inflation.

THE LONG-RUN *AS* CURVE, POTENTIAL GDP, AND THE NATURAL RATE OF UNEMPLOYMENT

13. Those who believe the *AS* curve is vertical in the long run also believe the Phillips Curve is vertical in the long run at the *natural rate of unemployment*. The natural rate is generally the sum of the frictional and structural rates. If the Phillips Curve is vertical in the long run, then there is a limit to how low government policy can push the unemployment rate without setting off inflation.

14. The NAIRU theory says that the price level will accelerate when the unemployment rate is below the NAIRU and decelerate when the unemployment rate is above the NAIRU.

REVIEW TERMS AND CONCEPTS

cost-of-living adjustments (COLAs), 706
cyclical unemployment, 702
efficiency wage theory, 706
explicit contracts, 706
frictional unemployment, 701
inflation rate, 709

labor demand curve, 703
labor supply curve, 702
minimum wage laws, 707
NAIRU, 715
natural rate of unemployment, 714
Phillips Curve, 709

relative-wage explanation of unemployment, 706
social, or implicit, contracts, 706
sticky wages, 705
structural unemployment, 701
unemployment rate, 701

PROBLEM SET

1. Obtain monthly data on the unemployment rate and the inflation rate for the last two years. (These data can be found in a recent issue of the *Survey of Current Business* or in the *Monthly Labor Review* or *Employment and Earnings*, all published by the government and available in many college libraries.)
   a. What trends do you observe? Can you explain what you see using aggregate supply and aggregate demand curves?
   b. Plot the 24 monthly rates on a graph with the unemployment rate measured on the X axis and the inflation rate on the Y axis. Is there evidence of a trade-off between these two variables? Can you offer an explanation?

2. In 1998, the country of Ruba was suffering a period of high unemployment. The new president Clang appointed as his chief economist Laurel Tiedye. Ms. Tiedye and her staff

estimated these supply and demand curves for labor from data obtained from the secretary of labor, Robert Small:

$$Q_D = 100 - 5W$$
$$Q_S = 10W - 20,$$

where Q is the quantity of labor supplied/demanded in millions of workers and W is the wage rate in slugs, the currency of Ruba.
   a. Currently, the law in Ruba says no worker shall be paid less than nine slugs per hour. Estimate the quantity of labor supplied, the number of unemployed, and the unemployment rate.
   b. President Clang, over the objection of Secretary Small, has recommended to the Congress that the law be

changed to allow the wage rate to be determined in the market. If such a law were passed, and the market adjusted quickly, what would happen to total employment, the size of the labor force, and the unemployment rate? Show the results graphically.

   c. Will the Rubanese labor market adjust quickly to such a change in the law? Why or why not?

3. The following policies have at times been advocated for coping with unemployment. Briefly explain how each might work, and explain which type or types of unemployment (frictional, structural, or cyclical) each policy is designed to alter.

   a. A computer list of job openings and a service that matches employees with job vacancies (sometimes called an "economic dating service").

   b. Lower minimum wage for teenagers.

   c. Retraining programs for workers who need to learn new skills in order to find employment.

   d. Public employment for people without jobs.

   e. Improved information about available jobs and current wage rates.

   f. The president goes on nationwide TV and attempts to convince firms and workers that the inflation rate next year will be low.

4. Your boss offers you a wage increase of 10 percent. Is it possible that you are worse off, even with the wage increase, than you were before?

5. How will the following affect labor force participation rates? Labor supply? Unemployment?

   a. Because the retired elderly are a larger and larger fraction of the U.S. population, Congress and the president decide to raise the social security tax on individuals in order to continue paying benefits to the elderly.

   b. A national child care program is enacted, requiring employers to provide free child care services.

   c. The U.S. government reduces restrictions on immigration into the United States.

   d. The welfare system is eliminated.

   e. The government subsidizes the purchase of new capital by firms (an investment tax credit).

6. Draw a graph to illustrate the following:

   a. A Phillips Curve based on the assumption of a vertical long-run aggregate supply curve.

   b. The effect of a change in inflationary expectations on a recently stable Phillips Curve.

   c. Unemployment caused by a recently enacted minimum wage law.

7. Obtain data on "average hourly earnings of production workers" and the unemployment rate for your state or area over a recent two-year period. Has unemployment increased or decreased? What has happened to wages? Does the pattern of unemployment help explain the movement of wages? Can you offer an explanation?

8. Suppose the inflation-unemployment relationship depicted by the Phillips Curve was stable. Do you think the U.S. trade-off and the Japanese trade-off would be identical? If not, what kinds of factors might make the trade-offs dissimilar?

TAKE IT TO THE NET

We invite you to visit the Case and Fair page on the Prentice Hall Web site:

http://www.prenhall.com/casefair

for this chapter's World Wide Web exercise.

Chapter 31

DEFICIT REDUCTION, FED BEHAVIOR, STABILIZATION, STOCK MARKET EFFECTS, AND MACRO ISSUES ABROAD

NEWSPAPERS CARRY ARTICLES dealing with macro-economic problems daily, and macroeconomic issues are a heavy part of many political campaigns. Using what we've learned about how the macro-economy works, we now examine in greater depth some current issues and problems.

In this chapter, we take up five issues: (1) legislation concerned with setting targets for the federal deficit; (2) the way the Fed reacts to the state of the economy; (3) the lags in the economy's response to monetary and fiscal policy changes; (4) the effects of the stock market on the economy; and (5) the cyclical behavior since 1980 of the economies of Japan and five European countries.

DEFICIT REDUCTION AND MACROPOLICY

The federal government's deficit was a concern to policy makers for many years. As discussed in chapter 25, the deficit problem began in the early 1980s, when huge increases in the deficit occurred, and it continued until the late 1990s. When the deficit reached 4.7 percent of GDP in 1986, the U.S. Congress passed and President Reagan signed the **Gramm-Rudman-Hollings Bill** (named for its three congressional sponsors), referred to as GRH.

GRH set a target for reducing the federal deficit by a set amount each year. As Figure 31.1 shows, the deficit was to decline by $36 billion per year between 1987 and 1991, with a deficit of zero slated for fiscal year 1991. What was interesting about the GRH legislation was that the targets were not merely guidelines. If Congress, through its decisions about taxes and

Gramm-Rudman-Hollings Bill
Passed by the U.S. Congress and signed by President Reagan in 1986, this law set out to reduce the federal deficit by $36 billion per year, with a deficit of zero slated for 1991.

721

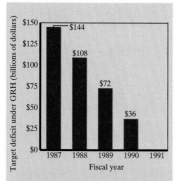

FIGURE 31.1

Deficit Reduction Targets under Gramm-Rudman-Hollings

The GRH legislation, passed in 1986, set out to lower the federal deficit by $36 billion per year. If the plan had worked, a zero deficit would have been achieved by 1991.

spending programs, produced a budget with a deficit larger than the targeted amount, GRH called for automatic spending cuts. The cuts were divided proportionately among most federal spending programs, so that a program that made up 5 percent of total spending was to endure a cut equal to 5 percent of the total spending cut.[1]

In 1986, the U.S. Supreme Court declared part of the GRH bill unconstitutional. In effect, the court said the Congress would have to approve the "automatic" spending cuts before they could take place. The law was changed in 1986 to meet the Supreme Court ruling and again in 1987, when new targets were established. The new targets had the deficit reaching zero in 1993 rather than 1991. The targets were changed again in 1991, when the year to achieve a zero deficit was changed from 1993 to 1996.

In practice, these targets never came close to being achieved. As time wore on, even the revised targets became completely unrealistic, and by the end of the 1980s the GRH legislation was not taken seriously.

The deficit problem continued in the 1990s, and one of President Clinton's goals when he took office in 1993 was to reduce the deficit. The first step was the Omnibus Budget Reconciliation Act of 1993. The act, which barely made it through Congress, was projected to reduce the deficit in the five fiscal years 1994 to 1998 by $504.8 billion—$254.7 billion would come from cuts in federal spending, and $250.1 billion would come from tax increases. Most of the tax increases were levied on high-income taxpayers.

There was also some sentiment in the mid 1990s for the passage of a "balanced-budget amendment," intended to prevent Congress from doing what it did in the 1980s. The balanced-budget amendment passed the House in early 1995, but it failed by one vote in the Senate. It turned out that the passage of the Omnibus Budget Reconciliation Act of 1993 and a robust economy from 1994 to 1997 was enough to lead to a roughly balanced budget by 1998. As of 1998, there was no longer a federal government deficit problem, although there was no assurance that the problem would not resurface in the future, especially as the baby boomers begin to retire and start drawing social security.

Although the government deficit is not currently a problem, it is instructive to see what the macroeconomic consequences are of legislation or amendments that target the deficit. Many economists who favored deficit reduction were opposed to the GRH legislation and the balanced-budget amendment, and we will now see why.

THE EFFECTS OF SPENDING CUTS ON THE DEFICIT

Suppose the terms of the balanced-budget amendment or some other deficit-reduction measure dictate that the deficit must be cut by $20 billion. By how much must government spending be cut to achieve this goal? You might be tempted to think the spending cuts should add up to the amount the deficit is to be cut—$20 billion. (This is what GRH dictated: If the deficit needed to be cut by a certain amount, automatic spending cuts were to be equal to this amount.) Seems reasonable! If you decrease your personal spending by $100 over a year, your personal deficit will fall by the full $100 of your spending cut.

But the government is not an individual household. A cut in government spending shifts the *AD* curve to the left and results in a decrease in aggregate output (income) (*Y*) and a contraction in the economy. When the economy contracts, both the taxable income of households and the profits of firms fall. This means revenue from the personal income tax and the corporate profits tax will fall.

How do these events affect the size of the deficit? To estimate the response of the deficit to changes in government spending, we need to go through two steps. First, we must decide how much a $1 change in government spending will change GDP. That means we need to know the size of the government spending multiplier. (Recall that the government spending multiplier measures the increase [or decrease] in GDP [*Y*]

[1]Programs like social security were exempt from cuts or were treated differently. Interest payments on the federal debt were also immune from cuts.

brought about by a $1 increase [or decrease] in government spending.) Based on empirical evidence, a reasonable value for the government spending multiplier seems to be around 1.4 after one year, and this is the value we will use. A $1 billion decrease in government spending lowers GDP by about $1.4 billion after one year.

Next, we must see what happens to the deficit when GDP changes. We have just noted that when GDP falls—the economy contracts—taxable income and corporate profits fall, so tax revenues fall. In addition, some categories of government expenditures tend to rise when the economy contracts. For example, unemployment insurance benefits (a transfer payment) rise as the economy contracts because more people become unemployed and eligible for benefits. Both the decrease in tax revenues and the rise in government expenditures cause the deficit to increase.

The deficit tends to rise when GDP falls, and tends to fall when GDP rises.

Assume the **deficit response index (DRI)** is −.22. That is, for every $1 billion decrease in GDP, the deficit rises by $0.22 billion. This number seems close to what is true in practice.

deficit response index (DRI)
The amount by which the deficit changes with a one-dollar change in GDP.

We can now use the multiplier and the DRI to answer the question that began this section. Suppose government spending is reduced by $20 billion, the exact amount of the necessary deficit reduction. This will lower GDP by 1.4 × $20 billion, or $28 billion, if the value of the multiplier is 1.4. A $28 billion fall in GDP will increase the deficit by .22 × $28 billion, or $6.2 billion, if the value of the DRI is −.22. Because we initially cut government spending (and therefore lowered the deficit from this source) by $20 billion, the net effect of the spending cut is to lower the deficit by $20 billion − $6.2 billion = $13.8 billion.

A $20 billion government spending cut does not lower the deficit by $20 billion. To lower the deficit by $20 billion, we need to cut government spending by about $30 billion. Using 1.4 as the value of the government spending multiplier and −.22 as the value of the DRI, we see that a spending cut of $30 billion lowers GDP by 1.4 × $30 billion, or $42 billion. This raises the deficit by .22 × $42 billion, or $9.2 billion. The net effect on the deficit is −$30 billion (from the government spending cut) + $9.2 billion, which is −$20.8 billion (slightly larger than the necessary $20 billion reduction). This means the spending cut must be nearly 50 percent larger than the deficit reduction we wish to achieve! Clearly, Congress would have had trouble achieving the deficit targets under the GRH legislation even if it had allowed GRH's automatic spending cuts to take place.

➤ **Monetary Policy to the Rescue?**   Was Congress so poorly informed about macroeconomics that it would pass legislation that could not possibly work? In other words, are there any conditions under which it would be reasonable to assume that a spending cut needs to be only as large as the desired reduction in the deficit? If the government spending multiplier is zero, government spending cuts will not contract the economy, and the cut in the deficit will be equal to the cut in government spending.

Could the government spending multiplier ever be zero? Before the GRH bill was passed, some argued it could. The argument went as follows: If households and firms are worried about the large government deficits and hold back on consumption and investment because of these worries, the passage of GRH might make them more optimistic and induce them to consume and invest more. This increased consumption and investment would offset the effects of the decreased government spending, and the net result would be a multiplier effect of zero.

Another argument in favor of the GRH bill centered on the Fed and monetary policy. We know from chapter 29 that an increase in the money supply shifts the *AD* curve to the right. Because a cut in government spending shifts the *AD* curve to the left, the Fed could respond to the spending cut by increasing the money supply enough to shift the *AD* curve back (to the right) to its original position, preventing any change in aggregate output (income). Some argued the Fed would behave in this way after the passage of the GRH bill because it would see that Congress finally "got its house in order."

From chapter 28 we know an increase in the money supply leads to a decrease in the equilibrium interest rate. If the Fed were to offset the effects of a decrease in government spending by increasing the money supply, the interest rate would fall, stimulating planned investment and offsetting the effects of the decrease in *G*. This would be a multiplier of zero. However, studies at the time of the original GRH bill showed the decrease in the interest rate that would be necessary to have the multiplier be zero (that is, for a government spending cut to have no effect on aggregate output [income]) is quite large. The Fed would have had to engage in extreme behavior with respect to interest rate changes for the multiplier to be zero.

> A zero multiplier can come about through renewed optimism on the part of households and firms or through very aggressive behavior on the part of the Fed. But because neither of these situations is very plausible, the multiplier is likely to be greater than zero. Thus, it is likely that to lower the deficit by a certain amount, the cut in government spending must be larger than that amount.

ECONOMIC STABILITY AND DEFICIT REDUCTION

So, lowering the deficit by a given amount is likely to require a government spending decrease larger than this amount. However, this is not the only point to learn from our analysis of deficit targeting. We will now show how deficit targeting can adversely affect the way the economy responds to a variety of stimuli.

In a world with no GRH, no balanced-budget amendment, no similar deficit-targeting measure, the Congress and the president make decisions each year about how much to spend and how much to tax. The federal government deficit is a result of these decisions and the state of the economy. But, with GRH or the balanced-budget amendment, the size of the deficit is set in advance. Taxes and government spending must be adjusted to produce the required deficit. In this situation, the deficit is no longer a consequence of the tax and spending decisions. Rather, taxes and spending become a consequence of the deficit decision.

What difference does it make whether Congress chooses a target deficit and adjusts government spending and taxes to achieve this target or decides how much to spend and tax and lets the deficit adjust itself? The difference may be substantial! Consider a leftward shift of the *AD* curve caused by some negative demand shock. A **negative demand shock** is something that causes a negative shift in consumption or investment schedules or that leads to a decrease in U.S. exports.

We know that a leftward shift of the *AD* curve lowers aggregate output (income), which causes the government deficit to increase. In a world without deficit targeting, the increase in the deficit during contractions provides an **automatic stabilizer** for the economy. (Review chapter 25 if this is hazy.) The contraction-induced decrease in tax revenues and increase in transfer payments tends to boost consumer incomes and stimulate consumer spending at a time when spending would otherwise be weak. Thus, the decrease in aggregate output (income) caused by the negative demand shock is lessened somewhat by the growth of the deficit (Figure 31.2a).

In a world with deficit targeting, the deficit is not allowed to rise. Some combination of tax increases and government spending cuts would be needed to offset what would have otherwise been an increase in the deficit. We know that increases in taxes or cuts in spending are contractionary in themselves. The contraction in the economy will therefore be larger than it would have been without deficit targeting, because the initial effect of the negative demand shock is worsened by the rise in taxes or the cut in government spending required to keep the deficit from rising. As Figure 31.2b shows,

negative demand shock
Something that causes a negative shift in consumption or investment schedules or that leads to a decrease in U.S. exports.

automatic stabilizers *Revenue and expenditure items in the federal budget that automatically change with the economy in such a way as to stabilize GDP.*

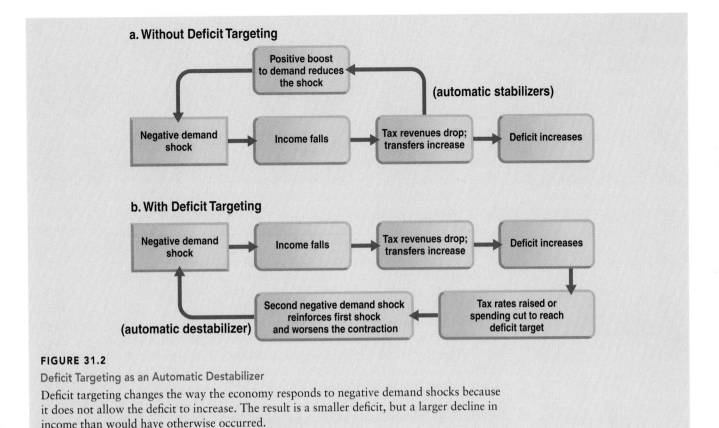

a. Without Deficit Targeting

Positive boost
to demand reduces
the shock

(automatic stabilizers)

Negative demand
shock → Income falls → Tax revenues drop;
transfers increase → Deficit increases

b. With Deficit Targeting

Negative demand
shock → Income falls → Tax revenues drop;
transfers increase → Deficit increases

(automatic destabilizer)

Second negative demand shock
reinforces first shock
and worsens the contraction ← Tax rates raised or
spending cut to reach
deficit target

FIGURE 31.2

Deficit Targeting as an Automatic Destabilizer

Deficit targeting changes the way the economy responds to negative demand shocks because it does not allow the deficit to increase. The result is a smaller deficit, but a larger decline in income than would have otherwise occurred.

deficit targeting acts as an **automatic destabilizer**. It requires taxes to be raised and government spending to be cut during a contraction. This reinforces, rather than counteracts, the shock that started the contraction.

▶ **Summary** It's clear the GRH legislation, the balanced-budget amendment, and similar deficit-targeting measures have some undesirable macroeconomic consequences. Deficit targeting requires cuts in spending or increases in taxes at times when the economy is already experiencing problems. This does not mean Congress should ignore the deficit. Rather, it means that locking the economy into spending cuts during periods of negative demand shocks, as deficit-targeting measures do, is not a good way to manage the economy.

automatic destabilizers
Revenue and expenditure items in the federal budget that automatically change with the economy in such a way as to destabilize GDP.

THE FED'S RESPONSE TO THE STATE OF THE ECONOMY

We know from chapter 26 that the Fed can control the money supply through open market operations, and from chapters 28 and 29 that changes in the money supply can affect aggregate output (income) (Y), the interest rate, and the price level. The Fed has the power to affect the economy through open market operations. But what factors affect its decisions? Why does the Fed sometimes increase the money supply and sometimes decrease the money supply?

Two of the Fed's main goals are high levels of output and employment and a low rate of inflation. From the Fed's point of view, the best situation is a fully employed economy with a low inflation rate. The worst situation is *stagflation*—high unemployment and high inflation.

FIGURE 31.3

The Fed's Response to Low
Output/Low Inflation

During periods of low
output/low inflation, the
economy is on the relatively
flat portion of the *AS* curve. In
this case, the Fed is likely to
expand the money supply. This
will shift the *AD* curve to the
right, from AD_0 to AD_1, and
lead to an increase in output
with very little increase in the
price level.

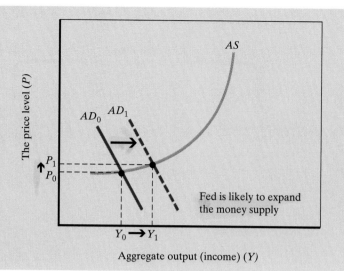

If the economy is in a low output/low inflation situation, it will be producing on
the relatively flat portion of the *AS* curve (Figure 31.3). In this case, the Fed can increase output by increasing the money supply with little effect on the price level. The
increase in the money supply will shift the *AD* curve to the right, leading to an increase
in output with little change in the price level.

> The Fed is likely to increase the money supply during times of low output and
> low inflation.

The opposite is true in times of high output and high inflation. In this situation, the
economy is producing on the relatively steep portion of the *AS* curve (Figure 31.4), and
the Fed can decrease the money supply with little effect on output. The decrease in the
money supply will shift the *AD* curve to the left, which will lead to a fall in the price
level and little effect on output.[2]

> The Fed is likely to decrease the money supply during times of high output and
> high inflation.

Stagflation is a more difficult problem to solve. If the Fed expands the money supply,
output will rise, but so will the inflation rate (which is already too high). If the Fed contracts the money supply, the inflation rate will fall, but so will output (which is already
too low). (You should be able to draw *AS/AD* diagrams to see why this is true.) The Fed
is faced with a trade-off. In this case, the Fed's decisions depend on how it weighs output
relative to inflation. If it dislikes high inflation more than low output, it will contract the
money supply; if it dislikes low output more than high inflation, it will expand the money
supply. In practice, the Fed probably dislikes high inflation more than low output, but
how the Fed behaves depends in part on the beliefs of the chair of the Fed.

The Fed sometimes "leans against the wind," meaning as the economy expands,
the Fed uses open market operations to raise interest rates gradually to try to prevent
the economy from expanding too quickly. Conversely, as the economy contracts, the

---

[2]In practice, the price level rarely falls. What the Fed actually achieves in this case is a decrease in the *rate
of inflation* (that is, in the percentage change in the price level), not a decrease in the price level itself. The
discussion here is sliding over the distinction between the price level and the rate of inflation. Recall our
discussion of this distinction in chapter 30.

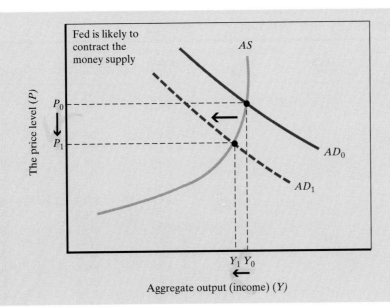

FIGURE 31.4

The Fed's Response to High Output/High Inflation

During periods of high output/high inflation, the economy is on the relatively steep portion of the *AS* curve. In this case, the Fed is likely to contract the money supply. This will shift the *AD* curve to the left, from AD_0 to AD_1, and lead to a decrease in the price level with very little decrease in output.

Fed lowers interest rates gradually to lessen (and eventually stop) the contraction. This type of stabilization is not easily achieved, as we will see later in this chapter.

> **The Behavior of the Fed During the 1990 to 1991 Recessions**   Table 31.1 presents data on selected variables for the 1989 I to 1997 IV period. We can use this table to see how the Fed behaved both before and after the 1990 to 1991 recession. In the first quarter of 1990 the growth rate was 3.9 percent, the unemployment rate 5.3 percent, the inflation rate 5.0 percent, and the three-month Treasury bill rate 7.8 percent. You can see that the Fed kept the bill rate fairly high in 1989. The economy was at or close to full employment, and the Fed wanted to keep the inflation rate in check.

In the second half of 1990, the economy went into a recession. Because inflation seemed to be under control at that time, experts expected the Fed would begin following an expansionary monetary policy to lessen the contraction of the economy. At the end of 1990, the Fed began to follow exactly this policy. Table 31.1 shows the three-month T-bill rate fell from 7.0 percent in the fourth quarter of 1990 to 6.1 percent in the first quarter of 1991. By the fourth quarter of 1991, the bill rate was down to 4.6 percent. This lowering of interest rates was designed to stimulate private spending and bring the economy out of the recession.

The Fed's behavior during the 1990 to 1991 recession is an example of its tendency to lean against the wind. After the Fed became convinced a recession was at hand, it responded by engaging in open market operations to lower interest rates. Inflation was not a problem, so the Fed could expand the economy in this way without worrying much about the inflationary consequences of its actions. Some argue that the Fed should have acted sooner, but with the Persian Gulf situation uncertain until February 1991, the Fed did not want to expand too much in the face of a possibly lengthy war that could have led to inflationary pressures. Once the outcome of the Persian Gulf War was known, the Fed responded rapidly.

> **The Behavior of the Fed in 1993 and 1994**   The economy was slow to recover from the 1990 to 1991 recession, and the growth rate did not pick up much until the beginning of 1992. Even at the end of 1992, the unemployment rate was still high at 7.4 percent (Table 31.1). The Fed kept the bill rate relatively low in 1992 and 1993 in an attempt to stimulate the economy. This was simply an extension of its expansionary policy in 1991. Again, inflation was not a problem in 1992 and 1993, so the Fed had room to stimulate.

TABLE 31.1 DATA FOR SELECTED VARIABLES FOR THE 1989–1997 PERIOD

QUARTER	REAL GDP GROWTH RATE (%)	UNEMPLOYMENT RATE (%)	INFLATION RATE (%)	THREE-MONTH T-BILL RATE	AAA BOND RATE	FEDERAL GOVERNMENT DEFICIT	DEFICIT/GDP
1989 I	4.0	5.2	4.7	8.5	9.7	92.1	0.017
II	3.0	5.2	4.3	8.4	9.5	100.3	0.019
III	2.2	5.3	3.3	7.8	9.0	124.8	0.023
IV	0.4	5.4	3.4	7.6	8.9	136.4	0.025
1990 I	3.9	5.3	5.0	7.8	9.2	154.1	0.027
II	1.2	5.3	5.2	7.8	9.4	144.2	0.025
III	−1.9	5.7	4.2	7.5	9.4	142.7	0.025
IV	−4.0	6.1	4.2	7.0	9.3	177.7	0.031
1991 I	−2.1	6.6	5.0	6.1	8.9	134.6	0.023
II	1.8	6.8	3.1	5.6	8.9	196.8	0.033
III	1.0	6.9	2.9	5.4	8.8	213.9	0.036
IV	1.0	7.1	2.5	4.6	8.4	238.9	0.040
1992 I	4.7	7.4	3.4	3.9	8.3	267.5	0.044
II	2.5	7.6	2.7	3.7	8.3	279.5	0.045
III	3.0	7.6	1.6	3.1	8.0	297.5	0.047
IV	4.3	7.4	2.9	3.1	8.0	278.9	0.044
1993 I	0.1	7.2	3.8	3.0	7.7	278.2	0.043
II	2.0	7.1	2.0	3.0	7.4	249.2	0.038
III	2.1	6.8	1.9	3.0	6.9	250.4	0.038
IV	5.3	6.6	2.7	3.1	6.8	224.7	0.034
1994 I	3.0	6.6	2.5	3.3	7.2	209.0	0.031
II	4.7	6.2	2.2	4.0	7.9	163.1	0.024
III	1.8	6.0	2.6	4.5	8.2	187.7	0.027
IV	3.6	5.6	2.7	5.3	8.6	186.9	0.026
1995 I	0.9	5.5	3.3	5.8	8.3	191.6	0.027
II	0.3	5.7	2.0	5.6	7.7	179.5	0.025
III	3.0	5.7	2.1	5.4	7.4	176.4	0.024
IV	2.2	5.6	2.2	5.3	7.0	150.3	0.020
1996 I	1.8	5.6	2.8	5.0	7.0	153.6	0.021
II	6.0	5.4	1.8	5.0	7.6	111.6	0.015
III	1.0	5.3	2.6	5.1	7.6	99.6	0.013
IV	4.3	5.3	1.8	5.0	7.2	77.0	0.010
1997 I	4.9	5.3	2.4	5.1	7.4	55.6	0.007
II	3.3	4.9	1.8	5.1	7.6	36.6	0.005
III	3.1	4.9	1.4	5.1	7.2	10.7	0.001
IV	3.9	4.7	1.4	5.1	6.9	8.3	0.001

Note: The inflation rate is the percentage change in the GDP price index.

By the fourth quarter of 1993 the unemployment rate had fallen to 6.6 percent and the growth rate was 5.3 percent.

At the end of 1993 the Fed decided to begin slowing down the economy. The bill rate rose from 3.1 percent in the fourth quarter of 1993 to 5.8 percent in the first quarter of 1995. Why was the Fed pursuing a contractionary policy? You can see from the table that the inflation rate in 1993 and 1994 was quite low, and there were no signs even at the end of 1994 of any inflationary pressures building in the economy. But the Fed was worried about inflation picking up in the future. The growth rate in 1994 was relatively high (about 3.3 percent) and the unemployment rate was down to 5.6 percent by the fourth quarter, and the Fed felt these trends might spell inflation problems in the future.

The Fed's behavior in 1994 is an example of leaning against the wind quite far in advance, long before any observed sign of increasing inflation. Some people felt that the Fed was acting too hastily and should have waited for direct signs of inflationary pressures before tightening.

> **The Behavior of the Fed in 1995–1997** Inflation in fact did not become a problem after 1994, and by 1997 the inflation rate was below 2 percent. After slow growth in the first half of 1995, the economy picked up the pace, and by the end of 1997, the unemployment rate was down to 4.7 percent. The Fed lowered the T-bill rate from 5.8 percent in the first quarter of 1995 to 5.0 percent in the first quarter of 1996, and then it kept the T-bill rate at roughly 5.0 percent throughout 1996 and 1997. You can see from Table 31.1 that the federal government deficit fell to essentially zero by the end of 1997. What better outcome could the Fed want: good growth, low unemployment, low inflation, and a balanced government budget!

Needless to say, Chairman Greenspan was fairly popular in 1997 (as was President Clinton). The economy was doing well. It was clear from Greenspan's testimony in 1996 and 1997, however, that he was nervous about the possibility of inflation increasing and that the Fed was watching very carefully for signs of this. It seemed very likely that the Fed would lean against wind (i.e., raise interest rates) at the first sign of inflation picking up. At the end of 1997, the Fed was also concerned about possible negative effects on the U.S. economy from the Asian crisis, and if the U.S. economy was adversely affected, the Fed would likely respond by lowering interest rates. Barring either inflation picking up or growth falling, the Fed seemed inclined to just sit and wait, as it had essentially done for all of 1996 and 1997.

LAGS IN THE ECONOMY'S RESPONSE TO MONETARY AND FISCAL POLICY

One of the objectives of monetary and fiscal policy is stabilization of the economy. Consider the two possible time paths for aggregate output (income) (Y) shown in Figure 31.5. In path B (the dashed line), the fluctuations in GDP are smaller than those in path A (the solid line). One aim of **stabilization policy** is to smooth out fluctuations in output, to try to move the economy along a path like B instead of A. Stabilization policy is also concerned with the stability of prices. Here the goal is not to prevent the overall price level from rising at all but rather to achieve an inflation rate that is as low as possible given the government's other goals of high and stable levels of output and employment.

Stabilization goals are not easy to achieve. The existence of various kinds of **time lags**, or delays in the response of the economy to stabilization policies, can make the economy difficult to control. Economists generally recognize three kinds of time lags: recognition lags, implementation lags, and response lags. We will consider each. But we will begin with an analogy.

stabilization policy *Describes both monetary and fiscal policy, the goals of which are to smooth out fluctuations in output and employment and to keep prices as stable as possible.*

time lags *Delays in the economy's response to stabilization policies.*

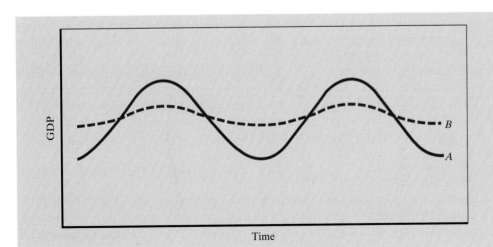

FIGURE 31.5

Two Time Paths for GDP

Path A is less stable—it varies more over time—than path B. Other things being equal, society prefers path B to path A.

THE GOVERNMENT'S ATTEMPTS
TO STABILIZE THE ECONOMY ARE
LIKE TRYING TO GET THE WATER
TEMPERATURE JUST RIGHT IN
THE SHOWER, ACCORDING TO
MILTON FRIEDMAN.

➤ "The Fool in the Shower" Milton Friedman, a leading critic of stabilization policy, likened the government's attempts to stabilize the economy to a "fool in the shower." The shower starts out too cold, because the pipes have not yet warmed up. So the fool turns up the hot water. Nothing happens, so he turns up the hot water further. The hot water comes on and scalds him. He immediately turns up the cold water. Nothing happens right away, so he turns up the cold further. When the cold water finally starts to come up, he finds the shower too cold. And so it goes.

In Friedman's view, the government is constantly behaving like the fool in the shower, stimulating or contracting the economy at the wrong time. How this might happen is shown in Figure 31.6. Suppose the economy reaches a peak and begins to slide into recession at point A (at time t_0). Policy makers do not observe the decline in GDP until it has sunk to point B (at time t_1). By the time they have begun to stimulate the economy (point C, time t_2), the recession is well advanced and the economy has almost bottomed out. When the policies finally begin to take effect (point D, time t_3), the economy is already on its road to recovery. The policies push the economy to point F'—a much greater fluctuation than point F, which is where the economy would have been without the stabilization policy. Sometime after point D, policy makers may begin to realize that the economy is expanding too quickly. But by the time they have implemented contractionary policies and the policies have made their effects felt, the economy is starting to weaken. The contractionary policies therefore end up pushing GDP to point G' instead of point G.

Because of the various time lags, the expansionary policies that should have been instituted at time t_0 do not begin to have an effect until time t_3, when they are no longer needed. The dashed lines in Figure 31.6 show how the economy behaves as a result of the "stabilization" policies; the solid lines show the time path of GDP if the economy had been allowed to run its course and no stabilization policies had been attempted. In this case, stabilization policy makes income more erratic, not less—the policy results in a peak income of F' as opposed to F and a trough income of G' instead of G.

Critics of stabilization policy argue that the situation in Figure 31.6 is typical of the interaction between the government and the rest of the economy. This is not necessarily true. We need to know more about the nature of the various kinds of lags before deciding whether stabilization policy is good or bad.

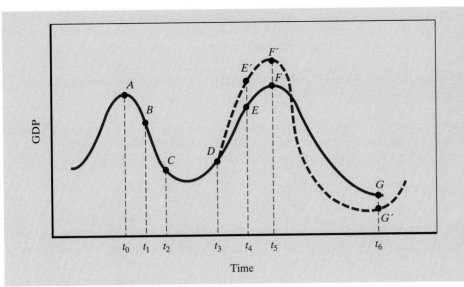

FIGURE 31.6

"The Fool in the Shower"—
How Government Policy Can
Make Matters Worse

Attempts to stabilize the economy
can prove destabilizing because of
time lags. An expansionary policy
that should have begun to take effect
at point A does not actually begin
to have an impact until point D,
when the economy is already on an
upswing. Hence the policy pushes the
economy to points F' and G' (rather
than points F and G). Income varies
more widely than it would have if no
policy had been implemented.

RECOGNITION LAGS

It takes time for policy makers to recognize a boom or a slump. Many important data—those from the national income and product accounts, for example—are available only quarterly. It usually takes several weeks to compile and prepare even the preliminary estimates for these figures. If the economy goes into a slump on January 1, the recession may not show up until the data for the first quarter are available at the end of April.

Moreover, the early national income and product accounts data are only preliminary, based on an incomplete compilation of the various data sources. These estimates can, and often do, change as better data become available. This makes the interpretation of the initial estimates difficult, and **recognition lags** result.

IMPLEMENTATION LAGS

The problems that lags pose for stabilization policy do not end once economists and policy makers recognize that the economy is in a slump or a boom. Even if everyone knows that the economy needs to be stimulated or reined in, it takes time to put the desired policy into effect, especially for actions that involve fiscal policy. **Implementation lags** result.

Each year Congress decides on the federal government's budget for the coming year. The tax laws and spending programs embodied in this budget are not subject to change once they are in place. If it becomes clear that the economy is entering a recession and is in need of a fiscal stimulus during the middle of the year, there is little that can be done. Until Congress authorizes more spending or a cut in taxes, changes in fiscal policy are not possible.[3]

Implementation lags vary in length. In May of 1975, for example, the U.S. economy was in a deep recession and needed immediate stimulation. Although many economists had called for government action earlier, general agreement that action was necessary did not come about until late spring. Once the consensus emerged, President Ford asked Congress for an immediate tax cut retroactive to 1974. (See Application box in chapter 25.) Congress responded, and rebate checks were mailed to millions of people within weeks. As those dollars were spent, the economy began to recover.

Monetary policy is less subject to the kinds of restrictions that slow down changes in fiscal policy. As we saw in chapter 26, the Fed's chief tool to control the supply of money

recognition lag *The time it takes for policy makers to recognize the existence of a boom or a slump.*

implementation lag *The time it takes to put the desired policy into effect once economists and policy makers recognize that the economy is in a boom or a slump.*

---

[3]Don't forget, however, about the existence of automatic stabilizers. Many programs contain built-in countercyclical features that expand spending or cut tax collections automatically (without the need for congressional or executive action) during a recession.

or the interest rate is open market operations—buying and selling government securities. Transactions in these securities take place in a highly developed market, and if the Fed wishes, it can buy or sell a large volume of securities in a very short period of time.

> The implementation lag for monetary policy is generally much shorter than for fiscal policy.

When the Fed wishes to increase the supply of money, it goes into the open market and purchases government securities. This instantly increases the stock of money (bank reserves held at the Fed), and an expansion of the money supply begins.

RESPONSE LAGS

response lag *The time that it takes for the economy to adjust to the new conditions after a new policy is implemented; the lag that occurs because of the operation of the economy itself.*

Even after a macroeconomic problem has been recognized and the appropriate policies to correct it have been implemented, there are **response lags**—lags that occur because of the operation of the economy itself. Even after the government has formulated a policy and put it into place, the economy takes time to adjust to the new conditions.

Although monetary policy can be adjusted and implemented more quickly than fiscal policy, it may actually take longer to make its effect felt on the economy because of response lags. What is most important is the total lag between the time a problem first occurs and the time the corrective policies are felt.

▶ **Response Lags for Fiscal Policy**   One way to think about the response lag in fiscal policy is through the government spending multiplier. This multiplier measures the change in GDP caused by a given change in government spending or net taxes. It takes time for the multiplier to reach its full value. The result is a lag between the time a fiscal policy action is initiated and the time the full change in GDP is realized.

The reason for the response lag in fiscal policy—the delay in the multiplier process—is simple. During the first few months after an increase in government spending or a tax cut, there is not enough time for the firms or individuals who benefit directly from the extra government spending or the tax cut to increase their own spending.

Suppose you are the owner of Transylvania Trucking, a small fleet of trucks. The government decides to increase its spending, and one of the things it spends more on is trucking services, including some extra purchases from your company. In the first months after you receive this extra business from the government, however, you are unlikely to increase your own purchases. Most of the things you buy—trucks, office furniture, stationery—are already contained in your inventories. It will generally take you some time before your own purchases are increased to reflect the extra income that you have received, and the multiplier effect of government spending will not be felt until this occurs.

> Neither individuals nor firms revise their spending plans instantaneously. Until they can make those revisions, extra government spending does not stimulate extra private spending.

Changes in government purchases are a component of aggregate expenditure. When G rises, aggregate expenditure increases directly; when G falls, aggregate expenditure decreases directly. When personal taxes are changed, however, an additional step intervenes, giving rise to another lag. Suppose a tax cut has lowered personal income taxes across the board. Each household must decide what portion of its tax cut to spend and what portion to save. This decision is the extra step. Before the tax cut gets translated into extra spending, households must take the step of increasing their spending, which usually takes some time.

With a business tax cut, there is a further complication. Firms must decide what to do with their added after-tax profits. If they pay out their added profits to households as dividends, the result is the same as with a personal tax cut. Households must decide whether to spend or to save the extra funds. Firms may also retain their added profits and use them for investment, but investment is a component of aggregate expenditure that requires planning and time.

In practice, it takes about a year for a change in taxes or in government spending to have its full effect on the economy. This means that if we increase spending to counteract a recession today, the full effects will not be felt for 12 months. By that time, the state of the economy might be very different.

▶ **Response Lags for Monetary Policy** Monetary policy works by changing interest rates, which then change planned investment. Interest rates can also affect consumption spending, as we discuss further in the next chapter. For now, it is enough to know that lower interest rates usually stimulate consumption spending and higher interest rates decrease consumption spending.

The response of consumption and investment to interest rate changes takes time. Even if interest rates were to drop by five percentage points overnight, firms would not immediately increase their investment purchases. Firms generally make their investment plans several years in advance. If General Motors wants to respond to a decrease in interest rates by investing more, it will take some time—perhaps up to a year—to come up with plans for a new factory or assembly line. While such plans are being drawn, GM may spend little on new investments. The effect of the decrease in interest rates may not make itself felt for quite some time.

It is likely that the response lags for monetary policy will be even longer than response lags for fiscal policy. When government spending changes, there is a direct change in the sales of firms, which sell more as a result of the increased government purchases. When interest rates change, however, the sales of firms do not change until households change their consumption spending and/or firms change their investment spending. It takes time for households and firms to respond to interest rate changes. In this sense, interest rate changes are like tax-rate changes. The resulting change in firm sales must wait for households and firms to change their purchases of goods.

▶ **Summary** Stabilization is not easily achieved. It takes time for policy makers to recognize the existence of a problem, more time for them to implement a solution, and yet more time for firms and households to respond to the stabilization policies taken. Monetary policy can be adjusted more quickly and easily than taxes or government spending, making it a useful instrument in stabilizing the economy. But because the economy's response to monetary changes is probably slower than its response to changes in fiscal policy, tax and spending changes can also play a useful role in macroeconomic management.

THE EFFECTS OF THE STOCK MARKET ON THE ECONOMY

We mentioned in chapter 24 that one of the factors that affects consumption is wealth, something we consider in more detail in chapter 32. If a household has a sudden increase in wealth, its current and future consumption levels will increase. One of the main components of household wealth is the value of stocks held by households. When stock prices rise, household wealth increases, and when stock prices fall, household wealth decreases. Stock prices affect the economy by affecting household wealth, which affects household consumption. (This chapter's Application boxes explain how to follow both the bond market and the stock market by reading the financial pages of the daily newspaper.)

As you should recall from chapter 3, one of the key aspects of the modern corporation is its limited liability. Stockholders are entitled to a share of the firm's profits, but if the firm incurs losses, stockholders' liability is limited to the amount of their initial contribution. This is not true with partnerships or proprietorships.

READING A BOND TABLE

WHAT IS A BOND?

When a business wishes to make a large purchase—to build a new factory, or to buy an expensive piece of machinery—it often cannot pay for the purchase all at once, entirely out of its normal revenues. The obvious solution is to borrow the money, make the purchase, and then repay the lender of the funds over a longer period of time. This is called "financing" an investment, and the "pieces of paper" that are involved in these transactions are called **financial instruments**. *Bonds* are one type of financial instrument that firms issue in exchange for cash. If you buy a bond, you are making a loan to the firm that sold it to you.

Bonds have several properties. First, they are issued with a *face value,* typically in denominations of $1,000, that represent the amount you (the buyer) agree to lend the bond issuer. They also come with a *maturity date* on which the firm promises to pay back the funds you lent it. (However, you can sell the bond to someone else before the maturity date if you want.) Finally, there is a fixed payment of a specified amount (usually made annually), paid by the bond issuer to the bondholder. This

payment, known as the *coupon,* is calculated using the prevailing interest rate at the time the bond is issued. Even if interest rates change over the life of the bond, which they almost always do, the amount you receive as interest on your bond remains fixed. (This is why bonds are sometimes referred to as fixed-income securities. The bondholder receives a set amount, known in advance, no matter what happens to interest rates, stock prices, and so on.)

If you bought a $10,000, 10 percent, 15-year bond from Company XYZ on January 1, 1998, this is what would happen. You would give XYZ, or perhaps your broker, a check for $10,000. Every January for the next 14 years, XYZ would send you a check for $1,000 (10 percent of the $10,000 face value). On January 1, 2013, XYZ would send you a check for the face value of the bond—$10,000—plus the interest for that year—$1,000—and that would square all accounts.

Does the fact that the annual interest payment (coupon) on a bond does not change with fluctuations in the interest rate mean that bonds are completely insulated from interest rate movements? Absolutely not!

Instead of the coupon responding to a change in the interest rate, it is the *price of the bond* that changes. To see why, suppose you had a choice of putting $10,000 into the bond described here or into a bank account that pays 10 percent per year interest. In either case, you would earn $1,000 per year in interest payments, so you should be indifferent between the two choices.

But now suppose that the interest rate on the bank account goes up to 20 percent instead of 10 percent. The bond still promises to pay $1,000 per year. If you want to earn $1,000 in interest, you need to put only $5,000 into the bank account (.20 × $5,000 = $1,000). You would obviously prefer to put $5,000 into the bank rather than tie up $10,000 in the bond. The only way anyone would willingly buy the bond is if it cost no more than other investments that yield the same stream of income in the future. The bond would thus be worth much less than $10,000 if the interest rate were 20 percent. It follows, then, that when interest rates rise, bond prices fall, and bondholders suffer a *capital loss*—that is, a reduction in the value of the securities they own.

▶ **The Crash of October 1987**   To see how events in the stock market affect the economy, let's consider a particular episode in the history of the stock market—the stock market crash of October 1987. The value of stocks in the United States fell by about a trillion dollars between August 1987 and the end of October 1987. In one day—October 19, 1987—the value of stocks fell nearly $700 billion. This corresponded to a large drop in household wealth.

In practice, it seems that a $1.00 decrease in wealth leads roughly to a $0.05 decrease in consumption spending per year. In other words, consumption seems to be lower in each future year by about 5 percent of the decrease in wealth. Using this estimate, we can see that the $1 trillion decrease in wealth in 1987 implies a $50 billion lower level of consumption in 1988. The level of GDP was around $4 trillion in 1987, so a $50 billion decrease in consumption is around 1.25 percent of GDP. A multiplier effect would also be at work here. A decrease in consumption spending leads to a

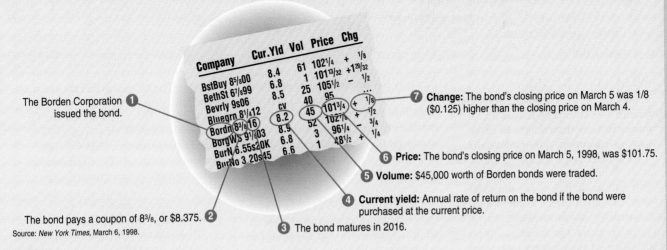

The Borden Corporation ❶ issued the bond.

❼ **Change:** The bond's closing price on March 5 was 1/8 ($0.125) higher than the closing price on March 4.

The bond pays a coupon of 8³/₈, or $8.375. ❷

Source: *New York Times*, March 6, 1998.

❻ **Price:** The bond's closing price on March 5, 1998, was $101.75.

❺ **Volume:** $45,000 worth of Borden bonds were traded.

❹ **Current yield:** Annual rate of return on the bond if the bond were purchased at the current price.

❸ The bond matures in 2016.

FIGURE 1

New York Stock Exchange Bonds

READING A BOND TABLE

Figure 1 shows a small section of the *New York Times*'s corporate bond price quotations for March 5, 1998. What do all these signs and symbols mean?

The first column, under "Company," gives the name of the corporation that issued the bond and certain information about the terms under which the bond was originally issued. Let's take the last bond listed in the figure as an example. This bond was issued by the Borden Corporation. The "8³/₈" means the bond pays a coupon of 8³/₈, or $8.375, per $100 of face

value of the bond. The "16" means the bond matures in 2016. The column titled "Cur. Yld" shows the annual rate of return on the bond if the bond were purchased at the current price. If the current price were $100, then the annual rate of return would be 8.375 percent. The bond yields 8.2 percent, however, so the current price of the bond must be higher than its face value of $100. (Remember: A decrease in the interest rate raises the value of a bond.) The column "Vol" tells how many thousands of dollars in bonds were traded during the day.

Here we see $45,000 (at face value) of the Borden bond was traded on March 5, 1998.

"Price" is the closing price of the bond. This is how much you would have to pay for the bond per $100 of face value. The Borden bond's closing price was 101³/₄, which means the bond was worth $101.75 at the end of the trading day. The last column, "Chg," tells us by how much the closing bond price differs from the closing price on the previous day. In this case, the price of the Borden bond rose by one eighth of a point—$0.125.

For more on bonds, see the Case and Fair Web page at
http://www.prenhall.com/casefair.

decrease in aggregate output (income), which leads to a further decrease in spending, and so on. The total decrease in GDP would be somewhat larger than the initial decrease in consumption of $50 billion. If the multiplier is 1.4, the total decrease in GDP would be about 1.4 × $50 billion = $70 billion, or about 1.75 percent of GDP.

Although 1.75 percent of GDP is a large amount, it is not large enough to imply that a recession would result from the crash. The life-cycle theory, which we discuss in chapter 32, helps explain why. If households are making lifetime decisions and want to have as smooth a consumption path as possible over their lifetimes, they will respond to a decrease in wealth by cutting consumption a little each year. They will *not* decrease their consumption in the current year by the full amount of the decrease in wealth. As we already noted, it has been estimated that households adjust their consumption by about 5 percent of the decrease in wealth each year.

Why were people predicting the economy would go into a recession, worse, a depression, after the crash? The reasons all pertain to expectations. If households and

READING THE STOCK PAGE

WHAT IS A STOCK?

In addition to issuing bonds, firms can finance investments by borrowing money directly from a bank or other lending institution. A third alternative is for firms to issue additional shares of stock. When a corporation issues new shares of stock, it does not add to its debt. Instead, it brings in additional "owners" of the firm, owners who agree to supply it with funds. The contributions of such owners are treated differently from loans made by outsiders, which are considered liabilities.

What is a share of stock? If you buy one share of Company QRS, and the firm has 1 million total shares outstanding, you have purchased a one-millionth ownership of the firm. You have a right—along with the owners of the other 999,999 shares—to select the management of the firm and to share in its profits. (This is not true of bondholders and other creditors of the firm, who have no say in its management.) Unlike bonds or direct borrowing, your stock does not promise a fixed annual payment. Rather, the returns you receive on your investment depend on how well Company QRS performs. If its profits are high, the firm may pay dividends to its shareholders, although it is not required to do so. If the firm does well, you may also find that the price of QRS stock has gone up, in which case you could realize a *capital gain* by selling your stock for more than you originally paid for it.

READING THE STOCK PAGES

Once you buy a stock, you are free to sell it to someone else at any time. Developments in the stock market, where such transactions take place, are constantly followed in the news.

Figure 1 reproduces part of the stock quotations from the *New York Times* for March 5, 1998. Let's take the stock of Chevron and see what information the stock pages provide.

The first two columns, under the heading "52-Week," give the stock's highest and lowest prices over the past year. The price of a share of Chevron stock reached a high of 89 3/16 and a low of 61 3/4 during this period. (Stock prices are quoted in dollars per share, so "61 3/4" means that the stock sold for $61.75 per share at its low point during the past 52 weeks.) The column "Div" gives the current annual rate of dividend payment. The "f" means that the rate was increased by the most recent dividend announcement. The current annual rate for Chevron is $2.44. What sort of return is this? The next column, "Yld %" (yield percent), takes the dividend as a percentage of the day's closing price. (The day's closing price in this case is 84 9/16, which is given in the column titled "Last.") For Chevron the yield is 2.9 percent.

The column "P/E" (price-earnings ratio) calculates the ratio of the price of a share of stock to the company's *total earnings per share* (which includes not only dividends paid to shareholders but also retained earnings). The PE ratio is a measure of how highly a stock is valued. Chevron's PE ratio is 17. The column "Sales 100s" tells how many hundreds of shares changed hands during the day's trading. On March 5, 1998, 1,958,600 shares of Chevron's stock were traded. The last four columns give the stock's highest, lowest, and closing price during the day's trading, as well as the change in the closing price from the closing price of the previous day.

Source: New York Times, March 6, 1998.

FIGURE 1

New York Stock Exchange Issues

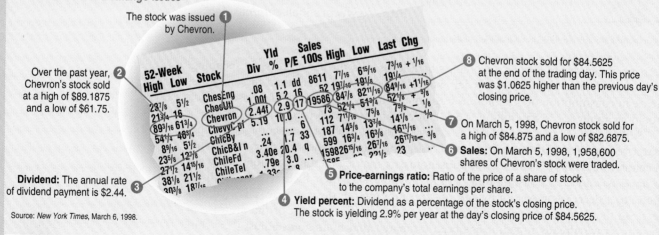

The stock was issued by Chevron. ①

Over the past year, ② Chevron's stock sold at a high of $89.1875 and a low of $61.75.

Dividend: The annual rate ③ of dividend payment is $2.44.

Source: *New York Times*, March 6, 1998.

⑧ Chevron stock sold for $84.5625 at the end of the trading day. This price was $1.0625 higher than the previous day's closing price.

⑦ On March 5, 1998, Chevron stock sold for a high of $84.875 and a low of $82.6875.

⑥ **Sales:** On March 5, 1998, 1,958,600 shares of Chevron's stock were traded.

⑤ **Price-earnings ratio:** Ratio of the price of a share of stock to the company's total earnings per share.

④ **Yield percent:** Dividend as a percentage of the stock's closing price. The stock is yielding 2.9% per year at the day's closing price of $84.5625.

firms expected the economy would contract sharply after the crash, they probably would have cut back on consumption and investment. (This would be Keynes's animal spirits at work.) These expectations would have become self-fulfilling in the sense that the economy would have gone into a recession because of the cuts in consumption and investment brought about by lowered expectations.

But, the economy did not go into a recession in 1988. Expectations were not changed drastically following the crash. The Fed helped out by easing monetary policy right after the crash to counteract any large negative reaction. The three-month Treasury bill rate fell from 6.4 percent to 5.8 percent between October and November of 1987. In addition, the value of stocks gradually increased over time to their earlier levels. Because the initial decrease in wealth turned out to be temporary, the negative wealth effect was not nearly as large as it otherwise would have been. The crash affected consumption only slightly.

► **The Stock Market Boom of 1995 to 1997**   Between the end of 1994 and the end of 1997, stock prices, on average, roughly doubled, adding over $3 trillion to household wealth. If this increase is sustained, and if households spend about 5 percent of the increase each year, we should expect to see consumption expenditures in the future about $150 billion higher per year than otherwise. This is a fairly large percentage of GDP. With GDP running around $8.5 trillion in 1998, the increased consumption would be about 1.8 percent of GDP, not counting any multiplier effects. Whether the stock market boom will have this much effect on GDP is hard to say. It may be that the 5 percent figure is a little high, but perhaps more importantly, it may be that not all of the increase in stock prices will be sustained. Even if only half of the increase is sustained, however, this should still have a fairly expansionary effect on the U.S. economy over the next few years.

BUSINESS CYCLES IN OTHER COUNTRIES

The United States is not the only developed nation to have business cycles. We now turn to inflation and unemployment in Japan, the United Kingdom, (West) Germany, France, Italy, and Spain. Figure 31.7 gives data for 1980 to 1996 for each country's (1) growth rate, (2) inflation rate, (3) unemployment rate, and (4) short-term interest rate.

The overall performance of the Japanese economy was quite good until 1992, when the growth rate slowed considerably. The slower growth led the unemployment rate to rise from 2.1 percent in 1991 to 3.4 percent in 1996. The Bank of Japan eased monetary policy during this period in an attempt to stimulate the economy, and by 1996 the short-term interest rate was down to 0.5 percent. This "leaning against the wind" behavior of the Bank of Japan is similar to the Fed's behavior discussed earlier in this chapter. Alas, this monetary-policy stimulus was not enough to prevent the slowdown from lasting a number of years.

The United Kingdom's economy shows distinct cycles. The U.K. growth rate was negative in 1980 to 1981 and then again in 1991 to 1992, whereas growth in the mid-1980s was strong. Note that inflation was very high in 1980 and 1981, even though growth was negative—a clear period of stagflation. By 1990, the unemployment rate had fallen to 7.1 percent, but it then began rising as the growth rate turned negative. The interest rate dropped substantially during the 1991 to 1993 period, which reflects the Bank of England's easing of monetary policy to try to stimulate the economy. The U.K. economy recovered moderately in 1994 to 1996, with the unemployment rate falling to 8.2 percent by 1996.

The general U.K. pattern of low or negative growth in the early 1980s and then again in the early 1990s also holds for the other four European countries in Figure 31.7. Also, the inflation rate has been generally falling over time in the European countries. Another trend is the fairly high level of unemployment across all of Europe for the period 1980 to 1996: Spain experienced the worst problems in this area.

There has been much discussion in Europe as to why the unemployment rates have remained so high for so long. Some say the problem is caused by the generous social welfare benefits in Europe—especially unemployment benefits—which may lead the

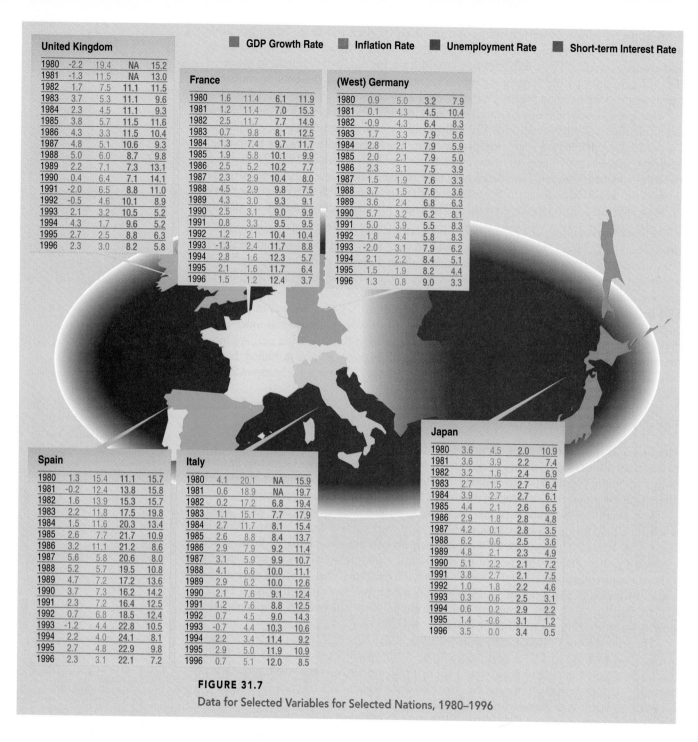

	GDP Growth Rate	Inflation Rate	Unemployment Rate	Short-term Interest Rate
United Kingdom				
1980	-2.2	19.4	NA	15.2
1981	-1.3	11.5	NA	13.0
1982	1.7	7.5	11.1	11.5
1983	3.7	5.3	11.1	9.6
1984	2.3	4.5	11.1	9.3
1985	3.8	5.7	11.5	11.6
1986	4.3	3.3	11.5	10.4
1987	4.8	5.1	10.6	9.3
1988	5.0	6.0	8.7	9.8
1989	2.2	7.1	7.3	13.1
1990	0.4	6.4	7.1	14.1
1991	-2.0	6.5	8.8	11.0
1992	-0.5	4.6	10.1	8.9
1993	2.1	3.2	10.5	5.2
1994	4.3	1.7	9.6	5.2
1995	2.7	2.5	8.8	6.3
1996	2.3	3.0	8.2	5.8

	GDP Growth Rate	Inflation Rate	Unemployment Rate	Short-term Interest Rate
France				
1980	1.6	11.4	6.1	11.9
1981	1.2	11.4	7.0	15.3
1982	2.5	11.7	7.7	14.9
1983	0.7	9.8	8.1	12.5
1984	1.3	7.4	9.7	11.7
1985	1.9	5.8	10.1	9.9
1986	2.5	5.2	10.2	7.7
1987	2.3	2.9	10.4	8.0
1988	4.5	2.9	9.8	7.5
1989	4.3	3.0	9.3	9.1
1990	2.5	3.1	9.0	9.9
1991	0.8	3.3	9.5	9.5
1992	1.2	2.1	10.4	10.4
1993	-1.3	2.4	11.7	8.8
1994	2.8	1.6	12.3	5.7
1995	2.1	1.6	11.7	6.4
1996	1.5	1.2	12.4	3.7

	GDP Growth Rate	Inflation Rate	Unemployment Rate	Short-term Interest Rate
(West) Germany				
1980	0.9	5.0	3.2	7.9
1981	0.1	4.3	4.5	10.4
1982	-0.9	4.3	6.4	8.3
1983	1.7	3.3	7.9	5.6
1984	2.8	2.1	7.9	5.9
1985	2.0	2.1	7.9	5.0
1986	2.3	3.1	7.5	3.9
1987	1.5	1.9	7.6	3.3
1988	3.7	1.5	7.6	3.6
1989	3.6	2.4	6.8	6.3
1990	5.7	3.2	6.2	8.1
1991	5.0	3.9	5.5	8.3
1992	1.8	4.4	5.8	8.3
1993	-2.0	3.1	7.9	6.2
1994	2.1	2.2	8.4	5.1
1995	1.5	1.9	8.2	4.4
1996	1.3	0.8	9.0	3.3

	GDP Growth Rate	Inflation Rate	Unemployment Rate	Short-term Interest Rate
Japan				
1980	3.6	4.5	2.0	10.9
1981	3.6	3.9	2.2	7.4
1982	3.2	1.6	2.4	6.9
1983	2.7	1.5	2.7	6.4
1984	3.9	2.7	2.7	6.1
1985	4.4	2.1	2.6	6.5
1986	2.9	1.8	2.8	4.8
1987	4.2	0.1	2.8	3.5
1988	6.2	0.6	2.5	3.6
1989	4.8	2.1	2.3	4.9
1990	5.1	2.2	2.1	7.2
1991	3.8	2.7	2.1	7.5
1992	1.0	1.8	2.2	4.6
1993	0.3	0.6	2.5	3.1
1994	0.6	0.2	2.9	2.2
1995	1.4	-0.6	3.1	1.2
1996	3.5	0.0	3.4	0.5

	GDP Growth Rate	Inflation Rate	Unemployment Rate	Short-term Interest Rate
Spain				
1980	1.3	15.4	11.1	15.7
1981	-0.2	12.4	13.8	15.8
1982	1.6	13.9	15.3	15.7
1983	2.2	11.8	17.5	19.8
1984	1.5	11.6	20.3	13.4
1985	2.6	7.7	21.7	10.9
1986	3.2	11.1	21.2	8.6
1987	5.6	5.8	20.6	8.0
1988	5.2	5.7	19.5	10.8
1989	4.7	7.2	17.2	13.6
1990	3.7	7.3	16.2	14.2
1991	2.3	7.2	16.4	12.5
1992	0.7	6.8	18.5	12.4
1993	-1.2	4.4	22.8	10.5
1994	2.2	4.0	24.1	8.1
1995	2.7	4.8	22.9	9.8
1996	2.3	3.1	22.1	7.2

	GDP Growth Rate	Inflation Rate	Unemployment Rate	Short-term Interest Rate
Italy				
1980	4.1	20.1	NA	15.9
1981	0.6	18.9	NA	19.7
1982	0.2	17.2	6.8	19.4
1983	1.1	15.1	7.7	17.9
1984	2.7	11.7	8.1	15.4
1985	2.6	8.8	8.4	13.7
1986	2.9	7.9	9.2	11.4
1987	3.1	5.9	9.9	10.7
1988	4.1	6.6	10.0	11.1
1989	2.9	6.2	10.0	12.6
1990	2.1	7.6	9.1	12.4
1991	1.2	7.6	8.8	12.5
1992	0.7	4.5	9.0	14.3
1993	-0.7	4.4	10.3	10.6
1994	2.2	3.4	11.4	9.2
1995	2.9	5.0	11.9	10.9
1996	0.7	5.1	12.0	8.5

FIGURE 31.7

Data for Selected Variables for Selected Nations, 1980–1996

unemployed not to search very hard for a job. Others say the problem has mushroomed as people who are laid off lose more work skills the longer they remain unemployed and over time suffer a lower likelihood of being hired again. Others say because of union power the real wage rate has been kept too high to allow full employment to be achieved. Finally, some say monetary and fiscal policies, especially monetary policies, have not been expansionary enough. They argue, for example, that more expansionary monetary policies could have led to lower unemployment rates without much of an increase in inflation. (Note that short-term interest rates were fairly high in Europe throughout the period, even after the inflation rates fell substantially.)

It is hard to resolve these debates, and it could be that each explanation has some validity. Although customs and institutions differ across countries, the basic tools of macroeconomics can be applied to many countries.

SUMMARY

DEFICIT REDUCTION AND MACROPOLICY: GRAMM-RUDMAN-HOLLINGS

1. In fiscal year 1986, Congress passed and President Reagan signed the *Gramm-Rudman-Hollings Bill,* which set out to reduce the federal deficit by $36 billion per year, with a zero deficit slated for fiscal year 1991. If Congress passed a budget with a deficit larger than the targeted amount, the law called for automatic spending cuts. A Supreme Court ruling later overturned this provision, and the actual figures for each year never came close to the targets. Thanks to the Omnibus Budget Reconciliation Act of 1993, and a robust economy, there was roughly a balanced federal budget in 1998.

2. The deficit tends to rise when GDP falls, and to fall when GDP rises. The *deficit response index (DRI)* is the amount by which the deficit changes with a one-dollar change in GDP.

3. For spending cuts of a certain amount to reduce the deficit by the same amount, the government spending multiplier must be zero. Before GRH was passed, some argued that a government spending multiplier of zero can be achieved through renewed optimism on the part of households or through very aggressive behavior by the Fed to decrease the interest rate. Empirical evidence has shown that neither situation is very plausible, so to lower the deficit by a certain amount, government spending cuts must be larger than that to lower the deficit.

4. Deficit-targeting measures that call for automatic spending cuts to eliminate or reduce the deficit may have the effect of destabilizing the economy because they prevent automatic stabilizers from working.

THE FED'S RESPONSE TO THE STATE OF THE ECONOMY

5. Because the Fed can control the money supply through open market operations, it has the ability to affect aggregate output (income) (Y), the interest rate, and the price level. The Fed is likely to increase the money supply during times of low output and low inflation, and to decrease the money supply during periods of high output and high inflation. The Fed's behavior during stagflation (periods of high unemployment and high inflation) depends on how the Fed weighs output relative to inflation.

6. As the economy expands, the Fed tends to use open market operations to raise interest rates gradually to try to prevent the economy from expanding too quickly. The Fed lowers interest rates gradually to lessen (and eventually stop) a contraction. This is called "leaning against the wind."

LAGS IN THE ECONOMY'S RESPONSE TO MONETARY AND FISCAL POLICY

7. *Stabilization policy* describes both fiscal and monetary policy, the goals of which are to smooth out fluctuations in output and employment and to keep prices as stable as possible. Stabilization goals are not necessarily easy to achieve because of the existence of certain *time lags*, or delays in the response of the economy to macropolicies.

8. A *recognition lag* is the time it takes for policy makers to recognize the existence of a boom or slump. An *implementation lag* is the time it takes to put the desired policy into effect once economists and policy makers recognize that the economy is in a boom or a slump. A *response lag* is the time that it takes for the economy to adjust to the new conditions after a new policy is implemented—in other words, a lag that occurs because of the operation of the economy itself. In general, monetary policy can be implemented more rapidly than fiscal policy, but fiscal policy generally has a shorter response lag than monetary policy.

THE EFFECTS OF THE STOCK MARKET ON THE ECONOMY

9. When stock prices rise, household wealth increases. When stock prices fall, household wealth decreases. Stock prices affect the economy by affecting household wealth, which affects household consumption.

BUSINESS CYCLES IN OTHER COUNTRIES

10. Since 1980, the nations of Europe have shown considerable fluctuation in growth rates, unemployment rates, and inflation rates. Japan suffered a slowdown in 1992–1995.

11. Explanations offered for the persistence of high unemployment in Europe are: (1) generous social welfare benefits, (2) structural unemployment as workers lose more skills the longer they are laid off, (3) union-imposed above-equilibrium wages, and (4) monetary and fiscal policies that have not been expansionary enough. Each explanation may have some validity.

REVIEW TERMS AND CONCEPTS

automatic destabilizer, 725
automatic stabilizer, 724
deficit response index (DRI), 723
Gramm-Rudman-Hollings Bill, 721
implementation lag, 731
negative demand shock, 724
recognition lag, 731
response lag, 732
stabilization policy, 729
time lag, 729

PROBLEM SET

1. What is meant by an automatic destabilizer?

2. The term *fine tuning* was sometimes used during the 1950s and 1960s to describe federal monetary and fiscal policy. At the time the U.S. economy was on a fairly steady growth path with little inflation. The term went out of fashion during the 1970s and 1980s when the economy experienced severe inflation followed by a deep recession twice within a decade. Between 1991 and 1998, the economy once again returned to steady growth with little inflation and the term came back into use. Explain what is meant by fine tuning. During the fall of 1993, growth accelerated. What moves would you anticipate by the Fed in early 1994? During 1995, growth slowed considerably. What would you expect the Fed to do?

3. During 1997, stock markets in Asia collapsed. Hong Kong's was down nearly 30 percent, Thailand's down 62 percent, Malaysia's down 60 percent. Big drops were also experienced in Japan and Korea. What impacts would these events have on the economies of the countries themselves? Explain your answer. In what ways would you have expected these events to influence the U.S. economy? How might the spending of Asians on American goods be affected? What about Americans who have invested in these countries?

4. Explain carefully why the government deficit rises as the economy contracts.

5. You are given the following information about the economy in 1996 (all in billions of dollars):

   (1) Consumption function: $C = 100 + (0.8 \times Y_d)$
   (2) Taxes: $T = -150 + (0.25 \times Y)$
   (3) Investment function: $I = 60$
   (4) Disposable income: $Y_d = Y - T$
   (5) Government spending: $G = 80$
   (6) Equilibrium: $Y = C + I + G$
   Hint: Deficit is $D = G - T = G - [-150 + (0.25 \times Y)]$

   a. Find equilibrium income. Show that the government budget deficit (the difference between government spending and tax revenues) is $5 billion.
   b. Congress passes the Foghorn-Leghorn amendment, which requires that the deficit be zero this year. If the budget adopted by Congress has a deficit that is larger than zero, the deficit target must be met by cutting spending. Suppose spending is cut by $5 billion (to $75 billion). What is the

new value for equilibrium GDP? What is the new deficit? Explain carefully why the deficit is not zero.
   c. What is the deficit response index and how is it defined? Explain why the DRI must equal 0.25 in this example. Using this information, by how much must we cut spending to achieve a deficit of zero?
   d. Suppose the Foghorn-Leghorn amendment was not in effect and planned investment falls to $I = 55$. What is the new value of GDP? What is the new government budget deficit? What happens to GDP if the F-L amendment is in effect and spending is cut to reach the deficit target? (*Hint:* Spending must be cut by $21.666 billion to balance the budget.)

6. During the first six months of 1995, the U.S. economy appeared to slow significantly. Many people point to Federal Reserve decisions made during 1994. What specific actions did the Fed take that might have caused economic slowing during 1995? Why were such actions taken? In retrospect, was the Fed right or wrong in doing what it did? Was the Fed a "fool in the shower"?

7. Some states are required to balance their budgets. Is this measure stabilizing or destabilizing? Suppose all states were committed to a balanced-budget philosophy and the economy moved into a recession. What effects would this philosophy have on the size of the federal deficit?

8. Describe the Fed's tendency to "lean against the wind." Do the Fed's policies tend to stabilize or destabilize the economy?

9. Explain why stabilization policy may be difficult to carry out. How is it possible that stabilization policies can actually be destabilizing?

10. It takes about one year for the multiplier to reach its full value. Explain this phenomenon? Does this have any implications for fiscal policy?

11. The unemployment rate in Japan has been much lower than the unemployment rate in the United States, and the unemployment rate in the United States has been much lower than unemployment rates in European countries. Look up the most recent unemployment figures for Europe, Japan, and the United States. Does this pattern still hold? Why might unemployment rates be consistently lower in one country *vis-à-vis* another?

TAKE IT TO THE NET

We invite you to visit the Case and Fair page on the Prentice Hall Web site:
http://www.prenhall.com/casefair
for this chapter's World Wide Web exercise.

Chapter 32

H OUSEHOLD AND FIRM BEHAVIOR IN THE MACROECONOMY

IN CHAPTERS 24 through 30, we considered the interactions of households, firms, the government, and the rest of the world in the goods, money, and labor markets. The macroeconomy is complicated, and there is a lot to learn about these interactions. To keep our discussions as uncomplicated as possible, we have so far assumed simple behavior of households and firms—the two basic decision-making units in the economy. We assumed household consumption (C) depends only on income and firms' planned investment (I) depends only on the interest rate. We did not consider that households make consumption and labor supply decisions simultaneously and that firms make investment and employment decisions simultaneously.

Now that we understand the basic interactions in the economy, we must relax these assumptions. In the first part of this chapter, we present a more realistic picture of the influences on households' consumption and labor supply decisions. In the second part, we present a more detailed and realistic picture of the influences on firms' investment and employment decisions. We then use what we have learned to analyze more macroeconomic issues.

HOUSEHOLDS: CONSUMPTION AND LABOR SUPPLY DECISIONS

Before discussing household behavior, let's review what we have learned so far.

THE KEYNESIAN THEORY OF CONSUMPTION: A REVIEW

The assumption that household consumption (C) depends on income, which we have used as the basis of our analysis so far, is one that Keynes stressed in his *General Theory of Employment, Interest, and Money*. While Keynes believed many factors, including interest rates and wealth, are likely to influence the level of consumption spending, he focused on current income:

The amount of aggregate consumption depends mainly on the amount of aggregate income. The fundamental psychological law, upon which we are entitled to depend with great confidence both . . . from our knowledge of human nature and from the detailed facts of experience, is that men [and women, too] are disposed, as a rule and on average, to increase their consumption as their incomes increase, but not by as much as the increase in their income.[1]

Keynes is making two points here. First, he suggests that consumption is a positive function of income. The more income you have, the more consuming you are likely to do. Except for a few rich misers who save scraps of soap and bits of string despite million-dollar incomes, this proposition makes sense. Rich people typically consume more than poor people.

Second, Keynes suggests, high-income households consume a smaller proportion of their income than low-income households. (If rich households consume relatively less of their incomes, then by definition they save a higher proportion of their incomes than poor households.) The proportion of income that households spend on consumption is measured by the **average propensity to consume (APC)**.[2] The APC is defined as consumption divided by income:

$$APC \equiv \frac{C}{Y}$$

If a household earns $30,000 per year and spends $25,000 (saving $5,000), it has an *APC* of $25,000/$30,000, or 0.833. Keynes argues that someone who earns, say, $30,000 is likely to spend a larger portion of his or her income than is someone who earns $100,000.

Although the idea that consumption depends on income is a useful starting point, it is far from a complete description of the consumption decision. We need to consider other theories of consumption.

THE LIFE-CYCLE THEORY OF CONSUMPTION

The **life-cycle theory of consumption** is an extension of Keynes's theory. The idea of the life-cycle theory is that people make lifetime consumption plans. Realizing that they are likely to earn more in their prime working years than they earn earlier or later, they make consumption decisions based on their expectations of lifetime income. People tend to consume less than they earn during their main working years—they *save* during those years—and they tend to consume more than they earn during their early and later years—they *dissave*, or use up savings, during those years. Students in medical school generally have very low current incomes, but few live in the poverty that those incomes might predict. Instead, they borrow now and plan to pay back later when their incomes improve.

The lifetime income and consumption pattern of a representative individual is shown in Figure 32.1. As you can see, this person has a low income during the first part of her life, high income in the middle, and low income again in retirement. Her income in retirement is not zero because she has income from sources other than her own labor—social security payments, interest and dividends, and the like.

The consumption path as drawn in Figure 32.1 is constant over the person's life. This is an extreme assumption, but it illustrates the point that the path of consumption over a lifetime is likely to be much more stable than the path of income. We consume an amount

---

average propensity to consume (APC) *The proportion of income households spend on consumption. Determined by dividing consumption (C) by income (Y).*

life-cycle theory of consumption *A theory of household consumption: Households make lifetime consumption decisions based on their expectations of lifetime income.*

---

[1]John Maynard Keynes, *The General Theory of Employment, Interest, and Money* (1936), First Harbinger Ed. (New York: Harcourt Brace Jovanovich, 1964), p. 96.

[2]Whereas the *APC* measures the proportion of total income households spend on consumption, the marginal propensity to consume (*MPC*), which we introduced in chapter 24, measures the proportion of a *change* in income that households spend on consumption. We could interpret Keynes's theory as implying that the marginal propensity to consume falls as income rises. If the *MPC* falls as income rises, it follows that the average propensity to consume (*APC*) falls also.

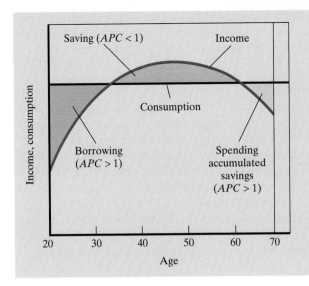

FIGURE 32.1

Life-Cycle Theory of Consumption

In their early working years, people consume more than they earn. This is also true in the retirement years. In between, people save (consume less than they earn) to pay off debts from borrowing and to accumulate savings for retirement.

greater than our incomes during our early working careers. We do this by borrowing against future income, by taking out a car loan, a mortgage to buy a house, or a loan to pay for college. This debt is repaid when our incomes have risen and we can afford to use some of our income to pay off past borrowing without substantially lowering our consumption. The reverse is true for our retirement years. Here, too, our incomes are low. But because we consume less than we earn during our prime working years, we can save up a "nest egg" that allows us to maintain an acceptable standard of living during retirement.

Fluctuations in wealth are also an important component of the life-cycle story. Many young households borrow in anticipation of higher income in the future. Some households actually have *negative wealth*—the value of their assets is less than the debts they owe. A household in its prime working years saves to pay off debts and to build up assets for its later years, when income typically goes down. Households whose assets are greater than the debts they owe have *positive wealth*. With its wage earners retired, a household consumes its accumulated wealth. Generally speaking, wealth starts out negative, turns positive, and then approaches zero near the end of life. Wealth, therefore, is intimately linked to the cumulative saving and dissaving behavior of households.

The key difference between the Keynesian theory of consumption and the life-cycle theory is that the life-cycle theory suggests consumption and saving decisions are likely to be based not just on current income but on expectations of future income as well. The consumption behavior of households immediately following World War II clearly supports the life-cycle story. Just after the war ended, income fell as wage earners moved out of war-related work. However, consumption spending did not fall commensurately, as Keynesian theory would predict. People expected to find jobs in other sectors eventually, and they did not adjust their consumption spending to the temporarily lower incomes they were earning in the meantime.

The phrase **permanent income** is sometimes used to refer to the average level of a person's expected future income stream. If you expect your income will be high in the future (even though it may not be high now), your permanent income is said to be high. With this concept, we can sum up the life-cycle theory by saying that current consumption decisions are likely to be based on permanent income rather than on current income.[3] This means that policy changes like tax-rate changes are likely to have more of an effect on household behavior if they are expected to be permanent rather than temporary.

permanent income *The average level of one's expected future income stream.*

---

[3]The pioneering work on this topic was done by Milton Friedman, *A Theory of the Consumption Function* (Princeton, N.J.: Princeton University Press, 1957). In the mid-1960s, Franco Modigliani did closely related work that included the formulation of the life-cycle theory.

But although this insight enriches our understanding of the consumption behavior of households, the analysis is still missing something. What's missing is the other main decision of households: the labor supply decision.

THE LABOR SUPPLY DECISION

The size of the labor force in an economy is of obvious importance. A growing labor force is one of the ways in which national income/output can be expanded, and the larger the percentage of people who work, the higher is the potential output per capita.

So far, we have said little about the things that determine the size of the labor force. Of course, demographics are a key; the number of children born in 2000 will go a long way toward determining the potential number of 20-year-old workers in 2020. In addition, immigration, both legal and illegal, plays a role.

But so does behavior. Households make decisions about whether to work and how much to work. These decisions are closely tied to consumption decisions, because for most households the bulk of their spending is financed out of wages and salaries.

> Households make consumption and labor supply decisions simultaneously. Consumption cannot be considered separately from labor supply, because it is precisely by selling your labor that you earn income to pay for your consumption.

As we discussed in chapter 4, the alternative to supplying your labor in exchange for a wage or a salary is leisure or other nonmarket activities. Nonmarket activities include raising a child, going to school, keeping a house, or, in a developing economy, working as a subsistence farmer.

But what determines the quantity of labor supplied by a household? Among the list of factors are the wage rate, prices, wealth, and nonlabor income.

▶ **The Wage Rate** A changing wage rate can affect labor supply, but whether the effect is positive or negative is ambiguous. For example, an increase in the wage rate affects a household in two ways. First, work becomes more attractive relative to leisure and other nonmarket activities. Because every hour spent in leisure now requires giving up a higher wage, the opportunity cost of leisure is higher. As a result, you would expect a higher wage would lead to a larger labor supply—a larger workforce. This is called the *substitution effect of a wage rate increase.*

On the other hand, households who work are clearly better off after a wage rate increase. By working the same number of hours as they did before, they will earn more income. If we assume that leisure is a normal good, people with higher income will spend some of it on leisure by working less. This is the *income effect of a wage rate increase.*

When wage rates rise, the substitution effect suggests that people will work more, while the income effect suggests that they will work less. The ultimate effect depends on which separate effect is more powerful. The data suggest that the substitution effect seems to win in most cases. That is, higher wage rates usually lead to a larger labor supply, while lower wage rates usually lead to a lower labor supply.

▶ **Prices** Prices also play a major role in the consumption/labor supply decision. In our discussions of the possible effects of an increase in the wage rate, we have been assuming that the prices of goods and services do not rise at the same time. If the wage rate and all other prices rise simultaneously, the story is different. To make things clear we need to distinguish between the nominal wage rate and the real wage rate.

The **nominal wage rate** is the wage rate in current dollars. When we adjust the nominal wage rate for changes in the price level, we obtain the **real wage rate**. The real wage rate measures the amount that wages can buy in terms of goods and services. Workers do not care about their nominal wage—they care about the purchasing power of this wage—the real wage.

nominal wage rate *The wage rate in current dollars.*

real wage rate *The amount that the nominal wage rate can buy in terms of goods and services.*

Suppose skilled workers in Indianapolis were paid a wage rate of $15 per hour in 1995. Now suppose that their wage rate rose to $18 in 1996, a 20 percent increase. If the prices of goods and services were exactly the same in 1996 as they were in 1995, the real wage rate would have increased by 20 percent. An hour of work in 1996 ($18) buys 20 percent more than an hour of work in 1995 ($15).

But what if the prices of all goods and services also increased by 20 percent between 1995 and 1996? The purchasing power of an hour's wages has not changed. The real wage rate has not increased at all. Eighteen dollars in 1996 buys the same quantity of goods and services that $15 bought in 1995.

To measure the real wage rate, we adjust the nominal wage rate with a price index. As we saw in chapter 23, there are several such indexes that we might use, including the consumer price index and the GDP price index.[4]

We can now apply what we have learned from the life-cycle theory to our wage/price story. Recall the life-cycle theory says people look ahead in making their decisions. Translated to real wage rates, this idea says:

> Households look at expected future real wage rates as well as the current real wage rate in making their current consumption and labor supply decisions.

Consider the medical student who expects his or her real wage rate will be higher in the future. This expectation obviously has an effect on current decisions about things like how much to buy and whether or not to take a part-time job.

➤ **Wealth and Nonlabor Income** Life-cycle theory says wealth fluctuates over the life cycle. Households accumulate wealth during their working years to pay off debts accumulated when they were young and to support themselves in retirement. This role of wealth is clear, but the existence of wealth poses another question. Consider two households that are at the same stage in their life cycle and have pretty much the same expectations about future wage rates, prices, and so forth. They expect to live the same length of time, and both plan to leave the same amount to their children. They differ only in their wealth. Because of a past inheritance, Household 1 has more wealth than Household 2. Which household is likely to have a higher consumption path for the rest of its life? Household 1, because it has more wealth to spread out over the rest of its life.

> Holding everything else constant (including the stage in the life cycle), the more wealth a household has, the more it will consume, both now and in the future.

Now consider a household that has a sudden unexpected increase in wealth, perhaps an inheritance from a distant relative. How will the household's consumption pattern be affected? The household will increase its consumption, both now and in the future, as it spends the inheritance over the course of the rest of its life.

An increase in wealth can also be looked upon as an increase in nonlabor income. **Nonlabor**, or **nonwage**, **income** is income received from sources other than working—inheritances, interest, dividends, and transfer payments such as welfare payments and social security payments. As with wealth:

nonlabor, or nonwage, income
Any income received from sources other than working—inheritances, interest, dividends, transfer payments, and so on.

> An unexpected increase in nonlabor income will have a positive effect on a household's consumption.

---

[4]To calculate the real wage rate, we divide the nominal wage rate by the price index. Suppose the wage rate rose from $5.00 per hour in 1984 to $9.00 per hour in 1994 and the price level rose 50 percent during the same period. Using 1984 as the base year, the price index would be 1.00 in 1984 and 1.50 in 1994. The real wage rate is W/P, where W is the nominal wage rate and P is the price level. The real wage rate is $5.00 in 1984 ($5.00/$1.00) and $6.00 in 1994 ($9.00/$1.50), using 1984 as the base year.

But what about the effect of an increase in wealth or nonlabor income on labor supply? We already know an increase in income results in an increase in the consumption of normal goods, including leisure. Therefore, an unexpected increase in wealth or nonlabor income results in both an increase in consumption and an increase in leisure. With leisure increasing, labor supply must fall, so:

> An unexpected increase in wealth or nonlabor income leads to a *decrease* in labor supply.

This point should be obvious. If I suddenly win a million dollars in the state lottery or make a killing in the stock market, I will probably work less in the future than I otherwise would have.

INTEREST RATE EFFECTS ON CONSUMPTION

Recall from the last few chapters that the interest rate affects a firm's investment decision. A higher interest rate leads to a lower level of planned investment, and vice versa. This was a key link between the money market and the goods market, and it was the channel through which monetary policy had an impact on planned aggregate expenditure.

We can now expand on this link: The interest rate also affects household behavior. Consider the effect of a fall in the interest rate on consumption. A fall in the interest rate lowers the reward to saving. If the interest rate falls from 10 percent to 5 percent, I earn 5 cents instead of 10 cents per year on every dollar saved. This means that the opportunity cost of spending a dollar today (instead of saving it and consuming it plus the interest income a year from now) has fallen. I will substitute toward current consumption and away from future consumption when the interest rate falls: I consume more today and save less. A rise in the interest rate leads me to consume less today and save more. This effect is called the *substitution effect*.

There is also an *income effect* of an interest rate change on consumption. If a household has positive wealth and is earning interest on that wealth, a fall in the interest rate leads to a fall in interest income. This is a decrease in its nonlabor income, which, as we just saw, will have a negative effect on consumption. For households with positive wealth, the income effect works in the opposite direction from the substitution effect. On the other hand, if a household is a debtor and is paying interest on its debt, a fall in the interest rate leads to a fall in interest payments. The household is better off in this case and will consume more. In this case the income and substitution effects work in the same direction. The total household sector in the United States has positive wealth, and so in the aggregate the income and substitution effects work in the opposite direction.

On balance, the data suggest that the substitution effect dominates the income effect, so that the interest rate has a negative net effect on consumption. There is also some evidence, however, that the income effect is getting larger over time. U.S. households own most of the U.S. government debt, and the size of this debt has increased dramatically in the last 20 years. This means the change in government interest payments, and so the change in household interest income, is now larger for a given change in interest rates than before, which leads to a larger income effect than before for a given change in interest rates. This may help explain why the easing of monetary policy in 1991 and 1992 was not very effective in stimulating the economy: The negative income effect from the falling interest rates nearly offset the positive substitution effect.

GOVERNMENT EFFECTS ON CONSUMPTION AND LABOR SUPPLY: TAXES AND TRANSFERS

The government influences household behavior mainly through income tax rates and transfer payments.

MORTGAGE REFINANCING GETS HOT IN 1997

One of the ways lower interest rates may affect consumption is that home owners may take advantage of lower rates to lower the monthly payments on the loans they used to finance their home purchases.

When most people purchase a home, they finance the purchase by borrowing most of the money through a *mortgage*. A mortgage loan is a long-term loan secured with real estate. The borrower secures the loan with the real estate purchased. In the case of a single family home purchase, if the borrower does not pay back the loan, the lender can "foreclose" (take possession of the house).

Houses are expensive, so most people spread their payments over long periods. Most loans are for 30 years. Because the loan is for a long time, small changes in interest rates can make a big difference. For example, the following table gives the approximate monthly payment required to finance a $100,000, 30-year-fixed-rate mortgage at various interest rates:

RATE	MONTHLY PAYMENT
10%	$878
9%	$805
8%	$734
7%	$665
6%	$600
5%	$537

When interest rates fall, as they did during 1997, some people take advantage of the lower rates by "refinancing." That is, they borrow the same amount of money at a lower rate and pay off the older, higher-rate loan. They end up with a lower monthly payment. The result may well be higher consumption spending on other goods and services.

During 1997, mortgage interest rates dropped steadily from over 8 percent to under 7 percent at the end of the year. At the same time, according to the Mortgage Bankers Association of the United States, the percentage of U.S. mortgage applications that were for refinancing of existing loans grew from 19.4 percent in April to 41.6 percent in November.

The following appeared in the *Boston Globe* on November 23, 1997:

When Maryanne Palladino discovered that interest rates were falling, she decided it was time to refinance the mortgage on her four-bedroom home in North Andover.

It would be Palladino's third time refinancing the $213,000 mortgage in the three-and-a-half years since she purchased the Cape Cod-style house.

With competition for customers growing, lenders are using other methods to attract business. They may waive the application fee, throw in a free appraisal, or hawk a slightly lower interest rate, especially for first-time buyers. Many have launched aggressive advertising campaigns, using radio, television, or direct-mail to catch the attention of consumers. And an increasing number of homeowners are refinancing over the Internet, though experts don't recommend that method for most consumers.[a]

---

[a]Jennifer Babson, "Refinancing Frenzy," *Boston Globe*, November 23, 1997, p. G1.

For more on refinancing loans, see the Case and Fair Web page at
http://www.prenhall.com/casefair.

When the government raises income tax rates, after-tax real wages decrease, lowering consumption. When the government lowers income tax rates, after-tax real wages increase, raising consumption.

A change in income tax rates also affects labor supply. If the substitution effect dominates, as we are generally assuming, then an increase in income tax rates, which lowers after-tax wages, will lower labor supply. A decrease in income tax rates will increase labor supply.

Transfer payments are payments such as social security benefits, veterans benefits, and welfare benefits. An increase in transfer payments is an increase in nonlabor income, which we have seen has a positive effect on consumption and a negative effect on labor supply. Increases in transfer payments thus increase consumption and decrease labor supply, while decreases in transfer payments decrease consumption and increase labor supply. Table 32.1 summarizes these results.

TABLE 32.1 THE EFFECTS OF GOVERNMENT ON HOUSEHOLD CONSUMPTION AND LABOR SUPPLY

| | INCOME TAX RATES | | TRANSFER PAYMENTS | |
	Increase	Decrease	Increase	Decrease
Effect on consumption	Negative	Positive	Positive	Negative
Effect on labor supply	Negative*	Positive*	Negative	Positive

*If the substitution effect dominates.

Note: The effects are larger if they are expected to be permanent rather than temporary.

FAST FACTS

unconstrained supply of labor
The amount a household would like to work within a given period at the current wage rate if it could find the work.

constrained supply of labor
The amount a household actually works in a given period at the current wage rate.

A POSSIBLE EMPLOYMENT CONSTRAINT ON HOUSEHOLDS

Our discussion of the labor supply decision has so far proceeded as if households were free to choose how much to work each period. If a member of a household decides to work five additional hours a week at the current wage rate, we have assumed the person *can* work five hours more—that work is available. If someone who has not been working decides to work at the current wage rate, we have assumed that the person *can find a job*.

There are times when these assumptions do not hold. The Great Depression, when unemployment rates reached 25 percent of the labor force, led to the birth of macroeconomics in the 1930s. Since the mid-1970s, the United States has experienced three recessions, with millions of unemployed workers unable to find work.

All households face a budget constraint, regardless of the state of the economy. This budget constraint, which separates those bundles of goods that are available to a household from those that are not, is determined by income, wealth, and prices. When there is unemployment, some households feel an additional constraint on their behavior. Some people may want to work 40 hours per week at the current wage rates but can find only part-time work. Others may not find any work at all.

How does a household respond when it is constrained from working as much as it would like? It consumes less. If your current wage rate is $10 per hour and you normally work 40 hours a week, your normal income from wages is $400 per week. If your average tax rate is 20 percent, your after-tax wage income is $320 per week. You are likely to spend much of this income during the week. If you are prevented from working, this income will not be available to you, and you will have less to spend.

You will spend something, of course. You may receive some form of nonlabor income, and you may have assets, such as savings deposits or stocks and bonds, that can be withdrawn or sold. You may also be able to borrow during your period of unemployment. But even though you will spend something during the week, it is almost certain that you will spend less than you would have if you had your usual income of $320 in after-tax wages.

Households consume less if they are constrained from working.

A household constrained from working as much as it would like at the current wage rate faces a different decision from the decision facing a household that can work as much as it wants. The work decision of the former household is, in effect, forced on it. The household works as much as it can—a certain number of hours per week or perhaps none at all—but this amount is less than the household would choose to work at the current wage rate if it could find more work. The amount that a household would like to work at the current wage rate if it could find the work is called its **unconstrained supply of labor**. The amount that the household actually works in a given period at current wage rates is called its **constrained supply of labor**.

A household's constrained supply of labor is not a variable over which it has any control. The amount of labor the household supplies is imposed on it from the outside by the workings of the economy. However, the household's consumption *is* under its control. We have just seen that the less a household works—that is, the smaller the household's constrained supply of labor—the lower is its consumption. Constraints on the supply of labor are an important determinant of consumption when there is unemployment.

➤ **Keynesian Theory Revisited**   Recall the Keynesian theory that current income determines current consumption. We now know the consumption decision is made jointly with the labor supply decision and the two depend on the real wage rate. It is incorrect to think consumption depends only on income, at least when there is full employment. But if there is unemployment, Keynes is closer to being correct because income is not determined by households. When there is unemployment, the level of income (at least workers' income) depends exclusively on the employment decisions made by firms. There are unemployed workers who are willing to work at the current wage rate, and their income is in effect determined by firms' hiring decisions. This income affects current consumption, which is consistent with Keynes's theory. This is one of the reasons Keynesian theory is considered to pertain to periods of unemployment. It was, of course, precisely during such a period that the theory was developed.

A SUMMARY OF HOUSEHOLD BEHAVIOR

This completes our discussion of household behavior in the macroeconomy. Clearly, household consumption depends on more than current income. Households determine consumption and labor supply simultaneously, and they look ahead in making their decisions.

> The following factors affect household consumption and labor supply decisions:
>
> - current and expected future real wage rates
> - the initial value of wealth
> - current and expected future nonlabor income
> - interest rates
> - current and expected future tax rates and transfer payments

If households are constrained in their labor supply decisions, income is directly determined by firms' hiring decisions. In this case, we can say (in the traditional, Keynesian way) that "income" affects consumption.

THE HOUSEHOLD SECTOR SINCE 1970

To better understand household behavior, let's examine how some of the aggregate household variables have changed over time. We will discuss the period 1970 I to 1997 IV. (Remember, Roman numerals refer to quarters. 1970 I means the first quarter of 1970.) Within this span, there have been three recessionary periods, 1974 I to 1975 IV, 1980 II to 1983 I, and 1990 III to 1991 I. How did the household variables behave during each period?

➤ **Consumption**   Data on the total consumption of the household sector are in the national income accounts. As we saw in Table 32.2, personal consumption expenditures accounted for 67.9 percent of GDP in 1997. The three basic categories of consumption expenditures are services, nondurable goods, and durable goods.

Figure 32.2 presents the data for consumption of services and nondurable goods combined and for durable goods. The variables are in real terms. You can see that expenditures on services and nondurable goods are "smoother" over time than expenditures on durable goods. For example, the decrease in expenditures on services and nondurable goods was much smaller during the three recessionary periods than the decrease in expenditures on durable goods.

Why do expenditures on durables fluctuate more than expenditures on services and nondurables? When times are bad, people can postpone the purchase of durable

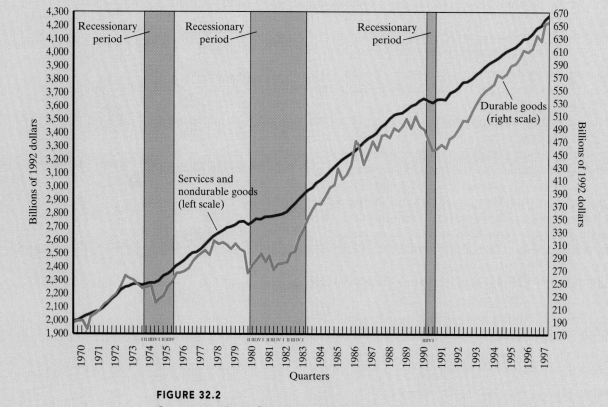

FIGURE 32.2

Consumption Expenditures, 1970 I to 1997 IV

Over time, expenditures for services and nondurable goods are "smoother" than expenditures for durable goods.

goods, and they do. It follows that expenditures on these goods change the most. When times are tough, you do not *have* to have a new car or a new washer-dryer; you can make do with your old Chevy or Maytag until things get better. But when your income falls, it is less easy to postpone the service costs of day care or health care. Nondurables fall into an intermediate category, with some items (like new clothes) easier to postpone than others (like food).

➤ **Housing Investment**   Another important expenditure of the household sector is housing investment (purchases of new housing), plotted in Figure 32.3. This variable fluctuates greatly, for at least two reasons. Housing investment is the most easily postponable of all household expenditures. Also, housing investment is sensitive to the general level of interest rates, and interest rates fluctuate considerably over time. When interest rates are low, housing investment is high, and vice versa.

➤ **Labor Supply**   As we noted in chapters 23 and 30, a person is considered a part of the labor force when he or she either is working or has been actively looking for work in the past few weeks. The ratio of the labor force to the total working-age population—those 16 and over—is the *labor-force participation rate*.

It is informative to divide the labor force into three categories: males 25 to 54, females 25 to 54, and all others 16 and over. Ages 25 to 54 are sometimes called "prime" ages, presuming that a person is in the prime of working life during these ages. The participation rates for these three groups are plotted in Figure 32.4.

As the figure shows, most men of prime age are in the labor force, although the participation rate has fallen slightly since 1970—from .961 in 1970 I to .920 in 1997 IV.

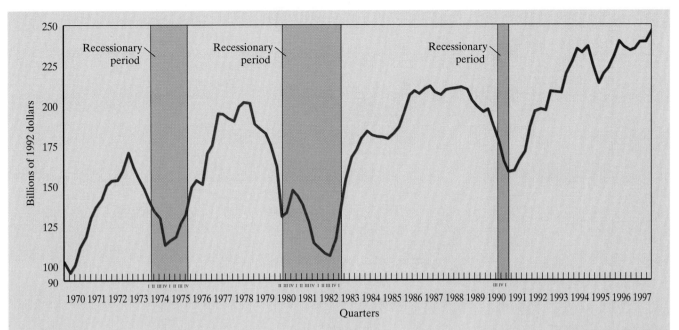

FIGURE 32.3

Housing Investment of the Household Sector, 1970 I to 1997 IV

Housing investment fell sharply during the three recessionary periods since 1970. Like expenditures for durable goods, expenditures for housing investment are postponable.

(A rate of .920 means that 92.0 percent of prime-age men were in the labor force.) The participation rate for prime-age women, on the other hand, has risen dramatically since 1970—from .501 in 1970 I to .766 in 1997 IV. Although economic factors account for some of this increase, a change in social attitudes and preferences probably explains much of the increase. Although the participation rate of prime-age women is still below the rate for prime-age men, this difference will narrow even further in the future if the rate for men keeps falling and the rate for women keeps rising.

Figure 32.4 also shows the participation rate for all individuals 16 and over except prime-age men and women. This rate has some cyclical features—it tends to fall in recessions and to rise or fall less during expansions. These features reveal the operation of the *discouraged-worker effect*, discussed in chapter 23. During recessions, some people get discouraged about ever finding a job. They stop looking and are then not considered a part of the labor force. During expansions, people become encouraged again. Once they begin looking for jobs, they are again considered a part of the labor force. Because prime-age women and men are likely to be fairly attached to the labor force, the discouraged-worker effect for them is quite small.

The participation rate for non-prime-age men and women has fallen since 1970. Part of this decrease reflects an increase in early retirement. When someone retires, he or she is no longer considered a part of the labor force.

FIRMS: INVESTMENT AND EMPLOYMENT DECISIONS

Having taken a closer look at the behavior of households in the macroeconomy, we now look more closely at the behavior of firms—the other major decision-making unit in the economy. In discussing firm behavior earlier, we assumed that planned investment depends only on the interest rate. However, there are several other determinants

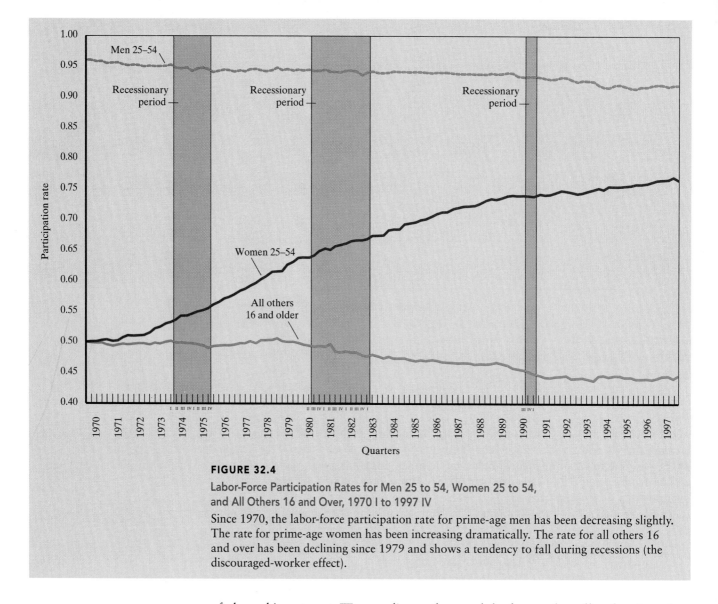

FIGURE 32.4

Labor-Force Participation Rates for Men 25 to 54, Women 25 to 54, and All Others 16 and Over, 1970 I to 1997 IV

Since 1970, the labor-force participation rate for prime-age men has been decreasing slightly. The rate for prime-age women has been increasing dramatically. The rate for all others 16 and over has been declining since 1979 and shows a tendency to fall during recessions (the discouraged-worker effect).

of planned investment. We now discuss them and the factors that affect firms' employment decisions. Once again, microeconomic theory can help us gain some insights into the working of the macroeconomy.

In a market economy, firms determine which goods and services are available to consumers today and which will be available in the future, how many workers are needed for what kinds of jobs, and how much investment will be undertaken. Stated in macroeconomic terms, the decisions of firms, taken together, determine output, labor demand, and investment.

inputs *The goods and services that firms purchase and turn into output.*

In this section, we concentrate on the input choices made by firms. By **inputs**, we mean the goods and services that firms purchase and turn into output. Two important inputs that firms use are capital and labor. (Other inputs are energy, raw materials, and semifinished goods.) Each period, firms must decide how much capital and labor to use in producing output. Let's look first at the decision about how much capital to use.

▶ **Investment Decisions** At any point in time a firm has a certain stock of capital on hand. *Stock of capital* means the factories and buildings (sometimes called "plants") firms own, the equipment they need to do business, and their inventories of partly or wholly finished goods. There are two basic ways a firm can add to its capital stock.

One is to buy more machinery or build new factories or buildings. This kind of addition to the capital stock is **plant-and-equipment investment.**

The other way a firm adds to its capital stock is to increase its inventories. When a firm produces more than it sells in a given period, the firm's stock of inventories increases.[5] This type of addition to the capital stock is **inventory investment.** Recall from chapter 24 that unplanned inventory investment is different from planned inventory investment. When a firm sells less than it expected to, it experiences an unplanned increase in its inventories and is forced to invest more than it planned to. Unplanned increases in inventories result from factors beyond the firm's control. (We take up inventory investment in detail later in this chapter.)

▶ **Employment Decisions**   In addition to investment decisions, firms make *employment* decisions. At the beginning of each period, a firm has a certain number of workers on its payroll. On the basis of its current situation and its upcoming plans, the firm must decide whether to hire additional workers, keep the same number, or reduce its workforce by laying off some employees.

Until this point, our description of firm behavior has been quite simple. In chapter 24 we argued that firms increase production when they experience unplanned decreases in inventory and reduce production when they experience unplanned increases in inventory. We have also alluded to the fact that the demand for labor increases when output grows. In reality, the set of decisions facing firms is much more complex. A decision to produce additional output is likely to involve additional demand for both labor *and* capital.

The demand for labor is quite important in macroeconomics. If the demand for labor increases at a time of less-than-full employment, the unemployment rate will fall. If the demand for labor increases when there is full employment, wage rates will rise. The demand for capital (which is partly determined by the interest rate) is important as well. Recall, planned investment spending is a component of planned aggregate expenditure. When planned investment spending (*I*, the demand for new capital) increases, the result is additional output (income). We discussed the investment multiplier effect in chapter 24.

▶ **Decision Making and Profit Maximization**   To understand the complex behavior of firms in input markets, we must assume that firms make decisions to maximize their profits. One of the most important profit-maximizing decisions that a firm must make is how to produce its output. In most cases, a firm must choose among alternative methods of production, or *technologies*. Different technologies generally require different combinations of capital and labor.

Consider a factory that manufactures shirts. Shirts can be made entirely by hand, with workers cutting the pieces of fabric and sewing them together. But shirts exactly like those can be made on huge complex machines that cut and sew and produce shirts with very little human supervision. Between these two extremes are dozens of alternative technologies. Shirts can be partly hand sewn, with the stitching done on electric sewing machines.

Firms' decisions regarding the amount of capital and labor that they will use in production are closely related. If firms maximize profits, they will choose the technology that minimizes the cost of production. That is, it is logical to assume that firms will choose the technology that is most efficient.

The most efficient technology depends on the relative prices of capital and labor. A shirt factory in the Philippines that decides to increase its production faces a large supply of relatively inexpensive labor. Wage rates in the Philippines are quite low. Capital equipment must be imported and is very expensive. A shirt factory in the Philippines is likely to choose a **labor-intensive technology**—a large amount of labor relative to capital.

plant-and-equipment investment *Purchases by firms of additional machines, factories, or buildings within a given period.*

inventory investment *Occurs when a firm produces more output than it sells within a given period.*

labor-intensive technology *A production technique that uses a large amount of labor relative to capital.*

---

[5]The change in inventories is exactly equal to the difference between production and sales. If a firm sells 20 units more than it produces in the course of a month, its inventories fall by 20 units; if it produces 20 units more than it sells, its inventories rise by 20 units.

capital-intensive technology
A production technique that uses a large amount of capital relative to labor.

When labor-intensive technologies are used, expansion is likely to increase the demand for labor substantially while increasing the demand for capital only modestly.

A shirt factory in Germany that decides to expand production is likely to buy a large amount of capital equipment and to hire relatively few new workers. It will probably choose a **capital-intensive technology**—a large amount of capital relative to labor. German wage rates are quite high, higher in many occupations than in the United States. Capital, however, is plentiful.

> Firms' decisions about labor demand and investment are likely to depend on the relative costs of labor and capital. The relative impact of an expansion of output on employment and on investment demand depends on the wage rate and the cost of capital.

EXPECTATIONS AND ANIMAL SPIRITS

In addition to the cost of capital and the cost of labor, firms' expectations about the future play a big role in investment and employment decisions.

Time is a key factor in investment decisions. Capital has a life that typically extends over many years. A developer who decides to build an office tower is making an investment that will be around (barring earthquakes, floods, or tornadoes) for several decades. In deciding where to build a plant, a manufacturing firm is committing a large amount of resources to purchase capital that will presumably yield services over a long time. Furthermore, the decision to build a plant or to purchase large equipment must often be made years before the actual project is completed. While the acquisition of a small business computer may take only a few days, the planning process for downtown developments in large U.S. cities has been known to take decades.

For these reasons, investment decisions require looking into the future and forming expectations about it. In forming their expectations, firms consider numerous factors. At a minimum, they gather information about the demand for their specific products, about what their competitors are planning, and about the macroeconomy's overall health. A firm is not likely to increase its production capacity if it does not expect to sell more of its product in the future. Hilton will not put up a new hotel if it does not expect to fill the rooms at a profitable rate. Ford will not build a new plant if it expects the economy to enter a long recession.

Forecasting the future is fraught with dangers. Many events cannot be foreseen. Investments are therefore always made with imperfect knowledge. Keynes pointed this out in 1936:

> The outstanding fact is the extreme precariousness of the basis of knowledge on which our estimates of prospective yield have to be made. Our knowledge of the factors which will govern the yield of an investment some years hence is usually very slight and often negligible. If we speak frankly, we have to admit that our basis of knowledge for estimating the yield ten years hence of a railway, a copper mine, a textile factory, the goodwill of a patent medicine, an Atlantic liner, a building in the City of London amounts to little and sometimes nothing.

animal spirits of entrepreneurs
A phrase coined by Keynes to describe investors' feelings.

Keynes concludes from this that much investment activity depends on psychology and on what he calls the **animal spirits of entrepreneurs**:

> Our decisions . . . can only be taken as a result of animal spirits. In estimating the prospects of investment, we must have regard, therefore, to nerves and hysteria and even the digestions and reactions to the weather of those upon whose spontaneous activity it largely depends.[6]

[6]John Maynard Keynes, *The General Theory of Employment, Interest, and Money* (1936), First Harbinger Ed. (New York: Harcourt Brace Jovanovich, 1964), pp. 149, 152.

Because expectations about the future are, as Keynes points out, subject to great uncertainty, they may change often. Thus animal spirits help to make investment a volatile component of GDP.

▶ **The Accelerator Effect** Expectations, at least in part, determine the level of planned investment spending. At any interest rate, the level of investment is likely to be higher if businesses are optimistic. If businesses are pessimistic, the level of planned investment will be lower. But what determines expectations?

One possibility borne out empirically is that expectations are optimistic when aggregate output (Y) is rising and pessimistic when aggregate output is falling.

> At any given level of the interest rate, expectations are likely to be more optimistic and planned investment is likely to be higher when output is growing rapidly than when it is growing slowly or falling.

It is easy to see why. If firms expect future output to grow, they must plan now to add productive capacity. One indicator of future prospects is the current growth rate.

If this is the case in reality, and evidence indicates it is, the ultimate result will be an **accelerator effect**. If aggregate output (income) (Y) is rising, investment will increase even though the level of Y may be low. Higher investment spending leads to an added increase in output, further "accelerating" the growth of aggregate output. If Y is falling, expectations are dampened, and investment spending will be cut even though the level of Y may be high, accelerating the decline.

accelerator effect *The tendency for investment to increase when aggregate output increases and decrease when aggregate output decreases, accelerating the growth or decline of output.*

EXCESS LABOR AND EXCESS CAPITAL EFFECTS

We need to make one more point about firms' investment and employment decisions: Firms may sometimes choose to hold **excess labor** and/or **excess capital**. A firm holds excess labor (or capital) if it could reduce the amount of labor it employs (or capital it holds) and still produce the same amount of output.

Why would a firm want to employ more workers or have more capital on hand than it needs? Both labor and capital are costly—a firm has to pay wages to its workers, and it forgoes interest on funds tied up in machinery or buildings. Why would a firm want to incur costs that do not yield revenue?

To see why, suppose a firm suffers a sudden and large decrease in sales, but it expects the lower sales level to last only a few months, after which it believes sales will pick up again. In this case, the firm is likely to lower production in response to the sales change to avoid too large an increase in its stock of inventories. This decrease in production means the firm could get rid of some workers and some machines, because it now needs less labor and less capital to produce the now-lower level of output.

Alas, things are not this simple. Decreasing its workforce and capital stock quickly can be costly for a firm. Abrupt cuts in the workforce hurt worker morale and may increase personnel administration costs, and abrupt reductions in capital stock may be disadvantageous because of the difficulty of selling used machines. These types of costs are sometimes called **adjustment costs** because they are the costs of adjusting to the new level of output. There are also adjustment costs to increasing output. For example, it is usually costly to recruit and train new workers.

Adjustment costs may be large enough that a firm chooses not to decrease its workforce and capital stock when production falls. The firm may at times choose to have more labor and capital on hand than it needs to produce its current amount of output, simply because it would be more costly to get rid of them than to keep them. In practice, excess labor takes the form of workers not working at their normal level of activity (more coffee breaks and more idle time, for instance). Some of this excess labor may receive new training so that productivity will be higher when production picks up again.

excess labor, excess capital *Labor and capital that are not needed to produce the firm's current level of output.*

adjustment costs *The costs that a firm incurs when it changes its production level—for example, the administration costs of laying off employees or the training costs of hiring new workers.*

The existence of excess labor and capital at any given moment is likely to affect future employment and investment decisions. Suppose a firm already has excess labor and capital due to a fall in its sales and production. When production picks up again, the firm will not need to hire as many new workers or acquire as much new capital as it otherwise would need to.

> The more excess capital a firm already has, the less likely it is to invest in new capital in the future. The more excess labor it has, the less likely it is to hire new workers in the future.

INVENTORY INVESTMENT

We now turn to a brief discussion of the inventory investment decision. This decision is quite different from the plant-and-equipment investment decision.

➤ **The Role of Inventories** Recall the distinction between a firm's sales and its output. If a firm can hold goods in inventory, which is usually the case unless the good is perishable or unless the firm produces services, then within a given period it can sell a quantity of goods that differs from the quantity of goods it produces during that period. When a firm sells more than it produces, its stock of inventories decreases; when it sells less than it produces, its stock of inventories increases.

> Stock of inventories (end of period) = Stock of inventories (beginning of period)
> + Production − Sales

If a firm starts a period with 100 umbrellas in inventory, produces 15 umbrellas during the period, and sells 10 umbrellas in this same interval, it will have 105 umbrellas (100 + 15 − 10) in inventory at the end of the period. A change in the stock of inventories is actually investment because inventories are counted as part of a firm's capital stock. In our example, inventory investment during the period is a positive number, 5 umbrellas (105 − 100). When the number of goods produced is less than the number of goods sold, inventory investment is negative.

➤ **The Optimal Inventory Policy** We can now consider firms' inventory decisions. Firms are concerned with what they are going to sell and produce in the future, as well as what they are selling and producing currently. At each point in time, a firm has some idea of how much it is going to sell in the current period and in future periods. Given these expectations and its knowledge of how much of its good it already has in stock, a firm must decide how much to produce in the current period.

Inventories are costly to a firm because they take up space and they tie up funds that could be earning interest. However, if a firm's stock of inventories gets too low, the firm may have difficulty meeting the demand for its product, especially if demand increases unexpectedly. The firm may lose sales. The point between too low and too high a stock of inventory is called the **desired, or optimal, level of inventories**. This is the level at which the extra cost (in lost sales) from decreasing inventories by a small amount is just equal to the extra gain (in interest revenue and decreased storage costs).

A firm that had no costs other than inventory costs would always aim to produce in a period exactly the volume of goods necessary to make its stock of inventories at the end of the period equal to the desired stock. If the stock of inventory fell lower than desired, the firm would produce more than it expected to sell to bring the stock up. If the stock of inventory grew above the desired level, the firm would produce less than it expected to sell to reduce the stock.

desired, or **optimal, level of inventories** *The level of inventory at which the extra cost (in lost sales) from lowering inventories by a small amount is just equal to the extra gain (in interest revenue and decreased storage costs).*

There are other costs to running a firm besides inventory costs. In particular, large and abrupt changes in production can be very costly because it is often disruptive to change a production process geared to a certain rate of output. If production is to be increased, there may be adjustment costs for hiring more labor and increasing the capital stock. If production is to be decreased, there may be adjustment costs in laying off workers and decreasing the capital stock.

Because holding inventories and changing production levels are both costly, firms face a trade-off between them. Because of adjustment costs, a firm is likely to smooth its production path relative to its sales path. This means a firm is likely to have its production fluctuate less than its sales, with changes in inventories to absorb the difference each period. However, because there are incentives not to stray too far from the optimal level of inventories, fluctuations in production are not eliminated completely. Production is still likely to fluctuate, just not as much as sales fluctuate.

Two other points need to be made here. First, if a firm's stock of inventories is unusually or unexpectedly high, the firm is likely to produce less in the future than it would have, to decrease its high stock of inventories. In other words, although the stock of inventories fluctuates over time because production is smoothed relative to sales, at any point in time inventories may be unexpectedly high or low because sales have been unexpectedly low or high. An unexpectedly high stock will have a negative effect on production in the future, and an unexpectedly low stock will have a positive effect on production in the future.

> An unexpected increase in inventories has a negative effect on future production, and an unexpected decrease in inventories has a positive effect on future production.

Second, firms do not know their future sales exactly. They have expectations of future sales, and these expectations may not turn out to be exactly right.

This has important consequences. If sales turn out to be less than expected, inventories will be higher than expected, and there will be less production in the future. Furthermore, *future* sales expectations are likely to have an important effect on *current* production. If a firm expects its sales to be high in the future, it will adjust its planned production path accordingly. Even though a firm smoothes production relative to sales, over a long time it must produce as much as it sells. If it did not, it would eventually run out of inventories.

> The level of a firm's planned production path depends on the level of its expected future sales path. If a firm's expectations of the level of its future sales path decrease, the firm is likely to decrease the level of its planned production path, including its actual production in the current period. Current production depends on expected future sales.

Because production is likely to depend on expectations of the future, animal spirits may play a role. If firms become more optimistic about the future, they are likely to produce more now. Keynes's view that animal spirits affect investment is also likely to pertain to output.

A SUMMARY OF FIRM BEHAVIOR

The following factors affect firms' investment and employment decisions:

- the wage rate and the cost of capital. (An important component of the cost of capital is the interest rate.)
- firms' expectations of future output.
- the amount of excess labor and excess capital on hand.

The most important points to remember about the relationship between production, sales, and inventory investment are:

- inventory investment (that is, the change in the stock of inventories) equals production minus sales.
- an unexpected increase in the stock of inventories has a negative effect on future production.
- current production depends on expected future sales.

THE FIRM SECTOR SINCE 1970

To close our discussion of firm behavior, we now examine some aggregate investment and employment variables for the period 1970 I to 1997 IV.

➤ **Plant and Equipment Investment**   Plant and equipment investment by the firm sector is plotted in Figure 32.5. Investment fared poorly in the three recessionary periods after 1970. This observation is consistent with the observation that investment depends in part on output. An examination of the plot of real GDP in Figure 21.6 and the plot of investment in Figure 32.5 shows investment generally does poorly when GDP does poorly and investment generally does well when GDP does well.

Figure 32.5 also shows that investment fluctuates greatly. Not surprising! The animal spirits of entrepreneurs are likely to be volatile, and if animal spirits affect investment, it follows that investment too will be volatile.

Despite the volatility of plant and equipment investment, however, it is still true that housing investment fluctuates more than plant and equipment investment (as you can see by comparing Figures 32.3 and 32.5). Plant and equipment investment is not the most volatile component of GDP.

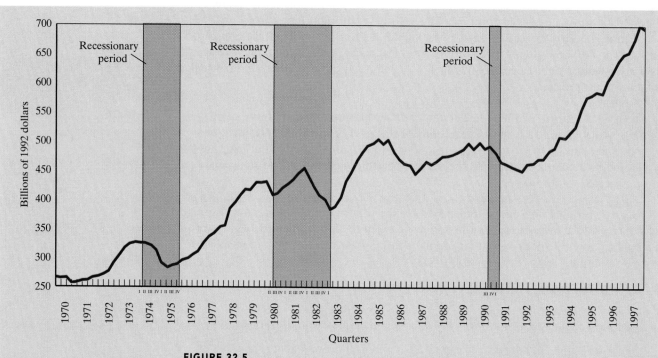

FIGURE 32.5

Plant and Equipment Investment of the Firm Sector, 1970 I to 1997 IV

Overall, plant and equipment investment declined in the three recessionary periods since 1970.

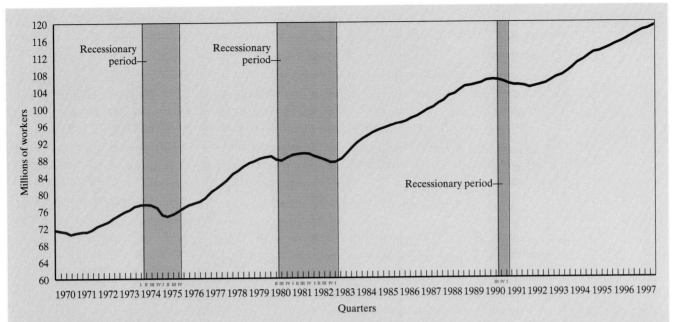

FIGURE 32.6

Employment in the Firm Sector, 1970 I to1997 IV

Growth in employment was generally negative in the three recessions the U.S. economy has experienced since 1970.

> **Employment**   Employment in the firm sector is plotted in Figure 32.6, which shows that employment fell in all three recessionary periods. This is consistent with the theory that employment depends in part on output. Otherwise, employment has grown over time in response to the growing economy. Employment in the firm sector rose from 71.4 million in 1970 I to 118.9 million in 1997 IV.

> **Inventory Investment**   Recall that *inventory investment* is the difference between the level of output and the level of sales. Recall also that some inventory investment is usually unplanned. This occurs when the actual level of sales is different from the expected level of sales.

Inventory investment of the firm sector is plotted in Figure 32.7. Also plotted in this figure is the ratio of the stock of inventories to the level of sales—the *inventory/sales ratio*. The figure shows that inventory investment is very volatile—more volatile than housing investment and plant and equipment investment. Some of this volatility is undoubtedly due to the unplanned component of inventory investment, which is likely to fluctuate greatly from one period to the next.

When the inventory/sales ratio is high, the actual stock of inventories is likely to be larger than the desired stock. In such a case, firms have overestimated demand and produced too much relative to sales, and they are likely to want to produce less in the future to draw down their stock. You can find several examples of this in Figure 32.7—the clearest occurred during the 1974 to 1975 period. At the end of 1974, the stock of inventories was very high relative to sales, which means that firms probably had undesired inventories at the end of 1974. In 1975, firms worked off these undesired inventories by producing less than they sold. Thus inventory investment was very low in 1975. The year 1975 is clearly a year in which output would have been higher had the stock of inventories at the beginning of the year not been so high.

On average the inventory/sales ratio has been declining over time, which suggests that firms are becoming more efficient in their management of inventory stocks. They

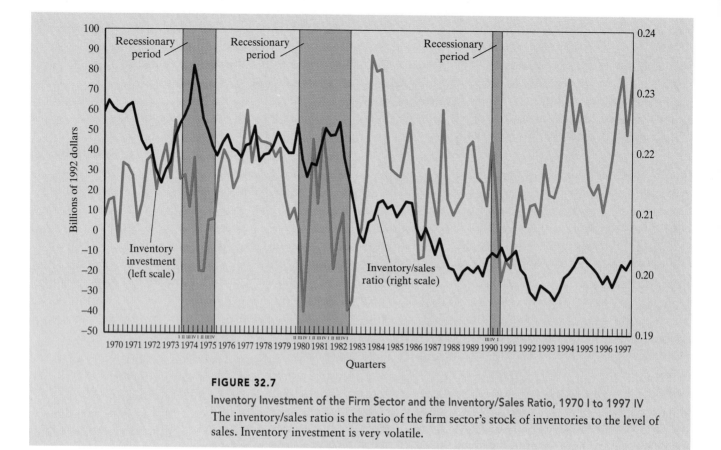

FIGURE 32.7

Inventory Investment of the Firm Sector and the Inventory/Sales Ratio, 1970 I to 1997 IV
The inventory/sales ratio is the ratio of the firm sector's stock of inventories to the level of sales. Inventory investment is very volatile.

are becoming more efficient in the sense of being able (other things equal) to hold smaller and smaller stocks of inventories relative to sales.

PRODUCTIVITY AND THE BUSINESS CYCLE

We can now use what we have just learned about firm behavior to analyze movements in productivity. **Productivity**, sometimes called **labor productivity**, is defined as output per worker hour. If output is Y and the number of hours worked in the economy is H, then productivity is Y/H. Simply stated, productivity measures how much output an average worker produces in one hour.

Productivity fluctuates over the business cycle, tending to rise during expansions and fall during contractions. The fact that firms at times hold excess labor explains why productivity fluctuates in the same direction as output.

Figure 32.8 shows the pattern of employment and output for a hypothetical economy over time. Employment does not fluctuate as much as output over the business cycle. It is precisely this pattern that leads to higher productivity during periods of high output and lower productivity during periods of low output. During expansions in the economy, output rises by a larger percentage than employment, and the ratio of output to workers rises. During downswings, output falls faster than employment and the ratio of output to workers falls.

The existence of excess labor when the economy is in a slump means productivity as measured by the ratio Y/H tends to fall at such times. Does this mean labor is in some sense "less productive" during recessions than before? Not really: It means only that firms choose to employ more labor than they need. For this reason, some workers are in effect idle some of the time, even though they are considered employed. They are not

productivity, or **labor productivity** *Output per worker hour; the amount of output produced by an average worker in one hour.*

PART SEVEN
*Macroeconomic
Analysis and Issues*

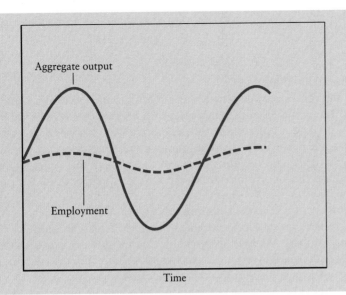

FIGURE 32.8

Employment and Output
over the Business Cycle

In general, employment does
not fluctuate as much as output
over the business cycle. As a
result, measured productivity
(the output-to-labor ratio)
tends to rise during expansionary periods and decline during
contractionary periods.

less productive in the sense of having less potential to produce output; they are merely not working part of the time that they are *counted* as working.

▶ **Productivity in the Long Run**   Theories of long-run economic behavior, which attempt to explain how and why economies grow over time, focus on productivity, usually mea-sured in this case as *output per worker*, or its closely related measure, *GDP per capita*. Productivity defined this way is a key index of an economy's performance over the long run. For example, in comparing how the economies of the United States and Japan have performed over the past 90 years, we would probably begin by noting that although the United States had a substantially higher income per person in 1900, the two countries' in-comes per person are now comparable. As we shall see in chapter 34, the growth of out-put per worker depends on technological progress and on the growth of the capital stock, both of which have been more rapid in Japan than in the United States.

Productivity figures can be misleading when used to diagnose the health of the economy over the short run, because business cycles can distort the meaning of productivity measurements. Output per worker falls in recessions because firms hold excess labor during slumps. Output per worker rises in expansions because firms put the excess labor back to work. Neither of these conditions has anything to do with the economy's long-run potential to produce output.

THE RELATIONSHIP BETWEEN OUTPUT AND UNEMPLOYMENT

We can also use what we have learned about household and firm behavior to analyze the relationship between output and unemployment. When we discussed the connec-tions between the *AS/AD* diagram and the Phillips Curve in chapter 30, we mentioned that output (*Y*) and the unemployment rate (*U*) are inversely related. When output rises, the unemployment rate falls, and when output falls, the unemployment rate rises. At one time, it was believed that the relationship between the two variables was fairly stable. **Okun's Law** (after Arthur Okun, who first studied the relationship) stated that the unemployment rate decreased about one percentage point for every 3 percent increase in real GDP. As with the Phillips Curve, Okun's Law has not turned out to be a "law." The economy is far too complex for there to be such a simple and stable relationship between two macroeconomic variables.

Okun's Law *The theory, put forth by Arthur Okun, that the unemployment rate decreases about one percentage point for every 3 percent increase in real GDP. Later research and data have shown that the relationship between output and unemployment is not as stable as Okun's "law" predicts.*

Although the relationship between output and the unemployment rate is not the simple relationship Okun believed, it is true that a 1 percent increase in output tends to correspond to a less than 1 percentage point decrease in the unemployment rate. In other words, there are a number of "slippages" between changes in output and changes in the unemployment rate.

The first slippage is between the change in output and the change in the number of jobs in the economy. When output increases by 1 percent, the number of jobs does not tend to rise by 1 percent in the short run. There are two reasons for this. First, a firm is likely to meet some of the increase in output by increasing the number of hours worked per job. Instead of having the labor force work 40 hours per week, the firm may pay overtime and have the labor force work 42 hours per week. Second, if a firm is holding excess labor at the time of the output increase, at least part of the increase in output can come from putting the excess labor back to work. For both reasons, the number of jobs is likely to rise by a smaller percentage than the increase in output.

The second slippage is between the change in the number of *jobs* and the change in the *number of people employed*. If I have two jobs, I am counted twice in the job data but only once in the persons-employed data. Because some people have two jobs, there are more jobs than there are people employed. When the number of jobs increases, some of the new jobs are filled by people who already have one job (rather than by people who are unemployed). This means the increase in the number of people employed is less than the increase in the number of jobs. This is a slippage between output and the unemployment rate because the unemployment rate is calculated from data on the number of people employed, not the number of jobs.

The third slippage concerns the response of the labor force to an increase in output. Let E denote the number of people employed, let L denote the number of people in the labor force, and let u denote the unemployment rate. In these terms, the unemployment rate is

$$u = 1 - E/L.$$

The unemployment rate is one minus the employment rate, E/L.

discouraged-worker effect
The decline in the measured unemployment rate that results when people who want to work but cannot find work grow discouraged and stop looking for jobs, dropping out of the ranks of the unemployed and the labor force.

When we discussed how the unemployment rate is measured in chapter 23, we introduced the **discouraged-worker effect**. A discouraged worker is one who would like a job but has stopped looking for one because the prospects seem so bleak. When output increases, job prospects begin to look better, and some people who had stopped looking for work begin looking again. When they do, they are once again counted as part of the labor force. The labor force increases when output increases because discouraged workers are moving back into the labor force. This is another reason the unemployment rate does not fall as much as might be expected when output increases.

These three slippages show that the link from changes in output to changes in the unemployment rate is complicated. All three combine to make the change in the unemployment rate less than the percentage change in output in the short run. They also show that the relationship between changes in output and changes in the unemployment rate is not likely to be stable. The size of the first slippage, for example, depends on how much excess labor is being held at the time of the output increase, and the size of the third slippage depends on what else is affecting the labor force (like changes in real wage rates) at the time of the output increase.

> The relationship between output and unemployment depends on the state of the economy at the time of the output change.

THE SIZE OF THE MULTIPLIER

We can finally bring together the material in this chapter and in previous chapters to consider the size of the multiplier. We mentioned in chapter 24 that much of the analysis we would do after deriving the simple multiplier would have the effect of decreasing the size of the multiplier. We can now summarize why.

- First, there are *automatic stabilizers*. We saw in the appendix to chapter 25 that if taxes are not a fixed amount but rather depend on income (which is surely the case in practice), the size of the multiplier is decreased. When the economy expands and income increases, the amount of taxes collected increases. This acts to offset some of the expansion (thus a smaller multiplier). When the economy contracts and income decreases, the amount of taxes collected decreases. This helps to lessen the contraction. Some transfer payments also respond to the state of the economy and act as automatic stabilizers, lowering the value of the multiplier. Unemployment benefits are the best example of transfer payments that increase during contractions and decrease during expansions.

- Second, there is the *interest rate*. We saw in chapter 28 that if government spending increases and the money supply remains unchanged, the interest rate increases, which decreases planned investment and aggregate output (income). This *crowding out* of planned investment decreases the value of the multiplier. And, as we saw in chapter 32, increases in the interest rate also have a negative effect on consumption. Consumption is also crowded out in the same way that planned investment is, and this lowers the value of the multiplier even further.

- Third, there is the response of the *price level*. We saw in chapter 29 that some of the effect of an expansionary policy is to increase the price level. The multiplier is smaller because of this price response. The multiplier is particularly small when the economy is on the steep part of the *AS* curve, where most of the effect of an expansionary policy is to increase prices.

- Fourth, there are *excess capital* and *excess labor*. If firms are holding excess labor and capital, then part of any output increase can come from putting the excess labor and capital back to work rather than from increasing employment and investment. This lowers the value of the multiplier because (1) investment increases less than it would have if there were no excess capital, and (2) consumption increases less that it would have if employment (and thus household income) had increased more.

- Fifth, there are *inventories*. Part of any initial increase in sales can come from drawing down inventories rather than increasing output. To the extent that firms draw down their inventories in the short run, the value of the multiplier is lower because output does not respond as quickly to demand changes.

- Sixth, there are the *life-cycle story* and *expectations*. People look ahead, and they respond less to temporary changes than to permanent changes. The multiplier effects for policy changes perceived to be temporary are smaller than those for policy changes perceived to be permanent.

- Finally, the fact that the United States imports a good deal of what it consumes makes the multiplier smaller than it would be if the U.S. economy were closed. Consider the effects of an increase in government purchases. Initially, most government spending is spending on domestically produced goods and services. But the multiplier effect results from consumption spending by those who earn more income as a result of the additional government spending. Consumers in the United States buy automobiles from Germany and Japan, electronics from Korea, and textiles from the Philippines. When spending "leaks" into imports, the size of the multiplier is reduced. (We discuss this in chapter 36.)

> **The Size of the Multiplier in Practice**   In practice, the multiplier probably has a value of around 1.4. Its size also depends on how long ago the spending increase began. For example, in the first quarter of an increase in government spending, the multiplier is only about 1.1. If government spending rises by $1 billion, then GDP increases by only about $1.1 billion during the first quarter. In the second quarter, the multiplier rises to about 1.3. The multiplier then rises to its peak of about 1.4 in the third or fourth quarter.

One of the main points to remember here is that if the government is contemplating a monetary or fiscal policy change, the response of the economy to the change is not likely to be large and quick. It takes time for the full effects to be felt, and in the final analysis the effects are much smaller than the simple multiplier we discussed in chapter 24 would lead one to believe.

A good way to review much of the material since chapter 24 is to make sure that you clearly understand how the value of the multiplier is affected by each of the additions to the simple model in chapter 24. We have come a long way since then, and this review may help you to put all the pieces together.

SUMMARY

HOUSEHOLDS: CONSUMPTION AND LABOR SUPPLY DECISIONS

1. The Keynesian theory of consumption holds that household consumption (C) is positively related to current income: The more income you have, the more you are likely to consume. Keynes also believed high-income households consume a smaller proportion of their income than low-income households. The proportion of income households spend on consumption is measured by the *average propensity to consume (APC)*, which is equal to consumption divided by income (C/Y).

2. The *life-cycle theory of consumption* says households make lifetime consumption decisions based on their expectations of lifetime income. Generally, households consume an amount less than their incomes during their prime working years and an amount greater than their incomes during their early working years and after they have retired.

3. Households make consumption and labor supply decisions simultaneously. Consumption cannot be considered separately from labor supply, because it is precisely by selling your labor that you earn the income that makes consumption possible.

4. There is a trade-off between the goods and services that wage income will buy and leisure or other nonmarket activities. The wage rate is the key variable that determines how a household responds to this trade-off.

5. Changes in the wage rate have both an income effect and a substitution effect. The evidence suggests the substitution effect seems to dominate for most people, which means the aggregate labor supply responds positively to an increase in the wage rate.

6. Consumption increases when the wage rate increases.

7. The *nominal wage rate* is the wage rate in current dollars. The *real wage rate* is the amount the nominal wage can buy in terms of goods and services. Households look at expected future real wage rates as well as the current real wage rate in making their consumption and labor supply decisions.

8. Holding all else constant (including the stage in the life cycle), the more wealth a household has, the more it will consume, both now and in the future.

9. An unexpected increase in *nonlabor income* (any income received from sources other than working, such as inheritances, interest, and dividends) will have a positive effect on a household's consumption and will lead to a decrease in labor supply.

10. The interest rate also affects consumption, although the direction of the total effect depends on the relative sizes of the income and substitution effects. There is some evidence the income effect is larger now than it used to be, making monetary policy less effective than it used to be.

11. The government influences household behavior mainly through income tax rates and transfer payments. If the substitution effect dominates, an increase in tax rates lowers after-tax income, decreases consumption, and decreases the labor supply; a decrease in tax rates raises after-tax income, increases consumption, and increases labor supply. Increases in transfer payments increase consumption and decrease labor supply; decreases in transfer payments decrease consumption and increase labor supply.

12. During times of unemployment, households' labor supply may be constrained. Households may wish to work a certain number of hours at current wage rates but may not be allowed to do so by firms. In this case, the level of income (at least workers' income) depends exclusively on the employment decisions made by firms. Households consume less if constrained from working.

FIRMS: INVESTMENT AND EMPLOYMENT DECISIONS

13. Firms purchase *inputs* and turn them into outputs. Each period, firms must decide how much capital and labor (two major inputs) to use in producing output. Firms can invest in plants and equipment or in inventory.

14. Because output can be produced using many different technologies, firms must make capital and labor decisions simultaneously. A *labor-intensive technique* uses a large amount of labor relative to capital. A *capital-intensive technique* uses a large amount of capital relative to labor. Which technology to use depends on the wage rate and the cost of capital.

15. Expectations affect investment and employment decisions. Keynes used *animal spirits of entrepreneurs* to refer to investors' feelings.

16. At any level of the interest rate, expectations are likely to be more optimistic and planned investment is likely to be higher when output is growing rapidly than when it is growing slowly or falling. The result is an *accelerator effect* that can cause the economy to expand more rapidly during an expansion and contract more quickly during a recession.

17. *Excess labor and capital* are labor and capital not needed to produce a firm's current level of output. Holding excess labor and capital may be more efficient than laying off workers or selling used equipment. The more excess capital a firm has, the less likely it is to invest in new capital in the future. The more excess labor it has, the less likely it is to hire new workers in the future.

18. Holding inventories is costly to a firm because they take up space and they tie up funds that could be earning interest. Not holding inventories can cause a firm to lose sales if demand increases. The *desired*, or *optimal*, *level of inventories* is the level at which the extra cost (in lost sales) from lowering inventories by a small amount is equal to the extra gain (in interest revenue and decreased storage costs).

19. An unexpected increase in inventories has a negative effect on future production, and an unexpected decrease in inventories has a positive effect on future production.

20. The level of a firm's planned production path depends on the level of its expected future sales path. If a firm's expectations of its future sales path decrease, the firm is likely to decrease the level of its planned production path, including its actual production in the current period.

PRODUCTIVITY AND THE BUSINESS CYCLE

21. *Productivity*, or *labor productivity*, is output per worker hour—the amount of output produced by an average worker in one hour. Productivity fluctuates over the business cycle, tending to rise during expansions and fall during contractions. That workers are less productive during contractions does not mean they have less potential to produce output; it means excess labor exists and workers are not working at their capacity.

THE RELATIONSHIP BETWEEN OUTPUT AND UNEMPLOYMENT

22. There is a negative relationship between output and unemployment: When output (Y) rises, the unemployment rate (U) falls, and when output falls, the unemployment rate rises. *Okun's Law* stated that the unemployment rate decreases about one percentage point for every 3 percent increase in GDP. Okun's Law is not a "law"—the economy is too complex for there to be a stable relationship between two macroeconomic variables. In general, the relationship between output and unemployment depends on the state of the economy at the time of the output change.

THE SIZE OF THE MULTIPLIER

23. There are several reasons why the actual value of the multiplier is smaller than the size that would be predicted by a simple model of a closed economy: (1) Automatic stabilizers help to offset contractions or limit expansions. (2) When government spending increases, the increased interest rate crowds out planned investment and consumption spending. (3) Expansionary policies increase the price level. (4) Firms sometimes hold excess capital and excess labor. (5) Firms may meet increased demand by drawing down inventories rather than increasing output. (6) Households and firms change their behavior less when they expect changes to be temporary rather than permanent. (7) A significant portion of spending is spent on foreign-produced goods.

24. In practice, the size of the multiplier at its peak is about 1.4.

REVIEW TERMS AND CONCEPTS

accelerator effect, 755

adjustment costs, 755

animal spirits of entrepreneurs, 754

average propensity to consume (*APC*), 742

capital-intensive technology, 754

constrained supply of labor, 748

desired, or optimal, level of inventories, 756

discouraged-worker effect, 762

excess capital, 755

excess labor, 755

income effect of a wage rate increase, 744

inputs, 752

inventory investment, 753

labor-intensive technology, 753

life-cycle theory of consumption, 742

nominal wage rate, 744

nonlabor, or nonwage, income, 745

Okun's law, 761

permanent income, 743

plant-and-equipment investment, 753

productivity, or labor productivity, 760

real wage rate, 744

substitution effect of a wage rate increase, 744

unconstrained supply of labor, 748

$$APC \equiv \frac{C}{Y}$$

PROBLEM SET

1. In October 1997, the unemployment rate hit a 24-year low of 4.7 percent. Partly as a result of very tight labor markets, wages rose 4.2 percent and were expected to rise further. What effect would rising wages likely have on the labor supply? Explain your answer using income and substitution effects. If rising wages and welfare reform succeeded in increasing the labor force, how would this affect the unemployment rate relative to what would have happened without the labor force increase? What about the rate of growth in real output/income (Y)?

2. The year 2000 is a presidential election year. What happens to the economy may have a large impact on the outcome. Candidates and the Congress will be taking positions that depend on the state of the economy. Get a copy of the latest employment release from the Bureau of Labor Statistics (their web site is: http://stats.bls.gov). What has happened to employment and wages during the last year? The last month? Is the labor force growing or shrinking? Can you say why? From the newspapers, what has been happening to real GDP? How fast is it growing or shrinking? What position has the Federal Reserve been taking most recently? Are interest rates up or down relative to six months ago? Explain the logic of what the Fed is doing using the concepts explored in this chapter.

3. At the beginning of 1998, the Federal Reserve Bank was poised to raise interest rates in an effort to slow the U.S. economy's rate of growth. Its goal: to prevent inflation.
   a. What direct effects do higher interest rates have on household and firm behavior?
   b. One of the consequences of higher interest rates was that the value of existing bonds (both corporate bonds and government bonds) fell by more than $1.7 trillion. Explain why higher interest rates would reduce the value of existing fixed rate bonds held by the public.
   c. Some economists argue that the wealth effect of higher interest rates on consumption is as important as the direct effect of higher interest rates on consumption. Explain what economists mean by "wealth effects on consumption" and illustrate with *AS/AD* curves.

4. In 1993, President Clinton proposed and Congress enacted an increase in taxes. One of the increases was in the income tax rate for higher-income wage earners. Republicans claimed that reducing the rewards for working (the net after-tax wage rate), would lead to less work effort and a lower labor supply. Supporters of the tax increase replied that this criticism was baseless because it "ignored the income effect of the tax increase (net wage reduction)." Explain what these supporters meant.

5. Graph the following two consumption functions:
   (1) $C = 300 + 0.5Y$
   (2) $C = 0.5Y$.
   a. For each function, calculate and graph the average propensity to consume (*APC*) when income is $100, $400, and $800.
   b. For each function, what happens to the *APC* as income rises?
   c. For each function, what is the relationship between the *APC* and the marginal propensity to consume?
   d. Under consumption function (1), a family with income of $50,000 consumes a smaller proportion of its income

than a family with income of $20,000; yet if we take a dollar of income away from the rich family and give it to the poor family, total consumption by the two families does not change. Explain how this could be.

6. During the late 1990s the price of houses increased steadily around the country.
   What impact would you expect increases and decreases in home value to have on the consumption behavior of home owners? Explain. In what ways might events in the housing market have influenced the rest of the economy through their effects on consumption spending? Be specific.

7. Adam Smith is 45 years old. He has assets (wealth) of $20,000 and has no debts or liabilities. He knows he will work for 20 more years and will live 5 years after that when he will earn nothing. His salary each year for the rest of his working career is $14,000. (There are no taxes.) He wants to distribute his consumption over the rest of his life in such a way that he consumes the same amount each year. He cannot consume in total more than his current wealth plus the sum of his income for the next 20 years. Assume the rate of interest is zero and Smith decides not to leave any inheritance to his children.
   a. How much will Adam consume this year? Next year? How did you arrive at your answer?
   b. Plot on a graph Adam's income, consumption, and wealth from the time he is 45 until he is 70 years old. What is the relationship between the annual increase in his wealth and his annual saving (income minus consumption)? In what year does Adam's wealth start to decline? Why? How much wealth does he have when he dies?
   c. Suppose Adam receives a tax rebate of $100 per year, so his income is $14,100 per year for the rest of his working career. By how much does his consumption increase this year? Next year?
   d. Now suppose Adam receives a one-year-only tax refund of $100—his income this year is $14,100, but in all succeeding years his income is $14,000. What happens to his consumption this year? In succeeding years?

8. Explain why a household's consumption and labor supply decisions are interdependent. What impact does this interdependence have on the way in which consumption and income are related?

9. Why do expectations play such an important role in investment demand? How, if at all, does this explain why investment is so volatile?

10. How can a firm maintain a smooth production schedule even when sales are fluctuating? What are the benefits of a smooth production schedule? What are the costs?

TAKE IT TO THE NET

We invite you to visit the Case and Fair page on the Prentice Hall Web site:
http://www.prenhall.com/casefair
for this chapter's World Wide Web exercise.

WHAT WOULD YOU DO WITH A BUDGET SURPLUS?

In February 1998 President Clinton submitted the first balanced budget to Congress in 30 years. The proposed $1.7 trillion in federal spending for fiscal year 1999 would result in a surplus of nearly $10 billion—if the Administration's economic projections come true. Many analysts believe that a budget surplus during the next fiscal year is possible, provided Congress and the Administration can avoid the temptation to create new ways to spend the increase in revenue that has resulted from a booming economy. However, this raises an interesting question. If we can't spend it, what should we do with it? After all, it has been so long since the United States has had a federal budget surplus.

Federal budget deficits are not a new phenomenon. The government incurred its first deficit in 1792, and has produced 70 annual deficits since 1900. Historically, deficits were the result of either wars or recessions. Wars required increased amounts of military spending, whereas recessions reduced Federal income tax revenues from households and businesses.

The government ran budget deficits during the War of 1812, the recession of 1837, the Civil War, the depression of the 1890s, and World War I. Each time, after the war was over or the economy recovered, the government used the budget surpluses that followed to pay down the debt it had accumulated.

During the Great Depression, and the increase in spending associated with President Roosevelt's New Deal, the government ran up sizable deficits once again. Then, World War II forced the government to spend more than ever before on defense—and the deficit grew to unprecedented levels. Since the end of World War II, the government has balanced its books only eight times—primarily because spending has grown faster than revenues. The total amount of accumulated deficits at the end of 1997 totaled $5.4 trillion.

During the 1990s, the Bush and Clinton Administrations, together with the Congress, finally began to enact serious deficit reduction measures, and their efforts have begun to pay off. Although the government held the line on spending, an expanding economy began to yield dividends in the form of increased revenues. According to the most recent estimates from the Office of Management and Budget, there was a cyclical surplus of $21 billion in 1997 that, when added to the actual deficit of $22 billion, amounted to an estimated structural deficit of $43 billion.

The rapid return to fiscal prosperity has surprised many, including analysts at the U.S. Treasury who watched their coffers fill with unexpected revenues. According to the 1998 *Economic Report of the President*, the deficit projections for fiscal 1997 were off by more than $100 billion. Roughly three-quarters of the forecast error was due to higher than expected revenues. A complete understanding of this revenue surprise will have to wait until the 1997 tax returns are completely processed, but a large share of it undoubtedly can be attributed to better-than-expected economic growth in 1997.

The prospect of an estimated $1 trillion in total surpluses over the next 10 years has some members of Congress scrambling for creative ways to spend it. It's clear that these days, using the surplus as a payment on past debt does not seem to have the same appeal it did at the turn of the century. We've lived with deficits for so long that the $5.4 trillion accumulated thus far doesn't seem to be an impediment to growth, and $10 billion is so small relative to the debt outstanding that it feels like a waste of resources to many people. Besides, there's some evidence that some predictable level of government securities in circulation are a good thing because they provide risk-free assets with which to balance a portfolio of financial assets.

Many Republicans are proposing a reduction in income taxes—giving back to the tax payers the surplus the government collected. Democrats are proposing increases in social spending as a way to take advantage of the windfall. Economists warn, however, that a reduction in tax rates hurts the government's ability to fund existing programs during times of economic recession, when incomes fall.

A *rainy-day* fund, where money is set aside for use during hard economic times, is popular with many citizens and indeed exists in many state budgets. State revenues have also enjoyed surprisingly strong growth during the past few years and the debates going on in state legislatures today mirror those at the federal level. Some states have decided to increase their rainy-day funds, whereas others are rolling back taxes.

One thing is clear, you can't just leave the money in the bank. Treasury deposits are held by the

Federal Reserve, but generally earn no interest.[1]

Increasingly, the proposal that gets the most favorable reviews is to use the forthcoming surpluses to fix the social security system. The number of baby boomers approaching retirement age threatens to bankrupt the social security system early in the next century unless something is done to make sure the system can afford to finance them. According to the Administration, simply transferring the projected surpluses to the social security trust fund would delay the fund's depletion by 10 years.

There are no easy answers, and the projected surpluses could vanish just as quickly as they came if an unexpected shock should drive the economy into recession. However,

the debate is certain to be full of interesting proposals . . . which is one of the things that makes economics so interesting.

Questions for Analytical Thinking

1. Write a memo to the President describing your proposals for the projected budget surplus.

2. Suppose you had $5,000 worth of credit card debt and you suddenly inherited $500. Would you spend it, save it, or retire some of your debt? Suppose, instead, you received a promotion in your first job and a $500 per month raise. Now what would you do?

3. Although the government is projecting a budget surplus for fiscal year 1999, the structural budget is projected to be in deficit until fiscal year 2001. Explain what these estimates imply about

the government's projections of the gap between actual and potential GDP.

4. Many members of Congress support a balanced budget amendment to the Constitution. What impact would a balanced budget amendment have on fiscal automatic stabilizers and business cycles in this country.

Sources: Jacob Schlesinger and Christopher Georges, "Uses of Surpluses to Save Social Security Gains Fed Chairman's Support," *The Wall Street Journal*, January 30, 1998, p. A2; David Wessel and Christopher Georges, "Federal Overhaul," *The Wall Street Journal*, February 3, 1998, p. A1; Jackie Calmes, "Clinton's Plan to Put 'Social Security First' Took Months of Debate and Changes Budget Politics," *The Wall Street Journal*, January 29, 1998, p. A20; *The Budget of the United States Government, FY 1999, Analytical Perspectives*, Office of Management and Budget, Washington, D.C., 1998; *A Citizen's Guide to the Federal Budget, FY 1999*, Office of Management and Budget, Washington, D.C., 1998; *Economic Report of the President*, President's Council of Economic Advisers, 1998.

---

[1] *In some instances, Treasury deposits are lent out via so-called "Repurchase Agreements" with brokers of government securities, and the yield on these loans are deposited in the Treasury's accounts.*

DEBATES IN MACROECONOMICS: MONETARISM, NEW CLASSICAL THEORY, AND SUPPLY-SIDE ECONOMICS

THROUGHOUT THIS BOOK, we have noted there are many disagreements and questions in macroeconomics. For example, economists disagree on whether the aggregate supply curve is vertical, either in the short run or the long run. Some even doubt that the aggregate supply curve is a useful macroeconomic concept! There are different views on whether cyclical employment exists and, if it does, what causes it. Economists disagree about whether monetary and fiscal policies are effective at stabilizing the economy, and they support different views on the primary determinants of consumption and investment spending.

We discussed some of these disagreements in previous chapters, but only briefly. In this chapter, we discuss in more detail a number of alternative views of how the macroeconomy works.

KEYNESIAN ECONOMICS

John Maynard Keynes's *General Theory of Employment, Interest and Money*, published in 1936, remains one of the most important works in economics. While a great deal of the material in the previous 10 chapters is drawn from modern research that postdates Keynes, much of it is built around a framework constructed by Keynes.

But what exactly is *Keynesian economics*? In one sense, it is the foundation of all of macroeconomics. Keynes was the first to stress aggregate demand and the links between the money market and the goods market. And it was Keynes who stressed the possible problem of sticky wages. Virtually all the debates in this chapter can be understood in terms of the aggregate output/aggregate expenditure framework suggested by Keynes.

In recent years, the term *Keynesian* has been used narrowly. Keynes believed in an activist federal government. He believed the government had a role to play in fighting inflation and unemployment, and he believed monetary and fiscal policy should be used to manage the macroeconomy. This is why *Keynesian* is sometimes used to refer to economists who advocate active government intervention in the macroeconomy.

During the 1970s and 1980s, it became clear that managing the macroeconomy was more easily accomplished on paper than in practice. The inflation problems of the 1970s and early 1980s and the seriousness of the recessions of 1974 to 1975 and 1980 to 1982 led many economists to challenge the idea of active government intervention in the economy. Some were simple attacks on the bureaucracy's ability to act in a timely manner. Others were theoretical assaults that claimed to show that monetary and fiscal policy could have *no effect whatsoever* on the economy, even if it were efficiently managed.

Two major schools decidedly *against* government intervention have developed: monetarism and new classical economics.

MONETARISM

The debate between "monetarist" and "Keynesian" economics is complicated because they mean different things to different people. If we consider the main monetarist message to be that "money matters," then almost all economists would agree. In the *AS/AD* story, for example, an increase in the money supply shifts the *AD* curve to the right, which leads to an increase in both aggregate output (Y) and the price level (P). Monetary policy thus has an effect on output and the price level. **Monetarism**, however, is usually considered to go beyond the notion that money matters.

THE VELOCITY OF MONEY

velocity of money *The number
of times a dollar bill changes
hands, on average, during a year;
the ratio of nominal GDP to the
stock of money.*

To understand monetarist reasoning, you must understand the **velocity of money**. Think of velocity as the number of times a dollar bill changes hands, on average, during a year.

Suppose on January 1 you buy a new ballpoint pen with a $5 bill. The owner of the stationery store does not spend your $5 right away. She may hold it until, say, May 1, when she uses it to buy a dozen doughnuts. The doughnut store owner does not spend the $5 he receives until July 1, when he uses it (along with other cash) to buy 100 gallons of oil. The oil distributor uses the bill to buy an engagement ring for his fiancée on September 1, but the $5 bill is not used again in the remaining three months of the year. Because this $5 bill has changed hands four times during the year, its velocity of circulation is four. A velocity of four means the $5 bill stays with each owner for an average of three months, or one quarter of a year.

In practice, we use GDP, rather than the total value of all transactions in the economy, to measure velocity,[1] because GDP data are more available. The income velocity of money (V) is the ratio of nominal GDP to the stock of money (M):

$$V \equiv \frac{GDP}{M}$$

If $6 trillion worth of final goods and services are produced in a year and if the money stock is $1 trillion, then the velocity of money is $6 trillion ÷ $1 trillion, or 6.0.

---

[1]Recall GDP does not include transactions in intermediate goods (e.g., flour sold to a baker to be made into bread) or in existing assets (the sale of a used car). If these transactions are made using money, however, they do influence the number of times money changes hands during the course of a year. GDP is an imperfect measure of transactions to use in calculating the velocity of money.

We can expand this definition slightly by noting that nominal income (GDP) is equal to real output (income) (Y) times the overall price level (P):

$$GDP \equiv P \times Y$$

Through substitution,

$$V \equiv \frac{P \times Y}{M}$$

or

$$M \times V \equiv P \times Y$$

At this point, it is worth pausing to ask if our definition has provided us with any insights into the workings of the economy. The answer is no. Because we defined V as the ratio of GDP to the money supply, the statement $M \times V \equiv P \times Y$ is an identity—it is true by definition. It contains no more useful information than the statement "a bachelor is an unmarried man." The definition does not, for example, say anything about what will happen to $P \times Y$ when M changes. The final value of $P \times Y$ depends on what happens to V. If V falls when M increases, the product $M \times V$ could stay the same, in which case the change in M would have had no effect on nominal income. To give monetarism some economic content, we turn to a simple version of monetarism known as the **quantity theory of money.**

quantity theory of money
The theory based on the identity $M \times V \equiv P \times Y$ *and the assumption that the velocity of money* (V) *is constant (or virtually constant).*

THE QUANTITY THEORY OF MONEY

The key assumption of the quantity theory of money is that the velocity of money is constant (or virtually constant) over time. If we let $\overline{V}$ denote the constant value of V, the equation for the quantity theory can be written:

$$M \times \overline{V} = P \times Y_{GDP}$$

Note the double equal sign has replaced the triple equal sign because the equation is no longer an identity. The equation is true if velocity is constant (and equal to $\overline{V}$), but not otherwise. If the equation is true, it provides an easy way to explain nominal GDP. Given M, which can be considered a policy variable set by the Federal Reserve, nominal GDP is just $M \times \overline{V}$. In this case, the effects of monetary policy are clear. Changes in M cause equal percentage changes in nominal GDP. For example, if the money supply doubles, nominal GDP also doubles. If the money supply remains unchanged, nominal GDP remains unchanged.

The key is whether the velocity of money is really constant. Early economists believed the velocity of money was determined largely by institutional considerations, such as how often people are paid and how the banking system clears transactions between banks. Because these factors change gradually, early economists believed velocity was essentially constant.

If there is equilibrium in the money market, then the quantity of money supplied is equal to the quantity of money demanded. That could mean M in the quantity-theory equation equals both the quantity of money supplied and the quantity of money demanded. If the quantity-theory equation is looked on as a demand-for-money equation, it says that the demand for money depends on nominal income (GDP, or $P \times Y$), but *not* on the interest rate.[2] If the interest rate changes and nominal income does not, the equation says that the quantity of money demanded will not change. This is contrary to the theory of the demand for money in chapter 27, which had the demand for money depending on both income and the interest rate.

---

[2]In terms of the appendix to chapter 28, this means the *LM* curve is vertical.

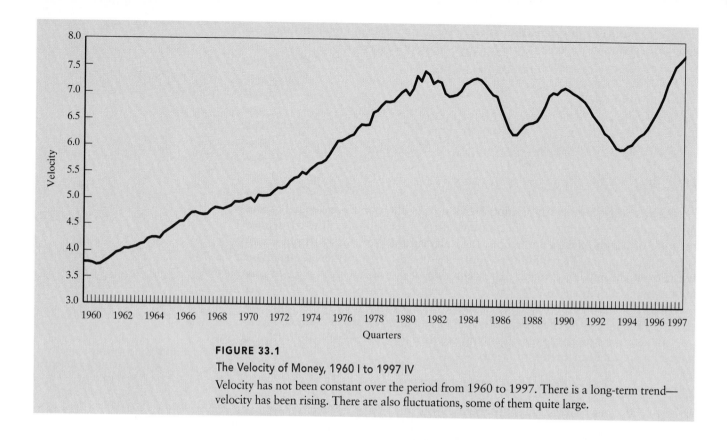

FIGURE 33.1

The Velocity of Money, 1960 I to 1997 IV

Velocity has not been constant over the period from 1960 to 1997. There is a long-term trend—velocity has been rising. There are also fluctuations, some of them quite large.

▶ **Testing the Quantity Theory of Money** One way to test the validity of the quantity theory of money is to look at the demand for money using recent data on the U.S. economy. The key is: Does money demand depend on the interest rate? Most empirical work says yes. When demand-for-money equations are estimated (or "fit to the data"), the interest rate usually turns out to be a factor. The demand for money does not appear to depend only on nominal income.

Another way of testing the quantity theory is to plot velocity over time and see how it behaves. Figure 33.1 plots the velocity of money for the 1960 I to 1997 IV period. The data show that velocity is far from constant. There is a long-term trend—on average, velocity has been rising during these years—but fluctuations around this trend have also occurred, and some have been quite large. Velocity rose from 6.8 in 1980 III to 7.2 in 1981 III; fell to 6.7 in 1983 I; rose to 7.0 in 1984 III; and fell to 6.1 in 1986 IV. Changes of a few tenths of a point may seem small, but they are actually large. For example, the money supply in 1986 IV was $709 billion. If velocity changes by 0.3 with a money supply of this amount, and if the money supply is unchanged, we have a change in nominal GDP ($P \times Y$) of $213 billion (0.3 × $709 billion), which is about 5 percent of GDP.

The debate over monetarist theories is more subtle than our discussion so far indicates. First, there are many definitions of the money supply. $M1$ is the money supply variable used for the graph in Figure 33.1, but there may be some other measure of the money supply that would lead to a smoother plot. For example, many people shifted their funds from checking account deposits to money market accounts when the latter became available in the late 1970s. Because GDP did not change as a result of this shift while $M1$ decreased, velocity—the ratio of GDP to $M1$—must have gone up. But suppose instead we measured the supply of money by $M2$ (which includes both checking accounts and money market accounts). In this case, the decrease in checking deposits would be exactly offset by the rise in money market account deposits, and $M2$ would not change. With no change in GDP and no change in $M2$, the velocity of money would not change. Whether velocity is constant or not may depend partly on how we measure the money supply.

Second, there may be a time lag between a change in the money supply and its effects on nominal GDP. Suppose we experience a 10 percent increase in the money supply today, but it takes one year for nominal GDP to increase by 10 percent. If we measured the ratio of today's money supply to today's GDP, it would seem that velocity had fallen by 10 percent. But if we measured today's money supply against GDP one year from now, when the increase in the supply of money had its full effect on income, then velocity would have been constant.

The debate over the usefulness of monetarist theory is primarily empirical. It is a debate that can be resolved by looking at facts about the real world and seeing whether they are in accord with the predictions of theory. Is there a measure of the money supply and a choice of the time lag between a change in the money supply and its effects on nominal GDP such that V is in effect constant? If so, then the monetarist theory is a useful approach to understanding how the macroeconomy works. If not, then some other theory is likely to be more appropriate. (We discuss the testing of alternative theories at the end of this chapter.)

INFLATION AS A PURELY MONETARY PHENOMENON

So far we have talked only about nominal output ($P \times Y$). We have said nothing about how a monetarist would break down a change in nominal output (due to a money-supply change) into a change in P and a change in Y. Here again it is not possible to make a general statement about what all monetarists believe. Some may believe that all of the change occurs in P, and others may believe that at least sometimes some of the change occurs in Y. If all of the change occurs in P, then there is a proportional relationship between changes in the money supply and changes in the price level. For example, a 10 percent change in M will lead to a 10 percent change in P if Y remains unchanged. In this case, inflation (an increase in P) is always a purely monetary phenomenon. The price level will not change if the money supply does not change. We will call this view, that changes in M affect only P and not Y, the "strict monetarist" view.

There is considerable disagreement as to whether the strict monetarist view is a good approximation of reality. For example, the strict view is not compatible with a nonvertical AS curve in the AS/AD model in chapter 29. In the case of a nonvertical AS curve, an increase in M, which shifts the AD curve to the right, increases both P and Y. (You may want to review why.)

Almost all economists agree, however, that *sustained* inflation—inflation that continues over many periods—is a purely monetary phenomenon. We pointed out in chapter 14

⏱ **F A S T**
FACTS

Monetarists say figures like these support their contention that inflation is a monetary phenomenon:

| Country | *Annual average percentage change 1985 to 1995 in:* | |
	Money Supply	Prices (GDP Deflator)
Brazil	995.5%	875.3%
Peru	388.5	398.5
Sierra Leone	51.4	61.6
Jamaica	32.8	28.3
Israel	22.1	17.1
United States	3.9	3.2

Source: World Bank, *World Development Report,* 1997, Table 2.

in the context of the *AS/AD* framework that inflation cannot continue indefinitely unless the Fed "accommodates" it by increasing the money supply. Let's review this.

Consider a continuously increasing level of government spending (*G*) without any corresponding increase in taxes. The increases in *G* keep shifting the *AD* curve to the right, which leads to an increasing price level (*P*). (You may find it useful to draw a graph here.) With a fixed money supply, the increases in *P* lead to a higher and higher interest rate, but there is a limit to how far this can go. Because taxes are unchanged, the government must finance the increases in *G* by issuing bonds, and there is a limit to how many bonds the public is willing to hold regardless of how high the interest rate goes. At the point at which the public cannot be induced to hold any more bonds, the government will be unable to borrow any more to finance its expenditures. Only if the Fed is willing to increase the money supply (buy some of the government bonds) can the government spending (with its inflationary consequences) continue.

> Inflation cannot continue indefinitely without increases in the money supply.

THE KEYNESIAN/MONETARIST DEBATE

The leading spokesman for monetarism over the last few decades has been Professor Milton Friedman, formerly of the University of Chicago and currently at the Hoover Institute in California. Most monetarists, including Friedman, blame most of the instability in the economy on the federal government, arguing that the inflation the United States encountered over the years could have been avoided if only the Fed had not expanded the money supply so rapidly.

Most monetarists do not advocate an activist monetary stabilization policy—expanding the money supply during bad times and slowing the growth of the money supply during good times. Monetarists tend to be skeptical of the government's ability to "manage" the macroeconomy. The most common argument against such management is the one expressed in chapter 31: Time lags make it likely that conscious attempts to stimulate and contract the economy make the economy more, not less, unstable.

Friedman has for many years advocated a policy of steady and slow money growth—specifically, that the money supply should grow at a rate equal to the average growth of real output (income) (*Y*). That is, the Fed should pursue a constant policy that accommodates real growth but not inflation.

Keynesianism and monetarism are at odds with each other. Many Keynesians advocate the application of coordinated monetary and fiscal policy tools to reduce instability in the economy—to fight inflation and unemployment. But not all Keynesians advocate an activist federal government. Some reject the strict monetarist position that changes in money only affect the price level in favor of the view that both monetary and fiscal policies make a difference and *at the same time* believe the best possible policy for government to pursue is basically noninterventionist.

Most Keynesians agree after the experience of the 1970s that monetary and fiscal tools are not finely calibrated. The notion that monetary and fiscal expansions and contractions can "fine-tune" the economy is gone forever. Still, many feel the experiences of the 1970s also show that stabilization policies can help prevent even bigger economic disasters. Had the government not cut taxes and expanded the money supply in 1975 and in 1982, they argue, the recessions of those years might have been significantly worse. The same people would argue that had the government not resisted the inflations of 1974 to 1975 and 1979 to 1981 with tight monetary policies, they would probably have become much worse.

Thirty years ago, the debate between Keynesians and monetarists was the central controversy in macroeconomics. That controversy, while still alive today, is no longer at the forefront. For the past two decades, the focus of current thinking in macroeconomics has been on the new classical macroeconomics.

NEW CLASSICAL MACROECONOMICS

The challenge to Keynesian and related theories has come from a school sometimes referred to as the **new classical macroeconomics**.[3] Like *monetarism* and *Keynesianism*, this term is vague. No two new classical macroeconomists think exactly alike, and no single model completely represents this school. The following discussion, however, conveys the flavor of the new classical views.

THE DEVELOPMENT OF NEW CLASSICAL MACROECONOMICS

New classical macroeconomics has developed from two different, though related, sources. These sources are the theoretical and the empirical critiques of existing, or traditional, macroeconomics.

On the theoretical level, there has been growing dissatisfaction with the way traditional models treat expectations. Keynes himself recognized that expectations (in the form of "animal spirits") play a big part in economic behavior. The problem is, traditional models have assumed that expectations are formed in naive ways. A common assumption, for example, is that people form their expectations of future inflation by assuming present inflation will continue. If they turn out to be wrong, they adjust their expectations by some fraction of the difference between their original forecast and the actual inflation rate. Suppose I expect 10 percent inflation next year. When next year comes, the inflation rate turns out to be only 5 percent, so I have made an error of 5 percent. I might then predict an inflation rate for the following year of 7.5 percent, halfway between my earlier expectation (10 percent) and actual inflation last year (5 percent).

The problem with this treatment of expectations is that it is not consistent with the assumptions of microeconomics. It implies people systematically overlook information that would allow them to make better forecasts, even though there are costs to being wrong. If, as microeconomic theory assumes, people are out to maximize their satisfaction and firms are out to maximize their profits, they should form their expectations in a smarter way. Instead of naively assuming the future will be like the past, they should actively seek to forecast the future. Any other behavior is not in keeping with the microeconomic view of the forward-looking, rational people who compose households and firms.

On the empirical level, there was stagflation in the U.S. economy during the 1970s. Remember, stagflation is simultaneous high unemployment and rising prices. The Phillips Curve theory of the 1960s predicted that demand pressure pushes up prices, so that when demand is weak—in times of high unemployment, for example—prices should be stable (or perhaps even falling). The new classical theories were an attempt to explain the apparent breakdown in the 1970s of the simple inflation-unemployment trade-off predicted by the Phillips Curve. Just as the Great Depression of the 1930s motivated the development of Keynesian economics, so the stagflation of the 1970s helped motivate the formulation of new classical economics.

RATIONAL EXPECTATIONS

In previous chapters, we stressed households' and firms' expectations about the future. A firm's decision to build a new plant depends on its expectations of future sales. The amount of saving a household undertakes today depends on its expectations about future interest rates, wages, and prices.

How are expectations formed? Do people assume things will continue as they are at present? (Like predicting rain tomorrow because it is raining today.) What information

---

[3]The term *new classical* is used because many of the assumptions and conclusions of this group of economists resemble those of the classical economists—that is, those who wrote before Keynes.

do people use to make their guesses about the future? Questions like these have become central to current macroeconomic thinking and research. One theory, the **rational-expectations hypothesis**, offers a powerful way of thinking about expectations.

Suppose we want to forecast inflation. What does it mean to say that my expectations of inflation are "rational"? The rational-expectations hypothesis assumes people know the "true model" that generates inflation—they know how inflation is determined in the economy—and they use this model to forecast future inflation rates. If there were no random, unpredictable events in the economy, and if people knew the true model generating inflation, their forecasts of future inflation rates would be perfect. Because it is true, the model would not permit mistakes, and thus the people using it would not make mistakes.

However, many events that affect the inflation rate are not predictable—they are random. By "true" model, then, we mean a model that is *on average* correct in forecasting inflation. Sometimes the random events have a positive effect on inflation, which means the model underestimates the inflation rate, and sometimes they have a negative effect, which means the model overestimates the inflation rate. On average, the model is correct. Therefore, rational expectations are correct on average, even though their predictions are not exactly right all the time.

To see this, suppose you have to forecast how many times a fair coin will come up heads out of 100 tosses. The true model in this case is that the coin has a 50–50 chance of coming up heads on any one toss. Because the outcome of the 100 tosses is random, you cannot be sure of guessing correctly. If you know the true model—that the coin is fair—your rational expectation of the outcome of 100 tosses is 50 heads. You are not likely to be exactly right—the actual number of heads is likely to be slightly higher or slightly lower than 50—but *on average* you will be correct.

Sometimes people are said to have rational expectations if they use "all available information" in forming their expectations. This definition is vague, because it is not always clear what "all available information" means. The definition is precise, if by "all available information" we mean that people know and use the true model. We cannot have more or better information than the true model.

If information can be obtained at no cost, then someone is not behaving rationally if he or she fails to use all available information. Because there are almost always costs to making a wrong forecast, it is not rational to overlook information that could help improve the accuracy of a forecast as long as the costs of acquiring that information do not outweigh the benefits of improving its accuracy.

EVEN THOUGH UNCERTAINTY EXISTS, IF YOU KNOW THE "MODEL" GENERATING THE UNCERTAINTY, IT IS POSSIBLE TO HAVE EXPECTATIONS ABOUT THE FUTURE THAT ARE "ON AVERAGE" CORRECT. YOU DON'T KNOW WHETHER A RANDOM COIN TOSS WILL COME UP HEADS OR TAILS. BUT YOU DO KNOW THAT IF YOU TOSS A FAIR COIN 1,000 TIMES, IT WILL COME UP HEADS ABOUT 500 TIMES.

► **Rational Expectations and Market Clearing**   If firms have rational expectations and if they set prices and wages on this basis, then, on average, prices and wages will be set at levels that ensure equilibrium in the goods and labor markets. When a firm has rational expectations, it knows the demand curve for its output and the supply curve of labor that it faces, except when random shocks disrupt those curves. Therefore, on average the firm will set the market-clearing prices and wages. The firm knows the true model, and it will not set wages different from those it expects will attract the number of workers it wants. If all firms behave this way, then wages will be set in such a way that the total amount of labor supplied will, on average, be equal to the total amount of labor that firms demand. In other words, on average there will be no unemployment.

In chapter 30, we argued that there might be disequilibrium in the labor market (either in the form of unemployment or in excess demand for workers) because firms may make mistakes in their wage-setting behavior due to expectation errors. If, on average, firms do not make errors, then, on average, there is equilibrium. When expectations are rational, disequilibrium exists only temporarily as a result of random, unpredictable shocks—obviously an important conclusion. If true, it means disequilibrium in any market is only temporary, because firms, on average, set market-clearing wages and prices.

The assumption that expectations are rational radically changes the way we can view the economy. We go from a world in which unemployment can exist for substantial periods and the multiplier can operate to a world in which (on average) all markets clear and there is full employment. In this world there is no need for government stabilization policies. Unemployment is not a problem that governments need to worry about; if it exists at all, it is because of unpredictable shocks that, on average, amount to zero. There is no more reason for the government to try to change the outcome in the labor market than there is for it to change the outcome in the banana market. On average, prices and wages are set at market-clearing levels.

THE LUCAS SUPPLY FUNCTION

The **Lucas supply function**, after Robert E. Lucas of the University of Chicago, is an important part of a number of new classical macroeconomic theories. It yields, as we shall see, a surprising policy conclusion. The function is deceptively simple. It says real output (Y) depends on (is a function of) the difference between the actual price level (P) and the expected price level (P^e):

$$Y = f(P - P^e)$$

Lucas supply function *The supply function embodies the idea that output (Y) depends on the difference between the actual price level and the expected price level.*

The actual price level minus the expected price level ($P - P^e$) is the **price surprise**. Before considering the policy implications of this function, we should look at the theory behind it.

price surprise *Actual price level minus expected price level.*

Lucas begins by assuming people and firms are specialists in production but generalists in consumption. If someone you know is a manual laborer, the chances are she sells only one thing—labor. If she is a lawyer, she sells only legal services. In contrast, people buy a large bundle of goods—ranging from gasoline to ice cream and pretzels—on a regular basis. The same is true for firms. Most companies tend to concentrate on producing a small range of products, but they typically buy a larger range of inputs—raw materials, labor, energy, capital. According to Lucas, this divergence between buying and selling creates an asymmetry. People know much more about the prices of the things they sell than they do about the prices of the things they buy.[4]

At the beginning of each period, a firm has some expectation of the average price level for that period. If the actual price level turns out to be different, there is a price surprise. Say the average price level is higher than expected. Because the firm learns about the actual price level slowly, some time goes by before it realizes all prices have gone up. The firm *does* learn *quickly* that the price of its *output* has gone up. The firm perceives—incorrectly, it turns out—that its price has risen relative to other prices, and this leads it to produce more output.

A similar argument holds for workers. When there is a positive price surprise, workers at first believe their "price"—their wage rate—has increased relative to other prices. Workers believe their real wage rate has risen. We know from theory that an increase in the real wage is likely to encourage workers to work more hours.[5] The real wage has not actually risen, but it takes workers a while to figure this out. In the meantime, they supply more hours of work than they would have. This means the economy will produce more output when prices are unexpectedly higher than when prices are at their expected level.

This is the rationale for the Lucas supply function. Unexpected increases in the price level can fool workers and firms into thinking relative prices have changed, causing them to alter the amount of labor or goods they choose to supply.

---

[4]It is not entirely obvious why this should be true, and some critics of the new classical school have argued that this is unrealistic. Some have also criticized the Lucas supply function as too simple, arguing that other things besides price surprises affect aggregate output.

[5]This is true if we assume that the substitution effect dominates the income effect (see chapter 32).

➤ Policy Implications of the Lucas Supply Function

The Lucas supply function in combination with the assumption that expectations are rational implies that anticipated policy changes have no effect on real output. Consider a change in monetary policy. In general, the change will have some effect on the average price level. If the policy change is announced to the public, then people know what the effect on the price level will be, because they have rational expectations (and know the way changes in monetary policy affect the price level). This means the change in monetary policy affects both the actual price level and the expected price level in the same way. The new price level minus the new expected price level is zero—no price surprise. In such a case, there will be no change in real output, because the Lucas supply function states that real output can change from its fixed level only if there is a price surprise.

The general conclusion is that *any* announced policy change—in fiscal policy or any other policy—has no effect on real output, because the policy change affects both actual and expected price levels in the same way. If people have rational expectations, known policy changes can produce no price surprises—and no increases in real output. The only way any change in government policy can affect real output is if it is kept in the dark so it is not generally known. Government policy can affect real output only if it surprises people; otherwise, it cannot. Rational-expectations theory combined with the Lucas supply function proposes a very small role for government policy in the economy.

EVALUATING RATIONAL-EXPECTATIONS THEORY

What are we to make of all this? It should be clear that the key question regarding the new classical macroeconomics is how realistic is the assumption of rational expectations. If it approximates the way expectations are actually formed, then it calls into question any theory that relies at least in part on expectation errors for the existence of disequilibrium. The arguments in favor of the rational-expectations assumption sound persuasive from the perspective of microeconomic theory. If expectations are not rational, there are likely to be unexploited profit opportunities—most economists believe such opportunities are rare and short-lived.

The argument *against* rational expectations is that it requires households and firms to know too much. This argument says it is unrealistic to think these basic decision-making units know as much as they need to know to form rational expectations. People must know the true model (or at least a good approximation of the true model) to form rational expectations, and this is a lot to expect. Even if firms and households are capable of learning the true model, it may be costly to take the time and gather the relevant information to learn it. The gain from learning the true model (or a good approximation of it) may not be worth the cost. In this sense, there may not be unexploited profit opportunities around. Gathering information and learning economic models may be too costly to bother with, given the expected gain from improving forecasts.

Although the assumption that expectations are rational seems consistent with the satisfaction-maximizing and profit-maximizing postulates of microeconomics, the rational-expectations assumption is more extreme and demanding because it requires more information on the part of households and firms. Consider a firm engaged in maximizing profits. In some way or other, it forms expectations of the relevant future variables, and given these expectations, it figures out the best thing to do from the point of view of maximizing profits. Given a set of expectations, the problem of maximizing profits may not be too hard. What may be hard is forming accurate expectations in the first place. This requires firms to know much more about the overall economy than they are likely to, so the assumption that their expectations are rational is not necessarily realistic. Firms, like the rest of us—so the argument goes—grope around in a world that is difficult to understand, trying to do their best but not always understanding enough to avoid mistakes.

In the final analysis, the issue is empirical. Does the assumption of rational expectations stand up well against empirical tests? This is difficult to answer. Much work is currently being done to answer it. There are no conclusive results yet, but it is one of the questions that makes macroeconomics an exciting area of research.

REAL BUSINESS CYCLE THEORY

Recent work in new classical macroeconomics has been concerned with whether the existence of business cycles can be explained under the assumptions of complete price and wage flexibility (market clearing) and rational expectations. This work is called **real business cycle theory**. As we discussed in chapter 29, if prices and wages are completely flexible, then the *AS* curve is vertical, even in the short run. If the *AS* curve is vertical, then events or phenomena that shift the *AD* curve (such as changes in the money supply, changes in government spending, and shocks to consumer and investor behavior) have no effect on real output. Real output does fluctuate over time, so the puzzle is how these fluctuations can be explained if they are not due to policy changes or other shocks that shift the *AD* curve. Solving this puzzle is one of the main missions of real business cycle theory.

It is clear that if shifts of the *AD* curve cannot account for real output fluctuations (because the *AS* curve is vertical), then shifts of the *AS* curve must be responsible. However, the task is to come up with convincing stories as to what causes these shifts and why they persist over a number of periods. The problem is particularly difficult when it comes to the labor market. If prices and wages are completely flexible, then there is never any unemployment aside from frictional unemployment. For example, because the measured U.S. unemployment rate was 9.7 percent in 1982 and 4.9 percent in 1997, the puzzle is to explain why so many more people choose not to work in 1982 than in 1997.

Early real business cycle theorists emphasized shocks to the production technology. Say there is a negative shock in a given year that causes the marginal product of labor to decline. This leads to a fall in the real wage, which leads to a decrease in labor supply. People have been led to work less because the negative technology shock has led to a lower return from working. The opposite happens when there is a positive shock: The marginal product of labor rises, the real wage rises, and people choose to work more. This early work was not as successful as some had hoped because it required what seemed to be unrealistically large shocks to explain the observed movements in labor supply over time.

Since this initial work, different types of shocks have been introduced, and work is actively continuing in this area. To date, fluctuations of some variables, but not all, have been explained fairly well. Some argue that this work is doomed to failure because it is based on the unrealistic assumption of complete price and wage flexibility, while others hold more hope. Real business cycle theory is another example of the current state of flux in macroeconomics.

SUPPLY-SIDE ECONOMICS

From our discussion of equilibrium in the goods market, beginning with the simple multiplier in chapter 24 and continuing through chapter 29, we have focused primarily on *demand*. Supply increases and decreases in response to changes in aggregate expenditure (which is closely linked to aggregate demand). Fiscal policy works by influencing aggregate expenditure through tax policy and government spending. Monetary policy works by influencing investment and consumption spending through

real business cycle theory
An attempt to explain business cycle fluctuations under the assumptions of complete price and wage flexibility and rational expectations. It emphasizes shocks to technology and other shocks.

increases and decreases in the interest rate. The theories we have been discussing are "demand oriented."

The 1970s were difficult times for the U.S. economy. The United States found itself in 1974 to 1975 with stagflation—high unemployment and inflation. The late 1970s saw inflation return to the high levels of 1974 to 1975. It seemed as if policy makers were incapable of controlling the business cycle.

As a result of these seeming failures, orthodox economics came under fire. One assault was from a group of economists who expounded **supply-side economics**. The argument of the supply-siders was simple. Basically, they said, all the attention to demand in orthodox macro theory distracted our attention from the real problem with the U.S. economy. The real problem, said supply-siders, was that high rates of taxation and heavy regulation had reduced the incentive to work, to save, and to invest. What was needed was not a demand stimulus but better incentives to stimulate *supply*.

If we cut taxes so people take home more of their paychecks, the argument continued, they will work harder and save more. If businesses get to keep more of their profits and can get away from government regulations, they will invest more. This added labor supply and investment, or capital supply, will lead to an expansion of the supply of goods and services, which will reduce inflation and unemployment at the same time. The ultimate solution to the economy's woes, the supply-siders concluded, was on the *supply side* of the economy.

At their most extreme, supply-siders argued that the incentive effects of supply-side policies were likely to be so great that a major cut in tax rates would actually *increase* tax revenues. Even though tax *rates* would be lower, more people would be working and earning income and firms would earn more profits, so that the increases in the *tax bases* (profits, sales, and income) would outweigh the decreases in rates, resulting in increased government revenues.

> **The Laffer Curve** Figure 33.2 presents a key diagram of supply-side economics. The tax rate is measured on the vertical axis, and tax revenue is measured on the horizontal axis. The assumption behind this curve is that there is some tax rate beyond which the supply response is large enough to lead to a decrease in tax revenue for further increases in the tax rate. There is obviously some tax rate between zero and 100 percent at which tax revenue is at a maximum. At a tax rate of zero, work effort is high, but there is no tax revenue. At a tax rate of 100, the labor supply is presumably zero, because no one is allowed to keep any of his or her income. Somewhere in between zero and 100 is the maximum-revenue rate.

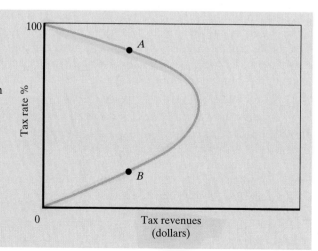

FIGURE 33.2

The Laffer Curve

The Laffer Curve shows the amount of revenue the government collects is a function of the tax rate. It shows that when tax rates are very high, an increase in the tax rate could cause tax revenues to fall. Similarly, under the same circumstances, a cut in the tax rate could generate enough additional economic activity to cause revenues to rise.

The big debate in the 1980s was whether tax rates in the United States put the country on the upper or lower part of the curve in Figure 33.2. The supply-side school claimed the United States was around *A* and taxes should be cut. Others argued that the United States was nearer *B* and tax cuts would lead to lower tax revenue.

The diagram in Figure 33.2 is the **Laffer Curve**, after Arthur Laffer, who, legend has it, first drew it on the back of a napkin at a cocktail party. The Laffer Curve had some influence on the passage of the Economic Recovery Tax Act of 1981, the tax package put forward by the Reagan administration that brought with it substantial cuts in both personal and business taxes. The individual income tax was to be cut 25 percent over three years. Corporate taxes were cut sharply in a way designed to stimulate capital investment. The new law allowed firms to depreciate their capital at a rapid rate for tax purposes, and the bigger deductions led to taxes that were significantly lower than before.

Laffer Curve *With the tax rate measured on the vertical axis and tax revenue measured on the horizontal axis, the Laffer Curve shows there is some tax rate beyond which the supply response is large enough to lead to a decrease in tax revenue for further increases in the tax rate.*

EVALUATING SUPPLY-SIDE ECONOMICS

Among the criticisms of supply-side economics is that it is unlikely a tax cut would substantially increase the supply of labor.

Supporters of supply-side economics claim that Reagan's tax policies were successful in stimulating the economy. They point to the fact that almost immediately after the tax cuts of 1981 were put into place, the economy expanded and the recession of 1980 to 1982 came to an end. In addition, inflation rates fell sharply from the high rates of 1980 and 1981. And, except for one year, federal receipts continued to rise throughout the 1980s despite the cut in tax rates.

Critics of supply-side policies do not dispute these facts but offer an alternative explanation of how the economy recovered. The Reagan tax cuts were enacted just as the U.S. economy was in the middle of its deepest recession since the Great Depression. The unemployment rate stood at 10.8 percent in the fourth quarter of 1982. It was the recession, critics argue, that was responsible for the reduction in inflation—not the supply-side policies. In addition, in theory, a tax cut could even lead to a *reduction* in labor supply. Recall our discussion of income and substitution effects in chapter 4. Although it is true a higher after-tax wage rate provides a higher reward for each hour of work and thus more incentive to work, a tax cut also means households receive a higher income for a given number of hours of work. Because they can earn the same amount of money working fewer hours, households might actually choose to work *less*. They might spend some of their added income on leisure. Research done during the 1980s suggests tax cuts seem to increase the supply of labor somewhat but the increases are very modest.

But what about the recovery from the recession? Why did real output begin to grow rapidly in late 1982, precisely when the supply-side tax cuts were taking effect? Two reasons have been suggested. First, the supply-side tax cuts had large *demand*-side effects that stimulated the economy. Second, the Federal Reserve pumped up the money supply and drove interest rates down at the same time that the tax cuts were being put into effect. The money supply expanded about 20 percent between 1981 and 1983, and interest rates succumbed. In 1981, the average three-month U.S. Treasury bill paid 14 percent interest. In 1983, the figure had dropped to 8.6 percent.

Certainly, traditional theory suggests that a huge tax cut will lead to an increase in disposable income and, in turn, an increase in consumption spending (a component of aggregate expenditure). In addition, although an increase in planned investment (brought about by a lower interest rate) leads to added productive capacity and added supply in the long run, it also increases expenditures on capital goods (new plant and equipment investment) in the short run.

THE SUPPLY-SIDE DEBATE: THEN AND NOW

THEN

In 1979 the Consumer Price Index rose 11.3 percent and in 1980 it rose 13.5 percent. So, in 1980 the Fed began pursuing a policy of slowing the rate of money growth to fight inflation. As the Fed tightened, interest rates rose. In 1978 the 90-day T-Bill interest rate was 7.2 percent. It rose to an average level of 10.0 percent in 1979, to 11.5 percent in 1980, and over 14 percent in 1981.

Ronald Reagan was elected in 1980 on an economic platform based on supply-side principles, promising to get the economy under control. Because Keynesian economics focuses on demand, Keynesian economists believe the appropriate fiscal-policy response to inflation is to increase taxes and reduce government spending. The idea is to reduce aggregate expenditure and shift the aggregate demand curve to the left. But supply-siders believe the policy prescription is exactly the opposite: *Cut* taxes and shift the aggregate supply curve to the right! The clearest statement of this logic is contained in the following excerpt from the *Joint Economic Report* of the 96th Congress:

[The policy of the United States should be to increase] real economic growth through tax reductions designed, not to pump money into the economy, but to restructure the tax code to increase the reward to additional saving, investment and employment. . . . The tax cuts to stimulate saving, investment, and competitiveness will put more goods on the shelves and lower prices, thus reinforcing anti-inflation monetary policy.[a]

NOW

In 1993, the Congress passed and the president signed the Omnibus Budget Reconciliation Act of 1993 that raised taxes substantially as part of a deficit reduction package. There were dire warnings from the supply-siders. But by 1997, the performance of the economy was cited by the administration in its critique of the supply-side position:

In 1993 the President submitted to the Congress a package of measures to reduce the Federal budget deficit that cut Federal spending and raised

income tax rates for the roughly 1.2 percent of taxpayers with the highest incomes. At the time, some critics said that these higher tax rates could hurt the economy by blunting incentives to work and to save. Adherents of supply-side theory went further, arguing that a combination of weaker economic performance and increased tax avoidance would result in little or no additional revenue from these higher tax rates. The 1994 Report explored this issue and concluded that the proposed increases in tax rates for high-income taxpayers would increase tax revenue without adversely affecting the economy. Three years later this conclusion has been justified. Between 1993 and 1994, households with adjusted gross incomes of $100,000 or more saw those incomes increase by an average of 9.0 percent while their income tax liability increased by 8.9 percent.[b]

Sources: [a]*Joint Economic Report*, 96th Congress, March 1980. [b]*Economic Report of the President*, 1997, p. 43.

For more on supply-side economics, see the Case and Fair Web page at
http://www.prenhall.com/casefair.

Whether the recovery from the 1981 to 1982 recession was the result of supply-side expansion or supply-side policies that had demand-side effects, one thing is clear: The extreme promises of the supply-siders did not materialize. President Reagan argued that because of the effect depicted in the Laffer Curve, the government could maintain expenditures (and even increase defense expenditures sharply), cut tax rates, *and* balance the budget. This was clearly not the case. Government revenues fell sharply from levels that would have been realized without the tax cuts. After 1982, the federal government ran huge deficits, with nearly $2 trillion added to the national debt between 1983 and 1992.

For more on the supply-side story, see the Issues and Debates box, "The Supply-Side Debate: Then and Now."

TESTING ALTERNATIVE MACRO MODELS

You may wonder why there is so much disagreement in macroeconomics. Why cannot macroeconomists test their models against one another and see which performs best?

One problem is that macroeconomic models differ in ways that are hard to standardize. If one model takes the price level to be given, or not explained within the model, and another one does not, the model with the given price level may do better in, say, predicting output—not because it is a better model but simply because the errors in predicting prices have not been allowed to affect the predictions of output. The model that takes prices as given has a head start, so to speak.

Another problem arises in the testing of the rational-expectations assumption. Remember, if people have rational expectations, they are using the true model to form their expectations. Therefore, to test this assumption we need the true model. But there's no way to be sure that whatever model is taken to be the true model is in fact the true one. Any test of the rational-expectations hypothesis is therefore a *joint* test (1) that expectations are formed rationally, and (2) that the model being used is the true one. If the test rejects the hypothesis, it may be that the model is wrong rather than that expectations are not rational.

Another problem for macroeconomists is the small amount of data available. Most empirical work uses data beginning about 1950, which in 1998 was about 49 years' (196 quarters) worth of data. While this may seem like a lot of data, it is not. Macroeconomic data are fairly "smooth," which means a typical variable does not vary much from quarter to quarter or year to year. For example, the number of business cycles within this 49-year period is small, about seven. Testing various macroeconomic hypotheses on the basis of seven business cycle observations is not easy, and any conclusions must be interpreted with caution.

To give an example of the problem of a small number of observations, consider trying to test the hypothesis that import prices affect domestic prices. Import prices changed very little in the 1950s and 1960s. Therefore, it would have been very difficult at the end of the 1960s to estimate the effect of import prices on domestic prices. The variation in import prices was not great enough to show any effects. We cannot demonstrate that changes in import prices explain changes in domestic prices if import prices do not change! The situation was different by the end of the 1970s, because by then import prices had varied considerably. By the end of the 1970s, there were good estimates of the import price effect, but not before. This kind of problem is encountered again and again in empirical macroeconomics. In many cases there are not enough observations for much to be said, hence considerable room for disagreement.

We said in chapter 1 that it is difficult in economics to perform controlled experiments. Economists are for the most part at the mercy of the historical data. If we were able to perform experiments, we could probably learn more about the economy in a shorter time. Alas, we must wait. In time, the current range of disagreements in macroeconomics should be considerably narrowed.

SUMMARY

KEYNESIAN ECONOMICS

1. In a broad sense, Keynesian economics is the foundation of modern macroeconomics. In a narrower sense, *Keynesian* refers to economists who advocate active government intervention in the economy.

MONETARISM

2. The monetarist analysis of the economy places a great deal of emphasis on the *velocity of money*, which is defined as the number of times a dollar bill changes hands, on average, during the course of a year. The

velocity of money is the ratio of nominal GDP to the stock of money, or $V \equiv GDP/M \equiv P \times Y/M$. Alternately, $M \times V \equiv P \times Y$.

3. The *quantity theory of money* assumes that velocity is constant (or virtually constant). This implies that changes in the supply of money will lead to equal percentage changes in nominal GDP. The quantity theory of money equation is $M \times V = P \times Y$. The equation says demand for money does not depend on the interest rate.

4. Most economists believe sustained inflation is a purely monetary phenomenon. Inflation cannot continue indefinitely unless the Fed "accommodates" it by expanding the money supply.

5. Most monetarists blame most of the instability in the economy on the federal government and are skeptical of the government's ability to manage the macroeconomy. They argue that the money supply should grow at a rate equal to the average growth of real output (income) (Y)—the Fed should expand the money supply to accommodate real growth but not inflation.

NEW CLASSICAL MACROECONOMICS

6. The *new classical macroeconomics* has developed from two different but related sources: the theoretical and the empirical critiques of traditional macroeconomics. On the theoretical level, there has been growing dissatisfaction with the way traditional models treat expectations. On the empirical level, the stagflation in the U.S. economy during the 1970s caused many people to look for alternative theories to explain the breakdown of the Phillips Curve.

7. The *rational-expectations hypothesis* assumes people know the "true model" that generates economic variables. For example, rational expectations assumes that people know how inflation is determined in the economy and use this model to forecast future inflation rates.

8. The *Lucas supply function* assumes that real output (Y) depends on the actual price level minus the expected price level, or the *price surprise*. This function combined with the assumption that expectations are rational implies that anticipated policy changes have no effect on real output.

9. *Real business cycle theory* is an attempt to explain business-cycle fluctuations under the assumptions of complete price and wage flexibility and rational expectations. It emphasizes shocks to technology and other shocks.

SUPPLY-SIDE ECONOMICS

10. *Supply-side economics* focuses on incentives to stimulate supply. Supply-side economists believe that if we lower taxes, workers will work harder and save more and firms will invest more and produce more. At their most extreme, supply-siders argue that incentive effects are likely to be so great that a major cut in taxes will actually increase tax revenues.

11. The *Laffer Curve* shows the relationship between tax rates and tax revenues. Supply-side economists use it to argue that it is possible to generate higher revenues by cutting tax rates, but evidence does not appear to support this. The lower tax rates by the Reagan administration decreased tax revenues significantly and contributed to the massive increase in the federal debt during the 1980s.

TESTING ALTERNATIVE MACRO MODELS

12. Economists disagree about which macroeconomic model is best for several reasons: (1) macroeconomic models differ in ways that are hard to standardize; (2) when testing the rational-expectations assumption, we are never sure that whatever model is taken to be the true model is the true one; (3) the amount of data available is fairly small.

REVIEW TERMS AND CONCEPTS

$$V \equiv \frac{GDP}{M}$$

$$M \times V \equiv P \times Y$$

$$M \times \overline{V} = P \times Y$$

PROBLEM SET

1. The table gives estimates of the rate of money supply growth and the rate of real GDP growth for six countries in 1997:

	RATE OF GROWTH IN MONEY SUPPLY (M1)	RATE OF GROWTH OF REAL GDP
Britain	+6.1%	+3.9%
Canada	+13.8	+3.7
Japan	+8.1	−0.3
Netherlands	+9.8	+3.1
Spain	+12.8	+3.1
United States	−2.1	+4.0

   a. If you were a monetarist, what would you predict about the rate of inflation across the six countries?
   b. If you were a Keynesian, and assuming activist central banks, how might you interpret the same data?

2. The three diagrams in Figure 1 represent in a simplified way the predictions of the three theories presented in this chapter about the likely effects of a major tax cut.
   a. Match each of the following theories with a graph: (1) Keynesian economics, (2) supply-side economics, (3) rational expectations/monetarism. Explain the logic behind the three graphs.
   b. Which theory do you find the most convincing? Explain.

3. In 1998, a well-known economist was heard to say, "The problem with supply-side economics is that when you cut taxes, they have both supply and demand side effects and you can't separate them." Explain what he meant. Be specific and use either the 1997 tax cuts or the Reagan tax cuts of 1981 as an example.

4. A cornerstone of new classical economics is the notion that expectations are "rational." What do you think will happen to the prices of single-family homes in your community over the next several years? On what do you base your expectations? Is your thinking consistent with the notion of rational expectations? Explain.

5. You are a monetarist given the following information. The money supply is $1,000. The velocity of money is 5. What is nominal income? Real income? What happens to nominal income if the money supply is doubled? What happens to real income?

6. When Bill Clinton took office in January 1993, he faced two major economic problems: a large federal budget deficit and high unemployment resulting from a very slow recovery from the recession of 1990 to 1991. In his first State of the Union message, the president called for spending cuts and substantial tax increases to reduce the deficit. Most of these proposed spending cuts were in the defense budget. The following day, Alan Greenspan, chair of the Federal Reserve Board of Governors, signaled his support for the president's plan. Many elements of the president's original plan were later incorporated into the deficit reduction bill passed in 1993.
   a. Some said at the time that without the Fed's support, the Clinton plan would be a disaster. Explain this argument.
   b. Supply-side economists and monetarists were very worried about the plan and the support it received from the Fed. What specific problems might a monetarist worry about? A supply-side economist?
   c. Suppose you were hired by the Fed Bank of St. Louis to report on the events of 1995 and 1996. What specific evidence would you look for to see if the Clinton plan was effective or whether the critics were right to be skeptical?

7. "In an economy with reasonably flexible prices and wages, full employment is almost always maintained." Explain why this is true.

FIGURE 1

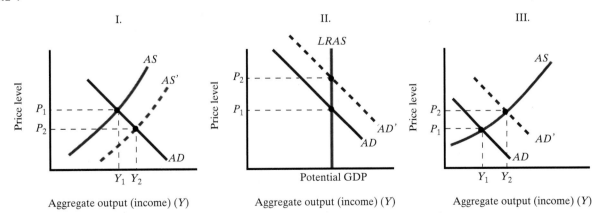

8. During the 1980 presidential campaign, Ronald Reagan promised to cut taxes, increase expenditures on national defense, and balance the budget. During the New Hampshire primary of 1980, George Bush called this policy "voodoo economics." The two men were arguing about the relative merits of supply-side economics. Explain their disagreement.

*9. In a hypothetical economy there is a simple proportional tax on wages imposed at a rate t. There are plenty of jobs around so if people enter the labor force they can find work. We define total government receipts from the tax as

$$T = t \times W \times L$$

where t = the tax rate, W = the gross wage rate, and L = the total supply of labor. The net wage rate is

$$W_n = (1 - t)W.$$

The elasticity of labor supply is defined as

$$\frac{\text{percentage change in } L}{\text{percentage change in } W_n} = \frac{\Delta L / \Delta L}{\Delta W_n / W_n}$$

Suppose t were cut from .25 to .20. For such a cut to *increase* total government receipts from the tax, how elastic must the supply of labor be? (Assume a constant gross wage.) What does your answer imply about the supply-side assertion that a cut in taxes can increase tax revenues?

TAKE IT TO THE NET

We invite you to visit the Case and Fair page on the Prentice Hall Web site:

http://www.prenhall.com/casefair

for this chapter's World Wide Web exercise.

Chapter 34

ECONOMIC GROWTH
AND PRODUCTIVITY

RECALL FROM CHAPTER 1 that **economic growth** occurs when an economy experiences an increase in total output. The increase in real output that began in the Western World with the Industrial Revolution and continues today has been so sustained and so rapid that economists refer to this as the period of **modern economic growth**. These three simple words describe the complex phenomenon that is the subject of this chapter.

It is through economic growth that living standards improve. But growth brings change. New things are produced, while others become obsolete. Some believe growth is the fundamental objective of a society, because it lifts people out of poverty and enhances the quality of their lives. Others say economic growth erodes traditional values and leads to exploitation, environmental destruction, and corruption.

The first part of this chapter describes economic growth in some detail and identifies sources of economic growth. After a review of the U.S. economy's growth record since the nineteenth century, we examine the role of public policy in the growth process. We conclude with a review of the debate over the benefits and costs of growth.

THE GROWTH PROCESS:
FROM AGRICULTURE TO INDUSTRY

The easiest way to understand the growth process and to identify its causes is to think about a simple economy. Recall from chapter 2 Colleen and Bill, washed up on a deserted island. At first they had only a few simple tools and whatever human capital they brought with them to the island. They gathered nuts and berries and built a small cabin. Their "GDP" consisted of basic food and shelter.

Over time, things improved. The first year, they cleared some land and began to cultivate a few vegetables that they found growing on the island. They made some tools and dug a small reservoir to store rainwater. As their agricultural efforts became more efficient, they shifted their resources—their time—into building a larger, more comfortable home.

Colleen and Bill were accumulating capital in two forms. First, they built *physical capital*, material things used in the production of goods and

economic growth *An increase in the total output of an economy. Defined by some economists as an increase of real GDP per capita.*

modern economic growth *The period of rapid and sustained increase in real output per capita that began in the Western World with the Industrial Revolution.*

services—a better house, tools, and a water system. Second, they acquired more *human capital*—knowledge, skills, and talents. Through trial and error, they learned about the island, its soil and its climate, what worked and what didn't. Both kinds of capital made them more efficient and increased their productivity. Because it took less time to produce the food they needed to survive, they could devote more energy to producing other things or to leisure.

At any given time, Colleen and Bill faced limits on what they could produce. These limits were imposed by the existing state of their technical knowledge and the resources at their disposal. Over time, they expanded their possibilities, developed new technologies, accumulated capital, and made their labor more productive. In chapter 2 we defined a society's *production possibilities frontier (ppf)*, which shows all possible combinations of output that can be produced given present technology and if all available resources are fully and efficiently employed. Economic growth expands those limits and shifts society's production possibilities frontier out to the right, as Figure 34.1 shows.

> **From Agriculture to Industry: The Industrial Revolution** Before the Industrial Revolution in Great Britain, every society in the world was agrarian. Towns and cities existed here and there, but almost everyone lived in rural areas. People spent most of their time producing food and other basic subsistence goods. Then, beginning in England around 1750, technical change and capital accumulation increased productivity significantly in two important industries: agriculture and textiles. New and more efficient methods of farming were developed. New inventions and new machinery in spinning, weaving, and steel production meant that more could be produced with fewer resources. Just as new technology, capital equipment, and the resulting higher productivity made it possible for Colleen and Bill to spend time working on other projects and new "products," the British turned from agricultural production to industrial production. In both cases, growth meant new products, more output, and wider choice.

There was one big difference. Colleen and Bill were fully in charge of their own lives. Peasants and workers in eighteenth-century England ended up with a very different set of choices. It was no longer possible to make a living as a peasant farmer. The cities offered the only real alternative, and a rural agrarian society was very quickly transformed into an urban industrial society.

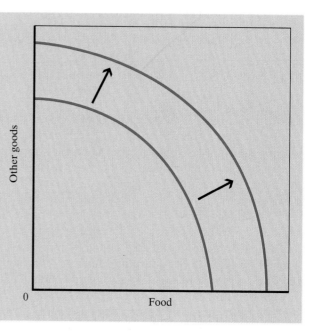

FIGURE 34.1

Economic Growth Shifts Society's Production Possibility Frontier Up and to the Right
The production possibility frontier shows all the combinations of output that can be produced if all of society's scarce resources are fully and efficiently employed. Economic growth expands society's production possibilities, shifting the ppf up and to the right.

Small changes in growth rates can make a big difference over time. Here's what can happen to an income of $10,000 over 10- and 20-year periods at various growth rates:

| | The value of $10,000: | |
Growth rate	after 10 years	after 20 years
1%	$11,046	$12,202
3%	13,439	18,061
5%	16,289	26,533
10%	26,931	67,275

▶ **Growth in an Industrial Society**   The process of economic growth in an industrial society such as the United States is more complex but follows the same steps we have just described for growth in an agrarian society.

Consider the development of the electronic calculator. Prior to 1970, calculators that could add, subtract, multiply, and divide weighed fifty pounds, performed calculations slowly, and were expensive (a good calculator cost hundreds of dollars). Today, electronic calculators retail for as low as $3 or come free with a magazine subscription. Some are small enough to fit into a wristwatch.

During the past 15 years, the growth of computing technology has changed the way we live and do business. Access to the World Wide Web is becoming cheaper and easier. Computers with Pentium processors and massive memory and storage capacity are selling for the price of small electronic calculators 25 years ago.

Technological change, innovation, and capital production (calculators, computers, and software) have increased productivity. If a diner spends less on accounting, its sandwiches will cost less. Sandwich buyers thus may go to see another movie or have another soda. The entertainment and soft drink sectors expand, and so on. That is economic growth.

THE SOURCES OF ECONOMIC GROWTH

Economic growth occurs either when (1) society acquires more resources, or (2) society discovers ways of using available resources more efficiently. For economic growth to increase living standards, the rate of growth must exceed the rate of population increase. Economic growth is generally defined as *an increase in real GDP per capita*.

As we discuss the factors that contribute to economic growth, it will be helpful to think of an **aggregate production function**. An individual firm's production function is a mathematical representation of the relationship between the firm's inputs and its output. Output for an aggregate production function is national output, or gross domestic product. Stated simply, gross domestic product (output) (Y), depends upon the amount of labor (L) and the amount of capital (K) available in the economy (assuming the amount of land is fixed).[1]

If you think of GDP as a function of both labor and capital, you can see that:

> An increase in GDP can come about through:
>
> 1. an increase in the labor supply,
> 2. an increase in physical or human capital, or
> 3. an increase in productivity (the amount of product produced by each unit of capital or labor).

aggregate production function
The mathematical representation of the relationship between inputs and national output, or gross domestic product.

---

[1]All the numbers in the tables to follow were derived from the simple production function: $Y = 3 \times K^{1/3}L^{2/3}$.

AN INCREASE IN LABOR SUPPLY

Consider what would happen if another person joined Colleen and Bill on the island. She would join in the work and produce, and so GDP would rise. Or suppose that a person who had not been a part of the labor force were to begin to work and use his time and energy to produce pottery. Real output would rise in this case also. An increasing labor supply can generate more output.

Whether output *per capita* rises when the labor supply increases is another matter. If the capital stock remains fixed while labor increases, the new labor will likely be less productive than the old labor. This is called *diminishing returns*, and it worried Thomas Malthus, David Ricardo, and other early economists.

Malthus and Ricardo, who lived in England during the nineteenth century, were concerned that the fixed supply of land would lead to diminishing returns. With land in strictly limited supply, the ppf could be pushed out only so far as population increased. To increase agricultural output, people would be forced to farm less productive land or to farm land more intensively. In either case, the returns to successive increases in population would diminish. Both Malthus and Ricardo predicted a gloomy future as population outstripped the land's capacity to produce. What both economists left out of their calculations was technological change and capital accumulation. New and better farming techniques have raised agricultural productivity so much that less than 3 percent of the U.S. population now provide enough food for the country's entire population.

Diminishing returns can also occur if a nation's capital stock grows more slowly than its workforce. Capital enhances workers' productivity. A person with a shovel digs a bigger hole than a person without one, and a person with a steam shovel outdoes them both. If a society's stock of plant and equipment does not grow and the technology of production does not change, additional workers will not be as productive, because they do not have machines to work with.

Table 34.1 illustrates how growth in the labor force, without a corresponding increase in the capital stock or technological change, might lead to growth of output but declining productivity and a lower standard of living. As labor increases, output rises from 300 units in Period 1 to 320 in Period 2, to 339 in Period 3, and so forth, but **labor productivity** (output per worker hour) falls. Output per worker hour, Y/L, is a measure of labor's productivity.

The fear that new workers entering the labor force will displace existing workers and generate unemployment has been with us for a long time. New workers can come from many places. They might be immigrants, young people looking for their first jobs, or older people entering the labor force for the first time. Between 1947 and 1997, the number of women in the labor force more than tripled, jumping from

labor productivity *Output per worker hour; the amount of output produced by an average worker in one hour.*

TABLE 34.1 ECONOMIC GROWTH FROM AN INCREASE IN LABOR— MORE OUTPUT BUT DIMINISHING RETURNS AND LOWER LABOR PRODUCTIVITY

PERIOD	QUANTITY OF LABOR L (HOURS)	QUANTITY OF CAPITAL K (UNITS)	TOTAL OUTPUT Y (UNITS)	MEASURED LABOR PRODUCTIVITY Y/L
1	100	100	300	3.0
2	110	100	320	2.9
3	120	100	339	2.8
4	130	100	357	2.7

TABLE 34.2 **EMPLOYMENT, LABOR FORCE, AND POPULATION GROWTH, 1947 TO 1997**

	CIVILIAN NONINSTITUTIONAL POPULATION OVER 16 YEARS OLD (MILLIONS)	CIVILIAN LABOR FORCE		EMPLOYMENT (MILLIONS)
		NUMBER (MILLIONS)	PERCENTAGE OF POPULATION	
1947	101.8	59.4	58.3	57.0
1960	117.3	69.6	59.3	65.8
1970	137.1	82.8	60.4	78.7
1980	167.7	106.9	63.7	99.3
1990	189.2	125.8	66.5	118.8
1997	203.1	136.3	67.1	129.6
Percentage change, 1947–1997	+99.5	+129.5		+127.4
Annual Rate	+1.4%	+1.7%		+1.7%

Source: Economic Report of the President, 1998, Table B-35.

17 million to 63 million. Table 34.2 shows that in the United States since World War II, the civilian noninstitutional population (those not in jails or mental institutions) over 16 years of age roughly doubled, while the labor force grew by 129.5 percent. The U.S. economy, however, has shown a remarkable ability to expand right along with the labor force. The number of persons employed jumped by 72.6 million—127.4 percent—during the same period.

> As long as the economy and the capital stock are expanding rapidly enough, new entrants into the labor force do not displace other workers.

INCREASES IN PHYSICAL CAPITAL

An increase in the stock of capital can also increase output, even if it is not accompanied by an increase in the labor force. Physical capital both enhances the productivity of labor and provides valuable services directly.

It is easy to see how capital provides services directly. Consider what happened on Bill and Colleen's island. In the first few years, they built a house, putting many hours of work into it that could have gone into producing other things for immediate consumption. With the house for shelter, Colleen and Bill can spend time on other things. In the same way, capital equipment produced in one year can add to the value of a product over many years. For example, we still derive use and value from bridges and tunnels built decades ago.

It is also easy to see how capital used in production enhances the productivity of labor. Computers enable us to do almost instantly tasks that once were impossible or might have taken years to complete. An airplane with a small crew can transport hundreds of people thousands of miles in a few hours. A bridge over a river at a critical location may save thousands of labor hours that would be spent transporting materials and people the long way around. It is precisely this yield in the form of future valuable services that provides both private and public investors with the incentive to devote resources to capital production.

Table 34.3 shows how an increase in capital without a corresponding increase in labor might increase output. Observe several things about these numbers. First, additional capital increases measured productivity; output per worker hour (Y/L) increases from 3.0 to 3.1, to 3.2, and finally to 3.3 as the quantity of capital (K)

TABLE 34.3 ECONOMIC GROWTH FROM AN INCREASE IN CAPITAL—MORE OUTPUT, DIMINISHING RETURNS TO ADDED CAPITAL, HIGHER MEASURED LABOR PRODUCTIVITY

PERIOD	QUANTITY OF LABOR L (HOURS)	QUANTITY OF CAPITAL K (UNITS)	TOTAL OUTPUT Y (UNITS)	MEASURED LABOR PRODUCTIVITY Y/L
1	100	100	300	3.0
2	100	110	310	3.1
3	100	120	319	3.2
4	100	130	327	3.3

WORKERS REPAIR THE BROOKLYN BRIDGE, WHICH CONNECTS THE NEW YORK CITY BOROUGHS OF MANHATTAN AND BROOKLYN. MAINTENANCE AND DEVELOPMENT OF INFRASTRUCTURE PLAY AN IMPORTANT ROLE IN ECONOMIC GROWTH.

increases. Second, there are diminishing returns to capital. Increasing capital by 10 units first increases output by 10 units—from 300 in Period 1 to 310 in Period 2. But the second increase of 10 units yields only 9 units of output, and the third increase yields only 8 units.

Table 34.4 shows the values of the private nonresidential capital stock in the United States since 1960. The increase in capital stock is the difference between gross investment and depreciation. (Remember, some capital becomes obsolete and some wears out every year.) Between 1960 and 1995, the stock of equipment has increased at a rate of 4.3 percent per year and the stock of structures has increased at a rate of 2.6 percent per year.

By comparing Tables 34.2 and 34.4, you can see that capital has been increasing faster than labor since 1960. In all economies experiencing modern economic growth, capital expands at a more rapid rate than labor. That is, the ratio of capital to labor (K/L) increases, and this too is a source of increasing productivity. Another source of increased productivity is public capital, the subject of the Application "Infrastructure and Economic Growth."

INCREASES IN HUMAN CAPITAL

Investment in human capital is another source of economic growth. People in good health are more productive than people in poor health; people with skills are more productive than people without them.

TABLE 34.4 FIXED PRIVATE NONRESIDENTIAL NET CAPITAL STOCK, 1960 TO 1995 (BILLIONS OF 1992 DOLLARS)

	EQUIPMENT	STRUCTURES
1960	660.6	1,768.8
1970	1,117.3	2,419.9
1980	1,855.4	3,176.9
1990	2,507.3	4,142.2
1995	2,885.5	4,399.1
Percentage change, 1960–1995	+336.8	+148.7
Annual rate	+4.3%	+2.6%

Source: Survey of Current Business, May 1997, Table 15, p. 92.

TABLE 34.5 YEARS OF SCHOOL COMPLETED BY PEOPLE OVER 25 YEARS OLD, 1940 TO 1996

	PERCENTAGE WITH LESS THAN FIVE YEARS OF SCHOOL	PERCENTAGE WITH FOUR YEARS OF HIGH SCHOOL OR MORE	PERCENTAGE WITH FOUR YEARS OF COLLEGE OR MORE
1940	13.7	24.5	4.6
1950	11.1	34.3	6.2
1960	8.3	41.1	7.7
1970	5.5	52.3	10.7
1980	3.6	66.5	16.2
1990	NA	77.6	21.3
1996	NA	81.7	23.6

Source: Statistical Abstract of the United States, 1990, Table 215; and *1997*, Table 243.
NA = not available.

Human capital can be produced in many ways. Individuals can invest in themselves by going to college or vocational training programs. Firms can invest in human capital through on-the-job training. The government invests in human capital with programs to improve health and to provide schooling and job training.

Table 34.5 shows the level of educational attainment has risen significantly since 1940. The percentage of the population with at least four years of college rose from under 5 percent in 1940 to 23.6 percent in 1996. In 1940 fewer than 1 person in 4 had completed high school; in 1996, more than 8 in 10 had.

INCREASES IN PRODUCTIVITY

Growth that cannot be explained by increases in the *quantity* of inputs can be explained only by an increase in the *productivity* of those inputs—each unit of input must be producing more output. The **productivity of an input** can be affected by factors including technological change, other advances in knowledge, and economies of scale.

productivity of an input *The amount of output produced per unit of an input.*

▶ **Technological Change**   The Industrial Revolution was in part sparked by new technological developments. New techniques of spinning and weaving—the invention of the "mule" and the "spinning jenny," for example—were critical. The high-tech boom that swept the United States in the early 1980s was driven by the rapid development and dissemination of semiconductor technology.

Technological change affects productivity in two stages. First, there is an advance in knowledge, or an **invention**. But knowledge by itself does nothing unless it is used. When new knowledge is used to produce a new product or to produce an existing product more efficiently, there is **innovation**.

invention *An advance in knowledge.*

innovation *The use of new knowledge to produce a new product or to produce an existing product more efficiently.*

Technological change cannot be measured directly. Some studies have presented data on "indicators" of the rate of technical change—the number of new patents, for example—but none are satisfactory. Still, we know technological changes that have improved productivity are all around us. Computer technology has revolutionized the office, hybrid seeds have increased the productivity of land, and more efficient and powerful aircraft have made air travel routine and inexpensive.

▶ **Other Advances in Knowledge**   Over and above invention and innovation, advances in other kinds of knowledge can also improve productivity. One is what we might call "managerial knowledge." For example, because of the very high cost of capital during

INFRASTRUCTURE AND ECONOMIC GROWTH

A major source of economic growth is the accumulation of capital. When we think of capital's role in economic growth, we tend to focus on private capital—the plant, equipment, and inventory of business firms. But what about *public* capital?

Recall from our earlier discussions that *capital goods* are used to produce other goods and services over time. One form of capital is infrastructure. **Infrastructure**, also called **public capital**, refers to the roads, bridges, water treatment plants, fire stations, and so on that collectively contribute to the public good.

Infrastructure has the potential for increasing productivity and growth. Good highways and bridges reduce transportation costs and make it easier to transport goods. Readily available clean water improves health and is often essential for production.

Governments are usually responsible for putting public capital into place. Throughout the 1980s, however, there was strong pressure to reduce government spending and to increase growth in the private sector. One of the consequences of these pressures was a significant slowdown in public infrastructure investment. Some have pointed to this slowdown as a cause of the slower economic growth in the 1980s.

In June 1990, the Federal Reserve Bank of Boston held a conference on the topic of infrastructure and growth. Professor David Aschauer of Bates College opened the conference with the following challenge:

As the decade of the 1990s begins, new challenges present themselves to the citizenry of the United States. Among the most important are concerns about the environment, economic productivity, and international competitiveness, and a rearrangement of standing strategic military relationships. Our future quality of life, economic prosperity, and security depend crucially on how we choose to meet these new challenges. . . .

The first direction, expenditure reduction, certainly has merit to a broad class of individuals. Many would point to the fact that total federal government outlays, expressed relative to gross national product, rose from 14.8 percent in 1950 to 21.6 percent in 1980 and, in 1989, to 21.8 percent. Others would point to the persistence of federal budget deficits. To both groups, expenditure reduction would be of benefit to economic performance, either by reducing the overall scale of government activity in the economy or by allowing a reduction in interest rates and an expansion in domestic investment activity.

But the second direction, expenditure reorientation, may also have merit. It could well be the case that quality of life and economic performance would be best served by retaining the resources within the public sector and expanding expenditure in certain critical areas. One candidate area is infrastructure, the public stock of social and economic overhead capital. Indeed, it has been claimed in the popular press that "it's hard to escape America's crumbling infrastructure" and that "even though the deterioration of U.S. highways, bridges, airports, harbors, sewage systems, and other building blocks of the economy has been exhaustively documented in recent years, there has been scant progress" in addressing the postulated need to renew the public capital stock (Industry Week, May 21, 1990).[a]

Clearly, someone was listening. Prior to taking office, President Bill Clinton held an economic summit to discuss ideas for stimulating economic growth. A major focus of the discussion was infrastructure, and it led to Clinton's call for $16 billion in public works spending in his 1993 State of the Union address.

The president's proposal was defeated by Congress, which argued that the infrastructure's role in economic growth is not significant enough to justify spending such huge sums of money. The debate continues to rage. In his 1995 *Economic Report*, Clinton summarized this situation as follows: "Declining trends in public capital suggest that infrastructure investment has been a net drag on the growth of productivity since 1970, but there is no consensus as to the quantitative importance of this effect."

---

[a]"Is There a Shortfall in Public Capital Investment?" Proceedings of a Conference sponsored by the Federal Reserve Bank of Boston, Alicia Munnell, Editor, June 1990.

For more on economic growth, see the Case and Fair Web page at http://www.prenhall.com/casefair.

the early 1980s, firms learned to manage their inventories much better. Many were able to keep production lines and distribution lines flowing with a much lower stock of inventories. Inventories are part of a firm's capital stock, and trimming them reduces costs and raises productivity. This is an example of a *capital-saving* innovation; many of the advances that we are used to thinking about, such as the introduction of robotics, are *labor-saving*.

In addition to managerial knowledge, improved personnel management techniques, accounting procedures, data management, and the like can also make production more efficient, reduce costs, and increase measured productivity.

> **Economies of Scale**   *External economies of scale* are cost savings that result from increases in the size of industries. The economies that accompany growth in size may arise from a variety of causes. For example, as firms in a growing industry build plants at new locations, they may lower transport costs. There may also be some economies of scale associated with R&D (research and development) spending and job-training programs.

> **Other Influences on Productivity**   In addition to technological change, other advances in knowledge, and economies of scale, other forces may affect productivity. During the 1970s and 1980s, the U.S. government required many firms to reduce the air and water pollution they were producing. These requirements diverted capital and labor from the production of measured output, therefore *reducing* measured productivity. Similarly, in recent years requirements imposed by the Occupational Safety and Health Act (OSHA) have required firms to protect workers better from accidental injuries and potential health problems. These laws also divert resources from measured output.

Negative effects such as these are more a problem of *measurement* than of truly declining productivity. The EPA (Environmental Protection Agency) regulates air and water quality because clean air and water presumably have a value to society. The resources diverted to produce that value are not wasted. A perfect measure of output produced that is of value to society would include environmental quality and good health.

The list of factors that can affect productivity is large. Weather can have a big impact on agricultural productivity. The early 1990s saw huge floods and massive crop losses in the Midwest. Floods in California in 1995 had similar effects.

Having presented the major factors that influence productivity, we now turn to the growth record for the United States and how these factors have combined to produce a record of steady growth that has lasted over 100 years.

GROWTH AND PRODUCTIVITY IN THE UNITED STATES

Modern economic growth in the United States began in the middle of the nineteenth century. After the Civil War, the railroads spread across the country and the economy took off. Table 34.6 shows the growth rate of real output in the United States since 1871.

Over the long haul, real output in the United States has been growing at about 3.3 percent annually. Between 1871 and 1909, the growth rate was very healthy, ranging from 4.0 percent to 5.5 percent per year. Because of the dislocations of the Great Depression, growth was slower during the 1930s and 1940s, but the 1950s and 1960s saw renewed growth and vigor in the economy. Although the 1970s contained some good years and some bad, during the decade output rose by an average of 3.1 percent per year, a credible performance. In the 1990 to 1997 period, the rate of growth was only 2.3 percent; it was brought down by the recession from 1990 to 1991.

TABLE 34.6 GROWTH OF REAL GDP IN THE UNITED STATES, 1871 TO 1997

PERIOD	AVERAGE GROWTH RATE PER YEAR	PERIOD	AVERAGE GROWTH RATE PER YEAR
1871–1889	5.5	1960–1970	4.1
1889–1909	4.0	1970–1980	3.1
1909–1929	2.8	1980–1990	2.9
1929–1950	3.4	1990–1997	2.3
1950–1960	3.5	1950–1997	3.2

Sources: Historical Statistics of the United States: Colonial Times to 1970, Tables F47-70, F98-124; U.S. Department of Commerce, Bureau of Economic Analysis.

Figure 34.2 shows growth rates of real GDP since 1961 for the United States and several other countries. Growth has been slowing everywhere. Virtually all the countries in the table experienced less growth during the 1970s than during the 1960s and continued to grow more slowly during the 1980s. The early 1990s saw a recession sweep across the world; in 1991, GDP declined in many countries, including the

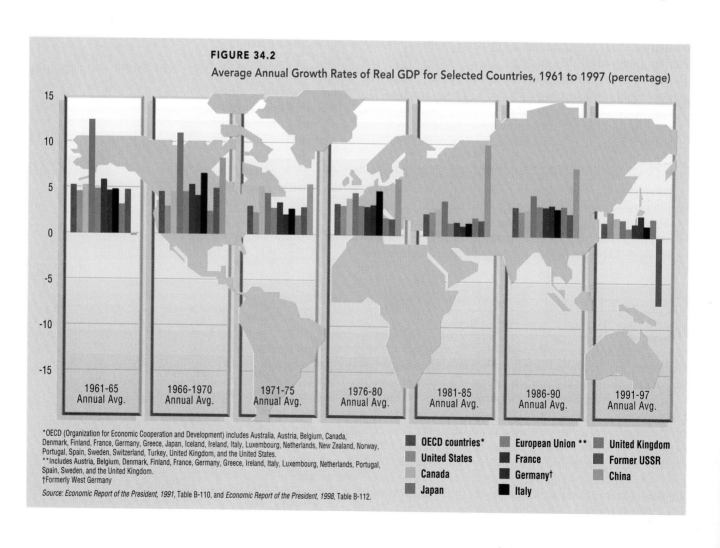

FIGURE 34.2

Average Annual Growth Rates of Real GDP for Selected Countries, 1961 to 1997 (percentage)

*OECD (Organization for Economic Cooperation and Development) includes Australia, Austria, Belgium, Canada, Denmark, Finland, France, Germany, Greece, Japan, Iceland, Ireland, Italy, Luxembourg, Netherlands, New Zealand, Norway, Portugal, Spain, Sweden, Switzerland, Turkey, United Kingdom, and the United States.
**Includes Austria, Belgium, Denmark, Finland, France, Germany, Greece, Ireland, Italy, Luxembourg, Netherlands, Portugal, Spain, Sweden, and the United Kingdom.
†Formerly West Germany

Source: Economic Report of the President, 1991, Table B-110, and Economic Report of the President, 1998, Table B-112.

- OECD countries*
- United States
- Canada
- Japan
- European Union **
- France
- Germany†
- Italy
- United Kingdom
- Former USSR
- China

United States. In most of the countries of the European Union, recession lasted through 1993, but by 1994 virtually all of the world's industrial countries were growing again. The economies of the former Soviet Union did very poorly in the 1991 to 1997 period, with real GDP falling at an annual rate of 7.3 percent.

SOURCES OF GROWTH IN THE U.S. ECONOMY SINCE 1929

For many years, Edward Denison of the Brookings Institution in Washington has been studying the growth process in the United States and sorting out the relative importance of the various causal factors. Table 34.7 presents the results of his most recently published major work.

Denison estimates that about half of U.S. growth in output over the entire period from 1929 to 1982 has come from increases in factors of production and the other half from increases in productivity. Growth in the labor force accounted for about 20 percent of overall growth, while growth in capital stock (both human and physical) accounted for 33 percent. Of the capital stock growth figure, human capital (education and training) accounted for 19 percent of the total, and physical capital accounted for 14 percent. Growth of knowledge was the most important factor contributing to increases in the productivity of inputs.

The relative importance of these causes of growth varied considerably over the years. Between 1929 and 1948, for example, physical capital played a much smaller role than it did in other periods. But each period included times that were atypical for one reason or another. The period between 1929 and 1948 included the dislocations and uncertainties of the Great Depression and World War II. From 1948 to 1973, the economy enjoyed a period of unusual stability and expansion.

A 1997 study by Charles Jones comes to the gloomy conclusion that a slowdown of growth in the United States is imminent. Jones's paper finds that much of the post WWII growth in the United States comes from three factors: (1) an increase in educational attainment, (2) a sharp increase in the share of the labor force devoted to

---

TABLE 34.7 **SOURCES OF GROWTH IN THE UNITED STATES, 1929 TO 1982**

	PERCENT OF GROWTH ATTRIBUTABLE TO EACH SOURCE			
	1929–1982	1929–1948	1948–1973	1973–1982
Increases in inputs	53	49	45	94
Labor	20	26	14	47
Capital	14	3	16	29
Education (human capital)	19	20	15	18
Increases in productivity	47	51	55	6
Advances in knowledge	31	30	39	8
Other factors*	16	21	16	−2
Total	100	100	100	100
Annual growth rate in real national income	2.8	2.4	3.6	2.6

*Note: Economies of scale, weather, pollution abatement, worker safety and health, crime, labor disputes, and so forth.

Source: Edward Denison, *Trends in American Economic Growth, 1929–1982* (Washington: Brookings Institution, 1985).

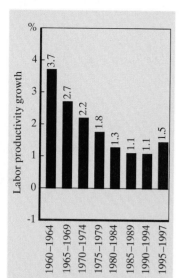

FIGURE 34.3

Labor Productivity Growth:
Rate of Change of Real
Output per Hour of Labor
in the United States,
1960–1997

*Source: Economic Report of
the President, 1998*, Table B-50.

research, and (3) an increase in the openness of the world economy—the expansion of trade. He concludes that these increases must ultimately level off, and when they do, the growth rate in the United States could fall by as much as 75 percent.[2]

THE PRODUCTIVITY "PROBLEM"

The years since 1973 have deserved the attention they received. During the early years of the Reagan administration, the "productivity problem" was much discussed. Some economics textbooks published in the early 1980s had entire chapters discussing the decline in productivity that seemed to be taking place during the late 1970s. In January of 1981, the Congressional Budget Office published a report, "The Productivity Problem: Alternatives for Action."

What exactly is this productivity problem? Figure 34.3 shows that the growth rate of *output per hour of labor* has generally fallen since 1960, and in the 1980s and early 1990s it was only slightly above 1 percent.

Many explanations were offered for the productivity decline of the late 1970s and early 1980s. Some economists pointed to the low rate of saving in the United States compared to other parts of the world. Others blamed increased environmental and government regulation of U.S. businesses. Still others argued that the country was not spending as much on research and development as it should have been. Finally, some suggested, high energy costs in the 1970s led to investment designed to save energy rather than to enhance productivity. (We discuss exactly how each of these factors influence growth later in this chapter.)

During the 1980s many of these factors seemed to turn around. Private investment in plant and equipment increased from long-run levels of under 8 percent of GDP to nearly 10 percent during the decade. Energy prices cascaded. There was some reduction in regulation under the Reagan administration. Research and development spending rose to its highest percentage of GDP since 1970. Productivity, on the other hand, did not respond; the growth rate of productivity remained low in the last half of the 1980s.

The late 1990s have seen a slight upward trend, with the growth rate of productivity averaging 1.5 percent in the 1995 to 1997 period.

To conclude our discussion of productivity, we must point out that the productivity statistics we have been examining are hotly debated. For more details, see Issues and Debates box "Can We Really Measure Productivity Changes?"

ECONOMIC GROWTH AND PUBLIC POLICY

The decline in productivity that has caused so much concern has led to a protracted national discussion about the role of government in stimulating economic growth. This debate was spurred in part by increasing concern in the United States that the United States was not doing as well as Japan. The enormous success of the Japanese in world markets and their extraordinary postwar annual rates of growth have led more and more people to look to the Far East for economic instruction.

Several strategies for increasing the rate of growth in the United States have been suggested, and some have been enacted into law. These strategies include policies aimed toward improving the quality of education, increasing the saving rate, stimulating

[2]Charles I. Jones, "The Coming Slowdown in U.S. Economic Growth," mimeo, Stanford University, September 15, 1997.

CAN WE REALLY MEASURE PRODUCTIVITY CHANGES?

When the government publishes numbers like those in Figure 19.3, most people take them as "true." Even though we don't really know much about how they are constructed, we assume they are the best measurements we can get.

Yet such data are often the source of controversy. Some have argued that the mix of products produced in the United States and the increased pace of technological change in recent years have made it increasingly difficult to measure productivity changes accurately. The observed productivity decline in recent decades may be measurement error.

These arguments make a certain amount of sense at an intuitive level. Even in agriculture, where it is relatively easy to measure productivity growth, the possibility of mismeasurement exists. The output of a soybean farm can be measured in bushels, and labor, capital, and land inputs present no serious measurement problems. So, over time, as farming techniques improved and farmers acquired new and better machinery, output per acre and output per worker rose and have continued to rise. But today we have biotechnology. Genetic engineering now makes it possible to make soybeans higher in protein and more disease resistant. Technology has improved and "output" has increased, but these increases do not show up in the data because of crude measures of output.

A similar problem exists with computers. If you simply counted the number of personal computers produced and measured the cost of the inputs used in their production, you would no doubt see some productivity advances. But computers being produced for under $1,000 in 1998 contained processors capable of performing tasks literally thousands of times faster than computers produced a few years earlier. If we were to measure computer outputs not in terms of units produced but in terms of the actual "services" they provide to users, we would find massive productivity advances. Most new PCs now contain CD-ROM slots and can be easily connected to the new and growing "information superhighway," a source of cheap and plentiful information. In short, the problem is that many of the products we now use are qualitatively different from the comparable products we used only a few years ago, and the standard measures of productivity miss much of these quality changes.

The problems are greater in the service sector, where output is extremely difficult to measure. It is easy to understand the problem if you think of what information technology has done for legal services. As recently as 10 years ago, a lawyer doing research to support a legal case might spend hundreds of hours looking through old cases and public documents. Today's lawyers can log on to a computer and in seconds do a key word search on a massive legal database. Such time- and labor-saving productivity advances are not counted in the official data.

One of the leading experts on technology and productivity estimates that we have reasonably good measures of output and productivity in only about 31 percent of the U.S. economy. Does this mean that productivity is not a problem? On this topic economists have agreed to disagree.[a]

---

[a]This argument was described most clearly by Professor Zvi Grilliches of Harvard in his presidential address to the American Economic Association in January 1994. The full text, entitled "Productivity, R&D, and the Data Constraint," is published in the *American Economic Review*, March 1994. The counterargument is best advanced by Professor Dale Jorgenson in *Productivity* (Harvard University Press, 1995).

For more on measuring productivity, see the Case and Fair Web page at
http://www.prenhall.com/casefair.

---

investment, increasing research and development, reducing regulation, and pursuing an industrial policy.

▶ **Policies to Improve the Quality of Education** The Denison study shows that the contribution of education and training (human capital production) to growth in the United States has remained relatively constant at about 20 percent since 1929.

During the 1970s, public education was criticized. Teachers' salaries declined sharply in real terms, while property tax limitations and cuts in federal programs forced the curtailment of school budgets. In the last few years, battles have been waged

CHAPTER THIRTY-FOUR
*Economic Growth
and Productivity*

in Congress over the amount of federal dollars set aside for scholarships and loans to college students. Whatever the policies of the moment, however, all federal, state, and local expenditures on education acknowledge the need to build the nation's stock of human capital.

The Taxpayer Relief Act of 1997 contained provisions that focused on education. First, the HOPE Scholarship credit allows taxpayers to claim a credit up to $1,500 for postsecondary education expenses on behalf of any family member. Other provisions include a new Education Individual Retirement Account that allows savings to earn tax free returns as long as the balance is used to pay educational expenses.

➤ **Policies to Increase the Saving Rate**　The amount of capital accumulation in an economy is ultimately constrained by its rate of saving. The more saving in an economy, the more funds are available for investment. The national saving rate in Japan is twice as high as in the United States, and investment is a much higher fraction of GDP in Japan than in the United States. Many people have argued that the tax system and the social security system in the United States are biased against saving. Some public finance economists favor shifting to a system of consumption taxation rather than income taxation to reduce the tax burden on saving.

Others claim the social security system, by providing guaranteed retirement incomes, reduces the incentive for people to save. Private pension plans make deposits to workers' accounts, the balances of which are invested in the stock market and bond market and are made available to firms for capital investment. Social security benefits, in contrast, are paid out of current tax receipts, and no such accumulations are available for investment. Thus, the argument goes, if social security substitutes for private saving, the national saving rate is reduced. Evidence on the extent to which taxes and social security reduce the saving rate has not been clear to date.

A provision of the 1997 Taxpayer Relief Act allowed for new "backloaded" retirement accounts (the so-called Roth IRAs) to stimulate savings. Individuals can deposit up to $2,000 annually to specified retirement accounts that accumulate earnings without paying income tax. Withdrawals made after age 59½ or for the purchase of a first home can be made tax free.

➤ **Policies to Stimulate Investment**　For the growth rate to increase, saving must be used to finance new investment. In an effort to revive a slowly growing economy in 1961, President Kennedy proposed and the Congress passed the *investment tax credit*. The ITC provided a tax reduction for firms that invest in new capital equipment. For most investments, the reduction took the form of a direct credit equal to 10 percent of the investment. A firm investing in a new computer system costing $100,000 would have its tax liability reduced by $10,000. The investment tax credit was changed periodically over the years, and it was on the books until it was repealed in 1986. Many states have adopted investment tax credits against their state corporation taxes.

In 1982, the federal Economic Recovery Tax Act contained a number of provisions designed to encourage investment. Among them was the *Accelerated Cost Recovery System (ACRS)*, which gave firms the opportunity to reduce their taxes by using artificially rapid rates of depreciation for purposes of calculating taxable profits. While these rules were complicated, their effect was similar to the effect of the investment tax credit. The government effectively reduced the cost of capital to firms that undertook investment in plant or equipment.

Another provision of the 1997 Taxpayer Relief Act cut the rate of taxation of income earned in the form of capital gains (taxes on increases in the value of assets such as shares of stock). For asset sales after May 6, 1997, the maximum rate of tax is 20 percent, down from 28 percent. The hope is to stimulate investment, especially in new start-up companies, but the evidence on the likely effects of such changes is mixed.

> **Policies to Increase Research and Development**   As Table 34.7 shows, increases in knowledge accounted for 31 percent of total growth in the United States between 1929 and 1982. Although not shown in the table, during the years of high R&D expenditures, 1953 to 1973, the figure reached 40 percent. Research also shows that the rate of return on investment in R&D is quite high. Estimates place the rate of return at around 30 percent.[3]

It can be argued that new knowledge is like a public good. Although the United States has a patent system to protect the gains of R&D for inventors and innovators, many of the benefits flow to imitators and others, including the public. This logic has been used to justify public subsidization of R&D spending.

> **Reduced Regulations**   The Reagan and Bush administrations, and the Republicans' "Contract with America" in 1995, were committed to reducing government regulation, which many believe stands in the way of U.S. industry.

Critics of these policies say many regulations on the books serve legitimate economic purposes. For example, environmental regulations, if properly administered, improve efficiency. Judicious use of antitrust laws can also improve the allocation of resources and stimulate investment and production.

Denison estimated that regulation of occupational health and safety, and of the environment, reduced the annual growth rate between 1973 and 1979 by 0.13 percentage points, from 2.74 percent to 2.61 percent per year. But has the value of the improved environment and increased safety been worth it?

> **Industrial Policy**   In the last few years, a number of economists have called for increased government involvement in the allocation of capital across manufacturing sectors, a practice known as **industrial policy**. Those who favor industrial policy believe that because governments of other countries are "targeting" industries for special subsidies and rapid investment, the United States should do likewise to avoid losing out in international competition. The Japanese Ministry of Trade and Industry, for example, picked the automobile industry very early on and decided to expand its role in world markets. The strategy succeeded very well; the Japanese auto industry has been remarkably successful.

Critics of industrial policy argue that having the government involved in the allocation of capital would be disastrous. Investment always involves risk, they believe, and the best people to judge the extent and appropriateness of that risk are those making the investments and those actually involved in the industry.

industrial policy *Government involvement in the allocation of capital across manufacturing sectors.*

GROWTH POLICY: A LONG-RUN PROPOSITION

When President Ford and Congress passed the dramatic tax cuts of 1975 to stimulate the economy and end the deep recession, the results were observable within a few months. Fiscal and monetary policies designed to counteract the cyclical up-and-down swings in the economy can produce measurable results in a short time.

However, the effects of policies designed to increase the rate of growth may not have observable effects for many years—they are by definition designed to mold the economy's long-run growth path. For example, a policy that succeeded in raising the rate of growth by one percentage point, say from 2.5 percent to 3.5 percent, would be viewed by all as a tremendous success. Yet it would be almost a decade before such a policy would raise GDP by 10 percent.

---

[3]See M. Nadiri, "Contributions and Determinants of Research and Development Expenditures in the U.S. Manufacturing Industries," in *Capital Efficiency and Growth*, ed. George M. von Furstenberg, (Cambridge, Mass.: Ballinger Press, 1980).

The fact that pro-growth policies can be costly in the short run and do not produce measurable results for a long time often pushes them far down on politicians' lists of priorities. Some economists who opposed the Tax Reform Act of 1986 argued that the elements of the tax code that had been favorable to capital investment and growth were cut for precisely these reasons. Defenders of the Tax Reform Act claim that it is indeed possible to oversubsidize investment and that the pre-1986 tax code had been doing just that.

Not everyone agrees that the top priority in a developed economy should be continued growth. We'll see why as we close the chapter.

THE PROS AND CONS OF GROWTH

There are those who believe growth should be the primary objective of any society and those who believe the costs of growth are too great.

THE PRO-GROWTH ARGUMENT

Advocates of growth believe growth *is* progress. Resources in a market economy are used to produce what people want; if you produce something people do not want, you are out of business. Even in a centrally planned economy, resources are targeted to fulfill needs and wants. If a society is able to produce those things more efficiently and at less cost, how can that be bad?

By applying new technologies and better production methods, resources are freed to produce new and better products. For Colleen and Bill accumulation of capital—a house, a water system, and so forth—and advancing knowledge were necessary to improve life on a formerly uninhabited island. In a modern industrial society, capital accumulation and new technology improve the quality of life.

One way to think about the benefits of growth is to compare two periods, say 1950 and 1995. In 1995, real GDP per capita was more than twice what it was in 1950. This means incomes have grown twice as fast as prices so that we can buy that much more. (Remember, no one is telling anyone what to buy, and most people can spend much more now than they could then.)

Although things available in both periods are not exactly the same, growth has given us *more* choice, not less. Consider transportation. In the 1950s, the interstate highway system (social capital) had not been built. Driving from Chicago to New York took several days. We had automobiles, but the highway system did not compare to what we have today. And greater advances have been made in air travel. Flying between the two cities was possible, but more costly, less comfortable, and slower in 1950 than it is today.

Do these changes improve the quality of life? Yes, because they give us more freedom. We can travel more frequently. I can see my mother more often. I spend less time getting where I want to go so I can spend more time there. People are able to get to more places for less money.

What about consumer durables—dishwashers, microwave ovens, compact disc players, power lawn mowers, and so forth? Do they enhance the quality of life? If not, why do we buy them? In 1950, about 3 percent of all homes had dishwashers; today it's close to 50 percent. In 1950, fewer than 2 percent of all homes had air conditioners; today over 60 percent do.

What makes a dishwasher worthwhile? It saves the most valuable commodity—*time*. Many consumer durables have no intrinsic value—they don't provide satisfaction directly. They free us from tasks and chores that are not fun (no one likes to wash clothes or dishes). If a product allows us to perform these tasks more easily and quickly, it gives us more time for other things.

And think of the improvement in the *quality* of things that yield satisfaction directly. Record players in the 1950s reproduced sound imperfectly; high fidelity was just being developed, and stereo was in the future. Today you can get a compact disc player for your car. Small "boxes" available at discount stores for under $30 reproduce sound far better than the best machines available in the early 1950s. And the range of tapes and compact discs available is extraordinary.

Growth also makes it possible to improve conditions for the less fortunate. The logic is simple: When there is more to go around, the sacrifice required to help the needy is smaller. With higher incomes, we can better afford the sacrifices needed to help the poor. Growth also produces jobs. When population growth is not accompanied by growth in output, unemployment and poverty increase.

Those in advanced societies can be complacent about growth, or critical of it. But leaders of developing countries understand its benefits. When 75 percent of a country's population is poor, redistributing existing incomes does not do much. The only hope for improvement in the long run is economic growth.

THE ANTI-GROWTH ARGUMENT

Those who argue against economic growth generally make four major points:

1. Any measure of output measures only the value of things exchanged in the market. Many things that affect the quality of life are not traded in the market, and those things generally lose value when growth occurs.
2. For growth to occur, industry must cause consumers to develop new tastes and preferences. Therefore, we have no real need for many of the things we now consume. Wants are created, and consumers have become the servants, rather than the masters, of the economy.
3. The world has a finite quantity of resources, and rapid growth is consuming them at a rate that cannot continue. Because the available resources impose limits to growth, we should begin now to plan for the future, when growth will be impossible.
4. Growth requires that income be distributed unfairly.

▶ **Growth Has Negative Effects on the Quality of Life** Perhaps the most significant "unmeasurable" changes that affect the quality of life occur in the early stages of growth when societies become industrialized. More is produced: Agricultural productivity is higher, more manufactured goods are available, and so forth. But most people are crowded into cities, and their lives change drastically.

Before industrialization, most people in the Western World lived in small towns in the country. Most were poor, and they worked long hours to produce enough food to survive. After industrialization and urbanization in eighteenth-century England, men, women, and children worked long hours at routine jobs in hot, crowded factories. They were paid low wages and had very little control over their lives.

Even today, growth continues to change the quality of life in ways that are observable but not taken into account when we calculate growth rates. U.S. agriculture, for example, is becoming more productive every year. As productivity goes up, food prices drop, and fewer resources are needed in the agricultural sector. States in New England that once had thriving farms have found their climates and soils not good enough to compete anymore. In 1959, 56,000 farms covered 9.3 million acres in the six New England states; in 1998, fewer than 30,000 farms covered fewer than 5 million acres. The agricultural sector had been cut in half.

During the early 1970s, small family farmers all over the United States found that making a living was becoming nearly impossible. The villain? Growth and progress. The cost? The decline of a lifestyle that many people want to maintain and that many others think of as an important part of America.

Following industrial mercury dumping into the waters of Minimata Bay, Japan, there were considerable numbers of birth defects.

There are other consequences of growth that are not counted in the growth calculation. Perhaps the most significant is environmental damage. As the industrial engine is fed, waste is produced. Often both the feeding and the waste cause massive environmental damage. A dramatic example is the surface, or strip, mining of coal that has ravaged many parts of the United States. Another is the uncontrolled harvesting of U.S. forests. Modern growth requires paper and wood products, and large areas of timber in many states have been cleared and never replanted.

The disposal of industrial wastes has not begun to keep pace with industrial growth. It is now clear that growing and prosperous chemical companies have for decades been dumping hazardous, often carcinogenic, waste products into the nation's soil and water. It is costing billions to clean them up. Those costs were never taken into account when the market was allocating resources to the growing chemical industry.

Growth-related problems are everywhere. Japan paid little attention to the environment during the early years of its rapid economic growth. Many of the results were disastrous. The best known of these results were the horrifying birth defects following the dumping of industrial mercury into the waters of Minamata Bay. In addition to birth defects, thousands of cases of "Minamata disease" in adults have been documented, and hundreds have died.

➤ **Growth Encourages the Creation of Artificial Needs** The nature of preferences has been debated within the economics profession for many years. The orthodox view, which lies at the heart of modern welfare economics, is that preferences exist among consumers and that the economy's purpose is to serve those needs. According to the notion of **consumer sovereignty**, people are free to choose, and things that people do not want will not sell. The consumer rules.

The opposite view is that preferences are formed within the economic system. To continue growing, firms need a continuously expanding set of demands. To ensure that demand grows, firms create it by managing our minds and manipulating our behavior with elaborate advertising, fancy packaging, and other marketing techniques that persuade us to buy things for which we have no intrinsic need.

➤ **Growth Means the Rapid Depletion of a Finite Quantity of Resources** In 1972, the Club of Rome, a group of "concerned citizens," contracted with a group at MIT to do a study entitled *The Limits to Growth*.[4] The book-length final report presented the

consumer sovereignty
The notion that people are free to choose, and that things that people do not want will not sell. "The customer rules."

---

[4]Dennis L. Meadows, et al., *The Limits to Growth* (Washington: Potomac Associates, 1972).

results of computer simulations that assumed present growth rates of population, food, industrial output, and resource exhaustion. According to these data, sometime after the year 2000 the limits will be reached, and the entire world economy will come crashing down:

> Collapse occurs because of nonrenewable resource depletion. The industrial capital stock grows to a level that requires an enormous input of resources. In the very process of that growth, it depletes a large fraction of the resource reserves available. As resource prices rise and mines are depleted, more and more capital must be used for obtaining resources, leaving less to be invested for future growth. Finally, investment cannot keep up with depreciation and the industrial base collapses, taking with it the service and agricultural systems, which have become dependent on industrial inputs (such as fertilizers, pesticides, hospital laboratories, computers, and especially energy for mechanization. . . . Population finally decreases when the death rate is driven upward by the lack of food and health services.[5]

This argument is similar to one offered almost 200 years ago by Thomas Malthus, mentioned earlier in this chapter.

In the early 1970s, many thought that the Club of Rome's predictions had come true. It seemed the world was starting to run up against the limits of world energy supplies; the prices of energy products shot up, and there were serious shortages. But in the years since, new reserves have been found, new sources of energy have been discovered and developed, and conservation measures have been tremendously successful (automobile gas mileage has been pushed up to levels that were inconceivable 15 years ago). Energy prices have fallen to levels that in real terms are about the same as they were before the oil price shocks of the 1970s.

A variation of the depletion-of-resources argument stops short of predicting doomsday. It does point out that unchecked growth in the developed world may have undesirable distributional consequences. To fuel our growth, we are buying vast quantities of minerals and other resources from the developing countries, which have become dependent on the proceeds of those sales to buy food and other commodities on world markets. If this continues, by the time these countries have grown to the point that they need mineral resources, their resources may be gone.

▶ **Growth Requires an Unfair Income Distribution and Propagates It** One cause of growth is capital accumulation. Capital investment requires saving, and saving comes mostly from the rich. The rich save more than the poor, and in the developing countries most people are poor and need to use whatever income they have for survival.

Critics also claim that the real beneficiaries of growth are the rich. Choices open to the "haves" in society are greatly enhanced, but the choices open to the "have-nots" remain severely limited. If the benefits of growth trickle down to the poor, why are there more homeless today than there were 20 years ago?

▶ **Summary: No Right Answer** We have presented the arguments for and against economic growth in simple terms. In reality, even those who take extreme positions in this debate acknowledge there is no "right answer." To suggest that all economic growth is bad is wrong; to suggest that economic growth should run unchecked is equally wrong. The question is: How can we derive the benefits of growth and at the same time minimize its undesirable consequences?

Society must make some hard choices, and there are many trade-offs. For example, we can grow faster if we pay less attention to environmental concerns. But how much environmental damage should we accept to get how much economic growth? Many

---

[5]Meadows, *Limits*, pp. 131–132.

argue that we can achieve an acceptable level of economic growth *and* protect the environment at the same time. There is also a trade-off between growth and the distribution of income. More financial inequality would probably lead to more saving and ultimately to more capital and faster growth. Using taxes and income transfers to redistribute some of the benefits of growth to the poor probably does slow the rate of growth. But it is not a question of all or nothing; society must decide how much inequality is desirable.

As long as these trade-offs exist, people will disagree. The debate in contemporary politics is largely about the costs and benefits of shifting more effort toward the goal of economic growth and away from environmental and social welfare goals.

SUMMARY

1. *Modern economic growth* is the period of rapid and sustained increase in real output per capita that began in the Western World with the Industrial Revolution.

THE GROWTH PROCESS: FROM AGRICULTURE TO INDUSTRY

2. All societies face limits imposed by the resources and technologies available to them. Economic growth expands these limits and shifts society's production possibilities frontier up and to the right.

THE SOURCES OF ECONOMIC GROWTH

3. If growth in output outpaces growth in population, and if the economic system is producing what people want, growth will increase the standard of living. Growth occurs when (1) society acquires more resources, or (2) society discovers ways of using available resources more efficiently.

4. An *aggregate production function* embodies the relationship between inputs—the labor force and the stock of capital—and total national output.

5. A number of factors contribute to *economic growth:* (1) an increase in the labor supply; (2) an increase in physical capital—plant and equipment—and/or human capital—education, training, and health; (3) an increase in productivity brought about by technological change; other advances in knowledge (managerial skills and so forth); and/or economies of scale.

GROWTH AND PRODUCTIVITY IN THE UNITED STATES

6. Modern economic growth in the United States dates to the middle of the nineteenth century. For the last 100 years, the nation's growth in real output has averaged about 3.0 percent per year. Between 1929 and 1982, about half of U.S. growth in output came from

increases in factors of production and half from increases in productivity.

7. There has been much concern that the rate of growth in the United States is slowing. The growth rate of measured labor productivity decreased from 3.7 percent in the 1960 to 1964 period to 1.1 percent in the 1985 to 1989 period.

ECONOMIC GROWTH AND PUBLIC POLICY

8. A number of public policies have been pursued with the aim of improving the growth of real output. These policies include efforts to improve the quality of education, to encourage saving, to stimulate investment, to increase research and development, and to reduce regulation. Some economists also argue for increased government involvement in the allocation of capital across manufacturing sectors, a practice known as *industrial policy*.

THE PROS AND CONS OF GROWTH

9. Advocates of growth argue that growth is progress. Growth gives us more freedom—meaning more choices. It saves time, improves the standard of living, and is the only way to improve conditions for the poor. Growth creates jobs and increases income simply because there is more to go around.

10. Those who argue against growth make four points. First, many things that affect the quality of life are not traded in the market, and these things generally lose value when there is growth. Second, to have growth, industry must cause consumers to develop new tastes and preferences for many things that they have no real need for. Third, the world has a finite quantity of resources, and rapid growth is eating them up at a rate that cannot continue. Fourth, growth requires that income be distributed inequitably.

REVIEW TERMS AND CONCEPTS

aggregate production function, 789
consumer sovereignty, 804
economic growth, 787
industrial policy, 801

infrastructure, or public capital, 794
innovation, 793
invention, 793

labor productivity, 790
modern economic growth, 787
productivity of an input, 793

PROBLEM SET

1. During 1997, real GDP in the United States was growing at a rate of about 4 percent per year. The Federal Reserve was contemplating an increase in interest rates to slow the growth rate to about 2.5 percent per year. If growth is a good thing for an economy, why would the Fed try to slow it down?

2. Tables 1, 2, and 3 present some data on three hypothetical economies. Complete the tables by figuring the measured productivity of labor and the rate of output growth. What do the data tell you about the causes of economic growth? (*Hint:* How fast are *L* and *K* growing?)

TABLE 1

PERIOD	L	K	Y	Y/L	GROWTH RATE OF OUTPUT
1	1,052	3,065	4,506		
2	1,105	3,095	4,674		
3	1,160	3,126	4,842		
4	1,218	3,157	5,019		

TABLE 2

PERIOD	L	K	Y	Y/L	GROWTH RATE OF OUTPUT
1	1,052	3,065	4,506		
2	1,062	3,371	4,683		
3	1,073	3,709	4,866		
4	1,084	4,079	5,055		

TABLE 3

PERIOD	L	K	Y	Y/L	GROWTH RATE OF OUTPUT
1	1,052	3,065	4,506		
2	1,062	3,095	4,731		
3	1,073	3,126	4,967		
4	1,084	3,157	5,216		

3. Between 1995 and 1998, according to the Departments of Commerce and Labor, measured productivity growth (the increase in Y/L) was less than the rate of growth of real output (the increase in Y). Explain this seeming paradox. Be specific. Provide any statistical evidence to support your theory.

4. One of the provisions of the Taxpayer Relief Act of 1997 was a reduction in the rate of income taxation on capital gains to 20 percent from 28 percent. The hope is that lower capital gains taxation will lead to a higher rate of growth. How might a lower rate of tax on capital gains affect household behavior? Firm behavior? In what ways are these changes in behavior likely or not likely to lead to more growth?

5. In earlier chapters, you learned that aggregate expenditure (C + I + G) must equal aggregate output for the economy to be in equilibrium. You also saw that when consumption spending rises, C + I + G increases, inventories fall, and aggregate output rises. Thus, policies that simultaneously increase consumer spending and reduce saving would lead to a higher level of GDP. In this chapter, we have argued that a higher saving rate, even with lower consumption spending, is the key to long-run GDP growth. How can both arguments be correct?

6. Suppose you have just been elected to Congress and you find yourself on the Ways and Means Committee—the committee in the House that decides on tax matters. The committee is debating a bill that would make major changes in tax policy. First, the corporate tax would be lowered substantially in an effort to stimulate investment. The bill contains a 15 percent investment tax credit—firms would be able to reduce their taxes by 15 percent of the value of investment projects that they undertake. To keep revenues constant, the bill would impose a national sales tax that would raise the price of consumer goods and reduce consumption. What trade-offs do you see implied in this bill? What are the pros and cons? How would you vote?

7. If you wanted to measure productivity (output per worker) in the following sectors over time, how would you measure "output"? How easy is it to measure productivity in each of the sectors?

a. Software
b. Vegetable farming
c. Education
d. Airline transportation

8. Economists generally agree high budget deficits today will reduce the growth rate of the economy in the future. Why? Do the reasons for the high budget deficit matter? In other words, does it matter whether the deficit is caused by lower taxes, increased defense spending, more job-training programs, and so on?

9. Why can growth lead to a more unequal distribution of income? Assuming this is true, how is it possible for the poor to benefit from economic growth?

TAKE IT TO THE NET

 We invite you to visit the Case and Fair page on the Prentice Hall Web site:

http://www.prenhall.com/casefair

for this chapter's World Wide Web exercise.

NEW IDEAS ABOUT ECONOMIC GROWTH

The data reported for the U.S. economy during the current expansion continues to confound traditional theories about the way mature economies are supposed to behave. In 1997 real GDP grew by nearly 4 percent over the year, the strongest annual rate of growth in nearly a decade. Even more surprising was that, during that same year, the GDP price index rose by less than 2 percent, the smallest annual rate of inflation since 1964, whereas the overall unemployment rate for 1997 was 4.9 percent, its lowest annual average since 1973.

Traditional economic theory about the business cycle says that tight labor markets are supposed to lead to higher prices, which then leads the Federal Reserve to raise interest rates and slow down the expansion, or even bring about a modest recession. But few economists are predicting anything like a traditional boom-bust cycle for the U.S. economy in the near future. In fact, more and more economists are coming to believe that we've entered a new era of economic growth—one in which the traditional theories no longer apply.

One of the key differences underlying this expansion has been the rapid developments in the high technology sectors of the economy, particularly in the area of computer hardware and software. According to traditional theorists, over the course of a business cycle prices rise and productivity slows as businesses bump up against their capacity constraints—that is, diminishing returns represent a speed limit to economic growth. In high-tech industries, however, although investments in microprocessor technology and computer software require large initial outlays, the costs of production and distribution are relatively small and decline over time. Such technological improvements lead to higher productivity and declining prices—a phenomenon that spreads as the new technology is adopted across industries.

Add to this increased global competitiveness and the growing importance of international financial markets and you have the seeds for a new era of economic growth. The changing complexion of the economy has led many economists to rethink their ideas about economic growth and its causes.

One of the leading proponents of what has become known as New Growth Theory is Paul Romer, an economist at Stanford University. Romer believes that the reason per capita GDP is so much higher in the United States than in other developed countries is because the United States has invested proportionately more in knowledge and discovery during the last century, leading to innovations and technological advancements that have paid significant dividends in terms of prospects

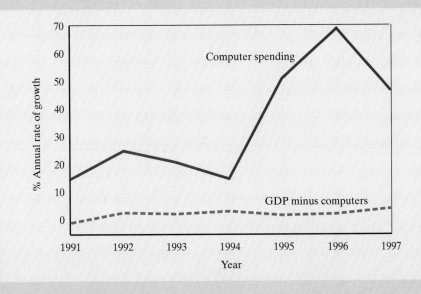

FIGURE 1

Computer Spending's Share of GDP Growth

Source: U.S. Department of Commerce, Bureau of Economic Analysis.

for long-term economic growth. Rather than focusing on the stock of capital and the supply of labor as primary determinants of growth, Romer believes that the keys to economic growth are a well-educated workforce and an adequate stock of ideas and innovation. New Growth Theory thus offers the promise of *increasing returns* as knowledge feeds on itself, enabling the rate of economic growth to actually increase over time.

Romer uses companies like Microsoft Corporation as an example of his New Growth Theory. Microsoft produces computer software—literally "bits" of information consisting of the ones and zeros that make up the instructions that make computers work. The company occupies just a handful of buildings and employs a few thousand people, yet it produces billions of dollars worth of output. Although the cost of the design and development of these computer applications was significant, the physical product itself is relatively unimportant, because it is inexpensive to replicate and can be distributed over the Internet at almost no cost. Microsoft is just one of hundreds of high-tech companies in the information processing and telecommunications industries that have accounted for roughly one-third of total GDP growth in recent years.

Questions for Analytical Thinking

1. Just as technological progress improves the prospects for employment in certain industries, it also makes other jobs obsolete. Should university professors be concerned about "technological unemployment"?

2. According to the U.S. Department of Labor, farmers and textile workers are two of the occupations projected to decline by the greatest amount between 1994 and 2005. What factors might be responsible for the decline in these occupations?

3. What sort of government policies could you recommend that might promote the growth of ideas in this country?

4. It's been argued that jobs in high-tech industries like the design of new microprocessors or computer software have a larger multiplier effect on the economy than traditional manufacturing industries like automobile production. Why?

Sources: Michael Mandel, "The New Business Cycle," *Business Week*, March 31, 1997; Thomas I. Palley, "Growth theory in a Keynesian Mode: Some Keynesian Foundations for New Endogenous Growth Theory," *Journal of Post Keynesian Economics*, Fall 1996, Vol. 19, No. 1; Paul M. Romer, "The Origins of Economic Growth," *The Journal of Economic Perspectives*, Winter 1994, Vol. 8, No. 1; Bernard Wysocki, Jr., "For Economist Paul Romer, Prosperity Depends on Ideas," *The Wall Street Journal*, January 21, 1997; U.S. Bureau of Labor Statistics, *Occupational Outlook Handbook*, available on-line at *http://www.bls.gov*.

INTERNATIONAL TRADE, COMPARATIVE ADVANTAGE, AND PROTECTIONISM

OVER THE LAST 25 YEARS, international transactions have become increasingly important to the U.S. economy. In 1970, imports represented only about 7 percent of U.S. gross domestic product. It's now around 13 percent. In 1997, the United States imported $1,058 billion worth of goods and services.

The "internationalization" or "globalization" of the U.S. economy has occurred in the private and public sectors, in input and output markets, and in business firms and households. Once uncommon, foreign products are now everywhere, from the utensils we eat with to the cars we drive. In 1970, foreign-produced cars made up only a small percentage of all the cars in the United States. At that time, it was difficult to find mechanics who knew how to repair foreign cars, and replacement parts were hard to obtain. Today the roads are full of Toyotas and Nissans from Japan, Volvos from Sweden, and BMWs from Germany, and any service station that cannot repair foreign-produced automobiles probably won't get much business. Half of all the cars and 80 percent of all the consumer electronics (televisions, CD players, and so forth) that U.S. consumers buy are produced abroad.

At the same time, the United States exports billions of dollars worth of agricultural goods, aircraft, and industrial machinery. Financial capital flows smoothly and swiftly across international boundaries in search of high returns. In 1997, for example, a downturn in some Asian economies, including Korea and Thailand, caused an outflow of international capital and a sharp decline in stock market prices.

The inextricable connection of the U.S. economy to the economies of the rest of the world has had a profound impact on the discipline of economics and is the basis of one of its most important insights:

All economies, regardless of their size, depend to some extent on other economies and are affected by events outside their borders.

TABLE 35.1

U.S. BALANCE OF
TRADE (EXPORTS
MINUS IMPORTS),
1929 TO 1997 (BILLIONS
OF DOLLARS)

	EXPORTS MINUS IMPORTS
1929	+0.4
1933	+0.1
1945	−0.9
1955	+0.4
1960	+2.4
1965	+3.9
1970	+1.2
1975	+13.6
1976	−2.3
1977	−23.7
1978	−26.1
1979	−24.0
1980	−14.9
1981	−15.0
1982	−20.5
1983	−51.7
1984	−102.0
1985	−114.2
1986	−131.5
1987	−142.1
1988	−106.1
1989	−80.4
1990	−71.3
1991	−20.5
1992	−29.5
1993	−60.7
1994	−90.9
1995	−86.0
1996	−94.8
1997	−101.1

Source: U.S. Department of Commerce, Bureau of Economic Analysis.

trade surplus *The situation when a country exports more than it imports.*

trade deficit *The situation when a country imports more than it exports.*

Corn Laws *The tariffs, subsidies, and restrictions enacted by the British Parliament in the early nineteenth century to discourage imports and encourage exports of grain.*

To get you more acquainted with the international economy, this chapter discusses the economics of international trade. First, we describe the recent tendency of the United States to import more than it exports. Next, we explore the basic logic of trade. Why should the United States or any other country engage in international trade? Finally, we address the controversial issue of protectionism. Should a country provide certain industries with protection in the form of import quotas, tariffs, or subsidies?

TRADE SURPLUSES AND DEFICITS

Until the 1970s, the United States generally exported more than it imported. When a country exports more than it imports, it runs a **trade surplus**. When a country imports more than it exports, it runs a **trade deficit**. Table 35.1 shows that before 1975 the United States generally ran a trade surplus. This changed in 1976, and since 1976 the United States has run a trade deficit. The deficit reached a peak of $142.1 billion in 1987, fell to $20.5 billion in 1991, and then rose again to $101.1 billion in 1997.

The large trade deficits in the middle and late 1980s touched off political controversy that continues today. Foreign competition hit U.S. markets hard. Less expensive foreign goods—among them steel, textiles, and automobiles—began driving U.S. manufacturers out of business, and thousands of jobs were lost in important industries. Cities such as Pittsburgh, Youngstown, and Detroit had major unemployment problems.

The natural reaction was to call for protection of U.S. industries. Many people wanted the president and Congress to impose taxes and import restrictions that would make foreign goods less available and more expensive, protecting U.S. jobs. This argument was not new. For hundreds of years, industries have petitioned governments for protection, and societies have debated the pros and cons of free and open trade. For the last century and a half, the principal argument against protection has been the theory of comparative advantage, first discussed in chapter 2.

THE ECONOMIC BASIS FOR TRADE: COMPARATIVE ADVANTAGE

Perhaps the best-known debate on the issue of free trade took place in the British Parliament during the early years of the nineteenth century. At that time, the landed gentry—the landowners—controlled Parliament. For a number of years, imports and exports of grain had been subject to a set of tariffs, subsidies, and restrictions collectively called the **Corn Laws**. Designed to discourage imports of grain and encourage exports, the Corn Laws' purpose was to keep the price of food high. The landlords' incomes, of course, depended on the prices they got for what their land produced. The Corn Laws clearly worked to the advantage of those in power.

With the Industrial Revolution, a class of wealthy industrial capitalists began to emerge. The industrial sector had to pay workers at least enough to live on, and a living wage depended greatly on the price of food. Tariffs on grain imports and export subsidies that kept grain and food prices high increased the wages that capitalists had to pay, cutting into their profits. The political battle raged for years. But as time went by, the power of the landowners in the House of Lords was significantly reduced. When the conflict ended in 1848, the Corn Laws were repealed.

On the side of repeal was David Ricardo, a businessman, economist, member of Parliament, and one of the fathers of modern economics. Ricardo's principal work, *Principles of Political Economy and Taxation*, was published in 1817, two years before he entered Parliament. Ricardo's **theory of comparative advantage**, which he used to argue against the Corn Laws, claimed that trade enables countries to specialize in producing the products they produce best. According to the theory:

> Specialization and free trade will benefit all trading partners (real wages will rise), even those that may be absolutely less efficient producers.

This basic argument remains at the heart of free-trade debates even today. It was invoked numerous times by Presidents Reagan and Bush as they wrestled with Congress over various pieces of protectionist legislation.

▶ **Specialization and Trade: The Two-Person Case** The easiest way to understand the theory of comparative advantage is to examine a simple two-person society. Suppose Bill and Colleen, stranded on a deserted island in chapter 2, have only two tasks to accomplish each week: gathering food to eat and cutting logs that will be used in constructing a house. If Colleen could cut more logs than Bill in a day and Bill could gather more berries and fruits, specialization would clearly benefit both of them.

But suppose Bill is slow and clumsy and Colleen is better at both cutting logs *and* gathering food. Ricardo's point is that it still pays for them to specialize. They can produce more in total by specializing than they can by sharing the work equally. (It may be helpful to review the discussion of comparative advantage in chapter 2 before proceeding.)

ABSOLUTE ADVANTAGE VERSUS COMPARATIVE ADVANTAGE

A country enjoys an **absolute advantage** over another country in the production of a product if it uses fewer resources to produce that product than the other country does. Suppose country A and country B produce wheat, but A's climate is more suited to wheat and its labor is more productive. Country A will produce more wheat per acre than country B and use less labor in growing it and bringing it to market. Country A enjoys an absolute advantage over country B in the production of wheat.

A country enjoys a **comparative advantage** in the production of a good if that good can be produced at lower cost *in terms of other goods*. Suppose countries C and D both produce wheat and corn and C enjoys an absolute advantage in the production of both—that is, C's climate is better than D's, and fewer of C's resources are needed to produce a given quantity of both wheat and corn. Now C and D must each choose between planting land with either wheat or corn. To produce more wheat, either country must transfer land from corn production; to produce more corn, either country must transfer land from wheat production. The cost of wheat in each country can be measured in bushels of corn, and the cost of corn can be measured in bushels of wheat.

Suppose that in country C, a bushel of wheat has an opportunity cost of two bushels of corn. That is, to produce an additional bushel of wheat, C must give up two bushels of corn. At the same time, producing a bushel of wheat in country D requires the sacrifice of only one bushel of corn. Even though C has an *absolute* advantage in the production of both products, D enjoys a *comparative* advantage in the production of wheat because the *opportunity cost* of producing wheat is lower in D. Under these circumstances, Ricardo claims, D can benefit from trade if it specializes in the production of wheat.

▶ **Gains from Mutual Absolute Advantage** To illustrate Ricardo's logic in more detail, suppose Australia and New Zealand each have a fixed amount of land and do not trade with the rest of the world. There are only two goods—wheat, to produce bread, and cotton, to produce clothing. This kind of two-country/two-good world does not exist, but its operations can be generalized to many countries and many goods.

To proceed, we have to make some assumptions about the preferences of the people living in New Zealand and the people living in Australia. If the citizens of both countries go around naked, there is no need to produce cotton; all the land can be used to produce wheat. However, assume that people in both countries have similar preferences

TABLE 35.2　YIELD PER ACRE OF WHEAT AND COTTON

	NEW ZEALAND	AUSTRALIA
Wheat	6 bushels	2 bushels
Cotton	2 bales	6 bales

Australia and New Zealand are more heavily trade dependent than the United States. In 1995 trade accounted for 40% of GDP in Australia and 62% of GDP in New Zealand.

Source: World Bank, *World Development Report 1997.*

with respect to food and clothing: The populations of both countries use both cotton and wheat. And preferences for food and clothing are such that both countries consume equal amounts of wheat and cotton.

Finally, we assume that each country has only 100 acres of land for planting and land yields are given in Table 35.2. New Zealand can produce three times the wheat that Australia can on one acre of land, and Australia can produce three times the cotton that New Zealand can in the same space. New Zealand has an absolute advantage in the production of wheat, and Australia has an absolute advantage in the production of cotton. In cases like this, we say the two countries have *mutual absolute advantage.*

If there is no trade and each country divides its land to obtain equal units of cotton and wheat production, each country produces 150 bushels of wheat and 150 bales of cotton. New Zealand puts 75 acres into cotton but only 25 acres into wheat, while Australia does the reverse. (See Table 35.3.)

We can organize the same information in graphical form as production possibility frontiers for each country. In Figure 35.1, which presents the positions of the two countries before trade, each country is constrained by its own resources and productivity. If Australia put all its land into cotton, it would produce 600 bales of cotton (100 acres × 6 bales/acre) and no wheat; if it put all its land into wheat, it would produce 200 bushels of wheat (100 acres × 2 bushels/acre) and no cotton. The opposite is true for New Zealand. Recall from chapter 2, a country's production possibility frontier represents all combinations of goods that can be produced, given the country's resources and state of technology. Each country must pick a point along its own production possibility curve.

Because both countries have an absolute advantage in the production of one product, specialization and trade will benefit both. Australia should produce cotton, New Zealand should produce wheat. Transferring all land to wheat production in New Zealand yields 600 bushels; transferring all land to cotton production in Australia yields 600 bales. An agreement to trade 300 bushels of wheat for 300 bales of cotton would double both wheat and cotton consumption in both countries. (Remember, before trade both countries produced 150 bushels of wheat and 150 bales of cotton. After trade, each country will have 300 bushels of wheat and 300 bales of cotton to consume. Final production and trade figures are in Table 35.4 and Figure 35.2.)

Trade enables both countries to move beyond their previous resource and productivity constraints.

TABLE 35.3　TOTAL PRODUCTION OF WHEAT AND COTTON ASSUMING NO TRADE, MUTUAL ABSOLUTE ADVANTAGE, AND 100 AVAILABLE ACRES

	NEW ZEALAND	AUSTRALIA
Wheat	25 acres × 6 bushels/acre 150 bushels	75 acres × 2 bushels/acre 150 bushels
Cotton	75 acres × 2 bales/acre 150 bales	25 acres × 6 bales/acre 150 bales

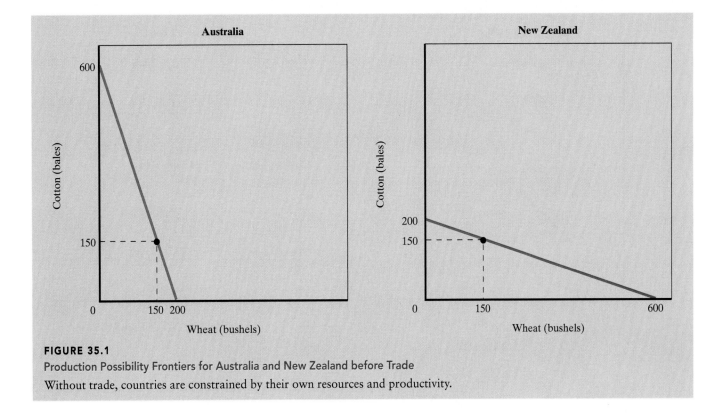

FIGURE 35.1

Production Possibility Frontiers for Australia and New Zealand before Trade

Without trade, countries are constrained by their own resources and productivity.

The advantages of specialization and trade seem obvious when one country is technologically superior at producing one product and another country is technologically superior at producing another product. But, let us turn to the case in which one country has an absolute advantage in the production of *both* goods.

➤ **Gains from Comparative Advantage** Table 35.5 contains different land yield figures for New Zealand and Australia. Now New Zealand has a considerable absolute advantage in the production of both cotton and wheat, with one acre of land yielding six times as much wheat and twice as much cotton as one acre in Australia. Ricardo would argue that *specialization and trade are still mutually beneficial.*

Again, preferences imply consumption of equal units of cotton and wheat in both countries. With no trade, New Zealand would divide its 100 available acres evenly, or 50/50, between the two crops. The result would be 300 bales of cotton and 300 bushels of wheat. Australia would divide its land 75/25. Table 35.6 shows that final production in Australia would be 75 bales of cotton and 75 bushels of wheat. (Remember, we are assuming that in each country, people consume equal amounts of

| **TABLE 35.4** | **PRODUCTION AND CONSUMPTION OF WHEAT AND COTTON AFTER SPECIALIZATION** |

| | PRODUCTION | | | CONSUMPTION | |
	New Zealand	Australia		New Zealand	Australia
Wheat	100 acres × 6 bu/acre 600 bushels	0 acres 0	Wheat	300 bushels	300 bushels
Cotton	0 acres 0	100 acres × 6 bales/acre 600 bales	Cotton	300 bales	300 bales

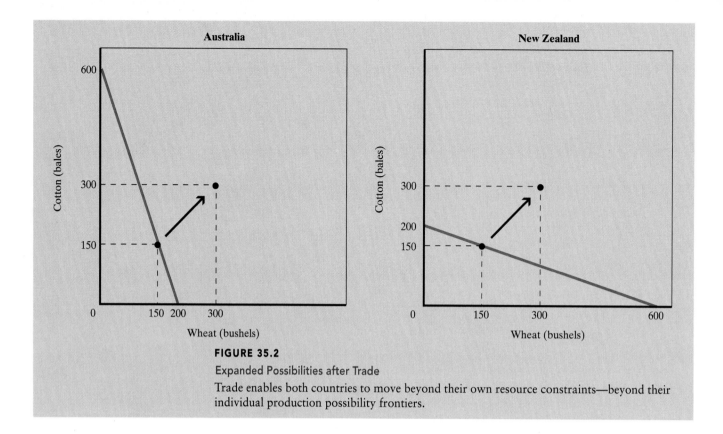

FIGURE 35.2

Expanded Possibilities after Trade

Trade enables both countries to move beyond their own resource constraints—beyond their individual production possibility frontiers.

cotton and wheat.) Again, before any trade takes place each country is constrained by its own domestic production possibilities curve.

Imagine we are at a meeting of trade representatives of both countries. As a special adviser, David Ricardo is asked to demonstrate that trade can benefit both countries. He divides his demonstration into three stages, which you can follow in Table 35.7.

In stage 1, Australia transfers all its land into cotton production. It will have no wheat and 300 bales of cotton. New Zealand cannot completely specialize in wheat because it needs 300 bales of cotton and will not be able to get enough cotton from Australia. This is because we are assuming that each country wants to consume equal amounts of cotton and wheat.

In stage 2 New Zealand transfers 25 acres out of cotton and into wheat. Now New Zealand has 25 acres in cotton that produce 150 bales and 75 acres in wheat that produce 450 bushels.

Finally, the two countries trade. We assume New Zealand ships 100 bushels of wheat to Australia in exchange for 200 bales of cotton. After the trade, New Zealand has 350 bales of cotton and 350 bushels of wheat; Australia has 100 bales of cotton and 100 bushels of wheat. Both countries are better off than they were before the trade (Table 35.6), and both have moved beyond their own production possibility frontiers.

TABLE 35.5 YIELD PER ACRE OF WHEAT AND COTTON

	NEW ZEALAND	AUSTRALIA
Wheat	6 bushels	1 bushel
Cotton	6 bales	3 bales

TABLE 35.6 TOTAL PRODUCTION OF WHEAT AND COTTON ASSUMING NO TRADE AND 100 AVAILABLE ACRES

	NEW ZEALAND	AUSTRALIA
Wheat	50 acres × 6 bushels/acre 300 bushels	75 acres × 1 bushels/acre 75 bushels
Cotton	50 acres × 6 bales/acre 300 bales	25 acres × 3 bales/acre 75 bales

➤ **Why Does Ricardo's Plan Work?**   To understand why Ricardo's scheme works, let us return to the definition of comparative advantage.

The real cost of producing cotton is the wheat that must be sacrificed to produce it. *When we think of cost this way, it is less costly to produce cotton in Australia than to produce it in New Zealand, even though an acre of land produces more cotton in New Zealand.* Consider the "cost" of three bales of cotton in the two countries. In terms of opportunity cost, three bales of cotton in New Zealand cost three bushels of wheat; in Australia, three bales of cotton cost only one bushel of wheat. Because three bales are produced by one acre of Australian land, to get three bales an Australian must transfer one acre of land from wheat to cotton production. And because an acre of land produces a bushel of wheat, losing one acre to cotton implies the loss of one bushel of wheat. *Australia has a comparative advantage in cotton production* because its opportunity cost, in terms of wheat, is lower than New Zealand's. This is illustrated in Figure 35.3.

Conversely, New Zealand has a comparative advantage in wheat production. A unit of wheat in New Zealand costs one unit of cotton; a unit of wheat in Australia costs three units of cotton.

> When countries specialize in producing goods in which they have a comparative advantage, they maximize their combined output and allocate their resources more efficiently.

TABLE 35.7 REALIZING A GAIN FROM TRADE WHEN ONE COUNTRY HAS A DOUBLE ABSOLUTE ADVANTAGE

	STAGE 1			STAGE 2	
	NEW ZEALAND	AUSTRALIA		NEW ZEALAND	AUSTRALIA
Wheat	50 acres × 6 bushels/acre 300 bushels	0 acres 0	Wheat	75 acres × 6 bushels/acre 450 bushels	0 acres 0
Cotton	50 acres × 6 bales/acre 300 bales	100 acres × 3 bales/acre 300 bales	Cotton	25 acres × 6 bales/acre 150 bales	100 acres × 3 bales/acre 300 bales

	STAGE 3	
	NEW ZEALAND	AUSTRALIA
Wheat	100 bushels (trade) ⟶ 350 bushels	100 bushels (after trade)
Cotton	200 bales (trade) ⟵ 350 bales	100 bales (after trade)

FIGURE 35.3

Comparative Advantage Means Lower Opportunity Cost

The real cost of cotton is the wheat sacrificed to obtain it. The cost of three bales of cotton in New Zealand is three bushels of wheat (one-half acre of land must be transferred from wheat to cotton—refer to Table 35.5). But the cost of three bales of cotton in Australia is only one bushel of wheat. Australia has a comparative advantage over New Zealand in cotton production, and New Zealand has a comparative advantage over Australia in wheat production.

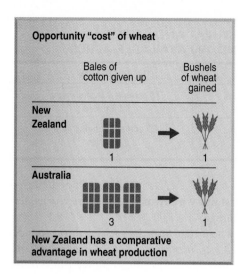

Opportunity "cost" of wheat

New Zealand has a comparative advantage in wheat production

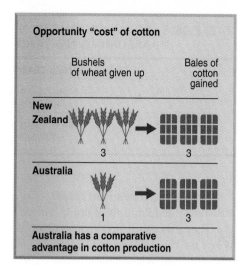

Opportunity "cost" of cotton

Australia has a comparative advantage in cotton production

TERMS OF TRADE

Ricardo might suggest a number of options open to the trading partners. The one we just examined benefited both partners; in percentage terms, Australia made out slightly better. Other deals might have been more advantageous to New Zealand.

terms of trade *The ratio at which a country can trade domestic products for imported products.*

The ratio at which a country can trade domestic products for imported products is the **terms of trade**. The terms of trade determine how the gains from trade are distributed among trading partners. In the case just considered, the agreed-upon terms of trade were one bushel of wheat for two bales of cotton. Such terms of trade benefit New Zealand, which can get two bales of cotton for each bushel of wheat. If it were to transfer its own land from wheat to cotton, it would get only one. The same terms of trade benefit Australia, which can get one bushel of wheat for two bales of cotton. A direct transfer of its own land would force it to give up three bales of cotton for one bushel of wheat.

If the terms of trade changed to three bales of cotton for every bushel of wheat, only New Zealand would benefit. At those terms of trade *all* the gains from trade would flow to New Zealand. Such terms do not benefit Australia at all because the opportunity cost of producing wheat domestically is *exactly the same* as the trade cost: One bushel of wheat costs three bales of cotton. If the terms of trade went the other way—one bale of cotton for each bushel of wheat—only Australia would benefit. New Zealand gains nothing, because it can already substitute cotton for wheat at that ratio. To get a bushel of wheat domestically, however, Australia must give up three bales of cotton, and one-for-one terms of trade would make wheat much less costly for Australia.

Both parties must have something to gain for trade to take place. In this case, you can see that both Australia and New Zealand will gain when the terms of trade are set between 1:1 and 3:1, cotton to wheat.

EXCHANGE RATES

The examples we have used thus far have shown that trade can result in gains to both parties. We have not yet discussed how trade actually comes about.

When trade is free—unimpeded by government-instituted barriers—patterns of trade and trade flows result from the independent decisions of thousands of importers and exporters and millions of private households and firms.

Private households decide whether to buy Toyotas or Chevrolets, and private firms decide whether to buy machine tools made in the United States or machine tools made in Taiwan, raw steel produced in Germany or raw steel produced in Pittsburgh.

Before a citizen of one country can buy a product made in, or sold by, someone in another country, a currency swap must take place. Consider Shane, who buys a Volkswagen from a dealer in Boston. He pays in dollars, but the German workers who made the car receive their salaries in deutsche marks. Somewhere between the buyer of the car and the producer, a currency exchange must be made. The regional distributor probably takes payment in dollars and converts them into marks before remitting the proceeds to Germany.

To buy a foreign-produced good, then, I in effect have to buy foreign currency. The price of Shane's Volkswagen in dollars depends on both the price of the car stated in deutsche marks and the price of deutsche marks. You probably know the ins and outs of currency exchange very well if you have ever traveled in another country. In December 1987, a dollar exchanged for 5.9 French francs, making each franc worth $0.168. Now suppose that you are in France, and you see a nice bottle of Bordeaux wine for 120 francs. How can you figure out whether you want to buy it? You know what dollars will buy you in the United States, so you have to convert the price into dollars. Each franc will cost you $0.168, so 120 francs is worth 120 × $0.168, or $20.16.

The attractiveness of foreign goods to U.S. buyers, and of U.S. goods to foreign buyers, depends in part on **exchange rates**, the ratio at which two currencies are traded. If the rate at which dollars could be converted into francs jumped to 10 francs for every dollar, that same bottle of wine would cost only $12.

To understand the patterns of trade that result from the actions of hundreds of thousands of independent buyers and sellers—households and firms—we must know something about the factors that determine exchange rates. Exchange rate determination is very complicated. Here, however, we can demonstrate two things:

> First, for any pair of countries, there is a range of exchange rates that can lead automatically to both countries realizing the gains from specialization and comparative advantage. Second, within that range, the exchange rate will determine which country gains the most from trade. In short, exchange rates determine the terms of trade.

exchange rate *The ratio at which two currencies are traded. The price of one currency in terms of another.*

► Trade and Exchange Rates in a Two-Country/Two-Good World

Consider first a simple two-country/two-good model. Suppose both the United States and Germany produce only two goods—raw timber and rolled steel. Table 35.8 gives the current prices of both goods as domestic buyers see them. In Germany timber is priced at 3 deutsche marks (DM) per foot, and steel is priced at 4 DM per meter. In the United States, timber costs $1 per foot and steel costs $2 per meter.

Suppose U.S. and German buyers have the option of buying at home or importing to meet their needs. The options they choose will depend on the exchange rate. For the time being, we will ignore transportation costs between countries and assume that German and U.S. products are of equal quality.

Let us start with the assumption that the exchange rate is $1 = 1 DM. From the standpoint of U.S. buyers, neither German steel nor German timber is competitive at this exchange rate. A dollar buys a foot of timber in the United States, but if converted into a mark, it will buy only one third of a foot. The price of German timber to an American is $3 because it will take $3 to buy the necessary three DM. Similarly, $2 buys a meter of rolled steel in the United States, but the same $2 buys only half a meter of German steel. The price of German steel to an American is $4, twice the price of domestically produced steel.

At this exchange rate, however, Germans find that U.S.-produced steel and timber are both less expensive than steel and timber produced in Germany. Timber at

TABLE 35.8

DOMESTIC PRICES OF TIMBER (PER FOOT) AND ROLLED STEEL (PER METER) IN THE UNITED STATES AND GERMANY

	UNITED STATES	GERMANY
Timber	$1	3 DM
Rolled steel	$2	4 DM

home—Germany—costs 3 DM, but 3 DM buys $3, which buys three times as much timber in the United States. Similarly, steel costs 4 DM at home, but 4 DM buys $4, which buys twice as much U.S.-made steel. At an exchange rate of $1 = 1 DM, Germany will import steel and timber and the United States will import nothing.

But now suppose the exchange rate is 1 DM = $0.25. We could say the "price" of a DM is $0.25. This means a dollar buys 4 DM. At this exchange rate, the Germans buy timber and steel at home and the Americans import both goods. At this exchange rate, Americans must pay a dollar for a foot of U.S. timber, but the same amount of timber can be had in Germany for the equivalent of $0.75. (Because 1 DM costs $0.25, 3 DM can be purchased for $0.75.) Similarly, steel that costs $2 per meter in the United States costs an American half as much in Germany, because $2 buys 8 DM, which buys two meters of German steel. At the same time, Germans are not interested in importing, because both goods are cheaper when purchased from a German producer. In this case, the United States imports both goods and Germany imports nothing.

So far, we can see that at exchange rates of $1 = 1 DM and $1 = 4 DM we get trade flowing in only one direction. Let's now try an exchange rate of $1 = 2 DM, or 1 DM = $0.50. First, Germans will buy timber in the United States. German timber costs 3 DM per foot, but 3 DM buys $1.50, which is enough to buy one and one half feet of U.S. timber. Buyers in the United States will find German timber too expensive, but Germany will import timber from the United States. At this same exchange rate, however, both German and U.S. buyers will be indifferent between German and U.S. steel. To U.S. buyers, domestically produced steel costs $2. Because $2 buys 4 DM, a meter of imported German steel also costs $2. German buyers also find that steel costs 4 DM, whether domestically produced or imported. Thus, there is likely to be no trade in steel.

But what happens if the exchange rate changes so that $1 buys 2.1 DM? While U.S. timber is still cheaper to both Germans and Americans, German steel begins to look good to U.S. buyers. Steel produced in the United States costs $2 per meter, but $2 buys 4.2 DM, which buys more than a meter of steel in Germany. When $1 buys more than 2 DM, trade begins to flow in both directions: Germany will import timber and the United States will import steel.

If you examine Table 35.9 carefully, you will see that trade flows in both directions as long as the exchange rate settles between $1 = 2 DM and $1 = 3 DM. Stated the other way around, trade will flow in both directions if the price of a DM is between $0.33 and $0.50.

▶ **Exchange Rates and Comparative Advantage**   If the foreign exchange market drives the exchange rate to anywhere between 2 and 3 DM per dollar, the countries will automatically adjust and comparative advantage will be realized. At these exchange rates,

TABLE 35.9   TRADE FLOWS DETERMINED BY EXCHANGE RATES

EXCHANGE RATE	PRICE OF DM	RESULT
$1 = 1 DM	$ 1.00	Germany imports timber and steel.
$1 = 2 DM	$.50	Germany imports timber.
$1 = 2.1 DM	$.48	Germany imports timber; United States imports steel.
$1 = 2.9 DM	$.34	Germany imports timber; United States imports steel.
$1 = 3 DM	$.33	United States imports steel.
$1 = 4 DM	$.25	United States imports timber and steel.

U.S. buyers begin buying all their steel in Germany. The U.S. steel industry finds itself in trouble. Plants close, and U.S. workers begin to lobby for tariff protection against German steel. At the same time, the U.S. timber industry does well, fueled by strong export demand from Germany. The timber-producing sector expands. Resources, including capital and labor, are attracted into timber production.

The opposite occurs in Germany. The German timber industry suffers losses as export demand dries up and Germans turn to cheaper U.S. imports. In Germany, lumber companies turn to the government and ask for protection from cheap U.S. timber. But steel producers in Germany are happy. Not only are they supplying 100 percent of the domestically demanded steel, but they are selling to U.S. buyers as well. The steel industry expands, and the timber industry contracts. Resources, including labor, flow into steel.

With this expansion-and-contraction scenario in mind, let's look again at our original definition of comparative advantage. If we assume that prices reflect resource use and resources can be transferred from sector to sector, we can calculate the opportunity cost of steel/timber in both countries. In the United States, the production of a meter of rolled steel consumes twice the resources that the production of a foot of timber consumes. Assuming that resources can be transferred, the opportunity cost of a meter of steel is two feet of timber (Table 35.8). In Germany, a meter of steel uses resources costing 4 DM, while a unit of timber costs 3 DM. To produce a meter of steel means the sacrifice of only four thirds, or one and one third, feet of timber. Because the opportunity cost of a meter of steel (in terms of timber) is lower in Germany, we say Germany has a comparative advantage in steel production.

Conversely, consider the opportunity cost of timber in the two countries. Increasing timber production in the United States requires the sacrifice of half a meter of steel for every foot of timber—producing a meter of steel uses $2 worth of resources, while producing a foot of timber requires only $1 worth of resources. But each foot of timber production in Germany requires the sacrifice of three fourths of a meter of steel. Because the opportunity cost of timber is lower in the United States, the United States has a comparative advantage in the production of timber.

> If exchange rates end up in the right ranges, the free market will drive each country to shift resources into those sectors in which it enjoys a comparative advantage. Only those products in which a country has a comparative advantage will be competitive in world markets.

THE SOURCES OF COMPARATIVE ADVANTAGE

Specialization and trade can benefit all trading partners, even those that may be inefficient producers in an absolute sense. If markets are competitive, and if foreign exchange markets are linked to goods-and-services exchange, countries will specialize in producing products in which they have a comparative advantage.

So far, we have said nothing about the sources of comparative advantage. What determines whether a country has a comparative advantage in heavy manufacturing or in agriculture? What explains the actual trade flows observed around the world? Various theories and empirical work on international trade have provided some answers. Most economists look to **factor endowments**—the quantity and quality of labor, land, and natural resources—as the principal sources of comparative advantage. Factor endowments seem to explain a significant portion of actual world trade patterns.

THE HECKSCHER-OHLIN THEOREM

Eli Heckscher and Bertil Ohlin, two Swedish economists who wrote in the first half of this century, expanded and elaborated on Ricardo's theory of comparative advantage. The **Heckscher-Ohlin theorem** ties the theory of comparative advantage to factor

factor endowments *The quantity and quality of labor, land, and natural resources of a country.*

Heckscher-Ohlin theorem *A theory that explains the existence of a country's comparative advantage by its factor endowments: A country has a comparative advantage in the production of a product if that country is relatively well endowed with inputs used intensively in the production of that product.*

endowments. It assumes that products can be produced using differing proportions of inputs and that inputs are mobile between sectors in each economy, but that factors are not mobile *between* economies. According to this theorem:

> A country has a comparative advantage in the production of a product if that country is relatively well endowed with inputs used intensively in the production of that product.

This idea is simple. A country with a lot of good fertile land is likely to have a comparative advantage in agriculture. A country with a large amount of accumulated capital is likely to have a comparative advantage in heavy manufacturing. A country with a lot of human capital is likely to have a comparative advantage in highly technical goods.

After an extensive study, Edward Leamer of UCLA has concluded that a short list of factors accounts for a large portion of world trade patterns. Natural resources, knowledge capital, physical capital, land, and skilled and unskilled labor, Leamer believes, explain "a large amount of the variability of net exports across countries."[1]

OTHER EXPLANATIONS FOR OBSERVED TRADE FLOWS

Comparative advantage is not the only reason countries trade. It does not explain why many countries both import and export the same kinds of goods. The United States, for example, both exports and imports automobiles.

And, just as industries within a country differentiate their products to capture a domestic market, so too do they differentiate their products to please the wide variety of tastes that exists worldwide. The Japanese automobile industry, for example, began producing small, fuel-efficient cars long before U.S. automobile makers did. In doing so, they developed expertise in creating products that attracted a devoted following and considerable brand loyalty. BMWs, made only in Germany, and Volvos, made only in Sweden, also have their champions in many countries. Just as product differentiation is a natural response to diverse preferences within an economy, it is also a natural response to diverse preferences across economies.

This idea is not inconsistent with the theory of comparative advantage. If the Japanese have developed skills and knowledge that gave them an edge in the production of fuel-efficient cars, that knowledge can be thought of as a very specific kind of capital not currently available to other producers. The Volvo company invested in a form of intangible capital that we call *goodwill*. That goodwill, which may come from establishing a reputation for safety and quality over the years, is one source of the comparative advantage that keeps Volvos selling on the international market. Some economists distinguish between gains from *acquired comparative advantages* and those from *natural comparative advantages*.

Another explanation for international trade is that some economies of scale may be available when producing for a world market that would not be available when producing for a more limited domestic market. But because the evidence suggests that economies of scale are exhausted at relatively small size in most industries, it seems unlikely that they constitute a valid explanation of world trade patterns.

TRADE BARRIERS: TARIFFS, EXPORT SUBSIDIES, AND QUOTAS

protection *The practice of shielding a sector of the economy from foreign competition.*

Trade barriers—also called *obstacles to trade*—take many forms; the three most common are tariffs, export subsidies, and quotas. All are forms of **protection** shielding some sector of the economy from foreign competition.

[1]Edward E. Leamer, *Sources of International Comparative Advantage: Theory and Evidence* (Cambridge, Mass: MIT Press, 1984), p. 187.

A **tariff** is a tax on imports. The average tariff on imports into the United States is about 5 percent. Certain protected items have much higher tariffs. For example, the tariff rate on concentrated orange juice is a flat $0.35 per gallon. On rubber footwear, the tariff ranges from 20 percent to 48 percent, and on canned tuna it is 35 percent.

Export subsidies—government payments made to domestic firms to encourage exports—can also act as a barrier to trade. One of the provisions of the Corn Laws that stimulated Ricardo's musings was an export subsidy automatically paid to farmers by the British government when the price of grain fell below a specified level. The subsidy served to keep domestic prices high, but it flooded the world market with cheap subsidized grain. Foreign farmers who were not subsidized were driven out of the international marketplace by the artificially low prices.

Farm subsidies remain a part of the international trade landscape today. Many countries, especially in Europe, continue to appease their farmers by heavily subsidizing exports of agricultural products. The political power of the farm lobby in many countries has had an important effect on recent international trade negotiations aimed at reducing trade barriers.

Closely related to subsidies is **dumping**. Dumping takes place when a firm or an industry sells products on the world market at prices *below* the cost of production. The charge has been leveled against several specific Japanese industries, including automobiles, consumer electronics, and silicon computer chips.

Generally, a company dumps when it wants to dominate a world market. After the lower prices of the dumped goods have succeeded in driving out all the competition, the dumping company can exploit its position by raising the price of its product. A U.S. firm attempting to monopolize a domestic market violates the Sherman Antitrust Act of 1890, prohibiting predatory pricing.

The current U.S. tariff laws contain several provisions aimed at counteracting the effects of dumping. The 1974 Trade Act contains a clause that qualifies an industry for protection if it has been "injured" by foreign competition. Building on that legislation, more recent trade bills, including the Comprehensive Trade Act of 1988, contain clauses that permit the president to impose trade sanctions when investigations reveal dumping by foreign companies or countries.

A **quota** is a limit on the quantity of imports. Quotas can be mandatory or voluntary, and they may be legislated or negotiated with foreign governments. The best-known voluntary quota, or "voluntary restraint," was negotiated with the Japanese government in 1981. Japan agreed to reduce its automobile exports to the United States by 7.7 percent, from the 1980 level of 1.82 million units to 1.68 million units. In 1985, President Reagan decided not to ask Japan to continue its restraints—auto imports jumped to 2.3 million units, nearly 20 percent of the U.S. market. Quotas currently apply to products like mushrooms, heavy motorcycles, and color TVs.

▶ **U.S. Trade Policies and GATT** The United States has been a high-tariff nation, with average tariffs of over 50 percent for much of its history. The highest were in effect during the Great Depression following the **Smoot-Hawley tariff**, which pushed the average tariff rate to 60 percent in 1930. The Smoot-Hawley tariff set off an international trade war when U.S. trading partners retaliated with tariffs of their own. Many economists say the decline in trade that followed was one of the causes of the worldwide depression of the 1930s.[2]

In 1947 the United States, with 22 other nations, agreed to reduce barriers to trade. It also established an organization to promote liberalization of foreign trade. This **General Agreement on Tariffs and Trade (GATT)**, at first considered to be an interim arrangement, continues today and has been quite effective. The most recent round of world trade talks sponsored by GATT, the "Uruguay Round," began in

tariff *A tax on imports.*

export subsidies *Government payments made to domestic firms to encourage exports.*

dumping *A firm or industry sells products on the world market at prices below the cost of production.*

quota *A limit on the quantity of imports.*

Smoot-Hawley tariff *The U.S. tariff law of the 1930s, which set the highest tariffs in U.S. history (60 percent). It set off an international trade war and caused the decline in trade that is often considered a cause of the worldwide depression of the 1930s.*

General Agreement on Tariffs and Trade (GATT) *An international agreement signed by the United States and 22 other countries in 1947 to promote the liberalization of foreign trade.*

---

[2]See especially Charles Kindleberger, *The World in Depression 1929–1939* (London: Allen Lane, 1973).

Uruguay in 1986. It was initialed by 116 countries on December 15, 1993, and was formally approved by the U.S. Congress after much debate following the election in 1994. The "Final Act" of the Uruguay Round of negotiations is the most comprehensive and complex multilateral trade agreement in history. See Global Perspective "A New World Trade Agreement: GATT and the Final Act."

Every president who has held office since the first round of the General Agreement was signed has argued for free-trade policies, yet each used his powers to protect one sector or another. Eisenhower and Kennedy restricted U.S. imports of Japanese textiles; Johnson restricted meat imports; Nixon restrained imports of steel and tightened restrictions on textiles; Carter protected steel, textiles, and footwear; Reagan restricted imports of sugar and automobiles. Both Bush and Clinton imposed new tariffs as well.

Nevertheless, the movement in the United States has been away from tariffs and quotas and toward freer trade. The Reciprocal Trade Agreements Act of 1934 authorized the president to negotiate trade agreements on behalf of the United States. As part of trade negotiations, the president can confer *most-favored-nation status* on individual trading partners. Imports from countries with most-favored-nation status are taxed at the lowest negotiated tariff rates. In addition, in recent years several successful rounds of tariff-reduction negotiations have reduced trade barriers to their lowest levels ever.

economic integration *Occurs when two or more nations join to form a free-trade zone.*

> **Economic Integration** Economic integration occurs when two or more nations join to form a free-trade zone. In 1991, the European Community (EC, or the Common Market) began forming the largest free-trade zone in the world. The economic integration process began that December, when the 12 original members (the United Kingdom, Belgium, France, Germany, Italy, the Netherlands, Luxembourg, Denmark, Greece, Ireland, Spain, and Portugal) signed the Maastricht Treaty. The treaty called for the end of border controls, a common currency, an end to all tariffs, and the coordination of monetary and even political affairs. In 1995, Austria, Finland, and Sweden became members of this **European Union (EU)**, as the EC is now called, bringing the number of member countries to 15.

European Union (EU)
The European trading bloc composed of Austria, Belgium, Denmark, Finland, France, Germany, Greece, Ireland, Italy, Luxembourg, the Netherlands, Portugal, Spain, Sweden, and the United Kingdom.

On January 1, 1993, all tariffs and trade barriers were dropped among the member countries. Border checkpoints were closed in early 1995. Citizens can now travel among member countries without passports. The most difficult step will be a common currency. The goal is to have it in place by 1999. Many economists believe the advantages of free trade within the bloc, a reunited Germany, and the ability to work well as a bloc will make the EU the most powerful player in the international marketplace in the coming decades.

The United States is not a part of the EU. However, in 1988 the United States (under President Reagan) and Canada (under Prime Minister Mulroney) signed the **U.S.-Canadian Free-Trade Agreement**, which will remove all barriers to trade, including tariffs and quotas, between the two countries by 1998.

U.S.-Canadian Free-Trade Agreement *An agreement in which the United States and Canada agreed to eliminate all barriers to trade between the two countries by 1998.*

During the last days of the Bush administration, the United States, Mexico, and Canada signed the **North American Free-Trade Agreement (NAFTA)**, the three countries agreeing to establish all of North America as a free-trade zone. The North American free-trade area will include 360 million people and a total output of over $7 trillion—larger than the output of the European Union. The agreement will eliminate all tariffs over a 10- to 15-year period and remove restrictions on most investments.

North American Free-Trade Agreement (NAFTA) *An agreement signed by the United States, Mexico, and Canada in which the three countries agreed to establish all of North America as a free-trade zone.*

During the presidential campaign of 1992, NAFTA was hotly debated. Both Bill Clinton and George Bush supported the agreement. Industrial labor unions that might be affected by increased imports from Mexico (like those in the automobile industry) opposed the agreement, while industries whose exports to Mexico might increase as a result of the agreement (for example, the machine tool industry) supported it. Another concern was that Mexican companies were not subject to the same environmental regulations as U.S. firms, so U.S. firms might move to Mexico for this reason.

NAFTA was ratified by the U.S. Congress in late 1993 and went into effect on the first day of 1994. The U.S. Department of Commerce has estimated that

A NEW WORLD TRADE AGREEMENT: GATT AND THE FINAL ACT

Launched in Punta del Este, Uruguay, in 1986, the Uruguay Round of multinational trade negotiations was concluded in Geneva on December 15, 1993, when 116 nations initialed what was called the "Final Act." In December 1994, a lame-duck U.S. Congress acted to approve the agreement for the United States.

The Final Act is a document of over 26,000 pages—the most comprehensive and complex trade agreement in history. Proponents say its implementation will increase the volume of world merchandise trade by 9 percent to 24 percent over what it would have been without the agreement.*

The provisions of the Final Act are: First, it reduces tariffs and protection for agricultural products. Throughout history, agricultural goods have been the target of high import duties, large domestic subsidies, and outright trade restrictions. In many cases this was due to the farmers' political power. Talk of reducing subsidies going to agriculture in France led, on several occasions in the last decade, to highway blockades and violent demonstrations by French farmers. The agreement calls for an end to many agricultural subsidies, an end to nontariff barriers, such as quantitative restrictions and bans, and an average tariff reduction of 37 percent on agricultural imports. In general, developed countries have agreed to reduce tariffs on 64 percent of their imports by about 40 percent, from an average rate of 6.3 percent to 3.8 percent. The percentage

of industrial imports allowed to enter the developed countries with no duties at all will increase from 20 percent to 44 percent. The developing countries have agreed to lower tariffs on about 33 percent of their imports.

Second, the Uruguay round is the first multilateral negotiation to reach a comprehensive agreement on international trade in services. It outlaws restrictions on the import of services such as banking, legal services, insurance, accounting, and computer consulting.

Third, the Final Act makes provisions for the protection of intellectual property. While existing patent and copyright laws usually protect artists, designers, computer software producers, authors, and the like from "theft" within their own countries, foreign pirating is common. Though it is usually illegal to reproduce and sell pirated CDs, videotapes, books, and computer software packages produced within a country, there were no internationally applicable rules about pirating across borders before the new agreement was signed. The new trade agreement requires all signatory countries to apply copyright and patent laws equally to foreign owners of intellectual property.

In addition, the Final Act established a Dispute Settlement Body designed to ensure compliance and to resolve conflicts between member countries. Some members of the U.S. Congress argued (in vain) that by signing the treaty the United States would be giving up its sovereignty to an international body.

THE NEW TRADE AGREEMENT REQUIRES ALL SIGNATORY COUNTRIES TO APPLY COPYRIGHT AND PATENT LAWS EQUALLY TO FOREIGN OWNERS OF INTELLECTUAL PROPERTY, SUCH AS THE CONTENT OF THE CDs AND VIDEO TAPES SHOWN HERE.

*Source: See Norman S. Fieleke, "The Uruguay Round of Trade Negotiations: An Overview," *New England Economic Review*, May–June 1995.

For more on trade agreements, see the Case and Fair Web page at **http://www.prenhall.com/casefair.**

as a result of NAFTA trade between the United States and Mexico increased by nearly $16 billion in 1994. In addition, exports from the United States to Mexico outpaced imports from Mexico during 1994. In 1995, however, the agreement fell under the shadow of a dramatic collapse of the value of the peso. U.S. exports to Mexico dropped sharply, and the United States shifted from a trade surplus to a large trade deficit with Mexico. By 1998, a general consensus emerged among economists that NAFTA had led to expanded employment opportunities on both sides of the border.

FREE TRADE OR PROTECTION?

One of the great economic debates of all time revolves around the free-trade-versus-protection controversy. We briefly summarize the arguments in favor of each.

THE CASE FOR FREE TRADE

In one sense, the theory of comparative advantage *is* the case for free trade. Trade has potential benefits for all nations. A good is not imported unless its net price to buyers is below the net price of the domestically produced alternative. When the Germans in our earlier example found U.S. timber less expensive than their own, they bought it, yet they continued to pay the same price for homemade steel. Americans bought less-expensive German steel, but they continued to buy domestic timber at the same lower price. Under these conditions, *both Americans and Germans ended up paying less and consuming more.*

At the same time, resources (including labor) move out of steel production and into timber production in the United States. In Germany, resources (including labor) move out of timber production and into steel production. The resources in both countries are more efficiently used. Tariffs, export subsidies, and quotas, which interfere with the free movement of goods and services around the world, reduce or eliminate the gains of comparative advantage.

We can use supply and demand curves to illustrate this. Suppose Figure 35.4a shows domestic supply and demand for textiles. In the absence of trade, the market clears at a price of $4.20. At equilibrium, 450 million yards of textiles are produced and consumed.

Assume now that textiles are available at a world price of $2. This is the price in dollars that Americans must pay for textiles from foreign sources. If we assume an unlimited amount of textiles is available at $2 and there is no difference in quality between domestic and foreign textiles, no domestic producer will be able to charge more than $2. In the absence of trade barriers, the world price sets the price in the United States. As the price in the United States falls from $4.20 to $2.00, the quantity demanded by consumers increases from 450 million yards to 700 million yards, but the quantity supplied by domestic producers drops from 450 million yards to 200 million yards. The difference, 500 million yards, is the quantity of textiles imported.

The argument for free trade is that each country should specialize in producing the goods and services in which it enjoys a comparative advantage. If foreign producers can produce textiles at a much lower price than domestic producers, they have a comparative advantage. As the world price of textiles falls to $2, domestic (U.S.) supply drops and resources are transferred to other sectors. These other sectors, which may be export industries or domestic industries, are not shown in Figure 35.4a. It is clear that the allocation of resources is more efficient at a price of $2. Why should the United States use domestic resources to produce what foreign producers can produce at a lower cost? U.S. resources should move into the production of the things it produces best.

Now consider what happens to the domestic price of textiles when a trade barrier is imposed. Figure 35.4b shows the effect of a set tariff of $1 per yard imposed on imported textiles. The tariff raises the domestic price of textiles to $2 + $1 = $3. The result is that some of the gains from trade are lost. First, consumers are forced to pay a higher price for the same good; the quantity of textiles demanded drops from 700 million yards under free trade to 600 million yards because some consumers are not willing to pay the higher price.

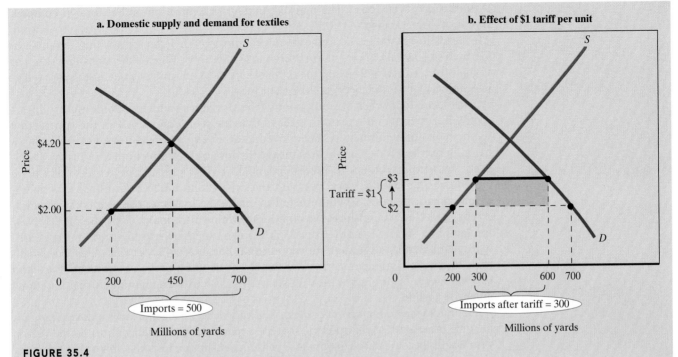

a. Domestic supply and demand for textiles

b. Effect of $1 tariff per unit

FIGURE 35.4

The Gains from Trade and Losses from the Imposition of a Tariff

A tariff of $1 increases the market price facing consumers from $2 per yard to $3 per yard. The government collects revenues equal to the gray shaded area. The loss of efficiency has two components. First, consumers must pay a higher price for goods that could be produced at lower cost. Second, marginal producers are drawn into textiles and away from other goods, resulting in inefficient domestic production.

At the same time, the higher price of textiles draws some marginal domestic producers who could not make a profit at $2 into textile production. (Recall, domestic producers do not pay a tariff.) As the price rises to $3, the quantity supplied by producers rises from 200 million yards to 300 million yards. The result is a decrease in imports from 500 million yards to 300 million yards.

Finally, the imposition of the tariff means the government collects revenue equal to the shaded gray area in Figure 35.4b. This shaded area is equal to the tariff rate per unit ($1) times the number of units imported after the tariff is in place (300 million yards). Thus, receipts from the tariff are $300 billion.

What is the final result of the tariff? Domestic producers receiving revenues of only $2 per unit before the tariff was imposed now receive a higher price and earn higher profits. But these higher profits are achieved at a loss of efficiency.

Trade barriers prevent a nation from reaping the benefits of specialization, push it to adopt relatively inefficient production techniques, and force consumers to pay higher prices for protected products than they would otherwise pay.

THE CASE FOR PROTECTION

Arguments can also be made in favor of tariffs and quotas. Over the course of U.S. history, these arguments have been made so many times by so many industries before so many congressional committees that it seems all pleas for protection share the same themes. We describe the most frequently heard pleas next.

> **Protection Saves Jobs** The main argument for protection is that foreign competition costs Americans their jobs. When Americans buy Toyotas, U.S. cars go unsold. This leads to layoffs in the domestic auto industry. When Americans buy Japanese or German steel, steelworkers in Pittsburgh lose their jobs. When Americans buy shoes or textiles from Korea or Taiwan, the millworkers in Maine and Massachusetts, as well as in South Carolina and Georgia, lose their jobs.

It is true that when we buy goods from foreign producers, domestic producers suffer. But there is no reason to believe that the workers laid off in the contracting sectors will not be ultimately reemployed in other expanding sectors. Foreign competition in textiles, for example, has meant the loss of U.S. jobs in that industry. Thousands of textile workers in New England lost their jobs as the textile mills there closed over the last 35 years. But with the expansion of high-tech industries, the unemployment rate in Massachusetts fell to one of the lowest in the country in the mid-1980s, and New Hampshire, Vermont, and Maine also boomed. By the 1990s, New England had suffered another severe downturn, due partly to high-technology hardware manufacturing that had moved abroad. But in 1994 it became clear that small-to medium-sized companies in such newly developing areas as biotechnology and software were beginning to pick up steam just as hardware manufacturing had done a decade earlier.

The adjustment is far from costless. The knowledge that some other industry, perhaps in some other part of the country, may be expanding is of little comfort to the person whose skills become obsolete or whose pension benefits are lost when his or her company abruptly closes a plant or goes bankrupt. The social and personal problems brought about by industry-specific unemployment, obsolete skills, and bankruptcy as a result of foreign competition are significant.

These problems can be addressed in two ways. We can ban imports and give up the gains from free trade, acknowledging that we are willing to pay premium prices to save domestic jobs in industries that can produce more efficiently abroad. Or we can aid the victims of free trade in a constructive way, helping to retrain them for jobs with a future. In some instances, programs to relocate people in expanding regions may be in order. Some programs deal directly with the transition without forgoing the gains from trade.

> **Some Countries Engage in Unfair Trade Practices** Attempts by U.S. firms to monopolize an industry are illegal under the Sherman and Clayton acts. If a strong company decides to drive the competition out of the market by setting prices below cost, it would be aggressively prosecuted by the Antitrust Division of the Justice Department. But, the argument goes, if we won't allow a U.S. firm to engage in predatory pricing or monopolize an industry or market, can we stand by and let a German firm or a Japanese firm do so in the name of free trade? This is a legitimate argument and one that has gained significant favor in recent years. How should we respond when a large international company or a country behaves strategically against a domestic firm or industry? Free trade may be the best solution when everybody plays by the rules, but sometimes we have to fight back.

> **Cheap Foreign Labor Makes Competition Unfair** Let's say that a particular country gained its "comparative advantage" in textiles by paying its workers low wages. How can U.S. textile companies compete with companies that pay wages that are less than a quarter of what U.S. companies pay?

First, remember that wages in a competitive economy reflect productivity. Workers in the United States earn higher wages because they are more productive. The United States has more capital per worker, and its workers are better trained. Second, trade flows not according to *absolute* advantage but according to *comparative* advantage: All countries benefit, even if one country is more efficient at producing everything.

➤ **Protection Safeguards National Security** Beyond saving jobs, certain sectors of the economy may appeal for protection for other reasons. The steel industry has argued for years with some success that it is vital to national defense. In the event of a war, the United States would not want to depend on foreign countries for products as vital as steel. Even if we acknowledge another country's comparative advantage, we may want to protect our own resources.

No industry has ever asked for protection without invoking the national defense argument. The testimony on behalf of the scissors and shears industry argued that "in the event of a national emergency and imports cutoff, the United States would be without a source of scissors and shears, basic tools for many industries and trades essential to our national defense." The question, then, lies not in the merit of the argument but in just how seriously it can be taken if *every* industry uses it.

➤ **Protection Discourages Dependency** Closely related to the national defense argument is the claim that countries, particularly small or developing countries, may come to rely too heavily on one or more trading partners for many items. If a small country comes to rely on a major power for food or energy or some important raw material in which the large nation has a comparative advantage, it may be difficult for the smaller nation to remain politically neutral. Some critics of free trade argue that the superpowers have consciously engaged in trade with smaller countries to create these kinds of dependencies.

Therefore, should small independent countries consciously avoid trading relationships that might lead to political dependence? This may involve developing domestic industries in areas where a country has a comparative disadvantage. To do so would mean protecting that industry from international competition.

➤ **Protection Safeguards Infant Industries** Young industries in a given country may have a difficult time competing with established industries in other countries. And in a dynamic world, a protected **infant industry** might mature into a strong one worldwide because of an acquired, but real, comparative advantage. If such an industry is undercut and driven out of world markets at the beginning of its life, that comparative advantage might never develop.

infant industry *A young industry that may need temporary protection from competition from the established industries of other countries in order to develop an acquired comparative advantage.*

Yet efforts to protect infant industries can backfire. In July 1991, the U.S. government imposed a 62.67 percent tariff on imports of active-matrix liquid crystal display screens (also referred to as "flat-panel displays" and primarily used for laptop computers) from Japan. The Commerce Department and the International Trade Commission agreed that Japanese producers were selling their screens in the U.S. market at a price below cost and that this "dumping" threatened the survival of domestic laptop screen producers. The tariff was meant to protect the infant U.S. industry until it could compete head-on with the Japanese.

Unfortunately for U.S. producers of laptop computers and for consumers who purchase them, the tariff had an unintended (though predictable) effect on the industry. Because U.S. laptop screens were generally recognized to be of lower quality than their Japanese counterparts, imposition of the tariff left U.S. computer manufacturers with three options: (1) They could use the screens available from U.S. producers and watch sales of their final product decline in the face of *higher quality* competition from abroad; (2) they could pay the tariff for the higher quality screens and watch sales of their final product decline in the face of *lower priced* competition from abroad; or (3) they could do what was the most profitable for them to do—move their production facilities abroad to avoid the tariff completely. The last is exactly what both Apple and IBM announced they would do. In the end, not only were the laptop industry and its consumers hurt by the imposition of the tariff (due to higher costs of production and to higher laptop computer prices), but the U.S. screen industry was hurt as well (due to its loss of buyers for its product) by a policy specifically designed to help it.

An Economic Consensus

You now know something about how international trade fits into the structure of the economy.

Critical to our study of international economics is the debate between free-traders and protectionists. On one side is the theory of comparative advantage, formalized by David Ricardo in the early part of the nineteenth century. According to this view, all countries benefit from specialization and trade. The gains from trade are real, and they can be large; free international trade raises real incomes and improves the standard of living.

On the other side are the protectionists, who point to the loss of jobs and argue for the protection of workers from foreign competition. But although foreign competition can cause job loss in specific sectors, it is unlikely to cause net job loss in an economy, and workers will over time be absorbed into expanding sectors.

> Foreign trade and full employment can be pursued simultaneously. Although economists disagree about many things, the vast majority of them favor free trade.

SUMMARY

1. All economies, regardless of their size, depend to some extent on other economies and are affected by events outside their borders.

Chapter 35

TRADE SURPLUSES AND DEFICITS

2. Until the 1970s, the United States generally exported more than it imported—it ran a *trade surplus*. In the mid-1970s, the United States began to import more merchandise than it exported—a *trade deficit*.

THE ECONOMIC BASIS FOR TRADE: COMPARATIVE ADVANTAGE

3. The *theory of comparative advantage*, dating to David Ricardo in the nineteenth century, holds that specialization and free trade will benefit all trading partners, even those that may be absolutely less efficient producers.

4. A country enjoys an *absolute advantage* over another country in the production of a product if it uses fewer resources to produce that product than the other country does. A country has a *comparative advantage* in the production of a product if that product can be produced at a lower cost in terms of other goods.

5. Trade enables countries to move beyond their previous resource and productivity constraints. When countries specialize in producing those goods in which they have a comparative advantage, they maximize their combined output and allocate their resources more efficiently.

6. When trade is free, patterns of trade and trade flows result from the independent decisions of thousands of importers and exporters and millions of private households and firms.

7. The relative attractiveness of foreign goods to U.S. buyers and of U.S. goods to foreign buyers depends in part on *exchange rates*, the ratios at which two currencies are traded for each other.

8. For any pair of countries, there is a range of exchange rates that will lead automatically to both countries realizing the gains from specialization and comparative advantage. Within that range, the exchange rate will determine which country gains the most from trade. This leads us to conclude that exchange rates determine the terms of trade.

9. If exchange rates end up in the right range (that is, in a range that facilitates the flow of goods between nations), the free market will drive each country to shift resources into those sectors in which it enjoys a comparative advantage. Only those products in which a country has a comparative advantage will be competitive in world markets.

THE SOURCES OF COMPARATIVE ADVANTAGE

10. The *Heckscher-Ohlin theorem* looks to relative *factor endowments* to explain comparative advantage and trade flows. According to the theorem, a country has a comparative advantage in the production of a product if that country is relatively well endowed with the inputs that are used intensively in the production of that product.

11. A relatively short list of inputs—natural resources, knowledge capital, physical capital, land, and skilled and unskilled labor—explains a surprisingly large portion of world trade patterns. But the simple version of the theory of comparative advantage cannot explain why many countries import and export the same goods.

12. Some theories argue that comparative advantage can be acquired. Just as industries within a country differentiate their products to capture a domestic market, so too do they differentiate their products to please the wide variety of

tastes that exists worldwide. This theory is not inconsistent with the theory of comparative advantage.

TRADE BARRIERS: TARIFFS, EXPORT SUBSIDIES, AND QUOTAS

13. Trade barriers take many forms; the three most common are *tariffs, export subsidies,* and *quotas.* All are forms of *protection* through which some sector of the economy is shielded from foreign competition.

14. Although the United States has historically been a high-tariff nation, the general movement is now away from tariffs and quotas. The *General Agreement on Tariffs and Trade (GATT),* signed by the United States and 22 other countries in 1947, continues in effect today; its purpose is to reduce barriers to world trade and keep them down. Also important are the *U.S.-Canadian Free Trade Agreement,* signed in 1988, and the *North American Free-Trade Agreement,* signed by the United States, Mexico, and Canada in the last days of the Bush administration, taking effect in 1994.

15. The *European Union (EU)* is a free-trade bloc composed of 15 nations: Austria, Belgium, Denmark, Finland, France, Germany, Greece, Ireland, Italy, Luxembourg, the Netherlands, Portugal, Spain, Sweden, and the United Kingdom.

Many economists believe that the advantages of free trade within the bloc, a reunited Germany, and the ability to work well as a bloc will make the EU the most powerful player in the international marketplace in the coming decades.

FREE TRADE OR PROTECTION?

16. In one sense, the theory of comparative advantage is the case for free trade. Trade barriers prevent a nation from reaping the benefits of specialization, push it to adopt relatively inefficient production techniques, and force consumers to pay higher prices for protected products than they would otherwise pay.

17. The case for protection rests on a number of propositions, one of which is that foreign competition results in a loss of domestic jobs. But there is no reason to believe that the workers laid off in the contracting sectors will not be ultimately reemployed in other expanding sectors. This adjustment process is far from costless, however.

18. Other arguments for protection hold that cheap foreign labor makes competition unfair; that some countries engage in unfair trade practices; that it protects the national security and discourages dependency; and that it protects *infant industries.* Despite these arguments, most economists favor free trade.

REVIEW TERMS AND CONCEPTS

absolute advantage, 813
comparative advantage, 813
Corn Laws, 812
dumping, 823
economic integration, 824
European Union (EU), 824
exchange rate, 819
export subsidies, 823
factor endowments, 821

General Agreement on Tariffs and Trade (GATT), 823
Heckscher-Ohlin theorem, 821
infant industry, 829
North American Free-Trade Agreement (NAFTA), 824
protection, 822
quota, 823

Smoot-Hawley tariff, 823
tariff, 823
terms of trade, 818
theory of comparative advantage, 813
trade deficit, 812
trade surplus, 812
U.S.-Canadian Free-Trade Agreement, 824

PROBLEM SET

1. Suppose Germany and France each produce only two goods, guns and butter. Both are produced using labor alone and the value of a good is equal to the number of labor units required to produce it. Assuming both countries are at full employment, you are given the following information:

Germany: 10 units of labor required to produce 1 gun
         5 units of labor required to produce 1 pound of butter
         Total labor force: 1,000,000 units
France: 15 units of labor required to produce 1 gun
         10 units of labor required to produce 1 pound of butter
         Total labor force: 750,000 units

  a. Draw the production possibility frontiers for each country in the absence of trade.

b. If transportation costs are ignored and trade is allowed, will France and Germany engage in trade? Explain.

c. If a trade agreement were negotiated, at what rate (number of guns per unit of butter) would they agree to exchange?

2. The United States and Russia each produce only bearskin caps and wheat. Domestic prices are given in the following table:

	RUSSIA	UNITED STATES	
Bearskin Caps	10 Ru	$ 7	Per hat
Wheat	15 Ru	$10	Per quart

On April 1, the Zurich exchange listed an exchange rate of $1 = 1 Ru.

a. Which country has an absolute advantage in the production of bearskin caps? Wheat?

b. Which country has a comparative advantage in the production of bearskin caps? Wheat?

c. If the United States and Russia were the only two countries engaging in trade, what adjustments would you predict, assuming exchange rates are freely determined by the laws of supply and demand?

3. The United States imported $27.9 billion worth of "food, feeds, and beverages" in 1996 and exported $40.7 billion worth.

a. Name some of the imported items that you are aware of in this category. Also name some of the exported items.

b. The United States is said to have a comparative advantage in the production of agricultural goods. How would you go about testing this proposition? What data would you need?

c. Are the foregoing numbers consistent with the theory of comparative advantage? Suppose you had a more detailed breakdown of which items the United States imports and which it exports. What would you look for?

d. What other theories of international trade might explain why the same goods are imported and exported?

4. The following table gives 1990 figures for yield per acre in Illinois and Kansas:

	WHEAT	SOYBEANS
Illinois	48	39
Kansas	40	24

Source: U.S. Dept. of Agriculture, *Crop Production*, 1992.

a. If we assume that farmers in Illinois and Kansas use the same amount of labor, capital, and fertilizer, which state has an absolute advantage in wheat production? Soybean production?

b. If we transfer land out of wheat into soybeans, how many bushels of wheat do we give up in Illinois per additional bushel of soybeans produced? In Kansas?

c. Which state has a comparative advantage in wheat production? In soybean production?

The following table gives the distribution of land planted for each state in millions of acres in 1990:

	TOTAL ACRES UNDER TILL	WHEAT	SOYBEANS
Illinois	22.9	1.9 (8.3%)	9.1 (39.7%)
Kansas	20.7	11.8 (57.0%)	1.9 (9.2%)

Are these data consistent with your answer to part c? Explain.

5. The U.S. Congress ratified the North American Free-Trade Agreement (NAFTA) in September of 1993 by a very slim vote. The agreement took effect on January 1, 1994. The same Congress ratified the Final Act of the Uruguay Round of the General Agreement on Tariffs and Trade (GATT) in December 1994, and that agreement took effect on January 1, 1995. Both were ratified over very strong political opposition from lobby groups. Using newspaper articles and periodicals from the time, write a short report about the opposition to each of these agreements. Who opposed them? Can you offer an explanation for their opposition? What logic did the Congress rely on to vote in favor?

6. You can think of the United States as a set of 50 separate economies with no trade barriers. In such an open environment, each state specializes in the products that it produces best.

a. What product or products does your state specialize in?

b. Can you identify the source of the comparative advantage that lies behind the production of one or more of these products (a natural resource, plentiful cheap labor, a skilled labor force, etc.)?

c. Do you think that the theory of comparative advantage and the Heckscher-Ohlin theorem help to explain why your state specializes in the way that it does?

7. Germany and France produce white and red wines. Current domestic prices for each are given in the following table:

	GERMANY	FRANCE
White wine	5 DM	10 francs
Red wine	10 DM	15 francs

Suppose that the exchange rate is 1 deutsche mark = 1 franc.

a. If the price ratios within each country reflect resource use, which country has a comparative advantage in the production of red wine? White wine?

b. Assume there are no other trading partners and that the only motive for holding foreign currency is to buy foreign goods. Will the current exchange rate lead to trade flows in both directions between the two countries?

c. What adjustments might you expect in the exchange rate? Be specific.

d. What would you predict about trade flows between Germany and France in the long run?

8. The European Union (EU) is scheduled to remove all trade barriers within its member countries in the next 5 years. Its goal is to become one "common market" with one uniform currency. Explain the likely benefits and costs to the EU's member countries. Should the United States be concerned about the new common market? Why or why not?

TAKE IT TO THE NET

We invite you to visit the Case and Fair page on the Prentice Hall Web site:

http://www.prenhall.com/casefair

for this chapter's World Wide Web exercise.

Chapter 36

OPEN-ECONOMY MACROECONOMICS: THE BALANCE OF PAYMENTS AND EXCHANGE RATES

THE ECONOMIES OF THE WORLD have become increasingly interdependent over the last two decades. No economy operates in a vacuum, and economic events in one country can have repercussions on the economies of other countries.

International trade is a major part of today's world economy. U.S. imports now account for over 13 percent of U.S. GDP, and billions of dollars flow through the international capital market each day. In chapter 35 we explored the main reasons why there is international exchange. Countries trade with each other to obtain goods and services they cannot produce themselves or because other nations can produce goods and services at a lower cost than they can. You can see the various connections between the domestic economy and the rest of the world in Figure 21.2. Foreign countries supply goods and services, labor, and capital to the United States, and the United States supplies goods and services, labor, and capital to the rest of the world.

From a macroeconomic point of view, the main difference between an international transaction and a domestic transaction concerns currency exchange:

> When people in different countries buy from and sell to each other, an exchange of currencies must also take place.

French wine exporters cannot spend U.S. dollars in France—they need French francs. Nor can a U.S. wheat exporter use French francs to buy a tractor from a U.S. company or to pay the rent on her warehouse. Somehow, international exchange must be managed in a way that allows each partner in the transaction to wind up with his or her own currency.

REPRESENTATIVES OF THE 44 COUNTRIES THAT MET IN BRETTON WOODS, NEW HAMPSHIRE, IN 1944 TO ALLAY THE IMPENDING CHAOS IN THE INTERNATIONAL MONETARY SYSTEM AS WORLD WAR II WAS ENDING.

exchange rate *The price of one country's currency in terms of another country's currency; the ratio at which two currencies are traded for each other.*

As you know from chapter 35, the direction of trade between two countries depends on **exchange rates**—the price of one country's currency in terms of the other country's currency. If the German deutsche mark were very expensive, (making the dollar cheap), both Germans and Americans would buy from U.S. producers. If the deutsche mark were very cheap (making the U.S. dollar expensive), both Germans and Americans would buy from German producers. Within a certain range of exchange rates, trade flows in both directions, each country specializes in producing the goods in which it enjoys a comparative advantage, and trade is mutually beneficial.

Because exchange rates are a factor in determining the flow of international trade, the way they are determined is very important. Since the turn of the century, the world monetary system has been changed several times by international agreements and events. Early in the century, nearly all currencies were backed by gold. Their values were fixed in terms of a specific number of ounces of gold, which determined their values in international trading—exchange rates.

In 1944, with the international monetary system in chaos as the end of World War II drew near, a large group of experts unofficially representing 44 countries met in Bretton Woods, New Hampshire, and drew up a number of agreements. One of these agreements established a system of essentially fixed exchange rates under which each country agreed to intervene by buying and selling currencies in the foreign exchange market when necessary to maintain the agreed-upon value of its currency.

In 1971, most countries, including the United States, gave up trying to fix exchange rates formally and began allowing them to be determined essentially by supply and demand. For example, without government intervention in the marketplace, the price of British pounds in dollars is determined by the interaction of those who want to exchange dollars for pounds (those who "demand" pounds) and those who want to exchange pounds for dollars (those who "supply" pounds). If the quantity of pounds demanded exceeds the quantity of pounds supplied, the price of pounds will rise, just as the price of peanuts or paper clips would rise under similar circumstances. A more detailed discussion of the various monetary systems that have been in place since 1900 is in the appendix to this chapter.

In this chapter, we explore what has come to be called "open-economy macroeconomics" in more detail. First, we discuss the *balance of payments*—the record of a nation's transactions with the rest of the world. We then go on to consider how the analysis we presented in chapters 24 through 32 changes when we allow for the international exchange of goods, services, and capital.

THE BALANCE OF PAYMENTS

We sometimes lump all foreign currencies—Swiss francs, Japanese yen, Brazilian cruzeiros, and so forth—together as "foreign exchange." **Foreign exchange** is simply all currencies other than the domestic currency of a given country (in the case of the United States, the U.S. dollar). U.S. demand for foreign exchange arises because its citizens want to buy things whose prices are quoted in other currencies, such as Australian jewelry, vacations in France, and bonds or stocks issued by Sony Corporation of Japan. Whenever U.S. citizens make these purchases, Australians, French, and Japanese gain U.S. dollars, which, from their point of view, are foreign exchange.

But where does the *supply* of foreign exchange come from? Simple: The United States (actually, U.S. citizens or firms) earns foreign exchange when it sells products, services, or assets to another country. Just as France earns foreign exchange when U.S. tourists go to visit the Eiffel Tower, the United States earns foreign exchange (in this case, French francs) when French tourists come to the United States to visit the Statue of Liberty. Similarly, Saudi Arabian purchases of stock in General Motors or Colombian purchases of real estate in Miami increase the U.S. supply of foreign exchange.

The record of a country's transactions in goods, services, and assets with the rest of the world is its **balance of payments**. The balance of payments is also the record of a country's sources (supply) and uses (demand) of foreign exchange.[1]

THE CURRENT ACCOUNT

The balance of payments is divided up into two major accounts, the *current account* and the *capital account*. These are shown in Table 36.1, which provides data on the U.S. balance of payments for 1997. We begin with the current account.

The first item in the current account is U.S. trade in goods. This category includes exports of computer chips, potato chips, and Sting records and imports of Scotch whiskey, Japanese calculators, and Mexican oil. United States exports *earn* foreign exchange for the United States and are a credit (+) item on the current account. United States imports *use up* foreign exchange and are a debit (−) item. In 1997, the United States imported $206.2 billion more in goods than it exported.

Next in the current account is services. Like most other countries, the United States buys services from and sells services to other countries. For example, a U.S. firm shipping wheat to England might purchase insurance from a British insurance company. A Dutch flower grower may fly flowers to the United States aboard an American airliner. In the first case, the United States is importing services and therefore using up foreign exchange; in the second, it is selling services to foreigners and earning foreign exchange. In 1997, the United States exported $87.6 billion more in services than it imported.

The difference between a country's exports of goods and services and its imports of goods and services is its **balance of trade**. If exports of goods and services are less than imports of goods and services, a country has a **trade deficit**.

The third item concerns *investment income*. U.S. citizens hold foreign assets (stocks, bonds, and real assets like buildings and factories). Dividends, interest, rent, and profits paid to U.S. asset holders are a source of foreign exchange. Conversely, when foreigners earn dividends, interest, and profits on assets held in the United States,

foreign exchange *All currencies other than the domestic currency of a given country.*

balance of payments *The record of a country's transactions in goods, services, and assets with the rest of the world; also the record of a country's sources (supply) and uses (demand) of foreign exchange.*

balance of trade *A country's exports of goods and services minus its imports of goods and services.*

trade deficit *Occurs when a country's exports of goods and services are less than its imports of goods and services in a given period.*

---

[1]Bear in mind the distinction between the balance of payments and a balance sheet. A *balance sheet* for a firm or a country measures that entity's stock of assets and liabilities at a moment in time. The *balance of payments*, by contrast, measures *flows*, usually over a period of a month, a quarter, or a year. Despite its name, the balance of payments is *not* a balance sheet.

TABLE 36.1 UNITED STATES BALANCE OF PAYMENTS, 1997

ALL TRANSACTIONS THAT BRING FOREIGN EXCHANGE INTO THE UNITED STATES ARE CREDITED (+) TO THE CURRENT ACCOUNT; ALL TRANSACTIONS THAT CAUSE THE UNITED STATES TO LOSE FOREIGN EXCHANGE ARE DEBITED (−) TO THE CURRENT ACCOUNT.

CURRENT ACCOUNT

Goods exports	682.3
Goods imports	−888.5
(1) Net export of goods	−206.2
Exports of services	257.6
Imports of services	−170.0
(2) Net export of services	87.6
Income received on investments	242.4
Income payments on investments	−255.7
(3) Net investment income	−13.3
(4) Net transfer payments and other	−36.8
(5) Balance on current account (1 + 2 + 3 + 4)	−168.7

CAPITAL ACCOUNT

(6) Change in private U.S. assets abroad (increase is −)	−405.3
(7) Change in foreign private assets in the United States	588.2
(8) Change in U.S. government assets abroad (increase is −)	−1.0
(9) Change in foreign government assets in the United States	90.0
(10) Balance on capital account (6 + 7 + 8 + 9)	271.9
(11) Statistical discrepancy	−103.2
(12) Balance of Payments (5 + 10 + 11)	0

Source: U.S. Department of Commerce, *Survey of Current Business*, March 1998. Data are for the third quarter of 1997, seasonally adjusted at annual rates.

foreign exchange is used up. In 1997, investment income paid to foreigners exceeded investment income received from foreigners by $13.3 billion.

The fourth item in Table 36.1 is *net transfer payments and other*. Transfer payments from the United States to foreigners are another use of foreign exchange. Some of these transfer payments are from private U.S. citizens and some are from the U.S. government. You may send a check to your aunt in Spain or the government may send a social security check to a retiree living in Italy. Conversely, some foreigners make transfer payments to the United States. "Net" refers to the difference between payments from the United States to foreigners and payments from foreigners to the United States.

If we add the balance of trade, net export of services, net investment income, and net transfer payments and other,[2] we get the **balance on current account**. The balance on current account shows how much a nation has spent on foreign goods, services, investment income payments, and transfers relative to how much it has earned from other countries. When the balance is negative, which it was for the United States in 1997, a

balance on current account
The balance of trade plus net exports of services, plus net investment income, plus the category "net transfer payments and other."

---

[2]"Other" includes interest paid by the U.S. government to foreigners. Contrary to the treatment of private interest payments, government interest payments are not counted as income payments on investments. (This treatment is similar to that for government interest payments to domestic citizens, as discussed in chapter 22.) These payments are a use of funds, however, so they must be included in computing the balance on current account.

nation has spent more on foreign goods and services (plus investment income and transfers paid) than it has earned through the sales of its goods and services to the rest of the world (plus investment income and transfers received). If a nation has spent more on foreign goods, services, investment income payments, and transfers than it has earned, its net wealth position vis-à-vis the rest of the world must decrease. By "net" we mean a nation's assets abroad minus its liabilities to the rest of the world. The capital account of the balance of payments records the changes in these assets and liabilities. We now turn to the capital account.

THE CAPITAL ACCOUNT

For each transaction recorded in the current account, there is an offsetting transaction recorded in the capital account. Consider the purchase of a Japanese car by a U.S. citizen. Say that the yen/dollar exchange rate is 125 yen to a dollar, and the yen price of the car is 2.5 million yen, which is $20,000. The U.S. citizen (probably an automobile dealer) takes $20,000, buys 2.5 million yen, and then buys the car. In this case, U.S. imports are increased by $20,000 in the current account and foreign assets in the United States (in this case, Japanese holdings of dollars) are increased by $20,000 in the capital account. The net wealth position of the United States vis-à-vis the rest of the world has decreased by $20,000. The key point to realize is that an increase in U.S. imports results in an increase in foreign assets in the United States. The United States must "pay" for the imports, and whatever it pays with (in this example, U.S. dollars) is an increase in foreign assets in the United States. Conversely, an increase in U.S. exports results in an increase in U.S. assets abroad, because foreigners must pay for the U.S. exports.

Table 36.1 shows that U.S. assets abroad are divided into private holdings (line 6) and U.S. government holdings (line 8). Similarly, foreign assets in the United States are divided into foreign private (line 7) and foreign government (line 9). The sum of lines 6, 7, 8, and 9 is the **balance on capital account** (line 10). If there were no errors of measurement in the data collection, the balance on capital account would equal the negative of the balance on current account, because, as mentioned above, for each transaction in the current account there is an offsetting transaction in the capital account. Another way of looking at the balance on capital account is that it is the decrease in the net wealth position of the country vis-à-vis the rest of the world. If the balance on capital account is positive, this means that the change in foreign assets in the country is greater than the change in the country's assets abroad, which is a decrease in the net wealth position of the country.

Table 36.1 shows that in 1997 the U.S. balance on current account was −$168.7 billion, which means that the United States spent considerably more than it made vis-à-vis the rest of the world. If the balance on current account is measured correctly, then the net wealth position of the United States vis-à-vis the rest of the world decreased by $168.7 billion in 1997. In this case, the balance on capital account should be $168.7 billion. The balance on capital account (line 10) is in fact $271.9 billion, and so the error of measurement, called the statistical discrepancy, is $103.2 billion (line 11) in 1997. The balance of payments (line 12) is the sum of the balance on current account, the balance on capital account, and the statistical discrepancy. By construction, it is always zero.

It is important to note from Table 36.1 that even though the net wealth position of the United States decreased in 1997, the change in U.S. assets abroad increased considerably ($405.3 billion private and $1.0 billion government). How can this be? Because there was an even larger increase in foreign assets in the United States ($588.2 billion private and $90.0 billion government). It is the *net* change (i.e., the change in foreign assets in the United States minus the change in U.S. assets abroad)

During the second quarter of 1997, U.S. purchases on foreign stock exchanges were $13.9 billion and U.S. purchases of foreign bonds were $7.4 billion. During the same quarter foreign purchases of U.S. Treasury securities were $46 billion. Foreign purchases of U.S. stocks were $21.7 billion in the second quarter, a record.

Source: Survey of Current Business, October 1997.

balance on capital account
In the United States, the sum of the following (measured in a given period): the change in private U.S. assets abroad, the change in foreign private assets in the United States, the change in U.S. government assets abroad, and the change in foreign government assets in the United States.

that is equal to the negative of the balance on current account (aside from the statistical discrepancy), not the change in just U.S. assets abroad.

There are many transactions that get recorded in the capital account that do not pertain to the current account. Consider a purchase of a U.K. security by a U.S. citizen. This is done by the U.S. citizen selling dollars for pounds and using the pounds to buy the U.K. security. After this transaction, U.S. assets abroad have increased (the United States now holds more U.K. securities) and foreign assets in the United States have increased (foreigners now hold more dollars). The purchase of the U.K. security is recorded as a minus item in line 6 in Table 36.1, and the increase in foreign holdings of dollars is recorded as a plus item in line 7. These two balance out. This happens whenever there is a switch of one kind of asset for another vis-à-vis the rest of the world. When a Japanese company bought Rockefeller Center in New York City in 1990, this was an increase in foreign assets in the United States (the Japanese then owned Rockefeller Center) and an increase in U.S. assets abroad (the United States then had the yen that was used to pay for the Center). If the United States then took the yen and bought Japanese securities, this was simply a switch of one kind of U.S. asset abroad (yen) for another (Japanese securities).

THE UNITED STATES AS A DEBTOR NATION

If a country has positive net wealth position vis-à-vis the rest of the world, it can be said to be a creditor nation. Conversely, if it has negative net wealth position, it can be said to be a debtor nation. Remember that a country's net wealth position increases if it has a positive current account balance and decreases if it has a negative current account balance. It is important to realize that the *only* way a country's net wealth position can change is if its current account balance is nonzero. Simply switching one form of asset for another, such as switching Rockefeller Center for Japanese securities in the above example, is not a change in a country's net wealth position. Another way of putting this is that a country's net wealth position is the sum of all of its past current account balances.

Prior to the mid-1970s, the United States had generally run current account surpluses, and thus its net wealth position was positive. It was a creditor nation. This began to turn around in the mid-1970s, and by the mid-1980s, the United States was running large current account deficits. Some time during this period the United States changed from having a positive net wealth position vis-à-vis the rest of the world to having a negative position. In other words, the United States changed from a creditor nation to a debtor nation. The current account deficits persisted into the 1990s, and the United States is now the largest debtor nation in the world. In 1996, foreign assets in the United States totaled $5.1 trillion and U.S. assets abroad totaled $4.3 trillion. The U.S. net wealth position was thus −$0.8 trillion. This large negative position is the result of the United States having spent much more in the 1980s and 1990s on foreign goods and services (plus investment income and transfers paid) than it earned through the sales of its goods and services to the rest of the world (plus investment income and transfers received).

EQUILIBRIUM OUTPUT (INCOME) IN AN OPEN ECONOMY

Everything we have said so far has been descriptive. Now we turn to analysis. How are all these trade and capital flows determined? What impacts do they have on the economies of the countries involved? To simplify our discussion here, we will assume that exchange rates are fixed. We will relax this assumption later.

THE INTERNATIONAL SECTOR AND PLANNED AGGREGATE EXPENDITURE

Our earlier descriptions of the multiplier took into account the consumption behavior of households (C), the planned investment behavior of firms (I), and the spending of the government (G). We defined the sum of these three components as planned aggregate expenditure (AE).

To analyze the international sector, we must include the goods and services a country exports to the rest of the world, as well as what it imports. If we call our exports of goods and services EX, it should be clear that EX is a component of total output and income. A U.S. razor blade sold to a buyer in Mexico is as much a part of U.S. production as a similar blade sold in Pittsburgh. Exports simply represent demand for domestic products not by domestic households and firms and the government but by the rest of the world.

What about imports? Remember, imports are *not a part of domestic output* (Y). By definition, imports are not produced by the country that is importing them. Remember also, when we look at households' total consumption spending, firms' total investment spending, and total government spending, imports are included. Therefore, to calculate domestic output correctly, we must subtract the parts of consumption, investment, and government spending that constitute imports. The definition of planned aggregate expenditure becomes:

Planned aggregate expenditure in an open economy:

$$AE \equiv C + I + G + EX - IM$$

The last two terms ($EX - IM$) together are the country's **net exports of goods and services**.

▶ **Determining the Level of Imports** What determines the level of imports and exports in a country? For now, we assume that the level of imports is a function of income (Y). The rationale is simple: When U.S. income increases, U.S. citizens buy more of everything, including U.S. cars and peanut butter, Japanese TV sets, and Korean steel and videocassette recorders. When income rises, imports tend to go up. Algebraically,

$$IM = mY$$

where Y is income and m is some positive number.[3] Recall from chapter 24 that the marginal propensity to consume (MPC) measures the change in consumption that

net exports of goods and services ($EX - IM$) *The difference between a country's total exports and total imports.*

FAST FACTS

Trade was a smaller part of U.S. output in the past. Here are estimates of annual GNP and exports over two historical decades:

Years	GNP	Exports	as % of GNP
	in billions of dollars		
1889–1898	12.73	.91	7.1%
1919–1928	81.20	5.26	6.4%

Source: Historical Statistics of the United States.

---

[3]*m* is assumed to be less than 1. Otherwise, a $1 increase in income generates an increase in imports of more than $1, which does not make sense.

results from a $1 change in income. Similarly, the **marginal propensity to import,** abbreviated as *MPM* or *m*, is the change in imports caused by a $1 change in income. If $m = 0.2$, or 20 percent, and income is $1,000, then imports, *IM*, are equal to $0.2 \times \$1,000 = \$200$. If income rises by $100 to $1,100, then the change in imports will equal $m \times$ (the change in income) $= 0.2 \times \$100 = \$20$.

For now we will assume that exports (EX) are given, i.e., that they are not affected, even indirectly, by the state of the economy. This assumption is relaxed later in this chapter.

▶ **Solving for Equilibrium**   Given the assumption about how imports are determined, we can solve for equilibrium income. This procedure is illustrated in Figure 36.1. Starting from the consumption function (blue line) in Figure 36.1a, we gradually build up the components of planned aggregate expenditure (brown line). Assuming for simplicity that planned investment, government purchases, and exports are all constant and do not depend on income, we move easily from the blue line to the brown line by adding the fixed amounts of *I*, *G*, and *EX* to consumption at every level of income. In this example, we take $I + G + EX$ to equal 80.

$C + I + G + EX$, however, includes spending on imports, which are not part of domestic production. To correct this, we must subtract the amount that is imported at each level of income. In Figure 36.1b, we assume $m = .25$, or 25 percent of total income is spent on goods and services produced in foreign countries. Imports are a constant fraction of total income; therefore at higher levels of income a larger amount is spent on foreign goods and services. For example, at $Y = 200$, $IM = .25Y$, or 50. Similarly, at $Y = 400$, $IM = .25Y$, or 100.

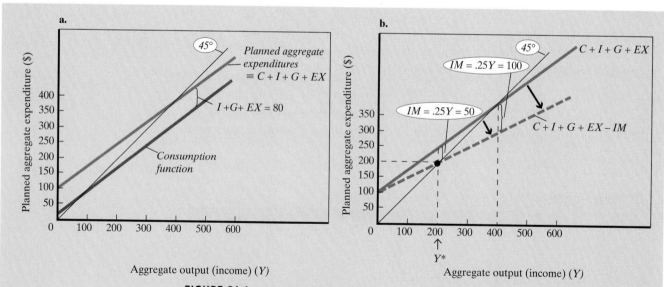

FIGURE 36.1

Determining Equilibrium Output in an Open Economy

In **a**, planned investment spending (*I*), government spending (*G*), and total exports (*EX*) are added to consumption (*C*) to arrive at planned aggregate expenditure. But $C + I + G + EX$ includes spending on imports because imports are part of planned aggregate expenditure. In **b**, the amount imported at every level of income is subtracted from planned aggregate expenditure. Equilibrium output occurs at $Y^* = 200$, the point at which planned domestic aggregate expenditure crosses the 45° line.

Remember that the *AE* function in Figure 36.1 must be planned aggregate expenditure on *domestically* produced goods and services. As income rises, some of the additional income is saved and the rest is spent. But not all of that added spending is on domestically produced goods and services. As income rises, some is saved and some is spent on imports. The brown dashed line in Figure 36.1b shows imports subtracted out of the *AE* function.

Equilibrium is reached when planned aggregate expenditure on domestic output equals aggregate domestic output (income). This is true at only one level of aggregate output, $Y^* = 200$, in Figure 36.1b. If Y were below Y^*, planned expenditure would exceed output, inventories would be lower than planned, and output would rise. At levels above Y^*, output would exceed planned expenditure, inventories would be larger than planned, and output would fall.

▶ **The Open-Economy Multiplier**   All of this has implications for the size of the multiplier. Recall the multiplier, introduced in chapter 24, and consider a sustained rise in government purchases (G). Initially, the increase in G will cause planned aggregate expenditure to be greater than aggregate output. Domestic firms will find their inventories to be lower than planned and thus will increase their output. But added output means more income. More workers are hired and profits are higher. Some of the added income is saved, and some is spent. The added consumption spending leads to a second round of inventories being lower than planned and raising output. Equilibrium output rises by a multiple of the initial increase in government purchases. This is the multiplier.

In chapters 24 and 25, we showed that the simple multiplier equals $1/(1 - MPC)$, or ($1/MPS$). That is, a sustained increase in government purchases equal to ΔG will lead to an increase in aggregate output (income) of $\Delta G[1/(1 - MPC)]$. If the MPC were .75 and government purchases rose by $10 billion, equilibrium income would rise by $4 \times$ $10 billion, or $40 billion. The multiplier is $[1/(1 - .75)] = [1/.25] = 4.0$.

In an open economy, some of the increase in income brought about by the increase in G is spent on imports rather than on domestically produced goods and services. The part of income spent on imports does not increase domestic income (Y) because imports are produced by foreigners. To compute the multiplier we need to know how much of the increased income is used to increase domestic consumption. (We are assuming all imports are consumption goods. In practice, some imports are investment goods and some are goods purchased by the government.) In other words, we need to know the marginal propensity to consume *domestic* goods. Domestic consumption is $C - IM$. So the marginal propensity to consume domestic goods is the marginal propensity to consume all goods (the MPC) minus the marginal propensity to import (the MPM). The marginal propensity to consume domestic goods is ($MPC - MPM$). Consequently,

$$\text{Open-economy multiplier} = \frac{1}{1 - (MPC - MPM)}$$

If the MPC is .75 and the MPM is .25, then the multiplier is $1/.5$, or 2.0. This multiplier is smaller than the multiplier in which imports are not taken into account, which is $1/.25$, or 4.0.

The message of the open-economy multiplier model, put succinctly:

The effect of a sustained increase in government spending (or investment) on income—that is, the multiplier—is smaller in an open economy than in a closed economy. The reason: When government spending (or investment) increases and income and consumption rise, some of the extra consumption spending that results is on foreign products and not on domestically produced goods and services.

THE DETERMINANTS OF IMPORTS AND EXPORTS

For simplicity, we have so far assumed that the level of imports depends only on income and that the level of exports is fixed. In reality the amount of spending on imports depends on factors other than income and exports are not fixed. We will now consider the more realistic picture.

> ▶ **The Determinants of Imports** The same factors that affect households' consumption behavior and firms' investment behavior are likely to affect the demand for imports because some imported goods are consumption goods and some are investment goods. For example, anything that increases consumption spending is likely to increase the demand for imports. We saw in chapters 24 and 32 that such factors as the after-tax real wage, after-tax nonlabor income, and interest rates affect consumption spending, and so these should also affect spending on imports. Similarly, anything that increases investment spending is likely to increase the demand for imports. A decrease in interest rates, for example, should encourage spending on both domestically produced goods and foreign-produced goods.

There is one additional consideration in determining spending on imports: the *relative prices* of domestically produced and foreign-produced goods. If the prices of foreign goods fall relative to the prices of domestic goods, people will consume more foreign goods relative to domestic goods. When Japanese cars are cheap relative to U.S. cars, consumption of Japanese cars should be high, and vice versa.

> ▶ **The Determinants of Exports** We now relax our assumption that exports are fixed. The demand for U.S. exports by other countries is identical to their demand for imports from the United States. Germany imports goods, some are U.S. produced. So do France, Spain, and so on. Total expenditure on imports in Germany is a function of the factors we have just discussed, except that the variables are German variables rather than U.S. variables. This is true for all other countries as well. The demand for U.S. exports depends on economic activity in the rest of the world—rest-of-the-world real wages, wealth, nonlabor income, interest rates, and so on—as well as on the prices of U.S. goods relative to the price of rest-of-the-world goods.

If foreign output increases, U.S. exports tend to increase. U.S. exports also tend to increase when U.S. prices fall relative to those in the rest of the world.

> ▶ **The Trade Feedback Effect** We can now combine what we know about the demand for imports and the demand for exports to discuss the **trade feedback effect**. Suppose the United States finds its exports increasing, perhaps because the world suddenly decides it prefers U.S. computers to other computers. This will lead to an increase in U.S. output (income), which leads to an increase in U.S. imports. Here is where the trade feedback begins. Because U.S. imports are somebody else's exports, the extra import demand from the United States raises the exports of the rest of the world. When other countries' exports to the United States go up, their output and incomes also rise, which leads to an increase in the demand for imports from the rest of the world. Some of the extra imports demanded by the rest of the world come from the United States, so U.S. exports increase. The increase in U.S. exports stimulates U.S. economic activity even more, which leads to a further increase in the U.S. demand for imports, and so on.

trade feedback effect *The tendency for an increase in the economic activity of one country to lead to a worldwide increase in economic activity, which then feeds back to that country.*

An increase in U.S. imports increases other countries' exports, which stimulates those countries' economies and increases their imports, which increases U.S. exports, which stimulates the U.S. economy and increases its imports, and so on. This is the trade feedback effect. In other words, an increase in U.S. economic activity leads to a worldwide increase in economic activity, which then "feeds back" to the United States.

> **Import and Export Prices** We have talked about the price of imports, but we have not yet discussed the factors that influence import prices. The consideration of import prices is complicated because more than one currency is involved. When we talk about "the price of imports," do we mean the price in dollars, in francs, or in yen? And because the exports of one country are the imports of another, the same question holds for the price of exports. When France exports wine to the United States, French wine growers are interested in the price of wine in terms of francs, because francs are what they use for transactions in France. U.S. consumers are interested in the price of wine in dollars, because dollars are what they use for transactions in the United States. The link between the two prices is the dollar/franc exchange rate.

Suppose France is experiencing an inflation and the price of wine in French francs rises from 20 francs to 30 francs per bottle. France's export price for wine (in terms of francs) will in general go up by the same amount.[4] If the dollar/franc exchange rate remains unchanged at, say, $0.20 per franc, then France's export price for wine in terms of dollars will also rise, from $4 to $6 per bottle. Because France's exports to the United States are by definition U.S. imports from France, an increase in the dollar prices of French exports to the United States means an increase in the prices of U.S. imports from France. Therefore, when France's export prices rise with no change in the dollar/franc exchange rate, U.S. import prices rise. This holds for any country that trades with France.

> Export prices of other countries affect U.S. import prices.

A country's export prices tend to move fairly closely with the general price level in that country. If France is experiencing a general increase in prices, it is likely this change will be reflected in price increases of all domestically produced goods, both exportable and nonexportable.

> The general rate of inflation abroad is likely to affect U.S. import prices. If the inflation rate abroad is high, U.S. import prices are likely to rise.

> **The Price Feedback Effect** We have just seen that when a country experiences an increase in domestic prices, the prices of its exports will increase. But it is also true that when the prices of a country's *imports* increase, the prices of domestic goods may increase in response. There are at least two ways this can occur.

First, an increase in the prices of imported inputs will shift a country's aggregate supply curve to the left. In chapter 29 we discussed the macroeconomy's response to a cost shock. Recall that a leftward shift in the aggregate supply curve due to a cost increase causes aggregate output to fall and prices to rise (stagflation).

Second, if import prices rise relative to domestic prices, households will tend to substitute domestically produced goods and services for imports. This is equivalent to a rightward shift of the aggregate demand curve. If the domestic economy is operating on the upward-sloping part of the aggregate supply curve, the overall domestic price level will rise in response to an increase in aggregate demand. Perfectly competitive firms will see market-determined prices rise, and imperfectly competitive firms will experience an increase in the demand for their products. Studies have shown, for example, that the price of automobiles produced in the United States moves closely with the price of imported cars.

---

[4]France's wine exporters could raise the export price but keep it less than the domestic price (to try to stay competitive with the rest of the world), but we ignore this possibility here.

Still, this is not the end of the story. Suppose a country—say, Germany—experiences an increase in its domestic price level. This will increase the price of its exports to France (and to all other countries). The increase in the price of French imports from Germany will lead to an increase in domestic prices in France. But France also exports to Germany. The increase in French prices causes an increase in the price of French exports to Germany, which then further increases the German price level.

This is called the **price feedback effect**, in the sense that inflation is "exportable." An increase in the price level in one country can drive up prices in other countries, which in turn further increases the price level in the first country. Through export and import prices, a domestic price increase can "feed back" on itself.

It is important to realize that the discussion so far has been based on the assumption of fixed exchange rates. Life is more complicated under flexible exchange rates, to which we now turn.

THE OPEN ECONOMY WITH FLEXIBLE EXCHANGE RATES

To a large extent, the fixed exchange rates set by the Bretton Woods agreements served as international monetary arrangements until 1971. Then, in 1971 the United States and most other countries decided to abandon the fixed exchange rate system in favor of **floating**, or **market-determined, exchange rates**. While governments still intervene to ensure that exchange rate movements are "orderly," exchange rates today are largely determined by the unregulated forces of supply and demand.

Understanding how an economy interacts with the rest of the world when exchange rates are not fixed is not as simple as when we assume fixed exchange rates. Exchange rates determine the price of imported goods relative to domestic goods and can have significant effects on the level of imports and exports. Consider a 20 percent drop in the value of the dollar against the deutsche mark. Dollars buy fewer marks and marks buy more dollars. Both Germans, who now get more dollars for marks, and U.S. citizens, who get fewer marks for dollars, find that U.S. goods and services are more attractive. Exchange rate movements have important impacts on imports, exports, and the movement of capital between countries.

THE MARKET FOR FOREIGN EXCHANGE

What determines exchange rates under a floating rate system? To explore this, we assume there are just two countries, the United States and Great Britain. It is easier to understand a world with only two countries, and most of the points we will make can be generalized to a world with many trading partners.

➤ **The Supply of and Demand for Pounds** Governments, private citizens, banks, and corporations exchange pounds for dollars and dollars for pounds every day. In our two-country case, those who *demand* pounds are holders of dollars seeking to exchange them for pounds. Those who *supply* pounds are holders of pounds seeking to exchange them for dollars. It is important not to confuse the supply of dollars (or pounds) on the foreign exchange market with the U.S. (or British) money supply. The latter is the sum of all the money currently in circulation. The supply of dollars on the foreign exchange market is the number of dollars that holders seek to exchange for pounds in a given time period. The demand for, and supply of, dollars on foreign exchange markets determines *exchange* rates; the demand for money balances and the total domestic money supply determine the *interest* rate.

The common reason for exchanging dollars for pounds is to buy something produced in Great Britain. U.S. importers who purchase Jaguar automobiles or

price feedback effect
The process by which a domestic price increase in one country can "feed back" on itself through export and import prices. An increase in the price level in one country can drive up prices in other countries. This in turn further increases the price level in the first country.

floating, or market-determined, exchange rates *Exchange rates that are determined by the unregulated forces of supply and demand.*

EXCHANGE RATES ARE POSTED DAILY AT BANKS AND OTHER FINANCIAL INSTITUTIONS. THEY ARE ALSO AVAILABLE IN NEWSPAPERS, FROM ELECTRONIC INFORMATION SERVICES, AND ON THE INTERNET.

Scotch whiskey must pay with pounds. U.S. citizens traveling in Great Britain who want to ride the train, stay in a hotel, or eat at a restaurant must acquire pounds for dollars to do so. If a U.S. corporation builds a plant in Great Britain, it must pay for that plant in pounds.

At the same time, some people may want to buy British stocks or bonds. Implicitly, when a U.S. citizen buys a bond issued by the British government or by a British corporation, he or she is making a loan, but the transaction requires a currency exchange. The British bond seller must ultimately be paid in pounds.

On the supply side of the market, the situation is reversed. Here we find people—usually British citizens—holding pounds they want to use to buy dollars. Again, the common reason is to buy things produced in the United States. If a British importer decides to import golf carts made in Georgia, the producer must be paid in dollars. British tourists visiting New York may ride in cabs, eat in restaurants, and tour Ellis Island. Doing these things requires dollars. When a British firm builds an office complex in Los Angeles, it must pay the contractor in dollars.

In addition to buyers and sellers who exchange money to engage in transactions, some people and institutions hold currency balances for speculative reasons. If I think the U.S. dollar is going to decline in value relative to the pound, I may want to hold some of my wealth in the form of pounds. Table 36.2 summarizes some of the major

---

TABLE 36.2 SOME PRIVATE BUYERS AND SELLERS IN INTERNATIONAL EXCHANGE MARKETS: UNITED STATES AND GREAT BRITAIN

THE DEMAND FOR POUNDS (SUPPLY OF DOLLARS)

1. Firms, households, or governments that import British goods into the United States or wish to buy British-made goods and services
2. U.S. citizens traveling in Great Britain
3. Holders of dollars who want to buy British stocks, bonds, or other financial instruments
4. U.S. companies that want to invest in Great Britain
5. Speculators who anticipate a decline in the value of the dollar relative to the pound

THE SUPPLY OF POUNDS (DEMAND FOR DOLLARS)

1. Firms, households, or governments that import U.S. goods into Great Britain or wish to buy U.S.-made goods and services
2. British citizens traveling in the United States
3. Holders of pounds who want to buy stocks, bonds, or other financial instruments in the United States
4. British companies that want to invest in the United States
5. Speculators who anticipate a rise in the value of the dollar relative to the pound

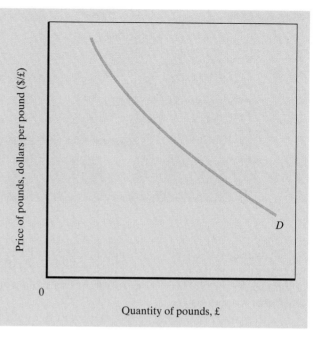

FIGURE 36.2

The Demand for Pounds in the Foreign Exchange Market

When the price of pounds falls, British-made goods and services appear less expensive to U.S. buyers. If British prices are constant, U.S. buyers will buy more British goods and services, and the quantity of pounds demanded will rise.

The Wall Street Journal reported on December 4, 1997, that speculative traders were selling yen for dollars in large quantities, "testing the resolve" of the Bank of Japan, which had been buying yen with dollars to hold up the value of the yen.

categories of private foreign exchange demanders and suppliers in the two-country case of the United States and Great Britain.

Figure 36.2 shows the demand curve for pounds in the foreign exchange market. When the price of pounds (the exchange rate) is lower, it takes fewer dollars to buy British goods and services, to build a plant in Liverpool, to travel to London, and so forth. Lower net prices (in dollars) should increase the demand for British-made products and encourage investment and travel in Great Britain. If prices (in pounds) in Britain do not change, an increase in the quantity of British goods and services demanded by foreigners will increase the quantity of pounds demanded. The demand-for-pounds curve in the foreign exchange market has a negative slope.

Figure 36.3 shows a supply curve for pounds in the foreign exchange market. At a higher exchange rate, each pound buys more dollars, making the price of U.S.-produced

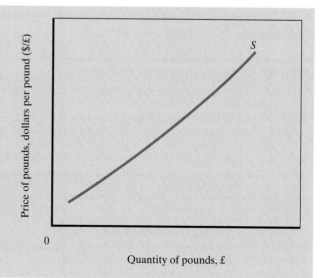

FIGURE 36.3

The Supply of Pounds in the Foreign Exchange Market

When the price of pounds rises, the British can obtain more dollars for each pound. This means that U.S.-made goods and services appear less expensive to British buyers. Thus, the quantity of pounds supplied is likely to rise with the exchange rate.

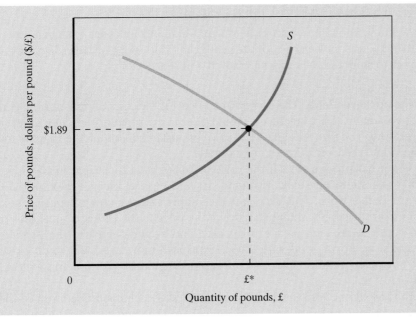

goods and services lower to the British. The British are more apt to buy U.S.-made goods when the price of pounds is high (the value of the dollar is low). An increase in British demand for U.S. goods and services is likely to increase the quantity of pounds supplied. The curve representing the supply of pounds in the foreign exchange market has a positive slope.

▶ **The Equilibrium Exchange Rate** When exchange rates are allowed to float, they are determined the same way other prices are determined:

> The equilibrium exchange rate occurs at the point at which the quantity demanded of a foreign currency equals the quantity of that currency supplied.

This is illustrated in Figure 36.4. An excess demand for pounds (quantity demanded in excess of quantity supplied) will cause the price of pounds to rise—the pound will **appreciate** with respect to the dollar. An excess supply of pounds will cause the price of pounds to fall—the pound will **depreciate** with respect to the dollar.[5]

appreciation of a currency
The rise in value of one currency relative to another.

depreciation of a currency
The fall in value of one currency relative to another.

---

[5]Although Figure 36.3 shows the supply-of-pounds curve in the foreign exchange market with a positive slope, under certain circumstances the curve may bend back. Suppose the price of a pound rises from $1.50 to $2.00. Consider a British importer who buys 10 Chevrolets each month at $15,000 each, including transportation costs. When a pound exchanges for $1.50, he will supply 100,000 pounds per month to the foreign exchange market—100,000 pounds brings $150,000, enough to buy 10 cars. Now suppose the cheaper dollar causes him to buy 12 cars. Twelve cars will cost a total of $180,000, but at $2.00 = 1 pound, he will spend only 90,000 pounds per month. The supply of pounds on the market falls when the price of pounds rises. The reason for this seeming paradox is simple. The number of pounds a British importer needs to buy U.S. goods depends on both the quantity of goods he buys and the price of those goods in pounds. If demand for imports is inelastic so that the percentage decrease in price resulting from the depreciated currency is greater than the percentage increase in the quantity of imports demanded, importers will spend fewer pounds and the quantity of pounds supplied in the foreign exchange market will fall. The supply of pounds will slope upward as long as the demand for U.S. imports is elastic.

FACTORS THAT AFFECT EXCHANGE RATES

We now know enough to discuss the factors likely to influence exchange rates. Anything that changes the behavior of the people in Table 36.2 can cause demand and supply curves to shift and the exchange rate to adjust accordingly.

law of one price *If the costs of transportation are small, the price of the same good in different countries should be roughly the same.*

▶ **Purchasing Power Parity: The Law of One Price** If the costs of transporting goods between two countries are small, we would expect the price of the same good in both countries to be roughly the same. The price of basketballs should be roughly the same in Canada and the United States, for example.

It is not hard to see why. If the price of basketballs is cheaper in Canada, it will pay for someone to buy balls in Canada at a low price and sell them in the United States at a higher price. This decreases the supply and pushes up the price in Canada and increases the supply and pushes down the price in the United States. This process should continue as long as the price differential, and therefore the profit opportunity, persists. For a good with trivial transportation costs, we would expect this **law of one price** to hold. The price of a good should be the same regardless where we buy it.

If the law of one price held for all goods, and if each country consumed the same market basket of goods, the exchange rate between the two currencies would be determined simply by the relative price levels in the two countries. If the price of a basketball were $10 in the United States and $12 in Canada, then the U.S.-Canada exchange rate would have to be $1 U.S. per $1.20 Canadian. If the rate were instead one-to-one, it would pay people to buy the balls in the United States and sell them in Canada. This would increase the demand for U.S. dollars in Canada, thereby driving up their price in terms of Canadian dollars to one U.S. dollar per 1.2 Canadian dollars, at which point no one could make a profit shipping basketballs across international lines, and the process would cease.[6]

purchasing-power-parity theory *A theory of international exchange holding that exchange rates are set so that the price of similar goods in different countries is the same.*

The theory that exchange rates are set so that the price of similar goods in different countries is the same is known as the **purchasing-power-parity theory**. According to this theory, if it takes five times as many French francs to buy a pound of salt in France as it takes U.S. dollars to buy a pound of salt in the United States, then the equilibrium exchange rate should be five francs per dollar.

In practice, transportation costs for many goods are quite large, and the law of one price does not hold for these goods. (Haircuts are often cited as a good example. The transportation costs for a U.S. resident to get a French haircut are indeed large unless that person is an airline pilot!) Also, many products that are potential substitutes for each other are not precisely identical. For instance, a Rolls Royce and a Mercedes Benz are both cars, but there is no reason to expect the exchange rate between the British pound and the deutsche mark to be set so that the prices of the two are equalized. In addition, countries consume different market baskets of goods, so we would not expect the aggregate price levels to follow the law of one price. Nevertheless,

> A high rate of inflation in one country relative to another puts pressure on the exchange rate between the two countries, and there is a general tendency for the currencies of relative high-inflation countries to depreciate.

---

[6]Of course, if the rate were $1 U.S. to $2 Canadian, then it would pay people to buy basketballs in Canada (at $12 Canadian, or $6 U.S.) and sell them in the United States. This would weaken demand for the U.S. dollar, and its price would fall from $2 Canadian until it reached $1.20 Canadian.

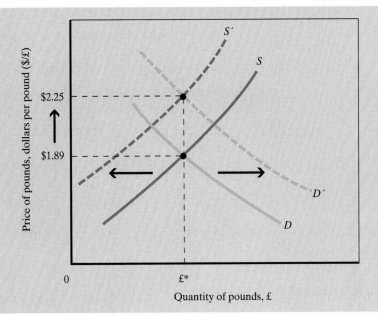

FIGURE 36.5

Exchange Rates Respond to
Changes in Relative Prices

The higher price level in the
United States makes imports
relatively less expensive. U.S.
citizens are likely to increase their
spending on imports from Britain,
shifting the demand for pounds to
the right, from D to D'. At the
same time, the British see U.S.
goods getting more expensive and
reduce their demand for exports
from the United States. The
supply of pounds shifts to the left,
from S to S'. The result is an
increase in the price of pounds.
The pound appreciates and the
dollar is worth less.

Figure 36.5 shows the adjustments likely to occur following an increase in the U.S.
price level relative to the price level in Great Britain. This change in relative prices will
affect citizens of both countries. Higher prices in the United States make imports relatively less expensive. U.S. citizens are likely to increase their spending on imports from
Britain, shifting the demand for pounds to the right, from D to D'. At the same time, the
British see U.S. goods getting more expensive and reduce their demand for exports from
the United States. Consequently, the supply of pounds shifts to the left, from S to S'. The
result is an increase in the price of pounds. Before the change in relative prices, 1 pound
sold for $1.89; after the change, 1 pound costs $2.25. The pound appreciates and the
dollar is worth less.

➤ **Relative Interest Rates**　Another factor that influences a country's exchange rate is
the level of its interest rate relative to other countries' interest rates. If the interest rate
is 7 percent in the United States and 9 percent in Germany, people with money to lend
have an incentive to buy German securities rather than U.S. securities. Although it is
sometimes difficult for individuals in one country to buy securities in another country,
it is easy for international banks and investment companies to do so. If the interest rate
is lower in the United States than in Germany, there will be a movement of funds out of
U.S. securities into German securities as banks and firms move their funds to the
higher-yielding securities.

How does a U.S. bank buy German securities? It takes its dollars, buys German
deutsche marks, and uses the marks to buy the German securities. The bank's purchase
of marks drives up the price of marks in the foreign exchange market. The increased
demand for marks increases the price of the mark (and decreases the price of the dollar). A high interest rate in Germany relative to the interest rate in the United States
tends to depreciate the dollar.

Figure 36.6 shows the effect of rising interest rates in the United States on the
pound-dollar exchange rate. Higher interest rates in the United States attract British investors. To buy U.S. securities, the British need dollars. The supply of pounds (the demand for dollars) shifts to the right, from S to S'. The same relative interest rates affect

If all goes as planned, on January 1, 1999, a number of European countries, including France, Germany and Italy, will shift to a common currency—called the "Euro"—with other countries to follow later. A common currency is yet another step on the long road to a unified European economy, as agreed to in the Maastricht Treaty signed in 1992. Already, steps have been taken to free the movement of goods and workers across borders in Europe. You no longer need a passport to travel from France to Germany, for example. The goal is to achieve the kind of smooth flow of resources that occurs across state lines in the United States. Can you imagine driving across the United States and having to show your passport and change currency at every state line? It certainly would be more difficult to run a multistate business.

One of the stumbling points in the negotiations that led to the European Monetary Union (EMU) was the fact that countries participating in the common currency will no longer be able to exercise independent monetary policy. This argument played a role in Britain's choice not to be among the first group to convert to a common currency. In June of 1998, the countries finally chosen to participate will form a European Central Bank that will regulate the supply of Euros and determine the common monetary policy of the EMU. There will be one common interest rate and bond market.

The fact that countries were giving up the freedom to exercise independent monetary policy continued

to be a sensitive issue right into 1998. In February, a large group of economists signed a petition urging German Chancellor Helmut Kohl to delay the implementation of the EMU because of the very high unemployment rate in Germany—close to 12 percent. Kohl, however, the strongest proponent of the EMU in Europe, was unmoved, arguing there was no turning back.

The following was the timetable for the first group of member countries:

TIME LINE FOR INTRODUCING THE EURO

May 1–8, 1998—Participating member states chosen and bilateral exchange rates announced

June 1, 1998—European Central Bank established

Dec. 31, 1998—"Conversion weekend"

Jan. 1, 1999—Economic and monetary union (EMU) begins; irrevocable conversion rates established; the euro becomes legal currency; single monetary policy starts

Jan. 4, 1999—The markets reopen

1999–2001—National notes and coins remain legal tender

Jan. 1, 2002—Introduction of euro notes and coins; mass changeover of retail activity to euro

Jan. 1–June 30, 2002—Maximum dual legal-tender period

June 30, 2002—Latest date for withdrawal of legal-tender status from national currency

Source: From Craig R. Whitney, "Ready or Not, Europe Draws Closer to One Currency," *The New York Times*, January 5, 1998.

For more on this subject matter, see the Case and Fair Web page at http://www.prenhall.com/casefair.

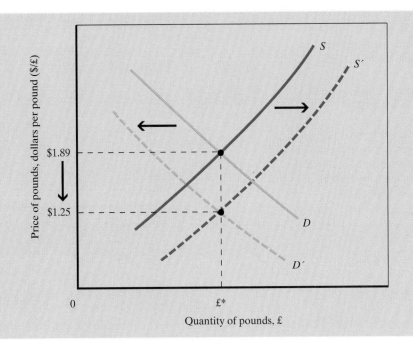

FIGURE 36.6

Exchange Rates Respond to Changes in Relative Interest Rates

If U.S. interest rates rise relative to British interest rates, British citizens holding pounds may be attracted into the U.S. securities market. To buy bonds in the United States, British buyers must exchange pounds for dollars. The supply of pounds shifts to the right, from S to S'. But U.S. citizens are less likely to be interested in British securities, because interest rates are higher at home. The demand for pounds shifts to the left, from D to D'. The result is a depreciated pound and a stronger dollar.

the portfolio choices of U.S. banks, firms, and households. With higher interest rates at home, there is less incentive for U.S. residents to buy British securities. The demand for pounds drops at the same time as the supply increases and the demand curve shifts to the left, from D to D'. The net result is a depreciating pound and an appreciating dollar. The price of pounds falls from $1.89 to $1.25.

THE EFFECTS OF EXCHANGE RATES ON THE ECONOMY

We are now ready to discuss some of the implications of floating exchange rates. Recall, when exchange rates are fixed, households spend some of their incomes on imports and the multiplier is smaller than it would otherwise be. Imports are a "leakage" from the circular flow, much like taxes and saving. Exports, in contrast, are like investment and government purchases; they represent spending on U.S.-produced goods and services ("injections" into the circular flow) and can stimulate output.

The world is far more complicated when exchange rates are allowed to float. First, the level of imports and exports depends on exchange rates as well as on income and other factors. When events cause exchange rates to adjust, the levels of imports and exports will change. Changes in exports and imports can in turn affect the level of real GDP and the price level. Further, exchange rates themselves also adjust to changes in the economy. Suppose the government decides to stimulate the economy with an expansionary monetary policy. This will affect interest rates, which may affect exchange rates.

▶ **Exchange Rate Effects on Imports, Exports, and Real GDP** As we already know, when a country's currency depreciates (falls in value), its import prices rise and its export prices (in foreign currencies) fall. When the U.S. dollar is cheap, U.S. products are more competitive with products produced in the rest of the world, and foreign-made goods look expensive to U.S. citizens.

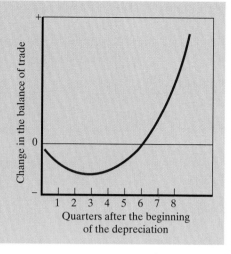

FIGURE 36.7

The Effect of a Depreciation on the Balance of Trade (the J Curve)

Initially, a depreciation of a country's currency may worsen its balance of trade. The negative effect on the price of imports may initially dominate the positive effects of an increase in exports and a decrease in imports.

A depreciation of a country's currency can serve as a stimulus to the economy. Suppose the U.S. dollar falls in value, as it did sharply between 1985 and 1988. If foreign buyers increase their spending on U.S. goods, and domestic buyers substitute U.S.-made goods for imports, aggregate expenditure on domestic output will rise, inventories will fall, and real GDP (Y) will increase.

> A depreciation of a country's currency is likely to increase its GDP.[7]

▶ **Exchange Rates and the Balance of Trade: The J Curve**   Because a depreciating currency tends to increase exports and decrease imports, you might think it will also reduce a country's trade deficit. In fact, the effect of a depreciation on the balance of trade is ambiguous.

Many economists believe when a currency starts to depreciate, the balance of trade is likely to worsen for the first few quarters (perhaps three to six). After that, the balance of trade may improve. This effect is graphed in Figure 36.7. The curve in this figure resembles the letter J, and the movement in the balance of trade that it describes is sometimes called the **J-curve effect**. The point of the J shape is that the balance of trade gets worse before it gets better following a currency depreciation.

How does the J curve come about? Recall that the balance of trade is equal to export revenue minus import costs, including exports and imports of services:

$$\text{Balance of trade} = \text{Dollar price of exports} \times \text{Quantity of Exports} - \text{Dollar price of imports} \times \text{Quantity of Imports}.$$

J-curve effect *Following a currency depreciation, a country's balance of trade may get worse before it gets better. The graph showing this effect is shaped like the letter J, hence the name "J-curve effect."*

---

[7]For this reason, some counties are tempted at times to intervene in foreign exchange markets, depreciate their currencies, and stimulate their economies. If all countries attempted to lower the value of their currencies simultaneously, there will be no gain in income for any of them. Although the exchange rate system at the time was different, such a situation actually occurred during the early years of the Great Depression. So-called *Beggar-thy-neighbor* policies of competitive devaluations were practiced by many countries in a desperate attempt to maintain export sales and employment.

THE IMF'S RESPONSE TO CRISES

In 1997 and 1998, there were severe economic problems in a number of Asian countries including Malaysia, Thailand, the Philippines, South Korea, and Indonesia. In each case, there was eventually a sharp depreciation of the country's currency, just like there was for Mexico in 1994 and 1995. Also, in each case, the International Monetary fund (IMF) stepped in to loan money to the country to help get it through the crisis. In many cases, the conditions imposed by the IMF for these loans were harsh, and a number of economists have criticized the IMF for doing more harm than good. The following article from *The New York Times* summarizes the IMF's response to three cases: Mexico, Indonesia, and South Korea.

MEXICO, 1994–95

SYMPTOMS *Collapse of the peso amid rampant imports, dwindling foreign reserves and high inflation in an overheated economy.*

PRESCRIPTION *Austerity, including a clampdown on credit and wages, in exchange for loans and guarantees led by the United States and backed up by the IMF and other institutions.*

CONSEQUENCES *Widespread bankruptcies. Huge job losses. Increased income inequality, poverty and social strife. But the peso stabilized relatively quickly, and within months Mexico regained the trust of foreign lenders.*

INDONESIA, 1997–98

SYMPTOMS *Collapse of the rupiah amid an explosion of foreign debt and a sharp stock market slide.*

PRESCRIPTION *Austerity and economic restructuring—including an end to special deals for businesses linked to President Suharto's family, the forced breakup of monopolies, the closing of failing banks and tight spending limits—in exchange for billions from the IMF, the United States and other industrial nations.*

CONSEQUENCES *Remain to be seen. Analysts expect inflation, unemployment and bankruptcies to skyrocket. The military stands ready to put down social unrest as political opposition begins to emerge. The IMF projects a stagnant economy this year, but renewed growth in 1999. Meanwhile, the rupiah continues to fall.*

SOUTH KOREA, 1997–98

SYMPTOMS *Collapse of the won and stock market under staggering foreign debt in a sheltered economy built on crony capitalism.*

PRESCRIPTION *Austerity and economic restructuring—including deep cuts in public spending, tight credit, markets thrown open to imports and foreign investment and the removal of government props for bloated conglomerates—in return for the biggest IMF-led bailout ever.*

CONSEQUENCES *Remain to be seen. Growth in screeching to a halt, and analysts expect a boom in unemployment and bankruptcies. Social unrest remains possible, but the stock market has rebounded and the won has steadied.*

Source: David E. Sanger and Richard W. Stevenson, "Second-Guessing the Economic Doctor," *The New York Times*, February 1, 1998.

For more on this subject matter, see the Case and Fair Web page at
http://www.prenhall.com/casefair.

A currency depreciation affects the items on the right side of this equation as follows. First, the quantity of exports increases and the quantity of imports decreases; both have a *positive* effect on the balance of trade (lowering the trade deficit or raising the trade surplus). Second, the dollar price of exports is not likely to change very much, at least not initially. The dollar price of exports changes when the U.S. price level changes, but the initial effect of a depreciation on the domestic price level is not likely to be large. Third, the dollar price of imports increases. Imports into the United States are more expensive, because one dollar buys fewer French francs and German deutsche marks than before. An increase in the dollar price of imports has a *negative* effect on the balance of trade.

An example to clarify this last point: The dollar price of a Japanese car that costs 2,000,000 yen rises from $10,000 to $15,000 when the exchange rate moves from 200 yen per dollar to 133 yen per dollar. After the currency depreciation, the United States ends up spending more (in dollars) for the Japanese car than it did before. Of course, the United States will end up buying fewer Japanese cars than it did before. But does the number of cars drop enough so the quantity effect is bigger than the price effect, or vice versa? Does the value of imports increase or decrease?

The net effect of a depreciation on the balance of trade could go either way. The depreciation stimulates exports and cuts back imports, but it also increases the dollar price of imports. It seems that the negative effect dominates initially. The impact of a depreciation on the price of imports is generally felt quickly, while it takes time for export and import quantities to respond to price changes. In the short run, the value of imports increases more than the value of exports, so the balance of trade worsens. The initial effect is likely to be negative; but after exports and imports have had time to respond, the net effect turns positive. The more elastic the demand for exports and imports, the larger the eventual improvement in the balance of trade.

> **Exchange Rates and Prices**   The depreciation of a country's currency tends to increase its price level. There are two reasons for this. First, when a country's currency is less expensive, its products are more competitive on world markets, so exports rise. In addition, domestic buyers tend to substitute domestic products for the now-more-expensive imports. This means planned aggregate expenditure on domestically produced goods and services rises, and the aggregate demand curve shifts to the right. The result is a higher price level, higher output, or both. (You may want to draw an *AS/AD* diagram to verify this.) If the economy is close to capacity, the result is likely to be higher prices. Second, a depreciation makes imported inputs more expensive. If costs increase, the aggregate supply curve shifts to the left. If aggregate demand remains unchanged, the result is an increase in the price level.

> **Monetary Policy with Flexible Exchange Rates**   Let's now put everything in this chapter together and consider what happens when monetary policy is used first to stimulate the economy and then to contract the economy.

Suppose the economy is below full employment and the Fed decides to expand the money supply. The volume of reserves in the system is expanded, perhaps through open market purchases of U.S. government securities by the Fed. This results in a decrease in the interest rate. The lower interest rate stimulates planned investment spending and consumption spending.

This added spending causes inventories to be lower than planned and aggregate output (income) (Y) to rise. But there are two additional effects. One, the lower interest rate has an impact in the foreign exchange market. A lower interest rate means a lower demand for U.S. securities by foreigners, so the demand for dollars drops. Two, U.S. investment managers will be more likely to buy foreign securities (which are now paying relatively higher interest rates), so the supply of dollars rises. Both events push down the value of the dollar.

A cheaper dollar is a good thing if the goal of the monetary expansion is to stimulate the domestic economy, because a cheaper dollar means more U.S. exports and fewer imports. If consumers substitute U.S.-made goods for imports, both the added exports and the decrease in imports mean more spending on domestic products, so the multiplier actually increases.

Now suppose inflation is a problem and the Fed wants to slow it down with tight money. Here again, floating exchange rates help. Tight monetary policy works through a higher interest rate. A higher interest rate lowers investment and consumption spending, reducing aggregate expenditure, reducing output, and lowering the price level. The higher interest rate also attracts foreign buyers into U.S. financial markets, driving up the value of the dollar, which reduces the price of imports. The reduction in the price of imports shifts the aggregate supply curve to the right, which helps fight inflation.

> **Fiscal Policy with Flexible Exchange Rates**   The openness of the economy and flexible exchange rates do not always work to the advantage of policy makers. Consider a policy of cutting taxes to stimulate the economy. Suppose Congress enacts a major tax cut designed to raise output. Spending by households rises, but not all of this added spending is on domestic products—some leaks out of the U.S. economy, reducing the multiplier.

As income rises, so does the demand for money (M^d)—not the demand for dollars in the foreign exchange market, but the amount of money people desire to hold for transactions. Unless the Fed is fully accommodating, the interest rate will rise. A higher interest rate tends to attract foreign demand for U.S. securities. This tends to drive the price of the dollar up, which further blunts the effectiveness of the tax cut. If the value of the dollar rises, U.S. exports are less competitive in world markets, and the quantity of exports will decline. Similarly, a strong dollar makes imported goods look cheaper, and U.S. citizens spend more on foreign goods and less on U.S. goods, again reducing the multiplier.

Another caveat to the multiplier story of chapters 24 and 25: Without a fully accommodating Fed, three factors work to reduce the multiplier: (1) A higher interest rate from the increase in money demand may crowd out private investment and consumption; (2) some of the increase in income from the expansion will be spent on imports; and (3) a higher interest rate may cause the dollar to appreciate, discouraging exports and further encouraging imports.

AN INTERDEPENDENT WORLD ECONOMY

The increasing interdependence of countries in the world economy has made the problems facing policy makers more difficult. We used to be able to think of the United States as a relatively self-sufficient region. Thirty years ago, economic events outside U.S. borders had relatively little effect on its economy. This is no longer true. The events of the past three decades have taught us that the United States is a part of a global economy and the performance of the U.S. economy is heavily dependent on events outside its borders.

This chapter and the previous one have provided only the bare bones of open-market macroeconomics. If you continue your study of economics, more will be added to the basic story we have presented.

Keeping us in the international arena, chapter 37 deals with the problems of developing countries, and chapter 38 explores special features of the economies of the former republics of the Soviet Union and some other nations.

SUMMARY

1. The main difference between an international transaction and a domestic transaction concerns currency exchange: When people in different countries buy from and sell to each other, an exchange of currencies must also take place.

2. The *exchange rate* is the price of one country's currency in terms of another country's currency.

THE BALANCE OF PAYMENTS

3. *Foreign exchange* is all currencies other than the domestic currency of a given country. The record of a nation's transactions in goods, services, and assets with the rest of the world is its *balance of payments*. The balance of payments is also the record of a country's sources (supply) and uses (demand) of foreign exchange.

EQUILIBRIUM OUTPUT (INCOME) IN AN OPEN ECONOMY

4. In an open economy, some income is spent on foreign-produced goods rather than domestically produced goods. To measure planned aggregate expenditure in an open economy, we add total exports but subtract total imports: $AE \equiv C + I + G + EX - IM$. The open economy is in equilibrium when aggregate output (income) (Y) equals planned aggregate expenditure (AE).

5. In an open economy, the multiplier equals $1/[1 - (MPC - MPM)]$, where MPC is the marginal propensity to consume and MPM is the marginal propensity to import. The *marginal propensity to import* is the change in imports caused by a $1 change in income.

6. In addition to income, other factors that affect the level of imports are the after-tax real wage rate, after-tax nonlabor income, interest rates, and the relative prices of domestically produced and foreign-produced goods. The demand for exports is determined by economic activity in the rest of the world and by relative prices.

7. An increase in U.S. economic activity leads to a worldwide increase in economic activity, which then "feeds back" to the United States. An increase in U.S. imports increases other countries' exports, which stimulates economies and increases their imports, which increases U.S. exports, which stimulates the U.S. economy and increases its imports, and so on. This is the *trade feedback effect*.

8. Export prices of other countries affect U.S. import prices. The general rate of inflation abroad is likely to affect U.S. import prices. If the inflation rate abroad is high, U.S. import prices are likely to rise.

9. Because one country's exports are another country's imports, an increase in export prices increases other countries' import prices. An increase in other countries' import prices leads to an increase in their domestic prices—and their export prices. In short, export prices affect import prices, and vice versa. This *price feedback effect* shows that inflation is "exportable"; an increase in the price level in one country can drive up prices in other countries, making inflation in the first country worse.

THE OPEN ECONOMY WITH FLEXIBLE EXCHANGE RATES

10. The equilibrium exchange rate occurs when the quantity demanded of a foreign currency in the foreign exchange market equals the quantity of that currency supplied in the foreign exchange market.

11. *Depreciation of a currency* occurs when a nation's currency falls in value relative to another country's currency. *Appreciation of a currency* occurs when a nation's currency rises in value relative to another country's currency.

12. According to the *law of one price*, if the costs of transportation are small, the price of the same good in different countries should be roughly the same. The theory that exchange rates are set so that the price of similar goods in different countries is the same is known as *purchasing-power-parity theory*. In practice, transportation costs are significant for many goods, and the law of one price does not hold for these goods.

13. A high rate of inflation in one country relative to another puts pressure on the exchange rate between the two countries. There is a general tendency for the currencies of relatively high-inflation countries to depreciate.

14. A depreciation of the dollar tends to increase U.S. GDP by making U.S. exports cheaper (hence more competitive abroad) and by making U.S. imports more expensive (encouraging consumers to switch to domestically produced goods and services).

15. The effect of a depreciation of a nation's currency on its balance of trade is unclear. In the short run, a currency depreciation may increase the balance-of-trade deficit, because it raises the price of imports. Although this price increase causes a decrease in the quantity of imports demanded, the impact of a depreciation on the price of imports is generally felt quickly, but it takes time for export and import quantities to respond to price changes. The initial effect is likely to be negative; but after exports and imports have had time to respond, the net effect turns positive. The tendency for the balance-of-trade deficit to widen and then to decrease as the result of a currency depreciation is known as the *J-curve effect*.

16. The depreciation of a country's currency tends to raise its price level for two reasons. First, a currency depreciation increases planned aggregate expenditure, which shifts the aggregate demand curve to the right. If the economy is close to capacity, the result is likely to be higher prices. Second, a depreciation makes imported inputs more expensive. If costs increase, the aggregate supply curve shifts to the left. If aggregate demand remains unchanged, the result is an increase in the price level.

17. When exchange rates are flexible, a U.S. expansionary monetary policy decreases the interest rate and stimulates planned investment and consumption spending. The lower interest rate leads to a lower demand for U.S. securities by foreigners, and a higher demand for foreign securities by U.S. investment-fund managers. As a result, the dollar depreciates. A U.S. contractionary monetary policy appreciates the dollar.

18. Flexible exchange rates do not always work to the advantage of policy makers. An expansionary fiscal policy can appreciate the dollar and work to reduce the multiplier.

REVIEW TERMS AND CONCEPTS

appreciation of a currency, 847

balance of payments, 835

balance of trade, 835

balance on capital account, 837

balance on current account, 836

depreciation of a currency, 847

exchange rate, 834

floating, or market-determined, exchange rates, 844

foreign exchange, 835

J-curve effect, 852

law of one price, 848

marginal propensity to import (MPM), 840

net exports of goods and services (EX − IM), 839

price feedback effect, 844

purchasing-power-parity theory, 848

trade deficit, 835

trade feedback effect, 842

Planned aggregate expenditure in an open economy:

$$AE \equiv C + I + G + EX - IM$$

Open-economy multiplier:

$$\frac{1}{1 - (MPC - MPM)}$$

PROBLEM SET

1. During 1997, a series of events rocked the economies of Asia. Describe the effects of each event if they had occurred at separate times on: the exchange rate of the U.S. dollar versus the Japanese yen; and the balance of trade between the United States and Japan.
  a. U.S. holders of Japanese stocks and bonds get spooked and sell their holdings, reinvesting the proceeds in U.S. stock and bond markets.
  b. Japan finds itself in recession with GDP falling sharply.
  c. The Japanese Ministry of Finance decides to balance the budget and to counteract the contractionary effects by expansionary monetary policy, pushing interest rates to under 1 percent.

2. Suppose the following prevailed on the foreign exchange market in 1998 with floating exchange rates:
  a. Name three phenomena that might shift the demand curve to the right.

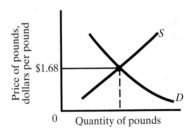

  b. Which, if any, of these three might cause a simultaneous shift of the supply curve to the left?
  c. What effects might the three phenomena have on the balance of trade if the exchange rate floats?

3. Explain how each of the following transactions would be treated in the U.S. balance of payments account. (Remember that there are two entries per transaction.)

a. You vacation in Mexico, spending $300 there on a hotel room, food, transportation, and so on.

b. You bring back an Oriental carpet that you bought in the Middle East. The carpet is worth $10,000, but you do not declare it at customs, and no official record of the transaction exists.

c. You buy a new Toyota (made in Japan) for $15,000.

d. You send your cousin in Canada a birthday present worth $50.

e. Volkswagen Inc. of Germany buys a factory in the United States for $100 million.

f. Toyota of Japan buys 10 percent of all the shares in General Motors.

g. You loan your uncle in Canada $5,000.

h. Your uncle pays you $500 in interest on the money you previously loaned him. He also repays $1,000 of the principal.

4. During 1981 and 1982, the president and the Congress were pursuing a very expansionary *fiscal* policy. In 1980 and 1981, the Federal Reserve was pursuing a very restrictive *monetary* policy in an attempt to rid the economy of inflation. Ultimately, the economy went into a deep recession, but before it did interest rates went to record levels with the prime rate topping out at over 21 percent.

a. Explain how this policy mix led to very high interest rates.

b. Show graphically the effect of the high interest rates on the foreign exchange market. What do you think would happen to the value of the dollar under these circumstances?

c. What impact was such a series of events likely to have on the trade balance in countries like Japan? Explain your answer.

5. The exchange rate between the U.S. dollar and the Japanese yen is floating freely—neither government intervenes in the market for either currency. Suppose a large trade deficit with Japan prompts the United States to impose quotas on certain Japanese products imported into the United States and, as a result, the quantity of these imports falls.

a. The decrease in spending on Japanese products increases spending on U.S.-made goods. Why? What effect will this have on U.S. output and employment? On Japanese output and employment?

b. What happens to U.S. imports from Japan when U.S. output (or income) rises? If the quotas initially reduce imports from Japan by $25 billion, why is the final reduction in imports likely to be less than $25 billion? Explain in terms of the trade feedback effect.

c. Suppose the quotas do succeed in reducing imports from Japan by $15 billion. What will happen to the demand for yen? Why?

d. What will happen to the dollar-yen exchange rate, and why? (*Hint:* There is an excess supply of yen, or an excess demand for dollars.) What effects will the change

in the value of each currency have on employment and output in the United States? What about the balance of trade? (Ignore complications such as the J curve.)

e. Considering the macroeconomic effects of a quota on Japanese imports, could a quota actually reduce employment and output in the United States, or have no effect at all? Explain.

6. What effect will each of the following events have on the current account balance and the exchange rate if the exchange rate is fixed? If it is floating?

a. The U.S. government cuts taxes, and income rises.

b. The U.S. inflation rate increases, and prices in the United States rise faster than those in the countries with which the United States trades.

c. The United States adopts an expansionary monetary policy. Interest rates fall (and are now lower than those in other countries), and income rises.

d. Textile companies' "Buy American" campaign is successful, and U.S. consumers switch from purchasing imported products to those made in the United States.

*7. You are given the following model, which describes the economy of Hypothetica.

(1) Consumption function: $C = 100 + .8Y_d$
(2) Planned investment: $I = 38$
(3) Government spending: $G = 75$
(4) Exports: $EX = 25$
(5) Imports: $IM = .05Y_d$
(6) Disposable income: $Y_d \equiv Y - T$
(7) Taxes: $T = 40$
(8) Planned aggregate expenditure:
   $AE \equiv C + I + G + (EX - IM)$
(9) Definition of equilibrium income: $Y = AE$.

a. What is equilibrium income in Hypothetica? What is the government deficit? What is the current account balance?

b. If government spending is increased to $G = 80$, what happens to equilibrium income? Explain, using the government spending multiplier. What happens to imports?

   Now suppose the amount of imports is limited to $IM = 40$ by a quota on imports. If government spending is again increased from 75 to 80, what happens to equilibrium income? Explain why the same increase in G has a bigger effect on income in the second case. What is it about the presence of imports that changes the value of the multiplier?

c. If exports are fixed at $EX = 25$, what must income be to ensure a current account balance of zero? (*Hint:* Imports depend on income, so what must income be for imports to be equal to exports?) By how much must we cut government spending to balance the current account? (*Hint:* Use your answer to the first part of this question to determine how much of a decrease in income is needed. Then use the multiplier to calculate the decrease in *G* needed to reduce income by that amount.)

8. The following table shows that over the course of a decade, the U.S. dollar has remained virtually constant against the British pound. In the same time frame, the dollar fell dramatically against the yen; the price of yen rose 160 percent between 1983 and 1995. Explain why this might be so.

	MAY 1983	MARCH 1995
Pound sterling	$1.56	$1.58
Yen	.0042	.0111

TAKE IT TO THE NET

We invite you to visit the Case and Fair page on the Prentice Hall Web site:

http://www.prenhall.com/casefair

for this chapter's World Wide Web exercise.

WORLD MONETARY SYSTEMS SINCE 1900

Since the beginning of the twentieth century, the world has operated under a number of different monetary systems. This appendix provides a brief history of each and a description of how they worked.

THE GOLD STANDARD

The gold standard was the major system of exchange rate determination before 1914. All currencies were priced in terms of gold—an ounce of gold was worth so much in each currency. When all currencies exchanged at fixed ratios to gold, exchange rates could be determined easily. For instance, one ounce of gold was worth $20 U.S.; that same ounce of gold exchanged for 4 British pounds. Because $20 and £4 were each worth one ounce of gold, the exchange rate between dollars and pounds was $20/£4, or $5 to £1.

For the gold standard to be effective it had to be backed up by the country's willingness to buy and sell gold at the determined price. As long as countries maintain their currencies at a fixed value in terms of gold *and* as long as each is willing to buy and sell gold, exchange rates are fixed. If at the given exchange rate the number of U.S. citizens who want to buy things produced in Great Britain is equal to the number of British citizens who want to buy things produced in the United States, the currencies of the two countries will simply be exchanged. But what if U.S. citizens suddenly decide they want to drink imported Scotch instead of domestic bourbon? If the British do not have an increased desire for U.S. goods, they would still accept U.S. dollars because they could be redeemed in gold. This gold could then be immediately turned into pounds.

As long as a country's overall balance of payments remained in balance, no gold would enter or leave the country, and the economy would be in equilibrium. If U.S. citizens bought more from the British than the British bought from the United States, however, the U.S. balance of payments would be in deficit, and the U.S. stock of gold would begin to fall. Conversely, Britain would start to accumulate gold because it would be exporting more than it spent on imports.

But under the gold standard, gold was a big determinant of the money supply.[1] An inflow of gold into a country caused that country's money supply to expand, and an outflow of gold caused that country's money supply to contract. If gold were flowing from the United States to Great Britain, the British money supply would expand and the U.S. money supply would contract.

Now recall from earlier chapters the impacts of a change in the money supply. An expanded money supply in Britain will lower British interest rates and stimulate aggregate demand. As a result, aggregate output (income) and the price level in Britain will increase. Higher British prices will discourage U.S. citizens from buying British goods. At the same time, British citizens will have more income and will face relatively lower import prices, causing them to import more from the States.

On the other side of the Atlantic, U.S. citizens will face a contracting domestic money supply. This will cause higher interest rates, declining aggregate demand, lower prices, and falling output (income). This will lower demand in the United States for British goods. Thus, changes in relative prices and incomes that resulted from the inflow and outflow of gold would automatically bring trade back into balance.

PROBLEMS WITH THE GOLD STANDARD

Two major problems were associated with the gold standard. First, the gold standard implied that a country had little control over its money supply. The reason, as we have just seen, is that the money stock increased when the overall balance of payments was in surplus (gold inflow) and decreased when the overall balance was in deficit (gold outflow). A country that was experiencing a balance-of-payments deficit could correct the problem only by the painful process of allowing its money supply to contract. This brought on a slump in economic activity, a slump that would eventually restore balance-of-payments equilibrium, but only after reductions in income and employment. Countries could (and often did) act to protect their gold reserves, and this prevented the adjustment mechanism from correcting the deficit.

Making the money supply depend on the amount of gold available had another disadvantage. When major new gold fields were discovered (as in California in 1849 or South Africa in 1886), the world's supply of gold (and therefore of money) increased. The price level rose and income increased. When no new gold was discovered, the supply of money remained unchanged and prices and income tended to fall.

When President Reagan took office in 1981, he established a commission to consider returning the nation

---

[1]In the days when currencies were tied to gold, changes in the amount of gold influenced the supply of money in two ways. A change in the quantity of gold coins in circulation had a direct effect on the supply of money; indirectly, gold served as a backing for paper currency. A decrease in the central bank's gold holdings meant a decline in the amount of paper money that could be supported.

to the gold standard. The final commission report recommended against such a move. An important part of the reasoning behind this was that the gold standard puts enormous economic power in the hands of gold-producing nations.

FIXED EXCHANGE RATES AND THE BRETTON WOODS SYSTEM

As World War II drew to a close, a group of economists from the United States and Europe met to formulate a new set of rules for exchange rate determination that they hoped would avoid the difficulties of the gold standard. The rules they designed became known as the **Bretton Woods system**, after the town in New Hampshire where the delegates met. The Bretton Woods system was based on two (not necessarily compatible) premises. First, countries were to maintain fixed exchange rates with each other. Instead of pegging their currencies directly to gold, however, currencies were fixed in terms of the U.S. dollar, which was fixed in value at $35 per ounce of gold. The British pound, for instance, was fixed at roughly $2.40, which meant that an ounce of gold was worth approximately 14.6 pounds. As we shall see, the pure system of fixed exchange rates would work in a manner very similar to the pre-1914 gold standard.

The second aspect of the Bretton Woods system added a new wrinkle to the operation of the international economy. Countries experiencing a "fundamental disequilibrium" in their balance of payments were allowed to change their exchange rates. (The term *fundamental disequilibrium* was necessarily vague, but it came to be interpreted as a large and persistent current account deficit.) Exchange rates were not really fixed under the Bretton Woods system; they were, as someone remarked, only "fixed until further notice."

The point of allowing countries with serious current account problems to alter the value of their currency was to avoid the harsh recessions that the operation of the gold standard would have produced under these circumstances. But the experience of the European economies in the years between World War I and World War II suggested it might not be a good idea to give countries complete freedom to change their exchange rates whenever they wished.

During the Great Depression, many countries undertook so-called competitive devaluations to protect domestic output and employment. That is, countries would try to encourage exports—a source of output growth and employment—by attempting to set as low an exchange rate as possible, thereby making their exports competitive with foreign-produced goods. Unfortunately, such policies had a built-in flaw. A devaluation

of the pound against the French franc may help encourage British exports to France, but if those additional British exports cut into French output and employment, France is likely to respond by devaluing the franc against the pound, which, of course, undoes the effects of the pound's initial devaluation.

To solve this exchange rate rivalry, the Bretton Woods agreement created the International Monetary Fund (IMF). Its job was to assist countries experiencing temporary current account problems.[2] It was also supposed to certify that a "fundamental disequilibrium" existed before a country was allowed to change its exchange rate. The IMF was like an international economic traffic cop whose job is to ensure that all countries are playing the game according to the agreed-upon rules and to provide emergency assistance where needed.

"PURE" FIXED EXCHANGE RATES

Under a pure fixed exchange rate system, governments set a particular *fixed* rate at which their currencies will exchange for each other and then commit themselves to maintaining that rate. A true fixed exchange rate system is like the gold standard in that exchange rates are supposed to stay the same forever.[3] Because currencies are no longer backed by gold, they have no fixed, or standard, value relative to each other. There is therefore no automatic mechanism to keep exchange rates aligned with each other, as with the gold standard.

The result is that under a pure fixed exchange rate system, governments must at times intervene in the foreign exchange market to keep currencies aligned at their established values. Economists define government intervention in the foreign exchange market as the buying or selling of foreign exchange for the purpose of manipulating the exchange rate. What kind of intervention is likely to occur under a fixed exchange rate system, and how does it work?

We can see how intervention works by looking at Figure 36A.1. Initially, the market for Italian lira is in equilibrium. At the fixed exchange rate of $0.02 per lira, the supply of lira is exactly equal to the demand for lira. No government intervention is necessary to maintain the exchange rate at this level. Now suppose Italian wines are found to be contaminated with antifreeze, and U.S.

---

[2]The idea was that the IMF would make short-term loans to a country with a current account deficit. The loans would enable the country to correct the current account problem gradually, without bringing on a deep recession, running out of foreign exchange reserves, or devaluing the currency.

[3]"Forever" is a very long time. Some countries in Central America have maintained fixed exchange rates with the U.S. dollar for almost 30 years, practically forever in the world of international finance!

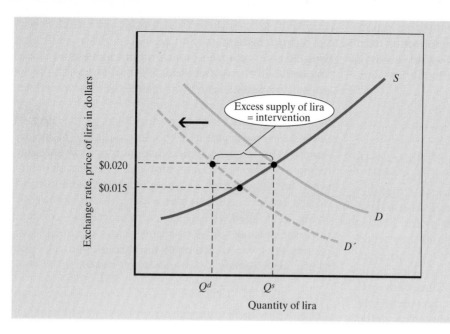

FIGURE 36A.1

Government Intervention in the Foreign Exchange Market

If the price of lira was set by a completely unfettered market, the price of a lira would be .020 when demand is D and .015 when demand is D'. If the government has committed itself to keeping the value of a lira at .020, it must buy up the excess supply of lira ($Q^s - Q^d$).

citizens switch to California wines. This substitution away from the Italian product shifts the U.S. demand curve for lira to the left: The United States demands fewer lira at every exchange rate (cost of a lira) because it is purchasing less from Italy than it did before.

If the price of lira were set by a completely unfettered market, the shift in the demand curve would lead to a fall in the price of lira, just the way the price of wheat would fall if there was an excess supply of wheat. Remember, the Italian and U.S. governments have committed themselves to maintaining the rate at $0.02 per lira. To do this, either the U.S. government or Italian government (or both) must buy up the excess supply of lira to keep the price of the lira from falling. In essence, the fixed exchange rate policy commits governments to making up any difference between the supply of a currency and the demand so as to keep the price of the currency (exchange rate) at the desired level. The government promises to act as the supplier (or demander) of last resort, who will ensure that the amount of foreign exchange demanded by the private sector will equal the supply at the fixed price.

PROBLEMS WITH THE BRETTON WOODS SYSTEM

As it developed after the end of World War II, the system of more-or-less fixed exchange rates had some flaws that led to its abandonment in 1971.

First, there was a basic asymmetry built into the rules of international finance. Countries experiencing large and persistent current account deficits—what the Bretton

Woods agreements termed "fundamental disequilibria"—were obliged to devalue their currencies and/or take measures to cut their deficits by contracting their economies. Both of these alternatives were unpleasant, because devaluation meant rising prices and contraction meant rising unemployment. But a country with a current account deficit had no choice, since it was losing its stock of foreign exchange reserves. When its stock of foreign currencies became exhausted, it had to change its exchange rate, because further intervention (selling off some of its foreign exchange reserves) became impossible.

Countries experiencing current account surpluses were in a different position, since they were gaining foreign exchange reserves. Although these countries were supposed to stimulate their economies and/or revalue their currencies to restore balance to their current account, they were not obliged to do so. They could easily maintain their fixed exchange rate by buying up any excess supply of foreign exchange with their own currency, of which they had plentiful supply.

In practice, this meant some countries—especially Germany and Japan—tended to run large and chronic current account surpluses and were under no compulsion to take steps to correct the problem. The U.S. economy, stimulated by expenditures on the Vietnam War, experienced a large and prolonged current account deficit (capital outflow) in the 1960s, which was the counterpart of these surpluses. The United States was, however, in a unique position under the Bretton Woods system. The value of gold was fixed in terms of the U.S. dollar at $35 per ounce of gold. Other countries fixed their exchange rates in terms of U.S. dollars (and therefore only indirectly in terms of gold). This meant the United States could never accomplish anything by devaluing its currency in terms of gold. If the dollar was devalued from $35 to $40 per ounce of gold, the yen, pegged at 200 yen per dollar, would move in parallel with the dollar (from 7,000 yen per ounce of gold to 8,000 yen per ounce), with the dollar-yen exchange rate unaffected. To correct its current account deficits vis-á-vis Japan and Germany, it would be necessary for those two countries to adjust their currencies' exchange rates with the dollar. But these countries were reluctant to do so for a variety of reasons. As a result, the U.S. current account was chronically in deficit throughout the late 1960s.

A second flaw in the Bretton Woods system was that it permitted devaluations only if a country had a "chronic" current account deficit and was in danger of running out of foreign exchange reserves. This meant devaluations could often be predicted quite far in advance, and they usually had to be rather large if they were to correct any serious current account problem. The situation made it tempting for speculators to "attack" the currencies of countries with current account deficits.

Problems like these eventually led the United States to abandon the Bretton Woods rules in 1971. The U.S. government refused to continue pegging the value of the dollar in terms of gold. This meant the prices of all currencies were free to find their own levels.

The alternative to fixed exchange rates is a system that allows exchange rates to move freely or flexibly in response to market forces. Two types of flexible exchange rate systems are usually distinguished. In a *freely floating system*, governments do not intervene at all in the foreign exchange market.[4] They do not buy or sell currencies with the aim of manipulating the rates. In a *managed floating system*, governments intervene if markets are becoming "disorderly"—fluctuating more than a government feels is desirable. Governments may also intervene if they think a currency is increasing or decreasing too much in value, even though the day-to-day fluctuations may be small.

Since the demise of the Bretton Woods system in 1971, the world's exchange rate system can be described as "managed floating." One of the important features of this system has been times of large fluctuations in exchange rates. For example, the yen-dollar rate went from 347 in 1971 to 210 in 1978, to 125 in 1988, to 80 in 1995. These are very large changes, changes that have important effects on the international economy, some of which we have covered in this text.

---

[4]However, governments may from time to time buy or sell foreign exchange for their own needs (rather than to influence the exchange rate). For example, the U.S. government might need British pounds to buy land for a U.S. embassy building in London. For our purposes, we ignore this behavior because it is not "intervention" in the strict sense of the word.

SUMMARY

1. The gold standard was the major system of exchange rate determination before 1914. All currencies were priced in terms of gold. Difficulties with the gold standard led to the *Bretton Woods* agreement following World War II. Under this system, countries maintained fixed exchange rates with each other and fixed the value of their currencies in terms of the U.S. dollar. Countries experiencing a "fundamental disequilibrium" in their current accounts were permitted to change their exchange rates.

2. The Bretton Woods system was abandoned in 1971. Since then, the world's exchange rate system has been one of managed floating rates. Under this system, governments intervene if foreign exchange markets are fluctuating more than the government thinks desirable.

REVIEW TERMS AND CONCEPTS

Bretton Woods The site in New Hampshire where a group of experts from 44 countries met in 1944 and agreed on an international monetary system of fixed exchange rates. 861

1. The currency of Atlantis is the wimp. In 1998, Atlantis developed a balance-of-payments deficit with the United States as a result of an unanticipated decrease in exports; U.S. citizens cut back on the purchase of Atlantean goods. Assume Atlantis is operating under a system of fixed exchange rates.

   a. How does the drop in exports affect the market for wimps? Identify the deficit graphically.

   b. How must the government of Atlantis act (in the short run) to maintain the value of the wimp?

   c. If originally Atlantis was operating at full employment (potential GDP), what impact will these events have on its economy? Explain your answer.

   d. The chief economist of Atlantis suggests expansionary monetary policy to restore full employment; the secretary of commerce suggests a tax cut (expansionary fiscal policy). Given the fixed exchange rate system, describe the effects of these two policy options on Atlantis's current account.

   e. How would your answers to a, b, and c change if the two countries operated under a floating rate system?

Chapter 37

ECONOMIC GROWTH
IN DEVELOPING NATIONS

OUR PRIMARY FOCUS in this text has been on economic issues facing the United States. Welfare and health-care reform, slow economic growth in recent years, antitrust action against Microsoft, and worries about the deficit are familiar to Americans. But the economics we have been studying also applies to other countries: Welfare reform is a big issue in the Netherlands, Japan is facing major fiscal deficits, and the German central bank has been wrestling with slow economic growth. We can analyze these and other issues in the Netherlands, Japan, and Germany with some confidence because these countries have so much in common with the United States. In spite of differences in languages and cultures, all these countries have modern industrialized economies that rely heavily on markets to allocate resources. But what about the economic problems facing Somalia or Haiti? Can we apply the same economic principles that we have been studying to these less-developed countries (sometimes called LDCs)?

Yes. All economic analysis deals with the problem of making choices under conditions of scarcity, and the problem of satisfying their citizens' wants and needs is as real for Somalia and Haiti as it is for the Netherlands, Germany, and Japan. The universality of scarcity is what makes economic analysis relevant to all nations, regardless of their level of material well-being or ruling political ideology.

The basic tools of supply and demand, theories about consumers and firms, and theories about the structure of markets all contribute to an understanding of the economic problems confronting the world's developing nations. However, these nations often face economic problems quite different from those faced by richer, more developed countries. In the developing nations, the economist may have to worry about chronic food shortages, explosive population growth, and hyperinflations that reach triple, and even quadruple, digits. The United States and other industrialized economies rarely encounter such difficulties.

The instruments of economic management also vary from nation to nation. The United States has well-developed financial market institutions and a strong central bank (the Federal Reserve) through which the government can control the macroeconomy to some extent. But even limited intervention is impossible in some of the developing countries. In the United States, tax laws can be changed to stimulate saving, to encourage particular kinds of investments, or to redistribute income. In most developing countries, there are neither meaningful personal income taxes nor effective tax policies.

But even though economic problems and the policy instruments available to tackle them vary across nations, economic thinking about these problems can be transferred easily from one setting to another. In this chapter we discuss several of the economic problems specific to developing nations in an attempt to capture some of the insights that economic analysis can offer.

LIFE IN THE DEVELOPING NATIONS: POPULATION AND POVERTY

By the year 2000, the population of the world will reach over 6.1 billion people. Most of the world's more than 200 nations belong to the developing world, in which about three-fourths of the world's population lives.

In the early 1960s, the nations of the world could be assigned rather easily to categories: The *developed countries* included most of Europe, North America, Japan, Australia, and New Zealand; the *developing countries* included the rest of the world. The developing nations were often referred to as the "Third World" to distinguish them from the Western industrialized nations (the "First World") and the former Socialist bloc of Eastern European nations (the "Second World").

In the 1990s the world does not divide easily into three neat parts. Rapid economic progress has brought some developing nations closer to developed economies. Countries such as Argentina and Korea, still considered to be "developing," are often referred to as middle-income, or newly industrialized, countries. Other countries, such as much of sub-Saharan Africa and some of South Asia, have stagnated and fallen so far behind the economic advances of the rest of the world that the "Fourth World" has been used to describe them. It is not clear yet where the republics of the former Soviet Union and other formerly Communist countries of Eastern Europe will end up. Production has fallen sharply in many of them. For example, between 1990 and 1997, real GDP fell about 40 percent in the transition economies and by over 50 percent in Russia and Central Asia. One estimate puts current per capita GDP in Russia at around $2,500. Some of the new republics now have more in common with developing countries than with developed countries.

Although the countries of the developing world exhibit considerable diversity, both in their standards of living and in their particular experiences of growth, marked differences continue to separate them from the developed nations. The developed countries have a higher average level of material well-being (the amounts of food, clothing, shelter, and other commodities consumed by the average person). Comparisons of gross domestic product (GDP) per capita—the value of goods and services produced per person in an economy—are often used as a crude index of the level of material well-being across nations. See Table 37.1 where GDP per capita in the industrial market economies significantly exceeds GDP of both the low- and middle-income developing economies.

Other characteristics of economic development include improvements in basic health and education. The degree of political and economic freedom enjoyed by individual citizens might also be part of what it means to be a developed nation. Some of these criteria are easier to quantify; Table 37.1 presents data for different types of economies according to some of the more easily measured indexes of development. As you see, the industrial market economies enjoy higher standards of living according to whatever indicator of development is chosen.

TABLE 37.1 INDICATORS OF ECONOMIC DEVELOPMENT

COUNTRY GROUP	POPULATION (MILLIONS) 1995	GDP PER CAPITA, 1995 (DOLLARS)	LIFE EXPECTANCY, 1995 (YEARS)	INFANT MORTALITY, 1995 (DEATHS BEFORE AGE ONE PER 1,000 BIRTHS)	PERCENTAGE OF POPULATION IN URBAN AREAS, 1995
Low-income (e.g., China, Ethiopia, Haiti, India)	3,180	430	63	69	29
Lower middle-income (e.g., Guatemala, Poland, Philippines, Thailand)	1,153	1,670	67	41	56
Upper middle-income (e.g., Brazil, Malaysia, Mexico)	438	4,260	69	35	73
Industrial market economies (e.g., Japan, Germany, New Zealand, United States)	902	24,930	77	7	75

Source: World Bank, *World Development Report, 1997.* Note that all numbers refer to weighted averages for each country group, where the weights equal the populations of each nation in a specific country group.

Behind these statistics lies the reality of the very difficult life facing the people of the developing world. For most, meager incomes provide only the basic necessities. Most meals are the same, consisting of the region's food staple—rice, wheat, or corn. Shelter is primitive. Many people share a small room, usually with an earthen floor and no sanitary facilities. The great majority of the population lives in rural areas where agricultural work is hard and extremely time-consuming. Productivity (output produced per worker) is low because household plots are small and only the crudest of farm implements are available. Low productivity means farm output per person is barely sufficient to feed a farmer's own family, with nothing left to sell to others. School-age children may receive some formal education, but illiteracy remains chronic for young and old. Infant mortality runs 10 times higher than in the United States. Although parasitic infections are common and debilitating, there is only one physician per 5,000 people. In addition, many developing nations are engaged in civil and external warfare.

Life in the developing nations is a continual struggle against the circumstances of poverty, and prospects for dramatic improvements in living standards for most people are dim. As with all generalizations, there are exceptions. Some nations are better off than others, and in any given nation an elite group always lives in considerable luxury. Income distribution in developing countries is often so skewed that the richest households surpass the living standards of many high-income families in the advanced economies. Table 37.2 presents some data on the distribution of income in some developing countries.

Clearly, poverty—not affluence—dominates the developing world. Recent studies suggest that 40 percent of the population of the developing nations have annual incomes insufficient to provide for adequate nutrition.

While the developed nations account for only about one-quarter of the world's population, they are estimated to consume three-quarters of the world's output. This leaves the developing countries with about three-fourths of the world's people, but only one-fourth of the world's income. The simple result is that most of our planet's population is poor.

In 1995, the poorest country in the world was Mozambique with per capita GDP of $80.

TABLE 37.2 INCOME DISTRIBUTION IN SOME DEVELOPING COUNTRIES

	UNITED STATES	SRI LANKA	BRAZIL	PAKISTAN	INDONESIA	KENYA
Per Capita GDP 1995	$26,980	$700	$3,640	$460	$980	$280
Bottom 20%	4.7	8.9	2.1	8.4	8.7	3.4
Second 20%	11.0	13.1	4.9	12.9	12.3	6.7
Third 20%	17.4	16.9	8.9	16.9	16.3	10.7
Fourth 20%	25.0	21.7	16.8	22.2	16.3	17.0
Top 20%	41.9	39.3	67.5	39.7	40.7	62.1
Top 10%	25.0	25.2	51.3	25.2	25.6	47.7

Source: World Bank, *World Development Report, 1997.*

In the United States, the poorest one-fifth (bottom 20 percent) of the families receives just under 5 percent of total income; the richest one-fifth receives about 42 percent. But the inequality in the world distribution of income is much greater. When we look at the world population, the poorest one-fifth of the families earns about 0.5 percent and the richest one-fifth earn 79 percent of total world income!

ECONOMIC DEVELOPMENT: SOURCES AND STRATEGIES

Economists have been trying to understand economic growth and development since Adam Smith and David Ricardo in the eighteenth and nineteenth centuries, but the study of development economics as it applies to the developing nations has a much shorter history. The geopolitical struggles that followed World War II brought increased attention to the developing nations and their economic problems. During this period, the new field of development economics asked simply: Why are some nations poor and others rich? If economists could understand the barriers to economic growth that prevent nations from developing and the prerequisites that would help them to develop, they could prescribe strategies for achieving economic advancement.

THE SOURCES OF ECONOMIC DEVELOPMENT

Although a general theory of economic development applicable to all nations has not emerged and probably never will, some basic factors that limit a poor nation's economic growth have been suggested. These include insufficient capital formation, a shortage of human resources and entrepreneurial ability, a lack of social overhead capital, and the constraints imposed by dependency on the already developed nations.

▶ **Capital Formation**   One explanation for low levels of output in developing nations is insufficient quantities of necessary inputs. Developing nations have diverse resource endowments—Congo, for instance, is abundant in natural resources, while Bangladesh is resource poor. Almost all developing nations have a scarcity of physical capital relative to other resources, especially labor. The small stock of physical capital (factories, machinery, farm equipment, and other productive capital) constrains labor's productivity and holds back national output.

But citing capital shortages as the cause of low productivity does not explain much. We need to know why capital is in such short supply in developing countries. There are

The following is an excerpt from a speech given by World Bank president James D. Wolfensohn on the challenge facing the world in 1997:

Our goal must be to reduce these disparities across and within countries, to bring more and more people into the economic mainstream, to promote equitable access to the benefits of development regardless of nationality, race, or gender. This—the Challenge of Inclusion—is the key development challenge of our time.

You and I and all of us in this room—the privileged of the developing and the industrial world—can choose to ignore it. We can focus only on the successes. We can live with a little more crime, a few more wars, air that is a little bit dirtier. We can insulate ourselves from whole sections of the world for which crisis is real and daily but which to the rest of us is largely invisible. But we must recognize that we are living with a time bomb, and unless we take action now, it could explode in our children's faces.

If we do not act, in thirty years the inequities will be greater. With population growing at 80 million a year, instead of 3 billion living on under $2 a day, it could be as high as 5 billion. In thirty years, the quality of our environment will be worse. Instead of 4 percent of tropical forests lost since Rio, it could be 24 percent.

In thirty years, the number of conflicts may be higher. Already

we live in a world which last year alone saw twenty-six interstate wars and 23 million refugees. One does not have to spend long in Bosnia or Gaza or the Lakes District in Africa to know that without economic hope we will not have peace. Without equity we will not have global stability. Without a better sense of social justice our cities will not be safe, and our societies will not be stable. Without inclusion, too many of us will be condemned to live separate, armed, and frightened lives.

And economics is fundamentally changing the relationships between the rich and the poor nations. Over the next twenty-five years, growth in China, India, Indonesia, Brazil, and Russia will likely redraw the economic map of the world, as the share in global output of the development and transition economies doubles. Today these countries represent 50 percent of the world's population but only 8 percent of its GDP. Their share in world trade is a quarter that of the European Union. By the year 2020, their share in world trade could be 50 percent more than Europe's.

We share the same world, and we share the same challenge. The fight against poverty is the fight for peace, security, and growth for us all.

How, then, do we proceed? This much we know: No country has been successful in reducing poverty without sustained economic growth. Those countries that have been most successful—

including, most notably, many here in East Asia—have also invested heavily in their people, have put in place the right policy fundamentals, and have not discriminated against their rural sectors. The results have been dramatic: large private capital inflows, rapid growth, and substantial poverty reduction.

The message for countries is clear: Educate your people; ensure their health; give them voice and justice, financial systems that work, and sound economic policies, and they will respond, and they will save, and they will attract the investment, both domestic and foreign, that is needed to raise living standards and fuel development.

But another message is also emerging from recent developments. We have seen in recent months how financial markets are demanding more information disclosure, and how they are making swift judgments about the quality and sustainability of government policies based on that information. We have seen that without sound organization and supervision a financial system can falter, with the poor hurt the most. We have seen how corruption flourishes in the dark, how it prevents growth and social equity, and how it creates the basis for social and political instability.

Source: "The Challenge of Inclusion," address by James D. Wolfensohn, president of the World Bank Group to the Board of Governors, Hong Kong, China, September 23, 1997.

For more on economic development, see the Case and Fair Web page at **http://www.prenhall.com/casefair.**

vicious-circle-of-poverty hypothesis *Suggests that poverty is self-perpetuating because poor nations are unable to save and invest enough to accumulate the capital stock that would help them grow.*

many explanations. One, the **vicious-circle-of-poverty hypothesis**, suggests that a poor nation must consume most of its income just to maintain its already low standard of living. Consuming most of national income implies limited saving, and this implies low levels of investment. Without investment, the capital stock does not grow, income remains low, and the vicious circle is complete. Poverty becomes self-perpetuating.

The difficulty with the vicious-circle argument is that if it were true, no nation could ever develop. For example, Japanese GDP per capita at the turn of the century was well below that of many of today's developing nations. The vicious-circle argument fails to recognize that every nation has some surplus above consumption needs that is available for investment. Often this surplus is most visible in the conspicuous-consumption habits of the nation's richest families.

> Poverty alone cannot explain capital shortages, nor is poverty necessarily self-perpetuating.

In a developing economy, scarcity of capital may have more to do with a lack of incentives for citizens to save and invest productively than with any absolute scarcity of income available for capital accumulation. Many of the rich in developing countries invest their savings in Europe or in the United States rather than risk holding them in what is often an unstable political climate. Savings transferred to the United States do not lead to physical capital growth in the developing countries. The term **capital flight** refers to the fact that both human capital and financial capital (domestic savings) leave developing countries in search of higher rates of return elsewhere. In addition, government policies in the developing nations—including price ceilings, import controls, and even outright appropriation of private property—tend to discourage investment.

capital flight *The tendency for both human capital and financial capital to leave developing countries in search of higher rates of return elsewhere.*

Whatever the causes of capital shortages, it is clear that the absence of productive capital prevents income from rising in any economy. The availability of capital is a necessary, but not a *sufficient*, condition for economic growth. The Third World landscape is littered with idle factories and abandoned machinery. Clearly, other ingredients are required to achieve economic progress.

> **Human Resources and Entrepreneurial Ability** Capital is not the only factor of production required to produce output. Labor is equally important. But the quantity of available labor rarely constrains a developing economy. In most developing nations, rapid population growth for several decades has resulted in rapidly expanding labor supplies. The *quality* of available labor, however, may pose a serious constraint on the growth of income. The stock of knowledge and skill embodied in the workforce may act as a barrier to economic growth.

Human capital may be developed in a number of ways. Programs to improve nutrition and health represent one kind of human capital investment that can lead to increased productivity and higher incomes. The more familiar forms of human capital investment, including formal education and on-the-job training, may also play a role. Basic literacy, as well as specialized training in farm management, for example, can yield high returns to both the individual worker and the economy. Education has grown to become the largest category of government expenditure in many developing nations, in part because of the belief that human resources are the ultimate determinant of economic advance.

Just as financial capital seeks the highest and safest return, so does human capital. Thousands of students from developing countries, many of whom were supported by their governments, graduate every year from U.S. colleges and universities as engineers, doctors, scientists, economists, and the like. After graduation, these people face a difficult choice: to remain in the United States and earn a high salary or to return home and accept a job at a much lower salary. Many remain in the United States. This **brain drain** siphons off many of the most talented minds from developing countries.

Innovative entrepreneurs who are willing to take risks are an essential human resource in any economy. In a developing nation, new techniques of production rarely need to be invented, because they can usually be adapted from the technology already developed by the technologically advanced nations. But entrepreneurs who are willing and able to organize and carry out economic activity appear to be in short supply. Family and political ties often seem to be more important than ability when it comes to securing positions of authority. Whatever the explanation:

> Development cannot proceed without human resources capable of initiating and managing economic activity.

> **Social Overhead Capital** Anyone who has spent time in a developing nation knows how difficult it can be to send a letter, make a local phone call, or travel within the country itself. Add to this problems with water supplies, frequent electrical power outages—in the few areas where electricity is available—and often ineffective mosquito and pest control, and you soon realize how deficient even the simplest, most basic government-provided goods and services can be.

In any economy, Third World or otherwise, the government has considerable opportunity and responsibility for involvement where conditions encourage natural monopoly (as in the utilities industries) and where public goods (such as roads and pest control) must be provided. In a developing economy, the government must put emphasis on creating a basic infrastructure—roads, power generation, irrigation systems. There are often good reasons why such projects, referred to as **social overhead capital**, cannot successfully be undertaken by the private sector. First, many of these projects operate with economies of scale, which means they can be efficient only if they are very large. In that case, they may be too large for any private company or group of companies to carry out.

Second, many socially useful projects cannot be undertaken by the private sector because there is no way for private agents to capture enough of the returns to make such projects profitable. This so-called *free-rider problem* is common in the economics of the developed world. Consider national defense: Everyone in a country benefits from national defense, whether they have paid for it or not. Anyone who attempted to go into the private business of providing national defense would go broke. Why should I buy any national defense if your purchase of defense will also protect me? Why should you buy any if my purchase will also protect you?

> The governments of developing countries can do important and useful things to encourage development, but many of their efforts must be concentrated in areas that the private sector would never touch. If government action in these realms is not forthcoming, economic development may be curtailed by a lack of social overhead capital.

brain drain *The tendency for talented people from developing countries to become educated in a developed country and remain there after graduation.*

In 1995, Nepal had a population of 22 million and a per capita GDP of $200. Only 48% of the population had access to safe water and just 6% had access to sanitation.

Source: World Bank, *World Development Report,* 1997.

social overhead capital *Basic infrastructure projects such as roads, power generation, and irrigation systems.*

STRATEGIES FOR ECONOMIC DEVELOPMENT

Just as no single theory appears to explain lack of economic advancement, no one development strategy will likely succeed in all nations. Many alternative development strategies have been proposed over the past 40 years. Although these strategies have been very different, they all recognize that a developing economy faces basic trade-offs. An insufficient amount of both human and physical resources dictates that choices must be made, including those between agriculture and industry, exports and import substitution, and central planning and free markets.

➤ **Agriculture or Industry?**   Most Third World countries began to gain political independence just after World War II. The tradition of promoting industrialization as the solution to the problems of the developing world dates from this time. The early five-year development plans of India called for promoting manufacturing; the current government in Ethiopia (an extremely poor country) has similar intentions.

Industry has several apparent attractions over agriculture. First, if it is true that capital shortages constrain economic growth, then the building of factories is an obvious step toward increasing a nation's stock of capital. Second, and perhaps most important, one of the primary characteristics of more developed economies is their structural transition away from agriculture and toward manufacturing and modern services. As Table 37.3 shows, agriculture's share in GDP declines substantially as per capita incomes increase. The share of services increases correspondingly, especially in the early phases of economic development.

Many economies have pursued industry at the expense of agriculture. In many countries, however, industrialization has been either unsuccessful or disappointing—that is, it has not brought the benefits that were expected. Experience suggests that simply trying to replicate the structure of developed economies does not in itself guarantee, or even promote, successful development.

Since the early 1970s, the agricultural sector has received considerably more attention. Agricultural strategies have had numerous benefits. Although some agricultural projects (such as the building of major dams and irrigation networks) are very capital intensive, many others (such as services to help teach better farming techniques and small-scale fertilizer programs) have low capital and import requirements. Programs like these can affect large numbers of households, and because their benefits are directed at rural areas, they are most likely to help a country's poorest families.

TABLE 37.3   THE STRUCTURE OF PRODUCTION IN SELECTED DEVELOPED AND DEVELOPING ECONOMIES, 1995

COUNTRY	PER CAPITA INCOME	PERCENTAGE OF GROSS DOMESTIC PRODUCT		
		AGRICULTURE	INDUSTRY	SERVICES
Tanzania	$120	58	17	24
Bangladesh	$240	31	18	52
China	$620	21	48	31
Colombia	$1,910	14	32	54
Thailand	$2,740	11	40	49
Brazil	$3,640	14	37	49
Korea (Rep.)	$9,700	7	43	50
Japan	$39,640	2	38	60

Source: World Bank, *World Development Report*, 1997, Tables 1 and 12.

Experience over the last three decades suggests that some balance between these approaches leads to the best outcome—that is, it is important and effective to pay attention to both industry and agriculture. The Chinese have referred to this dual approach to development as "walking on two legs."

➤ **Exports or Import Substitution?** As developing nations expand their industrial activities, they must decide what type of trade strategy to pursue, usually one of two alternatives: import substitution or export promotion.

Import substitution is an industrial trade strategy to develop local industries that can manufacture goods to replace imports. For example, if fertilizer is imported, import substitution calls for a domestic fertilizer industry to produce replacements for fertilizer imports. This strategy gained prominence throughout South America in the 1950s. At that time, most developing nations exported agricultural and mineral products, goods that faced uncertain and often unstable international markets. Furthermore, the *terms of trade* for these nations—the ratio of export to import prices—seemed to be on a long-run decline.[1] A decline in a country's terms of trade means its imports of manufactured goods become relatively expensive in the domestic market, while its exports—mostly primary goods such as rubber and wheat and oil—become relatively inexpensive in the world market.

Under these conditions, the call for import-substitution policies was understandable. Special government actions, including tariff and quota protection and subsidized imports of machinery, were set up to encourage new domestic industries. Multinational corporations were also invited into many countries to begin domestic operations.

Most economists believe import-substitution strategies have failed almost everywhere they have been tried. With domestic industries sheltered from international competition by high tariffs (often as high as 200 percent), major economic inefficiencies were created. For example, Peru has a population of just over 24 million, only a tiny fraction of whom could afford to buy an automobile. Yet at one time the country had five or six different automobile manufacturers, each of which produced only a few thousand cars per year. Because there are substantial economies of scale in automobile production, the cost per car was much higher than it needed to be, and valuable resources that could have been devoted to another, more productive, activity were squandered producing cars.

Furthermore, policies designed to promote import substitution often encouraged capital-intensive production methods, which limited the creation of jobs and hurt export activities. A country like Peru could not export automobiles, because it could produce them only at a cost far greater than their price on the world market. Worse still, import-substitution policies encouraged the use of expensive domestic products, such as tractors and fertilizer, instead of lower-cost imports. These policies taxed the sectors that might have successfully competed in world markets. To the extent that the Peruvian sugar industry had to rely on domestically produced, high-cost fertilizer, for example, its ability to compete in international markets was reduced, because its production costs were artificially raised.

As an alternative to import substitution, some nations have pursued strategies of export promotion. **Export promotion** is simply the policy of encouraging exports. As an industrial market economy, Japan is a striking example to the developing world of the economic success that exports can provide. With an average annual per capita real GDP growth rate of roughly 6 percent per year since 1960, Japan's achievements are in part based on industrial production oriented toward foreign consumers.

import substitution *An industrial trade strategy that favors developing local industries that can manufacture goods to replace imports.*

export promotion *A trade policy designed to encourage exports.*

---

[1] It now appears that the terms of trade for Third World countries as a group were not actually on a long-run decline. Of course, the prices of commodities have changed, with some doing very well and others doing quite poorly. During the 1950s, however, many policy makers believed that the purchasing power of developing-country exports was in a permanent slump.

Several countries in the developing world have attempted to emulate Japan's success. Starting around 1970, Hong Kong, Singapore, Korea, and Taiwan (the "four little dragons" between the two big dragons, China and Japan) all began to pursue export promotion of manufactured goods. Today their growth rates have surpassed Japan's. Other nations, including Brazil, Colombia, and Turkey, have also had some success at pursuing an outward-looking trade policy.

Government support of export promotion has often taken the form of maintaining an exchange rate favorable enough to permit exports to compete with products manufactured in developed economies. For example, many people believe Japan kept the value of the yen artificially low during the 1970s. Because "cheap" yen means inexpensive Japanese goods in the United States, sales of Japanese goods (especially automobiles) increased dramatically. Governments also have provided subsidies to export industries.

In 1997 Japan was in a serious recession. Overall, Japan's performance since 1990 has not been as strong as before 1990. But its recent troubles do not diminish the incredible performance of the Japanese economic machine between 1960 and 1990.

> **Central Planning or the Market?** As part of its strategy for achieving economic development, a nation must decide how its economy will be directed. Its basic choices lie between a market-oriented economic system and a centrally planned one.

In the 1950s and into the 1960s, development strategies that called for national planning commanded wide support. The rapid economic growth of the Soviet Union, a centrally planned economy, provided an example of how fast a less developed agrarian nation could be transformed into a modern industrial power. (The often appalling costs of this strategy—severe discipline, gross violation of human rights, and environmental damage—were less widely known.) In addition, the underdevelopment of many commodity and asset markets in the Third World led many experts to believe that market forces could not direct an economy reliably and that major government intervention was therefore necessary. Even the United States, with its commitment to free enterprise in the marketplace, supported early central planning efforts in many developing nations.

Today, planning takes many forms in the developing nations. In some, central planning has replaced market-based outcomes with direct, administratively determined controls over such economic variables as prices, output, and employment. In others, national planning amounts to little more than the formulation of general 5- or 10-year goals as rough blueprints for a nation's economic future.

The economic appeal of planning lies theoretically in its ability to channel savings into productive investment and to coordinate economic activities that private actors in the economy might not otherwise undertake. The reality of central planning, however, is that it is technically difficult, highly politicized, and a nightmare to administer. Given the scarcity of human resources and the unstable political environment in many developing nations, planning itself—let alone the execution of the plan—becomes a formidable task.

The failure of many central planning efforts has brought increasing calls for less government intervention and more market orientation in developing economies. The elimination of price controls, privatization of state-run enterprises, and reductions in import restraints are examples of market-oriented reforms recommended by such international agencies as the **International Monetary Fund**, whose primary goals are to stabilize international exchange rates and to lend money to countries that have problems financing their international transactions, and the **World Bank**, which lends money to a country for projects that promote economic development.

Members' contributions to both organizations are determined by the size of their

International Monetary Fund *An international agency whose primary goals are to stabilize international exchange rates and to lend money to countries that have problems financing their international transactions.*

World Bank *An international agency that lends money to individual countries for projects that promote economic development.*

economies. Only 20 percent of the World Bank's funding comes from contributions; 80 percent comes from retained earnings and investments in capital markets. The developing world is increasingly recognizing the value of market forces in determining the allocation of scarce resources. Nonetheless, government still has a major role to play. In the decades ahead, the governments of developing nations will need to determine those situations where planning is superior to the market and those where the market is superior to planning.

GROWTH VERSUS DEVELOPMENT: THE POLICY CYCLE

Until now, we have used *growth* and *development* as if they meant the same thing. But this may not always be the case. You can easily imagine instances in which a country has achieved higher levels of income (growth) with little or no benefit accruing to most of its citizens (development). Thus, the question is whether economic growth necessarily brings about economic development.

In the past, most development strategies were aimed at increasing the growth rate of income per capita. Many still are, based on the theory that benefits of economic growth will "trickle down" to all members of society. If this theory is correct, then growth should promote development.

By the early 1970s, the relationship between growth and development was being questioned more and more. A study by the World Bank in 1974 concluded

> it is now clear that more than a decade of rapid growth in underdeveloped countries has been of little or no benefit to perhaps a third of their population. . . . Paradoxically, while growth policies have succeeded beyond the expectations of the first development decade, the very idea of aggregate growth as a social objective has increasingly been called into question.

The World Bank study indicated that increases in GDP per capita did not guarantee significant improvements in such development indicators as nutrition, health, and education. Although GDP per capita did rise, its benefits trickled down to a small minority of the population. This prompted new development strategies that would directly address the problems of poverty. Such new strategies favored agriculture over industry, called for domestic redistribution of income and wealth (especially land), and encouraged programs to satisfy such basic needs as food and shelter.

In the late 1970s and early 1980s, the international macroeconomic crises of high oil prices, worldwide recession, and Third World debt forced attention away from programs designed to eliminate poverty directly. Then, during the 1980s and 1990s, the policy focus turned 180 degrees. The World Bank and the United States began demanding "structural adjustment" in the developing countries as a prerequisite for sending aid to them. **Structural adjustment** programs entail reducing the size of the public sector through privatization and/or expenditure reductions, substantially cutting budget deficits, reining in inflation, and encouraging private saving and investment with tax reforms. These pro-market demands were an attempt to stimulate growth; distributional consequences took a back seat.

In recent years, foreign aid has become a source of controversy. How much foreign aid does the United States provide, and who gets it? For the answers, see the Issues and Debates box "Where Does U.S. Foreign Aid Go?"

structural adjustment *A series of programs in developing nations designed to (1) reduce the size of their public sectors through privatization and/or expenditure reductions, (2) decrease their budget deficits, (3) control inflation, and (4) encourage private saving and investment through tax reform.*

ISSUES IN ECONOMIC DEVELOPMENT

Every developing nation has a cultural, political, and economic history all its own and therefore confronts a unique set of problems. Still, it is possible to discuss common economic issues that each nation must face in its own particular way. These issues

WHERE DOES U.S. FOREIGN AID GO?

Many developed countries provide direct assistance in the form of grants and loans to developing nations. This aid is used to build infrastructure (roads, power plants, and such), drill wells, improve medical care facilities, teach everything from crop management to business development, help rural credit banks grow, and (when necessary) provide food and medical services directly to the people.

Many people think foreign aid is a major part of U.S. government expenditures, and campaign rhetoric is often directed against it because the United States should "help its own people first." In fact, the total amount of direct development assistance in the *world* in 1997 was $55 billion, of which the United States contributed $9.5 billion. This figure amounted to only 6¢ out of every $10 of federal expenditures and only 1.3 percent of domestic transfer payments.

Table 1 shows the top 10 countries that benefit from U.S. economic aid. Israel is the only country that receives more than $1 billion, and most countries receive only a small amount.

TABLE 1	FOREIGN AID, 1997—DESTINATION OF DIRECT U.S. ECONOMIC ASSISTANCE, BY COUNTRY	
	COUNTRY	**MILLIONS OF DOLLARS**
	Israel	$1,200
	Egypt	815
	Bosnia	240
	Ukraine	227
	Peru	99
	Russia	99
	Haiti	96
	South Africa	79
	West Bank/Gaza	75
	Ethiopia	72

Source: U.S. Agency for International Development.

For more on economic development and foreign aid, see the Case and Fair Web page at **http://www.prenhall.com/casefair.**

include rapid population growth, food shortages, agricultural output and pricing policies, and the Third World debt problem.

POPULATION GROWTH

The populations of the developing nations are estimated to be growing at about 1.7 percent per year. (Compare this with a population growth rate of only 0.5 percent per year in the industrial market economies.) If the Third World's population growth rate remains at 1.7 percent, within 41 years the population of the Third World will double from its 1990 level of 4.1 billion to over 8 billion by the year 2031. It will take the industrialized nations 139 years to double their populations. What is so immediately alarming about these numbers is that given the developing nations' current economic problems, it is hard to imagine how they can possibly absorb so many more people in such a relatively short period.

Concern over world population growth is not new. The Reverend Thomas Malthus (who became England's first professor of political economy) expressed his fears about the population increases he observed 200 years ago. Malthus believed populations grow geometrically (at a constant growth rate: thus the absolute size of the increase each year gets larger and larger), but that food supplies grow much more slowly because of the diminishing marginal productivity of land.[2] These two phenomena led Malthus to predict the increasing impoverishment of the world's people unless population growth could be slowed.

Malthus's fears for Europe and America proved unfounded. He neither anticipated the technological changes that revolutionized agricultural productivity nor the eventual decrease in population growth rates in Europe and North America. But Malthus's prediction may have been right, only premature. Do the circumstances in the developing world now fit his predictions? Although some contemporary observers believe the Malthusian view is correct and the earth's population will eventually grow to a level that the world's resources cannot support, others say technological change and demographic transitions (to slower population growth rates) will permit further increases in global welfare.

➤ **The Consequences of Rapid Population Growth**   We know far less about the economic consequences of rapid population growth than you might expect. Conventional wisdom warns of dire economic consequences from the developing nations' "population explosion," but these predictions are difficult to substantiate with the available evidence. The rapid economic growth of the United States, for example, was accompanied by relatively rapid population growth by historical standards. Nor has any slowing of population growth been necessary for the economic progress achieved by many of the newly industrialized countries. Nonetheless, population expansion in many of today's poorest nations is of a magnitude unprecedented in world history, as Figure 37.1 clearly shows. From the year A.D. 1 until the mid-1600s, populations grew slowly, at rates of only about 0.04 percent per

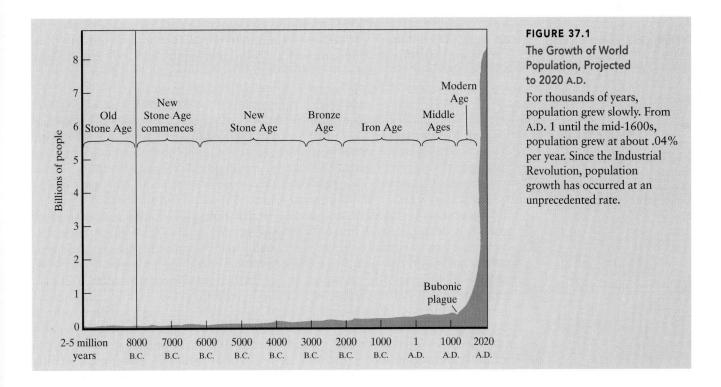

FIGURE 37.1

The Growth of World Population, Projected to 2020 A.D.

For thousands of years, population grew slowly. From A.D. 1 until the mid-1600s, population grew at about .04% per year. Since the Industrial Revolution, population growth has occurred at an unprecedented rate.

---

[2]The law of diminishing marginal productivity says that with a fixed amount of a resource (land), additions of more and more of a variable resource (labor) will produce smaller and smaller gains in output.

year. Since then, and especially since 1950, rates have skyrocketed. Today, populations are growing at rates of 1.5 percent to 4.0 percent per year throughout the developing world.

Because growth rates like these have never occurred before the twentieth century, no one knows what impact they will have on future economic development. But a basic economic concern is that such rapid population growth may limit investment and restrain increases in labor productivity and income. Rapid population growth changes the age composition of a population, generating many dependent children relative to the number of productive working adults. Such a situation may diminish saving rates, and hence investment, as the immediate consumption needs of the young take priority over saving for the future.

Even if low saving rates are not a necessary consequence of rapid population growth, as some authorities contend, other economic problems remain. The ability to improve human capital through a broad range of programs, from infant nutrition to formal secondary education, may be severely limited if the population explosion continues. Such programs are most often the responsibility of the state, and governments that are already weak cannot be expected to improve their services under the burden of population pressures that rapidly increase demands for all kinds of public goods and services.

For example, Mozambique's population growth rate—3.7 percent—is one of the highest in the world. It is likely that its 1997 population of over 17 million people will grow by about 3.4 million in the next five years and by 7.5 million in the next decade. This is a daunting prospect, and it is hard to imagine how in so little time Mozambique, with per capita GNP under $100, will be able to provide its population with the physical and human capital needed to maintain, let alone improve, already low standards of living.

> **Causes of Rapid Population Growth**   Population growth is determined by the relationship between births and deaths—that is, between **fertility rates** and **mortality rates**. The **natural rate of population increase** is defined as the difference between the birth rate and the death rate. If the birth rate is 4 percent, for example, and the death rate is 3 percent, the population is growing at a rate of 1 percent per year.

Historically, low rates of population growth were maintained because of high mortality rates despite high levels of fertility. That is, families had many children, but average life expectancies were low, and many children (and adults) died young. In Europe and North America, improvements in nutrition, in public health programs (especially those concerned with drinking water and sanitation services), and in medical practices have led to a drop in the mortality rate and hence to more rapid population growth. Eventually fertility rates also fell, returning population growth to a low and stable rate.

Public health programs and improved nutrition over the past 30 years have brought about precipitous declines in mortality rates in the developing nations also. But fertility rates have not declined as quickly, and the result has been high natural rates of population growth. Reduced population growth depends to some extent on decreased birth rates, but attempts to lower fertility rates must take account of how different cultures feel and behave with regard to fertility.

Family planning and modern forms of birth control are important mechanisms for decreasing fertility, but by themselves have had rather limited success in most countries where they have been tried. If family planning strategies are to be successful, they must make sense to the people who are supposed to benefit from them. The planners of such strategies must understand why families in developing nations have so many children.

To a great extent, in developing countries people want large families because they

fertility rate *The birth rate. Equal to (the number of births per year divided by the population) × 100.*

mortality rate *The death rate. Equal to (the number of deaths per year divided by the population) × 100.*

natural rate of population increase *The difference between the birth rate and the death rate. It does not take migration into account.*

believe they need them. Economists have attempted to understand fertility patterns in the developing countries by focusing on the determinants of the demand for children. In agrarian societies, children are sources of farm labor, and they may make significant contributions to household income. In societies without public old-age support social security programs, children may also provide a source of income for parents who are too old to support themselves. With the high value of children enhanced by high rates of infant mortality, it is no wonder that families try to have many children to ensure that a sufficient number will survive into adulthood.

Cultural and religious values also affect the number of children families want to have, but the economic incentives to have large families are extremely powerful. Only when the relationship between the costs and benefits of having children changes will fertility rates decline. Expanding employment opportunities for women in an economy increases the opportunity costs of child rearing (by giving women a more highly valued alternative to raising children) and often leads to lower birth rates. Government incentives for smaller families, such as subsidized education for families with fewer than three children, can have a similar effect. In general, rising incomes appear to decrease fertility rates, indicating that economic development itself reduces population growth rates.

Economic theories of population growth suggest that fertility decisions made by poor families should not be viewed as uninformed and uncontrolled. An individual family may find that having many children is a rational strategy for economic survival given the conditions in which it finds itself. This does not mean, however, that having many children is a net benefit to society as a whole. When a family decides to have a large number of children, it imposes costs on the rest of society; the children must be educated, their health provided for, and so forth. In other words, what makes sense for an individual household may create negative effects for the nation as a whole.

SEVERAL AFRICAN NATIONS HAVE COME TO RELY ON FOREIGN SUPPORT TO HELP PROVIDE FOOD FOR THEIR PEOPLE. HERE, YOU SEE GRAIN RECEIVED FROM THE FRENCH RED CROSS BY PEOPLE IN RWANDA.

> Any nation that wants to slow its rate of population growth will probably find it necessary to have in place economic incentives for fewer children as well as family planning programs.

FOOD SHORTAGES: ACTS OF NATURE OR HUMAN MISTAKES?

Television footage and newspaper photos portraying victims of the famine in Somalia burned indelible images of starving people into the minds of most Americans. No other recent event so forcefully dramatized the ongoing food crisis in many developing nations. The famines that have struck various parts of Africa and Asia in the past 15 years represent the most acute form of the chronic food shortage confronting the developing nations.

Pictures of the parched Somalian countryside might lead an observer to conclude that famines are acts of nature—if the rains do not come or the locusts do, human beings can do little. But this simplistic view of food shortages fails to recognize the extent to which contemporary food crises are the result of human behavior. Even such natural events as severe flooding can often be traced to the overharvesting of firewood, which denudes the landscape, increases soil erosion, and exacerbates spring floods.

Human behavior is a very strong factor in the inadequate distribution of available food to those who need it. India now grows enough grains to feed its vast population, for example, but malnutrition remains widespread because many people cannot afford to feed themselves. Other parts of the distribution problem involve failures to stockpile adequate food reserves in years of good harvests and transportation and communication barriers that prevent supplies from reaching those in need. World and domestic politics also heavily influence where, how, and whether food is available. During the Ethiopian famine in 1988, for example, the Ethiopian government blocked relief agencies from delivering food and medical supplies to the famine area because a civil war was being waged there. Similar events occurred when the United Nations attempted to aid Somalia in 1992. This led to U.S. military intervention in 1992 and 1993. War between the Hutu and the Tutsis in Rwanda in 1994 led to mass exodus into Zaire, loss of crops, and starvation. In 1997, a bitter civil war in the Congo (formerly Zaire) left millions in refugee camps.

Severe food shortages are recognized chronic problems, but developing nations often pursue farm policies that actually discourage agricultural production. Agricultural production in sub-Saharan Africa today is lower than it was 20 years ago, and economists believe that misguided agricultural policies are responsible for much of this decline.

AGRICULTURAL OUTPUT AND PRICING POLICIES

Few governments in either industrialized or developing nations have permitted market forces alone to determine agricultural prices. In the United States and much of Europe, farm subsidies often encourage production that results in food surpluses rather than shortages. Some developing nations follow similar policies, maintaining high farm prices both to increase agricultural production and to maintain farm incomes. However, many developing nations follow a different route, offering farmers low prices for their output.

produce-marketing boards
The channels through which the governments of some developing countries buy domestic farm output and then sell it to urban residents at government-controlled prices.

To appreciate the motives behind different pricing policies, you need to understand several things about the structure of agricultural markets in many developing nations. Often the government is the primary purchaser of both basic foodstuffs and export crops. Through **produce-marketing boards**, the governments of some developing countries buy farm output and sell it to urban residents at government-controlled prices. By setting the prices they pay to farmers at low levels, the government can afford to sell basic foodstuffs to urban consumers at low prices. Governments often find this an attractive course of action because the direct political influence of the relatively small urban population typically far outweighs the influence of the majority who live in the countryside. Because most city dwellers spend about half their incomes on food, low consumer prices bolster the real incomes of the urban residents and help keep them content. Urban food riots have been common in developing nations over the years, and whether a government is allowed to exist may hinge on its food-pricing strategy.

Although we can easily appreciate the political motives behind food pricing, policies that set artificially low prices have significant pitfalls. Farmers react to these prices—often set so low that farmers cannot cover their production costs—by reducing the amount of output they produce. In the city, meanwhile, excess demand for food at the artificially low ceiling prices imposed by the government may promote the emergence of black markets.

Many developing economies that have followed low agricultural pricing policies have experienced exactly these results. Until recently, for example, Mexico kept corn prices low to hold down the price of tortillas, the staple in the diet of much of Mexico's urban population. Corn production fell as farmers switched to crops whose prices the government did not control. Domestic corn shortages became widespread, and corn had to be imported to sustain urban demand.

► **Agricultural Output: The Supply Side** In 1998, a single U.S. farmer could provide enough food to feed 80 people. In most developing economies, a single farmer can provide barely enough food to feed his or her own family. Though differences in agricultural pricing policies account for a part of this gap, there are other factors. Low agricultural productivity in the developing world was blamed on the ignorance and laziness of peasant farmers. Today's more enlightened view recognizes a shortage of inputs, including land, fertilizer, irrigation, machinery, new seed varieties, and agricultural extension services (credit and technical advice).

Modern agricultural science has created a so-called **Green Revolution** (not to be confused with the "environmental revolution") based on new, high-yield varieties of wheat, rice, and other crops. Using new, faster-growing varieties instead of the single-crop plants they have relied upon for centuries, some farmers can now grow three crops of rice a year. In Mexico, under ideal conditions, "miracle" wheat has produced 105 bushels of grain per acre, compared with traditional varieties that yield only 11.5 bushels per acre.

If the Green Revolution suggests that science can, in principle, solve world food shortages, the developing countries' experiments with scientific agriculture offers a less optimistic outlook. Economic factors have greatly limited the adoption of Green Revolution techniques in developing countries. New seeds are expensive, and their cultivation requires the presence of many complementary inputs, including fertilizers and irrigation. With poorly developed rural credit markets, farmers often face interest rates so high that new technologies, regardless of their promise of higher crop yields, are out of reach or ultimately unprofitable. Although the reluctance of peasant farmers to adopt new agricultural techniques has often been blamed on superstition or lack of education, such decisions typically reflect a rational choice. Given the costs and benefits of new inputs and the inherent riskiness of any new method of cultivation, it is not surprising that it has been difficult to get farmers in the developing nations to accept the advances of the Green Revolution.

Peasant farmers in developing nations are also constrained by the amount of land they have to work. In some countries, high population density in the rural areas requires highly labor-intensive cultivation. In others, poor distribution of land decreases agricultural output. Throughout Latin America, for example, it is estimated that less than 2 percent of all landowners control almost 75 percent of the land under cultivation. Improved crop yields often follow land reforms that redistribute holdings, because owner households are often more productive than tenant farmers. Land reform has had positive effects on output in countries with economic systems as diverse as those of Korea and the People's Republic of China.

Green Revolution *The agricultural breakthroughs of modern science, such as the development of new, high-yield crop varieties.*

> Although acts of nature will always threaten agricultural production, human actions, especially policies designed to support the agricultural sector, can have a major impact on reducing the food problems of the developing world.

THIRD WORLD DEBT

In the 1970s, development experts worried about many crises facing the developing world, but not the debt crisis. Within a decade, this changed dramatically. The financial plight of nations such as Brazil, Mexico, and the Philippines has become front-page news. What alarmed those familiar with the debt situation was not only its potential impact on the developing nations, but a belief that it threatened the economic welfare of the developed nations as well.

Between 1970 and 1984, developing nations borrowed so much money from other nations that their combined debt increased by 1,000 percent, to almost $700 billion. Three nations alone—Brazil, Mexico, and Venezuela—had outstanding loans to three major U.S. banks (Citibank, Chase-Manhattan, and Manufacturer's Hanover, now part of Chemical) that were more than double the net worth of those financial institutions. As recession took hold in the economically advanced countries during the early 1980s, growth in the exports of the debtor countries slowed, and many found they could no longer pay back the money they owed.

As the situation continued to deteriorate, many feared that debtor nations might repudiate their debts outright and default on their outstanding loans. When *default* (nonpayment) occurs with domestic loans, some collateral is usually available to cover all or part of the remaining debt. For loans to another country, such collateral is virtually impossible to secure. Given their extensive involvement with Third World borrowers, Western banks did not want to set in motion a pattern of international default. Nor did borrowers want to default. Leaders of the developing nations recognized that default might result in the denial of access to developed-country banking facilities and to markets in the industrial countries, posing major obstacles to further development efforts.

Various countries rescheduled their debt as an interim solution. Under a **debt rescheduling** agreement, banks and borrowers negotiate a new schedule for the repayment of existing debt, often with some of the debt written off and with repayment periods extended. In return, borrowing countries are expected to sign an agreement with the International Monetary Fund to revamp their economic policies to provide incentives for higher export earnings and lower imports. This kind of agreement, referred to as a **stabilization program**, usually requires austerity measures such as currency devaluations, a reduction in government expenditures, and an increase in tax revenues.

By the early 1990s, the debt crisis was not over but it had lessened, mainly as a result of macroeconomic events that led to reduced interest rates. The international economy has revived somewhat, helping some nations to increase their export earnings. Other nations have benefited from new domestic policies. Still others, including Panama, and many African nations, however, continue to face debt burdens that

debt rescheduling *An agreement between banks and borrowers through which a new schedule of repayments of the debt is negotiated; often some of the debt is written off and the repayment period is extended.*

stabilization program *An agreement between a borrower country and the International Monetary Fund in which the country agrees to revamp its economic policies to provide incentives for higher export earnings and lower imports.*

TABLE 37.4   TOTAL (PUBLIC AND PRIVATE) EXTERNAL DEBT FOR SELECTED COUNTRIES, 1995 (BILLIONS OF DOLLARS)

COUNTRY	TOTAL EXTERNAL DEBT	TOTAL DEBT AS A PERCENTAGE OF GDP
Mexico	$165.7	69.9
Brazil	159.1	24.0
Russian Federation	120.5	37.6
China	118.1	17.2
Indonesia	107.8	56.9
India	93.8	28.2
Argentina	89.7	33.1
Turkey	73.6	44.1
Thailand	56.8	34.9
Peru	30.8	54.1
Nicaragua	9.3	589.7

Source: World Bank, World Development Report, 1997.

are unmanageable in the short run. Table 37.4 presents figures for selected countries in 1995.

Of concern in recent years has been Mexico's monetary and debt situation. Mexico's total external debt in 1995, $166 billion, was highest in the world. Following approval of the North American Free-Trade Agreement (NAFTA), there was great optimism about Mexico, and massive amounts of capital flowed to Mexico to take advantage of the relatively high interest rates available on Mexican debt. As a result, Mexico's total external debt increased dramatically. Though the flow of capital pushed up the value of the peso during 1993 and early 1994, by mid-1994 investors had become nervous about the possibility of a decline in the peso's value and began to pull out of Mexico. The peso's value finally collapsed in early 1995, and the Mexican government's inability to get investors to buy Mexican bonds pushed it to the brink of defaulting on its obligations. A loan guarantee of $37 billion from the United States and the International Monetary Fund at least temporarily restored confidence and may have saved Mexico the embarrassment of a default in 1995.

In 1997, several Asian countries including Korea and Thailand had financial problems that led to loan guarantee funds from the International Monetary Fund. Korea's package totaled over $50 billion.

One economic lesson of the last two decades is that proper management of foreign capital in developing countries is essential. Much foreign borrowing was wasted on projects that had little chance of generating the returns necessary to pay back their initial costs. In other cases, domestic policies that used debt as a substitute for adjusting to new economic circumstances proved to be harmful in the long run. And, overall, much optimism about the prospects of the developing economies was inappropriate. Whatever else we may have learned from these mistakes, the debt crisis underscored the growing interdependence of all economies—rich and poor, large and small.

SUMMARY

1. The economic problems facing the developing countries are often quite different from those confronting industrialized nations. The policy options available to governments may also differ. Nonetheless, the tools of economic analysis are as useful in understanding the economies of less developed countries as in understanding the U.S. economy.

LIFE IN THE DEVELOPING NATIONS: POPULATION AND POVERTY

2. The central reality of life in the developing countries is poverty. Although there is considerable diversity across the developing nations, most of the people in most developing countries are extremely poor by U.S. standards.

ECONOMIC DEVELOPMENT: SOURCES AND STRATEGIES

3. Almost all developing nations have a scarcity of physical capital relative to other resources, especially labor. The *vicious-circle-of-poverty hypothesis* says poor countries cannot escape from poverty because they cannot afford to postpone consumption (that is, to save) to make investments. In its crude form, the hypothesis is wrong inasmuch as some prosperous countries were at one time poorer than many developing countries are today. However, it is often difficult to mobilize savings efficiently in many developing nations.

4. Human capital—the stock of education and skills embodied in the workforce—plays a vital role in economic development.

5. Developing countries are often burdened by inadequate *social overhead capital*, ranging from poor public health and sanitation facilities to inadequate roads, telephones, and court systems. Such social overhead capital is often expensive to provide, and many governments are simply not in a position to undertake many useful projects because they are too costly.

6. Because developed economies are characterized by a large share of output and employment in the industrial sector, many developing countries seem to believe that development and industrialization are synonymous. In many cases, developing countries have pursued industry at the expense of agriculture, with mixed results. Recent evidence suggests that some balance between industry and agriculture leads to the best outcome.

7. *Import substitution* policies, a trade strategy that favors developing local industries that can manufacture goods to replace imports, were once very common in the developing nations. In general, such policies have not succeeded as well as those promoting open, export-oriented economies.

8. The failure of many central planning efforts has brought increasing calls for less government intervention and more market orientation in developing economies.

ISSUES IN ECONOMIC DEVELOPMENT

9. Rapid population growth is characteristic of many developing countries. Large families can be economically rational for parents who need support in their old age, or because children offer an important source of labor. But having many children does not mean a net benefit to society as whole. Rapid population growth can put a strain on already overburdened public services, such as education and health.

10. Food shortages in developing countries are not simply the result of bad weather. Public policies that depress the prices of agricultural goods, thereby lowering farmers' incentives to produce, are common throughout the developing nations, and in such countries, human behavior is very much behind the inadequate distribution of available food to those who need it.

11. Between 1970 and 1984 the debts of the developing countries grew tenfold. As recession took hold in the advanced countries during the early 1980s, growth in the exports of the debtor countries slowed, and many found they could no longer pay back money they owed. The prospect of loan defaults by Third World nations threatened the entire international financial system and transformed the debt crisis into a global problem.

REVIEW TERMS AND CONCEPTS

PROBLEM SET

1. Two developing countries that have been in the news lately are Thailand and Indonesia. Both countries were experiencing excellent growth during the early 1990s but fell on hard times in 1997. Choose either country and, using indexes to the popular press (like the *Wall Street Journal* or the *New York Times*), write a chronology of events starting in 1997. Using what you have learned in economics, what explanations can you offer for what happened? Were the problems that arose problems of mismanagement by governments, or were they the result of the way the markets worked (or failed to work)? What lessons have we learned?

2. For a developing country to grow, it needs capital. The major source of capital in most countries is domestic saving. But the goal of stimulating domestic saving usually is in conflict with government policies aimed at reducing inequality in the distribution of income. Comment on this trade-off between equity and growth. How would you go about resolving the issue if you were the president of a small, poor country?

3. Financial markets have become increasingly international. Savings flows very quickly between countries as investment opportunities arise or expectations change. International investors are reluctant to invest in countries where there is political or economic instability, and domestic investors, faced with uncertainty at home, are likely to protect their wealth by investing it in safe countries. During 1997 and 1998, there was much uncertainty and instability in many parts of the developing world. At the same time, the United States economy was very stable. What effect was this likely to have had on the value of the dollar? Explain. Verify what actually happened to the value of the dollar during 1997 (see, for example, the *Economic Report of the President*). What are the short- and long-term implications for the developing countries?

4. The GDP of any country can be divided into two kinds of goods: capital goods and consumption goods. The proportion of national output devoted to capital goods determines, to some extent, the nation's growth rate.

   a. Explain how capital accumulation leads to economic growth.
   b. Briefly describe how a market economy determines how much investment will be undertaken each period.
   c. "Consumption versus investment is a more painful conflict to resolve for developing countries." Comment on this statement.
   d. If you were the benevolent dictator of a developing country, what plans would you implement to increase per capita GDP?

5. "The main reason developing countries are poor is that they don't have enough capital. If we give them machinery, or build factories for them, we can greatly improve their situation." Comment.

6. "Poor countries are trapped in a vicious circle of poverty. For output to grow, they must accumulate capital. To accumulate capital, they must save (consume less than they produce). But because they are poor, they have little or no extra output available for savings—it must all go to feed and clothe the present generation. Thus they are doomed to stay poor forever." Comment on each step in this argument.

7. If children are an "investment in the future," why do some developing nations offer incentives to households that limit the size of their families? Why are these incentives often ignored?

8. If you were in charge of economic policy for a developing country and wanted to promote rapid economic growth, would you choose to favor industry over agriculture? What about exports versus import substitution? In each case, briefly explain your reasoning. How do you explain the fact that many countries chose industry and a protectionist import-substitution policy?

9. "Famines are acts of God, resulting from bad weather or other natural disasters. There is nothing we can do about them except to send food relief after they occur." Explain why this position is inaccurate. Concentrate on agricultural pricing policies and distributional issues.

We invite you to visit the Case and Fair page on the Prentice Hall Web site:

http://www.prenhall.com/casefair

for this chapter's World Wide Web exercise.

Chapter 38

ECONOMIES IN TRANSITION AND ALTERNATIVE ECONOMIC SYSTEMS

FOR 40 YEARS, between the end of World War II and the mid-1980s, a powerful rivalry existed between the Soviet Union and the United States. This "cold war" pitted the two superpowers against each other in a struggle for influence and fueled the nuclear arms race. At one time the mutual distrust between them was so strong that the concept of "mutual assured destruction" dominated international relations.

But the world began to change in the mid-1980s as the political and economic structures of the Soviet Union and the Eastern European Communist countries started to crumble. In 1989, relatively peaceful revolutions took place in rapid succession in Poland, Hungary, and Czechoslovakia (now the Czech Republic). A bloody revolution in Romania toppled Nicolae Ceausescu, who had ruled with an iron fist for 24 years. The Berlin Wall, which had separated Berlin since 1961, was knocked down and Germany was reunited. Then, in August 1991, after a failed coup attempt by hard-line Communists, the Soviet Union itself began to come apart. By the end of 1991, the Soviet Union had dissolved into 15 independent states, the largest is the Russian Republic. Ten of these 15 republics formed the Commonwealth of Independent States (CIS) in December 1991. The Cold War was over.

We reflect on historical political rivalries in an economics text for two reasons. First, the 40-year struggle between the United States and the Soviet Union was fundamentally a struggle between two economic systems: market-based capitalism (the U.S. system) and centrally planned socialism (the Soviet system). Second, the Cold War ended so abruptly in the late 1980s because the Soviet and Eastern European economies virtually collapsed during that period. In a sense, we could say 1991 was the year that the market triumphed.

What now? The independent states of the former Soviet Union and the other former Communist economies of Eastern Europe are struggling to make the transition from centrally planned socialism to some form of market-based capitalism. In some countries, such as Serbia and Bosnia-Herzegovina, economic reforms have taken a back seat to bitter and violent ethnic and political rivalries that have been simmering for decades. In other countries, like Poland and Russia, the biggest issue continues to be economic transformation.

The success or failure of this transition from centrally planned socialism to market-based capitalism will determine the course of history. Although many countries have made the transition from a market-based system to a centrally planned system, the opposite has never occurred. The process has been and will continue to be painful and filled with ups and downs. Between 1989 and 1997, industrial production fell more than 40 percent in countries like the former East Germany, Albania, Poland, and Romania. In Russia, production decreased about 30 percent. In all these nations, fairly prosperous people suddenly found themselves with annual real incomes closer to those of people in developing countries. For many people, the issue became survival: how to get enough food and fuel to get through the winter.

By 1995, things had turned around, and though uncertainty and problems remained, output was rising in much of Eastern and Central Europe. A growing optimism seemed to be spreading. The biggest success story was in East Germany, where real output in 1994 grew by over 9 percent, the fastest growth rate of any region of Europe. A construction boom, rapid development of infrastructure, low inflation, and rising exports all contributed to the region's success. But East Germany's situation is unique because it was absorbed by a prosperous, fully developed, and modern West Germany that has made development in the East its primary goal.

Central Europe, including Hungary, Poland, the Czech Republic, Bulgaria, and Romania, also achieved basic macroeconomic stability and began to grow in 1993 and 1994. Poland enjoyed the most rapid economic growth in the group (around 4.5 percent). Fueled by foreign investment, privatization, and entrepreneurship, the Polish private sector by 1992 accounted for well over one-third of the nation's total output, although many problems persist. (See Global Perspective "The Challenges to Private Enterprise in Poland.") Russia and the former countries of the Soviet Union have achieved less through 1997. Nonetheless, conditions have improved and prospects for success are greater than they were only a few years ago.

In this chapter, we focus on the ongoing debate over economic reform. How to make the transition from socialism to capitalism successful? In what sequence should changes be made? How quickly can markets be established? How much help from the United States and the rest of the world will be required?

To understand the transformation process, it is necessary to begin with some history. From what are these countries making a transition? Our chapter starts with a discussion of alternative economic systems, the vision of communism, and a brief description of the economic structure of the former Soviet Union. We then turn to the current debate over the transition process, focusing on the experiences of Poland and Russia. We end the chapter by examining a different kind of economic transformation that has been ongoing for some time in China and discussing the performance of the Japanese economy since World War II.

POLITICAL SYSTEMS AND ECONOMIC SYSTEMS: SOCIALISM, CAPITALISM, AND COMMUNISM

Every society has both a political system and an economic system. Unfortunately, the political and economic dimensions of a society are often confused.

The terms *democracy* and *dictatorship* refer to *political* systems. A *democracy* is a system of government in which ultimate power rests with the people, who make

THE CHALLENGES TO PRIVATE ENTERPRISE IN POLAND

Since 1991 the private sectors of most of the countries of the former Soviet Union and the formerly Communist countries of Central and Eastern Europe have expanded dramatically. Outside of East Germany, Poland's private sector has expanded the most, and it now accounts for well over a third of the economy's production.

This private expansion comes from four sources:

■ FIRST, thousands of entrepreneurs have started new businesses. It is estimated that more than 2 million Polish entrepreneurs have formed businesses, and small business in Poland is growing at about 10 percent per year.

■ SECOND, foreign investment is flowing into the region, although not at the pace once anticipated.

■ THIRD, "spontaneous privatizations," initiated by managers of state-owned enterprises, have converted many firms to private ownership without a great deal of state participation. The earliest forms of spontaneous privatization in Russia took the form of managers setting up parallel private firms opposite or even inside state-owned enterprises. The new private firm would buy the product of the state-owned enterprise at a controlled price and then resell it at the market price.

■ FOURTH, most countries have been selling off state-owned private enterprises directly or indirectly to private shareholders.[a]

Because the process of selling off state-owned assets has been slow, much of the economic action has occurred in entrepreneurial businesses.

Start-ups are the engine of Poland's post-communist boom. A book published this month by the Economist Intelligence Unit, a sister company of The Economist, calculates that private firms have trebled their share in industrial output since the transition began, from 16% of gross sales at the end of 1989 to 45% in 1995—an annual growth rate of more than a fifth. Since small businesses have every incentive to understate their performance, the real picture is probably even brighter.

Of course not every post-communist start-up is successful. Mr. Kunsch, at Creditanstalt in Budapest, reckons that the failure rate in Hungary is around 30%—one reason why his own and other banks are so cautious about lending to them. But all the post-communist economies have their quota of success stories, in both manufacturing and service industries. Euronet, a Hungarian operator of bank teller machines, is already listed on Nasdaq, America's small-company stock exchange, PCs, a software developer which started in Prague with

$3,000 in 1990, now has over 100 employees and sales of $30m.

The success of these companies (some of which have annual rates of return on capital of several hundred per cent) is all the more remarkable seen against the uphill struggle of their early years. Premises were cramped, working capital scarce, infrastructure fragile and the bureaucracy tiresome. Many entrepreneurs say that it is only now—with finance becoming easier and their credibility with foreign partners rising—that their businesses can really take off.

The start-ups have done so well for two main reasons. First, they were expanding into a vacuum. The collapse of communism created new markets overnight. Even when competing products or services existed, the locals often turned out to be more knowledgeable, hard-working, flexible and cost-effective.

The second reason has to do with human nature. For Eastern Europeans who had seen large chunks of their working lives wasted by communism, starting a business offered the chance to catch up. . . . Self-employment, therefore, has attracted a large number of Eastern Europe's brightest and best, with impressive results.[b]

Sources: [a]Olivier Jean Blanchard, Kenneth A. Froot, and Jeffrey D. Sachs, eds., *The Transition in Eastern Europe* (Chicago: University of Chicago Press, 1994), [b]*The Economist*, November 22–28, 1997, "Survey: Business in Eastern Europe," p. 10.

For more on economies in transition, see the Case and Fair Web page at
http://www.prenhall.com/casefair.

governmental decisions either directly through voting or indirectly through representatives. A *dictatorship* is a political system in which ultimate power is concentrated in either a small elite group or a single person.

Historically, two major *economic* systems have existed: socialism and capitalism. A **socialist economy** is one in which most capital—factories, equipment, buildings, railroads, and so forth—is owned by the government rather than by private

socialist economy *An economy in which most capital is owned by the government rather than by private citizens. Also called social ownership.*

capitalist economy *An economy in which most capital is privately owned.*

communism *An economic system in which the people control the means of production (capital and land) directly, without the intervention of a government or state.*

citizens. *Social ownership* is another term that is used to describe this kind of system. A **capitalist economy** is one in which most capital is privately owned. Beyond these systems is a purely theoretical economic system called *communism*.

Communism is an economic system in which the people control the means of production (land and capital) directly, without the intervention of a government or state. In the world envisioned by communists, the state would wither away and society would plan the economy in the same way a collective would. Although some countries still consider themselves communist—including China, North Korea, Cuba, and Tanzania—economic planning is done by the government in all of them.

> Comparing economies today, the real distinction is between centrally planned socialism and capitalism, not between capitalism and communism.

No pure socialist economies and no pure capitalist economies exist. Even the Soviet Union, which was basically socialist, had a large private sector. Fully one-fourth of agricultural output in what was the USSR was legally produced on private plots and sold, and in a large "second economy" private citizens provided goods and services to each other, sometimes in violation of the law. Conversely, the strongly capitalistic United States supports many government enterprises, including the postal system. Nonetheless, public ownership is the exception in the United States and private ownership was the exception in the Soviet Union.

Whether particular kinds of political systems tend to be associated with particular kinds of economic systems is debated. The United States and Japan are countries with essentially capitalist economic systems and essentially democratic political institutions. China and North Korea have basically socialist economies with political power highly concentrated in a single political party. These observations do not imply that all capitalist countries have democratic political institutions, nor that all socialist countries are subject to totalitarian party rule.

Many countries—Indonesia, for example—have basically capitalist economies without democratic political systems. Many other countries that are much closer to the socialist end of the economic spectrum also maintain strong democratic traditions. The people of France, for instance, elected the socialist government of François Mitterrand in 1981, and that government promptly nationalized several major industries. Great Britain and Sweden are other examples of democratic countries that support certain strong socialist institutions.

But do certain kinds of economic systems lead to repressive governments? Austrian economist Friedrich Hayek argues yes:

> Economic reforms and government coercion are the road to serfdom. . . . Personal and economic freedoms are inseparable. Once you start down the road to government regulation and planning of the economy, the freedom to speak minds and select political leaders will be jeopardized.[1]

The recent events in Eastern Europe and Russia seem to support Hayek's thesis. There, economic and political reforms are proceeding side by side, and the evidence is mounting that the heart of both the market system *and* democracy is individual freedom.

Nonetheless, some counter Hayek's argument by claiming that social reform and active government involvement in the economy are the only ways to prevent the rise of a totalitarian state. They argue that free and unregulated markets lead to inequality

---

[1]Friedrich Hayek, *The Road to Serfdom* (Chicago: University of Chicago Press, 1944).

and the accumulation of economic power. Accumulated economic power, in turn, leads to political power that is inevitably used in the interests of the wealthy few, not in the interests of all.

CENTRAL PLANNING VERSUS THE MARKET

In addition to ownership of capital, economic systems also differ in the extent to which economic decisions are made through central planning rather than through a market system. In some socialist economies, the allocation of resources, the mix of output, and the distribution of output are determined centrally according to a plan. The former Soviet Union, for example, generated one-year and five-year plans laying out specific production targets in virtually every sector of the economy. In market economies, decisions are made independently by buyers and sellers responding to market signals. Producers produce only what they expect to sell. Labor is attracted into and out of various occupations by wages that are determined by the forces of supply and demand.

Just as there are no pure capitalist and no pure socialist economies, there are no pure market economies and no pure planned economies. Even in the former Soviet Union markets existed and determined, to a large extent, the allocation of resources. Production targets in the United States are set by many agencies, including the Pentagon.

Generally, socialist economies favor central planning over market allocation, while capitalist economies rely to a much greater extent on the market. Nonetheless, some variety exists. The former Yugoslavia was a socialist country that made extensive use of the market. Ownership of capital and land rested with the government, but individual firms determined their own output levels and prices and made their own investment plans. Yugoslavian firms borrowed from banks to finance investments and paid interest on their loans. This type of system, which combines government ownership with market allocation, is referred to as a **market-socialist economy**.

market-socialist economy
An economy that combines government ownership with market allocation.

THE ECONOMIC THEORIES OF KARL MARX

The conflict between economic systems has taken place on two levels. On one, there are alternative economic *theories* that lead to very different conclusions about the relative merits of market-capitalist and planned socialist systems. On the other, the actual *performance* of these different economies must be considered.

The events of the early 1990s in Eastern Europe provide strong evidence that central planning has come up a big loser on the basis of performance. Why, then, should we spend time studying the theoretical underpinnings of communism and socialism? There are at least three reasons. First, for over 70 years in the Soviet Union, and for over 40 years in most parts of Eastern Europe and China, socialist ideology was dominant. Until very recently, about one-third of the world's population lived in countries whose economies were based on socialist and communist philosophies. Second, even though the economies of the republics of the former Soviet Union and the economies of Eastern Europe are moving rapidly toward a market-based system, a number of other countries remain firmly committed to the ideas of centrally planned socialism. Finally, to understand the capitalist system, one must understand the criticisms that have been leveled against it.

➤ **Marxian Economics: An Overview** Perhaps no single modern thinker has had a greater impact on the world in the twentieth century than Karl Marx, whose work is the basis of the communist ideology. Marxian economic analysis concludes that the capitalist system is morally wrong and doomed to ultimate failure.

The most common misconception about Marx's work is that it contains a blueprint for the operation of a socialist or communist economy. In fact, Marx did not write much about socialism; he wrote about capitalism. Published mostly after his death in 1883, his major work, the three-volume *Das Kapital*, is an extensive analysis of how capitalist economies function and how they are likely to develop over time. *The Communist Manifesto* (written with Friedrich Engels and published in 1848) and his other writings contain only a rough sketch of the socialist and communist societies that Marx predicted would ultimately replace capitalism.

Marx's economic theories lie at the root of his interpretation of history. In examining his work, let us begin with what might be called "Marxian microeconomics" and then turn to the macroeconomic conclusions that emerge from it.

> **The Labor Theory of Value**   The center of Marx's economic theories is the **labor theory of value**. Marx argued that the value of a commodity depends exclusively upon the amount of labor required to produce it. Commodities are thus the physical embodiment of the labor that produced them:

labor theory of value *Marx's theory that the value of a commodity depends exclusively upon the amount of labor required to produce it. Commodities are the physical embodiment of the labor that produced them, and capital is the physical embodiment of the past labor used to produce it.*

> A commodity has value, because it is a crystallization of social labor. The greatness of its value, of its relative value, depends upon the greater or less amount of that social substance contained in it. . . .The relative values of commodities are, therefore, determined by the respective quantities or amounts of labor, worked up, realized, fixed in them.[2]

The labor theory of value also addresses the nature and uses of capital. Goods can be produced with a variety of combinations of capital and labor. Are goods produced with a lot of capital and little labor worth less than goods produced with a lot of labor and little capital? No. Capital, according to Marx, is the physical embodiment of the *past labor* that was used to produce it. When used in production, capital contributes value by passing that past labor through to the final product. A machine that took 100 hours to build contributes 100 hours of value to final products over its lifetime. The value of a commodity is the sum of the values contributed by present labor and past labor (capital).

> **The Nature of Profit: The Marxian View**   If, as Marx believed, commodity values depend only on labor's contribution, where does profit come in? The answer: Capitalists own the **means of production**, Marx's term for land and capital. They hire individual workers who have no way to make a living except by selling their labor power. Capitalists make a profit by paying workers a daily wage that is less than the value that workers contribute to final products in a day.

means of production *Marx's term for land and capital.*

The wage rate is the **value of labor power**, and it is determined in the same way as the value of any other commodity. That is, the value of labor power depends on the amount of labor required to "produce" it. To produce and sustain labor power requires food, clothing, shelter, basic education, medical care, and so forth. The value of labor power, then, is determined by the amount of labor it takes to produce those things necessary to sustain a worker and his or her family. In essence, Marx was proposing a *subsistence theory of wages*: Capitalists will pay a wage that is just enough for laborers to live on.

value of labor power *The wage rate, dependent on the amount of clothing, shelter, basic education, medical care, and so on required to produce and sustain labor power.*

Suppose it takes 4 hours to produce everything necessary to sustain a worker for a day. Marx would argue that a day's wage paid by capitalists will be the equivalent of 4 hours' worth of value. If a worker is employed for 12 hours, the capitalist ends up with a final product containing 12 hours of value but needs to give only four hours' worth of value—or wages—to the worker. The difference (8 hours), which Marx called **surplus value**, is profit.

surplus value *The profit a capitalist earns by paying workers less than the value of what they produce.*

PART NINE
The Global Economy

---

[2]Karl Marx, *Wages, Price and Profit* (Beijing: Foreign Languages Press, 1975), pp. 34–35.

Profit is value created by workers but "expropriated" by capitalists. Capitalists are able to expropriate surplus value because they own the means of production and control access to them. Profit is not a reward for any productive activity; it is extracted solely by virtue of ownership. Marx referred to the ratio of surplus value to the value of labor power as the **rate of exploitation**.

rate of exploitation *The ratio of surplus value to the value of labor power.*

▶ The Nature of Profit: The Neoclassical View

The bulk of this text has presented mainstream, or neoclassical, economic theory, with its deep roots in nineteenth-century philosophy. At this point we reflect briefly on the nature of profit in that model, because it is so different from the Marxian notion of surplus value.

Neoclassical economics views both capital and labor as productive factors of production. If you have one worker digging a hole and you want a bigger hole faster, you can accomplish your goal by hiring a second worker *or* by giving the first worker a better shovel. Add labor and you get more product; add capital and you also get more product. According to neoclassical theory, every factor of production in a competitive market economy ends up being paid in accordance with the market value of its product. Profit-maximizing firms hire labor and capital as long as both contribute more to the final value of a product than they cost.

> Neoclassical theory views profit as the legitimate return to capital. Marx, however, saw profit as value created by labor and unjustly expropriated by nonproductive capitalists, who own the means of production and thus are able to exploit labor.

▶ Marx's Predictions

The labor theory of value led Marx to conclude that capitalism was doomed. The essence of his argument was that the rate of profit has a natural tendency to fall over time. With the rate of profits falling, capitalists increase the rate of exploitation, pushing workers deeper and deeper into misery. At the same time, the ups and downs of business cycles become more and more extreme. Ultimately, Marx believed, workers would rise up and overthrow the repressive capitalist system.

The theory that capitalism would ultimately collapse was part of Marx's longer view of history. Capitalism had emerged naturally from a previous stage (*feudalism*), which had emerged from an even earlier stage (*ancient slavery*), and so forth. In the economic evolutionary process, Marx believed, capitalism would be replaced by socialism, which ultimately would be replaced by communism.

At each stage of economic evolution, Marx said, a set of rules called the *social relations of production* defines the economic system. Contradictions and conflicts inevitably arise at each stage, and these problems are ultimately resolved in the establishment of a new set of social relations. The conflicts in capitalism include alienation, increasing exploitation, misery (or, as Marx called it, "emiserization"), and deeper and deeper business cycles.

It is clear that Marx was eager for the demise of capitalism. He advocated strong and powerful labor unions for two reasons. First, unions would push wages above subsistence and transfer some surplus value back to workers. Second, unions were a way of raising the consciousness of workers about their condition. Only through class consciousness, Marx believed, would workers be empowered to throw off the shackles of capitalism.

At the heart of Marx's ideas is the argument that private ownership and profit are unfair and unethical. Even if it could be demonstrated that the incentives provided by the institution of private property result in faster economic growth or improved living standards, anyone who accepts Marx's interpretation has to reject capitalism on moral grounds, on ideological grounds, or on both.

TABLE 38.1

PER CAPITA INCOME (RUBLES)

	1861	1913
Russia	71	119
U.K.	323	580
France	150	303
Germany	175	374
U.S.	450	1,033
Netherlands	—	366
Norway	166	659
Sweden	112	340
Italy	183	261
Spain	—	199
Austria-Hungary	—	190

Source: Paul Gregory and Robert Stuart, *Soviet Economic Structure and Performance,* 2nd ed. (New York: Harper & Row, 1981), p. 20.

ECONOMIES IN TRANSITION: EXPERIENCES OF RUSSIA AND EASTERN EUROPE

The Eastern European nations' transitions to market systems were largely the result of the economic failures of centrally planned socialism, which had ultimately failed to "deliver the goods." To understand the failure of the Eastern European socialist economies and the difficult process of transition that lies ahead for them, students of economics must be aware of these countries' economic histories. Here, we briefly describe the Soviet system as it existed for nearly 75 years and the changes taking place today. Although the transformation process is well under way, it will be some time before the process of dismantling the old system is complete.

THE SOVIET UNION: HISTORY AND REFORM

Marx believed that socialist revolution would occur in advanced capitalist states where a repressive industrial society would push workers to unite and rise up against their industrialist masters. The Russian nation in 1913 had experienced the beginnings of modern economic growth, but it could hardly have been called an advanced capitalist system. Table 38.1 shows that its relative position in terms of per capita income had improved in the half century prior to 1913, but that it still lagged far behind the other industrial countries of the world.

When the Bolsheviks took power after the October Revolution in 1917, they found themselves without the advanced industrial base that Marx had envisioned and with no real blueprint for running a socialist or communist state. Marx's writings provided only the broadest guidelines. Undaunted, the new government immediately abolished private land ownership and ordered that the land be distributed to those who worked on it. It also established worker control of industry and nationalized the banks. Sweeping nationalization of industry began in June 1918. Money, private trade, and wage differentials were abolished. All decisions were made centrally.

The rush into uncharted waters was too much too soon. Between 1921 and 1928 Soviet leaders retreated from their initial hard line back toward a market orientation. The **New Economic Policy** of the period was characterized by decentralization. Most smaller industrial enterprises were denationalized, although the peasants remained in control of agriculture. State control of production was replaced by market links between consumers and industry and between industry and agriculture.

The relative merits and demerits of these two periods, 1917 to 1921 and 1921 to 1928, were debated among the Soviet leadership. In 1928, the Soviet Union settled on an economic structure that lasted into the 1980s: comprehensive central planning and collectivization of agriculture. In 1928, under the leadership of Joseph Stalin, the first of many **five-year plans** was approved. The plan emphasized rapid industrialization and the production of industrial capital; the plan called for a doubling of the fixed capital stock of the Soviet Union in five years. Consumer goods were to be produced only when all other needs of the new industrial structure had been met.

The industrialization program depended on a steady flow of food and agricultural raw materials from the countryside, and that did not come easily. As a result, Stalin was forced to rely more and more on coercion. In 1929 the land holdings of the peasants were organized into collective farms that were obligated to deliver state-ordered quotas of farm products. Repression was severe, and millions of peasants perished.[3]

New Economic Policy *The Soviet economic policy in effect between 1921 and 1928; characterized by decentralization and a retreat to a market orientation.*

five-year plans *Plans developed in the Soviet Union that provided general guidelines and directions for the next five years.*

---

[3]George Orwell's novel *Animal Farm* is a parable of this period in Soviet history.

No serious debate about economic matters took place in the Soviet Union until after Stalin's death in 1953. In 1965 official reforms were introduced by the government of Alexei Kosygin. Mikhail Gorbachev announced a series of reforms in 1986 and in 1987, but the structure of the economy was not changed fundamentally.

Since 1991, Boris Yeltsin has been president of the Russian Republic and the champion of reform. Yeltsin has deregulated most prices, begun the privatization process, and attempted to stabilize the macroeconomy. By 1995 progress had been slow but significant. Privatization had made steady progress, reaching a point in 1994 where the private sector was generating 60 percent of personal income. Inflation was down, and a new "economic constitution" in the form of revised laws to establish property rights and stimulate economic activity went into effect in 1995. But things were not going well across the board.

Most observers estimate that Russian GDP began to grow in the spring of 1997, after falling by about 50 percent from its 1989 level. However, problems remained severe into 1998. The biggest problem was attracting investment, and the biggest barrier was crime and corruption. The Russian government was finding it very difficult to enforce the rule of law. The term *cowboy capitalism* is often used to describe the situation in Russia today.

➤ **Economic Performance** The Stalinist/Soviet strategy to achieve high rates of growth worked for many years. The highest rates of growth in Soviet GNP were during the 1950s. Official Soviet statistics put the real growth rate during that decade at over 10 percent, an extraordinary rate at which real output would double every seven years. Even the CIA's more conservative estimates, shown in Table 38.2, estimated the Soviet growth rate at 5.7 percent, nearly 80 percent above the U.S. average for the decade.

In 1957, the Soviet Union's GNP stood at about 39 percent of the U.S. GNP. A year later, Soviet GNP had jumped to nearly 44 percent of U.S. GNP. The rate at which the Soviet Union was catching up was so remarkable that it prompted Soviet premier Nikita Khrushchev to promise, "We will bury you!" If the Soviet growth rate estimates had been correct, and if both countries had continued to grow at the same rates as during the 1950s, Soviet GNP would have surpassed U.S. GNP by 1970.

TABLE 38.2 ECONOMIC GROWTH AND INVESTMENT IN THE SOVIET UNION AND THE UNITED STATES, 1950–1990

	ANNUAL AVERAGE RATE OF GROWTH				
	USSR NET MATERIAL PRODUCT (USSR, OFFICIAL FIGURES)	USSR REAL GNP (CIA)	USA REAL GNP	USSR CAPITAL STOCK	USA CAPITAL STOCK
1950–1960	10.3	5.7	3.2	9.5	3.6
1960–1970	7.1	5.1	4.0	8.0	4.0
1970–1975	5.7	3.7	2.6	7.9	4.0
1975–1980	4.3	2.7	3.7	6.8	3.9
1980–1984	—	2.6	2.7	6.3*	3.6
1984–1987	—	1.8	2.4	NA	NA
1988–1990	—	0.0	2.4	NA	NA

Note: *1980–1983. NA = not available. GDP data not available.

Sources: Abram Bergson, "Gorbachev Calls for Intensive Growth," *Challenge,* November–December 1985. For the United States, *Statistical Abstract of the United States, 1986* and *1990; Historical Statistics of the United States,* and *Economic Report of the President, 1990.*

The primary force behind Soviet growth was capital accumulation. During the 1950s, the capital stock of the USSR grew at 9.5 percent annually; in the United States, the corresponding figure was only 3.6 percent. Through 1975 Soviet capital stocks grew at twice the rate of capital accumulation in the United States. But these growth rates did not continue, and during the late 1970s they slowed down. Between 1975 and 1985, even the slowly growing U.S. economy outperformed the Soviet Union. In 1975, per capita GNP in the Soviet Union stood at 48.2 percent of per capita GNP in the United States. In 1985 the figure was 48.1 percent.

➤ **Gorbachev and *Perestroika***   In March 1985, Mikhail Gorbachev became general secretary of the Soviet Communist Party and almost immediately began to press for reforms that had an enormous impact on the world. In 1990, Gorbachev won the Nobel Peace Prize for ending the Cold War and was named "Man of the Decade" by *Time* magazine. Despite his enormous popularity around the world and his political successes, one prize continued to elude Gorbachev: improved economic performance in the Soviet Union.

Gorbachev's reforms fell into two categories: *glasnost* ("openness") and *perestroika* ("restructuring"). *Glasnost* led to the almost completely open discussion of every aspect of political and economic reform in the Soviet Union. It also led to a new set of political institutions, including an end to the power monopoly of the Communist party[4] and more free elections. Glasnost was relatively easy to achieve, but the establishment of new economic structures—the key element of Gorbachev's *perestroika*—was more difficult.

The initial goal of *perestroika* was to increase workers' responsibilities and discipline by attacking corruption and alcoholism. In these arenas, Gorbachev met with some success. Numerous bureau chiefs were replaced, alcoholism was reduced through strict law enforcement, absenteeism declined, and productivity increased. Then, in 1986, the focus of reform shifted to the performance of agriculture. In that year, Gorbachev restructured the agricultural sector giving local farm units and the peasantry new freedoms. Local farm units, for example, were allowed to use the market to dispose of any surplus over five-year plan levels. Payments to state and collective farm workers were tied to productivity and profits, and local directors were given more authority over management and investment decisions.

The best was yet to come. In June 1987, Gorbachev announced another series of reforms. The package included some surprising changes. First, price subsidies were to be drastically reduced or eliminated, even on such items as meat, bread, dairy products, and housing. Second, all limits on what workers could earn were to be removed, and salaries were to be tied directly to performance. Third, the decision-making authority of the farms and enterprises was to be greatly expanded. Central plans were to contain far less detail than in previous years. At the same time, Gorbachev called for sharp increases in small-scale family farming and for a "competitive atmosphere" among enterprises to ensure that goods were sold to consumers at the lowest possible prices that would still cover costs of production.

---

[4]For many years, membership in and loyalty to the Communist party were the ticket to the good life in the Soviet Union. Under the *nomenklatura* party patronage system, Communist party leaders received power and privilege in exchange for loyalty to the party. In addition to determining the staffing of government and industrial posts (a practice that led to a good deal of favoritism and nepotism), party members also enjoyed the right to shop at special state-run stores stocking luxury items not available to the general public. Travel privileges, admissions to the best colleges and universities, larger apartments, and bigger cars also went to members of the *nomenklatura*. In 1990, the Central Committee of the Soviet Communist Party approved a proposal by President Gorbachev calling for an end to the party's constitutional guarantee of power, ending the *nomenklatura*. After the failed August 1991 coup, the Communist party was completely dismantled.

Perhaps the most radical of the 1987 reforms was that job security, a sacred tenet of the Soviet system, would be reduced. For the first time, enterprises could fire lazy workers, and unproductive enterprises could be shut down.

▶ **Economic Crisis and Collapse**   Although Gorbachev's ideas seemed promising, the situation in the Soviet Union deteriorated sharply after 1987. The attempted transition from central planning to a partly free-market system caused major problems. Growth of output slowed to a crawl in 1989 and 1990, and in 1991 the economic system collapsed. Industrial production dropped sharply, food shortages grew worse, inflation became serious, and external debt increased rapidly.

Gorbachev ran out of time in August 1991 as the struggle between the hard-liners and the radical reformers came to a head. The hard-liners took Gorbachev prisoner and assumed control of the government. The coup lasted only three days. People took to the streets of Moscow and resisted the tanks, the Soviet army refused to obey orders, and the hard-liners were out.

But the end was near for both Gorbachev and the Soviet Union. In December 1991, the Soviet Union was dissolved, 10 of the former Soviet republics formed the Commonwealth of Independent States (CIS), and Boris Yeltsin became president of the Russian Republic as Gorbachev became part of history. From the beginning, Yeltsin showed himself to be a reformer committed to converting the Russian economy rapidly into a market system while maintaining hard-won political freedoms for the people. His reform plan called for deregulating prices, privatizing public enterprises, and stabilizing the macroeconomy.

THE TRANSITION TO A MARKET ECONOMY

The reforms under way in the Russian Republic and in the other formerly Communist countries of Eastern Europe have taken shape very slowly and amid debate about how best to proceed. Remember: there is absolutely no historical precedent to provide lessons. Despite this lack of precedent, however, there is substantial agreement among economists about what needs to be done.

> Economists generally agree on six basic requirements for a successful transition from socialism to a market-based system: (1) macroeconomic stabilization; (2) deregulation of prices and liberalization of trade; (3) privatization of state-owned enterprises and development of new private industry; (4) the establishment of market-supporting institutions, such as property and contract laws, accounting systems, and so forth; (5) a social safety net to deal with unemployment and poverty; and (6) external assistance.

We now discuss each component. Although we focus on the experience of the Russian Republic, these principles apply to all economies in transition.

▶ **Macroeconomic Stabilization**   Virtually every one of the countries in transition has had a problem with inflation, but nowhere has it been worse than in Russia. As economic conditions worsened, the government found itself with serious budget problems. As revenue flows slowed and expenditure commitments increased, large budget deficits resulted. At the same time, each of the new republics established its own central bank. Each central bank began issuing "ruble credits" to keep important enterprises afloat and to pay the government's bills. The issuance of these credits, which were generally accepted as a means of payment throughout the country, led to a dramatic expansion of the money supply.

IF THE GOVERNMENT SETS PRICES BELOW MARKET-CLEARING LEVELS, BLACK MARKETS ARE LIKELY TO DEVELOP. IN UKRAINE, IT IS SOMETIMES EASIER TO BUY POTS AND PANS ON THE STREET THAN IT IS TO FIND THEM IN STORES.

Almost from the beginning, the expanded money supply meant too much money was chasing too few goods. This was made worse by government-controlled prices set substantially below market-clearing levels. The combination of monetary expansion and price control was deadly. Government-run shops that sold goods at controlled prices were empty. People waited in line for days and often became violent when their efforts to buy goods at low official prices were thwarted. At the same time, suppliers found that they could charge much higher prices for their products on the black market—which grew bigger by the day, further exacerbating the shortage of goods at government shops. Over time, the ruble became worth less and less as black market prices continued to rise more rapidly. Russia found itself with near hyperinflation in 1992.

To achieve a properly functioning market system, prices must be stabilized. To do so, the government must find a way to move toward a balanced budget and to bring the supply of money under control.

> **Deregulation of Prices and Liberalization of Trade** To move successfully from central planning to a market system, individual prices must be deregulated. A system of freely moving prices forms the backbone of a market system. When people want more of a good than is currently being produced, its price will rise. This higher price increases producers' profits and provides an incentive for existing firms to expand production and for new firms to enter the industry. Conversely, if an industry is producing a good for which there is no market or a good that people no longer want in the same quantity, the result will be excess supply and the price of that good will fall. This reduces profits or creates losses, providing an incentive for some existing firms to cut back on production and for others to go out of business. In short, an unregulated price mechanism ensures an efficient allocation of resources across industries. Until prices are deregulated, this mechanism cannot function.

Trade barriers must also be removed. Reform-minded countries must be able to import capital, technology, and ideas. In addition, it makes no sense to continue to subsidize industries that cannot be competitive on world markets. If it is cheaper to buy steel from an efficient West German steel mill than to produce it in a subsidized antiquated Russian mill, the Russian mill should be modernized or shut down. Ultimately, as the theory of comparative advantage suggests, liberalized trade will push each country to produce the products it produces best.

FAST FACTS

While real GDP in Russia began to grow slowly during 1997, inflation remained at 13% and short-term interest rates were 28%.

Deregulating prices and eliminating subsidies can bring serious political problems. Many products in Russia and the rest of the socialist world were priced below market-clearing levels for equity reasons. Housing, food, and clothing were considered by many to be entitlements. Making them more expensive, at least relative to their prices in previous times, is not likely to be popular. In addition, forcing inefficient firms to operate without subsidies will lead many to go out of business, and jobs will be lost. So while price deregulation and trade liberalization are necessary, they are very difficult politically.

▶ **Privatization** One problem with a system of central ownership is a lack of accountability. Under a system of private ownership, owners reap the rewards of their successes and suffer the consequences of their failures. Private ownership provides a strong incentive for efficient operation, innovation, and hard work that is lacking when ownership is centralized and profits are distributed to the people.

The classic story to illustrate this is called the **tragedy of commons**. Suppose an agricultural community has 10,000 acres of grazing land. If the land were held in common so that all farmers had unlimited rights to graze their animals, each farmer would have an incentive to overgraze. He or she would reap the full benefits from grazing additional calves while the costs of grazing the calves would be borne collectively. The system provides no incentive to manage the land efficiently. Similarly, if the efficiency and benefits of my hard work and managerial skills accrue to others or to the state, what incentive do I have to work hard or to be efficient?

One solution to the tragedy of commons attempted in eighteenth-century Britain was to divide up the land into private holdings. Today, many economists argue, the solution to the incentive problem encountered in state-owned enterprises is to privatize them and let the owners compete.

In addition to increasing accountability, privatization means creating a climate in which new enterprises can flourish. If there is market demand for a product not currently being produced, individual entrepreneurs should be free to set up a business and make a profit. During the last months of the Soviet Union's existence, private enterprises such as taxi services, car repair services, restaurants, and even hotels began to spring up all over the country.

Like deregulation of prices, privatization is difficult politically. Privatization means many protected enterprises will go out of business because they cannot compete at world prices, resulting in a loss of jobs, at least temporarily.

▶ **Market-Supporting Institutions** Between 1991 and 1997, U.S. firms raced to Eastern Europe in search of markets and investment opportunities and immediately became aware of a major obstacle. The institutions that make the market function relatively smoothly in the United States do not exist in Eastern Europe.

For example, the capital market, which channels private saving into productive capital investment in developed capitalist economies, is made up of hundreds of different institutions. The banking system, venture capital funds, the stock market, the bond market, the commodity exchanges, brokerage houses, investment banks, and the like have all developed in the United States over hundreds of years, and they will not simply be replicated overnight in the formerly Communist world.

Many market-supporting institutions are so basic that Americans take them for granted. The institution of private property, for example, is a set of rights that must be protected by laws that the government must be willing to enforce. Suppose that the French hotel chain Novotel decides to build a new hotel in Moscow. Novotel must first acquire land. Then it will construct a building based on the expectation of renting rooms to customers. These investments are made with the expectation that the owner has a right to use them and a right to the profits that they produce. For such investments to be undertaken, these rights must be guaranteed by a set of property laws. This

tragedy of commons *The idea that collective ownership may not provide the proper private incentives for efficiency because individuals do not bear the full costs of their own decisions but do enjoy the full benefits.*

is equally true for large business firms and for Russian entrepreneurs who want to start their own enterprises.

Similarly, the law must provide for the enforcement of contracts. In the United States, a huge body of law determines what happens to you if you break a formal promise made in good faith. Businesses exist on promises to produce and promises to pay. Without recourse to the law when a contract is breached, contracts will not be entered into, goods will not be manufactured, and services will not be provided.

Another seemingly simple matter that turns out to be quite complex is the establishment of a set of accounting principles. In the United States, the rules of the accounting game are embodied in a set of Generally Accepted Accounting Principles (GAAP) that carry the force of law. Companies are required to keep track of their receipts, expenditures, and liabilities so their performance can be observed and evaluated by shareholders, taxing authorities, and others who have an interest in the company. If you have taken a course in accounting, you know how detailed these rules have become. Imagine trying to do business in a country operating under hundreds of different sets of rules. That's what has been happening in Russia.

Another institution is insurance. Whenever a venture undertakes a high-risk activity, it buys insurance to protect itself. Several years ago, Amnesty International (a nonprofit organization that works to protect civil liberties around the world) sponsored a worldwide concert tour with a number of well-known rock bands and performers. The most difficult part of organizing the tour was obtaining insurance for the artists and their equipment when they played in the then-Communist countries of Eastern Europe.

➤ **Social Safety Net** In a centrally planned socialist economy, the labor market does not function freely. Everyone who wants a job is guaranteed one somewhere. The number of jobs is determined by a central plan to match the number of workers. There is essentially no unemployment. This, it has been argued, is one of the great advantages of a planned system. In addition, a central planning system provides basic housing, food, and clothing at very affordable levels for all. With no unemployment and necessities available at very low prices, there is no need for unemployment insurance, welfare, or other social programs.

Transition to a free labor market and liberalization of prices means that some workers will end up unemployed and everyone will pay higher prices for necessities. Indeed, during the early phases of the transition process, unemployment will be high. Inefficient state-owned enterprises will go out of business; some sectors will contract while others expand. As more and more people experience unemployment, popular support for reform is likely to drop unless some sort of social safety net is erected to ease the transition. This social safety net might include unemployment insurance, aid for the poor, and food and housing assistance. The experiences of the developed world have shown that such programs are expensive.

➤ **External Assistance** Very few believe the transition to a market system can be achieved without outside support and some outside financing. Knowledge of and experience with capitalist institutions that exist in the United States, Western Europe, and Japan are of vital interest to the Eastern European nations. The basic skills of accounting, management, and enterprise development can be taught to Eastern Europe; many say it is in everyone's best interest to do so. Many also argue that the world's biggest nightmare is an economically weak or desperate Russia armed with nuclear weapons, giving up on reform or falling to a dictator.

There is little agreement about the extent of *financial* support that should be given, however. The United States has pushed for a worldwide effort to provide billions of dollars in aid. This aid, many argue, will help Russia stabilize its macroeconomy and buy desperately needed goods from abroad. But critics in the United States and other potential donor countries say pouring money into Russia now is like pouring it into a black hole—no matter how much we donate, it will have little impact on the ultimate success or failure of the reforms.

SHOCK THERAPY OR GRADUALISM?

Although economists generally agree on what the former socialist economies need to do, they debate the sequence and timing of specific reforms.

The popular press describes the debate as one between those who believe in "shock therapy" (sometimes called the "Big Bang" approach) and those who prefer a more gradual approach. Advocates of **shock therapy** believe that the economies in transition should proceed immediately on all fronts. They should stop printing money, deregulate prices and liberalize trade, privatize, develop market institutions, build a social safety net, and acquire external aid—all as quickly as possible. The pain will be severe, the argument goes, but in the end it will be forgotten as the transition raises living standards. Advocates of a *gradualist* approach believe the best course is to build up market institutions first, gradually decontrol prices, and privatize only the most efficient government enterprises first.

Those who favor moving quickly point to the apparent success of Poland, which moved rapidly through the first phases of reform. Russia's experience during the first years of its transition have demonstrated that, at least in that country, change must be to some extent gradual. In theory, stabilization and price liberalization can be achieved instantaneously. But to enjoy the benefits of liberalization, a good deal of privatization must have taken place—and that will take more time. One analyst has said, privatization means "selling assets with no value to people with no money." Some estimates suggest half of Russian state-owned enterprises are incapable of making a profit at world prices. Simply cutting them loose would create chaos. In a sense, Russia has no choice but to move slowly.

ALTERNATIVE ECONOMIC SYSTEMS

We now discuss two alternative economic systems: that of China and that of Japan.

THE PEOPLE'S REPUBLIC OF CHINA

Eastward around the globe from the Russian Republic lies China, the world's most populous country. With 1.2 billion people, mainland China accounts for one out of every five people in the world. And China is very poor, with per capita GDP around $850 in 1998.

China remains a country in which political dissent is not tolerated and the economic system remains Communist but in which private enterprise is permitted and even encouraged. This seemingly incongruous system is performing, at least for now, as well as any economy in the world. China, like Russia, is an enormously important power in the world, and understanding its history and the nature of its economic institutions is an essential part of understanding economics.

Compared to the United States, the People's Republic of China is very large and very poor. Per capita income in China is about one-twentieth of per capita income in the United States. The history of the People's Republic, established after the Communist victory in the revolution of 1949, has been marked by wild gyrations of policy and some extraordinary economic experiments.

▶ **Socialization under Mao Zedong**   Soon after gaining power, the Chinese Communists, led by Chairman Mao Zedong, became involved in the Korean War and found themselves

shock therapy *The approach to transition from socialism to market capitalism that advocates rapid deregulation of prices, liberalization of trade, and privatization.*

heavily dependent on the Soviet Union. That's why the early structure of the Chinese economic system was built on the Soviet-Stalinist model. China's first five-year plan, from 1953 to 1957, focused on developing capital-intensive heavy industries. Agriculture was collectivized, household farming was eliminated, and compulsory output quotas were put in place.

In 1958 China departed sharply from the Soviet model and launched a new economic strategy called the **Great Leap Forward**. The focus of production shifted from large-scale, capital-intensive industry to small-scale, labor-intensive industry scattered across the countryside. In addition, material incentives were reduced and replaced by the motivating power of revolutionary ideology and inspiration. Although initially successful, the strategy ultimately failed. In the early 1960s, output fell below 1958 levels. Between 1961 and 1965, material incentives were restored and a period of relative calm followed.

During the late 1960s and 1970s, economic development in China suffered a blow from the **Great Proletarian Cultural Revolution** that began in 1966. For almost a decade, the rule was ideological purity. The faithful—almost everyone—denounced those who favored material incentives and reform, and scientists, engineers, managers, and scholars whose views were out of favor were sent to the countryside to work in the fields. The universities were essentially closed down. Untrained revolutionary *cadres* (small groups of leaders) replaced trained specialists in almost all jobs, and the economy suffered terribly. Most estimates place per capita income and consumption in the late 1970s at levels only slightly above the levels of 1956 to 1957.[5]

> ### ▶ The Reforms of Deng Xiaoping

When Chairman Mao died in September 1976, the Cultural Revolution formally ended. Meanwhile, China watched as its once poor neighbors—Japan, South Korea, Taiwan, and Singapore—enjoyed extraordinary growth and prosperity.

In December 1978, the Chinese Central Committee, under Deng Xiaoping, announced sweeping reforms. These early reforms focused on agriculture, and they signaled the beginning of profound changes in the Chinese economy that would continue over the next 10 years.

Prior to 1978, each agricultural commune had distributed the harvest equally among its members. Incentives were purely collective, with everything done for the glory of the revolution. Because the cadres often overstated harvests, the state raised local delivery quotas, leaving the peasants with barely enough to go around. The new system begun under Deng Xiaoping gave individual families, through a 15-year family contract, formal rights to the land they worked. Families were also given the rights to dispose of any surpluses and to hire out part of the family labor force to enterprises outside the family plot. Deng gave the Chinese peasants permission to enrich themselves. And they did!

Output of grain and other basic necessities, such as cotton, increased substantially. More importantly, rural industry grew dramatically, employing over 20 percent of the rural labor force by 1985. From 1978 through 1983, wheat production increased at an annual rate of 8.6 percent, rice at 4.3 percent, and cotton at 16.4 percent. From 1981 to 1984, the growth rate of all agricultural output reached 11.0 percent annually. In 1984 China became an exporter of food, despite a population of over one billion. Peasant income more than doubled in less than a decade, and private consumption and housing construction increased sharply.[6]

Great Leap Forward *The economic strategy in the People's Republic of China that began in 1958 when it departed from the Soviet model and shifted from large-scale, capital-intensive industry to small-scale, labor-intensive industry scattered across the countryside. Material incentives were reduced and replaced by the motivating power of revolutionary ideology and inspiration.*

Great Proletarian Cultural Revolution (1966–1976) *A period of ideological purity in the People's Republic of China: Material incentives and reforms were denounced and highly trained specialists were sent to work in the fields. The effect of the Cultural Revolution on the Chinese economy was catastrophic.*

---

[5]See Nicholas Lardy, "Agricultural Reform," *Journal of International Affairs*, Winter 1986.

[6]"China: Economic Performance in 1985, A Report to the Subcommittee on Economic Resources, Competitiveness and Security of the Joint Economic Committee," The Central Intelligence Agency, Washington, D.C.: March 17, 1986 (mimeo), p. 2.

Similar reforms were implemented in Chinese industry on an experimental basis. Initially, enterprises were able to retain 15 percent to 25 percent of any profits above those specified by the plan. By 1984, Chinese enterprises were retaining over 85 percent of increased profits. As with agricultural reform, the goals of industrial reform were to increase the role of the producing unit, to increase individual incentives, and to reduce the role of the state and the central planners.

The most significant element of these reforms was the Chinese government's support of the expansion of enterprise rights. In the spirit of the Soviet New Economic Policy of the 1920s, the Chinese are actively encouraging small private trade and manufacturing. Today there is an increasingly important Chinese private sector competing with state stores in style, service, quality, and price. By 1986, 480,000 "new economic associations" were employing 4.2 million people.[7] China is now encouraging foreign investment. Initially only joint ventures with the government were permitted, but now foreigners retain 100 percent ownership in several projects.

➤ **China after Tiananmen Square**   Despite the economic advances that China has made in the last decades, there is a great deal of political unrest in the country. In May 1989, university students openly challenged the authority of the government by occupying Tiananmen Square in Beijing. Many went on hunger strikes to protest China's lack of democracy. The "democracy movement" was crushed on June 3, 1989, when the government cleared the square with troops and tanks as the world watched.

The events of 1989 turned world opinion against the Chinese and at least temporarily slowed the movement toward economic reform. A number of joint ventures were canceled, and the amount of direct aid flowing into China was reduced. But even before Tiananmen Square, Chinese economic reforms were beginning to encounter difficulty.

In 1988, China experienced serious inflation for the first time. By late 1988, prices were rising in historically unprecedented amounts, nearly 30 percent per year. In September, the government began implementing an austerity program that included strict price controls, reduced state investment, and reduced imports. The rate of inflation had dropped by 1989, but output of goods and services in China fell in 1989 and grew only slightly in 1990.

The years 1991 to 1995 saw a dramatic turnaround for China. While the current Communist government has retained power and maintained a hard line on the political front, economic freedoms have been extended into every sphere. Private enterprise continues to be encouraged (see Global Perspective box "China: Free Enterprise in a Communist Country"). A stock market was established and stock prices have boomed. Everyone in China wants a piece of the action. In October 1992, First Boston Corporation, Merrill Lynch and Co., and Salomon Brothers offered five million shares in and raised more than $75 million for the JinBei Vehicle Manufacturing Company in the city of Shenyang. Hundreds of billions of dollars in foreign investment are now flowing into China from the United States, Japan, Singapore, Taiwan, and Korea.

Some problems and challenges remain. Many fear that food shortages are imminent. While the Chinese population has continued to grow, the country's expanding industrial and housing sectors have led to a declining amount of land under cultivation. (China contains 20 percent of the world's population but only 7 percent of the world's arable land.) Also, over 50,000 state-owned enterprises continue to operate, although the process of selling these enterprises to foreign investors and allowing them to go into a form of bankruptcy continues.

FAST FACTS

One of the engines of recent Chinese growth has been exports. But the huge fall in the value of the Korean and Thai currencies in 1997 makes them more competitive with China. Some fear further slowdown for China as its neighbors recover.

[7]*Beijing Review*, no. 25, June 23, 1986.

CHINA: FREE ENTERPRISE IN A COMMUNIST COUNTRY

The following excerpt from a recent *New York Times* article summarizes nicely what seems to be happening in a rapidly changing China:

QIAOTOU, China—For a glimpse into China's economic revolution, it is useful to stroll down the main street of this humble little town. . . [which] has propelled itself over the last dozen years into the button capital of the world.

Each year, the privately run factories of Qiaotou produce about 12 billion buttons. . . . This button boom, amounting to two buttons annually per inhabitant on earth, has transformed rice paddies into factory districts, and peasants into tycoons.

One of them is Zhan Yusheng, a 27-year-old who began making buttons in his home 10 years ago. Today he owns a button factory with 100 employees, and last year he had sales of nearly $200,000.

"Now we need to upgrade our quality and produce more high-quality buttons," said Chen Jianlin, Qiaotou's Communist Party secretary. "Then we can expand on the

international market.". . . Mr. Chen sees his mission primarily as promoting private enterprise.

"My most important job is building up the economy," Mr. Chen said as he sipped tea at the conference table in his office. "People here say: 'If you push the economy along, you're a good leader. Otherwise, you're not.' "

While his salary is only $20 a month, about a third as much as the 20,000 migrant workers employed in Qiaotou's factories, . . . the party covers most of his expenses, supplies him with a house, a chauffered Audi, a phone with international direct dialing, a beeper, and a Mastercard.

"A lot of people here now carry credit cards when they travel," Mr. Chen said, beaming as he passed around his Mastercard for inspection. "Credit cards are very convenient and you don't have to carry so much cash."

Source: Nicholas D. Kristof, "Free Enterprise Encouraged," *The New York Times*, Jan. 18, 1993. Copyright © 1993 by The New York Times Co. Reprinted by permission.

EACH YEAR, THE PRIVATELY RUN FACTORIES OF QIAOTOU, CHINA, PRODUCE ABOUT 12 BILLION BUTTONS, PRIMARILY OF THE INEXPENSIVE KIND FOUND ON DISCOUNT-PRICED CLOTHING.

For more on what's happening in other economic systems, see the Case and Fair Web page at http://www.prenhall.com/casefair.

In July 1997, Hong Kong, previously a British colony, was returned to China with great fanfare. Hong Kong, boasting one of the most successful capitalist economies in the world, would continue to exist as a capitalist enclave albeit under rule of a Communist government. No one knows what the future holds for Hong Kong, although most analysts are optimistic.

At the end of 1997, there were a few signs of potential trouble for the former colony. The Hong Kong stock market fell over 20 percent during the year, and property values, which had been bid up wildly just before the turnover, fell significantly.

In China as a whole, growth cooled to under 8 percent during 1997, but the country seemed to hold its own amid deep troubles around Asia in countries like Korea, Thailand, and Japan. China continues to grow but remains very poor, with per capita GDP around $850 in 1998.

JAPAN

No country in history has accomplished what the Japanese economy has during the post–World War II period. Japan's economic progress over the last several decades is, with good reason, called the "Japanese economic miracle." Between 1951 and 1973, real GNP in Japan grew at an average annual rate of over 10 percent—in just over two decades, a seven-and-a-half-fold increase. Since the mid-1970s, economic growth in Japan has slowed, but until very recently the Japanese economy still significantly outperformed the U.S. economy.

What led to the Japanese "miracle"? Was it culture? Japan is a disciplined society with a strong work ethic and a tradition of cooperation. But although cultural differences may be part of the story, there is far more to it than that.

Structurally, Japan's is essentially a free-market capitalist economy. No industrialized country in the world has a smaller public sector, and none has a more "pro-business" government. To a very large extent, the private decisions of households and firms produced the miracle.

To explain Japan's success more specifically, analysts point to four major factors: (1) very high rates of saving and investment, (2) a highly trained labor force, (3) rapid absorption and effective utilization of technology, much of it imported, and (4) a pro-growth government policy.[8] Of these, perhaps the single most important cause of Japan's growth has been its incredible rate of investment. Between 1951 and 1973, the capital stock of Japan grew by more than 9 percent per year, and for a substantial period investment approached 40 percent of GNP. Between 1960 and 1980, the capital stock in the United States increased at about 4 percent per year, while gross investment fluctuated between 15 percent and 17 percent per year. Virtually all of Japan's investment was financed with domestic saving. Japan's rate of saving by households has been the highest in the world.

Until recent years, rates of return on new investment in Japan were high. But today Japan faces a new problem. Its high rates of investment have virtually exhausted the investment opportunities in the nation and pushed rates of return on saving to very low levels. The saving rate has remained high, however, and this has led many Japanese citizens to look abroad to place their savings. Much of those savings flowed to the United States during the 1980s. Real interest rates are much higher in the United States than in Japan, and a considerable number of new U.S. government bonds are now being sold to the Japanese. The Japanese are also investing billions in U.S. common stocks and real estate.

The second factor contributing to Japan's economic success is the quality of the Japanese labor force. As early as 1950, Japan had an education level comparable to that of the United States, despite a much lower level of economic development. Most Japanese workers were employed in jobs that demanded extremely low productivity relative to the education and training of those holding them. As the country's capital stock grew, workers moved easily into higher-productivity jobs.

Japan also consciously adopted the most advanced industrial technologies in the world. Much of the knowledge necessary to do this was available in technical journals or obtainable in U.S. graduate schools, and some came embodied in machinery and equipment imported into Japan. The Japanese were extremely effective at improving upon and commercializing what they imported. By importing technology, Japan did not have to develop it on its own; and, until recently, Japan devoted a smaller portion of its GNP to research and development than did the United States.

---

[8]This discussion owes much to an excellent paper by Hugh Patrick and Henry Rosovsky, "Japan's Economic Performance: An Overview" in *Asia's New Giant*, eds. Hugh Patrick and Henry Rosovsky (The Brookings Institution, 1976).

Ministry of Trade and Industry (MITI) *The agency of the Japanese government responsible for industrial policy. It uses tariffs and subsidies to protect and subsidize key industries and helps some sectors plan orderly reductions in capacity.*

The role of government in the Japanese economy is certainly different from the role of government in the United States. Economists disagree about the importance of government as an instrument of growth in Japan. It is clear the main source of growth has been the private sector, but the government has played a supportive role. For example, after World War II, the Japanese government, through the **Ministry of Trade and Industry (MITI)**, used tariffs and quotas to protect and subsidize a number of key industries, including coal, steel, electric power, and shipbuilding. During the 1960s, chemicals and machinery were added to the list. In the mid-1980s, the government and the private sector launched a partnership designed to develop and market the next generation of computers. MITI also helps some sectors of the economy plan orderly reductions in capacity. In short, the Japanese government is actively involved in the allocation process and has much to say about which industries will grow and which will not.

▶ **Japan in the 1990s**　The enormous success of the Japanese economy led to seemingly unbounded optimism at the end of the 1980s. Spurred by the profitability of Japanese firms, the market prices of Japanese stocks raced to unprecedented levels. At the same time, Japanese land values boomed. At one point, land in Tokyo was trading for as much as $6,000 per square foot. At that price, a small 100 by 100 foot plot of land (less than a quarter of an acre) was worth $60 million!

Then, in 1992, the Japanese stock market fell dramatically and land prices began to fall. For the first time in the history of modern Japan, confidence in the future was shaken. Beginning in 1992, real growth slowed considerably, and unemployment began to rise. In early 1998, recovery was still not in sight, and the unemployment rate had reached a post–War high.

Despite these setbacks, Japan remains an enormous economic power and a vital U.S. trading partner. As the economy becomes even more globalized in the coming years, it will be essential to understand more fully the successes and failures of Japanese industrial policy.

CONCLUSION

This chapter has introduced very briefly the structure, history, and performance of several different economic systems. It has also discussed the enormous problems of transforming a socialist economy into a market-based economy.

Studying alternative economic systems is a fitting way to conclude an introduction to economics. One of the themes running through this book has been the role of government in a market economy. We have tried to present a balanced description of how economies function, both in theory and in the real world. Throughout, we have focused on the potential benefits and problems associated with public-sector involvement. Eastern Europe, Russia, China, and Japan present very different perspectives on the interaction between the private and public sectors.

Concluding with this chapter is also, we hope, an enticement to further study. This is an exciting time in the world's economic history. Never before have systems changed so dramatically in such a short time. Many believe the reforms in China, Eastern Europe, and Russia have brought the world much closer together and that the time is ripe for a significant reduction in world political tensions. Others believe that the problems of transition are so difficult that the whole process will disintegrate into chaos. Only time will tell.

SUMMARY

POLITICAL SYSTEMS AND ECONOMIC SYSTEMS: SOCIALISM, CAPITALISM, AND COMMUNISM

1. In a *socialist economy* most capital is owned by the government rather than by private citizens. In a *capitalist economy* most capital is privately owned. *Communism* is a theoretical economic system in which the people directly control the means of production (capital and land) without the intervention of a government or state.

2. Economies differ in the extent to which decisions are made through central planning rather than through a market system. Generally, socialist economies favor central planning over market allocation, and capitalist economies rely to a much greater extent on the market. Nonetheless, there are markets in all societies, and planning takes place in all economies.

THE ECONOMIC THEORIES OF KARL MARX

3. According to Marxian thought, private ownership and profit are both unfair and unethical. Profit is value that is created by labor but expropriated by nonproductive capitalists, who are able to exploit labor by virtue of their ownership of the means of production (land and capital).

4. Marx predicted that falling rates of profit, increasing exploitation, and deeper business cycles would eventually cause capitalism to collapse.

5. Neoclassical economics sees profit as a return to a productive factor (capital) just as wages are the return to another productive factor (labor).

ECONOMIES IN TRANSITION: THE EXPERIENCES OF RUSSIA AND EASTERN EUROPE

6. When the Bolsheviks took power in Russia after the October Revolution in 1917, they found themselves without the advanced industrial base that Marx had envisioned and with no real blueprint for running a socialist or communist state. Marx had written mainly about capitalism, not socialism.

7. In 1928, the Soviet Union settled into central planning and collectivization of agriculture, an economic structure that lasted into the 1980s. Virtually all productive assets, including most land and capital, were publicly owned. There was no formal private business sector, no market for capital goods, and no income from property.

8. The Soviet Union grew rapidly through the mid-1970s. During the late 1950s, the Soviet Union's economy was growing much faster than that of the United States. The key to early Soviet success was rapid planned capital accumulation. The late 1970s saw things begin to deteriorate.

Dramatic reforms were finally introduced by Mikhail Gorbachev after his rise to power in 1985. Nonetheless, the Soviet economy collapsed in 1991. The Soviet Union was dissolved, and the new president of the Russian Republic, Boris Yeltsin, was left to start the difficult task of transition to a market system.

9. Economists generally agree on six requirements for a successful transition from socialism to a market-based system: (1) macroeconomic stabilization, (2) deregulation of prices and liberalization of trade, (3) privatization, (4) the establishment of market-supporting institutions, (5) a social safety net, and (6) external assistance.

10. Much debate exists about the sequence and timing of specific reforms. The idea of *shock therapy* is to proceed immediately on all six fronts, including rapid deregulation of prices and privatization. The *gradualist* approach is to build up market institutions first, gradually decontrol prices, and privatize only the most efficient government enterprises first.

ALTERNATIVE ECONOMIC SYSTEMS

11. China, the largest country in the world, became Communist following the revolution of 1949. In its early years under Chairman Mao Zedong, China organized under the Soviet model of central planning and rapid capital accumulation in heavy industry. In 1958, China departed sharply from the Soviet model, shifting instead to emphasis on small-scale, labor-intensive industry scattered around the countryside.

12. In 1978 Deng Xiaoping instituted sweeping reforms in the organization of the Chinese economy, particularly in agriculture. These reforms moved China away from central planning toward a system driven by market incentives.

13. China remains a country in which political dissent is not tolerated and the economic system remains Communist, but in which private enterprise is permitted and even encouraged. In the last several years the country has enjoyed rapid growth and substantial outside investment. However, inflation has been a problem, a fear of food shortages remains, and more than 50,000 state-owned enterprises continue to operate.

14. No country in history has accomplished what the Japanese economy has during the postwar period. Four major factors to explain Japan's success: (1) a very high rate of saving and investment, (2) a highly trained labor force, (3) rapid absorption and effective utilization of technology, much of it imported, and (4) a pro-growth government policy. Despite some setbacks in the 1990s, Japan remains an important economic power.

REVIEW TERMS AND CONCEPTS

capitalist economy, 890

communism, 890

five-year plans, 894

Great Leap Forward, 902

Great Proletarian Cultural Revolution, 902

labor theory of value, 892

market-socialist economy, 891

means of production, 892

Ministry of Trade and Industry (MITI), 906

New Economic Policy, 894

rate of exploitation, 893

shock therapy, 901

socialist economy, 889

surplus value, 892

tragedy of commons, 899

value of labor power, 892

PROBLEM SET

1. Choose one of the transitional economies of Central Europe (Poland, Hungary, Bulgaria, the Czech Republic, or Romania) or one of the 10 countries of the Commonwealth of Independent States (Armenia, Azerbaijan, Ukraine, Uzbekistan, Russia, etc.). Write a brief paper on how the transition to a market economy was proceeding in 1998 and 1999. Has the economy (prices, employment, etc.) stabilized? Has there been economic growth? How far has privatization progressed? What problems have been encountered? (A good source of information would be the chronological index to a publication like *The Economist* or the *New York Times*.)

2. In 1997, the Japanese economy was not recovering well from past low growth rates.
   a. What has happened to the Japanese economy since 1997? Has real GDP increased or decreased? At what rate?
   b. What has happened to the value of the yen (the number of yen per dollar at current exchange rates)?
   c. What steps have the Japanese taken to "restructure" their economy?
   Again, good sources for such information include *The Economist,* the *New York Times*, or *The Wall Street Journal*. Another source is the Web site of the Organization for Economic Cooperation and Development (OECD).

3. "The difference between the United States and the Soviet Union is that the United States has a capitalist economic system and the Soviet Union had a totalitarian government." Explain how this comparison confuses the economic and political aspects of the two societies. What words describe the former economic system of the Soviet Union?

4. What is the "tragedy of commons"? Suppose that all workers in a factory are paid the same wage and have no risk of being fired. Use the logic of the "tragedy of commons" to predict the result. How would you expect workers to behave?

5. You are assigned the task of debating the strengths of a socialist economy (regardless of your own viewpoint). Outline the points that you would make in the debate. Be sure to define socialism carefully in your presentation.

6. "The U.S. government should institute a policy of subsidizing those firms that are likely to be successful competitors in the international economic wars! Such an 'industrial policy' should have the authority to override the antitrust laws." Agree or disagree? Explain your answer.

7. Explain why Karl Marx thought profit was unjustified. Be sure to specifically define the labor theory of value. Contrast the Marxian view with the neo-classical view of profit.

8. Do you agree or disagree with each of the following statements? Explain your answers.
   a. Over time, the Chinese have shifted from a decentralized approach to economic development to a more centrally planned system. Since the events of 1989 in Tiananmen Square, there has been a severe crackdown on private businesses.
   b. Both Japan and the Soviet Union grew rapidly during the 1950s and 1960s. Growth in the Soviet Union was based on rapid accumulation of capital forced by the central plan under Stalin and Khrushchev. In Japan, the growth was not due to capital accumulation.
   c. Although economists generally agree that transition from socialism to a market-based system must proceed rapidly, there is little agreement about what must be done to make the transition successful.

9. The distribution of income in a capitalist economy is likely to be more unequal than it is in a socialist economy. Why is this so? Is there a tension between the goal of limiting inequality and the goal of motivating risk taking and hard work? Explain your answer in detail.

10. "There is no doubt that a centrally planned socialist system has the potential to grow faster than a market-oriented capitalist system." Do you agree or disagree? What are some of the trade-offs facing socialist planners who set target growth rates?

11. In the 1990s the world witnessed the rapid decline of several Eastern European governments (East Germany, Poland, and Romania, to name just a few). Poland immediately began moving its socialist economy toward a capitalist economy. Some of the effects of this transition have been increased unemployment and price inflation. Can you explain why? (*Hint:* Focus on differences between socialist and capitalist systems regarding the determination of prices and production levels.)

TAKE IT TO THE NET

We invite you to visit the Case and Fair page on the Prentice Hall Web site:

http://www.prenhall.com/casefair

for this chapter's World Wide Web exercise.

INTERNATIONAL INTEGRATION AND LABOR MARKET CONDITIONS: IS THERE A LINK?

Economies have become increasingly integrated over the past several decades. This increased international economic integration has taken the form of greater movements of goods and services, greater flows of financial capital, and the increased movement of labor (i.e., migration) between countries. Since the early 1970s, the continued international integration has coincided with two disturbing labor market developments. First, despite overall increases in economic activity, unemployment in Europe remains high. Second, the gap between the wages of skilled and unskilled workers has risen in a number of industrial countries (e.g., United States, United Kingdom, and Canada). Some analysts attribute much of the persistent unemployment in Europe and the recent increases in wage inequality to increased international integration. Others believe that the effects of integration on these two labor market trends are small.

The flow of goods and services among countries represents the "main channel of economic integration." The trade of goods and services among countries rose from 23 percent of world gross domestic product (GDP) in 1970 to approximately 40 percent of world GDP in 1990. Both exports and imports of goods and services have also risen significantly for the United States during the past four decades (see Table 1), most of the more recent increases resulting from trade with developing and transition economies.

Some say this increase in trade has caused reductions in the demand for unskilled labor in industrial economies. This decrease in demand can occur as imports of goods produced in low-wage economies compete with domestically produced goods. As the consumption of foreign-produced goods increases, some domestic firms are forced to cut back production and reduce their demand for labor. This reduction, particularly for unskilled labor, can have two effects. In economies where labor markets are not flexible and, therefore, where wages do not adjust quickly to changing labor supply and demand conditions (e.g., Europe), the drop in demand has a smaller effect on wages and wage inequality but has a greater effect on the number of unemployed individuals. In countries where labor markets and wage structures are more flexible, the drop in demand for unskilled labor has a greater effect on wages and on wage inequality and a smaller effect on the number of unemployed individuals. Today, many workers, politicians, and union officials fear that increased international integration (of trade, financial capital, and migration) causes job losses and/or reductions in wages.

Increased trade creates distributional effects as the *relative* demand for goods and services changes between economies. These adjustments can be painful for those workers adversely affected by increased trade. For example, approximately 150,000 U.S. garment workers lost their jobs since the North American Free Trade Agreement went into effect in January 1994. Many of these job losses were attributed to increased competition from Mexican imports. Although these adjustment costs should not be ignored, economists emphasize that increased trade yields benefits that exceed these costs. First, increased trade benefits all consumers as increased competition drives down the prices of goods and services. Second, many workers become more productive as the value of the goods

TABLE 1

YEAR	U.S. EXPORTS AS A PERCENTAGE OF U.S. GDP	U.S. IMPORTS AS A PERCENTAGE OF U.S. GDP	U.S. CIVILIAN EMPLOYMENT
1960	3.6	4.9	65,347,000
1965	3.7	4.6	69,997,000
1970	4.5	6.5	78,780,000
1975	6.1	6.2	85,627,000
1980	7.0	7.4	99,879,000
1985	6.4	8.9	106,302,000
1990	9.0	10.1	119,081,000
1995	11.3	13.0	124,766,000
1997	13.0	14.8	128,580,000

Note: *The percentages represent the first-quarter observations of the variables for each year. The employment data represent the number of civilian individuals employed in January of each year.*

Source: *Federal Reserve Bank of St. Louis.*

and services they produce increases. Third, increased trade increases the income and, therefore, consumption of individuals in developing and transition economies, resulting in an increase in the export of goods and services to those countries. Transition economies are in the process of substituting central planning systems with market systems. Fourth, the larger, global markets might create economies of scale, further depressing the prices of some goods.

Some argue that increased financial flows to developing and transition economies will cause a reduction in the amount of financial capital in (i.e., a "decapitalization" of) industrial economies; financial capital flows to developing and transition economies have increased from $42 billion in 1989 to $175 billion in 1994. This increased demand for financial capital may also cause a "capital shortage" and subsequent increase in world interest rates. Both concerns appear unwarranted. First, the net capital outflows from industrial economies represent a small percentage of their total savings. Second, even if world interest rates increase as the demand for funds rises, the increase in interest rates is a result of firms increasing the demand for funds to finance increasingly more productive activities. Third, the increased capital flows benefit investors and borrowers (i.e., recipients of the funds). Investors can take advantage of possibly higher returns and lower risk through increased portfolio diversification. Fourth, workers in developing and transition economies will also benefit as they obtain additional equipment (financed with these funds).

The flow of migrants to industrial economies has also increased over the past 30 years. The percentage of immigrants in the labor force in Europe increased from 3.5 percent in 1965 to 5.0 percent in 1990; in the United

TRADE BETWEEN QUEBEC AND ANOTHER PROVINCE IS APPROXIMATELY 20 TIMES GREATER THAN TRADE BETWEEN QUEBEC AND A STATE OF SIMILAR SIZE AND DISTANCE IN THE UNITED STATES. PHOTO DEPICTS THE ST. LAWRENCE SEAWAY AT QUEBEC.

States, this percentage increased from 6.0 percent to 8.0 percent during the same period. Increased immigration can have negative effects on workers in the host country as wages in certain sectors fall and unemployment among displaced workers occurs. There are, however, some benefits of increased migration. Migrants are generally more productive in the host country, raising world output. For firms, the increased migration can also cause a reduction in labor costs as wages adjust to the increase in labor supply. More generally, the increased migration can result in a more efficient, global allocation of labor resources.

In addition to changes in the flow of trade, financial capital, and migration, we have also witnessed changes in national borders (e.g. the unification of East and West Germany) and continued debates about the possible separation of the province of Quebec from Canada. Recent research indicates that the effects of national borders on the amount of trade between countries are significant. For example, the trade of goods and services between Quebec and another province

in Canada is approximately 20 times greater than between Quebec and a state of similar economic size and distance in the United States. This suggests that the formation of a European Union that would reduce the importance of national borders might have significant positive effects on trade among its members and on employment in these economies.

A number of policies have been proposed to limit the distributional effects of increased integration. Some argue that trade restrictions are needed to protect workers from the effects of job losses and lower wages, whereas most economists believe that any protectionist policies that restrict trade (e.g. tariffs and quotas) will reduce economic activity and have net negative effects on all workers. Still others argue that trade agreements should be linked to labor standard agreements. For example, because minimum wage legislation exists in the United States, they say all countries should adopt similar minimum wage legislation. There are two problems with linking trade agreements with labor standard issues. Those who favor protectionist policies will use the different labor standards of a country's trading partners as a means of limiting trade and preventing future gains from increased integration. Furthermore, it is the low labor costs in developing and transition economies that provide them with a comparative advantage in global markets. Agreements that force these countries to adopt policies that raise their labor costs will effectively reduce trade.

A more effective approach would be to increase integration among developing, transition, and industrial economies while simultaneously implementing domestic policies like placement services that ease the transition of workers from declining industries to expanding industries. Continued efforts to raise the skill level of unskilled workers will also potentially offset any increases in wage inequality and reductions in employment caused by increased integration.

Questions for Analytical Thinking

1. Suppose restrictions are imposed on the flow of financial capital to developing and transition economies. First, what effect might these restrictions have on economic activity in these countries? Explain. Second, how might these restrictions affect trade between these economies and industrial economies? Explain.

2. The North American Free Trade Agreement reduced tariffs on a number of goods and services. Explain how this reduction in tariffs might have affected consumers, firms, workers, and trade in the United States

3. Explain how the existence of a minimum wage and the extent to which this minimum wage applies to workers in an economy (i.e., the percentage of employed workers paid the minimum wage) can determine the *size* of the effects of increased trade on (1) wage inequality and (2) unemployment.

4. a. Based on your analysis of the data in Table 1, in which year, if any, did the United States experience a trade surplus (exports exceeding imports)? In which year was the trade deficit the largest share of U.S. GDP? Do the data in Table 1 indicate that the United States has become more or less integrated with the rest of the world? Explain.

   b. Between 1960 and 1965, U.S. imports as a percentage of U.S. GDP fell. Does this suggest that the *level* of imports fell during this period? Explain.

   c. U.S. civilian employment increased between each of the years in Table 1. Does this suggest that increases in U.S. trade had no negative effect on wages and employment in the United States during this period? Explain.

Sources: Helen Cooper and Scott Kilman, "Trade Wars Aside, U.S. and Europe Buy More of Each Other's Foods," *The Wall Street Journal*, November 4, 1997; Bob Davis, "At the Heart of the Trade Debate: Inequity," *The Wall Street Journal*, October 31, 1997; Robert S. Greenberger, "As U.S. Exports Rise, More Workers Benefit, and Favor Free Trade," *The Wall Street Journal*, September 10, 1997; John F. Helliwell, "Do National Borders Matter For Quebec's Trade?" *Canadian Journal of Economics*, August 1996, pp. 507–522; John McCallum, "National Borders Matter: Canada–U.S. Regional Trade Patterns," *American Economic Review*, June 1995, pp. 615–623; Ana Ravenga, "The Employment Crisis in Industrial Countries: Is International Integration to Blame?" *Regional Perspectives on World Development Report 1995*, Washington, D.C.: The World Bank.

CONCISE DICTIONARY OF ECONOMIC TERMINOLOGY

ability-to-pay principle   A theory of taxation holding that citizens should bear tax burdens in line with their ability to pay taxes.

absolute advantage   The advantage in the production of a product enjoyed by one country over another when it uses fewer resources to produce that product than the other country does.

accelerator effect   The tendency for investment to increase when aggregate output increases and decrease when aggregate output decreases, accelerating the growth or decline of output.

actual investment   The actual amount of investment that takes place; it includes items such as unplanned changes in inventories.

adjustment costs   The costs that a firm incurs when it changes its production level—for example, the administration costs of laying off employees or the training costs of hiring new workers.

adverse selection   An imperfect-information problem that can occur when a buyer or seller enters into an exchange with another party who has more information.

aggregate behavior   The behavior of all households and firms together.

aggregate demand   The total demand for goods and services in the economy.

aggregate demand (AD) curve   A curve that shows the negative relationship between aggregate output (income) and the price level. Each point on the AD curve is a point at which both the goods market and the money market are in equilibrium.

aggregate income   The total income received by all factors of production in a given period.

aggregate output   The total quantity of goods and services produced (or supplied) in an economy in a given period.

aggregate output (income) (Y)   A combined term used to remind you of the exact equality between aggregate output and aggregate income.

aggregate production function   The mathematical representation of the relationship between inputs and national output, or gross domestic product.

aggregate supply   The total supply of all goods and services in an economy.

aggregate supply (AS) curve   A graph that shows the relationship between the aggregate quantity of output supplied by all firms in an economy and the overall price level.

American Federation of Labor (AFL)   Founded in 1881, the AFL was successfully led by Samuel Gompers from 1886 until 1924. A practical, nonideological union, the AFL existed as a "confederation" of individual craft unions representing skilled workers, each with an independent organization and an exclusive jurisdiction. Now merged with the CIO, the AFL maintains a preeminent position among unions today.

animal spirits of entrepreneurs   A phrase coined by Keynes to describe investors' feelings.

Antitrust Division (of the Department of Justice)   One of two federal agencies empowered to act against those in violation of antitrust laws. It initiates action against those who violate antitrust laws and decides which cases to prosecute and against whom to bring criminal charges.

appreciation of a currency   The rise in value of one currency relative to another.

asymmetric information   A situation in which the participants in an economic transaction have different information about the transaction.

automatic destabilizers   Revenue and expenditure items in the federal budget that automatically change with the economy in such a way as to destabilize GDP.

automatic stabilizers   Revenue and expenditure items in the federal budget that automatically change with the economy in such a way as to stabilize GDP.

autonomous variable   A variable that is assumed not to depend on the state of the economy—that is, it is taken as given.

average fixed cost (AFC)   Total fixed cost divided by the number of units of output; a per-unit measure of fixed costs.

average product   The average amount produced by each unit of a variable factor of production.

average propensity to consume (APC)   The proportion of income households spend on consumption. Determined by dividing consumption (C) by income (Y).

average total cost (ATC)   Total cost divided by the number of units of output.

average variable cost (AVC)   Total variable cost divided by the number of units of output.

Averch-Johnson effect   The tendency for regulated monopolies to build more capital than they need. Usually occurs when allowed rates of return are set by a regulatory agency at some percent of fixed capital stocks.

balanced-budget multiplier   The ratio of change in the equilibrium level of output to a change in government spending where the change in government spending is balanced by a change in taxes so as not to create any deficit. The balanced-budget multiplier is equal to one: The change in Y resulting from the change in G and the equal change in T is exactly the same size as the initial change in G or T itself.

balance of payments   The record of a country's transactions in goods, services, and assets with the rest of the world; also the record of a country's sources (supply) and uses (demand) of foreign exchange.

balance of trade   A country's exports of goods and services minus its imports of goods and services.

balance on capital account   In the United States, the sum of the following (measured in a given period): the change in private U.S. assets abroad, the change in foreign private assets in the United States, the change in U.S. government assets abroad, and the change in foreign government assets in the United States.

balance on current account   The balance of trade plus net exports of services, plus net investment income, plus the category "net transfer payments and other."

barrier to entry   Something that prevents new firms from entering and competing in imperfectly competitive industries.

barter   The direct exchange of goods and services for other goods and services.

base-year   The year chosen for the weights in a fixed-weight procedure.

benefits-received principle   A theory of fairness holding that taxpayers should contribute to government (in the form of taxes) in proportion to the benefits that they receive from public expenditures.

black market   A market in which illegal trading takes place at market-determined prices.

bond   A contract between a borrower and a lender, in which the borrower agrees to pay the loan at some time in the future, along with interest payments along the way.

brain drain   The tendency for talented people from developing countries to become educated in a developed country and remain there after graduation.

breaking even   The situation in which a firm is earning exactly a normal rate of return.

budget constraint   The limits imposed on household choices by income, wealth, and product prices.

budget deficit   The difference between what a government spends and what it collects in taxes in a given period: $G - T$.

business cycle   The cycle of short-term ups and downs in the economy.

capital   Those goods produced by the economic system that are used as inputs to produce other goods and services in the future.

capital flight   The tendency for both human capital and financial capital to leave developing countries in search of higher rates of return elsewhere.

capital income   Income earned on savings that have been put to use through financial capital markets.

capital-intensive technology   A production technique that uses a large amount of capital relative to labor.

capital market   The input/factor market in which households supply their savings, for interest or for claims to future profits, to firms that demand funds in order to buy capital goods.

capital stock   For a single firm, the current market value of the firm's plant, equipment, inventories, and intangible assets.

capitalist economy   An economy in which most capital is privately owned.

cartel   A group of firms that gets together and makes joint price and output decisions to maximize joint profits.

Celler-Kefauver Act (1950)   Extended the government's authority to ban vertical and conglomerate mergers.

ceteris paribus, or all else equal   A device used to analyze the relationship between two variables while the values of other variables are held unchanged.

change in business inventories   The amount by which firms' inventories change during a period. Inventories are the goods that firms produce now but intend to sell later.

change in inventory   Production minus sales.

choice set or opportunity set   The set of options that is defined and limited by a budget constraint.

circular flow A diagram showing the income received and payments made by each sector of the economy.

Clayton Act Passed by Congress in 1914 to strengthen the Sherman Act and clarify the rule of reason, the act outlawed specific monopolistic behaviors such as tying contracts, price discrimination, and unlimited mergers.

Coase theorem Under certain conditions, when externalities are present, private parties can arrive at the efficient solution without government involvement.

collective bargaining The process by which union leaders bargain with management as the representatives of all union employees.

collusion The act of working with other producers in an effort to limit competition and increase joint profits.

command economy An economy in which a central government either directly or indirectly sets output targets, incomes, and prices.

commodity monies Items used as money that also have intrinsic value in some other use.

communism An economic system in which the people control the means of production (capital and land) directly, without the intervention of a government or state.

community rating A system in which insurance providers must accept all applicants and charge premiums based only on age, location, and perhaps some elements of behavior (such as smoking).

comparative advantage The advantage in the production of a product enjoyed by one country over another when that product can be produced at lower cost in terms of other goods than it could be in the other country.

compensating differentials Differences in wages that result from differences in working conditions. Risky jobs usually pay higher wages, and highly desirable jobs usually pay lower wages.

compensation of employees Includes wages, salaries, and various supplements—employer contributions to social insurance and pension funds, for example— paid to households by firms and by the government.

complements, complementary goods Goods that "go together"; a decrease in the price of one results in an increase in demand for the other, and vice versa.

Congress of Industrial Organizations (CIO) Founded by John L. Lewis, president of the United Mine Workers, after the AFL rejected his plan to organize the steel, rubber, automobile, and chemical industries in 1935. The CIO was the first union to organize semiskilled laborers in the mass production industries. After 20 years of independence, it merged with the AFL in 1955.

consent decrees Formal agreements on remedies between all the parties to an antitrust case that must be approved by the courts. Consent decrees can be signed before, during, or after a trial.

constant returns to scale An increase in a firm's scale of production has no effect on average costs per unit produced.

constrained supply of labor The amount a household actually works in a given period at the current wage rate.

consumer goods Goods produced for present consumption.

consumer price index (CPI) A price index computed each month by the Bureau of Labor Statistics using a bundle that is meant to represent the "market basket" purchased monthly by the typical urban consumer.

consumer sovereignty The notion that people are free to choose, and that things that people do not want will not sell. "The customer rules."

consumer surplus The difference between the maximum amount a person is willing to pay for a good and its current market price.

consumption function The relationship between consumption and income.

contraction, recession, or **slump** The period in the business cycle from a peak down to a trough, during which output and employment fall.

contractionary fiscal policy A decrease in government spending or an increase in net taxes aimed at decreasing aggregate output (income) (Y).

contractionary monetary policy A decrease in the money supply aimed at decreasing aggregate output (income) (Y).

copayment A fixed amount of money that an insured person pays for each visit to a doctor's office.

Corn Laws The tariffs, subsidies, and restrictions enacted by the British Parliament in the early nineteenth century to discourage imports and encourage exports of grain.

corporate bonds Promissory notes issued by corporations when they borrow money.

corporate income taxes Taxes levied on the net incomes of corporations.

corporate profits The income of corporate businesses.

corporation A form of business organization resting on a legal charter that establishes the corporation as an entity separate from its owners. Owners hold shares and are liable for the firm's debts only up to the limit of their investment, or share, in the firm.

cost-benefit analysis The formal technique by which the benefits of a public project are weighed against its costs.

cost-of-living adjustments (COLAs) Contract provisions that tie wages to changes in the cost of living. The greater the inflation rate, the more wages are raised.

cost-push, or **supply-side, inflation** Inflation caused by an increase in costs.

cost shock, or **supply shock** A change in costs that shifts the aggregate supply (AS) curve.

Cournot model A model of a two-firm industry (duopoly) in which a series of output-adjustment decisions leads to a final level of output between the output that would prevail if the market were organized competitively and the output that would be set by a monopoly.

cross-price elasticity of demand A measure of the response of the quantity of one good demanded to a change in the price of another good.

crowding-out effect The tendency for increases in government spending to cause reductions in private investment spending.

currency debasement The decrease in the value of money that occurs when its supply is increased rapidly.

current dollars The current prices that one pays for goods and services.

cyclical deficit The deficit that occurs because of a downturn in the business cycle.

cyclical unemployment The increase in unemployment that occurs during recessions and depressions.

debt rescheduling An agreement between banks and borrowers through which a new schedule of repayments of the debt is negotiated; often some of the debt is written off and the repayment period is extended.

decreasing returns to scale, or **diseconomies of scale** An increase in a firm's scale of production leads to higher average costs per unit produced.

deductible An annual out-of-pocket expenditure that an insurance policy holder must make before the insurance plan makes any reimbursement.

defensive medicine Ordering medical tests, procedures, or treatments that are not cost-effective to protect oneself from being sued for malpractice later on.

deficit response index (DRI) The amount by which the deficit changes with a one-dollar change in GDP.

deflation A decrease in the overall price level.

demand curve A graph illustrating how much of a given product a household would be willing to buy at different prices.

demand determined price The price of a good that is in fixed supply; it is determined exclusively by what firms and households are willing to pay for the good.

demand-pull inflation Inflation that is initiated by an increase in aggregate demand.

demand schedule A table showing how much of a given product a household would be willing to buy at different prices.

depreciation The decline in an asset's economic value over time.

depreciation of a currency The fall in value of one currency relative to another.

depression A prolonged and deep recession.

derived demand The demand for resources (inputs) that is dependent on the demand for the outputs those resources can be used to produce.

descriptive economics The compilation of data that describe phenomena and facts.

desired, or **optimal, level of inventories** The level of inventory at which the extra cost (in lost sales) from lowering inventories by a small amount is just equal to the extra gain (in interest revenue and decreased storage costs).

desired, or **planned, investment** Those additions to capital stock and inventory that are planned by firms.

diamond/water paradox A paradox stating that (1) the things with the greatest value in use frequently have little or no value in exchange, and (2) the things with the greatest value in exchange frequently have little or no value in use.

discount rate Interest rate that banks pay to the Fed to borrow from it.

discouraged-worker effect The decline in the measured unemployment rate that results when people who want to work but cannot find jobs grow discouraged and stop looking, thus dropping out of the ranks of the unemployed and the labor force.

discretionary fiscal policy Changes in taxes or spending that are the result of deliberate changes in government policy.

disposable, or after-tax, income (Y_d) Total income minus net taxes: $Y - T$.

disposable personal income or after-tax income Personal income minus personal income taxes. The amount that households have to spend or save.

dividends The portion of a corporation's profits that the firm pays out each period to shareholders. Also called *distributed profits*.

dominant strategy In game theory, a strategy that is best no matter what the opposition does.

drop-in-the-bucket problem A problem intrinsic to public goods: The good or service is usually so costly that its provision generally does not depend on whether or not any single person pays.

dumping A firm or industry sells products on the world market at prices below the cost of production.

durable goods Goods that last a relatively long time, such as cars and household appliances.

easy monetary policy Fed policies that expand the money supply in an effort to stimulate the economy.

economic growth An increase in the total output of an economy. It occurs when a society acquires new resources or when it learns to produce more using existing resources.

economic income The amount of money a household can spend during a given period without increasing or decreasing its net assets. Wages, salaries, dividends, interest income, transfer payments, rents, and so forth are sources of economic income.

economic integration Occurs when two or more nations join to form a free-trade zone.

economic problem Given scarce resources, how exactly do large, complex societies go about answering the three basic economic questions?

economics The study of how individuals and societies choose to use the scarce resources that nature and previous generations have provided.

economic theory A statement or set of related statements about cause and effect, action and reaction.

efficiency The condition in which the economy is producing what people want at least possible cost.

efficiency wage theory An explanation for unemployment that holds that the productivity of workers increases with the wage rate. If this is so, firms may have an incentive to pay wages above the market-clearing rate.

efficient market A market in which profit opportunities are eliminated almost instantaneously.

elastic demand A demand relationship in which the percentage change in quantity demanded is larger in absolute value than the percentage change in price (a demand elasticity with an absolute value greater than 1).

elasticity A general concept used to quantify the response in one variable when another variable changes.

elasticity of labor supply A measure of the response of labor supplied to a change in the price of labor.

elasticity of supply A measure of the response of quantity of a good supplied to a change in price of that good. Likely to be positive in output markets.

empirical economics The collection and use of data to test economic theories.

employed Any person 16 years old or older (1) who works for pay, either for someone else or in his or her own business for one or more hours per week, (2) who works without pay for 15 or more hours per week in a family enterprise, or (3) who has a job but has been temporarily absent, with or without pay.

employer mandate A system of health-care insurance provision in which all employers are required to provide health insurance and to pay on average 80 percent of the community-rated premiums.

entrepreneur A person who organizes, manages, and assumes the risks of a firm, taking a new idea or a new product and turning it into a successful business.

equilibrium Occurs when there is no tendency for change. In the macroeconomic goods market, equilibrium occurs when planned aggregate expenditure is equal to aggregate output.

equilibrium price level The point at which the aggregate demand and aggregate supply curves intersect.

equity Fairness.

European Union (EU) The European trading bloc composed of Austria, Belgium, Denmark, Finland, France, Germany, Greece, Ireland, Italy, Luxembourg, the Netherlands, Portugal, Spain, Sweden, and the United Kingdom.

excess burden The amount by which the burden of a tax exceeds the total revenue collected. Also called *dead weight losses*.

excess demand or **shortage** The condition that exists when quantity demanded exceeds quantity supplied at the current price.

excess labor, excess capital Labor and capital that are not needed to produce the firm's current level of output.

excess reserves The difference between a bank's actual reserves and its required reserves.

excess supply or **surplus** The condition that exists when quantity supplied exceeds quantity demanded at the current price.

exchange rate The price of one country's currency in terms of another country's currency; the ratio at which two currencies are traded for each other.

excise taxes Taxes on specific commodities.

expansion or **boom** The period in the business cycle from a trough up to a peak, during which output and employment rise.

expansionary fiscal policy An increase in government spending or a reduction in net taxes aimed at increasing aggregate output (income) (Y).

expansionary monetary policy An increase in the money supply aimed at increasing aggregate output (income) (Y).

expected rate of return The annual rate of return that a firm expects to obtain through a capital investment.

expenditure approach A method of computing GDP that measures the amount spent on all final goods during a given period.

experience rating The insurance-company practice of charging individuals or groups of individuals premiums that are linked to their current state of health or to the probability that they will become sick.

explicit contracts Employment contracts that stipulate workers' wages, usually for a period of one to three years.

export promotion A trade policy designed to encourage exports.

export subsidies Government payments made to domestic firms to encourage exports.

externality A cost or benefit resulting from some activity or transaction that is imposed or bestowed upon parties outside the activity or transaction. Sometimes called *spillovers* or *neighborhood effects*.

factor endowments The quantity and quality of labor, land, and natural resources of a country.

factor substitution effect The tendency of firms to substitute away from a factor whose price has risen and toward a factor whose price has fallen.

factors of production The inputs into the production process. Land, labor, and capital are the three key factors of production.

fallacy of composition The erroneous belief that what is true for a part is necessarily true for the whole.

favored customers Those who receive special treatment from dealers during situations of excess demand.

featherbedding The common union practice of preserving jobs even when it is inefficient to do so.

federal budget The budget of the federal government.

federal debt The total amount owed by the federal government.

federal deficit Federal government expenditures minus receipts.

Federal Open Market Committee (FOMC) A group composed of the seven members of the Fed's Board of Governors, the president of the New York Federal Reserve Bank, and four of the other eleven district bank presidents on a rotating basis; it sets goals regarding the money supply and interest rates and directs the operation of the Open Market Desk in New York.

Federal Reserve System (the Fed) The central bank of the United States.

Federal Trade Commission (FTC) A federal regulatory group created by Congress in 1914 to investigate the structure and behavior of firms engaging in interstate commerce, to determine what constitutes unlawful "unfair" behavior, and to issue cease-and-desist orders to those found in violation of antitrust law.

fee-for-service reimbursement A program in which insurance companies reimburse health-care providers for the services they've rendered.

fertility rate The birth rate. Equal to (the number of births per year divided by the population) × 100.

fiat, or token, money Items designated as money that are intrinsically worthless.

filtering The process whereby the newest and best housing goes to the wealthy, whose former housing passes down to those of middle income, whose former housing passes down to those of low income. Thus housing "filters" down the income-distribution ladder.

final goods and services Goods and services produced for final use.

financial capital market The part of the capital market in which savers and investors interact through intermediaries.

financial intermediaries Banks and other institutions that act as a link between those who have money to lend and those who want to borrow money.

fine tuning The phrase used by Walter Heller to refer to the government's role in regulating inflation and unemployment.

firm An organization that comes into being when a person or a group of people decides to produce a good or service to meet a perceived demand. Most firms exist to make a profit.

fiscal drag The negative effect on the economy that occurs when average tax rates increase because taxpayers have moved into higher income brackets during an expansion.

fiscal policy The government's spending and taxing policies.

five-year plans Plans developed in the Soviet Union that provided general guidelines and directions for the next five years.

fixed cost Any cost that does not depend on the firm's level of output. These costs are incurred even if the firm is producing nothing. There are no fixed costs in the long run.

fixed-weight procedure A procedure that uses weights from a given base year.

floating, or **market-determined, exchange rates** Exchange rates that are determined by the unregulated forces of supply and demand.

food stamps Vouchers that have a face value greater than their cost and that can be used to purchase food at grocery stores.

foreign exchange All currencies other than the domestic currency of a given country.

free-rider problem A problem intrinsic to public goods: Because people can enjoy the benefits of public goods whether they pay for them or not, they are usually unwilling to pay for them.

frictional unemployment The portion of unemployment that is due to the normal working of the labor market; used to denote short-run job/skill matching problems.

full-employment budget What the federal budget would be if the economy were producing at a full-employment level of output.

game theory Analyzes oligopolistic behavior as a complex series of strategic moves and reactive countermoves among rival firms. In game theory, firms are assumed to anticipate rival reactions.

General Agreement on Tariffs and Trade (GATT) An international agreement signed by the United States and 22 other countries in 1947 to promote the liberalization of foreign trade.

general equilibrium The condition that exists when all markets in an economy are in simultaneous equilibrium.

ghetto premiums Evidence suggests that during the 1960s and 1970s housing in sections of U.S. cities inhabited predominantly by African Americans was more expensive than comparable housing in white neighborhoods. The price difference came to be called a ghetto premium.

Gini coefficient A commonly used measure of inequality of income derived from a Lorenz Curve. It can range from zero to a maximum of 1.

goods market The market in which goods and services are exchanged and in which the equilibrium level of aggregate output is determined.

government consumption and investment (G) Expenditures by federal, state, and local governments for final goods and services.

government failure Occurs when the government becomes the tool of the rent seeker and the allocation of resources is made even less efficient by the intervention of government.

government franchise A monopoly by virtue of government directive.

government interest payments Cash payments made by the government to those who own government bonds.

government spending multiplier The ratio of the change in the equilibrium level of output to a change in government spending.

government transfer payments Cash payments made by the government directly to households for which no current services are received in return. They include social security benefits, unemployment compensation, and welfare payments.

Gramm-Rudman-Hollings Bill Passed by the U.S. Congress and signed by President Reagan in 1986, this law set out to reduce the federal deficit by $36 billion per year, with a deficit of zero slated for 1991.

Great Depression The period of severe economic contraction and high unemployment that began in 1929 and continued throughout the 1930s.

Great Leap Forward The economic strategy in the People's Republic of China that began in 1958 when it departed from the Soviet model and shifted from large-scale, capital-intensive industry to small-scale, labor-intensive industry scattered across the countryside. Material incentives were reduced and replaced by the motivating power of revolutionary ideology and inspiration.

Great Proletarian Cultural Revolution (1966–1976) A period of ideological purity in the People's Republic of China: Material incentives and reforms were denounced and highly trained specialists were sent to work in the fields. The effect of the Cultural Revolution on the Chinese economy was catastrophic.

Green Revolution The agricultural breakthroughs of modern science, such as the development of new, high-yield crop varieties.

gross domestic product (GDP) The total market value of all final goods and services produced within a given period by factors of production located within a country.

gross investment The total value of all newly produced capital goods (plant, equipment, housing, and inventory) produced in a given period.

gross national product (GNP) The total market value of all final goods and services produced within a given period by factors of production owned by a country's citizens, regardless of where the output is produced.

gross private investment (I) Total investment in capital—that is, the purchase of new housing, plants, equipment, and inventory by the private (or nongovern-ment) sector.

Hart-Scott-Rodino Act The 1980 antitrust legislation that extended the antitrust laws to proprietorships and partnerships and requires that all proposed mergers be reported to the Department of Justice.

health maintenance organization (HMO) A health-care plan that provides comprehensive medical services for employees and their families at a flat fee.

Heckscher-Ohlin theorem A theory that explains the existence of a country's comparative advantage by its factor endowments: A country has a comparative advantage in the production of a product if that country is relatively well endowed with inputs used intensively in the production of that product.

Herfindahl-Hirschman Index (HHI) A mathematical calculation that uses market share figures to determine whether or not a proposed merger will be challenged by the government.

homogeneous products Undifferentiated outputs; products that are identical to, or indistinguishable from, one another.

households The consuming units in an economy.

human capital A form of intangible capital that includes the skills and other knowledge that workers have or acquire through education and training and that yields valuable services to a firm over time.

hyperinflation A period of very rapid increases in the overall price level.

identity Something that is always true.

Immigration Act of 1990 Increased the number of legal immigrants allowed into the United States each year by 150,000.

Immigration Reform and Control Act (1986) Granted amnesty to about 3 million illegal aliens and imposed a strong set of employer sanctions designed to slow the flow of immigrants into the United States.

imperfect competition An industry in which single firms have some control over price and competition. Imperfectly competitive industries give rise to an inefficient allocation of resources.

imperfect information The absence of full knowledge regarding product characteristics, available prices, and so forth.

imperfectly competitive industry An industry in which single firms have some control over the price of their output.

implementation lag The time it takes to put the desired policy into effect once economists and policy makers recognize that the economy is in a boom or a slump.

import substitution An industrial trade strategy that favors developing local industries that can manufacture goods to replace imports.

impossibility theorem A proposition demonstrated by Kenneth Arrow showing that no system of aggregating individual preferences into social decisions will always yield consistent, nonarbitrary results.

income The sum of all a household's wages, salaries, profits, interest payments, rents, and other forms of earnings in a given period of time. It is a flow measure.

income approach A method of computing GDP that measures the income—wages, rents, interest, and profits—received by all factors of production in producing final goods.

income effect of higher wages When wages rise, people are better off. If leisure is a normal good, they may decide to consume more of it and to work less.

income elasticity of demand Measures the responsiveness of demand to changes in income.

increasing returns to scale, or **economies of scale** An increase in a firm's scale of production leads to lower average costs per unit produced.

indirect taxes Taxes like sales taxes, customs duties, and license fees.

Industrial Revolution The period in England during the late eighteenth and early nineteenth centuries in which new manufacturing technologies and improved transportation gave rise to the modern factory system and a massive movement of the population from the countryside to the cities.

industrial policy Government involvement in the allocation of capital across manufacturing sectors.

industry A group of firms that produce a similar product. The boundaries of a "product" can be drawn very widely ("agricultural products"), less widely ("dairy products"), or very narrowly ("cheese"). The term industry can be used interchangeably with the term market.

inelastic demand Demand that responds somewhat, but not a great deal, to changes in price. Inelastic demand always has a numerical value between zero and −1.

infant industry A young industry that may need temporary protection from competition from the established industries of other countries in order to develop an acquired comparative advantage.

inferior goods Goods for which demand tends to fall when income rises.

inflation An increase in the overall price level.

inflation rate The percentage change in the price level.

injunction A court order forbidding the continuation of behavior that leads to damages.

innovation The use of new knowledge to produce a new product or to produce an existing product more efficiently.

input or **factor markets** The markets in which the resources used to produce products are exchanged.

inputs The goods and services that firms purchase and turn into output.

intangible capital Nonmaterial things that contribute to the output of future goods and services.

interest The fee that a borrower pays to a lender for the use of his or her funds.

interest rate The annual interest payment on a loan expressed as a percentage of the loan. Equal to the amount of interest received per year divided by the amount of the loan.

interest sensitivity or **insensitivity of planned investment** The responsiveness of planned investment spending to changes in the interest rate. *Interest sensitivity* means that planned investment spending changes a great deal in response to changes in the interest rate; *interest insensitivity* means little

or no change in planned investment as a result of changes in the interest rate.

intermediate goods Goods that are produced by one firm for use in further processing by another firm.

International Monetary Fund An international agency whose primary goals are to stabilize international exchange rates and to lend money to countries that have problems financing their international transactions.

international sector From any one country's perspective, the economies of the rest of the world.

Interstate Commerce Commission (ICC) A federal regulatory group created by Congress in 1887 to oversee and correct abuses in the railroad industry.

invention An advance in knowledge.

inventory investment Occurs when a firm produces more output than it sells within a given period.

investment New capital additions to a firm's capital stock. Although capital is measured at a given point in time (a stock), investment is measured over a period of time (a flow). The flow of investment increases the capital stock.

J-curve effect Following a currency depreciation, a country's balance of trade may get worse before it gets better. The graph showing this effect is shaped like the letter J, hence the name "J-curve effect."

job search The process of gathering information about job availability and job characteristics.

kinked demand curve model A model of oligopoly in which the demand curve facing each individual firm has a "kink" in it. The kink follows from the assumption that competitive firms will follow if a single firm cuts price but will not follow if a single firm raises price.

Knights of Labor One of the earliest successful labor organizations in the United States, it recruited both skilled and unskilled laborers. Founded in 1869, the power of the Knights declined after the Chicago Haymarket bombing in 1886.

labor demand curve A graph that illustrates the amount of labor that firms want to employ at the particular wage rate.

labor force The number of people employed plus the number of unemployed.

labor-force participation rate The ratio of the labor force to the total population 16 years old or older.

labor-intensive technology A production technique that uses a large amount of labor relative to capital.

labor market The input/factor market in which households supply work for wages to firms that demand labor.

labor market discrimination Occurs when one group of workers receives inferior treatment from employers because of some characteristic irrelevant to job performance.

labor productivity Output per worker hour; the amount of output produced by an average worker in one hour.

labor supply curve A diagram that shows the quantity of labor supplied at different wage rates. Its shape depends on how households react to changes in the wage rate.

labor theory of value Marx's theory that the value of a commodity depends exclusively upon the amount of labor required to produce it. Commodities are the physical embodiment of the labor that produced them, and capital is the physical embodiment of the past labor used to produce it.

Laffer Curve With the tax rate measured on the vertical axis and tax revenue measured on the horizontal axis, the Laffer Curve shows there is some tax rate beyond which the supply response is large enough to lead to a decrease in tax revenue for further increases in the tax rate.

laissez-faire economy Literally from the French: "allow [them] to do." An economy in which individual people and firms pursue their own self-interests without any central direction or regulation.

land market The input/factor market in which households supply land or other real property in exchange for rent.

law of demand The negative relationship between price and quantity demanded: As price rises, quantity demanded decreases. As price falls, quantity demanded increases.

law of diminishing marginal utility The more of any one good consumed in a given period, the less satisfaction (utility) generated by consuming each additional (marginal) unit of the same good.

law of diminishing returns When additional units of a variable input are added to fixed inputs after a certain point, the marginal product of the variable input declines.

law of one price If the costs of transportation are small, the price of the same good in different countries should be roughly the same.

law of supply The positive relationship between price and quantity of a good supplied: An increase in market price will lead to an increase in quantity supplied, and a decrease in market price will lead to a decrease in quantity supplied.

legal tender Money that a government has required to be accepted in settlement of debts.

lender of last resort One of the functions of the Fed: It provides funds to troubled banks that cannot find any other sources of funds.

liability rules Laws that require A to compensate B for damages imposed.

life-cycle theory of consumption A theory of household consumption: Households make lifetime consumption decisions based on their expectations of lifetime income.

liquidity property of money The property of money that makes it a good medium of exchange as well as a store of value: It is portable and readily accepted and thus easily exchanged for goods.

logrolling Occurs when congressional representatives trade votes, agreeing to help each other get certain pieces of legislation passed.

long run That period of time for which there are no fixed factors of production. Firms can increase or decrease scale of operation, and new firms can enter and existing firms can exit the industry.

long-run average cost curve (*LRAC*) A graph that shows the different scales on which a firm can choose to operate in the long run.

long-run competitive equilibrium When P = SRMC = SRAC = LRAC and profits are zero.

Lorenz Curve A widely used graph of the distribution of income, with cumulative percentage of families plotted along the horizontal axis and cumulative percentage of income plotted along the vertical axis.

Lucas supply function The supply function embodies the idea that output (Y) depends on the difference between the actual price level and the expected price level.

M1, or transactions money Money that can be directly used for transactions.

M2, or broad money M1 plus savings accounts, money market accounts, and other near monies.

macroeconomics The branch of economics that deals with the economy as a whole. Macroeconomics focuses on the determinants of total national income, deals with aggregates such as aggregate consumption and investment, and looks at the overall level of prices rather than individual prices.

marginal cost (MC) The increase in total cost that results from producing one more unit of output. Marginal costs reflect changes in variable costs.

marginal damage cost (MDC) The additional harm done by increasing the level of an externality-producing activity by one unit. If producing product X pollutes the water in a river, MDC is the additional cost imposed by the added pollution that results from increasing output by one unit of X per period.

marginal factor cost (MFC) The additional cost of using one more unit of a given factor of production.

marginal private cost (MPC) The amount that a consumer pays to consume an additional unit of a particular good.

marginal product The additional output that can be produced by adding one more unit of a specific input, *ceteris paribus*.

marginal product of labor (MP_L) The additional output produced by one additional unit of labor.

marginal productivity theory of income distribution At equilibrium, all factors of production end up receiving rewards determined by their productivity as measured by marginal revenue product.

marginal propensity to consume (MPC) That fraction of a change in income that is consumed, or spent.

marginal propensity to import (MPM) The change in imports caused by a $1 change in income.

marginal propensity to save (MPS) That fraction of a change in income that is saved.

marginal revenue (MR) The additional revenue that a firm takes in when it increases output by one additional unit. In perfect competition, $P = MR$.

marginal revenue product (MRP) The additional revenue a firm earns by employing one additional unit of input, *ceteris paribus*.

marginal revenue product of labor (MRP_L) The additional revenue that a firm will take in by hiring one additional unit of labor, *ceteris paribus*. For perfectly competitive firms, the marginal revenue product of labor is equal to the marginal physical product of labor times the price of output.

marginal social cost (MSC) The total cost to society of producing an additional unit of a good or service. MSC is equal to the sum of the marginal costs of producing the product and the correctly measured damage costs involved in the process of production.

marginal utility (MU) The additional satisfaction gained by the consumption or use of *one more* unit of something.

market The institution through which buyers and sellers interact and engage in exchange.

market demand The sum of all the quantities of a good or service demanded per period by all the households buying in the market for that good or service.

market failure Occurs when resources are misallocated, or allocated inefficiently. The result is waste or lost value.

market organization The way an industry is structured. Structure is defined by how many firms there are in an industry, whether products are differentiated or are virtually the same, whether or not firms in the industry can control prices or wages, and whether or not competing firms can enter and leave the industry freely.

market power An imperfectly competitive firm's ability to raise price without losing all demand for its product.

market-socialist economy An economy that combines government ownership with market allocation.

market supply The sum of all that is supplied each period by all producers of a single product.

maximin strategy In game theory, a strategy chosen to maximize the minimum gain that can be earned.

means of production Marx's term for land and capital.

Medicaid and Medicare In-kind government transfer programs that provide health and hospitalization benefits: Medicare to the aged and their survivors and to certain of the disabled, regardless of income, and Medicaid to people with low incomes.

medium of exchange, or means of payment What sellers generally accept and buyers generally use to pay for goods and services.

microeconomic foundations of macroeconomics The microeconomic principles underlying macroeconomic analysis.

microeconomics The branch of economics that examines the functioning of individual industries and the behavior of individual decision-making units—that is, business firms and households.

midpoint formula A more precise way of calculating percentages by using the value halfway between P_1 and P_2 for the base in calculating the percentage change in price, and the value halfway between Q_1 and Q_2 as the base for calculating the percentage change in quantity demanded.

minimum wage The lowest wage that firms are permitted to pay workers.

minimum wage laws Laws that set a floor for wage rates—that is, a minimum hourly rate for any kind of labor.

Ministry of Trade and Industry (MITI) The agency of the Japanese government responsible for industrial policy. It uses tariffs and subsidies to protect and subsidize key industries and helps some sectors plan orderly reductions in capacity.

model A formal statement of a theory. Usually a mathematical statement of a presumed relationship between two or more variables.

modern economic growth The period of rapid and sustained increase in real output per capita that began in the Western World with the Industrial Revolution.

monetary policy The behavior of the Federal Reserve regarding the nation's money supply.

money income The measure of income used by the Census Bureau. Because it excludes noncash transfer payments and capital gains income, it is less inclusive than "economic income."

money market The market in which financial instruments are exchanged and in which the equilibrium level of the interest rate is determined.

money multiplier The multiple by which deposits can increase for every dollar increase in reserves; equal to one divided by the required reserve ratio.

monocentric models Models of residential location that assume central employment. As people move farther from the center, their costs of commuting increase. Equilibrium in the housing market exists only where land prices just offset the lower transport costs closer to the center.

monopolistic competition A common form of industry (market) structure in the United States, characterized by a large number of firms, none of which can influence market price by virtue of size alone. Some degree of market power is achieved by firms producing differentiated products. New firms can enter and established firms can exit such an industry with ease.

monopoly An industry structure in which there is only one large firm that produces a product for which there are no close substitutes. Monopolists can set prices but are subject to market discipline. For a monopoly to continue to exist, something must prevent potential competitors from entering the industry and competing for profits.

monopsony A market in which there is only one buyer for a good or service.

moral hazard Arises when one party to a contract passes the cost of his or her behavior on to the other party to the contract.

moral suasion The pressure exerted by the Fed on member banks to discourage them from borrowing heavily from the Fed.

mortality rate The death rate. Equal to (the number of deaths per year divided by the population) × 100.

movement along a demand curve The change in quantity demanded brought about by a change in price.

multiplier The ratio of the change in the equilibrium level of output to a change in some autonomous variable.

NAIRU The non-accelerating inflation rate of unemployment.

Nash equilibrium In game theory, the result of all players playing their best strategy given what their competitors are doing.

national income The total income earned by the factors of production owned by a country's citizens.

national income and product accounts Data collected and published by the government describing the various components of national income and output in the economy.

National Labor Relations Board (NLRB) A watchdog board established by the Wagner Act in 1935. Its duties include ensuring that all workers are guaranteed the right to join unions and that firm managers participate fairly in collective bargaining if so requested by a majority of their employees.

natural monopoly An industry that realizes such large economies of scale in producing its product that single-firm production of that good or service is most efficient.

natural rate of population increase The difference between the birth rate and the death rate. It does not take migration into account.

natural rate of unemployment The unemployment that occurs as a normal part of the functioning of the economy. Sometimes taken as the sum of frictional unemployment and structural unemployment.

near monies Close substitutes for transactions money, such as savings accounts and money market accounts.

negative demand shock Something that causes a negative shift in consumption or investment schedules or that leads to a decrease in U.S. exports.

net exports $(EX - IM)$ The difference between exports (sales to foreigners of U.S.-produced goods and services) and imports (U.S. purchases of goods and services from abroad). The figure can be positive or negative.

net exports of goods and services $(EX - IM)$ The difference between a country's total exports and total imports.

net factor payments to the rest of the world Payments of factor income to the rest of the world minus the receipt of factor income from the rest of the world.

net income The profits of a firm.

net interest The interest paid by business.

net investment Gross investment minus depreciation.

net national product (NNP) Gross national product minus depreciation; a nation's total product minus what is required to maintain the value of its capital stock.

net taxes (T) Taxes paid by firms and households to the government minus transfer payments made to households by the government.

New Economic Policy The Soviet economic policy in effect between 1921 and 1928; characterized by decentralization and a retreat to a market orientation.

nominal GDP Gross domestic product measured in current dollars.

nominal wage rate The wage rate in current dollars.

nondurable goods Goods that are used up fairly quickly, such as food and clothing.

nonexcludable A characteristic of most public goods: Once a good is produced, no one can be excluded from enjoying its benefits.

nonlabor, or nonwage, income Any income received from sources other than working—inheritances, interest, dividends, transfer payments, and so on.

nonresidential investment Expenditures by firms for machines, tools, plants, and so on.

nonrival in consumption A characteristic of public goods: One person's enjoyment of the benefits of a public good does not interfere with another's consumption of it.

nonsynchronization of income and spending The mismatch between the timing of money inflow to the household and the timing of money outflow for household expenses.

normal goods Goods for which demand goes up when income is higher and for which demand goes down when income is lower.

normal rate of return A rate of return on capital that is just sufficient to keep owners and investors satisfied. For relatively risk-free firms, it should be nearly the same as the interest rate on risk-free government bonds.

normative economics An approach to economics that analyzes outcomes of economic behavior, evaluates them as good or bad, and may prescribe courses of action. Also called policy economics.

North American Free-Trade Agreement (NAFTA) An agreement signed by the United States, Mexico, and Canada in which the three countries agreed to establish all of North America as a free-trade zone.

not in the labor force People who are not looking for work, either because they do not want a job or because they have given up looking.

Ockham's razor The principle that irrelevant detail should be cut away.

Okun's Law The theory, put forth by Arthur Okun, that the unemployment rate decreases about one percentage point for every 3 percent increase in real GDP. Later research and data have shown that the relationship between output and unemployment is not as stable as Okun's "law" predicts.

oligopoly An industry structure with a small number of (usually) large firms producing products that range from highly differentiated (automobiles) to standardized (copper). In general, entry of new firms into an oligopolistic industry is difficult but possible.

on-the-job training The principal form of human capital investment financed primarily by firms.

Open Market Desk The office in the New York Federal Reserve Bank from which government securities are bought and sold by the Fed.

open market operations The purchase and sale by the Fed of government securities in the open market; a tool used to expand or contract the amount of reserves in the system and thus the money supply.

operating profit (or loss) or net operating revenue Total revenue minus total variable cost $(TR - TVC)$.

opportunity cost That which we give up, or forgo, when we make a choice or a decision.

optimal level of provision for public goods The level at which resources are drawn from the production of other goods and services only to the extent that people want the public good and are willing to pay for it. At this level, society's willingness to pay per unit is equal to the marginal cost of producing the good.

optimal method of production The production method that minimizes cost.

optimal scale of plant The scale of plant that minimizes average cost.

outputs Usable products.

Pareto efficiency or Pareto optimality A condition in which no change is possible that will make some members of society better off without making some other members of society worse off.

partial equilibrium analysis The process of examining the equilibrium conditions in individual markets and for households and firms separately.

partnership A form of business organization in which there is more than one proprietor. The owners are responsible jointly and separately for the firm's obligations.

patent A barrier to entry that grants exclusive use of the patented product or process to the inventor.

per capita GDP or GNP A country's GDP or GNP divided by its population.

perfect competition An industry structure in which there are many firms, each small relative to the industry, producing virtually identical products and in which no firm is large enough to have any control over prices. In perfectly competitive industries, new competitors can freely enter and exit the market.

perfect knowledge The assumption that households possess a knowledge of the qualities and prices of everything available in the market, and that firms have all available infor-mation regarding wage rates, capital costs, and output prices.

perfectly contestable market A market in which entry and exit are costless.

perfectly elastic demand Demand in which quantity demanded drops to zero at the slightest increase in price.

perfectly inelastic demand Demand in which quantity demanded does not respond at all to a change in price.

perfect substitutes Identical products.

permanent income The average level of one's expected future income stream.

per se rule A rule enunciated by the courts declaring a particular action or outcome to be a per se (intrinsic) violation of antitrust law, whether the result is reasonable or not.

personal consumption expenditures (C) A major component of GDP: expenditures by consumers on goods and services.

personal income The total income of households. Equals (national income) minus (corporate profits minus dividends) minus (social insurance payments) plus (interest income received from the government and households) plus (transfer payments to households). The income received by households after paying social insurance taxes but before paying personal income taxes.

personal saving The amount of disposable income that is left after total personal spending in a given period.

personal saving rate The percentage of disposable personal income that is saved. If the personal saving rate is low, households are spending a large amount relative to their incomes; if it is high, households are spending cautiously.

Phillips Curve A graph showing the relationship between the inflation rate and the unemployment rate.

physical or tangible, capital Material things used as inputs in the production of future goods and services. The major categories of physical capital are nonresidential structures, durable equipment, residential structures, and inventories.

planned aggregate expenditure (AE) The total amount the economy plans to spend in a given period. Equal to consumption plus planned investment: $AE \equiv C + I$.

plant-and-equipment investment Purchases by firms of additional machines, factories, or buildings within a given period.

policy mix The combination of monetary and fiscal policies in use at a given time.

positive economics An approach to economics that seeks to understand behavior and the operation of systems without making judgments. It describes what exists and how it works.

post hoc, ergo propter hoc Literally, "after this (in time), therefore because of this." A common error made in thinking about causation: If Event A happens before Event B, it is not necessarily true that A caused B.

potential output, or potential GDP The level of aggregate output that can be sustained in the long run without inflation.

poverty line The officially established income level that distinguishes the poor from the nonpoor. It is set at three times the cost of the Department of Agriculture's minimum food budget.

preferred provider organization (PPO) A managed health-care plan in which an employer or insurance company establishes a network of doctors and hospitals to provide a broad set of medical services for a flat fee per participant. In return for the lower fee, the doctors and hospital who join the PPO network expect to receive a larger volume of patients.

price The amount that a product sells for per unit. It reflects what society is willing to pay.

price ceiling A maximum price that sellers may charge for a good, usually set by government.

price discrimination Occurs when a firm charges different buyers different prices for the same product. Such strategies are illegal if they drive out competition.

price elasticity of demand The ratio of the percentage change in quantity demanded to the percentage change in price; measures the responsiveness of demand to changes in price.

price feedback effect The process by which a domestic price increase in one country can "feed back" on itself through export and import prices. An increase in the price level in one country can drive up prices in other countries. This in turn further increases the price level in the first country.

price leadership A form of oligopoly in which one dominant firm sets prices and all the smaller firms in the industry follow its pricing policy.

price rationing The process by which the market system allocates goods and services to consumers when quantity demanded exceeds quantity supplied.

price surprise Actual price level minus expected price level.

principle of neutrality All else equal, taxes that are neutral with respect to economic decisions (that is, taxes that do not distort economic decisions) are generally preferable to taxes that distort economic decisions. Taxes that are not neutral impose excess burdens.

principle of second best The fact that a tax distorts an economic decision does not always imply that such a tax imposes an excess burden. If previously existing distortions exist, such a tax may actually improve efficiency.

private good A product produced by firms for sale to individual households. People can be excluded from the benefits of a private good if they do not pay for it.

private sector Includes all independently owned profit-making firms, nonprofit organizations, and households; all the decision-making units in the economy that are not part of the government.

privately held federal debt The privately held (non-government-owned) debt of the U.S. government.

privatization The transfer of government business to the private sector.

produce-marketing boards The channels through which the governments of some developing countries buy domestic farm output and then sell it to urban residents at government-controlled prices.

producer price indexes (PPIs) Measures of prices that producers receive for products at all stages in the production process.

producers Those people or groups of people, whether private or public, who transform resources into usable products.

product differentiation A strategy that firms use to achieve market power. Accomplished by producing products that have distinct positive identities in consumers' minds.

product, or output, markets The markets in which goods and services are exchanged.

production The process by which inputs are combined, transformed, and turned into outputs.

production function or **total product function** A numerical or mathematical expression of a relationship between inputs and outputs. It shows units of total product as a function of units of inputs.

production possibility frontier (ppf) A graph that shows all the combinations of goods and services that can be produced if all of society's resources are used efficiently.

production technology The quantitative relationship between inputs and outputs.

productivity, or labor productivity Output per worker hour; the amount of output produced by an average worker in one hour.

productivity of an input The amount of output produced per unit of an input.

profit The difference between total revenue and total cost.

progressive tax A tax whose burden, expressed as a percentage of income, increases as income increases.

property income Income from the ownership of real property and financial holdings. It takes the form of profits, interest, dividends, and rents.

proportional tax A tax whose burden is the same proportion of income for all households.

proprietorship A form of business organization in which a person simply sets up a business to provide goods or services at a profit. In a proprietorship, the proprietor (or owner) is the firm. The assets and liabilities of the firm are the owner's assets and liabilities.

proprietors' income The income of unincorporated businesses.

protection The practice of shielding a sector of the economy from foreign competition.

public assistance, or welfare Government transfer programs that provide cash benefits to (1) families with dependent children whose incomes and assets fall below a very low level and (2) the very poor regardless of whether or not they have children.

public choice theory An economic theory that the public officials who set economic policies and regulate the players act in their own self-interest, just as firms do.

public goods, or social goods Goods or services that bestow collective benefits on members of society. Generally, no one can be excluded from enjoying their benefits. The classic example is national defense.

public sector Includes all agencies at all levels of government—federal, state, and local.

purchasing-power-parity theory A theory of international exchange holding that exchange rates are set so that the price of similar goods in different countries is the same.

pure monopoly An industry with a single firm that produces a product for which there are no close substitutes and in which significant barriers to entry prevent other firms from entering the industry to compete for profits.

pure rent The return to any factor of production that is in fixed supply.

quantity demanded The amount (number of units) of a product that a household would buy in a given period if it could buy all it wanted at the current market price.

quantity supplied The amount of a particular product that a firm would be willing and able to offer for sale at a particular price during a given time period.

quantity theory of money The theory based on the identity $M \times V; P \times Y$ and the assumption that the velocity of money (V) is constant (or virtually constant).

queuing Waiting in line as a means of distributing goods and services; a nonprice rationing mechanism.

quota A limit on the quantity of imports.

racial covenants Provisions spelled out in property deeds that prohibit sale of that property to members of specific racial or ethnic groups.

rate of exploitation The ratio of surplus value to the value of labor power.

rational-expectations hypothesis The hypothesis that people know the "true model" of the economy and that they use this model to form their expectations of the future.

ration coupons Tickets or coupons that entitle individuals to purchase a certain amount of a given product per month.

Rawlsian justice A theory of distributional justice that concludes that the social contract emerging from the "original position" would call for an income distribution that would maximize the well-being of the worst-off member of society.

real business cycle theory An attempt to explain business cycle fluctuations under the assumptions of complete price and wage flexibility and rational expectations. It emphasizes shocks to technology and other shocks.

real interest rate The difference between the interest rate on a loan and the inflation rate.

real wage rate The amount that the nominal wage rate can buy in terms of goods and services.

real wealth, or real balance, effect The change in consumption brought about by a change in real wealth that results from a change in the price level.

recession A period during which aggregate output declines. Conventionally, a period in which aggregate output declines for two consecutive quarters.

recognition lag The time it takes for policy makers to recognize the existence of a boom or a slump.

regressive tax A tax whose burden, expressed as a percentage of income, falls as income increases.

relative-wage explanation of unemployment An explanation for sticky wages (and therefore unemployment): If workers are concerned about their wages relative to other workers in other firms and industries, they may be unwilling to accept a wage cut unless they know that all other workers are receiving similar cuts.

rental income The income received by property owners in the form of rent.

rent-seeking behavior Actions taken by households or firms to preserve positive profits.

required reserve ratio The percentage of its total deposits that a bank must keep as reserves at the Federal Reserve.

reserves The deposits that a bank has at the Federal Reserve bank plus its cash on hand.

residential investment Expenditures by households and firms on new houses and apartment buildings.

resources or inputs Anything provided by nature or previous generations that can be used directly or indirectly to satisfy human wants.

response lag The time that it takes for the economy to adjust to the new conditions after a new policy is implemented; the lag that occurs because of the operation of the economy itself.

retained earnings The profits that a corporation keeps, usually for the purchase of capital assets. Also called undistributed profits.

rule of reason The criterion introduced by the Supreme Court in 1911 to determine whether a particular action was illegal ("unreasonable") or legal ("reasonable") within the terms of the Sherman Act.

run on a bank Occurs when many of those who have claims on a bank (deposits) present them at the same time.

saving (S) The part of its income that a household does not consume in a given period. Distinguished from savings, which is the current stock of accumulated saving.

services The things we buy that do not involve the production of physical things, such as legal and medical services and education.

share of stock A certificate of partial ownership of a corporation. Entitles the holder to a portion of the corporation's profits.

Sherman Act Passed by Congress in 1890, the act declared every contract or conspiracy to restrain trade among states or nations illegal and declared any attempt at monopoly, successful or not, a misdemeanor. Interpretation of which specific behaviors were illegal fell to the courts.

shift of a demand curve The change that takes place in a demand curve corresponding to a new relationship between quantity demanded of a good and the price of that good. The shift is brought about by a change in the original conditions.

shock therapy The approach to transition from socialism to market capitalism that advocates rapid deregulation of prices, liberalization of trade, and privatization.

short run The period of time for which two conditions hold: The firm is operating under a fixed scale (fixed factor) of production, and firms can neither enter nor exit an industry.

short-run industry supply curve The sum of marginal cost curves (above *AVC*) of all the firms in an industry.

shut-down point The lowest point on the average variable cost curve. When price falls below the minimum point on *AVC*, total revenue is insufficient to cover variable costs and the firm will shut down and bear losses equal to fixed costs.

Smoot-Hawley tariff The U.S. tariff law of the 1930s, which set the highest tariffs in U.S. history (60 percent). It set off an international trade war and caused the decline in trade that is often considered a cause of the worldwide depression of the 1930s.

social capital, or infrastructure Capital that provides services to the public. Most social capital takes the form of public works (roads and bridges) and public services (police and fire protection).

social choice The problem of deciding what society wants. The process of adding up individual preferences to make a choice for society as a whole.

social, or implicit, contracts Unspoken agreements between workers and firms that firms will not cut wages.

social insurance, or payroll, taxes Taxes levied at a flat rate on wages and salaries. Proceeds support various government-administrated social-benefit programs, including the social security system and the unemployment benefits system.

socialist economy An economy in which most capital is owned by the government rather than by private citizens. Also called social ownership.

social overhead capital Basic infrastructure projects such as roads, power generation, and irrigation systems.

social security system The federal system of social insurance programs. It includes three separate programs that are financed through separate trust funds: the Old Age and Survivors Insurance program (OASI), the Disability Insurance program (DI), and the Health Insurance program (HI, or Medicare).

sources side/uses side The impact of a tax may be felt on one or the other or on both sides of the income equation. A tax may cause net income to fall (damage on the sources side), or it may cause prices of goods and services to rise so that income buys less (damage on the uses side).

speculation motive One reason for holding bonds instead of money: Because the market value of interest-bearing bonds is inversely related to the interest rate, investors may wish to hold bonds when interest rates are high with the hope of selling them when interest rates fall.

spreading overhead The process of dividing total fixed costs by more units of output. Average fixed cost declines as quantity rises.

stability A condition in which output is steady or growing, with low inflation and full employment of resources.

stabilization policy Describes both monetary and fiscal policy, the goals of which are to smooth out fluctuations in output and employment and to keep prices as stable as possible.

stabilization program An agreement between a borrower country and the International Monetary Fund in which the country agrees to revamp its economic policies to provide incentives for higher export earnings and lower imports.

stagflation Occurs when the overall price level rises rapidly (inflation) during periods of recession or high and persistent unemployment (stagnation).

sticky prices Prices that do not always adjust rapidly to maintain equality between quantity supplied and quantity demanded.

sticky wages The downward rigidity of wages as an explanation for the existence of unemployment.

store of value An asset that can be used to transport purchasing power from one time period to another.

structural adjustment A series of programs in developing nations designed to (1) reduce the size of their public sectors through privatization and/or expenditure reductions, (2) decrease their budget deficits, (3) control inflation, and (4) encourage private saving and investment through tax reform.

structural deficit The deficit that remains at full employment.

structural unemployment The portion of unemployment that is due to changes in the structure of the economy that result in a significant loss of jobs in certain industries.

subsidies Payments made by the government for which it receives no goods or services in return.

substitutes Goods that can serve as replacements for one another; when the price of one increases, demand for the other goes up.

substitution effect of higher wages Consuming an additional hour of leisure means sacrificing the wages that would be earned by working. When the wage rate rises, leisure becomes more expensive, and households may "buy" less of it. This means working more.

sunk costs Costs that cannot be avoided, regardless of what is done in the future, because they have already been incurred.

supply curve A graph illustrating how much of a product a firm will supply at different prices.

supply schedule A table showing how much of a product firms will supply at different prices.

supply-side policies Government policies that focus on aggregate supply and increasing production rather than stimulating aggregate demand.

surplus value The profit a capitalist earns by paying workers less than the value of what they produce.

sustained inflation An increase in the overall price level that continues over a significant period.

tacit collusion Collusion occurs when price- and quantity-fixing agreements among producers are explicit. *Tacit collusion* occurs when such agreements are implicit.

tariff A tax on imports.

tax base The measure or value upon which a tax is levied.

tax incidence The ultimate distribution of tax's burden.

tax multiplier The ratio of change in the equilibrium level of output to a change in taxes.

tax rate structure The percentage of a tax base that must be paid in taxes—25% of income, for example.

tax shifting Occurs when households can alter their behavior and do something to avoid paying a tax.

technological change The introduction of new methods of production or new products intended to increase the productivity of existing inputs or to raise marginal products.

terms of trade The ratio at which a country can trade domestic products for imported products.

theory of comparative advantage Ricardo's theory that specialization and free trade will benefit all trading partners (real wages will rise), even those that may be absolutely less efficient producers.

three basic questions The questions that all societies must answer: (1) What will be produced? (2) How will it be produced? (3) Who will get what is produced?

Tiebout hypothesis An efficient mix of public goods is produced when local land/housing prices and taxes come to reflect consumer preferences just as they do in the market for private goods.

tight monetary policy Fed policies that contract the money supply in an effort to restrain the economy.

time lags Delays in the economy's response to stabilization policies.

total cost The total of (1) out-of-pocket costs, (2) a normal rate of return on capital, and (3) the opportunity cost of each factor of production.

total fixed costs (*TFC*) or overhead The total of all costs that do not change with output, even if output is zero.

total revenue (*TR*) The total amount that a firm takes in from the sale of its product: The price per unit times the quantity of output the firm decides to produce ($P \times q$).

total utility The total amount of satisfaction obtained from consumption of a good or service.

total variable cost (*TVC*) The total of all costs that vary with output in the short run.

total variable cost curve A graph that shows the relationship between total variable cost and the level of a firm's output.

trade deficit Occurs when a country's exports of goods and services are less than its imports of goods and services in a given period.

trade feedback effect The tendency for an increase in the economic activity of one country to lead to a worldwide increase in economic activity, which then feeds back to that country.

trade surplus The situation when a country exports more than it imports.

tragedy of commons The idea that collective ownership may not provide the proper private incentives for efficiency because individuals do not bear the full costs of their own decisions but do enjoy the full benefits.

transaction motive The main reason that people hold money—to buy things.

transfer payments Cash payments made by the government to people who do not supply goods, services, or labor in exchange for these payments. They include social security benefits, veterans' benefits, and welfare payments.

Treasury bonds, notes, and bills Promissory notes issued by the federal government when it borrows money.

trust An arrangement in which shareholders of independent firms agree to give up their stock in exchange for trust certificates that entitle them to a share of the trust's common profits. A group of trustees then operates the trust as a monopoly, controlling output and setting price.

unconstrained supply of labor The amount a household would like to work within a given period at the current wage rate if it could find the work.

underground economy The part of the economy in which transactions take place and in which income is generated that is unreported and therefore not counted in GDP.

unemployed A person 16 years old or older who is not working, is available for work, and has made specific efforts to find work during the previous four weeks.

unemployment compensation A state government transfer program that pays cash benefits for a certain period of time to laid-off workers who have worked for a specified period of time for a covered employer.

unemployment rate The ratio of the number of people unemployed to the total number of people in the labor force.

unitary elasticity A demand relationship in which the percentage change in quantity of a product demanded is the same as the percentage change in price in absolute value (a demand elasticity of −1).

unit of account A standard unit that provides a consistent way of quoting prices.

urban decline The deterioration of the private and social capital stock of a city that results from the lack of investment by both private and public sectors.

U.S.-Canadian Free-Trade Agreement An agreement in which the United States and Canada agreed to eliminate all barriers to trade between the two countries by 1998.

utilitarian justice The idea that "a dollar in the hand of a rich person is worth less than a dollar in the hand of a poor person." If the marginal utility of income declines with income, transferring income from the rich to the poor will increase total utility.

utility The satisfaction, or reward, a product yields relative to its alternatives. The basis of choice.

utility possibilities frontier A graphical representation of a two-person world that shows all points at which A's utility can be increased only if B's utility is decreased.

value added The difference between the value of goods as they leave a stage of production and the cost of the goods as they entered that stage.

value of labor power The wage rate, dependent on the amount of clothing, shelter, basic education, medical care, and so on required to produce and sustain labor power.

variable A measure that can change from time to time or from observation to observation.

variable cost A cost that depends on the level of production chosen.

velocity of money The number of times a dollar bill changes hands, on average, during a year; the ratio of nominal *GDP* to the stock of money.

vicious-circle-of-poverty hypothesis Suggests that poverty is self-perpetuating because poor nations are unable to save and invest enough to accumulate the capital stock that would help them grow.

voting paradox A simple demonstration of how majority-rule voting can lead to seemingly contradictory and inconsistent results. A commonly cited illustration of the kind of inconsistency described in the impossibility theorem.

wealth or net worth The total value of what a household owns minus what it owes. It is a stock measure.

weight The importance attached to an item within a group of items.

Wheeler-Lea Act (1938) Extended the language of the Federal Trade Commission Act to include "deceptive" as well as "unfair" methods of competition.

Willis-Graham Act (1921) Declared the telephone industry a natural monopoly and exempted telephone mergers from review.

World Bank An international agency that lends money to individual countries for projects that promote economic development.

yellow-dog contracts Contracts in which workers agree not to join unions.

SOLUTIONS TO EVEN-NUMBERED PROBLEMS

CHAPTER 1

2. a. Pos. **b.** Norm. **c.** That Chile should not be allowed to join NAFTA is a normative statement. However, the reasons given are examples of positive economic analysis. **d.** Pos. **e.** Pos. **f.** Norm

4. Answers will vary.

6. a. Shopkeepers would gain by greater access to customers and higher profits. All city residents would gain, because greater access will generate higher sales and greater sales tax revenues. Consumers gain due to the opportunity cost of time not spent waiting in traffic jams.

b. Losers would include shopkeepers closer to the other, older bridge whose customers choose to shop closer to the new bridge. Any taxpayers for whom the extra taxes exceed the added benefit of the new bridge would also lose.

c. The gains/losses could be measured by adding up the value of all the time saved not waiting in line. We might say the bridge is efficient if the value of the time saved were greater than the cost of building the bridge.

8. a. Tuition (which could have been spent on other things), forgone wages, study time, etc.

b. All the money (gas, depreciation of the car, etc.) could have been spent on other items; time spent en route could have been used for other activities.

c. A better grade, no headache, perhaps admission to a better grad school, a higher paying job. He has traded off an investment in human capital (staying in to study) for present consumption (going to the party).

d. The other things that $200 could buy.

e. The $1 million could have been invested in other profit-making ventures or projects or it simply could have been put into the bank or loaned out to someone else at interest.

f. From the standpoint of the store, Alex is free. From Alex's standpoint he gives up other uses of time and wages that could be earned elsewhere.

Appendix

2. a. Negative slope. As price rises, quantity of apples purchased falls.

b. Positive (and declining) slope. As income rises, taxes rise, but the rise in taxes is less at higher incomes than at lower incomes.

c. Negative (and declining slope). As mortgage rates fall, home sales increase, but the increase in home sales is more at lower mortgage rates than at higher mortgage rates.

d. Negative, then positive slope. As young children get older, they run faster, but as adults get older (beyond a certain age), they run slower.

e. Positive slope. Greater sunshine leads to greater corn yield.

f. Positive, then negative slope. Up to a point, more fertilizer increases corn yield, but beyond a certain point, adding more fertilizer actually decreases the yield.

CHAPTER 2

2. Presumably studying means producing human capital, which will be used in the future to produce other things. Studying entails shifting benefits from the present into the future. The yield comes later in the form of higher productivity or a higher-paying job. Similarly, building a boat entails trading present consumption for a higher level of consumption later. The boat, like the knowledge gained while studying, is capital.

4. a. Depends on her state of mind and income. If she will be paying for college, she may have to work more later. In a sense, she is trading future work for present consumption. On the other hand, if she is really stressed out, taking time off may well make her a more productive student and earn her higher grades later on.

b. Sacrificing present consumption for the future benefits of losing weight. For most people, dieting and working out are difficult. The future benefits of feeling well and being healthy make it worthwhile for many.

c. Time and money spent today on maintenance can be thought of as an investment in the future—avoiding costly repair bills and/or the inconvenience of breaking down on the road. ("Pay me now or pay me later.")

d. Present time saved vs. risk of an accident or a ticket, which could be costly.

6. a. A straight-line ppf curve intersecting the Y axis at 1,000 units of luxury goods and intersecting the X axis at 500 units of necessity goods. These are the limits of production if all resources are used to produce only one good.

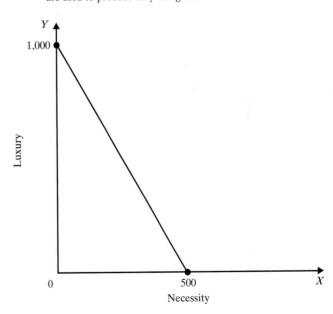

b. Unemployment or underemployment of labor would put the society inside the ppf. Full employment would move the society to some point on the ppf.

c. Answers will vary, but the decision should be based on the relative value of necessities and luxuries, and the degree of concern that all fellow citizens have enough necessities.

d. If left to the free market, prices would (at least ideally) be determined by market forces; incomes would be determined by a combination of ability, effort, and inheritance. It would be up to each individual to find a job and determine how to spend the income.

8. a. c **b.** a, d, e, f **c.** clearly d, probably e **d.** e **e.** all but a **f.** b

CHAPTER 3

2. Various. Some obvious examples are telecommunications, television broadcasting, electricity (coming), computer systems and software, etc.

4. Unions were the key opponents of GATT, especially unions in industries vulnerable to foreign competition (for example, sugar producers). Export industries, including the National Association of Manufacturers, favored GATT. Their reason: the theory of comparative advantage. (See chapter 2.)

6. Various.

8. Disagree. Change the word *corporations* to *sole proprietorships* and the statement is true (see Table 3.1).

10. No matter how much the firm produces, it is so small relative to the total market that its output has no effect on the market price. Therefore, the firm must be a "price taker"; it accepts the market-determined price charged by all other firms as a given that it cannot influence.

12. Government spending could increase while taxes are decreasing due to deficit spending (borrowing). Government spending could increase while government employment is decreasing if government is purchasing goods and services from the private sector that it formerly produced itself.

14. Answers will vary.

CHAPTER 4

2. a.

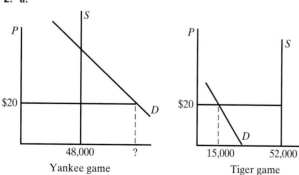

Yankee game / Tiger game

b. It depends on how responsive demand is to lower ticket prices. The way the curves are drawn in the figures, if the tickets were given away *free*, the stadium wouldn't fill up. If demand were

more responsive, the quantity demanded might equal the quantity supplied at a price above zero. Even if the quantity demanded is below the quantity supplied at a price of zero, a *negative* price might fill the stadium! That is, fans might have to be paid to endure such a bad game. This could be done by giving away free prizes to attendees.

c. Some demand was unsatisfied—price was below equilibrium, quantity demanded was below quantity supplied. The most common method of nonprice rationing is first-come, first-served. Sometimes people wait in line. Also, some firms have favored customers. See chapter 5.

4. a. Disagree. They are complements. **b.** Agree. **c.** Disagree. A rise in income will cause the demand for inferior goods to fall, pushing prices down. **d.** Disagree. Sure they can. Steak and lobster are both normal goods. **e.** Disagree. Price could go down if the shift of supply is larger than the shift of demand. **f.** Agree.

6.

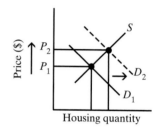

a. A simple demand shift: same diagram for both cities.

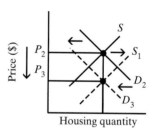

b. Rightward shift of supply with new development; leftward shift of demand with falling incomes: same diagram for both cities.

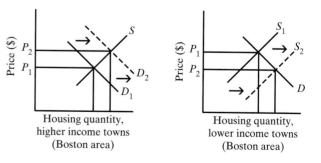

Housing quantity, higher income towns (Boston area) / Housing quantity, lower income towns (Boston area)

c. Trade-up buyers shift demand in the higher-income towns and supply in the lower-income towns.

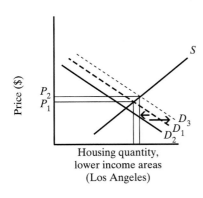

Housing quantity,
lower income areas
(Los Angeles)

d. Falling income pushes demand to the left; more households push demand to the right. The rightward shift is stronger.

8.

a. P decreases, Q decreases

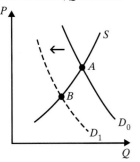

b. and **d.** P increases, Q increases

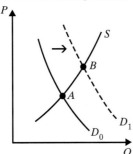

c. P increases, Q decreases

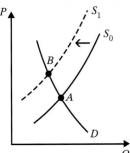

e. P decreases, Q increases

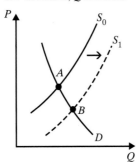

10. a.

PRICE	QUANTITY DEMANDED (IN MILLIONS)	QUANTITY SUPPLIED (IN MILLIONS)
$ .50	90	30
$1.00	80	50
$1.50	70	70
$2.00	60	90
$2.50	50	110

b. Quantity demanded equals quantity supplied at $P = \$1.50$, with quantity = 70 million dozen eggs.

c.

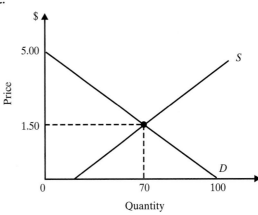

12. a.

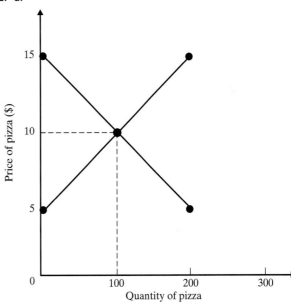

b. $Q_d = Q_s \rightarrow 300 - 20P = 20P - 100 \rightarrow P = \$10$. Substitute $P = \$10$ into either the demand or supply equation to get $Q = 100$.

c. With $P = \$15$, producers would want to supply $20(15) - 100 = 200$ pizzas, but consumers would want to buy $300 - 20(15) = 0$ pizzas. There would be an excess supply of pizzas, which would bring the price down. As the price decreased, quantity supplied would decrease while quantity demanded would increase until both were equal at a price of $10 and quantity of 100.

d. The new market demand for pizzas would be $Q_d = 600 - 40P$.

e. $Q_d = Q_s \rightarrow 600 - 40P = 20P - 100 \rightarrow P = 700/60 = \$11.67$. Substitute $P = \$11.67$ into either the demand or supply equation to get $Q = 133$.

CHAPTER 5

2. Answers will vary. But scalping—regardless of its morality—helps to eliminate shortages by creating a "market" where the price can rise to its equilibrium value. Anyone willing to pay the equilibrium price should be able to obtain a ticket. Also, by allowing price rationing to work somewhat, scalping reduces the need for waiting in line, and so results in less wasted time.

c. Rental housing

d. Plants

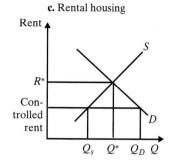

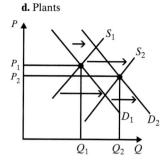

4.

a. Wheat market

b. Hamburger market

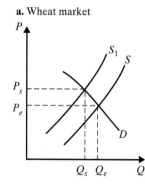

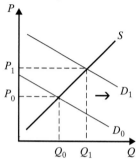

c. Gasoline market

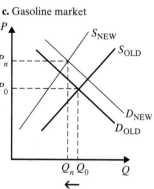

8. a. Using demand and supply data for the United States only, equilibrium price is $22 and equilibrium quantity is 12 million barrels.

b. With a price ceiling of $18, quantity demanded equals 14 million barrels, while quantity supplied equals 8 million barrels. There is an excess demand of 6 million barrels.

c. Quantity supplied will determine the quantity purchased. In a market system, no one can be forced to buy or sell more than he or she wants to. Under conditions of excess demand, suppliers will supply only as much as they want, and some consumer demand will go unsatisfied.

10. The key here is that total revenue is equal to $P \times Q$. When price rises (cab fares go up), quantity demanded goes down, depending on the elasticity of demand. Cab drivers who were expecting a 10% increase in revenues were expecting *no* loss of riders. They expected demand to be perfectly inelastic. But while fares did not go up 10%, they did go up. Thus, the increase in price was *more* than the decrease in riders, thus the percentage decrease in Q was less than the percentage increase in price: Demand in fact was *inelastic*.

12. a. −1.2 **b.** +10% **c.** +15% **d.** +12% **e.** .67

14. a. % ΔQ ÷ % ΔP = 0.2
Thus % ΔP = % $0\Delta Q$ ÷ 0.2 = 10% ÷ 0.2 = 50%.

b. A price ceiling at $1.40 per gallon would create a shortage of gasoline. The result might be long lines at gas stations and perhaps a black market in gasoline.

6.

a. Housing

b. Beef in Continental Europe

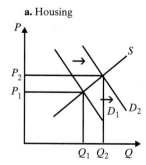

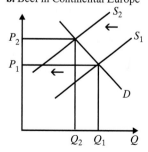

CHAPTER 6

2.

# of cookies	Marginal utility
1	100
2	100
3	75
4	50
5	25
6	10
7	0

The maximum that he would buy would be 6, because the seventh yields no marginal utility.

4.

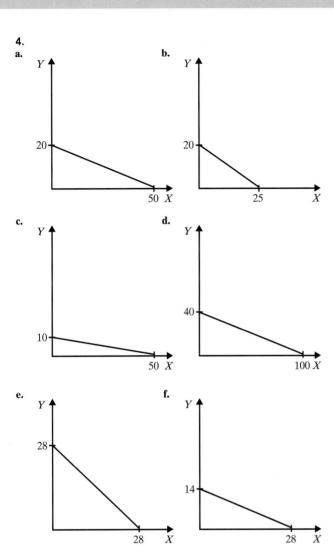

a.

b.

c.

d.

e.

f.

g.

6. The substitution effect is that leisure was less costly—each hour of leisure requires a smaller sacrifice of income because working gains only $.20 on the dollar. Thus, you would tend to work less after the cuts. However, the decline in welfare benefits also causes a decrease in purchasing power (for any given amount of leisure, you have less income than before). If leisure is a normal good, you would buy less of it. The income effect thus suggests working more. The two effects work in opposite directions, and the net result is ambiguous.

8. Demand shifts to the left, causing price to fall. The lower price causes the quantity demanded to rise *along* the new demand curve as consumers react to lower prices.

10. a.

# PER MONTH	MOVIES			# PER MONTH	BOOKS		
	TU	MU	MU/$		TU	MU	MU/$
1	50	50	6.25	1	22	22	1.10
2	80	30	3.75	2	42	20	1.00
3	100	20	2.50	3	52	10	.50
4	110	10	1.25	4	57	5	.25
5	116	6	.75	5	60	3	.15
6	121	5	.63	6	62	2	.10
7	123	2	.25	7	53	1	.05

b. Yes, these figures are consistent with the law of diminishing marginal utility, which states that as the quantity of a good consumed increases, utility also increases, but by less and less for each additional unit. In the tables, the *TU* figures for both books and movies are increasing, but as more movies or more books are consumed, the MU diminishes.

c. Five movies and two books. To maximize utility, the individual should allocate income toward those goods with the highest marginal utility per dollar. The first four movies have a higher marginal utility per dollar than the first book, so the person begins by seeing four movies for $32. The first book has a higher marginal utility than the fifth movie, so now the person should buy a book, for total expenditure of $52. Next, the second book, for total spending of $72. And finally, the fifth movie, for total spending of $80.

d. See graph in h below.

e. If the price of books falls to $10, only the *MU/$* column for books needs to be recalculated:

# PER MONTH	BOOKS		
	TU	MU	MU/$
1	22	22	2.20
2	42	20	2.00
3	52	10	1.00
4	57	5	.50
5	60	3	.30
6	62	2	.20
7	63	1	.10

f. Now, using the same logic as in c. above, this individual should purchase six movies and three books, for a total expenditure of 6($8) + 3($10) = $78.

g. See graph in h. below.

h. The decrease in the price of books increases the purchasing power of the individual's income. This increase in purchasing power—or income effect—will be used to purchase more of one or both goods, depending on the individual's tastes. In this case, the individual chooses to use his or her "increased income" to buy more of both goods.

(Note: Another answer to **f.** is 5 movies and 4 books. This choice uses up the entire $80, and it results in the same total utility as 6 movies and 3 books.)

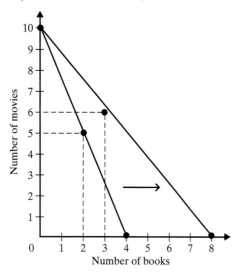

12. If leisure is a normal good, a large inheritance will be used to purchase more leisure, reducing the number of hours a person wants to work.

We might be tempted to conclude that taxing away all inheritances would increase desired working hours, but this is not necessarily the case. We must also consider the impact such large taxes would have on the desired working hours of those leaving the bequests. With a 100% tax rate, wealthy individuals would probably decide there is no point in leaving a bequest at all, therefore decreasing their need to work while they are alive. The final impact on desired working hours in the economy must take into account the effects on both bequest leavers and bequest receivers, and could go either way.

Appendix

2. $I/P_{x1} = 100$ and $I = 100$, thus $P_{x1} = \$1.00$ (Point A on demand curve).
$I/P_{x2} = 200$ and $I = 100$, thus $P_{x2} = \$.50$ (Point B on demand curve).
$I/P_{x3} = 300$ and $I = 100$, thus $P_{x3} = \$.33$ (Point C on demand curve).

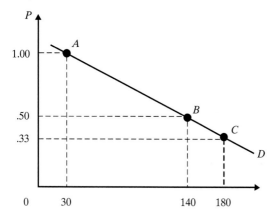

4. a. We know that $P_A A + P_N N = 100 \rightarrow 5N + 10A = 100$. We also know that $MU_N/MU_A = A/N = P_N/P_A = 5/10 \rightarrow N = 2A$. Substituting, we find that $5(2A) + 10A = 100 \rightarrow A = 5$; $N = 10$.

b. If $P_N = 10$, $N = 5$ and if $P_N = 2$, $N = 25$.

c. Answers will vary, but graph should show an indifference curve tangent to a budget constraint drawn for $P_A = \$10$ and P_N equal to one of the prices given in the answer to b.

CHAPTER 7

2. The size of the theater is the fixed factor. Decisions include how to divide up the tickets, what price to charge, what shows to put on, what kind of stage sets to use. All are constrained by the scale of the theater. In the long run you might be able to raise money and build or acquire a bigger theater. There is no fixed factor in the long run; you can think big!

4. a. The marginal product decreases as a single variable factor increases, holding all other factors constant.

b. The table does exhibit diminishing returns because the marginal product of labor falls as labor increases:

L	TP	MP
0	0	—
1	5	5
2	9	4
3	12	3
4	14	2
5	15	1

6. Clearly the labor-intensive way would be to carry the boxes down the hall and up the stairs one at a time. She could get a friend or two to help. If the dorm has an elevator and she can borrow a hand truck, the job would be a piece of cake. She would be using capital to raise her productivity. To go three miles across campus, a car (capital) or a truck (more capital) would be nice, although she could carry them one at a time across campus as well. In the developing world, where capital is scarce, people carry a lot of stuff. To get the boxes to a new campus, she would probably mail them or send them UPS. In this case, they would go in a big truck or in an airplane (a whole lot of capital).

8. a.

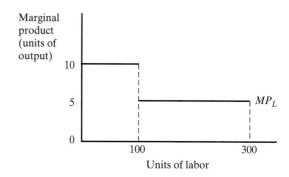

b. Yes, the marginal product drops from $10 to $5 after 100 units of labor have been used.

10. a. Tall buildings—skyscrapers.

b. Product usually has to move along an assembly line and out into a warehouse. An assembly line usually takes a lot of space on a single floor. (Can you imagine a vertical assembly line?)

c. Offices can be "stacked up." People can move by stairs or elevators easily.

d. Accessibility!

e. The area of land increases with the square of distance from the center: When a city grows from a radius of 1 mile to a radius of 5 miles, the new area is 25 times as large as the original (Area $= \pi R^2$).

12. a. The first step is to calculate the cost for each level of output using each of the three technologies. With capital costing $100 per day, and labor costing $80 per day, the results are as follows:

DAILY OUTPUT	TECHNOLOGY 1	TECHNOLOGY 2	TECHNOLOGY 3
100	860	800	820
150	1,100	960	900
200	1,280	1,140	1,080
250	1,540	1,400	1,340

From the table, we can see that for output of 100, Technology 2 is the cheapest. For output levels of 150, 200, and 250, Technology 3 is cheapest.

b. In a low-wage country, where capital costs $100 per day and labor costs only $40 per day, the cost figures are as follows:

DAILY OUTPUT	TECHNOLOGY 1	TECHNOLOGY 2	TECHNOLOGY 3
100	580	600	660
150	700	680	700
200	840	820	840
250	1,020	1,000	1,020

From the table, we can see that for output of 100, Technology 1 is now cheapest. For output levels of 150, 200, or 250, Technology 2 is now cheapest.

c. If the firm moves from a high-wage to a low-wage country and continues to produce 200 units per day, it will change from technology 3 (with six workers) to technology 2 (with eight workers). Employment increases by two workers.

Appendix

2. At A, $MP_L/MP_K > P_L/P_K$ because the slope of the isoquant is greater than the slope of the isocost. That means that $MP_L/P_L > MP_K/P_K$; thus the firm can cut costs by hiring more labor and less capital. At B, $MP_L/MP_K < P_L/P_K$ because the slope of the isoquant is less than the slope of the isocost. That means that $MP_K/P_K > MP_L/P_L$; thus the firm can cut costs by hiring more capital and less labor.

CHAPTER 8

2. a. False. MC may be rising, but if it is below AC, then AC will still be falling.

b. False. At the level of output where ATC is minimized, if $P > MC$, the firm should increase production even if this decision raises ATC. As long as $P > MC$, a competitive firm will increase its profits by increasing production (with one exception, as explained in chapter 9).

c. False. $AFC = $ Total fixed cost/Output $= TFC/q$. As q rises, fixed cost remains constant, so AFC must decrease.

4. a. Marginal cost is a constant $1 from one unit of output up to 100 units because the most efficient machine will be used. From the 101st unit to the 300th unit, MC is constant at $2. From the 301st unit to the 800th unit, MC is constant at $3.

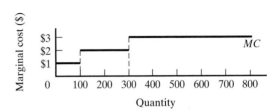

Total cost is $100 at zero units of output and rises by $1 per unit to a total of $200 at 100 units of output. From 101 units of output up to 300 units, total cost increases by $2 per unit up to a total of $600. After that it rises at $3 per unit to a total of $2,100 at 800 units of output.

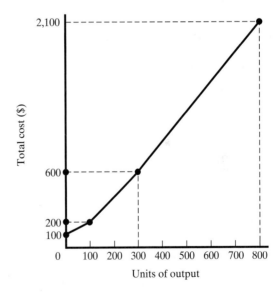

b. At a price of $2.50, the company should produce 300 books.

$$TR = \$750, TC = \$600, \text{ so profit} = \$150$$

6. a. The table gives the marginal product from each day's efforts: 100, 80, 60, and 40 kg.

b. Marginal cost of a kg of fish is the change in cost divided by the change in q. During prime season, each day brings in 100 kg of fish at a cost of 6,000 levs, or $MC = 6,000/100 = 60$ levs. During month 7, it's $6,000/80 = MC = 75$ levs. During month 8, it's $6,000/60 = MC = 100$ levs. During the rest of the year it's $6,000/40 = 150$ levs.

c. Produce as long as price, which is marginal revenue (80 levs), is greater than MC. Thus, the boat should be in the water fishing during prime season and month 7, but should not fish during month 8 or during the rest of the year.

8. a.

Q	L	TFC	TVC	TC	AFC	AVC	ATC	MC
0	0	$200	$0	$200	—	—	—	—
1	10	$200	$500	$700	$200	$500	$700	$500
2	15	$200	$750	$950	$100	$375	$475	$250
3	18	$200	$900	$1,100	$67	$300	$367	$150
4	22	$200	$1,100	$1,300	$50	$275	$325	$200
5	28	$200	$1,400	$1,600	$40	$280	$320	$300
6	36	$200	$1,800	$2,000	$33	$300	$333	$400
7	48	$200	$2,400	$2,600	$29	$343	$372	$600

b. (Student verification)

c. From 0 to 3 units of output, there are increasing returns to labor and (therefore) decreasing marginal costs. From 3 to 7 units of output, there are diminishing returns to labor and (therefore) increasing marginal costs.

d. AVC is minimized at 4 units of output. ATC is minimized at 5 units of output.

e. Under perfect competition, $MR = \$410$, so the firm should produce 6 units of output. (Note that $MR > MC$ for units 2–6, while $MR < MC$ for the first unit and the seventh. Thus, the profit-maximizing output could be either 0 units or 6 units, but nothing in between. A quick check tells us that profits at 0 units would be $-\$200$, and profits at 6 units would be $\$410(6) - \$2,000 = \$460$. The firm should produce 6 units.)

f. ATC is minimized at 5 units, but profits are maximized at 6 units. The firm is, indeed, "minimizing costs" in the sense that it is producing any given level of output at the lowest possible cost. But its goal in choosing among different output levels is to maximize profits, not to minimize average costs. Because $MR > MC$ for the sixth unit, producing the sixth unit adds to profits, even though it also raises ATC.

CHAPTER 9

2. One could make a case that some economies probably exist in all seven, but the case is much stronger in electric power (needs a big power plant or dam) and aircraft manufacturing (requires a big assembly line and a great deal of cooperation).

Home Building: Home building is usually done by very small independent contractors, although there are some big tract developers (like Ryan Homes) that produce tens of thousands of homes each year. They do quantity buying and use mass-produced parts.

It is hard to find economies of much significance in *software development* and *vegetable farming.* Although some firms in those industries are large, many are quite small and quite competitive.

4. a. Not true. A firm will never sell its output for less than the *marginal* cost of producing it, but may indeed sell at less than *average* total cost, as long as it can earn an operating profit.

b. Not true. The short-run marginal cost curve assumes at least one input is fixed. The long-run average cost curve allows all inputs to vary. For example, the short-run MC curve for each fixed level of capital could be U-shaped, and yet the $LRAC$ curve could be flat (constant returns to scale).

6. a. Disagree. Constant returns to scale means that the long-run average cost curve is flat over most of its range.

b. Disagree. Firms earning profits will produce to the right of the minimum point on the average total cost function. See the following diagram:

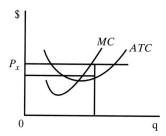

c. Disagree. The supply curve of a competitive firm is its marginal cost curve above the average *variable* cost curve. At any point above AVC, total revenue is greater than total variable cost and firms will choose to operate.

d. Disagree. A firm suffering losses will continue to operate as long as total revenue covers variable cost.

8. The enterprise is suffering a $1,000 loss. $TR = \$30,000$, $TC = \$29,000$, accounting profit $= \$1,000$. But the opportunity cost of capital is 10% or $2,000. When the $2,000 is added to cost the result is a $1,000 loss.

10. a. and **b.**

Industry

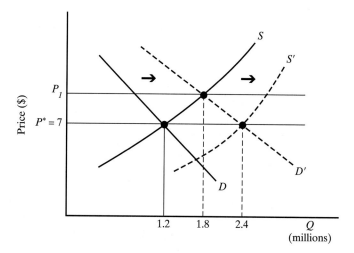

Representative firm

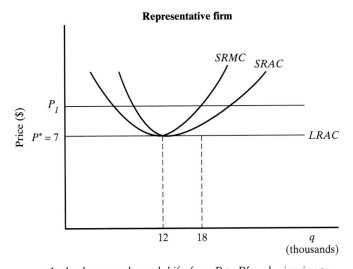

c. In the short run, demand shifts from D to D', and price rises to P_1. Firms are making profits, and they raise output to 18.

In the long run, 100 new firms enter the industry. Supply shifts from S to S', and price falls back to $7.

Appendix

2. See the story in the text and Figure 9A.2 for an increasing-cost industry.

CHAPTER 10

2.

WORKERS	BUSHELS	MP	MRP
0	0	—	—
1	40	40	$80
2	70	30	$60
3	90	20	$40
4	100	10	$20
5	105	5	$10
6	102	−3	−$6

The firm should hire workers as long as $MRP > W$. When $W = \$30$, the firm should hire three workers. If W increases to $50, the firm should cut back to only two workers, because the MRP of the third worker ($40) is now less than the cost of hiring him/her ($50).

4. a. Demand curve for construction workers shifts leftward; wage decreases; employment decreases.

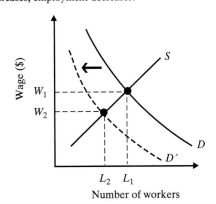

Number of workers

b. and **c.** Demand curve for construction workers shifts rightward; wage increases; employment increases.

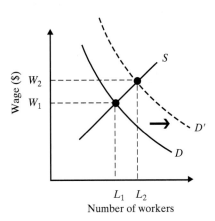

Number of workers

6. Investment tax credits reduce the cost of capital relative to the cost of labor. To the extent that capital is a substitute for labor, these credits can lead to layoffs and slower employment growth.

8. The company makes, among other things, airplanes. With no demand for airplanes there would be no salaries for anyone. The demand for Mr. Lanza's services is derived from the demand for airplanes. Also, most of Mr. Lanza's compensation was in the form of stock options. The value of those options was directly tied to the market price of Lockheed stock, which did very well (along with many other stocks during 1985 to 1987). One could argue that his leadership was responsible for the company's outstanding performance, and because his compensation was directly tied to performance, he was getting what he deserved. In a sense he was paid his marginal revenue product. Of course, it is very difficult to figure out how much of Lockheed's performance was the result of his own efforts and skills.

10. a.

NUMBER OF WORKERS	NUMBER OF SHIRTS PRODUCED PER DAY	MP_L	TR	MRP_L
0	0	—	$0	—
1	30	30	$90	$90
2	80	50	$240	$150
3	110	30	$330	$90
4	135	25	$405	$75
5	155	20	$465	$60
6	170	15	$510	$45
7	180	10	$540	$30
8	185	5	$555	$15

b. (1) $TR(170) = \$3 \times 170 = \$510$ and $TR(180) = \$3 \times 180 = \$540$, ∴ MR from selling the output produced by the seventh worker = ($\$540 − 810$) = $30

(2) $MRP(7) = \$3 \times 10 = \$30$

c. The firm should hire workers as long as $MRP_L > W$, subject to the shut-down condition. In this case, if the firm stays open, it should hire six workers. (If labor is the only variable cost, then the firm should indeed stay open, because in this case $TR > TVC$.)

d. Now the firm should hire only five workers, because the MRP of the sixth worker is only $45, which is less than the wage.

e. The new technology will double both *MPL* and *MRPL* at each number of workers. Now, at a wage of $50, the firm should hire seven workers (because the *MRP* of the seventh worker will be $60, but the *MRP* of the eighth worker will be only $30).

CHAPTER 11

2. No. The total capital cost of the station is $1 million. With revenues of $420,000 and costs of $360,000, profit is just $60,000, which is a 6% yield on an investment of $1 million. If I can get 7.5% by investing in perfectly safe government securities, why buy a gas station?

4.

Total investment (Singapore dollars)

Quando Company should invest in all projects that have a rate of return greater than the interest rate. Therefore, it should invest a total of $48,820,600.

6. Total profits are taxed; what is left is split between dividends paid out to owners and retained earnings held internally for investment.

8. Answers will vary. Interest rates differ because of the terms of the loan (how long before the loan is due) and the risk associated with the loan. Longer term interest rates may reflect expectations about future short-term rates. The federal government is considered a safe borrower and pays low interest rates.

10. Stockholders have put up $100,000 and receive dividends of $30,000. With an interest rate of 10%, $10,000 of this is the normal rate of return. The other $20,000 is profit, earned by the stockholders.

12. Disagree. Lower interest rates actually make households invest more (in human capital, durable goods, etc.), but might make them save less.

Appendix

2. Disagree. The bridge cannot be justified on efficiency grounds, because simply investing the $25,000 in the financial markets would generate a stream of income worth more to citizens than the benefits from the bridge. However, at substantially lower interest rates, the *PDV* of the benefits would be higher and might exceed $25,000. In that case, the bridge should be built.

4. a. $3,000/(1.05) = $2,857.14.

b. $3,000/(1.05)^2 = $2,721.09.

c. $1,000/(1.05) + $1,000/(1.05)^2 + $1,000/(1.05)^3 = $2723.24.

6. a. False; **b.** True.

CHAPTER 12

2. Let sector X be the new lower-cost stores and home shopping firms. Let sector Y be smaller specialty stores and traditional shops that provide more service. Note that these two are substitutes for one another, but they are not perfect substitutes. People have different preferences. Some people do not have computers and some like service. Also they may not be at the same location. You may have to drive a long way to a big box.

The *LRAC* shifts down as changing technology brings with it lower costs in sector X. That creates profits in X. New entry and expansion of existing firms drive supply to the right in X. Prices fall in X, reflecting the new supply in response to lower costs. Consumers respond to the lower prices in X; they shop at traditional stores less frequently. Demand for Y shifts to the left, causing prices to fall. Lower prices lead to losses and some stores respond in the long run by going out of business. Supply in Y shifts back to the left, holding prices in Y at *LRAC*.

Since fewer workers are required in the expanding part of the retail sector, the demand for labor falls. This leads to lower wages and a lower quantity of labor supplied.

4. By taxes we mean taxes on imports, which are called "tariffs." After trade is opened country A will specialize in the production of corn and country B will specialize in the production of soybeans. They will trade. The same acreage will produce more soybeans and more corn. With more output from the same inputs it is clearly possible to make some people better off without harming others.

6. All are examples of potentially Pareto efficient changes.

a. Both parties better off; no one else worse off.

b. Monopolist is hurt but gains to consumers are greater—enough to compensate losers.

c. If we assume that the taxes were being used wisely, this still might be an efficient change. Let's assume that the revenues are made up by a new tax that does not distort consumer choices. The argument here is that taxes produce extra or excess burdens when they distort consumer choices. As the result of the repeal some people buy sweaters, gaining utility over what they were buying before.

d. Simple elimination of waste is clearly efficient.

8. The coin toss is more "equitable," because both parties have the same chance of winning, regardless of their income. But with the coin toss, there is no guarantee that the party who values the ticket most would get it. Selling the ticket to the higher bidder is more "efficient," because whoever places the higher money value on the ticket will get it, but less equitable, because it favors those with larger incomes.

10. a. Pareto efficient. Both you and the street vendor benefit.

b. Pareto efficient. You are better off (you don't die) and the vagabond is better off (by $10,000). Given your circumstances, this is a voluntary exchange.

c. Not Pareto efficient. Not a voluntary exchange, and you are worse off.

d. Not Pareto efficient. You and the cab driver are better off, but you are also adding to traffic congestion that will make other rush-hour travelers worse off.

12. The allocation of labor is inefficient. Because each factory is hiring the profit maximizing number of workers (where $W = P_X \times MP_L$), the value of the marginal product of labor in factory A is \$10, while that in factory B is only \$6. If workers were moved from factory B to factory A, the value of total output would rise.

CHAPTER 13

2. A competitive firm can sell all the output it wants without having any impact on market price. For each additional unit sold, its revenue will rise by the market price. Hence, MR is the same at all levels of output.

Each time a monopolist increases output by one unit, the market price falls. The additional revenue the monopolist receives is actually less than the price, because consumers who were already buying the output get a price break too. MR is thus lower than price, and as output increases, both price and MR decline.

4.

INTERVAL	MARGINAL REVENUE
0–5	+90
5–10	+70
10–15	+50
15–20	+30
20–25	+10
25–30	−10
30–35	−30
35–40	−50

Produce as long as $MR > MC$; thus if $MC = \$20$, optimal output = 20 units. Profits are $TR = \$1,200$ ($20 \times \$60$) minus $TC = \$100$ $FC + \$400$ VC ($20 \times \$20$) = \$500. Thus profit = \$700.

When $MC = \$40$, optimal output = 15 units, $TR = \$1,050$ ($15 \times \$70$), $TC = \$100$ $FC + \$600$ VC ($15 \times \$400$). And, finally, profit = \$350 ($\$1,050 – \$700$).

6. a. and b.

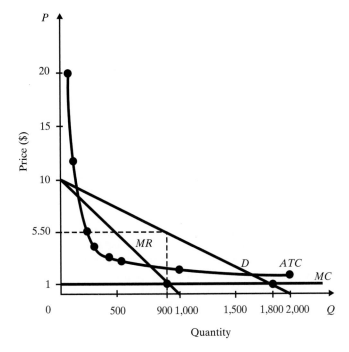

c. Profit-maximizing output is 900; profit-maximizing price is \$5.50.

d. Efficient price would be \$1, where the demand curve intersects the marginal cost curve. At this price, $Q = 1,800$.

e. Long-run output would be zero, because losses would cause the monopoly to exit the industry.

f. Alternatively, regulators could require the monopoly to charge a price equal to marginal cost and then subsidize the monopoly's loss.

CHAPTER 14

2. a. Monopolistic competition: free entry, lots of firms, product differentiation, close substitutability.

b. As new establishments open, demand curves for existing firms shift left. Price of admission falls and profits drop to zero at the tangency of demand and ATC (see Figure 14.3).

4. a. A good example was AT&T when it held a dominant position in the U.S. telecommunications market. At the same time it had little competition in the United States, other countries had big, powerful telecommunications firms producing equipment (telephones, etc.) and services for the world market. World competition was fierce.

b. The key is the availability of substitutes. A monopoly is a firm producing a product for which there is no close substitute. When they were just another band, clubs could hire a cheap band and consumers didn't know the difference or care. With their success, there became fewer substitutes in the minds of consumers.

6. Both A's and B's potential losses are minimized by cheating. To minimize the maximum loss, A should cheat, because it yields higher profit regardless of what B does. The same is true for B. If A cheats, so will B, and if B cheats, so will A. Most likely outcome: Both will cheat.

8. a. 30 units.

b. $P = \$14$.

c. $TR = 30 \times \$14 = \$420$.

$TC = \$9 \times 30 = \$270$.

Profit = \$420 – \$270 = \$150.

d. In the long run, entry will shift the demand and marginal revenue curves leftward until normal profit is earned at the profit-maximizing output level. This occurs when the demand curve is tangent to the ATC curve.

10. a. Both have dominant strategies in Game 1—charge the low price. Neither has a dominant strategy in Game 2.

b. You might try tit for tat (match the competitor's move) to signal the opposition that if she prices high, you might do so also.

c. If you are risk averse, you would probably swerve to guarantee a gain of 3. This minimizes your losses from the worst thing that can happen to you (a *maximum* strategy).

CHAPTER 15

2.

a. P_u
b. $TR=P_u a Q_u 0$
$TC=Cb Q_u 0$
$Profit=P_U abC$
c. P_e
d. $TR=P_e f Q_e 0$
$TC=de Q_e 0$
$LOSS=def P_e$
e. where ATC
intersects Demand

4. The "rule of reason" was the Supreme Court's guideline for interpreting the Sherman Act of 1890. The court declared that a monopoly would violate the law only if its conduct were unreasonable. The problem with the rule was that "unreasonable conduct" remained undefined, so businesses could not know in advance which behavior would be in violation of the law. The Clayton Act outlawed specific behavior, such as tying contracts, mergers that restrict competition, and price discrimination.

6. The HHI for this market is

$$5(15^2) + 5(5^2) = 1{,}125 + 125 = 1{,}250$$

Increase in HHI due to merger:

$$(30^2) - 2(15^2) = 450$$

Under current guidelines, the Justice Department will challenge any merger in an industry with an HHI between 1,000 and 1,800 that increases the HHI by more than 100 points. Because this merger does so, the Justice Department will challenge it.

8. Different answers.

10. Defining market share is a problem. Products of different firms may be slightly or greatly differentiated, and an arbitrary line must be drawn to define "the market." One must also (arbitrarily) decide the geographic size of the market. A firm might dominate the market within a single state or city, and yet have a small share of the national market. Mergers that would be forbidden with one definition of the product or the market-size might be permitted under alternative definitions. In addition, there is a special problem for multiproduct firms: The HHI criterion might forbid merger for some product lines and permit it for others. In this case, there is no clearly defined criterion for allowing merger even if there is agreement on how to calculate market share.

12. See Figure 13.9 in the text. In the competitive industry, output expands until $P = MC$. Under monopoly, output is smaller, and $P > MC$.

CHAPTER 16

2. a. With private goods, we each get to choose what quantity of each good we want. If I don't like a good, I don't buy it. But with public goods, we all get the same level of output. We all breathe better air if it is cleaned up, and we all get the same amount of national defense. When public goods are produced locally we have more choice (see discussion of the Tiebout hypothesis).

b. Representative democracy is not guaranteed to produce the socially optimal mix of public goods. Some problems are logrolling, a poorly informed electorate, poor incentives for people to become informed and vote, and the fact that votes are limited to *bundles* of public goods. Also, Arrow's theorem implies that there is no consistent, nonarbitrary way to agree on what the socially optimal mix is. The voting paradox is an example of why majority voting does not provide a consistent social choice mechanism.

c. An example might be a bureaucrat who is motivated just to increase the power, prestige, and budget of her bureau. This might lead to bloated bureaucracies. Clearly there has been great pressure in recent years to keep politicians and bureaucrats honest. The press plays an enormous role. House speaker Newt Gingrich's $4.5 million book deal in 1995 caused a public outcry.

4. a. *Elementary and secondary education:* Private aspects—substantial benefits accrue to the individual, and those who do not pay could, in theory, be excluded from receiving them. Also rivalry, in that there is a limited number of students one teacher can effectively teach. Public aspects—there are substantial benefits to the public at large (more informed voting, more socialized behavior). It is impossible to limit these benefits to those who pay.

b. *Higher education:* Same as above, but here even more of the benefits accrue to the individual, and the costs are often borne by those who benefit.

c. *Medical care:* Private aspects—most of the benefits of good health are enjoyed by the individual, and in theory we could exclude those who won't or can't pay. Also, high degree of rivalry. Public aspects—substantial public benefits when communicable diseases are reduced or public health is improved.

d. *Air-traffic control:* Private aspects—there is certainly rivalry, as shown by the congested skies over urban airports and the ulcers suffered by overworked air-traffic controllers. Public aspects—all air traffic in a given area must be controlled from a single set of controllers. Competing firms would not be able to supply this service effectively. Also, substantial benefits to the public at large, which are nonexcludable (e.g., reduced probability of a plane crashing into one's home).

6. a. People disagree about this. There are private aspects of housing for the poor: excludability and rivalry. There may also be substantial benefits for society at large when everyone has a place to sleep at night.

b. Disagree. An unregulated market economy tends to *under*produce public goods, because nonexcludability and the free-rider problem prevent the private sector from charging for these goods.

8. Most economists would argue that the patent system is, on balance, a good thing. True, patent holders—as monopolies—charge a higher-than-efficient price for the technology. But without such monopolies, the new technologies would not have been developed in the first place. Still, government involvement in research may be justified on several grounds. It might be better to have the government fund the research and make the results widely available than to encourage research via patents that impart monopoly control over new ideas. Also, patents may not be sufficient to keep new technology from being imitated once developed. In this case, the private sector has little incentive to develop the new technology.

10. **a.** *imperfect information:* impossible to verify who is faking. Also, *moral hazard:* less reason to avoid injury due to benefits received.

 b. *Adverse selection:* disproportionate number of damaged computers will be sold.

 c. *Imperfect information:* difficult to know how well a company's system will work until after it is in place. Hard to evaluate competing bids.

 d. *Adverse selection:* The worst drivers will buy more insurance, forcing up rates and causing better drivers to choose between subsidizing bad drivers or doing without insurance. Also, *moral hazard:* less reason to avoid collisions if insurance company will bear the costs.

12. Depends on what happened.

CHAPTER 17

2. The arguments in favor of Clinton's tax policy are primarily equity arguments. Higher tax rates for those with the highest incomes help to make the after-tax income distribution more equal. The arguments against the policy are both philosophical (government attempts to redistribute income are an unjustified interference with personal freedom) and practical (redistribution reduces rewards for those who contribute needed resources to production; with lower rewards, there will be fewer resources, less production, and lower average standard of living).

4. The biggest reason was that the economy was expanding at a rapid pace during this period. Millions of new jobs had to be filled; employment and labor force participation increased dramatically. In addition, welfare reform was passed and federal law made benefits temporary. In addition, real benefit levels have been falling steadily for years, making the opportunity cost of leisure significantly higher. In other words, the trade-off between work and welfare shifted toward work. The new welfare bill also provided more money for child care and medical insurance. There are many other possible explanations.

6. Computer programming requires a great deal of skill and training. Those who get such jobs have a lot of human capital. Working in a gas station or a car wash does not require great skill. Logging and heavy construction require some skills and are dangerous occupations requiring employers to pay compensation differentials to attract workers.

8. Disagree. The statement ignores different working conditions, differing vacations, and differing time available for other income opportunities (writing books, consulting). Also, choices reveal preferences for various jobs. Academic jobs must yield more utility to some or no one would be an academic.

10. Social security, Medicare, private pensions, and the availability of secure vehicles for saving (like FDIC-protected bank accounts) have all contributed to the reduction of poverty among the elderly.

CHAPTER 18

2.

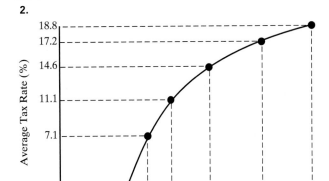

The tax is progressive because the first $25,000 is taxed at a marginal rate of zero. As income rises, the part subject to the 0% rate shrinks as a percentage of total income and the part subject to the 25% marginal rate rises as a percentage of total income.

4. Answers will vary. See Box in 1997 tax bill.

6. Disagree. Excess burdens come about because of distortions in behavior. If a good has a low demand elasticity, the tax will have a relatively small effect on quantity demanded, and the excess burden will be relatively small.

8. If one thinks of the social security tax as a payment for future entitlements, it would be correct to list it as part of employee compensation. However, Congress could always change the law so that those "entitlements" aren't received, and faculty may prefer to receive cash rather than future benefits; to this extent, the full value of the payroll tax should not be counted as compensation. Also, it must be pointed out that the imposition of the tax does not raise overall employee compensation. If it really is just another form of compensation, wages will simply fall by the amount of the tax. To the extent that it is a tax because workers prefer to be compensated in a different way, if the supply of labor is inelastic workers will bear the burden of the tax and their compensation will be reduced.

10. If the cost of one's car is proportional to one's income, then the tax would be proportional. If high-income people spend a smaller (larger) *percentage* of their income on cars, then the tax would be regressive (progressive). The tax would distort by discouraging automobile ownership (especially ownership of expensive cars) but might also correct for existing externalities (congestion, air pollution, noise).

CHAPTER 19

2. There was no change in her wage rate, thus the opportunity cost of leisure remained the same before and after her inheritance. Thus, there is no substitution effect. Her behavior changed because she was better off after the inheritance and she decided to "buy" some more leisure. It was a pure income effect!

4.

a.
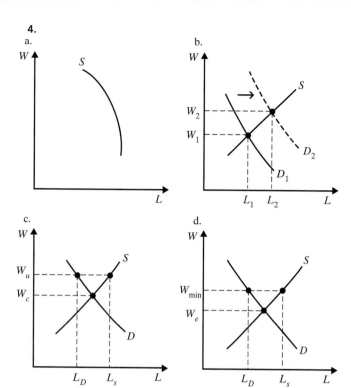

b.

c.

d.

6. Answers will vary. A progovernment answer might stress the "public goods" aspects of reducing the unemployment rate (see chapter 16), because we all benefit when unemployment decreases, regardless of our contribution to the effort. There is also an information problem (chapter 16), in that the unemployed in one region of the country may not be able to find out about job vacancies in another region.

An anti-intervention argument might stress the adequacy of wages as "signals" to reallocate labor where it is needed most, and the ability to obtain job-market training privately.

8. Income testing means benefits are withdrawn if income rises to a certain level. This is true for all programs designed to aid "the poor." The biggest problem is Medicaid. If Medicaid eligible people take jobs, they may well lose their eligibility—it is an implicit tax. When you add the benefits lost, you can get very high implicit tax rates. Even if the IRS doesn't tax the income of the poor, the fact that I will lose benefits if I work discourages work. It reduces the opportunity cost of leisure.

10.
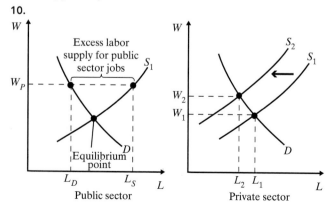

Public sector   Private sector

S-14

12. Answer should include compensating differentials, differences in human capital (which explains the lower wages of teenagers), occupational segregation (which explains in part the lower wages of women), and labor market discrimination (which explains in part the lower wages of African Americans).

CHAPTER 20

2. a. Should reduce costs by reducing the incentive to overprovide care. With fixed per-member fees, the incentive is to keep members healthy and to do procedures only when necessary.

b. Covering everyone will not be costless. Clearly, when some people are brought into the system who would otherwise go without care, more is spent. But some of the uninsured may be healthy and uninsured as a result of adverse selection. To the extent that this is true, the premiums would reflect the higher quality of the newly insured and could drop. Finally, community rating would bring in some of the less healthy who had been priced out. The likely result is a higher average premium.

c. Copayments makes the moral hazard problem less severe and patients would have a lower incentive to overuse medical providers' services.

4. Answers will vary.

6. *Location A annual costs:*

$ 50,000 (operating costs)
$ 25,000 (opportunity cost of land @ 10%)
$30,000 (opportunity cost of building @ 10%)
Total cost: $105,000.
Total revenue on gasoline turnover: $100,000.
   (10 cents per gallon markup on 1,000,000 gallons)
Net profit: –$5,000. Do not invest in "A."

Location B annual costs:

$ 50,000 (operating costs)
$100,000 (opportunity cost of land @ 10%)
$ 30,000 (opportunity cost of building @ 10%)
Total cost: $180,000.
Total revenue on gasoline turnover: $200,000.
   (10 cents per gallon markup on 2,000,000 gallons)
Net profit: $20,000. Invest in "B."

8. You would expect to see accessible locations increase in value. More remote locations would fall in value. Over time, you'd expect people to live closer to their workplaces. This might reduce urban sprawl and increase downtown development.

10. City dwellers face the negative externalities of more congestion, pollution, noise, and crime, and the positive externalities of more consumer choice in goods and services, and a greater quantity and quality in the arts. Suburb dwellers face negative externalities of greater travel requirements and social isolation, but enjoy the positive externalities of better schools, more parks and open spaces, and fewer conflicts with neighbors over noise and other disturbances.

CHAPTER 21

2. The unemployed are those who are not working for pay or profit but who have made specific efforts to find a job during the week of the employment survey. In simple terms it is the excess of labor supplied over labor demanded in the market. The labor demand curve measures the quantity of labor (workers or hours) demanded by firms at each possible wage rate. Firms' demand for labor is derived from the demand for products. Firms will hire workers as long as the product of their labor sells for a price high enough to produce a profit. Thus, the "productivity" of workers is critical. Labor supply reflects the choices made by households to work and how much to work. The alternative to working is leisure or "home production." Home production can include child rearing, subsistence farming, or other unpaid work. The value of leisure and home production is the opportunity cost of working.

4. The problem was that while output was rising, employment was not. The recovery doesn't really have much of an impact on people in general until new jobs begin to appear, reducing unemployment. The unemployment rate actually did not reach its highest level until the third quarter of 1992, just in time for the election.

6. Macro looks at aggregates in the total economy, while micro looks at individual markets and individual economic agents. It is often helpful (and more accurate) to base macroeconomics theories on the behavior of the individuals who make up the macroeconomy.

8. Wars result in high levels of government spending, which helps to increase total spending in the economy.

10. When demand shifts to the right in a market, prices tend to rise. Higher interest rates make buying a car or a home more expensive to those who must borrow to finance those items. Thus, high interest rates tend to shift demand curves back to the left, taking pressure off prices.

CHAPTER 22

2. Every payment made by a buyer becomes income for the seller. Thus, the dollar value of the purchases of new goods and services in a year must be the dollar value of the income generated in that year.

4. With fixed-weight indexes, the percentage change in the index from year to year depends on the weights chosen and thus on the base year.

Goods whose output decreases (or increases slowly) because of slowly- or backward-shifting supply curves will have their relative prices increase. If we use the old prices as weights, we will tend to understate the importance of this decrease. Likewise, if we use the new prices as weights, we overstate the importance of the production decline.

Fixed-weight price indexes that use old quantities as weights are generally taken as overestimates of the increase in the price level, because these indexes ignore consumers' opportunities to find substitutes for goods whose relative prices rise. Those that use current-year quantities as weights are taken to underestimate changes in the price level because they implicitly assume that the substitutes people chose for the goods whose relative prices rose are considered just as good as the "real thing."

The use of fixed-weight indexes poses special problems when used to make measurements over long periods of time, because the use of, say, 1950 weights for 1995's economy is not desirable.

The BEA's new approach does two things: First, it takes the (geometric) average of fixed-weight indexes, to deal with the overestimation and underestimation issues. Second, it "updates" the base years for the fixed-weight indexes every time it makes a new calculation, to ensure that the weights remain appropriate. That is, the indexes whose average it takes are those whose base years are the previous year and the current year.

6. You can't tell how much inflation is forecast. If you knew the forecast for "nominal" GDP (for GDP in current dollars) in addition to the forecast for real GDP, you could figure out how much of the forecast change was due to inflation. The 1998 per capita GDP: $26,943; 1999 per capita GDP: $27,355. Forecast for real GDP: +2.39%. Forecast for per capita real GDP: +1.53%.

8. Consumption as measured by retail sales is just part of GDP. Using the expenditure approach, real GDP is made up of consumption plus investment plus net exports plus government purchases. If the sum of I, G, and $(X - M)$ grows more rapidly than C, real GDP will rise more rapidly than retail sales.

10. The pizza is entirely consumed in the year it was produced, while the car will last many years. To correct for this, we could count just the value of the services provided by the car *each year*. For example, if the car lasts 5 years, then 20% of its value could be counted in each year's GDP.

12. There is no right or wrong answer here. But counting environmental damage requires a dollar estimate of this damage, about which there will be little consensus.

CHAPTER 23

2. *Full employment* is another term for the natural rate of unemployment. The idea behind this terminology is that if the only unemployment in the economy is the unemployment that comes about as the result of the normal working of the labor market, then there is no "unnecessary" unemployment. Labor is being "fully" utilized because the only unemployment that exists is the natural consequence of an efficiently working market. Thus the economy can be at full employment with a 4.9% unemployment rate, provided that the 4.9% unemployment is frictional and structural only.

4. This is structural unemployment, which can sometimes exist for long periods, especially when workers must learn new skills to find jobs. The social costs of this unemployment might be greater than the costs of retraining these workers, providing some justification for government assistance.

6. Yes, inflation would still be a problem. There are other costs of inflation besides the redistribution of income that occurs when incomes are not indexed. One example is the waste of time and resources spent coping with inflation. See the section on "Administrative Costs and Inefficiences" under the heading "Costs of Inflation."

8. Yes, both statements can be true. The labor force of Tappania may have grown faster than the number of employed, implying an increase in the number who are looking for work but not working, and an increase in the unemployment rate.

10. Answers will vary.

CHAPTER 24

2. We know that $C = .75Y = 150$ billion. $C + I = 150 + 75 = 225$ billion. Thus, $C + I > Y$ ... aggregate spending is greater than aggregate output. Inventories will fall and in the coming months Y (real GDP) will rise. GDP will stop rising when $C + I = Y$. That is when $.75Y + 75 = Y$ or $75 = .25Y$ or $Y = 300$ billion Yuck dollars.

4. Think of the adjustment that occurs when, with the economy at the equilibrium level of output, an increase in planned investment occurs. Inventories are drawn down, and output increases. If firms increase output by the amount of the increase in planned investment, equilibrium will not be reestablished. The increased output (income) will also

increase consumption. Thus there will have been an increase in Y of ΔI, but an increase in aggregate expenditure of more than ΔI. Y must increase further to establish equilibrium. The multiplier is finite because a fraction of income is saved. Thus, as Y grows, S grows; so we will eventually reach a level of Y at which the new planned investment just offsets the leakage into savings. This will be a new equilibrium. At this point, $\Delta S = \Delta I$. Because $\Delta S = MPS \times \Delta Y$, we can solve for ΔY:

$$\Delta Y = \frac{1}{MPS} \times \Delta I.$$

6. a. $MPC = .8$; $MPS = .2$.

b.

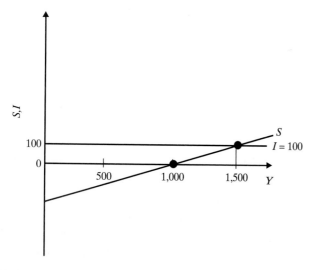

c. $\Delta Y = (1/MPS)\Delta I$. Multiplier $= 1/MPS = 1/.2 = 5$. In this case, with the multiplier equal to 5 and an increase in investment of 10, $\Delta Y = (5)(10) = 50$. Equilibrium Y increases from 1,500 to 1,550.

d. $S = Y - C$
   $= Y - (200 + .8Y)$
   $= -200 + .2Y$

The equilibrium must be the same in both graphs because $Y = C + I$ and $S = I$ are the same condition. To see this, remember that $Y = C + S$ always. Substitute $C + S$ for Y in the equilibrium condition $Y = C + I$ to obtain $C + S = C + I$, which simplifies to $S = I$.

8. No. AE is *planned* aggregate expenditure. If you add unplanned changes in inventory to it, the sum equals aggregate output (income).

CHAPTER 25

2. $Y = 1,000$, $Y_d = 800$, $C = 600$, $S = 200$, $I = 100$, $G = 200$. Because total spending $= C + I + G = 600 + 100 + 200 = 900$ is less than total output of 1,000, one would predict that inventories will pile up, and firms will decide to reduce output.

   b. Y would settle at 600. At this level of output, we would have $C = 300$, $I = 100$, and $G = 200$ so that $Y = C + I + G = 600$.

   c. Cutting government purchases would make the fall in output worse! In particular, a cut of 25 would cause equilibrium Y to decline by $25(1/MPS) = (25)(4) = 100$. This would mean Y would decline to 500 instead of 600.

4. The statement is true if one only cares about the budget deficit. But there are also political controversies about the efficiency and appropriate size of the government sector that would lead some to favor the tax cut even though it raises the deficit by more.

6. If G goes up and T does not, the equilibrium level of Y rises. $C + I + G > Y$, inventories fall, and Y increases! In 1946 gross federal debt was 127.5% of GDP. Recent figures put the figure at just under 70%.

8. a. Govt. spending multiplier $= 1/.4 = 2.5$.

   b. Govt. spending multiplier $= 1/(1 - .9) = 10$.

   c. Govt. spending multiplier $= 1/(1 - .5) = 2$.

   d. Tax multiplier $= -.75/(1 - .75) = -3$.

   e. Tax multiplier $= -.9/(1 - .9) = -9$.

   f. MPC must be .833. Tax multiplier $= -.833/(1 - .833) = -5.0$.

   g. MPC must be .666. Government spending multiplier $= 1/(1 - .666) = 3.0$.

   h. Output will increase by $100 billion (use the balanced-budget multiplier, which has a value of 1).

CHAPTER 26

2. *Cash:* Asset—Bank has it on hand.
   Demand Deposits: Liability—claims by depositors can be withdrawn at any time.
   Savings deposits: Liability—same logic.
   Reserves: Assets—They are in the vault as cash or on deposit with the Fed.
   Loans: Assets—They represent claims of the *bank* on borrowers.
   Deposits at the Fed: Assets—They can be withdrawn at any time; they are owned by the bank.

4. Before the change, the banks are holding $67.2 billion (10% of demand deposits) in reserve assets against demand deposits. Changing the reserve requirement does not increase or decrease the quantity of reserves. Rather, it changes the volume of deposits that can be held for each dollar of reserves. At an 11% reserve requirement, $61 billion can support only about $611 billion in demand deposits. Thus, the money supply would have to shrink by $61 billion ($672 billion – $611 billion) to restore banks to compliance with the reserve requirement.

6. M2 includes everything in M1, plus savings accounts, money market accounts, and some other categories. A shift of funds between, say, savings accounts and checking accounts will affect M1 but not M2, because both savings accounts and checking accounts are part of M2.

8. Money injected through open market operations results in a multiple expansion of the money supply only if it leads to loans, and loans can be made only if the new money ends up in banks as reserves. If the Fed buys a bond from James Q. Public, who immediately deposits the proceeds into a dollar-denominated Swiss bank account, the U.S. money supply won't expand at all. If the money ends up in his pockets or in his mattress, the expansion of the money supply will stop right there. If he had deposited the proceeds in a U.S. bank, excess reserves would have been created, stimulating lending and further money creation.

10. In addition to controlling the money supply, the Fed clears interbank payments, is responsible for many of the regulations governing banking practices and standards, and is the lender of last resort for the banking system. It is also responsible for managing exchange rates and the nation's foreign exchange reserves.

Answers to the second part of the question will vary.

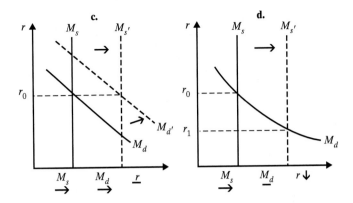

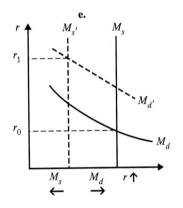

CHAPTER 27

2. If households believe that interest rates will rise, why should they lend money now? They will desire to hold more of their wealth as money for the time being, betting that they can get a higher interest rate if they wait. If they buy bonds now, they risk a capital loss (a decrease in the value of their assets), because bond prices fall when interest rates rise. When households hold money to speculate in this way, we call their motive for holding money the "speculation motive."

6. *Ceteris paribus,* an expansionary fiscal policy at a time when the Fed want to hold the rate of growth of the money supply steady will drive up interest rates. First, the added expenditure will push up the growth of real GDP. The increased spending and GDP would increase the demand for money, M_d. If the Fed holds the line, $M_d > M_s$ and rates will rise. At the same time these policies hit taxpayers, the Asia crisis of 1998 hit the U.S. economy and slowed down the growth of real GDP as exports to Asia fell. By early 1998, the Fed was even thinking of expanding M_s to push r down to restore GDP growth.

4.

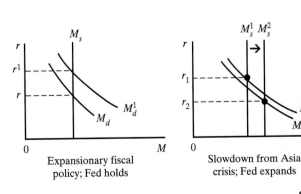

CHAPTER 28

2. Taxes (T) rise, causing disposable income (Y_d) to fall. When Y_d falls, C falls, causing $AE < Y$. When $AE < Y$, inventories rise and firms cut back on output/income: Y falls and unemployment rises. If I were the central bank and I wanted to counteract these effects, I might lower interest rates to try to stimulate investment with expansionary monetary policy.

4. a. In 1998, the tax cuts cause disposable income to rise. When Y_d rises, C increases and $C + I + G > Y$. Inventories contract, causing Y to rise. Higher Y causes money demand M_d to rise. If M^s is fixed, that will cause r to rise. In 1999–2000 the story is reversed. The expenditure cuts kick in, causing G to fall. $C + I + G < Y$, inventories rise, Y falls. That causes money demand to fall and with M^s constant, r will fall.

b. The tax increase reduced disposable income and thus consumption $C + I + G < Y$, so inventories build and output falls. A lower Y means lower money demand. At the same time that the Fed is increasing the money supply, interest rates will fall sharply, causing I to rise, perhaps offsetting the effects of the initial tax increase on Y. (Final result: ambiguous Y, lower r.)

c. The drop in consumption cuts aggregate expenditure: $C + I + G < Y$, so inventories rise and Y falls. As Y falls, money demand drops. If the Fed holds M^s constant, r will fall. Here again, the lower r may stimulate I, causing I to rise, partially offsetting the initial decline in Y. (Final result: lower Y, lower r.)

d. The Fed expands the money supply. $M^s > M^d$, so r falls. Normally, the lower r might be expected to cause I to rise, but gloomy expectations and no need for new plant and equipment keep I low. Thus the link to the goods market is broken, and the monetary policy doesn't have much impact. (Final result: lower r, little or no change in Y.)

6. a. The decline in investment would be a reduction in aggregate expenditure, causing equilibrium output (income) to decrease in the goods market. In the money market, the drop in income would decrease the demand for money (shift the M^d curve to the left), causing the interest rate to fall and investment spending to rise back up somewhat. But the net effect would be a decline in output (income) and the interest rate.

b. Option 3 is the most expansionary, because the increase in the money supply works to offset the crowding-out effect. Option 2 would come next, but would involve some crowding out. Option 1 would be least expansionary, because the tax increase would decrease consumption spending. (Option 1 relies on the balanced-budget multiplier, which has a value of 1. Option 2 relies on the government spending multiplier, which is larger than 1.)

8. The Fed's tight monetary policy would drive up interest rates, discouraging investment and causing aggregate output to fall. The simultaneous expansionary fiscal policy would increase the government spending and consumption components of aggregate output, increasing money demand and driving up interest rates further. The policies have opposing effects on aggregate output, so the ultimate effect on Y depends on which effect is stronger. But both policies drive interest rates higher. (In 1981, as a result of this policy, the prime interest rate rose to 21.5%!)

CHAPTER 29

2. a.

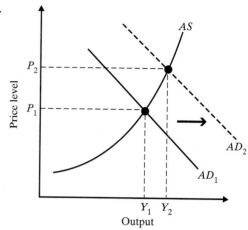

The price level will rise considerably; equilibrium GDP will rise only a little.

b.

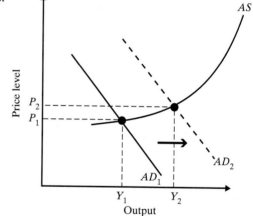

GDP will rise considerably; prices will rise only a little.

c.

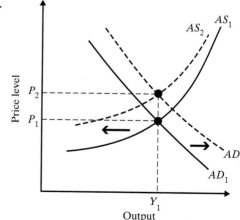

The price level will rise considerably. Equilibrium GDP may fall, but by less than it would if the Fed did not accommodate.

d.

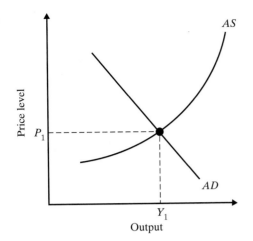

Neither the price level nor output would change. The fiscal and monetary policies have opposing effects on the AD curve. If they are of equal strength, there will be no shift in the curve.

4. a. Expansionary fiscal policy shifts the AD curve to the right if the Fed expands the money supply to accommodate the expansion and prevent crowding out. If it pushes us beyond potential GDP, inflation could be the result.

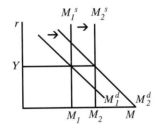

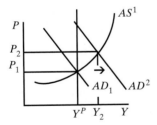

b. Contractionary monetary policy shifts the AD curve to the left.

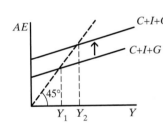

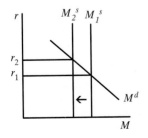

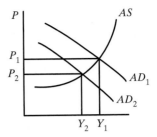

6. The actual physical capacity of existing plants represents the maximum output level the economy could produce in the short run. It is where the short-run AS curve becomes vertical. Potential GDP is the maximum output the economy could maintain in the long run without exacerbating inflation. It is less than full-capacity output because the bottlenecks and labor shortages that would exist at full-capacity output would cause wages and input prices to rise, leading to worsening inflation.

8.

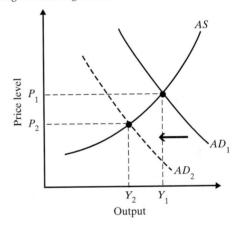

The government expected the decrease in the money supply to shift the aggregate demand curve to the left by raising interest rates and reducing planned investment. The shift should have caused aggregate output to fall from Y_1 to Y_2 and the price level to fall from P_1 to P_2.

Prices could have continued to increase because (a) there were expectations of continuing inflation, causing input prices to rise despite the fall in output; (b) OPEC increased the cost of oil to the United States during this period. Both explanations would be represented by a leftward shift in the AS curve.

CHAPTER 30

2. a. If the minimum wage is 9 slugs per hour, then:

$$Q_D = 100 - 5(9) = 55 \text{ million workers};$$
$$Q_S = 10(9) - 20 = 70 \text{ million workers}.$$

The excess supply of labor (number of unemployed) would be $70 - 55 = 15$ million workers. The unemployment rate would be $15/70 = .214$ or 21.4%.

b. With no minimum wage, the equilibrium wage is found by setting labor demand equal to labor supply:

$$100 - 5W = 10W - 20 \rightarrow 120 = 15W \rightarrow W = 8 \text{ slugs per hour.}$$

Equilibrium employment is found by substituting $W = 8$ into either the labor-demand or labor-supply equation:

$$Q_D = 100 - 5(8) = 60 \text{ million workers};$$
$$Q_S = 10(8) - 20 = 60 \text{ million workers}.$$

The labor force shrinks from 70 million to 60 million workers. Total employment rises from 55 million to 60 million workers. The unemployment rate shrinks from 21.4% to zero. (The model assumes no frictional unemployment.)

c. The labor market might not adjust so quickly due to wage rigidity, which has a number of possible causes, including implicit and explicit contracts, worker concerns over their relative wages, and firms' concerns over the decline in productivity that might follow a wage cut.

4. The point here is simple: If inflation is running at more than 10%, your real wage will decrease, and you will be less well off in terms of purchasing power.

6. a.

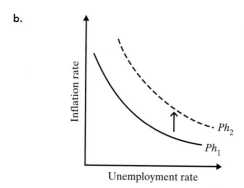

b.

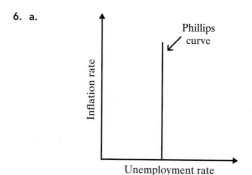

Here, it is assumed that inflationary expectations have increased.

c.

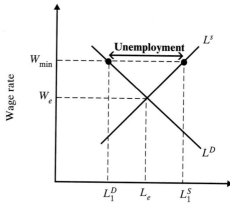

8. The trade-offs might be different for the two countries because social contracts and long-term explicit and implicit contracts may keep Japanese firms from laying off workers. Because the labor force in the United States is more transient, layoffs may be more likely. In Japan, a given reduction in inflation would probably require a smaller increase in unemployment.

CHAPTER 31

2. Fine-tuning means using monetary and fiscal policy to make adjustments to keep growth from going too fast (inflation) or drifting into recession. Many economists are skeptical of the government's ability to do this. Nevertheless, the 1990s were a very stable period, and the Fed made a number of seemingly effective monetary policy changes then. During the spring of 1994, the Fed tightened credit and drove up interest rates. The economy responded just as chapter 28 would suggest, and the growth of GDP slowed markedly. Then when things got too slow in 1995, the Fed expanded the money supply, dropping rates, and the economy seemed to respond by growing more rapidly a few months later.

4. When the economy contracts, both taxable income and corporate profits fall, causing a decrease in tax revenues. In addition, some government expenditure categories, such as unemployment insurance benefits, tend to rise. With decreased tax revenues and increased government expenditures, the government deficit typically rises when the economy contracts.

6. The Federal Reserve increased short-term interest rates seven times during 1994 by directly raising the discount rate and by using open-market operations to raise the federal funds rate. With a lag, such moves have an effect on aggregate expenditure (investment spending and consumption spending). The purpose was to prevent inflation. As unemployment fell below 6% in 1994, the Fed's Board of Governors decided that the United States was getting close to the natural rate of unemployment, or to "potential GDP." As GDP expands above potential GDP, inflation occurs. Inflation was not in fact a problem after 1994, and so it is not clear with hindsight that the Fed needed to tighten.

8. The Fed "leans against the wind" when it increases the money supply to lower interest rates to counteract contraction of the economy, and decreases the money supply to raise interest rates to counteract rapid expansion. These policies are designed to stabilize the economy.

10. It takes a full year for the spending multiplier to take effect because neither individuals nor firms alter their spending plans immediately. It takes time for the additional income derived from increased government spending to be translated into additional purchases, and when taxes are cut there are also decisions to be made about what portion of the tax cut to spend and what to spend it on. This makes correct timing of fiscal policy more difficult.

CHAPTER 32

2. Answers will vary.

4. When taxes increase (net wages decrease), one of the impacts is a reduction in income. If leisure is a normal good, the decrease in income will lead to less consumption of leisure, and therefore an increase in desired work hours. This serves to counteract the substitution effect of a decrease in wages, which lowers the opportunity cost of leisure and tends to decrease desired work hours.

6. The value of homes is an important component of household wealth. When home prices rise, household wealth rises and consumption tends to increase. When home prices fall, household wealth falls and consumption decreases. Because changes in consumption are changes in aggregate expenditure, they lead to changes in output and employment in the same direction.

8. A given consumption path requires a given amount of lifetime income to pay for it. But, given initial wealth, lifetime income is determined by working hours. This implies that income is not really an "independent" variable in the consumption function. Rather, the desire to consume and the desire to enjoy leisure together will determine how much income one will earn.

10. Maintaining inventory stocks helps a firm maintain a smooth production level. When sales unexpectedly increase, goods can be sold out of inventory. When sales unexpectedly decrease, goods can be added to inventories. By smoothing production, a firm can save on the adjustment costs associated with frequent changes in capital stock and employment levels. The cost of this policy is the forgone interest from investing funds in inventory stocks instead of lending out the money in financial markets.

CHAPTER 33

2. a. Graph I: Supply-side economics; it focuses on the supply-side effects of a tax cut and tends to ignore the demand-side impacts. Tax cuts should increase the incentive to work, save, and invest. If work effort, saving, and investment all increase, the AS curve will shift to the right, increasing output and reducing the price level. The extent to which the supply curve is likely to shift depends on the responsiveness of behavior to the tax cuts. This is the subject of much controversy.

Graph II: Monetarism/New classical economics. Both schools believe that fiscal policy cannot have an impact on the level of real output. Monetarism believes that nominal GDP cannot change as long as the money supply and the velocity of money remain constant. Thus real GDP will not respond to a tax cut. New classical theories predict that "anticipated" fiscal policies will have no effect on real GDP, which remains at the potential output level determined in the long run in markets such as the labor market.

Graph III: Keynesian economics. As long as the economy is not operating at capacity, and as long as the Fed accommodates

somewhat by increasing the money supply, a permanent tax cut can increase the level of real GDP and is likely to be inflationary. The impact on the price level is determined by how close to capacity the economy is operating.

b. Individual response.

4. Individual response.

6. a. Clinton's tax increases and spending cuts would be a fiscal contraction. With no change in Fed policy, output would decrease and unemployment would increase. If the Fed matches the fiscal contraction with a monetary expansion, lowering interest rates to stimulate investment, the decline in output could be avoided.

b. Monetarists would worry about imperfect policy timing. Fed stimulation might take effect at the wrong time (e.g., after the economy has recovered from the impact of the fiscal contraction). Supply-siders would worry that higher tax rates would decrease the incentive to work and invest. Extreme supply-siders might worry that an increase in tax rates would decrease tax revenue and result in an even larger budget deficit.

c. To evaluate the supply-side argument, you would need to see what happened to tax revenues and labor supply after the taxrate increases. An increase in tax revenues, *ceteris paribus*, would contradict the view of extreme supply-siders. If labor supply did not decrease much, general supply-side arguments would be weakened. To evaluate the monetarist argument, you would need to see if investment spending increased as consumption spending declined (proper policy timing), or only after consumption began to recover (poor timing).

8. Reagan believed that the lower tax rates would provide incentives for households to work more hours and to save more and for firms to invest more. These actions would expand the supply of goods and services and, thus, expand aggregate income and the tax base. The tax base would rise by so much that tax revenues would actually rise despite the lower tax rates. Bush believed that incentives were important, but that the effects would not be large enough to raise revenues and reduce the deficit.

CHAPTER 34

2. *TABLE 1*

Y/L	GROWTH RATE
4.28	—
4.23	3.7
4.17	3.6
4.12	3.7

TABLE 2

Y/L	GROWTH RATE
4.28	—
4.41	3.9
4.53	3.9
4.66	3.9

TABLE 3

	Y/L	GROWTH RATE
	4.28	—
	4.45	5.0
	4.63	5.0
	4.81	5.0

In Table 1, L is growing rapidly while K is growing slowly. It is likely that much of the growth in Y is due to growth in L. Because of diminishing returns to L, it is not surprising that Y/L is declining.

In Table 2, L is growing slowly while K is growing rapidly. In this case it seems that the growth in Y is caused mainly by growth in K. The ratio Y/L is increasing because each worker has more capital with which to work.

Finally, in Table 3, both L and K are growing slowly relative to Y. Technology must be the cause of most of the growth in Y in this case. This technological improvement also has the effect of increasing the amount of output per worker (Y/L).

4. Households would receive a higher after-tax rate of return on their stock portfolios. It could lead to higher saving. It could also lead households to shift their portfolios toward stocks and away from bonds. Some argue it could lead to more frequent trading among stockholders, leading to a more efficient stock market. Firms would be more likely to retain earnings for investment purposes because paid-out dividends would be taxed at a higher rate than capital gains. Some argue that it would lead to more start-up companies. When a small firm goes "public," successful entrepreneurs who cash in have to pay capital gains rates on the proceeds of their stock sale; lower CG rates increase the incentive to start a firm. Empirical research suggests that these effects are small.

6. Assuming that the economy stays at full employment, the bill would cause the economy to produce more capital goods and fewer consumption goods. This would lead to a higher growth rate over time. The trade-off is less consumption today. There are also distributional consequences. Capital income earners (who have higher incomes on average) would benefit. The members of the higher-income households (who spend a smaller fraction of their incomes) would bear relatively less of the consumption-tax burden, while the members of the low-income households (who spend a higher fraction of their incomes) would bear relatively more of the consumption-tax burden.

8. High budget deficits are financed with private saving. That saving otherwise would have found its way through financial markets into private capital production. If the deficit is used to finance current expenditures like paying judges and congresspeople, it is not contributing to an expansion of output in the long run. The same is true of a tax cut, which is used to increase current consumption expenditures. But if the government used the money to build capital such as roads and bridges or to increase human capital through better education and job training, it would at least offset part of the reduction in private investment spending. Whether the net result for output growth is positive or negative depends on whether private capital or public capital has a higher rate of return. This is a subject of much debate, and would depend on the specific capital expenditures undertaken by the government.

CHAPTER 35

2. **a.** You cannot tell from the information given which country has an absolute advantage because you are not given any information that would indicate the actual quantities of inputs used in production in either country.

   b. If resources are fully mobile between sectors the opportunity cost of a cap is 2/3 of a quart of wheat in Russia; the opportunity cost of a cap is 7/10 of a quart of wheat in the United States. Russia has a comparative advantage in cap production. The opportunity cost of a quart of wheat in Russia is 1.5 caps. The opportunity cost of a quart of wheat in the United States is 10/7 or 1.43 caps. The United States has a comparative advantage in wheat.

   c. At $1 = 1 Ru, both goods in the United States are cheaper to everyone. That would mean that there was a big demand for dollars and no supply on foreign exchange markets. The price of the dollar would rise. When a dollar was valued at between 1.43 and 1.50 Ru, caps would be cheaper in Russia and wheat would be cheaper in the United States. If the price of a dollar rises to more than 1.50 Ru, everyone would buy both goods in Russia.

4. **a.** Illinois would have an absolute advantage in both wheat and soybeans.

   b. In Illinois, taking 1 acre out of wheat and moving it into soybeans sacrifices 48 bushels of wheat for 39 bushes of soybeans. This is 48/39 = 1.23 bushels of wheat for each bushel of soybeans. In Kansas, the sacrifice is 40/24 = 1.67 bushels of wheat for each bushel of soybeans.

   c. Based on the calculations in b. above, Kansas has a comparative advantage in wheat, and Illinois has a comparative advantage in soybeans.

   d. Yes, the data are consistent with the conclusions in c. above. Kansas has more acreage devoted to wheat than soybeans, while in Illinois there is more acreage devoted to soybeans than to wheat. Although neither state completely "specializes," each state seems to be devoting more of its resources to producing the good in which it has a comparative advantage.

6. Answers will vary.

8. EC members will clearly benefit, because the volume of trade will increase, and the pattern of production in each country will conform more closely to comparative advantage. Initially, the EC will be a powerful trading bloc concerned with improvements of trade within its own unified area. This may mean it will conduct less trade with the United States, especially if trade barriers between the United States and the EC remain in place. Eventually, however, we would expect comparative advantage to bring about efficient trade flows between the United States and the new unified Europe.

CHAPTER 36

2. **a.** Answers can include an increase in U.S. incomes, an increase in British interest rates, a decrease in U.S. interest rates, a decrease in the British price level, and an increase in the U.S. price level.

   b. All of the above, except for the increase in U.S. incomes, would also cause the supply curve to shift to the left.

   c. The two changes in interest rates listed in a. and b. above— which would raise the value of the pound without any other simultaneous change in import or export demand—would make British goods relatively more expensive and decrease Britain's trade balance (shrink the surplus, or increase the deficit).

4. **a.** The expansionary fiscal policy increased incomes and the demand for money. This in itself would cause U.S. interest rates to rise. In addition, the contractionary monetary policy caused interest rates to rise further.

   b. The supply curve for dollars would shift to the left, and the demand curve would shift to the right. The value of the dollar would rise.

   c. The rise in the value of the dollar—with no other change in the desire to buy imports or exports—would make U.S. goods relatively more expensive. The U.S. trade deficit would worsen, and the trade balance of other countries with the United States would rise.

6. **a.** Under fixed rates, higher U.S. income would increase the demand for imports. The U.S. current account balance would decrease (i.e., the trade surplus would decrease or the trade deficit would increase). Under floating rates, there would be two forces acting on the exchange rate. Higher U.S. income would increase the demand for imports, increasing the supply of dollars on foreign exchange markets and causing the dollar to depreciate. However, with higher income, assuming the Fed is not fully accommodating, the interest rate in the United States would rise due to the higher demand for money. This increase in the interest rate would increase the demand for (and decrease the supply of) dollars in foreign exchange markets, causing an appreciation of the dollar. The net effect on the value of the dollar is ambiguous. However, because of the increased U.S. income, the demand for imports would increase and the current account balance would decrease, although this change in the current account balance may be partially offset if the dollar depreciated.

   b. Under fixed rates, higher U.S. prices would make U.S. goods less attractive. U.S. imports would increase, and exports would decrease, causing a decrease in the current account balance. Under floating rates, the dollar would depreciate, with no effect on the current account balance.

   c. Because U.S. interest rates fall, foreigners will take their money out of U.S. financial markets and the demand for dollars will decrease. U.S. citizens will find foreign financial markets more attractive, so the supply of dollars will increase. At the same time, U.S. income increases so the demand for foreign goods also increases, further increasing the supply of dollars. Under fixed rates, all this would decrease the current account balance. Under floating rates, the dollar would depreciate, causing a decrease in imports and increase in exports. Since imports would increase due to the higher U.S. income, the net effect on the current account balance is ambiguous.

   d. Imports will decrease and consumers will buy more domestic goods, so the demand for foreign currency decreases. Under fixed rates, this would increase the current account balance. Under floating rates, this would cause the dollar to appreciate, and the impact on the current account balance would be ambiguous.

8. Possible reasons are lower Japanese inflation rates and higher interest rates during much of the period.

CHAPTER 37

2. Answers will vary. There is no clearly "right answer" to this problem, only trade-offs. Capital accumulation requires saving (reduced consumption), and when most citizens are earning subsistence wages, reducing consumption is not an option for many.

4. **a.** Capital increases the productivity of labor. A given-sized labor force can produce more output, and output per capita rises.

   b. In a market economy, individual household savings decisions determine the pool of aggregate savings. Aggregate savings, in turn, is the amount made available for firms to purchase capital. Savings are matched to investment projects in financial markets, where the interest rate adjusts to equate total desired investment with total desired savings.

   c. In developing countries, a greater fraction of output is needed just to ensure the current population's survival. An increase in investment—which requires a decrease in current consumption—cuts dangerously close to this survival level of consumption, and at a minimum causes more discomfort than it would in developed countries.

   d. Answers will vary. Market-oriented economists would stress increased incentives for private investment (political stability, lower government budget deficit, and perhaps loans from abroad). Planning-oriented economists might stress government-directed projects, taxes on luxury goods, and capital controls designed to prevent capital flight to developed countries.

6. It is true that poor countries must accumulate capital in order to grow, but many poor countries do indeed have extra output available for savings. The problem is often that the available savings goes abroad (capital flight). Increased political stability and a more stable investment climate would help investment in the domestic economy. In addition, poor countries can get loans and other assistance from developed countries to help them accumulate capital.

8. A country should work to develop both its agricultural and its industrial sectors. Development of the agricultural sector can have high payoffs because it often requires little capital investment and directly benefits the poorest (rural) segment of society. Experience has shown that import substitution is a poor development policy. Its disadvantages include lessened competition in the domestic market, fewer jobs created, and expensive inputs for domestic industries.

   Many countries favor industry as a more direct route to growth in the capital stock, and also to emulate the production pattern of already developed countries. Import substitution is attractive because it lessens dependence on unstable foreign demand for exports.

CHAPTER 38

2. It depends on what happened. As of February 6, 1998, the yen had regained some of its value, closing at 123 yen = $1. There were signs that real growth, albeit slow, was returning to Japanese GDP.

4. The "tragedy of the commons" occurs when the costs or benefits of individual action are widely dispersed, rather than concentrated on the individual taking the action. In the case of a guaranteed job at a guaranteed wage, the benefits of doing one's job are dispersed widely among the other workers, and so are the costs of shirking. If workers follow narrow self-interest, we would expect productive behavior to decrease, and all workers would suffer.

6. There are arguments on both sides. Firms that acquire market power tend to overprice and underproduce relative to the efficient price and output levels. Market power, it is argued, stifles both price and quality competition. Microsoft was charged with anticompetitive behavior by packaging its web browser with its dominant operating system, Windows. After knocking out the competition, the story goes, they can raise prices without competitive pressure. But what about foreign competition? Isn't it a bigger, tougher game when the competition is a foreign firm receiving government support? The real problem is that the government is likely to be lousy at picking winners. What makes us think that the government can pick winners better than the market? Even recent Japanese attempts to subsidize a winner (fifth-generation computer) have failed.

8. **a.** Disagree. Exactly the opposite has occurred. Since 1958, China has moved toward a decentralized industrial base. Since Tiananmen Square, China has cracked down on political dissent but it has encouraged private enterprise.

b. The first two sentences are correct, the third is not. Japan's growth was primarily due to very high rates of saving and investment—capital accumulation.

c. Disagree. The opposite is true. Economists agree about the six components of transition, but disagree about the sequencing and speed.

10. Disagree. Though it is true that central planners can command a higher rate of national saving and capital accumulation, central planning requires keen and virtuous planners to ensure that scarce capital flows to where it is needed most. In a capitalist market economy, the self-interest of capital owners steers capital to those sectors where it is needed most—that is, those sectors offering the highest rate of return. Thus, although under central planning there might be more capital accumulation, it will not necessarily be the right kind of capital and will not necessarily find its way to the right places. Empirically, the United States grew faster than the USSR in the 1970s and 1980s.

PHOTO CREDITS

Chapters

Case Studies